MCAD/MCSD.NET

Developing and Implementing Web Applications with Visual Basic .NET and Visual Studio® .NET

Exam 70-305

Training Guide

MCAD/MCSD.NET Training Guide: Developing and Implementing Web Applications with Visual Basic .NET and Visual Studio® .NET (Exam 70-305)

International Standard Book Number: 0-7897-2818-4

Library of Congress Catalog Card Number: 2002114426

Printed in the United States of America

First Printing: December 2002

05 04 03 02 4 3 2 1

Trademarks

All terms mentioned in this book that are known to be trademarks or service marks have been appropriately capitalized. Que Certification cannot attest to the accuracy of this information. Use of a term in this book should not be regarded as affecting the validity of any trademark or service mark.

Warning and Disclaimer

Every effort has been made to make this book as complete and as accurate as possible, but no warranty or fitness is implied. The information provided is on an "as is" basis. The author and the publisher shall have neither liability nor responsibility to any person or entity with respect to any loss or damages arising from the information contained in this book.

PUBLISHER
Paul Boger

EXECUTIVE EDITOR
Jeff Riley

DEVELOPMENT EDITOR
Steve Rowe

MANAGING EDITOR
Charlotte Clapp

PROJECT EDITOR
Sheila Schroeder

COPY EDITOR
Michael Dietsch

INDEXER
John Sleeva

PROOFREADER
Linda Seifert

TECHNICAL EDITORS
Ken Cox
Emmett Dulaney

TEAM COORDINATORS
Rosemary Lewis
Kimberley Herbert

INTERIOR DESIGNER
Louisa Klucznik

COVER DESIGNER
Charis Ann Santillie

PAGE LAYOUT
Cheryl Lynch

Que Certification • 201 West 103rd Street • Indianapolis, Indiana 46290

A Note from Series Editor Ed Tittel

Congratulations on your purchase of the 70-305 Training Guide, the finest exam preparation book in the marketplace!

As Series Editor of the highly regarded Training Guide series, I can assure you that you won't be disappointed. You've taken your first step toward passing the 70-305 exam, and we value this opportunity to help you on your way!

As a "Favorite Study Guide Author" finalist in a 2002 poll of CertCities readers, I know the importance of delivering good books. You'll be impressed with Que Certification's stringent review process, which ensures the books are high-quality, relevant, and technically accurate. Rest assured that at least a dozen industry experts—including the panel of certification experts at CramSession—have reviewed this material, helping us deliver an excellent solution to your exam preparation needs.

We've also added a preview edition of PrepLogic's powerful, full-featured test engine, which is trusted by certification students throughout the world.

As a 20-year-plus veteran of the computing industry and the original creator and editor of the Exam Cram series, I've brought my IT experience to bear on these books. During my tenure at Novell from 1989 to 1994, I worked with and around its excellent education and certification department. At Novell, I witnessed the growth and development of the first really big, successful IT certification program—one that was to shape the industry forever afterward. This experience helped push my writing and teaching activities heavily in the certification direction. Since then, I've worked on more than 70 certification related books, and I write about certification topics for numerous Web sites and for *Certification* magazine.

In 1997 when Exam Cram was introduced, it quickly became the best-selling computer book series since "*...For Dummies*," and the best-selling certification book series ever. By maintaining an intense focus on the subject matter, tracking errata and updates quickly, and following the certification market closely, Exam Cram was able to establish the dominant position in cert prep books.

You will not be disappointed in your decision to purchase this book. If you are, please contact me at etittel@jump.net. All suggestions, ideas, input, or constructive criticism are welcome!

Ed Tittel

Contents at a Glance

PART IV Final Review

PART III Appendixes

Table of Contents

PART I: Developing Web Applications

PART IV: Final Review

PART V: Appendixes

About the Author

Mike Gunderloy pursued his first Microsoft certification the year that the program was introduced, and has earned the MCP, MCT, MCSE, MCDBA, and MCSD credentials in the decade since. As lead developer for Lark Group, Inc., Mike has worked with small businesses and Fortune 500 corporations alike, as well as trained many other developers in the use of Microsoft products. He got hooked on computers when you still had to build your own out of parts, and is still passionately interested in cutting-edge software technology. As a long-time member of the editorial staff of *MCP Magazine*, Mike has remained in close touch with the certification community.

Mike lives on a farm in eastern Washington state, along with his wife and children and an ever-changing array of horses, sheep, llamas, geese, turkeys, chickens, ducks, peacocks, cats, dogs, and guinea fowl. When he's not busy testing and writing about software, Mike can usually be found in his garden or greenhouse, trying to persuade recalcitrant vegetables to grow.

You can reach Mike at `MikeG1@larkfarm.com` or `http://www.larkware.com/`.

Dedication

For Mary Chipman, who knows what careers are made from.

Acknowledgments

It's never possible to thank everyone who contributed to a book in some way, but it's always fun to try. I'd like to start with Robert Shimonski, who first put me in touch with Que when this project was still being hatched. From there, it's been a treat to work with the editorial staff at Que, including Jeff Riley, Steve Rowe, and Sheila Schroeder, who helped turn a mass of manuscript into a book. Technical editors Emmett Dulaney and Ken Cox deserve special mention for wading through this entire book and pointing out the things that I missed.

Of course no book ever happens without a production staff. I'm happy that Michael Dietsch, Linda Seifert, Cheryl Lynch, and John Sleeva were working behind the scenes to take the final manuscript and put it between covers and on the shelf.

I've benefited over the years from many people in the wider development community. The editorial staff at *MCP Magazine*, including Dian Schaffhauser, Keith Ward, Michael Domingo, Becky Nagel, and Kris McCarthy, have helped me stay in touch with certification issues, and were very understanding when I trimmed my magazine duties to be able to tackle this project. Steve Bogart provided essential HTML advice and pointers.

Many people helped me develop some of my .NET skills; of these, Ken Getz, Mary Chipman, and Steve White deserve special mention. Let's tackle some development projects together again in the future, folks!

Although his name isn't on the cover, in many ways Amit Kalani is a co-author of the book you're holding now. Amit wrote the C# version of this book, and generously shared chapter drafts with me as both projects moved forward. This book benefited immensely from his insights into .NET. An added bonus for me was the chance to see step by step how C# handles some of the same topics tackled in this book.

Finally, and as always, I'd like to thank my family for supporting me through another book. My wonderful wife Dana always listened patiently when I ranted about stupid bugs, which of course were usually my own fault. And her constant encouragement keeps me going, no matter what obstacles lie in the road. Adam kept me entertained and challenged to be the best parent I possibly can at all times. Kayla was on her way out just as this introduction is on its way in to the publisher, but she's already helped make life even more exciting.

We Want to Hear from You!

As the reader of this book, *you* are our most important critic and commentator. We value your opinion and want to know what we're doing right, what we could do better, what areas you'd like to see us publish in, and any other words of wisdom you're willing to pass our way.

As an executive editor for Que, I welcome your comments. You can email or write me directly to let me know what you did or didn't like about this book—as well as what we can do to make our books better.

Please note that I cannot help you with technical problems related to the *topic* of this book. We do have a User Services group, however, where I will forward specific technical questions related to the book.

When you write, please be sure to include this book's title and author as well as your name, email address, and phone number. I will carefully review your comments and share them with the author and editors who worked on the book.

Email: `feedback@quepublishing.com`

Mail: Jeff Riley
Executive Editor
Que Certification
201 West 103rd Street
Indianapolis, IN 46290 USA

For more information about this book or another Que title, visit our Web site at `www.quepublishing.com`. Type the ISBN (excluding hyphens) or the title of a book in the Search field to find the page you're looking for.

We Want to Hear from You!

How to Use This Book

Que Certification has made an effort in its Training Guide series to make the information as accessible as possible for the purposes of learning the certification material. Here, you have an opportunity to view the many instructional features that have been incorporated into the books to achieve that goal.

Chapter Opener

Each chapter begins with a set of features designed to allow you to maximize study time for that material.

List of Objectives: Each chapter begins with a list of the objectives as stated by the exam's vendor.

Objective Explanations: Immediately following each objective is an explanation of it, providing context that defines it more meaningfully in relation to the exam. Because vendors can sometimes be vague in their objectives list, the objective explanations are designed to clarify any vagueness by relying on the authors' test-taking experience.

Objectives

This chapter covers the following Microsoft-specified objectives for the Creating User Services section of the exam 70-305 [Developing and Implementing Web-based Applications with Microsoft Visual Basic .NET and Microsoft Visual Studio .NET]:

Implement error handling in the user interface.

- **Configure custom error pages.**
- **Implement global.asax, application, page-level, and page event error handling.**

▸ When you run a Web application, it might encounter problems that should not occur in the normal course of operations. For example, a database server may be down, a file might be missing, or a user may enter nonsensical values. A good Web application must recover gracefully from these problems rather than abruptly terminating the page execution. The Microsoft .NET Framework provides structured exception handling through the use of try, catch, and finally blocks to help you catch these exceptional situations in your programs. There are predefined exception classes to represent different types of exceptions. You can also define your own exception handling classes and error messages that are specific to your own application.

▸ Exceptions that are not handled by structured exception handling are called unhandled exceptions. When such errors are unhandled, the Web page displays the raw error messages to the user. This is not user-friendly (and may be a source of a security leak). The .NET Framework allows you to create custom error pages to be displayed to the user. These custom error pages can be configured at both the Page and Application level. Objects such as the Page or Application object have an Error event that can be a suitable place to trap unmanaged errors.

CHAPTER 4

Error Handling for the User Interface

OUTLINE

STUDY STRATEGIES

- Review the "Performance Tips and Tricks in .NET Applications" White paper from the Visual Studio .NET Combined Help Collection. This paper is also available online at `http://msdn.microsoft.com/library/en-us/dndotnet/html/dotnetperftips.asp`.
- Try out the walkthrough exercises related to the Process, EventLog, and PerformanceCounter classes from the "Visual Basic and Visual C# Walkthroughs" section of the Visual Studio .NET Combined Help Collection.
- Review the Design Goals - Performance section of the Designing Distributed Applications topic from the Visual Studio .NET Combined Help Collection.

Chapter Outline: Learning always gets a boost when you can see both the forest and the trees. To give you a visual image of how the topics in a chapter fit together, you will find a chapter outline at the beginning of each chapter. You will also be able to use this for easy reference when looking for a particular topic.

OUTLINE

STUDY STRATEGIES

- Be sure to read the sections on data binding carefully, even if you think you already know all about data binding. In the .NET world, the concept of data binding has been generalized and improved from what existed in earlier Microsoft development environments. Data binding in ASP.NET bears little resemblance to what was available in classic ASP.
- In previous Microsoft development environments, many writers and trainers recommended avoiding data binding due to performance issues and a lack of flexibility. Microsoft has removed the bulk of these limitations in Visual Studio .NET. Even if you ignored data binding in the past, you should expect to be tested on it this time.
- Make sure you understand the difference between *simple* and *complex data binding*, and the syntax used for each.
- Carefully review the use of the DataBind() method and understand how it offers you control over data binding.
- Practice working with Server Explorer. You should know how to connect your application to any data source and how to select and display the data that you want to show to the end user.
- Build several templated controls (Repeater, DataList, DataGrid) and know which one is appropriate for which situations.

Study Strategies: Each topic presents its own learning challenge. To support you through this, Que Certification has included strategies for how to best approach studying in order to retain the material in the chapter, particularly as it is addressed on the exam.

INSTRUCTIONAL FEATURES WITHIN THE CHAPTER

These books include a large amount and different kinds of information. The many different elements are designed to help you identify information by its purpose and importance to the exam and also to provide you with varied ways to learn the material. You will be able to determine how much attention to devote to certain elements, depending on what your goals are. By becoming familiar with the different presentations of information, you will know what information will be important to you as a test-taker and which information will be important to you as a practitioner.

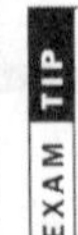

EXAM TIP

Database Terminology In some literature you'll see the rows of a database table referred to as records or tuples and the columns referred to as fields or attributes.

Exam Tip: Exam Tips appear in the margins to provide specific exam-related advice. Such tips may address what material is covered (or not covered) on the exam, how it is covered, mnemonic devices, or particular quirks of that exam.

Note: Notes appear in the margins and contain various kinds of useful information, such as tips on the technology or administrative practices, historical background on terms and technologies, or side commentary on industry issues.

NOTE

Microsoft Windows Installer Although the Windows Installer Service is included in all current versions of Windows, you may need to install a redistributable to have its latest version. Later in this chapter you will see how to create a Windows Installer bootstrapper to ensure that the Windows Installer Service is updated (if necessary) on target machines.

CREATING INSTALLATION COMPONENTS

Create a Setup program that installs a Web application and allows for the application to be uninstalled.

When you develop an application using Visual Studio .NET, you may use several resources at the time of development, such as databases, event logs, performance counters, message queues, and so on. However, when you install the program on a user's machine, these resources might not be present there. A good installation program ensures that all necessary resources that are required by an application exist on the target machine.

The .NET Framework provides you with an Installer class that is defined in the System.Configuration.Install namespace. This class is specifically designed to help you perform customized installation actions like those mentioned previously. In this section I will explore various ways in which you can use the Installer class to create powerful installation programs.

I will show you how to use the predefined installation classes that are available with several components of Visual Studio .NET. I will also show you how to create your own classes that extend the Install class to perform specialized tasks at the time of installation.

Objective Coverage Text: In the text before an exam objective is specifically addressed, you will notice the objective is listed to help call your attention to that particular material.

Understanding the Installer Class

The System.Configuration.Install.Installer class works as a base class for all the custom installers in the .NET Framework. Some of the important members of Installer class that I will discuss in this chapter are listed in Table 13.2.

TABLE 13.2

IMPORTANT MEMBERS OF THE INSTALLER CLASS

Member Name	*Type*	*Description*
`Commit`	Method	The code in the `Commit()` method is executed if the `Install()` method executes successfully.
`Install`	Method	Performs the specified actions during an application's installation.

continues

WARNING

Event Log Security Allowing event log access to ASP.NET forms can be a security risk. If you're running ASP.NET as the untrusted machine account, this code won't run. You'll need to configure ASP.NET to use the trusted System account to complete this example. See Chapter 15, "Configuring a Web Application," for more details.

Warning: In using sophisticated information technology, there is always potential for mistakes or even catastrophes that can occur through improper application of the technology. Warnings appear in the margins to alert you to such potential problems.

STEP BY STEP

10.1 Running ASP and ASP.NET Pages Together

1. Open a Visual Basic ASP.NET Web Application in the Visual Studio .NET IDE.
2. Add a new Web Form to your Visual Basic .NET project. Name the new Web Form `StepByStep10-1.aspx`.
3. Add two `Label` controls and a `HyperLink` control to the Web Form. Set the ID properties of the `Label` controls to `lblDate` and `lblSession`. Set the Text property of the `HyperLink` control to "Go to Classic ASP page" and set its `NavigateUrl` property to `StepByStep10-1.asp`.
4. Add a new text file to your Visual Basic .NET project. Name the new text file `StepByStep10-1.asp`. This will make the file an ASP file.

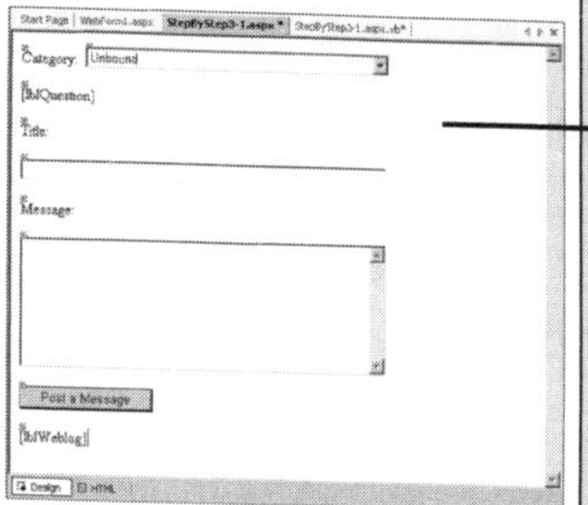

FIGURE 3.1
A design of a form that allows you to post messages to a Web log.

Figure: To improve readability, the figures have been placed in the margins wherever possible so they do not interrupt the main flow of text.

Step by Step: Step by Steps are hands-on tutorial instructions that walk you through a particular task or function relevant to the exam objectives.

EXTENSIVE REVIEW AND SELF-TEST OPTIONS

At the end of each chapter, along with some summary elements, you will find a section called "Apply Your Knowledge" that gives you several different methods with which to test your understanding of the material and review what you have learned.

CHAPTER SUMMARY

KEY TERMS

- Postback
- Round trip
- Session
- ASP.NET Application

In this chapter, you learned about how to deal with the disconnected nature of Web application by using the state management techniques provided by ASP.NET. In addition to the traditional client-side state management techniques such as query strings, cookies, and hidden variables, ASP.NET provides a new technique called as ViewState. When used carefully, ViewState can give great benefits. However careless use of ViewState can significantly increase the download size of the rendered HTML file.

You also learned about various server side state management techniques. In particular, ASP.NET provides great improvements over the session state of ASP. Session state in ASP.NET is highly configurable. With small configuration changes, you can support Web farms and cookie-less sessions.

Key Terms: A list of key terms appears at the end of each chapter. These are terms that you should be sure you know and are comfortable defining and understanding when you go in to take the exam.

Chapter Summary: Before the Apply Your Knowledge section, you will find a chapter summary that wraps up the chapter and reviews what you should have learned.

APPLY YOUR KNOWLEDGE

Exercises

15.1 Variable Caching with the Cache Object

You've already seen that you can use an `@OutputCache` directive to dictate caching that varies by input parameter. In this exercise, you'll learn how to implement the same feature by using the `Cache` object.

Estimated Time: 15 minutes.

1. Open a Visual Basic ASP.NET Web Application in the Visual Studio .NET IDE. Add a new Web Form to the application. Name the new Web Form `Exercise15-1.aspx`.
2. Place a `Label` control with the ID of `lblGenerateTime` and two `HyperLink` controls (`hlCache1` and `hlCache2`) on the form. Set the `NavigateUrl` property of the `hlCache1` control to `Exercise15-1.aspx?Cache=1` . Set the `NavigateUrl` property of the `hlCache2` control to `Exercise15-1.aspx?Cache=2`.
3. Double-click the form to open its module. Add this code to run when you load the form:

```
Private Sub Page_Load( _
 ByVal sender As System.Object, _
 ByVal e As System.EventArgs) _
 Handles MyBase.Load
    lblGenerateTime.Text = _
     DateTime.Now.ToLongTimeString()
    Response.Cache.SetExpires( _
     DateTime.Now.AddSeconds(15))
    Response.Cache.SetCacheability( _
     HttpCacheability.Public)
    Response.Cache.VaryByParams( _
     "Cache") = True
    Response.Cache. _
     SetValidUntilExpires(True)
End Sub
```

4. Set the Web Form as the start page for the project.
5. Run the project. Click the first `HyperLink` control and note the displayed time. Now click the second `HyperLink` control. Note that the displayed time is updated. Click the first `HyperLink` control again and the original displayed time will be returned from the cache. You'll find that both versions of the page are cached for 15 seconds each.

The `Cache.VaryByParams` property specifies the parameters that this page's caching depends on. By setting this to the "`Cache`" query parameter, you've caused ASP.NET to cache two separate versions of the page. You can also vary by multiple parameters by separating names with a semicolon:

```
Response.Cache.VaryByParams("City;State") =
True
```

Or you can tell ASP.NET to vary with every parameter it receives by specifying an asterisk:

```
Response.Cache.VaryByParams("*") = True
```

15.2 Application Data Caching

Caching is not limited to the output of ASP.NET pages. Because you have programmatic access to the `Cache` object, you can place anything you like in the cache. You can set time-based expiration policies, or (as in the following exercise) you can tie the expiration of a cached item to an external resource such as a file

Review Questions

1. How many configuration files can apply to a single ASP.NET page?
2. Explain the use of the `allowDefinition` and `allowLocation` attributes in configuration file section tags.
3. What is the purpose of `allowOverride="False"` in a configuration file?
4. What are authentication and authorization?

Exercises: These activities provide an opportunity for you to master specific hands-on tasks. Our goal is to increase your proficiency with the product or technology. You must be able to conduct these tasks in order to pass the exam.

Review Questions: These open-ended, short-answer questions allow you to quickly assess your comprehension of what you just read in the chapter. Instead of asking you to choose from a list of options, these questions require you to state the correct answers in your own words. Although you will not experience these kinds of questions on the exam, these questions will indeed test your level of comprehension of key concepts.

Exam Questions: These questions reflect the kinds of questions that appear on the actual vendor exam. Use them to become familiar with the exam question formats and to help you determine what you know and what you need to review or study more.

APPLY YOUR KNOWLEDGE

5. What are the default accounts for the ASP.NET process?
6. Name four types of authentication that you can specify in an ASP.NET configuration file.
7. What is meant by impersonation in ASP.NET?
8. Name three types of caching.
9. Name three places that you can store session state information in ASP.NET.
10. What do the `WindowsIdentity` and `WindowsPrincipal` objects represent?

Exam Questions

1. You are adding a section to the `machine.config` file on your ASP.NET Web server. You want to ensure that this section cannot be defined in any other configuration file. Which declaration should you use?

   A.

```
<section name="customSection"
     type="CustomConfiguration Handler"
     allowDefinition=
     "MachineToApplication"/>
```

   B.

```
<section name="customSection"
     type="CustomConfiguration Handler"
     allowLocation="false"/>
```

   C.

```
<section name="customSection"
     type="CustomConfiguration Handler" />
```

   D.

```
<section name="customSection"
     type="CustomConfiguration Handler"
     allowOverride="false"/>
```

2. You have adjusted a setting in one of your ASP.NET application's configuration files by editing the file with Notepad. What must you do to have the new setting take effect?

   A. Restart the Web server.

   B. Reboot the computer that hosts the Web server.

   C. Open the file in Visual Studio .NET.

   D. Save the file.

3. Your ASP.NET application requires users to be authenticated with a strong identity. You must allow users with any version 4.x or better browser, and you want passwords to cross the network only with secure encryption. Which authentication should you use?

   A. Windows authentication with Basic IIS authentication.

   B. Windows authentication with digest IIS authentication.

   C. Windows authentication with integrated IIS authentication.

   D. Passport authentication with anonymous IIS authentication.

4. You have implemented forms-based authentication for your ASP.NET application. Some users report that they cannot access any resources on the site, even though you have verified that these users are entering correct authentication information. What could be the problem?

   A. These users are using a browser other than Internet Explorer.

   B. These users have disabled cookies for your Web site.

Answers and Explanations: For each of the Review and Exam questions, you will find thorough explanations located at the end of the section.

Suggested Readings and Resources: The very last element in every chapter is a list of additional resources you can use if you want to go above and beyond certification-level material or if you need to spend more time on a particular subject that you are having trouble understanding.

Suggested Readings and Resources

1. Visual Studio .NET Combined Help Collection
   - Designing Accessible Applications topic
2. W3C WAI Web site, `http://www.w3.org/WAI/`.
3. Section 508 Web site, `http://www.section508.gov/`.

Introduction

MCSD Training Guide: Visual Basic .NET Web-Based Applications is designed for developers who are pursuing the Microsoft Certified Application Developer (MCAD) or Microsoft Certified Solution Developer (MCSD) certifications from Microsoft. This book covers the Developing and Implementing Windows-based Applications with Microsoft Visual Basic .NET and Microsoft Visual Studio .NET exam (70-306), which is a core exam for both of those certifications. The exam is designed to measure your skill in developing Windows-based applications using Windows Forms and the other tools in the Microsoft .NET Framework, with Visual Basic .NET as your programming language.

This book is designed to cover all the objectives that Microsoft created for this exam. It doesn't offer end-to-end coverage of the Visual Basic .NET language or the .NET Framework; rather, it helps you develop the specific core competencies that Microsoft says VB .NET-based Web application developers need to master. You can pass the exam by learning the material in this book, without taking a class. Of course, depending on your own personal study habits and learning style, you might benefit from studying this book *and* taking a class.

Even if you're not planning to take the exam, you may find this book useful. Experienced Visual Basic and ASP developers looking for a reference on the new features of VB .NET and ASP.NET in particular should appreciate the coverage of topics here.

How This Book Helps You

This book gives you a self-guided tour of all the areas of the product that are covered by the VB .NET Web Applications exam. The goal is to teach you the specific skills that you need to achieve your MCAD or MCSD certification. You'll also find helpful hints, tips, examples, exercises, and references to additional study materials. Specifically, this book is set up to help you in the following ways:

Organization

This book is organized around the individual objectives from Microsoft's preparation guide for the VB .NET Web-based Applications exam. Every objective is covered in this book. They're not covered in exactly the same order that you'll find them on the official preparation guide (which you can download from `http://www.microsoft.com/traincert/exams/70-305.asp`), but reorganized for more logical teaching. I've also tried to make the information more accessible in several ways:

- This introduction includes the full list of exam topics and objectives.
- Read the "Study and Exam Tips" section early on to help you develop study strategies while using this Training Guide. It also provides you with valuable exam-day tips and information.
- Each chapter starts with a list of objectives that are covered in that chapter.

- Each chapter also begins with an outline that provides an overview of the material for that chapter as well as the page numbers where specific topics can be found.
- I've also repeated each objective in the text where it is covered in detail.

Instructional Features

This book has been designed to provide you with multiple ways to learn and reinforce the exam material. Here are some of the instructional features you'll find inside:

- *Objective Explanations.* As mentioned previously, each chapter begins with a list of the objectives covered in the chapter. In addition, immediately following each objective is a more detailed explanation that puts the objective in the context of the product.
- *Study Strategies.* Each chapter also offers a selected list of study strategies—exercises to try or additional material to read that will help you in learning and retaining the material that you'll find in the chapter.
- *Exam Tips.* Exam tips appear in the margin to provide specific exam-related advice. Such tips might address what material is likely to be covered (or not covered) on the exam, how to remember it, or particular exam quirks.
- *Review Breaks and Summaries.* Crucial information is summarized at various points in the book in lists of key points you need to remember. Each chapter ends with an overall summary of the material covered in that chapter as well.
- *Guided Practice Exercises.* These exercises offer you additional opportunities to practice the material within a chapter and to learn additional facets of the topic at hand.
- *Key Terms.* A list of key terms appears at the end of each chapter.
- *Notes.* These appear in the margin and contain various kinds of useful information such as tips on technology, historical background, side commentary, or notes on where to go for more detailed coverage of a particular topic.
- *Warnings.* When using sophisticated computing technology, there is always the possibility of mistakes or even catastrophes. Warnings appear in the margin to alert you of such potential problems, whether they're in following along with the text or in implementing VB .NET in a production environment.
- *Step by Steps.* These are hands-on, tutorial instructions that lead you through a particular task or function relevant to the exam objectives.
- *Exercises.* Found at the end of each chapter in the "Apply Your Knowledge" section, the exercises may include additional tutorial material and more chances to practice the skills that you learned in the chapter.

Extensive Practice Test Options

The book provides numerous opportunities for you to assess your knowledge and practice for the exam. The practice options include the following:

- *Review Questions.* These open-ended questions appear in the "Apply Your Knowledge" section at the end of each chapter. They allow you to quickly assess your comprehension of what you just read in the chapter. The answers are provided later in the section.
- *Exam Questions.* These questions also appear in the "Apply Your Knowledge" section. They reflect the kinds of multiple-choice questions that appear on the Microsoft exams. Use them to practice for the exam and to help you determine what you know and what you may need to review or study further. Answers and explanations are provided later in the section.
- *Practice Exam.* The "Final Review" section includes a complete practice exam. The Final Review section and the Practice Exam are discussed in more detail later in this chapter.
- *PrepLogic.* The *PrepLogic, Preview Edition* software included on the CD-ROM provides further practice questions.

> NOTE
>
> ***PrepLogic, Preview Edition Software***
> For a complete description of the PrepLogic test engine, please see Appendix D, "*Using the PrepLogic, Preview Edition Software.*"

Final Review

This part of the book provides you with two valuable tools for preparing for the exam:

- *Fast Facts.* This condensed version of the information contained in the book will prove extremely useful for last-minute review.
- *Practice Exam.* A full practice test for the exam is included, with questions written in the style and format used on the actual exam. Use it to assess your readiness for the real thing.

This book includes several valuable appendixes as well, including a glossary (Appendix A), an overview of the Microsoft certification program (Appendix B), and a description of what is on the CD-ROM (Appendix C). Appendix D covers the use of the *PrepLogic, Preview Edition* software. Finally, Appendix E provides you with a list of suggested readings and resources that contain useful information on Visual Basic .NET and the .NET Framework.

These and all the other book features mentioned previously will provide you with thorough preparation for the exam.

For more information about the exam or the certification process, you should contact Microsoft directly:

By email: mailto:*MCPHelp@microsoft.com*

By regular mail, telephone, or fax, contact the Microsoft Regional Education Service Center (RESC) nearest you. You can find lists of Regional Education Service Centers at `http://www.microsoft.com/traincert/support/northamerica.asp` (for North America) or `http://www.microsoft.com/traincert/support/worldsites.asp` (worldwide).

On the Internet: `http://www.microsoft.com/traincert/`

WHAT THE DEVELOPING AND IMPLEMENTING WEB APPLICATIONS WITH MICROSOFT VISUAL BASIC .NET AND MICROSOFT VISUAL STUDIO .NET EXAM (70-305) COVERS

The Developing and Implementing Web Applications with Microsoft Visual Basic .NET and Microsoft Visual Studio .NET exam covers seven major topic areas: Creating User Services, Creating and Managing Components and .NET Assemblies, Consuming and Manipulating Data, Testing and Debugging, Deploying a Web Application, Maintaining and Supporting a Web Application, and Configuring and Securing a Web Application. The exam objectives are listed by topic area in the following sections.

Creating User Services

Create ASP.NET Pages.

- Add and set directives on ASP.NET pages.
- Separate user interface resources from business logic.

Add Web server controls, HTML server controls, user controls, and HTML code to ASP.NET pages.

- Set properties on controls.
- Load controls dynamically.
- Apply templates.
- Set styles on ASP.NET pages by using cascading style sheets.
- Instantiate and invoke an ActiveX control.

Implement navigation for the user interface (UI).

- Manage the view state.
- Manage data during postback events.
- Use session state to manage data across pages.

Validate user input.

- Validate non-Latin user input.

Implement error handling in the user interface.

- Configure custom error pages.
- Implement Global.asax, application, page-level, and page event error handling.

Implement online user assistance.

Incorporate existing code into ASP.NET pages.

Display and update data.

- Transform and filter data.
- Bind data to the user interface.
- Use controls to display data.

Instantiate and invoke Web service or components.

- Instantiate and invoke a Web service.
- Instantiate and invoke a COM or COM+ component.
- Instantiate and invoke a .NET component.
- Call native functions by using platform invoke.

Implement globalization.

- Implement localizability for the UI.
- Convert existing encodings.
- Implement right-to-left and left-to-right mirroring.
- Prepare culture-specific formatting.

Handle events.

- Create event handlers.
- Raise events.

Implement accessibility features.

Use and edit intrinsic objects. Intrinsic objects include response, request, session, server, and application.

- Retrieve values from the properties of intrinsic objects.
- Set values on the properties of intrinsic objects.
- Use intrinsic objects to perform operations.

Creating and Managing Components and .NET Assemblies

Create and modify a .NET assembly.

- Create and implement satellite assemblies.
- Create resource-only assemblies.

Create Web custom controls and Web user controls.

Consuming and Manipulating Data

Access and manipulate data from a Microsoft SQL Server database by creating and using ad hoc queries and stored procedures.

Access and manipulate data from a data store. Data stores include relational databases, XML documents, and flat files. Methods include XML techniques and ADO .NET.

Handle data errors.

Testing and Debugging

Create a unit test plan.

Implement tracing.

- Add trace listeners and trace switches to an application.
- Display trace output.

Debug, rework, and resolve defects in code.

- Configure the debugging environment.
- Create and apply debugging code to components, pages, and applications.
- Provide multicultural test data to components, pages, and applications.
- Execute tests.
- Resolve errors and rework code.

Deploying a Web Application

Plan the deployment of a Windows-based application.

- Plan a deployment that uses removable media.
- Plan a Web-based deployment.

- Plan the deployment of an application to a Web garden, a Web farm, or a cluster.

Create a setup program that installs a Web application and allows for the application to be uninstalled.

Deploy a Web application.

Add assemblies to the Global Assembly Cache.

Maintaining and Supporting a Web Application

Optimize the performance of a Web application.

Diagnose and resolve errors and issues.

Configuring and Securing a Web Application

Configure a Web application.

- Modify the web.config file.
- Modify the Machine.config file.
- Add and modify application settings.

Configure security for a Web application.

- Select and configure authentication type. Authentication types include Windows Authentication, None, forms-based, Microsoft Passport, and custom authentication.

Configure authorization.

- Configure role-based authorization.
- Implement impersonation.

Configure and implement caching. Caching types include output, fragment, and data.

- Use a cache object.
- Use cache directives.

Configure and implement session state in various topologies such as a Web garden and a Web farm.

- Use session state within a process.
- Use session state with session state service.
- Use session state with Microsoft SQL Server.

Install and configure server services.

- Install and configure a Web server.
- Install and configure Microsoft FrontPage Server Extensions.

What You Should Know Before Reading This Book

The Microsoft Visual Basic .NET exams assume that you're familiar with the Visual Basic language and the use of Visual Studio .NET to create applications, even though there are no objectives that pertain directly to this knowledge. I'll show you tasks that are directly related to exam objectives, but this book does not include a tutorial in Visual Basic .NET itself. If you're just getting started with the language, you should check out some of the references in Appendix E for the information that you'll need to get you started. For beginners, I particularly recommend these references:

- The Samples and QuickStart Tutorials, which are installed as part of the .NET Framework SDK (a component of a full Visual Studio .NET installation) are an excellent starting point for information on Windows Forms and common tasks.

- *Special Edition Using Microsoft Visual Basic .NET*, by Brian Siler and Jeff Spotts (Que, 2002)
- *Visual Basic .NET: The Complete Reference*, by Jeffrey R. Shapiro (McGraw-Hill/Osborne, 2002)
- *Programming Visual Basic .NET*, by Dave Grundgeiger (O'Reilly, 2002)
- *Mastering ASP.NET with VB.NET*, by A. Russell Jones (Sybex, 2002)
- *VB.NET Language in a Nutshell*, by Steven Roman, Ron Petrusha and Paul Lomax (O'Reilly, 2002)

HARDWARE AND SOFTWARE YOU'LL NEED

Although you can build Visual Basic ASP.NET applications using nothing more than the tools provided in the free .NET Framework SDK, to pass the exam you'll need to have access to a copy of Visual Studio .NET, which includes many tools and features not found in the free command-line tools. There are three editions of Visual Studio .NET:

- *Professional*. Visual Studio .NET Professional is the entry-level product in the product line. This edition allows you to build Windows, ASP.NET, and Web services applications. It includes visual design tools, Crystal Reports, and the MSDE version of SQL Server 2000.
- *Enterprise Developer*. Building on the Professional edition, the Enterprise Developer edition adds the full version of SQL Server 2000, Visual SourceSafe, Application Center Test, Visual Studio Analyzer, and developer licenses for Exchange Server, Host Integration Server, and Commerce Server. It also contains additional samples and templates.
- *Enterprise Architect*. The high-end Enterprise Architect edition adds Visio Enterprise Architect, a development license for SQL Server, and high-end enterprise templates.

You should be able to complete all of the exercises in this book with any of the three editions of Visual Studio .NET. Your computer should meet the minimum criteria required for a Visual Studio .NET installation:

- Pentium II or better CPU running at 450 MHz or faster.
- Windows NT 4.0 or later.
- Memory depending on the operating system you have installed: 64MB for Windows NT 4.0 Workstation, 96MB for Windows 2000 Professional, 160MB for Windows NT 4.0 Server or Windows XP Professional, or 192MB for Windows 2000 Server.
- 3.5GB of disk space for a full installation.
- CD-ROM or DVD drive.
- Video card running at 800×600 with at least 256 colors.
- Microsoft or compatible mouse.

Of course, those are *minimum* requirements. I recommend the following more realistic requirements:

- Pentium III or better CPU running at 800 MHz or faster.
- Windows 2000.
- At least 256MB of RAM, and as much more as you can afford.
- 5GB of disk space for a full installation.
- CD-ROM or DVD drive.
- Video card running at 1280×1024 or higher with at least 65,000 colors.
- Microsoft or compatible mouse.

You may find it easier to obtain access to the necessary computer hardware and software in a corporate environment. It can be difficult, however, to allocate enough time within a busy workday to complete a self-study program. Most of your study time will probably need to occur outside of normal working hours, away from the everyday interruptions and pressures of your job.

Advice on Taking the Exam

You'll find more extensive tips in "Study and Exam Prep Tips," but keep this advice in mind as you study:

- Read all the material. Microsoft has been known to include material not expressly specified in the objectives for an exam. This book includes additional information not reflected in the objectives in an effort to give you the best possible preparation for the examination—and for the real-world experiences to come.
- Do the Step by Steps and complete the Exercises in each chapter. They will help you gain experience with Visual Basic .NET. All Microsoft exams are task- and experience-based and require you to have experience using the Microsoft products, not just reading about them.
- Use the questions to assess your knowledge. Don't just read the chapter content; use the questions to find out what you know and what you don't. Study some more, review, and then assess your knowledge again.
- Review the exam objectives. Develop your own questions and examples for each topic listed. If you can develop and answer several questions for each topic, you should not find it difficult to pass the exam.

Remember, the primary objective is not to pass the exam—it is to understand the material. After you understand the material, passing the exam should be simple. To really work with Visual Basic .NET, you need a solid foundation in practical skills. This book, and the Microsoft Certified Professional program, are designed to ensure that you have that solid foundation.

Good luck!

EXAM TIP

No Substitute for Experience The single best study tip that anyone can give you is to actually work with the product that you're learning! Even if you could become a "paper MCAD" simply by reading books, you wouldn't get the real-world skills that you need to be a Visual Basic .NET success.

Study and Exam Prep Tips

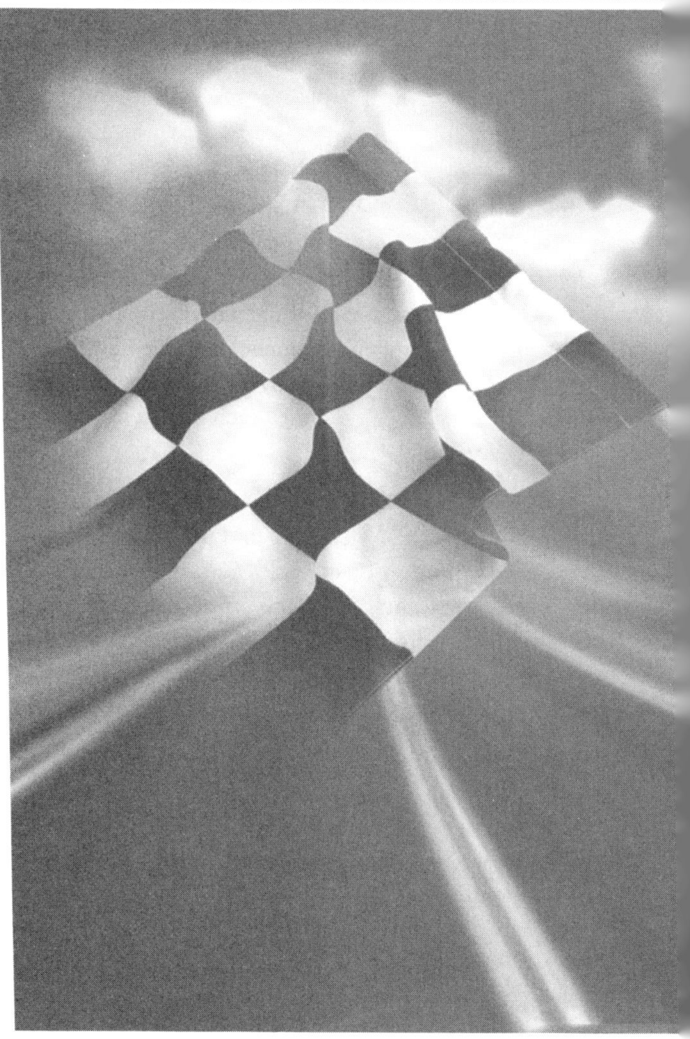

There are many ways to approach studying, just as there are many different types of material to study. However, the tips that follow should work well for the type of material covered on the certification exams.

STUDY STRATEGIES

Although individuals vary in the ways they learn information, some basic principles of learning apply to everyone. You should adopt some study strategies that take advantage of these principles. One of these principles is that learning can be broken into various depths. Recognition (of terms, for example) exemplifies a more surface level of learning in which you rely on a prompt of some sort to elicit recall. Comprehension or understanding (of the concepts behind the terms, for example) represents a deeper level of learning. The ability to analyze a concept and apply your understanding of it in a new way represents a further depth of learning.

Your learning strategy should enable you to know the material at a level or two deeper than mere recognition. This will help you do well on the exams. You will know the material so thoroughly that you can easily handle the recognition-level types of questions used in multiple-choice testing. You will also be able to apply your knowledge to solve new problems.

Macro and Micro Study Strategies

One strategy that can lead to this deeper learning includes preparing an outline that covers all the objectives and subobjectives for the particular exam you are working on. You should delve a bit further into the material and include a level or two of detail beyond the stated objectives and subobjectives for the exam. Then expand the outline by coming up with a statement of definition or a summary for each point in the outline.

An outline provides two approaches to studying. First, you can study the outline by focusing on the organization of the material. Work your way through the points and subpoints of your outline with the goal of learning how they relate to one another. For example, be sure you understand how each of the main objective areas is similar to and different from another. Then do the same thing with the subobjectives; be sure you know which subobjectives pertain to each objective area and how they relate to one another.

Next, you can work through the outline, focusing on learning the details. Memorize and understand terms and their definitions, facts, rules and strategies, advantages and disadvantages, and so on. In this pass through the outline, attempt to learn detail rather than the big picture (the organizational information that you worked on in the first pass through the outline).

Research has shown that attempting to assimilate both types of information at the same time seems to interfere with the overall learning process. Separate your studying into these two approaches and you will perform better on the exam.

Active Study Strategies

The process of writing down and defining objectives, subobjectives, terms, facts, and definitions promotes a more active learning strategy than merely reading the material. In human information-processing terms, writing forces you to engage in more active encoding of the information. Simply reading over it exemplifies more passive processing.

Next, determine whether you can apply the information you have learned by attempting to create examples and scenarios on your own. Think about how or where you could apply the concepts you are learning. Again, write down this information to process the facts and concepts in a more active fashion.

The hands-on nature of the Step by Step tutorials and the Exercises at the ends of the chapters provide further active learning opportunities that will reinforce concepts as well.

Common-Sense Strategies

Finally, you should also follow common-sense practices when studying. Study when you are alert, reduce or eliminate distractions, take breaks when you become fatigued, and so on.

Pre-Testing Yourself

Pre-testing enables you to assess how well you are learning. One of the most important aspects of learning is what has been called *meta-learning*. Meta-learning has to do with realizing when you know something well or when you need to study some more. In other words, you recognize how well or how poorly you have learned the material you are studying.

For most people, this can be difficult to assess objectively on their own. Practice tests are useful in that they reveal more objectively what you have learned and what you have not learned. You should use this information to guide review and further studying. Developmental learning takes place as you cycle through studying, assessing how well you have learned, reviewing, and assessing again until you feel you are ready to take the exam.

You may have noticed the practice exam included in this book, and the *PrepLogic, Preview Edition* software on the CD-ROM. These tools are excellent for providing extra exam preparation opportunities. Use these extensively as part of the learning process.

You should set a goal for your pre-testing. A reasonable goal would be to score consistently in the 90-percent range.

See Appendix D, "Using the *PrepLogic, Preview Edition Software*," for a more detailed explanation of the test engine.

Exam Prep Tips

Having mastered the subject matter, the final preparatory step is to understand how the exam will be presented. Make no mistake, a Microsoft Certified Professional (MCP) exam will challenge both your knowledge and test-taking skills. This section starts with the basics of exam design, reviews a new type of exam format, and concludes with hints targeted to each of the exam formats.

The MCP Exam

Every MCP exam is released in one of two basic formats. What's being called exam format here is really little more than a combination of the overall exam structure and the presentation method for exam questions.

Each exam format uses the same types of questions. These types or styles of questions include multiple-rating (or scenario-based) questions, traditional multiple-choice questions, and simulation-based questions. It's important to understand the types of questions you will be asked and the actions required to properly answer them.

Understanding the exam formats is key to good preparation because the format determines the number of questions presented, the difficulty of those questions, and the amount of time allowed to complete the exam.

Exam Format

There are two basic formats for the MCP exams: the traditional fixed-form exam and the adaptive form. As its name implies, the fixed-form exam presents a fixed set of questions during the exam session. The adaptive form, however, uses only a subset of questions drawn from a larger pool during any given exam session.

Fixed-Form

A fixed-form computerized exam is based on a fixed set of exam questions. The individual questions are presented in random order during a test session. If you take the same exam more than once you won't necessarily see the exact same questions. This is because two or three final forms are typically assembled for every fixed-form exam Microsoft releases. These are usually labeled Forms A, B, and C.

The final forms of a fixed-form exam are identical in terms of content coverage, number of questions, and allotted time, but the questions are different. You may notice, however, that some of the same questions appear on, or rather are shared among, different final forms. When questions are shared among multiple final forms of an exam, the percentage of sharing is generally small. Many final forms share no questions, but some older exams may have a 10 percent to 15 percent duplication of exam questions on the final exam forms.

Fixed-form exams also have a fixed time limit in which you must complete the exam. The *PrepLogic, Preview Edition* software on the CD-ROM that accompanies this book carries fixed-form exams.

Finally, the score you achieve on a fixed-form exam, which is always reported for MCP exams on a scale of 0 to 1,000, is based on the number of questions you answer correctly. The exam's passing score is the same for all final forms of a given fixed-form exam.

The typical format for the fixed-form exam is as follows:

- 50–60 questions.
- 75–90 minute testing time.
- Question review is allowed, including the opportunity to change your answers.

Adaptive Form

An adaptive-form exam has the same appearance as a fixed-form exam, but its questions differ in quantity and process of selection. Although the statistics of adaptive testing are fairly complex, the process is concerned with determining your level of skill or ability with the exam subject matter. This ability assessment begins by presenting questions of varying levels of difficulty and ascertaining at what difficulty level you can reliably answer them. Finally, the ability assessment determines if that ability level is above or below the level required to pass that exam.

Examinees at different levels of ability will see quite different sets of questions. Examinees who demonstrate little expertise with the subject matter will continue to be presented with relatively easy questions. Examinees who demonstrate a high level of expertise will be presented progressively more difficult questions. Individuals of both levels of expertise may answer the same number of questions correctly, but because the higher-expertise examinee can correctly answer more difficult questions, he or she will receive a higher score and is more likely to pass the exam.

The typical design for the adaptive form exam is as follows:

- 20–25 questions.
- 90 minute testing time, although this is likely to be reduced to 45–60 minutes in the near future.
- Question review is not allowed, providing no opportunity to change your answers.

The Adaptive-Exam Process

Your first adaptive exam will be unlike any other testing experience you have had. In fact, many examinees have difficulty accepting the adaptive testing process because they feel that they were not provided the opportunity to adequately demonstrate their full expertise.

You can take consolation in the fact that adaptive exams are painstakingly put together after months of data gathering and analysis and are just as valid as a fixed-form exam. The rigor introduced through the adaptive testing methodology means that there is nothing arbitrary about what you'll see. It is also a more efficient means of testing, requiring less time to conduct and complete.

As you can see from Figure 1, a number of statistical measures drive the adaptive examination process. The most immediately relevant to you is the ability estimate. Accompanying this test statistic are the standard error of measurement, the item characteristic curve, and the test information curve.

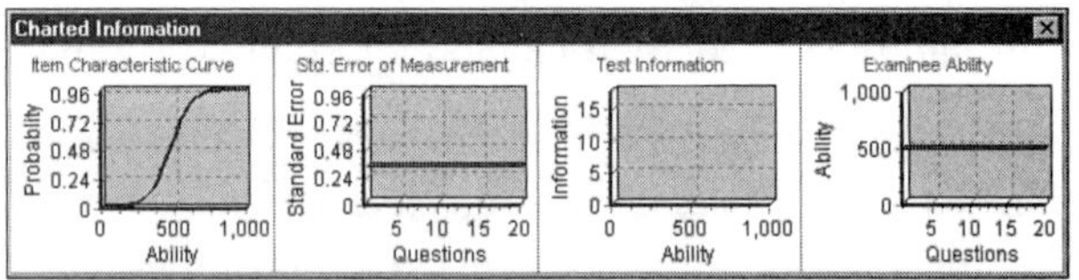

FIGURE 1
Microsoft's Adaptive Testing Demonstration Program.

The standard error, which is the key factor in determining when an adaptive exam will terminate, reflects the degree of error in the exam ability estimate. The item characteristic curve reflects the probability of a correct response relative to examinee ability. Finally, the test information statistic provides a measure of the information contained in the set of questions the examinee has answered, again relative to the ability level of the individual examinee.

When you begin an adaptive exam, the standard error has already been assigned a target value it must drop below for the exam to conclude. This target value reflects a particular level of statistical confidence in the process. The examinee ability is initially set to the mean possible exam score (500 for MCP exams).

As the adaptive exam progresses, questions of varying difficulty are presented. Based on your pattern of responses to these questions, the ability estimate is recalculated. Simultaneously, the standard error estimate is refined from its first estimated value of one toward the target value. When the standard error reaches its target value, the exam terminates. Thus, the more consistently you answer questions of the same degree of difficulty, the more quickly the standard error estimate drops, and the fewer questions you will end up seeing during the exam session. This situation is depicted in Figure 2.

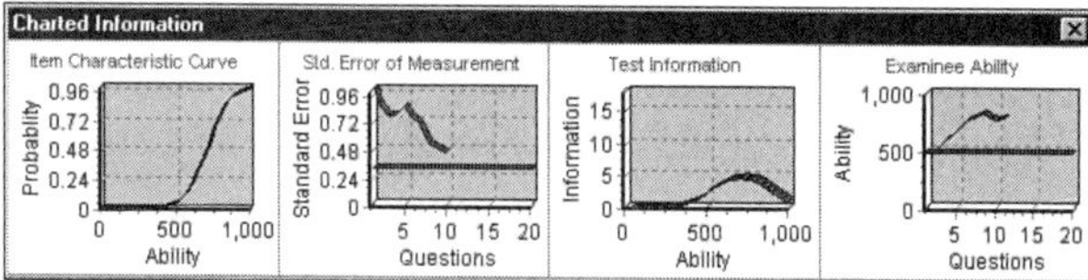

FIGURE 2
The changing statistics in an adaptive exam.

As you might suspect, one good piece of advice for taking an adaptive exam is to treat every exam question as if it is the most important. The adaptive scoring algorithm attempts to discover a pattern of responses that reflects some level of proficiency with the subject matter. Incorrect responses almost guarantee that additional questions must be answered (unless, of course, you get every question wrong). This is because the scoring algorithm must adjust to information that is not consistent with the emerging pattern.

New Question Types

A variety of question types can appear on MCP exams. Examples of multiple-choice questions and scenario-based questions appear throughout this book and the *PrepLogic, Preview Edition* software. Simulation-based questions are new to the MCP exam series.

Simulation Questions

Simulation-based questions reproduce the look and feel of key Microsoft product features for the purpose of testing. The simulation software used in MCP exams has been designed to look and act, as much as possible, just like the actual product. Consequently, answering simulation questions in a MCP exam entails completing one or more tasks just as if you were using the product itself.

The format of a typical Microsoft simulation question consists of a brief scenario or problem statement along with one or more tasks that must be completed to solve the problem.

A Typical Simulation Question

It sounds obvious, but your first step when you encounter a simulation is to carefully read the question. Do not go straight to the simulation application! You must assess the problem being presented and identify the conditions that make up the problem scenario. Note the tasks that must be performed or outcomes that must be achieved to answer the question and review any instructions on how to proceed.

The next step is to launch the simulator by using the button provided. After clicking the Show Simulation button, you will see a feature of the product presented in a dialog box. The simulation application will partially cover the question text on many test center machines. Feel free to reposition the simulation or move between the question text screen and the simulation by using hotkeys, point-and-click navigation, or even clicking the simulation launch button again.

It is important to understand that your answer to the simulation question will not be recorded until you move on to the next exam question. This gives you the added capability to close and reopen the simulation application (using the launch button) on the same question without losing any partial answer you may have made.

The third step is to use the simulator as you would the actual product to solve the problem or perform the defined tasks. Again, the simulation software is designed to function, within reason, just as the product does. But don't expect the simulation to reproduce product behavior perfectly. Most importantly, do not allow yourself to become flustered if the simulation does not look or act exactly like the product.

There are two final points that will help you tackle simulation questions. First, respond only to what is being asked in the question; do not solve problems that you are not asked to solve. Second, accept what is being asked of you. You may not entirely agree with conditions in the problem statement, the quality of the desired solution, or the sufficiency of defined tasks to adequately solve the problem. Always remember that you are being tested on your ability to solve the problem as it is presented. If you make any changes beyond those required by the question, the item will be scored as wrong on an MCP exam.

Putting It All Together

Given all these different pieces of information, the task now is to assemble a set of tips that will help you successfully tackle the different types of MCP exams.

More Pre-Exam Preparation Tips

Generic exam-preparation advice is always useful. Tips include the following:

- Become familiar with the product. Hands-on experience is one of the keys to success on any MCP exam. Review the exercises and the Step by Steps in the book.
- Review the current exam-preparation guide on the Microsoft MCP Web site. The documentation Microsoft makes available over the Web identifies the skills every exam is intended to test.
- Memorize foundational technical detail, but remember that MCP exams are generally heavy on problem solving and application of knowledge rather than just questions that require only rote memorization.
- Take any of the available practice tests. We recommend the one included in this book and the ones you can complete using the *PrepLogic, Preview Edition* software on the CD-ROM, and visiting the PrepLogic Web site for purchase of further practice exams if you feel the need for more examination practice. Although these are fixed-form exams, they provide preparation that is just as valuable for taking an adaptive exam. Because of the nature of adaptive testing, these practice exams cannot be done in the adaptive form. However, fixed-form exams use the same types of questions as adaptive exams and are the most effective way to prepare for either type.
- Look on the Microsoft MCP Web site for samples and demonstration items. These tend to be particularly valuable for one significant reason: They help you become familiar with any new testing technologies before you encounter them on a MCP exam.

During the Exam Session

The following generic exam-taking advice you've heard for years applies when taking a MCP exam:

- Take a deep breath and try to relax when you first sit down for your exam session. It is very important to control the pressure you may (naturally) feel when taking exams.
- You will be provided scratch paper. Take a moment to write down any factual information and technical detail that you committed to short-term memory.
- Carefully read all information and instruction screens. These displays have been put together to give you information relevant to the exam you are taking.
- Accept the Non-Disclosure Agreement and preliminary survey as part of the examination process. Complete them accurately and quickly move on.
- Read the exam questions carefully. Reread each question to identify all relevant detail.
- Tackle the questions in the order they are presented. Skipping around won't build your confidence; the clock is always counting down.
- Don't rush, but also don't linger on difficult questions. The questions vary in degree of difficulty. Don't let yourself be flustered by a particularly difficult or verbose question.

Fixed-Form Exams

Building from this basic preparation and test-taking advice, you also need to consider the challenges presented by the different exam designs. Because a fixed-form exam is composed of a fixed, finite set of questions, add these tips to your strategy for taking a fixed-form exam:

- Note the time allotted and the number of questions appearing on the exam you are taking. Make a rough calculation of how many minutes you can spend on each question and use this to pace yourself through the exam.
- Take advantage of the fact that you can return to and review skipped or previously answered questions. Record the questions you can't answer confidently, noting the relative difficulty of each question, on the scratch paper provided. Once you've made it to the end of the exam, return to the more difficult questions.
- If there is session time remaining once you have completed all questions (and if you aren't too fatigued!), review your answers. Pay particular attention to questions that seem to have a lot of detail or that require graphics.
- As for changing your answers, the general rule of thumb here is *don't*! If you read the question carefully and completely and you felt like you knew the right answer, you probably did. Don't second-guess yourself. If, as you check your answers, one clearly stands out as incorrectly marked, however, of course you should change it in that instance. If you are at all unsure, go with your first impression.

Adaptive Exams

If you are planning to take an adaptive exam, keep these additional tips in mind:

- Read and answer every question with great care. When reading a question, identify every relevant detail, requirement, or task that must be performed and double-check your answer to be sure you have addressed every one of them.
- If you cannot answer a question, use the process of elimination to reduce the set of potential answers, and then take your best guess. Stupid mistakes invariably mean additional questions will be presented.

- Forget about reviewing questions and changing your answers. Once you leave a question, whether you've answered it or not, you cannot return to it. Do not skip any questions either; once you do, they are counted as incorrect.

Simulation Questions

You may encounter simulation questions on either the fixed-form or adaptive-form exam. If you do, keep these tips in mind:

- Avoid changing any simulation settings that don't pertain directly to the problem solution. Solve the problem you are being asked to solve and nothing more.
- Assume default settings when related information has not been provided. If something has not been mentioned or defined, it is a noncritical detail that does not factor into the correct solution.
- Be sure your entries are syntactically correct, paying particular attention to your spelling. Enter relevant information just as the product would require it.
- Close all simulation application windows after completing the simulation tasks. The testing system software is designed to trap errors that could result when using the simulation application, but trust yourself over the testing software.
- If simulations are part of a fixed-form exam, you can return to skipped or previously answered questions and change your answer. However, if you choose to change your answer to a simulation question or even attempt to review the settings you've made in the simulation application, your previous response to that simulation question will be deleted. If simulations are part of an adaptive exam, you cannot return to previous questions.

Final Considerations

Finally, there are a number of changes in the MCP program that will impact how frequently you can repeat an exam and what you will see when you do.

- Microsoft has instituted a new exam retake policy. This new rule is "two and two, then one and two." That is, you can attempt any exam twice with no restrictions on the time between attempts. But after the second attempt, you must wait two weeks before you can attempt that exam again. After that, you will be required to wait two weeks between subsequent attempts. Plan to pass the exam in two attempts or plan to increase your time horizon for receiving a MCP credential.
- New questions are being seeded into the MCP exams. After performance data is gathered on new questions, the examiners will replace older questions on all exam forms. This means that the questions appearing on exams will be regularly changing.
- Many of the current MCP exams will be republished in adaptive form in the coming months. Prepare yourself for this significant change in testing as it is entirely likely that this will become the preferred MCP exam format.

These changes mean that the brute-force strategies for passing MCP exams are much less viable than they once were. So if you don't pass an exam on the first or second attempt, it is entirely possible that the exam's form will change significantly the next time you take it. It could be updated to adaptive form from fixed form or have a different set of questions or question types.

The intention of Microsoft is clearly not to make the exams more difficult by introducing unwanted change, but to create and maintain valid measures of the technical skills and knowledge associated with the different MCP credentials. Preparing for a MCP exam has always involved not only studying the subject matter, but also planning for the testing experience itself. With the recent changes, this is now truer than ever.

PART I

DEVELOPING WEB APPLICATIONS

OBJECTIVES

This chapter covers the following Microsoft-specified objectives for the "Creating User Services" section of Exam 70-305, "Developing and Implementing Web Applications with Microsoft Visual Basic .NET and Microsoft Visual Studio .NET":

Create ASP.NET pages.

- **Add and set directives on ASP.NET pages.**
- **Separate user interface resources from business logic.**

▶ ASP.NET pages are compiled into a class before they are executed. Directives in the page's code specify settings used by the page compiler when it processes ASP.NET pages. You should know what these directives are and how to use them in your programs.

▶ ASP.NET promotes separating the user-interface portion of the Web page from its business logic. This separation leads to development of Web pages that are easier to develop and maintain. This technique, also known as code-behind, is the preferred way of creating ASP.NET pages in Visual Studio .NET.

Handle events.

- **Create event handlers.**
- **Raise events.**

▶ Event handling is the core part of programming a user interface. An event enables a class to notify other classes when something of interest happens. Generating such notifications is also called *raising the event*. You should know about several events provided by the .NET Framework classes. In addition to this, you need to know how to raise a custom event.

▶ When an object takes some action in response to an event, it is said to *handle* the event. You are required to know several ways in which you can handle an event in an ASP.NET page.

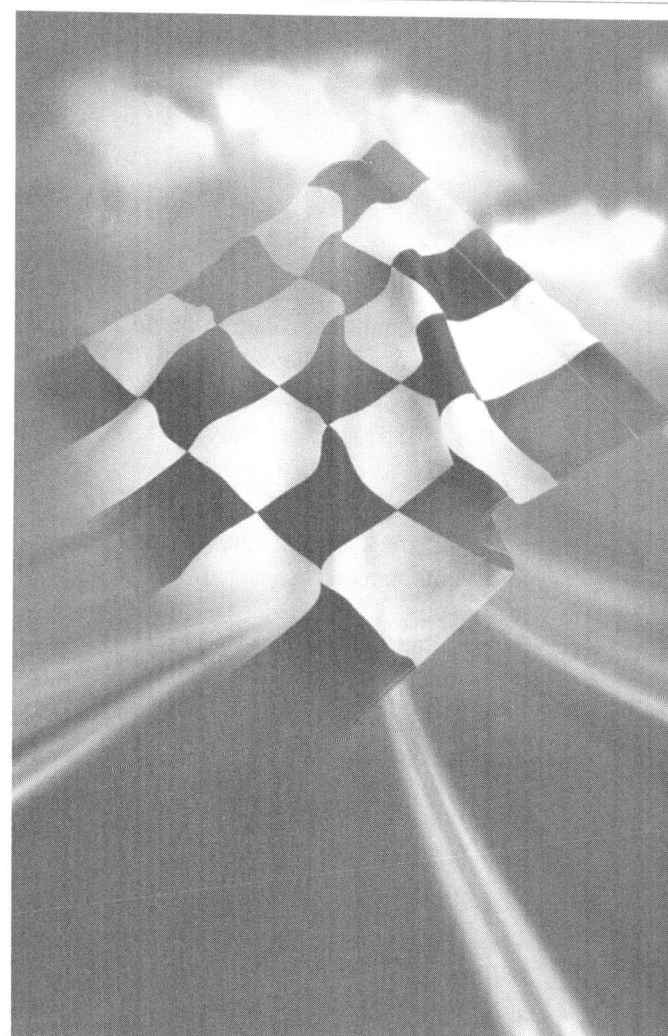

CHAPTER 1

Introducing Web Forms

OUTLINE

STUDY STRATEGIES

- Understand the execution of an ASP.NET page. Make sure that you complete Step by Step 1.1 and Step by Step 1.2.
- Use the ASP.NET Page directive and understand how it affects the compilation and execution of an ASP.NET page.
- Make sure you fully understand event handling. This will enable you to write interactive Web applications. Step by Steps 1.4, 1.5, and 1.6, and Guided Practice Exercise 1.2, will give you good practice on handling and raising events in an ASP.NET page.
- Appreciate the rationale behind the separation of code from the user interface. Make sure that you complete Guided Practice Exercise 1.3.
- If you are new to object-oriented programming, consider reading all or some of recommended material listed in the "Suggested Readings and Resources" section at the end of this chapter.

INTRODUCTION

As your first step toward passing Exam 70-305, in this chapter you will complete the groundwork required to build the foundation for the rest of this book.

This chapter starts with an overview of the .NET Framework and various development tools for developing applications for the .NET Framework. This overview will be enough to get you started; I will continually cover advanced features as they become important for meeting exam objectives.

Next, I will introduce ASP.NET. You will create an ASP.NET page and understand how it is processed. You will also understand the role of the Page class and some of its important members. You will learn that an ASP.NET page is compiled before it is executed, and you can use ASP.NET directives to change the behavior of the compilation process.

You follow an event-driven approach when programming ASP.NET applications. In this approach, you write code that executes in response to various events in the environment. In this chapter, you will learn how to write code that raises and handles events within ASP.NET pages.

ASP.NET supports a new way of developing Web pages called code-behind. It allows you to separate the code from the user-interface portion of your ASP.NET pages. This is the preferred approach for programming because it enables you to develop pages that are easier to develop, understand, and maintain. In this chapter, I will introduce various ways in which you can implement code-behind in your applications.

KEY CONCEPTS

You will develop a Web application using ASP.NET, but ASP.NET is part of larger framework called the .NET Framework. In this section, I'll give you an overview of the .NET Framework, various development tools, and basic object-oriented concepts that you will need right from the beginning.

An Overview of the .NET Framework

The Microsoft .NET Framework is a new computing platform for developing distributed applications. It provides several new features that enhance application development. Some of these features are

- **Consistent Development Model**—The .NET Framework proves an object-oriented and consistent development model. When you learn programming in the .NET Framework, you can use your skills in developing different types of applications such as desktop applications, Web applications, and Web services.
- **Robust Execution Environment**—The .NET Framework provides an execution environment that maximizes security, robustness and performance of applications while minimizing on deployment and versioning conflicts.
- **Support for Standards**—The .NET Framework is built around industry standards such as Extensible Markup Language (XML), Simple Object Access Protocol (SOAP), and the Common Language Infrastructure (CLI).

> NOTE
>
> **End Users Only Need a Web Browser**
>
> ASP.NET executes on the server side. The output of an ASP.NET application is in the form of HTML pages, which can be rendered correctly in all the popular Web browsers, such as Internet Explorer, Netscape Navigator, Opera, Mozilla, and so on. End users are not required to install the .NET Framework redistributable on their computers to access an ASP.NET Web application.

Because the .NET Framework provides a new execution environment for hosting the Web applications, you need to install the .NET Framework on the target Web server. The .NET Framework can be installed using the .NET Framework redistributable file (approx. 21MB). You can find the link to download this file from the Microsoft official ASP.NET site (`http://www.asp.net`).

The .NET Framework has two main components:

- The Common Language Runtime (CLR)
- The Framework Class Library (FCL)

The Common Language Runtime

The CLR provides a managed and language-agnostic environment for executing applications designed for the .NET Framework.

NOTE

C# and CLI Are ECMA Standards
The C# programming language as well as the CLI are ECMA standards. ECMA is an international association that coordinates standardization efforts in the computer industry. You can find them at `http://www.ecma.ch/`. The standardization has motivated a number of vendors to support and extend the .NET Framework in various ways. Some example includes the Mono project (`www.go-mono.com`), which is an open-source implementation of the .NET Framework, the Delphi 7 Studio (`www.borland.com/delphi`) that brings the Delphi language to the .NET Framework, and Covalent Enterprise Ready Servers (`www.covalent.net`) that supports ASP.NET on the Apache Web server.

The managed runtime environment provides a number of services to the executing code. These services include compilation, code safety verification, code execution, automatic memory management, and other system services. Applications designed to run under the CLR are known as managed applications because they enjoy the benefit of services offered by the managed execution environment provided by the CLR.

The CLR is based on the Common Language Infrastructure (CLI). The CLI provides a rich type system that supports the types and operations found in many programming languages. If a language compiler adheres to the CLI specifications, it can generate code that can run and interoperate with other code that executes on the CLR. This allows programmers to write applications using a development language of their choice and at the same time take full advantage of the CLR, FCL, and components written by other developers.

Microsoft provides five language compilers for the .NET Framework: C# .NET, Visual Basic .NET, Managed C++ .NET, Jscript .NET, and J# .NET. When you install the .NET Framework, you only get command-line compilers for C#, Visual Basic .NET, and Jscript .NET. The managed C++ compiler is part of .NET Framework SDK and Visual Studio .NET, whereas the J# .NET compiler can be separately downloaded from the Microsoft Web site. J# .NET will ship as a component of Visual Studio starting with version 1.1. In addition to the compilers available from Microsoft, you can obtain CLI-compliant compilers for languages such as COBOL, Delphi, Eiffel, Perl, Python, Smalltalk, and Haskell from various independent vendors or organizations.

CLI-compliant language compilers compile the source language to an intermediate format known as the Common Intermediate Language (CIL). At runtime, the CLR compiles the CIL code to the machine specific native code using a technique called just-in-time (JIT) compilation. Microsoft's implementation of CIL is the Microsoft Intermediate Language (MSIL).

The Framework Class Library

The FCL is an extensive collection of reusable types that allows you to develop a variety of applications, including

- Console applications
- Scripted or hosted applications

- Desktop applications (Windows Forms)
- Web applications (ASP.NET applications)
- XML Web services
- Windows services

The FCL organizes its classes in hierarchical namespaces so that they are logically grouped and easy to identify. You will learn about several of these namespaces and the classes that relate to the Web applications in this book.

An Overview of the Development Tools

Several tools are available to support development of Web applications that run on the .NET platform:

- The .NET Framework SDK
- ASP.NET Web Matrix Project
- Visual Studio .NET

I will discuss these tools in the following sections.

The .NET Framework SDK

The Microsoft .NET Framework Software Development Kit (SDK) is available as a free download. You can find the link to download it from `http://www.asp.net`. When you install the .NET Framework SDK you get a rich set of resources to help you develop applications for the Microsoft .NET Framework. This includes:

- **The .NET Framework**—This installs the necessary infrastructure of the .NET Framework including the CLR and the FCL.
- **Language compilers**—The command line–based compilers allow you to compile your applications. The language compilers installed with the SDK are C# .NET, Visual Basic .NET, Jscript.NET, and a nonoptimizing compiler for Managed C++ .NET.
- **Tools and debuggers**—Various tools installed with the .NET Framework SDK make it easy to create, debug, profile, deploy, configure, and manage applications and components. I will discuss most of these tools as I progress through this book.

- **Documentation**—The .NET Framework SDK installs a rich set of documentation to quickly get you up to speed on development using the .NET Framework. These include the QuickStart tutorials, product documentation, and samples.

It is possible to develop all your programs by using just a text editor and the command-line compilers and tools provided by the .NET Framework SDK. However, the GUI-based development environments such as ASP.NET Web Matrix and Visual Studio .NET provide productive development environment.

ASP.NET Web Matrix Project

To assist you with development using the .NET Framework SDK, Microsoft has released a free GUI-based Web application development tool called the Web Matrix Project. This tool itself is completely written using the .NET Framework and the C# programming language.

Although the Web Matrix Project is not close to the Visual Studio .NET in the number of features it offers, it still provides enough good features to simplify the development of Web applications. These features include a Web page designer, the ability to create and edit SQL Server and MSDE databases, ease of creating data-bound pages, support for application development for mobile devices, support for XML Web services, a development Web server, and an FTP tool for uploading the files to production Web server.

The Web Matrix Project can be downloaded from `http://www.asp.net`. With all the features listed earlier, its download size is amazingly small at about 1.2MB. To run the Web Matrix Project, you need to have the .NET Framework installed on your machine.

Visual Studio .NET

Visual Studio .NET provides developers with a full-service Integrated Development Environment (IDE) for building ASP.NET Web applications, XML Web services, desktop applications, and mobile applications for the .NET Framework. Visual Studio .NET supports multiple languages—Visual C# .NET, Visual Basic .NET, Visual C++ .NET, and Visual J# .NET, and provide transparent development and debugging facilities across these languages in a multi-language solution. Additional languages from other vendors can also be installed seamlessly into the Visual Studio .NET shell.

Visual Studio .NET installs the .NET Framework SDK as a part of its installation. In addition to the SDK features, some of important features of Visual Studio .NET are

- Integrated Development Environment (IDE)—Supports development, compilation, debugging, and deployment all from within the development environment.
- Editing Tools—Support language syntaxes for multiple languages. IntelliSense provides help with syntax. It also supports editing of XML, HTML, and Cascading Style Sheets (CSS) documents, among other types.
- Integrated Debugging—Supports cross-language debugging, including debugging of SQL Server Stored procedures. It can seamlessly debug applications running locally or on the remote server.
- Deployment Tools—Supports Windows Installer. It also provides graphical deployment editors that allow you to visually control various deployment settings for a Visual Studio .NET project.
- Automation—Provides tools for extending, customizing, and automating the Visual Studio .NET integrated development environment.

I'll cover all these features in the course of this book. As an exam requirement, this book uses Visual Studio .NET as its preferred tool for developing ASP.NET Web applications.

EXAM TIP

Use Visual Studio .NET for Developing Web Applications Exam 70-305 requires you to know Visual Studio .NET and the Visual Basic .NET programming language for developing Web applications. You might be asked questions about specific Visual Studio .NET features.

NOTE

Development Tools from Other Vendors Software vendors other than Microsoft have also released development tools to assist you in developing applications targeting the .NET Framework. One such tool is Macromedia Dreamweaver MX, which provides a highly productive environment for developing Web applications using ASP.NET. You can learn more about Dreamweaver MX from its Web site: `www.macromedia.com/software/dreamweaver`.

Understanding Classes, Inheritance, and Namespaces

The .NET Framework is designed to be object-oriented from the ground up. I'll cover the different elements of object-oriented programming as they come up, but before I start creating Web applications, you should know a few terms like *class*, *inheritance*, *namespace*, and so on that will be important right from the beginning. The following sections briefly explain these terms and their meanings.

Classes

Visual Basic .NET is an object-oriented programming language. One of the tasks of a VB .NET developer is to create user-defined types of data called classes. A class encapsulates data (such as constants and fields) and behavior (including methods, properties, constructors, and events) for your user-defined type. A class represents an abstract idea that you would like to include in your application. For example, the .NET Framework includes a Page class that represents an ASP.NET Web page. The Page class includes data fields for such things as the visibility of the page, its HTTP request, session variables, and so on. These data fields contain enough information for rendering a Page to a browser. The Page class also contains a set of methods that defines how a page behaves, such as a DataBind method that binds data to the page and a MapPath method that returns the physical path of the page.

A class functions as the blueprint of a concept. When you want to work with a class in your program, you create instances of the class. These instances are called objects. Objects are created from the blueprint defined by class but they physically exist in the sense that they have memory locations allocated to them and they will respond to your messages. For example, when you would like to create an actual Web page in your program, you create an instance of Page class. An instance of a class is also called an object. Once you have this instance available, you can actually work on it. You can set its properties and call its methods. Each object maintains its own copy of the data defined by the class. This allows different instances of a class to have different data values. The members of an object are accessed using the ObjectName.MemberName syntax, where ObjectName is name of the class instance and MemberName can be a field, property, method, or event. When an object is created, it will create its members in a special area in memory called the heap and will itself just store a pointer to that memory. Because they use pointers to refer to their data, classes are sometimes also called *reference types*. In contrast to this, Visual Basic .NET also has a structure type defined using the Structure keyword. These are almost like classes, but rather than storing a pointer to the memory location they use the memory location directly to store their members. A Structure is also referred to as a *value type*.

NOTE

Static Members A class can have static members (fields, methods, and so on). These are the members that belong to the class itself rather than to a particular instance. No instance of a class is required to access its static members. When you access a static member of a class, you do so by prefixing its name with the name of the class as in ClassName.StaticMemberName.

Among the members of a class, properties deserve special attention. A property provides access to the characteristics of a class or an instance of that class (an object). Examples of properties include the caption of a window, the name of an item, the font of a string, and so on. To the programs using a class, the property looks like a field—that is, a storage location. Properties and fields have the same usage syntax, but their implementation is different. In a class, a property is not a storage location but rather a set of accessors that contain code to be executed when property value is being read or written. This piece of code allows properties to preprocess the data before it is read or written and ensure integrity of a class. Properties are the preferred way of exposing attributes or characteristics of a class and you will see them being used extensively by various classes in this chapter.

Inheritance

Object-oriented programming languages such as VB.NET provide another feature called inheritance. Inheritance allows you to create new types that are based on already existing types. The original type is called a *base class* and the inherited class is called a *derived class*. When one class inherits from another class, the derived class gets all the functionality of the base class. The derived class can also choose to extend the base class by introducing new data and behavioral elements. In Windows Form development, you will frequently inherit from the Form class to create your own custom forms; these custom forms will be at least as functional as an object of the Form class even without writing any new code in the derived class. Value types like struct cannot be used for inheritance.

It is interesting to note that every single type (other than the Object itself) that you create or that is already defined in the framework is implicitly derived from the Object class of the System namespace. This is done to ensure that all classes provide a common minimum functionality. Also note that a VB.NET type can only inherit from a single parent class at a time.

Inheritance is widely used in the FCL, and you will come across classes (for example, Form) that get their functionality from other classes (for example, Control) as a result of a chain of inheritances.

NOTE

Access Modifiers A class can define the accessibility of its members by including an access modifier in their declarations. There are four different access modifiers in VB.NET:

- Public—Allows the member to be globally accessible
- Private—Limits access only to its containing type
- Protected—Limits access to the containing type and all classes derived from the containing type
- Friend—Limits access to classes within the current project

Namespaces

Several hundred classes are already available to you in the FCL. In addition to this, an increasingly large number of classes are available to you through third-party component vendors. These are all in addition to the classes that you develop on your own. A large number of classes not only makes organization difficult but can also create naming conflicts between various vendors. The .NET Framework provides you with a feature called a *namespace* that allows you to hierarchically organize these classes in logical groups based on what they do and where they originate. Not only does using namespaces organize your classes, but using them also helps you avoid naming conflicts between vendors because each class name is required to be unique only within its namespace. A general convention is to create a namespace like this:

```
CompanyName.ApplicationName
```

Here `CompanyName` is your unique company name, and `ApplicationName` is a unique application name within your company. All classes related to this application will belong to this namespace. A class is then identified as, for example, `QueCertifications.Exam70305.ExamQuestions` where `QueCertifications` is a unique name for a company, `Exam70305` is a unique application within this company, and `ExamQuestions` is the name of actual class. `QueCertifications` could have another class with the same name, `ExamQuestions`, as long as it belongs to a different application such as `QueCertifications.Exam70306`. The whole objective is to keep the complete naming hierarchy unique so that there are no naming conflicts.

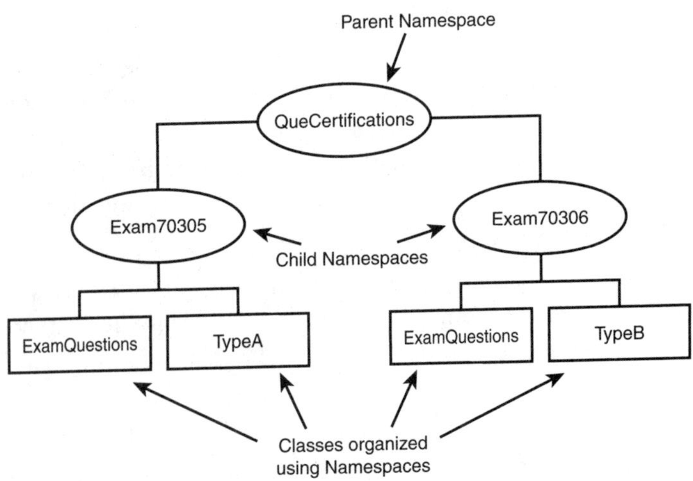

FIGURE 1.1
Use of namespace helps in avoiding naming conflicts between classes from different applications.

A namespace is just a string where a dot helps in creating a hierarchy. In the namespace QueCertifications.Exam70306, Exam70306 is called a child namespace of the QueCertifications namespace. You could organize your classes at two levels here: at the level of QueCertifications and also at the level of Exam70306. You can create as deep a hierarchy as you want.

A System namespace in the FCL acts as the root namespace for all the fundamental and base classes defined inside the library. One of the fundamental classes defined in the System namespace is Object class (uniquely identified as System.Object). This class acts as the ultimate base class for all other types in .NET Framework.

> NOTE
>
> **Two Hierarchies** A namespace hierarchy has nothing to do with inheritance hierarchy. When one class inherits from another, the base class and derived class may belong to different and unrelated namespaces.

The System.Web namespace organizes classes for creating Web applications. The System.Web.Services namespace organizes classes for creating XML-based Web Services. You will use many classes from these two namespaces in this book.

INTRODUCTION TO ASP.NET

> NOTE
>
> **Application Domains** Application domains provide a secure and versatile unit of processing that isolates running applications. The isolation between applications ensures that code running in one application cannot adversely affect any other unrelated application. Runtime hosts such as the ASP.NET worker process (aspnet_wp.exe) typically create application domains to isolate different running applications from one another.

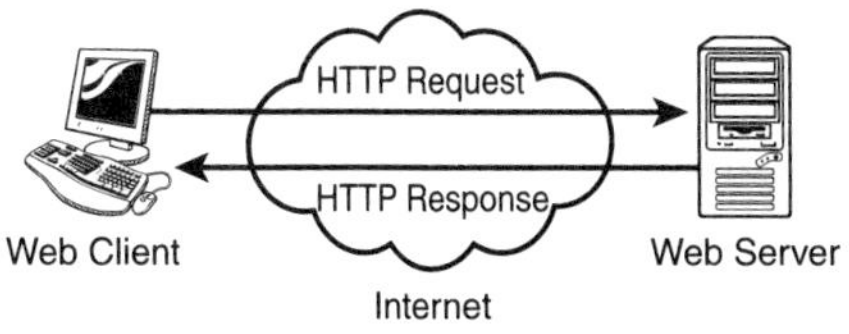

Active Server Pages .NET (ASP.NET) is the infrastructure built inside the .NET Framework for running Web applications. The ASP.NET infrastructure consists of two main parts:

- A set of classes and interfaces that enables communication between browser and Web server. These classes are organized in the System.Web namespace of the FCL.
- A runtime host that handles the Web request for ASP.NET resources. The ASP.NET runtime host (also known as the ASP.NET worker process) loads the CLR into a process, creates application domains within the process, and then loads and executes the requested code within the application domains.

At a higher level, an ASP.NET Web application is executed through a series of Hypertext Transfer Protocol (HTTP) request and response messages between the client browsers and the Web server (as shown in Figure 1.2):

FIGURE 1.2
User computers and the Web server communicate with each other using the HTTP protocol.

1. A user requests a resource from a Web server by typing a URL in her browser. The browser sends a HTTP request to the destination Web server.

2. The Web server analyzes the HTTP request and searches for a process capable of executing this request.

3. The results of the HTTP request are returned to the client browser in form of an HTTP response.

4. The browser reads the HTTP response and displays it as a Web page to the user.

As a Web programmer, you're probably more interested in knowing what goes on behind the scenes when a Web server executes a Web request for an ASP.NET page (.aspx file). Figure 1.3 represents the process of server-side execution with approximate details. (When I use the term *Web server* in this book, I am referring to a computer that is running Internet Information Services (IIS) and has the .NET Framework installed on it.)

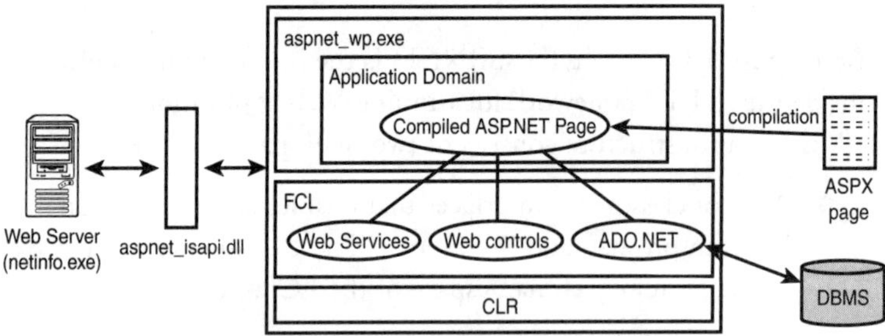

FIGURE 1.3
The ASP.NET worker process serves the requests to ASP.NET resources using the services provided by the .NET Framework.

The following list describes this process more fully:

1. When IIS (inetinfo.exe) receives an HTTP request, it uses the filename extension of the requested resource to determine which Internet Server Application Programming Interface (ISAPI) program to run to process the request. When the request is for an ASP.NET page (.aspx file), IIS passes the request to the ISAPI DLL capable of handling request for ASP.NET pages, which is aspnet_isapi.dll.

2. The aspnet_isapi.dll process passes the request to the ASP.NET worker process (aspnet_wp.exe), which fulfills the request.

NOTE

Application Mappings in IIS When ASP.NET is installed, it creates application mappings in IIS to associate the ASP.NET file extensions with the aspnet_isapi.dll. To view these settings, launch the IIS snap-in from the Windows Control Panel, access the properties of the default Web site, switch to the Home Directory tab, and click the Configuration button.

3. The ASP.NET worker process compiles the requested .aspx file into an assembly, creates an application domain, and instructs the CLR to execute the resulting assembly in the newly created application domain.
4. When the assembly containing the code for an ASP.NET page executes it uses of various classes in the FCL to accomplish its work and to generate response messages for the requesting client.
5. The ASP.NET worker process collects the response generated by the execution of the Web page, creates a response packet, and passes it to the IIS.
6. IIS forwards the response packet to the requesting client machine.

Advantages of ASP.NET

In some ways ASP.NET is just a successor to its previous version—ASP 3.0, but on the other hand, ASP.NET introduces so many new features for enhancing Web application development that it may be appropriate to call it a new product (which just happens to have some compatibility features with ASP 3.0). The following list summarizes some of the important features and benefit of ASP.NET over previous versions of ASP:

- **Enhanced Application Development Model**—ASP.NET supports the rapid application development (RAD) and object-oriented programming (OOP) techniques that were traditionally only available to the desktop applications. Two significant improvements in ASP.NET bring the development of Web applications close to that of desktop applications:
  - ASP.NET allows you to work with HTML elements, treating them as objects. Using properties, methods, and events associated with these objects greatly simplifies the programming model.
  - What distinguishes a Web application most from a desktop application is that the Web is stateless because of the inherent nature of HTTP protocol. To simplify the programming model, ASP.NET automatically maintains the state of a page and the controls on that page during the page-processing life cycle.

- **Rich Class Library Support**—In your ASP.NET programs you have access to all the classes of FCL. You can use these classes to accomplish complex tasks. For example, ADO.NET classes that belong to the System.Data namespace allow you to access data from different sources, whereas the classes in the System.Web. Services namespace allow you to create XML-based Web services.
- **Performance**—All ASP.NET pages are compiled before they can be executed. The overall performance of compiled code is much better than that of interpreted code. In addition to this, ASP.NET supports caching that allows ASP.NET to reuse the compiled version if there were no changes made to the source file since last compilation. Caching further increases the performance of ASP.NET by saving the time involved in repeated compilation of a page.
- **Scalability**—ASP.NET applications support running Web applications in a Web garden or Web farm. In a Web garden, processing work is distributed among several processors of a multiprocessor computer. In a Web farm, processing work is distributed among several computers making up the Web farm. Web gardens and Web farms allow increasing the scalability of a Web application by adding more processing power as the number of hits on the Web site increases.
- **Security**— As a part of the .NET Framework, ASP.NET has access to all the built-in security features of the .NET Framework, such as code access security and role-based user-access security. ASP.NET also offers various authentication modes for Web applications. In addition to Windows-based authentication, ASP.NET has two new modes of authentication—forms-based authentication and Passport authentication.
- **Manageability**—ASP.NET configuration files are stored as plain text. Applying new settings to a Web application is as simple as just copying the edited configuration files to the server. Most of the configuration changes do not even require a server restart.
- **Extensibility**—You can extend ASP.NET functionality by writing your own custom components. ASP.NET follows the object-oriented, component-based architecture of the .NET Framework that allows you to extend or replace any subcomponent of the ASP.NET runtime with your own custom-written component.

Creating an ASP.NET Page

Creating an ASP.NET page is easy. All you need to do is write the ASP.NET code in a text file with an ".aspx extension and place it in a virtual directory on the Web server from which it can be accessed. In Step by Step 1.1, I'll create a simple ASP.NET Web page that displays a Fahrenheit-to-Celsius temperature conversion chart. Although I can write this Web page using any text editor, I'll use Visual Studio .NET to accomplish my task because Visual Studio .NET also sets up the virtual directory required for accessing the Web application. Programmers who don't use Visual Studio .NET can of course manually create the virtual directory. Later on, in Exercise 1.1, I'll show you how to manually create and manage virtual directories.

NOTE

Web Site Structure A Web server can host one or more Web sites. Each Web site can have zero or more virtual directories defined inside it. A virtual directory maps a physical path to an alias within a Web site. A virtual directory is a convenient way to organize the contents of a Web site. A URL such as http://localhost/305C01 refers to a virtual directory with an alias of 305C01 and which is defined within the default Web site of the local Web server. The alias 305C01 by itself may point to a directory such as c:\inetpub\wwwroot\305C01, which is hidden from the user. You can use the Internet Information Service snap-in within the Windows Control Panel to administer the structure of a Web site. Refer to Exercise 1 in the "Apply Your Knowledge" section of this chapter for more information on virtual directory management.

STEP BY STEP

1.1 Creating an ASP.NET Page

1. Launch Visual Studio .NET. On the start page, click the New Project button (alternatively, you can select File, New, Project). In the New Project dialog box, select Visual Basic Projects as the project type and Empty Web Project as the template. Specify the location of the project as `http://localhost/305C01`, as shown in Figure 1.4, and click OK. This step will set up the project directory (`305C01`) as a virtual directory within the default Web site on the local Web server. The project directory will also be set up as an IIS application.

NOTE

Local Web Server In most of the examples in this book, I am using a Web server installed on my development machine (localhost). In some examples and screenshots and examples, you'll see the name of a particular Web server, when I've tested using a separate Web server. If you run the examples solely on your development machine, you should always use the localhost name. If you are using a remote Web server, you need to change the name of Web server accordingly.

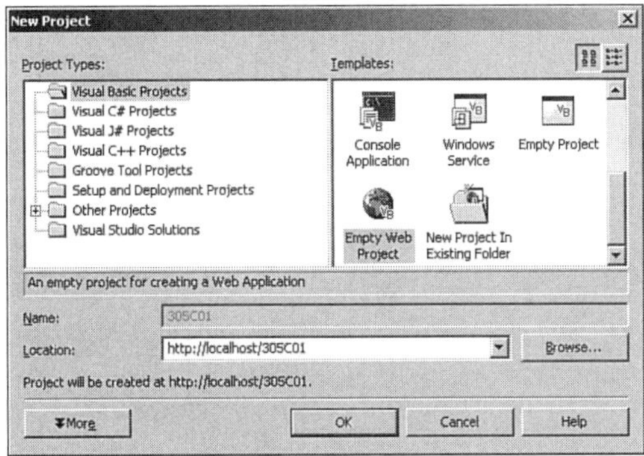

FIGURE 1.4
The Empty Web Project template sets up an application directory where you can create ASP.NET pages.

continues

NOTE

IIS Application When a virtual directory is set up as an IIS application, the files within it can share information such as context flow, session state, configuration, and other settings. A virtual directory marked as an IIS application is designated as the starting-point directory (also called an application root) for a Web application in your Web site. Every file and directory under the application root in your Web site is considered part of the application until another starting-point directory is found. That is, you can nest Web applications. You can use the Internet Information Services snap-in within the Windows Control Panel to manage IIS applications.

continued

2. Invoke the Solution Explorer window (by selecting View, Solution Explorer). Right-click the name of project and select Add, Add New Item from its shortcut menu as shown in Figure 1.5. Alternatively, you can also select Project, Add New Item from the Visual Studio .NET main menu. In the Add New Item dialog box select the Text File template and name the file `StepByStep1_1.aspx` as shown in Figure 1.6. Note that you may have various items in the Categories list in this dialog box, depending on what products you have installed on your computer.

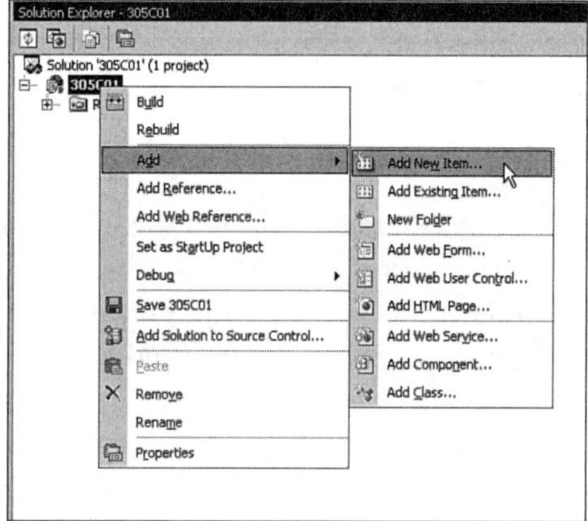

FIGURE 1.5
The Solution Explorer allows easy access to a project and its elements.

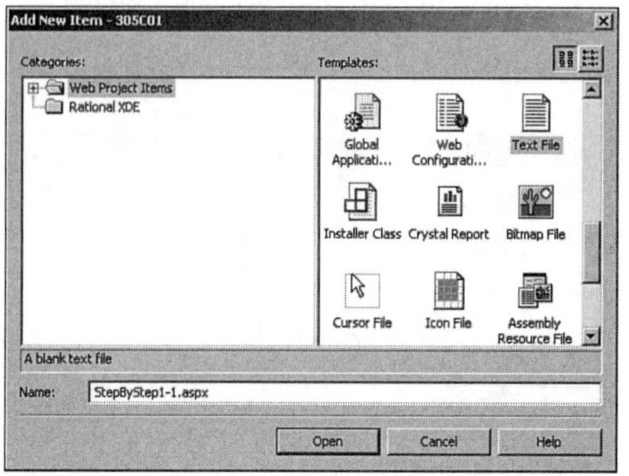

FIGURE 1.6
ASP.NET pages can be created by writing all the code in a text file.

NOTE

Projects and Solutions In Visual Studio .NET, a *solution* is used to group one or more projects. In a typical application, you first create a solution and then add projects to it. If you directly create a project, Visual Studio .NET automatically creates a solution for it. In that case, the name of the solution defaults to the name of project. For example, the project 305C01 is automatically created in solution 305C01.

3. When Visual Studio .NET creates the `.aspx` page, it detects that it is creating an ASP.NET Web page and displays the page with two available views: the Design view and the HTML view. Using the Design view, you can visually design a Web page by placing controls on it from the Visual Studio .NET Toolbox. Using the HTML view, you can view and modify the HTML code for a page. For now, you will restrain yourself to manually writing all the code, so switch to the HTML view by selecting View, HTML Source or by clicking on the HTML tab at the bottom of the designer window.

4. Add the following code to the HTML view of `StepByStep1_1.aspx` file. (Line numbers are for reference purposes only and are not part of the code.)

```
<!-- StepByStep1_1.aspx -->
<%@ Page Language='vb' %>
<html><head>
<script runat="server">
   Function ToCelsius(f As Double) As Double
       ToCelsius = (5.0/9.0)*(f-32.0)
   End Function
</script></head>
<body>
<h2>Fahrenheit to Celsius Conversion Chart</h2>
   <table border="2">
      <tr>
      <th>&deg Fahrenheit</th><th>&deg Celsius</th>
      </tr>
      <%
      Dim f As Double
      For f = 50.0 To 99.0 Step 1.0
         ' Sends formatted output to HTTP Response
    Response.Output.Write("<tr><td>{0}</td><td>" & _
              "{1:f}</td><tr>", f, ToCelsius(f))
      Next
      %>
  </table>
</body>
</html>
```

5. In the Solution Explorer, right-click `StepByStep1_1.aspx` and select View in Browser from its shortcut menu. A browser window opens in Visual Studio .NET and displays the page output as shown in Figure 1.7.

NOTE

Only One Language at a Time
ASP.NET supports the use of only one programming language for a single ASP.NET page. The Language attribute with the Page directive specifies which compiler ASP.NET should invoke to compile a page.

Additionally, when working with Visual Studio .NET, you must specify the same language for all ASP.NET page in a project.

NOTE

Response.Write() and Response.Output.Write()
The Response property of the Page class gives you access to the HTTP Response object. You can add content to the HTTP Response using the Response.Write() and Response. Output.Write() methods. The only difference between the two methods is that the latter allows you to write formatted output. I will discuss the HTTP Response object and its methods in Chapter 3, "Implementing Navigation for the User Interface."

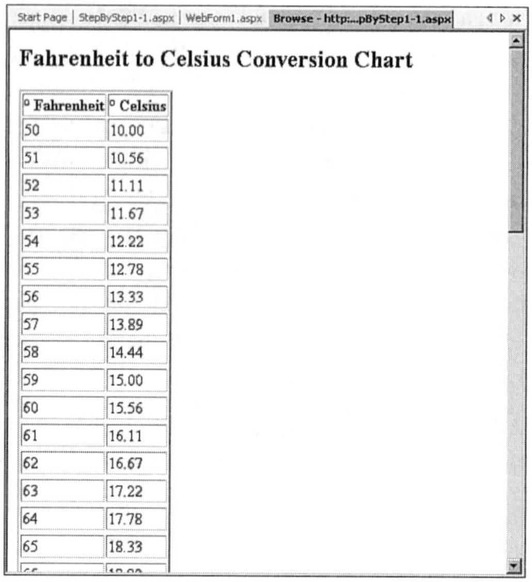

FIGURE 1.7
The temperature conversion chart is created by executing ASP.NET code on the Web server.

Start Page | StepByStep1-1.aspx | WebForm1.aspx | Browse - http:...pByStep1-1.aspx

Fahrenheit to Celsius Conversion Chart

° Fahrenheit	° Celsius
50	10.00
51	10.56
52	11.11
53	11.67
54	12.22
55	12.78
56	13.33
57	13.89
58	14.44
59	15.00
60	15.56
61	16.11
62	16.67
63	17.22
64	17.78
65	18.33

In the preceding code, line 1 is the HTML comment line. Line 2 is an ASP.NET directive that controls the behavior of the compiler translating the ASP.NET page to MSIL. All ASP.NET code in the page is enclosed in either the `<script runat=server>...</script>` tag (lines 4 to 9) or inside the `<%...%>` tag (lines 16 to 23). I'll explain the reason behind using two separate tags in the next section. All code outside these ASP.NET tags is just plain HTML. It is an interesting exercise to analyze the output HTML generated by the ASP.NET page. You can view the HTML source code of a Web page by right-clicking anywhere on the browser window and selecting View Source from its shortcut menu. In the following section you'll learn how exactly this ASP.NET page is executed.

Understanding ASP.NET Page Execution

Earlier in this chapter I mentioned that all ASP.NET code is compiled. In Step by Step 1.1, I also specified the language of the ASP.NET source code as Visual Basic .NET using the Page directive (I'll discuss the Page directive later in the chapter), but the structure of StepByStep1-1.aspx does not look like a valid Visual Basic .NET program. There is no class declaration and you have Visual Basic .NET code interspersed within the HTML code. Is the page actually compiled? If it does compile, then how does the compiler manage to compile the Visual Basic .NET code mixed in with the HTML code?

To answer these questions, I will introduce an error in the ASP.NET page! The error in the page will give you important information about how the page is compiled. Step by Step 1.2 lists the steps you need to take to achieve this.

> **NOTE**
>
> **Compilation Error Message** For security reasons the default setting in ASP.NET is to display the compiler error message, compiler output, and compilation source code only when you are running the Web page from the same machine that hosts the Web server. Remote users will not be able to see compiler error messages. You will see later in this book that you can override this setting using configuration files.

STEP BY STEP

1.2 Understanding ASP.NET Page Execution

1. Return to the HTML view of `StepByStep1-1.aspx`. Add the following line before the closing `%>` tag in line 23.

```
This line generates a compilation error
```

2. Using the Solution Explorer window, right-click `StepByStep1-1.aspx` and select View in Browser from its shortcut menu. Because the line of "code" that you just added is not a valid Visual Basic .NET statement, the browser window displays a compilation error as shown in Figure 1.8.

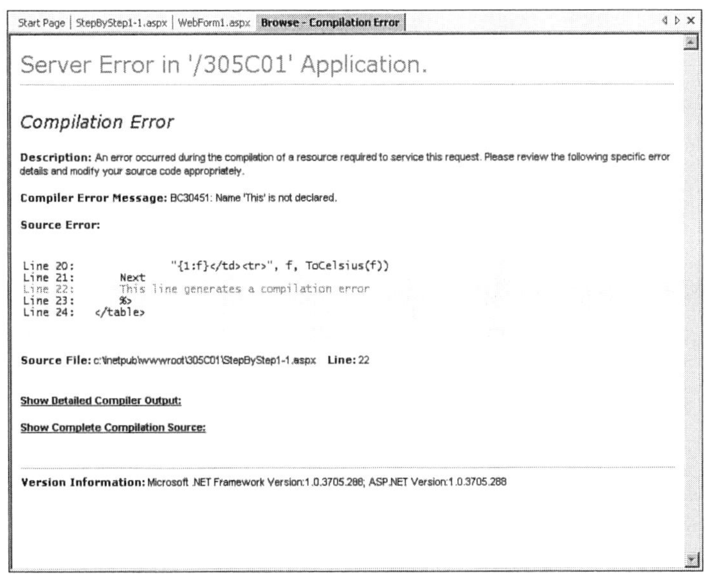

FIGURE 1.8
The Compilation Error page shows a descriptive error message and displays hyperlinks to the compiler output and compilation source.

continues

continued

3. Click the hyperlink titled "Show Detailed Compiler Output." You'll see the command line used by the VB complier (`vbc.exe`) to compile a `.vb` file. Analyze the command to note that the VB compiler is compiling a source file located at: `C:\WINNT\Microsoft.NET\Framework\v1.0.3705\Temporary ASP.NET Files\305c01\9fb707bc\85467d27\jkm0pkqn.0.vb` (the location will vary somewhat on your system). The output of compilation is a DLL file that is stored at `C:\WINNT\Microsoft.NET\Framework\v1.0.3705\Temporary ASP.NET Files\305c01\9fb707bc\85467d27\jkm0pkqn.dll`. (You will see a different path on your computer as some file and directory names are dynamically generated by ASP.NET.)

4. Click the hyperlink titled "Show Complete Compilation Source." This reveals the complete source code of the file (such as `jkm0pkqn.0.vb`) that was compiled in step 3.

5. Analyze the compilation source code. The Visual Basic .NET source code defines a class whose name is `StepByStep1_1_aspx`, which is same as the name of the corresponding `.aspx` file but with illegal characters (such as hyphens and periods) replaced by underscores. The class `StepByStep1_1_aspx` derives from the `System.Web.UI.Page` class. The method `ToCelsius()` defined in lines 5 to 8 of `StepByStep1_1.aspx` becomes a method of class `StepByStep1_1_aspx`. All the HTML code and the `for` loop defined in lines 20 to 24 in `StepByStep1_1.aspx` goes inside the `__Render__control1()` method of the class `StepByStep1_1_aspx`.

6. Remove the line of code from Step 1 that is causing the error and view the page in browser. The temperature conversion chart will be correctly displayed.

NOTE

ASP Namespace ASP.NET places the code for dynamically generated class corresponding to an ASPX file in a namespace named ASP.

Step by Step 1.2 reveals that an ASP.NET page is converted dynamically into a class file. The `Language` attribute of the `Page` directive used in line 2 of `StepByStep1_1.aspx` file specifies that the name of the dynamically compiled class file has a .vb extension and that the class is compiled using the Visual Basic .NET compiler (vbc.exe).

The compiler converts the source file to a DLL file. When an ASP.NET page is requested, instead of executing the .aspx file, the CLR actually executes the code in the compiled DLL file for that ASPX page.

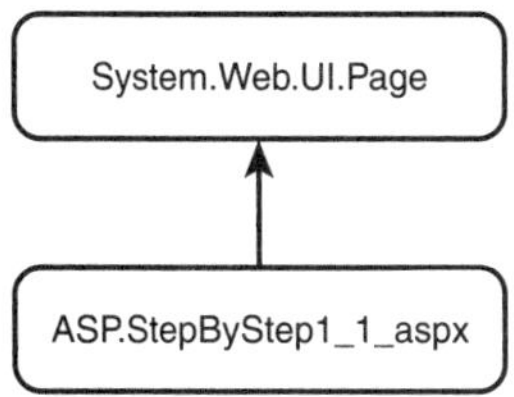

FIGURE 1.9
Each ASPX file is dynamically converted to a class that derives its major functionality from the System.Web.UI.Page class.

The dynamically generated class StepByStep1_1_aspx inherits from the Page class. Their inheritance relationship can be represented as shown in Figure 1.9.

Normally (when there are no errors in the ASP.NET code) the .vb source file is created and compiled into a DLL; the source file then is deleted. When there is an error, you get an opportunity to view the source code to assist you in finding the cause of the error.

To answer the question raised at the beginning of this section— Yes, each ASP.NET page is converted to a class file and is compiled into a DLL file. All the Visual Basic .NET code as well as the HTML in the .aspx file becomes part of the class file. The HTML elements are stored in strings and do not interfere the compilation process.

The compiled DLL files are managed by ASP.NET using a special directory structure within the Temporary ASP.NET Files directory. When the page is successfully compiled, if you navigate to this directory structure you will be able to locate the compiled DLL file in a directory with the same name as the virtual root of the ASP.NET project as shown in Figure 1.10.

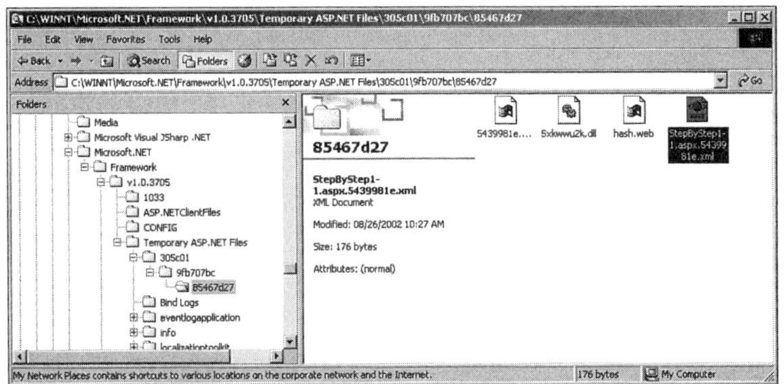

FIGURE 1.10
When an ASP.NET page is compiled, the resulting DLL file is stored in an ASP.NET managed directory structure.

ASP.NET maintains the reference between the source .aspx file and the DLL file. When an .aspx file is requested a second time, ASP.NET matches the timestamp of the .aspx file with the generated DLL file.

If the .aspx is newer (that is, it has been changed since last compilation), it is compiled again and the old DLL file is replaced with the new one. If the timestamp is not newer, ASP.NET knows that the .aspx file was not modified since the compilation; therefore, it saves time by skipping the compilation step and directly serves the HTTP request using the already-compiled version of the Web page.

Step by Step 1.2 made it clear that the code written in .aspx files in the <script runat=server>...</script> tags is placed directly in the class definition, whereas the code written in the <%...%> render blocks is placed inside a method that renders the user interface of the Web page. You should use this distinction to write only the appropriate type of code in each block. If you define a method inside the <%...%> render blocks, you will get a compilation error because that method will become part of another method in the generated source file and Visual Basic .NET does not allow you to define a method inside another method. Thus you need to take care not to define class level code between the <%...%> tags.

The Page Class

You now understand that each .aspx file is converted into a class. The class corresponding to the .aspx page derives most of its functionality from its base class, System.Web.UI.Page. If you look at the .NET Framework documentation, you'll see that the Page class itself derives from System.Web.UI.TemplateControl, System.Web.UI.Control, and System.Object, as shown in Figure 1.11.

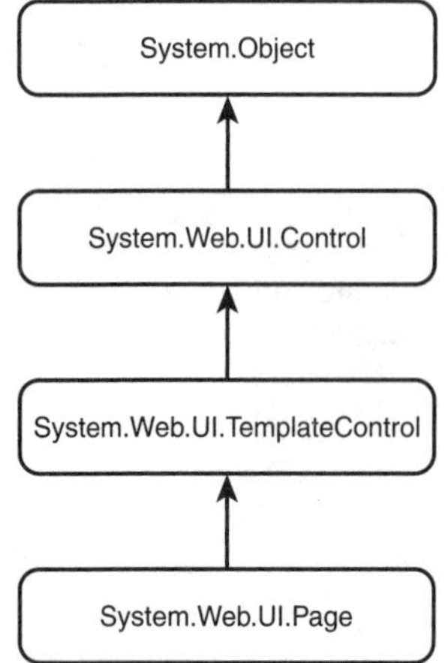

FIGURE 1.11
The System.Web.UI.Page class inherits from System.Object through a chain of inheritances.

Because of this inheritance relationship, you can also say that a Page is a Control, and as the Page class derives from the TemplateControl class, it derives extended capabilities such as hosting other controls on its surface.

The Page class provides a lot of functionality to your .aspx page such as capabilities for state management, access to intrinsic objects, information about the client, access to the controls placed on the Web page, and notifications for handling page-level events. Table 1.1 lists important members of the Page class. I won't use all these members in this chapter's code, but they'll turn up throughout the book.

TABLE 1.1

IMPORTANT MEMBERS OF PAGE CLASS

Member	*Type*	*Description*
`Application`	Property	Returns the application state object for the current HTTP request.
`Cache`	Property	Returns the cache object of the application to which the page belongs.
`ClientTarget`	Property	Provides information about the client browser and its capabilities. You can use this information to customize the rendering of a page for particular browser clients.
`Controls`	Property	Returns a `ControlCollection` object that represents the collection of controls placed on the page.
`EnableViewState`	Property	Indicates whether viewstate is maintained for the page and its container controls.
`Error`	Event	Occurs when an unhandled exception occurs in the page processing.
`ErrorPage`	Property	Specifies the error page where the user is redirected whenever an unhandled exception occurs in the page processing.
`Init`	Event	Occurs when the page is initialized. This event is the first step in the page lifecycle.
`IsPostBack`	Property	Indicates whether the page is loaded on a client postback.
`IsValid`	Property	Indicates whether all the validation controls on a page succeeded.
`Load`	Event	Occurs when the page is loaded in the memory.
`OnError()`	Method	Raises the `Error` event. It is a protected method derived from the `TemplateControl` class.
`MapPath()`	Method	Returns the actual physical path corresponding to a virtual path.
`OnInit()`	Method	Raises the `Init` event. It is a protected method derived from the `Control` class.
`OnLoad()`	Method	Raises the `Load` event. It is a protected method derived from the `Control` class.
`OnPreRender()`	Method	Raises the `PreRender` event. It is a protected method derived from the `Control` class.
`OnUnload()`	Method	Raises the `Unload` event. It is a protected method derived from the `Control` class.
`PreRender`	Event	Occurs when a page is about to render to its contents.
`RenderControl()`	Method	Outputs content of a page to a provided `HtmlTextWriter` object and stores tracing information about the control if tracing is enabled.
`Request`	Property	Returns the request object that contains information about the current HTTP request.
`Response`	Property	Returns the response object for the current HTTP request.
`Server`	Property	Provides an access to the server object associated to the page.
`Session`	Property	Returns the session state object applicable for the current HTTP request.
`SmartNavigation`	Property	Indicates whether smart navigation is enabled for the page.
`Trace`	Property	Returns the trace context object for the current HTTP request.
`Unload`	Event	Occurs when a page is unloaded from memory.
`Validators`	Property	Returns a collection of all validation controls contained in a page.
`Visible`	Property	Indicates whether the page should be displayed.

GUIDED PRACTICE EXERCISE 1.1

To understand the behavior of an ASP.NET page, you want to display values for some of its properties. In particular, you are interested in finding the following information:

- The physical location where the ASP.NET page is stored
- The total number of controls that are placed on the ASP.NET page
- Whether the page is loaded as a result of a client postback
- Whether ViewState is enabled for the page

How would you create such a Web page?

You should try working through this problem on your own first. If you are stuck, or if you'd like to see one possible solution, follow these steps:

1. Open the project `305C01`. Add a new text file with the name `GuidedPracticeExercise1-1.aspx` to the project.

2. Switch to the HTML view of the Web page and add the following code to it:

```
<%@ Page Language="vb"%>
<html>
    <body>
        <%
Response.Output.Write( _
 "Physical path of page is: {0}<br>", _
 MapPath("GuidedPracticeExercise1_1.aspx"))
Response.Output.Write("# of controls on page: {0}<br>", _
 Controls.Count)
Response.Output.Write( _
 "The value for IsPostback: {0}<br>", _
 IsPostBack)
If EnableViewState Then
    Response.Output.Write("View State is enabled<br>")
Else
    Response.Output.Write("View State is disabled<br>")
End if
%>
    </body>
</html>
```

3. View `GuidedPracticeExercise1-1.aspx` in the browser. You'll get a result similar to Figure 1.12.

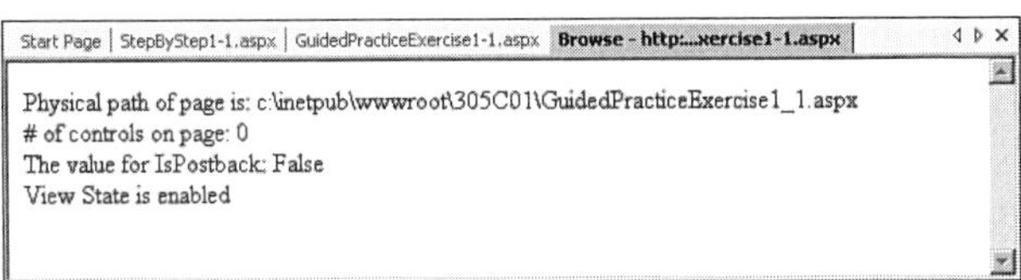

FIGURE 1.12
Use the methods and properties of the Page class to get information about the executing ASP.NET page.

If you have difficulty following this exercise, review the section "Creating an ASP.NET Page" earlier in this chapter. Perform Step by Step 1.1 and study the important members of the Page class given in Table 1.1. After doing this review, try this exercise again.

Stages in Page Processing

When ASP.NET processes a Web page, the page goes through distinct stages. Some of these common stages are listed in Table 1.2.

TABLE 1.2

THE STAGES OF ASP.NET PAGE PROCESSING

Stage	*Meaning*
Page Initialization	ASP.NET has done initialization of the page. The `Init` event is raised to indicate this stage. An `Init` event handler is the best place for code that you want to be executed before any page processing is done. You will see later in this chapter that Visual Studio .NET uses an `Init` event handler to attach event handlers for other events of a page.
User Code Initialization	The page initialization is complete at this stage. The page object indicates this stage by raising the `Load` event. A method that handles the `Load` event is the best place to store initialization code specific to this page.
PreRender	The page is just about to render its contents. This stage is indicated by raising the `PreRender` event. An event handler for the `PreRender` event has the last chance to modify a page's output before it is sent to the browser.
Page Cleanup	The page has finished rendering and is ready to be discarded. The `Unload` event is raised to indicate this stage.

As you can note from Table 1.2, the Page class raises a distinct event to indicate each processing stage. You can write event handling methods that respond to these events. You will learn about events and event handling in just a bit.

REVIEW BREAK

- Active Server Pages .NET (ASP.NET) is the infrastructure built inside the .NET Framework for running Web applications.
- An ASP.NET Web application is executed through a series of HTTP request and response messages between the client browser and the Web server.
- Some of the advantages of ASP.NET are an enhanced application development model, rich class library support, performance, scalability, security, manageability, and extensibility.
- An ASP.NET Web page should have an `.aspx` extension. Typically, you will place the Web page in a virtual directory of a Web server. The name of the Web server and the path of virtual directory makes up the URL that users will use to request the Web page from the Web server.
- Each ASPX file is dynamically converted to a class that derives its basic functionality from the `System.Web.UI.Page` class. This class is compiled into a DLL file when the ASPX page is opened in the browser for the first time.
- You should take care not to define class level code such as the declaration of variables, methods, and so on between the `<%...%>` render blocks in an ASPX page.

ASP.NET DIRECTIVES

ASP.NET pages allow you to specify various compiler options. You can specify these commands and options with the help of directives. A directive name begins with "@" character and is enclosed in <% and %> tags. A directive can be placed anywhere in a Web page, but directives are usually placed at the top of the Web page. Directives contain one or more attribute/value pairs. These attribute/value pairs are not case sensitive and they need not be placed in quotes.

Table 1.3 lists different types of directives, which can be added to an ASP.NET page.

TABLE 1.3

ASP.NET PAGE DIRECTIVES

Directive	*Description*
`Assembly`	Links an assembly to the application or a Web page during compilation. It is similar to the `/reference` command line switch of the VB.NET compiler (`vbc.exe`).
`Control`	Specifies user control related attributes that are used by the ASP.NET compiler when the user control (`ascx` file) is compiled. You will use this directive in Chapter 7.
`Implements`	Indicates that the Web page (`aspx` file) or the user control (`ascx` file) implements the interface specified by the `Interface` attribute of the directive.
`Import`	Imports a namespace into a page, user control, or application. It is similar to the Imports statement in VB.NET.
`OutputCache`	Controls the output caching of a Web page (`aspx` file) or user control (`ascx` file). You will use this directive in Chapter 15.
`Page`	Specifies page-related attributes that are used by the ASP.NET compiler when the Web client requests the ASPX page. Refer to Table 1.4 for list of attributes allowed in a Page directive.
`Reference`	Indicates a Web page or user control that should be compiled and linked during compilation of the aspx page that contains the `Reference` directive. It can contain either the `Page` attribute (`aspx` filename) or `Control` attribute (`ascx` filename).
`Register`	Registers a custom server control or a user control to be used within an ASP.NET page. You will use this directive in Chapter 7.

I will discuss these directives as I discuss related topics through the course of this book. For now, I will only discuss the Page directive in detail in the following section.

The Page Directive

The Page directive is used to specify page related attributes that control how an ASP.NET page is compiled and executed. An ASP.NET page can have only one Page directive. Table 1.4 lists the various attributes of the Page directive.

TABLE 1.4

ATTRIBUTES OF PAGE DIRECTIVE

Attributes	*Description*
`AspCompat`	Indicates whether the page is to be executed on a Single-Threaded Apartment (STA) thread model for backward compatibility. The default value is `False`.
`AutoEventWireUp`	Indicates whether ASP.NET should automatically connect methods with specific names such `Page_Init()`, `Page_Load()`, and so on with the page events. The default value is `True`. However, for Web pages created using Visual Studio .NET, the default value is `False`.
`Buffer`	Indicates whether the HTTP response buffer is enabled. The default value is `True`.
`ClassName`	Specifies the name for dynamically generated class file for the ASPX page.
`ClientTarget`	Represents the target user agent (such as Mozilla/4.0) or alias (such as IE4) according to which the ASP.NET page should be rendered.
`CodePage`	Indicates the culture codepage value for the ASP.NET page. Supports any valid codepage value. For example, the value "932" specifies a Japanese codepage.
`CompilerOptions`	Indicates the compiler options and switches to be passed to the language compiler.
`ContentType`	Indicates the MIME type for the page response.
`Culture`	Indicates the culture setting for the page. Supports any valid culture string.
`Debug`	Indicates whether the compilation should include debug symbols. The default value is `False`.
`Description`	Represents description of the page. The page compilers ignore this attribute.
`EnableSessionState`	Indicates whether the session state is enabled (`True`), read-only (`ReadOnly`), or disabled (`False`) for the page. The default value is `True`.
`EnableViewState`	Indicates whether the view state is maintained for the page and its container controls. The default value is `True`.
`EnableViewStateMac`	Indicates whether the encrypted view state should be verified against Machine Authentication Check (MAC) to assure that the view state is not tampered with.
`ErrorPage`	Specifies the error page where the user is redirected whenever an unhandled exception occurs in the page.
`Explicit`	Indicates whether all variables must be explicitly declared. The default is `False`.
`Inherits`	Represents the name of the code-behind class that contains code for the `aspx` page and from which the dynamically generated class inherits.
`Language`	Represents any .NET programming language used for inline coding in the page.
`LCID`	Defines the 32-bit locale identifier for code in the page.
`ResponseEncoding`	Defines the response encoding for the page such as UTF7Encoding, UTF8Encoding, ASCIIEncoding, UnicodeEncoding, and so on. You'll learn more about encodings in Chapter 9, "Globalization."
`Src`	Represents the source filename of the code-behind class that is dynamically compiled when the Web page is requested. Visual Studio .NET does not use this attribute as it precompiles the code behind class.

Attributes	*Description*
`SmartNavigation`	Indicates whether smart navigation is enabled for the page. The smart navigation feature preserves the scroll position and element focus whenever the page is refreshed. This feature is only supported in `IE5` or later browsers. The default value is `False`.
`Strict`	Indicates whether the page should be compiled using `Option Strict`. The default is `False`.
`Trace`	Indicates whether page-level tracing is enabled. The default value is `False`.
`TraceMode`	Indicates how trace messages are to be displayed when tracing is enabled. The default value is `SortByTime` and the other possible value is `SortByCategory`.
`Transaction`	Indicates whether transactions are supported on the page. The default value is `Disabled` and the other possible values are `NotSupported`, `Supported`, `Required`, and `RequiresNew`.
`UICulture`	Indicates the culture setting for the user interface of a page. Supports any valid culture string.
`WarningLevel`	Specifies the warning level at which page compilation should be stopped. The possible values are 0 through 4.

Step by Step 1.3 demonstrates how you can display information related to execution of a page by using the `Trace` attribute of the `Page` directive.

STEP BY STEP

1.3 Displaying Execution Information for an ASP.NET Page

1. Add a new text file to the project 305C01. Name the text file `StepByStep1-3.aspx`.

2. Switch to the HTML view and add the following code to the `StepByStep1-3.aspx` file.

```
<!--StepByStep1_3-->
<%@ Page Language="vb" Trace="true"%>
<html>
<body>
Trace Information
</body>
</html>
```

3. View `StepByStep1-3.aspx` in your browser. You'll see results similar to Figure 1.13.

FIGURE 1.13

Trace information allows you to analyze the execution information for a Page request.

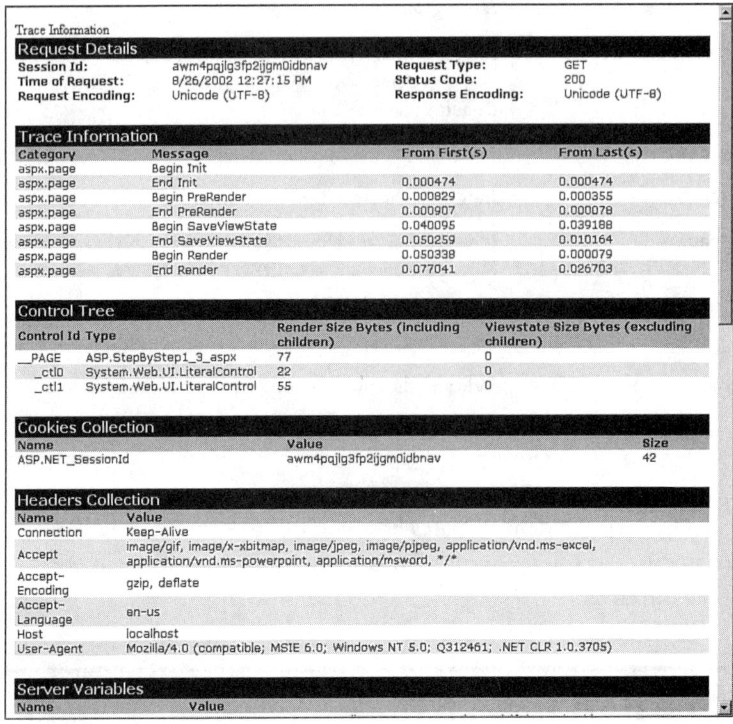

Trace Information

Request Details

Session Id:	awm4pqjlg3fp2ijgm0idbnav	**Request Type:**	GET
Time of Request:	8/26/2002 12:27:15 PM	**Status Code:**	200
Request Encoding:	Unicode (UTF-8)	**Response Encoding:**	Unicode (UTF-8)

Trace Information

Category	Message	From First(s)	From Last(s)
aspx.page	Begin Init		
aspx.page	End Init	0.000474	0.000474
aspx.page	Begin PreRender	0.000829	0.000355
aspx.page	End PreRender	0.000907	0.000078
aspx.page	Begin SaveViewState	0.040095	0.039188
aspx.page	End SaveViewState	0.050259	0.010164
aspx.page	Begin Render	0.050338	0.000079
aspx.page	End Render	0.077041	0.026703

Control Tree

Control Id	Type	Render Size Bytes (including children)	Viewstate Size Bytes (excluding children)
__PAGE	ASP.StepByStep1_3_aspx	77	0
_ctl0	System.Web.UI.LiteralControl	22	0
_ctl1	System.Web.UI.LiteralControl	55	0

Cookies Collection

Name	Value	Size
ASP.NET_SessionId	awm4pqjlg3fp2ijgm0idbnav	42

Headers Collection

Name	Value
Connection	Keep-Alive
Accept	image/gif, image/x-xbitmap, image/jpeg, image/pjpeg, application/vnd.ms-excel, application/vnd.ms-powerpoint, application/msword, */*
Accept-Encoding	gzip, deflate
Accept-Language	en-us
Host	localhost
User-Agent	Mozilla/4.0 (compatible; MSIE 6.0; Windows NT 5.0; Q312461; .NET CLR 1.0.3705)

Server Variables

Name	Value

The process of displaying execution information for an ASP.NET page is called *tracing*. Various sections in the tracing information display a wealth of information about the page execution. Tracing is an important tool for finding errors in ASP.NET page. I will discuss tracing in detail in Chapter 12, "Testing and Debugging a Web Application."

EVENT HANDLING

When you perform an action with an object, the object in turn raises events in the application. Clicking a button, for example, generates an event; loading a Web page generates another event. Not all events are triggered by user actions. Changes in the environment, such as the arrival of an email message, modifications to a file, changes in the time, and completion of program execution also trigger events.

Events are at the heart of graphical user interface (GUI)–based programming. A significant portion of code for a typical ASP.NET application is devoted to handling various events that are raised in the application. In the following sections, you will learn how to raise and handle events in an ASP.NET page.

Elements of Event Handling

Before I tell you how to raise and handle events in ASP.NET pages, I will introduce you to the basic elements of event handling that make up the event-handling infrastructure. I will talk about events, delegates, event handlers, event arguments, and methods that raise events. This information will help you understand how event handling works for the ASP.NET pages.

Event Arguments

An event argument specifies the data associated with an event. When an event is raised, the event arguments are passed to the event handlers so that they have enough information to handle the event.

Event arguments are of type EventArgs (or one of its derived types). As an example, all the events of the Page class pass an object of type EventArgs to their event handlers.

Event Handlers

An event handler is a method that performs custom actions in response to an event notification provided by the event of a class. An event handler must have a prototype compatible with the event that it is handling. That is, the event handler must take as parameters exactly the values that the event generates.

By convention, an event handler returns void and takes two arguments. The first argument specifying the object on which the event occurred (that is, the publisher of event) and the second argument specifies an event argument, which is an object of a type EventArgs or its derived classes.

As an example, an event handler method that handles the PreRender event of an ASP.NET page could have the following declaration:

```
Private Sub Page_PreRender(ByVal sender As Object, _
 ByVal e As System.EventArgs) Handles MyBase.PreRender
```

NOTE

Events with No Data If an event does not generate any data, you can use the predefined class EventArgs for the event data object, and the predefined EventHandler for the event delegate. These classes are already defined in the System namespace so you do not need to redefine them in your programs.

In case an event is generating data, you can extend the EventArgs class to store custom data and you can define a new delegate capable of storing references to event handlers receiving the custom event data.

Delegates

A delegate is a special class with an object capable of storing references to methods with a particular prototype. If you have a background of C/C++ programming, you can relate delegates with function pointers. The definition of a typical delegate looks like this:

```
Public Delegate Sub EventHandler( _
 ByVal sender As Object, _
 Byval e As EventArgs)
```

Here `EventHandler` is a delegate whose object is capable of storing references to any method that has void return type and that accepts two arguments: the first one of type `Object` and the other one of type `EventArgs`. ASP.NET uses delegates to attach code to events.

Events

An event in Visual Basic .NET is an abstraction of an incident that occurs in the environment. For example, the Click event of Button object is raised when a user clicks a button control.

An event enables a class to provide notifications to other objects that something of interest has happened. Events in Visual Basic .NET are based on a publisher-subscriber model. The class that implements an event is called the publisher of the event. A subscriber class can subscribe to a published event by registering an appropriate event handler with the published event. When an event is raised, the publisher notifies all registered objects about the event by invoking the registered event handlers.

As an example, the `Page` class notifies other objects that a page is about to render its content using the `PreRender` event. The definition of `PreRender` event in the `Page` is like this:

```
'Define the event
Public Event PreRender As EventHandler
```

An event is of the type of a delegate (in the preceding listing the type of the `PreRender` event is the `EventHandler` delegate). The delegate type determines the prototype of the event handlers that can be registered with an event.

As an example, you can attach the `Page_PreRender` method (discussed earlier) as an event handler to the `PreRender` event because the prototype of this method matches with the delegate that defines the `PreRender` event—`EventHandler`.

You can register an event handler with an event by encapsulating the event handler in a delegate object and adding the delegate to the event. For example, within an ASP.NET page you can code:

```
AddHandler Me.PreRender, AddressOf Me.Page_PreRender
```

The `Me` keyword represents the current instance of the `Page`. Note that there are no method call parentheses `()` after `MyPage_PreRender`; rather, a reference to the address of the method is passed to the event. The preceding statement first encapsulates the reference to the `Page_PreRender` method in a delegate object of compatible type and then uses the `AddHandler` syntax to add the delegate object to an event.

An event internally manages a linked list of delegates registered with it. The use of `AddHandler` in the preceding example ensures that if any event handlers are already attached to this event by other objects, they remain in the list. There is also a `RemoveHandler` keyword that you can use to drop a handler from the list for an event.

When the event is raised, its corresponding linked list of delegates is scanned to invoke the event handlers encapsulated in the delegate objects. Because the delegate object maintains the reference to the event handler method, it is capable of generating a callback on the event handler (in other words, is capable of invoking the event handler).

How does this work in practice? Usually you'll want to assign a single event handler to each event that you're interested in. In that case, that event handler is called when the event is raised. In some circumstances you may wish to associate multiple event handlers with a single event. In that case, you can use AddHandler more than once to create a list of handlers that will respond to the event.

Event Raising Methods

Each class that publishes an event also provides a protected, virtual method that raises the event. When a specific incident occurs in the environment, the publisher class invokes this method. The task of this method is to notify all the event-subscribers about the event.

You can easily identify these event-raising methods in a class declaration because their naming convention is the word "On" followed by the name of the event. For example, OnPreRender() is the method of the Control class that raises the PreRender event when the control is about to render its output. When the ASP.NET page is about to be rendered, the Page class notifies all its subscribers that the PreRender event has occurred by executing the event handlers attached to the PreRender event.

EXAM TIP

Overriding Protected Methods of a Base Class A derived class extends the functionality of its base class. It is generally a good idea to call the base class version of a method from an overridden method in a derived class. This way the derived class will have minimum level of functionality offered by the base class. You can of course write more code in the overridden method to achieve extended functionality of the derived class.

On the other hand, if a derived class does not call the base class version of a method from an overridden method in derived class, you will not be able to access all the functionality provided by the base class in the derived class.

Publishing and Subscribing to an Event

Now that you know the basic concepts involved with publishing and subscribing to an event, let me summarize the process for you.

Publishing an Event

When a publisher wants to publish and raise an event, it needs to take the following steps:

- Define a delegate type that specifies the prototype of the event handler. If the event generates no data, use the predefined EventHandler delegate.
- Define an event based on the delegate type defined in the preceding step.
- Define a protected, virtual method that raises the event.
- When the event occurs in the environment, invoke the protected, virtual method defined in the preceding step.

Subscribing to an Event

When a subscriber wants to subscribe to and handle an event, it needs to take the following steps:

- Implement an event handler with the signature specified by the delegate object of the event.
- Create a delegate object specified for the event. This delegate should refer to the event handler method.
- Attach the event handler to the event.

Event Handling in ASP.NET

Using the event handling concepts discussed so far, I will present the following three techniques to handle events in ASP.NET:

- Handling events by overriding the virtual, protected method of the base class
- Handling events by attaching a delegate to the event
- Handling events of the Page class through AutoEventWireup

Handling Events by Overriding the Virtual, Protected Method of the Base Class

When an ASP.NET page is dynamically compiled, it inherits from the `Page` class. By virtue of this inheritance, the ASP.NET page also derives a set of events and virtual protected methods for raising those events. For example, `OnInit()` is the method of the `Page` class that raises the `Init` event. When a Web page is first created and initialized, it automatically invokes the `OnInit()` method. The `OnInit()` method in turn raises the `Init` event corresponding to the recently initialized `Page` object and passes any required event related data to the `Init` event.

Step by Step 1.4 demonstrates event handling by overriding the virtual, protected method of the base class.

STEP BY STEP

1.4 Handling Events by Overriding the Virtual, Protected Method of the Base Class

1. Add a new text file to the project `305C01`. Name the text file `StepByStep1-4.aspx`.

2. Switch to the HTML view and add the following code to the `StepByStep1-4.aspx` file.

```
<!--StepByStep1_4.aspx-->
<%@ Page Language="vb"%>
<html><body>
<script runat=server>
    Protected Overrides Sub OnLoad(e As EventArgs)
        Response.Write("Message from OnLoad()
method.<br>")
        MyBase.OnLoad(e)
    End Sub
    Protected Overrides Sub OnInit(e As EventArgs)
        Response.Write("Message from OnInit()
method.<br>")
        MyBase.OnInit(e)
    End Sub
    Protected Overrides Sub OnPreRender(e As EventArgs)
        Response.Write( _
         "Message from OnPreRender() method.<br>")
```

continues

continued

```
        MyBase.OnPreRender(e)
    End Sub
</script>
<hr></body>
</html>
```

3. View `StepByStep1-4.aspx` in the browser. You'll see results similar to Figure 1.14.

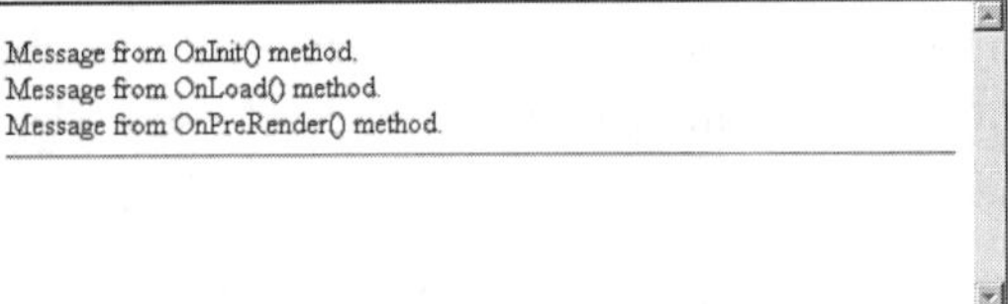

FIGURE 1.14
When an ASP.NET Page object is created, it invokes the OnInit(), OnLoad(), and OnPreRender() methods in order.

When an ASP.NET Page object is created it invokes the `OnInit()`, `OnLoad()`, and `OnPreRender()` methods in that order. You can write custom code in these methods in response to the specific events.

The predefined event handlers `OnInit()`, `OnLoad()`, and so on have more responsibility than just displaying a message. These methods must also bootstrap the event handling process for the events (`Init`, `Load`, and so on) of the Page class. You need not program this functionality again as it is already programmed in the base class, but to ensure that the base class version of an overridden method is also invoked, you need to explicitly call the base class version of a method by using the `MyBase.`*`MemberName`* syntax.

The event handling technique just presented takes advantage of the fact that the derived classes can override the event-raising protected method of the base class that publishes the event. Therefore, this technique of handling events can only be used in the derived class of the class that publishes the event.

If you want to subscribe to events from a class that does not derive from the class that publishes events, you have to use the other event handling scheme which handles events by attaching delegates.

Handling Events by Attaching Delegates

An alternative way of handling an event is by attaching a delegate object to the event. Although this scheme requires additional steps as compared to the event handling scheme described in the previous section, this event handling scheme is far more flexible because of the following reasons:

- Delegates allow you to attach a single event handler to several events. This technique eliminates extra coding efforts when you have to take similar actions when different events occur.
- Delegates allow you to dynamically add and remove event handlers for an event. You can also associate multiple event handlers with an event.
- The subscriber class is not required to derive from the class that publishes an event.

Because of these reasons, event handling using delegates is the preferred way of event handling in Visual Studio .NET. Visual Studio also automates the additional step of attaching the delegate and minimizes the net effort required for implementing event handling.

Step by Step 1.5 uses delegates to display messages when various events for a Page object are raised. I will restrict myself to manually coding the page for now so that you can understand the event handling technique. Once you are familiar with this technique, it will be easier to understand and appreciate Visual Studio .NET specific features for event handling that I'll cover later in this book.

STEP BY STEP

1.5 Handling Events by Attaching a Delegate

1. Add a new text file to the project `305C01`. Name the text file `StepByStep1-5.aspx`.
2. Switch to the HTML view and add the following code to the `StepByStep1-5.aspx` file.

continues

continued

```
<!--StepByStep1_5.aspx-->
<%@ Page Language="vb"%>
<html><body>
<script runat="server">
    Protected Sub StepByStep1_5_Load( _
     o As Object, e As EventArgs)
        Response.Write( _
         "Message from Load event handler.<br>")
    End Sub
    Protected Sub  StepByStep1_5_Init( _
     o As Object, e As EventArgs)
        Response.Write( _
         "Message from Init event handler.<br>")
    End Sub
    Protected Sub  StepByStep1_5_PreRender( _
     o As Object, e As EventArgs)
        Response.Write( _
         "Message from PreRender event handler.<br>")
    End Sub

    Protected Overrides Sub OnInit(e As EventArgs)
        AddHandler Me.Load, AddressOf
Me.StepByStep1_5_Load
        AddHandler Me.PreRender, _
         AddressOf Me.StepByStep1_5_PreRender
        AddHandler Me.Init, AddressOf
Me.StepByStep1_5_Init

        Mybase.OnInit(e)
    End Sub
</script>
<hr></body>
</html>
```

3. View `StepByStep1-5.aspx` in the browser. You'll see results similar to Figure 1.15.

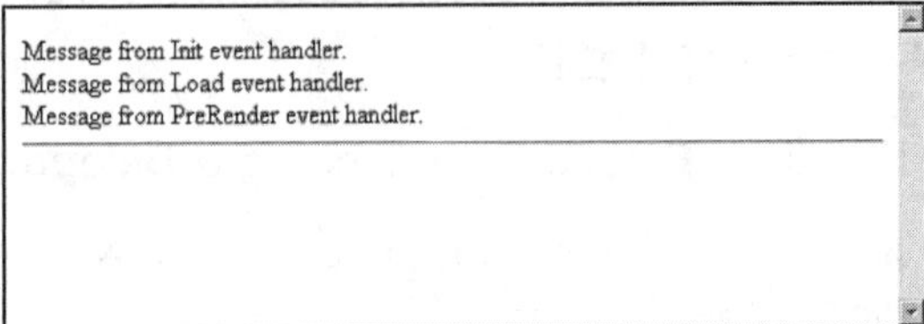

FIGURE 1.15
When an ASP.NET Page is loaded for the first time, the Init, Load, and PreRender events occur in that order.

The first question that might come to you is, if the technique explained used in Step by Step 1.4 is based on delegates, why am I still using the `OnInit()` method in my code? This is because when I attach delegates to an event, I must write that code somewhere.

The `OnInit()` method is an appropriate place to write such code because the `OnInit()` method for an ASP.NET page is executed when the page is initialized. Writing code in the `OnInit()` method ensures that the code will be executed before any other processing on the page.

The crux of the event handling technique used in Step by Step 1.5 lies in the first three lines of the `OnInit()` method. Each of these three lines work in the same way so I will pick up just the first line and explain it in detail:

```
AddHandler Me.Load, AddressOf Me.StepByStep1_5_Load
```

This looks like a complex statement but if you look at it carefully, you can see that there are three parts to it:

- `Load` is the name of an event.
- `Addhandler` is the keyword that hooks up the event.
- `StepByStep1_5_Load` is the name of an event handler.

And here is the role each of them is playing:

- The `Load` event is raised when an ASP.NET page is loaded. A set of event handlers can be attached to an event and when the event is fired, it invokes all the attached event handlers. An event handler can be attached to the `Load` event only through its delegate object. The `Me` keyword qualifies the `Load` event for the current instance of the Web page.
- `StepByStep1_5_Load` is the name of the method that is responding to the `Load` event. When a method name is used with the `AddressOf` operator, it works as a reference to the actual method definition.
- The delegate type of the `Load` event is `EventHandler`. You can add event handlers to a `Load` event only by adding new instances of the delegate to it. In the Visual Studio .NET documentation, the definition of `EventHandler` delegate looks like this:

  ```
  Public Delegate Sub EventHandler( _
  sender As Object, e As EventArgs)
  ```

- This means that EventHandler delegate is capable of storing references to any method that has no return value and that accepts two arguments: the first one of type System.Object and the other one of type EventArgs. The signature of the StepByStep1_5_Load event handler matches the criteria of this delegate, and hence a reference of StepByStep1_5_Load method can be stored in an instance of a delegate of type EventHandler.
- When you have an instance of the EventHandler delegate, you can attach it to the event by using the AddHandler keyword.
- At a later stage, when the Load event is raised, the StepByStep1_5_Load method is invoked through its reference that is maintained by the delegate object.

Handling Events of Page Class Through AutoEventWireup

ASP.NET supports an additional mechanism for handling events raised by the Page class. This technique is called AutoEventWireup.

AutoEventWireup relies on using specific names for the event handlers of Page class events. The name has to be of the type Page_*EventName*. For example, handling the Init, Load, and PreRender events, the name of the event handlers should be Page_Init, Page_Load, and Page_PreRender, respectively.

Event handling through AutoEventWireup only works when the AutoEventWireup attribute of the Page directive is True. The AutoEventWireup attribute is True by default so if you don't specify this attribute in the Page directive it's assumed to be True by ASP.NET. However, if you create your pages using Visual Studio .NET, it will automatically add AutoEventWireup=False to the Page directive.

Step by Step 1.6 demonstrates the use of predefined event handlers to handle various events of the Page class.

STEP BY STEP

1.6 Handling Events of Page Class Through AutoEventWireup

1. Add a new text file to the project `305C01`. Name the text file `StepByStep1-6.aspx`.

2. Switch to the HTML view and add the following code to the `StepByStep1-6.aspx` file.

```
<!--StepByStep1_6.aspx-->
<%@ Page Language="vb"%>
<html><body>
<script runat=server>
    Protected Sub Page_Load(o As Object, e As EventArgs)
        Response.Write( _
         "Message from Load event handler.<br>")
    End Sub
    Protected Sub Page_Init(o As Object, e As EventArgs)
        Response.Write( _
         "Message from Init event handler.<br>")
    End Sub
    Protected Sub Page_PreRender( _
     o As Object, e As EventArgs)
        Response.Write( _
         "Message from PreRender event handler.<br>")
    End Sub
</script>
<hr></body>
</html>
```

3. View `StepByStep1-6.aspx` in the browser. You see the results similar to Step by Step 1.5 as shown in Figure 1.15.

For handling events in Step by Step 1.6, you do not need to explicitly attach any delegates or override any predefined event handlers. Convenient as it may sound, this scheme is not as flexible as event handling through delegates because when you use `AutoEventWireup`, the page event handlers must have specific names. This limits your flexibility in naming the event handlers.

Because of this, event handling using `AutoEventWireup` is not used when creating Web Forms using Visual Studio .NET. You will note later in this chapter that when Visual Studio .NET automatically generates code, it always sets the `AutoEventWireup` attribute of the `Page` directive to `False` by default.

GUIDED PRACTICE EXERCISE 1.2

You need to publish a custom event in your ASP.NET page. The Name of this event is MyEvent and it generates no event-related data. The MyEvent event should be generated when a page is loaded.

To test that the event is published correctly, you also need to subscribe to the event and when the MyEvent event is raised, display the Web server's current date and time.

How would you create a Web page that publishes and subscribes to a custom event?

You should try working through this problem on your own at first. If you are stuck, or if you'd like to see one possible solution, follow these steps:

1. Open the project `305C01`. Add a new text file with the name `GuidedPracticeExercise1-2.aspx` to the project.

2. Switch to the HTML view of the Web page and add the following code to it:

```
<%@ Page Language="vb"%>
<html>
<body>
<script runat="server">
' Begin publishing MyEvent

' Define the event
Public Event MyEvent As EventHandler

' Notify the registered objects of the event
Protected Overridable Sub OnMyEvent(e As EventArgs)
    ' Raise the event
    RaiseEvent MyEvent(Me, e)
End Sub

' Raise MyEvent when the page is loaded
Protected Overrides Sub OnLoad(e As EventArgs)
    ' Raise MyEvent
    OnMyEvent(e)
    Mybase.OnLoad(e)
End Sub

' End publishing MyEvent
```

```
' Begin Subscribing to MyEvent
' Define event handler for MyEvent
Protected Sub RaisingEvents_MyEvent( _
 sender As Object, e As EventArgs)
    Response.Output.Write( _
     "Current date and time: {0}<hr>", _
     DateTime.Now.ToString())
End Sub

' Subscribe to the MyEvent Handler
Protected Overrides Sub OnInit(e As EventArgs)
    AddHandler Me.MyEvent, _
     AddressOf Me.RaisingEvents_MyEvent
    MyBase.OnInit(e)
End Sub

' End Subscribing to MyEvent

</script>
</body></html>
```

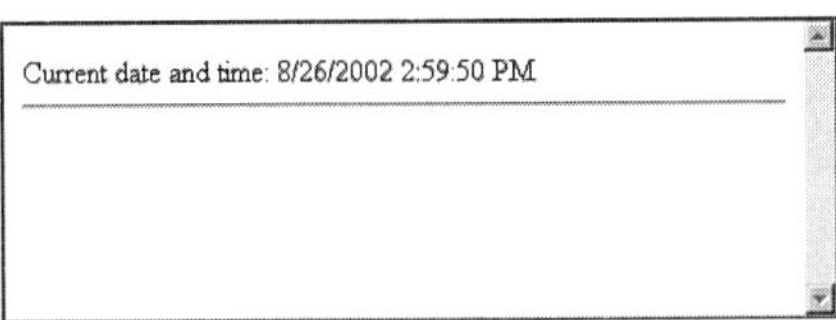

FIGURE 1.16
You can publish custom events in an ASP.NET Web page.

3. View `GuidedPracticeExercise1-2.aspx` in browser. You'll get a result similar to Figure 1.16.

If you have difficulty following this exercise, review the sections "Elements of Event Handling" and "Publishing and Subscribing to an Event" earlier in this chapter. After doing this review, try this exercise again.

REVIEW BREAK

- ASP.NET directives allow you to specify various compiler options.
- The `Page` directive is used to specify page-related attributes that help compilers know how an ASP.NET page is to be compiled and executed.
- Event handling allows a program to respond to changes in the environment. Events in Visual Basic .NET are based on a publisher-subscriber model. The class that creates and implements an event is called the publisher of the event. A class that subscribes a published event by registering an appropriate event handler with the published event is called a subscriber of the event.

continues

continued

- You can respond to an event by overriding the `On` method corresponding to an event. When you use this method, you should be sure to call the corresponding `On` method for the base class so that you don't miss any of the functionality of the base class when the event is raised.
- Custom code can be executed when an event occurs if the code is registered with the event. The pieces of code that respond to an event are called event handlers. An event handler must have a prototype compatible with the event that it is handling.
- Event handlers can be registered with events through delegate objects. Delegates are special objects that are capable of storing references to methods with a particular prototype.
- You can also register events of `Page` class by defining event handlers with specific names such as `Page_Init()`, `Page_Load()`, and so on and setting the `AutoEventWireup` attribute to true in the `Page` directive.

SEPARATING USER INTERFACE FROM BUSINESS LOGIC

In the ASP.NET pages created so far in this chapter you must have noted that the Visual Basic .NET code is interspersed between the HTML code. This is not much of a problem in a simple Web page but for complex Web pages this is not a good idea. Mixing both HTML and ASP.NET code makes Web pages difficult to understand, maintain, and debug. HTML code represents the user interface (UI) of the application while the ASP.NET code defines the business logic for that page. These are two different ideas and often need to be handled differently.

ASP.NET provides a mechanism to separate the user interface portion of a Web page from the business logic. This mechanism is known as code-behind. To implement code-behind, you will write all the user interface related code in one file (.aspx) and the business logic in another file (.vb for VB) and then link these two files using the Page directive in the .aspx file. The linking is provided in the .aspx file instead of the .vb file because the user requests the .aspx file. When ASP.NET compiles the .aspx file, it will look up the `Page` directive to locate the business logic associated with the user interface in the .aspx. There are different ways in which you can use the `Page` directive to link the code to the UI. I'll explain these ways in the following sections.

NOTE

Code-behind Facilitates Team-based Development Often Web designers and programmers will work together to create a Web page. The Web designers work on layout and content to create the visual look and feel for the Web page. Programmers add the business logic that provides the Web page with functionality. Using code-behind when the layout and content is separated from the business logic, allows the Web designers and programmers to independently accomplish their tasks more effectively.

Using Code-behind Without Precompilation

When you write both the UI and business logic in separate files, one way to link them is via the `Src` and `Inherits` attributes of the `Page` directive. Step by Step 1.7 uses the code of Step by Step 1.1 and converts it into the code-behind version. In the new version, I'll store the UI in `StepByStep1-7.aspx` while I store the code in `TemperatureCB.vb`.

STEP BY STEP

1.7 Using Code-behind Without Precompiling

1. Add a new text file to Web project `305C01`. Name the new file `StepByStep1-7.aspx`. Switch to its HTML view and add the following code to the Web page:

```
<!-StepByStep1_7.aspx -->
<%@ Page Language="vb"
 Inherits="Temperature.TemperatureCB"
 Src="TemperatureCB.vb"%>
<html>
<body>
    <h2>Fahrenheit to Celsius Conversion Chart</h2>
    <table border="2">
        <tr>
            <th>&deg Fahrenheit</th><th>&deg
Celsius</th>
        </tr>
```

continues

continued

```
        <%CreateTemperatureTable()%>
    </table>
</body>
</html>
```

2. Right-click the project in the Solution Explorer, and select Add, Add New Item. This opens the Add New Item dialog box. Select the Code File template and name the file `TemperatureCB.vb` as shown in Figure 1.17.

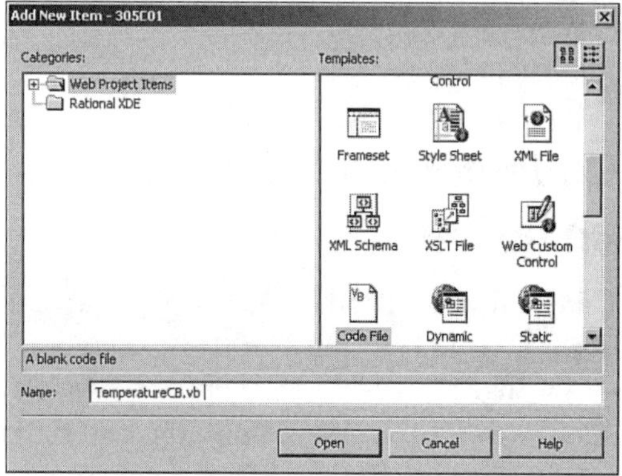

FIGURE 1.17
The code file template allows you to create code files.

3. Add the following code to the file:

```
' TemperatureCB.vb
' Define a namespace
Namespace Temperature
    ' Define TemperatureCB class
    Public Class TemperatureCB
        Inherits System.Web.UI.Page
        ' Define ToCelsius() method
        Function ToCelsius(ByVal f As Double) As Double
            ' Calculate and return the
            ' temperature in Celsius
            ToCelsius = (5.0 / 9.0) * (f - 32.0)
        End Function

        ' Define CreateTemperatureTable() method
        Public Sub CreateTemperatureTable()
            Dim f As Double
            For f = 50.0 To 99.0 Step 1.0
                Response.Output.Write( _
                 "<tr><td>{0}</td><td>" & _
                 "{1:f}</td><tr>", f, ToCelsius(f))
            Next
        End Sub
    End Class
End Namespace
```

4. View StepByStep1_7.aspx file in the browser. You see that the temperature table is created just as it was when you viewed StepByStep1-1.aspx in Step by Step 1.1, shown in Figure 1.7.

In Step by Step 1.7, all the code is enclosed in a namespace. The use of namespaces is a good practice to organize classes and other programming elements. All the code required to generate a temperature table is written in a separate class—TemperatureCB. The source code of the TemperatureCB class is physically present in TemperatureCB.vb.

The Page directive in the StepByStep1_7.aspx file provides the linking mechanism for the UI and the code-behind. The Inherits attribute specifies that when the .aspx file is dynamically compiled, it inherits its functionality from the TemperatureCB class of the Temperature namespace. The Src attribute specifies that the source code for TemperatureCB class is stored in TemperatureCB.vb file.

When the StepByStep1_7.aspx file is requested from the Web server, two files are dynamically compiled—the dynamically generated class file for StepByStep1_7.aspx and the code-behind source code file, TemperatureCB.vb.

In the case of code-behind, the inheritance relationship between the dynamically generated class StepByStep1_7_aspx and the Page class can be represented as shown in Figure 1.18.

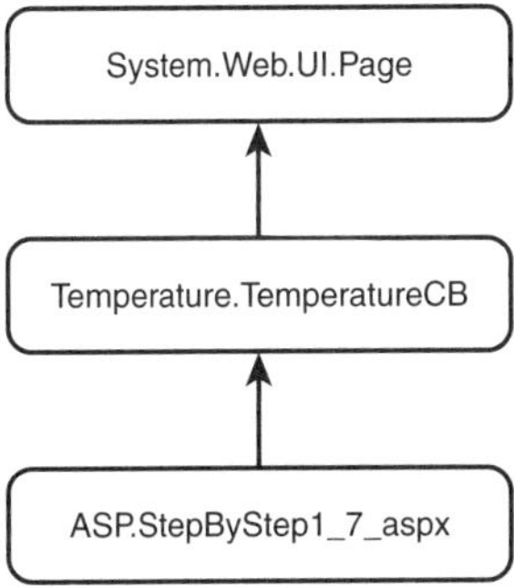

FIGURE 1.18
In the case of code-behind, the ASPX page inherits from the code behind class that usually in turn inherits from the Page class.

Using Code-behind With Precompilation

Another way in which you can use code-behind is by precompiling the code-behind class. Although this technique requires an additional step as compared to the dynamically generated class file, precompilation delivers at least the following three benefits:

- Precompiling a class file ensures that you catch any compilation errors before deploying the Web page.
- You do not have to distribute the source code for the code-behind file.

- If the development and deployment computers use different versions of .NET Framework, precompilation ensures that a class file is compiled using the desired version of the .NET Framework libraries.

Step by Step 1.8 demonstrates how to implement code-behind by precompiling a class.

NOTE

Framework Path Depending on your operating system, you may have to modify the paths in the preceding command to include the proper path to the .NET Framework files.

STEP BY STEP

1.8 Using Code-behind With Precompiling

1. Open the file `StepByStep1_7.aspx`. Switch to its HTML view and remove the `Src` attribute from the Page directive. The `Page` directive should now look like this:

```
<%@ Page Language="vb"
 Inherits="Temperature.TemperatureCB"%>
```

2. Open Visual Studio .NET Command Prompt (Start, Program Files, Visual Studio .NET, Visual Studio .NET Tools, Visual Studio .NET Command Prompt). Change the directory to your project's directory (such as `c:\inetpub\wwwroot\305C01`). Make sure you have a `bin` subdirectory inside the project's directory. Use the following command to compile the code-behind file as shown in Figure 1.19:

```
vbc /t:library /r:C:\WINNT\Microsoft.NET\Framework\
➥ v1.0.3705\System.dll /r:C:\WINNT\Microsoft.NET\
➥ Framework\v1.0.3705\System.Web.dll
➥ /out:bin\305C01.dll TemperatureCB.vb
```

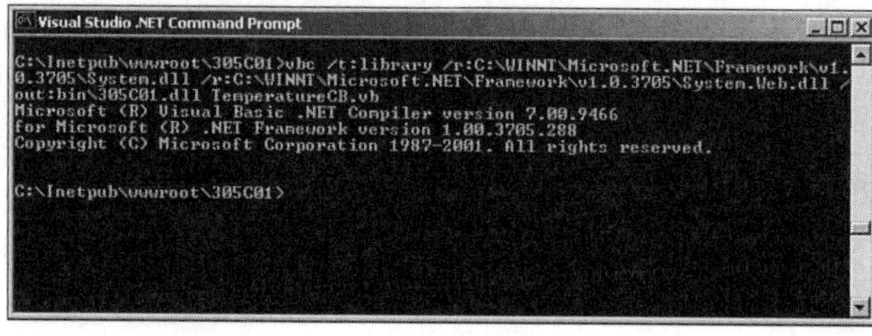

FIGURE 1.19
To precompile a code-behind file, compile it using the VB compiler and place the output in the bin subdirectory of the Web application.

3. Switch to Visual Studio .NET window and view `StepByStep1_7.aspx` file in the browser. You'll see that the temperature table is created just as it was in Step by Step 1.1 and Step by Step 1.7, shown in Figure 1.7.

In the modified `StepByStep1_7.aspx` file, no `Src` attribute is associated with the `Page` directive. Only the `Inherits` attribute of the `Page` directive is used, which specifies the base class for the `.aspx` page. How does ASP.NET locate its base class, `TemperatureCB`, while dynamically compiling the `.aspx` file? ASP.NET is able to locate the class because in step 2 of Step by Step 1.8, the DLL file containing the class is copied to the `bin` subdirectory of the application directory. When ASP.NET compiles the machine-generated class file corresponding to the `.aspx` file, it includes reference to all the DLL files present in the `bin` subdirectory. If you want to confirm this behavior, you can see the detailed compiler output of the `StepByStep1_7.aspx` file using the technique explained in Step by Step 1.2.

Creating a Web Form Using Visual Studio .NET

Web Forms are the preferred way of creating ASP.NET pages using Visual Studio .NET. Web Forms provide three distinct benefits over simple ASP.NET pages:

- Support code-behind by separating contents from business logic. Web Forms created in Visual Studio .NET use the technique of code-behind with precompilation discussed in the previous section.
- Provide an event-based programming model for designing Web pages.
- Support for RAD tools such as Visual Studio .NET.

Because Web Forms are the preferred way of creating Web pages in Visual Studio .NET, I will mostly use this technique for the rest of this book. Step by Step 1.9 demonstrates how to create a Web Form using Visual Studio .NET.

STEP BY STEP

1.9 Creating a Web Form Using Visual Studio .NET.

1. Open Solution Explorer window for project `305C01`. Right-click the project name and select Add, Add Web Form. In the Add New Item dialog box, name the file `StepByStep1-9.aspx`. The Web Form is in Design view. In the background of the form, you'll see a message as shown in Figure 1.20 asking you to select between grid layout mode and flow layout mode.

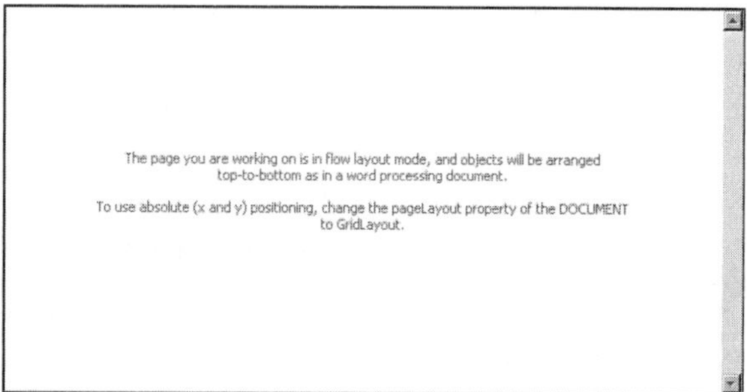

FIGURE 1.20
The Web Form Designer supports two layout modes: grid layout and flow layout.

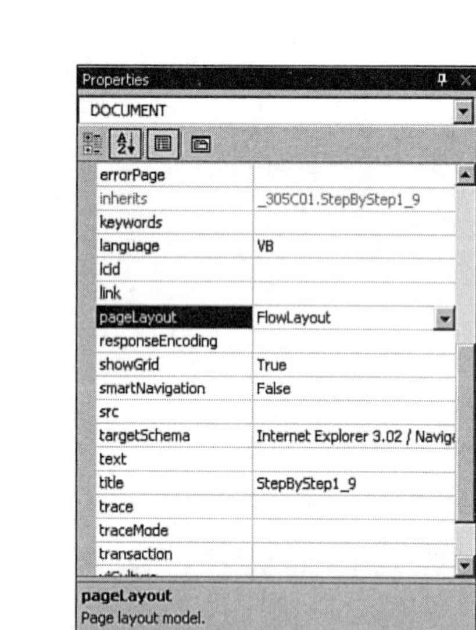

FIGURE 1.21
The Properties window shows the properties of an object.

2. Open the Properties window by selecting View, Properties Window. Change the `pageLayout` property of `DOCUMENT` to `FlowLayout`. (See Figure 1.21.)

3. In the flow layout mode, type "Fahrenheit to Celsius Conversion Chart" on the page. Select the text and change its block format to Heading 2 using the Block Format combo box on the formatting toolbar.

4. Press Enter to move to a new line on the Web form. Select Table, Insert, Table. In the Insert Table dialog box select options to make a table that is size 1 row and 2 columns. Set the Width attribute to 200 pixels (see Figure 1.22).

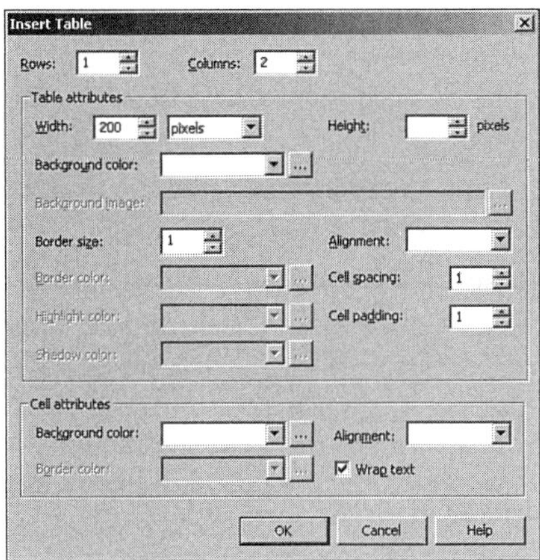

FIGURE 1.22
Tables are useful in aligning text and controls on a page in the flow layout mode.

5. Switch to the HTML view of StepByStep1_9.aspx file. Modify the code in the `<TABLE>` tag as shown here:

```
<TABLE id="Table1" cellSpacing="1" cellPadding="1"
        width="200" border="1">
    <TR>
        <TD>&deg Fahrenheit</TD>
        <TD>&deg Celcius</TD>
    </TR>
    <%CreateTemperatureTable()%>
</TABLE>
```

6. Invoke Solution Explorer, right-click `StepByStep1_9.aspx`, and select View Code. This will open the code-behind file `StepByStep1-9.aspx.vb`. Add the following code just above the Web Form Designer generated code region:

```
' Define ToCelsius() method
Function ToCelsius(ByVal f As Double) As Double
    ' Calculate and return the temperature in Celsius
    ToCelsius = (5.0 / 9.0) * (f - 32.0)
End Function

' Define CreateTemperatureTable() method
Public Sub CreateTemperatureTable()
    Dim f As Double
    For f = 50.0 To 99.0 Step 1.0
        Response.Output.Write( _
         "<tr><td>{0}</td><td>" & _
         "{1:f}</td><tr>", f, ToCelsius(f))
    Next
End Sub
```

7. In the Solution Explorer, right-click `StepByStep1_9.aspx` and select Set As Start Page.

continues

continued

8. Compile the page by selecting Build, Build 305C01. Run the page by selecting Debug, Start Without Debugging. You see that the temperature table is created just as it was in Step by Steps 1.1, 1.7, and 1.8, shown in Figure 1.7.

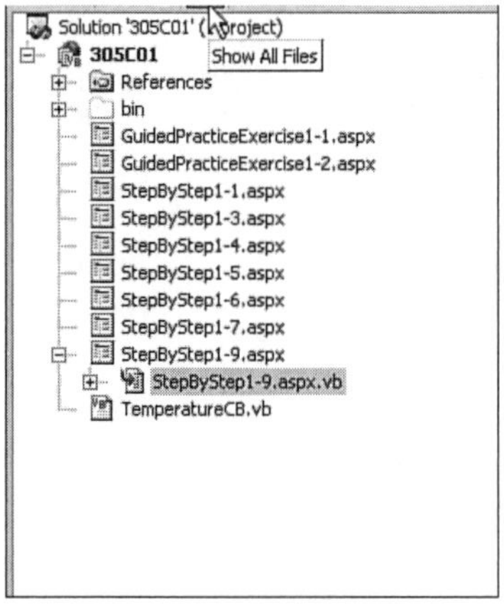

FIGURE 1.23
You can see the code-behind file for a Web Form by clicking on the Show All Files toolbar button.

An ASP.NET Web Form is made up of two distinct pieces:

- The user interface piece stored in the .aspx file
- The business logic piece stored in a .vb file

Visual Studio keeps the name of the .vb file synchronized with the name of .aspx file. If you can't find the .vb file corresponding to a Web Form listed in the Solution Explorer, that's because Visual Studio .NET hides it in the default view. To display the code-behind .vb file, select the project and click the "Show All Files" toolbar button in the Solution Explorer Window as shown in Figure 1.23.

Analyzing the User Interface Piece of a Web Form

The code-behind technique used in Step by Step 1.5 is similar to that discussed in the previous section, but some differences in the code should draw your attention. First, in the `StepByStep1-9.aspx` file, the `Page` directive is written as

```
<%@ Page Language="vb" AutoEventWireup="false"
Codebehind="StepByStep1-9.aspx.vb"
Inherits="_305C01.StepByStep1_9"%>
```

This usage of the `Page` directive has two new attributes—`AutoEventWireup` and `Codebehind`. `AutoEventWireup` is used for event handling. The `Codebehind` attribute is used by Visual Studio .NET to track the location of the source code of code behind file. ASP.NET does not understand the `Codebehind` attribute and therefore ignores it. This attribute does not play any role in the execution of the ASP.NET page.

EXAM TIP

The Codebehind Attribute Does Not Work Like the Src Attribute
In the `Page` directive, when the name of a source code file is specified using the Src attribute, the source code file is dynamically compiled at the runtime. This isn't true for the `Codebehind` attribute, which is just necessary for design time support in Visual Studio .NET. The `Codebehind` attribute plays no role at runtime because it's actually not at all recognized by ASP.NET.

Analyzing the Business Logic Piece of a Web Form

When you analyze the file storing the business logic piece (such as StepByStep1-9.aspx.vb) for a Web form, you'll observe that the source code generated by Visual Studio .NET is much more detailed than the earlier version of the code-behind file that I created manually (TemperatureCB.vb). Although all this code is not required for a simple program such as a temperature conversion chart, it might be useful when you add more functionality to the program.

The first thing you will notice in StepByStep1-9.aspx.vb is that Visual Studio .NET groups code into blocks. This feature is called *code outlining*. You can expand and collapse code blocks by using the + and – signs near the left margin of the window in code view. (See Figure 1.24.) Code outlining is especially helpful when you are working with large code files. You can collapse certain areas of code that you do not want to focus on at that time and continue editing the expanded sections that interest you.

EXAM TIP

Visual Studio .NET Sets AutoEventWireup to False for a Web Page If you are handling events in your program by attaching the delegates, you should set `AutoEventWireup` attribute to `False`. If you keep it `True`, as the page runs some of the event handlers may be called twice.

To understand why, assume that you want to handle the Load event for the Page object. You create a method named `Page_Load` and attach it to the Load event of the Page using a delegate object. Now, because `AutoEventWireup` attribute is true, the ASP.NET page framework will also automatically attach `Page_Load` as an event handler for `Load` event of the page. This results into registration of same event handler twice and hence the event handler will be also invoked twice when the event is raised.

This is why Visual Studio .NET always keeps `AutoEventWireup` set to `False`.

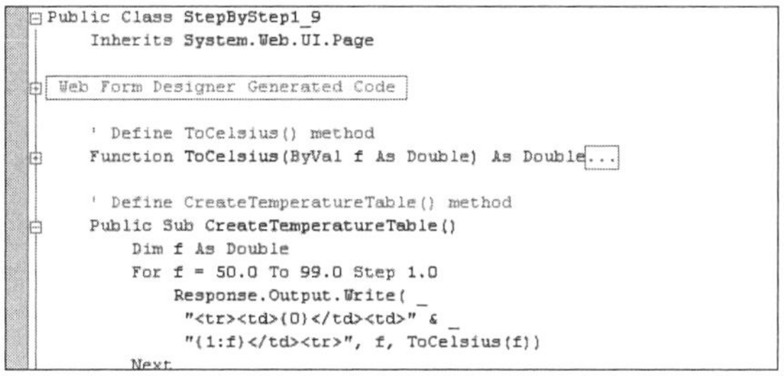

```
Public Class StepByStep1_9
    Inherits System.Web.UI.Page

 Web Form Designer Generated Code

    ' Define ToCelsius() method
    Function ToCelsius(ByVal f As Double) As Double...

    ' Define CreateTemperatureTable() method
    Public Sub CreateTemperatureTable()
        Dim f As Double
        For f = 50.0 To 99.0 Step 1.0
            Response.Output.Write( _
             "<tr><td>{0}</td><td>" & _
             "{1:f}</td><tr>", f, ToCelsius(f))
        Next
```

FIGURE 1.24
Code outlining and grouping allows you to focus on the piece of code that interests you while collapsing others that do not want your attention.

StepByStep1-9.aspx.vb also shows a rectangular block marked as "Web Form Designer generated code." This is a block of collapsed code with a name. When you expand the block, you'll see a set of statements included between #region and #endregion directives. These directives mark the beginning and end of a named code block. You can specify a name after the #region directive to identify the code block with a name. When you collapse this region, you can easily figure out what the collapsed code block does by looking at the name associated with the region. These directives are only useful in visual designers such as Visual Studio .NET, for effective presentation of your code. When code is compiled, these directives are not present in the executable code.

WARNING

Web Form Designer Generated Code The code enclosed in the code block titled "Web Form Designer generated code" is required for Designer support and you should not generally modify it.

The class definition for the `StepByStep1_9` class looks like this:

```
Public Class StepByStep1_9
    Inherits System.Web.UI.Page
    ...
End Class
```

In the file `StepByStep1_9.aspx.vb`, you can also write this definition as

```
Imports System.Web.UI
Public Class StepByStep1_9
    Inherits Page
    ...
End Class
```

How does the compiler locate a class if its full namespace qualified name is not provided? The VB.NET language designers noted that typing the full namespace with a class every time it is used is a lot of typing, so they provided a shortcut for this via the `Imports` directive.

The inclusion of `Imports` statements directs the VB compiler to search for each class that you are using in the namespaces specified in the `Imports` statement. The compiler looks up each namespace one by one, and when it finds the given class in one of the namespaces, it internally replaces the reference of the class with *`NamespaceName.ClassName`* in the code.

This Web Form in Step by Step 1.9 is inheriting its functionality from the StepByStep1_9 class. You know that the code for the StepByStep1_9 class is stored in compiled form in StepByStep1_9.dll file that is stored in the bin subdirectory within the Web application's folder. The class StepByStep1-9 derives its functionality from the System.Web.UI.Page class. Where is the code for the System.Web.UI.Page class and other classes in FCL? Code for various classes in the FCL is packaged as libraries (that is, .dll files), and Visual Studio .NET is smart enough to automatically include references to commonly used library in your project. Visual Studio .NET also lets you include references to other libraries. You can see what libraries are included with a project by opening the Solution Explorer and navigating to the References hierarchy within the project (refer to Figure 1.25).

NOTE

Don't Confuse Library Names with Namespaces The name of a library doesn't map directly to the name of a namespace. For example, classes in the namespace System.Web.UI, are not stored in System.Web.UI.dll, instead they are packaged in a file named System.Web.dll. In fact, the name of a library file and the name of a namespace are very different concepts. A library is a physical unit that stores classes as a single deployment unit. A library exists as a file and can contain code for one or more classes. Those classes may belong to different namespaces. A namespace is just a logical organization of classes and has no physical form. Creation of code libraries is discussed in more detail in Chapter 7, "Creating and Managing Components and .NET Assemblies."

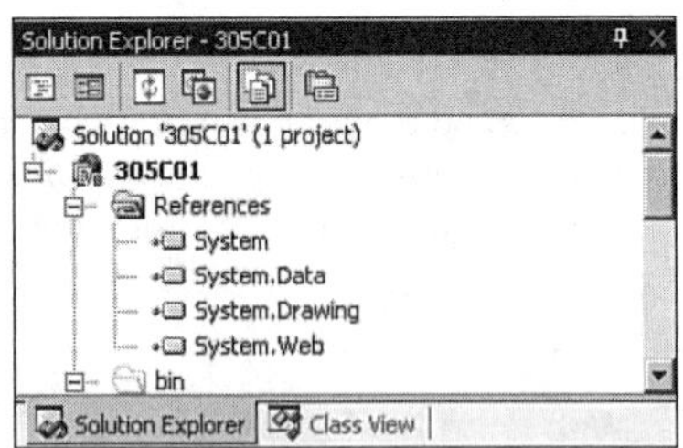

FIGURE 1.25
You can add or remove references to FCL and other libraries using the References node in the Solution Explorer window.

GUIDED PRACTICE EXERCISE 1.3

You are developing a Web site for providing ASP.NET related information to your friends and peers. You want a Web page that displays one of the few selected sites as a Features site when the user visits your page. The featured site is randomly selected from a list of Web sites.

How would you create such a Web page?

You should try working through this problem on your own first. If you are stuck, or if you would like to see one possible solution, follow these steps:

1. Open the project `305C01`. Add a new Web Form with the name `GuidedPracticeExercise1-3.aspx` to the project.
2. Switch to the Code view of the Web Form and add the following code to its `Page_Load` event handler:

```
Private Sub Page_Load( _
 ByVal sender As System.Object, _
 ByVal e As System.EventArgs) Handles MyBase.Load
    Dim WebSites() As String
    WebSites = New String() _
       {"http://www.asp.net", _
        "http://msdn.microsoft.com/net", _
        "http://www.gotdotnet.com", _
        "http://www.aspfriends.com", _
        "http://www.asptoday.com", _
        "http://www.aspfree.com", _
        "http://www.4guysfromrolla.com"}
    Dim randomNumber As Random = New Random()
    Response.Write("<h2>Featured Website:</h2><br>")
    Response.Output.Write("<a href='{0}'>{0}</a>", _
     Websites(randomNumber.Next(0, 7)))
End Sub
```

3. In the Solution Explorer, right-click `GuidedPracticeExercise1-3.aspx` and select Set As Start Page.
4. Run the page by selecting Debug, Start Without Debugging. You will get a randomly selected Web site as shown in Figure 1.26.

FIGURE 1.26
A site is selected from a list of sites using the random number generation capabilities of the System.Random class.

If you have difficulty following this exercise, review the section "Creating a Web Form Using Visual Studio .NET" earlier in this chapter. Also, look at the .NET Framework documentation for System.Random class. After doing this review, try this exercise again.

REVIEW BREAK

- ASP.NET provides a technique called code-behind to separate the user interface portion of a Web page from the business logic. The user interface is written in an aspx page (.aspx) and the business logic code is written in a Visual Basic .NET code file (.vb).
- The Inherits attribute of the Page directive specifies the name of the class. The Src attribute allows you to specify the name of the code-behind file that contains the code for the aspx page so that it can be compiled when the page is requested. If you are precompiling the code-behind file, you need not specify the Src attribute.
- Visual Studio .NET uses code-behind with precompilation as the preferred way of creating Web forms.

CHAPTER SUMMARY

KEY TERMS

- ASP.NET
- Class
- CLR (Common Language Runtime)
- Delegate
- Event
- Event handling
- FCL (Framework Class Library)
- Field
- Inheritance
- IL
- JIT (just-in-time) compilation
- Managed code
- Namespace
- .NET Framework
- Property
- Structure

The .NET Framework is a standards-based multilanguage platform for developing next-generation distributed applications. ASP.NET, which is a subset of the .NET Framework, provides classes that enable you to develop Web-based applications. Visual Studio .NET provides a productive IDE for developing .NET Framework applications.

Event handling plays a key role in user interface–based programming; through event handling, you respond to various events that are fired as a result of user actions or through the changes in the environment. This chapter discusses various ways to handle events.

ASP.NET encourages the separation of user interface from the business logic and enables you to develop Web pages that are easier to develop, understand, and maintain. This technique is called *code-behind* and it is the preferred way of creating Web Forms in Visual Studio .NET.

In this chapter, you have learned about the basics of the Page class and its execution process. In the next chapter you will learn how to create user interface for an ASP.NET page using various controls.

APPLY YOUR KNOWLEDGE

Exercises

1.1 Creating and Managing Virtual Directories

A virtual directory is a directory that is not stored at the same place as it would appear to client browsers. A virtual directory is identified by an alias, a name that Web browsers use to access a directory. An alias has three advantages over the actual path name:

- An alias is more convenient to type as it is usually shorter than the path name of the actual directory.
- An alias is more secure because it hides the actual directory location from the users.
- Use of an alias gives you the liberty to freely reorganize the directory structure on your computer as long as you point the alias to the desired directory.

In this exercise, you will learn how to create and manage virtual directories using Internet Information Services.

Estimated time: 10 minutes

1. Use Windows Explorer to create a directory on your hard drive that will correspond to the virtual directory to be created.
2. Right-click the My Computer icon and select Manage from its shortcut menu. Navigate to Internet Information Services under the Services and Application hierarchy.
3. Expand the Internet Information Services node. You will see a node named Default Web Site as shown in Figure 1.27.

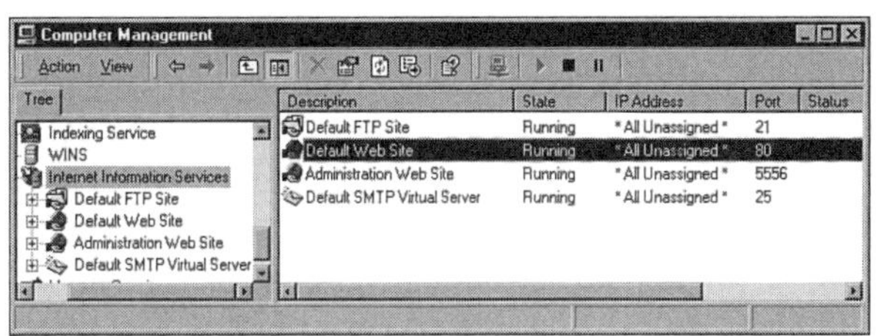

FIGURE 1.27
Use Internet Information Services to manage the Web applications on the Web server.

4. Right-click the Default Web Site icon and select New, Virtual Directory from its shortcut menu. This starts the Virtual Directory Creation Wizard. Click Next on the welcome screen.
5. The next screen as shown in Figure 1.28, prompts you to enter an alias for the virtual directory. Enter Chapter01. This is the path that users will attach to your Web server name to access the contents of a directory. As a developer, you will use this path to specify the location of a project in Visual Studio .NET.

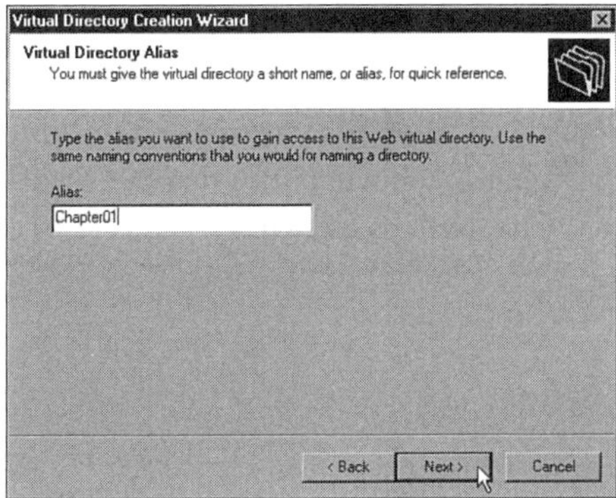

FIGURE 1.28
The Virtual Directory Alias screen allows you to specify an alias for the virtual directory.

APPLY YOUR KNOWLEDGE

6. Click Next to proceed to the Web Site Content Directory screen, shown in Figure 1.29. Here you specify the actual path on your hard drive that maps to the virtual directory specified in the previous step. I decided to specify the directory C:\inetpub\wwwroot\Chapter01. You can choose any path that you like. Make sure that the specified path already exists.

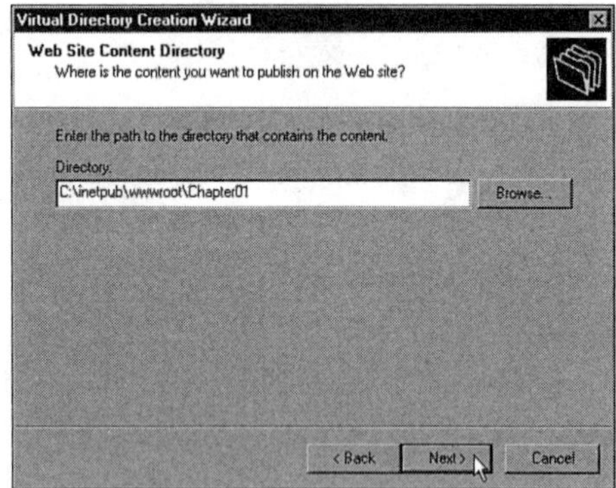

FIGURE 1.29
The Web Site Content Directory screen allows you to specify the directory on the Web server.

7. Click Next to proceed to the Access Permissions screen. Keep the default permissions as shown in Figure 1.30 and click Next button to complete the Wizard. You will notice that the virtual directory Chapter01 is created.

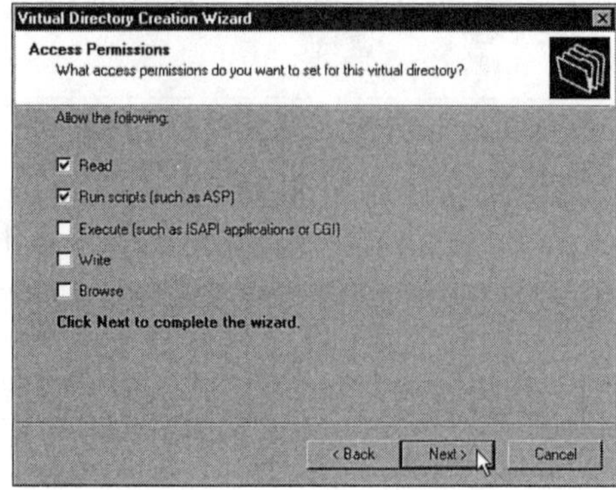

FIGURE 1.30
The Access Permissions screen allows you to specify the permissions for the virtual directory.

Virtual directories allow you to organize your projects by storing them into separate folders. Internet Information Services allows you to create and manage the virtual folders even when Visual Studio .NET is not installed on the Web server, which is especially true for the production Web servers.

1.2 Using Reflection to Find Information About the Page Class

Reflection is a technique that allows you to dynamically get information about types. It also allows you to dynamically create and invoke types at runtime. The System.Type class represents a type inside your program and is root of all reflection operations. In this exercise, you will use the Type class to list all the base types of the Page class.

Estimated time: 15 minutes

1. Create a new Visual Basic .NET project. Select ASP.NET Web Application as the template for the project and create the project at the location— http://localhost/305C01Exercises as shown in Figure 1.31.

APPLY YOUR KNOWLEDGE

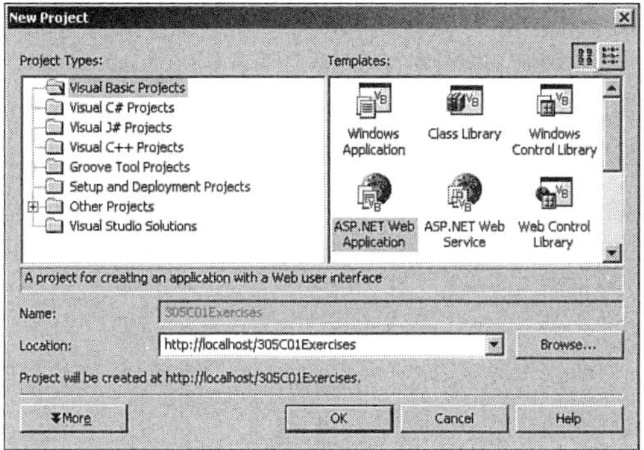

FIGURE 1.31
Create a new ASP.NET Web Application project to organize the Web Forms.

2. Using Solution Explorer, delete the default Web Form. Add a new Web Form named Exercise2.aspx.

3. Right-click the Web Form and select View Code. Add a line of code at the top of the module:

```
Imports System.Reflection
```

4. Add the following code to the Page_Load() method of Exercise2 class:

```
Private Sub Page_Load( _
ByVal sender As System.Object, _
 ByVal e As System.EventArgs) _
 Handles MyBase.Load
    Dim t As Type = Me.GetType()
    Do
        Response.Output.Write( _
             "{0}<BR>", t.Name)
        t = t.BaseType
    Loop While Not t Is Nothing
End Sub
```

5. Build the project. Right-click the page in Solution Explorer and select View in Browser.

6. You will see a list of all the classes showing the inheritance hierarchy for Exercise2.aspx as shown in Figure 1.32.

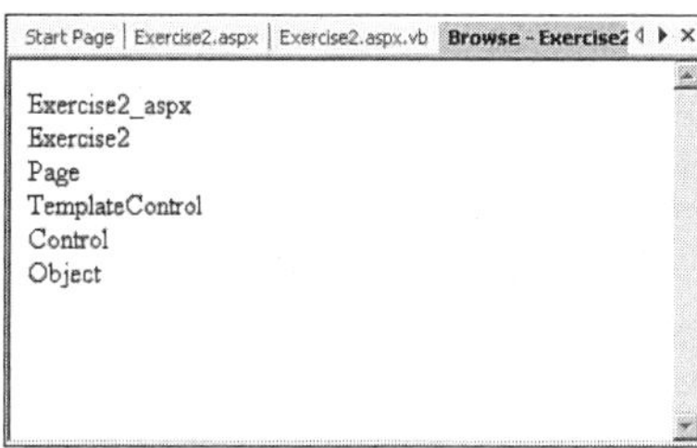

FIGURE 1.32
You can use reflection classes to get type information at runtime.

1.3 Using the MSIL Disassembler (ildasm.exe)

The .NET Framework SDK provides a tool called the MSIL Disassembler (Ildasm.exe). Ildasm.exe can parse any EXE or DLL file created using the .NET Framework, and shows the information contained in it in a user-friendly format. You can use Ildasm.exe to display type information about programs that you write as well as to examine native .NET Framework assemblies, such as Mscorlib.dll. As you learn more about the .NET Framework, Ildasm.exe will be great learning tool to understand and debug programs.

Estimated time: 10 minutes

1. Launch a Visual Studio .NET Command Prompt. Type the following command on the command line:

```
ildasm
```

APPLY YOUR KNOWLEDGE

2. This will open the MSIL Disassembler. Select File, Open, and browse to the directory where the .NET Framework is installed (it is something like, c:\WINNT\Microsoft.NET\Framework\v1.0.3705). Open System.Web.dll file.

3. Navigate to the System.Web.UI.Page class and look for the MapPath() method as shown in Figure 1.33. Methods are identified using a magenta rectangle.

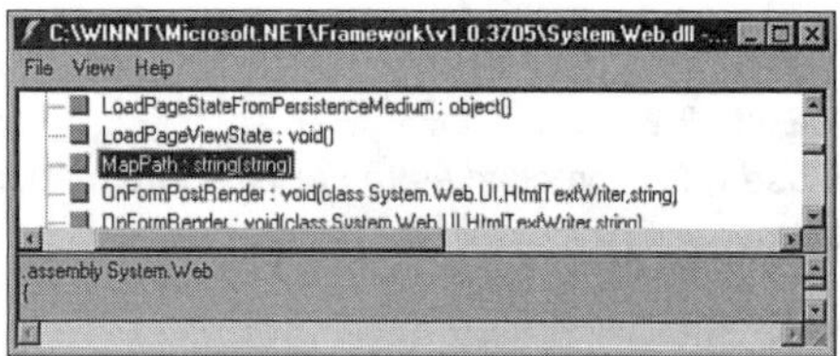

FIGURE 1.33
Use Ildasm.exe to analyze the information in the .NET Framework EXE or DLL file.

4. Double-click the MapPath() method. Another window opens as shown in Figure 1.34, that shows the disassembled Microsoft Intermediate Language (MSIL) code for the MapPath() method. MSIL is the universal format that pre-compiling a class produces in .NET.

Page::MapPath : string(string)

```
.method public hidebysig instance string
        MapPath(string virtualPath) cil managed
{
  // Code size       13 (0xd)
  .maxstack  8
  IL_0000:  ldarg.0
  IL_0001:  ldfld      class System.Web.HttpRequest System.Web.U
  IL_0006:  ldarg.1
  IL_0007:  callvirt   instance string System.Web.HttpRequest::M
  IL_000c:  ret
} // end of method Page::MapPath
```

FIGURE 1.34
Ildasm.exe can display MSIL code corresponding to methods in a class.

You can also use ildasm.exe to display information about the compiled files corresponding to your ASP.NET pages or the code-behind files. Although you won't get exam questions on the MSIL code, analyzing the generated MSIL for your own VB program is a good learning exercise to develop insights about the .NET Framework.

Review Questions

1. Describe the difference between a public field and a public property.
2. What is the purpose of organizing classes in namespaces?
3. Does Visual Basic .NET support multiple inheritance?
4. What are the benefits of deriving from the Page class?
5. What can you achieve with the Page directive?
6. What is the usual signature of an event handler?
7. What are the steps involved in publishing an event?
8. What are the steps to be performed in order to handle an event?
9. How does ASP.NET allow you to separate user interface from the business logic?
10. What are the advantages of precompiling the code-behind class?

APPLY YOUR KNOWLEDGE

Exam Questions

1. You are developing a Web Form to display weather information. When a user requests the Web Form, the form needs to do some initializations that will change the appearance of the form and assign values to some controls. Where should you put the code?

   A. In the InitializeComponent() method

   B. In the event handler for the Load event of the page

   C. In the event handler for the Init event of the page

   D. In the event handler for the PreRender event of the page

2. You are developing an online gaming application. The application provides a rich interface to the user and takes several actions when the user interacts with the Web page. You put several controls on the Web page. Each of these controls publishes some events that you need to handle in the page. In which of the following method of the ASP.NET page should you attach event handlers to the events?

   A. OnInit()

   B. OnLoad()

   C. OnPreRender()

   D. OnUnload()

3. You are developing a Web Form using Visual Studio .NET. You have placed the initialization code in the Page_Load() method of the form. You have then attached this method to the Load event of the Web Form. When you execute the program you note that the Page_Load() method is executing twice instead of executing just once. What should you do to correct this problem?

   A. Set AutoEventWireup to True in the Page directive of the Web Form.

   B. Set AutoEventWireup to False in the Page directive of the Web Form.

   C. Set SmartNavigation to True in the Page directive of the Web Form.

   D. Set SmartNavigation to False in the Page directive of the Web Form.

4. Part of your Web page looks like this:

```
<%@ Page Language="vb"%>
<html>
    <body>
        <script runat="server">
    Protected Sub Page_Load(o As Object, e As
EventArgs)
        ' Call procedure to load customers
        LoadCustomers()
        ' Call procedure to load orders
        LoadOrderss()
    End Sub
        </script>
        ... other code omitted ...
    </body>
</html>
```

   Now you've decided that you need to perform the same processing that your code does in the Page_Load event handler from several other events on the page. What strategy should you use? (select two)

   A. Call the Page_Load procedure from within the other event handlers.

   B. Copy the code from the Page_Load procedure to the other event handlers.

APPLY YOUR KNOWLEDGE

C. Disable AutoEventWireup.

D. Use AddHandler to associate a single procedure with multiple events.

5. Your colleague is designing an event-driven Web page. This Web page will be used by the material management group of your company. She needs to handle an event named LowInventory in the Web page and change the color of a Label control to red whenever LowInventory event is raised. She has written the following code in an ASP.NET Web Form to attach an event handler with the LowInventory event:

```
Protected Overrides Sub OnInit( _
 e As EventArgs)
    AddHandler Me.LowInventory _
     AddressOf Me.Inventory_LowInventory
End Sub
```

When she executes the page, she notes that although the LowInventory event is handled properly, other events that were previously raised by the page have stopped occurring. Which of the following options would you recommend to her to resolve this problem?

A. Change the method definition to

```
Protected Overrides Sub OnLoad( _
 e As EventArgs)
    AddHandler Me.LowInventory _
     AddressOf Me.Inventory_LowInventory
End Sub
```

B. Change the method definition to

```
Protected Overrides Sub OnLoad( _
 e As EventArgs)
    AddHandler Me.LowInventory _
     AddressOf Me.Inventory_LowInventory
    MyBase.OnInit(e)
End Sub
```

C. Change the method definition to

```
Protected Overrides Sub OnInit( _
 e As EventArgs)
    AddHandler Me.LowInventory _
     AddressOf Me.Inventory_LowInventory
    MyBase.OnInit(e)
End Sub
```

D. Change the method definition to

```
Protected Overrides Sub OnInit( _
 e As EventArgs)
    AddHandler Me.LowInventory _
     AddressOf Me.Inventory_LowInventory
    MyBase.OnLoad(e)
End Sub
```

6. You are developing a library of useful classes that you plan to sell over the Internet to other developers. In one of the classes, CommercePage, you have a method named Render(). You would like users of the library to be able to change the definition of the Render () method in a class that derives from CommercePage. You do not want to make the Render() method visible to those classes that do not derive from CommercePage. Which of the following modifiers should be applied to the Render() method while defining it in the CommercePage class?

A. Public

B. Protected

C. Friend

D. Overrides

7. You want to implement your Web page using the code-behind technique. You place the user interface in a file named WeatherPage.aspx and the business logic in another file named WeatherPage.aspx.vb. The WeatherPage.aspx.vb file contains the definition for a class that derives from the Page class. You want to link the user interface file with the code-behind file.

APPLY YOUR KNOWLEDGE

You do not want to compile the business logic before you deploy it on the Web server. Which of the following attributes will you use for the Page directive in WeatherPage.aspx file? (Select two.)

A. Src

B. Inherits

C. Codebehind

D. Class

8. You are designing a Web application that contains several Web Forms. One of the Web Forms, Catalog.aspx, displays catalogs to the users and performs several actions based on user input. You have used event handling extensively to make Catalog.aspx responsive to the user. When Catalog.aspx is loaded you need to invoke a method name PerformInitializations(). What statement should you use in the Web Form to achieve this?

A.

```
Me.Init = EventHandler( _
 PerformInitializations)
```

B.

```
Me.Init = New EventHandler( _
 PerformInitializations)
```

C.

```
Me.Load = New EventHandler( _
 PerformInitializations)
```

D.

```
AddHandler Me.Load, AddressOf _
 Me.EventHandler(PerformInitializations)
```

9. You want to display values of VB.NET expressions in an ASPX page. Which of the following types of code block would you use to enclose the expression in an ASPX file?

A. <script runat=server>…</script>

B. <script>…</script>

C. <%…%>

D. <form>…</form>

10. You have developed and deployed a Web application on a Web server. When users request the default.aspx file from the Web server from their browser, they are being prompted to download the default.aspx file on their computer. Which of the following components is having problems on the Web server?

A. aspnet_wp.exe

B. InetInfo.exe

C. aspnet_isapi.dll

D. csc.exe

11. Which of the following steps is not required for subscribing to an event?

A. Implement an event handler with the signature specified by the delegate object of the event.

B. Create a delegate object specified for the event. This delegate should refer to the event handler method.

C. Attach the event handler to the event. Remember to use the AddHandler method for attaching the delegate so that you don't cancel any of the previously registered delegates.

APPLY YOUR KNOWLEDGE

D. Define a protected, virtual method that raises the event.

12. You have developed a timesheet entry application that will be used by all employees in your company. You have used ASP.NET to develop this application and have deployed it on the company's Web server. What should you recommend to all the employees of the company to install on their computers before accessing the timesheet entry application?

    A. .NET Framework Redistributable

    B. .NET Framework SDK

    C. Visual Studio .NET

    D. Web Browser

13. You have created a Web page that users will use to register on the Web site. Inside the event handler for the Load event of the Page, you want to access the data entered by the user on the Web page. Which of the following property of the Page class can give you access to this data?

    A. ClientTarget

    B. Request

    C. Response

    D. Trace

14. You have created an ASP.NET Web Form using the code-behind technique. The user interface is stored in DisplayCatalog.aspx and the business logic is stored in DisplayCatalog.aspx.vb. You want to compile the code-behind file before you deploy it on the Web server. Which of the following commands will you use at the command line?

    A. vbc /t:library DisplayCatalog.aspx.vb

    B. vbc DisplayCatalog.aspx.vb

    C. vbc /t:library DisplayCatalog.aspx

    D. vbc DisplayCatalog.aspx

15. You have created an ASP.NET Web Form using the code-behind technique. The user interface is stored in DisplayCatalog.aspx and the business logic is stored in DisplayCatalog.aspx.vb. You have compiled the business logic and created a file named DisplayCatalog.dll. Where should you keep this file so that it can located by ASP.NET at runtime when a user requests DisplayCatalog.aspx?

    A. Store DisplayCatalog.dll in the same directory as DisplayCatalog.aspx.

    B. Store DisplayCatalog.dll in the System directory of the Web server.

    C. Store DisplayCatalog.dll in a subdirectory named DLL inside the Web application.

    D. Store DisplayCatalog.dll in a subdirectory named BIN inside the Web application.

Answers to Review Questions

1. A property, unlike a field, does not have any storage location associated with it. Generally (but not necessarily), a property would use a private field to store its data and expose its value through a pair of accessors named `Get` and `Set` that are used for read and write operations, respectively. These accessors can encapsulate program logic that runs when the property is read or written. A property is the preferred way to expose class characteristics.

2. Namespaces serve two purposes: They help organize classes by logically grouping them and they allow you to uniquely identify classes, thereby avoiding any naming conflicts that might otherwise occur.

APPLY YOUR KNOWLEDGE

3. Multiple inheritance is not supported in Visual Basic .NET. A class can inherit from only one base class. However, it can have many base classes through a chain of inheritance.

4. When you derive from the Page class, you automatically provide the derived class with the following benefits—capabilities for state management, access to the intrinsic objects, information about client, access to the controls placed on Web page, and notifications for handling page-level events.

5. The Page directive can be used to specify page related attributes that can control the way an ASP.NET page should be compiled and executed.

6. The event handler method usually contains two parameters the first being the object on which the event occurred and the second is the object of type System.EventArgs or its derived class that contains event related data.

7. The steps involved in publishing an event are

    - Define a delegate type that specifies the prototype of the event handler. If the event is generating no data then use the predefined EventHandler delegate.

    - Define an event based on the delegate type defined in the preceding step.

    - Define a protected, virtual method that raises the event.

    - When the event occurs in the environment, invoke the protected, virtual method defined in the preceding step.

8. To handle an event, you need to take care of the following steps:

    - Implement an event handler with the signature specified by the delegate object of the event.

    - Create a delegate object specified for the event. This delegate should refer to the event handler method.

    - Attach the event handler to the event. You should use the AddHandler statement for attaching the delegate so that you don't cancel any of the previously registered delegates.

9. ASP.NET provides a technique called code-behind to separate the user interface portion of a Web page from the business logic. The user interface portion of code is written in an ASPX page and the business logic code is written in a Visual Basic code file (.vb).

10. Precompiling a class file ensures that you catch any compilation errors before deploying the Web page. Also, once the code-behind file are compiled, you just need to deploy the compiled DLL files on the Web server. The source files need not be deployed.

Answers to Exam Questions

1. **B**. The most appropriate place to put these types of initialization is the Load event handler.

2. **A**. You would like to attach event handlers with the event before any other code is executed. Most appropriate place for placing this code is within the OnInit() method because the OnInit() method is called when an ASP.NET page is initialized.

APPLY YOUR KNOWLEDGE

3. **B**. When AutoEventWireup is set to true, ASP.NET will automatically register the Page_Load() method as an event handler for the Load event of the Page class. When you use Visual Studio .NET to attach Page_Load() with the Load event you end up getting Page_Load() registered twice for the Load event. It is because of this reason that Page_Load() is executing twice in your programs.

4. **C, D**. When you need to run the same code from more than one event, you should disable AutoEventWireup and use AddHandler to attach a single delegate to multiple events.

5. **C**. When you override a method of a base class, be sure to call the base class version of the same method. Otherwise you will lose some of the functionality offered by the base class.

6. **B**. The method in the base class should be declared with the Protected modifier. This will ensure that only classes derived from this class are able to change the method definition.

7. **A, B**. Because you do not want to precompile the business logic file before you deploy it to the Web server, you need to specify both the Inherits as well as Src attribute with the page directive of the WeatherPage.aspx.

8. **D**. You want to invoke PerformInitializations() when the Web Form is loaded, so you would attach to the Load event of the Web Form. Using the AddHandler syntax adds this delegate to the specified event.

9. **C**. Only two of the given choices execute code on the server side: the <script runat=server>...</script> block and the <%...%> block. The statement included in the latter block is executed while the page is rendered and therefore you should display the values of VB expressions in the <%...%> block.

10. **C**. This behavior means that although the request is going to the IIS (inetinfo.exe) it is not being executed by the ASP.NET worker process because IIS is not sure what to do with this file. This is due to problems with aspnet_isapi.dll on the Web server.

11. **D**. When you subscribe to an event, you are not required to define a protected, virtual method that raises the event.

12. **D**. Users accessing an ASP.NET Web application just need to have a Web browser on their computer.

13. **B**. The Request property contains information about the current HTTP request, which contains all the data entered by the user on a Web page.

14. **A**.You need to compile only the file that contains the business logic of the Web Form. You will need to compile the file into a DLL file using the following command:

    ```
    vbc /t:library DisplayCatalog.aspx.vb
    ```

    If you do not specify the /t switch, the default is to generate an EXE file which is not desired. The user interface file DisplayCatalog.aspx will be dynamically compiled by ASP.NET when the user first accesses it.

15. **D**. Store DisplayCatalog.dll in a subdirectory named BIN inside the Web application.

APPLY YOUR KNOWLEDGE

Suggested Readings and Resources

1. *The Visual Studio .NET Combined Help Collection*, including the following:
   - *Introducing Visual Studio .NET*
   - *Visual Basic Programmer's Reference*
   - *Introduction to ASP.NET*
   - *Handling and Raising Events*
   - *Managing Solutions, Projects, and Files*
2. Fred Barwell et al. *Professional Visual Basic .NET.* Wrox, 2002.
3. David Chappell. *Understanding .NET.* Addison-Wesley, 2001.
4. The Official Microsoft ASP.NET Site, `www.asp.NET`.
5. The .NET Framework Community Web site, `www.gotdotnet.com`.

OBJECTIVES

This chapter covers the following Microsoft-specified objectives for the "Creating User Services" section of Exam 70-305, "Developing and Implementing Web Applications with Microsoft Visual Basic .NET and Microsoft Visual Studio .NET":

Add Web server controls, HTML server controls, user controls, and HTML code to ASP.NET pages.

- **Set properties on controls.**
- **Load controls dynamically.**
- **Set styles on ASP.NET pages by using cascading style sheets.**

▶ Controls have a prominent place in a Web application. The purpose of this objective is to test your knowledge of working with the most common Web Forms controls, including working with their properties, methods, and events.

Validate user input.

▶ This exam objective tests your ability to effectively use controls to validate data entered by the user. In this chapter, you will learn about the various validation controls offered by ASP.NET to simplify this task.

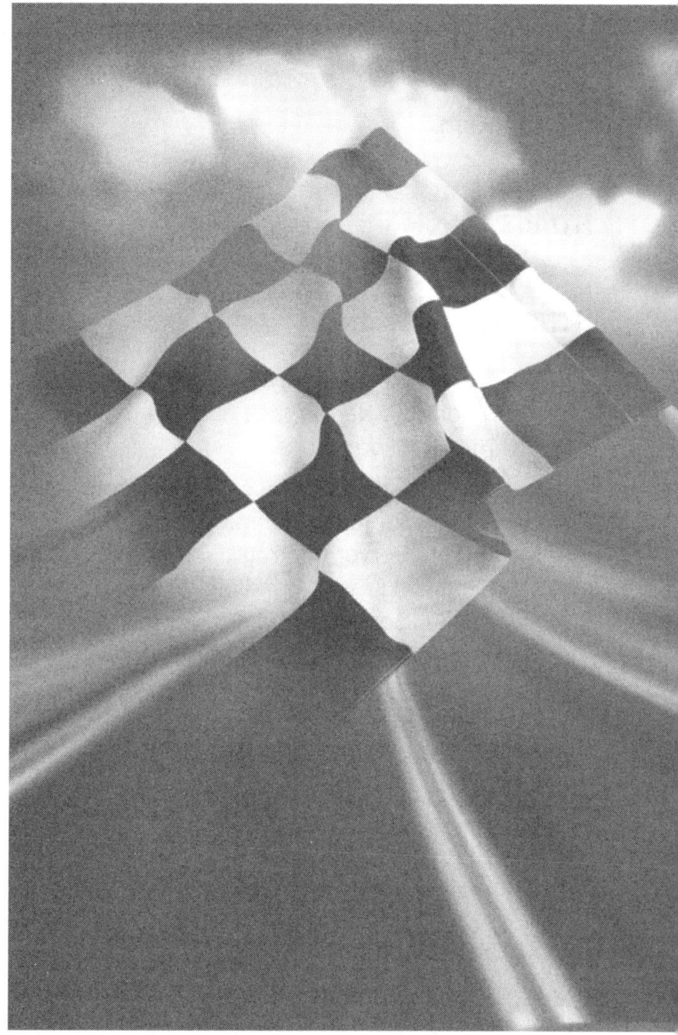

CHAPTER 2

Controls

OUTLINE

STUDY STRATEGIES

- Experiment with the controls that are available in the Visual Studio .NET toolbox. Knowing their properties, methods, and events well will help you answer several exam questions. You will find the important members of the various controls listed in tables throughout the chapter.
- Know how to handle events for Web Forms controls. Make sure you read the section "Event Handling" in Chapter 1, "Introducing Web Forms."
- Understand how to create controls dynamically. See Step by Step 2.7 and Step by Step 2.8 to get hands-on experience in loading controls dynamically.
- Work thoroughly with validation Web server controls. You should be able to answer questions that ask you to choose the most appropriate validation control for a given scenario.

INTRODUCTION

This chapter extends the concepts presented in Chapter 1, "Introducing Web Forms," and discusses various aspects of graphical user interface (GUI) programming in more detail.

Controls are the building blocks of a GUI. Visual Studio .NET allows you to work with the following types of controls on Web Forms:

- **HTML Controls** These controls are nothing but HTML elements. HTML controls have traditionally been used in Web programming and are still supported in ASP.NET.
- **HTML Server Controls** HTML server controls map one-to-one with the HTML controls but are programmatically accessible on the Web server. Any HTML control can be converted into an HTML server control by applying a runat="server" attribute to the control. HTML server controls provide an easy migration path for existing Web Forms because of their compatibility with HTML controls.
- **Web Server Controls** Web server controls are specifically designed to integrate well with the ASP.NET programming model. Web server controls provide various simple controls as well as some controls that provide advanced level of functionality such as Calendar and DataGrid.
- **Validation Controls** Validation Controls are Web server controls that contain logic to validate input in other server controls. You can use validation controls to perform a variety of checks. For example, you can tell whether a value has been entered, whether the value is in a given range, whether the value contains specific patterns of characters, and so on.
- **Web User Controls and Web Custom Controls** ASP.NET allows you to create new controls by extending existing controls. Depending on how these controls are created, they are known as Web user controls or Web custom controls. This topic is covered in Chapter 7, "Creating and Managing Components and .NET Assemblies."

As you learn to use these controls in this chapter, you will also learn how to set properties and handle various events associated with these controls.

In addition to various types of controls, I'll also discuss the use of cascading style sheets (CSS). You will learn how to use CSS styles to provide an attractive and consistent appearance for Web Forms.

HTML Controls

HTML controls represent common HTML elements. You can access all the commonly used HTML controls through the Visual Studio .NET Toolbox. The IDE allows you to visually work with HTML controls. Some of the typical operations that you can perform include dragging controls to the Web Form, setting the properties for controls, and visually arranging them on a Web Form.

Step by Step 2.1 demonstrates how to use the Visual Studio .NET IDE to work with HTML controls.

STEP BY STEP

2.1 Using HTML Controls

1. Launch Visual Studio .NET. Create a new Visual Basic Project based on the ASP.NET Web Application template. Specify the location of the project as `http://localhost/305C02`.
2. Add a new Web Form to the project. Name the Web Form `StepByStep2-1.aspx`.
3. Switch to the Design View of the Web Form. Invoke the Toolbox window by selecting Toolbox from the View menu. In the Toolbox window, select the HTML tab as shown in Figure 2.1.
4. Scroll down the HTML tab and drag an Image control to the Web Form. Select the Image control and select View, Properties Window (alternatively, press the F4 key) to invoke the Properties window (see Figure 2.2). Select the `src` property and click the ellipsis (...) button. This will open the Create URL dialog box, as shown in Figure 2.3. Select an image file and click OK.

continues

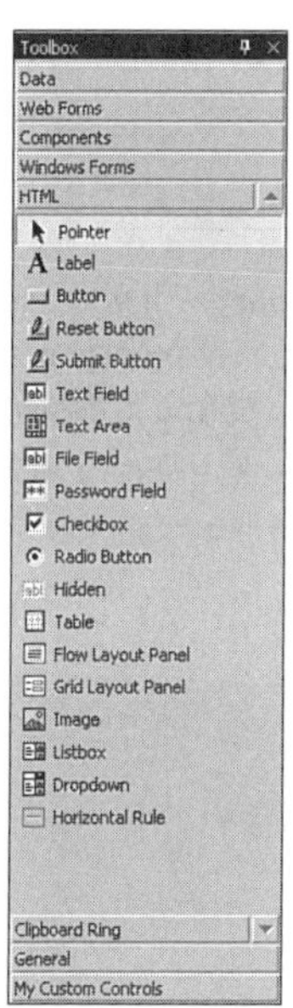

FIGURE 2.1
You can select and drag items from the Toolbox onto a Web Form to design the user interface.

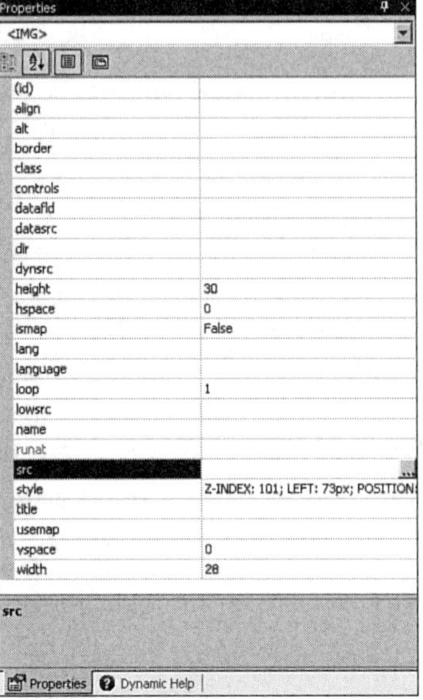

FIGURE 2.2
Use the Properties window to view and change the design-time properties of selected objects that are located in editors and designers.

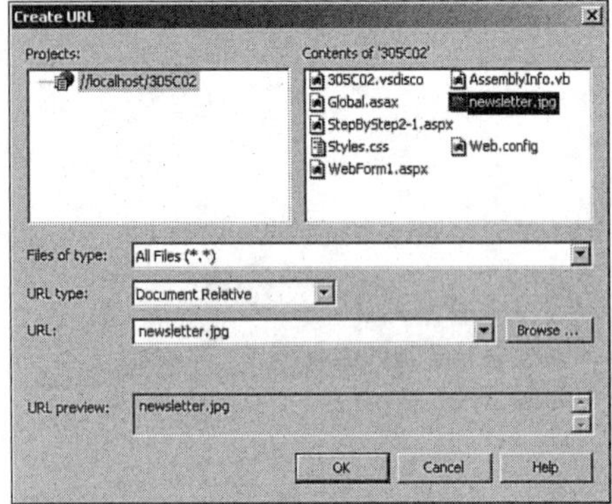

FIGURE 2.3
Use the Create URL dialog box to create a URL for a server resource.

> **NOTE**
>
> **The id Property** If you use or intend to use a control programmatically in a Web Form, you must assign a unique value to the id property of the control.

5. Drag a Horizontal Rule control and a `Label` control to the Web Form. Select the `Label` control and then click in it. You are now able to change its text. Change the text to "Subscribe to our Newsletter." Select the text and change its format from `Normal` to `Heading2` from the Formatting toolbar. If the Formatting tool bar is not visible, you can make it visible by selecting View, Toolbars, Formatting.

6. Add a Submit `Button` control to the form. Set the `id` property to `btnSubscribe` and value to `Subscribe`.

7. Drag thirteen `Label` controls; one Text Field control with `id` property set to `txtName`; one Text Area control with `id` `txtAddress`; four Check Box controls with their `id` properties set to `cbWinForms`, `cbWebForms`, `cbWebServices`, and `cbRemoting`; four `RadioButton` controls with their `id` properties set to `rbCSharp`, `rbVB`, `rbJShard`, and `rbCPlusPlus`; and a Dropdown control with its `id` set to `ddlNewsletter` to the form. Select Format, Snap to Grid. Arrange and label the controls as shown in Figure 2.4.

FIGURE 2.4
When Snap to Grid is enabled, elements dragged across the Design view surface automatically align with the nearest positioning grid guideline.

8. Select the four `RadioButton` controls by holding down the Ctrl key and clicking each one in turn. Invoke the Properties window by pressing the F4 key. Set the `name` property to `Language` to include them in a group and make them behave mutually exclusive.

9. Right-click the `ddlNewsletter` control and select Properties from the context menu. This opens Property Pages dialog box for this control as shown in Figure 2.5. Add options to the control by entering the text in the `Text` textbox and clicking `Insert` button. Add the options shown in Figure 2.5. Click OK to save your changes.

10. Switch to the HTML view of StepByStep2_1.aspx in the Web Forms designer. Analyze the code and compare it with the visual tasks that you have performed in the preceding steps.

11. Right-click the `StepByStep2-1.aspx` page in the Solution Explorer and select `Set as Start Page` from the context menu.

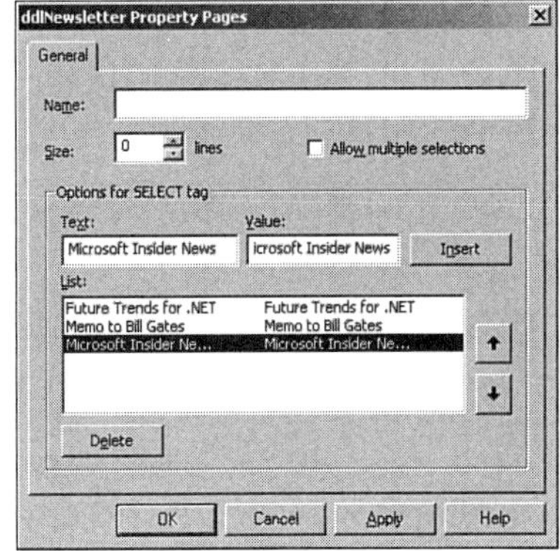

FIGURE 2.5
The Property Pages dialog box allows you to add options to the control.

continues

NOTE **Unable to Start Debugging on the Web Server** You may get this error when you try running the project in Step 11. This error can occur because the Web application project is not configured to run in Debug mode. To configure the project for debugging, open the Web.config file from the Solution Explorer and change the debug attribute in the <compilation> element to true:

```
<compilation
 defaultLanguage="vb"
 debug="true"
/>
```

You may also need to change IIS authentication on your server to remove Anonymous access and allow Integrated Windows Authentication. You will learn about Debugging techniques in Chapter 12, "Testing and Debugging a Web Application."

NOTE **HTML Control Reference** Although I'll occasionally use HTML controls for rendering a user interface on a Web page, they are not the main focus of this book. If you are new to HTML and Web programming, I would recommend that you read a good primer on HTML and JavaScript.

continued

12. Run the project by selecting Debug, Start. When the Web page opens in a Web browser window, fill some values in the form and click the Subscribe button.
13. View the HTML source for the browser window; compare the HTML rendered to the browser with the HTML code in the `StepByStep2-1.aspx` file.

You should observe the following important things from Step by Step 2.1:

- The controls from the Toolbox such as Text Field and Label are converted to their appropriate HTML equivalents such as <INPUT> and <DIV> elements, respectively, in the source code of the ASPX file. All the HTML controls are automatically placed inside an HTML <FORM> element.
- The code corresponding to the HTML controls in the ASPX file is rendered as it is to the browser.
- When you fill in the form and click the Subscribe button, the form is posted to the Web server. When the Web server sends the result back, the originally entered values disappear. This indicates that HTML controls do not maintain their states across page postback.

The HTML controls are available specifically for rendering them to the Web browser. The HTML controls are not directly accessible on the Web server. If you want to access the values posted by the user in the ASPX page, you must retrieve them by analyzing the HTTP request. Although this is a clumsy process that requires a lot of coding, this process has traditionally been the standard way used by the Web developers (in technologies such as ASP, CGI, and so on) to retrieve data posted to the Web server.

To simplify this process, ASP.NET introduces controls that are accessible on the Web server. These controls are called *server controls*. Server controls are directly accessible on the Web server. This cuts down on the amount of code that you need to write to retrieve their values.

HTML SERVER CONTROLS

You can mark any HTML control to run as an HTML server control. Unlike regular HTML controls, HTML server controls are programmable on the Web server. You can access properties and events for the HTML server control just as you do for controls in Windows desktop-based applications.

As discussed before, ASP.NET also provides you with another set of server controls known as Web server controls. Web server controls do almost everything that HTML server controls can do. They can also do much more and provide a better and more consistent programming model.

If Web server controls can do so much then why did the ASP.NET designers choose to include HTML server controls with ASP.NET? One of the main reasons for including HTML server controls with ASP.NET is to provide an easy migration path for existing Web Forms. You will see in this section that it is very easy to change an HTML control to run as a server control.

Step by Step 2.2 creates a copy of the Web Form created in Step by Step 2.1 and converts all of the HTML controls to HTML Server Controls.

STEP BY STEP

2.2 Using HTML Server Controls

1. In the Solution Explorer, right-click StepByStep2-1.aspx and select Copy. Then right-click the project name and select Paste. Rename the pasted Web Form to StepByStep2-2.aspx. Open the aspx (HTML view) and vb (code view) files of the new Web Form and change all references to `StepByStep2_1` to refer to `StepByStep2_2`.

2. Right-click the `txtName` text box and select Run As Server Control from the shortcut menu.

continues

continued

3. Convert the text area, check box controls, `RadioButton` controls, drop-down list, and submit button to HTML server controls. You can use Shift-click or Ctrl-click to select them all. Right-click and select Run As Server Control from the context menu. This will make all these controls HTML server controls.

4. Before the Name label and text box on the page, drag a `Label` control from the HTML tab to the form. Click the `Label` control and remove the text. Set the `id` property to `lblMessage`. Set the `lblMessage` HTML control to run as an HTML server control.

NOTE **HTML Idiosyncrasies** HTML server controls retain the idiosyncrasies of HTML. The contents of a label control are accessed using the InnerText property while the contents of a textbox are accessed using the Value property. You will see later in this chapter that the other set of server controls provided by ASP.NET—the Web server controls—removes these idiosyncrasies and provides a much more consistent model for programming.

5. Double-click the Submit button. You are taken to the code view where an event handler for the `btnSubscribe`'s `ServerClick` event is added. Add the following code in the event handler:

```
Private Sub btnSubscribe_ServerClick( _
 ByVal sender As System.Object, _
 ByVal e As System.EventArgs) _
 Handles btnSubscribe.ServerClick
    ' Display a thank you message with the
    ' Name entered and Newsletter selected
    lblMessage.InnerText = txtName.Value & _
        ", thank you for subscribing to """ & _
        ddlNewsletter.Value & """."
End Sub
```

6. Right-click the `StepByStep2-2.aspx` page in the Solution Explorer and select `Set as Start Page` from the context menu.

7. Run the project by selecting Debug, Start. You should see the Web page opened in a Web browser.

8. Fill the form and submit the details by clicking the Subscribe button. You should see a thank you message along with the name of subscriber and the newsletter as show in Figure 2.6. You should also notice that when the Web server returns the form after postback, all the controls maintain their state unlike the results in the Step by Step 2.1.

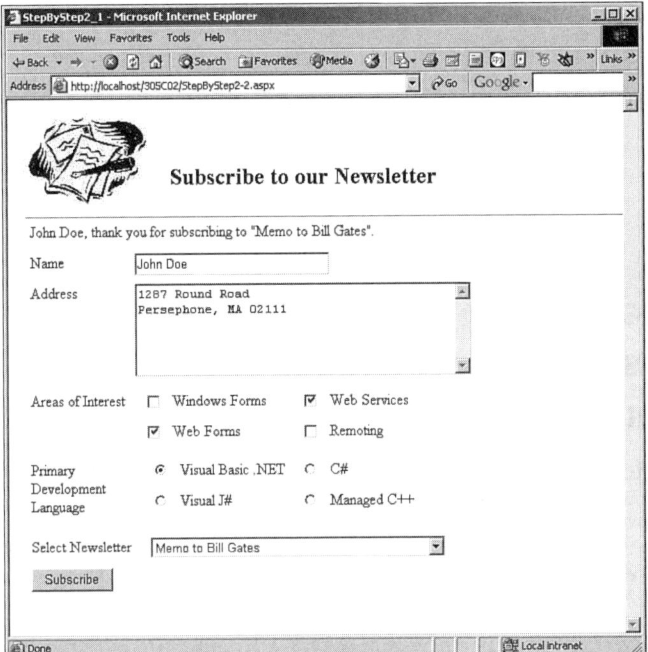

FIGURE 2.6
The HTML server controls maintain their state across page postback and are programmatically accessible on the Web server.

NOTE

State Management for Server Controls You will learn how server controls are able to manage their state across a page postback in Chapter 3, "Implementing Navigation for the User Interface."

When you create an HTML server control (that is, set an HTML control to "Run As Server Control" in the design view), two things happen:

1. The control is marked with the `runat="server"` attribute in the user interface code (ASPX file) of the Web Form. For example:

```
<INPUT id="txtName" style="Z-INDEX: 110; LEFT: 162px;
       POSITION: absolute; TOP: 144px"
       type="text" runat="server">
```

2. A data field is created corresponding to each HTML server control in the code-behind file (.vb file) of the Web Form. The data fields have the same name as the id property of its respective HTML server control. For example, corresponding to a Text Field txtName, the following data field is added to the class definition:

```
Protected WithEvents txtName As _
 System.Web.UI.HtmlControls.HtmlInputText
```

The preceding two points distinguish an HTML control from an HTML server control and ensure that the HTML server controls are programmatically accessible on the Web server.

I'll use the program in Step by Step 2.2 as the base example and will answer the following questions in the next couple of sections:

- What are the classes that represent HTML server controls in a Visual Basic .NET program?
- How does event handling work with HTML server controls?

The Classes in System.Web.UI.HtmlControls Namespace

In Step by Step 2.2, when you mark an HTML control to run as a server control, the Web Forms designer creates a data field in the code-behind file corresponding to each server control. According to the semantic requirements of Visual Basic .NET, each data field must be an object of some class. Fortunately, the FCL provides a number of classes in its System.Web.UI.HtmlControls namespace that directly map to the HTML controls. Table 2.1 shows the mapping between various HTML server controls and the classes in System.Web.UI.HtmlControls namespace.

TABLE 2.1

HTML SERVER CONTROLS

HTML Elements	*Class*
`<a runat="server">`	`HtmlAnchor`
`<button runat="server">`	`HtmlButton`
`<form runat="server">`	`HtmlForm`
`<img runat="server">`	`HtmlImage`
`<input type="button" runat="server">`	
`<input type="reset" runat="server">`	
`<input type="submit" runat="server">`	`HtmlInputButton`
`<input type="checkbox" runat="server">`	`HtmlInputCheckBox`
`<input type="file" runat="server">`	`HtmlInputFile`

HTML Elements	*Class*
`<input type="hidden" runat="server">`	HtmlInputHidden
`<input type="image" runat="server">`	HtmlInputImage
`<input type="radio" runat="server">`	HtmlInputRadioButton
`<input type="text" runat="server">`	HtmlInputText
`<select runat="server">`	HtmlSelect
`<table runat="server">`	HtmlTable
`<td runat="server">`	
`<th runat="server">`	HtmlTableCell
`<textarea runat="server">`	HtmlTextArea
`<tr runat="server">`	HtmlTableRow
All other HTML server controls not listed in any rows above such as: `<body runat="server">`	
`<div runat="server">`	
`<h1 runat="server">`	
`<span runat="server">`	HtmlGenericControl

One interesting thing to note in Table 2.1 is that all HTML controls that do not have a distinct class associated with them become objects of the HtmlGenericControl class. This arrangement allows HTML server controls to work well with future HTML extensions as well as browser-specific extensions to HTML.

In fact, the classes corresponding to HTML server controls are also robust enough to live along with browser specific or future changes in properties of any existing HTML controls. ASP.NET does this to leave the interpretation of any property it does not understand on the Web browser. So any properties that are not recognized by ASP.NET are rendered as is to the Web browser rather than causing a program error.

Figure 2.7 shows the hierarchy of HTML server control classes. Note that all the classes corresponding to HTML controls derive their functionality from a common base class—System.Web.UI.HtmlControls.HtmlControl.

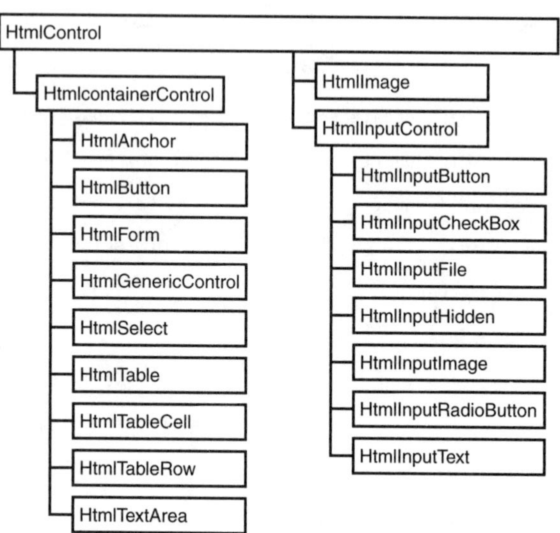

FIGURE 2.7
The collection of classes in the System.Web.UI.HtmlControls namespace allows you to programmatically control the HTML elements on a Web Forms page.

Analyzing Figure 2.7 and Table 2.1, you can find that three classes from the HtmlControl hierarchy do not map directly to any of the HTML controls:

- **HtmlControl** The HtmlControl class is the abstract base class of all HTML server controls. It provides the basic functionality to all the HTML server controls.
- **HtmlContainerControl** The HtmlContainerControl class is the abstract base class of all the HTML container server controls that is, all the HTML elements that should have a closing tag. This class contains two important properties, InnerText and InnerHtml, which set or retrieve the contents between the opening and closing tags of the server controls. InnerHtml returns the entire HTML part inside the closing tags and InnerText returns the data in text contained between the tags. In Step by Step 2.2, the ServerClick event handler used the InnerText property to set the text in the label control, which is represented as a <DIV> element.
- **HtmlInputControl** HtmlInputControl is the abstract base class of all the HTML input server controls. It has a special property called Value that returns the value of the control.

The HtmlForm Class

Whenever you add a Web Form to an ASP.NET Web application project, the user interface code in the ASPX file automatically includes a `<form runat="server">`. This is the most important server control. The form along with all its controls is only submitted to the ASP.NET server when the `<form>` element has a `runat="server"` attribute attached to it. There can be only one `<form runat="server">` control on a Web page. The `<form runat=s"server">` element corresponds to the HtmlForm class. Table 2.2 lists important members of the `HtmlForm` class.

TABLE 2.2

IMPORTANT MEMBERS OF THE HTMLFORM CLASS

Properties	*Description*
`EncType`	Specifies the encoding type that is used by the browsers to post the form's data. The supported encoding types are application/x-www-form-urlencoded (standard encoding, Internet media type), multipart/form-data(containing multiple type of data), text/plain (text or plain data), and image/jpeg (image files).
`Method`	Indicates how the form sends data to the server. It can be done either by GET or POST (the default).
`Name`	Specifies the name of the form.
`Target`	Specifies the target window or frame where the results in the browser will be displayed. Some of the possible values are _blank (new window), _parent (parent frameset), _self(current position in the window), _top (current window).

NOTE

GET and POST GET and POST are the two common techniques supported by all browsers to send form data to the Web server. GET attaches the data to the URL whereas POST embeds the data within an HTTP request body. Web Forms use the POST method as their default way to post the form's data. You can change the method to GET, but the GET method is limited in functionality and does not support several Web Form features such as the state management.

Event Handling for HTML Server Controls

When a user interacts with a page, the following steps are ordinarily involved:

- The user raises an event by performing actions on the client side.
- The browser executes event handling code (if any) at the client side in response to the events.

- The browser uses an HTTP request to transmit an event message to the server.
- ASP.NET analyzes the HTTP request to determine which event has occurred and on which HTML server control. ASP.NET then raises a server-side equivalent of that event. For example, in Step by Step 2.2, when the user clicks the subscribe button, the form is posted to the Web server. ASP.NET determines that the postback was due to the user clicking the Subscribe button and therefore raises the ServerClick event for btnSubscribe.
- The event-handling mechanism of ASP.NET invokes the event handlers registered to handle the raised event. For example, in Step by Step 2.2, the btnSubscribe_ServerClick method is the registered event handler for the ServerClick event of btnSubscribe object. ASP.NET therefore invokes the btnSubscribe_ServerClick method on the server side.

As is apparent from the preceding steps, the event handling model of Web Forms is quite different from that of desktop-based applications. In the case of Web Forms, although the events occur at the client side, you can handle them in two places:

- At the Web server where event handling code is executed by the CLR.
- At the client side where the event handling code is executed by the Web browser.

Server-side Event Handling for HTML Server Controls

The following list summarizes the events raised by the various HTML server controls on the server side when the user interacts with the controls on the client side:

- **ServerClick**—Raised for the HtmlAnchor, HtmlButton, HtmlInputButton, and HtmlInputImage controls.
- **ServerChange**—Raised for the HtmlInputCheckBox, HtmlInputHidden, HtmlInputRadioButton, HtmlInputText, HtmlSelect, and HtmlTextArea controls.

These two events are also the default events for the HTML server controls listed along with them. It is easy to create an event handler for a default event—just double-click the control in the Web Forms designer and the designer will create an empty event handler and attach it to the default event; you just need to fill in the code in the event handler.

These server-side events are only fired when a page postback occurs. If you are curious how the events are raised at server side, here's the scoop. You can assume that server-side events are cached while the page is at client side. When the page is submitted to the server, ASP.NET analyzes the HTTP request and determines which server-side events needs to be raised. ASP.NET then raises the server-side events and the registered server-side event handlers are executed in response.

Client-side Event Handling for HTML Server Controls

Because an HTTP postback is involved in transmitting the event information to the Web server, server-based event handling can be a slow operation. It is therefore not reasonable to use server events to respond to events such as MouseMove or KeyPress that happen frequently. These events are better suited for handling at the client side. When you use client-side event handling, you should note that:

- Client-side event handlers execute prior to server-side event handlers.
- Client-side events are handled using code running within the Web browser, so you must write the client side event handler in a language such as JavaScript that is generally understood by Web browsers.

Step by Step 2.3 demonstrates how you can execute both a client-side event handler and a server-side event handler when the user clicks a button.

STEP BY STEP

2.3 Using Both Server-side and Client-side Event Handling with HTML Server Controls

1. In the Solution Explorer, right-click StepByStep2-2.aspx and select Copy. Right-click the project name and select Paste. Rename the pasted Web Form to `StepByStep2-3.aspx`. Open the ASPX (HTML view) and VB (code view) files of the newly added Web Form and change all references to `StepByStep2_2` to refer to `StepByStep2_3`.

2. Switch to the HTML view of the Web Form. Insert a `<SCRIPT>` element under the `<HEAD>` element as shown here:

```
<HEAD>
 ...
    <SCRIPT language="javascript">
        function btnSubscribe_Click()
        {
            alert(document.Form1.txtName.value +
              ", thank you for subscribing to " +
              document.Form1.ddlNewsletter.value);
        }
    </SCRIPT>
</HEAD>
```

3. Add an `onclick` attribute to the `btnSubscribe` control definition to execute client-side function added in the step 2. This function will be executed when the button is clicked. The control definition in the HTML view should look like this (if your Web Form is in grid layout mode, there will be additional attributes specifying size and position):

```
<INPUT id="btnSubscribe" type="submit"
  value="Subscribe"
  runat="server" onclick="btnSubscribe_Click();">
```

4. Set `StepByStep2-3.aspx` as the start page in the project.

5. Run the project by selecting `Debug, Start`. Fill the form and submit the details by clicking the Subscribe button. You should see a message box with a thank you message along with the name of subscriber and the newsletter as shown in Figure 2.8. You will then see the same message displayed in the Web Form by the `ServerClick` event handler.

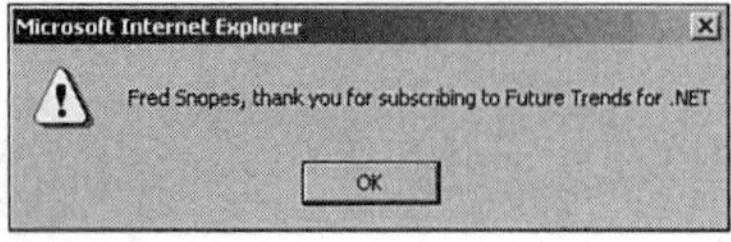

FIGURE 2.8
You can use traditional client-side scripting techniques to handle events for HTML server controls at the client side.

GUIDED PRACTICE EXERCISE 2.1

A common requirement for Web applications is to allow users to upload files from their local machines to the Web server. To achieve this functionality an ASP programmer traditionally had to depend on third-party controls, but now ASP.NET has native support available for such a common requirement.

You can use the HTML File Field (which is an object of type HtmlInputFile class) to achieve this functionality. The PostedFile property of the HtmlInputFile object gives you access to the uploaded file on the Web server.

The PostedFile property provides an HttpPostedFile object. You can use the SaveAs() method of HttpPostedFile object to save the uploaded file on the Web server.

You must also set the EncType property of the HtmlForm element to "multipart/form-data" to allow the form to post multiple types of data to the Web server.

How would you create a Web Form that allows users to upload files to the Web server?

You should try working through this problem on your own first. If you are stuck, or if you'd like to see one possible solution, follow these steps:

1. Open the project 305C02. Add a new Web Form named GuidedPracticeExercise2-1 to the project.
2. Drag three Label controls (one with id lblMessage), one File Field control with id set to filSource, one Text Field control with id set to txtTarget, and one Submit Button control with id set to btnUpload from the HTML tab of the toolbox on to the form. Set the lblMessage, filSource, txtTarget, and btnUpload controls as HTML server controls. Set the size property of the filSource control to 50. Figure 2.9 shows a possible design of the Web Form.

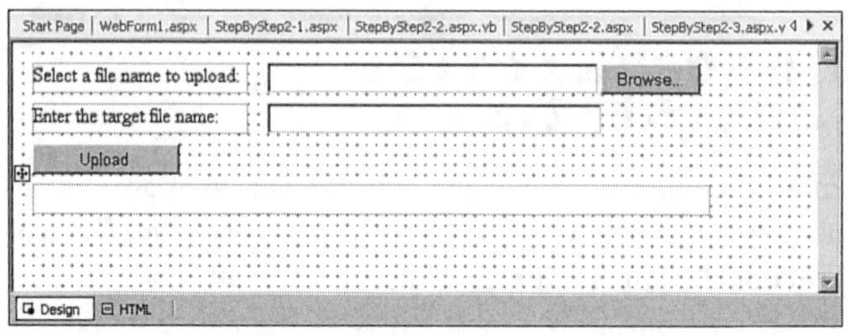

FIGURE 2.9
Use the HtmlInputFile HTML server control to upload files from client to the Web server.

3. Switch to the HTML view of the form. Add an enctype attribute to the form element with its value set to multipart/form-data as shown here:

```
<form id="Form1" method="post"
   runat="server" enctype="multipart/form-data">
...
</form>
```

4. Double-click the btnUpload control. You will be taken to the code view and an event handler for the btnUpload's ServerClick event will be added. Add the following code in the event handler:

```
Private Sub btnUpload_ServerClick( _
 ByVal sender As System.Object, _
 ByVal e As System.EventArgs) _
 Handles btnUpload.ServerClick
    ' Save the file
    filSource.PostedFile.SaveAs("C:\temp\" & _
        txtTarget.Value)
    ' Display the message
    lblMessage.InnerHtml = _
     "File uploaded from the client" & _
     " successfully: <br>" & _
     "C:\temp\" & txtTarget.Value
End Sub
```

5. Set the GuidedPracticeExercise2-1.aspx page as the start page of the project.

6. Run the project by selecting Debug, Start. Click the Browse button. This opens the Choose File dialog box. Select the file you want to upload. Enter the name of the target file in the text box and click Upload. The form will be submitted to the server and a successful upload message will be displayed.

If you have difficulty following this exercise, review the sections "The Classes in System.Web.UI.HtmlControls Namespace," "The HtmlForm Class," and "Event Handling for HTML Server Controls" earlier in this chapter. Perform Step by Steps 2.1 and 2.2. After doing this review, try this exercise again.

NOTE

MaxRequestLength ASP.NET includes a parameter named maxRequestLength that limits the size of files that can be uploaded. You can set this parameter in the web.config file for your application.

REVIEW BREAK

- HTML controls represent common HTML elements. You can access all the commonly used HTML controls through the HTML tab of the Visual Studio .NET Toolbox. The IDE allows you to visually work with HTML controls. However, HTML controls are not programmatically accessible on the Web server.
- ASP.NET provides server controls that are directly accessible on the Web server. There are two main categories of server controls—HTML server controls and Web server controls.
- The HTML server controls mainly exists to provide an easy migration path for existing Web Forms. It is very easy to change an HTML control to run as a server control because all you need to do is to apply the `runat="server"` attribute to every HTML control.
- For HTML server controls, ASP.NET analyzes the HTTP post to find if any events needs to be raised at server side and raises all such events. Only some HTML server controls raise events on the server side; an HTML control can raise either a ServerClick event or a ServerChange event.
- Client-side event handling still proves helpful for handling frequently occurring events such as MouseMove or KeyPress. The traditional JavaScript-based event handling techniques still apply for handling client-side events for HTML server controls.

WEB SERVER CONTROLS

So far, I have discussed both HTML controls and HTML server controls. You have noted that HTML server controls are just like the HTML controls with the added feature of server-side availability. By design, HTML server controls are compatible with HTML controls and therefore share the inconsistencies of HTML.

ASP.NET provides another set of classes that provides a simplified and consistent programming model. This set of classes is known as Web server controls. Web server controls provide a higher level of abstraction than the HTML server controls because their object model matches closely with the .NET Framework, rather than matching with the requirements of HTML syntax.

Some of the advantages of Web server controls that are not available with the HTML server controls are listed here:

- Web server controls provide a rich object model that closely matches the rest of the .NET Framework.
- Web controls have built-in automatic browser detection capabilities. They can render their output HTML correctly for both uplevel and downlevel browsers.
- Some Web server controls have capability to cause an immediate postback when users click, change, or select a value.
- Some Web server controls (such as the Calendar, and AdRotator controls) provide richer functionality than is available with HTML controls.
- Web server controls support event bubbling in the nested controls. Event bubbling is the ability to pass events from a nested control (such as a button in a table) to the container control.

> NOTE
> **Uplevel and Downlevel Browsers** ASP.NET treats browsers as either uplevel or downlevel. Uplevel browsers support HTML 4.0 or later and JavaScript 1.2 or later. Internet Explorer 4.0 or later is an example of an uplevel browser. Browsers with any lesser capabilities are considered to be downlevel browsers.

> NOTE
> **Mixing HTML Server Controls and Web Server Controls** You can freely mix and match HTML server controls with Web server controls in your code. You can choose whatever control is most appropriate for a requirement and then use it in your code.

Unlike HTML server controls where you use the `run="server"` attribute with the conventional HTML tag, Web server controls are declared in code explicitly by prefixing the class name of Web server control with asp: and of course including the runat="server" attribute in its definition. For example, a Label Web server control can be declared in code as `<asp:Label runat="server">`. If you are using Visual Studio .NET, you can just drag and drop these controls on a Web Form using the Web Forms tab of the Visual Studio .NET Toolbox.

Web server controls include not only form-type controls such as buttons and text boxes, but also include more advanced controls such as the AdRotator, Calendar, DataGrid, validation, and Xml controls. These advanced controls do not render a single HTML element but instead render several HTML elements to achieve the level of functionality that they offer.

Figure 2.10 shows the hierarchy of some of the most commonly used Web server controls.

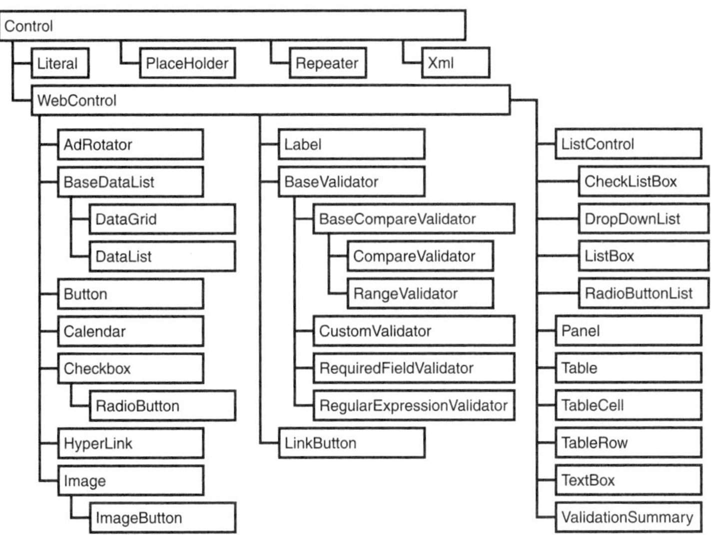

FIGURE 2.10
Inheritance hierarchy for the most commonly used Web server controls.

You'll see in Figure 2.10 that most of the Web server controls derive their functionality from the WebControl class of the System.Web.UI.WebControls namespace. However, some Web server controls such as the Repeater and Xml controls do not get their functionality from the WebControl class; they instead derive directly from the Control class of the System.Web.UI namespace.

Table 2.3 lists some of the common properties that all Web server controls derive from the WebControl class.

TABLE 2.3

Important Properties of the System.Web.UI.WebControls.WebControl Class

Properties	*Description*
`AccessKey`	Represents the single character keyboard shortcut key for quick navigation to the Web server control. The focus is moved to the Web server control when the Alt+AccessKey assigned to this property is pressed. For example, if S is the AccessKey for the Submit button, pressing Alt+S keys moves focus to the Submit button. This feature is only supported in uplevel browsers.
`Attributes`	Represents a collection of all attributes (name/value pairs) in the opening tag of a Web server control. All the attributes contained in this collection are rendered to the browser. You can add or remove attributes from the AttributeCollection object.
`BackColor`	Specifies the background color of the Web server control.
`BorderColor`	Specifies the border color of the Web server control.
`BorderStyle`	Specifies the border style of the Web server control. The possible values are defined in the BorderStyle enumeration—Dotted, Dashed, Double, Inset, NotSet, None, OutSet, Groove, Solid, and Ridge.
`BorderWidth`	Specifies the border width of the Web server control.
`Controls`	Represents the collection of controls added to the Web server control as child controls. The WebControl class inherits this property from the Control class.
`CssClass`	Represents the CSS class with which the Web server control is rendered.
`Enabled`	Indicates whether the Web server control is allowed to receive the focus.
`EnableViewState`	Indicates whether view state is enabled for the Web server control. The WebControl class inherits this property from the Control class.
`Font`	Specifies a FontInfo object that represents the font properties of a Web server control.
`ForeColor`	Specifies the color of text in the Web server control.
`Height`	Specifies the height of the Web server control.
`ID`	Specifies an identifier for the Web server control. The WebControl class inherits this property from the Control class.
`Parent`	Represents the parent control of the Web server control. The WebControl class inherits this property from the Control class.

Properties	*Description*
`Style`	Specifies the collection of CSS properties applied to the Web server control.
`TabIndex`	Specifies the tab order of a Web server control.
`ToolTip`	Specifies the pop-up text displayed by the Web server control when the mouse hovers over it.
`Visible`	Indicates whether the Web server control is visible on the rendered page. The WebControl class inherits this property from the Control class.
`Width`	Specifies the width of the Web server control.

Now that you have developed a basic understanding of Web server controls, it's time to discuss some important Web server controls and their workings in detail. I have divided the discussion of Web server controls into the following categories:

- Common Web server controls
- Event Handling with Web server controls
- List controls
- PlaceHolder and Panel controls
- Table, TableRow, and TableCell controls
- AdRotator control
- Calendar control

In addition to these, I will also discuss various Web server controls related to input data validation in the section titled "User Input Validation."

Common Web Server Controls

In this section, I'll discuss some simple but commonly used controls that are available in the Visual Studio .NET Toolbox. These controls are simple because they have a small number of properties and they are usually rendered as a single HTML element. Later in this chapter, you will learn about many advanced controls that provide more properties and render big chunks of HTML code.

The Label Control

A Label control is used to display read-only information to the user. It is generally used to label other controls and to provide the user with any useful messages or statistics. It exposes its text content through the Text property. This property can be used to manipulate its text programmatically. The control is rendered as a <span> HTML element on the Web browser.

The TextBox Control

A TextBox control provides an area that the user can use to input text. Depending on how you set the properties of this Web server control, you can use it for single or multiline text input, or you can use it as a password box that masks the characters entered by the user with the asterisk character (*). Thus this server control can be rendered as three different types of HTML elements—`<input type="text">`, `<input type="password">`, and `<textarea>`. Table 2.4 summarizes the important members of the TextBox class.

TABLE 2.4

IMPORTANT MEMBERS OF THE TEXTBOX CLASS

Member	*Type*	*Description*
`AutoPostBack`	Property	Indicates whether the Web Form should be posted to the server automatically whenever the data in the text box is changed. Works only if the browser supports client-side scripting.
`Columns`	Property	Specifies the width in characters of the text box.
`MaxLength`	Property	Specifies the maximum number of characters allowed to be entered by the user. The default value is `0`, which does not impose any limit.
`ReadOnly`	Property	Indicates whether the contents of the text box are read only—that is, they cannot be modified. The default value is `False`.
`Rows`	Property	Specifies the height in characters of the multiline text box. The default value is `0`. Works only if the `TextMode` property is set to `MultiLine`.
`Text`	Property	Specifies the text contained in the textbox.

Member	Type	Description
`TextChanged`	Event	Occurs when the value of the `Text` property changes. `TextChanged` is the default event for the `TextBox` class.
`TextMode`	Property	Represents the type of text box to be rendered in the Web page. It can be displayed in one of the three values of `TextBoxMode` enumeration—`MultiLine` (text box can accept multiple lines of input), `Password` (single-line text box with each character masked with an asterisk character; *) and `SingleLine` (single line text box with normal text displayed).
`Wrap`	Property	Specifies whether the control can automatically wrap words to the next line. The default value is `True`. Works only if the `TextMode` property is set to `MultiLine`.

The Image Control

The Image Web server control can display images from bitmap, JPEG, PNG, and GIF files. The control is rendered as an <img> HTML element on the Web page. Table 2.5 summarizes the important properties of the Image class.

TABLE 2.5

IMPORTANT MEMBERS OF THE IMAGE CLASS

Properties	Description
`AlternateText`	Specifies the text that is displayed in the place of `Image` Web server control when the image is being downloaded, or if the image is unavailable, or if the browser doesn't support images. The specified text is also displayed as a `ToolTip` if the browser supports the ToolTip feature.
`ImageAlign`	Indicates the alignment of the `Image` Web server control with reference to other elements in the Web page. It can be set to one of the `ImageAlign` values—`AbsBottom`, `AbsMiddle`, `Baseline`, `Bottom`, `Left`, `Middle`, `NotSet` (default value), `Right`, `TextTop`, and `Top`.
`ImageUrl`	Represents the URL (location) of the image that the Image Web server control displays. The URL can be both relative and absolute.

The Checkbox and RadioButton Controls

The CheckBox and RadioButton Web server controls represent a state. They can be on or off (that is, selected or not selected, checked or unchecked). These controls are generally used in groups. A CheckBox control allows you to select one or more options from a group of options, and a group of RadioButton controls is used to select one out of several mutually exclusive options. The RadioButton controls that need to be set mutually exclusive should belong to the same group specified by the GroupName property. If you want to place two groups of RadioButton controls on a form and have each group allow one selection, then RadioButton controls of each group should individually set their GroupName property to indicate the group that they belong to. The check box and radio button Web server controls are rendered as `<input type="checkbox">` and `<input type="radio">` HTML elements on the Web page.

The RadioButton class inherits from the CheckBox class and both of them share the same members, except for the GroupName property available in the RadioButton class.

Table 2.6 summarizes the important members of the CheckBox and RadioButton classes.

TABLE 2.6

IMPORTANT MEMBERS OF THE CHECKBOX AND RADIOBUTTON CLASSES

Member	*Member*	*Description*
`AutoPostBack`	Property	Indicates whether the Web Form should be posted to the server automatically when the check box is clicked. Works only if the browser supports client side scripting.
`Checked`	Property	Returns `True` if the check box or radio button has been checked. Otherwise, it returns `False`.
`CheckedChanged`	Event	Occurs every time a check box is checked or unchecked. `CheckedChanged` is the default event for the `CheckBox` class.
`Text`	Property	Specifies the text displayed along with the check box.

Member	*Member*	*Description*
`TextAlign`	Property	Specifies the alignment of the text displayed along with the check box. It can be one of the TextAlign enumeration values—`Left` (text is displayed on the left of the check box) and `Right` (default, text is displayed on the right of the check box).

The Button, LinkButton, and ImageButton Controls

A button is used to initiate a specific action when clicked by a user. There are three types of buttons. Each of these controls is different in its appearance and is rendered differently on the Web page:

- Button The Button control displays as a push button on the Web page and is rendered as an `<input type="submit">` HTML element
- LinkButton The LinkButton control displays as a hyperlink on the Web page and is rendered as an `<a>` HTML element.
- ImageButton The ImageButton control displays as an image button on the Web page and is rendered as an `<input type="image">` HTML element.

NOTE

LinkButton Control The LinkButton control works only if client-side scripting is enabled in the Web browser.

However, all three button Web server controls behave in the same way in that they all post the form data to the Web server when they are clicked.

Table 2.7 summarizes the important members that are applicable to the Button, LinkButton, and ImageButton classes.

TABLE 2.7

IMPORTANT MEMBERS OF THE BUTTON, LINKBUTTON, AND IMAGEBUTTON CLASSES

Member	*Type*	*Description*
`CausesValidation`	Property	Indicates whether validation should be performed when the button control is clicked. Validation is discussed in detail later in this chapter.

continues

TABLE 2.7 *continued*

IMPORTANT MEMBERS OF THE BUTTON, LINKBUTTON, AND IMAGEBUTTON CLASSES

Member	*Type*	*Description*
`Click`	Event	Occurs when the button control is clicked. `Click` is the default event of all the three classes. This event is mostly used for submit buttons.
`Command`	Event	Occurs when the button control is clicked. This event is mostly used for command buttons. The event handler receives an object of type `CommandEventArgs` that contains both the `CommandName` and `CommandArgument` properties containing event-related data.
`CommandArgument`	Property	Specifies the argument for a command. Works only if the `CommandName` property is set. The property is passed to the `Command` event when the button is clicked.
`CommandName`	Property	Specifies the command name for the button. The property is passed to the `Command` event when the button is clicked.
`Text`	Property	Specifies the text displayed on a button. The `ImageButton` class does not have this property.

All three button controls can behave in two different ways—submit button or command button. By default any type of button Web server control is a submit button. If you specify a command name via the CommandName property, the button controls also become a command button.

A command button raises the Command event when it is clicked. The button passes the CommandName and CommandArgument encapsulated in a CommandEventArgs object to the event handlers. A command button is useful when you wish to pass some event related information to the event handler.

Step by Step 2.4 creates a Web Form that uses some of the common Web server controls discussed in thc previous sections.

STEP BY STEP

2.4 Using Simple Web Server Controls

1. Add a new Web Form to the project. Name the form `StepByStep2-4.aspx`.
2. Switch to the Design View. Invoke the Toolbox window by selecting Toolbox from the View menu. In the Toolbox window, select the Web Forms.
3. Scroll down the Web Forms tab and drag an `Image` control to the Web Form. Select the `Image` control and invoke the Properties window by pressing the F4 key. Select the `ImageUrl` property and click the ellipsis (...) button. This opens the Select Image dialog box as shown in Figure 2.11. Select an image file and click OK.

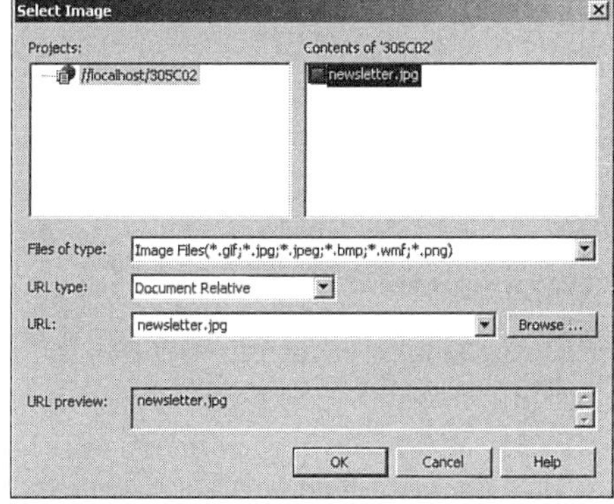

FIGURE 2.11
Use the Select Image dialog box to easily specify the URL of an image file.

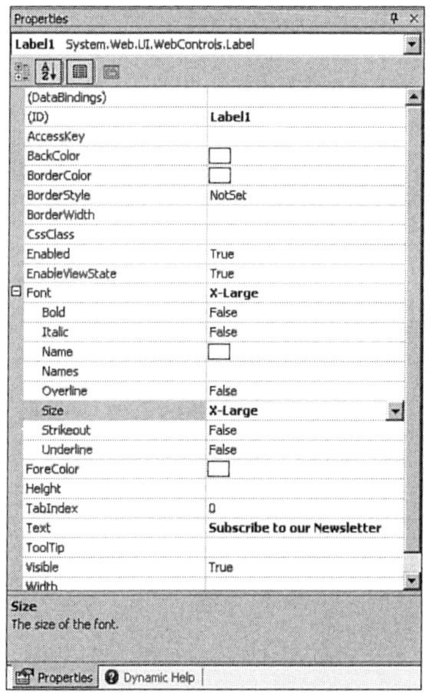

FIGURE 2.12
You can expand a property node in the Properties window to access its sub-properties.

4. Place a `Label` control on the Web Form. Invoke the Properties window and set the Text property to `Subscribe to our Newsletter`. Click the + node next to the Font property. You should see that the Font properties expand and there is a list of subproperties as shown in Figure 2.12. Set the Size subproperty to X-Large by selecting from the drop-down list.
5. Drag six `Label` controls from the toolbox. Set the `id` of one `Label` to `lblMessage` and empty out its Text property. Set the Text property of other `Label` controls as shown in Figure 2.13.

continues

continued

FIGURE 2.13
Web server controls can be added to the Web Form through the Web Forms tab of the toolbox.

6. Place two `TextBox` controls on the form. Set the `id` of the text box controls to `txtName` and `txtAddress`. Select the `txtAddress` text box and set the `TextMode` property to `MultiLine`, `Rows` to 4, and `Columns` to 40.

7. Place four CheckBox controls with their `id` set to `cbWinForms`, `cbWebForms`, `cbWebServices`, `cbRemoting` on the Web Form. Set the Text property of the CheckBox controls as shown in Figure 2.13.

8. Place four `RadioButton` controls with their `id` set to `rbCSharp`, `rbVB`, `rbJSharp`, `rbCPlusPlus` on the form. Set the Text property of the `RadioButton` controls as shown in Figure 2.13. Select all four `RadioButton` controls and invoke Properties window by pressing F4 key. Set the `GroupName` property to `Language` to include them in a group and make them behave mutually exclusive.

9. Place a `DropDownList` control with `id` `ddlNewsletter` on the Web Form. Select the Items property of the `ddlNewsletter` control and click the ellipsis (…) button in the Properties window. This opens the ListItem Collection Editor dialog box as shown in Figure 2.14.

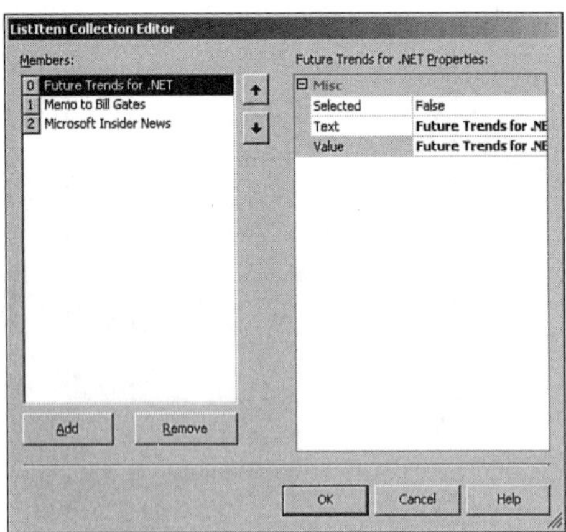

FIGURE 2.14
The ListItem Collection Editor dialog box allows you to add list items in all the list controls such as DropDownList or ListBox controls.

Click the Add button in the dialog box and enter the Text and Value of the list item in the right side of the dialog box. Add all the three list items shown in Figure 2.14.

10. Add a Button control named `btnSubscribe` to the Web Form. Double-click the Subscribe button. You will be taken to the code view where an event handler for the `btnSubscribe`'s `Click` event will be added. Add the following code in the event handler:

```
Private Sub btnSubscribe_Click( _
 ByVal sender As System.Object, _
 ByVal e As System.EventArgs) _
 Handles btnSubscribe.Click
    ' Display a thank you message with the
    ' Name entered and Newsletter selected
    lblMessage.Text = txtName.Text & _
        ", thank you for subscribing to """ & _
        ddlNewsletter.SelectedItem.Text & """."
End Sub
```

11. Switch to the HTML view of `StepByStep2-4.aspx` in the Web Forms designer. Analyze the code and compare it with the visual tasks that you have performed in the preceding steps.

12. Right-click the `StepByStep2-4.aspx` page in the Solution Explorer and select `Set as Start Page` from the context menu.

13. Run the project by selecting Debug, Start. Fill in details in the Web page and click the Subscribe button.

14. View the HTML source for the browser window; compare the HTML rendered to the browser with the HTML code in the `StepByStep2-4.aspx` file.

You can see from the `btnSubscribe_Click()` method that Web server controls provide a much more consistent model for programming than HTML controls do. The text of the label control can now be accessed using the obvious Text property rather than the InnerText property as in the case of HTML server controls. You can also see that the Web server controls have much better designer support. You have complete access to properties and events of a Web server control through the Properties window.

Event Handling with Web Server Controls

The basic mechanism for event handling in Web server controls is quite similar to that of HTML server controls. There are some differences though as listed here:

- **Intrinsic Events** The Web server controls have a set of intrinsic events available to them. The name and number of these events depend on the type of the Web server control. Some simple controls such as the Button control, just provide two native events—Click and Command—whereas advanced controls such as the DataGrid control provide as many as nine native events.
- **Event Arguments** By convention, all events in the .NET Framework pass two arguments to their event handler—the object that raised the event, and an object containing any event-specific information. Most events do not have any event-specific information and therefore just pass an object of type System.EventArgs as the second argument. Some Web server controls, however, do pass event-specific data to their event handlers by using a type extended from System.EventArgs. One such example is the ImageButton Web server control where the second argument is of the type ImageClickEventArgs. The ImageClickEventsArgs objects encapsulates information about the coordinates where the user has clicked the ImageButton.
- **AutoPostBack** Usually change events are cached and are fired on the Web server at a later stage when the page is posted back as a result of a click event. Some Web server controls such as DropDownList, CheckBox, and so on have a property named AutoPostBack. When this property is set to true, it causes an immediate postback of the page when the value of control is changed. This allows the Web server to immediately respond to change events without waiting for a click event to cause a page postback. In HTML, only a few controls inherently submit a form; to enable other controls to cause a postback, ASP.NET attaches a small client script with the control. This client side script causes the postback to occur with a change or click event.

- **Bubbled Events** Some advanced Web server controls such as the DataGrid control can also contain other controls such as a Button. DataGrid controls usually display dynamically generated data and if each row of DataGrid contains a Button, you may end up having a variable number of Button controls. Writing an individual event handler for each Button control in this case is a very tedious process. To simplify event handling, controls such as DataGrid support bubbling of events in which all events raised at the level of child control are bubbled up to the container control where container control can raise a generic event in response to the child events. You will learn about container controls such as the Repeater, DataList and DataGrid controls in Chapter 5, "Data Binding."

Client-Side Event Handling with Web Server Controls

In traditional ASP programming, client-side programming is used to validate user input in order to avoid frequent page postbacks. ASP.NET provides a set of validation controls that makes it easy to validate user input without manual client-side programming and without frequent round trips to the server.

Validation controls of course minimize the amount of client-side code that you may have to traditionally include. But still, you might like to use some amount of client-side programming in your code especially to handle frequently occurring events such as MouseMove or KeyPress.

Unlike the HTML server controls, for the Web server controls you cannot simply use the HTML syntax to add client-side event handling. The reason is that for some controls ASP.NET already uses the client-side event handling to perform automatic postback operation. The preferred way to add client side event handling code for Web server controls is via the use of the Attributes property of the Web server controls. For example, the following code fragment attaches the `someClientCode()` client-side method to the onMouseOver event of the btnSubmit button.

```
btnSubmit.Attributes.Add("onMouseOver", _
 "someClientCode();")
```

Step by Step 2.5 demonstrates the technique of mixing both client-side and server-side event handling for Web server controls.

STEP BY STEP

2.5 Adding Client-side Event Handling Code to the Web Server Controls

1. In the Solution Explorer, right-click `StepByStep2-4.aspx` and select Copy. Right-click the project name and select Paste. Rename the pasted Web Form to `StepByStep2-5.aspx`. Open the ASPX (HTML view) and VB (Code view) files of the new Web Form and change all references to `StepByStep2_4` to refer to `StepByStep2_5` instead.

2. Switch to the HTML view of the Web Form. Insert a `<SCRIPT>` element under the `<HEAD>` element as shown here:

```
<HEAD>
 ...
    <SCRIPT language="javascript">
        function btnSubscribe_ClientClick()
        {
            alert(document.Form1.txtName.value +
              ", thank you for subscribing to " +
              document.Form1.ddlNewsletter.value);
        }
    </SCRIPT>
</HEAD>
```

3. Switch to the code view of the page. Add code to hook up the script to the button:

```
Private Sub Page_Load(ByVal sender As System.Object, _
 ByVal e As System.EventArgs) Handles MyBase.Load
    ' Add the onclick attribute with value
    ' Set to the client-side event handler code
    btnSubscribe.Attributes.Add("onclick", _
       "btnSubscribe_ClientClick();")
End Sub
```

4. Set `StepByStep2-5.aspx` as the start page in the project.

5. Run the project by selecting Debug, Start. Fill the form and submit the details by clicking the Subscribe button.

You should see a message box with a thank you message along with the name of subscriber and the newsletter from the client-side event handling code. You should also notice the same message displayed in the Web Form by the ServerClick event handler.

As you can see in Step by Step 2.5, to specify a client-side event handler with a Web server control you need to add an event attribute to the control at runtime.

GUIDED PRACTICE EXERCISE 2.2

You are required to design a Web Form as shown in Figure 2.15. When the user clicks left-side buttons, specified odd numbers should be generated. If the user clicks the right-side buttons, specified even numbers should be generated. You should write the minimum code to achieve your solution.

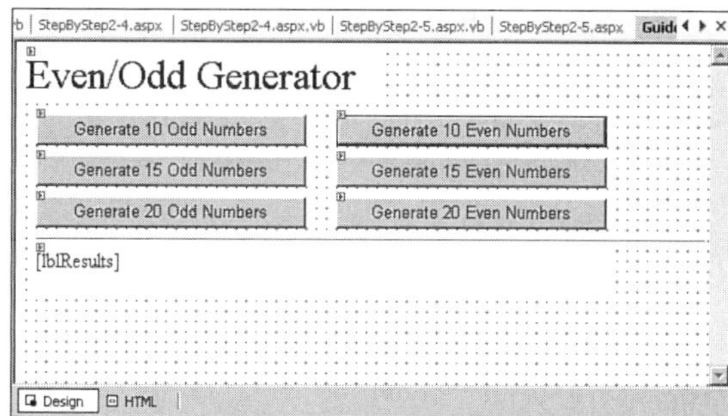

FIGURE 2.15
In the Even/Odd Generator page, some of the button controls generate specified even numbers whereas the other button controls generate specified odd numbers.

How would you create such a Web Form?

You should try working through this problem on your own first. If you are stuck, or if you'd like to see one possible solution, follow these steps:

1. Open the project 305C02. Add a new Web Form GuidedPracticeExercise2-2 to the project.

continues

continued

2. Add the Label controls, button controls, and a horizontal rule to the form. Set the text and arrange the controls as shown in Figure 2.15.

3. Select all three left-side button controls. Open the Properties window and set the CommandName property to Odd. Repeat this process with right side button controls and set their CommandName property to Even.

4. Select top two button controls and set their CommandArgument property to 10. Repeat the process for next two rows of button controls and set their CommandArgument property to 15 and 20, respectively.

5. Switch to the code view of the form. Add the following line of code at the top of the code-behind file.

```
Imports System.Text
```

6. Add the following method to the class:

```
' A generic event handler that handles the Command
' event for all the button controls
Private Sub EvenOdd_Command(ByVal sender As Object, _
 ByVal e As System.Web.UI. _
 WebControls.CommandEventArgs)
    ' Get the command specified for the Button
    Dim strEvenOdd As String = e.CommandName
    ' Get the command argument for the Button
    Dim intTimes As Integer = _
     Convert.ToInt32(e.CommandArgument)

    Dim sbResults As StringBuilder = _
     New StringBuilder()
    Dim i As Integer
    For i = 0 To intTimes
        ' Generate an Odd/Even number
        If strEvenOdd = "Odd" Then
            sbResults.Append(String.Format( _
             "{0} number {1} is: {2}<br>", _
             strEvenOdd, i + 1, i * 2 + 1))
        Else
            sbResults.Append(String.Format( _
             "{0} number {1} is: {2}<br>", _
             strEvenOdd, i + 1, i * 2))
        End If
    Next
    ' Store the final results in a label control
    lblResults.Text = sbResults.ToString()
End Sub
```

7. Add an event handler to hook up these events when the page is loaded:

```
Private Sub Page_Load(ByVal sender As System.Object, _
 ByVal e As System.EventArgs) Handles MyBase.Load
    AddHandler Button1.Command, _
     AddressOf EvenOdd_Command
    AddHandler Button2.Command, _
     AddressOf EvenOdd_Command
    AddHandler Button3.Command, _
     AddressOf EvenOdd_Command
    AddHandler Button4.Command, _
     AddressOf EvenOdd_Command
    AddHandler Button5.Command, _
     AddressOf EvenOdd_Command
    AddHandler Button6.Command, _
     AddressOf EvenOdd_Command
End Sub
```

8. Set the GuidedPracticeExercise2_2.aspx page as the start page of the project.

9. Run the project. Click the buttons; you should see that they generate the correct number of odd or even numbers, as shown in Figure 2.16.

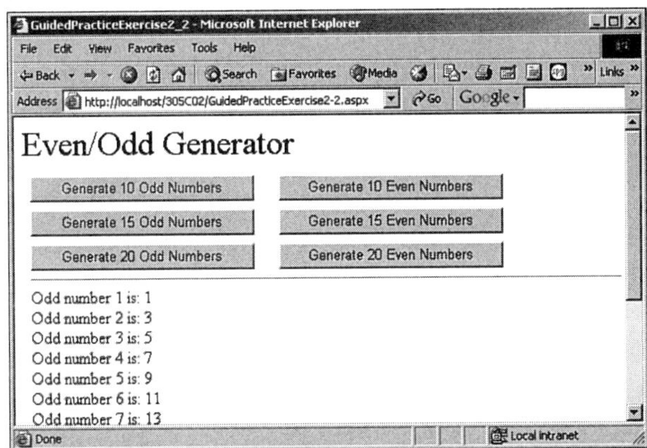

FIGURE 2.16
The results of clicking a command button on the Web Form.

In this exercise, some of the button controls do one task while the other button controls perform other tasks. It would obviously take lot of code to individually program the Click event of each button.

continues

continued

The CommandName and CommandArgument properties of Button control are designed specifically for these requirements. You can set a command name in the CommandName property and its associated argument in CommandArgument property for each of the buttons.

Finally, you can program a single event handler for the Command event of all the buttons and access the CommandName and CommandArgument properties of the button that was actually clicked by using the CommandEventArgs object.

If you have difficulty following this exercise, review the section "The Button, LinkButton, and ImageButton Controls " and "Event Handling with Web Server Controls" earlier in this chapter. After doing this review, try this exercise again.

REVIEW BREAK

- Web server controls provide a rich and consistent model of programming that integrates well with the rest of .NET Framework.
- Some Web server controls such as the DropDownList, RadioButton, and CheckBox have a property named AutoPostBack. When this property is set to True, it causes an immediate postback of the page when the value of control is changed. This allows the Web server to immediately respond to change events without waiting for a click event to cause a page postback.
- The preferred way to add client side event handling code for Web server controls is via the use of the Attributes property of the Web server controls.
- A button is used to initiate a specific action when clicked by the user. There are three types of buttons—Button, LinkButton, and ImageButton. Each of these buttons have similar functionality but is different in its appearance and is rendered differently on the Web page.

The List Controls

The category of list controls consists of the DropDownList, ListBox, CheckBoxList, and RadioButtonList controls. These controls display a list of items from which the user can select. These controls inherit from the abstract base ListControl class. The class provides the basic properties, methods, and events common to all the list controls. Items can be added to the list controls at design time using the <asp:ListItem> element. The list items in the list controls can be manipulated programmatically with the help of the ListItemCollection class or by specifying the data source using data binding. Data binding with list controls and their data-bound properties are discussed in detail in Chapter 5. Table 2.8 summarizes the important members of the ListControl class with which you should be familiar.

TABLE 2.8

IMPORTANT MEMBERS OF THE LISTCONTROL CLASS

Member	*Member*	*Description*
`AutoPostBack`	Property	Indicates whether the Web Form should be posted to the server automatically whenever the list selection is changed. Works only if the browser supports client-side scripting.
`Items`	Property	Specifies a collection of items in the list control.
`SelectedIndex`	Property	Specifies an index of the currently selected item. The default value is –1, which means no item is selected in the list control.
`SelectedIndexChanged`	Event	Occurs when the `SelectedIndex` property changes. `SelectedIndexChanged` is the default event for the list controls.
`SelectedItem`	Property	Specifies the currently selected item.

Although these controls inherit their basic functionality from the ListControl class, they display the list of items in different styles and allow single or multiple modes of selection.

A DropDownList Web server control allows you to select only a single item from the drop-down list. The DropDownList Web server control is rendered as <select> HTML element and its items are added as <option> elements within the HTML <select> element. The default value of the SelectedIndex property is 0, which means the first item is selected in the drop-down list. This overrides the default of the general ListControl class.

A ListBox Web server control allows you to select single or multiple items from the list of items displayed in the list box. The ListBox Web server control is rendered as <select> or <select multiple="multiple"> HTML element depending on whether single or multiple selections are allowed. The items are added as <option> elements within the HTML <select> element. The ListBox class adds two more properties to enable it to select multiple items:

1. **Rows**: This property represents the number of rows to be displayed in the list box. The default value is 4. The value of this property must be between 1 and 2000.

2. **SelectionMode**: This property indicates the mode of selection allowed in the list box. It can be one of the ListSelectionMode values—Multiple or Single (default).

The CheckBoxList and RadioButtonList Web server controls display lists of check boxes and radio buttons, respectively, where each check box or radio button represents a CheckBox or RadioButton Web server control. The CheckBoxList control allows you to select multiple check boxes in the list. The RadioButtonList control allows you to select only a single radio button from the list of radio buttons. The CheckBoxList and RadioButtonList render each list item as <input type="checkbox"> and <input type="radio"> HTML elements, respectively. The list items are displayed in a table or without a table structure depending on the layout selected.

Table 2.9 summarizes the important members of the CheckBoxList and RadioButtonList classes that enable you to format these Web server controls.

TABLE 2.9

IMPORTANT MEMBERS OF THE CHECKBOXLIST AND RADIOBUTTONLIST CLASS

Member	*Member*	*Description*
`CellPadding`	Property	Specifies the distance in pixels between the border and the contents (that is, checkbox or radio button) of the list control.
`CellSpacing`	Property	Specifies the distance in pixels between the items (that is, checkbox or radio button) of the list control.
`RepeatColumns`	Property	Specifies the number of columns to be displayed in the list control
`RepeatDirection`	Property	Specifies the direction of layout of the items in the list control. It can be one of the RepeatDirection enumeration—Horizontal or Vertical (default).
`RepeatLayout`	Property	Specifies the layout method of the items in the list control. It can be one of the RepeatLayout enumeration—Flow (items are not displayed in a table structure) or Table (default, items are displayed in a table structure).
`TextAlign`	Property	Specifies the alignment of the text displayed along with the individual items in the list control. It can be one of the TextAlign enumeration values—Left (text is displayed on the left of the item control) and Right (default, text is displayed on the right of the item control).

EXAM TIP

SelectedIndex The default value of the SelectedIndex property in a list control is –1, which indicates that no item is selected in the list control. However, the DropDownList control overrides this property and sets the default value to 0, which indicates the first item in the list. This ensures that an item is always selected in the drop-down list.

EXAM TIP

Multiple Selection The list controls like ListBox and CheckBoxList allow you to make multiple selections from the list controls. When these controls allow multiple selections, the SelectedIndex and SelectedItem properties return the index of the first selected item and the first selected item itself, respectively. You have to iterate through the Items collection and check that each item's Selected property is true, to retrieve the items selected by the user.

STEP BY STEP

2.6 Using List Controls

1. In the solution 315C02, add a new Web Form. Name the new form `StepByStep2_6.aspx`.
2. Add a `Label` control on the form. Change its Text property to "Tourist Interests Survey." Set the Font size to `Large`. Add another `Label` control and change its `Text` property to "Which national parks are you interested in visiting?" Set the Font size to `Medium`.

continues

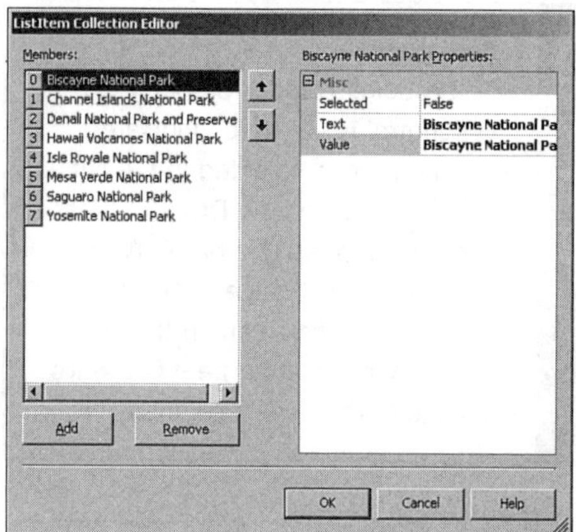

FIGURE 2.17
Use the ListItem Collection Editor dialog box to add list items to the lbParks control.

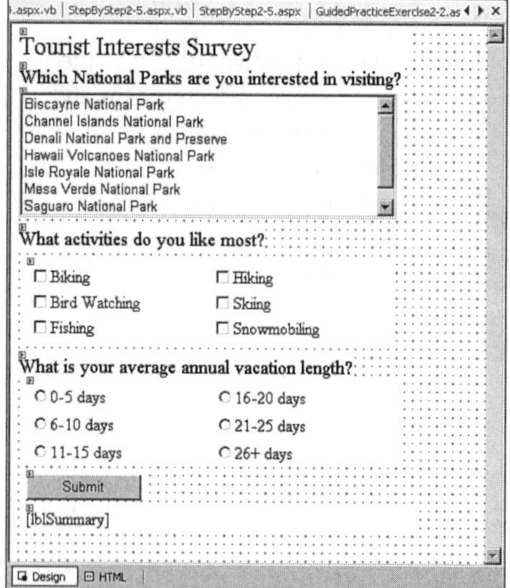

FIGURE 2.18
Use the RepeatColumn property to arrange the data in CheckBoxList and RadioButtonList in multiple columns.

continued

3. Drag a ListBox control to the Form. Change its `id` to `lbParks`. Using the Properties window, select the `Items` property and click the ellipsis button (...). This will open the ListItem Collection Editor. Enter the values as shown in Figure 2.17. Set the `SelectionMode` property of the `lbParks` list box to `Multiple`.

4. Drag a CheckBoxList control (`cblActivities`) and a `RadioButtonList` control (`rblVacation`) to the form. Set the `RepeatColumn` property for both the controls to `2`. Use the ListItem Collection Editor to add items to these controls. Add a couple of label controls and arrange the controls as shown in Figure 2.18.

5. Place a Button control (`btnSubmit`) on the Web Form. Place a `Label` control (`lblSummary`) at the bottom of the Web Form.

6. Add the following line of code at the top of the code-behind file.

```
Imports System.Text
```

7. Double-click the `btnSubmit` button to attach an event handler to its `Click` event. Add the following code to the event handler:

```
Private Sub btnSubmit_Click( _
 ByVal sender As System.Object, _
 ByVal e As System.EventArgs) Handles btnSubmit.Click
    ' Create a StringBuilder object that you
    ' will use to effieciently concatenate messages
    Dim sb As StringBuilder = New StringBuilder()
    sb.Append("<h3>Thank You! The following data ")
    sb.Append( _
     " entered by you has been recorded</h3>")
    sb.Append("<h4>Selected Parks: </h4>")

    ' Because the SelectionMode property of lbParks
    ' is Multiple, you need to iterate through its
    ' Items collection to individually gather the
    ' select national parks
```

```
    Dim li As ListItem
    For Each li In lbParks.Items
        If li.Selected Then
            sb.Append(li.Text)
            sb.Append("<BR>")
        End If
    Next

    sb.Append("<h4>Selected Activities: </h4>")

    ' Multiple activities can be selected by the
    ' user, therefore, you need to iterate through
    ' the complete Items collection to individually
    ' find the select activities
    For Each li In cblActivities.Items
        If li.Selected Then
            sb.Append(li.Text)
            sb.Append("<BR>")
        End If
    Next

    sb.Append("<h4>Average Vacation Size: </h4>")
    ' Only one item can be selected from a
    ' RadioButtonList
    sb.Append(rblVacation.SelectedItem.Text)

    ' Copy the messages to the bottom label control
    lblSummary.Text = sb.ToString()
End Sub
```

8. Set the `StepByStep2-6.aspx` as the start page of the project.

9. Run the project by selecting Debug, Start. Fill the form and submit the details by clicking the Submit image button. You should see a summary message displaying all the selected items displayed at the bottom of the form as shown in Figure 2.19.

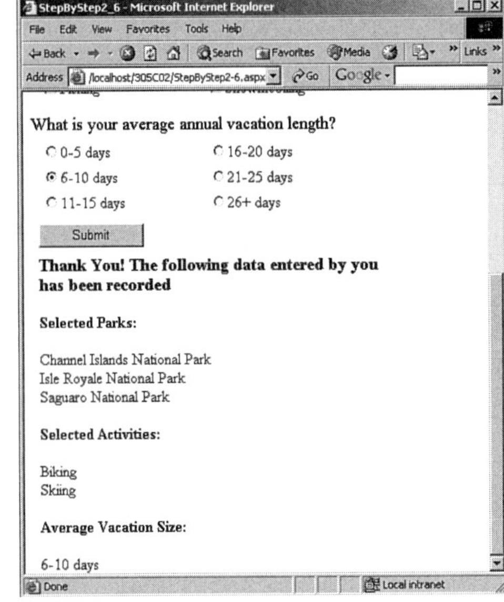

FIGURE 2.19
Message constructed from the value of other controls on the Web Form.

In Step by Step 2.6, to enumerate the selected items in the list controls where multiple items can be selected, you had to iterate through the entire Items collection of the list control. For those controls where only a single selection is allowed, you can simply use the SelectedItem property to find out the selected item.

Step by Step 2.6 also uses the StringBuilder object to combine strings. When multiple strings need to be concatenated, StringBuilder object provides much better performance than using concatenation with the String class.

The PlaceHolder and Panel Controls

A PlaceHolder Web server control allows you to hold an area on a Web page. The placeholder control allows you to add controls dynamically in a Web page at the area reserved by the placeholder control.

The PlaceHolder Web server control inherits from the System.Web.UI.Control class and does not share the common properties shared by the Web server controls that inherit from the WebControl class. The control does not define any new properties, events, or methods. It does not render any HTML element for itself.

A Panel Web server control acts as a container for other controls in the Web page. The Panel control can be used to organize controls in the Web page. It can be used to hide or show controls contained in the panel on the Web page. Controls can also be added programmatically to the panel control.

The Panel Web server control is rendered as a <div> HTML element on the Web page. Table 2.10 summarizes the important members of the Panel class with which you should be familiar.

TABLE 2.10

IMPORTANT MEMBERS OF THE PANEL CLASS

Member	*Member*	*Description*
`BackImageUrl`	Property	Specifies the URL of the background image to be displayed behind the contents of the panel control.
`HorizontalAlign`	Property	Specifies the horizontal alignment of the contents within the panel control. It can be assigned one of the `HorizontalAlign` enumeration—`Center`, `Justify`, `Left`, `NotSet` (default), and `Right`.
`Wrap`	Property	Indicates whether the contents in the panel can automatically wrap within the panel. The default value is `True`.

STEP BY STEP

2.7 Loading Controls Dynamically

1. In the solution 305C02, add a new Web Form. Name the new form StepByStep2-7.aspx.

2. Place a Label control on the Web Form. Set its Text property to "Travel Expense Calculator" and set the font size to Medium. Place a horizontal rule after the label.

3. Place two more Label controls on the Web Form and set their Text properties to "Associate Name" and "Number of days", respectively. Place a TextBox control on the Web Form and set its id property to txtName.

4. Add a DropDownList, and set its id property to ddlDays and the AutoPostBack property to true. Use the ListItem Collection Editor to add values 0 to 5 in the drop-down list.

5. At the bottom of the form, place a Panel control. Set its id property to pnlDynamic.

6. Switch to the code view and add the following code in the Page_Load event:

```
Private Sub Page_Load(ByVal sender As System.Object, _
 ByVal e As System.EventArgs) Handles MyBase.Load
    ' Use the Page_Load event to load the
    ' dynamically created controls so that
    ' they are available prior to rendering

    ' Get the value selected by
    ' user in the dropdown list
    Dim intDays As Integer = _
     Convert.ToInt32(ddlDays.SelectedItem.Value)
    ' Create textboxes to allow entering the
    ' travel expenses for each travel day
    Dim i As Integer
    For i = 1 To intDays
        Dim lcExpenseCaption As LiteralControl = _
         New LiteralControl()
        lcExpenseCaption.Text = _
         String.Format( _
         "Travel Expense for Day-{0} ", i)
        ' Create a textbox control
        Dim txtExpense As TextBox = New TextBox()
```

continues

continued

```
            ' Set the id property of the textbox
            txtExpense.ID = String.Format("Expense{0}", i)
            Dim lcBreak As HtmlControl = _
             New HtmlGenericControl("br")
            pnlDynamic.Controls.Add(lcExpenseCaption)
            ' Add the textbox to the panel
            ' if you omit this step, the textbox is
            ' created but not displayed
            pnlDynamic.Controls.Add(txtExpense)
            pnlDynamic.Controls.Add(lcBreak)
        Next
        ' Display a linkbutton that allow users to
        ' post the expenses after
        ' they have entered the data
        If (intDays > 0) Then
            Dim lbtnSubmit As LinkButton = _
             New LinkButton()
            lbtnSubmit.Text = "Submit Expenses"
            ' Add an event handler to
            ' the dynamically created
            ' link button
            AddHandler lbtnSubmit.Click, _
             AddressOf lbtnSubmit_Click
            pnlDynamic.Controls.Add(lbtnSubmit)
            Dim lcBreak As HtmlControl = _
             New HtmlGenericControl("br")
            pnlDynamic.Controls.Add(lcBreak)
        End If

End Sub
```

7. Add another method that handles the `Click` event for the dynamic link button:

```
' Handles the Click event for the dynamically
' created link button
Private Sub lbtnSubmit_Click( _
 ByVal sender As Object, _
 ByVal e As System.EventArgs)
    Dim dblExpenses As Double = 0
    Dim intDays As Integer = _
     Convert.ToInt32(ddlDays.SelectedItem.Value)
    ' Find sum of all expenses
    Dim i As Integer
    For i = 1 To intDays
        ' Find control in the collection of controls
        ' contained by the panel
        Dim txtExpense As TextBox = _
         CType(pnlDynamic.FindControl( _
         String.Format("Expense{0}", i)), TextBox)
        dblExpenses += _
         Convert.ToDouble(txtExpense.Text)
    Next
```

```
    ' Display the results
    Dim lblResults As Label = New Label()
    lblResults.Text = String.Format( _
     "{0}, your expenses are ${1}", _
     txtName.Text, dblExpenses)
    pnlDynamic.Controls.Add(lblResults)
End Sub
```

8. Set `StepByStep2-7.aspx` as the start page of the project.

9. Run the project. Enter a name for the associate and select 3 from the drop-down list. You will see that three `TextBox` controls have been created to enter travel expenses. A link button allows you to post the expenses to the Web server. Enter some values for the expenses and click the link button. You will see that the expenses were all summed up and a message displaying the credit to the account of the associate is shown as in Figure 2.20.

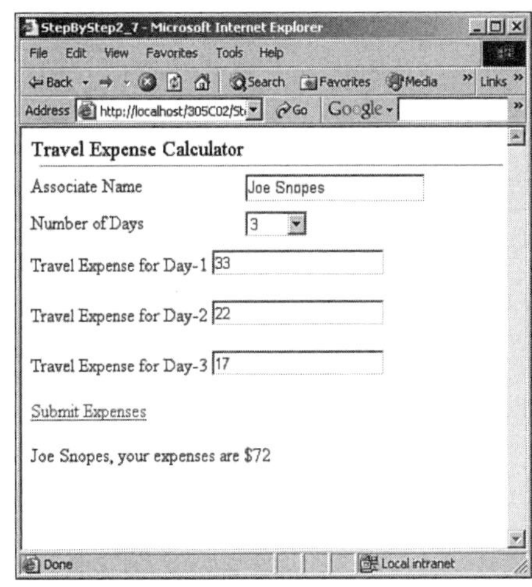

FIGURE 2.20
The fields for entering travel expenses and the Submit Expenses link button are dynamically generated.

In Step by Step 2.7, I am adding controls dynamically in the Load event handler of the Page class. You will recall from Chapter 1 that the Load event is called prior to page rendering. So adding controls in the Load events ensures that the controls are rendered properly and are available for access at a later stage when you would like to retrieve the value entered by the user in those dynamically created controls.

Another important thing to note is that, after you create a control, you must remember to add it to one of the container controls on the Web page. If you just create a control but forget to add it to the container control, your control will not be rendered with the page.

The Table, TableRow, and TableCell Controls

The Table Web server control allows you to build a table on the Web page. This control is very useful to display data in columnar format. The table control is rendered as a <table> HTML element on the Web page. Table 2.11 summarizes the important members of the Table class with which you should be familiar.

TABLE 2.11

IMPORTANT MEMBERS OF THE TABLE CLASS

Member	*Member*	*Description*
`BackImageUrl`	Property	Specifies the URL of the background image to be displayed behind the contents of the table.
`CellPadding`	Property	Specifies the distance in pixels between the border and the contents of a cell in the table control.
`CellSpacing`	Property	Specifies the width in pixels between the cells of the table control.
`GridLines`	Property	Indicates which cell borders to be displayed in the table control. It can be assigned one of the GridLines enumeration—`Both` (horizontal and vertical borders), `Horizontal`, `None` (default, no cell borders), and `Vertical`.
`HorizontalAlign`	Property	Specifies the horizontal alignment of the table within the Web page. It can be assigned one of the `HorizontalAlign` enumeration—`Center`, `Justify`, `Left`, `NotSet` (default), and `Right`.
`Rows`	Property	Specifies a collection of rows in the table control.

The TableRow class represents a row in a table control. The TableRow class is rendered as a <tr> HTML element on the Web page. Table 2.12 summarizes the important members of the TableRow class with which you should be familiar.

TABLE 2.12

IMPORTANT MEMBERS OF THE TABLEROW CLASS

Member	*Member*	*Description*
`Cells`	Property	Specifies a collection of the table cells contained in a table row.
`HorizontalAlign`	Property	Specifies the horizontal alignment of the cells within the table row. It can be one of the `HorizontalAlign` enumeration—`Center`, `Justify`, `Left`, `NotSet` (default), and `Right`.
VerticalAlign	Property	Specifies the vertical alignment of the cells within the table row. It can be one of the `VerticalAlign` enumeration—`Bottom`, `Middle`, `NotSet` (default), and `Top`.

The TableCell Web server control represents a cell in a table control. The Table Web server control is rendered as a <td> HTML element on the Web page. Table 2.13 summarizes the important members of the TableCell class with which you should be familiar.

TABLE 2.13

IMPORTANT MEMBERS OF THE TABLECELL CLASS

Member	*Member*	*Description*
`ColumnSpan`	Property	Specifies the number of columns occupied by a single table cell.
`HorizontalAlign`	Property	Specifies the horizontal alignment of the contents of the cells within the table cell. It can be one of the `HorizontalAlign` enumeration—`Center`, `Justify`, `Left`, `NotSet` (default), and `Right`.
`RowSpan`	Property	Specifies the number of rows occupied by a single table cell.
`Text`	Property	Specifies the text displayed on a table cell.
`VerticalAlign`	Property	Specifies the vertical alignment of the cells within the table row. It can be one of the `VerticalAlign` enumeration—`Bottom`, `Middle`, `NotSet` (default), and `Top`.
`Wrap`	Property	Indicates whether the contents in a cell can automatically wrap to the next line.

Step by Step 2.8 dynamically creates a table whose number of rows and columns are specified by the user at runtime.

STEP BY STEP

2.8 Using PlaceHolder, Table, TableRow, and TableCell Controls

1. In the solution `305C02`, add a new Web Form. Name the new form as `StepByStep2-8.aspx`. Change the `pageLayout` property for the document to `FlowLayout`.

continues

continued

2. Place a `Label` control on the Web Form. Set its Text property to "Enter number of rows and columns to create a table dynamically" and set the font size to Medium.

3. Place two more `Label` controls on the Web Form and set their Text properties to `"Rows"` and `"Columns"`. Place two `TextBox` controls on the Web Form and set their `id` property to `txtRows` and `txtColumns`.

4. Place a Button control on the Web Form. Set its `id` property to `btnSubmit` and Text property to `"Submit"`.

5. At the bottom of the Web Form, place a PlaceHolder control. Set its `id` property to `phTable`.

6. Double-click the submit button and write the following code to its `Click` event handler:

```
Private Sub btnSubmit_Click( _
 ByVal sender As System.Object, _
 ByVal e As System.EventArgs) _
 Handles btnSubmit.Click
    ' Create a new table
    Dim tblNew As Table = New Table()
    tblNew.GridLines = GridLines.Both
    tblNew.BorderStyle = BorderStyle.Solid

    Dim trRow As TableRow
    Dim tcCell As TableCell

    ' Iterate for the specified number of rows
    Dim intRow As Integer
    For intRow = 1 To Int32.Parse(txtRows.Text)
        ' Create a row
        trRow = New TableRow()
        If intRow Mod 2 = 0 Then
            trRow.BackColor = Color.LightBlue
        End If
        ' Iterate for the specified number of columns
        Dim intCell As Integer
        For intCell = 1 To _
         Int32.Parse(txtColumns.Text)
            ' Create a cell in the current row
            tcCell = New TableCell()
            tcCell.Text = "Cell (" & intRow & "," & _
             CStr(intCell) & ")"
            trRow.Cells.Add(tcCell)
        Next
        tblNew.Rows.Add(trRow)
```

```
        Next
        ' Add the newly created Table to the
        ' PlaceHolder control
        phTable.Controls.Add(tblNew)
    End Sub
```

7. Set the `StepByStep2-8.aspx` as the start page of the project.

8. Run the project by selecting Debug, Start. Enter a value of 4 for the Rows and 7 for the Columns field and press the Submit button. You should see that a table is dynamically drawn for the given size as shown in Figure 2.21.

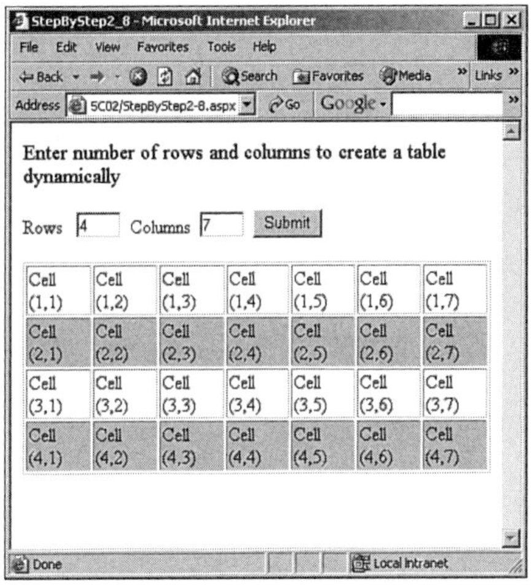

FIGURE 2.21
You can dynamically create a table by adding TableCell objects to a TableRow and then adding the TableRows objects to the Table.

A Table is a control that has one or more rows. Similarly, a TableRow control is a container for one or more cells. When you need to dynamically generate a table, you need to create the required number of cells to first create a row and then add rows to the table container.

The AdRotator Control

The AdRotator Web server control provides a convenient mechanism for displaying advertisements randomly selected from a list on a Web page. It fetches the images from a list stored in an Extensible Markup Language (XML) file and randomly loads an image in the AdRotator control every time the page is loaded. It allows you to specify a Web page whose contents will be displayed in the current window when the AdRotator control is clicked.

In the previous version of ASP, ActiveX objects were used to achieve rich features. In ASP.NET, the AdRotator control is a dream for developers and administrators alike.

The advertisements are detailed in an XML-based file, making advertisement management easy to administer. This listing shows a partial sample advertisement file:

```
<?xml version="1.0" ?>
<Advertisements>
    <Ad>
       <ImageUrl>que.gif</ImageUrl>
       <NavigateUrl>http://www.quepublishing.com
       </NavigateUrl>
```

```
    <AlternateText>Que Publishing</AlternateText>
    <Impressions>40</Impressions>
    <Keyword>Books</Keyword>
    <Specialization>Certification Books
    </Specialization>
  </Ad>
 <Ad>
  ...
  </Ad>
  ...
</Advertisements>
```

As is clear from the preceding listing, the <Advertisements> element is the root element of the advertisement's XML file. The advertisements are individually stored in an <Ad> element. The <Ad> element specifies the information for each advertisement by a collection of elements. There are some predefined elements listed in Table 2.14. However, you can add new elements within the <Ad> element to provide additional advertisement information. For example, the <Specialization> element added in the preceding listing provides the field in which the advertisement company specializes.

TABLE 2.14

PREDEFINED ELEMENTS WITHIN THE <AD> ELEMENT

Elements	*Description*
`<AlternateText>`	Specifies the text that is displayed in the place of the image in the advertisement, if the image of the advertisement is not available for any reason. This property is displayed as a `ToolTip` if the browser supports the ToolTip feature.
`<ImageUrl>`	Specifies the URL of the image to be displayed in the `AdRotator` control.
`<Impressions>`	Indicates how often the current advertisement should be displayed in relation to other advertisements specified by the advertisements file.
`<Keyword>`	Specifies the group to which a particular advertisement belongs.
`<NavigateUrl>`	Specifies the URL of the Web page that is to be displayed when the `AdRotator` control is clicked.

The AdRotator control is rendered as an <a> anchor HTML element with an embedded <img> image HTML element to display the image on the Web page. Table 2.15 summarizes the important members of the AdRotator class with which you should be familiar.

TABLE 2.15

IMPORTANT MEMBERS OF THE ADROTATOR CLASS

Member	*Member*	*Description*
`AdCreated`	Event	Occurs when the `AdRotator` control is created. This event occurs after the control is created but before the Web page is rendered. The `AdRotator` control is created whenever the page control is refreshed. `AdCreated` is the default event for the `AdRotator` control.
`AdvertisementFile`	Property	Specifies the location of an XML file that stores the advertisement information.
`KeywordFilter`	Property	Specifies the keyword (group name) on which the advertisements need to be filtered. The property relates to the `<Keyword>` element within an `<Ad>` element in the advertisement file.
`Target`	Property	Specifies the target window or frame where the contents of the linked Web page will be displayed when the `AdRotator` control is clicked. Some of the possible values are `_blank` (new window), `_parent` (parent frameset), `_self` (current position in the window), `_top` (current window).

EXAM TIP

The KeywordFilter Property When the KeywordFilter property of an AdRotator control is set to a keyword that does not correspond to any <Keyword> element in the XML advertisement file, the AdRotator will display a blank image in place of the advertisement and a trace warning will be generated.

The AdCreated event passes an object of type AdCreatedEventArgs that contains event-related data. This object exposes the following four properties: AdProperties, AlternateText, ImageUrl, and NavigateUrl. The AdProperties contains a collection of key-value pairs representing all the elements (including custom elements) defined for the current <Ad> element.

STEP BY STEP

2.9 Using the AdRotator Web Server Control

1. Add a new Web Form to the project `305C02`. Name the form `StepByStep2-9.aspx`.

continues

continued

2. In the Solution Explorer, right-click the project and select Add, Add New Item from the dialog box. The Add New Item dialog box opens as shown in Figure 2.22. Select an XML File template and name the XML file `advertisements.xml`.

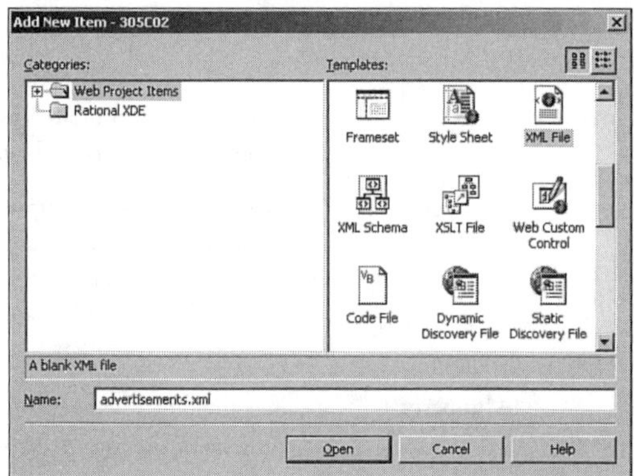

FIGURE 2.22
Using the Add New Item dialog box, add a new file based on the XML File template.

3. Open the `advertisements.xml` file and add the following data:

```
<?xml version="1.0" ?>
<Advertisements>
    <Ad>
       <ImageUrl>que.gif</ImageUrl>
       <NavigateUrl>http://www.quepublishing.com
       </NavigateUrl>
       <AlternateText>Que Publishing</AlternateText>
       <Impressions>40</Impressions>
       <Keyword>Books</Keyword>
       <Specialization>Certification Books
       </Specialization>
     </Ad>
    <Ad>
       <ImageUrl>awl.gif</ImageUrl>
       <NavigateUrl>http://www.awl.com</NavigateUrl>
       <AlternateText>Addison Wesley</AlternateText>
       <Impressions>30</Impressions>
       <Keyword>Books</Keyword>
       <Specialization>Books for Professionals
       </Specialization>
     </Ad>
    <Ad>
       <ImageUrl>prenhall.gif</ImageUrl>
       <NavigateUrl>http://www.prenhall.com
       </NavigateUrl>
```

```
      <AlternateText>Prentice Hall</AlternateText>
      <Impressions>30</Impressions>
      <Keyword>Books</Keyword>
      <Specialization>Academic Books</Specialization>
    </Ad>
</Advertisements>
```

4. Add images to the project as specified by the `<ImageUrl>` elements in the `advertisements.xml` file. To do this, right-click the project in Solution Explorer and select Add, Add Existing Item. Browse to each file and click OK to add it to the project.

5. Drag an `AdRotator` control with `id adrBooks` and a `Label` control with `id lblSpecialization` to the Web Form. Set the Target property of the `AdRotator` control to `_blank`. This will open the Web page linked to the advertisement in a new window.

6. Select the `AdvertisementFile` property of the `AdRotator` control in the Properties window and click the ellipsis (…) button. This opens Select XML file dialog box. Select the `advertisements.xml` file created in the step 2.

7. Double-click the `AdRotator` control and add the following code in the `AdCreated` event handler:

```
Private Sub adrBooks_AdCreated( _
 ByVal sender As System.Object, _
 ByVal e As System.Web.UI. _
 WebControls.AdCreatedEventArgs) _
 Handles adrBooks.AdCreated
    ' Fetch the value of the Specialization element
    ' through the AdProperties property of the
    ' AdCreatedEventArgs object
    lblSpecialization.Text = _
        e.AdProperties("Specialization")
End Sub
```

8. Set `StepByStep2-9.aspx` as the start page in the project.

9. Run the project. You will see the `AdRotator` control displaying an advertisement from the `advertisements.xml` file (see Figure 2.23). You should also see a label displaying the value of the custom `<Specialization>` element added to the advertisement file. Refresh the Web page and it will display a different advertisement.

FIGURE 2.23
The AdRotator control displays advertisements based on the settings in an XML advertisement file.

The Calendar Control

The Calendar Web server control displays a calendar on the Web page. It allows you to select a day, or a week, or a month, or even a range of days. You can customize the appearance of the control and even add custom content for each day. The control generates events when a selection changes or when the visible month is changed in the calendar control. Thus, the Calendar Web server control is an extremely sophisticated and powerful tool for Web application development. The Calendar control is rendered as a <table> HTML element on the Web page. Figure 2.24 shows a calendar control and its important elements.

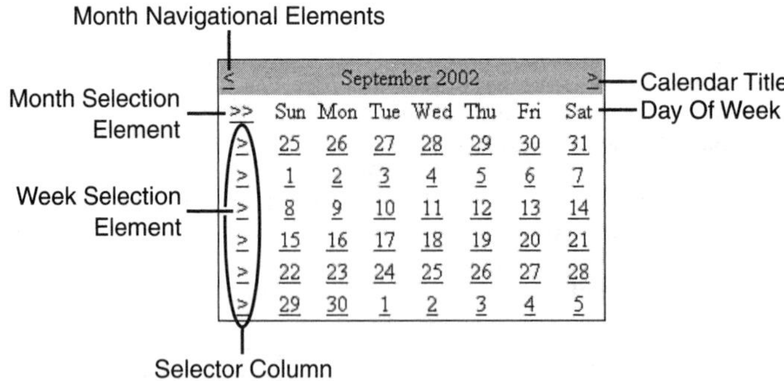

FIGURE 2.24
The Calendar control with its SelectionMode property set to DayWeekMonth.

Tables 2.16 and 2.17 summarizes the important properties and events of the Calendar class, respectively.

TABLE 2.16

IMPORTANT PROPERTIES OF THE CALENDAR CLASS

Properties	*Description*
`CellPadding`	Specifies the distance in pixels between the border and the contents of a cell in the calendar control.
`CellSpacing`	Specifies the width in pixels between the cells of the calendar control.
`DayHeaderStyle`	Specifies the style properties of the section where the days of the week are displayed. Works only if the `ShowDayHeader` property is `True`.
`DayNameFormat`	Specifies the name format for the days of the week. It can be one of the formats defined by the `DayNameFormat` enumeration—`FirstLetter`, `FirstTwoLetters`, `Full`, and `Short` (default). Works only if the `ShowDayHeader` property is `True`.
`DayStyle`	Specifies the style properties of the section where the days of the displayed month are displayed.
`FirstDayOfWeek`	Specifies the day of the week to be displayed in the first column of the calendar control. Values are specified by the `FirstDayOfWeek` enumeration—`Default` (default, picks the day specified by the system settings), `Monday`, `Tuesday`, `Wednesday`, `Thursday`, `Friday`, `Saturday`, and `Sunday`.
`NextMonthText`	Specifies the text for the navigational element to select the next month. The default value is `>` (>) sign. Works only if the `ShowNextPrevMonth` property is `True`.
`NextPrevFormat`	Specifies the text format for the navigational elements that select the previous and next months on the calendar control. Values are specified by the `NextPrevFormat` enumeration— `CustomText` (default, picks the value specified by the `PreviousMonthText` and `NextMonthText` property), `ShortMonth` (first three characters) and `FullMonth`. Works only if the `ShowNextPrevMonth` property is `True`.
`NextPrevStyle`	Specifies the style properties for the next and previous navigational elements. Works only if the `ShowNextPrevMonth` property is `True`.
`OtherMonthDayStyle`	Specifies the style properties for the days that do not belong to the displayed month.
`PrevMonthText`	Specifies the text for the navigational element to select the previous month. The default value is `<` (<) sign. Works only if the `ShowNextPrevMonth` property is `True`.
`SelectedDate`	Specifies the selected date.
`SelectedDates`	Specifies a collection of selected dates.
`SelectedDayStyle`	Specifies the style properties for the selected day in the calendar control.
`SelectionMode`	Specifies the mode of selection in the calendar. Values are specified by the `CalendarSelectionMode` enumeration—`Day` (default), `DayWeek` (day or week), `DayWeekMonth` (day, or week, or month) and `None`.
`SelectMonthText`	Specifies the text for the month selection element in the selector column. The default value is `>>` (>>) sign. Works only if the `SelectionMode` property is `DayWeekMonth`.
`SelectorStyle`	Specifies the style properties for the week and month selector column. Works only if the `SelectionMode` property is `DayWeek` or `DayWeekMonth`.
`SelectWeekText`	Specifies the text for the week selection element in the selector column. The default value is `>` (>) sign. Works only if the `SelectionMode` property is `DayWeek` or `DayWeekMonth`.

continues

TABLE 2.16 *continued*

IMPORTANT PROPERTIES OF THE CALENDAR CLASS

Properties	*Description*
ShowDayHeader	Indicates whether the row showing the name of the day of the week should be displayed. The default is True.
ShowGridLines	Indicates whether the cells of the calendar control should be separated with grid lines. The default is False.
ShowNextPrevMonth	Indicates whether the navigational elements for the next and previous month should be displayed. The default is True.
ShowTitle	Indicates whether to show the title of the calendar control.
TitleFormat	Specifies the format of the title of the calendar control. Values are specified by the TitleFormat enumeration—Month and MonthYear (default). Works only if the ShowTitle property is True.
TitleStyle	Specifies the style properties for the title of the calendar control. Works only if the ShowTitle property is True.
TodayDayStyle	Specifies the style properties for today's date in the calendar control.
TodaysDate	Specifies today's date. The default is picked up from the system.
VisibleDate	Specifies the month to be displayed on the calendar depending on the value of this property.
WeekendDayStyle	Specifies the style properties for the weekend days in the calendar control.

TABLE 2.17

IMPORTANT EVENTS OF THE CALENDAR CLASS

Event	*Description*
DayRender	Occurs when each day is created in the calendar control. This event occurs after the control is created but before is rendered to the Web page.
SelectionChanged	Occurs when the user changes the selection in the calendar control. SelectionChanged is the default event for the calendar control.
VisibleMonthChanged	Occurs when the month selection is changed when the user clicks the previous or next month navigational elements.

In Step by Step 2.10, you'll see how to customize the appearance of a calendar and how you program its SelectionChanged event to determine the dates selected by the user.

STEP BY STEP

2.10 Using the Calendar Web Server Control

1. Add a new Web Form to the project `305C02`. Name the form `StepByStep2-10.aspx`.

2. Drag a Calendar control to the Web Form and set its `id` to `calSelect`. Add two `Label` controls, one with `id` `lblMessage`. Set the `NextPrevFormat` property of the calendar to `ShortMonth`, the `SelectionMode` property to `DayWeekMonth`, the `SelectMonthText` property to Month, and the `SelectWeekText` property to Week.

3. Expand the node next to the `TitleStyle` property of the Calendar control in the Properties window and set different values for the subproperties to provide a custom style to the title of the Calendar as shown in Figure 2.25. Similarly, set other properties like `DayHeaderStyle`, `DayStyle`, `SelectorStyle`, `SelectedDayStyle` and so on to provide desired custom appearance to the Calendar control.

4. Switch to the code view of the form. Add the following line of code at the top of the code-behind file.

```
Imports System.Text
```

5. Double-click the Calendar control and add the following code in the `SelectionChanged` event handler:

```
Private Sub calSelect_SelectionChanged( _
 ByVal sender As System.Object, _
 ByVal e As System.EventArgs) _
 Handles calSelect.SelectionChanged
    Dim sbMessage As StringBuilder = _
     New StringBuilder()
    sbMessage.Append("The selected date(s) <br> ")
    ' Iterate through the SelectedDatesCollection
    ' And display the selected dates
    Dim i As Integer
    For i = 0 To calSelect.SelectedDates.Count - 1
        sbMessage.Append( _
         calSelect.SelectedDates(i). _
         ToShortDateString() & _
         "<br>")
    Next
    lblMessage.Text = sbMessage.ToString()
End Sub
```

continues

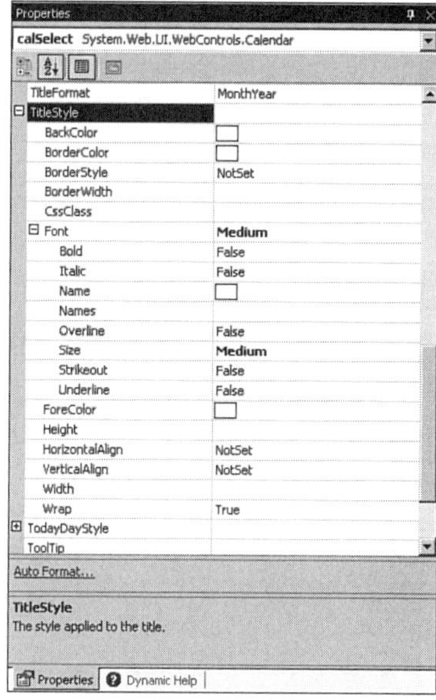

FIGURE 2.25
The Calendar control provides a large number of style properties that can be used to provide a custom appearance to the calendar.

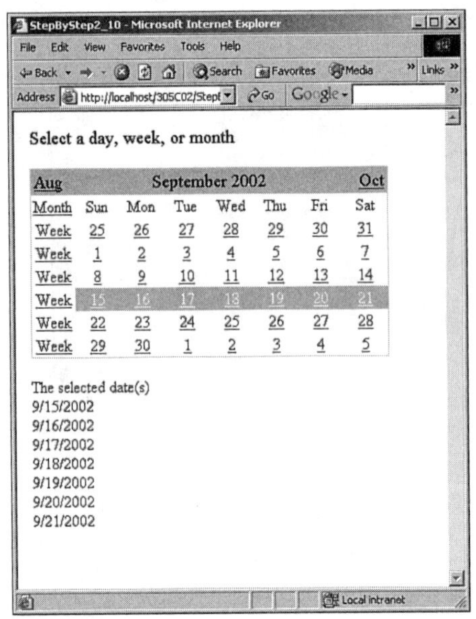

FIGURE 2.26
The SelectionChanged event occurs whenever the date selection is changed in the calendar control; the SelectedDate and SelectedDates property contain the new selected dates when the event occurs.

continued

6. Set `StepByStep2-10.aspx` as the start page in the project.

7. Run the project. You will see the Calendar control displayed. Click a day to select a day, on the Week link to select a week, or on the Month link to select the entire month. You should see a message showing the selected date(s) whenever the selection is changed in the calendar control as shown in Figure 2.26.

You can also auto format a calendar control by selecting a scheme from the Calendar Auto Format dialog box as shown in Figure 2.27. The Calendar Auto Format dialog box opens when the Auto Format link found in the lower portion of the Properties window (refer to Figure 2.25) is clicked.

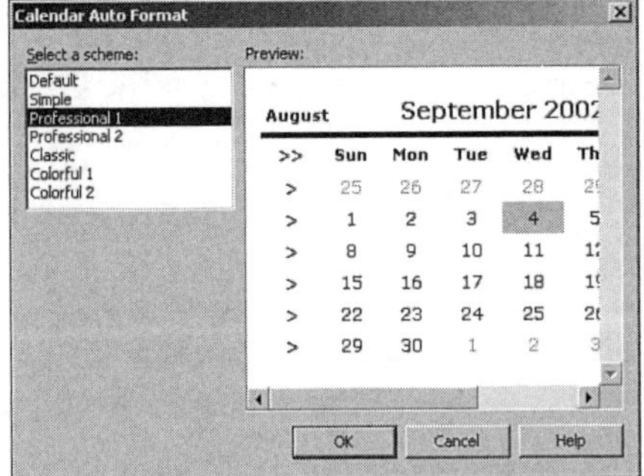

FIGURE 2.27
The Calendar Auto Format dialog box allows you to select a predefined set of colors, border styles, and other settings for a calendar control.

GUIDED PRACTICE EXERCISE 2.3

You are creating a class scheduling system for a school's intranet. You are using a Calendar control that helps users to select the dates for their schedules. The calendar allows users to select dates except for the calendar of vacation months such as June and July where no scheduling is required.

How would you create such a calendar?

You should try working through this problem on your own first. If you are stuck, or if you'd like to see one possible solution, follow these steps:

1. Open the project 3105C02. Add a new Web Form GuidedPracticeExercise2-3 to the project.

2. Drag a Calendar control with id calSchool to the Web Form. Add two Label controls, one with id lblMessage.

3. Switch to code view. Add the following code in the VisibleMonthChanged event handler:

```
Private Sub calSchool_VisibleMonthChanged( _
 ByVal sender As Object, _
 ByVal e As _
 System.Web.UI.WebControls.MonthChangedEventArgs) _
 Handles calSchool.VisibleMonthChanged
    ' If the Month of the new date selected is
    ' June (6) or July (7)
    ' Set the SelectionMode to None
    If e.NewDate.Month = 6 Or e.NewDate.Month = 7 Then
        calSchool.SelectionMode = _
         CalendarSelectionMode.None
        lblMessage.Text = _
         "You cannot select a date " & _
         "in a vacation month"
        ' othwerise set the SelectionMode to Day
    Else
    calSchool.SelectionMode = _
        CalendarSelectionMode.Day
        lblMessage.Text = ""
    End If
End Sub
```

4. Set GuidedPracticeExercise2-3.aspx as the start page of the project.

5. Run the project. Navigate to the June or July month in the calendar control. You should see a message that a date cannot be selected in the vacation month as shown in Figure 2.28. You should select other months to select a date.

If you have difficulty following this exercise, review the section "The Calendar Control" earlier in this chapter and Perform Step by Step 2.10. After doing this review, try this exercise again.

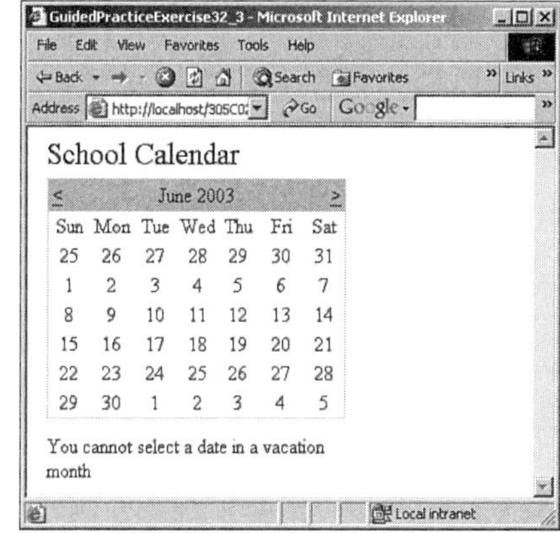

FIGURE 2.28
The VisibleMonthChanged event occurs when the user clicks the previous or next month navigational elements.

REVIEW BREAK

- There are four list Web server controls—ListBox, DropDownList, CheckBoxList, and RadioButtonList. These controls are used to present a list of items of the user.
- Use the Placeholder and Panel controls as container controls. These controls can be used to organize other controls either at design time or dynamically through a program.
- Use the AdRotator control to display a randomly selected advertisement banner on the Web page. The advertisement is selected based on the settings stored in an XML advertisement file.
- Use can the Calendar control to display a single month of a calendar on a Web page. The control allows you to select dates and move to the next or previous month.

USER INPUT VALIDATION

Validate user input.

Garbage-in is garbage-out. When designing a Web application that interacts with a user to accept data, you must ensure that the entered data is acceptable by the application.

The best place to ensure the validity of data is at the time of data entry itself. In Web applications, you have a choice of placing the validation logic at either the client side or server side:

- **Client-side Validation** When you place validation code at the client side, validation does not require postback operation and provides fast responses to the user. However, since the validation code is outside the Web server, it may be possible that client can spoof the Web server with invalid data. In addition to this, client-side validation requires the client to be capable of running scripts. That may be an issue with old browsers and some new browsers where users turn off script execution thinking it is unsafe.

- **Server-side Validation** When the validation code is placed at the server side, the process of validation may be slow as a form may involve multiple roundtrips to the Web server before all the data is validated. On the other hand, since the Web server is performing all the validation, you can trust the validated data. Server-side validation works well with even primitive browsers as it does not assume any specific browser capabilities.

ASP.NET provides a set of Web server controls called validation controls. These controls provide sophisticated validation on both the client-side and the server-side depending upon the validation settings and the browser capability.

The validation controls are usually associated with input server controls on which the validation needs to be performed. For validation to work properly, the validation control and the input server control must be placed in the same container control.

The input control associated with a validation control should have a ValidationProperty attribute applied to it. This attribute specifies the name of the server control's property that needs to be validated. Thus, validation can be performed only on those controls that can specify a single property that should be validated. Table 2.17 lists the standard input server controls that can be validated and their validation properties.

NOTE

Client-side Validation The client-side validation provided by ASP.NET validation controls works only with Internet Explorer 4.0 or higher.

EXAM TIP

Server-side Validation ASP.NET ensures that validations are performed on server side even if they were already performed at the client side. This ensures that validations are not bypassed if a malicious user tries to circumvent the client-side validation. Of course, if the client-side validation fails, the server-side validation is never performed.

TABLE 2.17

STANDARD INPUT SERVER CONTROLS

Class	*Validation Property*
`HtmlInputText`	`Value`
`HtmlInputFile`	`Value`
`HtmlSelect`	`Value`
`HtmlTextArea`	`Value`
`DropDownList`	`SelectedItem.Value`
`ListBox`	`SelectedItem.Value`
`RadioButtonList`	`SelectedItem.Value`
`TextBox`	`Text`

All the Validation controls derive their basic functionality from the BaseValidator abstract class available in the System.Web.UI. WebControls namespace. Table 2.18 lists some of the important members of the BaseValidator class that are inherited by the validation controls.

TABLE 2.18

IMPORTANT MEMBERS OF BASEVALIDATOR CLASS

Member	*Type*	*Description*
`ControlToValidate`	Property	Specifies the `id` of the input server control that needs to be validated. This property should be passed a valid `id`. However, it can be empty for a custom validator control.
`Display`	Property	Specifies how to display the inline error message contained in the `Text` property. It can be any of the `ValidatorDisplay` values—`Dynamic` (the space is dynamically added), `None` (the message is never displayed), and `Static` (the space is occupied when the validation control is rendered).
`EnableClientScript`	Property	Indicates whether the client-side validation is enabled. The default is `True`.
`Enabled`	Property	Indicates whether the validation control is enabled. If `False`, the validation is never performed.
`ErrorMessage`	Property	Represents the error message to be displayed when the validation fails by the `ValidationSummary` control. If the `Text` property is not set, this message is displayed inline.
`ForeColor`	Property	Specifies the foreground color in which the message is displayed when the validation fails. The default value is `Color.Red`.
`IsValid`	Property	Indicates whether the input control passes the validation.
`Text`	Property	Specifies the text of the error message that is displayed by the validation control inline.
`Validate`	Method	Performs the validation on the associated input control and then updates the `IsValid` property with the result of validation.

Each validation control maintains an IsValid property that indicates the status of the validation test. The Page control that hosts all the Web controls also contains a property called IsValid that indicates the status of the validation for the whole page. When all the validation controls on the Web Form set their IsValid properties to True, the Page.IsValid also becomes True. If any control has its IsValid property set to False, Page.IsValid will also return False.

> NOTE
> **The Display Property** The Display property of the BaseValidator class is only applicable when the client-side validation is performed.

ASP.NET provides the following validation controls that derive their functionality from the BaseValidator class:

- **RequiredFieldValidator**—Ensures that the data is not empty in the input control.
- **RegularExpressionValidator**—Ensures that the data in the input control matches a specific pattern.
- **RangeValidator**—Ensures that the data is within a specific range in the input control.
- **CompareValidator**—Compares the data against a given value.
- **CustomValidator**—Uses custom logic to validate data.

You can associate any number of validation controls with a single input server control. For example, the Date of Hire input field in an Add Employee form cannot be left empty (validated through the RequiredFieldValidator control) and should be less or equal to the current date (validated through the CompareValidator control).

The RequiredFieldValidator Control

The RequiredFieldValidator control can be used to check whether the input control contains an entry. It makes the associated input control a required field in the Web page and ensures some input data is passed to it. The control also trims whitespace in order to check for the required field entry.

The RequiredFieldValidator control contains a special property called InitialValue that can be passed the initial value of the associated input control. During validation, if the input control's validation property contains the same initial value or is empty, it sets IsValid property to False indicating that the validation failed.

EXAM TIP

RequiredFieldValidator The RequiredFieldValidator control is the only validation control that ensures that associated input control is a required field. Otherwise, the validation controls validate the input control only if some data is entered in the control, and assume that any empty control is valid.

For example, a drop-down list may allow users to select a state. When the page loads, the initial value in this control might be *Select a State*. If a RequiredFieldValidator control is associated with the drop-down list control, its InitialValue property can be set to the same initial value as the drop-down list, *Select a State*. When the validation occurs, the validation control will ensure that the item selected in the drop-down list is not the item set in the InitialValue property of the validation control.

The RegularExpressionValidator Control

The RegularExpressionValidator control checks whether the associated input control's validation property matches a specified pattern. This pattern is specified by the ValidationExpression property using a regular expression.

STEP BY STEP

2.11 Using the `RequiredFieldValidator` and `RegularExpressionValidator` Controls

1. Add a new Web Form to the project. Name the form `StepByStep2-11.aspx`.

2. Insert a table by selecting Table, Insert, Table. This opens the Insert Table dialog box. Create a table of three rows and two columns, with border size 0, on the form. Add three `Label` controls, two `TextBox` controls (`txtName`, `txtEmail`), and a `DropDownList` control (`ddlCountry`) to the table, as shown in Figure 2.29. Place two `Label` controls (one with the `id lblMessage`) and a `Button` control (`btnSubmit`) on the Web Form.

3. Select the Items property of the drop-down list in the Properties window and click the ellipsis (...) button to add items to the drop-down list. Add the first item as `<Select a Country>`. Add few more list items with different country names.

4. Place three `RequiredFieldValidator` controls on the form, one next to each of the input controls (refer to Figure 2.29).

Name them rfvName, rfvEmail, and rfvCountry and set their ControlToValidate property to txtName, txtEmail, and ddlCountry, respectively. Set their Display property to Dynamic and ErrorMessage property with an appropriate error message. Set the InitialValue property of the rfvCountry to <Select a Country>.

5. Place a RegularExpressionValidator control revEmail next to rfvEmail control on the form as shown in Figure 2.29. Set the ControlToValidate property of revEmail to txtEmail. Set its ErrorMessage property with an appropriate error message.

FIGURE 2.29◀
The RequiredFieldValidator control allows you to ensure that the input server control contains a value and the RegularExpressionValidator control ensures that the input control's value matches a particular pattern.

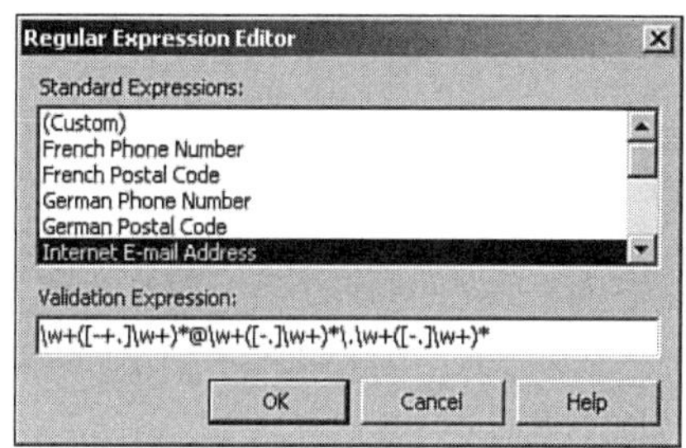

FIGURE 2.30▲
The Regular Expression Editor dialog box allows you to create a regular expression by selecting from an existing standard regular expression or creating a custom regular expression.

6. Select the ValidationExpression property of the revEmail RegularExpressionValidator control in the Properties window and click the ellipsis (...) button. This opens the Regular Expression Editor dialog box as shown in Figure 2.30. Select the Internet E-mail Address expression from the list of Standard Expressions and click OK.

7. Switch to the code view of the form. Add the following line of code at the top of the code-behind file:

```
Imports System.Text
```

8. Double-click the Button control and add the following code to the Click event handler:

```
Private Sub btnSubmit_Click( _
 ByVal sender As System.Object, _
 ByVal e As System.EventArgs) Handles btnSubmit.Click
```

continues

continued

```
        If Page.IsValid Then
            Dim sbText As StringBuilder = _
             New StringBuilder()
            sbText.Append("You entered <br>")
            sbText.Append(txtName.Text & "<br>")
            sbText.Append(txtEmail.Text & "<br>")
            sbText.Append(ddlCountry.SelectedItem.Text & _
             "<br>")
            lblMessage.Text = sbText.ToString()
        End If
    End Sub
```

9. Set `StepByStep2-11.aspx` as the start page in the project.

10. Run the project. Click the Submit button. You will see all three messages from the three `RequiredFieldValidator` controls. Enter the Name and an invalid Email Address and click the Submit button. You should notice error messages from the `RegularExpressionValidator` control in Figure 2.31. Now enter a valid email address and select a country from the drop-down list to post the form successfully.

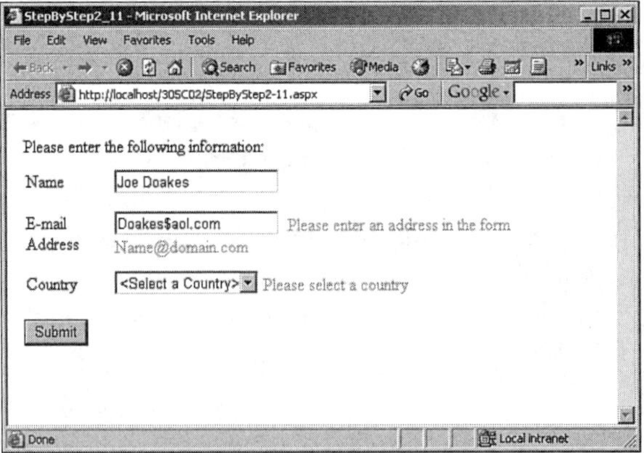

FIGURE 2.31
Setting the Display property to Dynamic of the rfvEmail control to not occupy any space in the Web page unless the validation fails.

In Step by Step 2.11, I selected an existing regular expression from the Regular Expression Editor. You can also assign custom regular expressions to the ValidationExpression property. For more information on the .NET regular expression grammar, refer to the Regular Expression Language Elements topic in the Reference section of the FCL help file.

The RangeValidator Control

The RangeValidator control is used to check whether the input control contains a value in the specified range. You can check the range of values against different data types like String, Date, and Integer.

Table 2.19 shows the important properties of the RangeValidator class.

TABLE 2.19

IMPORTANT PROPERTIES OF THE RANGEVALIDATOR CLASS

Property	*Description*
`MaximumValue`	Specifies the upper value of the validation range.
`MinimumValue`	Specifies the lower value of the validation range.
`Type`	Specifies the data type to be used when comparing the data. Values are specified by the `ValidationDataType` enumeration—`Currency`, `Date`, `Double`, `Integer`, and `String` (default).

The CompareValidator Control

The CompareValidator control is used to compare the input server control's value against another value. The CompareValidator control can compare against a value specified to the validator control or against the value of another input control. The comparison can be made with different comparison operators such as equal, greater than, and so on. A special comparison operation can be made to verify that the associated input control's value is of a specified data type. You can make comparisons against different data types like String, Date, and Integer.

Table 2.20 shows the important properties of the CompareValidator class.

NOTE

ControlToCompare Takes Precedence If both the ControlToCompare and ValueToCompare properties are set for a CompareValidator control, the ControlToCompare property takes precedence.

EXAM TIP

DataTypeCheck Operator Takes Precedence If the Operator property of a CompareValidator is set to DataTypeCheck, the ControlToCompare and ValueToCompare properties are ignored. The validator control tries to convert the input control value to the data type specified by the Type property and sets the IsValid property based on the result.

TABLE 2.20

IMPORTANT PROPERTIES OF THE COMPAREVALIDATOR CLASS

Property	*Description*
`ControlToCompare`	Specifies the input server control against whose value the associated input control is to be validated.
`Operator`	Specifies the comparison operation to be performed. Values are specified by the `ValidationCompareOperator` enumeration— `DataTypeCheck` (indicates whether the input control value can be converted to the data type mentioned by the Type property), `Equal` (==), `GreaterThan` (>), `GreaterThanEqual` (>=), `LessThan` (<), `LessThanEqual` (<=) and `NotEqual` (!=).
`Type`	Specifies the data type to be used when comparing the data. Values are specified by the `ValidationDataType` enumeration— `Currency`, `Date`, `Double`, `Integer`, and `String` (default).
`ValueToCompare`	Specifies the value against which the associated input control is to be validated.

STEP BY STEP

2.12 Using the `RangeValidator` and `CompareValidator` Controls

1. Add a new Web Form to the project. Name the form `StepByStep2-12.aspx`.

2. Insert a table by selecting Table, Insert, Table. This opens the Insert Table dialog box. Create a table of two rows and two columns of border size 0 in the form. Add two `Label` controls and two `TextBox` controls (`txtDate` and `txtTickets`) to the table. Drag three `Label` controls and a Button control (`btnSubmit`) on the Web Form and arrange the controls. Figure 2.32 shows a design for this form.

3. Place one `RangeValidator` control (`rvDate`) on the table next to `txtDate` control. Set its `ControlToValidate` property to `txtDate`, its `Type` property to `Date`, its `MinimumValue` property to `09/01/2003`, its `MaximumValue` property to `09/30/2003`, and its `ErrorMessage` property to an appropriate error message. Note that these values are culture-specific. For example, if you run this code on a system with European date settings, you'll see an error because those cultures expect the day before the month.

4. Place one `CompareValidator` control (`cvTickets`) on the table next to `txtTickets` control. Set its `ControlToValidate` property to `txtTickets`, its `Type` property to `Integer`, its `Operator` property to `GreaterThanEqual`, its `ValueToCompare` property to `2`, and its `ErrorMessage` property to an appropriate error message.

5. Set `StepByStep2-12.aspx` as the start page in the project.

6. Run the project. Enter an invalid date, or an invalid number of tickets, and click the Submit button. You will see the error messages from the `RangeValidator` and `CompareValiator` controls. Enter valid values and click the Submit button. The form posts back successfully.

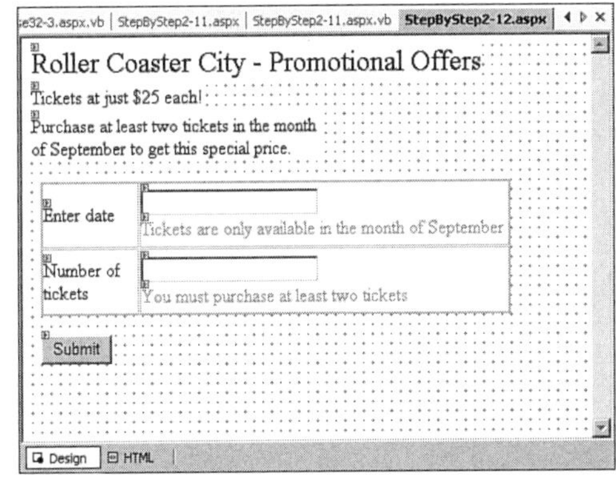

FIGURE 2.32
The RangeValidator control allows you to ensure that the input server control contains a value in the specified range and the CompareValidator control compares the input control's value with a specified value and comparison operator.

The CustomValidator Control

The validation controls discussed allow you to handle many different types of validations. However, you may want to perform a validation that cannot be achieved by any of these validation controls. The CustomValidator control allows you to build a validation control for a custom specification. You can perform any custom validation both at the server-side and client-side with the help of this validation control.

The validation control exposes a property called ClientValidationFunction that specifies the name of the client script function to be executed for validation on the client side.

This custom validation function will be passed two arguments, the first being the custom validator control and the second argument is an object that contains two properties: IsValid and Value. The Value property contains the value that is to be validated and the IsValid property is used to return the result of the validation.

At the server side, during the validation on the server, the validation control fires a ServerValidate event. An event handler containing the custom validation code is added to this event to perform validation on the server. The event sends a ServerValidateEventArgs object containing event related data. This object contains two properties—IsValid and Value. The Value property contains the value of the control that is to be validated and the IsValid property is used to set the result of the validation.

STEP BY STEP

2.13 Using the `CustomValidator` Control

1. Add a new Web Form to the project. Name the form `StepByStep2-13.aspx`.
2. Add one `Label` control, one `TextBox` control (`txtText`), and a Button control (`btnSubmit`) to the Web Form.
3. Place one `CustomValidator` control (`cuvPalindrome`) next to the `txtText` control. Set its `ControlToValidate` property to `txtText`, its `ClientValidationFunction` property to `palindrome`, and its `ErrorMessage` property to an appropriate error message.
4. Switch to the HTML view of the Web Form. Insert a `<SCRIPT>` element under the `<HEAD>` element as shown here:

```
<HEAD>
 ...
    <SCRIPT language="javascript">
        function palindrome(source, args)
        {
            var strReverse="";
            // Get the text entered
            // by the user from the
            // Value property of the ars object
            var strPalindrome = args.Value;
```

```
            // Reverse the string
            for(var intI=strPalindrome.length-1;
               intI >= 0; intI--)
                strReverse = strReverse +
                   strPalindrome.charAt(intI);
            // Check if the  string and the
            // reverse string are equal
            if(strReverse == strPalindrome)
            {
                // Set the IsValid to true as
                // the validation succeeds
                args.IsValid = true;
            }
            else
            {
                // Set the IsValid to false as
                // the validation fails
                args.IsValid = false;
            }
        }
    </SCRIPT>
</HEAD>
```

5. Double-click the `cuvPalindrome` `CustomValidator` control and add the following code to the `ServerValidate` event handler:

```
Private Sub cuvPalindrome_ServerValidate( _
 ByVal source As System.Object, _
 ByVal args As _
 System.Web.UI.WebControls.ServerValidateEventArgs) _
 Handles cuvPalindrome.ServerValidate
    ' Get the text entered by the user from the Value
    ' property of the ServerValidateEventArgs object
    Dim strPalindrome As String = args.Value
    Dim strReverse As String = ""
    ' Reverse the string
    Dim i As Integer
    For i = strPalindrome.Length To 1 Step -1
        strReverse = strReverse & _
         Mid(strPalindrome, i, 1)
    Next
    ' Check if the  string and the
    ' reverse string are equal
    If strReverse = strPalindrome Then
        ' Set the IsValid to true as
        ' the validation succeeds
        args.IsValid = True
    Else
        ' Set the IsValid to false as
        ' the validation fails
        args.IsValid = False
    End If
End Sub
```

continues

continued

6. Set `StepByStep2-13.aspx` as the start page in the project.
7. Run the project. Enter text in the text box and press the Tab key. You should see an error message if a palindrome is not entered in the text box as shown in Figure 2.33.

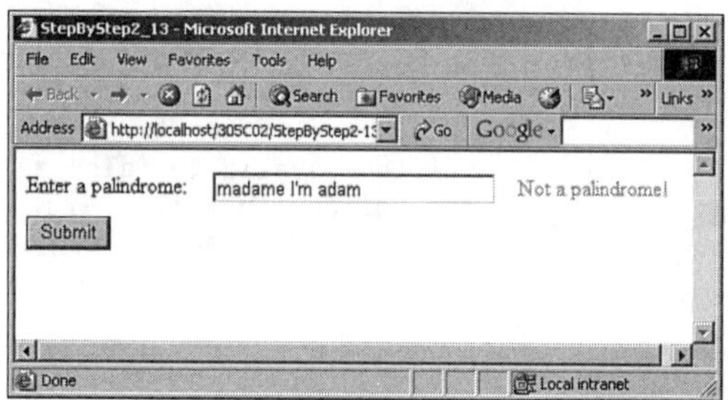

FIGURE 2.33
The CustomValidator control allows you to perform custom validation at both the client side and the server side.

The ValidationSummary Control

As the name implies, the ValidationSummary control is used to display a summary of all the validation errors on a Web page. It displays the ErrorMessage property of the validation controls in the summary. If the ErrorMessage property is not set, then the Text property is displayed as error messages for all the validation controls whose validation fails.

Table 2.21 shows the important properties of the ValidationSummary class.

TABLE 2.21

IMPORTANT PROPERTIES OF THE VALIDATIONSUMMARY CLASS

Property	*Description*
`DisplayMode`	Specifies the way in which the validation summary will be displayed. Values are defined by the `ValidationSummaryDisplayMode` enumeration—`BulletList` (default), `List`, and `SingleParagraph`.

Property	*Description*
`EnableClientScript`	Indicates whether the client-side validation is enabled. The default is `True`.
`ForeColor`	Specifies the fore color in which the message is displayed when the validation fails. The default value is `Color.Red`.
`HeaderText`	Specifies the header text of the validation summary control.
`ShowMessageBox`	Indicates whether the validation summary messages should be displayed in a message box. The default is `False`.
`ShowSummary`	Indicates whether the validation summary messages should be displayed inline in the validation summary control. The default is `True`.

STEP BY STEP

2.14 Using the ValidationSummary Control

1. In the Solution Explorer, right-click `StepByStep2-11.aspx` and select Copy. Right-click your project and select Paste. Rename the pasted Web Form to `StepByStep2-14.aspx`. Open the ASPX (HTML view) and VB (Code view) files of the new Web Form and change all references to `StepByStep2_11` to refer to `StepByStep2_14` instead.
2. Drag a `ValidationSummary` control on the Web Form. Set its `ShowMessageBox` property to `True`.
3. Set the `Text` property of all validation controls on the page to `*`.
4. Set `StepByStep2-14.aspx` as the start page in the project.
5. Run the project. Enter invalid values. You should see an asterisk (`*`) as you leave the invalid Web control. The error messages are displayed in the validation summary control when you click the button. You should also see a message box showing the error messages as shown in Figure 2.34.

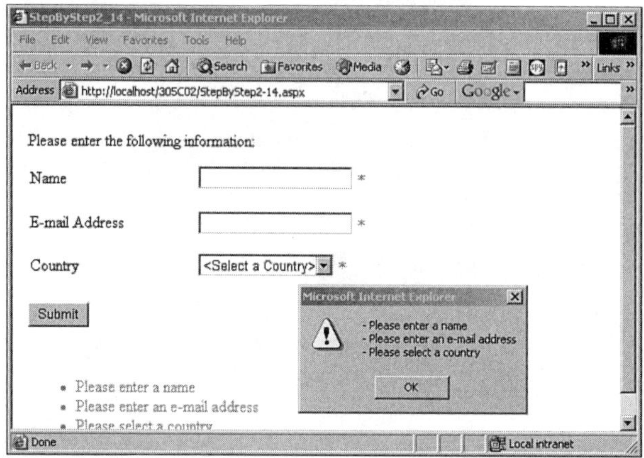

FIGURE 2.34
The ValidationSummary can display a summary of all validation error messages on the Web Form either inline in the control or in a message box.

GUIDED PRACTICE EXERCISE 2.4

You are a Web developer for a state-run agency. You are creating a Web site for senior welfare programs. You are designing a registration Web Form where senior citizens can register themselves for various benefits. The Web Form asks users to enter their names and dates of birth. The Web site should only register users if their age is 65 years or more.

How would you create such a Web Form?

You should try working through this problem on your own first. If you are stuck, or if you'd like to see one possible solution, follow these steps:

1. Open the project 305C02. Add a new Web Form GuidedPracticeExercise2-4 to the project.
2. Insert a table by selecting Table, Insert, Table. Create a table of two rows and two columns of border size 0 on the form. Add two Label controls and two TextBox controls (txtName and txtDOB) to the table. Drag two Label controls, a ValidationSummaryControl and a Button control (btnSubmit) to the Web Form and arrange the controls as shown in Figure 2.35.

3. Place two RequiredFieldValidator controls on the form, one next to each of the input controls. Name them rfvName and rfvDOB. Set their ControlToValidate property to txtName and txtDOB, respectively. Set their Display property to Dynamic, their Text property to * and ErrorMessage property with an appropriate error message.

4. Place one CompareValidator control (cmvDOB) on the table next to rfvDOB control. Set its ControlToValidate property to txtDOB, its Type property to Date, its Text property to * and its ErrorMessage property to an appropriate error message.

5. Double-click the form and add the following code in the Page_Load event handler:

```
Private Sub Page_Load(ByVal sender As System.Object, _
 ByVal e As System.EventArgs) Handles MyBase.Load
    ' Calculate the date which is
    ' 65 years before today
    cmvDOB.ValueToCompare = _
      DateTime.Now.AddYears(-65).ToShortDateString()
    ' Set the Operator to LessThanEqual
    cmvDOB.Operator = _
     ValidationCompareOperator.LessThanEqual
End Sub
```

6. Double-click the Button control and add the following code in the Click event handler:

```
Private Sub btnSubmit_Click( _
 ByVal sender As System.Object, _
 ByVal e As System.EventArgs) Handles btnSubmit.Click
    If Page.IsValid Then
        lblMessage.Text = _
           "Thank you for registering with us!"
    End If
End Sub
```

7. Set StepByStep2-12.aspx as the start page in the project.

8. Run the project. Enter a name and an invalid date and click the Submit button. You will see the error messages from the CompareValidator control as shown in Figure 2.35. Enter valid values and click the Submit button. The form posts back successfully.

If you have difficulty following this exercise, review the section "User Input Validation" earlier in this chapter. After doing this review, try this exercise again.

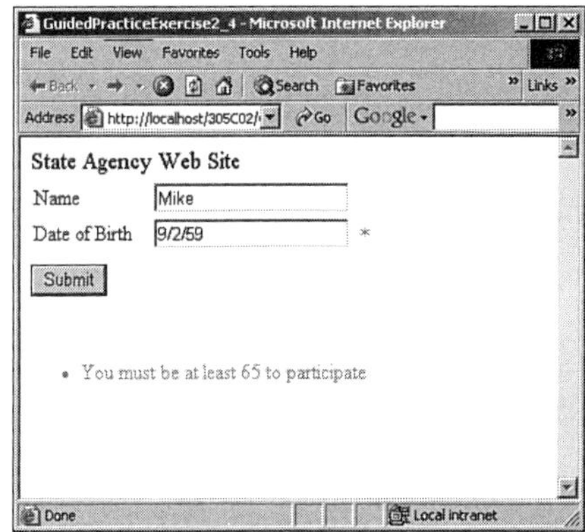

FIGURE 2.35
The validator controls provide a sophisticated way to validate controls in the Web Form.

REVIEW BREAK

- ASP.NET provides a set of Web server controls called validation controls that provide sophisticated validation on both the client side and the server side depending upon the validation settings and the browser's capabilities.
- The BaseValidator class serves as the base class for all the validation controls. This class provides the basic implementation of the validation controls.
- You can associate any number of validation controls to an input server control.
- The RequiredFieldValidator control can be used to check whether the input control contains an entry.
- The RegularExpressionValidator control ensures that the associated input control's value matches a specified regular expression.
- The RangeValidator control is used to check whether the input control contains a value in the specified range.
- The CompareValidator control is used to compare the input server controls value against a data type, a fixed value, or another input control.
- The CustomValidator control allows you to specify custom validation code to be executed during validation.
- The ValidationSummary control is used to display summaries of all the validation errors of a Web page.

CASCADING STYLE SHEETS

A cascading style sheet (CSS) contains style definitions that are applied to elements in an HTML document. The information inside a CSS defines how HTML elements are displayed and where they are positioned on a Web page. CSS offers the following advantages:

- **Uniform Look and Feel** With the help of CSS, it is easy to achieve a consistent appearance of Web Forms throughout a Web application. You can store all the formatting information for a Web application in a single CSS file and then instruct all Web Forms to use the CSS file for formatting settings.
- **Ease of Maintenance** With the help of CSS files you can store all the formatting information at a central place. With this scheme when you make changes in the CSS file, all Web pages linked to it will automatically pick up the changes. The use of CSS not only improves consistency across pages but also eases the maintenance of the Web site.

Both HTML server controls and Web server controls provide first-class support for CSS styles. In addition to this, Visual Studio .NET provides GUI-based style-editing tools, which makes it easy to work with CSS files.

NOTE

Browser Support for CSS CSS is only supported by Web browsers that support HTML 4.0 or higher. Older Web browsers that support only HTML 3.2 or earlier simply ignore CSS styles.

Using Style Sheets With Web Forms

When you create a Web application using Visual Basic .NET, Visual Studio .NET automatically creates a default style sheet named Styles.css for your Web application. You can also add additional style sheets for specific documents. In Step by Step 2.15, you will work with a new CSS file to control the formatting of a Web Form.

STEP BY STEP

2.15 Using Cascading Style Sheets

1. Add a new Web Form to the project. Name the form `StepByStep2-15.aspx`.
2. In the Solution Explorer window, right-click the project name and select Add, Add New Item. In the Add New Item dialog box, select the Style Sheet template and name the file `StepByStep2-15.css`.

continues

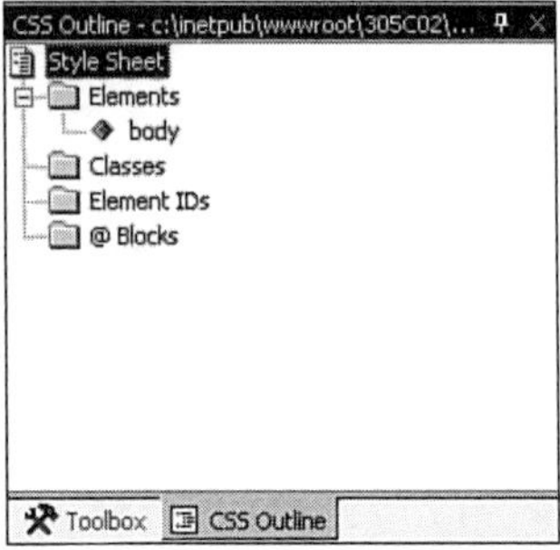

FIGURE 2.36▲
The CSS Outline Window allows you to work with the CSS document.

continued

3. When the CSS file is opened in the designer, you can click the CSS Outline tab beneath the Toolbox to see the CSS Outline window, as shown in Figure 2.36. Right-click the body element in the outline window and select Build Style from the shortcut menu.

4. In the Style Builder dialog box, enter "Verdana, Helvetica, sans-serif" as the name of the font family and specify the font size as 8 pt., as shown in Figure 2.37. Click OK to create the style.

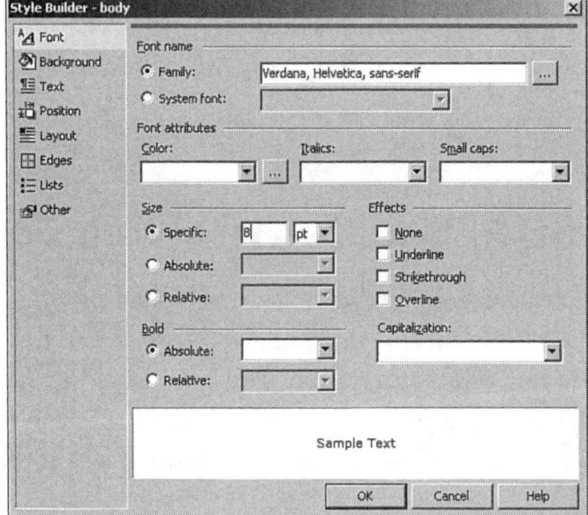

FIGURE 2.37▶
The Style Builder dialog box provides a visual interface to build a style.

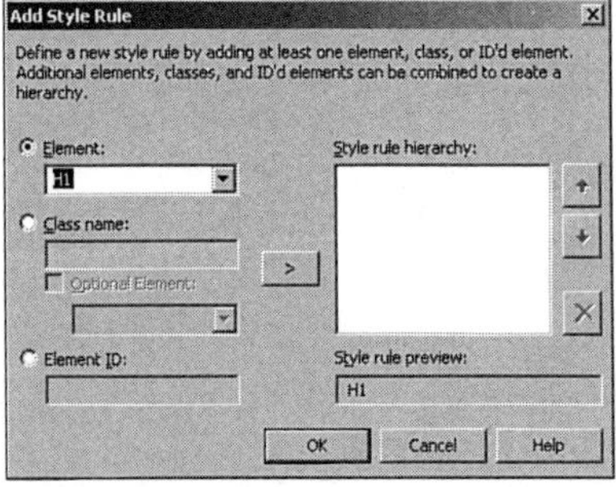

FIGURE 2.38
You can add a new style rule to the CSS file using the Add Style Rule dialog box.

5. In the CSS Outline window, right-click the Element node and select Add Style Rule from the shortcut menu. In the Add Style Rule dialog box, select the H1 element from the Element drop-down list and click OK (see Figure 2.38). This step adds a new H1 style in the CSS document.

6. In the CSS Outline window, right-click the H1 node and select Build Style from its shortcut menu. In the Style Builder dialog box, enter the name of the font family as "Verdana, Arial, Helvetica, sans-serif" and specify the font size as 2 em.

7. Add another style rule. Select the element as UL and click the ">" button. This moves the UL element to the Style Rule Hierarchy area. Select the LI element from the list and click the ">" button as shown in Figure 2.39. This action adds a UL LI item in the CSS file.

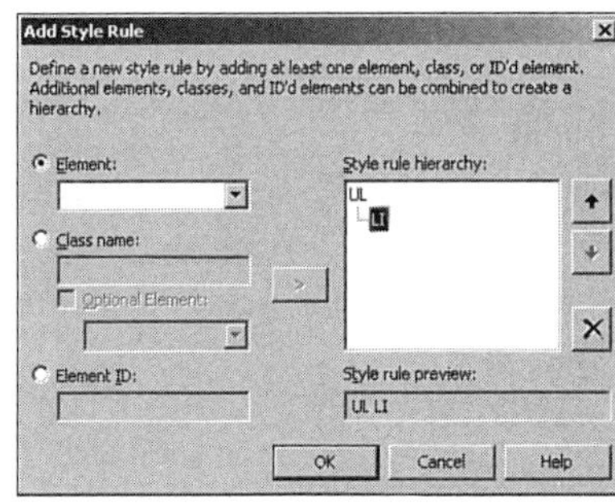

FIGURE 2.39
The Add Style Rule dialog box can be used to create a style rule hierarchy.

8. Invoke the Style Builder dialog box for UL LI element and select the Lists page. Select Bulleted from the first drop-down list and select Square as the bullet style as shown in Figure 2.40.

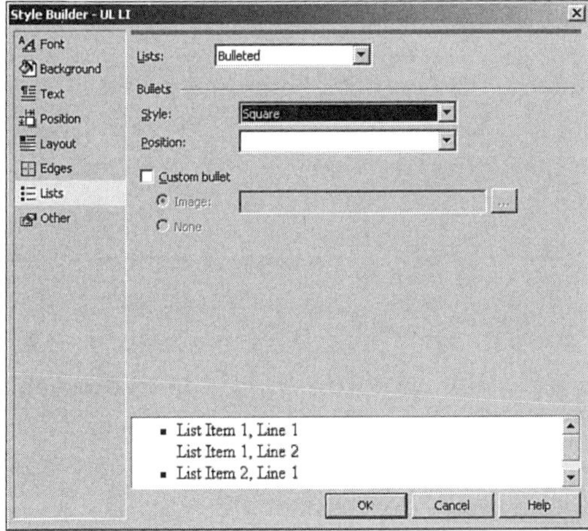

FIGURE 2.40
The Lists page of the Style Builder dialog box makes it possible for you to define CSS style attributes that format lists created using the <OL> and <UL> tags.

9. You can also edit the CSS file directly. Add styles for the following elements by typing into the designer window:

```
H2    {
   font-family: Verdana, Arial, Helvetica, sans-serif;
   font-size:1.75em;
}
UL UL LI {
   list-style-type:    disc;
}

UL UL UL LI    {
   list-style-type:    circle;
}
```

10. Save the `StepByStep2-15.css` file and switch to the `StepByStep2.15.aspx` file. Change the `pageLayout` of the Web Form to `FlowLayout`.

continues

continued

11. Switch to the HTML view of the Web Form and add the following code to the HTML `<HEAD>` element:

```
<LINK href="StepByStep2-15.css"
type="text/css" rel="stylesheet">
```

12. Switch to the design view. Type "Heading 1" on the form. Select the text and using the formatting toolbar, change its style to Heading1. Type "Heading 2" and change its style to Heading2. Type some more text in the Normal Style. Also add a nested bulleted list on the form.

13. Set `StepByStep2-15.aspx` as the start page in the project.

14. Run the project. The output looks similar to Figure 2.41. You can see that the text in the browser appears according to the settings that you specified in the `StepByStep2-15.css` file.

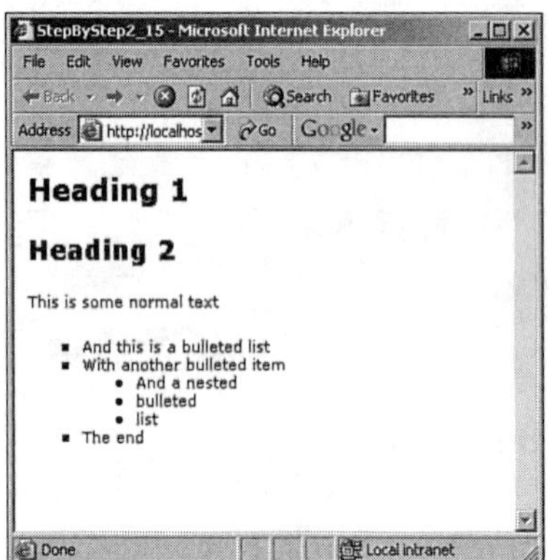

FIGURE 2.41
The style defined in CSS files can be used to format individual HTML elements.

As you can see in the code of StepByStep2-15.css file, each CSS style rule has two parts: a selector (such as H1) and a declaration (such as font-size: 2em). You can use the CSS designer to easily create the CSS files and attach them to your Web application. Web Forms do not automatically read the information in CSS files; you need to link a CSS file with the ASPX file by using the HTML <LINK> element.

Creating Styles to Format Web Controls

In the previous section, you noted that you could define CSS styles that apply to the HTML elements. However, when you are working with Web server controls you are enjoying the abstraction and do not necessary care about the HTML that is rendered by the Web server control.

For these cases, CSS allows you to define a custom style class. A custom style class is applied to a Web server control using the CssClass property or to a HTML server control using the Class property.

Step by Step 2.16 demonstrates the use of custom style classes to control the appearance of Web server controls.

STEP BY STEP

2.16 Using Cascading Style Sheets Classes

1. Add a new Web Form to the project. Name the form `StepByStep2-16.aspx`. Link the ASPX file with the `StepByStep2-15.css` file by adding the following code in the HTML `<HEAD>` element.

```
<LINK href="StepByStep2-15.css" type="text/css"
rel="stylesheet">
```

2. Add a style rule to the `StepByStep2-15.css` file. Name the class for the style rule `TextBoxStyle` as shown in Figure 2.42.

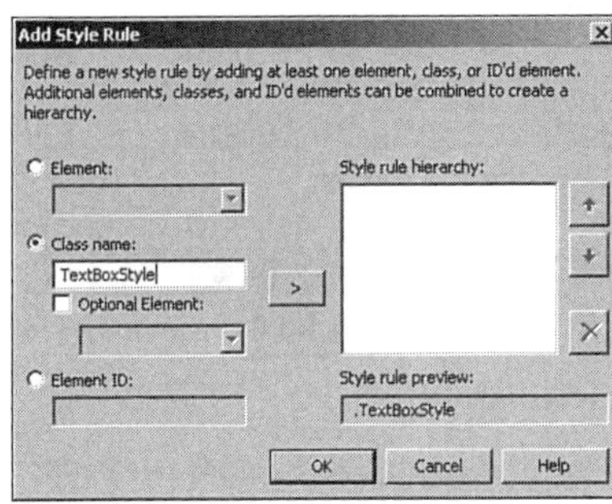

FIGURE 2.42
Add a new class name using the Add Style Rule dialog box.

3. Edit the definition for the `TextBoxStyle` class as follows:

```
.TextBoxStyle
{
    border-right: blue double;
    border-top: blue double;
    font-size: medium;
    border-left: blue double;
    color: white;
    border-bottom: blue double;
    background-color: #6699cc;
}
```

4. Add another CSS class named `ButtonStyle` and use the Style Builder dialog box to create a style that matches the following CSS definition:

```
.ButtonStyle
{
    border-right: white outset;
    border-top: white outset;
    border-left: white outset;
    cursor: hand;
    color: black;
    border-bottom: white outset;
    background-color: #cc9999;
    font-variant: small-caps;
}
```

> **NOTE**
> **Styles Sometimes Don't Show in Designer Right Away** Sometime the Web Form designer may not immediately show the styles `applied` to the controls. In that case, first make sure that you have saved the CSS file and then switch to the HTML view and then back to the Design view of the form.

continues

continued

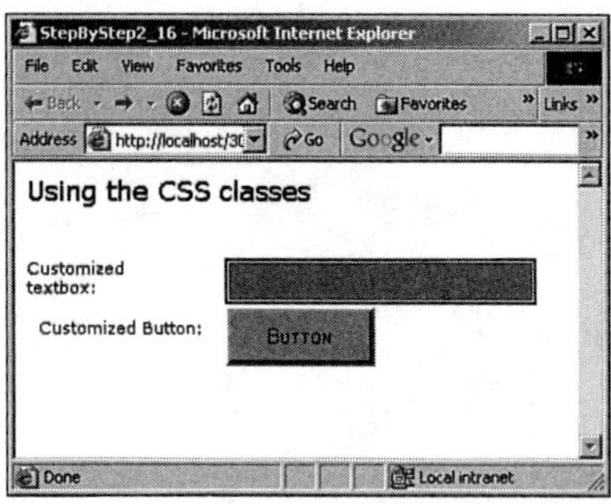

FIGURE 2.43
The style classes defined in CSS files can be used to format Web server controls.

5. Place a `Label` control on the top of the form. Change its `Text` property to "Using the CSS Classes" and set the font size to medium.

6. Place a `TextBox` Web server control on the Web Form, and set its `CssClass` property to `TextBoxStyle`. Place a Button control on the Web Form and change its `CssClass` property to `ButtonStyle`.

7. Place two more `Label` controls in the front of `TextBox` and Button controls. Set their `Text` properties to "A customized TextBox:" and "A customized Button:", respectively.

8. Set `StepByStep2-16.aspx` as the start page in the project.

9. Run the project. The output looks similar to Figure 2.43.

REVIEW BREAK

- ▶ The Style Builder dialog box provides a visual interface in Visual Studio .NET to build CSS styles.
- ▶ A custom style class is applied to the Web server control using the CssClass property and to the HTML server control using the Class property.

CHAPTER SUMMARY

Using Visual Studio .NET, you can add controls to a Web Form in two ways: Either you can use the convenient Web Forms Designer or you can hand-code the controls and load them dynamically in the Web Form.

Event handling is the key to interactive applications. In this chapter, you learned how to develop Web Forms capable of handling events at both the client and the server.

Visual Studio .NET allows you to work with three types of controls: HTML controls, HTML server controls, and Web server controls. Web server controls can be used directly from an ASP.NET program; they bring the model of Web programming close to that of desktop-based applications.

The Web server controls provide a rich set of controls and a consistent model of programming that looks similar to rest of the .NET Framework. You learned about various commonly used controls as well as some advanced controls like the AdRotator and Calendar controls.

I also discussed the validation controls. These controls significantly reduce the amount of code and efforts that you would have spent in user input validation if you would have used traditional development techniques.

This chapter presents the rich library of Web server controls. I discussed most of the common controls used by the applications. In fact, Visual Studio .NET also allows you to create your own controls. In addition, a large number of controls are available from third-party control vendors. Chapter 7, "Creating and Managing Components and .NET Assemblies," explains how to create Web user controls and Web custom controls and add them to the list of available controls.

KEY TERMS

- CSS (Cascading Style Sheets)
- HTML controls
- HTML server controls
- Input validation
- Web server controls

APPLY YOUR KNOWLEDGE

Exercises

2.1 Finding the Click Position in an Image

When you click an `ImageButton` Web server control, it causes a Click event to occur. The event handler for the Click event of an `ImageButton` control receives an argument of type `ImageClickEventArgs` containing data related to this event.

The `ImageClickEventArgs` provides the position of X and Y coordinates where the image was clicked. The origin coordinates (0,0) are assumed to be located at the upper-left corner of the image.

In this exercise, you will write an event handler for the Click event of the `ImageButton` class where you will read the `ImageClickEventArgs` object to determine the coordinates where the user clicked the image.

Estimated time: 10 minutes

1. Create a new Visual Basic ASP.NET Web Application project at the location http://localhost/305C02Exercises.

2. Add a Web Form to the project. Name it Exercise2-1.aspx.

3. Drag an `ImageButton` (`ibLocate`) and a `Label` (`lblMessage`) to the form. Set the `ImageUrl` property of the image button to point to an image and also set an appropriate value for the `AlternateText` property.

4. Double-click the `ImageButton` control and add the following code to the Click event handler:

```
Private Sub ibLocate_Click( _
 ByVal sender As System.Object, _
 ByVal e As System.Web.UI. _
 ImageClickEventArgs) _
 Handles ibLocate.Click
    ' Get the X and Y coordinates
    ' from the ImageClickEventArgs object
    lblMessage.Text = String.Format( _
     "You clicked at X:{0} and Y:{1}", _
     e.X, e.Y)
End Sub
```

5. Set the `Exercise2-1.aspx` page as the start page of the project.

6. Run the project. Click the image button and you should see a message displaying X and Y coordinates of the click position as shown in Figure 2.44.

FIGURE 2.44
The ImageButton control can be used to get the X and Y coordinates of the click position in the image.

2.2 Registering Client-side Script

The Page class provides a `RegisterClientScriptBlock()` method that allows ASP.NET to emit client-side script blocks while rendering a Web page.

APPLY YOUR KNOWLEDGE

This method takes two arguments, both of type string. The first argument uniquely identifies a string block in the program, while the second argument is the complete scripting code that you wish to register with the given unique identifier.

Another method that works in close conjunction with the `RegisterClientSideScriptBlock()` method is the `IsClientScriptBlockRegistered()` method. This method determines whether the client script block associated with a given unique identifier is already registered with the page.

In this exercise, you will learn how to use the `RegisterClientSideScriptBlock()` and `IsClientScriptBlockRegistered()` methods to programmatically inject client-side JavaScript code in an ASP.NET Web page.

Estimated time: 10 minutes

1. Add a Web Form to the project. Name it Exercise2_2.aspx.

2. Drag a `TextBox` control (`txtText`) and a `Label` control to the form.

3. Switch to the code view of the form. Add the following line of code at the top of the code-behind file.

   ```
   Imports System.Text
   ```

4. Add the following code in the `Page_Load` event handler to register the client script code and to add an attribute to the `txtText` control to execute client side code when the contents in the text box change:

   ```
   Private Sub Page_Load( _
    ByVal sender As System.Object, _
    ByVal e As System.EventArgs) _
    Handles MyBase.Load
       ' Create a StringBuilder object and
       ' Add client-side script to it
       Dim sbScript As StringBuilder = _
        New StringBuilder()
       sbScript.Append( _
        "<script language=javascript> ")
       sbScript.Append( _
        "function txtTextUpper()")
       sbScript.Append("{")
       sbScript.Append( _
       "document.forms[0].txtText.value =" & _
        " document.forms[0].txtText" & _
        ".value.toUpperCase();")
       sbScript.Append("} ")
       sbScript.Append("</script>")

       ' Check whether the block is registered
       If Not _
        Page.IsClientScriptBlockRegistered( _
        "Text Upper") Then
           ' Register the client script code
           Page.RegisterClientScriptBlock( _
            "Text Upper", _
            sbScript.ToString())
       End If
       ' Add the attribute to
       ' invoke client side code
       ' when the text changes
       ' in the text box.
       txtText.Attributes.Add( _
        "onchange", "txtTextUpper()")
   End Sub
   ```

5. Set the Exercise2-2.aspx page as the start page of the project.

6. Run the project. Enter some text in the text box and press the Tab key. You should see that all the text is converted to uppercase. The conversion was done by the client-side code that was registered in the `Page_Load` event handler.

APPLY YOUR KNOWLEDGE

2.3 Using the Xml Control

The Xml Web server control reads XML and XSLT information stored in external files and writes the formatted XML into a Web Form. The formatted XML is written at the location of the control. The Xml control provides the easiest way to render XML-based data on a Web page.

In this exercise, you will learn how to use Xml Web server control to display formatted XML content on a Web page.

Estimated time: 10 minutes

1. Add a Web Form to the project. Name it Exercise2-3.aspx.

2. Drag an Xml control and drop it on the Web Form.

3. Add a new XML file to your project. Name it `Books.xml`. Enter this text for the `Books.xml` file:

```
<?xml version="1.0" encoding="utf-8"
  standalone="yes"?>
<MCADBooks>
  <MCADBook>
    <Title>MCAD Training Guide (70-315):
    Developing and Implementing
    Web Applications with
    C# and Visual Studio.NET
    </Title>
    <ISBN>0789728222</ISBN>
    <PublicationDate>December 13, 2002
    </PublicationDate>
    <Author>Amit Kalani</Author>
  </MCADBook>
  <MCADBook>
    <Title>MCAD Training Guide (70-316):
    Developing and Implementing
    Windows-Based Applications
    with C# and Visual Studio.NET
    </Title>
    <ISBN>0789728230</ISBN>
    <PublicationDate>November 26, 2002
    </PublicationDate>
    <Author>Amit Kalani</Author>
  </MCADBook>
  <MCADBook >
    <Title>MCAD Training Guide (70-305):
    Developing and Implementing
    Web Applications with
    Visual Basic.NET and Visual Studio.NET
    </Title>
    <ISBN>0789728184</ISBN>
    <PublicationDate>December 10, 2002
    </PublicationDate>
    <Author>Mike Gunderloy</Author>
  </MCADBook>
  <MCADBook>
    <Title>MCAD Training Guide (70-306):
    Developing and Implementing
    Windows-Based Applications
    with Visual Basic.NET and
    Visual Studio.NET
    </Title>
    <ISBN>0789728192</ISBN>
    <PublicationDate>November 25, 2002
    </PublicationDate>
    <Author>Mike Gunderloy</Author>
  </MCADBook>
</MCADBooks>
```

4. Add a new XSLT file to your project. Name it `Books.xslt`. Enter this text for the `Books.xslt` file:

```
<?xml version="1.0" encoding="UTF-8" ?>
<xsl:stylesheet version="1.0"
xmlns:
xsl="http://www.w3.org/1999/XSL/Transform">
  <xsl:template match="/">
    <html>
    <body>
      <xsl:apply-templates
       select="//MCADBook" />
    </body>
    </html>
  </xsl:template>

  <xsl:template match="MCADBook">
    <xsl:value-of select="Category" />
    <div>Title:
    <xsl:value-of select="Title" /></div>
    <div>Publication Date:
    <xsl:value-of select=
     "PublicationDate" /></div>
    <div>ISBN:
    <xsl:value-of select="ISBN" /></div>
    <div>Author:
    <xsl:value-of select="Author" /></div>
    <hr />
  </xsl:template>
```

APPLY YOUR KNOWLEDGE

```
    <xsl:template match="*">
      <xsl:value-of select="." /><br />
    </xsl:template>

  </xsl:stylesheet>
```

5. Set the `DocumentSource` property of the Xml control to an `Books.xml` and the `TransformSource` property of the Xml control to `Books.xslt`.

6. Set the `Exercise2-3.aspx page` as the start page of the project.

7. Run the project. You should see the XML file being formatted using the style sheet provided to the control as shown in Figure 2.45.

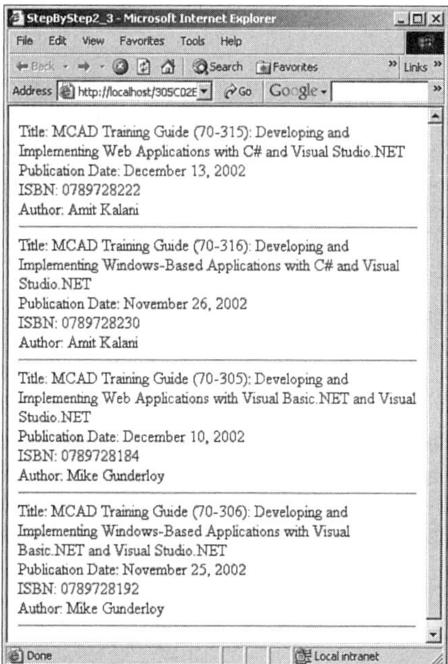

FIGURE 2.45
The Xml control provides an easy way to render XML-based data on a Web page.

2.4 Change Password Screen

The Change Password screen is commonly used by Web sites that allow users to manage their own account information. The Change Password screen typically asks the user to enter the old password as well as the new password. In order to avoid mistakes, it's a good idea to ask the user to retype the newly entered password. For security reasons, some Web sites also require that your new password should be different than the old password.

In this exercise, you will create a Web page that allows users to change passwords. You will ensure that the new password is not the same as old password. You will also ask the user to enter the new password twice. You will also generate a message if both the newly entered passwords don't match. You will use ASP.NET Validation Web server controls to perform this task.

Estimated time: 10 minutes

1. Add a Web Form to the project. Name it Exercise2-4.aspx.

2. Insert a table by selecting Table, Insert, Table. This opens the Insert Table dialog box. Create a table of four rows and two columns of border size 0 on the form. Add four `Label` controls and four `TextBox` controls (`txtUserName`, `txtOldPassword`, `txtNewPassword` and `txtReNewPassword`) to the table. Place a `Label` control, a `ValidationSummary` control and a `Button` control (`btnSubmit`) on the Web Form. Figure 2.46 shows a design for this form.

3. Place four `RequiredFieldValidator` controls on the form, each next to one of the input controls.

APPLY YOUR KNOWLEDGE

Name them rfvUserName, rfvOldPassword, rfvNewPassword and rfvReNewPassword and set their ControlToValidate properties with txtUserName, txtOldPassword, txtNewPassword, and txtReNewPassword, respectively. Set their Display property to Dynamic, Text property to * and ErrorMessage property with an appropriate error message.

4. Place two CompareValidator controls (cmvNewPassword and cmvReNewPassword) next to the rfvNewPassword and rfvReNewPassword controls on the form. Set their Text property to * and ErrorMessage property to an appropriate error message.
5. Select the cmvNewPassword control and set its ControlToCompare property to txtOldPassword, ControlToValidate property to txtNewPassword and Operator property to NotEqual.
6. Select the cmvReNewPassword control and set its ControlToCompare property to txtNewPassword, ControlToValidate property to txtReNewPassword and Operator property to Equal.
7. Set Exercise2-4.aspx as the start page in the project.
8. Run the project. Fill out the form and click the Submit button. You should see error messages from compare validation controls displayed if the old password and the new password entered are the same or if the new password is not entered the same in the re-enter new password field as shown in Figure 2.46.

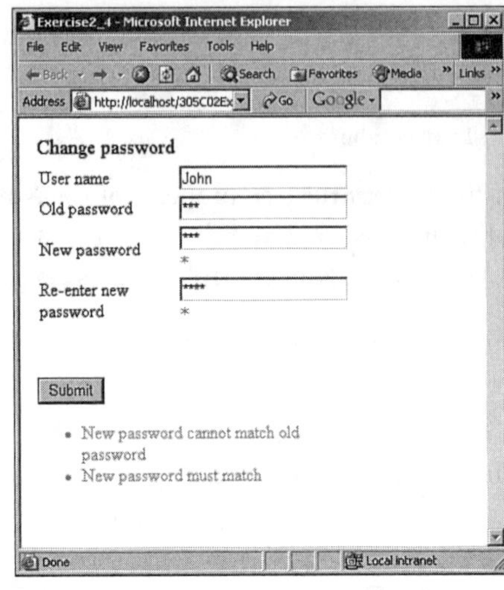

FIGURE 2.46
Use the ControlToCompare property of the CompareValidator to compare associated input control's value with another input control.

2.5 Using the Hyperlink Control

The HyperLink Web server control is used to create a link that moves you to another page or a location on the page.

In this exercise, you will learn how to use the HyperLink Web server control to navigate to other Web pages.

Estimated time: 15 minutes

1. Add a Web Form to the project. Name it Exercise2-5.aspx.
2. Drag two Hyperlink controls (hlExercise2_3 and hlExercise2_4) on the Web Form.

APPLY YOUR KNOWLEDGE

3. Set the `NavigateUrl` property of the `hlExercise2_3` to point to `Exercise2_3.aspx`. Set the `NavigateUrl` property of the `hlExercise2_4` to point to `Exercise2_4.aspx` and the Target property to `_blank` to open the linked Web page in a new window.

4. Set the `Exercise2_5.aspx` page as the start page of the project.

5. Run the project. You should see two hyperlinks on the Web page. Clicking the `hlExercise2_3` hyperlink navigates the browser to the linked Web page and clicking the `hlExercise2_4` hyperlink opens the linked Web page in a new window.

The target page can be specified using the `NavigateUrl` property. The link can be displayed either as text or as an image. You can use the Text property to set the text for the control or set the `ImageUrl` property to display an image. If you specify both then, the image takes precedence over the Text property.

Review Questions

1. What is the main difference between HTML controls and HTML server controls?

2. Why can't you write client side event handling code for a Web server control using the HTML syntax?

3. What is the difference between HTML server controls and Web server controls?

4. User interaction raises events at the client side. How does ASP.NET raise the equivalent events at the server side?

5. What is the difference between the Click and the Command events of a Button Web server control?

6. What is the use of AutoPostBack property of Web server controls?

7. How can you place controls dynamically on a Web page?

8. How can you disable client side scripting for a particular validation control?

9. What are the different data types on which the RangeValidator and CompareValidator controls can work?

10. What is the importance of the IsValid property of the validation and Page controls?

Exam Questions

1. Your company has recently decided to upgrade the supplier evaluation system from ASP to ASP.NET. You want to convert old ASP pages to Web Forms as quickly as possible. You have decided that you can keep the existing user interface but would like to move the business logic to code-behind files. Which of the following approaches provides you the smoothest migration path?

   A. Continue to use HTML controls on ASP.NET Web Forms. In the code behind files, rewrite all business logic using Visual Basic .NET.

   B. Apply the runat="server" attribute to all HTML controls. In the code-behind files, rewrite all business logic using Visual Basic .NET.

APPLY YOUR KNOWLEDGE

C. Use ASP.NET Web server controls instead of HTML controls. In the code-behind files, rewrite all business logic using Visual Basic .NET.

D. Continue to use HTML controls for labels and textboxes but convert all button controls to Web server controls. In the code-behind files, rewrite all business logic using Visual Basic .NET.

2. You are developing an online gaming application. In one of the games, users will click different areas of a screen. In the Web Form, you need to determine the exact location of a click. Which of the following controls would you use on the Web Form to display the image? (Select all that apply.)

   A. ImageButton

   B. Image

   C. <img runat="server">

   D. <input type="image" runat="server">

3. SurveyComm Inc. is a marketing company that organizes surveys on behalf of large consumer-goods companies. The surveys involve a large number of participants. SurveyComm recently decided to put its surveys online. You work as a Web developer for SurveyComm and your responsibility is to design one of the online survey forms using ASP.NET. One of the questions in the survey form has a large number of options and users can select multiple options as an answer to this question. You have used a CheckBoxList Web server control to display the options. In the code, you want to get all the options selected by the user so that you can store them in a database. Which of the following techniques should you use?

   A. Use the SelectedItem property of the CheckBoxList control.

   B. Use the SelectedIndex property of the CheckBoxList control.

   C. Use the DataValueField property of the CheckBoxList control.

   D. Use the Items property of the CheckBoxList control.

4. You are creating a free Web log service using ASP.NET. This service allows users to maintain their own online diaries on the Internet. You plan to earn revenue by selling advertisements when displaying a Web log. You understand that the advertising scheme is going to be effective only if targeted advertisements are shown. You use the AdRotator control with the Web page. You set the KeywordFilter property of the AdRotator control to "Books" if a Web log is about books and set the Keyword property to "Software" if the Web log is about software. You suspect that some of the keywords that you specify with the KeywordFilter property may not exist in the advertisement file. How will the AdRotator control behave in that case?

   A. The AdRotator control will display a blank image.

   B. The AdRotator control will display the first advertisement from the advertisement file.

   C. The AdRotator control will display any random advertisement from the advertisement file.

   D. Users will get an ASP.NET error message from the AdRotator control.

APPLY YOUR KNOWLEDGE

5. You want to create a client-side event handler for the click event of a Button Web server control. The client side event handler is written in JavaScript and is executed by the Web browser. The name of the Button control is btnSubmit and the name of the JavaScript event handler is GlowButton(). How should you accomplish this in your Web Form?

   A.

```
<INPUT id="btnSubmit"
 Type="Submit" Runat="Server"
 Value="Submit" onclick="GlowButton()">
```

   B.

```
<INPUT id="btnSubmit" Runat="Server"
Value="Submit" onclick="GlowButton();">
```

   C.

```
<asp:Button id="btnSubmit" Runat="Server"
Value="Submit" onclick="GlowButton();">
```

   D.

```
btnSubmit.Attributes.Add("onclick",
"GlowButton();")
```

6. You are using a DropDownList Web server control on a Web page that allows users to select a country name. Based on the user's selection of country, you want to display the drop-down list showing states in the selected country and several other country specific fields. You don't want users to click a button in order to submit country information to the Web server. All your users have JavaScript-enabled browsers. Which of the following techniques would you use?

   A. Use HTML server control instead of Web server controls.

   B. Write client side code in JavaScript to cause a postback when user selects country.

   C. Set the AutoPostBack property to true.

   D. Set the AutoEventWireup attribute to true.

7. You are creating a Web page that collects information about the various sports activities that interest the user. You want to display a sorted list of activities using a CheckBoxList as shown in Figure 2.47. Which of the following ways should you use to declare the CheckBoxList Web server control in your Web page?

☐ Biking	☐ Hiking
☐ Bird Watching	☐ Skiing
☐ Fishing	☐ Snowmobiling

FIGURE 2.47
How should you declare the CheckBoxList to display its items as shown in the figure?

   A.

```
<asp:CheckBoxList id="cblActivities"
runat="server"
RepeatColumns="2"
RepeatDirection="Vertical"
RepeatLayout="Table">
...
</asp:CheckBoxList>
```

   B.

```
<asp:CheckBoxList id="cblActivities"
runat="server"
RepeatColumns="2"
RepeatDirection="Horizontal"
RepeatLayout="Table">
...
</asp:CheckBoxList>
```

   C.

```
<asp:CheckBoxList id="cblActivities"
runat="server"
RepeatColumns="2"
RepeatDirection="Vertical"
RepeatLayout="Flow">
...
</asp:CheckBoxList>
```

APPLY YOUR KNOWLEDGE

D.

```
<asp:CheckBoxList id="cblActivities"
runat="server"
RepeatColumns="2"
RepeatDirection="Horizontal"
RepeatLayout="Flow">
...
</asp:CheckBoxList>
```

8. In a Web page, you are dynamically generating numerous Button controls. Each of the Button controls is titled as either Add or Update. You want to write a single event handler to handle events for all the Button controls. Which of the following options would you choose to ensure that you could take different actions when Add or Update buttons are clicked?

   A. Write an event handler for the Click event. Use the event arguments passed to the event handler to determine whether an Add button or an Update button was clicked, and take appropriate actions in the event handler.

   B. Write an event handler for the Command event. Use the event arguments passed to the event handler to determine whether an Add button or an Update button was clicked, and take appropriate actions in the event handler.

   C. Set the Command property for each button to either Add or Update. Write an event handler for the Click event. Use the event arguments passed to the event handler to determine whether an Add button or an Update button was clicked, and take appropriate actions in the event handler.

   D. Handle all the events in a Page level event handler such as Load event.

9. You have developed a Web page that uses Image controls to display images from various sources on the Internet. Sometimes an image may not be available because a Web site may be temporarily down for maintenance. For these situations, you are required to display a description for the image. Which of the following properties of the Image control would you use?

   A. ToolTip

   B. Attributes

   C. AlternateText

   D. ImageUrl

10. You want to keep consistent formatting for all the Web Forms in your application. To achieve this, you have created a cascading style sheet named style.css and have linked it to all the Web pages. You have defined a style class named TextBoxStyle in style.css to format textboxes on the Web Forms. Which of the following property settings would you use with the TextBox Web server control to use the TextBoxStyle style class?

    A. Class="TextBoxStyle"

    B. CssClass="TextBoxStyle"

    C. Class=".TextBoxStyle"

    D. CssClass=".TextBoxStyle"

11. You are a Web developer working for a state-run agency. You are creating a Web site for senior welfare programs. To register with the program, seniors must enter both their name as well as date of birth. The Web site should only register users if their age is 65 years or more. You want to write minimum validation code. How would you set up validation in the Web Form to achieve this objective? (Select all that apply.)

APPLY YOUR KNOWLEDGE

A. Use a RequiredFieldValidator control with name.

B. Use a RequiredFieldValidator control with date of birth.

C. Use a CompareValidator control with date of birth.

D. Use a RangeValidator control with date of birth.

E. Use a CustomValidator control with date of birth.

12. You are developing a scheduling application for your company's intranet. You are using a calendar control to enable easy and correct selection of dates. You want to mark holidays on the calendar so that users are aware of them while creating a schedule. For example, January 1 should be marked as "New Year's Day." You want to display the description of holiday in the same cell that displays the date. Which of the following calendar events would you use to achieve this?

    A. DayRender

    B. SelectionChanged

    C. VisibleMonthChanged

    D. Load

13. You are designing a Web site that allows users to file their taxes online. Users log in to the Web site using their tax identification number and a personal identification number. You want to ensure that users do not include spaces with the tax identification number. You want to achieve this by writing minimum amount of code. Which of the following validation controls would you choose?

    A. RequiredFieldValidator

    B. RangeValidator

    C. RegularExpressionValidator

    D. CustomValidator

14. You are designing a Web site that is used by your suppliers to quote their pricing for a product that your company will buy over the next quarter. The Web site will use data to calculate best possible purchase options. Your application displays three text boxes to the suppliers. The first text box (txtPrevQtrMax) allows suppliers to enter the maximum value charged by them for this product in the previous quarter. The second text box (txtPrevQtrMin) allows suppliers to enter the minimum value charged by them in the previous quarter. The third textbox (txtQuote) is for entering the proposed pricing of the product for the next quarter. You want suppliers to restrict the value of txtQuote field between txtPrevQtrMin and txtPrevQtrMax. The validation technique you use should use the minimum amount of code. Which validation control would you use to perform the validation?

    A. CompareValidator

    B. RangeValidator

    C. CustomValidator

    D. RegularExpressionValidator

15. Your Web application should allow users to upload files from their local computers to the Web server. You are using the following control to achieve this:

```
<input id="File1" type="file" runat="server">
```

APPLY YOUR KNOWLEDGE

What additional steps do you need to take in order for the file upload to work? (Select all that apply.)

A. Use the runat="server" attribute with the <FORM> element.

B. Use the EncType="multipart/form-data" attribute with the <FORM> element.

C. Use the EncType="multipart/form-data" attribute with the <input> element.

D. Use the Method="Get" attribute with the <FORM> element.

Answers to Review Questions

1. HTML server controls map one-to-one with HTML controls but are programmatically accessible on the Web server. Any HTML control can be converted into an HTML server control by applying a runat="server" attribute with the control. HTML server controls, because of their compatibility with HTML, provide an easy migration path for existing Web Forms.

2. Unlike HTML server controls, for Web server controls you cannot simply use the HTML syntax to add client-side event handling. The reason is that for some controls ASP.NET already uses the client-side event handling to perform automatic postback operation. The preferred way to add client-side event handling code for Web server controls is via the use of the Attributes property of the Web server controls. For example, the following code fragment attaches the someClientCode() client-side method to the onMouseOver event of the btnSubmit button.

```
btnSubmit.Attributes.Add( _
 "onMouseOver", "someClientCode();")
```

3. The main difference between HTML server controls and Web server controls is the model of programming. The HTML server controls are designed to provide an easier migration path for existing applications to ASP.NET; therefore HTML server controls use the programming model based on HTML. As opposed to this, Web server controls provide a much richer set of controls and consistent programming model that integrates well with the rest of .NET Framework.

4. When the events occur at the client side, their information is cached in the page itself. Finally, when the page is submitted to the server, ASP.NET analyzes the HTTP request and determines which server-side events need to be raised. ASP.NET then raises the server-side events and the registered server-side event handlers are executed in response.

5. The Click event does not pass any event related information to its event handler. As opposed to this, the Command event passed a CommandEventArgs object that contains two properties—CommandName and CommandArgument, which provides information about the event.

6. Some Web server controls such as DropDownList and CheckBox have a property named AutoPostBack. When this property is set to true, it causes an immediate postback of the page when the value of control is changed. This allows a Web server to immediately respond to change events without waiting for a click event to cause a page postback.

7. To place controls dynamically on the Web page, first you need to programmatically create them.

APPLY YOUR KNOWLEDGE

This can be done by creating an instance of the control's class. After setting the values of a control's object, you can add the control to one of the container controls such as a Panel or a Placeholder. The dynamically added controls are rendered as part of the container control's rendering logic.

8. The EnableClientScript property of a validation control indicates whether the client-side scripting should be performed. Setting this property to false will disable client-side scripting for a validation control.

9. The RangeValidator and CompareValidator controls can work on Currency, String, Date, Integer, and Double data types. These data types are defined in the ValidationDataType enumeration.

10. The IsValid property of the validation controls stores the result of the validation. The validation controls during validation set this property to true or false depending on whether the validation succeeded or failed. If at the end of the validation, all the validation controls have this property set to true, the Page.IsValid is also set to true; otherwise it's set to false. All other events execute in the same way in the server irrespective of the value of this property. Activities that require validation should always be enclosed in an IsValid check.

Answers to Exam Questions

1. **B**. Use of HTML server controls provides the easiest migration path for an existing HTML-based User interface. It does not take much effort to convert an HTML control to an HTML server control because all you need is to add a runat="server" attribute to it.

2. **A and D**. The ImageButton Web server control and the HtmlInputImage HTML server control pass the event related information to the Web server using an ImageClickEventArgs object.

3. **D**. You should use the Items property of the CheckBoxList control to iterate through the list items and then use the Selected property of ListItem object to find whether the item has been selected. The SelectedIndex and SelectedItem properties return only the index of the first selected item and the first selected item, respectively. DataValueField is the data source that provides item value. It is used for populating the contents of the CheckBoxList.

4. **A**. If no match exists in the advertisement file for a keyword, the AdRotator will display a blank image and a trace warning will be generated, but no error message will be generated.

5. **D**. The preferred way to add client-side event handling code for Web server controls is via the use of the Attributes property of the Web server controls.

6. **C**. You can specify a change event to cause a form post back by setting the AutoPostBack property of the DropDownList Web server control to True. This technique automatically generates the required client side code that causes the page postback when the user changes the selection.

7. **A**. The given list is sorted and you want to vertically organize the elements in a table of two columns. For achieving this, you should set the RepeatColumns property to "2," RepeatDirection property to "Vertical" and the RepeatLayout property to "Table."

Apply Your Knowledge

8. **B**. The Command event is raised when the Button control is clicked. You can use the CommandEventArgs object to find the CommandName and CommandArguments associated with the button that initiated the event.
9. **C**. You should use the AlternateText property to specify the text to display if the specified image is not available. In Internet Explorer, this text also displays as a ToolTip.
10. **B**. When you want a Web server control to use a style class defined in a CSS file, you use the CssClass property of the Web server control. Although the style itself may be defined as ".TextBoxStyle" in the CSS file, you only need to specify the name that is "TextBoxStyle" with the CssClass property. The Class property is only used with HTML server controls and not with the Web server controls.
11. **A**, **B**, **C**. It is required that both name and date of birth must be entered, so you must use RequiredFieldValidator for both the fields.

    In addition to this, you need to compare the date of birth entered by the user and compare it with the current date to check if they are 65 years or more apart. This can be easily done using the CompareValidator control by programmatically setting its ValueToCompare property.
12. **A**. The DayRender event is raised while the Calendar control is being rendered. The DayRender event is therefore the preferred place to write additional messages along with a day.
13. **C**. The question requires that the contents of a textbox match a given pattern, which in this case is that the value should not contain any space. The RegularExpressionValidator control is the best choice to perform this kind of validation. You can of course use CustomValidator control also but that will require you to write more code.
14. **A**. You would use two CompareValidator controls, one control compares that the value in control txtQuote is greater than or equal to PrevQtrMin whereas the other control compares that txtQuote is less than or equal to PrevQtrMax. You can also use CustomValidator but at the cost of writing more code.
15. **A and B**. You must use both runat="server" attribute and the EncType="multipart/form-data" with the <FORM> element.

APPLY YOUR KNOWLEDGE

Suggested Readings and Resources

1. *The Visual Studio .NET Combined Help Collection*, including the following:
   - *HTML Server Controls*
   - *ASP.NET Server Control Event Model*
   - *ASP.NET Server Controls*
   - *Web Forms Validation*
   - *ASP.NET Server Controls and CSS Styles*
2. Jesse Liberty, Dan Hurwitz. *Programming ASP.NET.* O'Reilly, 2002.
3. Amit Kalani et al. *ASP.NET 1.0 with C# Namespace Reference.* Wrox, 2002.
4. The Official Microsoft ASP.NET Site, `www.asp.NET`.
5. The .NET Framework Community Web site, `www.gotdotnet.com`.

OBJECTIVES

This chapter covers the following Microsoft-specified objectives for the "Creating User Services" section of Exam 70-305, "Developing and Implementing Web Applications with Microsoft Visual Basic .NET and Microsoft Visual Studio .NET":

Implement navigation for the user interface.

- **Manage the ViewState.**
- **Manage data during postback events.**
- **Use session state to manage data across pages.**

▶ The underlying protocol for communication between the Web browser and Web server is HTTP. Because of the stateless nature of the HTTP protocol, Web applications are also stateless. Traditionally, this has been one of the major challenges for developing rich and interactive Web applications.

▶ ASP.NET provides several features that help you in easily maintaining the state of a page across a page postback or during navigation. This exam objective requires you to know the various ways in which you can manage state using ASP.NET. In addition to this, you should also know the various ways in which you can navigate from one page to another in a Web application.

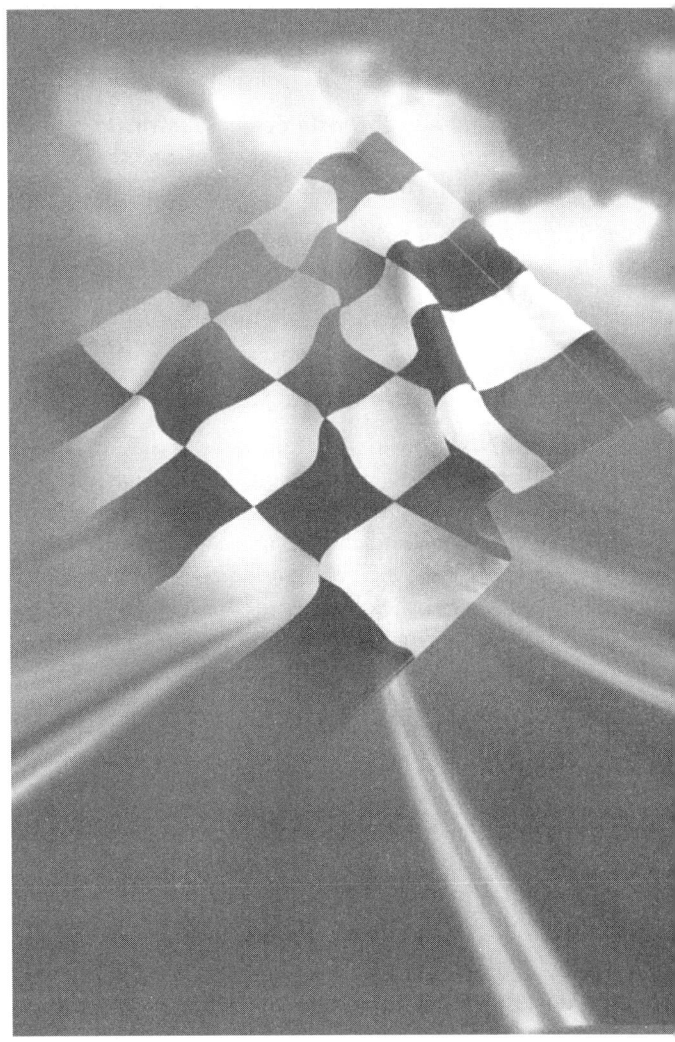

CHAPTER 3

Implementing Navigation for the User Interface

Objectives

Use and edit intrinsic objects. Intrinsic objects include response, request, session, server, and application.

- **Retrieve values from the properties of intrinsic objects.**
- **Set values on the properties of intrinsic objects.**
- **Use intrinsic objects to perform operations.**

▶ ASP.NET provides several classes, including HttpResponse, HttpRequest, HttpSessionState, HttpServerUtility, and HttpApplicationState that give you method and properties to access the underlying Web application's framework. You can easily access the object of these classes for the current HTTP request using the properties of the Page class such as Response, Request, Session, Server, and Application. This exam objective requires you to know about the various important properties and methods of these objects.

Outline

Outline

Study Strategies

- ▶ Experiment with different techniques for state management. You should understand their differences, advantages, and disadvantages so that you know which technique to use in a given scenario.
- ▶ Use the new features of ASP.NET such as ViewState and SmartNavigation to enhance the user experience for a Web page.
- ▶ Use Response.Redirect(), Server.Transfer(), and Server.Execute() in your programs and understand their differences. Be prepared to choose an appropriate navigation method for a given scenario.
- ▶ Know how to access and use various intrinsic objects from your Web Form. Use various properties and methods of these objects to understand how they can help you in Web development tasks.

INTRODUCTION

Developing Web application is a different activity from developing Windows applications. One of the major challenges that a Web developer faces while developing a Web application is the disconnected nature of Web applications. Traditionally, programmers had to write additional code to maintain state between page postback and navigation. ASP.NET provides a better model of programming by incorporating the tasks related to state management as part of the programming framework itself. This allows developers to spend less time in plumbing work and more on developing the actual business logic.

In this chapter, I'll present various state management features provided by ASP.NET. I'll discuss both client-side techniques and server-side techniques for state management.

I'll also discuss the ASP.NET intrinsic objects that are available to you via the Page class. You'll see how these objects can help you in various common Web development scenarios.

Finally, I'll use the intrinsic objects to demonstrate various ways that you can use to navigate from one page to another. I'll also compare various navigation techniques so that you can choose the appropriate technique for a given scenario.

ROUND TRIP AND POSTBACK

Web applications have a distributed execution model. When a user interacts with a Web Form, the browser may respond to some of the user actions by executing client-side scripts while some other actions that require server resources must be sent for processing to the Web server. When server-side processing is involved, a typical interactive user session with a Web Form consists of the following steps:

1. The user requests a Web Form from the Web server.
2. The Web server responds back with the requested Web Form.
3. The user enters the data and submits the form to the Web server.
4. The Web server processes the form, and sends the result back to the user.

Step 3 is also referred to as a page postback, whereas steps 3 and 4 are collectively referred to as a round trip. A round trip involves making a complete trip over the network to the Web server and getting back the response .

The Web applications use the HTTP protocol to establish communication between the Web browser and the Web server. The HTTP protocol is disconnected in nature, which means that the life cycle of a Web page is just a single round trip. Every time a Web server responds to a page request, it freshly creates the resources required to create the page, sends the page to the requesting client and destroys the page resources from the server. Between two page requests, Web servers and clients are disconnected from each other. The values of page variables and controls are not preserved between page requests.

This model of execution allows a Web server to support a large number of clients because each client request occupies the server resources only for a short duration. However, the disconnected nature of the HTTP protocol provides major challenges to the Web developer. It is difficult to implement the following functionality in Web applications:

- Maintain values of controls and variables across page postbacks.
- Distinguish the initial request of a page from the page postback.
- Provide smart navigation features similar to those of desktop applications

ASP.NET provides solutions to these problems built right into its framework. As an ASP.NET developer, you only need to write a small amount of code to implement these features in your applications. From my discussion about server controls in Chapter 2, "Controls," you already know that ASP.NET provides a set of server controls that automatically retain their value across page postbacks. You'll learn how ASP.NET actually retains the state for server controls, later in this chapter in a section titled "State Management." For now, I'll talk about two properties of the Page class, IsPostBack and SmartNavigation, that provide the other two functionalities from the preceding list.

The IsPostBack Property

The IsPostBack property of the Page class returns True when a page is being loaded in response to a client postback. If the page is being requested for the first time (that is, if you've requested the page by navigating to its URL, or by following a link), the value of the IsPostBack property is False.

You can use this when you do not want the server to execute some costly initialization operations for each page postback. Instead, you would like the initializations to be performed only with the first request to the page.

Step by Step 3.1 helps you in understanding round trip and postback operations and demonstrates the use of the `IsPostBack` property.

STEP BY STEP

3.1 Using the IsPostBack Property

1. Create a new Visual Basic ASP.NET Web application project. Name the project `305C03`.
2. Add a new Web Form to the project. Name the Web Form `StepByStep3-1.aspx`. Change the `pageLayout` property of `DOCUMENT` element to `FlowLayout`.
3. Add a `DropDownList` Web server control (`ddlCategories`) to the form. Set its `AutoPostBack` to `True` and `TabIndex` to `1`. Add a `Label` control next to the `DropDownList` control.
4. Add a `Label` control (`lblQuestion`) to the Web Form.
5. Add a `TextBox` control (`txtTitle`) and set its `AutoPostBack` to `True` and `TabIndex` to `2`. Add another `TextBox` (`txtMessage`) and set its `TabIndex` to `3` and `TextMode` to `MultiLine`. Add `Label` controls for both `TextBox` controls.
6. Add a `Button` control (`btnPost`) and set its `Text` to `Post A Message`. Place a `Label` control (`lblWeblog`) at the end of the form. Figure 3.1 shows a design for the completed form.

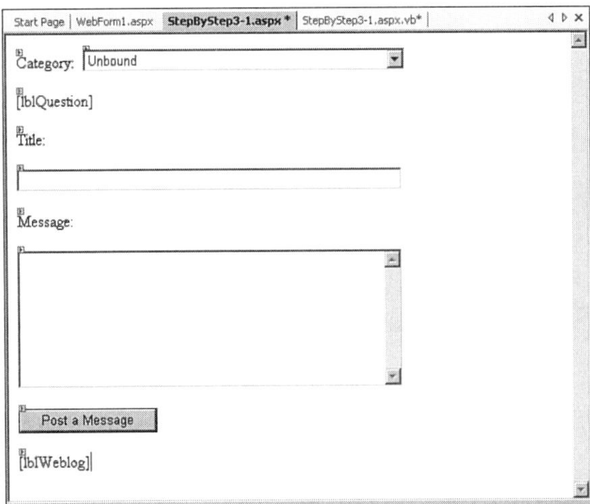

FIGURE 3.1
A design of a form that allows you to post messages to a Web log.

7. Switch to the code view of the Web Form and add the following code to the `Page_Load()` method:

```
Private Sub Page_Load( _
 ByVal sender As System.Object, _
 ByVal e As System.EventArgs) Handles MyBase.Load
    If Not Page.IsPostBack Then
        ' If page is requested for the first time
        ddlCategories.Items.Add("Web development")
        ddlCategories.Items.Add( _
         "Programming Languages")
        ddlCategories.Items.Add("Certifications")
    Else
        ' On postback, change the case of textbox
        txtTitle.Text = txtTitle.Text.ToUpper()
    End If
    ' Set the text of the label
    ' control on each page load
    lblQuestion.Text = _
     "What do you want to write about " & _
    ddlCategories.SelectedItem.Text + " today?"
End Sub
```

8. Attach the following event handler to the `Click` event of the Post button:

```
Private Sub btnPost_Click( _
 ByVal sender As System.Object, _
 ByVal e As System.EventArgs) Handles btnPost.Click
```

continues

continued

```
        ' Format the data entered by the user and
        ' append it to the existing contents of lblWeblog
        lblWeblog.Text = "<b>" & _
         ddlCategories.SelectedItem.Text & _
         " :: " + txtTitle.Text & "</b> (" & _
         DateTime.Now.ToString() & ")<HR>" & _
         txtMessage.Text & "<p>" & _
         lblWeblog.Text
    End Sub
```

9. Set `StepByStep3-1.aspx` as the start page for the project.

10. Run the project. Use the Tab key to navigate between various fields and publish a few entries to the Web log as shown in Figure 3.2.

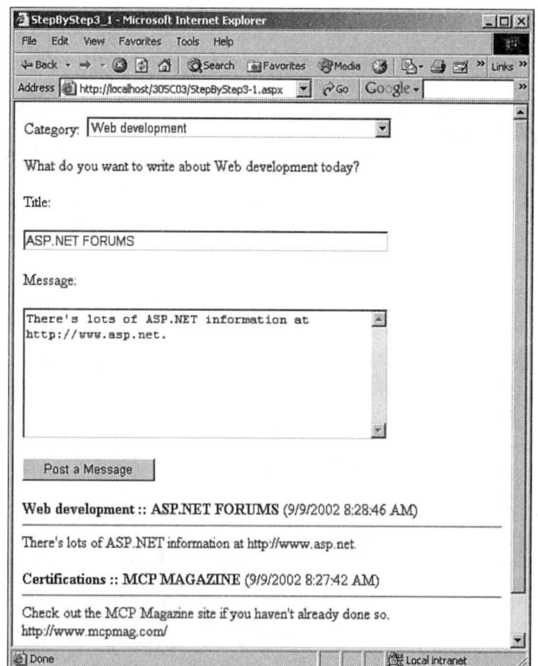

FIGURE 3.2
The Web Form retains state for both postback as well as non-postback controls.

In Step by Step 3.1, I use the event handler for the Load event to check whether the page is loaded by a postback operation. If that is the case, I skip executing the code for adding items to the drop-down list.

You will also note that the navigation between controls is not smooth. When the form returns after a postback, it does not remember the active control. However, there is a solution to this problem with the help of the SmartNavigation property.

The SmartNavigation Property

ASP.NET has a feature called smart navigation that can greatly enhance the user experience of a Web page for the users of Internet Explorer 5.0 or higher browsers. The following list summarizes the enhancements provided by smart navigation:

- **Persisting element focus between postbacks** When a postback occurs, the active control on the Web page loses its focus. Those using the keyboard for navigation will have to press the Tab key several times to return to their original position of data entry. However, when smart navigation is enabled information about the active control is persisted between postbacks to the server.
- **Persisting scroll position between postbacks** When a postback occurs, the browser loses the record of the scroll position of the page. This can be especially annoying in the case of large data entry forms because after postback, the form will be positioned at the beginning and the user will have to scroll down to find his last data entry position. However, when smart navigation is enabled, the scroll position persists between postbacks to the server.
- **Eliminate page flash caused by page postback** When users navigate from one page to another, the old page is destroyed and the new one is created on a blank screen. Depending on the user's video card and display setting, this operation can cause a small flash to occur. This flash is especially noticeable during the page postback operations where the visual contents of the page do not change significantly between the two page requests. When smart navigation is enabled, ASP.NET uses a technique called double buffering to eliminate this flash from occurring.

WARNING

Intranet Only Because smart navigation is limited to recent Internet Explorer versions, it's generally only useful in intranet scenarios. For Internet applications you can't be sure that any given visitor will see the benefits of smart navigation.

- **Prevents each postback from being saved in the browser history** Normally, every postback to an ASP.NET page causes an entry to be created in the browser's history. This defeats the purpose of the browser's back button because instead of going back to the previous page, users are taken to the previous state of the current page. Smart navigation prevents this from happening by saving only the latest state of the current page to be saved in the browser's history.

Smart navigation is specified by the SmartNavigation property of the Page class. The default value of this property is false, thereby disabling smart navigation for the Web Form.

You can set the SmartNavigation property to true through the Page directive on a Web page. This setting generates the correct code for setting the SmartNavigation property of the Page class to true, when the Web Form is compiled to create a Page derived class.

Step by Step 3.2 enhances the Web Form created in Step by Step 3.1 to use the smart navigation features.

STEP BY STEP

3.2 Using the Smart Navigation Features of ASP.NET

1. Make a copy of `StepByStep3-1.aspx` and save it as `StepByStep3-2.aspx`. Make sure that you change all references of `StepByStep3_1` to `StepByStep3_2` in both the ASPX and the VB files.

2. Switch to the HTML view of `StepByStep3_2.aspx` file and modify the `@Page` directive to the following:

```
<%@ Page Language="vb" AutoEventWireup="false"
 Codebehind="StepByStep3-2.aspx.vb"
 Inherits="_305C03.StepByStep3_2"
 SmartNavigation="true"%>
```

3. Set `StepByStep3-2.aspx` as the start page. Build the project and browse to `StepByStep3-2.aspx` using Internet Explorer 5.0 or higher.

4. Use the Tab key to navigate between various fields, publish a few messages, and observe the enhancements because of the smart navigation feature.

In a corporate scenario where you are sure about the browsers used by the users, you may want to turn on smart navigation for the complete Web application instead of individual files. In that case, you can make the following changes to the web.config file:

```
<configuration>
     <system.web>
          <pages smartNavigation="true"/>
     </system.web>
</configuration>
```

ASP.NET INTRINSIC OBJECTS

ASP.NET provides intrinsic objects to enable low-level access to the Web application framework. With the help of these intrinsic objects you can work directly with the underlying HTTP streams, server, session, and application objects. The intrinsic objects can be accessed in a Web Form through the properties of the Page class. Table 3.1 lists the important intrinsic objects and the properties of the Page class to which they are mapped.

TABLE 3.1

INTRINSIC OBJECTS AND THEIR MAPPINGS TO THE PAGE CLASS PROPERTIES

Intrinsic Object	*Property of the Page Class*
HttpRequest	Request
HttpResponse	Response
HttpServerUtility	Server
HttpApplicationState	Application
HttpSessionState	Session

I'll discuss the HttpRequest, HttpResponse, and HttpServerUtility objects in the following section. The other two objects, HttpApplicationState and HttpSessionState, are discussed later in this chapter in the section "State Management."

The HttpRequest Object

The HttpRequest object represents the incoming request from the client to the Web server. The request from the client can come in two ways—GET or POST. GET attaches the data with the URL whereas POST embeds the data within the HTTP request body.

The requested page and its details are encapsulated in an HttpRequest object. The HttpRequest intrinsic object can be accessed by the Request property of the Page class. Tables 3.2 and 3.3 list the properties and methods of the HttpRequest class. Because the HttpRequest class provides information about the request sent by the client, all the properties are read-only except the Filter property.

NOTE

CurrentExecutionFilePath This property of the HttpRequest class returns the file path of the currently executing page. When using the server-side redirection methods such as Server.Execute() and Server.Transfer(), the FilePath property returns the path to the original page whereas the CurrentExecutionFilePath returns the path to the redirected page.

TABLE 3.2

PROPERTIES OF HTTPREQUEST CLASS

Property	*Description*
`AcceptTypes`	Specifies the MIME types that the client browser accepts.
`ApplicationPath`	Represents the application's virtual application root path on the server.
`Browser`	Provides access to the abilities and characteristics of the requesting browser.
`ClientCertificate`	Represents the certificate, if any, sent by the client for secure communications.
`ContentEncoding`	Represents the character encoding (such as UTF7 or ASCII) for the entity body.
`ContentLength`	Specifies the length in bytes of the request.
`ContentType`	Specifies the MIME type of the incoming request.
`Cookies`	Represents the cookies collection that is sent by the client to the server.
`CurrentExecutionFilePath`	Specifies the virtual path of the current executing page on the Web server.
`FilePath`	Specifies the virtual path of the file on the Web server.
`Files`	Represents the file collection that is posted by the client to the Web server.
`Filter`	Represents a stream that is applied as a filter on the incoming request.
`Form`	Specifies the contents of a form posted to the server.

Property	*Description*
`Headers`	Represents the HTTP headers passed in with the incoming request.
`HttpMethod`	Represents the method of the HTTP request. For example, `GET`, `POST`, or `HEAD`.
`InputStream`	Represents the stream that contains the incoming HTTP request body.
`IsAuthenticated`	Indicates whether the client has been authenticated to the site.
`IsSecureConnection`	Indicates whether the client connection is over a secure HTTPS connection.
`Params`	Represents the form, query string, cookies, and server variables collections of the current request.
`Path`	Specifies the virtual path of the current request along with additional path information.
`PathInfo`	Specifies the additional path information of the current request.
`PhysicalApplicationPath`	Specifies the physical file system path of the application's root directory.
`PhysicalPath`	Specifies the physical file system path of the current request on the Web server.
`QueryString`	Represents the querystring collection sent by the client to the Web server through the URL.
`RawUrl`	Specifies the URL portion of the current request, excluding the domain information.
`RequestType`	Represents the type of request (`GET` or `POST`) made by the client.
`ServerVariables`	Represents the collection of Web server variables.
`TotalBytes`	Represents the total number of bytes posted to the server in the current request.
`Url`	Specifies information about the current URL request.
`UrlReferrer`	Specifies the URL of the client's previous request that linked to the current URL.
`UserAgent`	Represents the browser being used by the client.
`UserHostAddress`	Represents the IP address of the requesting client's machine.
`UserHostName`	Represents the DNS name of the requesting client's machine.
`UserLanguages`	Specifies the languages preferred by the client's browser.

TABLE 3.3

METHODS OF THE HTTPREQUEST CLASS

Method	*Description*
`BinaryRead()`	Reads specified number of bytes from the request stream. This method is provided for backward compatibility. You should use `InputStream` property instead.
`MapImageCoordinates()`	Returns the coordinates of a form image that is sent to the server in the current request.
`MapPath()`	Returns the physical file system path of the file for a specified virtual path of a Web server.
`SaveAs()`	Saves the current HTTP request into a disk file, with an option to include or exclude headers.

Step by Step 3.3 displays some of the path-related properties of the HttpRequest object and calls its MapPath() method to get the physical file system path for a specified virtual path. It also displays the header information sent by the client to the server when the StepByStep3-3.aspx page is requested from the server.

STEP BY STEP

3.3 Using the `HttpRequest` Intrinsic Object

1. Add a new Web Form to the project. Name the Web Form `StepByStep3-3.aspx`. Change the `pageLayout` property of `DOCUMENT` element to `FlowLayout`.

2. Add a `Label` control (`lblInfo`) to the Web Form.

3. Switch to the code view of the form. Add the following directives at the top of the code-behind file.

```
Imports System.Text
Imports System.Collections.Specialized
```

4. Add the following code to the `Page_Load()` event handler:

```
Private Sub Page_Load( _
 ByVal sender As System.Object, _
 ByVal e As System.EventArgs) Handles MyBase.Load
    Dim sbInfo As StringBuilder = New StringBuilder()

    ' Display some of the path related properties
    ' of the HttpRequest object
    sbInfo.Append("The Url of the ASPX page: " & _
     Request.Url.ToString & "<br>")
    sbInfo.Append("The Virtual File Path: " & _
     Request.FilePath & "<br>")
    sbInfo.Append("The Physical File Path: " & _
     Request.PhysicalPath & "<br>")
    sbInfo.Append("The Application Path: " & _
     Request.ApplicationPath & "<br>")
    sbInfo.Append( _
     "The Physical Application Path: " & _
     Request.PhysicalApplicationPath & "<br>")

' Display the request header
    sbInfo.Append("Request Header:")
    sbInfo.Append("<br>")
    Dim nvcHeaders As NameValueCollection = _
     Request.Headers
    Dim astrKeys() As String = nvcHeaders.AllKeys
```

```
    ' Iterate through all header keys
    ' and display their values
    Dim strKey As String
    For Each strKey In astrKeys
        sbInfo.Append(strKey & ": " & _
            nvcHeaders(strKey).ToString())
        sbInfo.Append("<br>")
    Next
    ' Call MapPath() method to find the physical path
    ' of the StepByStep3-3.aspx file
    sbInfo.Append( _
     "The physical path of StepByStep3-3.aspx: ")
    sbInfo.Append(Request.MapPath( _
     "StepByStep3-3.aspx"))
lblInfo.Text = sbInfo.ToString()
End Sub
```

5. Set `StepByStep3-3.aspx` as the start page for the project.

6. Run the project. You should see the Web Form displaying the properties for the current request as shown in Figure 3.3.

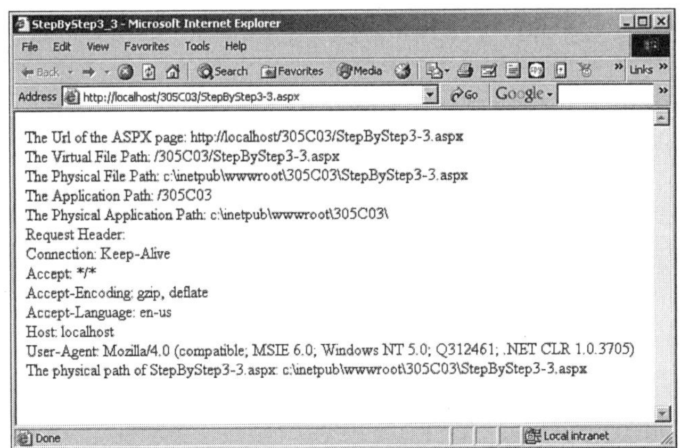

FIGURE 3.3
The Request property of the Page class returns an HttpRequest object that gives access to the HTTP values sent by a client during a Web request.

Some of the properties of the HttpRequest object such as Form, QueryString, and Headers return a NameValueCollection containing a collection of key-value pairs of their contents. Step by Step 3.3 shows how to iterate through this collection by iterating through the keys of the Headers collection and displaying the key and value of each header sent by the client.

The HttpResponse Object

The HttpResponse object represents the response sent back to the client from the Web server. It contains properties and methods that provide direct access to the response stream and allow you to set its behavior and operations. The Response property of the Page class provides access to the HttpResponse object. Tables 3.4 and 3.5 list the properties and the methods of the HttpResponse class.

TABLE 3.4

PROPERTIES OF THE HTTPRESPONSE CLASS

Property	*Description*
`Buffer`	Indicates whether the output to response stream needs to be buffered and sent to the client after the entire page is processed. This property is provided for backward compatibility. The `BufferOutput` property should be used instead.
`BufferOutput`	Indicates whether the output to response stream needs to be buffered and then sent to the client after the entire page is processed. The default is True.
`Cache`	Represents the caching policy of page. The policy controls where caching can be done, the expiration time, and so on.
`CacheControl`	Specifies where the caching should be done. The possible values `Public` and `Private`.
`Charset`	Represents the character set of the output stream. If set to null, the content-type header will be suppressed.
`ContentEncoding`	Represents the character set of the response output stream.
`ContentType`	Represents the MIME type for the outgoing response stream such as `text/html` or `text/xml`.
`Cookies`	Represents the cookies collection that is sent by the server to the client.
`Expires`	Indicates the number of minutes until which the page is cached by the client browser.
`ExpiresAbsolute`	Indicates the specific date and time until which the page is cached by the client browser.
`Filter`	Represents a stream that is applied as a filter to the outgoing response.
`IsClientConnected`	Indicates whether the client is connected to the server. This property is very helpful when running a lengthy request.
`Output`	Allows writing text output to the outgoing response.

Property	*Description*
`OutputStream`	Allows writing binary output to the outgoing response.
`Status`	Specifies the status of the HTTP output that is being sent to the client. This property returns both the status code and the text description of the status. For example, `200 OK`.
`StatusCode`	Specifies the numeric representation of the status of the HTTP output sent to the client. For example, `200` or `302`.
`StatusDescription`	Specifies the text representation of the status of the HTTP output sent to the client. For example, `OK` or `Redirect`.
`SupressContent`	Indicates whether the content in the page should be suppressed and not sent to the client.

NOTE

Caching Policy The properties CacheControl, Expires, and ExpiresAbsolute are provided for backward compatibility. You should instead use the HttpCachePolicy object's methods to set caching policy. This object is returned by the Cache property. Setting caching policy is discussed in Chapter 15, "Configuring a Web Application."

TABLE 3.5

METHODS OF THE HTTPRESPONSE CLASS

Method	*Description*
`AddCacheItemDependencies()`	Makes the validity of the cache item dependent on the other items in the cache.
`AddCacheItemDependency()`	Makes the validity of the cache item dependent on another item in the cache.
`AddFileDependencies()`	Adds group of files to the collection on which the current response depends.
`AddFileDependency()`	Adds a file to the collection on which the current response depends.
`AddHeader()`	Adds an HTTP header to the outgoing response stream. This method is provided for backward compatibility with ASP.
`AppendHeader()`	Adds an HTTP header to the outgoing response stream.
`AppendToLog()`	Adds information to the IIS Web log file.
`BinaryWrite()`	Allows writing binary data such as an image file, PDF file to the response stream.
`Clear()`	Clears the entire response stream buffer, including its contents and headers.
`ClearContent()`	Clears the entire content portion of the response stream buffer.

continues

TABLE 3.5 *continued*

METHODS OF THE HTTPRESPONSE CLASS

Method	*Description*
`ClearHeaders()`	Clears the headers portion of the response stream buffer.
`Close()`	Closes the response object and the socket connection to the client.
`End()`	Stops the execution of the page after flushing the output buffer to the client.
`Flush()`	Flushes the currently buffered content out to the client.
`Pics()`	Adds a `PICS-label` HTTP header to the outgoing response.
`Redirect()`	Redirects the client browser to any URL. This method requires an additional round trip to the browser.
`RemoveOutputCacheItem()`	Removes all cache items for the path specified.
`Write()`	Writes output to the outgoing response.
`WriteFile()`	Writes file to the outgoing response.

Step by Step 3.4 shows the use of the HttpResponse object methods and properties to create a response that displays the File Download dialog box and allows the user to download a text file from the Web server to the client's machine.

STEP BY STEP

3.4 Using the `HttpResponse` Intrinsic Object

1. Add a new Web Form to the project. Name the Web Form `StepByStep3-4.aspx`. Change the `pageLayout` property of `DOCUMENT` element to `FlowLayout`.

2. Add a text file to the project and add some random data to the file. Name it `Summary.txt`.

3. Add a `LinkButton` control (`lbtnDownload`) to the Web Form with its Text property set to `Download Summary.txt`.

4. Double-click the `lbtnDownload` control and add the following code to the `Click` event handler:

```
Private Sub lbtnDownload_Click( _
 ByVal sender As System.Object, _
 ByVal e As System.EventArgs) _
 Handles lbtnDownload.Click
    ' Append a Header to the response to force a
    ' Download of the Summary.txt as an attachment
    Response.AppendHeader("Content-Disposition", _
     "Attachment;FileName=" & "Summary.txt")

    ' Set the Content type to text/plain
    ' As the download file is a TXT file
    Response.ContentType = "text/plain"

    ' Write the file to the Response
    Response.WriteFile("Summary.txt")

    ' Stop the further execution of the page
    Response.End()
End Sub
```

5. Set `StepByStep3-4.aspx` as the start page for the project.

6. Run the project. Click the link button. You should see a File Download dialog box as shown in the Figure 3.4. After the download, open the file to verify that the file has been successfully downloaded.

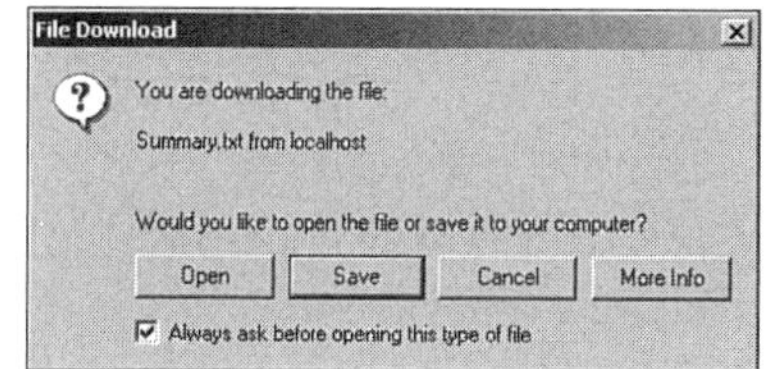

FIGURE 3.4
The File Download dialog box provides the interface to download a file from the Web server.

The HttpServerUtility Object

The HttpServerUtility object contains utility methods and properties to work with the Server object. It contains methods to enable HTML/URL encoding and decoding, execute or transfer to an ASPX page, create COM components, and so on. The Server property of the Page class provides access to the HttpServerUtility object. Tables 3.6 and 3.7 list the properties and methods of the of the HttpServerUtility class.

TABLE 3.6

PROPERTIES OF THE HTTPSERVERUTILITY CLASS

Property	*Description*
`MachineName`	Returns the name of the server that hosts the Web application.
`ScriptTimeout`	Indicates the number of seconds that are allowed to elapse to process the request before the timeout error is sent to the client.

TABLE 3.7

METHODS OF THE HTTPSERVERUTILITY CLASS

Method	*Description*
`ClearError()`	Clears the last exception from the memory. This method is discussed in Chapter 4, "Error Handling for the User Interface."
`CreateObject()`	Creates a COM object on the server. This method is discussed in Chapter 10, "Working with Legacy Code."
`CreateObjectFromClsid()`	Creates a COM object on the server identified by a specified class identifier (CLSID).
`Execute()`	Executes an ASPX page within the current requested page. This method is discussed later in the chapter.
`GetLastError()`	Returns the last exception that occurred on the Web server. This method is discussed in Chapter 4.
`HtmlDecode()`	Enables decoding a string that has been previously HTML encoded for sending over HTTP to a browser.
`HtmlEncode()`	Enables HTML encoding a string for sending over HTTP to a browser.
`MapPath()`	Returns the physical path for a specified virtual path for a Web server.
`Transfer()`	Allows the transfer of ASPX page execution from the current page to another ASPX page on the same Web server. This method is discussed later in the chapter.

Method	*Description*
`UrlDecode()`	Enables decoding a URL string that has been previously HTML encoded for sending over HTTP to a browser.
`UrlEncode()`	Enables encoding a URL string for safe transmission over HTTP.
`UrlPathEncode()`	Enables encoding of a path portion of the URL string for safe transmission over HTTP.

STEP BY STEP

3.5 Using the `HttpServerUtility` Object

1. Add a new Web Form to the project. Name the Web Form `StepByStep3-5.aspx`. Change the `pageLayout` property of the `DOCUMENT` element to `FlowLayout`.

2. Add the following code to the `Page_Load()` event handler:

```
Private Sub Page_Load(ByVal sender As System.Object, _
 ByVal e As System.EventArgs) Handles MyBase.Load
    ' Write to the response
    ' using the Server.HtmlEncode() method
    ' so that the browser does not parse
    ' the text into HTML elements
    Response.Write(Server.HtmlEncode( _
     "To include a title in the title bar, " & _
     "enclose your chosen title between the " & _
     "pairs of the <title>...</title> element " & _
     "in the HTML <head> element. "))

    Response.Write(Server.HtmlEncode( _
     "For example, " & _
     "<title> Using the HtmlEncode()" & _
     "method </title>"))
End Sub
```

3. Set `StepByStep3-5.aspx` as the start page for the project.

4. Run the project. You should see that the browser does not parse the HTML `<title>` elements written to the response, as shown in Figure 3.5. This is because of the use of `HtmlEncode()` method of the `HttpServerUtility` class.

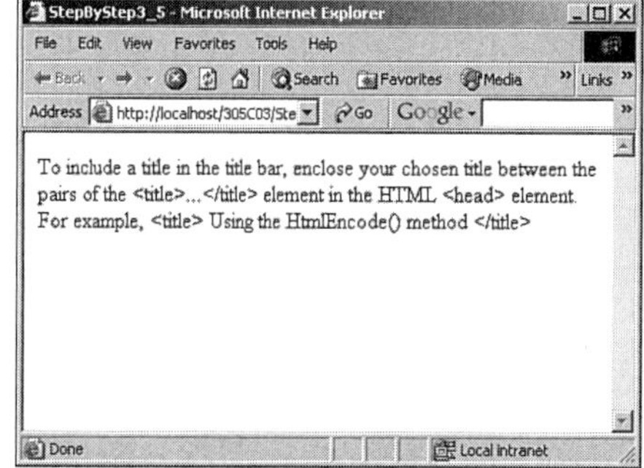

FIGURE 3.5
The HtmlEncode() method of the HttpServerUtility object HTML encodes a string to be displayed in the browser.

I will discuss various other methods of the HttpServerUtility object over the course of this book.

GUIDED PRACTICE EXERCISE 3.1

Several Web sites collect statistics about the browsers, operating systems, and other settings on their users' computers. This data helps the Web site in customizing content to target a large number of users. A common requirement for Web applications is to find out the browser version of their users and then serve them files that are optimized for that particular browser version.

In this exercise, you are required to create a Web Form that displays the following information about the client browser: the browser name and version, the platform of the client's computer, the CLR version installed, JavaScript support, ECMA version, MS DOM version, and the W3C XML DOM version supported by the browser.

You can use the Request.Browser property to get access to the HttpBrowserCapabilities object that provides various properties to gather information on the capabilities of the client's browser.

How would you create a Web Form that allows the Web page to get information about the browser?

You should try working through this problem on your own first. If you are stuck, or if you'd like to see one possible solution, follow these steps:

1. Open the project `315C03`. Add a new Web Form named `GuidedPracticeExercise3-1` to the project. Change the `pageLayout` property of the `DOCUMENT` element to `FlowLayout`.
2. Add a `Label` control (`lblInfo`) to the Web Form.
3. Switch to the code view of the form. Add the following `Imports` directive at the top of the code-behind file.

```
Imports System.Text
```

4. Add the following code to the `Page_Load()` event handler:

```
Private Sub Page_Load(ByVal sender As System.Object, _
 ByVal e As System.EventArgs) Handles MyBase.Load
    Dim sbText As StringBuilder = New StringBuilder()
```

```
        ' Get the reference to the
        ' HttpBrowserCapabilities object
        Dim browser As HttpBrowserCapabilities = _
         Request.Browser

        ' Display  the properties of the
        ' HttpBrowserCapabilities Class
        sbText.AppendFormat("Browser : " & _
         browser.Browser & "<br>")
        sbText.AppendFormat("Browser Version: " & _
         browser.Version & "<br>")
        sbText.AppendFormat("Client's Platform: " & _
         browser.Platform & "<br>")
        sbText.AppendFormat(".NET CLR Version: " & _
         browser.ClrVersion.ToString & "<br>")
        sbText.AppendFormat("ECMA Script Version: " & _
         browser.EcmaScriptVersion.ToString & "<br>")
        sbText.AppendFormat("JavaScript Support: " & _
         browser.JavaScript & "<br>")
        sbText.AppendFormat( _
         "Microsoft HTML Document " & _
         "Object Model Version: " & _
         browser.MSDomVersion.ToString & "<br>")
        sbText.AppendFormat( _
         "World Wide Web (W3C) " & _
         "XML Document Object Model " & _
         "Version: " & _
         browser.W3CDomVersion.ToString & "<br>")

        lblInfo.Text = sbText.ToString()
    End Sub
```

5. Set `GuidedPracticeExercise3_1.aspx` as the start page for the project.

6. Run the project. You should see the Web Form displaying the properties of the browser as shown in Figure 3.6.

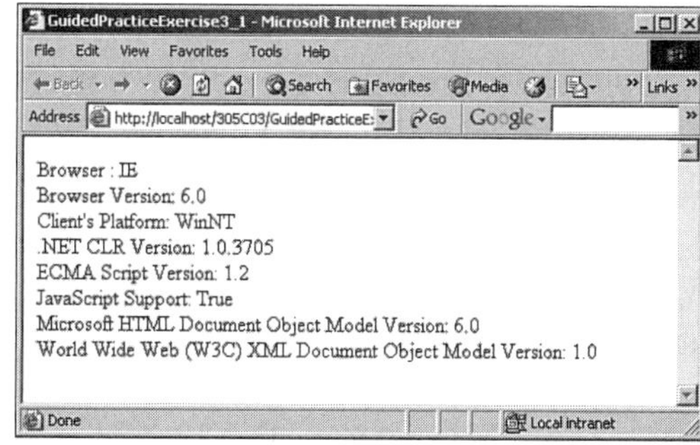

FIGURE 3.6
The HttpBrowserCapabilities object provides access to the capabilities of the client's browser.

If you have difficulty following this exercise, review the section "The HttpRequest Object" earlier in this chapter and perform Step by Step 3.3. After doing this review, try this exercise again.

REVIEW BREAK

- Web applications are disconnected in nature. That is, the values of a page's variables and controls are not preserved across the page requests.
- You can use the Page.IsPostBack property to determine whether a page is being loaded for the first time or in response to a postback operation.
- ASP.NET has a feature called smart navigation that can greatly enhance the user experience of a Web page for users of Internet Explorer 5.0 or higher browsers.
- ASP.NET provides intrinsic objects to enable low-level access to the Web application framework. With the help of these intrinsic objects you can work directly with the underlying HTTP request, HTTP response, server, session, and application objects.

ASP.NET Application

An ASP.NET application is made up of the Web Forms, assemblies, and other files stored within a virtual Web directory marked as an IIS application.

When ASP.NET receives the very first request for a resource in an ASP.NET application, it instantiates an HttpApplication object. This HttpApplication object then takes over the processing of incoming requests. For the sake of optimization, ASP.NET maintains a pool of HttpApplication objects. When a new HTTP request arrives, ASP.NET uses an object from this pool rather than creating an HttpApplication object from scratch.

The HttpApplication class defines the methods, properties, and events common to all application objects within an ASP.NET application. If you want to customize the behavior of an HttpApplication object, you can derive a class from the HttpApplication class and override the event handlers of the base class for various application-level events. An easy way to do this is by using the global.asax file.

The global.asax File

ASP.NET provides an easy way for application customization through the use of the global.asax file. This optional file resides in the root directory of an ASP.NET application. The global.asax file defines a class named Global that derives from the HttpApplication class. When ASP.NET notices that the global.asax file is present for an application, rather than using the implicitly created HttpApplication object, ASP.NET creates instances of the class defined in the global.asax file to handle requests for your application.

Visual Studio .NET automatically creates a global.asax file when you create an ASP.NET Web application project. As with Web Forms, Visual Studio .NET creates a code-behind version of the global.asax file. When you make any changes to the code-behind file for global.asax you must precompile the file before the server can detect those changes. However, it is also possible to create a single file implementation of global.asax file. In that case instead of using precompilation the global.asax file will be dynamically compiled at runtime by ASP.NET.

NOTE

The global.asax File Is Protected
You use global.asax file to provide event handlers for various application-level events. For security reasons, ASP.NET restricts users of your application from downloading any file with an extension of .asax.

Global Event Handlers

The global.asax file is an appropriate place to handle events that are not specific to a Web Form but rather apply to an application as a whole. I'll call these events global events and classify them in two categories: application- and session-level events, and per-request events.

Application- and Session-Level Events

Application- and session-level events are fired to signal the start and end of the application or a user session. These events can be handled using the following predefined event handlers in the global.asax file, as shown in Table 3.8.

TABLE 3.8

APPLICATION- AND SESSION-LEVEL EVENT HANDLERS IN THE GLOBAL.ASAX FILE

Event Handler	*Purpose*
`Application_Start()`	Called when an application receives its first request. Generally used to initialize data that is shared among all the users of an application.
`Application_End()`	Called when an application shuts down. Here you can write code to persist the information that you want to be reloaded when an application restarts.
`Session_Start()`	Called when ASP.NET application creates a new session for a user of the application.
`Session_End()`	Called when the user's session expires. By default, this happens 20 minutes after the last request of a page from a user.

Per-Request Events

Table 3.9 shows the event handlers that are invoked for each individual page request processed by the HttpApplication object.

TABLE 3.9

PER-REQUEST EVENT HANDLERS

Event Handler	*Purpose*
`Application_BeginRequest()`	Called at the beginning of each request.
`Application_AuthenticateRequest()`	Called when a security module has established the identity of the user.
`Application_AuthorizeRequest()`	Called when a security module has verified user authorization.
`Application_ResolveRequestCache()`	Called to resolve the current request by providing content from a cache.
`Application_AcquireRequestState()`	Called to associate the current request with the session state.

Event Handler	*Purpose*
`Application_PreRequestHandlerExecute()`	Called when ASP.NET begins executing a page.
`Application_PostRequestHandlerExecute()`	Called when ASP.NET finishes executing a page.
`Application_ReleaseRequestState()`	Called to save the current state data.
`Application_UpdateRequestCache()`	Called to update a cache with the responses.
`Application_EndRequest()`	Called at the end of each request.

You can see from Table 3.9 that you have complete control over how a request is processed. You can write code in any of these event handlers to modify the default behavior of ASP.NET. Step by Step 3.6 uses the Application_BeginRequest() and Application_EndRequest() methods to determine the time it took for each request to process and append this information with every page of the application.

STEP BY STEP

3.6 Handling Global Events Using the global.asax File

1. Open the `global.asax` file from the Solution Explorer. Click the `Click here to switch to code view` hyperlink to switch to the code view.

2. Add the following code to the `Application_BeginRequest()` event handler:

```
Sub Application_BeginRequest( _
 ByVal sender As Object, ByVal e As EventArgs)
    ' Store the begin time of the
    ' request in the HttpContext object
    Me.Context.Items.Add("BeginTime", DateTime.Now)
End Sub
```

3. Add the following code to the `Application_EndRequest()` event handler:

```
Sub Application_EndRequest(ByVal sender As Object, _
 ByVal e As System.EventArgs)
```

continues

continued

```
        ' Get the begin time from the HttpContext object
        Dim dtBeginTime As DateTime = _
         CType(Me.Context.Items("BeginTime"), DateTime)

        ' Calculate the time span between
        ' the start and end of request
        Dim tsProcessingTime As TimeSpan = _
         DateTime.Now.Subtract(dtBeginTime)

        ' Display the processing
        ' time taken in the response
        Me.Context.Response.Output.Write("<hr>")
        Me.Context.Response.Output.Write( _
          "{0} took {1} milliseconds to execute.", _
          Me.Request.Url, _
          tsProcessingTime.TotalMilliseconds)
    End Sub
```

4. Run the project. You should see that the page shows a message at the bottom indicating the processing time of the request as shown in Figure 3.7.

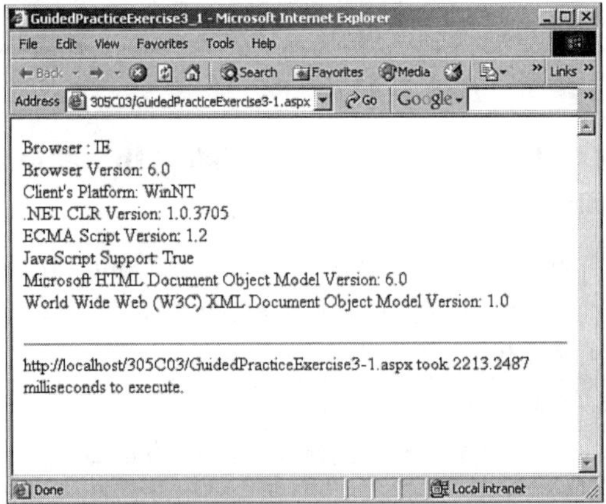

FIGURE 3.7
The global.asax file gives you access to application-level events that affect all the pages in an application.

The modification of the global.asax file in Step by Step 3.6 will affect all other Web Forms in the Web application 305C03. If at a later stage, you would like to disable the output generated by the global events, just comment the corresponding lines in the global.asax file.

REVIEW BREAK

- ASP.NET maintains a pool of HttpApplication objects. When a new HTTP request arrives, ASP.NET uses one of the objects from this pool rather than creating an HttpApplication object from scratch.
- The Global.asax file can be used to define a customized HttpApplication class. When a global.asax file exists in the Web application's root directory, ASP.NET uses the HttpApplication-derived class defined in the global.asax file to serve the Web application.
- The global.asax file is the appropriate place to handle global events that are not specific to a Web Form but rather apply to an application as a whole.

STATE MANAGEMENT

The values of the variables and controls collectively make up the state of a Web page. State management is the process of maintaining the state of a Web page across round trips.

State management is ubiquitous with desktop-based applications and programmers need not even care about it while developing their applications. However, because of the disconnected nature of the HTTP protocol, state management is a big issue for Web applications.

ASP.NET provides several techniques to preserve state information across page postbacks. I'll broadly categorize these techniques as either client-side or the server-side depending on where the resources are consumed for state management.

Client-side Techniques for State Management

Client-side techniques use the HTML code and the capabilities of the Web browser to store state related information. ASP.NET supports the following techniques for storing state information at the client-side:

- Query strings
- Cookies
- Hidden Fields
- ViewState

Query Strings

A query string maintains state by appending the state information to a page's URL. The state data is separated from the actual URL with a question mark (`?`). The data attached to the URL is usually a set of key-value pairs where each key-value pair is separated using an ampersand (`&`). For example, look at this URL that embeds two key-value pairs, name and city:

```
www.buddy.com/find.aspx?name=Bill+Gates&city=Redmond
```

Because of their simplicity, query strings are widely used for passing small amounts of information to the Web pages. However, query strings suffer from the following limitations:

- Most browsers restrict the length of the query string; this reduces the amount of data that you can embed to a URL.
- Query strings do not provide any support for structured data types.
- The information stored in query strings is not secure because they are directly visible to the users.

Reading information from query string in an ASP.NET program is easy. You can use the QueryString property of the current HttpRequest object. QueryString returns a NameValueCollection object representing the key-value pairs stored in the query string.

STEP BY STEP

3.7 Using Query Strings in a Web Application

1. Add a new Web Form to the project. Name the Web Form `StepByStep3-7.aspx`. Change the `pageLayout` property of the `DOCUMENT` element to `FlowLayout`.

2. Add two `Label` controls, two `TextBox` controls (`txtName`, `txtEmail`), and a `Button` control (`btnSubmit`) to the Web Form.

3. Double-click the `button` control and add the following code in the `Click` event handler:

```
Private Sub btnSubmit_Click( _
 ByVal sender As System.Object, _
 ByVal e As System.EventArgs) Handles btnSubmit.Click
    ' Redirect to a page with a query string
    ' containing name and email
    Response.Redirect("StepByStep3-7a.aspx?Name=" & _
     txtName.Text & "&Email=" & txtEmail.Text)
End Sub
```

4. Add a new Web Form to the project. Name the Web Form `StepByStep3-7a.aspx`. Change the `pageLayout` property of the `DOCUMENT` element to `FlowLayout`.

5. Add a `Label` control (`lblInfo`) on the Web Form.

6. Add the following code in the `Page_Load()` event handler:

```
Private Sub Page_Load(ByVal sender As System.Object, _
 ByVal e As System.EventArgs) Handles MyBase.Load
    ' If the query string collection contains Name
    If Not Request.QueryString("Name") Is Nothing Then
        ' Display a message by getting Name and Email
        ' from the query string collection
    lblInfo.Text = Request.QueryString("Name") & _
       ", thanks for registering with us! "
        lblInfo.Text &= "You are subscribed at " & _
            Request.QueryString("Email")
    End If
End Sub
```

7. Set `StepByStep3-7.aspx` as the start page for the project.

continues

continued

8. Run the project. Enter a name and email address in the text boxes and click the Submit button. You should see that the button redirects the response to the `StepByStep3-7a.aspx` with the name and email address data as the query string. The new form then displays a message along with the name and email address fetched from the query string as shown in Figure 3.8.

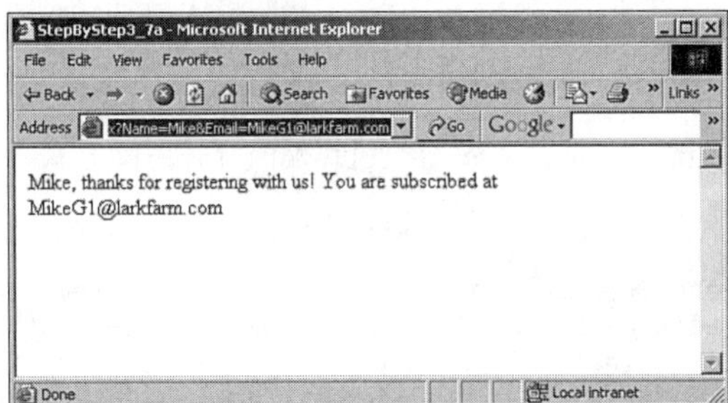

FIGURE 3.8
Query string is used to maintain state by appending the state information to a page's URL.

If you observe the URL in Figure 3.8, you'll note that the name and email address are embedded in the URL itself. The query string is a very easy way to pass small, nonsensitive pieces of information.

Cookies

Cookies are small packets of information, each storing a key-value pair, stored on the client's computer. These packets are associated with a specific domain and are sent along with each request to the associated Web server.

A cookie can be set to expire when a user session ends or you can request the browser to persist the cookies on the user's computer for a specified period. Cookies are commonly used to store a user's preferences and provide them personalized browsing experience on their repeated visits to a Web page.

Use of cookies suffers from the following limitations:

- Most browsers limit the size of information that you can store in a cookie. A typical size is 4096 bytes with older browser versions and 8192 bytes with the newer browser versions.
- Some users configure their browsers to refuse cookies.
- When you request the browser to persist a cookie on the user's computer for a specified period, browsers may override that request by using their own rules for cookie expiration.
- Because cookies are stored at the client, they may be tampered with. You cannot trust the data that you receive from a cookie.

You can use the Cookies property of the HttpRequest object to get an HttpCookieCollection object that represents the cookies sent by the client for the current HTTP request.

STEP BY STEP

3.8 Using Cookies to Maintain Client-side State

1. Copy the Web Form `StepByStep3-1.aspx` and change its name to `StepByStep3-8.aspx`. Open the ASPX file and the VB file and change all occurrences of `StepByStep3_1` to `StepByStep3_8`. Add a `Label` control with the `id` of `lblName` to the form.

2. Switch to the code view and modify the `Page_Load()` method as shown here:

```
Private Sub Page_Load( _
 ByVal sender As System.Object, _
 ByVal e As System.EventArgs) Handles MyBase.Load
    If Request.Cookies("Name") Is Nothing Then
        ' If the Name cookie does not exists
        ' ask user to enter name
        Response.Redirect("StepByStep3-8a.aspx")
    Else
```

continues

continued

```
        ' If cookie already exists then show
        ' a personalized welcome message to the user
        lblName.Text = "Welcome " & _
          Request.Cookies("Name").Value
    End If
    If Not Page.IsPostBack Then
        ' If page is requested for the first time
        ddlCategories.Items.Add("Web development")
        ddlCategories.Items.Add( _
         "Programming Languages")
        ddlCategories.Items.Add("Certifications")
    Else
        ' On postback, change the case of textbox
        txtTitle.Text = txtTitle.Text.ToUpper()
    End If
    ' Set the text of the label
    ' control on each page load
    lblQuestion.Text = _
     "What do you want to write about " & _
    ddlCategories.SelectedItem.Text + " today?"
End Sub
```

3. Double-click the Post `button` control and modify the `Click` event handler as follows:

```
Private Sub btnPost_Click( _
 ByVal sender As System.Object, _
 ByVal e As System.EventArgs) Handles btnPost.Click
    ' Format the data entered by the user and
    ' use the name of the user stored in a cookie
    ' append it all to the existing
    ' contents of lblWeblog
    lblWeblog.Text = "<b>" & _
     ddlCategories.SelectedItem.Text & _
     " :: " & txtTitle.Text & ":: by " & _
     Request.Cookies("Name").Value & "</b> (" & _
     DateTime.Now.ToString() & ")<HR>" & _
     txtMessage.Text & "<p>" & _
     lblWeblog.Text
End Sub
```

4. Add a new Web Form to the project. Name the Web Form `StepByStep3-8a.aspx`. Change the `pageLayout` property of the `DOCUMENT` element to `FlowLayout`.

5. Add a `Label` control, a `TextBox` control (`txtName`), a `Button` control (`btnSubmit`), and a `CheckBox` control (`cbRemember`) on the Web Form.

6. Double-click the Submit `button` control and add the following code in the `Click` event handler:

```
Private Sub btnSubmit_Click( _
 ByVal sender As System.Object, _
 ByVal e As System.EventArgs) Handles btnSubmit.Click
    ' Create a cookie called Name
    ' Set the cookie with the Text of the text box
    Dim cName As HttpCookie = New HttpCookie("Name")
    cName.Value = txtName.Text
    ' Check if the checkbox "remember me" is checked
    If cbRemember.Checked Then
        ' Set the expiration time of the cookie
        ' to 15 minutes from the current time
        cName.Expires = DateTime.Now.Add( _
           New TimeSpan(0, 0, 15, 0))
    End If
    ' Add the cookie to the response
    ' cookies collection
    ' To send it to the client's machine
    Response.Cookies.Add(cName)
    ' Redirect the response to the message post page
    Response.Redirect("StepByStep3-8.aspx")
End Sub
```

7. Set `StepByStep3-8.aspx` as the start page for the project.

8. Run the project. You should see that you have been redirected to `StepByStep3-8a.aspx`. Enter a name, select the checkbox, and click the Submit button. You'll now see `StepByStep3-8.aspx` with a personalized greeting. Post a message, and you should see that your name is now posted along with the title of the message as shown in Figure 3.9.

continues

continued

FIGURE 3.9
Cookies can be used to provide personalization settings for individual users.

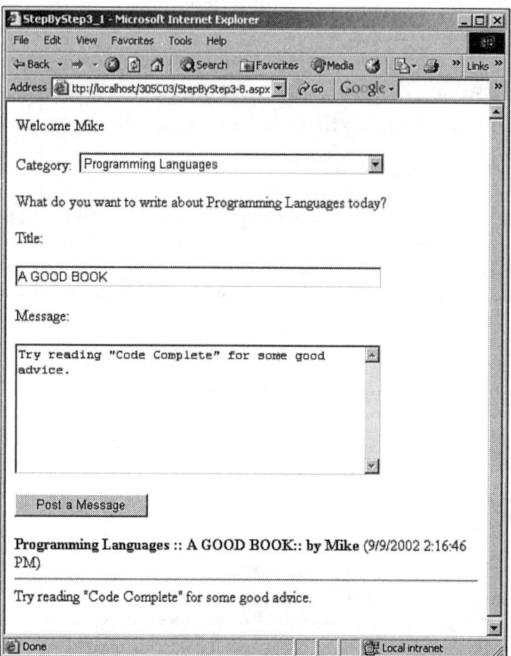

9. Close this browser window. Open another browser window and browse to `StepByStep3-8.aspx`. Assuming you checked the "Remember me" checkbox, the form will display your name immediately.

Step by Step 3.8 demonstrates how cookies can be used to persist state across browser restarts. If you don't select the checkbox, cookies will just be stored in the primary memory and will be destroyed when the browser window is closed. The program also demonstrates how you can request the browser to set an expiration date and time for the cookie. Step by Step 3.8 sets the expiration time of the cookie to 15 minutes from the current time. You should note that this is just a request; browsers are free to override this with their own settings.

Hidden Fields

Hidden fields contain information that is not visible on the page but is posted to the server along with a page postback. Most browsers support hidden fields on a Web page. However, hidden fields have some limitations as mentioned in the following list:

- Although the information stored in hidden fields is not visible on the page, it is still part of the page's HTML code and users can view them by viewing the HTML source of the page. Hidden fields are therefore not a good choice for storing information that you would like to keep secure.
- Hidden fields are part of the page HTML. If you store more information in hidden fields, it increases the size of HTML page making it slow for users to download.
- Hidden fields only allow you to store a single value in a field. If you want to store structured values such as a customer record, you'll have to use several hidden fields.

ASP.NET provides an HTML server control, HtmlInputHidden, that maps to the <input type="hidden"> HTML element. Step by Step 3.9 demonstrates the use of hidden fields to maintain the number of posts on the Web log page created in Step by Step 3.1.

STEP BY STEP

3.9 Using Hidden Fields to Maintain Client-side State

1. Copy the Web Form `StepByStep3-1.aspx` and change its name to `StepByStep3-9.aspx`. Open the ASPX file and the VB file and change all occurrences of `StepByStep3_1` to `StepByStep3_9`.
2. Place a `Label` control (`lblPosts`) and an HTML `Hidden` control (`txtPosts`) next to the Post `button` control on the form. Right-click the `txtPosts` control and select Run As Server Control. Set the `value` property of txtPosts to `0`.
3. Switch to the code view and modify the `Click` event handler of the `btnPost` control as shown here:

```
Private Sub btnPost_Click( _
 ByVal sender As System.Object, _
 ByVal e As System.EventArgs) Handles btnPost.Click
```

continues

continued

```
    ' Format the data entered by the user and
    ' append it to the existing contents of lblWeblog
    lblWeblog.Text = "<b>" & _
     ddlCategories.SelectedItem.Text & _
     " :: " + txtTitle.Text & "</b> (" & _
     DateTime.Now.ToString() & ")<HR>" & _
     txtMessage.Text & "<p>" & _
     lblWeblog.Text

    ' As one more post is added
    ' Increment the value of the hidden control
    Dim intPostCount As Int32 = _
     Int32.Parse(txtPosts.Value) + 1
    txtPosts.Value = intPostCount.ToString()
    lblPosts.Text = "Total Posts: (" & _
     txtPosts.Value & ")"
End Sub
```

4. Set `StepByStep3-9.aspx` as the start page for the project.

5. Run the project. Make a few entries in the Web log. You will see that with each entry in the Web log, the total posts value is increased by 1 as shown in Figure 3.10.

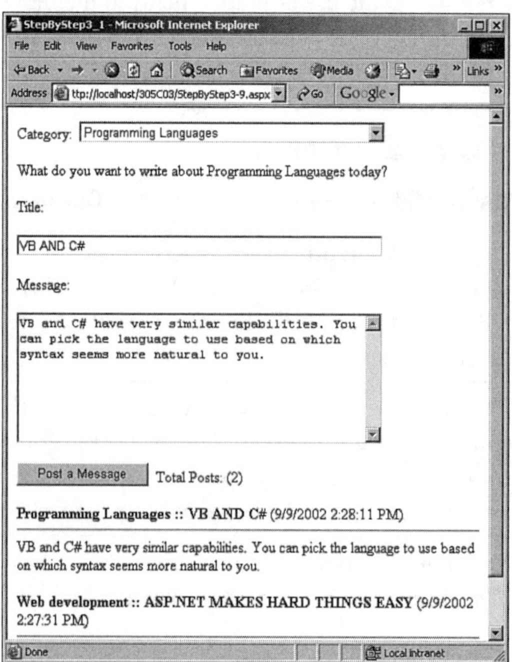

FIGURE 3.10
Contents of hidden fields are posted to the Web server with each page postback.

Step by Step 3.9 shows a typical example in which hidden fields can be used to maintain state information. Here, because a hidden field is an input type of control, its value is posted back to the Web server with each page postback. Hidden fields can be used to store page-scope values between round trips.

The `HtmlInputHidden` control is not available as a Web server control. This is mainly because ASP.NET uses a similar but more powerful technique called ViewState.

NOTE

Programmatic Hidden Fields If you only need a hidden field in some circumstances, you can create it programmatically. The RegisterHiddenField method of the Page object allows you to create hidden fields at runtime.

ViewState

ViewState is the mechanism that ASP.NET uses to maintain the state of controls across page postbacks. Just like hidden fields and cookies, you can also use ViewState to maintain state for noncontrol values in a page. You must keep in mind that ViewState works only when a page is posted back to itself.

The following sections explain how ViewState works in various scenarios.

ViewState for Postback Controls

Some server controls such as TextBox or CheckBox post their values as part of the postback operation. These types of controls are known as the postback controls. For postback controls, ASP.NET retrieves their values one-by-one from the HTTP Request and copies them to the control values while creating the HTTP response. Traditionally, Web developers had to write this code manually to maintain state for the postback controls but now ASP.NET does this automatically.

ViewState does not require any additional storage either on the client side or on the server side for maintaining state for postback controls.

ViewState for Non-postback Controls

In addition to the postback controls, the ViewState mechanism of ASP.NET also manages to retain values for non-postback controls (that is, the controls that do not post their values as part of the postback operation, such as Label controls). You may wonder how ASP.NET manages to maintain values for control even when the controls do not post their values. Actually, there is no magic involved; ASP.NET extends the concept of hidden fields to accomplish this.

When ASP.NET executes a page, it collects the value of all non-postback controls that are modified in the code and formats them into a single base64-encoded string. This string is then stored in a hidden field in a control named __VIEWSTATE, as in this example:

```
<input type="hidden" name="__VIEWSTATE"
value="dDwtMTg3NjA4ODA2MDs7PoY
➥LsizcOhkv2XeRfSJNPt12o1HP" />
```

The hidden input field is a postback control, and so in the next postback of the page, the encoded string stored in the __VIEWSTATE field is also posted. At the Web server, ASP.NET decodes the ViewState string at page initialization and restores the controls values in the page.

Maintaining state using this technique does not require many server resources but it definitely increases the size of the HTML file and therefore increases the amount of time it takes to load the page.

ViewState for Page-level Values

The ViewState property of the Page class is a great place to store page-level values. ViewState will save these values just prior to rendering that page and restore the values at the time of page initialization after the postback operation. This may sound like a cookie or hidden field but a major improvement is that you are not just limited to store simple values. You can use the ViewState to store any object as long as it is serializable.

A good practice is to expose a page level value as a property that internally manipulates the ViewState of the page. I'll use this technique in Step by Step 3.10 to maintain the number of posts on the Web log using ViewState.

STEP BY STEP

3.10 Using ViewState to Maintain State for Page-level Values

1. Make a copy the Web Form `StepByStep3-1.aspx` and change its name to `StepByStep3-10.aspx`. Open the ASPX file and the VB file and change all occurrences of `StepByStep3_1` to `StepByStep3_10`.

2. Place a `Label` control (`lblPosts`) next to the `button` control on the form.

3. Switch to the code view and the following property to the class `StepByStep3_10` definition:

```
' Get or set the number of posts in the Weblog
Protected Property NumberOfPosts() As Integer
    Get
        If ViewState("NumberOfPosts") Is Nothing Then
            ' The NumberOfPosts key is not
            ' present in the ViewState
            NumberOfPosts = 0
        Else
            ' Retrieve the NumberOfPosts
            ' from the ViewState
            Return Convert.ToInt32( _
                   ViewState("NumberOfPosts"))
        End If
    End Get
    Set(ByVal Value As Integer)
        ' Set the NumberOfPost in the ViewState
        ViewState("NumberOfPosts") = Value
    End Set
End Property
```

4. Modify the event handler for the `Click` event of `btnPost` control as shown below:

```
Private Sub btnPost_Click( _
 ByVal sender As System.Object, _
 ByVal e As System.EventArgs) Handles btnPost.Click
    ' Format the data entered by the user and
    ' append it to the existing contents of lblWeblog
    lblWeblog.Text = "<b>" & _
     ddlCategories.SelectedItem.Text & _
     " :: " + txtTitle.Text & "</b> (" & _
     DateTime.Now.ToString() & ")<HR>" & _
     txtMessage.Text & "<p>" & _
     lblWeblog.Text
    ' One more post is added
    ' Increment the value of NumberOfPost
    ' key in the Page's ViewState
    NumberOfPosts = NumberOfPosts + 1
    lblPosts.Text = "Total Posts : (" & _
     NumberOfPosts & ")"
End Sub
```

5. Set `StepByStep3-10.aspx` as the start page for the project.

continues

continued

6. Run the project. Make a few entries in the Web log. You should see that with each entry in the Web log, the total posts value is increased by 1, just as it did in Step by Step 3.10.

7. View the HTML code rendered in the Web browser. You'll note that the value associated with the __VIEWSTATE field changes as you post more messages to the Web log.

As you see from Step by Step 3.10, internally ViewState is also maintained as hidden field. However, ViewState provides a higher degree of customizability and other security features that you'll see shortly.

Disabling ViewState

By default, ViewState is enabled in an ASP.NET application. As you have observed in the previous examples, the size of information stored in ViewState can increase the size of HTML for a Web page. This is especially important when your application contains complex controls such as a DataList or DataGrid. To optimize a Web page size you may want to disable ViewState in the following cases:

- When a page does not postback to itself
- When there are no dynamically set control properties
- When the dynamic properties are set with each request of the page

ASP.NET provides you complete flexibility to disable ViewState at various levels as mentioned in the following list:

- **At the level of a control** If you populate the control's state on each request, you may disable `ViewState` at the control level by setting the `EnableViewState` property of the control to `false`:

```
<asp:DataGrid EnableViewState="false" …/>
```

- **At the level of a page** If the page doesn't post back to itself, you may disable `ViewState` at the page level by setting the `EnableViewState` attribute of the `@Page` directive to `false` in the ASPX file:

  ```
  <%@Page EnableViewState="false" %>
  ```

- **At the level of an application** If no page in an application posts back to itself, you may disable `ViewState` at the application level by adding the following line to the web.config file:

  ```
  <Pages enableViewState="false"/>
  ```

- **At the level of machine** In the unlikely case where you want to disable ViewState for all the applications running on a Web server, you can do so by adding the following statement to the machine.config file:

  ```
  <Pages enableViewState="false"/>
  ```

Protecting ViewState

By default the ViewState of a page is not protected. Although the values are not directly visible as in the case of query string or hidden variables, it is not difficult for determined users to decode the storage format.

> NOTE
> **ViewState Decoder** You can decode the contents stored in the __VIEWSTATE hidden input control using the ViewState Decoder utility written by Fritz Onion. You can download this utility from `http://www.develop.com/devresources/resourcedetail.aspx?type=t&id=827`.

However, only with a few configuration changes, ASP.NET allows you to store ViewState in a much more secure way. ASP.NET provides two ways to increase the security of ViewState:

> NOTE
> **Secure Only When Needed** Running security algorithms puts additional overhead on your Web server and makes applications slower. Therefore, you should enable security for ViewState only when it is a must.

- **Tamper-proofing the ViewState** Tamper-proofing does not protect against someone determining the contents of `ViewState`. It instead provides a way of knowing whether somebody has modified the contents of `ViewState` to fool your application. Using this technique, the `ViewState` is encoded using a hash code (using the SHA1 or MD5 algorithms) when it is sent to the browser. When the page is posted back, ASP.NET checks the encoded `ViewState` to verify that it has not been tampered with on the client. This type of check is called machine authentication check (MAC). By default, ASP.NET has the following entry in its machine.config file:

  ```
  <pages enableViewStateMac='true' />
  ```

EXAM TIP

ViewState Security on a Web Farm When securing the ViewState for applications running on a Web Farm configuration, you must use the same validation key for all the machines on a Web Farm. To do this use a manually assigned key instead of the default auto generated key with the <machineKey> setting in the machine.config file.

This enables tamper-proofing for all the applications running on a Web server. You can also manually enable or disable the tamper-proofing check at a page level by setting the `EnableViewStateMac` attribute of the `@Page` directive to `true` or `false` in the ASPX file:

```
<%@ Page EnableViewStateMac="true"%>
```

- **Encrypting the ViewState** This technique instructs ASP.NET to encrypt the contents of `ViewState` using Triple DES symmetric algorithm (3DES) making it extremely difficult for the client to decode the `ViewState`. This kind of encryption can be applied only at the machine level by specifying the following setting in machine.config file:

```
<machineKey validation='3DES' />
```

Choosing a Client-side State Management Technique

Table 3.10 lists the advantages and disadvantages of the various client-side state management techniques. This table will help you take a quick decision about which client-side state management technique to choose in a given scenario:

TABLE 3.10

COMPARING THE CLIENT-SIDE STATE MANAGEMENT TECHNIQUES

Technique	*Advantage*	*Disadvantage*
QueryString	Requires no postback operation.	Most browsers limit the length of data that can included in a query string. No security. No options for persistence. No support for storing structured values.
Cookies	State may be persisted on user's computer.	Requires no postback operation. Some users disable cookies in their browsers. Size restriction by browser (~4 to 8KB). No support for storing structured values. No security.
Hidden fields	Can be used for pages that post to themselves or to other pages.	Increases HTML size. No support for storing structured values. No security. No options for persistence.

Technique	*Advantage*	*Disadvantage*
ViewState	Support for structured values.	Involves less coding. Easy configuration options for security. Increases HTML size. Only works when a page posts back to itself. No options for persistence.

Server-side Techniques for State Management

Unlike client-side techniques for state management, server-side techniques use server resources for storing and managing state. One of the advantages of using server-side techniques for state management is that the possibility of user spoofing or reading the session data is eliminated, but there is a disadvantage too; because these techniques use server resources, they raise scalability issues.

ASP.NET supports server-side state management at two levels: at the level of the Web application using application state, and at the level of a user session using session state.

Session State

An ASP.NET application creates a session for each user that sends a request to the application. ASP.NET distinctly identifies each of these sessions by sending a unique SessionID to the requesting browser. This SessionID is sent as a cookie or is embedded to the URL depending on the application's configuration.

This mechanism of sending SessionID ensures that when the next request is sent to the server, the server can use the unique SessionID to distinctly identify the repeat visit of the user and both the user visits are considered to belong to the same session.

The capability of uniquely identifying and relating requests can be used by Web developers to store session specific data. A common example is to store the shopping cart contents for the users as they browse through the store. This session specific information is collectively known as the session state of a Web application.

Comparing ASP.NET Session State with ASP

The concept of SessionID and session state is not new to ASP.NET. ASP.NET's predecessor ASP also supported these features. ASP.NET comes with a new implementation of session state that removes all the old problems and provides several enhancements that are equally useful to small and very large Web sites. Table 3.11 compares these improvements.

TABLE 3.11

MANAGING THE SESSION STATE

The ASP Way	*The ASP.NET Way*
ASP maintains the state in the same process that hosts ASP. If the ASP process somehow fails, the session state is lost.	ASP.NET allows you to store session state out-of-process in a state service or in a database.
Each ASP Web server maintains its own session state. This creates a problem in Web Farm scenario where user's request can be dynamically routed to a different server in the Web farm.	Because ASP.NET can store its session state out-of-process, several computers in a Web Farm can use a common computer as their session state server.
ASP session does not work with browsers that don't support cookies or where the users have disabled the cookies.	ASP.NET supports cookie-less sessions by storing the SessionID in the URL itself (if the application is configured to do so).

Moreover, session state in ASP.NET is configurable. Depending on the requirements of your Web application, you can change the way the session state is maintained in your application by just changing a few lines in an XML based configuration file (web.config). You will learn about session state configuration in Chapter 15.

Using Session State

ASP.NET provides access to the session data for the user who originated the request using an instance of the HttpSessionState class. In an ASPX page, this object is accessible through the Session property of the Page class. This property provides access to the HttpSessionState object that stores the session state as a collection of key-value pairs, where the key is a string and the value can be any type derived from System.Object. Tables 3.12 and 3.13 explain the properties and methods of the HttpSessionState class.

TABLE 3.12

PROPERTIES OF HTTPSESSIONSTATE CLASS

Property	*Description*
`CodePage`	Specifies the code page identifier for the current session. This provides compatibility with ASP. `Response.ContentEncoding.CodePage` should be used instead.
`Contents`	Gets a reference to the session state (`HttpSessionState`) object. This provides compatibility with ASP.
`Count`	Gets the number of objects in the session state.
`IsCookieless`	Indicates whether the session is managed using a cookie-less session.
`IsNewSession`	Indicates whether the session has been created with the current request.
`IsReadOnly`	Indicates whether the session is read-only.
`IsSynchronized`	Indicates whether access to the session state is read-only (thread-safe).
`Keys`	Gets a collection of all session keys.
`LCID`	Specifies the locale identifier (LCID) of the current session.
`Mode`	Gets the current session state mode. The values are defined by the `SessionStateMode` enumeration—`Off` (disabled), `InProc` (session state is stored in process with aspnet_wp.exe), `SqlServer` (session state is stored in SQL Server) and `StateServer` (session state stored in state service).
`SessionID`	Represents the unique session identifier used to identify a session.
`StaticObjects`	Gets a collection of objects declared by `<object runat="server" scope="Session">` tags within the ASPX application file `global.asax`.
`SyncRoot`	Gets an object that can be used to synchronize access to the collection of session state values.
`Timeout`	Specifies the timeout period (in minutes) allowed between requests before the session state provider terminates the session.

TABLE 3.13

METHODS OF HTTPSESSIONSTATE CLASS

Property	*Description*
`Abandon`	Cancels the current session.
`Add`	Adds a new object to the session state.
`Clear`	Removes all objects from the session state.
`CopyTo`	Copies the session state values to a single-dimensional array at the specified index.
`GetEnumerator`	Gets an enumerator of all session state values in the current session.
`Remove`	Removes an object from the session state.
`RemoveAll`	Removes all the objects from the session state. Calls `Clear()` method internally.
`RemoveAt`	Removes an object from the session state at a particular index.

Step by Step 3.11 demonstrates the use of session state by upgrading the cookie example that you used in Step by Step 3.8 to maintain the session state at the server side instead of maintaining state at the client side.

STEP BY STEP

3.11 Using Session State

1. Copy the Web Form `StepByStep3-1.aspx` and change its name to `StepByStep3-11.aspx`. Open the ASPX file and the VB file and change all occurrences of `StepByStep3_1` to `StepByStep3_11`. Add a `Label` control named `lblName` to the form.

2. Switch to the code view and modify the `Page_Load()` method as shown here:

```
Private Sub Page_Load( _
 ByVal sender As System.Object, _
 ByVal e As System.EventArgs) Handles MyBase.Load
    If Session("Name") Is Nothing Then
```

```
        ' The Name key is not present in the session
        ' navigate to accept name of the the user
        Response.Redirect("StepByStep3-11a.aspx")
    Else
        ' The Name key is present in the session
        ' display a greeting
        lblName.Text = "Welcome " & _
           Session("Name").ToString()
    End If
    If Not Page.IsPostBack Then
        ' If page is requested for the first time
        ddlCategories.Items.Add("Web development")
        ddlCategories.Items.Add( _
         "Programming Languages")
        ddlCategories.Items.Add("Certifications")
    Else
        ' On postback, change the case of textbox
        txtTitle.Text = txtTitle.Text.ToUpper()
    End If
    ' Set the text of the label
    ' control on each page load
    lblQuestion.Text = _
     "What do you want to write about " & _
    ddlCategories.SelectedItem.Text + " today?"
End Sub
```

3. Double-click the Post `button` control and add the following code in the `Click` event handler:

```
Private Sub btnPost_Click( _
 ByVal sender As System.Object, _
 ByVal e As System.EventArgs) Handles btnPost.Click
    ' Format the data entered by the user and
    ' append it to the existing contents of lblWeblog
    lblWeblog.Text = "<b>" & _
     ddlCategories.SelectedItem.Text & _
    " :: " & txtTitle.Text & ":: by " & _
    Session("Name").ToString() & "</b> (" & _
    DateTime.Now.ToString() & ")<HR>" & _
    txtMessage.Text & "<p>" & _
   lblWeblog.Text
End Sub
```

4. Add a new Web Form to the project. Name the Web Form `StepByStep3-11a.aspx`. Change the `pageLayout` property of `DOCUMENT` element to `FlowLayout`.

5. Add a `Label` control, a `TextBox` control (`txtName`), and a `Button` control (`btnSubmit`) on the Web Form.

6. Double-click the Submit `button` control and add the following code in the `Click` event handler:

continues

continued

```
Private Sub btnSubmit_Click( _
 ByVal sender As System.Object, _
 ByVal e As System.EventArgs) Handles btnSubmit.Click
    ' Add the Name entered in the Session
    ' Redirect the response to the Weblog page
    Session("Name") = txtName.Text
    Response.Redirect("StepByStep3-11.aspx")
End Sub
```

7. Set `StepByStep3-11.aspx` as the start page for the project.

8. Run the project. You see that you have been redirected to `StepByStep3-11a.aspx`. Enter a name and click the Submit button. You'll now see `StepByStep3-11.aspx` page with a personalized greeting. Post a message; you should see that your name is now posted along with the title of the message (refer to Figure 3.9).

9. Close this browser window. Open another browser window and browse to `StepByStep3-11.aspx`. You should see that you have been again redirected to `StepByStep3-11a.aspx` to enter your name information.

Step by Step 3.11 demonstrates that session state is not persistently stored like cookies. The default technique of passing SessionID is with nonpersistent cookies, so this example only works if you are using a cookie-enabled browser. If you instead want to use a cookie-less session, you'll have to modify the web.config file associated with this application to set the cookie-less attribute to true in the <sessionState> element:

```
<?xml version="1.0" encoding="utf-8" ?>
<configuration>
    <system.web>
        <sessionState mode="Inproc" cookieless="true" />
    </system.Web>
</configuration>
```

Application State

Application state is used to store data that is globally used by the application. The application state is stored in memory, and unlike the session state, application state can't be configured for storage on another server or a SQL database. This limits the usefulness of the application state in Web farm scenarios.

Application state can be easily accessed through the Application property of the Page class. This property provides access to the HttpApplicationState object that stores the application state as a collection of key-value pairs, where the key is a string type while value can be any type derived from System.Object. Tables 3.14 and 3.15 discuss the properties and methods of the HttpApplicationState class.

TABLE 3.14

PROPERTIES OF THE HTTPAPPLICATIONSTATE CLASS

Property	*Description*
`AllKeys`	Gets the collection of all the key names in the application state in a string array.
`Contents`	Gets a reference to the application state (`HttpApplicationState`) object. This provides compatibility with ASP.
`Count`	Gets the number of objects in the application state.
`Keys`	Gets the NameObjectCollectionBase.KeysCollection collection of all the key names in the application state.
`StaticObjects`	Gets all objects declared via an `<object runat="server" scope="Application"></object>` tag within the ASP.NET application.

TABLE 3.15

METHODS OF HTTPAPPLICATIONSTATE CLASS

Methods	*Description*
`Add`	Adds a new object to the application state.
`Clear`	Removes all objects from the application state.
`Get`	Gets an object from the application state by key name or index.
`GetKey`	Gets an object from the application state by index.
`Lock`	Locks access to the application state object. This is used to prevent other clients from changing data stored in the application state.
`Remove`	Removes an object from the application state.
`RemoveAll`	Removes all the objects from the application state. Calls `Clear()` method internally.

TABLE 3.15 *continued*

METHODS OF HTTPAPPLICATIONSTATE CLASS

Methods	*Description*
`RemoveAt`	Removes an object from the application state at a particular index.
`Set`	Updates the value of an object stored in the application state.
`Unlock`	Unlocks the access to the application state.

Step by Step 3.12 demonstrates the use of `Application` property to store applicationwide data.

STEP BY STEP

3.12 Using the Application State

1. Add a new Web Form to the project. Name the Web Form `StepByStep3-12.aspx`. Change the `pageLayout` property of the `DOCUMENT` element to `FlowLayout`. Add a `Label` control named `lblInfo` to the Web Form.

2. Switch to the code view and add the following code in the `Page_Load()` event handler:

```
Private Sub Page_Load(ByVal sender As System.Object, _
 ByVal e As System.EventArgs) Handles MyBase.Load
    ' Lock the Application because the
    ' application state value needs to be modified
    Application.Lock()
    If Not Application("HitCount") Is Nothing Then
        ' Increment the HitCount variable
        ' stored in the application state
    Application("HitCount") = _
        CInt(Application("HitCount")) + 1
    Else
        Application("HitCount") = 1
    End If
    ' Unlock the application now
    ' that the changes are done
    Application.UnLock()
    ' Display the hit count of this page by
    ' fetching the value from the HitCount key
    ' in the application state
    lblInfo.Text = "This page has been accessed " & _
        Application("HitCount").ToString() + " times!"
End Sub
```

3. Set `StepByStep3-12.aspx` as the start page for the project.

4. Run the project. You should see that the page shows the number of times it is accessed. Refresh the page and you should see that the page accessed counter increments by 1 as shown in Figure 3.11.

5. Close this browser window. Open another browser window and browse to `StepByStep3-12.aspx`. You should see that the page retains the value of the counter and increments it by 1.

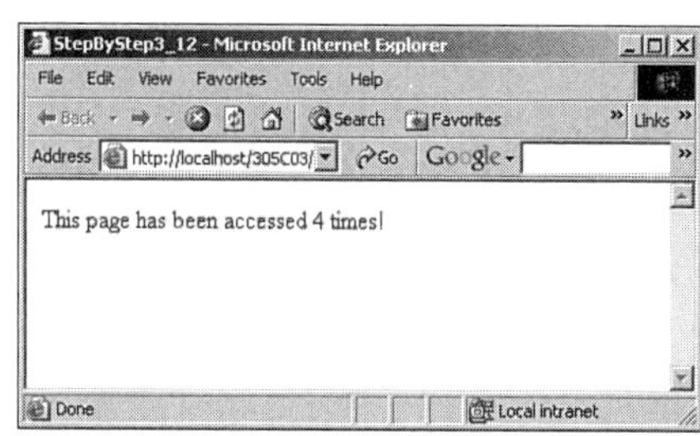

FIGURE 3.11
Application state allows you to store global information.

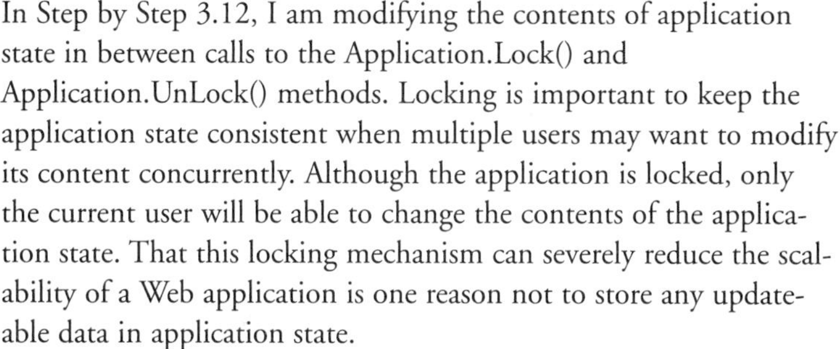

In Step by Step 3.12, I am modifying the contents of application state in between calls to the Application.Lock() and Application.UnLock() methods. Locking is important to keep the application state consistent when multiple users may want to modify its content concurrently. Although the application is locked, only the current user will be able to change the contents of the application state. That this locking mechanism can severely reduce the scalability of a Web application is one reason not to store any updateable data in application state.

In Chapter 15, you'll learn about an alternative way of maintaining global state for an application by using the application data cache. In fact, the application data cache provides all that application state offers and provides several other advanced features such as cache expiration policy. I recommend using application state only when you are migrating ASP applications to ASP.NET and want to write as little new code as possible. In all other cases and for all new ASP.NET application you should use the application data cache as your preferred choice for storing global data.

REVIEW BREAK

- ASP.NET uses a hidden input control named __VIEWSTATE to maintain state for all non-postback controls that are modified in the code. When ASP.NET executes a page, it collects values for all these controls and formats them into a single base64-encoded string. This string is then stored in the __VIEWSTATE control.

continues

- You can use the ViewState property of the Page class to store page level values. The ViewState property allows you to store structured data as long as the data is serializable.
- ViewState is easily configurable. ASP.NET provides configuration schemes for disabling, tamper-proofing, or protecting the contents of the ViewState.
- ASP.NET provides session state to store session specific data for each user. The session state can be scaled to support multiple Web servers in a Web farm with just minor configuration changes.
- ASP.NET provides two ways to store data that is globally used throughout the application. One is Application state and the other is Application data cache. The application data cache provides all that application state offers and also provides several other advanced features such as a cache expiration policy.

NAVIGATION BETWEEN PAGES

A typical Web application is a collection of Web pages linked with each other. In Chapter 2, I discussed the `HyperLink` control that allows a user to navigate to a different Web page when the hyperlink is clicked. However, there is frequently a need to navigate to a Web page programmatically. ASP.NET provides the following methods for programmatically navigating between pages.

- Response.Redirect()
- Server.Transfer()
- Server.Execute()

I'll discuss each of these techniques in turn.

The Response.Redirect() Method

The Response.Redirect() method causes the browser to connect to the specified URL. When the Response.Redirectc) method is called, it creates a response whose header contains a 302 (Object Moved) status code and the target URL. When the browser receives this response from the server, it uses the header information to generate another request to the new URL. When using the Response.Redirect() method, the redirection happens at the client side and involves two round trips to the server.

You should use the Response.Redirect() method in the following cases:

- You want to connect to a resource on *any* Web server.
- You want to connect to a non ASPX resource (such as an HTML file).
- You want to pass the query string as part of the URL.

The Server.Transfer() Method

The Server.Transfer() method transfers the execution from the current ASPX file to the specified ASPX file. The path specified to the ASPX file must be on the same Web server.

When the Server.Transfer() method is called from an executing ASPX page the current ASPX page terminates execution and the control is transferred to another ASPX page. The new ASPX page still uses the response stream created by the prior ASPX page. When this transfer occurs, the URL in the browser still shows the original page because the redirection occurs on the server side and the browser remains unaware of this transfer.

When you want to transfer the control to an ASPX page residing on the same Web server, you should use Server.Transfer() instead of Response.Redirect() because Server.Transfer() will avoid the unnecessary round trip and provide better performance and a better user experience.

The default use of the Server.Transfer() method does not pass the form data and the query string of the original page request to the transferred page. But, you can preserve the form data and query string of the original page by passing a True value to the optional second argument, preserveForm, of the Server.Transfer() method. The second argument takes a Boolean value that indicates whether to preserve form and query string collection.

When you set the second argument to True, you need to be aware of one thing: The destination page uses the same response stream that was created by the original page, and therefore the hidden _VIEWSTATE field of the original page is also preserved in the form collection. The ViewState is page-scoped and is valid for a particular page only. This causes the ASP.NET machine authentication check (MAC) to announce that the ViewState of the new page has been tampered with. Therefore, when you choose to preserve the form and query string collection of the original page, you must set the EnableViewStateMac attribute of the Page directive to false for the destination page.

The Server.Execute() Method

The Server.Execute() method allows the current ASPX page to execute a specified ASPX page. The path to the specified ASPX file must be on the same Web server.

After the specified ASPX page is executed, the control transfers back to the original page from which the Server.Execute() method was called. This technique of page navigation is analogous to making a function call to an ASPX page.

The called ASPX page has access to the form and query string collections of the calling page and thus for the reasons explained in the previous section, you need to set the EnableViewStateMac attribute of the Page directive to false on the executed page.

By default, the output of the executed page is added to the current response stream. This method also has an overloaded version in which the output of the redirected page can be fetched in a TextWriter object instead of adding the output to the response stream. This helps you to control where to place the output in the original page.

> **WARNING**
>
> **Bad HTML Code** The output returned to the browser by the Server.Execute() and Server.Transfer() may contain multiple <html> and <body> tags as the response stream remains the same while executing another ASPX pages. Therefore, the resulting output by calling these methods may contain bad HTML code.

STEP BY STEP

3.13 Using the Response.Redirect(), Server.Transfer(), and Server.Execute() Methods

1. Add a new Web Form named StepByStep3-13.aspx to your project. Add three `Label` controls, a `Literal` control (`litDynamic`), two `TextBox` controls (`txtRows`, `txtCells`) and three `button` controls (`btnTransfer`, `btnExecute`, and `btnRedirect`) to the new Web Form as shown in Figure 3.12.

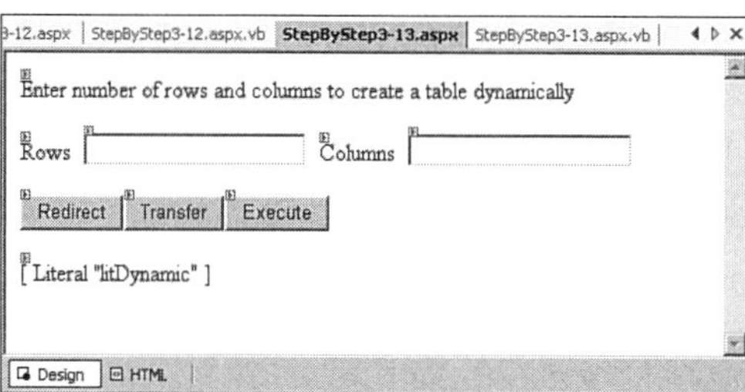

FIGURE 3.12
Design of a form that allows you to specify rows and columns to create a table dynamically.

2. Add a line of code at the top of the Web Form's module:

```
Imports System.IO
```

3. Add code to handle the events of the `Button` controls:

```
Private Sub btnRedirect_Click( _
 ByVal sender As System.Object, _
 ByVal e As System.EventArgs) _
 Handles btnRedirect.Click
    ' Calling Response.Redirect by passing
    ' Rows and Cells values as query strings
    Response.Redirect("StepByStep3-13a.aspx?Rows=" & _
     txtRows.Text + "&Cells=" + txtCells.Text)
End Sub

Private Sub btnTransfer_Click( _
 ByVal sender As System.Object, _
 ByVal e As System.EventArgs) _
 Handles btnTransfer.Click
    ' Writing into Response stream
    Response.Write( _
     "The following table is generated " & _
     "by the StepByStep3-13a.aspx page:")
```

continues

continued

```
    ' Calling the Server.Transfer method
    ' with the second argument set to true
    ' to preserve the form and query string data
    Server.Transfer("StepByStep3-13a.aspx", True)
    ' Control does not come  back here
End Sub

Private Sub btnExecute_Click( _
 ByVal sender As System.Object, _
 ByVal e As System.EventArgs) Handles btnExecute.Click
    ' Creating a StringWriter object
    Dim sw As StringWriter = New StringWriter()
    ' Calling the Server.Execute method by
    ' passing a StringWriter object
    Server.Execute("StepByStep3-13a.aspx", sw)
    ' Control comes back
    ' Displaying the output in the StringWriter
    ' object in a Literal control
    litDynamic.Text = sw.ToString()
End Sub
```

4. Add a new Web Form to the project. Name the Web Form `StepByStep3-13a.aspx`. Change the `pageLayout` property of the `DOCUMENT` element to `FlowLayout`.

5. Add a `Table` control (`tblDynamic`) from the Web Forms tab of the Toolbox on the Web Form.

6. Switch to the HTML view of `StepByStep3_11a.aspx` file and modify the `@Page` directive to add the `EnableViewStateMac="false"` attribute:

```
<%@ Page Language="vb" AutoEventWireup="false"
 Codebehind="StepByStep3-13a.aspx.vb"
 Inherits="_305C03.StepByStep3_13a"
 EnableViewStateMac="false"%>
```

7. Switch to code view and add the following method to the class definition:

```
Private Sub CreateTable(ByVal intRows As Int32, _
 ByVal intCells As Int32)
    ' Create a new table
    Dim trRow As TableRow
    Dim tcCell As TableCell

    ' Iterate for the specified number of rows
    Dim intRow As Integer
    Dim intCell As Integer
    For intRow = 1 To intRows
```

```
        '  Create a row
        trRow = New TableRow()
        If intRow Mod 2 = 0 Then
            trRow.BackColor = Color.LightBlue
        End If
        ' Iterate for the specified number of columns
        For intCell = 1 To intCells
            ' Create a cell in the current row
            tcCell = New TableCell()
            tcCell.Text = "Cell (" & _
             CStr(intRow) & "," & _
             CStr(intCell) & ")"
            trRow.Cells.Add(tcCell)
        Next
        ' Add the row to the table
        tblDynamic.Rows.Add(trRow)
    Next
End Sub
```

8. Add the following code in the `Page_Load()` event handler:

```
Private Sub Page_Load(ByVal sender As System.Object, _
 ByVal e As System.EventArgs) Handles MyBase.Load
    If Not Request.Form("txtRows") Is Nothing Then
        ' If the request contains form data then the
        ' page is called from the Server.Transfer or
        ' Server.Execute method from the
        ' StepByStep3_13.aspx page. Get the Rows and
        ' Cells value from the form collection and
        ' Create a table.
        CreateTable(Int32.Parse( _
         Request.Form("txtRows")), _
            Int32.Parse(Request.Form("txtCells")))
    ElseIf Not Request.QueryString("Rows") _
     Is Nothing Then
        ' If the request contains query string data
        ' that means the response is redirected from
        ' StepByStep3_14.aspx page. Get the Rows and
        ' Cells values from the query string and
        ' Create a table.
        Response.Write("StepByStep3_13a.aspx:")
        CreateTable( _
         Int32.Parse(Request.QueryString("Rows")), _
         Int32.Parse(Request.QueryString("Cells")))
    End If
End Sub
```

9. Set `StepByStep3_13.aspx` as the start page for the project.

continues

continued

10. Run the project. Enter the number of rows and cells and click all three buttons one by one. When you click the Redirect button, the browser is redirected to `StepByStep3-13a.aspx` and passes the rows and cells values as the query string data, as shown in Figure 3.13. When you click the Transfer button, the browser doesn't change the page name in the location bar but the control gets transferred to the `StepByStep3-13a.aspx` page as shown in Figure 3.14. Finally, when you click the Execute button, the `StepByStep3-13a.aspx` page is executed and control comes back to the calling page where the output of `Server.Execute()` method is displayed as shown in Figure 3.15.

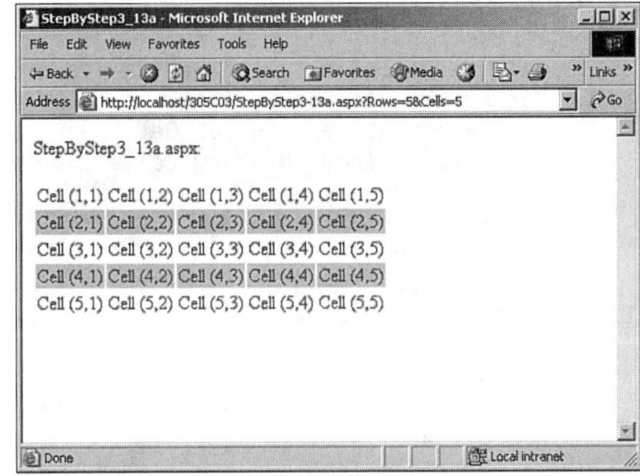

FIGURE 3.13
The Response.Redirect() method can be use to navigate to a URL that contains query strings.

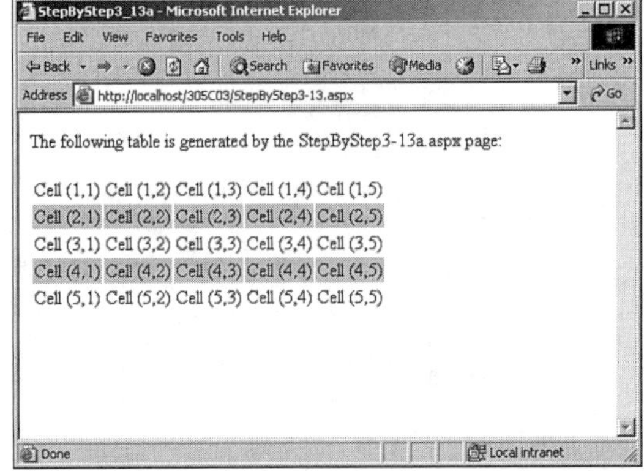

FIGURE 3.14
The Server.Transfer() method is used to navigate to an ASPX page on the same server without causing an additional round trip.

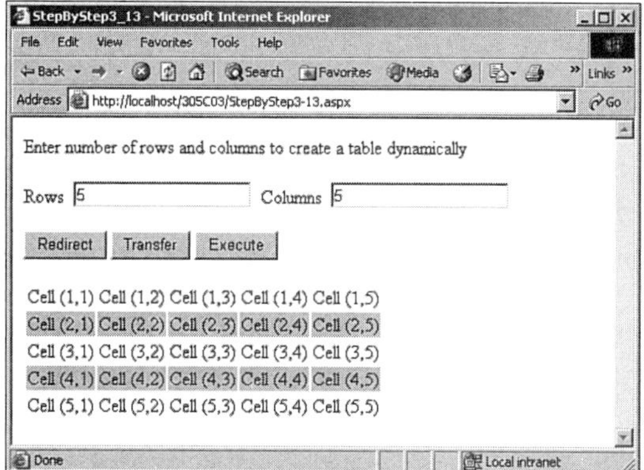

FIGURE 3.15
The Server.Execute() method executes the specified ASPX page and returns the control back to the calling page.

REVIEW BREAK

- The Response.Redirect() method can be used to connect to any specified URL. The specified URL can point to any resource and may also contain query strings. The use of Response.Redirect causes an additional round trip to the server.
- The Server.Transfer() method performs a server-side redirection of a page. The use of Server.Transfer() avoids an extra round trip but only works with an ASPX file residing in the same Web application on the same Web server. Also, when you use the Server.Transfer method, any query string on the original request is not automatically passed to the new page.
- The Server.Execute method is like a function call to an ASPX file. This method executes the specified ASPX file and then returns execution to the calling ASPX page. The file specified as an argument to the Server.Execute() must be an ASPX file residing on the same Web server and the argument should not contain query string data.

CHAPTER SUMMARY

KEY TERMS

- Postback
- Round trip
- Session
- ASP.NET Application

In this chapter, you learned about how to deal with the disconnected nature of Web application by using the state management techniques provided by ASP.NET. In addition to the traditional client-side state management techniques such as query strings, cookies, and hidden variables, ASP.NET provides a new technique called as ViewState. When used carefully, ViewState can give great benefits. However careless use of ViewState can significantly increase the download size of the rendered HTML file.

You also learned about various server side state management techniques. In particular, ASP.NET provides great improvements over the session state of ASP. Session state in ASP.NET is highly configurable. With small configuration changes, you can support Web farms and cookie-less sessions.

I also discussed the various ASP.NET intrinsic objects that can be accessed using the properties of the Page class such as the Request, Response, Session, Application, and Server objects. You experimented with several properties and methods of these objects in this chapter.

I also discussed the Response.Redirect( ), Server.Transfer( ), and Server.Execute( ) methods for implementing navigation from one page to another.

APPLY YOUR KNOWLEDGE

Exercises

3.1 Using Session State to Create a Shopping Cart

Online stores often use session state to maintain information about a user's shopping cart. This allows the site to keep track of a user's selection as he explores the store rather than requiring the user to add all the items at the same time.

In this exercise, you'll use a similar technique to manage a shopping cart. To keep the emphasis on session state, you'll keep the catalog smaller than you'll generally find at most stores.

Estimated time: 10 minutes

1. Create a new Visual Basic ASP.NET Web Application project at the location `http://localhost/305C03Exercises`.
2. Add a Web Form to the project. Name it `ShoppingPage.aspx`.
3. Add three `Label` controls, three `Textbox` controls (`txtNK`, `txtCF`, and `txtHA`) and three `Button` controls (`btnNK`, `btnCF`, and `btnHA`) to a table on the Web Form. Figure 3.16 shows a design for this Web Form.
4. Switch to the code view and add the following code to add selected items and their quantity to the session:

```
' Add the selected item to
' the session state
Private Sub AddToSession( _
 ByVal strProduct As String, _
 ByVal intQty As Integer)
    If Not Session(strProduct) _
     Is Nothing Then
        ' If the product already exist,
        ' increase its quantity
        Session(strProduct) = _
         CInt(Session(strProduct)) + intQty
    Else
        Session(strProduct) = intQty
    End If
End Sub
```

5. Double-click the three `button` controls and add the following code to their `Click` event handlers:

```
Private Sub btnNK_Click( _
 ByVal sender As System.Object, _
 ByVal e As System.EventArgs) _
 Handles btnNK.Click
    ' Add the selected item
    ' to the shopping cart
    AddToSession("NK", _
     Int32.Parse(txtNK.Text))
    ' Display shopping cart
    Server.Transfer("ShoppingCart.aspx")
End Sub

Private Sub btnCF_Click( _
 ByVal sender As System.Object, _
 ByVal e As System.EventArgs) _
 Handles btnCF.Click
    ' Add the selected item
    ' to the shopping cart
    AddToSession("CF", _
     Int32.Parse(txtCF.Text))
    ' Display shopping cart
    Server.Transfer("ShoppingCart.aspx")
End Sub

Private Sub btnHA_Click(
 ByVal sender As System.Object, _
 ByVal e As System.EventArgs) _
 Handles btnHA.Click
    ' Add the selected item
    ' to the shopping cart
    AddToSession("HA", _
     Int32.Parse(txtHA.Text))
    ' Display shopping cart
    Server.Transfer("ShoppingCart.aspx")
End Sub
```

6. Add a new Web Form to the project. Name the Web Form `ShoppingCart.aspx`.

Apply Your Knowledge

7. Drag a `Hyperlink` control (`hlShopping`) to the Web Form. Set its `NavigateUrl` property to `ShoppingPage.aspx`.

8. Switch to the code view and add the following code in the `Page_Load()` event handler:

```
Private Sub Page_Load( _
 ByVal sender As System.Object, _
 ByVal e As System.EventArgs) _
 Handles MyBase.Load
    Response.Write( _
     "The shopping cart contains " & _
     "the following items: <br>")
    ' Display the contents
    ' of the shopping cart
    Dim intI As Integer
    For intI = 0 To Session.Count - 1
        Select Case Session.Keys(intI)
            Case "NK"
                Response.Write( _
                 "New Kandy (" & _
                 Session(intI) & ")" _
                 & "<br>")
            Case "CF"
                Response.Write( _
                 "Chixen Fingerz (" _
                 & Session(intI) & _
                 ")" & "<br>")
            Case "HA"
                Response.Write( _
                 "Hairy Apples (" & _
                 Session(intI) & ")" _
                 & "<br>")
        End Select
    Next
End Sub
```

9. Set `ShoppingPage.aspx` as the start page for the project.

10. Run the project. You'll see a shopping page as shown in Figure 3.16. Enter quantity for a product and click the Add to Cart button. You'll be taken to the shopping cart as shown in Figure 3.17. Add a few more items to this cart, and you'll note that shopping cart remembers your selections.

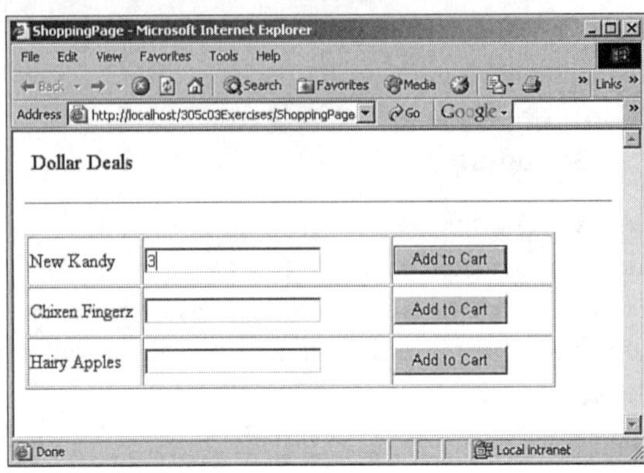

FIGURE 3.16
The Add to Cart button updates the session state with the corresponding item and its quantity.

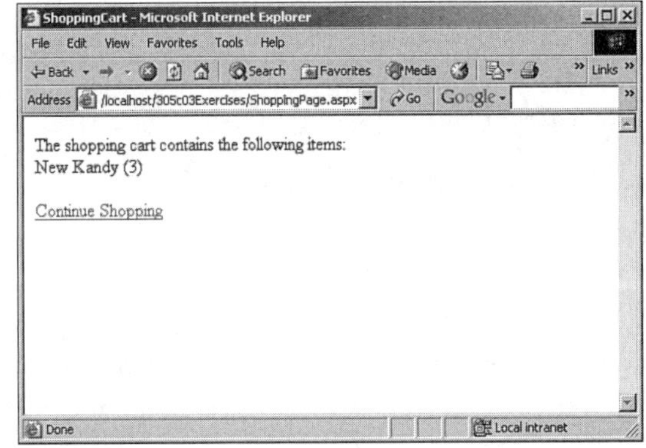

FIGURE 3.17
The shopping cart page summarizse user's selection by retrieving the information from the session state.

3.2 Creating a Wizardlike User Interface

When creating a wizardlike user interface, you need to access the information entered in one page from another page in the wizard.

APPLY YOUR KNOWLEDGE

In a wizardlike interface, all the Web Forms that make up the wizard are accessed in the same HTTP context. You can access this context in any page using the Context property of the Page class. The Context property provides access to the HttpContext object for the current request.

The HttpContext object gives access to all the information about the current HTTP request. It exposes an Items collection, in which you can add values that will be available for the life of the current request. The Page class contains a property called Context that provides access to the HttpContext object for the current request.

In this exercise, I'll show you how to use the Items collection of the HttpContext object to retrieve values from previous pages of a wizard.

Estimated time: 10 minutes

1. Add a Web Form to the project. Name it `Magazine1.aspx`.
2. Drag two `Label` controls, a `TextBox` control (`txtCode`) and a `Button` control (`btnCode`) to the Web Form.
3. Switch to the code view of the form. Add the following code in the class definition:

```
' Declaring a Code property to expose
' the txtCode control's value
Public ReadOnly Property Code() As String
    Get
        Code = txtCode.Text
    End Get
End Property
```

4. Double-click the `Button` control and add the following code in the `Click` event handler:

```
Private Sub btnCode_Click( _
 ByVal sender As System.Object, _
 ByVal e As System.EventArgs) _
 Handles btnCode.Click
    ' Adding the Code to the
    ' Items collection of the
    ' HttpContext object for
    ' the current request
    Context.Items.Add("Code", txtCode.Text)
    ' Calling the Server.Transfer method
    Server.Transfer("Magazine2.aspx")
End Sub
```

5. Add another Web Form to the project. Name it `Magazine2.aspx`.
6. Drag two `Label` controls, two `TextBox` controls (`txtName` and `txtAddress`) and a `Button` control (`btnFinish`) to the Web Form (see Figure 3.19).
7. Add the following code in the `Page_Load()` event handler:

```
Private Sub Page_Load( _
 ByVal sender As System.Object, _
 ByVal e As System.EventArgs) _
 Handles MyBase.Load
    If Not IsPostBack Then
        ' Fetch the Code value from the
        ' HttpContext object
        ' of the current request
        Dim strCode As String = _
         Context.Items("Code").ToString()
        Response.Write( _
         "Priority Code: " & strCode)
    End If
End Sub
```

8. Set the `Magazine1.aspx` page as the start page of the project.
9. Run the project. You will see the first page of the wizard as shown in Figure 3.18. Enter some text in the text box and click the Next button. You can see that the second page can retrieve the information entered in the first page of the wizard (see Figure 3.19).

APPLY YOUR KNOWLEDGE

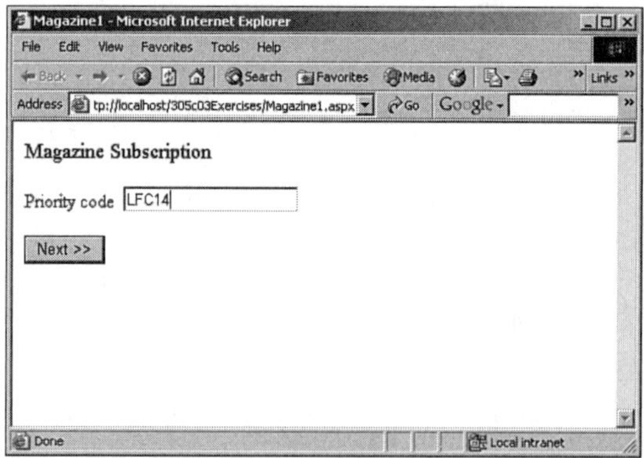

FIGURE 3.18
The first page of the wizard publishes its properties to another page by adding it to the HttpContext.Items collection.

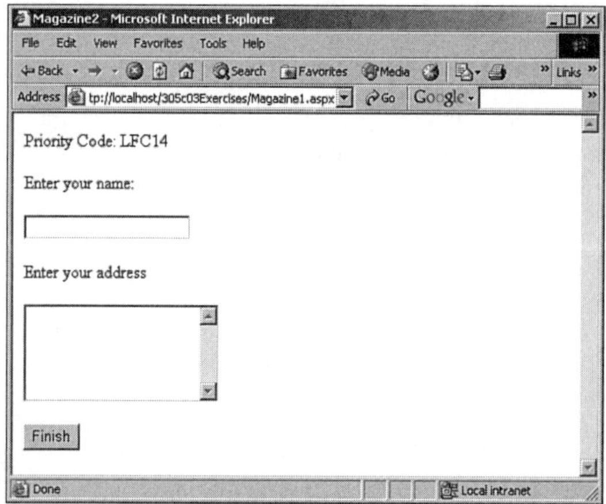

FIGURE 3.19
The second page of the wizard fetches the value of the first page in the wizard through the HttpContext.Items collection.

Review Questions

1. What is a postback? How can you determine when a postback occurs in an ASP.NET page?
2. What file do you use to handle Session and Application level events?
3. What are the classes mapped to the Response, Request, Server, Application, and Session properties of the Page class?
4. What are the client-side techniques available for state management?
5. What are the benefits of using ViewState in ASP.NET?
6. What can you achieve by setting the EnableViewStateMac property to true?
7. What is the difference between the client-side and the server-side state management techniques?
8. What type of data can be stored in session state and in application state?
9. When would you store an object in the session state instead of the application state?
10. What methods can be called to perform server-side redirection to an ASPX page?

Exam Questions

1. You are developing a Web Form to display weather information. On the initial requests to the Web Form, you need to do some initialization that will change the appearance of the form and assign values to some controls. However, this initialization should not be repeated again when the user submits the Web Form. Where should you put the code? (Select two.)

   A. In the Page_Init() method.

   B. In the Page_Load() method.

APPLY YOUR KNOWLEDGE

C. Execute the initialization code only when the Page.IsPostBack property is true.

D. Execute the initialization code only when the Page.IsPostBack property is false.

2. You have used ASP.NET to develop an inventory management system for your organization. Associates can access this application from the company's intranet. When analyzing users' feedback about the application, you found that users complain that they receive an annoying flash when they submit forms. They also complain that the data entry form sometimes does not remember the active controls and because of this, they have to press the Tab key several times before they can focus again on the desired control; this makes the data entry inconvenient and time-consuming. On analyzing further usage data, you found that all the users in your company use Internet Explorer 5.5 or above to access your application. What should you do to eliminate the problems reported by the users?

   A. Set SmartNavigation to true.

   B. Set AutoEventWireup to true.

   C. Set EnableViewState to true.

   D. Set ClientTarget to "ie5".

3. You are developing an ASP.NET Web site for a popular Web development magazine. You want to keep track of how many times each page of your Web application is accessed. This data will help your company to analyze the usage pattern and develop appropriate content. You want to write the minimum code to achieve this task; which of the following techniques will you use?

   A. Use the Page_Load() method to increment the usage counter of the page.

   B. Use the Application_BeginRequest() method to increment the usage counter of the page.

   C. Use the Session_Start() method to increment the usage counter of the page.

   D. Use the Application_Start() method to increment the usage counter of the page.

4. You are designing a Web application for a multinational company. When users access the Web site, they should be automatically redirected to a page specific to their country. Your colleague has developed a method that determines the user's country from the HTTP Request and does the redirection. Where should you call this method in your application?

   A. Session_Start() method of the global.asax file

   B. Begin_Request() method of the global.asax file

   C. Page_Load() method of the default.aspx file

   D. Application_Start()method of the global.asax file

5. Your ASP.NET page contains a page-level ArrayList variable. You want to preserve the value of this variable across page postbacks. You do not need this variable in any other page in the application, which of the following state management techniques provides you the best way to achieve this?

   A. Query strings

   B. Cookies

   C. Session

   D. ViewState

APPLY YOUR KNOWLEDGE

6. You are developing a Web application for an online bank. Your application allows users to access account information and transactions right from their desktops. When the user logs on to your application, you want to show the username and current balance on all the pages of the application, until the user logs off. You want your application to be safe from malicious users. Which of the following state management techniques should you use?

   A. Cookies

   B. ViewState

   C. ViewState with encryption

   D. Session

7. You are developing an online retail store using ASP.NET. Users can freely access the catalogs and add items to the shopping cart. Users are only required to log on to the Web site when they are ready to check out. However, you want to remember users' names and greet the users on their future visits to the retail store. Which of the following state management techniques helps you accomplish this?

   A. Hidden fields

   B. ViewState

   C. Cookies

   D. Session

8. You have developed and deployed a Web application for an online bank. This application allows users to access their account information and transactions right from their desktops. Because the application deals with financial data, you have enabled encryption for ViewState of all the pages. The bank business rapidly increased and the management decided to upgrade the single Web server to a Web Farm of Web servers. When you were testing the application for the Web Form, sometimes the application worked fine while other times it generated a ViewState error. What should you do to resolve this problem?

   A. Use same validation key for all the Web servers in the Web farm.

   B. Use different validation key for all the Web servers in the Web farm.

   C. Set EnableViewStateMac attribute to True for all the pages in the application.

   D. Set EnableViewStateMac attribute to False for all the pages in the application.

9. You have recently developed and deployed a Web application for a large automotive parts supplier. This application is used by users in the United States, and from several countries Europe, and Asia. You have received complaints from several users that the Web pages take very long to download. You did some research and found that an HTML element named __VIEWSTATE in your pages is storing a large amount of data and is responsible for bigger page sizes. Your manager recommended that you disable ViewState where ever it is not needed in the application. In which of the following cases can you safely disable ViewState in your application? (Select three.)

   A. Those pages that do not post back.

   B. Those pages that post back.

   C. Those controls that are not dynamically changed.

   D. Those controls that are dynamically changed.

APPLY YOUR KNOWLEDGE

E. Those controls are modified at every page load.

F. Those controls that are not modified at every page load.

10. You have recently developed and deployed a Web application for a large automotive parts supplier. This application is used by users from the United States, and several countries in Europe, and Asia. You have received complaints from several users that the Web pages take very long to download. You did some research and found that an HTML element named __VIEWSTATE in your pages is storing a large amount of data and is responsible for bigger page sizes. You have also found that some of your pages do not use ViewState. You want to do minimum modification to the code. How would you disable ViewState for such pages?

    A. Set the EnableViewState property for all the Web server controls to false.

    B. Set the EnableViewState attribute of the @Page directive to false.

    C. Set the EnableViewStateMac attribute of the @Page directive to false.

    D. Set the EnableViewState attribute to false for the <Pages> element in the web.config file.

11. In a Web page of your application, you allow users to select a product and its quantity. When the user has finished making selections, you want to transfer them to another page named "ShoppingCart.aspx" with the ProductId and Quantity as the query string parameters to the ASPX page. Which of the following methods would you use in your code to accomplish this?

    A. HyperLink control

    B. Response.Redirect() method

    C. Server.Transfer() method

    D. Server.Execute() method

12. You are using a DataGrid control in a Web Form "ShowData.aspx" of your Web application. You want to invoke another ASP.NET page "GetData.aspx" which returns the data to be displayed in the DataGrid control. Which of the following method would you use to invoke "GetData.aspx" from "ShowData.aspx"?

    A. HyperLink control

    B. Response.Redirect() method

    C. Server.Transfer() method

    D. Server.Execute() method

13. You are developing an online bill payment system using ASP.NET. When a user logs on to the application by entering her user name and password, you want to programmatically redirect the user to a page named accountdetails.aspx in the same Web application. You want an application that responds quickly to the users. Which of the following methods would you use to accomplish this?

    A. HyperLink control

    B. Response.Redirect() method

    C. Server.Transfer() method

    D. Server.Execute() method

14. You are using a DataGrid control in an ASP.NET page "ShowData.aspx" of your Web application. You want to invoke another ASP.NET page "GetData.aspx" which returns the data to be displayed in the DataGrid control. You are using Server.Execute() method to invoke "GetData.aspx" from "ShowData.aspx" page.

APPLY YOUR KNOWLEDGE

When you run the application, you get an Invalid ViewState error. Which option would you choose to resolve this error?

A. Use the Server.Transfer( ) method instead of the Server.Execute( ) method.

B. Set the EnableViewStateMac attribute to false in the @Page directive of GetData.aspx.

C. Set the EnableViewStateMac attribute to false in the @Page directive of ShowData.aspx.

E. Set the EnableViewState attribute to false in the @Page directive of GetData.aspx.

15. You are creating a Web site that allows users to create online communities to interact with their friends and families. The creation of a community requires a user to register with the Web site. You have created a user registration wizard that allows users to enter registration information in a step-by-step manner. The wizard consists of four ASPX files. You want all the data entered by a user in the first three ASPX files to be available in the fourth file. For security reasons, you are not allowed to disable the ViewState machine authentication check in your ASP.NET pages. Which of the following options would you use? (Select two.)

    A. For each screen add the collected data to Context.Items collection and retrieve the information from this collection in the last ASPX page.

    B. Use the Request.Form collection in the last ASPX page to retrieve the information entered by the user.

    C. Use the Server.Transfer() method to transfer the control from one wizard page to the next wizard page.

    D. Use the Server.Execute() method to transfer the control from one wizard page to the next wizard page.

Answers to Review Questions

1. When a user submits the form to the Web server, it is called a postback. The Page.IsPostBack property, when True, indicates that the page is loaded as a result of postback from the client.

2. The ASP.NET application file global.asax contains event handlers to handle Session and Application level events.

3. The classes that map to the Response, Request, Server, Application, and Session properties of the Page class are HttpResponse, HttpRequest, HttpServerUtility, HttpApplicationState, and HttpSessionState, respectively.

4. You can use Query strings, cookies, hidden fields, and ViewState for managing state at the client-side.

5. ViewState provides the following benefits:

    - It maintains the state of non-postback controls in a page across page postbacks.
    - You can store any object in the ViewState as long as it is serializable.
    - You can customize ViewState to enable protection and encryption.

6. When the EnableViewStateMac property is set to True, ASP.NET performs a machine authentication check (MAC) on the ViewState during postback to verify that the ViewState has not been tampered with at the client-side.

APPLY YOUR KNOWLEDGE

7. The client-side state management techniques consume client resources to manage state where as the server-side techniques consume server resources to manage state.
8. Any object that inherits from System.Object directly or indirectly by chain of its inheritance, can be stored in session state or application state.
9. When you need to store an object that does not apply to all the users of the application but only to specific users then you should choose session state instead of the application state to store the object.
10. Server.Transfer() and Server.Execute().

Answers to Exam Questions

1. **B** and **D.** The code for initialization of controls should be placed inside the Page_Load() method. If you want to execute the initialization code only when the page is first requested and do not want to run that code again at the time of page post-back then you must execute the code when the IsPostBack property of the Page class is false.
2. **A.** When all users are using Internet Explorer Versions 5.5 or later, you can set the SmartNavigation property to true. This will eliminate the flash and will cause Internet Explorer to focus active control.
3. **B.** Options C and D do not work with each page request, so only options A and B are the viable choices. Among these two choices, you should choose to write the code in the Application_BeginRequest() method of the global.asax file because if you use the Page_Load() method, you'll have to write code in each and every ASPX file in the application.
4. **A.**When a user visits the site, a browser establishes a new session with the Web server. At that time the Session_Start() method is executed. This method is executed only once for the user session and is an appropriate choice for the case in question. Page_Load() may not work in all cases because users might come to your Web site by clicking a link of some other file. Begin_Request() work for the entire HTTP request and not just the first request. Application_Start() method will only redirect the first user of the application.
5. **D.** Because the variable is only required on a single page, you may not want to consume server resources by storing the values in session. You can instead use a client-side technique for state management, but cookies and hidden fields do not allow you to stored structured data. Therefore, the best option is to use ViewState.
6. **D.** Cookies can be easily accessed and used by malicious users. ViewState with encryption does provide a high level of encryption but is only available on the same page. In the application, you want the name and current balance to be displayed on all the pages, so the correct choice is session. Sessions are stored at the server side and cannot be easily tampered with.
7. **C.** You want the information to be available across browser restarts. In this case, cookies are the right choice because they allow you to store small amount of information the user's computer.
8. **A.** When you use ViewState encryption in a Web farm, you must use the same validation key for all the Web servers. If the validation keys don't match, you will get an error when the user is directed to a different server in the Web farm.

APPLY YOUR KNOWLEDGE

9. **A, C, and E.** If the pages don't postback to themselves, they are not using ViewState; in that case, it's a good idea to disable ViewState for the whole of the page. For all other pages, the controls that are not dynamically changed need not have their ViewState enabled. Also, the controls whose value is modified at every page load need not store value in the ViewState.

10. **B.** Setting EnableViewState property for all the Web server controls to false does the trick but involves a lot of coding. An option that requires lesser code is to set the EnableViewState attribute of the @Page directive to false. Changing EnableViewState to false in web.config file will affect all the pages in the Web application, not just the one which use ViewState and is not recommended in the given case.

11. **B.** Query strings are not automatically passed with the Server.Transfer() and Server.Execute() methods. Hyperlink control does accept query strings but not when they are dynamically created as in the above question therefore the best choice is the use of Response.Redirect() method.

12. **D.** Only Server.Execute() method works like a function call. That is invoking the specified page and returns the control back to the original page.

13. **C.** Response.Redirect() involves additional round trips and therefore is not a good option when you want the application to be responsive at each level. You should instead use Server.Transfer() method to redirect your user to another ASPX page on the same Web server.

14. **B.** You get an error while executing Server.Execute() method because the ViewState of "ShowData.aspx" page is passed to "GetData.aspx" page causing the ASP.NET machine authentication check to fail. You need set EnableViewState attribute of the @Page directive in the "GetData.aspx" page to false in order to resolve this error.

15. **A** and **C.** You should use Context.Items to accumulate data from the previous pages, because neither the Server.Transfer() method nor the Server.Execute() method preserves the form data by default. When choosing between Server.Transfer() and Server.Execute(), you need Server.Transfer() in the case mentioned in the question as you'll progress from one page to another.

Suggested Readings and Resources

1. *The Visual Studio .NET Combined Help Collection*, including the following:
   - *Introduction to Web Forms State Management*
   - *Web Forms Page Processing*
2. ASP.NET/Visual Studio .NET Tips. `http://www.swarren.net`
3. Fritz Onion. *Essential ASP.NET.* Addison-Wesley, 2002
4. Jeff Prosise. *Programming Microsoft .NET.* Microsoft Press, 2002

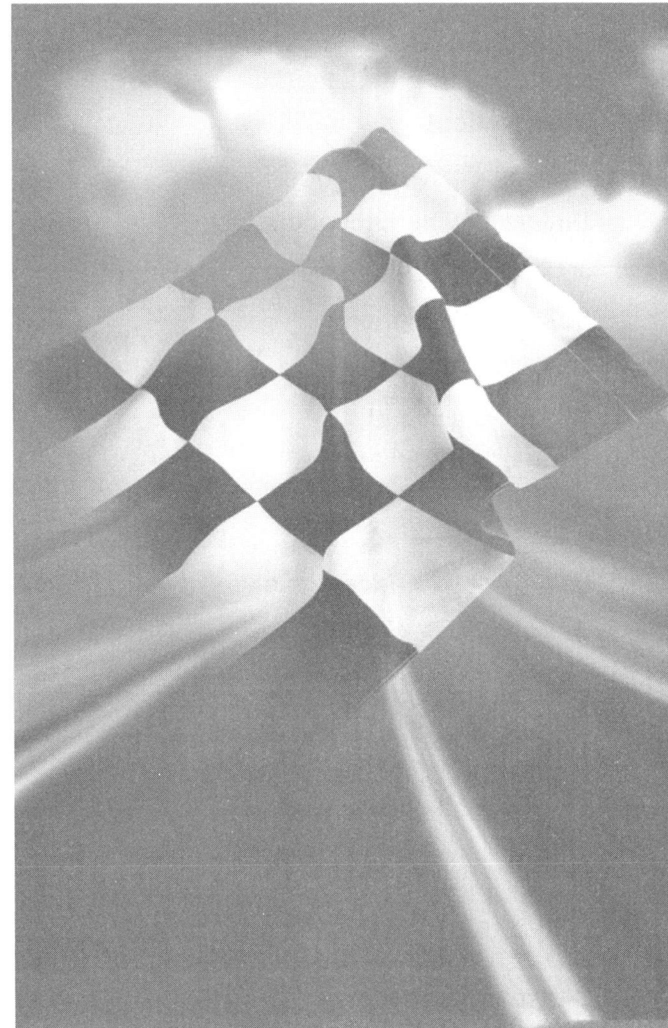

CHAPTER 4

Error Handling for the User Interface

OBJECTIVES

This chapter covers the following Microsoft-specified objectives for the Creating User Services section of the exam 70-305 [Developing and Implementing Web-based Applications with Microsoft Visual Basic .NET and Microsoft Visual Studio .NET]:

Implement error handling in the user interface.

- **Configure custom error pages.**
- **Implement global.asax, application, page-level, and page event error handling.**

▶ When you run a Web application, it might encounter problems that should not occur in the normal course of operations. For example, a database server may be down, a file might be missing, or a user may enter nonsensical values. A good Web application must recover gracefully from these problems rather than abruptly terminating the page execution. The Microsoft .NET Framework provides structured exception handling through the use of try, catch, and finally blocks to help you catch these exceptional situations in your programs. There are predefined exception classes to represent different types of exceptions. You can also define your own exception handling classes and error messages that are specific to your own application.

▶ Exceptions that are not handled by structured exception handling are called unhandled exceptions. When such errors are unhandled, the Web page displays the raw error messages to the user. This is not user-friendly (and may be a source of a security leak). The .NET Framework allows you to create custom error pages to be displayed to the user. These custom error pages can be configured at both the Page and Application level. Objects such as the Page or Application object have an Error event that can be a suitable place to trap unmanaged errors.

Outline

Study Strategies

- Review the "Exception Handling Statements" and the "Best Practices for Exception Handling" sections of the Visual Studio .NET Combined Help Collection. This Collection is installed as a part of the Visual Studio .NET installation.
- Experiment with code that uses Try, Catch, and Finally blocks. Use these blocks with various combinations and inspect the differences in your code's output.
- Know how to create custom exception classes and custom error messages in your program.
- Know how to configure custom error pages in the web.config file. Learn how to create a default error page for the application and some different error pages for various types of HTTP error codes.
- Experiment with code that performs error handling in the Page_Error or Application_Error events. Learn how to get the details of the error that occurred most recently in an application.

INTRODUCTION

Exception handling is an integral part of the .NET Framework. The framework classes as well as user-defined classes throw `Exception` objects to indicate unexpected problems in the code.

The Framework Class Library provides a huge set of exception classes representing various unforeseen conditions in the normal execution environment. If you feel the need to create custom exception classes to meet the specific requirements of your application, you can do so by deriving a class from the ApplicationException class. An exception can be explicitly generated using the Throw statement.

This chapter introduces the Try-Catch-Finally syntax that helps you in catching Exception objects to recover from error situations. Exceptions that are not handled by a Try-Catch block are called unhandled exceptions. When errors are unhandled, the Web page that caused the error displays the error messages to the user. The .NET Framework also allows you to create custom user-friendly error pages to be displayed to the user rather than the default error messages pages being displayed. These custom error pages can be configured at both the Page and Application levels.

You can trap unhandled exceptions at the level of objects including Page and Application. The Page_Error event handler can be used to trap unhandled exceptions in a page, whereas the Application_Error event handler can be used to trap unhandled exceptions thrown by all the Web pages of an application.

UNDERSTANDING EXCEPTIONS

An exception occurs when a program encounters any unexpected problems, such as running out of memory or attempting to read from a file that no longer exists. These problems are not necessarily caused by a programming error, but mainly occur due to the violation of an assumption that you might have made about the execution environment.

When a program encounters an exception, the default behavior is to stop processing and return an error message. This is not a characteristic of a robust application and it will not make your program popular among users. Your program should be able to handle exceptional situations and if possible gracefully recover from them.

This is called exception handling. The proper use of exception handling can make your programs robust, easy to develop, and easy to maintain. If you do not use exception handling properly, you might end up having a program that performs poorly, is harder to maintain, and may potentially mislead its users.

Step By Step 4.1 demonstrates how an exception may occur in your program. I will later explain how to handle these exceptions.

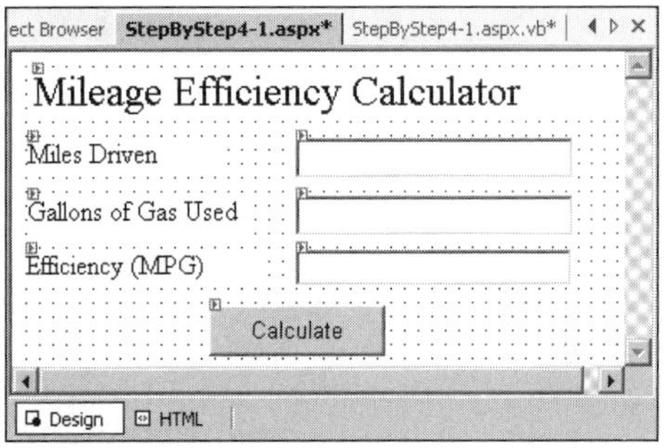

FIGURE 4.1
Design of the Mileage Efficiency Calculator form.

STEP BY STEP

4.1 Exception in a Web Application

1. Create a new Visual Basic ASP.NET Web Application project.
2. Add a new Web Form to the project. Name it `StepByStep4-1.aspx`.
3. Place three `TextBox` controls (`txtMiles`, `txtGallons`, and `txtEfficiency`) and a `Button` (`btnCalculate`) on the Web Form's surface and arrange them as shown in Figure 4.1. Add the label controls as necessary.
4. Add the following code to the `Click` event handler of `btnCalculate`:

```
Private Sub btnCalculate_Click( _
 ByVal sender As System.Object, _
 ByVal e As System.EventArgs) _
 Handles btnCalculate.Click
    ' This code has no error checking. If something
    ' goes wrong at run time,
    ' it will throw an exception.
    Dim decMiles As Decimal = _
     Convert.ToDecimal(txtMiles.Text)
    Dim decGallons As Decimal = _
     Convert.ToDecimal(txtGallons.Text)
    Dim decEfficiency As Decimal = _
     decMiles / decGallons
    txtEfficiency.Text = _
     String.Format("{0:n}", decEfficiency)
End Sub
```

5. Set the Web Form as the start page for the project.

6. Run the project in Debug mode. Enter values for miles and gallons and click the Calculate button. The form calculates the mileage efficiency as expected. Now enter the value `0` in the gallons field and run the program. The program abruptly terminates by displaying error details in the Web page as shown in Figure 4.2.

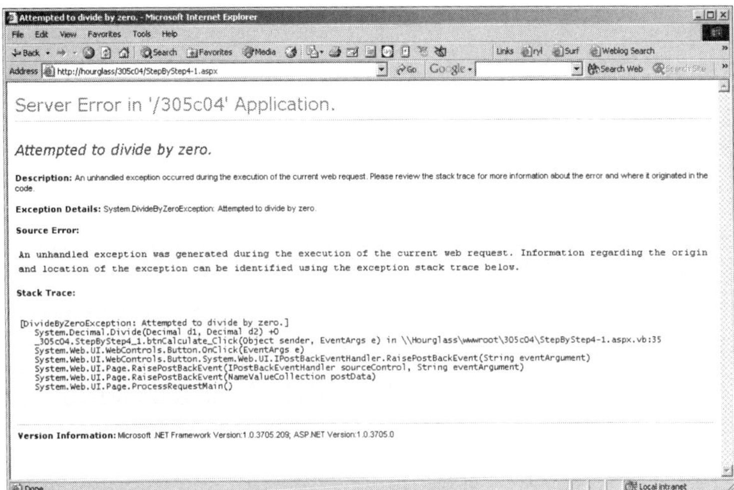

FIGURE 4.2
`DivideByZeroException` thrown in Debug mode.

When you run the program in debug mode and the program throws an exception, the Web page displays a detailed error. This is the default behavior of ASP.NET when the machine accessing the page is the Web server itself. If instead the page were accessed from a remote client, the default behavior of ASP.NET is to hide the details, as shown in Figure 4.3. If you need to see full error details from a remote browser, you can edit the customErrors mode setting in the projects web.config file to set the mode to "Off."

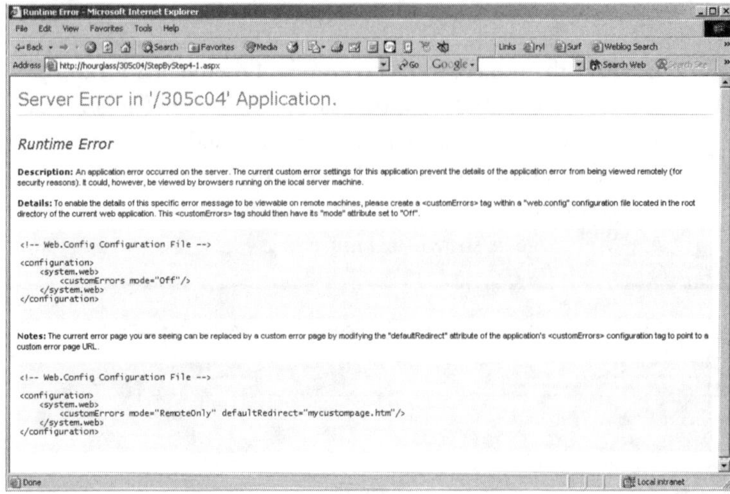

FIGURE 4.3
Details of the error are hidden from remote browsers.

The Common Language Runtime (CLR) views an exception as an object that encapsulates any information about the problems that occurred during program execution. The Framework Class Library (FCL) provides two categories of exceptions:

1. *ApplicationException*: Represents the exceptions thrown by the user programs.
2. *SystemException*: Represents the exceptions thrown by the CLR.

Both of these exception classes derive from the base Exception class. The Exception class implements the common functionality for exception handling. Neither the ApplicationException class nor the SystemException class adds any new functionality to the Exception class. These classes exist just to differentiate exceptions in user programs from exceptions in the CLR. Table 4.1 lists the important properties of all three of these classes.

TABLE 4.1

IMPORTANT MEMBERS OF THE EXCEPTION CLASS

Property	*Description*
`HelpLink`	A URL to the help file associated with this exception.
`InnerException`	Specifies an exception associated with this exception. This property is helpful when a series of exceptions are involved. Each new exception can preserve the information about the previous exception by storing it in the `InnerException` property.

Property	*Description*
`Message`	Textual information that specifies the reason for the error and possibly provides a way to resolve it.
`Source`	The name of the application that causes the error.
`StackTrace`	Specifies where an error occurred. If the debugging information is available, the stack trace includes the source file name and program line number.
`TargetSite`	The method that threw the current exception.

HANDLING EXCEPTIONS

Abruptly terminating the program when an exception occurs is not a good idea. Your application should be able to handle the exception and (if possible) try to recover from it. If recovery is not possible you may take other steps, such as notifying the user and then gracefully terminating the application.

The .NET Framework allows exception handling to interoperate among languages and across machines. You can throw an exception in code written in VB.NET and catch it in code written in C#, for example. In fact, the .NET framework also allows you to handle exceptions thrown by legacy COM applications and legacy non–COM Win32 applications.

Exception handling is such an integral part of .NET Framework that when you look up a method in the product documentation, there will always be a section specifying what exceptions a call to that method might throw.

You can handle exceptions in Visual Basic .NET programs by using a combination of the exception handling statements: `Try`, `Catch`, `Finally`, and `Throw`. In this section of the chapter I'll show you how these statements are used.

The Try Block

You should place the code that may cause exception in a `Try` block. A typical `Try` block will look like this:

```
Try
    ' Code that may cause an exception
End Try
```

You can place any valid Visual Basic .NET statements inside a `Try` block. Such statements might include another `Try` block or a call to a method that places some of its statement inside a `Try` block. Thus at runtime you might have a hierarchy of Try blocks placed inside each other. When an exception occurs at any point, the CLR searches for the nearest `Try` block that encloses this code. The CLR then passes control of the application to a matching `Catch` block (if any) and then to the Finally block associated with this `Try` block.

A `Try` block cannot exist on its own; it must be immediately followed either by one or more `Catch` blocks or by a `Finally` block.

The Catch Block

> NOTE
>
> **Exception Handling Hierarchy** If there is no matching Catch block for a particular exception, that exception becomes an unhandled exception. The unhandled exception is propagated back to the code that called the current method. If the exception is not handled there, it propagates farther up the hierarchy of method calls. If the exception is not handled anywhere, it goes to the CLR for processing. The CLR's default behavior is to terminate the program immediately.

You can have several `Catch` blocks immediately following a `Try` block. Each `Catch` block handles an exception of a particular type. When an exception occurs in a statement placed inside of a `Try` block, the CLR looks for a matching `Catch` block that is capable of handling that type of exception. The formula that CLR uses to match the exception is simple. It looks for the first `Catch` block with either an exact match for the exception or for any of the exception's base classes. For example, a DivideByZeroException matches with any of these exceptions: DivideByZeroException, ArithmeticException, SystemException, and Exception (progressively more general classes from which DivideByZeroException is derived). In the case of multiple `Catch` blocks, only the first matching `Catch` block is executed. All other `Catch` blocks are ignored.

When you write multiple `Catch` blocks, you need to arrange them from specific exception types to more general exception type. For example, the `Catch` block for catching DivideByZeroException should always precede the `Catch` block for catching ArithmeticException. This is because the DivideByZeroException derives from ArithmeticException and is therefore more specific then the latter. You'll get a compiler error if you do not follow this rule.

A `Try` block need not necessarily have a `Catch` block associated with it, but in that case it must have a `Finally` block associated with it.

STEP BY STEP

4.2 Handling Exceptions

1. Add a new Web Form to the project.

2. Create a form similar to the one created in Step By Step 4.1 (see Figure 4.1) with the same names for controls. Add a `Label` control (`lblMessage`) to the form.

3. Add the following code to the `Click` event handler of `btnCalculate`:

```
Private Sub btnCalculate_Click( _
 ByVal sender As System.Object, _
 ByVal e As System.EventArgs) _
 Handles btnCalculate.Click
    ' Put all the code that may require graceful error
    ' recovery in a try block
    Try
        Dim decMiles As Decimal = _
         Convert.ToDecimal(txtMiles.Text)
        Dim decGallons As Decimal = _
         Convert.ToDecimal(txtGallons.Text)
        Dim decEfficiency As Decimal = _
         decMiles / decGallons
        txtEfficiency.Text = _
         String.Format("{0:n}", decEfficiency)
        ' try block should at least have
        ' one catch or a finally block
        ' catch block should be in order
        ' of specific to the generalized
        ' exceptions otherwise compilation
        ' generates an error
    Catch fe As FormatException
        Dim msg As String = String.Format( _
         "Message: {0} Stack Trace: {1}", _
            fe.Message, fe.StackTrace)
        lblMessage.Text = fe.GetType().ToString() + _
         "<br>" + msg
    Catch dbze As DivideByZeroException
        Dim msg As String = String.Format( _
         "Message: {0} Stack Trace: {1}", _
            dbze.Message, dbze.StackTrace)
        lblMessage.Text = _
         dbze.GetType().ToString() + _
         "<br>" + msg
        ' catches all CLS-complaint exceptions
```

continues

continued

```
        Catch ex As Exception
            Dim msg As String = String.Format( _
             "Message: {0} Stack Trace: {1}", _
                ex.Message, ex.StackTrace)
            lblMessage.Text = ex.GetType().ToString() + _
             "<br>" + msg
            ' catches all other exception including
            ' the NON-CLS complaint exceptions
        Catch
            ' just rethrow the exception to the caller
            Throw
        End Try
    End Sub
```

4. Set the Web Form as the start page for the project.

5. Run the project. Enter values for miles and gallons and click the Calculate button. The form calculates the mileage efficiency as expected. Now enter the value `0` in the gallons field and run the program. You will see that instead of abruptly terminating and showing the error page (as in the earlier example), the program shows a message about a `DivideByZeroException` (as shown in Figure 4.4) and continues running. Now enter some alphabetic characters in the fields instead of numbers and click the Calculate button. This time you get a `FormatException` message and the program continues to run. Now try entering a large value for both the fields. If the values are large enough the program encounters an `OverflowException`, but because the program is catching all types of exceptions, it continues running.

EXAM TIP

CLS and Non-CLS Compliant Exceptions All languages that follow the Common Language Specification (CLS) throw exceptions with a type of System.Exception, or a type that derives from System.Exception. A language that is not CLS compliant might throw exceptions of other types as well. You can catch those types of exceptions by placing a general `Catch` block (one that does not specify any exception) within a `Try` block. In fact, a general `Catch` block can catch exceptions of all types, so it is most generic of all `Catch` blocks. This means that it should be the last `Catch` block among the multiple `Catch` blocks associated with a `Try` block.

The program in Step By Step 4.2 displays a message when an exception occurs. The `StackTrace` property lists the methods that led up to the exception in the reverse order of their calling sequence. This helps you in understanding the flow of logic of the program. In a real application you might choose to try to automatically fix the exceptions as well.

When you write a `Catch` block that catches exceptions of the general `Exception` type, it catches all CLS-compliant exceptions.

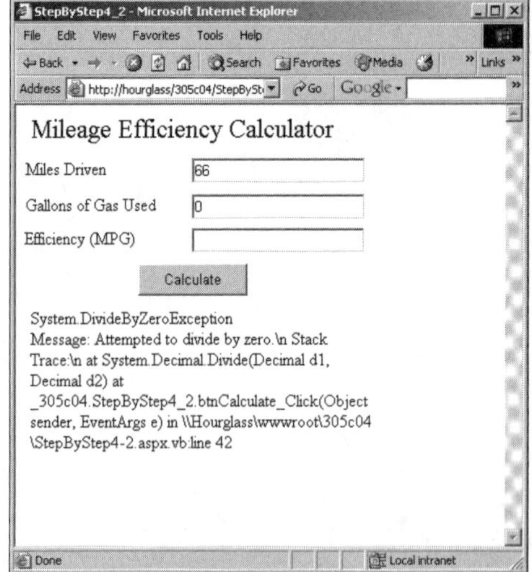

FIGURE 4.4
DivideByZeroException.

That includes all exceptions unless you're interacting with legacy COM or Win32 API code. If you want to catch all kinds of exceptions, whether CLS-compliant or not, you can use a `Catch` block with no specific type. A `Catch` block like this has to be the last in the list of `Catch` blocks because it is the most generic one.

If you are thinking that it's a good idea to catch all sorts of exceptions in your code and suppress them as soon as possible, think again. A good programmer catches an exception in code only if the answer is yes to one or more of these questions:

- Will I attempt to recover from this error in the `Catch` block?
- Will I log the exception information in system event log or any other log file?
- Will I add relevant information to the exception and rethrow it?
- Will I execute cleanup code that must run even if an exception occurs?

If you answered no to all these questions, you should not catch the exception but rather just let it go. In that case, the exception propagates up to the code that is calling your code. Possibly that code will have a better idea of what to do with the exception.

The Throw Statement

A `Throw` statement explicitly generates an exception in your code. You can use `Throw` to handle execution paths that lead to undesired results.

You should not throw an exception for anticipated cases such as the user entering an invalid username or password. This can be handled in a method that returns a value indicating whether the logon was successful. If you don't have enough permissions to read records from the user table, that's a better candidate to raise an exception because a method to validate users should normally have read access to the user table.

Using exceptions to control the normal flow of execution is bad for two reasons:

1. It might make your code difficult to read and maintain because the use of `Try-Catch` blocks to deal with exceptions forces you to separate the regular program logic between separate locations.
2. It might make your programs slower because exception handling consumes more resources than just returning values from a method.

You can use the `Throw` statement in two ways. First, in its simplest form, you can simply rethrow an exception that you've caught in a `Catch` block:

```
Catch ex As Exception
    ' TODO: Add code to write to the event log
    Throw
```

This usage of the `Throw` statement rethrows the exception that was just caught. It can be useful in situations where you don't want to handle the exception yourself but would like to take other actions (such as recording the error in an event log or sending an email notification about the error) when the exception occurs. Then you can pass the exception unchanged to the next method in the calling chain.

The second way of using a `Throw` statement is to use it to throw explicitly created exceptions. For example, this code creates and throws an exception:

```
Dim strMessage As String = _
 "EndDate should be greater than the StartDate"
Dim exNew As ArgumentOutOfRangeException = _
 New ArgumentOutOfRangeException(strMessage)
Throw exNew
```

> **EXAM TIP**
>
> **Custom Error Messages** When creating an exception class, you should use the constructor that allows you to associate a custom error message with the exception instead of the default constructor. The custom error message can pass specific information about the cause of the error and a possible way to resolve it.

In this example, I first created a new instance of the `Exception` object, associated a custom error message with it, and then threw the newly created exception.

You are not required to put this usage of the `Throw` statement inside of a `Catch` block, because you're just creating and throwing a new exception rather than rethrowing an existing one. You will typically use this technique in raising your own custom exceptions. I'll show how to do that later in this chapter.

An alternate way of throwing an exception is to throw it after wrapping it with additional useful information, for example:

```
Catch ane As ArgumentNullException
    ' TODO: Add code to create an entry in the log file
    Dim strMessage As String = _
     "CustomerID cannot be null"
    Dim aneNew As ArgumentNullException =
➥New ArgumentNullException(strMessage)
    Throw aneNew
```

You might need to catch an exception that you cannot handle completely. You would then perform any required processing and throw a more relevant and informative exception to the calling code so that it can perform the rest of the processing. In this case, you can create a new exception with a constructor that wraps the previously caught exception in the new exception's InnerException property. The calling code now has more information available to handle the exception appropriately.

It is interesting to note that because InnerException is also an exception, it might also store an exception object in its InnerException property, so what you are propagating up is a chain of exceptions. This information can be valuable at debugging time because it allows you to trace down the path of the problem to its origin.

The Finally Block

The `Finally` block contains the code that always executes whether or not any exception occurred. You can use the `Finally` block to write cleanup code that maintains your application in consistent state and preserves the external environment. As an example you can write code to close files, database connections, or related I/O resources in a `Finally` block.

It is not necessary for a `Try` block to have an associated `Finally` block. However, if you do write a `Finally` block you cannot have more than one and the `Finally` block must appear after all of the `Catch` blocks.

Step By Step 4.3 illustrates the use of the `Finally` block.

EXAM TIP

No Code in Between Try, Catch, and Finally Blocks When you write Try, Catch and Finally blocks, they must be in immediate succession of each other. You cannot write any other code between the blocks, although you can place comments between them.

STEP BY STEP

4.3 Using a Finally Block

1. Add a new Web Form to the project.

2. Place two TextBox controls (txtFileName and txtText), three Label controls (one being lblMessage), and a Button control (btnSave) on the form's surface and arrange them as shown in Figure 4.5. Set the TextMode property of the txtText control to MultiLine.

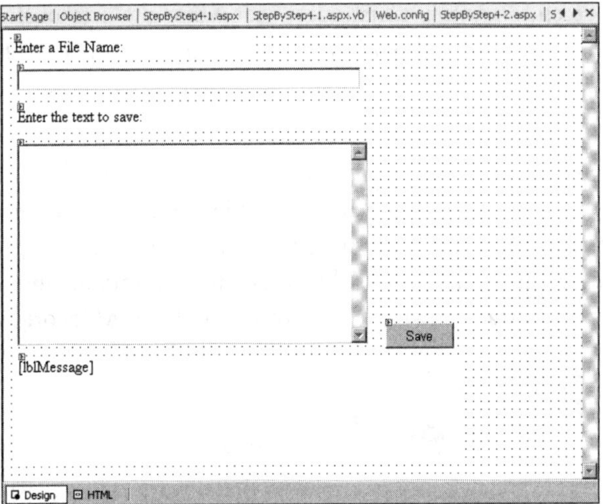

FIGURE 4.5
An application showing the usage of a Finally block.

3. Switch to code view and add the following statement at the top of the module:

```
Imports System.IO
```

4. Add the following code to the Click event handler of the btnSave control:

```
Private Sub btnSave_Click( _
 ByVal sender As System.Object, _
 ByVal e As System.EventArgs) Handles btnSave.Click
    ' A StreamWriter writes characters to a stream
    Dim sw As StreamWriter
    Try
        sw = New StreamWriter(txtFileName.Text)
        ' Attempt to write the textbox
        ' contents to a file
        sw.Write(txtText.Text)
```

```
        ' This line only executes if there were
        ' no exceptions so far
        lblMessage.Text = _
         "Contents written without any exceptions" _
         + "<br>"
        ' Catches all CLS-complaint exceptions
    Catch ex As Exception
        Dim msg As String = String.Format( _
         "Message: {0}\n Stack Trace:\n {1}", _
         ex.Message, ex.StackTrace)
        lblMessage.Text = ex.GetType().ToString() + _
         "<br>" + msg + "<br>"
        GoTo endit
        ' Finally block is always executed
        ' to make sure that the
        ' resources get closed whether or
        ' not the exception occurs.
        ' Even if there is any goto (control
        ' transfer) statement
        ' in catch or try block the finally
        ' block is first executed
        ' before the control goes to the goto label
    Finally
        If Not sw Is Nothing Then
            sw.Close()
        End If
        lblMessage.Text = lblMessage.Text & _
         "Finally block always " & _
         "executes" + _
         "<br>"
    End Try
EndIt:
    lblMessage.Text = lblMessage.Text & _
     "Control is at label: end"
End Sub
```

5. Set the Web Form as the start page for the project.

6. Run the project. You will see a Web Form as shown in Figure 4.5. Enter a filename and some text. Watch the order of messages. You will note that the message from the `Finally` block is always displayed prior to the message that appears in the code after the `EndIt` label.

Step By Step 4.3 illustrates that the `Finally` block always executes, even if there is a transfer-of-control statement such as `GoTo` within a `Try` or `Catch` block. The compiler does not allow a transfer-of-control statement within a `Finally` block.

EXAM TIP

Finally Block Always Executes If you have a Finally block associated with a Try block, the code in the Finally block always executes whether or not an exception occurs.

NOTE

Throwing Exceptions from a Finally Block Although it is perfectly legitimate to throw exceptions from a Finally block, you should avoid doing so. In a Finally block, there might already be an unhandled exception waiting to be handled.

The `Finally` statement can be used in a `Try` block with no `Catch` block. For example:

```
Try
    ' Write code to allocate some resources
Finally
    ' Write code to Dispose all allocated resources
End Try
```

This usage ensures that allocated resources are properly disposed of no matter what happens in the `Try` block.

REVIEW BREAK

- An exception occurs when a program encounters any unexpected problem during normal execution of the program.
- The Framework Class Library (FCL) provides two main types of exceptions—`SystemException` and `ApplicationException`. `SystemException` represents the exceptions thrown by the CLR, whereas `ApplicationException` represents the exceptions thrown by the user programs.
- The `System.Exception` class represents the base class for all CLS-compliant exceptions and provides the common functionality for exception handling.
- The `Try` block consists of code that may raise an exception. A `Try` block cannot exist on its own. It should be immediately followed by one or more `Catch` blocks or a `Finally` block.
- The `Catch` block handles any exception raised by the code in the `Try` block. The runtime looks for matching a `Catch` block to handle the exception, which is the first `Catch` block with either the exact same exception or any of the exception's base classes.
- If there are multiple `Catch` blocks associated with `Try` block, the `Catch` blocks should be arranged in top-to-bottom order of specific to general exception types.
- The `Throw` statement is used to raise an exception.
- The `Finally` block is used to enclose the code that needs to be run irrespective of whether the exception is raised.

CUSTOM EXCEPTIONS

In most cases, .NET's built-in exception classes, combined with custom messages that you create when instantiating a new exception, will satisfy your exception handling requirements. However, in some cases you'll need exception types that are specific to the problem you are solving.

The .NET Framework allows you to define custom exception classes. To make your custom Exception class work well with the .NET exception handling framework, Microsoft recommends that you consider the following when you're designing a custom exception class:

- Create an exception class only if there is no existing exception class that satisfies your requirement.
- Derive all programmer-defined exception classes from the System.ApplicationException class.
- End the name of custom exception class with the word Exception (for example, MyOwnCustomException).
- Implement three constructors with the signatures shown in the following code:

```
Public Class MyOwnCustomException
    Inherits ApplicationException

    ' Default constructor
    Public Sub New()

    End Sub

    ' Constructor accepting a single string message
    Public Sub New(ByVal message As String)
        MyBase.New(message)
    End Sub

    ' Constructor accepting a string message
    '  and an inner exception
    ' that will be wrapped by this
    ' custom exception class
    Public Sub New( _
     ByVal message As String, _
     ByVal inner As Exception)
        MyBase.new(message, inner)
    End Sub

End Class
```

Step By Step 4.4 shows you how to create a custom exception.

EXAM TIP

Use ApplicationException as Base Class for Custom Exceptions
Although you can derive directly from the Exception class, Microsoft recommends that you derive any custom exception class you create for your Windows application from the ApplicationException class.

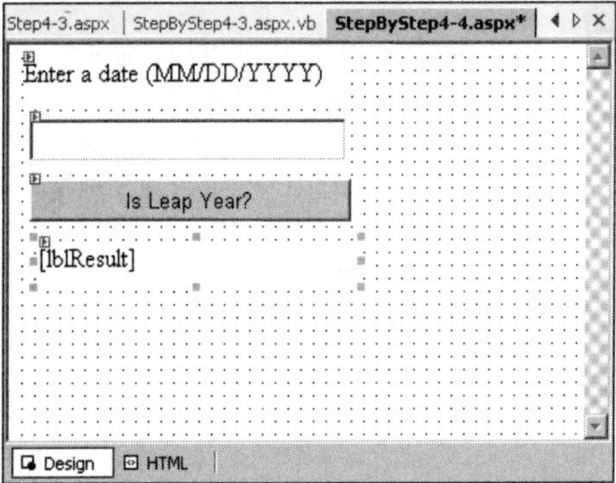

FIGURE 4.6
Designing a Web Form for the Leap Year Finder.

STEP BY STEP

4.4 Creating a Custom Exception

1. Add a new Web Form to the project.
2. Place two `Label` controls (one being `lblResult`), a `TextBox` control (`txtDate`), and a `Button` control (`btnIsLeap`) on the form, as shown in Figure 4.6.
3. Add a new class to your project. Add code to create a custom exception class:

```
Public Class MyOwnInvalidDateFormatException
    Inherits ApplicationException

    ' Default constructor
    Public Sub New()

    End Sub

    ' Constructor accepting a single string message
    Public Sub New(ByVal message As String)
        MyBase.New(message)
        Me.HelpLink = _
         "file://MyOwnInvalidDate" & _
         "FormatExceptionHelp.htm"
    End Sub

    ' Constructor accepting a string
    ' message and an inner exception
    ' that will be wrapped by this
    'custom exception class
    Public Sub New(ByVal message As String, _
     ByVal inner As Exception)
        MyBase.new(message, inner)
        Me.HelpLink = _
         "file://MyOwnInvalidDate" & _
         "FormatExceptionHelp.htm"
    End Sub

End Class
```

4. Add a second new class to your project. Add code to create a class named `LeapDate`:

```
Public Class LeapDate
    ' This class does elementary date handling for the
    ' leap year form
    Private day, month, year As Integer
```

```
    Public Sub New(ByVal strDate As String)
        If strDate.Trim().Length = 10 Then
            ' Input data might be in
            ' invalid format; in that case
            ' the Convert.ToDateTime method will fail
            Try
                Dim dt As DateTime = _
                 Convert.ToDateTime(strDate)
                day = dt.Day
                month = dt.Month
                year = dt.Year
                ' Catch any exception, attach it
                ' to the custom exception and
                ' throw the custom exception
            Catch e As Exception
                Throw New _
                 MyOwnInvalidDateFormatException( _
                 "Custom Exception: " & _
                 "Invalid Date Format", e)
            End Try
        Else
            ' bad input, throw a custom exception
            Throw New _
             MyOwnInvalidDateFormatException( _
             "The input does not match " & _
             " the required format: MM/DD/YYYY")
        End If
    End Sub

    ' Find if the given date belongs to a leap year
    Public Function IsLeapYear() As Boolean
        IsLeapYear = (year Mod 4 = 0) And _
         ((year Mod 100 <> 0) Or (year Mod 400 = 0))
    End Function
End Class
```

5. Add the following event handler for the `Click` event of `btnIsLeap`:

```
Private Sub btnIsLeap_Click( _
 ByVal sender As System.Object, _
 ByVal e As System.EventArgs) _
 Handles btnIsLeap.Click
    Try
        Dim dt As LeapDate = _
         New LeapDate(txtDate.Text)
        If dt.IsLeapYear() Then
            lblResult.Text = _
             "This date is in a leap year"
        Else
            lblResult.Text = _
             "This date is NOT in a leap year"
        End If
```

continues

continued

```
        ' Catch the custom exception and
        ' display an appropriate message
    Catch dte As MyOwnInvalidDateFormatException
        Dim msg As String
        ' If some other exception was also
        ' attached with this exception
        If Not dte.InnerException Is Nothing Then
            msg = String.Format("Message:" & _
             vbCrLf & "{0}" & _
             vbCrLf & vbCrLf & _
             "Inner Exception:" & vbCrLf & "{1}", _
             dte.Message, dte.InnerException.Message)
        Else
            msg = String.Format("Message:" & _
             vbCrLf & "{0}" & _
             vbCrLf & vbCrLf & "Help Link:" & _
             vbCrLf & "{1}", _
             dte.Message, dte.HelpLink)
        End If
    lblResult.Text = _
     dte.GetType().ToString() + "<br>" + msg
    End Try
End Sub
```

6. Set the Web Form as the start page for the project.

7. Run the project. Enter a date and click the button. If the date was in the native format for your computer (for example, 11/22/2002 for a computer running a US English version of the operating system), you'll see a result displayed in the Results group box. Otherwise you'll get a message showing the custom error message thrown by the custom exception as in Figure 4.7.

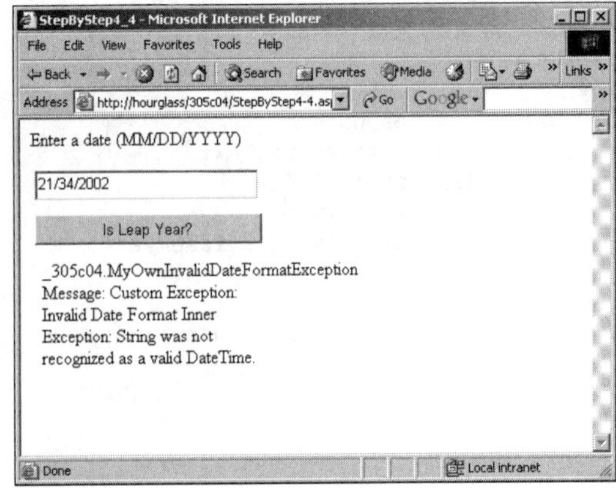

FIGURE 4.7
Custom Error Message thrown by the custom exception.

GUIDED PRACTICE EXERCISE 4.1

In this exercise, you will create a custom defined `Exception` class that helps you implement custom error messages and custom error handling in your programs.

You have to create a keyword-searching page. The page should ask the user to enter some text in a multi-line textbox, to enter a keyword, and to search for the keyword in the text of the multi-line textbox. The Web page should then display the number of lines containing the keyword. The Web page assumes that the entered keyword will be a single word. If it is not, you need to create and throw a custom exception for that case.

You should try doing this on your own first. If you get stuck, or you'd like to see one possible solution, follow these steps.

1. Add a new form to your Visual Basic ASP.NET Project.
2. Place and arrange the controls on the form as shown in Figure 4.8. Name the `TextBox` for accepting text to be searched as `txtText`. Set the `TextMode` property of `txtText` to `MultiLine`. Name the `TextBox` for accepting keywords as `txtKeyword` and the search button as `btnSearch`.

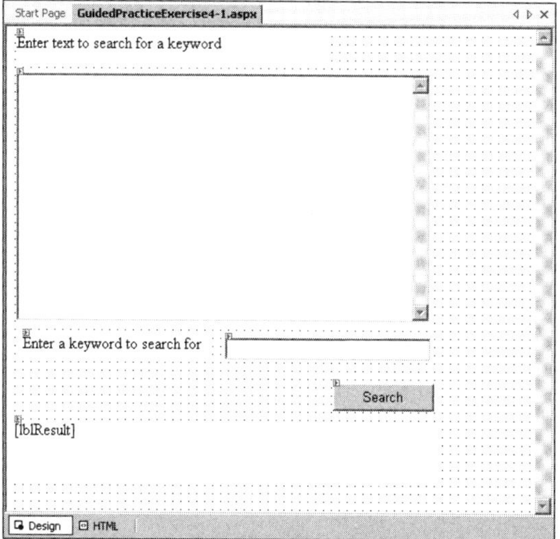

FIGURE 4.8
Form allowing keyword search in a textbox.

continues

continued

3. Create a new class named `BadKeywordFormatException` that derives from `ApplicationException` and place the following code in it:

```
Public Class BadKeywordFormatException
    Inherits ApplicationException

    ' Default constructor
    Public Sub New()

    End Sub

    ' Constructor accepting a string
    ' message and an inner exception
    ' that will be wrapped by this
    ' custom exception class
    Public Sub New(ByVal message As String, _
     ByVal inner As Exception)
        MyBase.new(message, inner)
    End Sub

End Class
```

4. Create a method named `GetKeywordFrequency` in the Web Form's module. This class returns the number of lines containing the keyword. Add the following code to the method:

```
Private Function GetKeywordFrequency() As Integer
    If Me.txtKeyword.Text.Trim(). _
     IndexOf(" ") >= 0 Then
        Throw New BadKeywordFormatException( _
         "The keyword must only have a single word")
    End If
    Dim intCount As Integer = 0

    Dim line As String() = txtText.Text.Split()
    Dim intI As Integer

    For intI = 0 To line.Length - 1
        If (line(intI). _
         IndexOf(txtKeyword.Text) >= 0) Then
            intCount += 1
        End If
    Next
    GetKeywordFrequency = intCount
End Function
```

5. Add the following code to the `Click` event handler of `btnSearch`:

```
Private Sub btnSearch_Click( _
 ByVal sender As System.Object, _
 ByVal e As System.EventArgs) _
 Handles btnSearch.Click
    If txtKeyword.Text.Trim().Length = 0 Then
        lblResult.Text = _
         "Please enter a keyword to search"
        Exit Sub
    ElseIf txtText.Text.Trim().Length = 0 Then
        lblResult.Text = "Please enter text to search"
        Exit Sub
    End If
    Try
        lblResult.Text = String.Format( _
         "The keyword: '{0}', " & _
          "was found in {1} lines", _
            txtKeyword.Text, GetKeywordFrequency())
    Catch bkfe As BadKeywordFormatException
        Dim msg As String = String.Format( _
         "Message: {0} " & vbCrLf & _
          "StackTrace:\n{1}", _
         bkfe.Message, bkfe.StackTrace)
        lblResult.Text = msg + "<br>" + _
         bkfe.GetType().ToString()
    Catch ex As Exception
        Dim msg As String = String.Format( _
          "Message: {0} " & vbCrLf & _
           "StackTrace:\n{1}", _
         ex.Message, ex.StackTrace)
        lblResult.Text = msg + "<br>" & _
         ex.GetType().ToString()
    End Try
End Sub
```

6. Set the Web Form as the start page for the project.

7. Run the project. Enter some text and the keyword to search for and press the Search button. If the keyword entered is in the wrong format (that is, if it contains two words), a custom exception is raised.

Managing Unhandled Exceptions

Unhandled exceptions are those exceptions that are not caught in a Try/Catch block in an application. Whenever an unhandled exception occurs, ASP.NET displays its default error page to the user.

The default page is not pretty and sometimes (depending on the settings in the web.config file) can provide enough details to be a security concern. You're usually better off displaying your own custom error messages instead.

ASP.NET stops processing a Web page after it encounters an unhandled exception. However, you can trap an unhandled exception at either the Page or Application level.

Using Custom Error Pages

Custom error pages are those Web pages that are displayed in the browser when an unhandled exception occurs. You can even display custom error pages whenever an HTTP error occurs (such as Page Not Found, Internal Server Error, and so on) while requesting a Web page from your ASP.NET application.

ASP.NET provides full built-in support to configure custom error pages in a Web application. element (web.config)>This configuration information is stored in an XML-based configuration file (web.config), where you use the <customErrors> element to configure custom error pages. The <customErrors> element consists of two attributes—mode and defaultRedirect. The mode attribute specifies how the custom error pages should be displayed. It can have one of the following three values:

1. On Display custom error pages at both the local and remote clients.
2. Off Disable custom error pages at both the local and remote clients.
3. RemoteOnly Display custom error pages only at remote clients. If you're running the page on the Web server itself, display the default ASP.NET error pages. This is the default setting in the web.config file.

The defaultRedirect attribute is an optional attribute that specifies the custom error page to be displayed when an error occurs. You can use either a static HTML page or a dynamic ASPX page as a custom error page. When the defaultRedirect attribute is not set to a custom error page, ASP.NET displays a generic error element (web.config)>message in the browser.

A specific element (web.config)>custom error page can be displayed for specific HTTP error codes by associating the error code with the Web page through the <error> element. There can be multiple <error> elements nested inside the <customErrors> element. They consist of the following two attributes:

- statusCode HTTP error status code. For example: 403 (Forbidden), 404 (Not Found), 500 (Internal Server Error), and so on.
- redirect The error page to which the browser should be redirected when the associated HTTP error occurs.

If an error occurs that has no specific page assigned, the custom error page specified by the defaultRedirect attribute of <customErrors> element element (web.config)>is displayed.

EXAM TIP

Configuring Custom Error Pages through IIS An alternate way of configuring custom error pages is through Internet Information Services (IIS). When given a choice between IIS and ASP.NET custom error pages you should prefer ASP.NET, because in ASP.NET the custom pages are configured in an XML-based web.config (application configuration) file, resulting in easy (`xcopy`) deployment and management.

STEP BY STEP

4.5 Setting Custom Error Pages for a Web Application

1. Open the `web.config` file in your project from Solution Explorer. Search for the `<customErrors>` element in the file. Modify the `<customErrors>` element with as follows:

```
<customErrors mode="On"
 defaultRedirect="ApplicationError.htm">
    <error statusCode="403"
redirect="Forbidden.htm" />
    <error statusCode="404" redirect="NotFound.htm" />
</customErrors>
```

2. Select Project, Add Html Page. This opens the Add New Item dialog box. Create a page with the name `ApplicationError.htm`. Switch to HTML view and enter the following code for this page:

```
<!DOCTYPE HTML PUBLIC "-//W3C//DTD
 HTML 4.0 Transitional//EN" >
<HTML>
    <HEAD>
        <TITLE>Application Error</TITLE>
        <META NAME="GENERATOR"
         Content="Microsoft Visual Studio 7.0">
    </HEAD>
```

continues

continued

```
    <BODY>
        <H1>Application Error</H1>
        <P>Sorry there is a server application error,
         and we are unable to
         process your request.</P>
    </BODY>
</HTML>
```

3. Select Project, Add Html Page. This opens the Add New Item dialog box. Add another page with the name `Forbidden.htm`. Switch to HTML view and enter the following code for this page:

```
<!DOCTYPE HTML PUBLIC "-//W3C//DTD
 HTML 4.0 Transitional//EN" >
<HTML>
    <HEAD>
        <TITLE>Page Forbidden</TITLE>
        <META NAME="GENERATOR"
         Content="Microsoft Visual Studio 7.0">
    </HEAD>
    <BODY>
        <H1>
            Page Forbidden</H1>
        Sorry this page is forbidden,
        so we cannot fulfill your request.
</BODY>
</HTML>
```

4. Select Project, Add Html Page. This opens the Add New Item dialog box. Add another page with the name `NotFound.htm`. Switch to HTML view and enter the following code for this page:

```
<!DOCTYPE HTML PUBLIC "-//W3C//DTD
 HTML 4.0 Transitional//EN" >
<HTML>
    <HEAD>
        <TITLE>Page Not Found</TITLE>
        <META NAME="GENERATOR"
         Content="Microsoft Visual Studio 7.0">
    </HEAD>
    <BODY>
        <h1>Page Not Found</h1>
        Sorry, we don't have the page you requested.
    </BODY>
</HTML>
```

5. Set `StepByStep4-1.aspx` as the start page for the project.

6. Run the project. Enter a value for Miles and `0` for Gallons, and click the Calculate button. The application displays the `ApplicationError.htm` page, as shown in Figure 4.9, because there is no code behind Step By Step 4.1 to display a custom error.

7. Now try displaying the code-behind file of the StepByStep4_1.aspx page by typing `http://localhost/305C04/StepByStep4-1.aspx.vb` (substitute the name of your Web server for `localhost` if the Web server is not on your development computer). You will see that this request generates an HTTP Page Forbidden (403) error. Because you have specified a different custom Web page for HTTP error code 403, the `PageForbidden.htm` page is now displayed as shown in Figure 4.10, rather than the default Web page `ApplicationError.htm`.

FIGURE 4.9
Custom Application Error page.

FIGURE 4.10
Custom Page Forbidden Error page.

8. Now try displaying a nonexistent page in the Web application. For example, make a typo by typing an underscore instead of a hyphen: `http://localhost/305C04/StepByStep4_1.aspx`. This request generates an HTTP Page Not Found (404) error. The custom error page is only displayed if the not-found page is one that would have been processed by ASP.NET. For example, if you tried to get to `StepByStep4-1.htm`, you wouldn't see the custom error page because IIS would never call the ASP.NET processor. Again, because you have specified a different custom Web page for HTTP error code 404, the `PageNotFound.htm` page is displayed as shown in Figure 4.11.

> NOTE
>
> **Forbidden Files** The `*.vb` files contain the source code for the application. Other files such as `*.config`, `*.resx`, `*.asax`, and so on also contain sensitive information. If the user could request these files through the browser, it could risk security and intellectual property of your application. Fortunately, ASP.NET restricts access to these files by generating a HTTP 403 Forbidden error.

continues

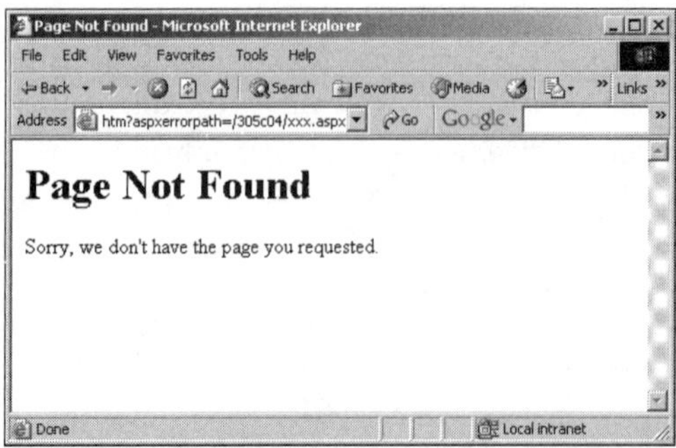

FIGURE 4.11
Custom Page Not Found Error page.

9. Repeat steps 6, 7, and 8, after changing the value of the mode attribute in the `web.config` file to `Off` (where no custom error pages will be displayed) and then to `RemoteOnly` (where custom error pages will be displayed in remote machine and default errors in local machines).

Setting a Custom Error Page for a Specific Page

Sometimes there may be a special need where a particular Web page in an application should display its own error page. This can be done by setting ErrorPage attribute of the @Page directive or the ErrorPage property of the Page class to the desired custom error page. When the custom error page is set using this technique, it overwrites the settings that apply to this Web page via web.config file.

Step By Step 4.6 shows how to set a custom error page for a specific Web page in a Web application.

STEP BY STEP

4.6 Setting a Custom Error Page for a Specific Web Page

1. In Solution Explorer, right-click `StepByStep4-1.aspx` and select Copy. Right-click your project and select Paste. Rename the pasted Web Form to `StepByStep4-6.aspx`.

Open the aspx (in HTML view) and vb files for the new Web Form and change all references to StepByStep4-1 to refer to StepByStep4-6 instead.

2. Open StepByStep4_6.aspx in HTML view. Add the ErrorPage="Error4-6.htm" attribute to the Page directive:

```
<%@ Page Language="vb" AutoEventWireup="false"
 Codebehind="StepByStep4-6.aspx.vb"
 Inherits="_305c04.StepByStep4_6"
 ErrorPage="Error4-6.htm" %>
```

3. Select Project, Add Html Page. This opens the Add New Item dialog box. Create a page with the name Error4-6.htm. Switch to HTML view and enter the following HTML code:

```
<!DOCTYPE HTML PUBLIC "-//W3C//DTD
 HTML 4.0 Transitional//EN" >
<HTML>
    <HEAD>
        <META NAME="GENERATOR"
        Content="Microsoft Visual Studio 7.0">
        <TITLE>Error in StepByStep4-6.aspx</TITLE>
    </HEAD>
    <BODY>
        <h1>
            Error in StepByStep4_6.aspx</h1>
        <p>Sorry, there was an error while
        processing the StepByStep4-6.aspx page. Please
        ensure that you enter numeric, greater than
        zero data in both the input fields.</p>
        <p>Please try again.</p>
    </BODY>
</HTML>
```

4. Set the StepByStep4-6.aspx page as the start page for the project.

5. Run the project. Enter invalid values for miles and gallons and click the Calculate button. You will notice that the Error4-6.htm page is displayed as shown in Figure 4.12. The ErrorPage attribute for this page overrides the setting for ApplicationError.htm defined in the web.config file.

6. Stop the project. Set the original StepByStep4-1.aspx page as the start page for the project. Enter invalid values for miles and gallons and click the Calculate button. You will notice that ApplicationError.htm page is displayed because this page does not have an ErrorPage attribute.

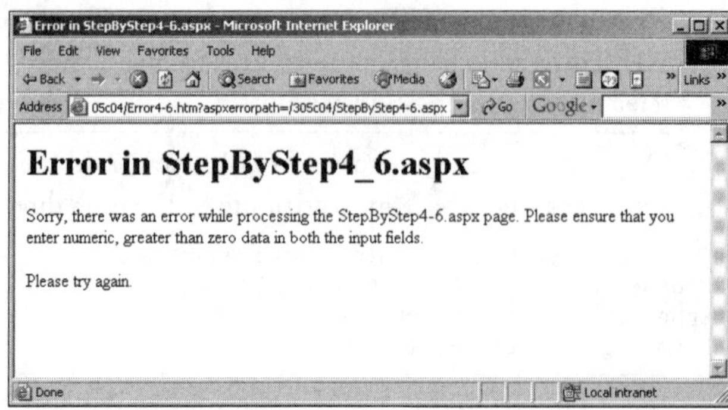

FIGURE 4.12
Custom Error page for StepByStep4_6 page.

Using Error Events

When an unhandled exception occurs in a Web application, the following events are fired in order:

1. `Page.Error` page-level event, handled by the `Page_Error` event handler
2. `Application.Error` application-level event, handled by `Application_Error` event handler

Either of these event handlers can be used to trap and work with unhandled exceptions.

Using Page.Error Event

The `Page_Error` event handler can be used to trap unhandled exceptions at a page level. Step By Step 4.7 shows how to handle unhandled exceptions in a page.

STEP BY STEP

4.7 Handling Unhandled Exceptions in a Page

1. In Solution Explorer, right-click `StepByStep4-1.aspx` and select Copy. Right-click your project and select Paste. Rename the pasted Web Form to `StepByStep4-7.aspx`. Open the `aspx` (in HTML view) and `vb` files for the new Web Form and change all references to StepByStep4-1 to refer to StepByStep4-7 instead.

2. Switch to code view for the page. Add an event handler for the `Page.Error` event:

```
Private Sub Page_Error(ByVal sender As Object, _
 ByVal e As System.EventArgs) Handles MyBase.Error
    ' Display error details
    ' Get the last error in the Server by calling
    ' the GetLastError(method)
    ' Clear the error to flush the new response
    ' and erase the default ASP.NET error page
    Response.Write("Error Details: <br>")
    Response.Write( _
     Server.GetLastError().Message + "<br>")
    Response.Write( _
     Server.GetLastError().StackTrace + _
     "<br>")
    Server.ClearError()
End Sub
```

3. Set the Web Form as the start page for the project.

4. Run the project. Enter wrong values for miles and gallons and click the Calculate button. The program displays the Error details in the Web page as shown in Figure 4.13.

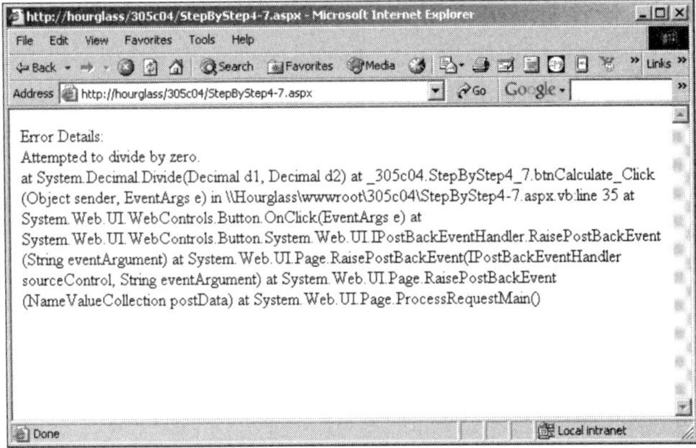

FIGURE 4.13
Handling an unhandled exception via the Page.Error event.

The `Page_Error` event handler in the previous example displays the details of the unhandled exception. This is achieved by calling the `Server` object's `GetLastError` method. The method returns an `Exception` object that is a reference to the last exception that occurred on the server.

The `ClearError` method of the `Server` object clears the last exception and does not fire subsequent error events (that is, `Application.Error`) for the exception. Because of this, the application-level custom error page is not displayed even though there is an unhandled error. Also for the same reason, the default ASP.NET error page will also not be displayed if there is no custom error page configured.

Using the Application.Error Event

You can also choose to trap unhandled exceptions that occur anywhere in the application in the `Application.Error` event. This event is handled by the Application_Error event handler available in the ASP.NET application file, global.asax. Handling exceptions at the application level can be really helpful if you are planning to handle exceptions from all pages in a similar fashion. Handling these events at the application level saves you from writing repetitive code for every page. For example, if you want to take custom actions like logging the exception-related information for all Web pages, your best bet is to trap the unhandled exceptions at the application level.

Logging exceptions is one of the best ways to keep track of the exceptions generated. A log maintained over a period of time may help you to analyze and find patterns that may give you useful debugging information. There are several ways you can log the information related to an event:

- System event log
- Custom log files
- Databases such as SQL Server 2000
- Email notifications

Among these ways, the Windows event log offers you a very robust way of event logging. It requires the minimum infrastructure for logging the event. The other cases are not as fail-safe because your application may lose connectivity with a database or with the SMTP server, or you might have problems writing an entry in a custom log file.

The .NET Framework provides you access to the Windows event log through the EventLog class. Windows 2000 and later versions have three default logs—Application, System, and Security.

You can use the EventLog class to create custom event logs. These event logs can be easily viewed using the Windows Event Viewer utility.

You should know about the important members of the EventLog class that are listed in Table 4.2.

TABLE 4.2

IMPORTANT MEMBERS OF THE EVENTLOG CLASS

Member	*Type*	*Description*
`Clear`	Method	Removes all entries from the event log and make it empty.
`CreateEventSource`	Method	Creates an event source that you can use to write to a standard or custom event log.
`Entries`	Property	Gets the contents of the event log.
`Log`	Property	The name of the log to read from or write to.
`MachineName`	Property	The name of the computer on which to read or write events.
`Source`	Property	The event source name to register and use when writing to the event log.
`SourceExists`	Method	Specifies whether the event source exists on a computer.
`WriteEntry`	Method	Writes an entry in the event log.

NOTE

Logging in a Web Farm In case of a Web Farm (where multiple computers do not share the same event log), you might want to log all the errors centrally in a SQL Server database. To make the scheme fail-safe you may choose to log locally if the database is not available and transfer the log to the central database when it is available again.

STEP BY STEP

4.8 Logging Unhandled Exceptions in the System Event Log

1. Open the `Global.asax` file in code view from Solution Explorer.

2. Add this statement at the top of the file:

```
Imports System.Diagnostics
```

continues

continued

3. Add the following code to the `Application_Error` event handler:

```
Sub Application_Error(ByVal sender As Object, _
 ByVal e As EventArgs)
    ' Get the Exception object wrapped in
    ' the InnerException property
    Dim unhandledException As Exception = _
     Server.GetLastError().InnerException

    ' If no event source exist, create an event source
    If Not EventLog.SourceExists( _
     "Mileage Efficiency Calculator") Then
        EventLog.CreateEventSource( _
          "Mileage Efficiency Calculator", _
          "Mileage Efficiency Calculator Log")
    End If

    ' Create an EventLog instance
    ' and assign its source.
    Dim el As EventLog = New EventLog()
    el.Source = "Mileage Efficiency Calculator"
    ' Write an informational entry to the event log.
    el.WriteEntry(unhandledException.Message)
    Response.Write("An exception occurred: " & _
     "Created an entry in the event log ")
    Server.ClearError()
End Sub
```

4. Set the form StepByStep4-1 as the start page for the project.

5. Run the project. You will see that when you enter invalid values, you get a message saying that an entry has been created in the event log. Thus unhandled exceptions of all the Web pages of an application are handled by the `Application_Error` event in the `global.asax`.

6. Stop the project. Set the form StepByStep4_7 as the start page for the project.

7. Run the project. You will notice that, when you enter invalid values, you get the error details displayed in the browser but no message about an entry in the event log. Thus only `Page_Error` event handler is being executed.

8. Stop the project. Open the form StepByStep4_7 in code-view. Comment the following line in the `Page_Error` event handler:

```
Server.ClearError()
```

9. Run the project. You will notice that when you enter invalid values, you get the error details displayed as in earlier steps along with a message saying that an entry has been created in the event log. Here, both the `Page` level and `Application` level events are fired.

10. You can view the logged messages by viewing Start, Programs, Administrative Tools, Event Viewer. The Event Viewer displays the Mileage Efficiency Calculator Log in the left pane of the window as shown in the Figure 4.14. The right pane of the window shows the events that have been logged. You can double-click the event to view the description and other properties of the event as shown in Figure 4.15.

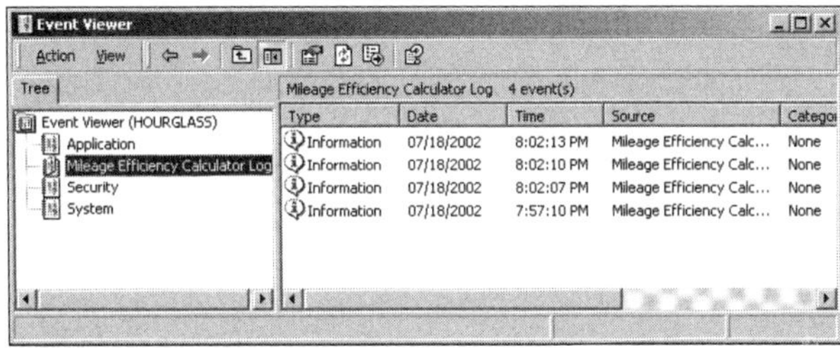

FIGURE 4.14
EventViewer showing the `MileageEfficiencyCalculatorLog`.

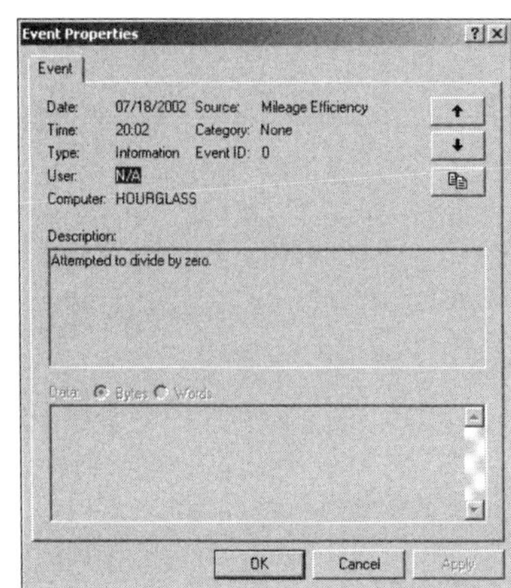

FIGURE 4.15
Event Properties of a particular event.

11. Stop the project. Open the file `Global.asax` in code-view. Comment out the following line in the `Application_Error` event handler:

```
Server.ClearError()
```

12. Run the project. You will notice that when you enter invalid values, you get the Custom or default error page (depending on your web.config settings) displayed in the browser. This is because the error is not cleared, although the exception is still logged in the system event log.

When ASP.NET propagates the unhandled exception to the `Application` object (`Application.Error` event), the exception object is wrapped into an `HttpUnHandledException` object. To see the original exception at the application level, you need to unpack the `Exception` object's `InnerException` property.

REVIEW BREAK

- If the existing exception classes do not meet your exception handling requirements, you can create new exception classes that are specific to your application by deriving from the `ApplicationException` class.
- Custom error pages can be used to display user-friendly messages rather than the default error page shown by ASP.NET. They can be set by configuring the `customErrors` element in the `web.config` file for all the Web pages in an application.
- You can set a custom error Web page for individual pages in your application by using the `ErrorPage` attribute of the `Page` directive or the `ErrorPage` property of the `Page` class.
- You can handle any unhandled error that occurs in a page in its `Error` event handler.
- Unhandled exceptions for an entire application can be trapped in the `Application_Error` event handler in the `global.asax` file.

GUIDED PRACTICE EXERCISE 4.2

In this exercise, you will create an `aspx` custom error page for a Web Form. The custom error page should display the error details when it loads.

You should try doing this on your own first. If you get stuck, or you'd like to see one possible solution, follow these steps.

1. In Solution Explorer, right-click `StepByStep4-1.aspx` and select Copy. Right-click your project and select Paste. Rename the pasted Web Form to `GuidedPracticeExercise4-2.aspx`.

Open the `aspx` (in HTML view) and `vb` files for the new Web Form and change all references to StepByStep4-1 to refer to GuidedPracticeExercise4-2 instead.

2. Open `GuidedPracticeExercise4-2.aspx` in HTML view. Add the `ErrorPage` attribute to the `Page` directive:

```
<%@ Page Language="vb" AutoEventWireup="false"
 Codebehind="GuidedPracticeExercise4-2.aspx.vb"
 Inherits="_305c04.GuidedPracticeExercise4_2"
 ErrorPage="ErrorGPE4-2.aspx" %>
```

3. Add this code to handle the `Page_Error` event:

```
Private Sub Page_Error(ByVal sender As Object, _
 ByVal e As System.EventArgs) Handles MyBase.Error
    ' Store the Error object in the Session
    Session("Error") = Server.GetLastError()
End Sub
```

4. Select Project, Add Web Form. This opens the Add New Item dialog box. Create a Web Form named ErrorGPE4-2.aspx.

5. Place a `Label` control with the ID of `lblError` on the form.

6. Add the following code to the `Page_Load` event handler for the new page:

```
Private Sub Page_Load(ByVal sender As System.Object, _
 ByVal e As System.EventArgs) Handles MyBase.Load
    lblError.Text = "Error Details: " & "<br>"
    ' Get the Exception object from the Session
    Dim ex As Exception = Session("Error")
    lblError.Text = lblError.Text & ex.ToString()
End Sub
```

7. Set `GuidedPracticeExercise4-2.aspx` as the start page for the project.

8. Run the project. Enter invalid values for miles and gallons and click the Calculate button. The ErrorGPE4-2.aspx page displays the error details.

CHAPTER SUMMARY

KEY TERMS

- Exception
- Exception handling
- Unhandled exceptions

The .NET Framework includes thorough support for exception handling. In fact, it allows you to raise exceptions in one language and catch them in a program written in another language. A Try block should enclose any code that may cause exceptions. A Catch block is used to handle the exceptions raised by the code in the Try block and the Finally block contains code that will be executed irrespective of the occurrence of an exception.

The Framework Class Library (FCL) provides a large number of Exception classes that represent most of the exceptions that your program might encounter. If you prefer to create your own custom exception class, you can do so by deriving your exception class from the ApplicationException class.

You also learned how to configure custom error pages at an application level using the <customErrors> element and at a page level using the ErrorPage property of the Page class or the ErrorPage attribute of the Page directive. You can set static HTML pages as well as dynamic ASPX pages as custom error pages. You also learned how to trap unhandled exceptions of a page in the Page_Error event handler. You can also trap unhandled exceptions of an application (that is, of all Web pages in an application) in the Application_Error event handler in the global.asax file.

APPLY YOUR KNOWLEDGE

Exercises

4.1 Emailing Unhandled Exceptions

The objective of this exercise is to send email notifications whenever an unhandled exception occurs in an application.

Estimated Time: 15 minutes.

1. Open a new Web Application in Visual Basic .NET. Name it 305C04Exercises.

2. Add a Web Form to the project. Name this form Exercise4-1.

3. Add the following code to the `Page_Load` event handler:

```
Private Sub Page_Load( _
 ByVal sender As System.Object, _
 ByVal e As System.EventArgs) _
 Handles MyBase.Load
    Throw New Exception( _
     "This exception needs to be emailed")
End Sub
```

4. Open the `global.asax` file in code view. Add a line of code at the top of the file:

```
Imports System.Web.Mail
```

5. Add the following code to the `Application_Error` event handler (change the To address to an actual email address to which you have access):

```
Sub Application_Error( _
 ByVal sender As Object, _
 ByVal e As EventArgs)
    ' Get the Exception object wrapped
    ' in the InnerException property
    Dim unhandledException As Exception = _
     Server.GetLastError().InnerException

    ' Create a MailMessage object
    Dim m As MailMessage = _
     New MailMessage()
    m.From = "errors@server.com"
    m.To = "admin@server.com"
    m.BodyFormat = MailFormat.Text
    m.Subject = _
     "unHandledException.Message"
    m.Body = unhandledException.ToString()

    ' Send the email
    SmtpMail.Send(m)
End Sub
```

6. Set the form as the start page for the project.

7. Run the project. You will see an error message from ASP.NET. At the same time, an email will also be sent to the email account specified in the code.

Review Questions

1. What is the default behavior of the .NET Framework when an exception is raised?

2. Which base class of all the exceptions provides the basic functionality for exception handling? What are the two main types of exception classes and their purpose?

3. Explain the Message and InnerException property of the Exception class.

4. What is the purpose of Try and Catch blocks?

5. How many Catch blocks can be associated with a single Try block? How should they be arranged?

6. What is the importance of the Finally block?

7. Can you associate custom error messages with the exception types defined by the CLR? If yes, how can you do this?

8. What are some of the points you should consider before creating custom exceptions?

APPLY YOUR KNOWLEDGE

9. What are custom error pages used for? What is the ASP.NET style of configuring them?
10. What is the purpose of the mode attribute in the <customErrors> element?
11. What are the events that are fired when an unhandled exception occurs in a Web application?
12. What is the importance of the GetLastError method?

Exam Questions

1. You are creating a data import utility for a personal information system that you designed recently. When the record in the source data file is not in the required format, your application needs to throw a custom exception. You will name this exception class InvalidRecordStructureException. Which of the following classes would you choose as the base class for your custom exception class?

   A. `ApplicationException`

   B. `Exception`

   C. `SystemException`

   D. `InvalidFilterCriteriaException`

2. You are assisting your colleague in solving the compiler error that his code is throwing. The problematic portion of his code is

```
Try
    Dim success As Boolean = _
     GenerateNewtonSeries(500, 0)
    ' more code here
Catch dbze As DivideByZeroException
    ' exception handling code
Catch nfne As NotFiniteNumberException
    ' exception handling code
Catch ae As ArithmeticException
    ' exception handling code
Catch e As OverflowException
    ' exception handling code
End Try
```

To remove the compilation error, which of the following ways would you modify the code?

A.

```
Try
    Dim success As Boolean = _
     GenerateNewtonSeries(500, 0)
    ' more code here
Catch dbze As DivideByZeroException
    ' exception handling code
Catch ae As ArithmeticException
    ' exception handling code
Catch e As OverflowException
    ' exception handling code
End Try
```

B.

```
Try
    Dim success As Boolean = _
     GenerateNewtonSeries(500, 0)
    ' more code here
Catch dbze As DivideByZeroException
    ' exception handling code
Catch ae As Exception
    ' exception handling code
Catch e As OverflowException
    ' exception handling code
End Try
```

C.

```
Try
    Dim success As Boolean = _
     GenerateNewtonSeries(500, 0)
    ' more code here
Catch dbze As DivideByZeroException
    ' exception handling code
Catch nfne As NotFiniteNumberException
    ' exception handling code
Catch e As OverflowException
    ' exception handling code
Catch ae As ArithmeticException
    ' exception handling code
End Try
```

APPLY YOUR KNOWLEDGE

D.

```
Try
    Dim success As Boolean = _
     GenerateNewtonSeries(500, 0)
    ' more code here
Catch dbze As DivideByZeroException
    ' exception handling code
Catch nfne As NotFiniteNumberException
    ' exception handling code
Catch ae As Exception
    ' exception handling code
Catch e As OverflowException
    ' exception handling code
End Try
```

3. You need to debug a program containing some exception handling code. To understand the program better, you created a stripped-down version of it and included some Response.Write statements that give you a clue about the flow of its execution. The program has the following code:

```
Try
    Dim num As Integer = 100
    dim den as Integer  = 0)
    Response.Write("Message1")
    Try
        Dim res As Integer = num / den
        Response.Write("Message2")
    Catch ae As ArithmeticException
        Response.Write("Message3")
    End Try
Catch dbze As DivideByZeroException
    Response.Write("Message4")
Finally
    Response.Write("Message5")
End Try
```

Which of these is the order of messages that you receive?

A.

```
Message1
Message2
Message3
Message4
Message5
```

B.

```
Message1
Message3
Message5
```

C.

```
Message1
Message4
Message5
```

D.

```
Message1
Message2
Message4
Message5
```

4. What is the output displayed by the Label control named lblResult in the following code segment?

```
Try
    Try
        Throw New _
         ArgumentOutOfRangeException()
    Catch ae As ArgumentException
        Throw New ArgumentException( _
         "Out of Range", ae)
    End Try
Catch ex As Exception
    lblResult.Text = _
     ex.InnerException.GetType().ToString()
End Try
```

A. System.Exception

B. System.ApplicationException

C. System.ArgumentException

D. System.ArgumentOutOfRangeException

5. You are designing a global Time-Entry system for a multinational company. It will be an ASP.NET application that will be served over the Internet through the company's Web server. You are designing an error handling mechanism for this application. You want the application to show a customized error page for all HTTP errors.

APPLY YOUR KNOWLEDGE

All unhandled exceptions caused by the ASP.NET pages should be logged in the Web server's event log. Which of the following places will be your preferred place to write this code? (Select two.)

A. web.config

B. global.asax

C. in the ASPX file, using the Page directive

D. machine.config

6. You have developed a global Time-Entry system for a multinational company. The system is an ASP.NET application served over the Internet through the company's Web server in New York. The first phase of testing is being performed in the Los Angeles offices where you are told that users are getting default ASP.NET error pages instead of customized error pages. Which of the following options settings you need to make to enable custom pages for those users? (Select two.)

   A. Set the mode attribute of the <customErrors> element in web.config file to `On`.

   B. Set the mode attribute of the <customErrors> element in web.config file to `Off`.

   C. Set the mode attribute of the <customErrors> element in web.config file to RemoteOnly.

   D. Set the defaultRedirect attribute of the <customErrors> element in web.config file to the location of custom error page.

7. You need to create a custom exception class in your Windows application. You have written the following code for the exception class:

```
Public Class KeywordNotFound
    Inherits ApplicationException

    Public Sub New()
        ' Code here
    End Sub

    Public Sub New(ByVal message As String, _
     ByVal inner As Exception)
        MyBase.New(message, inner)
        ' Code here
    End Sub

End Class
```

   A code review suggests that that you did not follow some of the best practices for creating a custom exception class. Which of these changes should you make (Select two.)?

   A. Name the exception class KeywordNotFoundException.

   B. Derive the exception class from the base class Exception instead of ApplicationException.

   C. Add one more constructor to the class with the following signature

```
Public Sub New(ByVal message As String)
    MyBase.New(message)
    ' Code here
End Sub
```

   D. Add one more constructor to the class with the following signature

```
Public Sub New(ByVal inner As Exception)
    MyBase.New(inner)
    ' Code here
End Sub
```

   E. Derive the exception class from the base class SystemException instead of ApplicationException.

8. You are writing the error handling code for an ASP.NET Web application. You want to display different custom error pages for different HTTP error codes in the application. Which one of the following options should you choose?

APPLY YOUR KNOWLEDGE

A. Set the ErrorPage attribute of the Page directive to the custom page.

B. Set the ErrorPage property of the Page class to the custom page.

C. Set the redirect attribute of the <error> element to the custom page.

D. Set the defaultRedirect attribute of the <customErrors> element to the custom page.

9. You are writing exception handling code for an order entry form. When the exception occurs, you want to get information about the sequence of method calls and the line number in the method where the exception occurs. Which property of your exception class can help you?

   A. HelpLink

   B. InnerException

   C. Message

   D. StackTrace

10. Your code uses the Throw statement in this fashion:

```
Catch e As Exception
    Throw
```

   Which of these statements is true about this code?

   A. The Throw statement catches and rethrows the current exception.

   B. The Throw statement catches, wraps, and then rethrows the current exception.

   C. The Throw statement must be followed by an exception object to be thrown.

   D. The Throw statement transfers control to the Finally block following the Catch block.

11. In your ASP.NET application, you are opening a file. You want to close the file whether or not an exception occurs in the program. Which of the following code blocks can help you to achieve this?

   A. Try

   B. Catch

   C. Finally

   D. Imports

12. You want to capture all the exceptions that escape from the exception handling code in your application and log them to the system event log. Which of the following techniques would you use?

   A. Program the Application_End event handler in the global.asax file.

   B. Program the Page_Unload event handler of the Page class.

   C. Program the Page_Error event handler of the Page class.

   D. Program the Application_Error event handler in the global.asax file.

13. Which of the following is generally the most robust way to record the unhandled exceptions in your application?

   A. Create an entry in the Windows event log.

   B. Create an entry in the application's custom event log.

   C. Create an entry in a table in Microsoft SQL Server 2000 database.

   D. Send an email using SMTP.

APPLY YOUR KNOWLEDGE

14. The structured exception handling mechanism of the .NET Framework allows you to handle which of the following types of exceptions? (Select all that apply.)

    A. Exceptions from all CLS-compliant languages.

    B. Exceptions from non-CLS-compliant languages.

    C. Exceptions from unmanaged COM code.

    D. Exceptions from unmanaged non-COM code.

15. What is the result of executing this code snippet?

```
Const someVal1 As Int32 = Int32.MaxValue
Const someVal2 As Int32 = Int32.MaxValue
Dim result As Int32

result = someVal1 * someVal2
```

    A. The code generates an OverflowException.

    B. The code executes successfully without any exceptions.

    C. The code causes a compile-time error.

    D. The code executes successfully but the value of the variable result is truncated.

Answers to Review Questions

1. When an Exception is raised, the .NET Framework stops processing the page after displaying an error.

2. The Exception class is the base class that provides common functionality for exception handling. The two main types of exceptions derived from Exception class are SystemException and `ApplicationException`. `SystemException` represents the exceptions thrown by the CLR, whereas ApplicationException represents the exceptions thrown by user code.

3. The Message property describes the current exception. The InnerException property represents an exception object associated with the exception object; this property is helpful when a series of exceptions are involved. Each new exception can preserve information about previous exception by storing it in InnerException property.

4. The Try block is used to enclose code that may raise an exception. The Catch block handles any exception raised by the code in the Try block.

5. Zero or more Catch blocks can be associated with a single Try block. If there is no Catch block associated with a Try block, a Finally block should follow the Try block; otherwise a compile-time error occurs. The Catch blocks should be arranged from top to bottom in the order of specific to general exception types; otherwise a compile time error occurs.

6. The code contained by the Finally block always executes whether or not any exception occurs in the application. Therefore you can use the Finally block to write cleanup code to do things such as closing data connections, closing files and so on, that needs to be performed whether or not an exception occurred.

7. Yes, you can associate custom error messages with the exception classes defined by the CLR to provide more meaningful information to the caller code.

APPLY YOUR KNOWLEDGE

The constructor of these classes that accepts the exception message as its parameter can be used to pass the custom error message.

8. Custom exceptions should be derived from ApplicationException and should be created only if existing classes do not meet the requirements of your application. They should have a name ending with the word Exception and should implement the three constructors (default, Message, Message and Exception) of their base class.

9. Custom error pages are used to show user-friendly error pages whenever an unhandled error occurs in an application. ASP.NET provides built-in support to configure custom error pages using the <customErrors> element.

10. The mode attribute in the <customErrors> element specifies the location (clients) where the custom error pages should be displayed. It can have one of three values—`On` (display custom error pages to both local and remote clients), `Off` (do not display custom error pages to any of the clients), and `RemoteOnly` (display custom error pages to only remote clients).

11. When an unhandled exception occurs in a Web application, the Page.Error and the Application.Error events are fired in that order.

12. The GetLastError method of the HttpServerUtility class returns an Exception object that encapsulates the error details of the last error that occurred on the server.

Answers to Exam Questions

1. **A.** When creating a class for handling custom exceptions in your programs, the best practice is to derive it from the ApplicationException class. The SystemException class is for system-defined exceptions. The Exception class is the base class for both ApplicationException and SystemException class and should not generally be derived from directly.

2. **C.**When you have multiple Catch blocks associated with a Try block, you must write them in the order of most specific to the most general. The Catch block corresponding to the ArithmeticException should come at the end as it is relatively more general class as compared to the other three—DivideByZeroException, NotFiniteNumberException, and the OverFlowException classes that are derived from it.

3. **B.** When an exception occurs in a Try block, it searches for a matching Catch block associated with that Try block. In this case, the `ArithmeticException` generates a match for DivideByZeroException because DivideByZeroException is derived from ArithmeticException, and the exception is handled right there. In all cases the Finally block is executed.

4. **D.** The Label control displays System.ArgumentOutOfRangeException because that is the exception that you caught and wrapped in the InnerException property of the exception that was caught later by the outer `Catch` block.

APPLY YOUR KNOWLEDGE

5. **A** and **B**. The customized error page for HTTP errors can be shown using the <error> element in the web.config file. To catch all unhandled exceptions in an application, the Application_Error event handler in the global.asax file needs to be programmed.

6. **C** and **D**. To set the custom error page you need to set the defaultRedirect attribute to the location of the custom error page and to enable custom error pages for LA testing team, you will have to set the mode attribute to RemoteOnly.

7. **A, C.** The best practices for exception handling recommend that you must end the name of your exception class with the word Exception. In addition to this, an exception class must implement three standard constructors. The missing constructor is the one given in option C.

8. **C**. The <error> element associates the HTTP error codes with custom error pages. The statusCode attribute holds the error code and the redirect attribute holds the location of the custom error page. The defaultRedirect attribute sets the custom error page for all types of errors that are not handled by the <error> element. The ErrorPage property and ErrorPage attribute only set the error page for a specific page that is displayed whenever an error occurs during the processing of that page request.

9. **D.** The StackTrace property of the Exception class and the classes that derive from it contains information about the sequence of method calls and the line numbers in which the exception occurred. Therefore, it is the right property to use.

10. **A.** The Throw statement just catches and throws the current exception.

11. **C**. The Finally block is the correct location for this purpose.

12. **D**. You need to handle unhandled exceptions in the Error events. Because you need to trap exceptions for the whole of application, Application_Error event handler is the best place to trap exceptions.

13. **A.** Logging to the Windows event handler is the most robust solution because the other solutions have more assumptions that may fail. Sometimes your application may lose connectivity with the database or with the SMTP server or you might have problems writing an entry in a custom log file.

14. **A, B, C, D.** The .NET Framework allows you to handle all kinds of exceptions, including cross-language exceptions for both CLS- and non–CLS-complaint languages. It also allows you to handle exceptions from unmanaged code, both COM and non-COM.

15. **C.** Because you are multiplying two maximum possible values for integer, the result can certainly be not stored inside an integer. The compiler will detect it and will flag a compile time error.

APPLY YOUR KNOWLEDGE

Suggested Readings and Resources

1. Visual Studio .NET Combined Help Collection
   - Exception Management in .NET
   - Exception Handling Statements
   - Best Practices for Exception Handling
2. Shapiro, Jeffrey R., *Visual Basic .NET: The Complete Reference.* McGraw-Hill/Osborne, 2002.
3. Richter, Jeffrey. *Applied Microsoft .NET Framework Programming.* Microsoft Press, 2001.
4. Mitchell, Scott, et al. *ASP.NET: Tips, Tutorials, and Code.* Sams Publishing, 2001.
5. Jones, A. Russell. *Mastering ASP.NET with VB.NET.* Sybex, 2002.

Objectives

This chapter covers the following Microsoft-specified objectives for the Creating User Services section of the Visual Basic .NET Web Applications exam:

Display and update data.

- **Transform and filter data.**
- **Bind data to the user interface.**
- **Use controls to display data.**

▶ Nearly every Web application deals with data in one way or another. The purpose of this objective is to teach you some of the skills involved in making this data available on the user interface (UI) of a Web application. That includes both getting the data that the user wants to see (transforming and filtering) and tying the data to the user interface (data binding). In Chapter 6, "Consuming and Manipulating Data," you'll learn more about programming with data; this objective deals with the parts of the process that you can actually see onscreen.

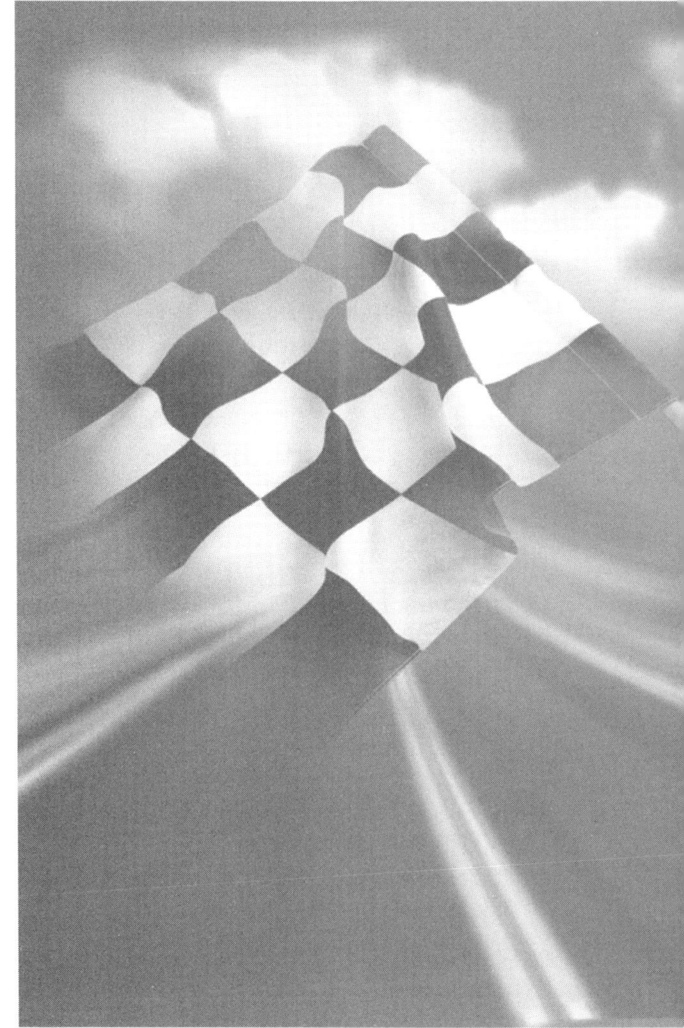

CHAPTER 5

Data Binding

Outline

Study Strategies

- Be sure to read the sections on data binding carefully, even if you think you already know all about data binding. In the .NET world, the concept of data binding has been generalized and improved from what existed in earlier Microsoft development environments. Data binding in ASP.NET bears little resemblance to what was available in classic ASP.
- In previous Microsoft development environments, many writers and trainers recommended avoiding data binding due to performance issues and a lack of flexibility. Microsoft has removed the bulk of these limitations in Visual Studio .NET. Even if you ignored data binding in the past, you should expect to be tested on it this time.
- Make sure you understand the difference between *simple* and *complex data binding*, and the syntax used for each.
- Carefully review the use of the DataBind() method and understand how it offers you control over data binding.
- Practice working with Server Explorer. You should know how to connect your application to any data source and how to select and display the data that you want to show to the end user.
- Build several templated controls (Repeater, DataList, DataGrid) and know which one is appropriate for which situations.

INTRODUCTION

Now that you know how to put together a user interface for an ASP.NET application, it's time to turn to the functionality behind that user interface. One of the most important parts of almost any application is to connect the *data model* of the application to the user interface. Data model is a general term: It might refer to data stored in a database, or to an array of values, or to items contained in an object from the System.Collections namespace. The data model is internal to the application. It contains information that is known to the application.

To be useful for the end users of your application, the data model must somehow be connected to the user interface. One of the easiest ways to make a connection between the data model and the user interface is to bind the data to the user interface. *Binding* refers to the process of making a link between controls on the user interface and data stored in the data model. As the user views and manipulates controls, the application takes care of translating his or her actions into reading and writing data from the data model.

Sometimes the data model contains more information than you want to show to the user. For example, you might have a list of 10,000 customers in the data model. Most likely the user wants to see the orders from a single customer or a small group of customers. So your application will need to filter (limit) the amount of information that it shows from the data model, in order to avoid overwhelming the user or (if your application delivers data over a slow network) his connection. You may also need to transform the data from an internal representation (for example, a customer code) to something more user-friendly (such as a customer name) in the process of moving it from the data model to the user interface.

In this chapter I'll cover all these topics using a very broad concept of data. In the next chapter, I'll drill into the use of ADO.NET, focusing on data stored in databases.

BIND DATA TO THE UI

Display and update data: Bind data to the UI.

Binding data (sometimes called *data binding*) refers to the process of creating a link between a data model and the user interface of an application. The data model can be any source of data within the application: It might be an array of values, an XML file, or data stored in a database. The user interface consists of the controls that are contained on the forms in your application.

ASP.NET includes extremely flexible data binding capabilities. In this section you'll learn about many of those capabilities:

- Simple Data binding
- Complex Data binding
- The DataBind method
- The DataForm Wizard

Simple Data Binding

Simple data binding means connecting a single value from the data model to a single property of a control. For example, you might bind the Vendor name returned by a VendorName property to text on the user interface of a Web Form.

STEP BY STEP

5.1 Using Simple Data Binding to Display a Property Value

1. Create a new Web Form. Set its `pageLayout` property to `FlowLayout`.
2. Switch to HTML view in the designer and add code to the `<body>` tag:

```
<body>
    Vendor:
    <%# VendorName %>
</body>
```

3. Open the Web Form's module and add code to create a public property:

```
Public ReadOnly Property VendorName()
    Get
        VendorName = "Microsoft"
    End Get
End Property
```

4. Add code to the Web Form's `Page_Load` event:

```
Private Sub Page_Load( _
 ByVal sender As System.Object, _
 ByVal e As System.EventArgs) Handles MyBase.Load
    'Put user code to initialize the page here
    DataBind()
End Sub
```

5. Set the Web Form as the start page for the project.

6. Run the project. The user interface is now bound to the property, and will display the value returned from the property.

Looking at the code, you can see that ASP.NET supplies a syntax for binding. The <%# … %> may remind you of the classic ASP syntax <%= … %>, but it works in a different way. The classic ASP version is simply a runtime shortcut for Response.Write(). The new ASP.NET version is evaluated when the DataBind method is called. You'll learn more about the DataBind method later in the chapter.

Binding to Public Members

In the example you just saw, the user interface was bound to a property of the Web Form. The ASP.NET data binding syntax can accept many other things as a data source. These include

- A public member, such as a variable, field, or method of the page.
- Properties of other controls.
- An instance of a collection class.
- The result of an expression.

Often the most convenient way to place a variable value on the user interface of a Web Form is to use simple data binding with a public variable.

STEP BY STEP

5.2 Using Simple Data Binding to a Method

1. Create a new Web Form. Set its `pageLayout` property to `FlowLayout`.
2. Switch to HTML view in the designer and add code to the `<body>` tag:

```
<body>
    The time is:
    <%# CurrentTime() %>
</body>
```

3. Open the Web Form's module and add code to create a public method:

```
Public Function CurrentTime() As String
        CurrentTime = DateTime.Now.ToLongTimeString()
End Function
```

4. Add code to the Web Form's `Page_Load` event:

```
Private Sub Page_Load( _
 ByVal sender As System.Object, _
 ByVal e As System.EventArgs) Handles MyBase.Load
    DataBind()
End Sub
```

5. Set the Web Form as the start page for the project.
6. Run the project. The user interface is now bound to the public method and will display the value calculated by the method when the call to `DataBind()` is executed in the `Page_Load` event. Note the parentheses in the data binding expression, which indicate that `CurrentTime` is a method call.

> **NOTE**
>
> **Controlling the Binding Time** This list of steps demonstrates that you can control the point in your code at which the data is bound to the user interface by explicitly calling the `DataBind()` method when you want the binding to occur.

Just as the .NET Framework allows flexibility in the source of bound data, it allows flexibility on the user interface side of the equation. You can use simple data binding to any property that you can set in the HTML for a Web Form. In practice, that's any property of any control that you can drop on a Web Form.

This gives you enormous flexibility in building a user interface that depends on data. For example, you can bind a DateTime value to the SelectedDate property of a Calendar control.

STEP BY STEP

5.3 Binding Data to a `Calendar` Control

1. Place a `Calendar` control on a new ASP.NET Form.
2. Place a `Button` control on the form. Set the ID of the control to `btnTomorrow` and set its `Text` property to `"Tomorrow"`.
3. Switch to HTML view and add a data binding marker to the `Calendar` control:

```
<asp:Calendar id="Calendar1" runat="server"
SelectedDate="<%# DateTime.Today.AddDays(1) %>">
</asp:Calendar></P>
```

4. Switch back to Design view and double-click the button. Enter code into the form's module to handle the `Click` event:

```
Private Sub btnTomorrow_Click( _
 ByVal sender As System.Object, _
 ByVal e As System.EventArgs) _
 Handles btnTomorrow.Click
    Page.DataBind()
End Sub
```

5. Set the Web Form as the start page for the project.
6. Run the project. When you click the button, the form will reload with tomorrow's date selected on the `Calendar` control. The syntax for simple data binding is the same no matter what property of what control you choose to bind.

Binding to Control Properties

You can also bind a property of one server control directly to a property of another server control. This provides you with an easy method to transfer information from one part of a Web Form to another.

STEP BY STEP

5.4 Binding a Control to Another Control

1. Place a `Calendar` control on a new ASP.NET Form. Set the ID of this control to `Calendar1`.

2. Place a `Label` control on the form (be sure to use the Web Forms `Label` control, not the HTML `Label` control). Set the ID of this control to `lblInfo`. Set the `Visible` property of this control to `False`. Switch to HTML view and enter a data-binding expression that refers to a property of the `Calendar` control as the text for the `Label` control:

```
<asp:Label id="lblInfo" runat="server"
 Visible="False">
   <%# Calendar1.SelectedDate.ToShortDateString %>
</asp:Label>
```

3. Double-click the `Calendar` control. Enter code into the form's module to handle the `SelectionChanged` event:

```
Private Sub Calendar1_SelectionChanged( _
 ByVal sender As System.Object, _
 ByVal e As System.EventArgs) _
 Handles Calendar1.SelectionChanged
    lblInfo.Visible = True
    lblInfo.DataBind()
End Sub
```

4. Set the Web Form as the start page for the project.

5. Run the project. When you click on a date in the `Calendar` control, the label control will be made visible, and it will display the selected date, because its `Text` property is bound directly to the `Calendar` control's `SelectedDate` property.

This example works because the value that you specified for the `Text` property of the Label control includes a data-binding expression that refers to a property of the Calendar control. When you activate data binding on the Label control (by invoking its DataBind method), ASP.NET evaluates this property and inserts it into the resulting HTML page.

If you think creatively, you can find many ways to use simple data binding beyond simple displaying text on a form. Some possibilities:

- Control the error message shown by a RequiredFieldValidator control by binding text to its ErrorMessage property.
- Show the relative magnitude of quantities with the Width property of a Panel control. For example, you might create a bar graph in which the bars are actually Panel control bound to the quantities that you want to graph.
- Color-code an area of a form by binding the BackColor property of a Panel control.

REVIEW BREAK

- Simple data binding refers to connecting a single entity in the data model to a single property of a control on the user interface.
- Anything that will deliver data can be bound. This includes public Page properties, methods, public variables, and properties of other controls.
- You can bind to almost any property of any control.

Complex Data Binding

In complex data binding, you bind a user interface control to an entire collection of data, rather than to a single data item. A good example of complex data binding is the DataGrid control. Figure 5.1 shows a bound DataGrid control displaying data from the Suppliers table in the SQL Server 2000 Northwind database.

FIGURE 5.1
By using complex data binding, you can see an entire collection of data on the user interface at one time. Here a DataGrid control displays the Northwind Suppliers table.

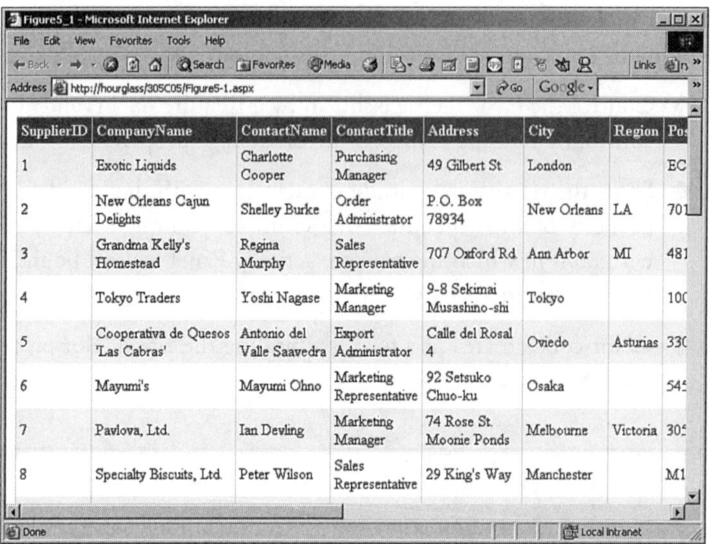

SupplierID	CompanyName	ContactName	ContactTitle	Address	City	Region	Pos
1	Exotic Liquids	Charlotte Cooper	Purchasing Manager	49 Gilbert St.	London		EC
2	New Orleans Cajun Delights	Shelley Burke	Order Administrator	P.O. Box 78934	New Orleans	LA	701
3	Grandma Kelly's Homestead	Regina Murphy	Sales Representative	707 Oxford Rd.	Ann Arbor	MI	481
4	Tokyo Traders	Yoshi Nagase	Marketing Manager	9-8 Sekimai Musashino-shi	Tokyo		10
5	Cooperativa de Quesos 'Las Cabras'	Antonio del Valle Saavedra	Export Administrator	Calle del Rosal 4	Oviedo	Asturias	33
6	Mayumi's	Mayumi Ohno	Marketing Representative	92 Setsuko Chuo-ku	Osaka		54
7	Pavlova, Ltd.	Ian Devling	Marketing Manager	74 Rose St. Moonie Ponds	Melbourne	Victoria	30
8	Specialty Biscuits, Ltd.	Peter Wilson	Sales Representative	29 King's Way	Manchester		M1

WARNING

Not All DataGrids Are the Same! You may already be familiar with the DataGrid control that you can place on a Windows form in a VB .NET Windows application. Although this DataGrid control is similar in appearance to that DataGrid control, they are not the same. Be sure to study the differences between the two controls.

EXAM TIP

Database Terminology In some literature you'll see the rows of a database table referred to as records or tuples and the columns referred to as fields or attributes.

NOTE

The Northwind Sample Database Whenever I've used data from a database in this book, I've used the Northwind sample database that comes as part of SQL Server 2000. Visual Studio .NET includes MSDE, a stripped-down version of SQL Server that you can use if you don't have the full version installed. See your Visual Studio CD's readme file for information on installing MSDE. You can also find the Northwind sample database in any version of Microsoft Access, but the Access version does not ship with Visual Studio .NET. The code in this book assumes that you're using the SQL Server version.

You'll learn how to build forms like this later in the chapter, but for now, just concentrate on its features. The DataGrid is a single control that displays many pieces of data. In this case, the data is taken from the rows and columns of the Suppliers table in a SQL Server 2000 database. With additional programming, you can add interactivity to the control. For example, you can make it possible to edit the displayed data and then write the changes back to the data model and from there to the underlying database.

Obviously, complex data binding is a powerful tool for transferring large amounts of data from a data model to a user interface. In this section we'll dig into the mechanics of complex data binding with three examples:

- Binding to a DropDownList or ListBox
- Binding to a CheckBoxList or RadioButtonList
- Binding to a DataGrid

Binding to a DropDownList or ListBox

The DropDownList and ListBox controls both provide ways for the user to select one item from a list of data. The difference between the two is that in the ListBox the list is visible at all times, whereas in the DropDownList the list is hidden until the user clicks the drop-down arrow at the end of the box. Either of these controls can be loaded with an entire list of data via complex data binding.

These controls can be bound to any collection that supports the IEnumerable, ICollection, or IListSource interface. This includes the ArrayList, HashTable, DataReader, and DataView classes.

STEP BY STEP

5.5 Binding Data to the List in a `ListBox` Control

1. Place a `ListBox` control on a new Web Form. Set the ID of the control to `lbExams`.

2. Add a new module named `Exam.vb` to your VB .NET project. Enter this code in the module:

```
Imports System.Data

Module Exam

    Public Function DataLoad() As ICollection
        Dim dt As DataTable = New DataTable()
        Dim dv As DataView
        Dim dr As DataRow

        ' Add two columns to the DataTable
        dt.Columns.Add(New DataColumn( _
         "ExamNumber", GetType(String)))
        dt.Columns.Add(New DataColumn( _
        "ExamName", GetType(String)))

        ' Put some data in
        dr = dt.NewRow()
        dr(0) = "305"
        dr(1) = "Web Applications With VB.NET"
        dt.Rows.Add(dr)

        dr = dt.NewRow()
        dr(0) = "306"
        dr(1) = "Windows Applications With VB.NET"
        dt.Rows.Add(dr)

        dr = dt.NewRow()
        dr(0) = "310"
        dr(1) = "XML With VB.NET"
        dt.Rows.Add(dr)

        dr = dt.NewRow()
        dr(0) = "315"
        dr(1) = "Web Applications With Visual C# .NET"
        dt.Rows.Add(dr)
```

continues

continued

```
        dr = dt.NewRow()
        dr(0) = "316"
        dr(1) = _
         "Windows Applications With Visual C# .NET"
        dt.Rows.Add(dr)

        dr = dt.NewRow()
        dr(0) = "320"
        dr(1) = "XML With Visual C# .NET"
        dt.Rows.Add(dr)

        ' And return the datatable
        ' wrapped in a dataview
        dv = New DataView(dt)
        Return dv

    End Function

End Module
```

3. Double-click the Web Form and enter code in the form's `Load` event:

```
Private Sub Page_Load( _
 ByVal sender As System.Object, _
 ByVal e As System.EventArgs) Handles MyBase.Load
    lbExams.DataSource = DataLoad()
    lbExams.DataTextField = "ExamName"
    DataBind()
End Sub
```

4. Set the Web Form as the start page for the project.

5. Run the project. The `ListBox` control will display the `ExamName` property of every object in the `DataView`. Note that the `DataLoad` function has a return value typed as `ICollection`, which is one of the types that the `ListBox` can use as a `DataSource`.

NOTE

About the Data Objects The DataLoad function uses four objects that you haven't seen before: DataRow, DataColumn, DataTable, and DataView. You'll meet these objects in detail in Chapter 6. But for now, you can just think of them in simple terms. The DataTable stores a table of data (a table, in this context, is a rectangular array of data). The DataColumn represents one column in a DataTable, and the DataRow represents one row in a DataTable. The DataView provides a way to deliver all or part of the contents of a DataTable through the bindable ICollection interface. You can also access the contents of a DataView as if it were a two-dimensional array. That is, dv(1)(1) returns the second item in the second row of the DataView (the subscripts are numbered starting with zero).

Frequently you'll use a complex data bound ListBox or DropDownList in conjunction with a simple data bound control such as a TextBox. By selecting a row in the ListBox, the user can choose a value for the TextBox.

You can think of the ListBox in this case as a little pump that moves data from one part of your application to another. Step By Step 5.6 shows how you can set this up.

STEP BY STEP

5.6 Using a `ListBox` With Two Data Bindings

1. Place a `ListBox` control on a new Web Form. Set the ID of the control to `lbExams` and the `AutoPostBack` property of the control to True. Add a `Label` control to the Web Form. Set the ID of the control to `lblSelected` and the `Text` property to

```
<%# lbExams.SelectedItem.Value %>
```

Figure 5.2 shows the Web Form open in the designer.

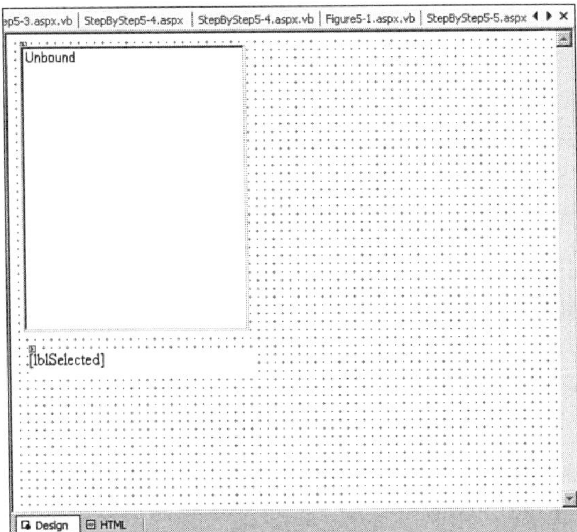

FIGURE 5.2
This Web Form will automatically look up data from the selected item in the ListBox control and place the results in the Label control.

2. You'll need the `Exam.vb` module from Step by Step 5.5, so enter it now if you didn't already create it.

3. Double-click the Web Form and enter code in the form's `Load` event:

```
Private Sub Page_Load(ByVal sender As System.Object, _
 ByVal e As System.EventArgs) Handles MyBase.Load
    If Not IsPostBack Then
        lbExams.DataSource = DataLoad()
        lbExams.DataTextField = "ExamName"
        lbExams.DataValueField = "ExamNumber"
        lbExams.DataBind()
    End If
End Sub
```

continues

continued

4. Enter code for the ListBox's SelectedIndexChanged event:

```
Private Sub lbExams_SelectedIndexChanged( _
 ByVal sender As System.Object, _
 ByVal e As System.EventArgs) _
 Handles lbExams.SelectedIndexChanged
    lblSelected.DataBind()
End Sub
```

5. Set the Web Form as the start page for the project.

6. Run the project. The ListBox control will display the ExamName property of every object in the DataView. When you select an exam name, the corresponding ExamNumber value will appear in the Label control.

Understanding this example is crucial for the effective use of DropDownList and ListBox controls in your applications. That can be a little tricky, because the ListBox control is bound to two different things. To review how it all fits together:

- The ListBox in this example draws the list of items to display from the DataView of exam information. The list portion of the listbox is complex bound to this object. The complex binding is managed by setting the DataSource, DataTextField, and DataValueField properties of the ListBox.
- When you first load the form, the data is loaded by calling the DataBind method of the ListBox itself. The check of the IsPostBack form variable makes sure that this only happens once. If you neglected to check, then the data would be loaded when the form was posted back, and you'd lose the information on which ListBox item was selected.
- When you click an item in the ListBox, it posts that information back to the server, because the AutoPostBack property of the ListBox is set to True.
- The SelectedIndexChanged event handles binding the currently selected row of the ListBox to the Label. The code for this calls the DataBind method of the Label control itself.
- You can use the DataTextField and DataValueField properties of the ListBox control to cause it to show one value while binding another, as in this example.

Binding to a CheckBoxList or RadioButtonList

There are two other controls in the Web Forms toolbox that function like the DropDownList and ListBox controls. These are the CheckBoxList and RadioButtonList controls. Figure 5.3 shows these two controls on a Web Form.

Although the RadioButtonList and CheckBoxList controls are rendered as groups of radio button or checkbox controls, they're designed as a single control. Step by Step 5.7 shows how you create a set of radio buttons dynamically by binding a RadioButtonList control to a DataView.

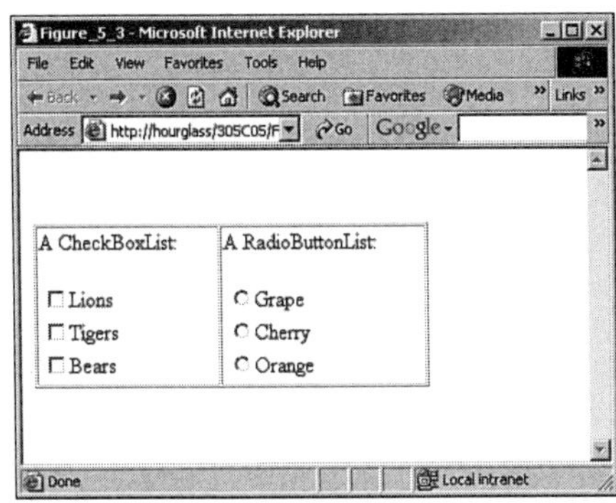

FIGURE 5.3
A CheckBoxList control and a RadioButtonList control. Though these controls are rendered as groups of other controls, you design each one as a single entity.

STEP BY STEP

5.7 Binding Data to the List in a `RadioButtonList` Control

1. Place a `RadioButtonList` control on a new Web Form. Set the ID of the control to `rblExams`.

2. If your sample project does not already contain the `Exam.vb` module, use the code in Step By Step 5.5 to create this module.

3. Double-click the Web Form and enter code in the form's `Load` event:

```
Private Sub Page_Load( _
 ByVal sender As System.Object, _
 ByVal e As System.EventArgs) Handles MyBase.Load
    rblExams.DataSource = DataLoad()
    rblExams.DataTextField = "ExamName"
    DataBind()
End Sub
```

4. Set the Web Form as the start page for the project.

5. Run the project. The `RadioButtonList` control will display the `ExamName` property of every object in the `DataView`. If you compare this Step by Step with the previous one, you'll see that the `RadioButtonList` functions exactly the same as the `ListBox`. The two controls just render the bound data in slightly different formats.

Binding to a DataGrid

The DataGrid also provides a way to display many rows from a data model at one time. The DataGrid is designed to let you see an entire collection of data (often called a *resultset*) at one time.

STEP BY STEP

5.8 Binding a `DataView` to a `DataGrid`

1. Place a `DataGrid` control on a new Web Form. Set the ID of the control to `dgExams`.
2. You'll need the `Exam.vb` module from Step By Step 5.5, so enter it now if you didn't already create it.
3. Double-click the form and enter code in the form's `Load` event:

```
Private Sub Page_Load( _
 ByVal sender As System.Object, _
 ByVal e As System.EventArgs) Handles MyBase.Load
    dgExams.DataSource = DataLoad()
    DataBind()
End Sub
```

4. Set the form as the startup object for the project.
5. Run the project. The `DataGrid` will display all the information from the exams `DataView`. Notice that you don't have to do anything to tell the `DataGrid` what data to display. It takes care of all of the details of turning rows and columns from the `DataView` into rows and columns in an HTML table.

The DataGrid control is a mainstay of data display for ASP.NET forms. As such, it is extremely configurable. Visual Studio .NET includes several interfaces for setting the display properties of a DataGrid. First, you can set individual properties to control the look of the DataGrid in the Properties Window. Second, you can use AutoFormats to apply a whole new look to a DataGrid quickly.

STEP BY STEP

5.9 Applying an AutoFormat to a `DataGrid`

1. Select a `DataGrid` control on a Visual Basic .NET form with the form open in the Visual Studio .NET Designer.
2. Click the AutoFormat hyperlink, located directly under the properties list in the Properties Window. This will open the Auto Format dialog box.
3. Select a Format from the list and click OK to apply the new format to the `DataGrid` control.

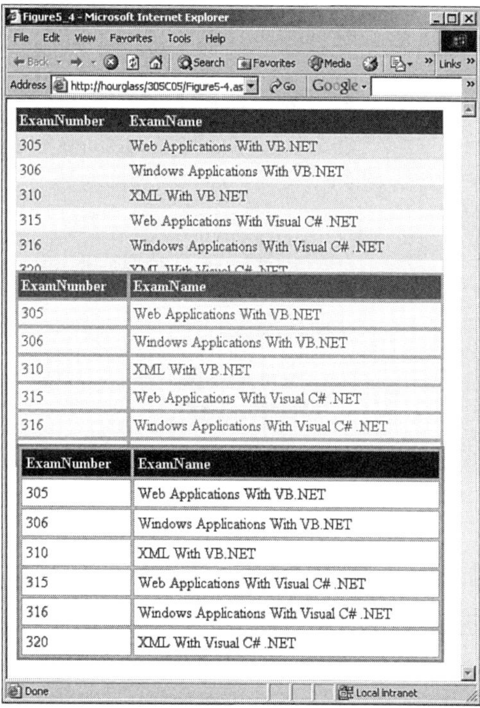

FIGURE 5.4
The three DataGrid controls on this Web Form have had three different AutoFormats applied. Though they are each bound to the same DataView, they all look different.

When you need more precise formatting for a DataGrid control than the Auto Format dialog box allows, or when you just don't care for the look of any of the AutoFormats, you can set individual display properties for the DataGrid control. Table 5.1 lists the properties that you can use to control the look of the DataGrid control.

TABLE 5.1

DATAGRID CONTROL DISPLAY PROPERTIES

Property	*Explanation*
`AllowCustomPaging`	Boolean property that controls whether you will write custom code to support moving between groups of records
`AllowPaging`	Boolean property that controls whether the grid supports moving between groups of records
`AllowSorting`	Boolean property that controls whether the grid allows sorting records by clicking on column headers
`AlternatingItemStyle`	Display style (font, color, and so on) to use for even-numbered rows in the grid
`AutoGenerateColumns`	Boolean property that controls whether the grid automatically includes one column for each column in the resultset
`BackColor`	Background color of the control
`BackImageUrl`	URL of an image to display in the background of the grid
`BorderColor`	Color to use for the control's border
`BorderStyle`	Select from None, Dotted, Dashed, and so on for the borders of the control
`BorderWidth`	Width of the border of the grid
`CellPadding`	Amount of space between the contents of a cell and the cell's border
`CellSpacing`	Amount of space between cells
`CssClass`	Cascading Style Sheet class used to render the control
`Font`	Font for text in the control
`ForeColor`	Foreground color for text in the control
`Gridlines`	Boolean property that controls whether the grid is displayed
`HeaderStyle`	Display style (font, color, and so on) to use for the header row
`ItemStyle`	Display style (font, color, and so on) to use for items in the grid
`PagerStyle`	Display style (font, color, and so on) to use for any paging controls

Property	*Explanation*
`SelectedItemStyle`	Display style (font, color, and so on) to use for any selected item in the grid
`ShowFooter`	Boolean property that controls whether the grid includes a footer row
`ShowHeader`	Boolean property that controls whether the grid includes a header row
`Style`	The style attribute for the Web control

EXAM TIP

Don't Memorize Properties You're not likely to need to know every single one of these properties for the exam. This list will give you a sense of the things that you can customize, but it's more important to learn the techniques for customization.

GUIDED PRACTICE EXERCISE 5.1

In this exercise, you'll be working with employee data from Skylark Spaceways. This exercise will help you review the basic syntax of both simple and complex data binding, as well as the use of the DataGrid control. Table 5.2 shows the data that you need to manage.

TABLE 5.2
SKYLARK SPACEWAYS EMPLOYEE ROSTER

Employee Number	*Employee Name*	*Position*	*Home Planet*
1	E.E. Smith	CEO	Earth
2	Melanie "Jets" Riggs	Chief Pilot	Mars
3	William Danforth	Pilot	Mars
4	Blaise Canton	Engineer	Luna
5	Amanda Timmel	CFO	Earth

The task you need to perform is to display this data in two different ways. First, you should create a Web Form that displays information about one employee at a time. This Web Form will include a DropDownList control that shows all the employee numbers; when you select an employee number, it should display the rest of the information on that employee. There should be a link on this Web Form to open a second Web Form. The second Web Form should display the entire employee roster in grid form.

continues

continued

You should try doing this on your own first. If you get stuck, or you'd like to see one possible solution, follow these steps:

1. Create a Web Form populated with a DropDownList control (ddlEmployeeNumber), three TextBox controls (txtEmployeeName, txtPosition, and txtHomePlanet), four Label controls, and a HyperLink control, arranged as shown in Figure 5.5. Set the AutoPostBack property of the DropDownList control to True. Set the NavigateUrl property of the HyperLink control to GuidedPraticeExercise5_1a.aspx.

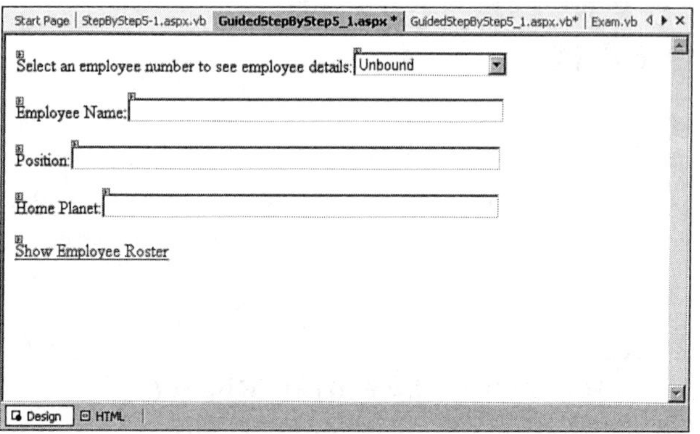

FIGURE 5.5
Designing a Web Form to display employee data.

2. Create a new module named Employee.vb in the project. Add this code to the module:

```
Imports System.Data
Module Employee

    Public Function RosterDataLoad() As ICollection
        Dim dt As DataTable = New DataTable()
        Dim dv As DataView
        Dim dr As DataRow

        ' Add four columns to the DataTable
        dt.Columns.Add(New DataColumn( _
         "EmployeeNumber", GetType(String)))
        dt.Columns.Add(New DataColumn( _
         "EmployeeName", GetType(String)))
        dt.Columns.Add(New DataColumn( _
         "Position", GetType(String)))
        dt.Columns.Add(New DataColumn( _
         "HomePlanet", GetType(String)))
```

```
        ' Put the data in
        dr = dt.NewRow()
        dr(0) = "1"
        dr(1) = "E.E. Smith"
        dr(2) = "CEO"
        dr(3) = "Earth"
        dt.Rows.Add(dr)

        dr = dt.NewRow()
        dr(0) = "2"
        dr(1) = "Melanie ""Jets"" Riggs"
        dr(2) = "Chief Pilot"
        dr(3) = "Mars"
        dt.Rows.Add(dr)

        dr = dt.NewRow()
        dr(0) = "3"
        dr(1) = "William Danforth"
        dr(2) = "Pilot"
        dr(3) = "Mars"
        dt.Rows.Add(dr)

        dr = dt.NewRow()
        dr(0) = "4"
        dr(1) = "Blaise Canton"
        dr(2) = "Engineer"
        dr(3) = "Luna"
        dt.Rows.Add(dr)

        dr = dt.NewRow()
        dr(0) = "5"
        dr(1) = "Amanda Timmel"
        dr(2) = "CFO"
        dr(3) = "Earth"
        dt.Rows.Add(dr)

        ' And return the datatable
        ' wrapped in a dataview
        dv = New DataView(dt)
        Return dv

    End Function

End Module
```

EXAM TIP

Quotes in Strings Remember, if you want to insert a quote mark (") into a string constant, you must use two quote marks in a row.

3. Add code behind this form to handle data creation and data binding:

```
Private Sub Page_Load(ByVal sender As System.Object, _
 ByVal e As System.EventArgs) Handles MyBase.Load
    If Not IsPostBack Then
```

continues

continued

```
            ' First time in, load the dropdownlist
            Dim dv As DataView
            dv = RosterDataLoad()
            With ddlEmployeeNumber
                .DataSource = dv
                .DataTextField = "EmployeeNumber"
                .DataBind()
                .SelectedIndex = 0
            End With
            ' and show the first employee
            txtEmployeeName.Text = dv(0)(1)
            txtPosition.Text = dv(0)(2)
            txtHomePlanet.Text = dv(0)(3)
        End If
    End Sub

    Private Sub ddlEmployeeNumber_SelectedIndexChanged( _
     ByVal sender As System.Object, _
     ByVal e As System.EventArgs) _
     Handles ddlEmployeeNumber.SelectedIndexChanged
        Dim i As Integer
        Dim dv As DataView
        ' figure out which row was selected
        i = ddlEmployeeNumber.SelectedIndex
        ' and load info from the
        ' corresponding dataview row
        dv = RosterDataLoad()
        txtEmployeeName.Text = dv(i)(1)
        txtPosition.Text = dv(i)(2)
        txtHomePlanet.Text = dv(i)(3)
    End Sub
```

4. Create a second Web Form and name it GuidedPracticeExercise5_1a (or give it any name you like, and revise the NavigateUrl of the HyperLink control in step 1 to match). Place a single DataGrid control on this form. Name the DataGrid Control dgEmployees.

5. Double-click the new Web Form and add code to its Load event:

```
Private Sub Page_Load(ByVal sender As System.Object, _
 ByVal e As System.EventArgs) Handles MyBase.Load
    dgEmployees.DataSource = RosterDataLoad()
    DataBind()
End Sub
```

6. Set the first Web Form as the project's start page and test your work. You should be able to choose an employee number to see the details of that employee. You should also be able to open a grid containing all the employee information.

7. If you had difficulty following this exercise, review the sections titled "Simple Data Binding" and "Complex Data Binding." The text and examples should help you in relearning this material and help you understand what just happened in this exercise. After review, try this exercise again.

REVIEW BREAK

- Complex data binding binds a user interface control to an entire collection of data.
- To use complex data binding with a list control (such as a ListBox, DropDownList, RadioButtonList, or CheckBoxList control), you set the control's DataSource and DataTextField properties.
- A list control can act to pull values from one data source and place them in another.
- You can cause a list control to display one value while binding another by using the DataTextField and DataValueField properties of the control.
- The DataGrid control displays an entire array of data in rows and columns. You specify the data to display by setting the DataSource property of the DataGrid control.
- The properties of the DataGrid control include many flexible formatting options.

The DataBind Method

DataBind is a method of the Page object (which, of course, represents the entire ASP.NET Web Form) and of all server controls. Data-binding expressions are not evaluated until you explicitly call the DataBind method. This gives you flexibility to decide when to bind things and lets you run preliminary code to calculate values if necessary.

The DataBind method cascades from parent controls to their children. If you call the DataBind method of the Page, then all data binding expressions on the page are evaluated. If you call the DataBind method of a control that has constituent controls, all data binding expressions in any of those controls are evaluated.

In addition to the design-time data binding expressions that you've already seen, you can perform runtime data binding by responding to the DataBinding event of a control. This event is raised by each control when its DataBind method is invoked.

STEP BY STEP

5.10 Responding to a `DataBinding` Event

1. Place a `Label` control on a new ASP.NET Form. Set the ID of this control to `lblRuntime`.

2. Double-click the form and enter code to handle the `Load` event:

```
Private Sub Page_Load(ByVal sender As System.Object, _
 ByVal e As System.EventArgs) Handles MyBase.Load
    lblRuntime.DataBind()
End Sub
```

3. Enter code for the `DataBinding` event of the label control:

```
Private Sub lblRuntime_DataBinding( _
 ByVal sender As Object, _
 ByVal e As System.EventArgs) _
 Handles lblRuntime.DataBinding
    lblRuntime.Text = "Runtime data binding"
End Sub
```

4. Set the Web Form as the start page for the project.

5. Run the project. The user interface will display "Runtime data binding" as the text of the label control.

NOTE

When Should You Use Runtime Data Binding? Anything you can do with runtime data binding you can also do with design-time data binding. That's because, as you saw earlier in the chapter, you can use design-time data binding with properties of the page. It's a matter of personal style whether you'd like to put code into a public property or into a DataBinding event.

Using the Data Form Wizard

Now that you've seen the mechanics of data binding, it's time to explore one of the tools that Visual Basic .NET offers for automatic data binding: the Data Form Wizard. In this section, you'll see how to use the wizard to build both a single-table form and a multiple-table form.

These will help us ease into the broad topic of using data from databases, which will occupy much of the rest of this chapter and all the next one.

IN THE FIELD

A CRASH COURSE IN DATABASES

Although this exam doesn't have any objectives that explicitly demand database knowledge, you can't pass it without knowing something about databases. These days, databases are part of the pervasive understructure of computing. You're expected to understand the basics, just as you understand the basics of files and folders.

We're interested in data stored in relational databases. A relational database (such as Microsoft SQL Server, which is used in the examples in this book) stores data in tables, each of which represents instances of a particular entity. An entity is anything that you're interested in tracking in the database: a customer, an order, an employee, or a supplier, for example. A single database can contain many tables; in this case, you might have tables named Customers, Orders, Employees, and Suppliers.

Each table contains one row (or record) for each instance of an entity: if you have 50 customers, the Customers table will have 50 rows. Each row consists of a number of columns (or fields) that describe the entity. For example, the fields in a Customers table might be:

- Customer Number
- Customer Name
- City
- State

In a well-designed database, each entity can be identified by a column or combination of columns called the primary key. For example, the primary key for the Customers table could be the Customer Number column. Each customer would then have a unique and unchanging Customer Number. If you knew the Customer Number, you could use it to look up all the other information that the database stores about that customer.

The reason that SQL Server is called a relational database is that it understands that there are relations between entities stored in different tables. Think about customers and orders, for example.

continues

continued

Each order is placed by a single customer. You can indicate this by storing the Customer Number (the primary key of the Customers table) in the Orders table. The columns of the Orders table might be:

- Order Number
- Customer Number
- Order Date
- Delivery Date

In this case, the Order Number would be the primary key (the unique identifying column) of the Orders table. The Customer Number in the Orders table serves to relate each order to a corresponding row in the Customers table. We call the Customer Number a foreign key in the Orders table. To specify a relation between tables, you name the two tables and the columns that match between them. Relations can be one-to-many (one customer can place many orders) or one-to-one (one employee has at most one pension).

In addition to tables, databases can contain other objects. These include views and stored procedures (which can provide a subset of information from one or more tables) and users and groups (which control the security of database objects).

If you've never worked with a database, you may find it a bit confusing at first. But if you work through the examples carefully, it should become clear to you.

NOTE

For more information on relational database design and terminology, refer to Que Publishing's *SQL Server 2000 Programming* by Carlos Rojas and Fernando Guerrero (ISBN 0789724499).

Building a Single-Table Data Form

We'll start by building a data form that displays data from a single table—the Customers table in the Northwind sample database.

STEP BY STEP

5.11 Building a Single-Table Data Form

1. Select Project, Add New Item. In the Add New Item dialog box (shown in Figure 5.6) select the Data Form Wizard. Name the new form `StepByStep5-11.aspx` and click Open.

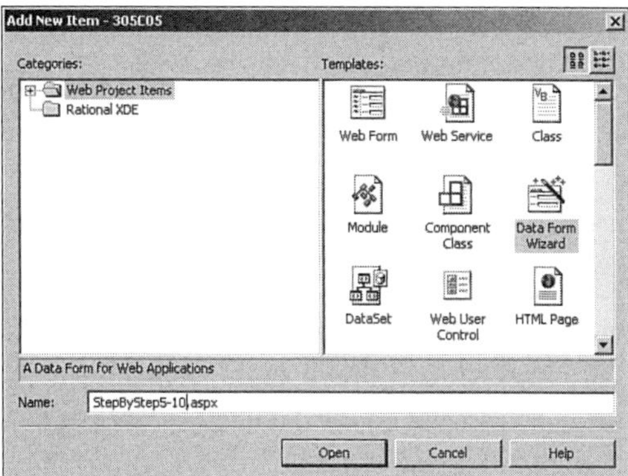

FIGURE 5.6◀
Launching the Data Form Wizard.

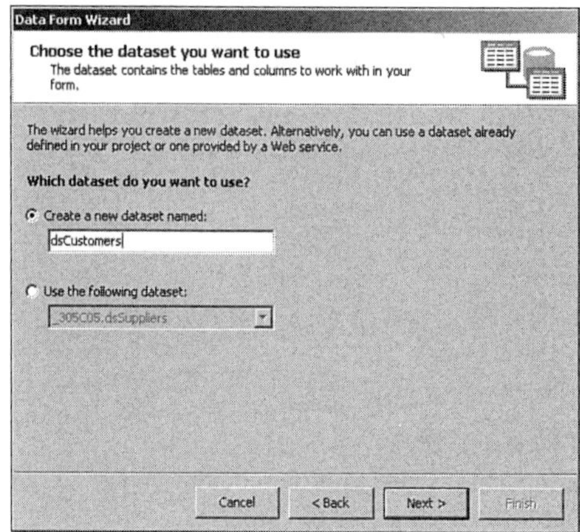

FIGURE 5.7▲
Creating a new Dataset.

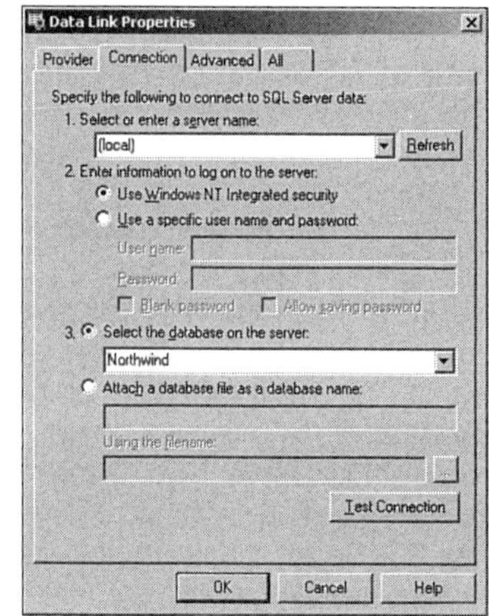

FIGURE 5.8▲
Connecting to the Northwind sample database.

2. Read the Welcome panel of the wizard and click Next.

3. The next panel helps you choose a Dataset to use with the Data Form. A Dataset is a .NET Framework object that you can think of as representing one or more tables from a database (it's actually more flexible than that, but that's enough for this example). On this panel, shown in Figure 5.7, choose to create a new Dataset named `dsCustomers`. Click Next.

4. The next panel helps you choose or build a Data Connection. A Data Connection tells Visual Basic .NET which database contains the data that you want to retrieve. You haven't set up any Data Connections yet, so click the New Connection button. This will open the Data Link Properties dialog box.

5. Click on the Provider tab of the Data Link Properties dialog box and select the Microsoft OLE DB Provider for SQL Server.

6. Click on the Connection tab of the Data Link Properties dialog box and enter the information that you need to use the Northwind Database, as shown in Figure 5.8.

continues

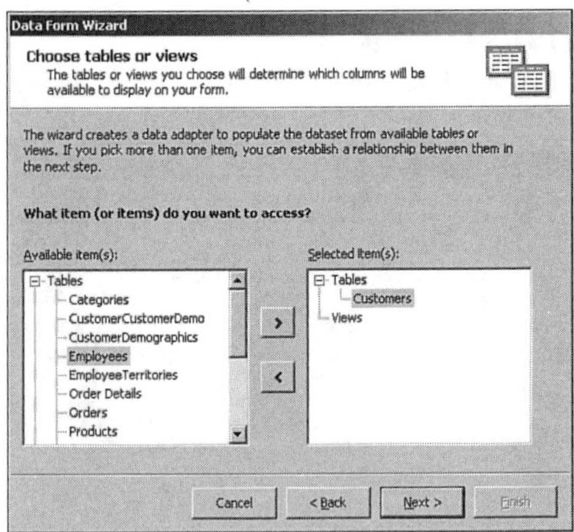

FIGURE 5.9
Choosing a table as a data source.

continued

7. Click OK on the Data Link Properties dialog box to create the connection and return to the Data Form Wizard. Select the new connection in the combo box (it will have a name such as `MACHINENAME.Northwind.dbo`) and click Next.

8. On the Choose Tables or Views panel, select the Customers table in the Available Items list and click the > button to move it to the Selected Items list, as shown in Figure 5.9. Click Next.

9. On the Choose Tables and Columns to Display on the Form panel, leave all the columns in the table selected, and click Finish.

10. Set the new form as the start page for the project and run the project to experiment with the Data Form.

Figure 5.10 shows the finished Data Form created by this Step By Step. When you first load the form, it will contain only the Load button. Clicking the Load button loads and binds the data to the user interface.

EXAM TIP

Specifying Connection Information You may have to try a few things to connect to the database. For the server name, you can use the name of a computer where SQL Server is running. If SQL Server is installed on the same computer where you're writing the code, you can use the special name "(local)" instead of entering a server name. For log on information, you should first try Windows NT Integrated Security, which logs on to SQL Server using your Windows identity. If that fails, try using the specific user name "sa" and a blank password. If that also fails, you'll need to check with the person responsible for the SQL Server to find out what login information to use. Note the Test Connection button at the bottom of the dialog box. This will come in handy as you're trying to get your login information correct.

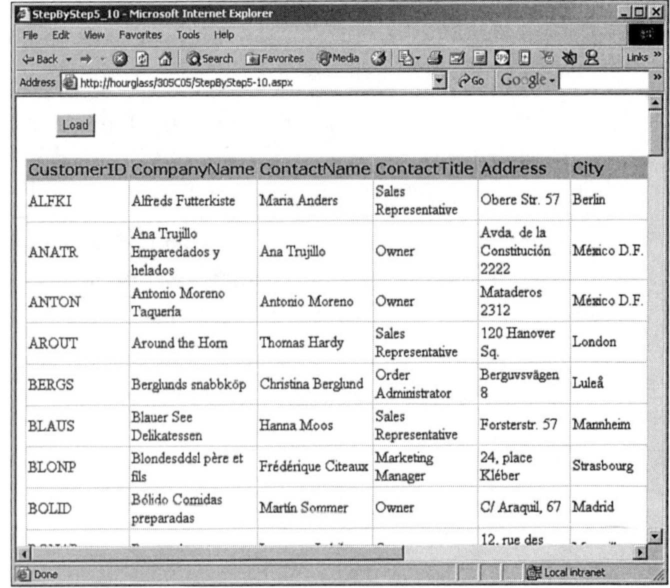

CustomerID	CompanyName	ContactName	ContactTitle	Address	City
ALFKI	Alfreds Futterkiste	Maria Anders	Sales Representative	Obere Str. 57	Berlin
ANATR	Ana Trujillo Emparedados y helados	Ana Trujillo	Owner	Avda. de la Constitución 2222	México D.F.
ANTON	Antonio Moreno Taquería	Antonio Moreno	Owner	Mataderos 2312	México D.F.
AROUT	Around the Horn	Thomas Hardy	Sales Representative	120 Hanover Sq.	London
BERGS	Berglunds snabbköp	Christina Berglund	Order Administrator	Berguvsvägen 8	Luleå
BLAUS	Blauer See Delikatessen	Hanna Moos	Sales Representative	Forsterstr. 57	Mannheim
BLONP	Blondesddsl père et fils	Frédérique Citeaux	Marketing Manager	24, place Kléber	Strasbourg
BOLID	Bólido Comidas preparadas	Martín Sommer	Owner	C/ Araquil, 67	Madrid
				12, rue des	

FIGURE 5.10
The finished Data Form displays all the data from the Customers table. It also provides a button to let you choose when to load the data.

You may want to browse through the code that the wizard created behind this form. Be warned, though, that there are over 200 lines of code involved in implementing this functionality! Obviously, the Data Form Wizard can save you a lot of time in building data bound forms. As you continue through the book, you'll learn more about database objects and the code that you can use to manipulate them. For now, we'll stick to the relatively easy user-interface tools as we explore what can be done with data binding.

Building a Multiple-Table Data Form

The Data Form Wizard can also build a form that displays data from more than one table.

STEP BY STEP

5.12 Building a Multiple-Table Data Form

1. Select Project, Add New Item. In the Add New Item dialog box, select the Data Form Wizard. Name the new form `StepByStep5-11.aspx` and click Open.
2. Read the Welcome panel of the wizard and click Next.
3. On the Choose a Dataset panel, choose to create a new Dataset named `dsCustOrders`. Click Next.
4. On the Choose a Data Connection panel, select the Data Connection that you created in the previous Step By Step and click Next.
5. On the Choose Tables or Views panel, select the Customers table in the Available Items list and click the > button to move it to the Selected Items list. Also select the Orders table and click the > button to move it to the Selected Items list. Click Next.
6. The next panel will help you specify the relationship between the two tables, Customers and Orders. Name the new relationship `relCustomerOrders`. Select Customers as the parent table and Orders as the child table. Select `CustomerID` as the key field in each table. Figure 5.11 shows the wizard at this point. Click the > button to create the new relationship, and then click Next.

continues

FIGURE 5.11
Creating a relationship between tables.

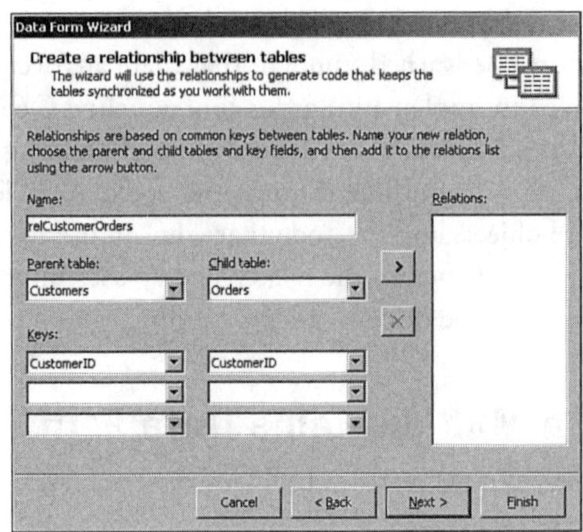

> **NOTE**
>
> **Relationships** Creating a relationship between tables tells the wizard which fields it should treat as primary and foreign keys. Refer back to the earlier "Crash Course in Relational Databases" section if you need to review this concept.

7. On the Choose Tables and Columns to Display on the Form panel, leave all the columns in both tables selected, and click Finish.

8. Set the new form as the start page for the project and run the project to experiment with the Data Form.

The Data Form initially opens with only a Load button visible. Clicking the button loads all the rows from the Customers table. Each row has a "Show Details" link in the first column. Clicking this link loads the orders for that customer. The form knows which orders go with which customer thanks to the relationship that you created between the two tables. Figure 5.12 shows an example.

Once again, you'll find a tremendous amount of code (about 400 lines) behind this form. And once again we'll leave it for future inspection.

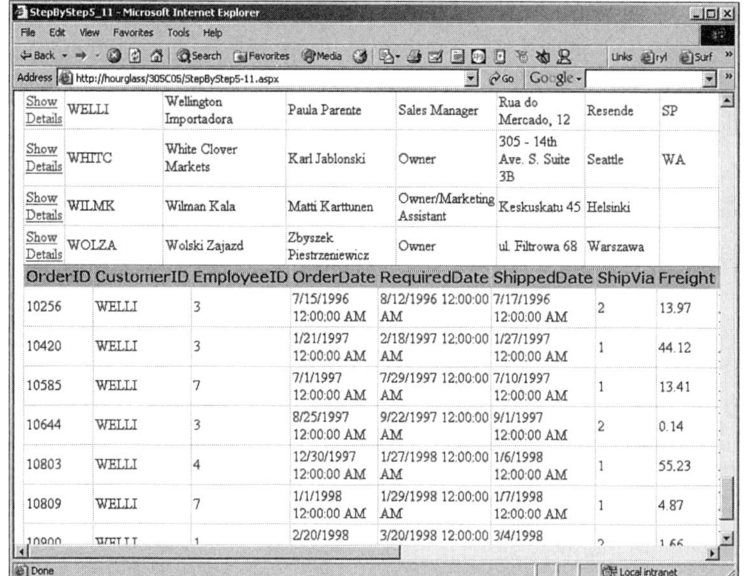

FIGURE 5.12
A two-table Data Form that uses one DataGrid control for each table and uses code to keep the two DataGrid controls synchronized.

REVIEW BREAK

- The DataBind method is used to bind data to an entire page or to any of the controls on the page. This method triggers a DataBinding event for the affected controls.
- The Data Form Wizard will help you create data-bound forms, both simple and complex, quickly. These forms will draw their data from a relational database such as SQL Server.

TRANSFORM AND FILTER DATA

Display and Update Data: Transform and Filter Data

The second test objective for this chapter covers transforming and filtering data. Especially when you're dealing with data from a database, you may find that it's not in the exact form that you'd like to display to the user. Perhaps there are 5,000 rows in the Customer table, and you'd like to pull out the single row that interests your users.

Perhaps you'd like to show customer names with orders, but the Orders table only stores the CustomerID. In this section, we'll look at a few of the tools that the .NET Framework offers for manipulating database data.

First, we'll dig into the Server Explorer, which allows you to interact directly with SQL Server or other databases. Then we'll look at some of the ways that you can filter and transform data.

Using Server Explorer

By default, the Server Explorer window in Visual Studio .NET is displayed as a small vertical tab to the left of the Toolbox. When you hover the mouse over this tab, the Server Explorer will slide out to cover the Toolbox. Figure 5.13 shows the two states of the Server Explorer window.

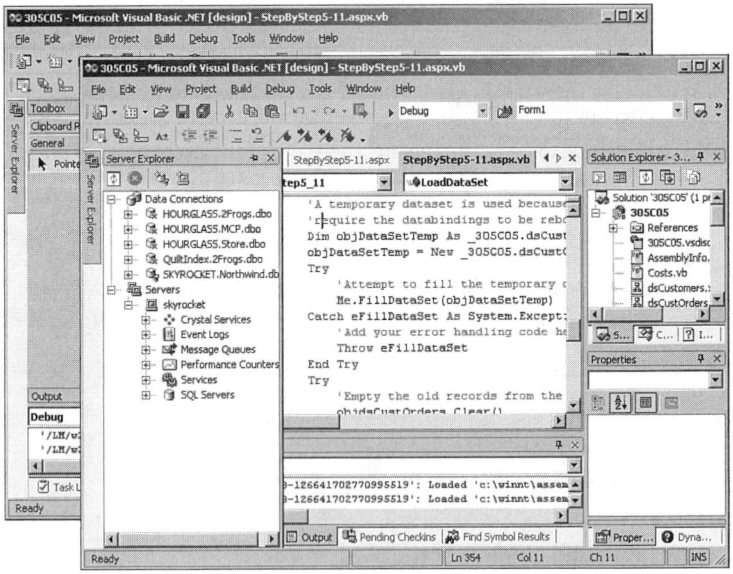

FIGURE 5.13
The Server Explorer is normally displayed as a small vertical tab. When you hover the mouse over this tab, the window slides out to cover the Toolbox.

Although we're going to use the Server Explorer to work with databases, it's really a general-purpose tool for managing server resources of many types. Table 5.3 lists the resources that you can manage with Server Explorer.

TABLE 5.3

RESOURCES THAT YOU CAN MANAGE WITH SERVER EXPLORER

Resource Type	*Represents*
Data Connection	A connection to a particular database
Crystal Services	Options for Crystal Reports
Event Logs	Windows event logs
Message Queues	Windows message queues
Performance Counters	Windows performance counters
Services	Windows services
SQL Servers	Microsoft SQL Servers

To work with bound data, you'll use the Data Connection node in Server Explorer and its children.

Adding a Data Connection

You've already seen that you can add a Data Connection to your project from within the Data Form Wizard. Those Data Connections are automatically available in Server Explorer as well. You can also add a Data Connection directly from Server Explorer.

STEP BY STEP

5.13 Adding a Data Connection from Server Explorer

1. Open Server Explorer.
2. Right-click the Data Connections node and then select Add Connection. This will open the Data Link Properties dialog box.
3. Fill in the connection information for your data source. The dialog box will default to using the Microsoft OLE DB Provider for SQL Server, but you can change that on the Provider tab if you like.
4. Click OK to create the Data Connection.

EXAM TIP

Supported Connection Types
You've probably noticed that the Data Link Properties dialog box gives you a great many choices on the Provider tab. In addition to SQL Server, connections using the Oracle or Jet providers are also fully supported by .NET, although you'll need to use slightly different code with those providers; I'll cover those differences in Chapter 6. Other providers may work, but there's no guarantee and you should test your application carefully if you decide to use another provider.

Visual Studio .NET remembers your Data Connections across sessions and projects. Any Data Connection that you've created will appear in Server Explorer in all your projects unless you right-click the Data Connection and choose Delete.

Object Design From Server Explorer

Even without bringing SQL Server objects into your Visual Basic .NET projects, you can manipulate them from Server Explorer. Visual Studio .NET provides wide-ranging design options for SQL Server objects. Table 5.4 summarizes your options in this area.

EXAM TIP

Visual Studio Focuses on Data, Not Management The objects that you can edit from Visual Studio are those that can bring back data to your application. SQL Server contains many other objects (such as users, groups, and alerts) that are used for server management. To work with these objects, you need to use SQL Server's own design tools.

TABLE 5.4

MANIPULATING SQL SERVER OBJECTS FROM SERVER EXPLORER

Object	*Edit Data?*	*Design?*	*Create New?*
Database Diagram	N/A	Yes	Yes
Table	Yes	Yes	Yes
View	Yes	Yes	Yes
Stored Procedure	Yes	Yes	Yes
Function	Yes	Yes	Yes

STEP BY STEP

5.14 Editing a SQL Server Table from Server Explorer

1. Open Server Explorer.
2. Expand the tree under Data Connections to show a SQL Server data connection that points to the Northwind sample database, then the Tables node of the SQL Server, and then individual tables.
3. Right-click on the Products table and select Retrieve Data From Table. The data stored in the table will appear within your Visual Studio .NET workspace, as shown in Figure 5.14.

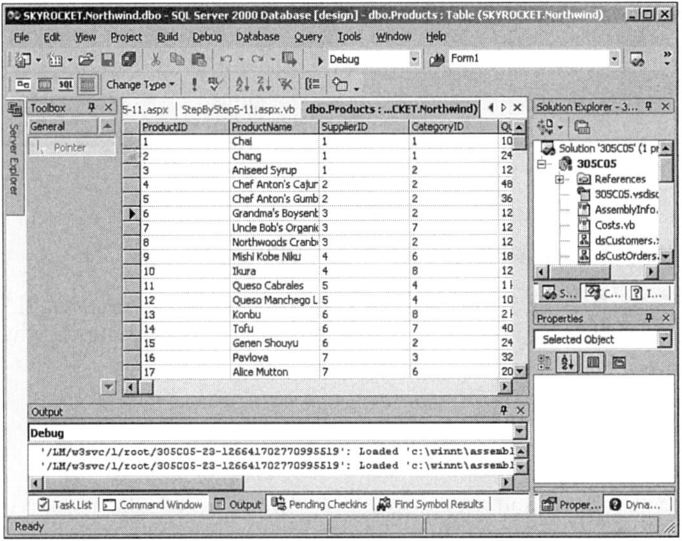

FIGURE 5.14
Editing SQL Server data directly within Visual Studio .NET.

4. As you work with the data, you'll find that you can edit, add, and delete values from the table.

5. Close the window that displays the Products data.

6. Reopen Server Explorer and find the Products table again. Right-click the table and select Design Table. Visual Studio .NET will display information relating to the design of the table, as show in Figure 5.15. This information includes such things as the name and data type of each column in the table.

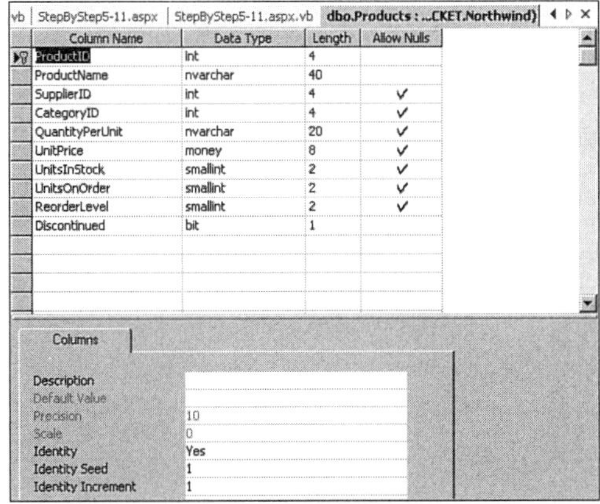

FIGURE 5.15
Designing a SQL Server table directly within Visual Studio .NET.

continues

continued

7. Close the editing window when you're done examining the design information for the table.

Drag-and-Drop from Server Explorer

The Server Explorer can also act as a source for drag-and-drop operations. Different visual data objects are created, depending on what sort of object you drag from Server Explorer:

- Dragging and dropping a database creates a SqlConnection object.
- Dragging and dropping a Table, View, Table Column, or View Column creates a SqlDataAdapter.
- Dragging and dropping a stored procedure or table-valued function creates a SqlCommand.

These three objects are members of the System.Data.SqlClient namespace. You'll learn more about this namespace in Chapter 6. In this chapter, we'll concentrate more on what you can do with the objects than with the code that creates and supports them.

Figure 5.16 shows the appearance of the created objects on a Web Form. This figure also includes a DataSet object; you'll see how to generate a DataSet object in the form designer shortly.

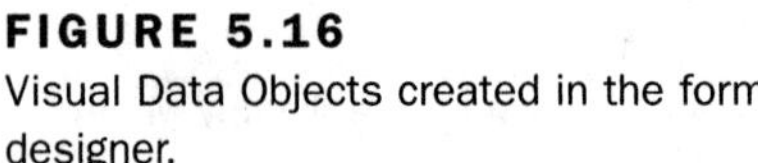

FIGURE 5.16
Visual Data Objects created in the form designer.

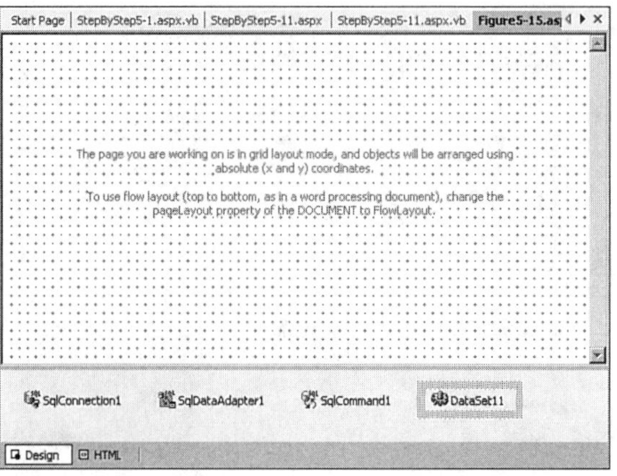

As you might guess from their placement below the form's design surface, these visual data objects are not visible at runtime. At design time, they provide access to instances of their underlying class. For example, the SqlConnection1 object in the designer is a visual representation of an instance of the SqlConnection class. If you view the code behind the form, you'll find the declaration that Visual Basic .NET created when you dropped the object on the form:

```
Protected WithEvents SqlConnection1 _
 As System.Data.SqlClient.SqlConnection
```

Expanding the "Web Form Designer generated code" region will reveal the code used to initialize this object.

What can you use these visual data objects for? They're ideal for any situation where you'd like to retrieve data from a database without writing a lot of code by hand. For example, you can use these objects to implement complex binding between a DataGrid control and a SQL Server table, as in the following Step by Step.

> **EXAM TIP**
>
> **Protected and WithEvents** The Protected keyword makes this object accessible from its own class or a class derived from this class. The WithEvents keyword makes it possible to connect event handlers to this object.

STEP BY STEP

5.15 Binding a `DataGrid` Control to a SQL Server Table

1. Place a `DataGrid` control on a new Web Form. Set the ID property of the control to `dgCustomers`.
2. Open Server Explorer.
3. Expand the tree under Data Connections to show a SQL Server data connection that points to the Northwind sample database, then the Tables node of the SQL Server, and then individual tables.
4. Drag the Customers table from Server Explorer and drop it on the form. This will create two visual data objects, `SqlConnection1` and `SqlDataAdapter1`.
5. Select the SqlDataAdapter1 object. Click the Generate Dataset link below the Properties window.
6. In the Generate Dataset window, choose to use the existing `dsCustomers` Dataset. Click OK. Figure 5.17 shows this dialog box.

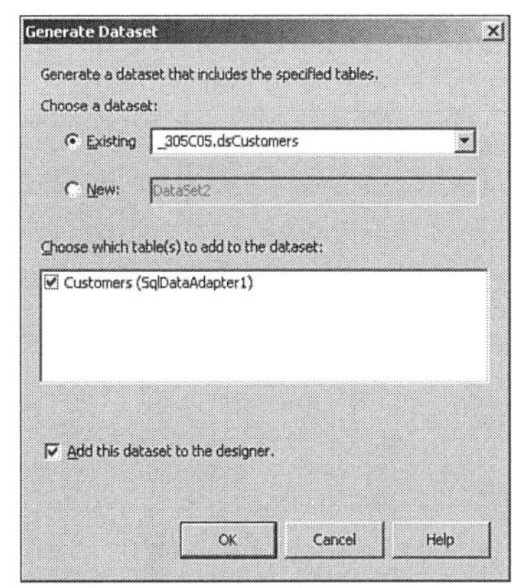

FIGURE 5.17
Generating a dataset.

continues

continued

7. Set the `DataSource` property of the `DataGrid` control to DsCustomers1. Set the `DataMember` property of the `DataGrid` control to Customers.

8. Double-click the form and enter code in the form's `Load` event:

```
Private Sub Page_Load(ByVal sender As System.Object, _
 ByVal e As System.EventArgs) Handles MyBase.Load
    ' Move the data from the database to the DataGrid
    SqlDataAdapter1.Fill(DsCustomers1, "Customers")
    dgCustomers.DataBind()
End Sub
```

9. Set the form as the start page for the project.

10. Run the project. The `DataGrid` will display all the data from the Customers table. The code uses the visual data objects that you created on the form to make the connection between the `DataGrid` and the table.

Although you only had to write two lines of code for this Step by Step, you actually created a number of ADO.NET objects along the way. Here's a rundown of how all the pieces fit together:

- The SqlConnection1 object is an instance of the SqlConnection class. This object represents a connection to the SQL Server database.
- The SqlDataAdapter1 object is an instance of the SqlDataAdapter class. This class encapsulates all the tools necessary to extract data via a SqlConnection, and to write changes back to the data source.
- The Generate Dataset dialog box created an XSD file, dsCustomers.xsd. This is an XML Schema Design file that represents the structure of the Customers table to the .NET Framework.
- The DsCustomers1 object is an instance of the DataSet represented by the dsCustomers.xsd file.

- The call to the Fill method of the SqlDataAdapter1 object tells it to extract all the rows from the Customers table and to place them in the DsCustomers1 object. You can think of the SqlDataAdapter class as a two-way pump that can move data from the underlying database to the data model within your application and back.
- Setting the DataSource and DataMember properties of the DataGrid control uses complex data binding to show the contents of the DsCustomers1 object on the user interface.

Filtering Data

Filtering data refers to the process of selecting only some data from a larger body of data to appear on the user interface of a form. This can be a critical part of avoiding information overload for end users of an application. In most cases, users are not going to need to see every row of data in a database or even every row from a specific table. More often, they are only going to need a small subset of the larger data body. In this section, we'll look at two different ways to filter data in your applications.

Filtering with a DataView

You've already seen the DataView in action as a way to add the ICollection interface to a DataTable. Now it's time to look at this object in a bit more depth. To understand the DataView, you need to know a little bit about the internal structure of the DataSet object. A DataSet contains two collections. The Tables collection is made up of DataTable objects, each one of which represents data from a single table in the datasource. The Relations collection is made up of DataRelation objects, each one of which represents the relation between two DataTable objects.

The DataView object supplies one more piece of this puzzle: it represents a bindable, customized view of a DataTable. You can sort or filter the records from a DataTable to build a DataView.

STEP BY STEP

5.16 Using a DataView to Filter Data

1. Place a `DataGrid` control on a new Web Form. Name the control `dgCustomers`.
2. Open Server Explorer.
3. Expand the tree under Data Connections to show a SQL Server data connection that points to the Northwind sample database, then the Tables node of the SQL Server, and then individual tables.
4. Drag the Customers table from Server Explorer and drop it on the form. This will create two visual data objects, `SqlConnection1` and `SqlDataAdapter1`.
5. Select the SqlDataAdapter1 object. Click the Generate Dataset link below the Properties window.
6. In the Generate Dataset window, choose to use the existing `dsCustomers` Dataset. Click OK.
7. Double-click the form and enter code in the pages's `Load` event:

```
Private Sub Page_Load(ByVal sender As System.Object, _
 ByVal e As System.EventArgs) Handles MyBase.Load
    ' Move the data from the database to the DataSet
    SqlDataAdapter1.Fill(DsCustomers1, "Customers")

    ' Create a dataview to filter the Customers table
    Dim dvCustomers As DataView = _
     New DataView(DsCustomers1.Tables("Customers"))
    ' Apply a sort to the dataview
    dvCustomers.Sort = "ContactName"
    ' Apply a filter to the dataview
    dvCustomers.RowFilter = "Country = 'France'"
    ' and bind the results to the grid
    dgCustomers.DataSource = dvCustomers
    dgCustomers.DataBind()
End Sub
```

8. Set the form as the startup object for the project.

9. Run the project. The `DataGrid` will display only the data from customers in France, because you set the `RowFilter` property of the `DataView` to an expression that retrieves only these customers. Note that they're also sorted by the `ContactName` column, because the Sort property of the `DataView species` that column for sorting, as shown in Figure 5.18.

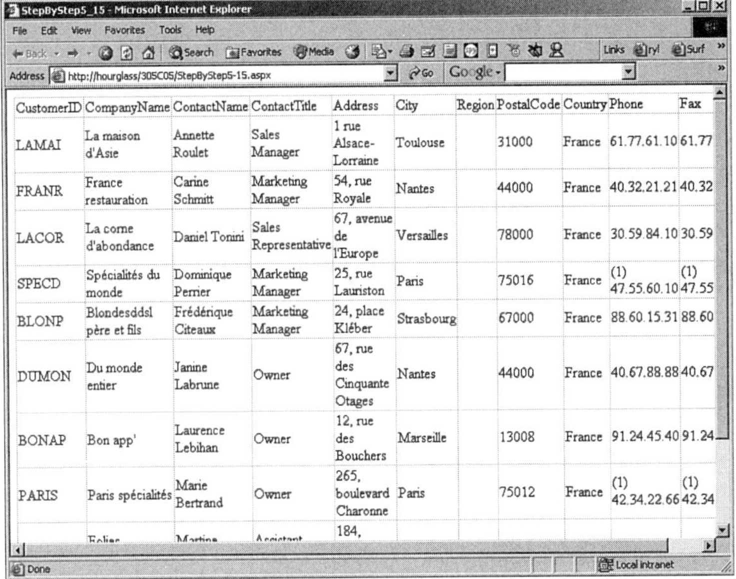

FIGURE 5.18
This DataGrid was populated by binding it to a DataView that filters and sorts the records from the Customers table.

Filtering at the Server

The DataView class provides a useful way to filter data, but it's inefficient for some purposes. That's because all the data is first retrieved from the database server and stored in memory on the client. So if there are 10 million rows of data on the server, a DataView will retrieve all ten million rows. After that, the DataView can be used to quickly select a subset of the data. But what if you're never going to need all of the data? In that case, you're better off filtering on the server, rather than retrieving all of that data that you'll never need. One way to do this is by basing a SqlDataAdapter object on a view The instead of a table.

STEP BY STEP

5.17 Using a Server-Side View to Filter Data

1. Place a `DataGrid` control on a new Web Form. Set the ID of the control to `dgCustomers`.
2. Open Server Explorer.
3. Expand the tree under Data Connections to show a SQL Server data connection that points to the Northwind sample database, and then the Views node of the SQL Server.
4. Right-click on the Views node and select New View.
5. In the Add Table dialog box, select the Customers table, click Add, and then click Close. This will put you in the view designer within Visual Studio .NET.
6. Click the checkboxes for All Columns, `ContactName`, and Country in the column listing.
7. Fill in the details of the view as shown in Figure 5.19. When you uncheck the Output column for ContactName and Country, they will be unchecked in the column listing, but they'll remain in the grid area. You can either edit properties in the grid, or simply edit the SQL statement to match the end result:

```
SELECT TOP 100 PERCENT dbo.Customers.*
FROM dbo.Customers
WHERE (Country='France')
ORDER BY ContactName
```

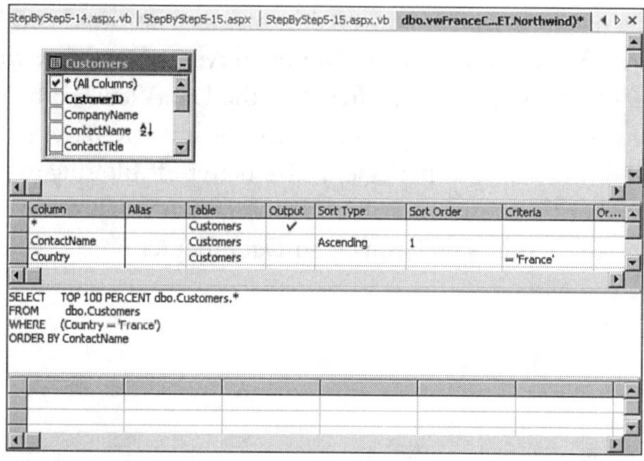

FIGURE 5.19
Creating a new SQL Server view using the design tools within Visual Studio .NET.

8. Click on the Save button and save the view as `vwFranceCustomers`. Close the design window for the view.

9. Drag the `vwFranceCustomers` view from Server Explorer and drop it on the form. You'll get a configuration error because the view is read-only. That's not a problem because we're not writing any data back to the database; click OK to create objects. This will create two visual data objects, `SqlConnection1` and `SqlDataAdapter1`.

10. Select the `SqlDataAdapter1` object. Click the Generate Dataset link below the Properties window.

11. In the Generate Dataset window, choose to use the existing `dsCustomers` Dataset. Click OK.

12. Set the `DataSource` property of the `DataGrid` control to `DsCustomers1`. Set the `DataMember` property of the `DataGrid` control to `vwFranceCustomers`.

13. Double-click the form and enter code in the page's `Load` event:

```
Private Sub Page_Load(ByVal sender As System.Object, _
 ByVal e As System.EventArgs) Handles MyBase.Load
    ' Move the data from the database to the DataGrid
    SqlDataAdapter1.Fill( _
     DsCustomers1, "vwFranceCustomers")
    dgCustomers.DataBind()
End Sub
```

14. Set the form as the start page for the project.

15. Run the project. The `DataGrid` will display only the data from customers in France, sorted by the `ContactName` column. This time the filtering and sorting is all done by the view that you created on the SQL Server.

This Step by Step will display the same results as the previous version. However, behind the scenes, things are different. Instead of retrieving all rows of the Customers table from the server, this version retrieves only the rows that belong on the display. If you're operating over a slow network or Internet connection, this sort of server-side filtering can save you a good deal of time.

Transforming Data

Finally, we'll take a brief look at another server-side technique: transforming data by applying lookups. A lookup is a technique for replacing one column of data with another column from the same table. For example, given a customer ID value, you could look up the corresponding customer name.

Figure 5.20 shows a DataGrid control bound to the Orders table.

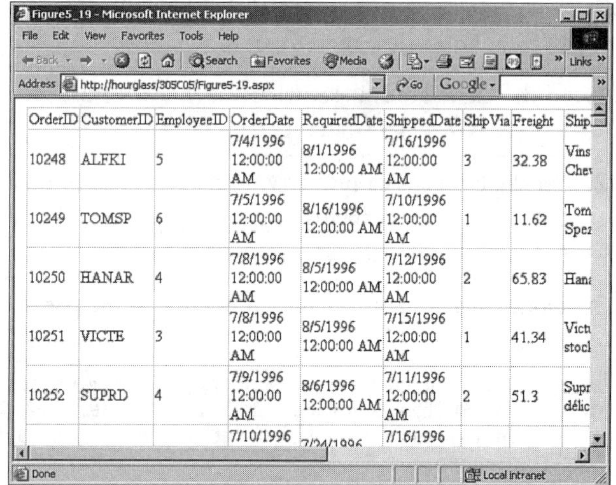

FIGURE 5.20
This DataGrid control is bound to the Orders table. Note that only the Customer ID is displayed to identify the customers.

One problem with this particular form is that it only displays Customer ID values, and no other information about the customers. What if you wanted to view customer names instead? The answer is to use a new view to retrieve data from the server.

STEP BY STEP

5.18 Using a Server-Side View to Transform Data

1. Place a `DataGrid` control on a new Web Form. Name the control `dgOrders`.
2. Open Server Explorer.
3. Expand the tree under Data Connections to show a SQL Server data connection that points to the Northwind sample database, and then the Views node of the SQL Server.

4. Right-click on the Views node and select New View.

5. In the Add Table dialog box, select the Customers table, and click Add. Select the Orders table, click Add, and then click Close. This will put you in the view designer within Visual Studio .NET.

6. Click the checkboxes for `CompanyName` in the Customers table, and all columns except for `CustomerID` in the Orders table.

7. In the grid, drag the `OrderID` column above the `CompanyName` column. Figure 5.21 shows the completed view.

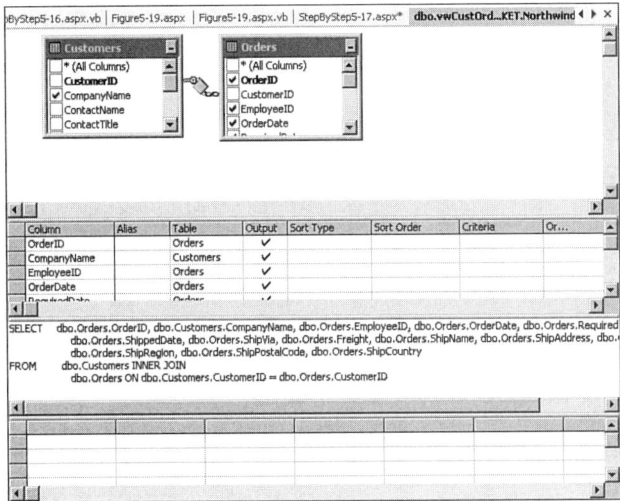

FIGURE 5.21
Creating a new SQL Server view that joins data from two tables.

8. Click the Save button and save the view as `vwCustOrders`. Close the design window for the view.

9. Drag the `vwCustOrders` view from Server Explorer and drop it on the form. You'll get a configuration error because the view is read-only. That's not a problem because we're not writing any data back to the database; click OK to create objects. This will create two visual data objects, `SqlConnection1` and `SqlDataAdapter1`.

continues

continued

10. Select the `SqlDataAdapter1` object. Click the Generate Dataset link below the Properties window.

11. In the Generate Dataset window, create a new Dataset named dsOrders2. Click OK.

12. Set the `DataSource` property of the `DataGrid` control to DsOrders21. Set the `DataMember` property of the `DataGrid` control to `vwCustOrders`.

13. Double-click the form and enter code in the page's `Load` event:

```
Private Sub Page_Load(ByVal sender As System.Object, _
 ByVal e As System.EventArgs) Handles MyBase.Load
    ' Load the data
    SqlDataAdapter1.Fill(DsOrders21, "vwCustOrders")
    DataBind()
End Sub
```

14. Set the form as the start page for the project.

15. Run the project. The `DataGrid` will display order data with full customer names, as shown in Figure 5.22. The lookup operation is performed by the SQL Server view before the data is even sent to your application.

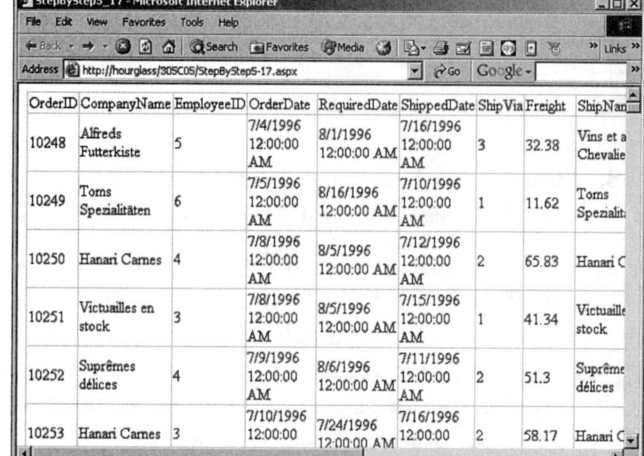

FIGURE 5.22
Customer IDs transformed into customer names.

GUIDED PRACTICE EXERCISE 5.2

In this exercise, you'll be working with Order and Order Detail data from the Northwind sample database. You need to design a form that lets the user select from a list of orders, and then displays all the order detail data for the selected order. The list of orders should be presented in a DropDownList control, and the corresponding order detail data should be shown on a DataGrid control.

You should try doing this on your own first. If you get stuck, or you'd like to see one possible solution, follow these steps:

1. Create a form populated with a DropDownList control. Set the ID of this control to ddlOrders and the AutoPostBack property to True. Add a DataGrid control and set its ID to dgOrderDetails.
2. Open Server Explorer.
3. Expand the tree under Data Connections to show a SQL Server data connection that points to the Northwind sample database, then the Tables node of the SQL Server, and then individual tables.
4. Drag the Orders table from Server Explorer and drop it on the form. This will create two visual data objects, SqlConnection1 and SqlDataAdapter1. Drag the Order Details table from Server Explorer and drop it on the form. This will create one more object, SqlDataAdapter2.
5. Select the SqlDataAdapter1 object. Click the Generate Dataset link below the Properties window.
6. In the Generate Dataset window, choose to use the existing dsOrders Dataset. Click OK
7. Select the SqlDataAdapter1 object. Click the Generate Dataset link below the Properties window.
8. In the Generate Dataset window, choose to create a new dsOrderDetails Dataset. Click OK.

continues

continued

9. Double-click the form and enter code for the form:

```
Private Sub Page_Load(ByVal sender As System.Object, _
 ByVal e As System.EventArgs) Handles MyBase.Load
    If Not IsPostBack Then
        ' Load the dataset for the dropdownlist
        SqlDataAdapter1.Fill(DsOrders1, "Orders")
        ' And bind it
        With ddlOrders
            .DataSource = DsOrders1
            .DataTextField = "OrderID"
            .DataValueField = "OrderID"
            .DataBind()
        End With
    End If
End Sub

Private Sub ddlOrders_SelectedIndexChanged( _
 ByVal sender As System.Object, _
 ByVal e As System.EventArgs) _
 Handles ddlOrders.SelectedIndexChanged
    Dim dvOrderDetails As DataView
    ' When a new item is selected in the
    ' listbox, filter the dataview
    SqlDataAdapter2.Fill(DsOrderDetails1, _
     "Order Details")
    ' and set up a dataview
    dvOrderDetails = New DataView( _
     DsOrderDetails1.Tables("Order Details"))
    dvOrderDetails.RowFilter = _
     "OrderID = " & ddlOrders.SelectedItem.Value
    dgOrderDetails.DataSource = dvOrderDetails
    dgOrderDetails.DataBind()
End Sub
```

10. Set the form as the start page for the project.

11. Run the project. The DropDownList control will display all order numbers from the database. The DataGrid will display the order details for the selected order. Figure 5.23 shows the final form.

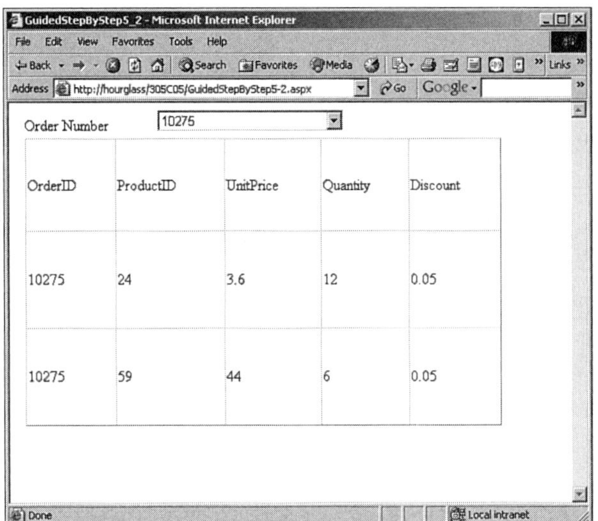

OrderID	ProductID	UnitPrice	Quantity	Discount
10275	24	3.6	12	0.05
10275	59	44	6	0.05

FIGURE 5.23
Order and Order Detail information on a single form.

12. If you had difficulty following this exercise, review the sections titled "Using Server Explorer" and "Filtering with a DataView," as well as the material earlier in the chapter on complex data binding. The text and examples should help you in relearning this material and help you understand what just happened in this exercise. After review, try this exercise again.

REVIEW BREAK

- The Server Explorer provides a powerful tool for working with SQL Server data.
- You can edit and design SQL Server objects directly within Visual Studio .NET.
- The DataView object offers client-side sorting and filtering capabilities for data bound objects.
- Views on the server can be an efficient way to filter or transform data.

USING CONTROLS TO DISPLAY DATA

Display and Update Data

- **Use Controls to Display Data**

The final test objective for this chapter covers the use of controls to display data. Of course, throughout the chapter you've seen data displayed in controls, ranging from simple Label controls through the complex DataGrid. In this section, you'll work specifically with data on templated controls: the Repeater and DataList controls. You'll learn how templated controls handle formatting data, and see the support that the DataList control offers for editing data.

The Repeater Control

A templated control is one whose display is entirely dictated by templates. These controls have no default rendering. Instead, it's up to you to supply templates for the items in the control. ASP.NET implements two templated controls, the Repeater and the DataList. We'll start with the simpler of the two, the Repeater control.

STEP BY STEP

5.19 Using the Repeater Control to Display Data

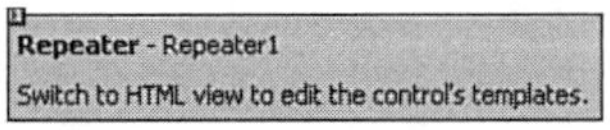

1. Place a Repeater control on a new Web Form. Set the ID of the control to `rptOrders`. Figure 5.24 shows the initial appearance of this control. As you can see, it begins by displaying a design-time placeholder.

2. Open Server Explorer.

3. Expand the tree under Data Connections to show a SQL Server data connection that points to the Northwind sample database, and then the Tables node of the SQL Server.

4. Drag the Orders table from Server Explorer and drop it on the form. This will create two visual data objects, `SqlConnection1` and `SqlDataAdapter1`.

5. Select the SqlDataAdapter1 object. Click the Generate Dataset link below the Properties window.

Repeater - Repeater1
Switch to HTML view to edit the control's templates.

FIGURE 5.24
The Repeater control displays a placeholder at design time.

6. In the Generate Dataset window, use the existing `dsOrders` dataset. Click OK

7. Set the `DataSource` property of the Repeater control to DsOrders1. Set the `DataMember` property of the Repeater control to Orders.

8. Switch to HTML view and enter code to customize the Repeater control:

```
<asp:Repeater id="rptOrders" runat="server"
 DataSource="<%# DsOrders1 %>" DataMember="Orders">
    <HeaderTemplate>
        <table>
            <thead bgcolor=#6699ff>
                <th>Order ID</th>
                <th>Customer ID</th>
                <th>Order Date</th>
                <th>Freight</th>
            </thead>
    </HeaderTemplate>
    <ItemTemplate>
        <tr bgcolor=#ccffff>
            <td><%# DataBinder.Eval(
Container.DataItem, "OrderID") %></td>
            <td><%# DataBinder.Eval(
Container.DataItem, "CustomerID") %></td>
            <td><%# DataBinder.Eval(
Container.DataItem, "OrderDate", "{0:d}") %></td>
            <td><%# DataBinder.Eval(
Container.DataItem, "Freight", "{0:c}") %></td>
        </tr>
    </ItemTemplate>
    <AlternatingItemTemplate>
        <tr bgcolor=#ffffff>
            <td><%# DataBinder.Eval(
Container.DataItem, "OrderID") %></td>
            <td><%# DataBinder.Eval(
Container.DataItem, "CustomerID") %></td>
            <td><%# DataBinder.Eval(
Container.DataItem, "OrderDate", "{0:d}") %></td>
            <td><%# DataBinder.Eval(
Container.DataItem, "Freight", "{0:c}") %></td>
        </tr>
    </AlternatingItemTemplate>
    <SeparatorTemplate>
        <tr height=4 bgcolor=#0000ff>
            <td></td><td></td><td></td><td></td>
        </tr>
    </SeparatorTemplate>
    <FooterTemplate>
        </table>
    </FooterTemplate>
</asp:Repeater>
```

continues

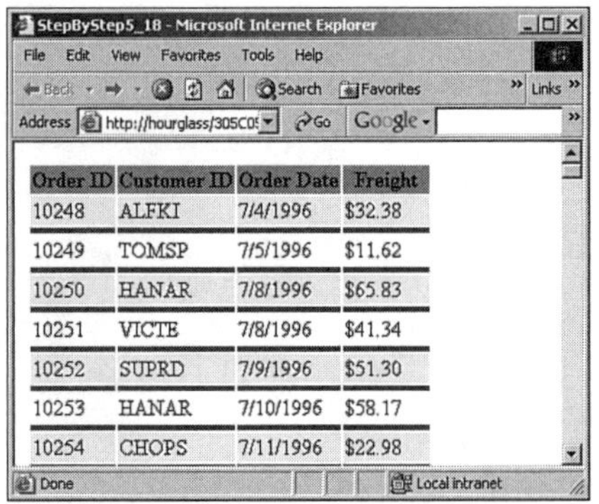

Order ID	Customer ID	Order Date	Freight
10248	ALFKI	7/4/1996	$32.38
10249	TOMSP	7/5/1996	$11.62
10250	HANAR	7/8/1996	$65.83
10251	VICTE	7/8/1996	$41.34
10252	SUPRD	7/9/1996	$51.30
10253	HANAR	7/10/1996	$58.17
10254	CHOPS	7/11/1996	$22.98

FIGURE 5.25
The Repeater control offers flexible formatting options for tabular data.

continued

9. Double-click the form and enter code in the page's `Load` event:

```
Private Sub Page_Load(ByVal sender As System.Object, _
 ByVal e As System.EventArgs) Handles MyBase.Load
    'Load the data
    SqlDataAdapter1.Fill(DsOrders1, "Orders")
    DataBind()
End Sub
```

10. Set the form as the start page for the project.

11. Run the project. The Repeater will display data from four columns of the Orders table, as shown in Figure 5.25.

If you inspect the HTML, you'll see that the Repeater control allows you to specify five templates:

- The HeaderTemplate is rendered once at the start of the control.
- The ItemTemplate is rendered once for every row of data in the data source of the control.
- The AlternatingItemTemplate is used instead of the ItemTemplate for every other row of data.
- The SeparatorTemplate is rendered once between each row of data.
- The FooterTemplate is rendered once at the end of the control.

The only one of these templates that you're required to implement for a Repeater control is the ItemTemplate. You can only perform data binding in the ItemTemplate and AlternatingItemTemplate templates.

You'll also see a new object in the HTML code: the DataBinder. The DataBinder exists to make formatting data in templated controls (and other controls that contain subcontrols) easy. The Eval method of the DataBinder object takes three arguments:

- The first argument specifies the source of the data. The templates are contained within the Repeater control, and it's the Repeater control itself that is bound to a collection of data. So in this case the source of the data is Container.DataItem, a single item of data from the containing control.
- The second argument is the name of a column within the data to bind at this position.
- The third (optional) argument is a format string, of the type that could be supplied to the String.Format method.

The DataBinder control handles all the necessary casting to make string formatting work properly with bound data, regardless of the data type of the underlying data.

NOTE

Pros and Cons of Using the DataBinder The best thing about the DataBinder.Eval method is that it saves you from writing complex expressions. However, using this method does impose a performance penalty on your code, because all the work it does is late-bound. If you want the fastest possible code, you can replace calls to DataBinder.Eval with explicit casts. For example, consider this binding expression:

```
<%# DataBinder.Eval(
Container.DataItem, "Freight",
"{0:c}") %>
```

An equivalent expression using casts would be this:

```
<%# String.Format("{0:c}",
(CType(
Container.DataItem,
DataRowView)("Freight"))) %>
```

The DataList Control

The DataList control is similar to the Repeater control, but it provides more flexible formatting options. The control handles the layout of items in rows and columns, so you don't have to supply <table> tags within its templates. It also lets you build data-editing capabilities into the Web Form.

STEP BY STEP

5.20 Using the `DataList` Control to Display Data

1. Place a `DataList` control on a new Web Form. Set the ID of the control to `dlOrders`. Set the `RepeatColumns` property of the control to 2 and the `CellSpacing` property of the control to 10.
2. Open Server Explorer.
3. Expand the tree under Data Connections to show a SQL Server data connection that points to the Northwind sample database, and then the Tables node of the SQL Server.

continues

continued

4. Drag the Orders table from Server Explorer and drop it on the form. This will create two visual data objects, `SqlConnection1` and `SqlDataAdapter1`.

5. Select the `SqlDataAdapter1` object. Click the Generate Dataset link below the Properties window.

6. In the Generate Dataset window, use the existing `dsOrders` dataset. Click OK

7. Set the `DataSource` property of the Repeater control to DsOrders1. Set the `DataMember` property of the Repeater control to Orders.

8. Switch to HTML view and enter code to customize the `DataList` control:

```
<asp:DataList id="dlOrders" runat="server"
 DataSource="<%# DsOrders1 %>" DataMember="Orders"
RepeatColumns="2" CellSpacing="10">
    <ItemTemplate>
        <b>Order ID: </b>
        <%# DataBinder.Eval(
Container.DataItem, "OrderID") %>
        <br>
        <b>Customer ID: </b>
        <%# DataBinder.Eval(
Container.DataItem, "CustomerID") %>
        <br>
        <b>Order Date: </b>
        <%# DataBinder.Eval(
Container.DataItem, "OrderDate", "{0:d}") %>
        <br>
        <b>Freight: </b>
        <%# DataBinder.Eval(
Container.DataItem, "Freight", "{0:c}") %>
        <br>
    </ItemTemplate>
</asp:DataList>
```

9. Double-click the form and enter code in the page's `Load` event:

```
Private Sub Page_Load(ByVal sender As System.Object, _
 ByVal e As System.EventArgs) Handles MyBase.Load
    'Load the data
    SqlDataAdapter1.Fill(DsOrders1, "Orders")
    DataBind()
End Sub
```

10. Set the form as the start page for the project.

11. Run the project. The `DataList` will display data from four columns of the Orders table, as shown in Figure 5.26. The number of columns of information on the display is controlled by the `RepeatColumns` property of the `DataList`. Each item is rendered according to the HTML code in the `ItemTemplate` template.

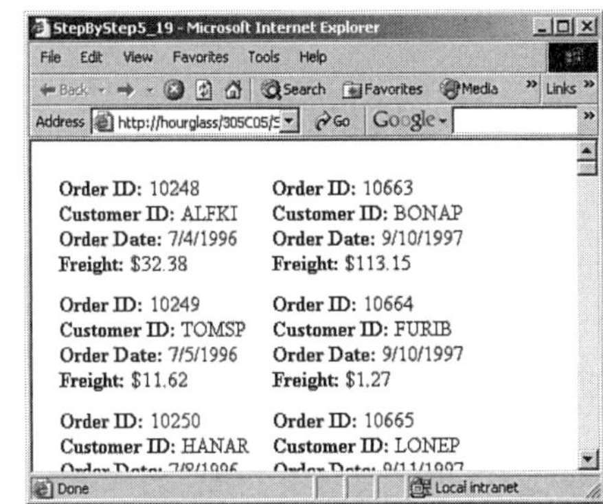

FIGURE 5.26
The DataList control lets you display multiple columns of formatted data.

Like the Repeater control, the `DataList` control supports multiple templates. In addition to the five templates supported by the Repeater control, the `DataList` also allows you to set a `SelectedItemTemplate` to indicate a current row in the data, and an `EditedItemTemplate` which is used to render data that's being edited by the user. Unlike the Repeater, the `DataList` supports formatting templates directly in the Visual Studio .NET IDE. Step by Step 5.21 will show you how.

STEP BY STEP

5.21 Adding Formatting to a `DataList` Control.

1. Place a `DataList` control on a new Web Form. Set the ID of the control to `dlOrders`. Set the `RepeatColumns` property of the control to 2 and the `CellSpacing` property of the control to 10.
2. Open Server Explorer.
3. Expand the tree under Data Connections to show a SQL Server data connection that points to the Northwind sample database, and then the Tables node of the SQL Server.
4. Drag the Orders table from Server Explorer and drop it on the form. This will create two visual data objects, `SqlConnection1` and `SqlDataAdapter1`.
5. Select the `SqlDataAdapter1` object. Click the Generate Dataset link below the Properties window.
6. In the Generate Dataset window, use the existing `dsOrders` dataset. Click OK.

continues

continued

7. Set the `DataSource` property of the Repeater control to `DsOrders1`. Set the `DataMember` property of the Repeater control to Orders.

8. Switch to HTML view and enter code to customize the `DataList` control. Note the `<DIV>` tags within the `ItemTemplate`, which are essential to preserve formatting:

```
<asp:DataList id="dlOrders" runat="server"
 DataSource="<%# DsOrders1 %>" DataMember="Orders"
RepeatColumns="2" CellSpacing="10">
    <ItemTemplate><DIV>
        <b>Order ID: </b>
        <%# DataBinder.Eval(
Container.DataItem, "OrderID") %>
        <br>
        <b>Customer ID: </b>
        <%# DataBinder.Eval(
Container.DataItem, "CustomerID") %>
        <br>
        <b>Order Date: </b>
        <%# DataBinder.Eval(
Container.DataItem, "OrderDate", "{0:d}") %>
        <br>
        <b>Freight: </b>
        <%# DataBinder.Eval(
Container.DataItem, "Freight", "{0:c}") %>
        <br>
    <DIV></ItemTemplate>
</asp:DataList>
```

9. Switch back to Design view. Right-click on the `DataList` control and select Edit Template, Item Templates.

10. Click in the `ItemTemplate` area, below the text, so that you can see the properties for the `<DIV>` tag that wraps this template in the Properties Window. Click in the Style property and click the builder (...) button to open the Style Builder dialog box. You can use the Style Builder to control the appearance of the item template. For example, you can go to the Background category to set a background color. Click OK when you're finished setting styles.

11. Select all of the text in the `ItemTemplate`, copy it, and paste a `copy` into the `AlternatingItemTemplate`. Use the Style Builder to set properties for the `AlternatingItemTemplate`. Figure 5.27 shows the formatted item templates.

FIGURE 5.27
The Visual Studio IDE supports formatting the templates in a DataList control visually.

12. Double-click the form and enter code in the page's `Load` event:

```
Private Sub Page_Load(ByVal sender As System.Object, _
 ByVal e As System.EventArgs) Handles MyBase.Load
    'Load the data
    SqlDataAdapter1.Fill(DsOrders1, "Orders")
    DataBind()
End Sub
```

13. Set the form as the start page for the project.

14. Run the project. The `DataList` will display data from four columns of the `Orders` table, as shown in Figure 5.28. The formatting will be as you specified in the Style Builder.

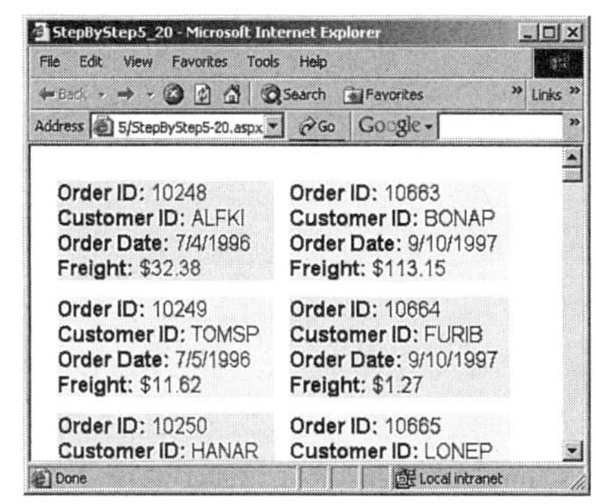

FIGURE 5.28
A DataList control with formatting on the ItemTemplate and AlternatingItemTemplate templates.

Editing Data With a DataList Control

The DataList control also offers support for editing data. To enable this support, you need to supply an EditItemTemplate and respond properly to several events.

STEP BY STEP

5.22 Editing Data in a `DataList` Control.

1. Place a `DataList` control on a new Web Form. Set the ID of the control to `dlOrders`. Set the `RepeatColumns` property of the control to `1` and the `CellSpacing` property of the control to `10`.

2. Open Server Explorer.

3. Expand the tree under Data Connections to show a SQL Server data connection that points to the Northwind sample database, and then the Tables node of the SQL Server.

4. Drag the Orders table from Server Explorer and drop it on the form. This will create two visual data objects, `SqlConnection1` and `SqlDataAdapter1`.

5. Select the `SqlDataAdapter1` object. Click the Generate Dataset link below the Properties window.

continues

continued

6. In the Generate Dataset window, use the existing `dsOrders` dataset. Click OK

7. Set the `DataSource` property of the Repeater control to DsOrders1. Set the `DataMember` property of the Repeater control to Orders.

8. Switch to HTML view and enter code to customize the `DataList` control. This code includes an `EditItemTemplate` with a control to edit the freight charge for a row.

```
<asp:DataList id="dlOrders" runat="server"
 DataSource="<%# DsOrders1 %>" DataMember="Orders"
RepeatColumns="1" CellSpacing="10">
    <ItemTemplate>
        <B>Order ID: </B>
        <%# DataBinder.Eval(
Container.DataItem, "OrderID") %>
        <BR>
        <B>Customer ID: </B>
        <%# DataBinder.Eval(
Container.DataItem, "CustomerID") %>
        <BR>
        <B>Order Date: </B>
        <%# DataBinder.Eval(
Container.DataItem, "OrderDate", "{0:d}") %>
        <BR>
        <B>Freight: </B>
        <%# DataBinder.Eval(
Container.DataItem, "Freight", "{0:c}") %>
        <BR>
        <asp:Button id="btnEdit"
         runat="server" Text="Edit"
         CommandName="Edit"></asp:Button>
    </ItemTemplate>
    <EditItemTemplate>
        <B>Order ID: </B>
        <%# DataBinder.Eval(
Container.DataItem, "OrderID") %>
        <BR>
        <B>Customer ID: </B>
        <%# DataBinder.Eval(
Container.DataItem, "CustomerID") %>
        <BR>
        <B>Order Date: </B>
        <%# DataBinder.Eval(
Container.DataItem, "OrderDate", "{0:d}") %>
        <BR>
        <B>Freight: </B><INPUT id=freight type=text
         value='<%# DataBinder.Eval(
Container.DataItem, "Freight") %>' runat="server">
```

```
        <BR>
        <asp:Button id="btnUpdate"
runat="server" Text="Update"
         CommandName="Update"></asp:Button>
        <asp:Button id="btnCancel"
runat="server" Text="Cancel"
         CommandName="Cancel"></asp:Button>
    </EditItemTemplate>
</asp:DataList>
```

9. Double-click the form and enter code to handle loading data, binding data, and editing data:

```
Private Sub Page_Load(ByVal sender As System.Object, _
 ByVal e As System.EventArgs) Handles MyBase.Load
    ' Load the data
    If Not IsPostBack Then
        SqlDataAdapter1.Fill(DsOrders1, "Orders")
        DataBind()
    End If
End Sub

Private Sub dlOrders_CancelCommand( _
 ByVal source As Object, _
 ByVal e As System.Web.UI.WebControls. _
 DataListCommandEventArgs) _
 Handles dlOrders.CancelCommand
    ' Turn off the editing controls
    dlOrders.EditItemIndex = -1
    ' Re-bind the data
    SqlDataAdapter1.Fill(DsOrders1, "Orders")
    DataBind()
End Sub

Private Sub dlOrders_EditCommand( _
 ByVal source As Object, _
 ByVal e As System.Web.UI.WebControls. _
 DataListCommandEventArgs) _
 Handles dlOrders.EditCommand
    ' Turn on the editing controls
    dlOrders.EditItemIndex = CInt(e.Item.ItemIndex)
    ' Re-bind the data
    SqlDataAdapter1.Fill(DsOrders1, "Orders")
    DataBind()
End Sub

Private Sub dlOrders_UpdateCommand( _
 ByVal source As Object, _
 ByVal e As System.Web.UI.WebControls. _
 DataListCommandEventArgs) _
 Handles dlOrders.UpdateCommand
    Dim htEdit As HtmlInputText
    ' Get the existing data
    SqlDataAdapter1.Fill(DsOrders1, "Orders")
```

continues

continued

```
        ' Get the changed data and put it in the dataase
        htEdit = e.Item.FindControl("freight")
        DsOrders1.Tables("Orders").Rows( _
         e.Item.ItemIndex)(7) = htEdit.Value
        ' Turn off editing
        dlOrders.EditItemIndex = -1
        ' re-bind the data
        DataBind()
    End Sub
```

10. Set the form as the start page for the project.

11. Run the project. The DataList will display data from four columns of the Orders table. Click the Edit button for any row, and you'll be able to edit the Freight value, as shown in Figure 5.29.

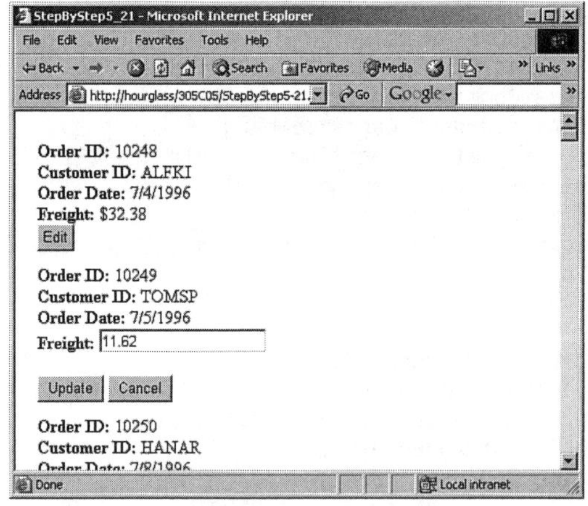

FIGURE 5.29
Editing data in a DataList control.

> **NOTE**
> **SelectedIndex** Although it's not used in this example, the DataGrid control also has a SelectedIndex property. Like the EditItemIndex property, SelectedIndex is zero-based. If you set the SelectedItemIndex to 3, for example, the third row in the DataGrid will be displayed using the SelectedItemTemplate. You can use this property to highlight a particular row in the DataGrid.

After you've created a DataList with an EditItemTemplate, you can tell the control to use that template for a specific row by supplying the (zero-based) index of that row. The CommandName tags in the HTML code correspond to the events that the DataList will raise in the VB code. For example, the CommandName="Edit" tag in the HTML corresponds to the EditCommand event in the VB .NET code. The Edit, Update, and Cancel commands are hardwired in this fashion.

When you raise an EditCommand event, the parameters passed to the event include the data item where the event was raised. The code uses the index of this item to determine which row to show in the edited state. Note that you need to rebind the data when you do this, because in reality you're rebuilding the entire page from scratch.

To cancel an edit, you just set the EditItemIndex property back to –1 and rebind the control.

To update the data, the code uses the FindControl method of the data item to find the input control where the freight value was edited. This control can be represented by an HtmlInputText object in the code. The code then uses the Value property of that object to update the corresponding row in the Dataset.

NOTE

Data Model and Database This example is a good demonstration of the difference between the data model and the database. If you edit the first row of data, you'll see the new value on the DataList. But if you then edit the second row, the first row will revert to its original value when the data is rebound. That's because changes are only being written to the data model and not back to the underlying database. In the next chapter, you'll see how to use the Update method of the DataAdapter object to write changes back to the database.

REVIEW BREAK

- The Repeater control uses templates to allow you to precisely format data from a collection.
- The DataBinder.Eval method is used to handle casts and formatting for data in a templated control.
- The DataList also uses templates, and supports formatting directly in the Visual Studio IDE.
- You can set the EditItemIndex property of a DataList control to show a particular row with edit controls.
- The EditCommand, UpdateCommand, and CancelCommand events of the DataList are used to control the editing process.

CHAPTER SUMMARY

KEY TERMS

- Data binding
- Simple data binding
- Complex data binding
- Resultset
- One-way data binding
- Two-way data binding
- Relational database
- Table
- Row
- Column
- Primary Key
- Relation
- Foreign Key
- Templated control

Nearly every Web-based application deals with data in one form or another. Often this data is contained in a database, but it may also be in a simple array, an array of objects, or many other forms. This data is known as the data model of the application.

Data binding gives you a way to connect data stored in the data model with the user interface of your application. In this chapter, you saw many of the tools that ASP.NET provides for data binding. This includes both simple and complex data binding, the Data Form Wizard, and the Server Explorer.

Data binding in the .NET Framework is much more flexible than it was in any previous development environment. You can bind to page properties, methods, collections, or properties of other controls.

You also saw some programmatic approaches to data, including the use of the DataView and DataSet classes and the creation of SQL Server views to filter or transform data. Templated controls provide you with additional control over data formatting, and the DataList control has built-in support for editing data on ASP.NET Web Forms.

APPLY YOUR KNOWLEDGE

Exercises

5.1 Using Simple Data Binding to Display Information from an Array

This exercise shows you how to populate an array in code and then use simple data binding to display the information on the user interface. A `DropDownList` control will enable the user to choose which member of the array to display.

Estimated Time: 20 minutes.

1. Create a new Visual Basic ASP.NET Web Application project to use for the Exercises in this chapter.

2. Add a new class file to the project. Name the class `Computer.vb`. Enter this code in the class file to create a class with three properties and a constructor:

```
Public Class Computer

    Private mstrComputerName As String
    Private mstrCPU As String
    Private mintRAM As Integer

    Public Property _
     ComputerName() As String
        Get
            ComputerName = mstrComputerName
        End Get
        Set(ByVal Value As String)
            mstrComputerName = Value
        End Set
    End Property

    Public Property CPU() As String
        Get
            CPU = mstrCPU
        End Get
        Set(ByVal Value As String)
            mstrCPU = Value
        End Set
    End Property

    Public Property RAM() As Integer
        Get
            RAM = mintRAM
        End Get
        Set(ByVal Value As Integer)
            mintRAM = Value
        End Set
    End Property

    Sub New(ByVal ComputerName As String, _
     ByVal CPU As String, _
     ByVal RAM As Integer)
        mstrComputerName = ComputerName
        mstrCPU = CPU
        mintRAM = RAM
    End Sub

End Class
```

3. Add a new Web Form to the project. Place a `DropDownList` and four `Label` controls on the form as shown in Figure 5.30. Set the ID property of the `DropDownList` control to `ddlComputerNumber` and set its `AutoPostBack` property to True. Set the ID properties of three of the `Label` controls to `lblComputerName`, `lblRAM`, and `lblCPU`.

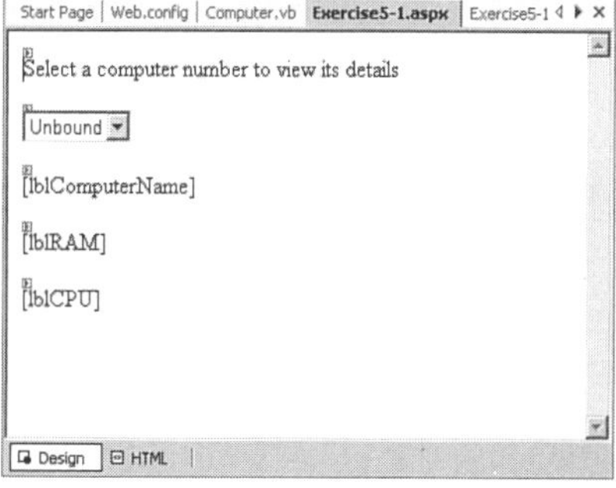

FIGURE 5.30
Design of the Web Form for Exercise 5.1.

APPLY YOUR KNOWLEDGE

4. Switch to HTML view and enter data-binding code for the three `Label` controls:

```
<P>
    <asp:Label id="lblComputerName"
runat="server" Width="284px">
     Computer Name:
<%# ComputerName %></asp:Label></P>
<P>
    <asp:Label id="lblRAM"
runat="server" Width="284px">
     RAM: <%# RAM %></asp:Label></P>
<P>
    <asp:Label id="lblCPU"
runat="server" Width="284px">
     CPU: <%# CPU %></asp:Label></P>
```

5. Add code to the form to create and initialize an array of `Computer` objects, and then to present information from the array as public properties:

```
Private maComputers() As Computer = _
         {New Computer( _
          "Frodo", "PIII-866", 512), _
          New Computer( _
           "Samwise", "PIII-500", 256), _
          New Computer( _
           "Meriadoc", "K6-350", 128), _
          New Computer( _
           "Peregrine", "K6-350", 128)}

Private mintComputerNumber As Integer

Public ReadOnly Property ComputerName()
    Get
        ComputerName = _
         maComputers( _
         mintComputerNumber).ComputerName
    End Get
End Property

Public ReadOnly Property RAM()
    Get
        RAM = maComputers( _
         mintComputerNumber).RAM
    End Get
End Property

Public ReadOnly Property CPU()
    Get
        CPU = maComputers( _
         mintComputerNumber).CPU
    End Get
End Property
```

6. Add code to the page load event to handle data binding:

```
Private Sub Page_Load( _
 ByVal sender As System.Object, _
 ByVal e As System.EventArgs) _
 Handles MyBase.Load
    Dim alNumbers As New ArrayList()
    If Not IsPostBack Then
        ' First time in,
        ' stock the DropDownList
        alNumbers.Add(0)
        alNumbers.Add(1)
        alNumbers.Add(2)
        alNumbers.Add(3)
        ddlComputerNumber. _
         DataSource = alNumbers
        ddlComputerNumber.DataBind()
        mintComputerNumber = 0
    Else
        mintComputerNumber = _
         ddlComputerNumber. _
          SelectedItem.Value
    End If
    ' Bind data to the Label controls
    lblComputerName.DataBind()
    lblRAM.DataBind()
    lblCPU.DataBind()
End Sub
```

7. Set the form as the start page for the project and run the project. The `DropDownList` will contain the computer numbers, and the user interface will show the information from the first computer. As you select values from the `DropDownList`, the user interface will be refreshed with the corresponding information from the array.

This exercise demonstrates one design pattern that you can use to allow the user to choose from a list of information. Remember, though, that in cases like this you end up sending the entire list to the server and back every time the user posts back to the page, due to the stateless nature of HTTP. You should be careful about how much information you're storing when you use this technique.

APPLY YOUR KNOWLEDGE

5.2 Use Simple Data Binding to Display Information from a Database

This exercise shows how you can connect to a database using Server Explorer, and then bind some of the information from the database to the user interface by using simple data binding.

Estimated Time: 20 minutes.

> NOTE
>
> **Creating the Database Connection** This exercise assumes that you've already used Server Explorer to connect to a copy of the SQL Server 2000 Northwind sample database. If you haven't yet done that, refer back to Step by Step 5.10, particularly steps 4 through 6 and the accompanying Exam Tip, to build a connection. After that, you can proceed with the exercise.

1. Add a new Web Form to the ASP.NET project.
2. Hover your cursor over the Server Explorer tab until the Server Explorer appears.
3. Expand the tree in the Server Explorer to locate the Orders table in the Northwind sample database. Drag the Orders table from Server Explorer and drop it on the form.
4. Click on the `SqlDataAdapter1` object. Click the Generate Dataset link in the Properties window. Create a new Dataset named `dsOrders` and click OK.
5. Place three `Label` and three `TextBox` controls on the form as shown in Figure 5.31. Assign IDs to the `TextBox` controls of `txtOrderID`, `txtCustomerID`, and `txtOrderDate`.

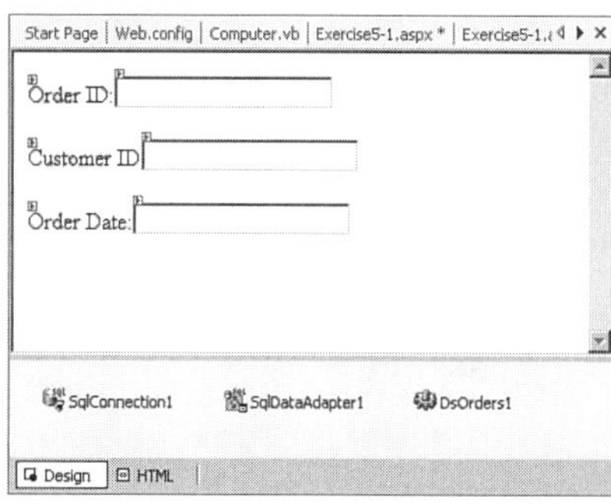

FIGURE 5.31
Design of the form for Exercise 5.2.

6. Switch to HTML view and enter data-binding tags for the TextBox controls:

```
<P>
    <asp:Label id="Label1"
runat="server">Order ID:
</asp:Label>
    <asp:TextBox id="txtOrderID"
runat="server"
     text='<%# dsOrders1.
Tables("Orders").Rows(0).
Item("OrderID") %>'>
    </asp:TextBox></P>
<P>
    <asp:Label id="Label2" runat="server">
Customer ID</asp:Label>
    <asp:TextBox id="txtCustomerID"
runat="server"
     text='<%# dsOrders1.
Tables("Orders").Rows(0).
Item("CustomerID") %>'>
    </asp:TextBox></P>
<P>
    <asp:Label id="Label3" runat="server">
Order Date:</asp:Label>
    <asp:TextBox id="txtOrderDate"
runat="server"
     text='<%# dsOrders1.
Tables("Orders").Rows(0).
Item("OrderDate") %>'>
    </asp:TextBox></P>
```

APPLY YOUR KNOWLEDGE

7. Add code to the form to fill the DataSet, and then bind selected items from the DataSet to the user interface:

```
Private Sub Page_Load( _
 ByVal sender As System.Object, _
 ByVal e As System.EventArgs) _
 Handles MyBase.Load
    ' Load the data
    SqlDataAdapter1.Fill( _
     DsOrders1, "Orders")
    DataBind()
End Sub
```

8. Set the form as the start page for the project and run the project. The information from the first row of the data model will appear on the user interface.

As this exercise shows, you're not forced to use complex data binding when you use data from a database. Simple data binding works just as well. However, there are some syntactical complexities introduced because the DataSet object can contain more than one bindable object (remember, a DataSet contains a collection of one or more DataTables). The code in this exercise shows you how to specify the database column to bind.

Also, you should be aware that this is not very efficient code. We loaded all the orders and only displayed one of them. In Chapter 6 you'll see how to use a SqlCommand object to load only the single order that you're interested in.

5.3 Use Complex and Simple Data Binding with a DropDownList

In this exercise, you'll use complex data binding to fill the list in a DropDownList control, and simple data binding to retrieve the value that the user selects from the list.

Estimated Time: 10 minutes.

1. Add a new form to the ASP.NET project. Place a `DropDownList` with the ID of `ddlComputers` and a `TextBox` control with the ID of txtRAM on the form. Set the `AutoPostBack` property of the `DropDownList` to true.

2. Switch to HTML view and enter data-binding code for the `TextBox` control:

```
<asp:TextBox id="txtOrderID" runat="server"
     text='<%# ddlComputers.
SelectedItem.Value %>'>
</asp:TextBox>
```

3. Add a new module to the project. Name the new module `Computers.vb` and enter this code:

```
Module Computers

    Public Function ComputerDataLoad() _
     As ICollection
        Dim dt As DataTable = _
        New DataTable()
        Dim dv As DataView
        Dim dr As DataRow

        ' Add two columns to the DataTable
        dt.Columns.Add(New DataColumn( _
         "ComputerName", GetType(String)))
        dt.Columns.Add( _
         New DataColumn("RAM", _
         GetType(String)))

        ' Put some data in
        dr = dt.NewRow()
        dr(0) = "Frodo"
        dr(1) = "512"
        dt.Rows.Add(dr)

        dr = dt.NewRow()
        dr(0) = "Samwise"
        dr(1) = "256"
        dt.Rows.Add(dr)

        dr = dt.NewRow()
        dr(0) = "Meriadoc"
        dr(1) = "128"
        dt.Rows.Add(dr)
```

Apply Your Knowledge

```
        dr = dt.NewRow()
        dr(0) = "Peregrine"
        dr(1) = "128"
        dt.Rows.Add(dr)

        ' And return the datatable
        ' wrapped in a dataview
        dv = New DataView(dt)
        Return dv

    End Function

End Module
```

4. Double-click the Web Form and enter code in the form's `Load` event:

```
Private Sub Page_Load( _
 ByVal sender As System.Object, _
 ByVal e As System.EventArgs) _
 Handles MyBase.Load
    If Not IsPostBack Then
        ddlComputers.DataSource = _
         ComputerDataLoad()
        ddlComputers.DataTextField = _
         "ComputerName"
        ddlComputers.DataValueField = "RAM"
        ddlComputers.DataBind()
    End If
End Sub
```

5. Enter code for the `DropDownList's` `SelectedIndexChanged` event:

```
Private Sub _
 ddlComputers_SelectedIndexChanged( _
 ByVal sender As System.Object, _
 ByVal e As System.EventArgs) _
 Handles ddlComputers.SelectedIndexChanged
    txtOrderID.DataBind()
End Sub
```

6. Set the Web Form as the start page for the project.

7. Run the project. As you select computer names from the `DropDownList`, the corresponding RAM values will appear in the `TextBox`.

5.4 Create a Master-Detail Data Form

This exercise will let you practice with the Visual Basic .NET Data Form Wizard. You'll build a Data Form that shows all of the employees in the Northwind sample database. When the user selects a particular employee, the form will display the orders that that employee has taken.

Estimated Time: 15 minutes.

1. Select Project, Add New Item. In the Add New Item dialog box, select the Data Form Wizard. Name the new form `Exercise5-4.aspx` and click Open.

2. Read the Welcome panel of the wizard and click Next.

3. On the Choose a Dataset panel, choose to create a new Dataset named `dsEmpOrders`. Click Next.

4. On the Choose a Data Connection panel, select the Data Connection to the Northwind sample database and click Next.

5. On the Choose Tables or Views panel, select the Employees table in the Available Items list and click the > button to move it to the Selected Items list. Also select the Orders table and click the > button to move it to the Selected Items list. Click Next.

6. On the Create a Relationship Between Tables panel, name the new relationship `relEmpOrders`. Select Employees as the parent table and Orders as the child table. Select `EmployeeID` as the key field in each table. Click the > button to create the new relationship, and then click Next.

7. On the Choose Tables and Columns to Display on the Form panel, leave all the columns in both tables selected, and click Finish.

APPLY YOUR KNOWLEDGE

8. Set the new Data Form as the start page for the project and run the project to experiment with the Data Form. Figure 5.32 shows the completed form.

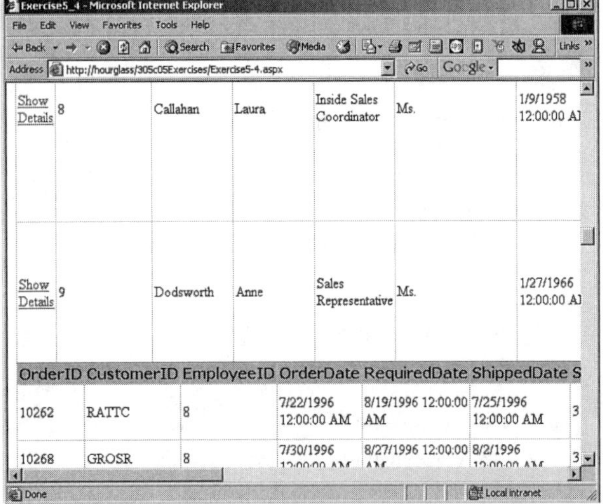

FIGURE 5.32
Browsing data with the form created in Exercise 5.4.

5.5 Use a DataView to Filter Data at Runtime

This exercise will guide you through the steps involved in building a form with a DataGrid whose display can be filtered at runtime. The DataGrid will display customers from a country selected by the user.

Estimated Time: 40 minutes.

1. Add a new form to the Visual Basic ASP.NET project.
2. Hover your cursor over the Server Explorer tab until the Server Explorer appears.
3. Expand the tree in the Server Explorer to locate the Customers table in the Northwind sample database. Drag the Customers table from Server Explorer and drop it on the form.
4. Click on the SqlDataAdapter1 object. Click the Generate Dataset link in the Properties window. Create a new Dataset named dsCustomers and click OK.
5. Reopen Server Explorer.
6. Right-click on the Views node and select New View.
7. In the Add Table dialog box, select the Customers table, click Add, and then click Close. This will put you in the view designer within Visual Studio .NET.
8. Click the checkbox for Country in the column listing.
9. Fill in the details of the view as shown in Figure 5.33.

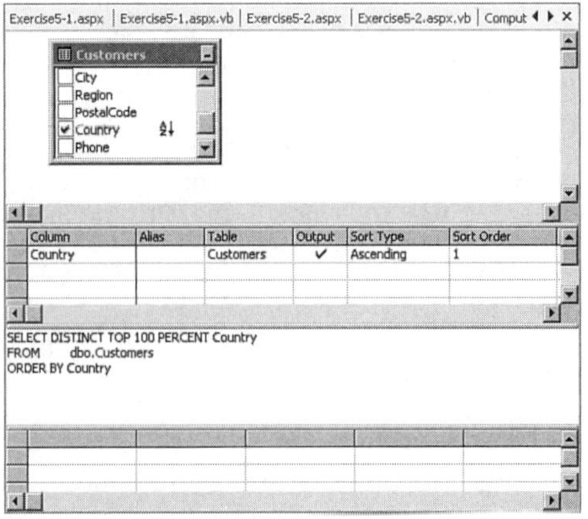

FIGURE 5.33
Creating a new SQL Server view to select the country names from the Customers table.

APPLY YOUR KNOWLEDGE

> **EXAM TIP**
>
> **SELECT DISTINCT** The use of the DISTINCT keyword in the SQL statement tells SQL Server to not return any duplicates when running this view. You'll need to add the DISTINCT keyword by typing it in to the SQL string.

10. Click on the Save button and save the view as `vwCustomerCountries`. Close the design window for the view.

11. Drag the `vwCustomerCountries` view from Server Explorer and drop it on the form. You'll get a configuration error because the view is read-only. That's not a problem because we're not writing any data back to the database; click OK to create objects. This will create one more visual data object, `SqlDataAdapter2`.

12. Select the `SqlDataAdapter2` object. Click the Generate Dataset link below the Properties window.

13. In the Generate Dataset window, choose to create a new `dsCountries` Dataset. Click OK.

14. Place a `DropDownList` control on the form. Set the ID of the control to `ddlCountries` and set its `AutoPostBack` property to `True`. Place a `DataGrid` control on the form and set its ID to `dgCustomers`.

15. Add code to the form to initialize the `DropDownList` when the page is first loaded:

```
Private Sub Page_Load( _
 ByVal sender As System.Object, _
 ByVal e As System.EventArgs) _
 Handles MyBase.Load
    If Not IsPostBack Then
        ' Fill the dataset of countries
        ' and bind it to the dropdownlist
        SqlDataAdapter2.Fill( _
         DsCountries1, "Countries")
        With ddlCountries
            .DataSource = _
             DsCountries1.Tables("Countries")
            .DataTextField = "Country"
            .DataValueField = "Country"
        End With
        ddlCountries.DataBind()
    End If
End Sub
```

16. Add code to the form to create a filtered `DataView` and bind that to the `DataGrid` whenever the selection in the `DropDownList` changes:

```
Private Sub _
 ddlCountries_SelectedIndexChanged( _
 ByVal sender As System.Object, _
 ByVal e As System.EventArgs) _
 Handles ddlCountries.SelectedIndexChanged
    ' Fill the dataset of customers
    ' and set up a dataview
    SqlDataAdapter1.Fill( _
     DsCustomers1, "Customers")
    Dim dvCustomers As DataView = _
     New DataView( _
      DsCustomers1.Tables("Customers"))
    ' Apply a filter to the dataview
    dvCustomers.RowFilter = _
     "Country = '" & _
     ddlCountries.SelectedItem.Value & "'"
    ' And bind the result to the datagrid
    dgCustomers.DataSource = dvCustomers
    dgCustomers.DataBind()
End Sub
```

17. Set the form as the start page for the project and run the project. As you select countries in the `DropDownList`, customers from the selected country will be displayed on the `DataGrid`.

APPLY YOUR KNOWLEDGE

5.6 Use SelectedIndex in a DataList

This exercise will guide you through the steps involved in building a form with a DataList that includes a SelectedItemTemplate. Buttons on the form enable the user to select different items at runtime.

Estimated Time: 35 minutes.

1. Add a new form to the Visual Basic ASP.NET project.

2. Place a `DataList` control on the new Web Form. Set the ID of the control to `dlEmployees`. Set the `RepeatColumns` property of the control to 2 and the `CellSpacing` property of the control to 10. Place two `Button` controls on the form. Set the ID properties of these controls to `btnPrevious` and `btnNext`.

3. Open Server Explorer.

4. Expand the tree under Data Connections to show a SQL Server data connection that points to the Northwind sample database, and then the Tables node of the SQL Server.

5. Drag the Employees table from Server Explorer and drop it on the form. This will create two visual data objects, `SqlConnection1` and `SqlDataAdapter1`.

6. Select the `SqlDataAdapter1` object. Click the Generate Dataset link below the Properties window.

7. In the Generate Dataset window, create a new `dsEmployees` dataset. Click OK.

8. Set the `DataSource` property of the `Repeater` control to `DsEmployees1`. Set the `DataMember` property of the `Repeater` control to `Employees`.

9. Switch to HTML view and enter code to customize the `DataList` control:

```
<asp:DataList id=DataList1 runat="server"
RepeatColumns="2"
  CellSpacing="10"
  DataSource="<%# DsEmployees1 %>
" DataMember="Employees">
<ItemTemplate>
<DIV>
<b>Employee ID:</b>
<%# DataBinder.Eval(
Container.DataItem, "EmployeeID") %>
<br>
<b>First Name:</b>
<%# DataBinder.Eval(
Container.DataItem, "FirstName") %><br>
<b>Last Name:</b>
<%# DataBinder.Eval(
Container.DataItem, "LastName") %><br>
</DIV>
</ItemTemplate>
</asp:DataList></P>
```

10. Switch back to Design view. Right-click on the `DataList` control and select Edit Template, Item `Templates`.

11. Click in the `ItemTemplate` area, below the text, so that you can see the properties for the `<DIV>` tag that wraps this template in the Properties Window. Click in the Style property and click the builder (…) button to open the Style Builder dialog box. Use the Style Builder to set font and color properties as you like and then click OK. For example, you might like to format the text as 12-point Arial on a tan background.

12. Select all the text in the `ItemTemplate`, copy it, and paste a copy into the `SelectedItemTemplate`. Use the Style Builder to set properties for the `SelectedItemTemplate` that contrast with those you chose for the `ItemTemplate`. For example, you might choose 12-point Arial bold in yellow on a blue background for the selected item.

APPLY YOUR KNOWLEDGE

13. Right-click in the control and select End Template Editing.

14. Double-click the form and enter code in the page's `Load` event:

```
Private Sub Page_Load( _
 ByVal sender As System.Object, _
 ByVal e As System.EventArgs) _
 Handles MyBase.Load
    'Load the data
    SqlDataAdapter1.Fill( _
     DsEmployees1, "Employees")
    DataBind()
End Sub
```

15. Enter code to handle the navigation buttons:

```
Private Sub btnPrevious_Click( _
 ByVal sender As System.Object, _
 ByVal e As System.EventArgs) _
 Handles btnPrevious.Click
    If dlEmployees.SelectedIndex > 0 Then
        dlEmployees.SelectedIndex -= 1
        DataBind()
    End If
End Sub

Private Sub btnNext_Click( _
 ByVal sender As System.Object, _
 ByVal e As System.EventArgs) _
 Handles btnNext.Click
    If dlEmployees.SelectedIndex < _
     dlEmployees.Items.Count Then
        dlEmployees.SelectedIndex += 1
        DataBind()
    End If
End Sub
```

16. Set the form as the start page for the project.

17. Run the project. The `DataList` will display data from three columns of the Employees table. The Next and Previous buttons will move a highlight through the list.

Review Questions

1. Describe the difference between a database and a data model.

2. Describe the difference between simple and complex data binding.

3. What is the purpose of the DataBind method?

4. What objects implement the DataBind method?

5. Name and briefly explain two different ways to filter data.

6. Name the templates available in the Repeater and DataList controls.

7. How do the DataSource, DataTextField, and DataValueField properties of the DropDownList work together?

8. Name at least two SQL Server objects that you can design from within Visual Studio .NET.

9. Which is more efficient for filtering data, a server-side view or a DataView object?

Exam Questions

1. The data model for your application includes an array of Product objects named Products. Each Product object exposes public properties named ProductNumber and ProductName. You'd like to provide an interface that allows users to select the ProductNumber and see the corresponding ProductName. What should you do?

   A. Create two TextBox controls. Bind the ProductNumber property to one TextBox control and the ProductNumber to the other TextBox control. Provide navigation buttons to allow the user to scroll through the data.

   B. Create a DataGrid control. Bind the Products array to the DataGrid control.

APPLY YOUR KNOWLEDGE

C. Create a DropDownList control. Set the Products array as the DataSource of the control. Bind the DataTextField property to the ProductNumber property, and bind the DataValue property to the ProductName property. Bind a TextBox on the form to the SelectedItem.Value property of the DropDownList control. Add Code to the SelectedIndexChanged property of the DropDownList control to invoke the DataBind method of the TextBox control.

D. Create a TextBox control and a Label control. Bind the ProductNumber property to the TextBox control and the ProductName property to the Label control.

2. Your application's data model represents orders as Order objects. You've created a function to return a DataView containing Order objects and used simple data binding to display the pertinent fields from the Order objects on a form. At runtime, the form does not display any data, even though you have confirmed that the DataView is not empty. What must you do?

   A. Change your function to return an ArrayList instead of a DataView.

   B. Create a DataSet from the DataView and bind the DataSet to the form.

   C. Drag and Drop a SqlConnection object representing the database containing the Orders to the form.

   D. Call the DataBind method of the form to bind the data to the user interface.

3. You have designed a Web Form that will use a Repeater control with the ID of rptEmployees to display employee information. The form includes a SqlDataAdapter object named SqlDataAdapter1 that draws data from the Employees table, and a DataSet object named dsEmployees1 that will contain the data. What code should you add to initialize the display when the page is loaded?

   A.

```
If Not IsPostBack Then
    SqlDataAdapter1.Fill( _
     DsEmployees1, "Employees")
    rptEmployees.DataSource = dsEmployees1
    rptEmployees.DataMember = "Employees"
    DataBind()
End If
```

   B.

```
If IsPostBack Then
    SqlDataAdapter1.Fill( _
     DsEmployees1, "Employees")
    rptEmployees.DataSource = dsEmployees1
    rptEmployees.DataMember = "Employees"
    DataBind()
End If
```

   C.

```
If Not IsPostBack Then
    SqlDataAdapter1.Fill( _
     DsEmployees1, "Employees")
    rptEmployees.DataSource = dsEmployees1
    rptEmployees. _
     DataTextField = "Employees"
    DataBind()
End If
```

   D.

```
If IsPostBack Then
    SqlDataAdapter1.Fill( _
     DsEmployees1, "Employees")
    rptEmployees.DataSource = dsEmployees1
    rptEmployees.DataTextField _
     = "Employees"
    DataBind()
End If
```

APPLY YOUR KNOWLEDGE

4. Your application includes a database table named Courses that contains a list of course numbers and course names. You've used Server Explorer to create a SqlConnection object and a SqlDataAdapter object to access this data. You've created a Dataset named dsCourses1 to hold this data. Your form includes code to fill the Dataset when it's loaded.

   Now you'd like to display the list of courses in a ListBox control named lbCourses on your form. The ListBox should show the course names and return the course numbers. Which of these code snippets should you use?

   A.

```
With lbCourses
    .DataSource = DsCourses1
    .DataTextField = "CourseName"
    .DataValueField = "CourseNumber"
    .DataBind
End With
```

   B.

```
With lbCourses
    .DataSource = _
     DsCourses1.Tables("Courses")
    .DataTextField = "CourseName"
    .DataValueField = "CourseNumber"
    .DataBind
End With
```

   C.

```
With lbCourses
    .DataSource = _
     DsCourses1.Tables("Courses")
    .DataTextField = "CourseName"
    .SelectedItem = "CourseNumber"
End With
```

   D.

```
With lbCourses
    .DataTextField = "CourseName"
    .DataValueField = "CourseNumber"
    .DataBind
End With
```

5. Your application includes a ListBox control named lbEmployees that displays a list of employees. The DataTextField property of the ListBox is bound to the EmployeeName column of the Employees database table. The DataValueField property of the ListBox is bound to the EmployeeNumber column of the Employees database table.

   Your form also contains a TextBox control named txtEmployeeNumber. This control uses simple data binding to display the SelectedItem.Value from the ListBox control.

   When the user selects a new employee name in the ListBox, you wish to display the corresponding EmployeeNumber value in the txtEmployeeNumber control. What should you do?

   A. Call the DataBind method of the ListBox control in the SelectedIndexChanged event of the Listbox.

   B. Create a public property named EmployeeNumber and return the SelectedItem.Value property of the Listbox as the value of the public property.

   C. Call the DataBind method of the TextBox control in the SelectedIndexChanged event of the Listbox.

   D. Use simple data binding to bind the SelectedValue property of the ListBox to the EmployeeNumber column of the Employees table.

6. Your application requires data from a database named College. The database includes two tables. The Departments table includes columns DepartmentID and DepartmentName.

APPLY YOUR KNOWLEDGE

The Courses table includes columns DepartmentID, CourseName, and CourseNumber. The DepartmentID column is a primary key for the Departments table and a foreign key for the Courses table.

A form in your application needs to display a list of CourseName values, together with the DepartmentName value for each course. This form does not need any other data. How should you retrieve only this data from the database.

A. Use Server Explorer to create a new SQL Server view that joins the two tables and returns only the required fields. Drag this view and drop it on a form to create a DataAdapter that returns the required data. Build a DataSet from the DataAdapter and bind the DataSet to your form.

B. Drag both the Departments table and the Courses table from Server Explorer and drop them on your form to create two separate DataAdapters. Use the DataAdapters to fill a single Dataset. Build a DataView from the Dataset and use the DataView to filter the data.

C. Drag both the Departments table and the Courses table from Server Explorer and drop them on your form to create two separate DataAdapters. Use the two DataAdapters to create two separate DataSets. Bind the DataSet of Course information to a DataGrid. Bind the DataSet of Department information to a DropDownList. Use the value in the DropDownList to filter the information displayed on the DataGrid.

D. Use Server Explorer to create a new SQL Server table that includes only the necessary information. Copy the data from the two separate tables to this table. Drag and drop this table from Server Explorer to your form to create a DataAdapter. Build a DataSet from the DataAdapter and bind the DataSet to your form.

7. Your application includes a SqlDataAdapter object named SqlDataAdapter1 that was created by dragging and dropping the Physicians table from a database to your form. Your application also includes a Dataset named dsPhysicians1, based on this SqlDataAdapter. What line of code should you use to load the data from the database into the Dataset?

   A. dsPhysicians = sqlDataAdapter1.Fill("Physicians")

   B. SqlDataAdapter1.Fill("DsPhysicians1", "Physicians")

   C. SqlDataAdapter1.Fill(DsPhysicians1)

   D. SqlDataAdapter1.Fill(DsPhysicians1, "Physicians")

8. The application that you're designing will display employee information on a DataGrid control using complex data binding. Your database contains a table of departments and a table of employees. The employees table has a foreign key that points back to the departments table. The application will communicate with the database via a slow WAN link. The list of departments changes approximately once every two months.

APPLY YOUR KNOWLEDGE

The form will display all the employees from a single department. Although users will only view one department at a time, they will frequently need to view several departments during the course of a session with the application.

How should you design the filtering for this form?

A. Build one view on the server for each department. At runtime, have the program use the appropriate view to retrieve the requested department.

B. Each time the user requests a department, retrieve all the data into a Dataset. Then delete all rows from the Dataset that do not apply to this department.

C. Retrieve all the data into a Dataset. Use a Dataview with its RowFilter property set at runtime to retrieve individual departments as needed.

D. Build one form for each department. Each form should be based on a view that returns only the employees for that department. At runtime, open the appropriate form. Hide the form when the user is done so that it can be opened more quickly if it's needed a second time.

9. Your application is connected to a SQL Server database that contains customer and order information. You have a form in your application that fills a Dataset with information from the Orders table that includes the CustomerID. The Dataset is displayed on the form by using complex data binding to a DataGrid.

Now you've been asked to display the CustomerName column from the Customers table in the DataGrid, instead of the CustomerID column. How should you proceed?

A. Create a view in the SQL Server database that combines the Customers and Orders tables. Replace the Dataset on the form with a new Dataset based on this new view. Bind the new Dataset to the DataGrid.

B. Add a second Dataset to the form. Base the second Dataset on the Customers table from the database. Use each Dataset to fill the appropriate columns of the DataGrid.

C. Create a DataView in code from the existing Dataset. Filter the DataView to remove the CustomerID column.

D. Add an array of Customer objects to your application and initialize it in code with customer names and IDs. Use a view to join this array to the existing Dataset.

10. Your application uses a DataList control to display course information. The information is supplied by a DataSet named DsCourses1. You want the user to be able to edit the CourseName field. You've created a Button control in the ItemTemplate with this code:

```
<asp:Button id="btnEdit"
runat="server" Text="Edit"
 CommandName="Edit"></asp:Button>
```

You've also created an EditItemTemplate that includes a TextBox control with the ID of txtCourseName for editing the CourseName field. What code should your application run when the user clicks the btnEdit button?

APPLY YOUR KNOWLEDGE

A.

```
Private Sub dlCourses_EditCommand( _
 ByVal source As Object, _
 ByVal e As System.Web.UI. _
 WebControls.DataListCommandEventArgs) _
 Handles dlCourses.EditCommand
    dlCourses.EditItemIndex = _
     CInt(e.Item.ItemIndex)
End Sub
```

B.

```
Private Sub dlCourses_EditCommand( _
 ByVal source As Object, _
 ByVal e As System.Web.UI. _
 WebControls.DataListCommandEventArgs) _
 Handles dlCourses.EditCommand
    dlCourses.EditItemIndex = _
     CInt(e.Item.ItemIndex)
    SqlDataAdapter1.Fill( _
     DsCourses1, "Courses")
    DataBind()
End Sub
```

C.

```
Private Sub dlCourses_EditCommand( _
 ByVal source As Object, _
 ByVal e As System.Web.UI. _
 WebControls.DataListCommandEventArgs) _
 Handles dlCourses.EditCommand
    dlCourses.EditItemIndex = -1
    SqlDataAdapter1.Fill( _
     DsCourses1, "Courses")
    DataBind()
End Sub
```

D.

```
Private Sub dlCourses_EditCommand( _
 ByVal source As Object, _
 ByVal e As System.Web.UI.WebControls. _
 DataListCommandEventArgs) _
 Handles dlCourses.EditCommand
    dlCourses.EditItemIndex = -1
End Sub
```

11. You have developed a form with a DataList control that displays order information. One of the database columns that you wish to display on this form is named Tax. This column contains a currency value. What binding expression should you use to display this value on the user interface, formatted as currency?

A.

```
<%# DataBinder.Eval(Container.DataItem,
"Tax") %>
```

B.

```
<%# "Tax" %>
```

C.

```
<%# "Tax", "{0:c}" %>
```

D.

```
<%# DataBinder.Eval(Container.DataItem,
"Tax", "{0:c}") %>
```

12. The data model of your application includes a task list that might have anywhere from one to eight items in it. Each item is characterized by five pieces of information. You need to display the entire task list on a single form. Your users want to be able to see all tasks at one time. What should you do?

   A. Use simple data binding to display a single task in individual TextBox controls. Provide a DropDownList control to allow the user to select the task to display.

   B. Use the System.Reflection.Emit namespace to create the appropriate number of TextBox controls at runtime. Use simple data binding to bind each task to a different set of controls.

   C. Use complex data binding to display the task list in a DropDownList control.

   D. Use complex data binding to display the task list in a DataGrid control.

APPLY YOUR KNOWLEDGE

13. You are designing a form to display information on customers. You want to show the customers in two columns on the form. Each customer will include name, address, and last order date information. You want to change the background color on alternate rows of customers so that it's easy to tell where one ends and another starts.

    What control should you use to display the customer information?

    A. DropDownList

    B. Repeater

    C. DataList

    D. DataGrid

14. You have an XML file containing information on customers. You plan to make this information available to your users by using simple data binding to controls on the user interface. What must you do?

    A. Transfer the data from the XML file to a data structure that implements the ICollection interface.

    B. Create an XML Web Service to retrieve information from the file.

    C. Store the XML file in a SQL Server database.

    D. Set the Tag property of each control that you will use for data binding to "XML."

15. Your Web Form includes a DropDownList control named ddlStudent that displays a list of students, and a DataGrid control named dgCourses that displays the courses that the selected student is enrolled in. When the page is loaded, you run code that includes the lines:

```
' Load the data
DataBind()
```

    When the user selects an entry in the DropDownList control, you create a DataView and then set the DataSource property of the DataGrid control to the DataView.

    You're receiving an error at page load. What is the most likely cause of this error?

    A. The DataBind method for the page is attempting to bind data to the DataGrid as well as to the DropDownList, and the data for the DataGrid does not exist yet.

    B. The DropDownList control is marked as read-only.

    C. There is no student information in the database.

    D. The DataBind method cannot be called in the Page_Load event, because there is no data available to the form in that event.

Answers to Review Questions

1. A database is a location, such as a SQL Server database, where you can store data outside of your application. A data model is the representation of data within your application.

2. Simple data binding means connecting a single value from the data model to a single property of a control. Complex data binding means connecting a user interface control to an entire collection of data, rather than to a single data item.

3. The DataBind method allows you to specify precisely when data should be bound to the controls on a Web Form.

4. DataBind is a method of all Web Forms controls and of the Page object. Calling DataBind on a containing object automatically binds the contained objects as well.

APPLY YOUR KNOWLEDGE

5. You can filter data by creating a DataView object and setting its RowFilter property, or by creating a view on the database server. In the first case, all of the data is returned from the server to your application, and then filtered in your application. In the second case, the data is filtered on the server, and only the filtered data is returned to your application.

6. Formatting of the Repeater control is handled by the HeaderTemplate, ItemTemplate, AlternatingItemTemplate, SeparatorTemplate, and FooterTemplate templates. The DataList control adds the SelectedItemTemplate and EditItemTemplate to this list.

7. The DataSource property of a DropDownList control specifies the data that will be displayed in the list portion of the DropDownList. The DataTextField property specifies the exact column of data that will be shown in the list. The DataValueField property specifies the exact column of data that will be returned by the SelectedItem.Value property of the DropDownList.

8. You can design SQL Server database diagrams, tables, views, stored procedures, and functions from within Visual Studio .NET.

9. Which alternative is more efficient depends on what your application is doing with the data. If you only need a small portion of the data, it's more efficient to filter the data on the server with a server-side view. But if your communications link with the server is slow, or you will need a variety of different subsets of the data, it can be more efficient to perform filtering on the client with a DataView.

Answers to Exam Questions

1. **C.** Binding the DropDownList control to the DataSource and responding to its SelectedIndexChanged event lets the DropDownList transfer data from the source to the TextBox. Answer A requires searching for the data rather than choosing it. Answer B displays all the data at once. Answer D does not have any provision for choosing a ProductNumber.

2. **D.** Unlike data binding on regular Windows Forms, data binding on Web Forms does not occur until you explicitly call the DataBind method.

3. **A.** To initialize data when the page is loaded, you want to check to be sure that you're not in a postback. Loading data requires a four-step process: fill the DataSet, set the DataSource and DataMember properties of the Repeater, and call DataBind to bind the data.

4. **B.** The code in B performs the required task. Answer A does not properly specify which data from the Dataset to use. Answer C neglects to bind the DataValueField property, which controls the value of the ListBox. Answer D neglects to set the DataSource property, without which there is no data to bind.

5. **C.** This is the only choice that will satisfy the conditions.

6. **A.** Answers B and C return too much data to the client. Answer D results in storing duplicate data on the server, which is inefficient and prone to error.

APPLY YOUR KNOWLEDGE

7. **D.** In a call to the Fill method of a SqlDataAdapter object, you must specify the Dataset to fill as an object and the table to fill as a string.

8. **C.** Answers A and D require maintenance programming every time that the list of departments changes. Answer B will retrieve more data than necessary over the slow WAN line.

9. **A.** Answers B and C are unworkable. Answer D requires you to maintain the code to synchronize the array with the actual data in the database. Only answer A lets you set up the DataGrid so that it's automatically kept up to date.

10. **B.** Answer B follows the correct steps to place the selected row into edit mode, including setting the EditItemIndex property to the row number and then rebinding the data so that the edit controls are initialized. Answer A fails because it doesn't rebind the data. Answers C and D set the EditItemIndex property to –1, which is how you end an edit, not how you begin one.

11. **D.** Answer D correctly uses the DataBinder object's Eval method to format the data. Answer A is syntactically correct, but won't apply any format. Answers B and C fail to retrieve the correct information.

12. **D.** Answers A and C result in only one task being visible at a time. Answer B uses much complicated programming where a single data binding call will suffice.

13. **C.** Only the Repeater and DataList control support the AlternatingItemTemplate template to handle the alternate-row formatting, and only the DataList can easily provide the two-column display.

14. **A.** Only this answer will produce data that can be bound.

15. **A.** Calling the DataBind method for the page will call the DataBind method for every control on the page as well, whether the data is available or not.

Suggested Readings and Resources

1. ASP.NET QuickStart Tutorial
   - Data Binding Server Controls
   - Server-Side Data Access
   - Web Forms Controls Reference.
2. Visual Studio .NET Combined Help Collection
   - Accessing Data With ASP.NET
3. .NET Framework SDK Documentation
   - System.Data Namespace
   - System.Web.UI.WebControls Namespace

OBJECTIVES

This chapter covers the following Microsoft-specified objectives for the Consuming and Manipulating Data section of the Visual Basic .NET Web Applications exam:

Consuming and Manipulating Data

- **Access and manipulate data from a Microsoft SQL Server(TM) database by creating and using ad hoc queries and stored procedures.**
- **Access and manipulate data from a data store. Data stores include relational databases, XML documents, and flat files. Methods include XML techniques and ADO .NET.**
- **Handle data errors.**

▶ Visual Basic .NET includes a variety of ways to manipulate data and to move it from place to place. The Visual Studio .NET IDE offers tight integration with Microsoft SQL Server, making it easy to work with SQL Server data, either interactively or programmatically. The .NET Framework also offers several entire namespaces to deal with data in its various forms. These include the following:

- **`System.IO` for dealing with file-based storage**
- **`System.Data`, `System.Data.SqlClient`, and `System.Data.OleDb` (which collectively make up ADO.NET) for using data from relational databases**
- **`System.Xml` for working with XML files**

In this chapter you'll learn about these many ways to manipulate data within your application.

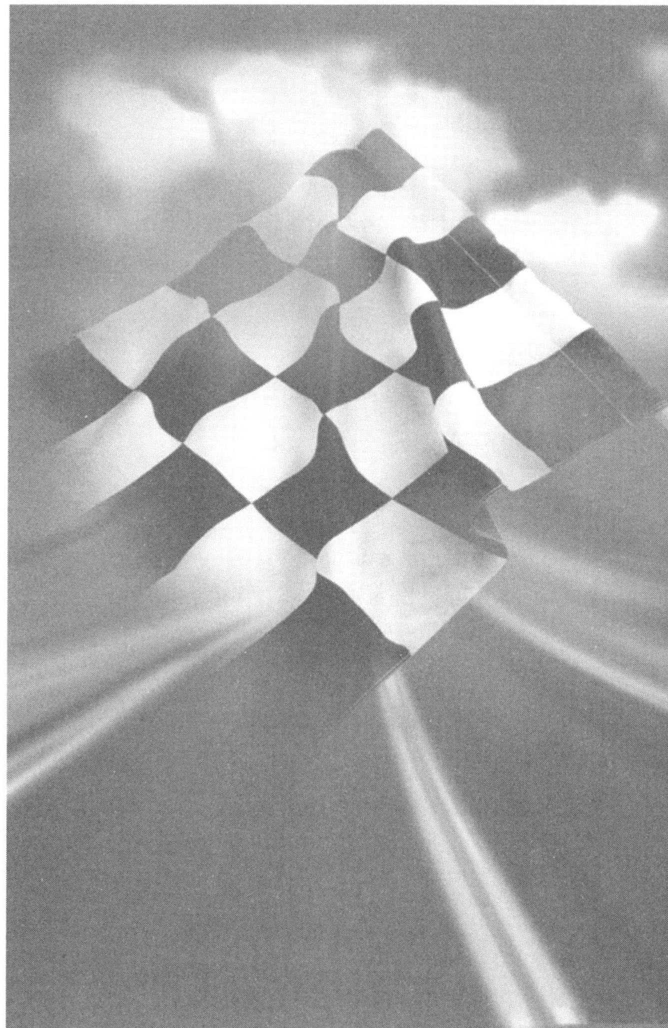

CHAPTER 6

Consuming and Manipulating Data

OUTLINE

STUDY STRATEGIES

- You should understand how to construct and interpret simple Transact SQL statements, including SELECT, INSERT, UPDATE, and DELETE, as well as SQL Server–stored procedures. Spend some time practicing with the Visual Data Tools inside of .NET or with another query front-end such as SQL Server Query Analyzer. Make sure you work with the raw T-SQL, not just the graphical tools.
- For file-based access, you should understand the difference between a stream and a backing store. Practice reading and writing data with FileStream, StreamReader, and StreamWriter objects.
- Sometimes you'll come across the claim that ADO.NET is just an evolutionary improvement on classic ADO, and that your knowledge of classic ADO will help you learn ADO.NET. This is not true! ADO.NET is an entirely new model for working with data. Make sure that you pay attention to the uses and functions of the ADO.NET objects, and don't get confused by the similarity of names between these objects and classic ADO objects.
- Know which objects are part of the System.Data namespace (and so shared by all data providers) and which are part of specific data provider namespaces such as System.Data.SqlClient and System.Data.OleDb.
- You'll need to know the objects that are contained within a DataSet and the methods that are available to manipulate those objects. Be sure to understand when to use a strongly typed DataSet and how this affects the syntax of DataSet operations.
- You should also know how to read and write XML data by using the classes from the System.Xml namespace. Understand how to synchronize an XML document with a DataSet and some of the reasons that you might want to do this.

INTRODUCTION

You've already seen techniques that are available for dealing with data directly from the user interface of a Visual Basic .NET Web application, and so now it's time to take a more detailed look at the facilities that the .NET Framework offers for working with data. Data is at the core of many .NET applications, and the Microsoft developers spent many hours building a flexible set of tools for working with data in your code.

I'll look at three main types of data in this chapter: data stored in databases such as Microsoft SQL Server, data stored in disk files, and data stored in XML. The .NET Framework offers specialized ways to deal with each of these types of data.

Many parts of ADO.NET are specially optimized to work with Microsoft SQL Server as a database, so you need to understand the language Transact-SQL (usually abbreviated as T-SQL), which is used to communicate with SQL Server. I'll start the chapter by reviewing the basic parts of the T-SQL language that you need to know to communicate effectively with SQL Server. You'll also see how you can use a small part of ADO.NET to send T-SQL statements to SQL Server and receive the results of the statements.

Once you know T-SQL, you can look at ways to manipulate a variety of data. Data stored in files is handled by the classes in the `System.IO` namespace. The .NET Framework handles file data as part of a more general concept of streams and backing stores. A backing store is any place that you can store data (including a disk file) and a stream represents that data moving from place to place.

Data stored in databases is the target of ADO.NET, a subset of the .NET Framework that uses objects from the `System.Data` namespace and related namespaces. The `DataSet` object is the central object here, representing an entire relational database in a single object (with many constituent objects). You'll see how to create `DataSet` objects and fill them with data and then some of the many ways that you can work with that data.

Data stored in XML is handled by the `System.Xml` namespace. XML is a key part of the .NET Framework, and the classes in this namespace give you flexibility to read and write such data.

I'll close the chapter with a look at handling data errors. In particular, you'll see how the .NET error-trapping mechanisms let you deal with common database and multi-user data errors.

ACCESS AND MANIPULATE SQL SERVER DATA

Consuming and Manipulating Data: Access and manipulate data from a Microsoft SQL Server(TM) database by creating and using ad hoc queries and stored procedures.

You might be a bit surprised to find a Microsoft SQL Server objective on a Visual Basic .NET certification exam, but this really makes perfect sense. Many Visual Basic .NET applications require a database to enable them to store data on a permanent basis, and SQL Server is one of the best databases to use with .NET. As you'll see later in this chapter, there's an entire namespace (`System.Data.SqlClient`) devoted to efficient communication between .NET applications and SQL Server.

The objects in `System.Data.SqlClient`, though, won't do you any good unless you understand the language used to communicate with SQL Server. This language is *Transact-SQL*, usually abbreviated T-SQL. T-SQL is Microsoft's implementation of SQL, the Structured Query Language, which is defined by a standard from the American National Standards Institute (ANSI). The core of T-SQL is based on the ANSI SQL-92 standard. SQL-92 defines a query-oriented language, in which you submit queries to the database and get back a result set consisting of rows and columns of data. Other queries cause changes to the database (for example, adding, deleting, or updating a row of data) without returning any result set.

There are two main ways to submit T-SQL to a SQL Server database for processing. First, you can write *ad-hoc queries*, SQL statements that are executed directly. Second, you can write *stored procedures*, SQL statements that are stored on the server as a named object. The .NET Framework includes facilities for running both ad-hoc queries and stored procedures.

EXAM TIP

SQL Statement Formatting You'll usually see SQL keywords (such as `SELECT`, `INSERT`, `UPDATE`, and `DELETE`) formatted entirely in uppercase. I'll follow that convention in this book, but uppercase formatting isn't required by SQL Server. You might see these same keywords in mixed case or lowercase on an exam. As far as SQL Server is concerned, there's no difference between `SELECT`, `Select`, and `select`.

NOTE

SQL Dialects Microsoft SQL Server isn't the only product that implements the SQL-92 standard. Other products, including Microsoft Access and Oracle, also use SQL-92–based query languages. However, different databases differ in their treatment of SQL in many subtle ways. Most databases contain extensions to SQL-92 (keywords that are understood only by that particular database) and most don't implement the entire SQL-92 standard. The SQL statements in this chapter are from the shared core of SQL-92 that's identical in nearly all database products, so they should work fine whether you're using SQL Server, Access, or Oracle (among others). But as you study the more advanced features of SQL Server, you should keep in mind that T-SQL statements will not necessarily run without changes on other database servers.

Using Ad Hoc Queries

Ad hoc T-SQL queries provide you with an extremely flexible way to retrieve data from a SQL Server database or to make changes to that database. In this section of the chapter, I'll show you several ways to send an ad hoc query to SQL Server. Then you'll learn the basics of the four main T-SQL statements that help you manipulate SQL Server data:

- `SELECT` statements allow you to retrieve data stored in the database.
- `INSERT` statements allow you to add new data to the database.
- `UPDATE` statements allow you to modify data that's already in the database.
- `DELETE` statements allow you to delete data from the database.

Running Queries

When you're learning T-SQL, it's useful to be able to send queries to a SQL Server database and to see the results (if any) that the server returns. You should be familiar with the many ways to communicate with SQL Server. I'll show you four of them in this section:

- Using the Visual Studio .NET IDE
- Using `osql`
- Using SQL Query Analyzer
- Using an ASP.NET Application

Using the Visual Studio .NET IDE

When you just need to run a query in the course of working with a project, you can run it directly from the Visual Studio .NET IDE. Step by Step 6.1 shows you how.

STEP BY STEP

6.1 Running a Query from the Visual Studio .NET IDE

1. Open a Visual Basic .NET Web Application in the Visual Studio .NET IDE.
2. Open Server Explorer.
3. Expand the tree under Data Connections to show a SQL Server data connection that points to the Northwind sample database, then the Views node of the SQL Server.
4. Right-click the Views node and select New View.
5. Click Close on the Add Table dialog box.
6. In the SQL pane of the View Designer (this is the area that starts by displaying the text SELECT FROM) type this SQL statement (replacing the existing text):

```
SELECT * FROM Employees
```

7. Select Query, Run from the Visual Studio menu, or click the Run Query button on the View toolbar. This sends the SQL statement to SQL Server and displays the results, as shown in Figure 6.1.

NOTE

The Northwind Sample Database
Whenever I've used data from a database in this book, I've used the Northwind sample database that comes as part of SQL Server 2000. Visual Studio .NET includes MSDE, a stripped-down version of SQL Server that you can use if you don't have the full version installed. See your Visual Studio CD's readme file for information on installing MSDE.

NOTE

Creating Data Connections If you need a refresher on creating SQL Server data connections, refer back to Chapter 5, "Data Binding"—especially Step By Step 5.11, "Building a Single-Table Data Form," and Step By Step 5.13, "Adding a Data Connection from Server Explorer."

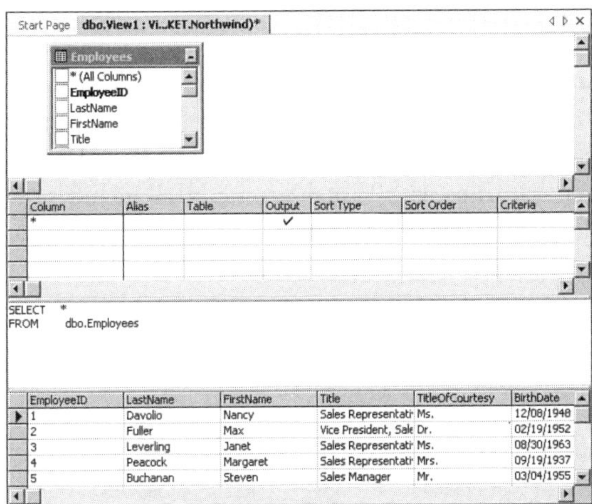

FIGURE 6.1
Running an ad hoc query directly from the Visual Studio .NET IDE.

When you run the query, Visual Studio .NET sends the SQL statement to the SQL Server that was specified by the database connection that you chose in Step 3. The server then processes the query (this particular query tells it to return all columns in all rows of the Employees table) and sends the results back to the client (in this case, Visual Studio .NET). The IDE then displays the results formatted as a grid.

EXAM TIP

SQL Statement Formatting If you look at Figure 6.1, you'll see that Visual Studio .NET made some changes to the SQL statement that you typed. The original statement was

```
SELECT * FROM Employees
```

The statement that Visual Studio .NET turns this into is

```
SELECT     *
FROM         dbo.Employees
```

Two things are going on here. First, SQL Server doesn't care about white space. You can insert spaces, tabs, or new lines between any SQL keywords without changing the statement. Second, every SQL Server object (such as the Employees table) has an owner. The default owner is a user named `dbo` (for database owner). You can add the name of the owner of an object to the object when referring to it. In the case of SQL statements on the exam, it's likely that every object will be owned by `dbo`, so don't get thrown if you see the `dbo` prefix on a table name.

The View Designer in Visual Studio .NET displays up to four panes, which I describe here in the order they appear onscreen, from top to bottom:

1. The Diagram pane displays the tables involved in the query, the relationships between these tables, and all the columns that the tables contain.
2. The Grid pane shows the columns that have been selected as part of the query, as well as additional sorting and filtering information.
3. The SQL pane shows the actual SQL statement that will be executed.
4. The Results pane shows the results (if any) after the query has been executed.

The View toolbar includes buttons that you can use to hide or show any of these four panes. For this chapter, you'll need only the SQL pane and the Results pane.

Using Osql

A second option for executing ad hoc queries is to use one of the utilities that ships as a part of SQL Server. The MSDE version of SQL Server that ships with Visual Studio .NET includes one of these utilities, `osql`, which is a command-line utility that can execute SQL Server queries.

STEP BY STEP

6.2 Running a Query from osql

1. Open a Windows command prompt.

2. To launch `osql` and log in using Windows integrated authentication, type

   ```
   osql -E
   ```

3. To execute a query in `osql`, you must first tell it which database to use. Type

   ```
   use Northwind
   ```

4. Next you must enter the query to execute. Type

   ```
   SELECT FirstName, LastName FROM Employees
   ```

5. Finally, you must tell `osql` to execute the SQL statements that you just entered. Type

   ```
   GO
   ```

6. When you're done with `osql`, type

   ```
   exit
   ```

   Here's the entire `osql` session, including the prompts from `osql`:

   ```
   C:\>osql -E
   1> use Northwind
   2> SELECT FirstName, LastName FROM Employees
   3> GO
    FirstName  LastName
    ---------- --------------------
    Nancy      Davolio
    Max        Fuller
    Janet      Leverling
    Margaret   Peacock
    Steven     Buchanan
    Michael    Suyama
    Robert     King
    Laura      Callahan
    Anne       Dodsworth

   (9 rows affected)
   1> exit

   C:\>
   ```

> **EXAM TIP**
>
> **Obtaining SQL Query Analyzer**
> SQL Query Analyzer is not included in the MSDE version of SQL Server. It's a part of all the other editions of SQL Server, so if you have another edition installed, you'll have SQL Query Analyzer available. Otherwise, you can download the 120-day trial version of SQL Server 2000 from `http://www.microsoft.com/sql/evaluation/trial/2000/default.asp`. This version also contains SQL Query Analyzer.

I chose a slightly different query for the `osql` session than I used in the first Step By Step. The `SELECT` query in Step By Step 5.2 specifies two columns from the table (`FirstName` and `LastName`), telling SQL Server to return only the contents of those two columns. If you execute `SELECT * FROM Employees` in `osql`, you may get a bit of a shock. That's because the Employees table includes a bitmap image column, and the contents of that column will fill a command session with junk characters.

Using SQL Query Analyzer

Although `osql` can be convenient for quick queries, it doesn't offer much in the way of tools. SQL Server also offers a full-featured query environment called SQL Query Analyzer.

STEP BY STEP

6.3 Running a Query from SQL Query Analyzer

1. Select Start, Programs, Microsoft SQL Server, Query Analyzer.
2. SQL Query Analyzer launches, displaying the Connect to SQL Server dialog box. To choose a SQL Server to work with, you can type the name of a SQL Server, or the special name `(local)` to use a SQL Server on the same computer as SQL Query Analyzer. You can also use the Browse button to list all servers on the network. After selecting a server and filling in your authentication information, click OK.
3. Select the Northwind database from the databases combo box on the SQL Query Analyzer toolbar.
4. Type a query in the Query window:

```
SELECT * FROM Employees
```

5. Select Query, Execute, click the Execute button on the toolbar, or click F5 to run the query. This sends the SQL statement to SQL Server and displays the results, as shown in Figure 6.2.

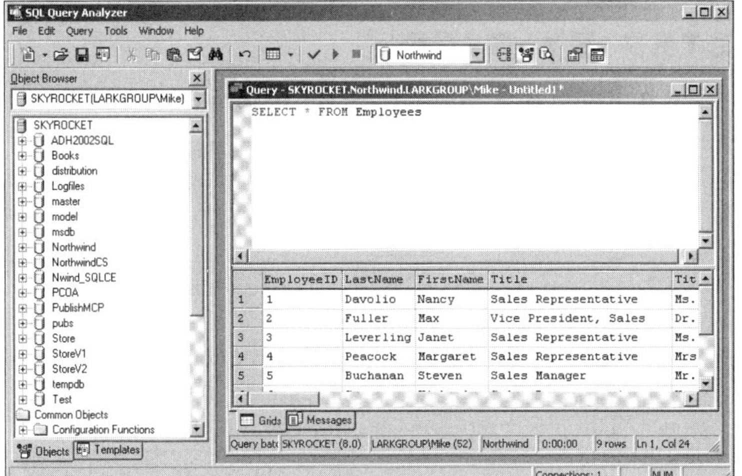

FIGURE 6.2
Running an ad hoc query in SQL Query Analyzer.

SQL Query Analyzer offers an extremely flexible environment for running ad hoc queries. The features of SQL Query Analyzer include

- Multiple open query windows
- An Object Browser to see the structure of SQL Server objects
- Performance analysis
- Templates for common queries

For more information on using SQL Query Analyzer, refer to SQL Server Books Online, the help file that is installed as part of SQL Server.

Using a Visual Basic .NET Application

As a final alternative for executing ad hoc queries, I'll show you how to build your own Visual Basic .NET form in an ASP.NET application to execute any query.

STEP BY STEP

6.4 Running a Query from a Custom Form

1. Add a new Web Form to your Visual Basic .NET web project.
2. Open Server Explorer.
3. Expand the tree under Data Connections to show a SQL Server data connection that points to the Northwind sample database. Drag and drop the data connection to the form. This creates a `SqlConnection1` object on the form. This object represents a connection to SQL Server.
4. Add a `TextBox` control with the ID of `txtQuery`, a `Button` control with the ID of `btnExecute`, and a `DataGrid` control with the ID of `dgResults` to the form. Set the `TextMode` property of the `TextBox` to `MultiLine`.
5. Double-click the `Button` control to open the form's module. Enter two statements at the top of the module to make the ADO.NET objects available:

```
Imports System.Data
Imports System.Data.SqlClient
```

6. Enter this code to execute the query when you click the `Button` control:

```
Private Sub Page_Load( _
 ByVal sender As System.Object, _
 ByVal e As System.EventArgs) Handles MyBase.Load
    ' Process queries when form is posted back
    If IsPostBack Then
        ' Create a SqlCommand to represent the query
        Dim cmd As SqlCommand = _
         SqlConnection1.CreateCommand
        cmd.CommandType = CommandType.Text
        cmd.CommandText = txtQuery.Text
        ' Create a SqlDataAdapter to
        ' talk to the database
        Dim da As SqlDataAdapter = _
         New SqlDataAdapter()
        da.SelectCommand = cmd
        ' Create a DataSet to hold the results
        Dim ds As DataSet = New DataSet()
        ' Fill the DataSet
        da.Fill(ds, ìResultsî)
        ' And bind it to the DataGrid
        dgResults.DataSource = ds
```

```
        dgResults.DataMember = "Results"
        dgResults.DataBind()
    End If
End Sub
```

7. Set the form as the start page for the project.

8. Run the project. Enter a query in the `TextBox`:

   `SELECT * FROM Employees`

9. Click the button. Even though there's no code attached to the button itself, clicking the button posts the form back to the server automatically. This runs the code, retrieving the results to the `DataGrid`, as shown in Figure 6.3.

You'll learn about the ADO.NET objects that this example uses later in this chapter, starting in the section "The ADO.NET Object Model." So for now I'll settle for a quick preview of the objects that I just used:

- The `SqlConnection` object represents a connection to a database.

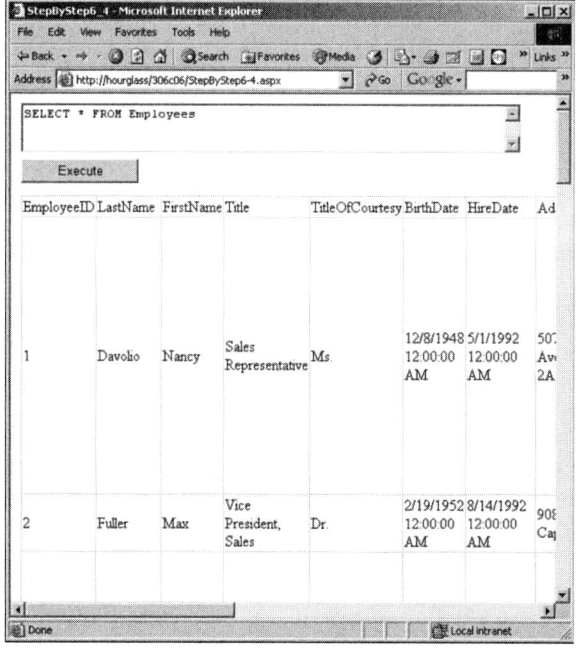

FIGURE 6.3
Running an ad hoc query from a custom form.

- The SqlCommand object represents a single query that you can send to the server.
- The DataSet object represents the results of one or more queries.
- The SqlDataAdapter object acts as a pipeline between the SqlConnection and DataSet objects.

The code uses these objects to retrieve data from the SQL Server to the DataSet and uses the SQL statement that you typed in to know which data to retrieve. It then uses complex data binding (which you learned about in Chapter 5) to display the results on the user interface in the DataGrid control.

EXAM TIP

Practice Using SQL You can use any of the methods that you saw in the preceding section to execute the statements that you're about to learn. You *should* execute enough of these statements to get a good idea of how the T-SQL language works. Just reading the descriptions here is no substitute for actually practicing with T-SQL. You're sure to see some SQL statements on the exam.

The SELECT Statement

Now that you know a variety of ways to execute ad hoc queries, it's time to dig into the T-SQL language to see some of the possible queries, starting with the SELECT statement.

The basic SQL statement is the SELECT statement. This statement is used to create a result set. In skeleton form, a SELECT looks like this:

```
SELECT field_list
FROM table_list
WHERE where_clause
GROUP BY group_by_clause
HAVING having_clause
ORDER BY sort_clause
```

Each of those lines of code is called a clause. The SELECT and FROM clauses are required, and the rest are optional. Here's an example of a SQL statement containing only the required clauses:

```
SELECT OrderID, CustomerID
FROM Orders
```

The result set for this statement contains the values of the OrderID and CustomerID field from every record in the Orders table.

There are other things you can do in the SELECT clause besides just list fields. You've already seen that there's a shortcut for all fields:

```
SELECT *
FROM Orders
```

You can also perform calculations in the SELECT clause:

```
SELECT OrderID,
CAST(ShippedDate - OrderDate AS integer) AS Delay
FROM Orders
```

The expression ShippedDate - OrderDate calculates the number of days between the two dates. The CAST function tells SQL Server to return the result as an integer. If you try that example, you'll see that the AS clause supplies a name for the calculated column. If you omit the AS Delay, the query will still work but SQL Server will return the calculation without assigning a name to the column.

You're also not limited to fields from a single table. For instance, you might try retrieving information from both the Customers and Orders table with this query:

```
SELECT OrderID, Customers.CustomerID
FROM Orders, Customers
```

Customers.CustomerID is what's known as a fully qualified name, specifying both the table name and the field name. This is necessary because both the Customers and the Orders tables contain fields named CustomerID, and you need to tell SQL Server which one you want to display.

If you try this last query, though, it will return more than 75,000 records. That's many more than the number of orders in the database! That's because the query as written, while it includes all the proper tables, doesn't tell SQL Server how to relate those tables.

The name for this sort of query is a "cross-product" query. SQL Server constructs the result set by including one row in the output for each row in each combination of input table rows. That is, there's an output row for the first order and the first customer, one for the first order and the second customer, and so on. A more useful query, of course, matches each order with the corresponding customer.

That's the job of the INNER JOIN keyword. INNER JOIN tells SQL Server how to match two tables. Here's how the syntax looks for a fixed version of the original query:

```
SELECT OrderID, Customers.CustomerID
FROM Orders INNER JOIN Customers
ON Orders.CustomerID = Customers.CustomerID
```

NOTE

One Keyword or Two? Even though it's two words, INNER JOIN is referred to as a single SQL keyword. That's because you can't have INNER in T-SQL unless you immediately follow it with JOIN.

This rewrite tells SQL Server to look at each row in the Orders table and match it with all rows in the Customers table where the `CustomerID` of the order equals the `CustomerID` of the Customer. Because `CustomerIDs` are unique in the Customers table, this is tantamount to including only a single row for each order in the result set.

The `INNER JOIN` keyword can appear more than once in a query if there are more than two tables to join. For example, here's a query to show Employee IDs along with Order and Customer IDs:

```
SELECT Orders.OrderID, Customers.CustomerID,
Employees.EmployeeID
FROM Employees INNER JOIN
(Customers INNER JOIN Orders
ON Customers.CustomerID = Orders.CustomerID)
ON Employees.EmployeeID = Orders.EmployeeID
```

Note the use of parentheses to specify the order in which the joins should be performed.

The basic `SELECT` query allows you to see all the data in a table. For example,

```
SELECT * FROM Orders
```

That query returns every bit of data in the Orders table: every column, every row. You've already seen that you can use a field list to limit the number of columns returned:

```
SELECT OrderID, CustomerID, EmployeeID FROM Orders
```

But what if you only want to see some of the rows in the table? That's where the `WHERE` clause comes into the picture. You can think of a `WHERE` clause as making a simple yes-or-no decision for each row of data in the original table, deciding whether or not to include that row in the result set.

The simplest form of the `WHERE` clause checks for the exact contents of a field. For example,

```
SELECT * FROM Orders
WHERE ShipCountry = 'Brazil'
```

This query looks at every row in the Orders table and determines whether the `ShipCountry` field contains the exact value "Brazil". If so, the row is included in the results. If not, it's discarded. However, `WHERE` clauses need not be exact. This is also a valid SQL statement:

```
SELECT * FROM Orders
WHERE Freight > 50
```

In this case, you'll get all the rows where the amount in the `Freight` field is greater than `50`.

Note, by the way, that `Brazil` goes in quotation marks whereas `50` doesn't. That's simply a syntax matter: Text and date data need the quote marks, numeric columns don't.

You're free to combine multiple tests in a single `WHERE` clause. For example,

```
SELECT * FROM Orders
WHERE ShipCountry = 'Brazil'
 AND Freight > 50
 AND OrderDate <= '12/31/97'
```

This retrieves all orders that went to Brazil, had more than $50 of freight charges, and were shipped before the end of 1997. The key is that the entire `WHERE` clause must be a single logical predicate. That is, by evaluating all the pieces, the result must be a True or False value. Rows for which the `WHERE` clause evaluates to True are included in the results; rows for which it evaluates to False are excluded.

You can also use wild cards in a `WHERE` clause. Consider this simple `SELECT` statement:

```
SELECT * FROM Customers
WHERE CustomerID = 'BLONP'
```

If you run that query, you'll find that it returns the record for Blondel pere et fils, the customer that is assigned the `CustomerID` of BLONP. So far, that's easy. But what if you remember that the `CustomerID` starts with B, but not what it is exactly? That's when you'd use a wildcard:

```
SELECT * FROM Customers
WHERE CustomerID LIKE 'B%'
```

The `%` wildcard matches zero or more characters—so the result of this query is to retrieve all customers whose `CustomerIDs` begin with "B". Note the switch from `=` to `LIKE` when using a wildcard (if you searched for `CustomerID = "B%"`, you'd only find a customer with that exact ID). Now suppose you almost remember the `CustomerID`, but not quite: Is it `BLOND` or `BLONP`? Try this query:

```
SELECT * FROM Customers
WHERE CustomerID LIKE 'BLON_'
```

The _ wildcard matches precisely one character—so that would match BLONA, BLONB, and so on. If you're sure that it's either BLOND or BLONP, you can match only those two possibilities with a character set wildcard:

```
SELECT * FROM Customers
WHERE CustomerID LIKE 'BLON"'
```

The " is a character set wildcard. The square brackets tell SQL Server to match any one of the characters listed in the set. You can also use a dash in a character set to indicate a range:

```
SELECT * FROM Customers
WHERE CustomerID LIKE 'BLON[D-P]'
```

That matches BLOND, BLONE, and so on, up to BLONP. You can also invert a character set with the ^ character. For example,

```
SELECT * FROM Customers
WHERE CustomerID LIKE 'BLON[^A-O]'
```

That matches BLONP, BLONQ, and so on—but not BLONA, BLONB, or anything else that would match on the character set without the ^ character.

SQL is a set-oriented language; by default, the database engine is free to return the set of results in any order it likes. The way to guarantee a sort order is to include an ORDER BY clause in your SQL statement. For example, to see the customers from Venezuela in Postal Code order, you could use this statement:

```
SELECT * FROM Customers
WHERE Country = 'Venezuela'
ORDER BY PostalCode
```

That's the basic ORDER BY clause: a field name to sort by. There are two keywords you can use to modify this: ASC, for ascending sort (the default), and DESC, for descending sort. So, you could equally well write the previous SQL statement as

```
SELECT * FROM Customers
WHERE Country = 'Venezuela'
ORDER BY PostalCode ASC
```

And you could get the customers sorted in reverse postal code order with this statement:

```
SELECT * FROM Customers
WHERE Country = 'Venezuela'
ORDER BY PostalCode DESC
```

You're not limited to sorting by a single field. For example, you might want to see the entire Customer list, sorted first by country and then by postal code within country:

```
SELECT * FROM Customers
ORDER BY Country, PostalCode
```

You can specify on a field-by-field basis the order of the sort:

```
SELECT * FROM Customers
ORDER BY Country ASC, PostalCode DESC
```

That would sort by country in ascending order, and then by postal code in descending order within each country.

You can also calculate a sort. For example, you can sort the customers by the length of their company name:

```
SELECT * FROM Customers
ORDER BY Len([CompanyName])
```

Here the square brackets tell the `Len()` function that it's being passed a column name, and to retrieve that column value for each row as the input to the function. In fact, the calculation need not have anything to do with the fields returned by the `SELECT` statement:

```
SELECT * FROM Customers
ORDER BY 2+2
```

That's a perfectly valid SQL statement, though the effect is to put the records in whatever order the database engine decides it wants to use.

So far, all the `SELECT` statements you've seen in this chapter have returned results where each row corresponds to one row in the underlying tables. However, it's possible (and indeed common) to use SQL to return aggregate, summarized information.

For example, suppose you want to know how many customers you have in each country. Here's a query that will give you the answer:

```
SELECT Count(CustomerID) AS CustCount, Country
FROM Customers
GROUP BY Country
```

You can think of the `GROUP BY` clause as creating "buckets," in this case, one for each country. As the database engine examines each record, it tosses it in the appropriate bucket. After this process is done, it counts the number of records that ended up in each bucket and outputs a row for each one. Figure 6.4 shows the start of the result set from this query.

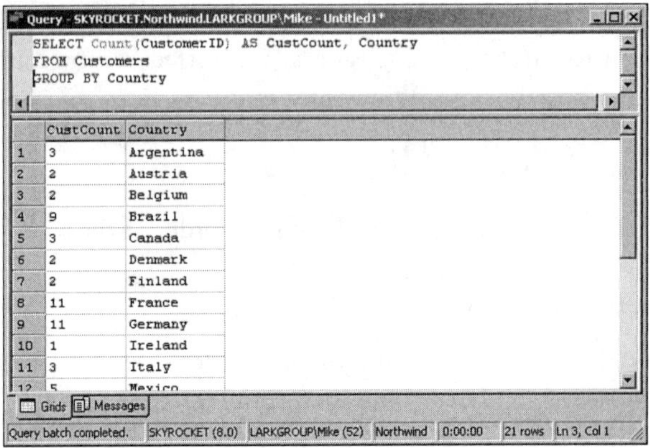

FIGURE 6.4
Result set from a query that includes a `GROUP BY` clause.

You can use `ORDER BY` in conjunction with `GROUP BY`. In this case, you could sort by the number of customers in each country:

```
SELECT Count(CustomerID) AS CustCount, Country
FROM Customers
GROUP BY Country
ORDER BY Count(CustomerID) DESC
```

Or by the country name:

```
SELECT Count(CustomerID) AS CustCount, Country
FROM Customers
GROUP BY Country
ORDER BY Country
```

`Count()` in these SQL statements is an *aggregate function*, one that returns a result based on a number of rows. T-SQL supports a number of aggregate functions. Here are some of the most common:

- `Count()`—Number of records
- `Sum()`—Total value of records
- `Avg()`—Average value of records
- `Min()`—Smallest record
- `Max()`—Largest record

You can also group on more than one field. For example,

```
SELECT Count(CustomerID) AS CustCount, Region, Country
FROM Customers
GROUP BY Region, Country
```

That statement sets up one "bucket" for each combination of Region and Country and categorizes the customers by both fields simultaneously.

So far, the GROUP BY statements you've seen have included all the records in the table. For example, consider this query:

```
SELECT ProductID,
Sum(Quantity) AS TotalSales
FROM [Order Details]
GROUP BY ProductID
ORDER BY Sum(Quantity) DESC
```

That query returns a result set that has one row for each Product found in the Order Details table, with the Product ID and the total quantity of that product that was ordered.

As stated, that query uses all the rows in the Order Details table to come up with its totals. There are two ways that you can limit this to use only part of the table.

First, you can use a WHERE clause to limit the rows from the original query that will be included in the totals:

```
SELECT ProductID,
Sum(Quantity) AS TotalSales
FROM [Order Details]
WHERE Quantity > 10
GROUP BY ProductID
ORDER BY Sum(Quantity) DESC
```

That will have the same effect as the first query, except that it will just ignore any row in the Order Details table that has a quantity of 10 or under.

The other way to limit the results is by filtering on the totals with a HAVING clause:

```
SELECT ProductID, Sum(Quantity) AS TotalSales
FROM [Order Details]
GROUP BY ProductID
HAVING Sum(Quantity) > 1000
ORDER BY Sum(Quantity) DESC
```

A HAVING clause filters on the results, rather than on the input. That is, the last query will sum everything from the Order Details table and then show you only rows where the total is greater than 1000.

You can also combine the two types of filtering:

```
SELECT ProductID, Sum(Quantity) AS TotalSales
FROM [Order Details]
WHERE Quantity > 10
GROUP BY ProductID
HAVING  Sum(Quantity) > 1000
ORDER BY Sum(Quantity) DESC
```

NOTE

Quoting Names This query uses square brackets to quote the name of the Order Details table. That's necessary because the table name has a space in it, and without the quoting, SQL Server would try to interpret it as two names.

That goes through the source table, sums up all the rows where Quantity is greater than 10, and then only keeps those rows where the total is over a thousand.

Note that WHERE and HAVING go in two different places in the SQL statement. The order of clauses is fixed, not optional.

The INSERT Statement

The purpose of the INSERT statement is to add a row or multiple rows to a table through executing a SQL statement. In its simplest form, the INSERT query lists a target table and a set of values to insert. For example, this query adds a new row to the Order Details table:

```
INSERT INTO [Order Details]
VALUES (10248, 1, 12.00, 5, 0)
```

There are two drawbacks to this simple form of the statement. First, it's very hard to tell which field is getting which piece of data; the values are inserted into the table fields in the order that the fields show up in design view, but you need to remember (in this example) that the quantity is the fourth field. Second, if you use this format, you need to supply a value for every field. This is a problem when you want the default value for a field or when a field can't have data inserted into it (for example, an identity field, with values that are automatically generated by SQL Server). To get around these problems, there is a second format that explicitly lists the fields for the target table:

```
INSERT INTO [Order Details]
  (OrderID, ProductID, UnitPrice, Quantity, Discount)
VALUES (10248, 2, 12.00, 5, 0)
```

Here, the first set of parentheses holds a column list, and the second set holds the values to insert. If a field has a default value, if it can be null, or if it is an identity field, you can leave it out of the field list:

```
INSERT INTO Products
  (ProductName, SupplierID, CategoryID)
VALUES ('Turnips', 25, 7)
```

This works even though no value is specified for most of the fields in the Products table. Also, you can rearrange the field list as long as you rearrange the value list to match:

```
INSERT INTO Products
  (SupplierID, ProductName, CategoryID)
VALUES (20, 'Lettuce',  7)
```

The INSERT query isn't limited to inserting a single record. There's a second format that inserts the results of a SELECT statement into the target table. For example, this query inserts a product from every supplier into the Products table:

```
INSERT INTO Products (SupplierID, ProductName,
CategoryID )
SELECT SupplierID, 'Trout', 8
FROM Suppliers
```

This works by building the results of the SELECT statement and then putting each row returned by the SELECT into the target table. Of course, the columns still need to match up properly.

The UPDATE Statement

Another very useful SQL statement is the UPDATE statement. As you can probably guess, the purpose of an UPDATE query is to update data. For example, you could update a field in a record in Northwind with this query:

```
UPDATE Customers
 SET ContactName = 'Maria Anderson'
 WHERE CustomerID = 'ALFKI'
```

In this query, the UPDATE keyword introduces an Update query. The SET keyword tells SQL Server what to update. Here it's setting a field equal to a literal value. The WHERE clause tells SQL Server which row in the table to update.

You're not limited to updating a single record. If the WHERE clause selects multiple records, they'll all be updated:

```
UPDATE Customers
 SET Country = 'United States'
 WHERE Country = 'USA'
```

You can even update every row in a table, by leaving out the WHERE clause:

```
UPDATE Products
 SET Discontinued = False
```

That will happily update every row in the Product table, even those where the Discontinued field already has the value False.

You can also update more than one field at a time with an UPDATE query:

```
UPDATE Customers
 SET ContactName = 'Maria Anders', City = 'Berlin'
 WHERE CustomerID = 'ALFKI'
```

And you can update with the result of an expression:

```
UPDATE Products
 SET UnitPrice = UnitPrice * 1.1
```

If only it were so simple to raise prices in real life!

The DELETE Statement

The DELETE statement removes data from a table. The rule for constructing a Delete query is simple: construct a Select query to select the records you want to delete, and then change the SELECT keyword to DELETE. Remove any "*" identifier from the SELECT clause as well. That's it!

To avoid destroying existing data, I'll use another query to set the stage. The SELECT INTO statement is used to create a new table. For example, this statement creates a table named BadCustomers with all the data from the existing Customers table:

```
SELECT * INTO BadCustomers
FROM Customers
```

Here's a Select query to select a single row from the new table:

```
SELECT * FROM BadCustomers WHERE CustomerID = 'GODOS'
```

Now change the SELECT * clause to DELETE:

```
DELETE FROM BadCustomers WHERE CustomerID = 'GODOS'
```

If you run this query, it will delete the specified row.

There's no need for a WHERE clause if you want to get really extreme:

```
DELETE FROM BadCustomers
```

That statement deletes all the rows from the BadCustomers table.

REVIEW BREAK

- Transact-SQL is the Microsoft SQL Server dialect of the ANSI SQL-92 standard query language.
- You can execute T-SQL statements from a variety of interfaces, including the Visual Studio .NET IDE, osql, SQL Query Analyzer, or custom applications.
- SELECT statements retrieve data from tables in a database.
- INSERT statements add new data to tables in a database.

- `UPDATE` statements modify existing data in tables in a database.
- `DELETE` statements remove data from tables in a database.

Using Stored Procedures

When you use an ad hoc query to interact with SQL Server, the SQL statements in the query are completely transient. They vanish as soon as you close whatever tool you've used to execute the query. By contrast, stored procedures are queries that are stored permanently on the SQL Server itself. Stored procedures have two main benefits. First, you can save complex SQL statements for future execution so that you don't have to re-create them from scratch. Second, SQL Server compiles stored procedures so that they run faster than ad hoc queries.

In this section, you'll see how you can create and run stored procedures. I'll also discuss parameters, which make stored procedures more flexible, and the `@@IDENTITY` variable, which can supply useful information any time that you use a stored procedure to insert data into a table with an identity column.

> **EXAM TIP**
>
> **When to use Stored Procedures**
> In almost every case, stored procedures are preferable to ad hoc queries in production applications. The only time you should consider using ad hoc queries is when you're writing an application that must allow completely freeform querying by the end user. Otherwise, the additional development time required to implement stored procedures will be worth it in the end.

Creating a Stored Procedure

T-SQL includes a `CREATE PROCEDURE` keyword that you use to create stored procedures. You can run `CREATE PROCEDURE` statements from any interface that allows you to enter and execute T-SQL.

STEP BY STEP

6.5 Creating a Stored Procedure from the Visual Studio .NET IDE

1. Open a Visual Basic ASP.NET Web Application in the Visual Studio .NET IDE.
2. Open Server Explorer.

continues

continued

3. Expand the tree under Data Connections to show a SQL Server data connection that points to the Northwind sample database, then the Views node of the SQL Server.
4. Right-click the Stored Procedures node and select New Stored Procedure.
5. Replace the boilerplate code in the Stored Procedure designer with this code:

```
CREATE PROCEDURE procFranceCustomers
AS
    SELECT * FROM Customers
    WHERE Country = 'France'
```

6. Click the Save button to save the stored procedure to the database.
7. Select Database, Run Stored Procedure to run the `CREATE PROCEDURE` statement. This creates the stored procedure in the database.
8. Now you can execute the new `procFranceCustomers` stored procedure from any tool that allows you to execute SQL statements. For example, Figure 6.5 shows the results of executing this stored procedure in the custom form that you build in Step By Step 6.4.

You can see that there are two separate executing steps in this process. Executing the `CREATE PROCEDURE` statement (which is itself an ad hoc query) is necessary to create the stored procedure. After that has been done, you can execute the stored procedure itself to return results.

Running Stored Procedures from .NET

Executing a stored procedure from .NET is very similar to executing an ad hoc query. The difference is that you supply the name of the stored procedure instead of the actual SQL as the `CommandText` property of a `SqlCommand` object.

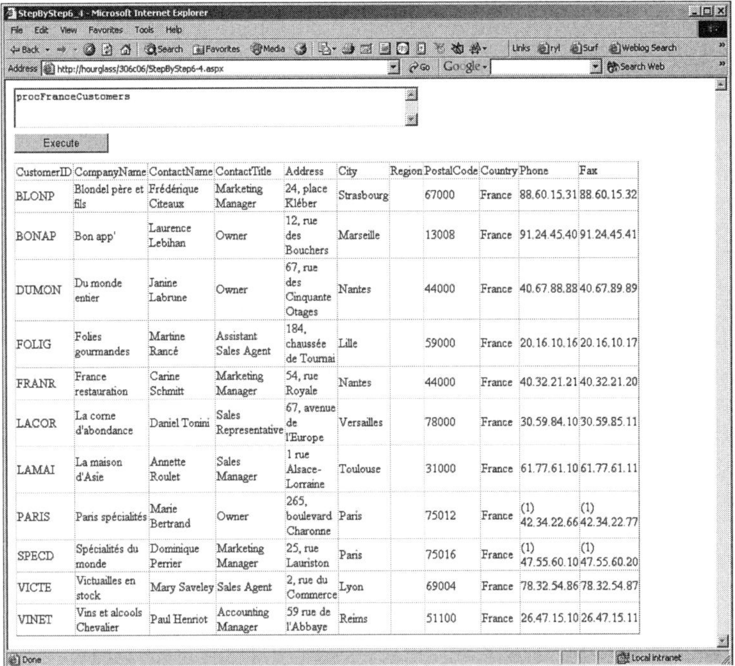

CustomerID	CompanyName	ContactName	ContactTitle	Address	City	Region	PostalCode	Country	Phone	Fax
BLONP	Blondel père et fils	Frédérique Citeaux	Marketing Manager	24, place Kléber	Strasbourg		67000	France	88.60.15.31	88.60.15.32
BONAP	Bon app'	Laurence Lebihan	Owner	12, rue des Bouchers	Marseille		13008	France	91.24.45.40	91.24.45.41
DUMON	Du monde entier	Janine Labrune	Owner	67, rue des Cinquante Otages	Nantes		44000	France	40.67.88.88	40.67.89.89
FOLIG	Folies gourmandes	Martine Rancé	Assistant Sales Agent	184, chaussée de Tournai	Lille		59000	France	20.16.10.16	20.16.10.17
FRANR	France restauration	Carine Schmitt	Marketing Manager	54, rue Royale	Nantes		44000	France	40.32.21.21	40.32.21.20
LACOR	La corne d'abondance	Daniel Tonini	Sales Representative	67, avenue de l'Europe	Versailles		78000	France	30.59.84.10	30.59.85.11
LAMAI	La maison d'Asie	Annette Roulet	Sales Manager	1 rue Alsace-Lorraine	Toulouse		31000	France	61.77.61.10	61.77.61.11
PARIS	Paris spécialités	Marie Bertrand	Owner	265, boulevard Charonne	Paris		75012	France	(1) 42.34.22.66	(1) 42.34.22.77
SPECD	Spécialités du monde	Dominique Perrier	Marketing Manager	25, rue Lauriston	Paris		75016	France	(1) 47.55.60.10	(1) 47.55.60.20
VICTE	Victuailles en stock	Mary Saveley	Sales Agent	2, rue du Commerce	Lyon		69004	France	78.32.54.86	78.32.54.87
VINET	Vins et alcools Chevalier	Paul Henriot	Accounting Manager	59 rue de l'Abbaye	Reims		51100	France	26.47.15.10	26.47.15.11

FIGURE 6.5
The results of running a stored procedure are the same as the results of running the T-SQL statements contained in the stored procedure.

STEP BY STEP

6.6 Running a Stored Procedure from ASP.NET

1. Add a new form to your Visual Basic web project.
2. Open Server Explorer.
3. Expand the tree under Data Connections to show a SQL Server data connection that points to the Northwind sample database. Drag and drop the data connection to the form. This creates a `SqlConnection1` object on the form.
4. Add a `DataGrid` control to the form. Set the ID property of the control to `dgResults`.
5. Double-click the form to open the form's module. Enter two statements at the top of the module to make the ADO.NET objects available:

```
Imports System.Data
Imports System.Data.SqlClient
```

continues

continued

6. Enter this code to execute the stored procedure when you first load the page:

```
Private Sub Page_Load(ByVal sender As System.Object, _
 ByVal e As System.EventArgs) Handles MyBase.Load
    If Not IsPostBack Then
        ' Create a SqlCommand to
        ' represent the stored procedure
        Dim cmd As SqlCommand = _
         SqlConnection1.CreateCommand
        cmd.CommandType = CommandType.StoredProcedure
        cmd.CommandText = "procFranceCustomers"
        ' Create a SqlDataAdapter
        ' to talk to the database
        Dim da As SqlDataAdapter = _
         New SqlDataAdapter()
        da.SelectCommand = cmd
        ' Create a DataSet to hold the results
        Dim ds As DataSet = New DataSet()
        ' Fill the DataSet
        da.Fill(ds, "Customers")
        ' And bind it to the DataGrid
        dgResults.DataSource = ds
        dgResults.DataMember = "Customers"
        dgResults.DataBind()
    End If
End Sub
```

7. Set the form as the start page for the project.

8. Run the project. This will run the code, retrieving the results from the stored procedure to the `DataGrid`, as shown in Figure 6.6.

Stored procedures are not limited to containing `SELECT` statements. You can place any SQL statement inside of a stored procedure. For example, you might use this SQL statement to create a stored procedure to update the Customers table:

```
CREATE PROCEDURE procExpandCountry
AS
UPDATE Customers
 SET Country = 'United States'
 WHERE Country = 'USA'
```

When your stored procedure doesn't return a result set, you need to use a slightly different code structure to execute it.

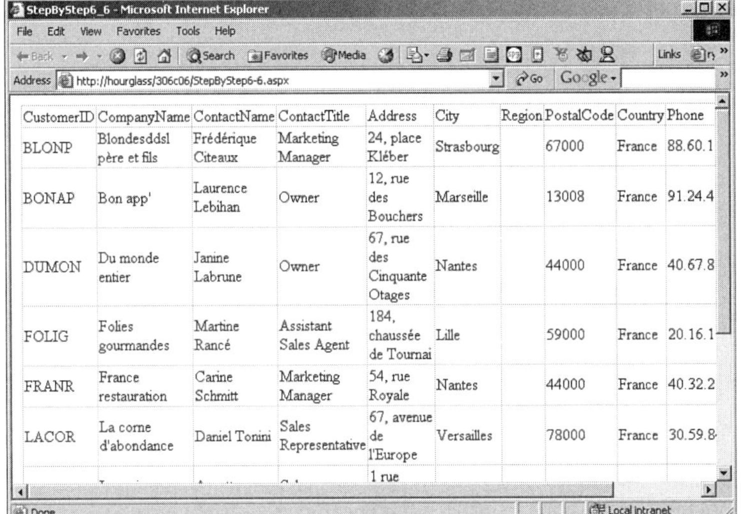

CustomerID	CompanyName	ContactName	ContactTitle	Address	City	Region	PostalCode	Country	Phone
BLONP	Blondesddsl père et fils	Frédérique Citeaux	Marketing Manager	24, place Kléber	Strasbourg		67000	France	88.60.1
BONAP	Bon app'	Laurence Lebihan	Owner	12, rue des Bouchers	Marseille		13008	France	91.24.4
DUMON	Du monde entier	Janine Labrune	Owner	67, rue des Cinquante Otages	Nantes		44000	France	40.67.8
FOLIG	Folies gourmandes	Martine Rancé	Assistant Sales Agent	184, chaussée de Tournai	Lille		59000	France	20.16.1
FRANR	France restauration	Carine Schmitt	Marketing Manager	54, rue Royale	Nantes		44000	France	40.32.2
LACOR	La corne d'abondance	Daniel Tonini	Sales Representative	67, avenue de l'Europe	Versailles		78000	France	30.59.8
				1 rue					

FIGURE 6.6
Displaying results from a stored procedure.

STEP BY STEP

6.7 Running a Stored Procedure That Does Not Return Results

1. Add a new Web Form to your Visual Basic .NET web project.

2. Open Server Explorer.

3. Expand the tree under Data Connections to show a SQL Server data connection that points to the Northwind sample database. Drag and drop the data connection to the form. This creates a `SqlConnection1` object on the form.

4. Use a tool such as SQL Query Analyzer or the Visual Studio .NET IDE to create a stored procedure with this code:

```
CREATE PROCEDURE procExpandCountry
AS
UPDATE Customers
 SET Country = 'United States'
 WHERE Country = 'USA'
```

continues

continued

5. Place a `Button` control on the form and set its ID to `btnExecute`. Place a `Label` control on the form, set its ID to `lblMessage`, and set its Visible property to False.

6. Double-click the `Button` control to open the form's module. Enter this statement at the top of the module to make the ADO.NET objects available:

```
Imports System.Data.SqlClient
```

7. Enter this code to execute the stored procedure when you click the button:

```
Private Sub Page_Load(ByVal sender As System.Object, _
 ByVal e As System.EventArgs) Handles MyBase.Load
    If IsPostBack Then
        ' Create a SqlCommand to
        ' represent the stored procedure
        Dim cmd As SqlCommand = _
         SqlConnection1.CreateCommand
        cmd.CommandType = CommandType.StoredProcedure
        cmd.CommandText = "procExpandCountry"
        ' Open the connection and
        ' execute the stored procedure
        SqlConnection1.Open()
        cmd.ExecuteNonQuery()
        ' Close the connection
        SqlConnection1.Close()
        ' And notify the user
        lblMessage.Text = "SQL statement was executed."
        lblMessage.Visible = True
    End If
End Sub
```

8. Set the form as the start page for the project.

9. Run the project and click the button. This executes the stored procedure and informs you of that fact by showing a message in the Label control.

EXAM TIP

Opening and Closing Connections When you call the methods of the `SqlDataAdapter` object, the .NET Framework automatically opens and closes the associated `SqlConnection` object as necessary. For any other operation (such as using the `SqlCommand.ExecuteNonQuery` method) you must explicitly call the `SqlConnection.Open` and `SqlConnection.Close` methods in your code.

The `ExecuteNonQuery` method of the `SqlCommand` object can be used to execute any ad hoc query or stored procedure that doesn't return any results.

Using Parameters in Stored Procedures

The examples that you've seen so far don't begin to tap the real power of stored procedures. SQL Server supports *parameterized stored procedures*, which allow you to pass information to the stored procedure at runtime (you can think of these as the T-SQL analog of Visual Basic .NET functions). For example, this SQL statement defines a stored procedure that returns the total sales for a particular customer, with the customer ID specified at runtime:

```
CREATE PROC procCustomerSales
  @CustomerID char(5),
  @TotalSales money OUTPUT
AS
  SELECT @TotalSales = SUM(Quantity * UnitPrice)
  FROM ((Customers INNER JOIN Orders
  ON Customers.CustomerID = Orders.CustomerID)
  INNER JOIN [Order Details]
  ON Orders.OrderID = [Order Details].OrderID)
  WHERE Customers.CustomerID = @CustomerID
```

In this SQL statement, both `@CustomerID` and `@TotalSales` are variables (called parameters in T-SQL). To use the stored procedure, you must supply a value for the `@CustomerID` parameter. The `@TotalSales` parameter is marked as an `OUTPUT` parameter; it returns a value from the stored procedure to the calling code.

In the .NET Framework, the `SqlCommand` object has a collection of parameters to let you manage parameterized stored procedures.

STEP BY STEP

6.8 Running a Parameterized Stored Procedure

1. Add a new Web Form to your Visual Basic .NET web project.
2. Open Server Explorer.
3. Expand the tree under Data Connections to show a SQL Server data connection that points to the Northwind sample database. Drag and drop the data connection to the form. This creates a `SqlConnection1` object on the form.

continues

continued

4. Use a tool such as SQL Query Analyzer or the Visual Studio .NET IDE to create a stored procedure with this code:

```
CREATE PROC procCustomerSales
  @CustomerID char(5),
  @TotalSales money OUTPUT
AS
  SELECT @TotalSales = SUM(Quantity * UnitPrice)
  FROM ((Customers INNER JOIN Orders
  ON Customers.CustomerID = Orders.CustomerID)
  INNER JOIN [Order Details]
  ON Orders.OrderID = [Order Details].OrderID)
  WHERE Customers.CustomerID = @CustomerID
```

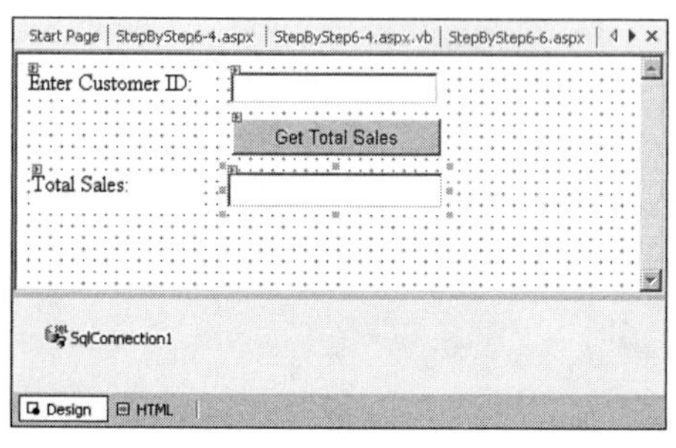

FIGURE 6.7
Designing a form to execute a parameterized stored procedure.

5. Place two label controls, two `TextBox` controls (`txtCustomerID` and `txtTotalSales`) and a `Button` control (`btnGetTotalSales`) on the form, as shown in Figure 6.7.

6. Double-click the form to open the form's module. Enter these two statements at the top of the module to make the ADO.NET objects available:

```
Imports System.Data.SqlClient
Imports System.Data.SqlTypes
```

7. Enter this code to execute the stored procedure when you click the button:

```
Private Sub Page_Load(ByVal sender As System.Object, _
 ByVal e As System.EventArgs) Handles MyBase.Load
    If IsPostBack Then
        ' Create a SqlCommand to
        ' represent the stored procedure
        Dim cmd As SqlCommand = _
         SqlConnection1.CreateCommand
        cmd.CommandType = CommandType.StoredProcedure
        cmd.CommandText = "procCustomerSales"
        ' Add the input parameter and set its value
        cmd.Parameters.Add(New SqlParameter( _
         "@CustomerID", SqlDbType.Text, 5))
        cmd.Parameters("@CustomerID").Value = _
         txtCustomerID.Text
        ' Add the output parameter and set its direction
        cmd.Parameters.Add(New SqlParameter( _
         "@TotalSales", SqlDbType.Money))
        cmd.Parameters("@TotalSales").Direction = _
         ParameterDirection.Output
        ' Execute the stored procedure and
        ' display the formatted results
        SqlConnection1.Open()
        cmd.ExecuteNonQuery()
```

```
        txtTotalSales.Text = String.Format("{0:c}", _
         cmd.Parameters("@TotalSales").Value)
        SqlConnection1.Close()
    End If
End Sub
```

8. Set the form as the start page for the project.

9. Run the project and enter a `CustomerID` (such as `ALFKI` or `BONAP`) from the Customers table in the first `TextBox`. Click the button. The form executes the stored procedure and returns the total sales for this customer in the second `TextBox`.

This example uses the SqlTypes namespace. This namespace includes types such as SqlDbType.Money that can be used to identify the type of data corresponding to a database parameter.

In ADO.NET, parameters are represented by `SqlParameter` objects. This code uses two different forms of the constructor for `SqlParameters`. The first takes the parameter name, the parameter data type, and the size of the parameter; the second omits the parameter size (because the money type has a fixed size). The code works by setting the Value property of the `@CustomerID` parameter, executing the `SqlCommand` object, and then retrieving the Value property of the `@TotalSales` parameter.

The `@@IDENTITY` Variable

A SQL Server table can have a single *identity* column. An identity column is a column with a value assigned by SQL Server itself whenever you add a new row to the table. The purpose of the identity column is to guarantee that each row in the table has a unique primary key.

If you're working with a table that contains an identity column, you'll often want to add a new row to the table and then immediately retrieve the value of the identity column for the new row. SQL Server provides a variable named `@@IDENTITY` for just this purpose. The `@@IDENTITY` variable returns the most recently assigned identity column value.

Step By Step 6.9 shows how you can use a stored procedure to insert a new row in a table and return the value of the identity column so that your code can continue to work with the new row.

STEP BY STEP

6.9 Retrieving a New Identity Value

1. Add a new Web Form to your Visual Basic .NET Web project.
2. Open Server Explorer.
3. Expand the tree under Data Connections to show a SQL Server data connection that points to the Northwind sample database. Drag and drop the data connection to the form. This creates a `SqlConnection1` object on the form.
4. Use a tool such as SQL Query Analyzer or the Visual Studio .NET IDE to create a stored procedure with this code:

```
CREATE PROC procInsertShipper
  @CompanyName nvarchar(40),
  @ShipperID int OUTPUT
AS
  INSERT INTO Shippers (CompanyName)
    VALUES (@CompanyName)
  SELECT @ShipperID = @@IDENTITY
```

   This stored procedure contains two SQL statements. The first inserts a row into the Shippers table, and the second retrieves the value of the identity column for the new row.
5. Place two label controls, two `TextBox` controls (`txtCompanyName` and `txtShipperID`), and a `Button` control (`btnAddShipper`) on the form.
6. Double-click the form to open the form's module. Enter these two statements at the top of the module to make the ADO.NET objects available:

```
Imports System.Data.SqlClient
Imports System.Data.SqlTypes
```

7. Enter this code to execute the stored procedure when you click the button:

```
Private Sub Page_Load(ByVal sender As System.Object, _
 ByVal e As System.EventArgs) Handles MyBase.Load
    If IsPostBack Then
        ' Create a SqlCommand to
        ' represent the stored procedure
        Dim cmd As SqlCommand = _
         SqlConnection1.CreateCommand
```

```
            cmd.CommandType = CommandType.StoredProcedure
            cmd.CommandText = "procInsertShipper"
            ' Add the input parameter and set its value
            cmd.Parameters.Add( _
             New SqlParameter("@CompanyName", _
             SqlDbType.VarChar, 40))
            cmd.Parameters("@CompanyName").Value = _
             txtCompanyName.Text
            ' Add the output parameter
            ' and set its direction
            cmd.Parameters.Add(New SqlParameter( _
             "@ShipperID", SqlDbType.Int))
            cmd.Parameters("@ShipperID").Direction = _
             ParameterDirection.Output
            ' Execute the stored procedure
            ' and display the result
            SqlConnection1.Open()
            cmd.ExecuteNonQuery()
            txtShipperID.Text = cmd.Parameters( _
             "@ShipperID").Value
            SqlConnection1.Close()
        End If
    End Sub
```

8. Set the form as the start page for the project.

9. Run the project and enter a company name for the new shipper in the first `TextBox`. Click the button. The form executes the stored procedure and returns the identity value assigned to the new shipper in the second `TextBox`.

This Step By Step uses the same code pattern as the previous one. The variable names and control names are different, but the two Step By Steps show a common pattern for using stored procedures in your code:

1. Create a `SqlCommand` object to represent the stored procedure.
2. Create `SqlParameter` objects to represent the parameters of the stored procedure.
3. Supply values for any input parameters.
4. Open the `SqlConnection` for this stored procedure.
5. Execute the stored procedure using the `ExecuteNonQuery` method of the `SqlCommand` object.
6. Retrieve values of any output parameters.
7. Close the `SqlConnection`.

GUIDED PRACTICE EXERCISE 6.1

In this exercise, you'll be designing a form to enter new products into the Northwind database. Table 6.1 shows the columns that the Products table contains.

TABLE 6.1

NORTHWIND PRODUCTS TABLE

Column Name	*Data Type*	*Nullable?*	*Identity?*
`ProductID`	`int`	No	Yes
`ProductName`	`nvarchar(40)`	No	No
`SupplierID`	`int`	Yes	No
`CategoryID`	`int`	Yes	No
`QuantityPerUnit`	`nvarchar(20)`	Yes	No
`UnitPrice`	`money`	Yes	No
`UnitsInStock`	`smallint`	Yes	No
`UnitsOnOrder`	`smallint`	Yes	No
`ReorderLevel`	`smallint`	Yes	No
`Discontinued`	`bit`	No	No

The task you need to perform is to allow the user to enter at least the `ProductName` and `CategoryID`, add the product to the table, and to see the `ProductID` that's assigned to the new row in the table. You may optionally allow the user to input any other data that you like.

Valid values for the `CategoryID` column can be determined by retrieving the `CategoryID` values from the Categories table, which also contains a `CategoryName` column. You should use a `DropDownList` control to display valid `CategoryID` values.

You should try doing this on your own first. If you get stuck, or if you'd like to see one possible solution, follow these steps:.

1. Add a new form to your Visual Basic .NET project.

2. Open Server Explorer.
3. Expand the tree under Data Connections to show a SQL Server data connection that points to the Northwind sample database. Drag and drop the data connection to the form. This creates a `SqlConnection1` object on the form.
4. Add Label controls, a `DropDownList` control (`ddlCategoryID`), a `Button` control (`btnAddProduct`), and two `TextBox` controls (`txtProductName` and `txtProductID`) to the form. Figure 6.8 shows a design for the form.

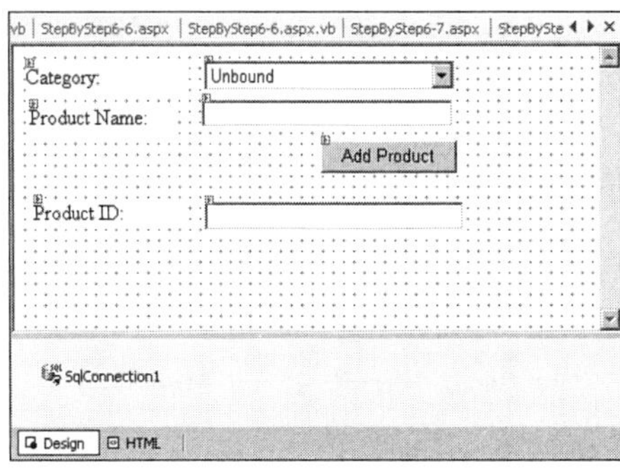

FIGURE 6.8
Designing a form to enter product information.

5. Use a tool such as SQL Query Analyzer or the Visual Studio .NET IDE to create a stored procedure with this code:

```
CREATE PROC procInsertProduct
  @ProductName nvarchar(40),
  @CategoryID int,
  @ProductID int OUTPUT
AS
  INSERT INTO Products (ProductName, CategoryID)
    VALUES (@ProductName, @CategoryID)
  SELECT @ProductID = @@IDENTITY
```

6. Double-click the form to open the form's module. Enter these three statements at the top of the module to make the ADO.NET objects available:

```
Imports System.Data
Imports System.Data.SqlClient
Imports System.Data.SqlTypes
```

7. Enter code to fill the list in the `DropDownList` control when the form is opened, and to execute the stored procedure on post-back:

```
Private Sub Page_Load(ByVal sender As System.Object, _
 ByVal e As System.EventArgs) Handles MyBase.Load
    If Not IsPostBack Then
        ' When the form is loaded,
        ' retrieve data for the combo box
        Dim cmdCategories As SqlCommand = _
         SqlConnection1.CreateCommand()
        cmdCategories.CommandType = CommandType.Text
        cmdCategories.CommandText = _
         "SELECT CategoryID, CategoryName " & _
         "FROM Categories ORDER BY CategoryName"
        Dim ds As DataSet = New DataSet()
        Dim da As SqlDataAdapter = _
         New SqlDataAdapter()
```

continues

continued

```
            da.SelectCommand = cmdCategories
            da.Fill(ds, "Categories")
            With ddlCategoryID
                .DataSource = ds.Tables("Categories")
                .DataTextField = "CategoryName"
                .DataValueField = "CategoryID"
                .DataBind()
            End With
        Else
            ' On postback, insert the new product
            ' Create a SqlCommand to
            ' represent the stored procedure
            Dim cmd As SqlCommand = _
             SqlConnection1.CreateCommand
            cmd.CommandType = CommandType.StoredProcedure
            cmd.CommandText = "procInsertProduct"
            ' Add the input parameters
            ' and set their values
            cmd.Parameters.Add(New SqlParameter( _
             "@ProductName", _
             SqlDbType.VarChar, 40))
            cmd.Parameters("@ProductName").Value = _
             txtProductName.Text
            cmd.Parameters.Add(New SqlParameter( _
             "@CategoryID", SqlDbType.Int))
            cmd.Parameters("@CategoryID").Value = _
             ddlCategoryID.SelectedItem.Value
            ' Add the output parameter
            ' and set its direction
            cmd.Parameters.Add(New SqlParameter( _
             "@ProductID", SqlDbType.Int))
            cmd.Parameters("@ProductID").Direction = _
             ParameterDirection.Output
            ' Execute the stored procedure and
            ' display the result
            SqlConnection1.Open()
            cmd.ExecuteNonQuery()
            txtProductID.Text = cmd.Parameters( _
             "@ProductID").Value
            SqlConnection1.Close()
        End If
    End Sub
```

8. Set the form as the startup object for the project.

9. Run the project. Select a category for the new product from the `DropDownList` control. Enter a name for the new product in the first `TextBox`. Click the button. The form executes the

stored procedure and returns the identity value assigned to the new shipper in the second `TextBox`.

10. If you had difficulty following this exercise, review the sections titled "Running Queries," "The `SELECT` Statement," "The `INSERT` Statement," and "Using Stored Procedures," as well as the material on "Complex Data Binding" in Chapter 5. The text and examples should help you in relearning this material and help you understand what just happened in this exercise. After review, try this exercise again.

REVIEW BREAK

- Stored procedures are queries that are stored permanently on the SQL Server itself. They run faster than ad-hoc statements and are easier to use in code.
- The `CREATE PROCEDURE` statement allows you to create stored procedures.
- To execute a stored procedure, you can use the `Execute` methods of the `SqlCommand` object.
- Stored procedures can accept input parameters that supply variables to the procedure. Output parameters can return information to the calling code.
- The `@@IDENTITY` variable returns the most recently assigned identity column value.

ACCESS AND MANIPULATE DATA

Consuming and Manipulating Data: Access and manipulate data from a data store. Data stores include relational databases, XML documents, and flat files. Methods include XML techniques and ADO .NET.

Although it's only a single test objective, this particular objective covers an immense amount of functionality within the .NET Framework. You'll need to know how to work with three types of data:

- File-based data
- Relational database data
- XML data

The .NET Framework includes namespaces and classes optimized for each of these types of data.

Data stored in files is handled by the classes in the `System.IO` namespace. The .NET Framework handles file data as part of a more general concept of streams and backing stores. A backing store is any place that you can store data (including a disk file) and a stream represents that data moving from place to place.

Data stored in databases is the target of ADO.NET, a subset of the .NET Framework that uses objects from the `System.Data` namespace and related namespaces. The `DataSet` object is the central object here, representing an entire relational database in a single object (with many constituent objects). You'll see how to create `DataSet` objects and fill them with data and then some of the many ways that you can work with that data.

Data stored in XML is handled by the `System.Xml` namespace. XML is a key part of the .NET Framework, and the classes in this namespace give you flexibility to read and write such data.

I'll cover the following major topics for this objective:

- Reading and writing disk files
- The ADO.NET object model
- Manipulating data with ADO.NET

- XML basics
- XML techniques

Working with Disk Files

The oldest form of data that you're likely to work with in the .NET Framework is the simple disk file. This is sometimes called a "flat file," to distinguish it from more structured forms of storage such as relational databases and XML files.

The .NET Framework includes complete support for working with flat files. In this section, I'll introduce the concepts of streams and backing stores and demonstrate the classes from the `System.IO` namespace that you can use to manipulate data stored in disk files.

Streams and Backing Stores

File-based input and output in the .NET Framework revolves around the twin concepts of *streams* and *backing stores*. A stream represents a flow of raw data. A backing store represents some place you can put data. A backing store might be a file—but it might also be a network connection, an Internet address, or even a section of memory. The .NET Framework contains classes to let you work with data from any of these backing stores.

You'll find classes for working with streams and backing stores in the `System.IO` namespace. In this section, I'll show you how to use five of these classes that apply directly to working with disk files. The `FileStream` class gives you a stream-oriented view of a disk file. The `FileStream` class treats files as a raw, typeless stream of bytes. For cases where you know more about the structure of the file, you may find the `BinaryReader` and `BinaryWriter`, or `StreamReader` and `StreamWriter` classes to be more convenient to use.

Using the `FileStream` Class

The `FileStream` class treats a file as a stream of bytes. For example, you can use this class as a way to make a backup copy of a file.

STEP BY STEP

6.10 Using FileStream Objects to Back Up a File

1. Add a new Web Form to your Visual Basic .NET Web project.

2. Place a `Button` control on the form. Set the ID of the `Button` control to `btnBackup`. Place a Label control on the form. Set the ID of the Label control to `lblMessage` and set its Visible property to False.

3. Add a new XML file to your Visual Basic .NET Web project. Name the new file `XMLFile1.xml`. Open the XML file in the designer and enter some sample text:

```
<?xml version="1.0" encoding="utf-8" ?>
<Root>
<Item1>Test Data</Item1>
</Root>
```

4. Double-click the form control to open the form's module. Enter this statement at the top of the module:

```
Imports System.IO
```

5. Enter this code to back up the file when the `Button` control is clicked:

```
Private Sub Page_Load(ByVal sender As System.Object,
 ByVal e As System.EventArgs) Handles MyBase.Load
    If IsPostBack Then
        ' Get the physical path of the file
        Dim strFileName = _
         Server.MapPath("XMLFile1.xml")
        ' Open the file for reading as a stream
        Dim fsIn As FileStream = _
         File.OpenRead(strFileName)
        ' Open the file for writing as a stream
        Dim fsOut As FileStream = _
         File.OpenWrite(strFileName & ".bak")
        ' Copy all data from in to out, byte-by-byte
        Dim b As Integer
        b = fsIn.ReadByte()
        Do While (b > -1)
            fsOut.WriteByte(CType(b, Byte))
            b = fsIn.ReadByte()
        Loop
        ' Clean up
        fsOut.Flush()
        fsOut.Close()
        fsIn.Close()
        ' Display the original and backup file names
```

```
            lblMessage.Text = "Backed up " & _
             strFileName & _
             " to " & strFileName & ".bak"
            lblMessage.Visible = True
        End If
    End Sub
```

6. Set the form as the startup object for the project.

7. You need to give the ASP.NET process permission to write to the server's hard drive for this and other Step By Steps in this section to work. On the Web server computer, launch Windows Explorer. Locate the folder that contains your Web site. Right-click the folder and select Properties. Click the Security tab. Click the Add Button and select the ASPNET user from the local computer. Click Add, and then click OK. Click the checkbox to allow the user to write to the folder, and then click OK again.

8. Run the project and click the button. The server backs up the file and shows you the filenames involved, as shown in Figure 6.9. If you check your hard drive, you'll find a copy of the file with the added extension `bak`.

WARNING

Data Loss Danger! Be very careful when using this code. It doesn't check for the existence of the backup file, so it will overwrite any existing file without warning.

EXAM TIP

Understanding `Server.MapPath` The `Server.MapPath` function takes a relative name for a file in the current web and returns its absolute name as a disk file. That's why this code can work no matter what your VB .NET project is named or where on your Web server it resides. Remember, all your VB .NET code is running on the server, so any file paths must make sense in the context of the server's file system.

The code creates two `FileStream` objects, one each for the input and output files, by using static methods of the File object (which represents a disk file). It then reads bytes from the input file and writes those bytes to the output file. Note the difference between the `ReadByte` method, which returns an `int`, and the `WriteByte` method, which writes a byte. That's because the `ReadByte` method uses the special value –1 (which can't be stored in a byte) to indicate that it's reached the end of the data.

EXAM TIP

ASP.NET Security Unlike previous versions of ASP, ASP.NET is designed to run under a user account with very low privileges. By default, the ASP.NET process cannot write any files to your Web server's hard drive.

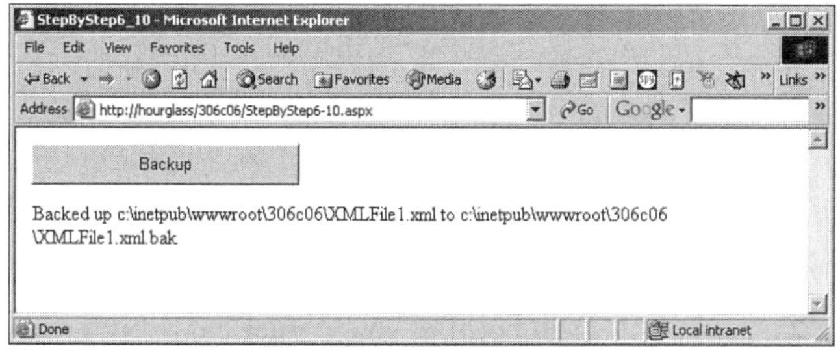

FIGURE 6.9
Results of backing up a file on the server.

When the code is done writing, it calls the Flush method of the output stream. That's necessary to be sure that all the data has actually been written to the disk. Then it closes both the input and output streams.

Table 6.2 shows some of the methods and properties of the `FileStream` object that you should be familiar with.

TABLE 6.2

`FileStream` OBJECT MEMBERS

Member	*Type*	*Description*
`CanRead`	Property	Indicates whether you can read from this `FileStream`
`CanSeek`	Property	Indicates whether you can seek to a particular location in this `FileStream`
`CanWrite`	Property	Indicates whether you can write to this `FileStream`
`Close`	Method	Closes the `FileStream` and releases associated resources
`Flush`	Method	Writes any buffered data to the backing store
`Length`	Property	Length of the `FileStream` in bytes
`Position`	Property	Gets the position within the `FileStream`
`Read`	Method	Reads a sequence of bytes
`ReadByte`	Method	Reads a single byte
`Seek`	Method	Sets the `FileStream` to a specified position
`Write`	Method	Writes a sequence of bytes
`WriteByte`	Method	Writes a single byte

Although the code in Step By Step 6.11 performs the desired task, it's not very efficient. Using a buffer to hold data allows the operating system to optimize file activity for increased speed.

STEP BY STEP

6.11 Using `FileStream` Objects with a Buffer

1. Add a new Web Form to your Visual Basic .NET web project.

2. Place a `Button` control on the form. Set the ID of the `Button` control to `btnBackup`. Place a Label control on the form. Set the ID of the Label control to `lblMessage` and set its Visible property to False.

3. Double-click the form to open the form's module. Enter this statement at the top of the module:

```
Imports System.IO
```

4. Enter this code to back up the file when the `Button` control is clicked:

```
Private Sub Page_Load(ByVal sender As System.Object, _
 ByVal e As System.EventArgs) Handles MyBase.Load
    If IsPostBack Then
        ' Get the physical path of the file
        Dim strFileName = _
         Server.MapPath("XMLFile1.xml")
        ' Open the file for reading as a stream
        Dim fsIn As FileStream = _
         File.OpenRead(strFileName)
        ' Open the file for writing as a stream
        Dim fsOut As FileStream = _
         File.OpenWrite(strFileName & ".bak")
        ' Copy all data from in to out, byte-by-byte
        Dim buf(4096) As Byte
        Dim intBytesRead As Integer
        intBytesRead = fsIn.Read(buf, 0, 4096)
        Do While intBytesRead > 0
            fsOut.Write(buf, 0, intBytesRead)
            intBytesRead = fsIn.Read(buf, 0, 4096)
        Loop
        ' Clean up
        fsOut.Flush()
        fsOut.Close()
        fsIn.Close()
        ' Display the original and backup file names
        lblMessage.Text = "Backed up " & _
         strFileName & _
         " to " & strFileName & ".bak"
        lblMessage.Visible = True
    End If
End Sub
```

5. Set the Web Form as the start page for the project.

6. Run the project and click the button. The server backs up the file and shows you the filenames involved. If you check your hard drive, you'll find a copy of the file with the added extension `bak`. If you experiment with large files, you should be able to see a speed difference between this version of the code and the one from the previous Step By Step.

The `FileStream.Read` method takes three parameters:

1. A buffer to hold the data being read.
2. An offset in the buffer where newly read bytes should be placed.
3. The maximum number of bytes to read.

The `Read` method returns the number of bytes that were actually read. Similarly, the `Write` method takes three parameters:

1. A buffer to hold the data being written
2. An offset in the buffer where bytes to write begin
3. The number of bytes to write

Using the `StreamReader` and `StreamWriter` Classes

The `FileStream` class is your best option when you don't care (or don't know) about the internal structure of the files with which you're working. But in many cases, you have additional knowledge that let you use other objects. Text files, for example, are often organized as lines of text separated by end of line characters. The `StreamReader` and `StreamWriter` classes provide you with tools for manipulating such files.

STEP BY STEP

6.12 Using `StreamWriter` and `StreamReader` Objects

1. Add a new Web Form to your Visual Basic .NET web project.
2. Place a `Button` control with the ID of `btnCreateFile` and a `ListBox` control with the ID of `lbLines` on the form.

3. Double-click the form to open the form's module. Enter this statement at the top of the module:

```
Imports System.IO
```

4. Enter this code to run when the user clicks the `Button` control:

```
Private Sub Page_Load(ByVal sender As System.Object, _
 ByVal e As System.EventArgs) Handles MyBase.Load
    If IsPostBack Then
        ' Create a new file to work with
        Dim fsOut As FileStream = _
         File.Create(Server.MapPath("test.txt"))
        ' Create a StreamWriter to handle writing
        Dim sw As StreamWriter = _
         New StreamWriter(fsOut)
        ' And write some data
        sw.WriteLine("There was a young " & _
         "lady named Bright")
        sw.WriteLine("Whose speed was much " & _
         "faster than light")
        sw.WriteLine("She set out one day")
        sw.WriteLine("In a relative way")
        sw.WriteLine("And returned on the " & _
         "previous night")
        sw.Flush()
        sw.Close()

        ' Now open the file for reading
        Dim fsIn As FileStream = _
         File.OpenRead(Server.MapPath("test.txt"))
        ' Create a StreamReader to handle reading
        Dim sr As StreamReader = New StreamReader(fsIn)
        ' And read the data
        Do While sr.Peek > -1
            lbLines.Items.Add(sr.ReadLine())
        Loop
        sr.Close()
    End If
End Sub
```

5. Set the Web Form as the start page for the project.

6. Run the project and click the button. The `test.txt` file is created in the root folder of the Web site on the server's hard drive, and the `ListBox` control shows the contents of the file, as shown in Figure 6.10.

FIGURE 6.10
Contents of a file written by a `StreamWriter` and then read by a `StreamReader`.

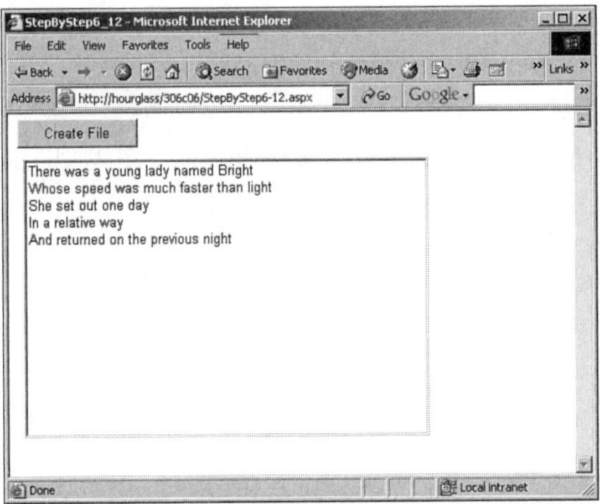

You can think of the `StreamWriter` and `StreamReader` classes as forming an additional layer of functionality on top of the `FileStream` class. The `FileStream` object handles opening a particular disk file and then serves as a parameter to the constructor of the `StreamWriter` or `StreamReader`. This code first opens a `StreamWriter` and calls its `WriteLine` method multiple times to write lines of text to the file. It then creates a `StreamReader` that uses the same text file. The code makes use of the Peek method of the `StreamReader` to watch for the end of the file. This method returns the next byte in the file without actually reading it, or –1 if there is no more data to be read. As long as there's data to read, the `ReadLine` method of the `StreamReader` can read it to place in the `ListBox`.

In addition to the methods that you see in this example, the `StreamWriter` has a `Write` method that writes output without adding a new line character. The `StreamReader` class implements `Read` and `ReadToEnd` methods which offer additional functionality for reading data. The `Read` method reads a specified number of characters. The `ReadToEnd` method reads all the remaining characters to the end of the stream.

Using the `BinaryReader` and `BinaryWriter` Classes

For files with a known internal structure, the `BinaryReader` and `BinaryWriter` classes offer streaming functionality that's oriented toward particular data types.

STEP BY STEP

6.13 Using BinaryWriter and BinaryReader Objects

1. Add a new Web Form to your Visual Basic .NET project.
2. Place a `Button` control with the ID of `btnCreateFile` and a `ListBox` control with the ID of `lbData` on the form.
3. Double-click the form to open the form's module. Enter this statement at the top of the module:

```
Imports System.IO
```

4. Enter this code to run when the user clicks the `Button` control:

```
Private Sub Page_Load(ByVal sender As System.Object, _
 ByVal e As System.EventArgs) Handles MyBase.Load
    If IsPostBack Then
        ' Create a new file to work with
        Dim fsOut As FileStream = _
         File.Create(Server.MapPath("test.dat"))
        ' Create a BinaryWriter to handle writing
        Dim bw As BinaryWriter = _
         New BinaryWriter(fsOut)
        ' And write some data
        Dim intData1 As Integer = 7
        Dim dblData2 As Decimal = 3.14159
        Dim strData3 As String = "Pi in the Sky"
        bw.Write(intData1)
        bw.Write(dblData2)
        bw.Write(strData3)
        bw.Flush()
        bw.Close()

        ' Now open the file for reading
        Dim fsIn As FileStream = _
         File.OpenRead(Server.MapPath("test.dat"))
        ' Create a BinaryReader to handle reading
        Dim br As BinaryReader = New BinaryReader(fsIn)
        ' And read the data
        lbData.Items.Add("Integer: " & br.ReadInt32())
        lbData.Items.Add("Decimal: " & _
         br.ReadDecimal())
        lbData.Items.Add("String: " & br.ReadString())
        br.Close()
    End If
End Sub
```

5. Set the Web Form as the start page for the project.

continues

continued

6. Run the project and click the button. The `test.dat` file is created on the server's hard drive, and the `ListBox` control shows the contents of the file, as shown in Figure 6.11.

WARNING

Don't Mix Up Data Types You must read exactly the same data types with the `BinaryReader` that you originally wrote with the `BinaryWriter`. Otherwise you'll get back garbage in your read data.

Like the `StreamWriter` and the `StreamReader`, the `BinaryWriter` and `BinaryReader` provide a layer on top of the basic `FileStream` object. `BinaryWriter` and `BinaryReader` are oriented toward writing and reading particular types of data. The `BinaryWriter.Write` method has overloads for many data types, so it can handle writing almost anything to a file. The `BinaryReader` class has methods for reading all those different data types; this code shows the `ReadInt32`, `ReadDecimal`, and `ReadStringmethods` in action.

GUIDED PRACTICE EXERCISE 6.2

In this exercise, you'll write a set of decimal numbers out to two different file formats: a text file with each number on a separate line, and a binary file. After writing the files, you can see which file format is more efficient for this particular data. Table 6.3 shows the values to write.

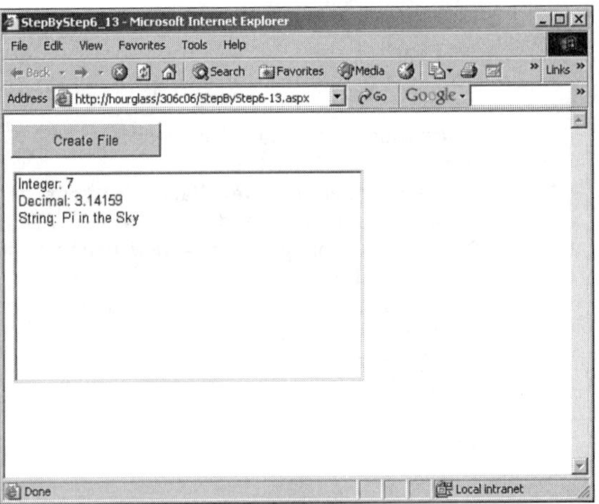

FIGURE 6.11
Contents of a file written by a `BinaryWriter` and then read by a `BinaryReader`.

TABLE 6.3

DATA TO BE WRITTEN TO TEXT AND BINARY FILES

Value
4.981273
45.92847
1.099
0.47162
2.44801
17.2323
490.00901
12.1234
23.022
1.034782

You should try doing this on your own first. If you get stuck, or you'd like to see one possible solution, follow these steps:

1. Add a new Web Form to your Visual Basic .NET web project.
2. Place a `Button` control with the ID of `btnCreateFiles` and a `ListBox` control with the ID of `lbResults` on the form.
3. Double-click the form to open the form's module. Enter this statement at the top of the module:

   ```
   Imports System.IO
   ```

4. Enter this code to run when the user clicks the `Button` control:

   ```
   Private Sub Page_Load(ByVal sender As System.Object, _
    ByVal e As System.EventArgs) Handles MyBase.Load
       If IsPostBack Then
           ' Create a new text file to work with
           Dim fsOut As FileStream = _
            File.Create(Server.MapPath("TextTest.txt"))
           ' Create a StreamWriter to handle writing
           Dim sw As StreamWriter = _
            New StreamWriter(fsOut)
           ' And write some data
           sw.WriteLine("4.981273")
           sw.WriteLine("45.92847")
           sw.WriteLine("1.099")
   ```

continues

continued

```
            sw.WriteLine("0.47162")
            sw.WriteLine("2.44801")
            sw.WriteLine("17.2323")
            sw.WriteLine("490.00901")
            sw.WriteLine("12.1234")
            sw.WriteLine("23.022")
            sw.WriteLine("1.034782")
            sw.Flush()
            lbResults.Items.Add( _
             "Text file length = " & fsOut.Length)
            sw.Close()

            ' Create a new binary file to work with
            fsOut = File.Create( _
             Server.MapPath("BinaryTest.dat"))
            ' Create a BinaryWriter to handle writing
            Dim bw As BinaryWriter = _
             New BinaryWriter(fsOut)
            ' And write some data
            bw.Write(4.981273)
            bw.Write(45.92847)
            bw.Write(1.099)
            bw.Write(0.47162)
            bw.Write(2.44801)
            bw.Write(17.2323)
            bw.Write(490.00901)
            bw.Write(12.1234)
            bw.Write(23.022)
            bw.Write(1.034782)
            bw.Flush()
            lbResults.Items.Add( _
             "Binary file length = " & fsOut.Length)
            bw.Close()
        End If
    End Sub
```

5. Set the Web Form as the start page for the web project.

6. Run the project and click the button. The two files are created on the Web server's hard drive, and the `ListBox` control shows the lengths of the files, as shown in Figure 6.12.

7. If you had difficulty following this exercise, review the sections titled "Using the `StreamReader` and `StreamWriter` Classes" and "Using the `BinaryReader` and `BinaryWriter` Classes." The text and examples should help you in relearning this material and help you understand what just happened in this exercise. After review, try this exercise again.

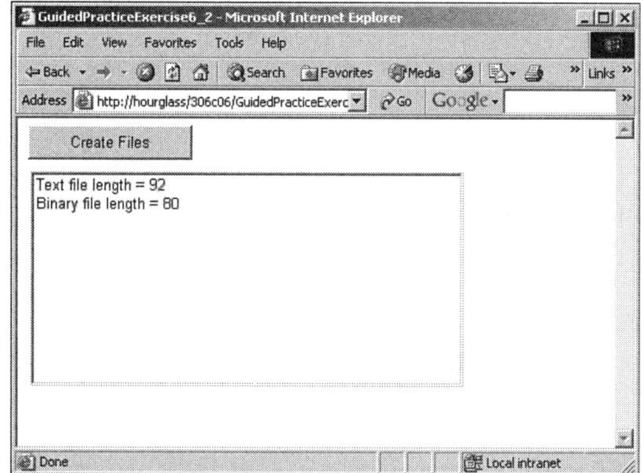

FIGURE 6.12
Relative lengths of the same data in a text file and in a binary file.

The ADO.NET Object Model

ADO.NET is the overall name for the set of classes (spread across a number of namespaces including `System.Data`, `System.Data.SqlClient`, and `System.Data.OleDb`) that the .NET Framework provides for working with data in relational databases.

The ADO.NET object model is broken up into two distinct sets of objects: data provider objects and `DataSet` objects. There are two sets of objects because the .NET Framework separates the task of using data from the task of storing data. The `DataSet` objects provide a memory-resident, disconnected set of objects that you can load with data. The data provider objects handle the task of working directly with data sources. One of the provider objects, the `DataAdapter` object, serves as a conduit between the two sets of objects. By using a `DataAdapter`, you can load data from a database into a `DataSet` and later save changes back to the original data source.

In generic terms, the data provider objects manage the database for your application, and the `DataSet` objects manage the data model for the application.

Data Providers and Their Objects

There are five main data provider objects that you should know about:

- `Connection`
- `Command`
- `Parameter`

- `DataReader`
- `DataAdapter`

You've actually seen most of these objects already, but not with these names. That's because those are generic names, and each data provider has implementations of these objects with specific names.

A *data provider* is a namespace that implements these five classes (and some other classes and enumerations) for use with a particular database. For example, I've been using the SQL Server data provider, which is implemented in the `System.Data.SqlClient` namespace. In this namespace, the object names are as follows:

- `SqlConnection`
- `SqlCommand`
- `SqlParameter`
- `SqlDataReader`
- `SqlDataAdapter`

EXAM TIP

Not All OLE DB Is Equal Though from the name it seems that the OLE DB data provider should work with any existing OLE DB provider, that's not the case. It's only designed to work with the SQL Server, Jet 4.0, and Oracle OLE DB providers. Other providers may work, but they are not supported.

But the SQL Server data provider is not the only alternative for retrieving data in ADO.NET. The .NET Framework also ships with the OLE DB data provider, implemented in the `System.Data.OleDb` namespace. In this namespace, the corresponding object names are as follows:

- `OleDbConnection`
- `OleDbCommand`
- `OleDbParameter`
- `OleDbDataReader`
- `OleDbDataAdapter`

Though the .NET Framework only includes two data providers, there are other alternatives. For example, Microsoft has made an ODBC data provider and an Oracle data provider available for download. Third parties are also planning to release other providers.

I'll continue to use the SQL Server data provider objects in all my examples. But you should keep in mind that the techniques you learn to work with objects from this namespace will also work with objects from other data provider namespaces.

The SqlConnection Object

The `SqlConnection` object represents a single persistent connection to a SQL Server data source. ADO.NET automatically handles connection pooling, which contributes to better application performance. When you call the `Close` method of a `SqlConnection` object, it is returned to a connection pool. Connections in a pool are not immediately destroyed by ADO.NET. Instead, they're available for reuse if another part of your application requests a `SqlConnection` that matches in details a previously closed `SqlConnection`.

Table 6.4 shows the most important members of the `SqlConnection` object.

TABLE 6.4

`SqlConnection` OBJECT MEMBERS

Member	*Type*	*Description*
`BeginTransaction`	Method	Starts a new transaction on this `SqlConnection`
`Close`	Method	Returns the `SqlConnection` to the connection pool
`ConnectionString`	Property	Specifies the server to be used by this `SqlConnection`
`CreateCommand`	Method	Returns a new `SqlCommand` object that executes via this `SqlConnection`
`Open`	Method	Opens the `SqlConnection`

So far, all the `SqlConnection` objects that you've seen in this book have been created by drag-and-drop from Server Explorer. But it's easy to create them in code yourself.

NOTE

Connection Strings The connection strings in code in this chapter assume that you have SQL Server installed on the same computer as your Web server, and that the ASP.NET user has permissions to access the Northwind database. You may need to modify the connection strings to include a different data source name or different authentication information if this is not the case.

EXAM TIP

The Parts of a Connection String You should know how to construct a SQL Server connection string for use with the `SqlConnection` object. There are three parts to the string. First is the Data Source, which is the name of the server to which you'd like to connect. You can use `(local)` as a shortcut name for the SQL Server instance running on the same computer as this code. Second is the Initial Catalog, which is the name of the database on the server to use. Third is authentication information. This can either be `Integrated Security=SSPI` to use Windows authentication, or `User ID=`*`username`*`;Password=`*`password`* to use SQL Server authentication. There are other optional parameters, but these three are the most important.

STEP BY STEP

6.14 Creating a `SqlConnection` in Code

1. Add a new Web Form to your Visual Basic .NET web project.

2. Place a `Button` control with the ID of `btnConnect` and a `TextBox` control with the ID of `txtConnectionString` on the form.

3. Double-click the form to open the form's module. Enter this statement at the top of the module:

```
Imports System.Data.SqlClient
```

4. Enter this code to handle the click event of the `Button` control:

```
Private Sub Page_Load(ByVal sender As System.Object, _
 ByVal e As System.EventArgs) Handles MyBase.Load
    If IsPostBack Then
        Dim cnn As SqlConnection = New SqlConnection()
        cnn.ConnectionString = _
         "Data Source=(local);" & _
         "Initial Catalog=Northwind;" & _
         "Integrated Security=SSPI"
        cnn.Open()
        txtConnectionString.Text = _
         cnn.ConnectionString
        cnn.Close()
    End If
End Sub
```

5. Set the Web Form as the start page for the project.

6. Run the project and click the button. The code connects to the SQL Server database on the Web server computer and echoes the connection string to the `TextBox` control.

You've already seen the `SqlCommand` and `SqlParameter` objects in use in quite a few examples. The `SqlCommand` represents something that can be executed. This could be an ad hoc query string or a stored procedure name. The `SqlParameter` object represents a single parameter to a stored procedure.

Table 6.5 shows the most important members of the `SqlCommand` object.

TABLE 6.5

SqlCommand OBJECT MEMBERS

Member	*Type*	*Description*
`CommandText`	Property	Statement to be executed by the `SqlCommand`
`CommandType`	Property	Enumeration indicating what type of command this `SqlCommand` represents
`Connection`	Property	`SqlConnection` through which this `SqlCommand` executes
`CreateParameter`	Method	Creates a new `SqlParameter` for this `SqlCommand`
`ExecuteNonQuery`	Method	Executes a `SqlCommand` that does not return a result set
`ExecuteReader`	Method	Executes a `SqlCommand` and places the results in a `SqlDataReader`
`ExecuteScalar`	Method	Executes a `SqlCommand` and returns the first column of the first row of the result set
`ExecuteXmlReader`	Method	Executes a `SqlCommand` and places the results in an `XmlReader` object
`Parameters`	Property	Collection of `SqlParameter` objects for this `SqlCommand`

Here's an example of using the `ExecuteScalar`, which provides you with an easy way to retrieve a single value (such as an aggregation) from a database.

STEP BY STEP

6.15 Using the `ExecuteScalar` Method

1. Add a new Web Form to your Visual Basic .NET Web project.

2. Place a `Button` control with the ID of `btnCount`, a `TextBox` control with the ID of txtCountry, and a `Label` control with the ID of `lblResults` on the form. Figure 6.13 shows the design of this form.

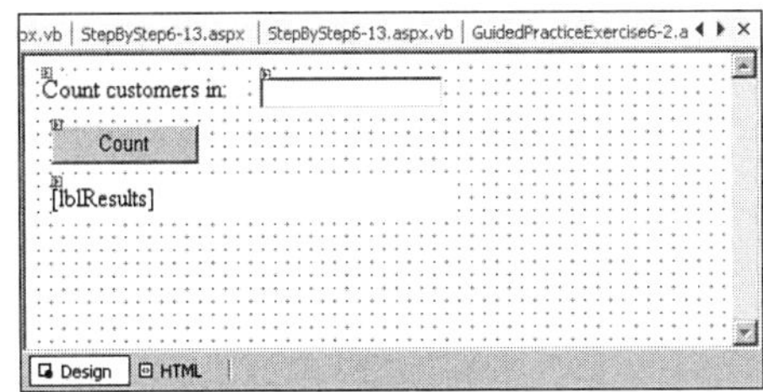

FIGURE 6.13
Designing a form to demonstrate the `ExecuteScalar` method.

continues

continued

3. Double-click the form to open the form's module. Enter this statement at the top of the module:

```
Imports System.Data.SqlClient
```

4. Enter this code to run when the user clicks the `Button` control:

```
Private Sub Page_Load(ByVal sender As System.Object, _
 ByVal e As System.EventArgs) Handles MyBase.Load
    If IsPostBack Then
        ' Connect to the database
        Dim cnn As SqlConnection = New SqlConnection()
        cnn.ConnectionString = _
         "Data Source=(local);" & _
         "Initial Catalog=Northwind;" & _
         "Integrated Security=SSPI"
        ' Create a new ad hoc query to
        ' count customers in the selected country
        Dim cmd As SqlCommand = cnn.CreateCommand
        cmd.CommandType = CommandType.Text
        cmd.CommandText = _
         "SELECT COUNT(*) FROM Customers " & _
         "WHERE Country = '" & _
         txtCountry.Text & "'"
        ' Use ExecuteScalar to return results
        cnn.Open()
        lblResults.Text = "There are " & _
         cmd.ExecuteScalar() & _
         " customers in " & txtCountry.Text
        cnn.Close()
    End If
End Sub
```

5. Set the form as the startup object for the project.

6. Run the project. Enter a country name such as `France` and click the button. The code connects to the SQL Server database on the Web server computer and fills in the Label control's text with a string that includes the results of the ad hoc query.

The SqlDataReader Object

The `SqlDataReader` object is designed to be the fastest possible way to retrieve a result set from a database. `SqlDataReader` objects can only be constructed by calling the `ExecuteReader` method of a `Command` object. The result set contained in a `SqlDataReader` is forward-only, read-only. That is, you can only read the rows in the result set sequentially from start to finish, and you can't modify any of the data.

STEP BY STEP

6.16 Using a SqlDataReader

1. Add a new Web Form to your Visual Basic .NET Web project.

2. Place a `Button` control with the ID of `btnGetCustomers` and a `ListBox` control with the ID of `lbCustomers` on the form.

3. Double-click the form to open the form's module. Enter this statement at the top of the module:

```
Imports System.Data.SqlClient
```

4. Enter this code to run when the user clicks the `Button` control:

```
Private Sub btnGetCustomers_Click( _
 ByVal sender As System.Object, _
 ByVal e As System.EventArgs) _
 Handles btnGetCustomers.Click
    ' Connect to the database
    Dim cnn As SqlConnection = New SqlConnection()
    cnn.ConnectionString = "Data Source=(local);" & _
     "Initial Catalog=Northwind;" & _
     "Integrated Security=SSPI"
    ' Create a new ad hoc query
    ' to retrieve customer names
    Dim cmd As SqlCommand = cnn.CreateCommand
    cmd.CommandType = CommandType.Text
    cmd.CommandText = _
     "SELECT CompanyName FROM Customers " & _
     "ORDER BY CompanyName"
    ' Dump the data to the user interface
    cnn.Open()
```

continues

continued

```
        Dim dr As SqlDataReader = cmd.ExecuteReader
        Do While dr.Read()
            lbCustomers.Items.Add(dr.GetString(0))
        Loop
        ' Clean up
        dr.Close()
        cnn.Close()
    End Sub
```

5. Set the Web Form as the start page for the project.
6. Run the project and click the button. The code connects to the SQL Server database on the Web server computer and fills the `ListBox` control with a list of customers from the Northwind database.

EXAM TIP

Stored Procedures for Speed You could improve the performance of this code even more by using a stored procedure instead of an ad hoc query to deliver the customer names.

You can think of the `SqlDataReader` as a data structure that can contain one row of data at a time. Each call to the `SqlDataReader.Read` method loads the next row of data into this structure. When there are no more rows to load, the `Read` method returns `False`, which tells you that you've reached the end of the data. To retrieve individual columns of data from the current row, the `SqlDataReader` provides a series of methods (such as the `GetString` method used in the code above) that take a column number and return the data from that column. There's also a `GetValue` method that you can use with any column, but the typed methods are faster.

Table 6.6 shows the most important members of the `SqlDataReader` object. There's no need to memorize all the data methods (and there are others that aren't shown in this table), but you should understand the pattern that they represent.

TABLE 6.6

`SqlDataReader` OBJECT MEMBERS

Member	*Type*	*Description*
`Close`	Method	Closes the `SqlDataReader`
`GetBoolean`	Method	Gets a Boolean value from the specified column
`GetByte`	Method	Gets a byte value from the specified column
`GetChar`	Method	Gets a character value from the specified column

Member	*Type*	*Description*
`GetDateTime`	Method	Gets a date/time value from the specified column
`GetDecimal`	Method	Gets a decimal value from the specified column
`GetDouble`	Method	Gets a double value from the specified column
`GetFloat`	Method	Gets a float value from the specified column
`GetGuid`	Method	Gets a GUID value from the specified column
`GetInt16`	Method	Gets a 16-bit integer value from the specified column
`GetInt32`	Method	Gets a 32-bit integer value from the specified column
`GetInt64`	Method	Gets a 64-bit integer value from the specified column
`GetString`	Method	Gets a string value from the specified column
`GetValue`	Method	Gets a value from the specified column
`GetValues`	Method	Gets an entire row of data and places it in an array of objects
`IsDbNull`	Method	Indicates whether a specified column contains a Null value
`Read`	Method	Loads the next row of data into the `SqlDataReader`

EXAM TIP

Close Your `SqlDataReaders`! The `SqlDataReader` makes exclusive use of its `SqlConnection` object as long as it is open. You won't be able to execute any other `SqlCommand` objects on that connection as long as the `SqlDataReader` is open. Always call `SqlDataReader.Close` as soon as you're done retrieving data.

The SqlDataAdapter Object

The final data provider object that I'll consider, the `SqlDataAdapter`, provides a bridge between the data provider objects and the `DataSet` objects that you'll learn about in the next section. You can think of the `SqlDataAdapter` as a two-way pipeline between the data in its native storage format and the data in a more abstract representation (the `DataSet`) that's designed for manipulation in your application.

Table 6.7 shows the most important members of the `SqlDataAdapter` object.

TABLE 6.7

`SqlDataAdapter` OBJECT MEMBERS

Member	*Type*	*Description*
`DeleteCommand`	Property	`SqlCommand` used to delete rows from the data source
`Fill`	Method	Transfers data from the data source to a `DataSet`

continues

TABLE 6.7 *continued*

`SqlDataAdapter` OBJECT MEMBERS

Member	*Type*	*Description*
`InsertCommand`	Property	`SqlCommand` used to insert rows into the data source
`SelectCommand`	Property	`SqlCommand` used to retrieve rows from the data source
`Update`	Method	Transfers data from a `DataSet` to the data source
`UpdateCommand`	Property	`SqlCommand` used to update rows in the data source

You've seen the `SqlDataAdapter` in use in many samples in Chapter 5 and earlier in this chapter. Later in this chapter (in the "Using `DataSets`" section) you'll learn more about using the `SqlDataAdapter` in conjunction with the `DataSet` to manipulate data.

The DataSet Objects

The second set of ADO.NET objects are the `DataSet` objects, which are all contained in the `System.Data` namespace. Unlike the data provider objects, there's only one set of `DataSet` objects. The `DataSet` objects represent data in an abstract form that's not tied to any particular database implementation. In this section, I'll introduce you to the `DataSet` and the other objects that it contains:

- `DataSet`
- `DataTable`
- `DataRelation`
- `DataRow`
- `DataColumn`
- `DataView`

The DataSet Object

The DataSet itself is a self-contained memory-resident representation of relational data. A DataSet contains other objects, such as DataTables and DataRelations, that hold the actual data and information about the design of the data. The DataSet is designed to be easy to move between components. In particular, there are methods to convert a DataSet to an XML file and vice versa. DataSet objects are created on the server but can be passed to the client like any other object.

Table 6.8 shows the most important members of the DataSet object.

TABLE 6.8

DataSet OBJECT MEMBERS

Member	*Type*	*Description*
AcceptChanges	Method	Marks all changes in the DataSet as having been accepted
Clear	Method	Removes all data from the DataSet
GetChanges	Method	Gets a DataSet that contains only the changed data in this DataSet
GetXml	Method	Gets an XML representation of the DataSet
GetXmlSchema	Method	Gets an XSD representation of the DataSet
Merge	Method	Merges two DataSets
ReadXml	Method	Loads the DataSet from an XML file
ReadXmlSchema	Method	Loads the DataSet's schema from an XSD file
Relations	Property	A collection of DataRelation objects
Tables	Property	A collection of DataTable objects
WriteXml	Method	Writes the DataSet to an XML file
WriteXmlSchema	Method	Writes the DataSet's schema to an XSD file

As you can see, several of the DataSet methods deal with XML and XSD files. You'll learn more about these files in the "XML Basics" section later in this chapter.

The DataTable Object

The `DataTable` object represents a single table within the `DataSet`. A single `DataSet` can contain many `DataTable` objects. Table 6.9 shows the most important members of the `DataTable` object.

TABLE 6.9

`DataTable` OBJECT MEMBERS

Member	*Type*	*Description*
`ChildRelations`	Property	A collection of `DataRelation` objects that refer to children of this `DataTable`
`Clear`	Method	Removes all data from the `DataTable`
`ColumnChanged`	Event	Fires when the data in any row of a specified column has been changed
`ColumnChanging`	Event	Fires when the data in any row of a specified column is about to be changed
`Columns`	Property	A collection of `DataColumn` objects
`Constraints`	Property	A collection of Constraint objects
`NewRow`	Method	Creates a new, blank row in the `DataTable`
`ParentRelations`	Property	A collection of `DataRelation` objects that refer to parents of this `DataTable`
`PrimaryKey`	Property	An array of `DataColumn` objects that provide the primary key for this `DataTable`
`RowChanged`	Event	Fires when any data in a `DataRow` has been changed
`RowChanging`	Event	Fires when any data in a `DataRow` is about to be changed
`RowDeleted`	Event	Fires when a row has been deleted
`RowDeleting`	Event	Fires when a row is about to be deleted
`Rows`	Property	A collection of `DataRow` objects
`Select`	Method	Selects an array of `DataRow` objects that meet specified criteria
`TableName`	Property	The name of this `DataTable`

As you can see, you can manipulate a DataTable as either a collection of DataColumn objects or a collection of DataRow objects. The DataTable also provides events that you can use to monitor data changes. For example, you might bind a DataTable to a DataGrid, and use these events to track the user's operations on the data within the DataGrid.

The DataRelation Object

As I mentioned previously, the DataSet can represent an entire relational database. The DataRelation object stores information on the relations between DataTables within a DataSet. Table 6.10 shows the most important members of the DataRelation object.

TABLE 6.10

DataRelation OBJECT MEMBERS

Member	*Type*	*Description*
ChildColumns	Property	Collection of DataColumn objects that define the foreign key side of the relation
ChildKeyConstraint	Property	Returns a ForeignKeyConstraint object for the relation
ChildTable	Property	DataTable from the foreign key side of the relation
ParentColumns	Property	Collection of DataColumn objects that define the primary key side of the relation
ParentKeyConstraint	Property	Returns a PrimaryKeyConstraint object for the relation
ParentTable	Property	DataTable from the primary key side of the relation
RelationName	Property	Name of the DataRelation

The DataRow Object

Continuing down the object hierarchy from the DataSet past the DataTable, you come to the DataRow. As you can guess by now, the DataRow represents a single row of data. When you're selecting, inserting, updating, or deleting data in a DataSet, you'll normally work with DataRow objects.

Table 6.11 shows the most important members of the `DataRow` object.

TABLE 6.11

`DataRow` OBJECT MEMBERS

Member	*Type*	*Description*
`BeginEdit`	Method	Starts editing the `DataRow`
`CancelEdit`	Method	Discards an edit in progress
`Delete`	Method	Deletes the `DataRow` from its parent `DataTable`
`EndEdit`	Method	Ends an edit in progress, saving the changes
`Item`	Property	Returns the data from a particular column in the `DataRow`
`IsNull`	Method	Returns `True` if a specified column contains a Null value
`RowState`	Property	Returns information on the current state of a `DataRow` (for example, whether it has been changed since it was last saved to the database)

The DataColumn Object

The `DataTable` also contains a collection of `DataColumn` objects. A `DataColumn` represents a single column in the `DataTable`. By manipulating the `DataColumn` objects, you can determine and even change the structure of the `DataTable`.

Table 6.12 shows the most important members of the `DataColumn` object.

TABLE 6.12

`DataColumn` OBJECT MEMBERS

Member	*Type*	*Description*
`AllowDbNull`	Property	Indicates whether the `DataColumn` can contain Null values
`AutoIncrement`	Property	Indicates whether the `DataColumn` is an identity column
`ColumnName`	Property	Name of the `DataColumn`

Member	*Type*	*Description*
`DataType`	Property	Data type of the `DataColumn`
`DefaultValue`	Property	Default value of this `DataColumn` for new rows of data
`MaxLength`	Property	Maximum length of a text `DataColumn`
`Unique`	Property	Indicates whether values in the `DataColumn` must be unique across all rows in the `DataTable`

The DataView Object

Finally, the `DataView` object represents a view of the data contained in a `DataTable`. A `DataView` might contain every `DataRow` from the `DataTable`, or it might be filtered to contain only specific rows. That filtering can be done by SQL expressions (returning, for example, only rows for customers in France) or by row state (returning, for example, only rows that have been modified).

Table 6.13 shows the most important members of the `DataView` object.

TABLE 6.13

`DataView` OBJECT MEMBERS

Member	*Type*	*Description*
`AddNew`	Method	Adds a new row to the `DataView`
`AllowDelete`	Property	Indicates whether deletions can be performed through this `DataView`
`AllowEdit`	Property	Indicates whether updates can be performed through this `DataView`
`AllowNew`	Property	Indicates whether insertions can be performed through this `DataView`
`Count`	Property	Number of rows in this `DataView`
`Delete`	Method	Deletes a row from this `DataView`
`Find`	Method	Searches for a row in the `DataView`
`FindRows`	Method	Returns an array of rows matching a filter expression
`Item`	Property	Returns a `DataRowView` object representing a particular row in the `DataView`
`Sort`	Method	Sorts the data in a `DataView`

REVIEW BREAK

- The ADO.NET object model includes both database-specific data provider classes and database-independent `DataSet` classes.
- Data providers contain implementations of the `Connection`, `Command`, `Parameter`, `DataReader`, and `DataAdapter` objects optimized for a particular database product.
- The `SqlConnection` object represents a connection to a database.
- The `SqlCommand` object represents a command that can be executed.
- The `SqlParameter` object represents a parameter of a stored procedure.
- The `SqlDataReader` object provides a fast way to retrieve a result set from a command.
- The `SqlDataAdapter` object implements a two-way pipeline between the database and the data model.
- The `DataSet` represents an entire relational database in memory. It's composed of `DataTable`, `DataRelation`, `DataRow`, and `DataColumn` objects.
- The `DataView` object provides a filtered row of the data from a `DataTable`.

Using `DataSets`

Now that you've seen the ADO.NET objects, it's time to see what you can do with them. Of course, in a single chapter I can't possibly cover everything that you can do with ADO.NET. So I'm going to concentrate on the following basic operations:

- Populating a `DataSet` From a database
- Moving around in `DataSets` and retrieving data
- Using strongly typed `DataSets`
- `DataSets` With multiple tables
- Finding and sorting data in `DataSets`

- Editing data with ADO.NET
- Updating data
- Adding data
- Deleting data

If you're interested in exploring ADO.NET in more depth, you'll find a list of references at the end of the chapter.

Populating a `DataSet` From a Database

Before you can do anything with data in a `DataSet`, you have to get that data into the `DataSet` somehow. In general, you can follow a four-step pattern to move data from the database to a `DataSet` object:

1. Create a `SqlConnection` object to connect to the database.
2. Create a `SqlCommand` object to retrieve the desired data.
3. Assign the `SqlCommand` to the `SelectCommand` property of a `SqlDataAdapter` object.
4. Call the `Fill` method of the `SqlDataAdapter` object.

STEP BY STEP

6.17 Filling a `DataSet`

1. Add a new Web Form to your Visual Basic .NET web project.
2. Place a `Button` control with the ID of `btnLoad` and a `DataGrid` control with the ID of `dgProducts` on the form.
3. Double-click the `Button` control to open the form's module. Enter these statements at the top of the module:

```
Imports System.Data
Imports System.Data.SqlClient
```

continues

continued

4. Enter this code to handle the `Load` event of the page:

```
Private Sub Page_Load(ByVal sender As System.Object, _
 ByVal e As System.EventArgs) Handles MyBase.Load
    If IsPostBack Then
        ' Create a SqlConnection
        Dim cnn As SqlConnection = _
         New SqlConnection("Data Source=(local);" & _
         "Initial Catalog=Northwind;" & _
         "Integrated Security=SSPI")
        ' Create a SqlCommand
        Dim cmd As SqlCommand = cnn.CreateCommand()
        cmd.CommandType = CommandType.Text
        cmd.CommandText = _
         "SELECT * FROM Products ORDER BY ProductName"
        ' Set up the DataAdapter and fill the DataSet
        Dim da As SqlDataAdapter = _
         New SqlDataAdapter()
        da.SelectCommand = cmd
        Dim ds As DataSet = New DataSet()
        ' Display the data on the user interface
        da.Fill(ds, "Products")
        dgProducts.DataSource = ds
        dgProducts.DataMember = "Products"
        dgProducts.DataBind()
    End If
End Sub
```

5. Set the Web Form as the start page for the project.

6. Run the project and click the button. The code connects to the SQL Server database on the Web server computer and fills the `DataGrid` control with the result of executing the SQL statement, as shown in Figure 6.14.

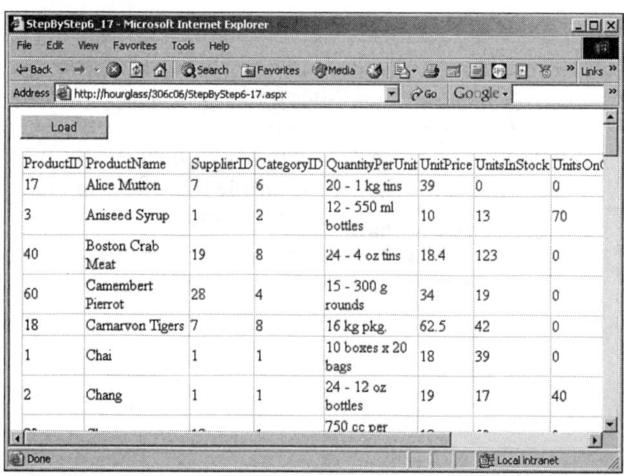

FIGURE 6.14
A `DataGrid` control bound to data stored in a `DataSet`.

This sample demonstrates a couple of shortcuts that you can use in your ADO.NET code. First, the constructor for the `SqlConnection` object has an overloaded form that lets you supply the connection string when you create the object. Second, this code doesn't call the `Open` and `Close` methods of the `SqlConnection` explicitly. Instead, it lets the `SqlDataAdapter` make those calls when it needs the data. Doing this not only cuts down the amount of code that you need to write, it also improves the scalability of your application by keeping the `SqlConnection` open for the shortest possible period of time.

EXAM TIP

Choose a Table Name The second parameter to the `DataAdapter.Fill` method is the name of the `DataTable` to create from the data supplied by the `SelectCommand`. The `DataTable` name does not have to match the table name in the underlying database. This example would work just as well if you placed data from the Products table into a `DataTable` named Starship (although that would be a pretty poor idea from the standpoint of code maintainability).

Moving Around in `DataSets` and Retrieving Data

If you're familiar with classic ADO, you're used to recordsets: collections of records that have a pointer to a current record. In classic ADO, you move through a recordset with code such as this:

```
Do Until rst.EOF
    rst.MoveNext
Loop
```

There's no equivalent to this code for `DataSets`, because `DataSets` have no concept of a current record pointer. Instead, you move through a `DataSet` by working with the collections that the `DataSet` contains.

STEP BY STEP

6.18 Moving Through a `DataSet`

1. Add a new Web Form to your Visual Basic .NET Web project.
2. Place a `Button` control with the ID of `btnLoadData` and a `ListBox` control with the ID of `lbData` on the form.
3. Double-click the form to open the form's module. Enter these statements at the top of the module:

```
Imports System.Data
Imports System.Data.SqlClient
```

continues

continued

4. Enter this code to run when the user clicks the `Button` control:

```
Private Sub btnLoadData_Click( _
 ByVal sender As System.Object, _
 ByVal e As System.EventArgs) _
 Handles btnLoadData.Click
    ' Create a SqlConnection
    Dim cnn As SqlConnection = _
     New SqlConnection("Data Source=(local);" & _
     "Initial Catalog=Northwind;" & _
     "Integrated Security=SSPI")
    ' Create a SqlCommand
    Dim cmd As SqlCommand = cnn.CreateCommand()
    cmd.CommandType = CommandType.Text
    cmd.CommandText = _
     "SELECT * FROM Customers " & _
     "WHERE Country = 'France'"
    ' Set up the DataAdapter and fill the DataSet
    Dim da As SqlDataAdapter = New SqlDataAdapter()
    da.SelectCommand = cmd
    Dim ds As DataSet = New DataSet()
    da.Fill(ds, "Customers")
    ' Dump the contents of the DataSet
    Dim dt As DataTable
    Dim dr As DataRow
    Dim dc As DataColumn
    lbData.Items.Add("DataSet: " & ds.DataSetName)
    For Each dt In ds.Tables
        lbData.Items.Add("  DataTable: " & _
         dt.TableName)
        For Each dr In dt.Rows
            lbData.Items.Add("    DataRow")
            For Each dc In dt.Columns
                lbData.Items.Add("      " & dr(dc))
            Next
        Next
    Next
End Sub
```

5. Set the Web Form as the start page for the project.

6. Run the project and click the button. The code will dump the contents of the `DataSet` to the `ListBox` control, as shown in Figure 6.15.

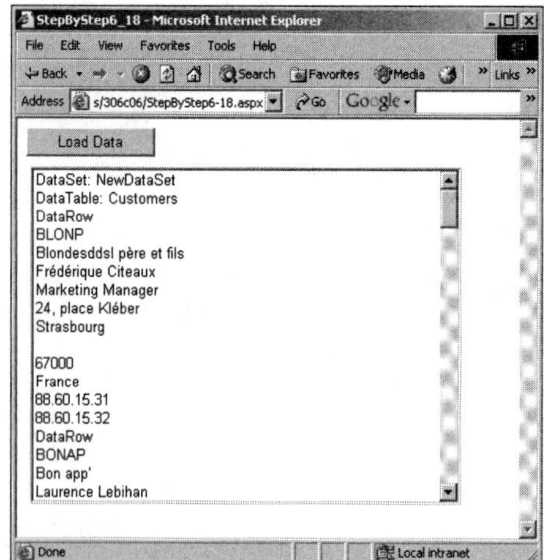

FIGURE 6.15
Dumping the contents of a `DataSet` to a `ListBox` control.

This sample shows how you can visit every piece of data in a DataSet by a proper selection of nested For Each loops. It also shows a general syntax for retrieving data: Locate the DataRow and DataColumn with an intersection containing the data that you're interested in, and use the dr(dc) syntax to retrieve the actual data value. You can use a variety of other syntaxes to retrieve data. Given a DataTable variable named dt that refers to the data from the Customer table, for example, any of these statements will retrieve the value in the first column of the first row of data in the DataTable:

```
dt.Rows(0).Item(0)
dt.Rows(0)(0)
dt.Rows(0).Item("CustomerID")
dt.Rows(0)("CustomerID")
dt.Rows(0)!CustomerID
```

Using Strongly Typed DataSets

All the syntaxes for retrieving data that you saw in the previous section have one thing in common: They're all late-bound. That is, the .NET Framework doesn't know until runtime that "CustomerID" is a valid column name. One of the innovations of ADO.NET is a provision to create strongly typed DataSets. In a strongly typed DataSet, columns actually become properties of the row. This allows you to write an early-bound version of the data-retrieval expression:

```
dt.Rows(0).CustomerID
```

In addition to being faster than the late-bound syntaxes, the early-bound syntax has the added advantage of making column names show up in IntelliSense tips as you type code.

You've already seen quite a few strongly typed DataSets, although I didn't emphasize this while I was using them. Any time that you use the "Generate DataSet" link in the Properties Window for a SqlDataAdapter object on a form, Visual Studio .NET builds a strongly typed DataSet. You can also build strongly typed DataSets by using the XSD designer.

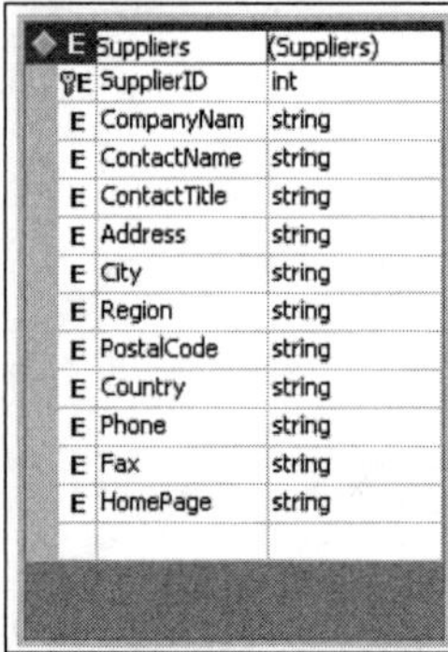

FIGURE 6.16
A strongly typed `DataSet` open in the XSD Designer.

STEP BY STEP

6.19 Designing a Strongly Typed DataSet

1. Select Project, Add New Item in your Visual Basic .NET project.
2. In the Add New Item dialog box, select the `DataSet` template. Name the new `DataSet` `Suppliers.xsd`. Click Open to create the XSD file and open it in the Designer.
3. Open Server Explorer.
4. Expand the tree under Data Connections to show a SQL Server data connection that points to the Northwind sample database, and then the Tables node of the SQL Server. Drag the Suppliers table from Server Explorer and drop it on the design surface for the `DataSet`. Figure 6.16 shows the resulting XSD design view. The "E" icons for each column of the table indicate that those columns have been rendered as XML elements.
5. Save the `DataSet`. At this point, your project contains a new class named Suppliers, which is a strongly typed `DataSet` that you can use in code.
6. Add a new Web Form to your Visual Basic .NET web project.
7. Place a `Button` control with the ID of `btnLoadData` and a `ListBox` control with the ID of `lbData` on the form.
8. Double-click the form to open the form's module. Enter these statements at the top of the module:

```
Imports System.Data
Imports System.Data.SqlClient
```

9. Enter this code to run when the user clicks the `Button` control:

```
Private Sub Page_Load(ByVal sender As System.Object, _
 ByVal e As System.EventArgs) Handles MyBase.Load
    If IsPostBack Then
        ' Create a SqlConnection
        Dim cnn As SqlConnection = _
         New SqlConnection("Data Source=(local);" & _
         "Initial Catalog=Northwind;" & _
         "Integrated Security=SSPI")
```

```
        ' Create a SqlCommand
        Dim cmd As SqlCommand = cnn.CreateCommand()
        cmd.CommandType = CommandType.Text
        cmd.CommandText = "SELECT * FROM Suppliers"
        ' Set up the DataAdapter and fill the DataSet
        Dim da As SqlDataAdapter = _
         New SqlDataAdapter()
        da.SelectCommand = cmd
        Dim ds As Suppliers = New Suppliers()
        da.Fill(ds, "Suppliers")
        ' Dump the contents of the DataSet
        Dim suppRow As Suppliers.SuppliersRow
        For Each suppRow In ds.Suppliers
            lbData.Items.Add(suppRow.SupplierID & _
             " " & suppRow.CompanyName)
        Next
    End If
End Sub
```

10. Set the Web Form as the start page for the project.

11. Run the project and click the button. The code displays two columns from the `DataSet` in the `ListBox` control, as shown in Figure 6.17.

FIGURE 6.17
Data dumped from a strongly typed `DataSet`.

Using the Suppliers class to define the `DataSet` in this case gives you several syntactical benefits. You can refer to the Suppliers `DataTable` as a property of the `DataSet`. You can also refer to the columns in the `DataRows` in this `DataTable` as properties of the `DataRow`. The strongly typed `DataSet` automatically defines a class named `SuppliersRow` to represent one `DataRow` with strong typing.

DataSets With Multiple Tables

Every `DataSet` that you've seen so far in this chapter has contained a single `DataTable`. But `DataSets` are not limited to a single `DataTable`; in fact, there's no practical limit on the number of `DataTables` that a `DataSet` can contain. By using multiple `DataAdapter` objects, you can connect a single `DataSet` to more than one table in the SQL Server database. You can also define `DataRelation` objects to represent the relationship between the `DataTables` in the `DataSet`.

STEP BY STEP

6.20 Building a DataSet Containing Multiple DataTables

1. Add a new Web Form to your Visual Basic .NET Web project.

2. Place two `DataGrid` controls on the form. Set the ID properties of the `DataGrid` control to `dgCustomers` and `dgOrders`.

3. Select the `dgCustomers` `DataGrid` control. Set its `DataKeyField` property to `CustomerID`.

4. Click the Property Builder hyperlink beneath the Properties window. Select the Columns section of the `dgCustomers` Properties dialog box. In the Available Columns list, expand the node for `Button` Column. Select the Select item. Click the > button to move this item to the Selected Columns list. Click OK. Figure 6.18 shows the form in design view, with the `dgOrders` control placed above the `dgCustomers` control.

5. Double-click the form to open the form's module. Enter these statements at the top of the module:

```
Imports System.Data
Imports System.Data.SqlClient
```

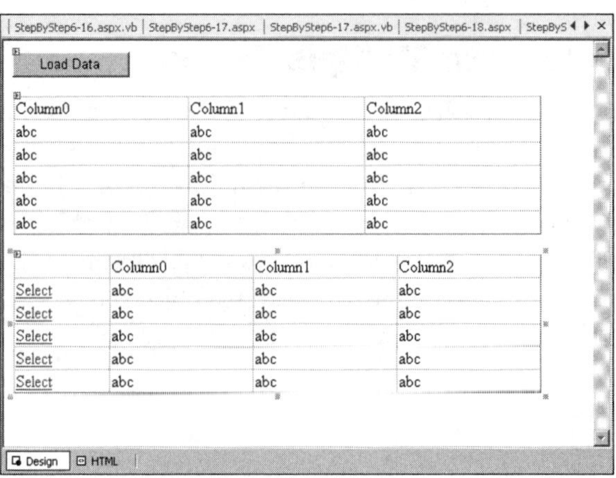

FIGURE 6.18
Designing a form to display data from a multi-table `DataSet`.

6. Enter this code in the form's module:

```
Dim mds As DataSet = New DataSet()

Private Sub Page_Load(ByVal sender As System.Object, _
 ByVal e As System.EventArgs) Handles MyBase.Load
    ' Initialize the DataSet
    LoadData()
    ' And show the data on the user interface
    dgCustomers.DataSource = mds
    dgCustomers.DataMember = "Customers"
    dgCustomers.DataBind()
End Sub

Private Sub dgCustomers_ItemCommand( _
 ByVal source As Object, _
 ByVal e As System.Web.UI. _
 WebControls.DataGridCommandEventArgs) _
 Handles dgCustomers.ItemCommand
    ' Create a DataView showing
    ' orders for the selected customer
    Dim dv As DataView = _
     New DataView(mds.Tables("Orders"))
    dv.RowFilter = "CustomerID = '" & _
     dgCustomers.DataKeys( _
      CInt(e.Item.ItemIndex)) & "'"
    ' And show the data on the user interface
    dgOrders.DataSource = dv
    dgOrders.DataBind()
End Sub

Private Sub LoadData()
    ' Create a SqlConnection and a DataSet
    Dim cnn As SqlConnection = _
     New SqlConnection("Data Source=(local);" & _
     "Initial Catalog=Northwind;" & _
     "Integrated Security=SSPI")

    ' Add the customers data to the DataSet
    Dim cmdCustomers As SqlCommand = _
     cnn.CreateCommand()
    cmdCustomers.CommandType = CommandType.Text
    cmdCustomers.CommandText = _
     "SELECT * FROM Customers"
    Dim daCustomers As SqlDataAdapter = _
     New SqlDataAdapter()
    daCustomers.SelectCommand = cmdCustomers
    daCustomers.Fill(mds, "Customers")

    ' Add the Orders data to the DataSet
    Dim cmdOrders As SqlCommand = cnn.CreateCommand()
    cmdOrders.CommandType = CommandType.Text
    cmdOrders.CommandText = "SELECT * FROM Orders"
```

continues

continued

```
        Dim daOrders As SqlDataAdapter = _
         New SqlDataAdapter()
        daOrders.SelectCommand = cmdOrders
        daOrders.Fill(mds, "Orders")

        ' Add Relation
        Dim relCustOrder As DataRelation = _
         mds.Relations.Add("CustOrder", _
         mds.Tables("Customers"). _
          Columns("CustomerID"), _
         mds.Tables("Orders").Columns("CustomerID"))

    End Sub
```

7. Set the form as the startup object for the project.

8. Run the project. The code loads both database tables into the `DataSet`, and then displays the Customers information on the `DataGrid`, as shown in Figure 6.19.

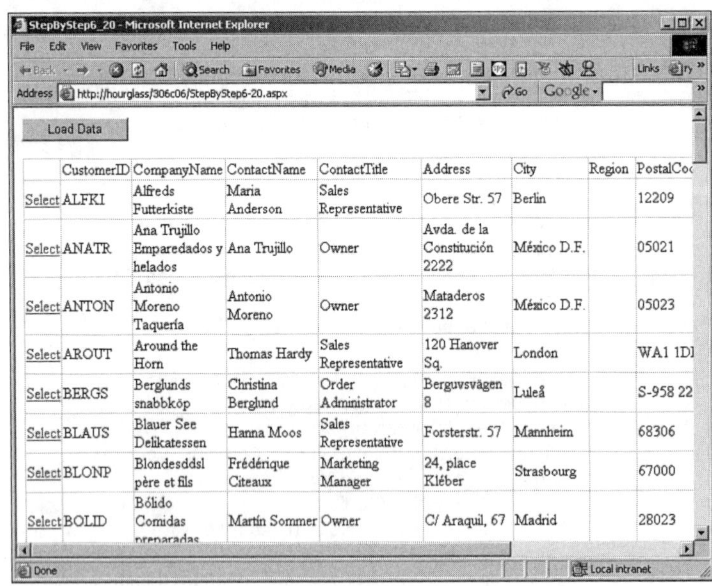

FIGURE 6.19
Customers data from a multi-table `DataSet`.

9. Click the Select hyperlink for one of the rows. This posts the form back to the server. First the Load event of the page fires, loading the `DataSet` and initializing the `dgCustomers` `DataGrid` control. Then the `ItemCommand` event of the `DataGrid` fires. In the handler for this event, the code retrieves the key from the selected row, and uses this key to build a `DataView` containing orders for the selected customer. The end result is that both `DataGrids` display information, as shown in Figure 6.20.

   You'll learn more about the `DataView` object in the next section of this chapter.

This code uses two different `SqlDataAdapter` objects to move data from two different database tables into a single `DataSet`. The data from each `SqlDataAdapter` is stored in a separate `DataTable`. The code then adds `DataRelation` objects to specify the relationships between these `DataTables`. The `Add` method of the `DataSet`.Relations collection takes three parameters:

1. A name for the `DataRelation` object to be created.

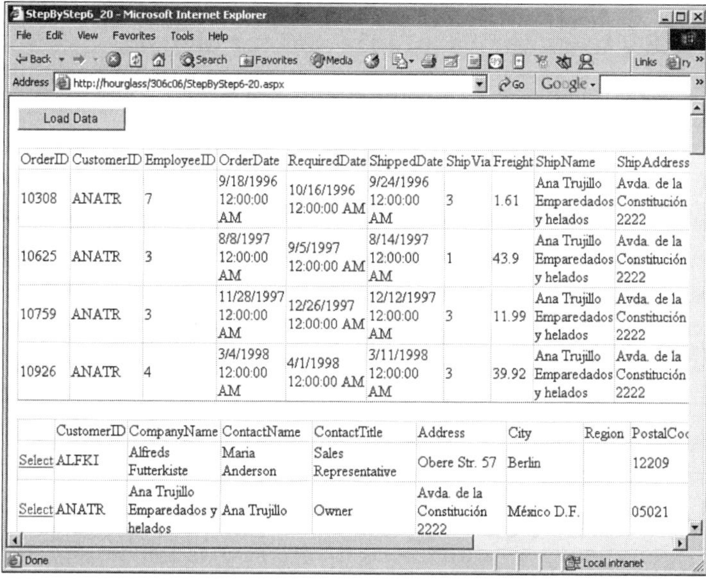

FIGURE 6.20
Customer and order data from a multi-table `DataSet`.

2. The DataColumn object representing the primary key side of the relationship.

3. The DataColumn object representing the foreign key side of the relationship.

Finding and Sorting Data in DataSets

The .NET Framework offers several object-oriented ways to find and sort data. In this section, I'll show you how to use two of these ways: the DataTable.Select method and the filtering and sorting capabilities of the DataView object.

The Select method of the DataTable object is a convenient way to find particular DataRow objects within the DataTable. This method extracts an array of DataRow objects that you can work with. This is useful when you're selecting data from a large DataTable that's already been returned to your code. If you know in advance which rows you want to work with, it's more efficient to do the selection in the WHERE clause of your SQL statement.

STEP BY STEP

6.21 Using the DataTable.Select Method

1. Add a new Web Form to your Visual Basic .NET Web project.

2. Place a Button control with the ID of btnSelect, a TextBox control with the ID of txtCountry, and a ListBox control with the ID of lbSelected on the form.

3. Double-click the form to open the form's module. Enter these statements at the top of the module:

```
Imports System.Data
Imports System.Data.SqlClient
```

4. Enter this code to handle the Click event of the Button control:

```
Private Sub Page_Load(ByVal sender As System.Object, _
 ByVal e As System.EventArgs) Handles MyBase.Load
    If IsPostBack Then
        ' Create a SqlConnection
        Dim cnn As SqlConnection = _
         New SqlConnection("Data Source=(local);" & _
```

```
            "Initial Catalog=Northwind;" & _
            "Integrated Security=SSPI")
           ' Create a SqlCommand
           Dim cmd As SqlCommand = cnn.CreateCommand()
           cmd.CommandType = CommandType.Text
           cmd.CommandText = "SELECT * FROM Customers"
           ' Set up the DataAdapter and fill the DataSet
           Dim da As SqlDataAdapter = _
            New SqlDataAdapter()
           da.SelectCommand = cmd
           Dim ds As DataSet = New DataSet()
           da.Fill(ds, "Customers")
           ' Use the Select method to get
           ' a sorted array of DataRows
           Dim adr() As DataRow = _
            ds.Tables("Customers").Select( _
            "Country = '" & txtCountry.Text & _
            "'", "ContactName ASC")
           ' Dump the result to the user interface
           lbSelected.Items.Clear()
           Dim dr As DataRow
           For Each dr In adr
               lbSelected.Items.Add(dr(0) & " " & _
                dr(1) & " " & dr(2))
           Next
       End If
   End Sub
```

5. Set the Web Form as the start page for the project.

6. Run the project. Enter a country name and click the button. You'll see the first three columns from `DataRows` for customers in that country, as shown in Figure 6.21.

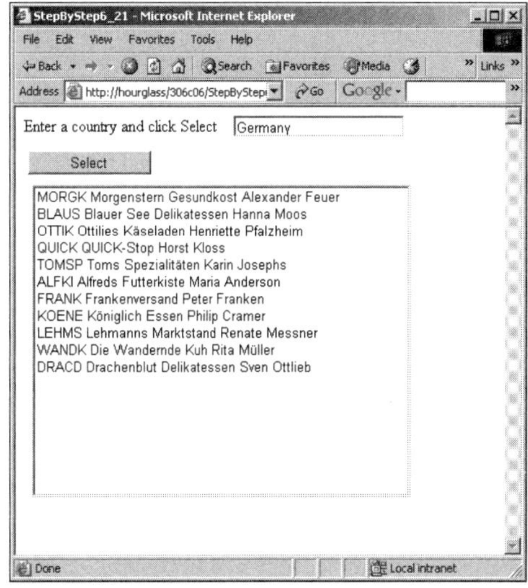

FIGURE 6.21
Results of using the `DataTable.Select` method.

The Select method of the `DataTable` constructs an array of `DataRows`, based on up to three factors: a filter expression, a sort expression, and a state constant.

Filter expressions are essentially SQL `WHERE` clauses constructed according to these rules:

- Column names containing special characters should be enclosed in square brackets.
- String constants should be enclosed in single quotes.
- Date constants should be enclosed in pound signs.
- Numeric expressions can be specified in decimal or scientific notation.

- Expressions can be created using AND, OR, NOT, parentheses, IN, LIKE, comparison operators, and arithmetic operators.
- The + operator is used to concatenate strings.
- Either * or % can be used as a wildcard to match any number of characters. Wildcards may be used only at the start or end of strings.
- Columns in a child table can be referenced with the expression Child.Column. If the table has more than one child table, use the expression Child(RelationName).Column to choose a particular child table.
- The Sum, Avg, Min, Max, Count, StDev, and Var aggregates can be used with child tables.
- Supported functions include CONVERT, LEN, ISNULL, IIF, and SUBSTRING.

In the sample code, the filter expression is built by concatenating the text from the txtCountry control with a column comparison.

If you don't specify a sort order in the Select method, the rows are returned in primary key order, or in the order of addition if the table doesn't have a primary key. You can also specify a sort expression consisting of one or more column names and the keywords ASC or DESC to specify ascending or descending sorts. For example, this is a valid sort expression:

```
Country ASC, CompanyName DESC
```

That expression will sort first by country in ascending order and then by company name within each country in descending order.

Finally, you can also select DataRows according to their current state by supplying one of the DataViewRowState constants. Table 6.14 shows these constants.

TABLE 6.14

DataViewRowState CONSTANTS

Constant	*Meaning*
`Added`	New rows that have not yet been committed
`CurrentRows`	All current rows, whether unchanged, modified, or new
`Deleted`	Deleted rows
`ModifiedCurrent`	Modified rows
`ModifiedOriginal`	Original data from modified rows
`None`	No rows
`OriginalRows`	Original data, including rows that have been modified or deleted
`Unchanged`	Rows that have not been changed

You can also sort and filter data by using a `DataView`. The `DataView` has the same structure of rows and columns as a `DataTable`, but it also lets you specify sorting and filtering options. Typically you'll create a `DataView` by starting with a `DataTable` and specifying options to include a subset of the rows in the `DataTable`.

EXAM TIP

`DataTable` to Array You can easily create an array that holds all the content of a `DataTable` by calling the `Select` method with no parameters:

```
Dim adr() As DataRow =
dt.Select()
```

STEP BY STEP

6.22 Using a `DataView` to Sort and Filter Data

1. Add a new Web Form to your Visual Basic .NET web project.
2. Place a `Button` control with the ID of `btnLoad` and a `DataGrid` control with the ID of `dgCustomers` on the form.
3. Double-click the form to open the form's module. Enter these statements at the top of the module:

```
Imports System.Data
Imports System.Data.SqlClient
```

continues

continued

4. Enter this code to run when the user clicks the `Button` control:

```
Private Sub Page_Load(ByVal sender As System.Object, _
 ByVal e As System.EventArgs) Handles MyBase.Load
    If IsPostBack Then
        ' Create a SqlConnection
        Dim cnn As SqlConnection = _
         New SqlConnection("Data Source=(local);" & _
         "Initial Catalog=Northwind;" & _
         "Integrated Security=SSPI")
        ' Create a SqlCommand
        Dim cmd As SqlCommand = cnn.CreateCommand()
        cmd.CommandType = CommandType.Text
        cmd.CommandText = "SELECT * FROM Customers"
        ' Set up the DataAdapter and fill the DataSet
        Dim da As SqlDataAdapter = _
         New SqlDataAdapter()
        da.SelectCommand = cmd
        Dim ds As DataSet = New DataSet()
        da.Fill(ds, "Customers")
        ' Create a DataView based on
        ' the Customers DataTable
        Dim dv As DataView = _
         New DataView(ds.Tables("Customers"))
        dv.RowFilter = "Country = 'France'"
        dv.Sort = "CompanyName ASC"
        dgCustomers.DataSource = dv
        dgCustomers.DataBind()
    End If
End Sub
```

5. Set the Web Form as the start page for the project.

6. Run the project and click the button. The `DataGrid` will display only the customers from France, sorted in ascending order by `CompanyName`.

The constructor for the `DataView` specifies the `DataTable` that includes the data from which the `DataView` can draw. By setting the `RowFilter`, `Sort`, and `RowStateFilter` properties of the `DataView`, you can control which rows are available in the `DataView`, as well as the order in which they are presented.

GUIDED PRACTICE EXERCISE 6.3

In this exercise, you'll fill a `DataSet` with customer and order data. Then you'll allow the user to select a customer and display a `DataView` containing only that customer's orders on the user interface.

Your form should include a bound `ComboBox` control to allow the user to select a `CustomerID` value. When the user selects a new value in the `ComboBox`, you should initialize the `DataView` and bind it to a `DataGrid` for display.

You should try doing this on your own first. If you get stuck, or you'd like to see one possible solution, follow these steps:

1. Add a new form to your Visual Basic .NET project.
2. Open Server Explorer.
3. Add a Label control, a `DropDownList` control (`ddlCustomers`) and a `DataGrid` control (`dgOrders`) to the form. Set the `AutoPostBack` property of the `DropDownList` control to True. Figure 6.22 shows a design for the form.
4. Double-click the form to open the form's module. Enter these two statements at the top of the module to make the ADO.NET objects available:

```
Imports System.Data
Imports System.Data.SqlClient
```

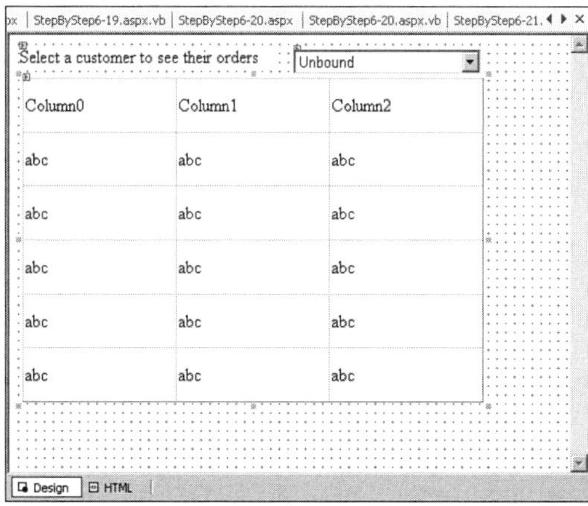

FIGURE 6.22
Designing a form to retrieve order information by customers.

5. Enter code to fill the list in the `DropDownList` control when the page is loaded, and to load the correct orders when the page is reloaded on postback:

```
Private Sub Page_Load(ByVal sender As System.Object, _
 ByVal e As System.EventArgs) Handles MyBase.Load
    ' Create a SqlConnection
    Dim cnn As SqlConnection = _
     New SqlConnection("Data Source=(local);" & _
     "Initial Catalog=Northwind;" & _
     "Integrated Security=SSPI")
    If Not IsPostBack Then
        ' Initial load - stock the DropDownList
        Dim cmdCustomers As SqlCommand = _
         cnn.CreateCommand()
        cmdCustomers.CommandType = CommandType.Text
        cmdCustomers.CommandText = _
         "SELECT CustomerID, CompanyName " & _
         "FROM Customers ORDER BY CompanyName"
        Dim ds As DataSet = New DataSet()
        Dim da As SqlDataAdapter = _
         New SqlDataAdapter()
        da.SelectCommand = cmdCustomers
        da.Fill(ds, "Customers")
        With ddlCustomers
            .DataSource = ds.Tables("Customers")
            .DataTextField = "CompanyName"
            .DataValueField = "CustomerID"
            .DataBind()
        End With
    Else
        ' Postback - get the right
        ' orders and show them
        Dim cmdOrders As SqlCommand = _
         cnn.CreateCommand
        cmdOrders.CommandType = CommandType.Text
        cmdOrders.CommandText = "SELECT * FROM Orders"
        Dim daOrders As SqlDataAdapter = _
         New SqlDataAdapter()
        Dim dsOrders As DataSet = New DataSet()
        daOrders.SelectCommand = cmdOrders
        daOrders.Fill(dsOrders, "Orders")
        ' Create a DataView containing the
        ' orders for the selected customer
        Dim dv As DataView = New DataView( _
         dsOrders.Tables("Orders"))
        dv.RowFilter = "CustomerID = '" & _
         ddlCustomers.SelectedItem.Value & "'"
        dgOrders.DataSource = dv
        dgOrders.DataBind()
    End If
End Sub
```

6. Set the Web Form as the start page for the project.

7. Run the project. Select a customer from the `ComboBox`. That customer's orders are displayed in the `DataGrid`.
8. If you had difficulty following this exercise, review the sections titled "Running Queries," "The `SELECT` Statement," and "Finding and Sorting Data in `DataSets`," as well as the material on "Complex Data Binding" in Chapter 5. The text and examples should help you in relearning this material and help you understand what just happened in this exercise. After review, try this exercise again.

There are many other ways that you could meet the requirements of this particular exercise. For example, you could create stored procedures to retrieve the customer or order information (or both), or you could use `DataSet.Select` whenever you need a set of orders rather than building a `DataView` on an existing `DataSet`. As you practice with ADO.NET, you'll find that it's so flexible that there are almost always alternative ways to do things.

Editing Data with ADO.NET

Now that you know how to retrieve data with ADO.NET, there's one other important database-related topic to cover: editing data. ADO.NET supports all the normal database operations of updating existing data, adding new data, and deleting existing data.

As you read this section, you need to keep in mind the distinction between the data model and the database. As you work with data in the `DataSet` and its subsidiary objects, you're altering the data in the data model. These changes will not be reflected in the underlying database until and unless you call the `Update` method of the `DataAdapter` method. So far I've only been using the `SqlDataAdapter` to move data from the database to the data model; in this section, you'll see how it works to move data back from the data model to the database.

Updating Data

Updating data is easy: Just assign a new value to the item in the `DataRow` that you want to change. But there's more to finishing the job. In order for the Update method of the `SqlDataAdapter` to write changes back to the database, you need to set its `UpdateCommand` property to an appropriate `SqlCommand` object. Step By Step 6.23 shows you how.

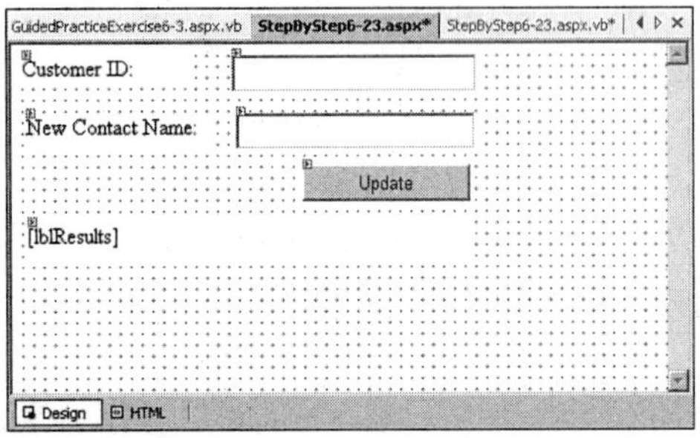

STEP BY STEP

6.23 Updating Data with a SqlDataAdapter

FIGURE 6.23
Designing a form to update contact information in the database.

1. Add a new Web Form to your Visual Basic .NET Web project.

2. Place a `Button` control with the ID of `btnUpdate`, three Label controls (one of which should have the id of `lblResults`), and two `TextBox` controls (`txtCustomerID` and `txtContactName`) on the form. Figure 6.23 shows the layout of this form in design mode.

3. Double-click the form to open the form's module. Enter these statements at the top of the module:

```
Imports System.Data
Imports System.Data.SqlClient
```

4. Enter this code to load and update data when the button is clicked:

```
Private Sub Page_Load(ByVal sender As System.Object, _
 ByVal e As System.EventArgs) Handles MyBase.Load
    If IsPostBack Then
        ' Create some ADO.NET objects
        Dim cnn As SqlConnection = _
         New SqlConnection("Data Source=(local);" & _
         "Initial Catalog=Northwind;" & _
         "Integrated Security=SSPI")
        Dim ds As DataSet = New DataSet()
        Dim da As SqlDataAdapter = _
         New SqlDataAdapter()
        ' Create a SqlCommand to select data
        Dim cmdSelect As SqlCommand = _
         cnn.CreateCommand()
        cmdSelect.CommandType = CommandType.Text
        cmdSelect.CommandText = _
         "SELECT CustomerID, ContactName " & _
         "FROM Customers"
```

```
        ' Create a SqlCommand to update data
        Dim cmdUpdate As SqlCommand = _
         cnn.CreateCommand()
        cmdUpdate.CommandType = CommandType.Text
        cmdUpdate.CommandText = _
         "UPDATE Customers SET " & _
         "ContactName = @ContactName " & _
         "WHERE CustomerID = @CustomerID"
        cmdUpdate.Parameters.Add("@ContactName", _
         SqlDbType.NVarChar, _
         30, "ContactName")
        cmdUpdate.Parameters.Add("@CustomerID", _
         SqlDbType.NChar, _
         5, "CustomerID")
        cmdUpdate.Parameters("@CustomerID"). _
         SourceVersion = _
         DataRowVersion.Original
        ' Set up the DataAdapter and fill the DataSet
        da.SelectCommand = cmdSelect
        da.UpdateCommand = cmdUpdate
        da.Fill(ds, "Customers")
        ' Get the DataRow to edit
        Dim adrEdit() As DataRow = _
         ds.Tables("Customers").Select( _
          "CustomerID = '" & _
          txtCustomerID.Text & "'")
        ' Make sure there's some data
        If UBound(adrEdit) > -1 Then
            ' Put in the edited data
            adrEdit(0)("ContactName") = _
             txtContactName.Text
            ' Save the changes
            da.Update(ds, "Customers")
            ' And make a note on the UI
            lblResults.Text = "Row has been updated"
        End If
    End If
End Sub
```

5. Set the Web Form as the start page for the project.

6. Run the project. Enter a customer ID (such as ALFKI) and a new contact name, and click OK. The code writes the change back to the database and shows the “Row has been updated” text on the form.

The `Update` method of the `SqlDataAdapter` is syntactically similar to the `Fill` method. It takes as its parameters the `DataSet` to be reconciled with the database and the name of the `DataTable` to be saved. You don't have to worry about which rows or columns of data were changed. The `SqlDataAdapter` automatically locates the changed rows. It executes the `SqlCommand` specified in its `UpdateCommand` property for each of those rows.

In this particular case, the command specified by the `UpdateCommand` property has two parameters. The `SqlParameter` objects are created using a version of the constructor that takes four parameters rather than the three that you saw earlier in the chapter. The fourth parameter is the name of a `DataColumn` which contains the data to be used in this particular parameter. Note also that you can specify whether a parameter should be filled in from the current data in the `DataSet` (the default), or the original version of the data before any edits were made. In this case, the `@CustomerID` parameter is being used to locate the row to edit in the database, so the code uses the original value of the column as the value for the parameter.

Adding Data

To add data to the database, you must supply a `SqlCommand` for the `InsertCommand` property of the `SqlDataAdapter`.

STEP BY STEP

6.24 Adding Data with a SqlDataAdapter

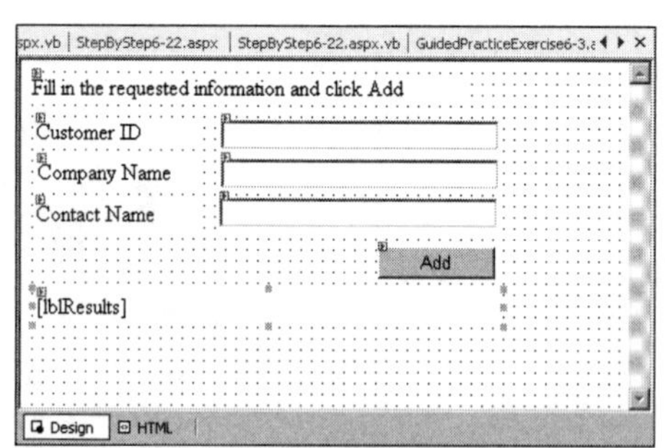

FIGURE 6.24
Designing a form to add new customers to the database.

1. Add a new Web Form to your Visual Basic .NET Web project.

2. Place five Label controls, three `TextBox` controls (`txtCustomerID`, `txtCompanyName`, and `txtContactName`) and a `Button` control (`btnAdd`) on the form. Figure 6.24 shows a design for the form.

3. Double-click the form to open the form's module. Enter these statements at the top of the module:

```
Imports System.Data
Imports System.Data.SqlClient
```

4. Enter this code to load data and add a new row when the user clicks the `Button` control:

```
Private Sub Page_Load(ByVal sender As System.Object, _
 ByVal e As System.EventArgs) Handles MyBase.Load
    If IsPostBack Then
        ' Create some ADO.NET objects
        Dim cnn As SqlConnection = _
         New SqlConnection("Data Source=(local);" & _
         "Initial Catalog=Northwind;" & _
         "Integrated Security=SSPI")
        Dim ds As DataSet = New DataSet()
        Dim da As SqlDataAdapter = _
         New SqlDataAdapter()
        ' Create a SqlCommand to select data
        Dim cmdSelect As SqlCommand = _
         cnn.CreateCommand()
        cmdSelect.CommandType = CommandType.Text
        cmdSelect.CommandText = _
         "SELECT CustomerID, CompanyName, " & _
         "ContactName FROM Customers"
        ' Create a SqlCommand to insert data
        Dim cmdInsert As SqlCommand = _
         cnn.CreateCommand()
        cmdInsert.CommandType = CommandType.Text
        cmdInsert.CommandText = _
         "INSERT INTO Customers " & _
         "(CustomerID, CompanyName, ContactName) " & _
         "VALUES(@CustomerID, @CompanyName, " & _
         "@ContactName)"
        cmdInsert.Parameters.Add("@CustomerID", _
         SqlDbType.NChar, _
         5, "CustomerID")
        cmdInsert.Parameters.Add("@CompanyName", _
         SqlDbType.NVarChar, _
         40, "CompanyName")
        cmdInsert.Parameters.Add("@ContactName", _
         SqlDbType.NVarChar, _
         30, "ContactName")
        cmdInsert.Parameters("@CustomerID"). _
         SourceVersion = _
         DataRowVersion.Original
        ' Set up the DataAdapter and fill the DataSet
        da.SelectCommand = cmdSelect
        da.InsertCommand = cmdInsert
        da.Fill(ds, "Customers")
        ' Create a new DataRow
        Dim dr As DataRow = ds.Tables( _
         "Customers").NewRow()
        ' Set values
        dr(0) = txtCustomerID.Text
        dr(1) = txtCompanyName.Text
        dr(2) = txtContactName.Text
```

continues

continued

```
            ' And append the new row to the DataTable
            ds.Tables("Customers").Rows.Add(dr)
            ' Now save back to the database
            da.Update(ds, "Customers")
            lblResults.Text = "Row added!"
        End If
    End Sub
```

5. Set the Web Form as the start page for the project.

6. Run the project. Enter data in the `TextBox` controls and click the button. The code adds the new row to the database.

As you can see, adding a new `DataRow` to a `DataTable` is a process that has several steps. First, you call the `NewRow` method of the `DataTable`. This returns a `DataRow` object that has the proper schema for that particular `DataTable`. Then you can set the values of the individual items in the `DataRow`. Finally, call the `Add` method of the `DataTable` to actually append this `DataRow` to the `DataTable`.

Of course, appending the `DataRow` to the `DataTable` doesn't make any changes to the database. For that, you need to call the `Update` method of the `SqlDataAdapter` once again. If the `SqlDataAdapter` finds any new rows in its scan of the database, it will call the `SqlCommand` specified by its `InsertCommand` property once for each new row. It's this `SqlCommand` that does the actual work of permanently saving the data.

Deleting Data

The `Rows` collection of the `DataTable` object supports a `Remove` method that deletes an entire `DataRow` from the `DataTable`. To persist the changes to the database, you'll need to call the Update method of the `SqlDataAdapter`.

STEP BY STEP

6.25 Deleting Data with a SqlDataAdapter

1. Add a new Web Form to your Visual Basic .NET web project.

2. Place a `Button` control with the ID of `btnDelete`, a `TextBox` control with the ID of `txtCustomerID`, and a `Label` control with the ID of `lblResults` on the form.

3. Double-click the form to open the form's module. Enter these statements at the top of the module:

```
Imports System.Data
Imports System.Data.SqlClient
```

4. Enter this code to delete data when the user clicks the `Button` control:

```
Private Sub Page_Load(ByVal sender As System.Object, _
 ByVal e As System.EventArgs) Handles MyBase.Load
    If IsPostBack Then
        ' Create some ADO.NET objects
        Dim cnn As SqlConnection = _
         New SqlConnection("Data Source=(local);" & _
         "Initial Catalog=Northwind;" & _
         "Integrated Security=SSPI")
        Dim ds As DataSet = New DataSet()
        Dim da As SqlDataAdapter = _
         New SqlDataAdapter()
        ' Create a SqlCommand to select data
        Dim cmdSelect As SqlCommand = _
         cnn.CreateCommand()
        cmdSelect.CommandType = CommandType.Text
        cmdSelect.CommandText = _
         "SELECT CustomerID, ContactName " & _
         "FROM Customers"
        ' Create a SqlCommand to delete data
        Dim cmdDelete As SqlCommand = _
         cnn.CreateCommand()
        cmdDelete.CommandType = CommandType.Text
        cmdDelete.CommandText = _
         "DELETE FROM Customers " & _
         "WHERE CustomerID = @CustomerID"
        cmdDelete.Parameters.Add("@CustomerID", _
         SqlDbType.NChar, _
         5, "CustomerID")
        cmdDelete.Parameters("@CustomerID"). _
         SourceVersion = _
         DataRowVersion.Original
```

continues

continued

```
            ' Set up the DataAdapter and fill the DataSet
            da.SelectCommand = cmdSelect
            da.DeleteCommand = cmdDelete
            da.Fill(ds, "Customers")
            ' Find the specified row and delete it
            Dim dr As DataRow
            For Each dr In ds.Tables("Customers").Rows
                If dr(0) = txtCustomerID.Text Then
                    ds.Tables("Customers").Rows.Remove(dr)
                    Exit For
                End If
            Next
            ' Save the changes
            da.Update(ds, "Customers")
            lblResults.Text = "Row deleted!"
        End If
    End Sub
```

5. Set the form as the startup object for the project.

6. Run the project. Enter a customer ID (such as ALFKI) in the `TextBox` control and click the `Button` control. That customer is deleted from the `DataSet` and from the database.

Note that the deletion command uses the original value of the `CustomerID` column to locate the correct row to delete from the database.

Editing With a `DataGrid`

The examples that you just saw of editing, adding, and deleting rows are functional, but somewhat tedious. Fortunately, there are easier ways to set these operations up in the user interface. If you bind a `DataSet` to a `DataGrid` control, you'll find that the `DataGrid` enables you to perform all three of the fundamental editing operations:

- To update the data in a row, click in the column to be updated and type a new value.
- To add a new row, scroll to the end of the list and type the values for the row into the last row of the `DataGrid`.
- To delete a row, click the record selector to the left of the row and click the Delete key on the keyboard.

If you do use a DataGrid for editing, you should supply SqlCommand objects to handle all the editing operations.

I covered the use of the DataList control to edit data in Chapter 5. Editing data via the DataGrid control is very similar. You might want to review the section "Editing Data With a DataList Control" in Chapter 5 to refresh your memory on the basic concepts.

STEP BY STEP

6.26 Editing Data Through a DataGrid Control

1. Add a new Web Form to your Visual Basic .NET web project.
2. Place a DataGrid control named dgCustomers on the form. Set the DataKeyField property of the DataGrid control to CustomerID.
3. Select the DataGrid control and click the Property Builder hyperlink underneath the Properties button. Click the Columns section of the dgCustomers Properties dialog box. Expand the Buttons node of the Available Columns list and add an Edit, Update, Cancel column and a Delete column to the Selected Columns List. Click OK.
4. Place three Label controls, three TextBox controls (txtCustomerID, txtCompanyName, and txtContactName), and a Button control (btnAdd) on the form. Figure 6.25 shows the form.
5. Double-click the form to open the form's module. Enter these statements at the top of the module:

```
Imports System.Data
Imports System.Data.SqlClient
```

6. Enter this code to load data when the page is loaded:

```
' Create some ADO.NET objects
    Dim cnn As SqlConnection = _
     New SqlConnection("Data Source=(local);" & _
     "Initial Catalog=Northwind;" & _
     "Integrated Security=SSPI")
Dim mds As DataSet = New DataSet()
Dim mda As SqlDataAdapter = New SqlDataAdapter()
```

continues

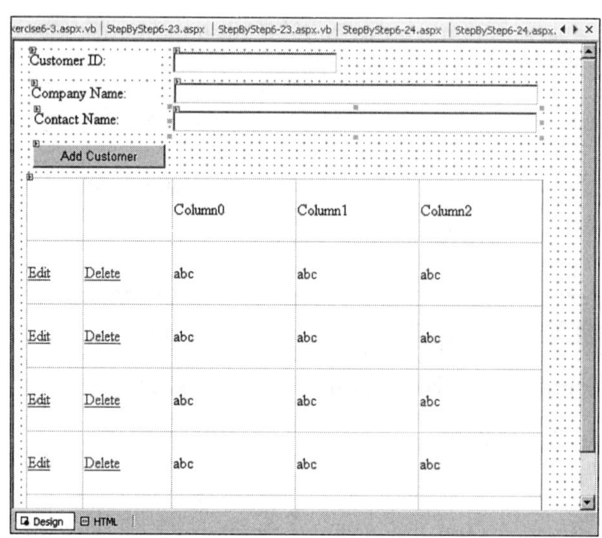

FIGURE 6.25
Designing a form to edit customers.

continued

```
Private Sub Page_Load(ByVal sender As System.Object, _
 ByVal e As System.EventArgs) Handles MyBase.Load
    ' Set up the SqlDataAdapter
    ' Create a SqlCommand to select data
    Dim cmdSelect As SqlCommand = mcnn.CreateCommand()
    cmdSelect.CommandType = CommandType.Text
    cmdSelect.CommandText = _
     "SELECT CustomerID, CompanyName, " & _
     "ContactName FROM Customers"
    ' Create a SqlCommand to update data
    Dim cmdUpdate As SqlCommand = mcnn.CreateCommand()
    cmdUpdate.CommandType = CommandType.Text
    cmdUpdate.CommandText = _
     "UPDATE Customers SET " & _
     "CompanyName = @CompanyName, ContactName " & _
     "= @ContactName " & _
     "WHERE CustomerID = @CustomerID"
    cmdUpdate.Parameters.Add("@ContactName", _
     SqlDbType.NVarChar, _
     30, "ContactName")
    cmdUpdate.Parameters.Add("@CompanyName", _
     SqlDbType.NVarChar, _
     40, "CompanyName")
    cmdUpdate.Parameters.Add("@CustomerID", _
     SqlDbType.NChar, _
     5, "CustomerID")
    cmdUpdate.Parameters("@CustomerID"). _
     SourceVersion = _
     DataRowVersion.Original
    ' Create a SqlCommand to insert data
    Dim cmdInsert As SqlCommand = mcnn.CreateCommand()
    cmdInsert.CommandType = CommandType.Text
```

```
    cmdInsert.CommandText = _
     "INSERT INTO Customers " & _
     "(CustomerID, CompanyName, ContactName) " & _
     "VALUES(@CustomerID, @CompanyName, @ContactName)"
    cmdInsert.Parameters.Add("@CustomerID", _
     SqlDbType.NChar, _
     5, "CustomerID")
    cmdInsert.Parameters.Add("@CompanyName", _
     SqlDbType.NVarChar, _
     40, "CompanyName")
    cmdInsert.Parameters.Add("@ContactName", _
     SqlDbType.NVarChar, _
     30, "ContactName")
    cmdInsert.Parameters("@CustomerID"). _
     SourceVersion = _
     DataRowVersion.Original
    ' Create a SqlCommand to delete data
    Dim cmdDelete As SqlCommand = mcnn.CreateCommand()
    cmdDelete.CommandType = CommandType.Text
    cmdDelete.CommandText = _
     "DELETE FROM Customers " & _
     "WHERE CustomerID = @CustomerID"
    cmdDelete.Parameters.Add( _
     "@CustomerID", SqlDbType.NChar, _
     5, "CustomerID")
    cmdDelete.Parameters("@CustomerID"). _
     SourceVersion = _
     DataRowVersion.Original
    ' Set up the DataAdapter and fill the DataSet
    mda.SelectCommand = cmdSelect
    mda.UpdateCommand = cmdUpdate
    mda.InsertCommand = cmdInsert
    mda.DeleteCommand = cmdDelete
    ' Get the current data from the database
    mda.Fill(mds, "Customers")
    ' At page load, fill the DataGrid
    If Not IsPostBack Then
        LoadData()
    End If
End Sub

Private Sub LoadData()
    ' Bind the data to the DataGrid
    dgCustomers.DataSource = mds
    dgCustomers.DataMember = "Customers"
    dgCustomers.DataBind()
End Sub
```

7. Enter this code to handle editing operations:

```
Private Sub dgCustomers_CancelCommand( _
 ByVal source As Object, _
 ByVal e As System.Web.UI.WebControls. _
 DataGridCommandEventArgs) _
 Handles dgCustomers.CancelCommand
```

continues

continued

```
        ' Cancel editing
        dgCustomers.EditItemIndex = -1
        LoadData()
    End Sub

    Private Sub dgCustomers_DeleteCommand( _
     ByVal source As Object, _
     ByVal e As System.Web.UI.WebControls. _
     DataGridCommandEventArgs) _
     Handles dgCustomers.DeleteCommand
        ' Find the specified row and delete it
        Dim strCustomerID As String = _
         dgCustomers.DataKeys(e.Item.ItemIndex)
        Dim dr As DataRow
        For Each dr In mds.Tables("Customers").Rows
            If dr(0) = strCustomerID Then
                mds.Tables("Customers").Rows.Remove(dr)
                Exit For
            End If
        Next
        ' Update the database
        mda.Update(mds, "Customers")
        ' And bind the data to the UI
        LoadData()
    End Sub

    Private Sub dgCustomers_EditCommand( _
     ByVal source As Object, _
     ByVal e As System.Web.UI.WebControls. _
     DataGridCommandEventArgs) _
     Handles dgCustomers.EditCommand
        ' Enter editing mode
        dgCustomers.EditItemIndex = CInt(e.Item.ItemIndex)
        LoadData()
    End Sub

    Private Sub dgCustomers_UpdateCommand( _
     ByVal source As Object, _
     ByVal e As System.Web.UI.WebControls. _
     DataGridCommandEventArgs) _
     Handles dgCustomers.UpdateCommand
        Dim adrEdit() As DataRow = _
         mds.Tables("Customers").Select( _
          "CustomerID = '" & _
          dgCustomers.DataKeys(e.Item.ItemIndex) & "'")
        ' Make sure there's some data
        If UBound(adrEdit) > -1 Then
            ' Put in the edited data
            Dim txtCompanyName As TextBox = _
             e.Item.Cells(3).Controls(0)
            adrEdit(0)("CompanyName") = _
             txtCompanyName.Text
            Dim txtContactName As TextBox = _
             e.Item.Cells(4).Controls(0)
```

```
            adrEdit(0)("ContactName") = _
             txtContactName.Text
        End If
        ' End editing
        dgCustomers.EditItemIndex = -1
        ' Update the database
        mda.Update(mds, "Customers")
        ' And bind the data to the UI
        LoadData()
    End Sub

    Private Sub btnAdd_Click(ByVal sender As Object, _
     ByVal e As System.EventArgs) Handles btnAdd.Click
        ' Add a new row to the DataSet
        Dim dr As DataRow = _
         mds.Tables("Customers").NewRow()
        ' Set values
        dr(0) = txtCustomerID.Text
        dr(1) = txtCompanyName.Text
        dr(2) = txtContactName.Text
        ' And append the new row to the DataTable
        mds.Tables("Customers").Rows.Add(dr)
        ' Update the database
        mda.Update(mds, "Customers")
        ' And bind the data to the UI
        LoadData()
        ' Clear the textboxes
        txtCustomerID.Text = ""
        txtCompanyName.Text = ""
        txtContactName.Text = ""
    End Sub
```

8. Set the Web Form as the start page for the project.

9. Run the project. You can enter new data and click the Add button, use the Delete button to delete a row, or use the Edit button to edit a row. As you work with the data, you'll see the changes reflected in the `DataGrid`.

Although there's a lot of code in this Step By Step, most of it is just a combination of the code that you saw in the previous three examples. To set up a `SqlDataAdapter` to handle all possible changes, you need to supply all the necessary `SqlCommand` objects. The `Update` method of the `SqlDataAdapter` takes care of calling the appropriate `SqlCommand` object for each change.

REVIEW BREAK

- Changing data in a `DataSet` can be done just by treating the items in the `DataSet` like any other variable.
- To persist changes from the data model to the underlying database you must call the `Update` method of the `SqlDataAdapter` object.
- The `UpdateCommand` property of the `SqlDataAdapter` object specifies a `SqlCommand` object to be executed for all changed rows.
- The `InsertCommand` property of the `SqlDataAdapter` object specifies a `SqlCommand` object to be executed for all new rows.
- The `DeleteCommand` property of the `SqlDataAdapter` object specifies a `SqlCommand` object to be executed for all deleted rows.
- The `DataGrid` control can provide a convenient way to handle data changes on the user interface.

Using XML Data

The final type of data that you'll learn about in this chapter is XML data. XML, the Extensible Markup Language, is an entire family of closely related standards. For example, an XSD file is a special type of XML file optimized for storing schema information. You saw XSD files in action in the section on strongly typed `DataSets` earlier in the chapter.

In this section of the chapter, I'll introduce you to the basic terminology and format of XML files. Then you'll see the `XmlDocument` and `XmlNode` classes, which are part of the `System.Xml` namespace. These classes provide an internal representation of XML that your .NET applications can use. Finally, to tie things together, you'll see how you can synchronize data in a `DataSet` with data in an `XmlDocument`.

XML Basics

If you're already familiar with XML, you might want to skip this section. But if you're still confused about the whole XML thing, follow along. You'll find that the basics are not that difficult, though some people seem determined to make XML harder than it has to be.

First, a definition: XML is just human-readable data combined with human-readable metadata. That is, XML files are in regular text, so you can read them. And they contain both data (such as customer ID values) and descriptions of that data.

Here's a concrete example to start with. This XML file represents data for two customers:

```
<?xml version="1.0" encoding="UTF-8"?>
<!-- Customer list for Bob's Tractor Parts -->
<Customers>
    <Customer CustomerNumber="1">
        <CustomerName>Lambert Tractor Works
        </CustomerName>
        <CustomerCity>Millbank</CustomerCity>
        <CustomerState>WA</CustomerState>
    </Customer>
    <Customer CustomerNumber="2">
        <CustomerName><![CDATA[Joe's Garage]]>
        </CustomerName>
        <CustomerCity>Doppel</CustomerCity>
        <CustomerState>OR</CustomerState>
    </Customer>
</Customers>
```

Even without knowing anything about XML, you can see some things just by looking at this file. In particular, XML consists of tags (which are contained within angle brackets) and data. Tags come in pairs, with each opening tag matched by a closing tag. The closing tag has the same text as the opening tag, prefixed with a forward slash.

The first thing that you'll find in an XML file is the *XML declaration*:

```
<?xml version="1.0" encoding="UTF-8"?>
```

The declaration tells you three things about this document:

- It's an XML document.
- It conforms to the XML 1.0 specification.
- It uses the UTF-8 character set (a standard set of characters for the western alphabet).

Tags in an XML document contain the names of elements. If you're familiar with HTML, you'll know that some elements have names dictated by the HTML specification. For example, the `<H1>` tag specifies a first-level heading. XML takes a different approach. You can make up any name you like for an element, subject to some simple naming rules:

- Names can contain any alphanumeric character.
- Names can contain underscores, hyphens, and periods.
- Names must not contain any white space.
- Names must start with a letter or underscore.

A start tag together with an end tag and the content between them defines an *element*. For example, here's a single element from the sample document:

```
<CustomerState>OR</CustomerState>
```

That defines an element with a name of `CustomerState` and with a value of `OR`.

Elements can be nested, but they cannot overlap. So this is legal XML, defining an element named `Customer` with three child elements:

```
<Customer CustomerNumber="1">
    <CustomerName>Lambert Tractor Works</CustomerName>
    <CustomerCity>Millbank</CustomerCity>
    <CustomerState>WA</CustomerState>
</Customer>
```

But this is not legal XML, because the `CustomerCity` and `CustomerState` elements overlap:

```
<Customer CustomerNumber="1">
    <CustomerName>Lambert Tractor Works</CustomerName>
    <CustomerCity>Millbank</CustomerState>
    <CustomerState>WA</CustomerCity>
</Customer>
```

Every XML document contains a single root element. The root element in the sample document is named `Customers`. The effect of these rules (nesting is OK, overlapping is not, and there is a single root element) is that any XML document can be represented as a tree of nodes.

Elements can contain *attributes*. An attribute is a piece of data that further describes an element. For example, the sample document includes this opening tag for an element:

```
<Customer CustomerNumber="1">
```

That declares an element named `Customer`. The `Customer` element includes an attribute with a name of `CustomerNumber` and with a value of 1.

XML documents can contain one or more *namespace* declarations. The sample document does not declare a namespace. Here's the syntax for a namespace declaration:

```
<Customers xmlns:tr="urn:schemas-tractor-repair">
```

The namespace is declared as part of the root tag for the document. In this particular case, the namespace (introduced with the special `xmlns` characters) defines a prefix of `tr` for tags within the namespace. The `urn` (Uniform Resource Name) is an arbitrary string, the purpose of which is to distinguish this namespace from other namespaces.

XML namespaces serve the same purpose as .NET namespaces: they help cut down on naming collisions. After declaring the `tr` namespace, an XML document could use a tag such as

```
<tr:CustomerState>OR</tr:CustomerState>
```

That indicates that this `CustomerState` tag is from the `tr` namespace, and should not be confused with any other `CustomerState` tag.

XML offers two ways to deal with special characters in data. First, for individual characters you can use entity references. There (closing angle bracket) entity reference>are five entity references defined in the XML standard:

- `<` translates to < (opening angle bracket)
- `>` translates to > (closing angle bracket)
- `&` translates to & (ampersand)
- `'` translates to ' (apostrophe)
- `"` translates to " (quotation mark)

You can also use a CDATA section to hold any arbitrary data, whether the data contains special characters or not. The sample document uses this approach to store a customer name containing an apostrophe:

```
<CustomerName><![CDATA[Joe's Garage]]></CustomerName>
```

Finally, an XML document can contain comments. Comments are set off by the opening string `<!--` and the closing string `-->`. Here's an example:

```
<!-- Customer list for Bob's Tractor Parts -->
```

There is a great deal more complexity available in XML than I've covered in this section. But these basics are more than enough to understand most of the XML that you're likely to run across until you start working with XML in depth.

Using the `XmlDocument` Class

XML documents on disk are just disk files, so you could read them with the `System.IO` classes that you learned about earlier in the chapter. But XML is so central to the .NET Framework that the Framework provides classes especially for working with XML.

To understand the .NET Framework representation of an XML document, you can start with the concept of a node. A node is one item in an XML document: it might be an attribute, a comment, an element, or something else. In the `System.Xml` namespace, nodes are represented by `XmlNode` objects. Table 6.15 shows the most important members of the `XmlNode` object.

TABLE 6.15

`XmlNode` OBJECT MEMBERS

Member	*Type*	*Description*
`AppendChild`	Method	Adds a new child node to the end of this node's list of children.
`Attributes`	Property	A collection of the attributes of this node.
`ChildNodes`	Property	A collection of child nodes of this node.
`FirstChild`	Property	The first child node of this node.
`InnerText`	Property	The value of this node and all its children.
`InnerXml`	Property	XML representing just the children of this node.
`InsertAfter`	Method	Inserts a new node after this node.
`InsertBefore`	Method	Inserts a new node before this node.
`LastChild`	Property	The last child node of this node.
`Name`	Property	The name of the node.
`NextSibling`	Property	The next child node of this node's parent node.
`NodeType`	Property	The type of this node. The `XmlNodeType` enumeration includes values for all possible node types.

Member	*Type*	*Description*
`OuterXml`	Property	XML representing this node and all its children.
`ParentNode`	Property	The parent of this node.
`PrependChild`	Method	Adds a new child node to the start of this node's list of children.
`PreviousSibling`	Method	The previous child node of this node's parent node.
`RemoveAll`	Method	Removes all children of this node.
`RemoveChild`	Method	Removes a specified child of this node.
`ReplaceChild`	Method	Replaces a child node with a new node.
`Value`	Property	Value of the node.

EXAM TIP

Get the Big Picture Don't worry about memorizing the complete list of `XmlNode` members. Instead, concentrate on understanding the big picture: There are rich methods for navigating the tree of nodes and for altering existing nodes.

`XmlNode` objects are collected into an `XmlDocument` object. As you can probably guess, `XmlDocument` is the object in the `System.Xml` namespace that represents an entire XML document. Table 6.16 shows the most important members of the `XmlNode` object.

TABLE 6.16

`XmlDocument` OBJECT MEMBERS

Member	*Type*	*Description*
`CreateAttribute`	Method	Creates a new attribute node.
`CreateElement`	Method	Creates a new element node.
`CreateNode`	Method	Creates a new `XmlNode` object.
`DocumentElement`	Property	Returns the `XmlNode` object that represents the root node of this document.
`GetElementsByTagName`	Method	Returns a list of all elements with the specified tag name.
`Load`	Method	Loads an XML document.
`LoadXml`	Method	Loads a string of XML.
`Save`	Method	Saves the `XmlDocument` as a file or stream.
WriteTo	Method	Saves the XmlDocument to an XmlWriter.

STEP BY STEP

6.27 Displaying the Contents of an XML Document

1. Add a new Web Form to your Visual Basic .NET Web project.

2. Add a new XML File to your Visual Basic .NET Web project. Name the new file `BobsTractors.xml`. Enter this text in the new file and save the file:

```
<?xml version="1.0" encoding="UTF-8"?>
<!-- Customer list for Bob's Tractor Parts -->
<Customers>
    <Customer CustomerNumber="1">
        <CustomerName>Lambert Tractor Works
        </CustomerName>
        <CustomerCity>Millbank</CustomerCity>
        <CustomerState>WA</CustomerState>
    </Customer>
    <Customer CustomerNumber="2">
        <CustomerName><![CDATA[Joe's Garage]]>
        </CustomerName>
        <CustomerCity>Doppel</CustomerCity>
        <CustomerState>OR</CustomerState>
    </Customer>
</Customers>
```

3. Place a `ListBox` control with the ID of `lbNodes` and a `Button` with the ID of `btnLoadXml` on the form.

4. Double-click the form to open the form's module. Enter this statement at the top of the module:

```
Imports System.Xml
```

5. Enter this code to load data when the button is clicked:

```
Private Sub Page_Load(ByVal sender As System.Object, _
 ByVal e As System.EventArgs) Handles MyBase.Load
    If IsPostBack Then
        ' Hook up to the disk file
        Dim xtr As New XmlTextReader( _
         Server.MapPath("BobsTractors.xml"))
        xtr.WhitespaceHandling = _
         WhitespaceHandling.None
        Dim xd As XmlDocument = New XmlDocument()
        ' Load the file into the XmlDocument
        xd.Load(xtr)
            ' Add an item representing the
            ' document to the ListBox
            lbNodes.Items.Add("XML Document")
```

```
            ' Find the root node, and add it
            ' together with its children
            Dim xnod As XmlNode = xd.DocumentElement
            AddWithChildren(xnod, 1)
        End If
End Sub

Private Sub AddWithChildren( _
 ByVal xnod As XmlNode, _
 ByVal intLevel As Integer)
    ' Adds a node to the ListBox,
    ' together with its children.
    ' intLevel controls the depth of indenting
    Dim xnodWorking As XmlNode
    Dim strIndent As String = _
     New String(" ", 2 * intLevel)
    ' Get the value of the node (if any)
    Dim strValue As String = _
     CType(xnod.Value, String)
    If Len(strValue) > 0 Then
        strValue = " : " & strValue
    End If
    ' Add the node details to the ListBox
    lbNodes.Items.Add(strIndent & _
     xnod.Name & strValue)
    ' For an element node, retrieve the attributes
    If xnod.NodeType = XmlNodeType.Element Then
        Dim mapAttributes As XmlNamedNodeMap = _
         xnod.Attributes
        Dim xnodAttribute As XmlNode
        ' Add the attrbutes to the ListBox
        For Each xnodAttribute In mapAttributes
            lbNodes.Items.Add(strIndent & "  " & _
             xnodAttribute.Name _
             & " : " & xnodAttribute.Value)
        Next
    End If
    ' If there are any child nodes,
    ' call this procedure recursively
    If xnod.HasChildNodes Then
        xnodWorking = xnod.FirstChild
        Do Until IsNothing(xnodWorking)
            AddWithChildren(xnodWorking, intLevel + 1)
            xnodWorking = xnodWorking.NextSibling
        Loop
    End If
End Sub
```

6. Set the Web Form as the start page for the project.

7. Run the project and click the button. The contents of the XML file will be dumped to the `ListBox` control, as shown in Figure 6.26.

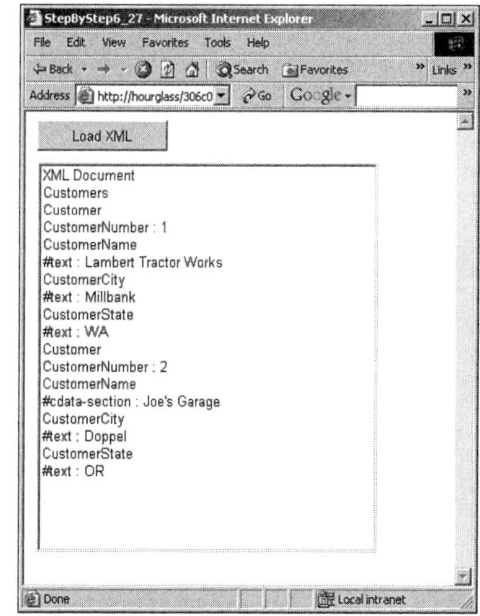

FIGURE 6.26
Viewing a list of nodes from an XML file.

As you can see in Figure 6.26, the object model implemented in the XmlDocument and XmlNode objects has access to the entire contents of the XML file. This code uses an XmlTextReader object to read the disk file into the XmlDocument object. The XmlTextReader has very similar functionality to the StreamReader and BinaryReader objects that you saw earlier in the chapter, except that it's designed to pipe data from a disk file to an XmlDocument object. The XmlTextReader also has other XML-specific features. For example, the WhitespaceHandling property setting in this code tells it not to create nodes for extra white space in the XML file.

The code uses the DocumentElement property of the XmlDocument object to find the node at the root of the tree representation of the XML. After that, it's just a matter of recursively calling a procedure that adds information about the node to the ListBox control.

One bit of added complexity in the code is necessary to deal with attributes. Attribute nodes are not included in the ChildNodes collection of a node in the XmlDocument. Instead, you can use the Attributes property of the XmlNode object to get a collection of attribute nodes only. The code uses an XmlNamedNodeMap object to hold this collection; this object can hold an arbitrary collection of XmlNode objects of any type.

You can also modify an XML document through the XmlDocument object. To do so, you need to modify the individual XmlNode objects and then write the file back out to disk.

STEP BY STEP

6.28 Modifying an XML File in Code

1. Add a new Web Form to your Visual Basic .NET Web project.

2. Place a Button control with the ID of btnModify and a Label control with the ID of lblResults on the form.

3. Double-click the form to open the form's module. Enter this statement at the top of the module:

```
Imports System.Xml
```

4. Enter this code to load and modify data when the button is clicked:

```
Private Sub Page_Load(ByVal sender As System.Object, _
 ByVal e As System.EventArgs) Handles MyBase.Load
    If IsPostBack Then
        ' Hook up to the disk file
        Dim xtr As New XmlTextReader( _
         Server.MapPath("BobsTractors.xml"))
        xtr.WhitespaceHandling = _
         WhitespaceHandling.None
        Dim xd As XmlDocument = New XmlDocument()
        ' Load the file into the XmlDocument
        xd.Load(xtr)
        xtr.Close()
        ' Find the root node, and modify it
        ' together with its children
        Dim xnod As XmlNode = xd.DocumentElement
        ModifyWithChildren(xnod)
        ' Write the modified file to disk
        Dim xtw As XmlTextWriter = _
         New XmlTextWriter(Server.MapPath( _
          "BobsTractors.new.xml"), _
          System.Text.Encoding.UTF8)
        xd.WriteTo(xtw)
        xtw.Flush()
        xtw.Close()
        lblResults.Text = "Done!"
    End If
End Sub

Private Sub ModifyWithChildren(ByVal xnod As XmlNode)
    ' Sets all CustomerCity nodes to uppercase
    Dim xnodWorking As XmlNode

    If xnod.Name = "CustomerCity" Then
        xnod.FirstChild.Value = _
         xnod.FirstChild.Value.ToUpper
    End If
    ' If there are any child nodes,
    ' call this procedure recursively
    If xnod.HasChildNodes Then
        xnodWorking = xnod.FirstChild
        Do Until IsNothing(xnodWorking)
            ModifyWithChildren(xnodWorking)
            xnodWorking = xnodWorking.NextSibling
        Loop
    End If
End Sub
```

5. Set the Web Form as the start page for the project.

continues

continued

6. Run the project and click the button. The code makes a copy of the XML file with the added extension ".new". The copy will have all the `CustomerState` values converted to uppercase.

Writing the XML file out uses one new class, the `XmlTextWriter`. This class connects an `XmlDocument` to a backing store for output, similar to the `StreamWriter` that you saw earlier in the chapter.

Treating XML as Relational Data

You can also treat an XML document as relational data. To do this, you can use an `XmlDataDocument` class, which inherits from `XmlDocument`. The key feature of the `XmlDataDocument` class is that it can be synchronized with a `DataSet`.

STEP BY STEP

6.29 Reading an XML Document into a DataSet

1. Add a new Web Form to your Visual Basic .NET Web project.
2. Place a `Button` control with the ID of `btnLoadXml` and a `DataGrid` with the ID of `dgXml` on the form.
3. Double-click the form to open the form's module. Enter these statements at the top of the module:

```
Imports System.Data
Imports System.Xml
```

4. Enter this code to load data when the button is clicked:

```
Private Sub Page_Load(ByVal sender As System.Object,
_
 ByVal e As System.EventArgs) Handles MyBase.Load
    If IsPostBack Then
        ' Hook up to the disk file
        Dim xtr As New XmlTextReader( _
         Server.MapPath("BobsTractors.xml"))
        Dim xdd As XmlDataDocument = _
         New XmlDataDocument()
```

```
        ' Get the DataSet
        Dim ds As DataSet = xdd.DataSet
        ' Read the schema of the file
        ' to initialize the DataSet
        ds.ReadXmlSchema(xtr)
        xtr.Close()
        xtr = New XmlTextReader( _
         Server.MapPath("BobsTractors.xml"))
        xtr.WhitespaceHandling = _
         WhitespaceHandling.None
        ' Load the file into the XmlDataDocument
        xdd.Load(xtr)
        xtr.Close()
        ' And display it on the DataGrid
        dgXML.DataSource = ds
        dgXML.DataBind()
    End If
End Sub
```

5. Set the Web Form as the start page for the project.

6. Run the project and click the button. The code loads the XML file into the `DataSet` and displays it on the user interface, as shown in Figure 6.27.

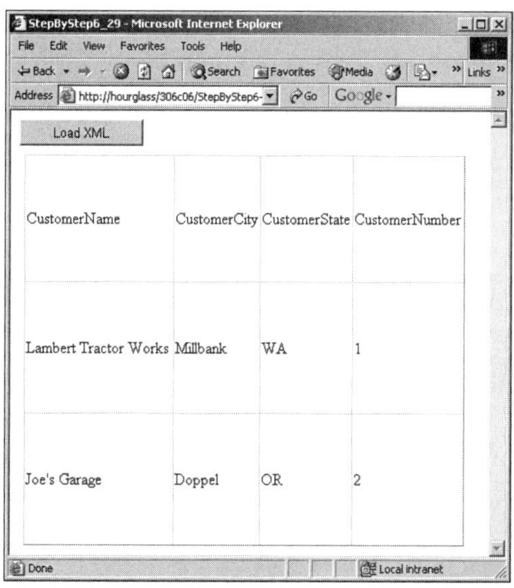

FIGURE 6.27
An XML file displayed as a `DataSet`.

NOTE

DataSet to XML You can also go in the other direction. If you've already got a DataSet in your code, you can create the equivalent XML document by calling an overloaded constructor of the XmlDataDocument class:

```
Dim xdd As XmlDataDocument = New
XmlDataDocument(ds)
```

For the DataSet to properly represent the XML, it must have the same schema (structure) as the XML file. In this example, I've ensured that by using the ReadXmlSchema method of the DataSet to load the schema from the same XML file that the XmlDataDocument holds. The XmlTextReader has to be closed and reopened after reading the schema, because it's a forward-only object.

The synchronization between the XmlDataDocument and the DataSet is two way. If you derive a DataSet from an XmlDataDocument, modify the DataSet, and then write the XmlDataDocument back to disk, the changes that you made in the DataSet will be reflected in the XML file.

GUIDED PRACTICE EXERCISE 6.4

Northwind Traders has a new European partner who doesn't use Microsoft SQL Server for its data storage. However, the European company can import an XML file to its system. In this exercise, you need to retrieve all the customers from France, allow the user to edit the customer information on a form, and then save the edited version as an XML file. Edits should consist of updates only; you do not have to support additions or deletions.

You should try doing this on your own first. If you get stuck, or you'd like to see one possible solution, follow these steps:

1. Add a new Web Form to your Visual Basic .NET web project.
2. Place a DataGrid control with the ID of dgCustomers and a Button control with the ID of btnSave on the form. Set the DataKeyField property of the DataGrid control to CustomerID.
3. Select the DataGrid control and click the Property Builder hyperlink underneath the Properties button. Click the Columns section of the dgCustomers Properties dialog box. Expand the Buttons node of the Available Columns list and add an Edit, Update, Cancel Column to the Selected Columns List. Click OK.
4. Double-click the Button control to open the form's module. Enter these statements at the top of the module:

```
Imports System.Data
Imports System.Data.SqlClient
Imports System.Xml
```

5. Enter this code to load the data when the page is opened and to manage editing operations:

```
' Create some ADO.NET objects
    Dim cnn As SqlConnection = _
     New SqlConnection("Data Source=(local);" & _
     "Initial Catalog=Northwind;" & _
     "Integrated Security=SSPI")
Dim mds As DataSet = New DataSet()
Dim mda As SqlDataAdapter = New SqlDataAdapter()

Private Sub Page_Load(ByVal sender As System.Object, _
 ByVal e As System.EventArgs) Handles MyBase.Load
    ' Set up the SqlDataAdapter
    ' Create a SqlCommand to select data
    Dim cmdSelect As SqlCommand = mcnn.CreateCommand()
    cmdSelect.CommandType = CommandType.Text
    cmdSelect.CommandText = _
     "SELECT * FROM Customers " & _
     "WHERE Country = 'France'"
    ' Create a SqlCommand to update data
    Dim cmdUpdate As SqlCommand = mcnn.CreateCommand()
    cmdUpdate.CommandType = CommandType.Text
    cmdUpdate.CommandText = _
     "UPDATE Customers SET " & _
     "CompanyName = @CompanyName, " & _
     "ContactName = @ContactName, " & _
     "ContactTitle = @ContactTitle, " & _
     "Address = @Address, " & _
     "City = @City, Region = @Region, " & _
     "PostalCode = @PostalCode, Country " & _
     "= @Country, " & _
     "Phone = @Phone, Fax = @Fax " & _
     "WHERE CustomerID = @CustomerID"
    cmdUpdate.Parameters.Add("@ContactName", _
     SqlDbType.NVarChar, _
     30, "ContactName")
    cmdUpdate.Parameters.Add("@CompanyName", _
     SqlDbType.NVarChar, _
     40, "CompanyName")
    cmdUpdate.Parameters.Add("@ContactTitle", _
     SqlDbType.NVarChar, _
     30, "ContactTitle")
    cmdUpdate.Parameters.Add("@Address", _
     SqlDbType.NVarChar, _
     60, "Address")
    cmdUpdate.Parameters.Add("@City", _
     SqlDbType.NVarChar, _
     15, "City")
    cmdUpdate.Parameters.Add("@Region", _
     SqlDbType.NVarChar, _
     15, "Region")
    cmdUpdate.Parameters.Add("@PostalCode", _
     SqlDbType.NVarChar, _
     10, "PostalCode")
```

continues

continued

```
    cmdUpdate.Parameters.Add("@Country", _
     SqlDbType.NVarChar, _
     15, "Country")
    cmdUpdate.Parameters.Add("@Phone", _
     SqlDbType.NVarChar, _
     24, "Phone")
    cmdUpdate.Parameters.Add("@Fax", _
     SqlDbType.NVarChar, _
     24, "Fax")
    cmdUpdate.Parameters.Add("@CustomerID", _
     SqlDbType.NChar, _
     5, "CustomerID")
    cmdUpdate.Parameters("@CustomerID"). _
     SourceVersion = _
     DataRowVersion.Original
    ' Set up the DataAdapter and fill the DataSet
    mda.SelectCommand = cmdSelect
    mda.UpdateCommand = cmdUpdate
    ' At page load, fill the DataGrid
    ' Get the current data from the database
    mda.Fill(mds, "Customers")
    If Not IsPostBack Then
        LoadData()
    End If
End Sub

Private Sub LoadData()
    ' Bind the data to the DataGrid
    dgCustomers.DataSource = mds
    dgCustomers.DataMember = "Customers"
    dgCustomers.DataBind()
End Sub

Private Sub dgCustomers_CancelCommand( _
 ByVal source As Object, _
 ByVal e As System.Web.UI.WebControls. _
 DataGridCommandEventArgs) _
 Handles dgCustomers.CancelCommand
    ' Cancel editing
    dgCustomers.EditItemIndex = -1
    LoadData()
End Sub

Private Sub dgCustomers_EditCommand( _
 ByVal source As Object, _
 ByVal e As System.Web.UI.WebControls. _
 DataGridCommandEventArgs) _
 Handles dgCustomers.EditCommand
    ' Enter editing mode
    dgCustomers.EditItemIndex = CInt(e.Item.ItemIndex)
    LoadData()
End Sub
```

```
Private Sub dgCustomers_UpdateCommand( _
 ByVal source As Object, _
 ByVal e As System.Web.UI.WebControls. _
 DataGridCommandEventArgs) _
 Handles dgCustomers.UpdateCommand
    Dim adrEdit() As DataRow = _
     mds.Tables("Customers"). _
      Select("CustomerID = '" & _
      dgCustomers.DataKeys(e.Item.ItemIndex) & "'")
    ' Make sure there's some data
    If UBound(adrEdit) > -1 Then
        ' Put in the edited data
        Dim txtCompanyName As TextBox = _
         e.Item.Cells(2).Controls(0)
        adrEdit(0)("CompanyName") = _
         txtCompanyName.Text
        Dim txtContactName As TextBox = _
         e.Item.Cells(3).Controls(0)
        adrEdit(0)("ContactName") = _
         txtContactName.Text
        Dim txtContactTitle As TextBox = _
         e.Item.Cells(4).Controls(0)
        adrEdit(0)("ContactTitle") = _
         txtContactTitle.Text
        Dim txtAddress As TextBox = _
         e.Item.Cells(5).Controls(0)
        adrEdit(0)("Address") = txtAddress.Text
        Dim txtCity As TextBox = _
         e.Item.Cells(6).Controls(0)
        adrEdit(0)("City") = txtCity.Text
        Dim txtRegion As TextBox = _
         e.Item.Cells(7).Controls(0)
        adrEdit(0)("Region") = txtRegion.Text
        Dim txtPostalCode As TextBox = _
         e.Item.Cells(8).Controls(0)
        adrEdit(0)("PostalCode") = txtPostalCode.Text
        Dim txtCountry As TextBox = _
         e.Item.Cells(9).Controls(0)
        adrEdit(0)("Country") = txtCountry.Text
        Dim txtPhone As TextBox = _
         e.Item.Cells(10).Controls(0)
        adrEdit(0)("Phone") = txtPhone.Text
        Dim txtFax As TextBox = _
         e.Item.Cells(11).Controls(0)
        adrEdit(0)("Fax") = txtFax.Text
    End If
    ' End editing
    dgCustomers.EditItemIndex = -1
    ' Save to the database
    mda.Update(mds, "Customers")
    ' And bind the data to the UI
    LoadData()
End Sub
```

continues

continued

6. Enter this code to save the file when the user clicks the button:

```
Private Sub btnSave_Click( _
 ByVal sender As System.Object, _
 ByVal e As System.EventArgs) Handles btnSave.Click
    ' Create an XmlDataDocument from the DataSet
    Dim xdd As XmlDataDocument = _
     New XmlDataDocument(mds)
    ' And save it to a disk file
    Dim xtw As XmlTextWriter = _
     New XmlTextWriter(Server.MapPath( _
      "FranceCust.xml"), _
     System.Text.Encoding.UTF8)
    xdd.WriteTo(xtw)
    xtw.Flush()
    xtw.Close()
End Sub
```

7. Run the project. The French customers appear on the user interface. Edit some of the data and then click the Save button. Open the `FranceCust.xml` file on your Web server to verify that it contains the edited data.

8. If you had difficulty following this exercise, review the sections titled "Using the `XmlDocument` Class" and "Treating XML as Relational Data," as well as Step By Step 6.26. The text and examples should help you in relearning this material and help you understand what just happened in this exercise. After review, try this exercise again.

There are several alternatives for meeting the requirements of this Guided Practice Exercise. You could choose to save the `DataSet` directly, instead of working with an `XmlDataDocument`, by working with the `DataSet.WriteXml` method. You might also like to let the user input a file name, instead of hard-coding the file name.

HANDLE DATA ERRORS

Consuming and Manipulating Data

- **Handle Data Errors.**

Although I've been leaving error trapping out of the code so far in this chapter for simplicity, in real life you can't afford to do that. You should always check for errors in any production code, so that you can take corrective action if something goes wrong. In this section I'll show you how to deal with two groups of data errors. First, you might attempt an operation that causes an error from the underlying database. Second, in a multiuser situation you can have errors caused by two or more users editing the same row of data.

Handling Database Errors

Many things can go wrong when you're working with a database. You might try to add a duplicate value to a column that only allows unique values, or you might try to write to a table that you don't have permission to modify. In serious cases, the database server itself might run out of disk space. These are just a few of the thousands of specific conditions that can trigger SQL Server errors.

The `System.Data.SqlClient` namespace includes two objects to help you handle SQL Server-specific errors. These are the `SqlException` class, which inherits from `System.Exception`, and the `SqlError` class, which represents a single SQL Server error.

STEP BY STEP

6.30 Trapping SQL Server Errors

1. Add a new Web Form to your Visual Basic .NET web project.
2. Place a `Button` control with the ID of `btnNew` and a `ListBox` control with the ID of `lbErrors` on the form.
3. Double-click the form to open the form's module. Enter this statement at the top of the module:

```
Imports System.Data.SqlClient
```

continues

continued

4. Enter this code to run when the user clicks the `Button` control:

```
Private Sub Page_Load(ByVal sender As System.Object, _
 ByVal e As System.EventArgs) Handles MyBase.Load
    If IsPostBack Then
        Try
            ' Create a SqlConnection
            Dim cnn As SqlConnection = _
             New SqlConnection( _
             "Data Source=(local);" & _
             "Initial Catalog=Northwind;" & _
             "Integrated Security=SSPI")
            ' Create a SqlCommand
            Dim cmd As SqlCommand = _
             cnn.CreateCommand()
            cmd.CommandType = CommandType.Text
            cmd.CommandText = _
             "INSERT INTO Customers (CompanyName) " & _
             "VALUES ('New Company')"
            ' And execute it
            cnn.Open()
            cmd.ExecuteNonQuery()
            cnn.Close()
        Catch SqlEx As SqlException
            ' Handle SQL Server specific errors
            Dim err As SqlError
            For Each err In SqlEx.Errors
                lbErrors.Items.Add("SQL Error " & _
                 err.Number & ": " & err.Message)
            Next
        Catch Ex As Exception
            ' Handle general errors
            lbErrors.Items.Add( _
             "Non-SQL Exception " & Ex.Message)
        End Try
    End If
End Sub
```

5. Set the form as the startup object for the project.

6. Run the project. Click the button. You'll get two items in the `ListBox`. The first informs you of error 515, "Cannot insert the value NULL into column '`CustomerID`', table 'Northwind.dbo.Customers'; column does not allow nulls. `INSERT` fails." The second message box informs you of error 3621, "The statement has been terminated."

As you can see in the code, the `SqlException` object exposes an Errors property. This property is a collection of `SqlError` objects, each of which contains a SQL Server error. A single SQL Server operation can raise multiple errors, as it did in this case. You should place a similar error trap in any procedure that uses the classes from `System.Data.SqlClient`.

> **EXAM TIP**
>
> **Trap All the Errors** This code actually has two different `Catch` statements. The first one will catch exceptions that are packaged as a `SqlException` object. But even if you're writing data access code, it's possible for non-data-related errors to occur. That's why there's a second `Catch` statement that uses the generic `Exception` object. Any time that you write code to catch exceptions of a specific type, you should remember to include a general-purpose `Catch` statement as well, just in case.

Handling Multi-User Errors

There's a second class of errors that you need to be aware of when you're writing database code—though actually, these are better thought of as "potentially unexpected outcomes" than as errors. Whenever you have more than one user updating the same data, concurrency issues can arise. The basic question is who wins in case of multiple updates.

Here's how the problem arises: suppose both Alice and Bob are working with data from the Customers table in a SQL Server database. They've both downloaded a `DataSet` containing the table to their local computers, and both are making edits in a `DataGrid` control. Alice changes the address of the first customer in the table, because she's working on a stack of change of address requests. Meanwhile, Bob changes the contact name for the first customer, because he's updating the sales records. So now there are three versions of the row: the original one that's still on the SQL Server, the one with a new address that's on Alice's computer, and the one with the new contact name that's on Bob's computer. Now Bob saves his changes by calling the `Update` method of the `SqlDataAdapter`, so the SQL Server database contains the new contact name.

What happens when Alice saves her changes?

The answer is, "It depends." When you're creating the `SqlCommand` object that will be used for the `UpdateCommand` property of a `SqlDataAdapter`, it's up to you to choose between two different strategies for dealing with such conflicts:

- With optimistic concurrency control, an update to a row will succeed only if no one else has changed that row after it was loaded into the `DataSet`.

- With "last one wins" concurrency control, an update to a row always succeeds, whether another user has edited the row or not (as long as the row still exists).

You've already seen how to implement "last one wins" concurrency control, in Step By Step 6.23. Consider the SQL statement that the code in that example uses to update the database:

```
UPDATE Customers
SET ContactName = @ContactName
WHERE CustomerID = @CustomerID
```

The key thing to look at here is the `WHERE` clause. The only column that it looks at is the `CustomerID` column. `CustomerID` is the primary key of this table, a value that should never change. As long as that one column has not been changed, the `UPDATE` statement will succeed, no matter what may have changed about other columns in the same table.

STEP BY STEP

6.31 Implementing Optimistic Concurrency Control

1. Add a new Web Form to your Visual Basic .NET Web project.

2. Place a `Button` control with the ID of `btnUpdate`, three Label controls, and two `TextBox` controls (`txtCustomerID` and `txtContactName`) on the form.

3. Double-click the form to open the form's module. Enter these statements at the top of the module:

```
Imports System.Data
Imports System.Data.SqlClient
```

4. Enter this code to load data when the form is opened:

```
Private Sub Page_Load(ByVal sender As System.Object, _
 ByVal e As System.EventArgs) Handles MyBase.Load
    If IsPostBack Then
        ' Create some ADO.NET objects
        Dim cnn As SqlConnection = _
         New SqlConnection("Data Source=(local);" & _
         "Initial Catalog=Northwind;" & _
         "Integrated Security=SSPI")
        Dim ds As DataSet = New DataSet()
        Dim da As SqlDataAdapter = _
         New SqlDataAdapter()
```

```
        ' Create a SqlCommand to select data
        Dim cmdSelect As SqlCommand = _
         cnn.CreateCommand()
        cmdSelect.CommandType = CommandType.Text
        cmdSelect.CommandText = _
         "SELECT CustomerID, ContactName " & _
         "FROM Customers"
        ' Create a SqlCommand to update data
        Dim cmdUpdate As SqlCommand = _
         cnn.CreateCommand()
        cmdUpdate.CommandType = CommandType.Text
        cmdUpdate.CommandText = _
         "UPDATE Customers SET " & _
         "ContactName = @ContactName WHERE " & _
         "CustomerID = @CustomerID AND " & _
         "ContactName = @ContactNameOrig"
        cmdUpdate.Parameters.Add("@ContactName", _
         SqlDbType.NVarChar, _
         30, "ContactName")
        cmdUpdate.Parameters.Add("@CustomerID", _
         SqlDbType.NChar, _
         5, "CustomerID")
        cmdUpdate.Parameters("@CustomerID"). _
         SourceVersion = _
         DataRowVersion.Original
        cmdUpdate.Parameters.Add( _
         "@ContactNameOrig", SqlDbType.NVarChar, _
         30, "ContactName")
        cmdUpdate.Parameters("@ContactNameOrig"). _
         SourceVersion = _
         DataRowVersion.Original
        ' Set up the DataAdapter and fill the DataSet
        da.SelectCommand = cmdSelect
        da.UpdateCommand = cmdUpdate
        da.Fill(ds, "Customers")
        ' Get the DataRow to edit
        Dim adrEdit() As DataRow = _
         ds.Tables("Customers").Select( _
          "CustomerID = '" & _
          txtCustomerID.Text & "'")
        ' Make sure there's some data
        If UBound(adrEdit) > -1 Then
            ' Put in the edited data
            adrEdit(0)("ContactName") = _
             txtContactName.Text
            ' Save the changes
            da.Update(ds, "Customers")
            ' And make a note on the UI
            lblResults.Text = "Row has been updated"
        End If
    End If
End Sub
```

5. Set the Web Form as the start page for the project.

continues

continued

6. Run the project. Enter a customer ID (such as ALFKI) and a new contact name, and click OK. The code writes the change back to the database and shows the "Row has been updated" text on the form.

The only difference between this version of the update code and the earlier version is in the `UPDATE` SQL statement, which now has a different `WHERE` clause:

```
UPDATE Customers
SET ContactName = @ContactName
WHERE CustomerID = @CustomerID AND
ContactName = @ContactNameOrig
```

The new `WHERE` clause will find a row to update only if both the `CustomerID` and `ContactName` are unchanged from what they were when the row was originally loaded. If you'd like to experiment with this, you can run two copies of the code at the same time. Load the data in both copies, then change the contact name with one copy. You'll find that you cannot then change the contact name with the second copy.

EXAM TIP

Retrieve Whole Tables Strictly speaking, you can only enforce optimistic concurrency control if you check every column of the table in the `WHERE` clause. If you only retrieve a few columns, it's possible to miss a change in a column that you didn't retrieve.

REVIEW BREAK

- Every real-world application should include error trapping. Data manipulation adds some special requirements to error trapping code.
- The `SqlException` and `SqlError` objects provide you with the means to retrieve SQL Server specific error information.
- You can choose when you're designing update commands between optimistic concurrency and "last one wins" concurrency.

CHAPTER SUMMARY

The .NET Framework offers an incredible amount of flexibility for consuming and manipulating data. In this chapter, you've seen a broad survey of various techniques for dealing with data. As you continue to work with Visual Basic .NET, you'll discover more advanced techniques in all these areas.

SQL Server is an important data source for .NET applications. To deal effectively with SQL Server data, you need to have an understanding of the T-SQL language. In this chapter you learned the basics of T-SQL, including the `SELECT`, `INSERT`, `UPDATE`, and `DELETE` statements. You also saw how to execute SQL in ad hoc queries and in stored procedures.

The .NET Framework also includes classes for manipulating disk files. These classes are part of the `System.IO` namespace, which treats data as streams that are supplied by backing stores. You learned how to browse for files as well as how to read and write files.

The major part of the chapter dealt with the ADO.NET objects, which span multiple namespaces. ADO.NET includes both data provider objects, which are tied to specific data sources, and `DataSet` objects, which provide a purely abstract view of relational data. After seeing the object model, you learned how to apply it to a number of problems, including loading and saving data, finding and sorting data, and editing data.

You also saw the key classes that are used for dealing with XML. These classes, `XmlNode` and `XmlDocument`, are contained in the `System.Xml` namespace. XML data can also be loaded into `DataSet` objects, allowing you to treat XML files as relational databases.

Finally, you learned about some of the key issues involved in error handling for data-oriented applications. This includes the classes that are available for catching SQL Server errors and the issues surrounding multi-user concurrency control.

KEY TERMS

- Transact-SQL
- SQL-92
- Ad-hoc query
- Stored procedure
- OSQL
- SQL Query Analyzer
- Parameter
- Identity
- Stream
- Backing store
- Data Provider
- DataSet
- Schema
- XML
- XML Declaration
- Element
- Attribute
- XML Namespace
- CDATA Section
- "Last one wins" concurrency control
- Optimistic concurrency control

APPLY YOUR KNOWLEDGE

Exercises

6.1 Preselecting Data with Parameterized Stored Procedures

One of the biggest issues in working with server-side data such as SQL Server data is to minimize the amount of data that you load into your application. That's because communications with such servers are typically comparatively slow, while the servers themselves have enough processing power to quickly locate the exact data that you want. In this exercise, you'll see how you can minimize the amount of data retrieved by using a series of stored procedures with parameters.

Estimated Time: 30 minutes.

1. Create a new Visual Basic .NET Web project to use for the exercises in this chapter.

2. Add a new Web Form to the project.

3. Place a `DropDownList` control with the ID of `ddlCustomers`, a `Button` control with the ID of `btnLoad`, and a `DataGrid` control with the ID of `dgMain` on the form.

4. Double-click the form to open the form's module. Enter these statements at the top of the module:

```
Imports System.Data
Imports System.Data.SqlClient
```

5. Use a tool such as SQL Query Analyzer to create this stored procedure:

```
CREATE PROC procCustomerList
AS
SELECT CustomerID, CompanyName
FROM Customers
ORDER BY CompanyName
```

6. Use a tool such as SQL Query Analyzer to create this stored procedure:

```
CREATE PROC procOrdersForCustomer
  @CustomerID char(5)
AS
SELECT * FROM Orders
WHERE CustomerID = @CustomerID
```

7. To minimize load time, the form will start by loading only the customer list into the `ComboBox` control. Enter this code to load the customer list:

```
Dim mcnn As SqlConnection = _
 New SqlConnection( _
 "Data Source=(local);" & _
 "Initial Catalog=Northwind;" & _
 "Integrated Security=SSPI")

Private Sub Page_Load( _
 ByVal sender As System.Object, _
 ByVal e As System.EventArgs) _
 Handles MyBase.Load
    If Not IsPostBack Then
        ' Load the customer list
        Dim cmdCustomers As SqlCommand = _
         mcnn.CreateCommand
        cmdCustomers.CommandType = _
         CommandType.StoredProcedure
        cmdCustomers.CommandText = _
         "procCustomerList"
        mcnn.Open()
        Dim ds As DataSet = New DataSet()
        Dim da As SqlDataAdapter = _
         New SqlDataAdapter()
        da.SelectCommand = cmdCustomers
        da.Fill(ds, "Customers")
        With ddlCustomers
            .DataSource = _
             ds.Tables("Customers")
            .DataTextField = "CompanyName"
            .DataValueField = "CustomerID"
            .DataBind()
        End With
        mcnn.Close()
    End If
End Sub
```

APPLY YOUR KNOWLEDGE

8. When the user clicks the Load button, you'll use the other stored procedures to load only the data of interest. Enter this code to build the `DataSet` and bind it to the `DataGrid`:

```
Private Sub btnLoad_Click( _
 ByVal sender As System.Object, _
 ByVal e As System.EventArgs) _
 Handles btnLoad.Click
    ' Create a new DataSet
    Dim ds As DataSet = New DataSet()
    ' Load the orders for the
    ' selected customer
    Dim cmdOrders As SqlCommand = _
     mcnn.CreateCommand()
    cmdOrders.CommandType = _
     CommandType.StoredProcedure
    cmdOrders.CommandText = _
     "procOrdersForCustomer"
    cmdOrders.Parameters.Add(New _
     SqlParameter("@CustomerID", _
     SqlDbType.Text, 5))
    cmdOrders.Parameters( _
     "@CustomerID").Value = _
     ddlCustomers.SelectedItem.Value
    Dim daOrders As SqlDataAdapter = _
     New SqlDataAdapter()
    daOrders.SelectCommand = cmdOrders
    daOrders.Fill(ds, "Orders")
    ' Bind the data to the user interface
    dgMain.DataSource = ds
    dgMain.DataMember = "Orders"
    dgMain.DataBind()
End Sub
```

9. Set the Web Form as the start page for the project.

10. Run the project. Select a customer from the list in the `DropDownList` and then press the Load button. The form will display only the orders for that customer, as shown in Figure 6.28.

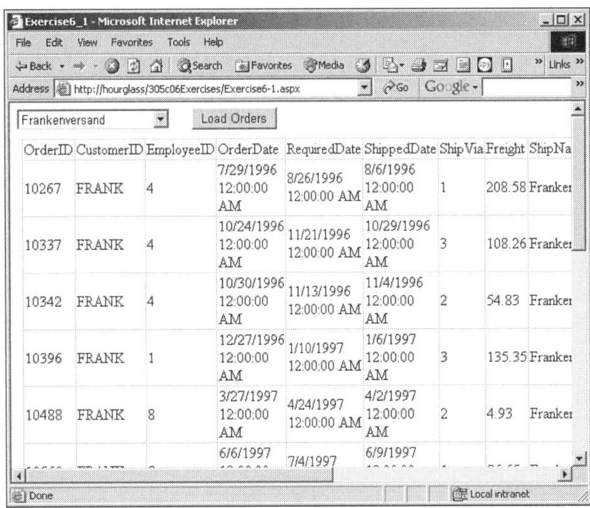

FIGURE 6.28
Retrieving data on a particular customer's orders.

6.2 Transferring Database Data to a Disk File

The `DataSet` object has facilities for saving data as XML. But sometimes file size is more important than the readability that XML brings to the table. In this exercise, you'll retrieve data from a database and then use the `BinaryWriter` class to write it out as a compact disk file.

Estimated Time: 20 minutes.

1. Add a new Web Form to your Visual Basic .NET web project.

2. Place a `DropDownList` control with the ID of `ddlProducts`, a `Label` control with the ID of `lblResults`, and a `Button` control with the ID of `btnWrite` on the form.

APPLY YOUR KNOWLEDGE

3. Double-click the `Button` to open the form's module. Enter these statements at the top of the module:

```
Imports System.Data
Imports System.Data.SqlClient
Imports System.IO
```

4. The form initializes the list of products at load time. Enter this code to load the list of products:

```
Dim mcnn As SqlConnection = _
 New SqlConnection( _
 "Data Source=(local);" & _
 "Initial Catalog=Northwind;" & _
 "Integrated Security=SSPI")

Private Sub Page_Load( _
 ByVal sender As System.Object, _
 ByVal e As System.EventArgs) _
 Handles MyBase.Load
    If Not IsPostBack Then
        ' Load the customer list
        Dim cmd As SqlCommand = _
         mcnn.CreateCommand()
        cmd.CommandType = CommandType.Text
        cmd.CommandText = _
         "SELECT ProductName, " & _
         "ProductID " & _
         "FROM Products " & _
         "ORDER BY ProductName"
        mcnn.Open()
        Dim ds As DataSet = New DataSet()
        Dim da As SqlDataAdapter = _
         New SqlDataAdapter()
        da.SelectCommand = cmd
        da.Fill(ds, "Products")
        With ddlProducts
            .DataSource = _
             ds.Tables("Products")
            .DataTextField = "ProductName"
            .DataValueField = "ProductID"
            .DataBind()
        End With
        mcnn.Close()
    End If
End Sub
```

5. Enter this code to handle the button's click event. This code retrieves the `DataRow` of interest and then uses a `BinaryWriter` to move it, field by field, to a disk file. The code uses the `SaveFileDialog` class to prompt for a filename.

```
Private Sub btnWrite_Click( _
 ByVal sender As System.Object, _
 ByVal e As System.EventArgs) _
 Handles btnWrite.Click
    ' Get the full data on
    ' the selected product
    Dim cmdProduct As SqlCommand = _
     mcnn.CreateCommand()
    cmdProduct.CommandType = _
     CommandType.Text
    cmdProduct.CommandText = _
     "SELECT * FROM Products " & _
     "WHERE ProductID = @ProductID"
        cmdProduct.Parameters.Add(New _
         SqlParameter("@ProductID", _
         SqlDbType.Int))
    cmdProduct.Parameters("@ProductID"). _
     Value = _
     ddlProducts.SelectedItem.Value
        ' Open a BinaryWriter
    Dim fsOut As FileStream = _
     New FileStream( _
     Server.MapPath(ddlProducts. _
     SelectedItem.Text & ".dat"), _
     FileMode.Create)
        Dim bw As BinaryWriter = _
         New BinaryWriter(fsOut)
        ' Get the data into a DataRow
        Dim da As SqlDataAdapter = _
         New SqlDataAdapter()
        da.SelectCommand = cmdProduct
        Dim ds As DataSet = New DataSet()
        da.Fill(ds, "Products")
        Dim dr As DataRow = ds.Tables( _
         "Products").Rows(0)
        ' And write the data
        Dim intI As Integer
        For intI = 0 To 9
            bw.Write(dr(intI))
        Next
        bw.Flush()
        bw.Close()
    lblResults.Text = "Data written"
End Sub
```

APPLY YOUR KNOWLEDGE

6. Set the Web Form as the start page for the project.

7. Run the project. Select a customer from the list in the `DropDownList` and click the Write button to save the corresponding `DataRow` through a `BinaryWriter` class. The file is saved to the root directory of the web project on your Web server.

Review Questions

1. Describe the difference between an ad hoc query and a stored procedure.

2. List and describe the four basic T-SQL statements.

3. Name four ways that you can execute SQL statements.

4. In a T-SQL `SELECT` statement, what is the difference between the `WHERE` clause and the `HAVING` clause?

5. What is the purpose of the `@@IDENTITY` variable?

6. What is a stream? What is a backing store?

7. How should you decide between using a `StreamReader` object and using a `BinaryReader` object?

8. Describe the difference between the data provider objects and the `DataSet` objects.

9. Which ADO.NET object do you use to execute a stored procedure?

10. Which ADO.NET object transfers data between the database and the data model?

11. What are the advantages of strongly typed `DataSets`?

12. Which XML object can you synchronize with a `DataSet` object?

13. Name and describe the two main types of concurrency control that you can implement in .NET.

Exam Questions

1. Your SQL Server database contains a table, Sales, with these columns:

   `SalesID` (`int`, `identity`)

   `StoreNumber` (`int`)

   `DailySales` (`int`)

   You want to see a list of each store, together with its total daily sales. The list should be filtered to only include stores with a total daily sale of more than 10. Which SQL statement should you use?

   A. `SELECT StoreNumber, DailySales FROM Sales WHERE DailySales > 10`

   B. `SELECT StoreNumber, SUM(DailySales) FROM Sales WHERE DailySales > 10 GROUP BY StoreNumber`

   C. `SELECT StoreNumber, SUM(DailySales) FROM Sales GROUP BY StoreNumber HAVING SUM(DailySales) > 10`

   D. `SELECT StoreNumber, SUM(DailySales) FROM Sales WHERE DailySales > 10 GROUP BY StoreNumber HAVING SUM(DailySales) > 10`

APPLY YOUR KNOWLEDGE

2. Your SQL Server database contains a table, Sales, with these columns:

   `SalesID` (int, identity)

   `StoreNumber` (int)

   `DailySales` (int)

   You want to see a list of each store, together with its total daily sales. The list should be filtered to only include rows from the table where the daily sales is more than 10. Which SQL statement should you use?

   A. `SELECT StoreNumber, DailySales FROM Sales WHERE DailySales > 10`

   B. `SELECT StoreNumber, SUM(DailySales) FROM Sales WHERE DailySales > 10 GROUP BY StoreNumber`

   C. `SELECT StoreNumber, SUM(DailySales) FROM Sales GROUP BY StoreNumber HAVING SUM(DailySales) > 10`

   D. `SELECT StoreNumber, SUM(DailySales) FROM Sales WHERE DailySales > 10 GROUP BY StoreNumber HAVING SUM(DailySales) > 10`

3. Your SQL Server database contains a table, Experiments, with the following columns:

   `ExperimentID` (int, identity)

   `ExperimentType` (char(1))

   `ExperimentDate` (datetime)

   You wish to delete all rows from the table where the `ExperimentType` value is either "A" or "C". You do not wish to delete any other rows. Which SQL statement should you use?

   A. `DELETE FROM Experiments WHERE ExperimentType LIKE '[AC]'`

   B. `DELETE FROM Experiments WHERE ExperimentType LIKE '[A-C]'`

   C. `DELETE FROM Experiments WHERE ExperimentType LIKE 'A' OR 'C'`

   D. `DELETE * FROM Experiments WHERE ExperimentType IN ('A', 'C')`

4. Your SQL Server database contains a table, Sales, with these columns:

   `SalesID` (int, identity)

   `StoreNumber` (int)

   `DailySales` (int)

   You wish to create a stored procedure that accepts as inputs the store number and daily sales, inserts a new row in the table with this information, and returns the new identity value. Which SQL statement should you use?

   A.

```
CREATE PROCEDURE procInsertSales
  @StoreNumber int,
  @DailySales int,
  @SalesID int
AS
  INSERT INTO Sales (
  StoreNumber, DailySales)
  VALUES (@StoreNumber, @DailySales)
  SELECT @SalesID = @@IDENTITY
```

   B.

```
CREATE PROCEDURE procInsertSales
  @StoreNumber int,
  @DailySales int,
  @SalesID int OUTPUT
AS
  INSERT INTO Sales (
  SalesID, StoreNumber, DailySales)
  VALUES (@SalesID, @StoreNumber,

  @DailySales)
```

APPLY YOUR KNOWLEDGE

C.

```
CREATE PROCEDURE procInsertSales
  @StoreNumber int,
  @DailySales int,
  @SalesID int OUTPUT
AS
  INSERT INTO Sales (
  SalesID, StoreNumber, DailySales)
  VALUES (0, @StoreNumber, @DailySales)
  SELECT @SalesID = @@IDENTITY
```

D.

```
CREATE PROCEDURE procInsertSales
  @StoreNumber int,
  @DailySales int,
  @SalesID int OUTPUT
AS
  INSERT INTO Sales (StoreNumber,
  DailySales)
  VALUES (@StoreNumber, @DailySales)
  SELECT @SalesID = @@IDENTITY
```

5. Your application has two `FileStream` objects. The `fsIn` object is open for reading, and the `fsOut` object is open for writing. Which code snippet will copy the contents of `fsIn` to `fsOut` using a 2KB buffer?

A.

```
Dim buf(2048) As Integer
Dim intBytesRead As Integer
Do While ((intBytesRead = _
 fsIn.Read(buf, 0, 2048)) > 0)
   fsOut.Write(buf, 0, intBytesRead)
Loop
' Clean up
fsOut.Flush()
fsOut.Close()
fsIn.Close()
```

B.

```
Dim buf(2048) As Integer
Dim intBytesRead As Integer
Do While ((intBytesRead = _
 fsIn.Read(buf, 0, 2048)) > 1)
   fsOut.Write(buf, 0, intBytesRead)
Loop
' Clean up
fsOut.Flush()
fsOut.Close()
fsIn.Close()
```

C.

```
Dim buf(2048) As Byte
Dim intBytesRead As Integer
Do While ((intBytesRead = _
 fsIn.Read(buf, 0, 2048)) > 0)
   fsOut.Write(buf, 0, intBytesRead)
Loop
' Clean up
fsOut.Flush()
fsOut.Close()
fsIn.Close()
```

D.

```
Dim buf(2048) As Byte
Dim intBytesRead As Integer
Do While ((intBytesRead = _
 fsIn.Read(buf, 0, 2048)) > 1)
   fsOut.Write(buf, 0, intBytesRead)
Loop
' Clean up
fsOut.Flush()
fsOut.Close()
fsIn.Close()
```

6. Your application includes 15 double-precision floating point numbers that you wish to write out to a disk file. You'd like to minimize the size of the disk file. Which object should you use to write the file?

   A. `FileStream`

   B. `StreamWriter`

   C. `BinaryWriter`

   D. `XmlTextWriter`

APPLY YOUR KNOWLEDGE

7. Your application needs to return the total number of customers in the database. What is the fastest way to do this?

   A. Write ad hoc SQL to return the total number of customers. Use the `SqlCommand.ExecuteScalar` method to execute the SQL statement.

   B. Write ad hoc SQL to return the total number of customers. Use the `SqlDataAdapter.Fill` method to execute the SQL statement.

   C. Create a stored procedure to return the total number of customers. Use the `SqlCommand.ExecuteScalar` method to execute the stored procedure.

   D. Create a stored procedure to return the total number of customers. Use the `SqlDataAdapter.Fill` method to execute the stored procedure.

8. Your application needs to retrieve a list of customer balances from a SQL Server database. The application moves through the list once, processing each balance in turn. The application does not need to write to the database. Which object should you use to hold the list in the data model?

   A. `DataSet`

   B. `SqlDataReader`

   C. `DataTable`

   D. `DataView`

9. Your SQL Server database contains customer and order information. The Order table includes a foreign key that refers to the Customer table. You have loaded the Customer and Order tables into a single `DataSet` through two separate `SqlDataAdapter` objects. The `DataSet` is bound to a `DataGrid` on your application's user interface. When you run the application, only customer information appears in the `DataGrid`. You have verified that there are orders in the database. What is the most likely cause of this problem?

   A. You must use a single `SqlDataAdapter` object to load both tables.

   B. The Web Forms `DataGrid` control can only display a single table at a time.

   C. There are no orders for the first customer displayed on the `DataGrid`.

   D. The `DataGrid` can only display information from a single table.

10. Your application uses a `SqlDataReader` object to retrieve information on customer balances. When you find a past-due balance, you wish to write a new entry to a billing table by executing a stored procedure in the same database. You have used a `SqlCommand` object to represent the stored procedure. Calling the `ExecuteNonQuery` method of the `SqlCommand` object is causing an error. What is the most likely cause of this error?

    A. You must use a `SqlDataAdapter` object to execute the stored procedure.

    B. You must use an ad hoc SQL statement rather than a stored procedure to insert new rows in a database.

APPLY YOUR KNOWLEDGE

C. You are using the `ExecuteNonQuery` method of the `SqlCommand` object, and should be using the `ExecuteScalar` method instead.

D. You are using the same `SqlConnection` object for both the `SqlDataReader` object and the `SqlCommand` object, and the `SqlDataReader` is still open when you try to execute the `SqlCommand`.

11. Your application allows the user to edit product data on a `DataGrid` control. The `DataGrid` is bound to a `DataSet`. The `DataSet` is filled through a `SqlDataAdapter` object. The `InsertCommand`, `UpdateCommand`, and `DeleteCommand` properties of the `SqlDataAdapter` are set to `SqlCommand` objects, and you have tested the SQL in those `SqlCommand` objects.

    When users exit the application, none of their changes are saved to the database, and they do not receive any errors. What could be the problem?

    A. You have neglected to call the `SqlDataAdapter.Update` method in your code.

    B. The users do not have permission to write to the database.

    C. You have neglected to fill the `DataSet` from the `DataGrid` after the users finish editing the data.

    D. The `DataSet` is a read-only object.

12. Your application includes a `DataSet` that contains a `DataTable` named Suppliers. This `DataTable` contains all rows from the Suppliers table in your database. You wish to bind an object to a `DataGrid` on a form such that the `DataGrid` displays only the Suppliers from Pennsylvania. What should you do?

    A. Create a filtered array by calling the `DataTable.Select` method on the Suppliers `DataTable` and bind the array to the `DataGrid`.

    B. Create a new `SqlCommand` object to retrieve only suppliers from Pennsylvania. Use a new `SqlDataAdapter` to fill a new `DataSet` with these suppliers. Bind the new `DataSet` to the `DataGrid`.

    C. Use a `For Each` loop to move through the entire Suppliers `DataTable`. Each time you find a `DataRow` representing a supplier from Pennsylvania, bind that `DataRow` to the `DataGrid`.

    D. Create a filtered `DataView` from the Suppliers `DataTable` and bind the `DataView` to the `DataGrid`.

13. You allow users to edit Product information on a `DataGrid` bound to a `DataSet`. When the user clicks the Update button on the form, you call the `SqlDataAdapter.Update` method to persist the changes from the `DataSet` to the underlying database.

    Users report that new records and updated rows are saved properly, but that deleted rows are reappearing the next time they run the application. What could be the problem?

    A. The users do not have permission to update the underlying table.

    B. The `Update` method does not delete rows.

    C. Someone is restoring an old version of the database between the two executions of the program.

    D. The `DeleteCommand` property of the `SqlDataAdapter` points to a `SqlCommand` object that does not properly delete rows.

APPLY YOUR KNOWLEDGE

14. Your application recursively calls the `FirstChild` and `NextChild` methods of `XmlNode` objects to visit every node in an XML file. When you find a node that includes customer name information, you store the information. The application is not returning all the customer names from the file. What could be the problem?

    A. The XML file is not well-formed.

    B. The XML file has more than one root node.

    C. The customer name information is stored in XML attributes.

    D. The `HasChildNodes` property is not properly set on all nodes.

15. Your application reads an XML file from disk into an `XmlDocument` object, and then modifies some of the nodes in the document. Which object should you use to write the modified `XmlDocument` object back to disk?

    A. `XmlTextWriter`

    B. `FileStream`

    C. `StreamWriter`

    D. `BinaryWriter`

16. You have designed your application to use optimistic concurrency control. Alice and Bob each retrieve the products table to the application at 8:00 AM. The initial price of a widget is $3. At 8:05 AM, Alice changes the price of a widget to $4 and saves her changes to the database. At 8:10 AM, Bob changes the price of a widget to $5 and saves his changes to the database. What will be the price of a widget in the database at 8:11 AM if no one makes any other changes?

    A. $3

    B. $4

    C. $5

    D. $9

Answers to Review Questions

1. An ad hoc query consists of SQL statements that are sent to the server. A stored procedure consists of SQL statements that are permanently stored on the server.
2. The `SELECT` statement retrieves data, the `UPDATE` statement updates existing data, the `INSERT` statement adds new data, and the `DELETE` statement deletes data.
3. Using the Visual Studio IDE, through `osql`, through Sql Query Analyzer, or with your own homegrown solutions.
4. The `WHERE` clause restricts the output of the statement. The `HAVING` clause restricts the rows that are used as input to an aggregate.
5. The `@@IDENTITY` variable returns the last identity value to have been assigned to a table.
6. A stream is a file viewed as a list of bytes. A backing store is a place where data can be stored.
7. The `StreamReader` is most useful when you're dealing with a line-oriented text file. The `BinaryWriter` is most useful when you're working with a file in a particular format.
8. There are multiple sets of platform- and product-specific data provider objects. There's a single set of `DataSet` objects which holds abstract data that's not directly associated with any database.

APPLY YOUR KNOWLEDGE

9. The `SqlCommand` object can be used to execute a stored procedure.
10. The `SqlDataAdapter` object is the pipeline between the data model and the `dataset`.
11. Strongly typed `datasets` give you the benefit of IntelliSense at design time. They also provide faster data binding than automatic `datasets`.
12. The `XmlDataDocument` object can be synchronized with a `DataSet`.
13. With optimistic concurrency control, an update to a row will succeed only if no one else has changed that row after it was loaded into the `DataSet`. With "last one wins" concurrency control, an update to a row always succeeds, whether another user has edited the row or not (as long as the row still exists).

Answers to Exam Questions

1. **C.** The `GROUP BY` clause is required to obtain aggregate numbers. The `HAVING` clause filters the results after the aggregation has been performed. The answers containing the `WHERE` clause are incorrect because `WHERE` filters the input to the aggregations.
2. **B.** The `GROUP BY` clause is required to obtain aggregate numbers. The `WHERE` clause filters rows before aggregating them. The answers containing the `HAVING` clause are incorrect because `HAVING` filters the results after aggregation.
3. **A.** Answer B would also delete rows with an `ExperimentType` of B. Answer C would take the `OR` of "A" and "C" before evaluating the `LIKE` clause. `DELETE *` is not valid T-SQL syntax.
4. **D.** Answer A does not indicate that `@SalesID` is an output parameter. Answers B and C attempt to insert values into the identity column, rather than letting SQL Server assign the new value.
5. **C.** The `Read` method returns the number of bytes read, so answers B and D fail when there is 1 byte in the file. The `Read` method reads to a byte array, so answers A and B will fail because the buffer has the wrong data type.
6. **B.** The `BinaryWriter` provides a compact format for data storage on disk, as long as you don't need the data to be human-readable. All the other objects will store the data as ASCII text, which will take more space.
7. **C.** Stored procedures execute faster than the corresponding ad hoc SQL statements because stored procedures are stored in the database in compiled form. The `ExecuteScalar` method is faster than filling a `DataSet` for returning a single value.
8. **B.** The `SqlDataReader` gives you a fast, forward-only, read-only view of the data. It's ideal for processing all rows once without extra overhead.
9. **B.** If you've worked extensively with the Windows Forms `DataGrid`, you're probably used to its feature of displaying multiple hierarchical tables in a single grid. The Web version of the control has no such feature. You'll need to implement a different interface (such as two different `DataGrid` controls) to show multiple tables.
10. **D.** While a `SqlDataReader` object is open, you cannot execute other commands on the `SqlConnection` that the `SqlDataReader` is using.

APPLY YOUR KNOWLEDGE

11. **A.** If you do not call the `SqlDataAdapter.Update` method, all changes to the data model will be lost. Answer B would return an error to the users. Answer C is incorrect because a bound `DataSet` automatically reflects changes to the `DataGrid`. Answer D is incorrect because `DataSets` are designed to be edited.

12. **D.** Answers A and C do not give you objects that can be bound to the `DataGrid`. Answer B will work, but retrieving the data from the database a second time will be slower than filtering it from the existing `DataTable`.

13. **D.** If answers A or C were the case, none of the changes would be saved. Answer B is simply incorrect.

14. **C.** By default, XML attributes do not appear as part of the `XmlNodes` collections that are traversed by the `FirstChild` and `NextChild` methods. If answers A or B were the case, then you would not be able to load the file into an `XmlDocument`. Answer D is incorrect because `HasChildNodes` is automatically set by the .NET Framework.

15. **A.** The `XmlTextWriter` is designed to write XML files, preserving the proper XML structure.

16. **B.** With optimistic concurrency control, Bob's change will not be written to the database.

Suggested Readings and Resources

1. SQL Server Books Online
   - Transact-SQL Reference
2. Visual Studio .NET Combined Help Collection
3. .NET Framework SDK Documentation
   - Accessing Data With ADO.NET
4. Gunderloy, Mike. *ADO and ADO.NET Programming*. Sybex, 2002.
5. Vaughn, Bill. *ADO.NET and ADO Examples and Best Practices for VB Programmers*. Apress, 2002.
6. Delaney, Kalen. *Inside SQL Server 2000*. Microsoft Press, 2000.
7. Jones, A. Russell. *Mastering ASP.NET with VB.NET*. Sybex, 2002.
8. Esposito, Dino. *Building Web Applications with ASP.NET and ADO.NET*. Microsoft Press, 2002.

OBJECTIVES

This chapter covers the following Microsoft-specified objective for the Creating User Services section of the Visual Basic .NET Web-Based Applications exam:

Instantiate and invoke a .NET component.

- One of the benefits of working with ASP.NET is that it encourages component-based development. Components allow you to write code once and use it many times. This objective requires you to understand the big picture of component use in the .NET Framework. You'll need to understand the overall component architecture of .NET, as well as how to create and consume components in your own applications.

- This chapter also covers the following Microsoft-specified objectives for the Creating and Managing Components and .NET Assemblies section of the Visual Basic .NET Web-Based Applications exam:

Create Web custom controls and Web user controls.

Create and modify a .NET assembly.

- **Create and implement satellite assemblies.**
- **Create resource-only assemblies.**

- Controls and assemblies are two particular types of components that you can create and use in ASP.NET.

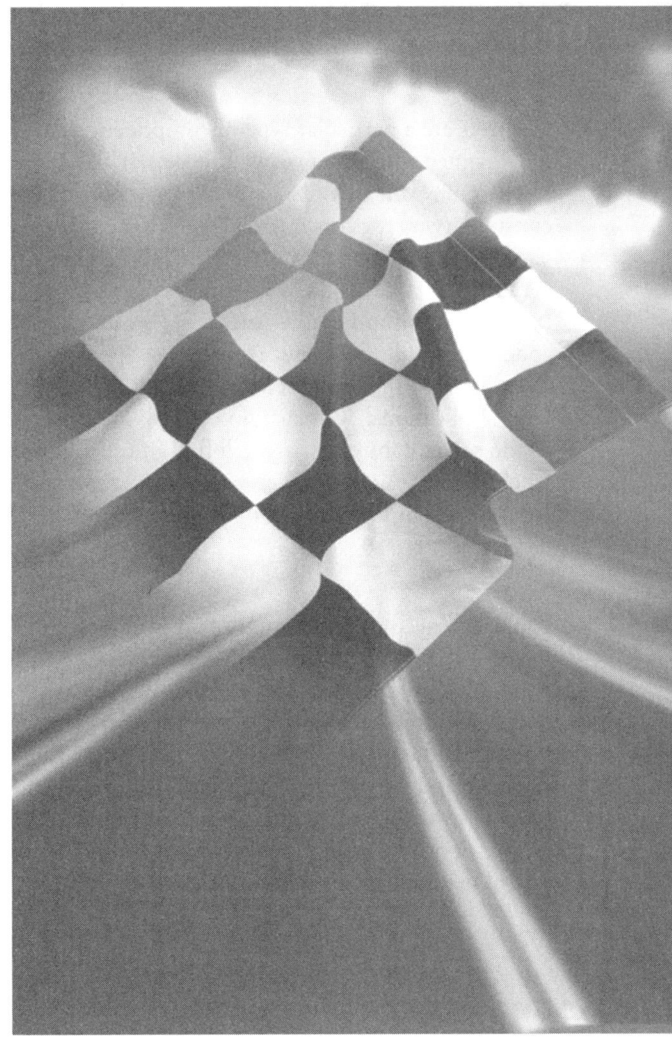

CHAPTER 7

Creating and Managing Components and .NET Assemblies

Objectives

- Controls are a particular type of component that are designed to be used on Web Forms. This objective requires you to understand how to create and consume two types of controls. Web user controls let you define new controls with an architecture very similar to that of a Web Form: Web user controls consist of both a user interface page and a code-behind file. Web user controls are appropriate for static information that is used frequently in your applications. Web custom controls are closer to the server controls that you'll find in the Toolbox when you're designing a web page. Web custom controls are appropriate for innovative dynamic displays.

- You'll also need to understand the role of assemblies in the .NET Framework for this objective. Assemblies are the fundamental unit of .NET for many purposes, including security boundaries, versioning, and deployment. You'll need to know how to create and use assemblies, including two special types of assemblies. Satellite assemblies contain localization information, while resource-only assemblies are used to add resources to applications.

Outline

Study Strategies

- Review the Component Authoring Walkthroughs topic in the Visual Studio .NET Combined Help Collection. Work through several of the walkthroughs to be sure that you understand the .NET component architecture.
- Review the Web Forms User Controls and Authoring Custom Controls QuickStart Tutorials from the .NET Framework SDK.
- Create your own user control and custom control and try hosting them on the same Web Form. Note the differences in both creating and using the two types of controls.

INTRODUCTION

Software development would be much more difficult than it actually is if we had to write the code for each new application from scratch. Fortunately, we don't have to do so. Code reuse is an important part of software engineering. You can reuse code by cutting and pasting, or by building it into a callable library of routines. This chapter covers another way to reuse code: by building it into reusable components.

By packaging your code as a component, you gain several benefits:

- Because the interfaces of components are standardized, your component can be easily used in many projects.
- Components can be tested and debugged once, and then used many times.
- Some components, such as user controls, can help provide a consistent visual interface across multiple applications.
- Components let your divide labor among developers of differing skills and experience more effectively.

In this chapter, you'll learn about several types of components supported by .NET. I'll begin by exploring components that derive from the Component class within the .NET Framework. Then I'll discuss Web user controls and Web custom controls, which provide two different reuse models for ASP.NET applications. Finally, I'll discuss assemblies, which can be used to group components together for security, deployment, and versioning.

CREATING AND USING .NET COMPONENTS

Instantiate and invoke a .NET component.

There are many ways to reuse code. For example, you might simply cut and paste code from one application to another. For more organized code reuse, you might create a class library that can be referenced from many different applications.

Although you can refer to any piece of reusable code as a component, the .NET Framework has formalized the notion of a component as a class that implements the IComponent interface (normally by inheriting from the base Component class). Components in this sense have advanced capabilities including a specified architecture for managing resources and support for use on containers such as forms.

In this section, you'll see how you can create a component with Visual Basic .NET, and how you can add properties and methods to the component. At the end of the section, you should understand the basic mechanics of component use in the .NET Framework. Other specialized components such as controls build on this foundation.

Creating a Component

To create a component, you derive a class from the System.Component base class. But to effectively program with components, you'll need to set up a class library to contain the component, and a project to test the component. Step by Step 7.1 shows you how to begin working with a component.

STEP BY STEP

7.1 Creating and Testing a Component

1. Launch Visual Studio .NET. Click the New Project button on the Start Page. Select the Visual Studio Solutions project type and create a new Blank Solution named 305C07.
2. Right-click the solution in Solution Explorer. Select Add, Add New Project. Add a new Visual Basic Class Library project named QueComponents.
3. Right-click the new project in Solution Explorer. Select Add, Add New Component. This will open the Add New Item dialog box with the Component Class template selected, as shown in Figure 7.1. Name the new component RandomNumber.vb and click Open.

continues

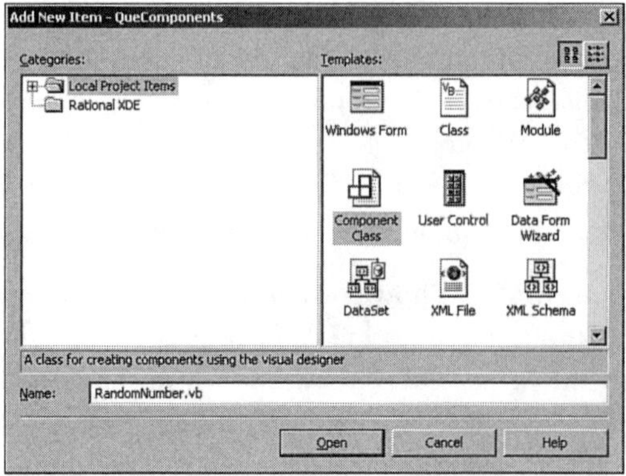

FIGURE 7.1
Creating a new Component class.

4. Delete the default Class1.vb class from the project.

5. The new component will open with a blank designer where you can drop other components. Right-click this design surface and select View Code. Expand the Component Designer generated code region. Modify the New and Dispose methods as follows:

```
Public Sub New()
    MyBase.New()

    'This call is required by
    'the Component Designer.
    InitializeComponent()

    'Add any initialization after
    ' the InitializeComponent() call
    StartRandom()
End Sub

'Component overrides dispose to clean
'up the component list.
Protected Overloads Overrides Sub Dispose( _
 ByVal disposing As Boolean)
    If disposing Then
        If Not (components Is Nothing) Then
            components.Dispose()
        End If
    End If
    mRandom = Nothing
    MyBase.Dispose(disposing)
End Sub
```

6. Add this code after the Component Designer generated code region:

```
Private mRandom As System.Random

Private Sub StartRandom()
    mRandom = New System.Random()
End Sub

Protected Overrides Sub Finalize()
    Dispose(False)
    MyBase.Finalize()
End Sub
```

7. Right-click the solution in Solution Explorer. Select Add, Add New Project. Add a new Visual Basic ASP.NET Web Application library project named RandomTimerTest.

8. Right-click the References folder in the new project and select Add Reference. Click the Projects tab of the Add Reference dialog box and select the QueComponents project, as shown in Figure 7.2. Click OK.

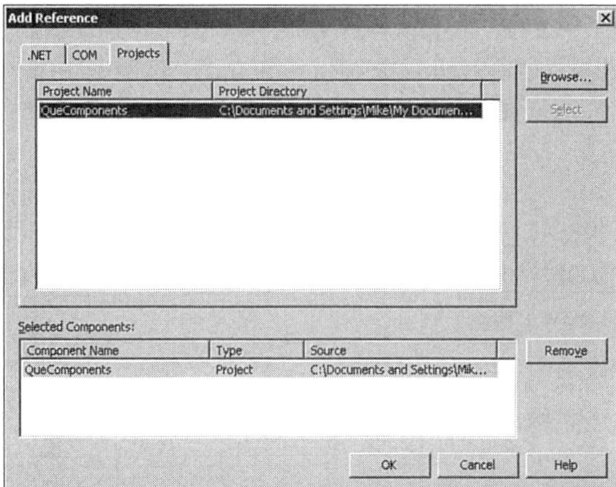

FIGURE 7.2
Setting a reference to the class library.

9. Switch to code view of the default WebForm1.aspx Web Form. Enter this code at the top of the module:

```
Imports QueComponents
```

10. Enter this code to handle the page's `Load` event:

```
Private Sub Page_Load( _
 ByVal sender As System.Object, _
 ByVal e As System.EventArgs) Handles MyBase.Load
    Dim rt As RandomNumber = New RandomNumber()
    Response.Write("Created RandomNumber component")
End Sub
```

continues

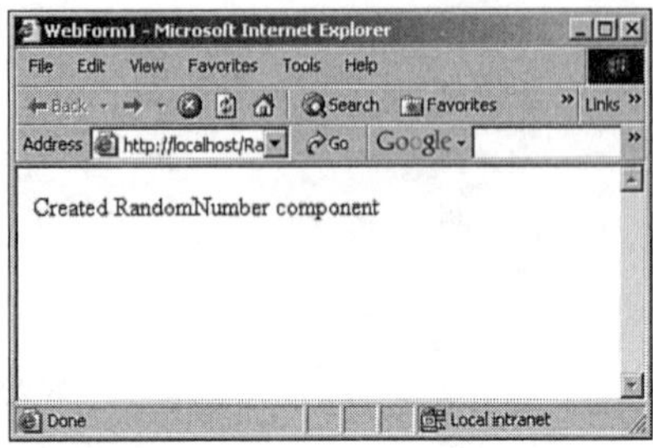

FIGURE 7.3
Component creation at runtime.

continued

11. Set RandomTimerTest as the startup project for the solution. Run the project. You'll see a notification that the form created an instance of the component, as shown in Figure 7.3.

Step by Step 7.1 shows how you can create a component at runtime. But it doesn't demonstrate the design-time support that components offer. Step by Step 7.2 shows how you can add your new component to the Visual Studio .NET Toolbox.

STEP BY STEP

7.2 Adding a Component to the Toolbox

1. Select the Components tab in the Visual Studio .NET Toolbox. Right-click the tab and select Customize Toolbox Select the .NET Framework Components tab in the Customize Toolbox dialog box. Click the Browse button and browse to the QueComponents.dll file in the bin directory under the QueComponents project. Check the RandomNumber component, as shown in Figure 7.4. Click OK.

FIGURE 7.4
Adding a component to the Toolbox.

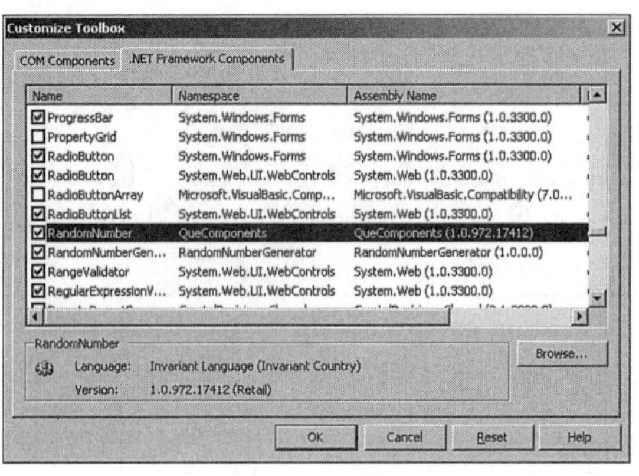

2. Add a new Web Form to the RandomTimerTest project. Name the new Web Form StepByStep7-2.aspx.

3. Drag a RandomNumber component from the Components tab of the Toolbox and drop it on the new Web Form. This will create a component named RandomNumber1 in the tray area of the designer.

4. Switch to code view of the new Web Form. Enter this code to handle the page's `Load` event:

```
Private Sub Page_Load( _
 ByVal sender As System.Object, _
 ByVal e As System.EventArgs) Handles MyBase.Load
    If Not RandomNumber1 Is Nothing Then
        Response.Write( _
         "Created RandomNumber component")
    End If
End Sub
```

5. Set the Web Form as the start page for the project. Run the project. Once again you'll see a message that the component was created.

In Step By Step 7.2, the new component is created even though you didn't explicitly include a call to its constructor. That's because the component support in .NET handles all the necessary connectivity code when you drop a component on a container such as a Web Form. If you expand the Web Form Designer generated code section behind StepByStep7-2.aspx, you'll find that the Page_Init event handler of the Web Form calls the Initialize_Component method to create the new component:

```
Private Sub Page_Init(ByVal sender As System.Object, _
 ByVal e As System.EventArgs) Handles MyBase.Init
    'CODEGEN: This method call is required
    'by the Web Form Designer
    'Do not modify it using the code editor.
    InitializeComponent()
End Sub

'This call is required by the Web Form Designer.
<System.Diagnostics.DebuggerStepThrough()> _
 Private Sub InitializeComponent()
    Me.components = New System.ComponentModel.Container()
    Me.RandomNumber1 = New QueComponents.RandomNumber( _
     Me.components)

End Sub
```

The creation code passes an instance of the Container class to an overloaded constructor for the RandomNumber class. This constructor in turn adds the component to the container and finishes initializing the component:

```
Public Sub New(ByVal Container As _
 System.ComponentModel.IContainer)
    MyClass.New()

    'Required for Windows.Forms Class
    'Composition Designer support
    Container.Add(Me)
End Sub

Public Sub New()
    MyBase.New()

    'This call is required by
    'the Component Designer.
    InitializeComponent()

    'Add any initialization after
    ' the InitializeComponent() call
    StartRandom()
End Sub
```

What about the other end of the component lifecycle? When ASP.NET finishes building the HTML response to the client, it will destroy the instance of the StepByStep7_2 class. This in turn will cause the .NET garbage collector to call the Finalize method of the component, which calls through to its Dispose method:

```
Protected Overrides Sub Finalize()
    Dispose(False)
    MyBase.Finalize()
End Sub

'Component overrides dispose to clean
'up the component list.
Protected Overloads Overrides Sub Dispose( _
 ByVal disposing As Boolean)
    If disposing Then
        If Not (components Is Nothing) Then
            components.Dispose()
        End If
    End If
    mRandom = Nothing
    MyBase.Dispose(disposing)
End Sub
```

Note that the Dispose method is responsible for freeing up the resources used by the component. If you're finished with a component that consumes potentially scarce resources such as database connections, you can call the Dispose method of the component explicitly to free those resources.

Implementing Properties in Components

So far, all I've done with the RandomNumber component is create and destroy it. But of course components can interact with their containers in a number of ways. Step By Step 7.3 demonstrates the use of properties in a component.

STEP BY STEP

7.3 Adding Properties to a Component

1. Open the `RandomNumber.vb` class that you created in Step by Step 7.1. Add three more module-level variables:

```
Private mMinValue As Integer
Private mMaxValue As Integer
Private mResult As Integer
```

2. Modify the `StartRandom` method as follows:

```
Private Sub StartRandom()
    mRandom = New System.Random()
    mMaxValue = 1000
    mResult = mRandom.Next()
End Sub
```

3. Add property procedures to the code to allow the component's container to set and read property values:

```
Public Property minValue() As Integer
    Get
        minValue = mMinValue
    End Get
    Set(ByVal Value As Integer)
        Value = mMinValue
    End Set
End Property
```

continues

continued

```
Public Property maxValue() As Integer
    Get
        maxValue = mMaxValue
    End Get
    Set(ByVal Value As Integer)
        mMaxValue = Value
    End Set
End Property

Public ReadOnly Property Result() As Integer
    Get
        Result = mResult
    End Get
End Property
```

4. Right-click the `QueComponents` project in Solution Explorer and select Build.

5. Add a new Web Form to the `RandomTimerTest` project. Name the new Web Form `StepByStep7-3.aspx`.

6. Drag a `RandomNumber` component from the Components tab of the Toolbox and drop it on the new Web Form. This will create a component named `RandomNumber1` in the tray area of the designer. The new component will expose its properties via the Properties window, as shown in Figure 7.5.

7. Switch to code view of the new Web Form. Enter this code to handle the page's `Load` event:

```
Private Sub Page_Load( _
 ByVal sender As System.Object, _
 ByVal e As System.EventArgs) Handles MyBase.Load
    Response.Write( _
     "Created RandomNumber component<br>")
    Response.Write("Random number is " & _
     RandomNumber1.Result)
End Sub
```

8. Set the Web Form as the start page for the project. Run the project. You'll see a page similar to that shown in Figure 7.6.

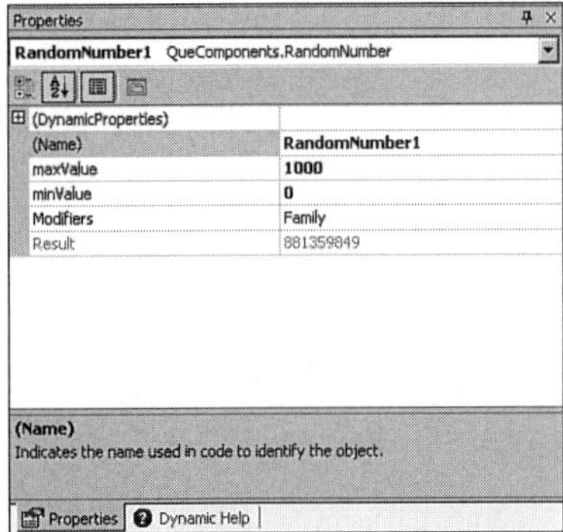

FIGURE 7.5
Setting properties of a component.

FIGURE 7.6
Retrieving a property of a component.

Implementing Methods in Components

Of course, you can also implement methods in your components. Methods are nothing more than public `Sub` or `Function` procedures, just as they are in any other class. Step by Step 7.4 demonstrates the implementation of an overloaded method in the `RandomNumber` class.

STEP BY STEP

7.4 Adding Methods to a Component

1. Open the `RandomNumber.vb` class that you created in Step by Step 7.1. Add two procedures to the module:

```
Public Function GetRandom() As Integer
    mResult = mRandom.Next(mMinValue, mMaxValue)
    GetRandom = mResult
End Function

Public Function GetRandom(ByVal minValue As Integer, _
 ByVal maxValue As Integer) As Integer
    mResult = mRandom.Next(minValue, maxValue)
    GetRandom = mResult
End Function
```

2. Right-click the `QueComponents` project in Solution Explorer and select Build.

3. Add a new Web Form to the `RandomTimerTest` project. Name the new Web Form `StepByStep7-4.aspx`.

4. Drag a `RandomNumber` component from the Components tab of the Toolbox and drop it on the new Web Form. This will create a component named `RandomNumber1` in the tray area of the designer.

5. Switch to code view of the new Web Form. Enter this code to handle the page's `Load` event:

```
Private Sub Page_Load( _
 ByVal sender As System.Object, _
 ByVal e As System.EventArgs) Handles MyBase.Load
    Response.Write( _
     "Created RandomNumber component<br>")
    Response.Write("Random number is " & _
     RandomNumber1.Result & "<br>")
    Response.Write("Random number is " & _
     RandomNumber1.GetRandom() & "<br>")
```

continues

continued

```
        Response.Write("Random number is " & _
         RandomNumber1.GetRandom(1000, 2000))
    End Sub
```

6. Set the Web Form as the start page for the project. Run the project. The page will display three different random numbers.

REVIEW BREAK

- Components provide a way to encapsulate reusable code for use in multiple projects.
- In the .NET Framework, components are classes that derive from System.Component.
- Component classes enjoy features such as container support and resource management because they derive from System.Component.
- You can add methods and properties to a component class just as you can add them to any other class.

CREATING AND USING WEB USER CONTROLS

Create Web custom controls and Web user controls.

A Web user control provides more specialized reuse than does the basic component class. Web user controls are designed to let you reuse common user interface functionality in a Web application. You can think of a Web user control as a chunk of your application's user interface packaged for easy reuse.

In this section of the chapter, you'll learn how to create a user control, how to set its properties, and how to react to its events from the hosting ASP.NET project.

Creating a Web User Control

The process of creating a Web user control is very similar to the process of creating a Web Form, as Step by Step 7.5 demonstrates.

STEP BY STEP

7.5 Creating a Web User Control

1. Add a new Visual Basic ASP.NET Web Application project to your solution. Name the new project `WebUserControlTest`.

2. Right-click the new project in Solution Explorer and select Add, Add Web User Control. Name the new Web user control `CompanyHeading.ascx`.

3. Add a `LinkButton` control with the ID of `lbCompanyName` and a `Label` control with the ID of `lblMotto` to the Web user control. Arrange the controls as shown in Figure 7.7.

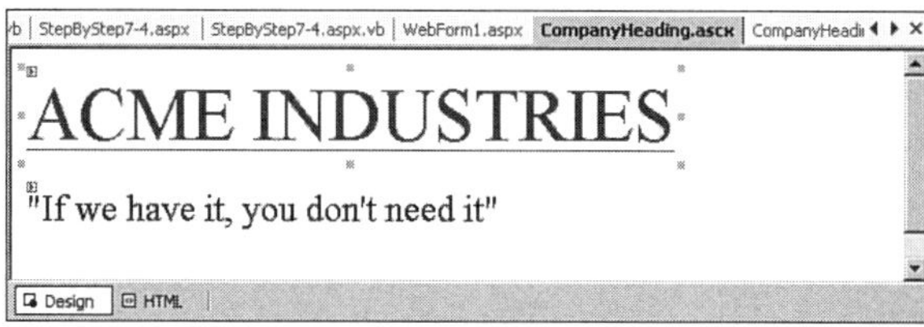

FIGURE 7.7
Designing a Web user control.

4. Add a Web Form to the project. Name the new Web Form `StepByStep7-5.aspx`. Switch the new Web Form to flow layout.

5. Drag `CompanyHeading.ascx` from Solution Explorer and drop it on the new Web Form. Add a `Label` control with text as shown in Figure 7.8.

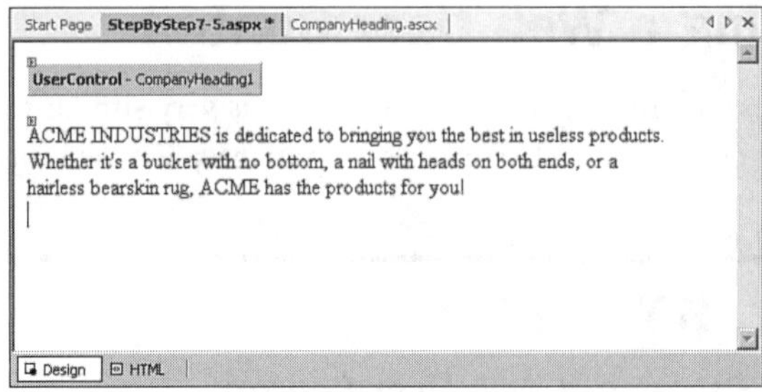

FIGURE 7.8
Web user control on a Web Form

6. Set the Web Form as the start page for the project and set the project as the startup project for the solution. Run the project. The page will be rendered as shown in Figure 7.9.

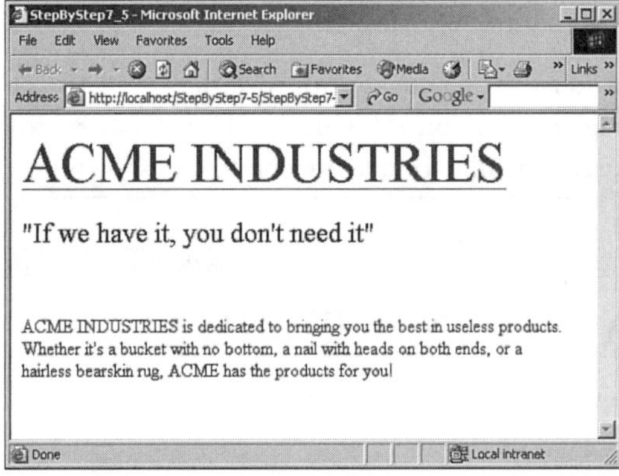

FIGURE 7.9
Web user control on a Web Form at runtime.

Note that in Figure 7.8, the Web user control is shown on the Web Form using a placeholder image. That's because the user control is not compiled until the project itself is compiled, so ASP.NET can't know how large the final control will be.

Implementing Properties in a Web User Control

Just like other server controls, Web user controls have properties that you can manipulate in code. You can expose properties as public members of the Web user control, or you can create Property procedures as shown in Step By Step 7.6.

STEP BY STEP

7.6 Using Properties of a Web User Control

1. Right-click the `CompanyHeading.ascx` Web user control in Solution Explorer and select View Code.

2. Add the following code after the Web Form Designer Generated Code region:

```
Public TargetUrl As String

Public WriteOnly Property ForeColor() As String
    Set(ByVal Value As String)
        lblMotto.ForeColor = _
         ColorTranslator.FromHtml(Value)
        lbCompanyName.ForeColor = _
         ColorTranslator.FromHtml(Value)
    End Set
End Property
```

3. Add a Web Form to the project. Name the new Web Form `StepByStep7-6.aspx`. Switch the new Web Form to flow layout.

4. Drag `CompanyHeading.ascx` from Solution Explorer and drop it on the new Web Form. Add a `Label` control with text as shown in Figure 7.8.

5. Switch to HTML view of the Web Form. Alter the tag for `CompanyHeading1` as follows:

```
<uc1:CompanyHeading id="CompanyHeading1"
 runat="server"
 ForeColor="Red" TargetUrl="http://www.larkware.com/">
 </uc1:CompanyHeading></P>
```

6. Set the Web Form as the start page for the project and set the project as the startup project for the solution. Run the project. The page will be rendered with both the `LinkButton` control and the `Label` control in red.

Note that the properties of the Web user control are set in the HTML, rather than in code. That's because the control is not compiled at design time, so its properties are not available to the code.

> **NOTE**
>
> **Compiled Web User Controls** It is possible to compile a Web user control into a separate assembly. If you do this, you can use the properties of the Web user control in code. However, the process is cumbersome, and you must still have the .ascx file containing the HTML available within the Web application. I don't recommend compiling Web user controls. If you want more information, see the topic "Manipulating User Control Properties" in the Visual Studio .NET Combined Help file.

Implementing Events in a Web User Control

Because they can contain server controls, Web user controls can participate in the ASP.NET event handling architecture. In fact, there's very little difference between events on a Web form and events in a Web user control, as Step by Step 7.7 demonstrates.

EXAM TIP

Web User Controls and Projects
A Web user control is only available to the project in which it is contained. To reuse a Web user control in another project, copy the ascx and associated vb files to the new project.

STEP BY STEP

7.7 Using Events of a Web User Control

1. Open the `CompanyHeading.ascx` Web user control in the designer in regular design view.

2. Double-click the `lbCompanyName` control. Add the following code to handle the `Click` event of this control:

```
Private Sub lbCompanyName_Click( _
 ByVal sender As System.Object, _
 ByVal e As System.EventArgs) _
 Handles lbCompanyName.Click
    Response.Redirect(TargetUrl)
End Sub
```

3. Run the project, leaving the `StepByStep7-6` page set as the start page. Click the `LinkButton` control when the page is displayed. The code in the `LinkButton`'s event handler will run and redirect your browser to the Larkware Web site.

REVIEW BREAK

- Web User Controls let you encapsulate common blocks of user interface functionality for reuse.
- You can create properties for a Web user control by creating public members for the control.
- Web user controls can handle the events of their own constituent controls in their own code-behind files.
- Web user controls must be contained within the project in which they are used.

CREATING WEB CUSTOM CONTROLS

Create Web custom controls and Web user controls.

Web custom controls provide a more flexible (and more complex) alternative to Web user controls for reusing user interface functionality on Web forms. With a Web custom control, you can provide complete design-time support, event handling, data binding, and other advanced features. However, you'll need to do quite a bit of work to properly implement a Web custom control. In this section, I'll show you the basics of three different ways to create a Web custom control:

- By combining two or more controls into a composite control
- By inheriting from a specific server control
- By inheriting from the generic System.Web.Ui.Control class

Creating a Composite Control

A composite control is a Web custom control composed of two or more standard Web server controls. In Step by Step 7.8, you'll create a new composite control consisting of a Label control and a Button control.

STEP BY STEP

7.8 Creating a Composite Control

1. Launch a new instance of Visual Studio .NET.
2. Click the New Project button on the Start Page. Select the Visual Basic Projects project type and create a new Web Control Library project named `WebCustomControls`.
3. Right-click the project in Solution Explorer and select Add, Add Class. Name the new class `CompositeControl.vb`.

continues

NOTE: **Separate Solution for Controls** You can add a Web Control Library project to an existing solution, but I've found that Visual Studio .NET can become confused as to which version of the controls to use in that case. Creating the control library as a separate solution seems to be more reliable.

continued

4. Enter the following code for the `CompositeControl.vb` class:

```
Imports System.Web.UI
Imports System.Web.UI.WebControls
Imports System.ComponentModel

Public Class CompositeControl
    Inherits Control
    Implements INamingContainer

    Public Sub New()
        ' Set default values for persisted properties
        ViewState("MinValue") = 0
        ViewState("MaxValue") = 1000
    End Sub

    Protected Overrides Sub CreateChildControls()
        ' Create the constituent controls
        Dim lbl As System.Web.UI.WebControls.Label = _
         New Label()
        Dim btn As _
         System.Web.UI.WebControls.Button = _
         New Button()
        ' Set initial properties
        With lbl
            .Height = Unit.Pixel(25)
            .Width = Unit.Pixel(75)
            .Text = "0"
        End With
        With btn
            .Height = Unit.Pixel(25)
            .Width = Unit.Pixel(75)
            .Text = "Go"
        End With
        ' Add them to the controls to be rendered
        Controls.Add(lbl)
        Controls.Add(btn)
        ' Hook up an event handler
        AddHandler btn.Click, AddressOf btnClick
    End Sub

    ' Public properties to display
    ' in the Properties Window
    <Category("Behavior"), _
    Description("Minimum value")> _
    Public Property MinValue() As Integer
        Get
            MinValue = _
             CType(ViewState("MinValue"), Integer)
        End Get
        Set(ByVal Value As Integer)
            ViewState("MinValue") = Value
        End Set
    End Property
```

```
    <Category("Behavior"), _
    Description("Maximum value")> _
    Public Property MaxValue() As Integer
        Get
            MaxValue = _
             CType(ViewState("MaxValue"), Integer)
        End Get
        Set(ByVal Value As Integer)
            ViewState("MaxValue") = Value
        End Set
    End Property

    ' Handle the constituent control event
    Public Sub btnClick(ByVal sender As Object, _
     ByVal e As EventArgs)
        Dim r As System.Random = New System.Random()
        Dim Value As Integer
        ' Generate a new random value based
        ' on the minimum and
        ' maximum stored in the state
        Value = CType(r.Next( _
         CType(ViewState("MinValue"), Integer), _
         CType(ViewState("MaxValue"), _
          Integer)), String)
        ' Find the constituent label control
        Dim lbl As Label = Controls(0)
        ' Make sure the controls really exist
        Me.EnsureChildControls()
        ' And set the text to display
        lbl.Text = Value.ToString
    End Sub

End Class
```

5. Save and build the `WebCustomControls` project.

6. Switch back to the 305C07 solution. Add a new Visual Basic ASP.NET Web Application project named `WebCustomControlTest`.

7. Delete the default `WebForm1.aspx` Web Form from the new project.

8. Add a Web Form named `StepByStep7-8.aspx` to the project.

9. Select the Components tab in the Visual Studio .NET Toolbox. Right-click the tab and select Customize Toolbox. Select the .NET Framework Components tab in the Customize Toolbox dialog box. Click the Browse button and browse to the `WebCustomControls.dll` file in the bin directory under the `WebCustomControls` project.

continues

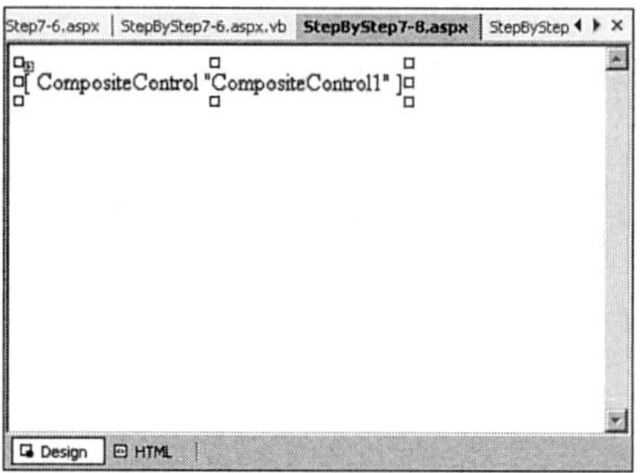

FIGURE 7.10
Composite control on a Web Form at design time.

> **NOTE**
>
> **Composite Controls at Design Time**
> Because the constituent controls in the composite control are dynamically created when the control is rendered in the browser, they aren't displayed at design time by default. Guided Practice Exercise 8.1 will show you how to add design-time support to this control.

continued

Click OK. This will add both the `CompositeControl` control and the `WebCustomControl1` control (which is a default part of the library template) to the Toolbox.

10. Drag the `CompositeControl` control from the Toolbox and drop it on the Web Form. Figure 7.10 shows the resulting Web Form.

11. Set the `MinValue` property of the new control to 500 and the `MaxValue` property of the new control to 1500 by changing the values in the Properties window.

12. Set the Web Form as the start page for the project and set the project as the startup project for the solution.

13. Run the solution. The composite control will render as a label and a button in the browser. Click the button to display a random number between 500 and 1500, as shown in Figure 7.11.

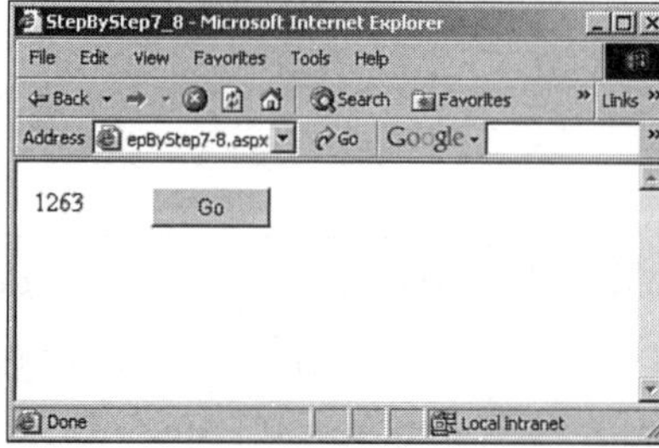

FIGURE 7.11
Composite control on a Web Form at runtime.

The composite control uses the ViewState container to store property values that need to be persisted across round-trips to the browser. Recall that ViewState allows you to automatically read existing values from a hidden value that is sent as part of a postback. Using ViewState is a necessity for values that are required for postback processing (such as the minimum and maximum values in this case).

ASP.NET automatically calls the CreateChildControls method when it's time to render the control. In this procedure, the composite control creates new instances of the server controls that it will contain, sets their properties, and adds them to its own Controls collection. This is also the point at which any event handlers can be hooked up.

Public properties of the composite control are displayed in the Properties window. The attributes of the properties control some Visual Studio .NET specific behavior. For example, this set of attributes marks the MinValue property to be displayed in the Behavior category and specifies descriptive text to show when the property is selected:

```
<Category("Behavior"), Description("Minimum value")>
```

Finally, the event handler in this example demonstrates how you can retrieve a control from the collection of constituent controls to continue working with it. Controls in the collection are numbered starting at zero, in the order that they were added to the collection. Note also the call to the EnsureChildControls method. This method should be used to protect any access to properties of the child controls; it will cause the code to exit if the control does not exist for some reason.

Creating a Derived Control

Another way to create a Web custom control is to subclass an existing Web server control. Step By Step 7.9 shows how you can use this technique to create a TextBox control that is automatically displayed with a red, dashed border.

STEP BY STEP

7.9 Creating a Subclassed Control

1. Open the `WebCustomControls` project.
2. Right-click the project in Solution Explorer and select Add, Add Class. Name the new class `CustomTextbox.vb`.
3. Enter the following code for the `CustomTextbox.vb` class:

```
Imports System.Web.UI
Imports System.Web.UI.WebControls
Imports System.ComponentModel

Public Class CustomTextBox
    Inherits System.Web.UI.WebControls.TextBox
```

continues

continued

```
        Public Sub New()
            Me.BorderColor = System.Drawing.Color.Red
            Me.BorderStyle = BorderStyle.Dashed
        End Sub
    End Class
```

4. Save and build the `WebCustomControls` project.

5. Switch back to the `305C07` solution.

6. Add a Web Form named `StepByStep7-9.aspx` to the project.

7. Select the Components tab in the Visual Studio .NET Toolbox. Delete the existing custom controls from the `WebCustomControls` project by selecting each one in the Toolbox and clicking Delete. Delete the reference to the `WebCustomControls` project from the references node in Solution Explorer.

8. Select the Components tab in the Visual Studio .NET Toolbox. Right-click the tab and select Customize Toolbox. Select the .NET Framework Components tab in the Customize Toolbox dialog box. Click the Browse button and browse to the `WebCustomControls.dll` file in the `bin` directory under the `WebCustomControls` project. Click OK.

9. Drag the `CustomTextbox` control from the Toolbox and drop it on the Web Form. Figure 7.12 shows the resulting Web Form.

10. Set the Web Form as the start page for the project and set the project as the startup project for the solution.

11. Run the solution. The derived control will behave like any other TextBox control at runtime.

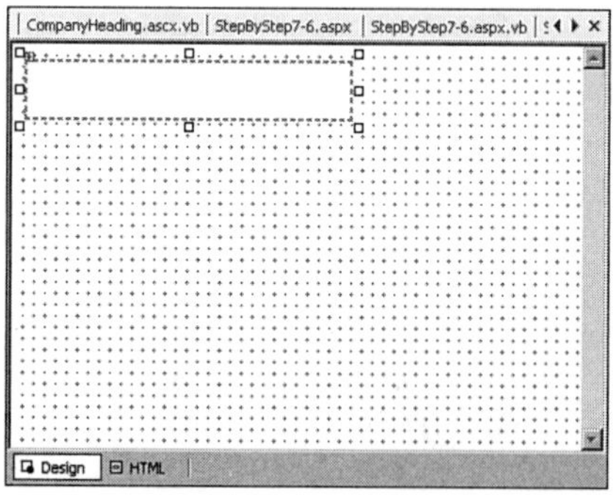

FIGURE 7.12
Derived control on a Web Form at design time.

Derived custom controls are useful in situations where you want behavior very much like that of a built-in server control. In this case, the only behavior added by the derived control is the specific default display of the control's border. All other methods, properties, and events are inherited directly from the original TextBox control.

Creating a Control From Scratch

The third way to create a Web custom control is to create the control "from scratch," by deriving it from the WebControl class and writing code to handle rendering and other tasks, rather than depending on existing controls. You probably noticed the WebCustomControl class that's automatically created as part of the Web Control Library project type. This class handles its own rendering. In Step by Step 7.10, you'll modify this class and use it on a Web Form.

STEP BY STEP

7.10 Creating a Control From Scratch

1. Open the `WebCustomControls` project.

2. Open the `WebCustomControl` class and modify its code as follows:

```
Imports System.ComponentModel
Imports System.Web.UI

<DefaultProperty("Text"), _
 ToolboxData("<{0}:WebCustomControl1 _
 runat=server>" & _
 "</{0}:WebCustomControl1>")> _
 Public Class WebCustomControl1
    Inherits System.Web.UI.WebControls.WebControl

    Dim _text As String
    Dim _bold As Boolean

    <Bindable(True), Category("Appearance"), _
     DefaultValue("")> _
     Property [Text]() As String
        Get
            Return _text
        End Get

        Set(ByVal Value As String)
            _text = Value
        End Set
    End Property

    <Category("Appearance")> _
     Property Bold() As Boolean
        Get
            Return _bold
        End Get
```

continues

continued

```
        Set(ByVal Value As Boolean)
            _bold = Value
        End Set
    End Property

    Protected Overrides Sub Render( _
     ByVal output As System.Web.UI.HtmlTextWriter)
        If _bold Then
            output.RenderBeginTag(HtmlTextWriterTag.B)
            output.Write([Text])
            output.RenderEndTag()
        Else
            output.Write([Text])
        End If
    End Sub

End Class
```

3. Save and build the `WebCustomControls` project.

4. Switch back to the `305C07` solution.

5. Add a Web Form named `StepByStep7-10.aspx` to the project.

6. Select the Components tab in the Visual Studio .NET Toolbox. Delete the existing custom controls from the `WebCustomControls` project by selecting each on in the Toolbox and clicking Delete. Delete the reference to the `WebCustomControls` project from the references node in Solution Explorer.

7. Select the Components tab in the Visual Studio .NET Toolbox. Right-click the tab and select Customize Toolbox. Select the .NET Framework Components tab in the Customize Toolbox dialog box. Click the Browse button and browse to the `WebCustomControls.dll` file in the bin directory under the `WebCustomControls` project. Click OK.

8. Drag the `WebCustomControl` control from the Toolbox and drop it on the Web Form.

9. Set the `Bold` property of the control to `True`. Set the `Text` property of the control to `This is my custom control`.

10. Set the Web Form as the start page for the project and set the project as the startup project for the solution.

11. Run the solution. You'll see the text from the control displayed in bold on the resulting HTML page, as shown in Figure 7.13.

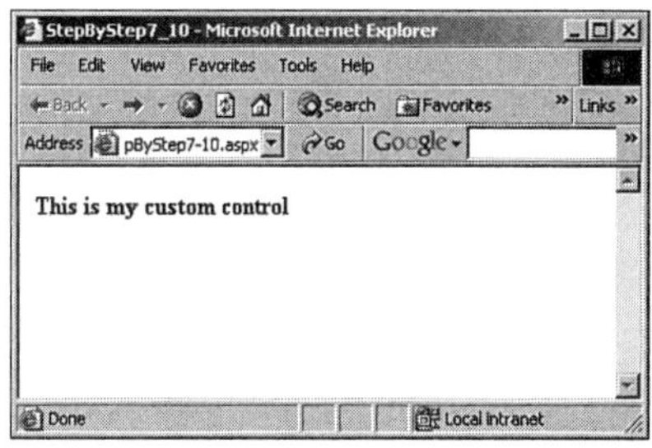

FIGURE 7.13
Rendered control on a Web Form at runtime.

This Step by Step demonstrates the Render method, which gets called to draw text in both design and run modes. Because this control implements its own version of Render, it can display text easily in either mode. Note also the use of the RenderBeginTag and RenderEndTag methods to add HTML markup to the control's output.

You can also see some new attributes at both the class and the property level here:

- The DefaultProperty attribute of the class specifies the name of a property that is the default property for the control.
- The ToolboxData attribute of the class provides the default HTML that the control will generate when it is dropped on a form.
- The Bindable attribute of a property specifies whether the property can participate in data binding.
- The DefaultValue attribute of a property specifies the default value for the property on a new instance of the control.

GUIDED PRACTICE EXERCISE 7.1

Although the simple composite control that you created in Step by Step 7.8 did not offer any support for design-time rendering, it's relatively easy to add such support. To add such support, you must create a custom designer class which derives from System.Web.UI.Design.ControlDesigner and override its GetDesignTimeHtml method. Then you specify the designer class using the Designer attribute of the control class.

You should try doing this on your own first. If you get stuck, or you'd like to see one possible solution, follow these steps:

1. Open the WebCustomControls project.
2. Right-click the References node in Solution Explorer and select Add Reference. Add a reference to System.Design.dll.
3. Right-click the Project and select Add, Add Class. Name the new class CompositeControlDesigner.vb. Modify the code for this class as follows:

```
Imports System
Imports System.IO
Imports System.Web
Imports System.Web.UI
Imports System.Web.UI.WebControls
Imports System.Web.UI.Design

Public Class CompositeControlDesigner
    Inherits System.Web.UI.Design.ControlDesigner

    Public Overrides Function _
     GetDesignTimeHtml() As String
        ' This shows how to get a reference to the
        ' actual control instance,
        ' though it's not used
        ' in this example
        Dim ctl As CompositeControl = _
         CType(Me.Component, _
            CompositeControl)
        ' Set up plumbing to write out HTML
        Dim sw As New StringWriter()
        Dim tw As New HtmlTextWriter(sw)
        ' Create controls that represent the composite
        ' control
        Dim lbl As System.Web.UI.WebControls.Label = _
         New Label()
        Dim btn As System.Web.UI. _
         WebControls.Button = _
         New Button()
        ' Set initial properties
        With lbl
            .Height = Unit.Pixel(25)
            .Width = Unit.Pixel(75)
            .Text = "0"
        End With
        With btn
            .Height = Unit.Pixel(25)
            .Width = Unit.Pixel(75)
            .Text = "Go"
        End With
```

```
        ' Cause them to render themselves to the HTML
        lbl.RenderControl(tw)
        btn.RenderControl(tw)
        ' And return the HTML to be
        ' used in design view
        Return sw.ToString()
    End Function
End Class
```

4. Save and build the WebCustomControls project.

5. Switch back to the 305C07 solution.

6. Add a Web Form named GuidedPracticeExercise7-1.aspx to the project.

7. Select the Components tab in the Visual Studio .NET Toolbox. Delete the existing custom controls from the WebCustomControls project by selecting each one in the Toolbox and clicking Delete. Delete the reference to the WebCustomControls project from the references node in Solution Explorer.

8. Select the Components tab in the Visual Studio .NET Toolbox. Right-click the tab and select Customize Toolbox. Select the .NET Framework Components tab in the Customize Toolbox dialog box. Click the Browse button and browse to the WebCustomControls.dll file in the bin directory under the WebCustomControls project. Click OK.

9. Drag the CompositeControl control from the Toolbox and drop it on the Web Form. After a pause while Visual Studio .NET instantiates the designer class, you'll see the control on the Web Form, as shown in Figure 7.14.

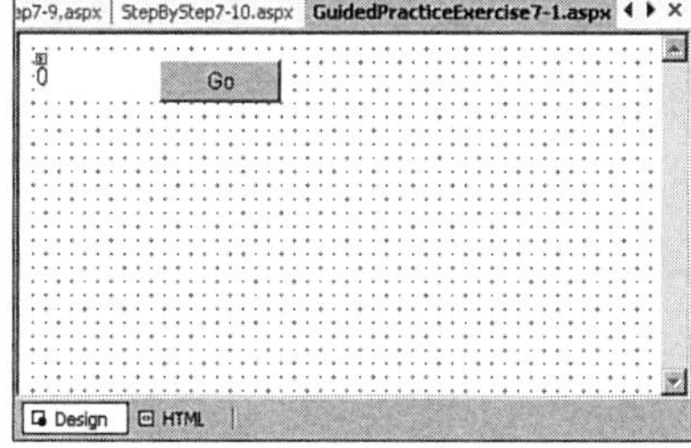

FIGURE 7.14
Composite control on a Web Form at design time.

Custom Control Choices

As you've seen, there are quite a few choices when you want to build a control for use in ASP.NET applications. Here are some points to keep in mind as you decide which architecture to implement for a particular control:

- Web user controls can only be used in the same project where their .ascx file is contained. So they're not well suited for controls that need to be used across many projects.
- Web user controls are much easier to create than Web custom controls.
- Web user controls don't support a good representation at design time. Web custom controls can be represented with high fidelity at design time, although you may need to write additional code to do so.
- Web user controls cannot be added to the Visual Studio .NET Toolbox. Web custom controls can be added to the Toolbox.
- Web custom controls are better suited than Web user controls to dynamic layout tasks where constituent controls must be created at runtime.
- Composite custom controls are a good choice when you have a group of controls that must be repeated consistently on the user interface of an application.
- Derived custom controls are a good choice when you want most of the functionality of an existing server control with only a few changes.
- Writing a Web custom control from scratch provides you with the most flexibility and control over the generated HTML.

REVIEW BREAK

- Web custom controls are compiled components that offer support for almost all the features of the server controls that ship with Visual Studio .NET.
- You can create a Web custom control by combining existing controls, by deriving from an existing control, or by inheriting directly from the WebControl class.
- Web custom controls offer full support for the Visual Studio .NET interface, including the Toolbox and the Properties window.
- You can create a designer class that handles the display of a Web custom control at design time.

CREATING AND MANAGING .NET ASSEMBLIES

Create and modify a .NET assembly.

A Web application usually consists of several different files; it typically includes the DLL and EXE files that contain the application code, the GIF, BMP, or JPG files that contain graphics, and other data files such as those storing strings in several languages for multilingual support. A Web application created using the .NET Framework groups a logical collection of such files into what is called an *assembly*. The reason I use the term *logical* here is that these files are not necessarily physically combined into a single large file. Even when these files are part of an assembly, they maintain their own physical existence. In fact, you can't tell by looking at a file that it belongs to a particular assembly.

One of the files in the assembly contains a special piece of information called the *assembly manifest*. The manifest contains the metadata for the assembly. When the common language runtime loads an assembly it first reads the manifest to get the following information:

- The name and version of the assembly.
- The files that make up the assembly, including their names and hash values.
- The compile-time dependency of this assembly on other assemblies.
- The culture or language that an assembly supports.
- The set of permissions required for the assembly to run properly.

An assembly is the basic unit of deployment, scoping, versioning and security in the .NET Framework. Microsoft uses assemblies to deliver these benefits to .NET:

- Each assembly has a version number. All the types and resources in an assembly share the same version number to make it easy for applications to refer to the correct version of files and avoid problems like the infamous "DLL Hell," where installing a new version of a shared library breaks older applications.

- The self-describing nature of assemblies makes it possible to deploy applications using the zero-impact XCOPY installation. There's nothing to register and no system files to change.
- Assemblies define a security boundary, allowing the Common Language Runtime to restrict a set of operations to be executed depending on the identity and origin of the assembly.

All .NET code executes as part of an assembly. When a user browses to a page on your ASP.NET Web site, the compiled class for the page is part of an assembly.

Assemblies exist in different forms depending on how they are used. One way to classify assemblies is with these categories:

- Single-file and multifile assemblies
- Static and dynamic assemblies
- Private and shared assemblies
- Satellite and resource-only assemblies

The following sections discuss each of these categories.

Single-file and Multifile Assemblies

A single-file assembly consists of a single EXE or DLL file. This file consists of code, any embedded resources, and the assembly manifest of the assembly. A single-file assembly is something you are already familiar with because when you were building your projects in the Step by Step exercises, the output DLL or EXE file was nothing but a single-file assembly. Step by Step 7.11 shows how to view the contents of an assembly file.

STEP BY STEP

7.11 Viewing Assembly Contents

1. Activate the Solution Explorer window. Select the `RandomTimerTest` project. Click the Show All Files toolbar button in Solution Explorer.

2. Right-click `RandomTimerTest.dll` it and select Open With from its shortcut menu. In the Open With dialog box (see Figure 7.15), select `Ildasm.exe` and click Open. If `Ildasm` is not on the list, click the Add button and browse for it; you'll find it in the `FrameworkSDK\bin` folder inside the Visual Studio .NET installation. This step will launch the Microsoft Intermediate Language Disassembler, showing the contents of `RandomTimerTest.dll` (see Figure 7.16).

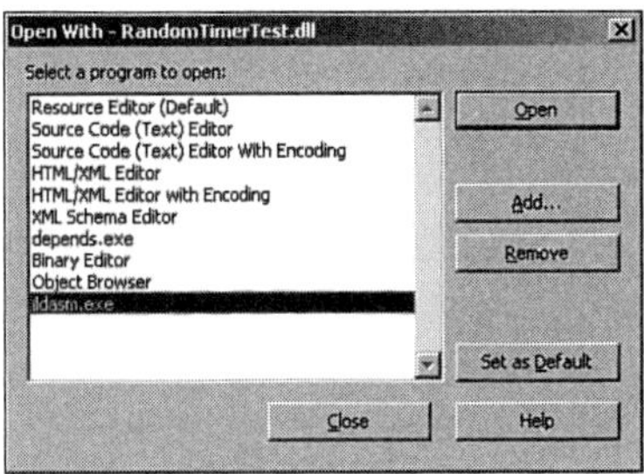

FIGURE 7.15
Selecting the application for opening a DLL file.

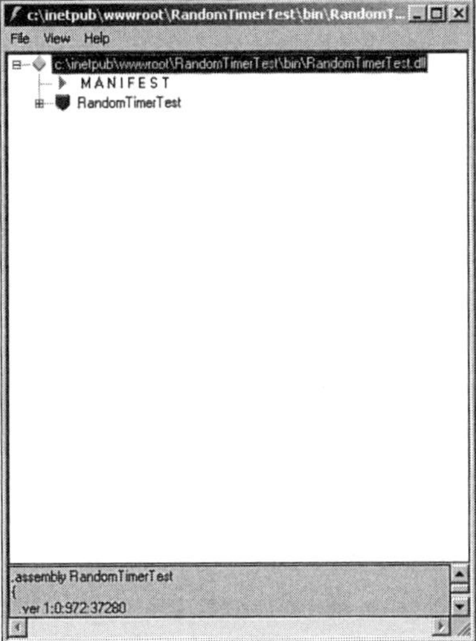

FIGURE 7.16
Microsoft Intermediate Language Disassembler.

3. Expand the nodes to see the methods, properties, constructors, and other members defined inside the assembly. Double-clicking a member node will open a window showing disassembled code for the member.

4. On the top of the hierarchy you will find a node titled MANIFEST. Double-click it to open the metadata information for this assembly, as shown in Figure 7.17. You will see that manifest contains references to other assemblies, version information, and values among other information.

NOTE

Microsoft Intermediate Language Disassembler The *MSIL Disassembler* can be used to view the metadata and disassembled code for .NET libraries, modules, and executables in a hierarchical Tree view. Looking at MSIL can reveal much information about the inner workings of a program or a component, and it can be a useful learning and debugging tool.

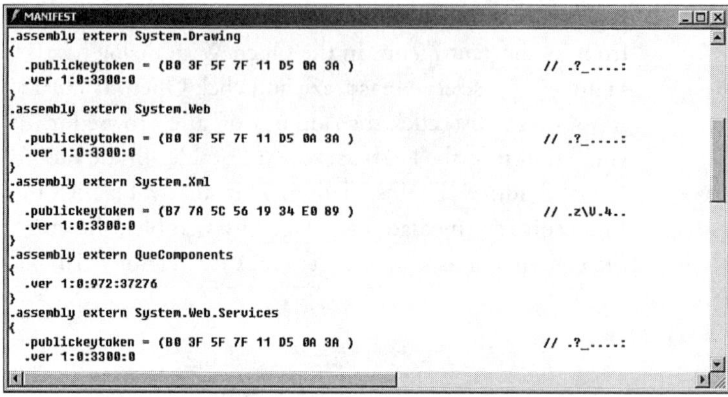

FIGURE 7.17
Assembly manifest.

You might also find it useful to add an Ildasm entry for EXE files as well as DLL files. Alternatively, you can launch Ildasm from the .NET Framework command prompt and use its menus to open any assembly that you wish to inspect.

The assemblies that ASP.NET creates are always single-file assemblies. The .NET Framework can also handle multifile assemblies. A multifile assembly can include multiple files in one assembly. You should have at least one DLL or EXE file among these files. You can choose to attach the assembly manifest with any of these files, or you can keep it in a separate file of its own. Because multifile assemblies aren't used in ASP.NET, I won't cover the details of their creation here. If you're interested, you can find full details in MCSD Training Guide: Visual Basic Windows-Based Applications 70-306.

Static and Dynamic Assemblies

When you compile programs using Visual Studio .NET or through the command-line compiler, it emits the files that make up an assembly. These files are physically stored on disk. Such an assembly is called a *static assembly*.

However, it is also possible to create and execute assemblies on-the-fly (while a program is still under execution). Such assemblies are called *dynamic assemblies*. In fact, dynamic assemblies are used extensively by ASP.NET. While executing ASPX files, the ASP .NET process creates the corresponding assemblies at runtime.

That's how ASP.NET automatically uses new files when you upload them, even if you don't supply the compiled version of the assemblies, If needed, dynamic assemblies can be saved to disk to be later loaded again. The classes used to create dynamic assemblies are available in the System.Reflection.Emit namespace. I won't cover that namespace in this text because it isn't required by the exam objectives, but if you are interested, you might want to look at the documentation for the System.Reflection.Emit namespace.

Private and Shared Assemblies

Assemblies can be deployed using two different approaches:

- You can deploy an assembly for use with a single application. When an assembly is deployed this way, it is called a *private assembly*.
- You can deploy an assembly for use with several applications. When an assembly is deployed in the shared mode, it is called a *shared assembly*.

Here are some fast facts about private assemblies:

- Private assemblies are intended to be only used by the application they are deployed with.
- Private assemblies are deployed in the directory (or a subdirectory) where the main application is installed.
- Typically, a private assembly is written by the same company that writes the main application that uses the private assembly.

Because of the localized nature of a private assembly, the runtime does not impose a strict versioning policy with them. How the application developers version and name their assembly is more or less left to them.

On the other hand, a shared assembly can be used by more than one application. All the shared assemblies on a computer are stored in a special place called the Global Assembly Cache (GAC) to be accessible by all applications. Because of the shared nature of the GAC, the common language runtime imposes special security and versioning requirements on any assembly installed in the GAC.

NOTE

XCOPY Deployment and the Global Assembly Cache When your application needs to refer to assemblies in the Global Assembly Cache, you can no longer deploy the applications using just the XCOPY command. Now you also need to install the assembly in the Global Assembly Cache of the target machine. In this case, you should use an installer program (such as Windows Installer 2.0) that understands how to work with the GAC. You'll learn about the Windows Installer in Chapter 13, "Deploying a Web Application."

NOTE

Private Assemblies Versus Shared Assemblies As a general rule of thumb, you should always deploy your assemblies as private assemblies. Install the assemblies in the Global Assembly Cache only if you are explicitly required to share them with other applications. One common use for shared assemblies in ASP.NET is to allow Web custom controls to be shared by multiple applications.

NOTE

Native Assembly Versus JIT-Compiled Assembly Assemblies store code in the MSIL (Microsoft Intermediate Language) format. When a method is invoked for the first time, the common language runtime will Just In Time–compile that method into native machine code. The native code is stored in memory and directly used for any subsequent calls to this method. In the JIT compilation mode, a method is slow when it is called for the first time because an additional step of compilation is involved, but any subsequent calls to that method will run as fast as native code itself.

When you view the GAC, note that some assemblies have their type marked as *native images*, meaning these assemblies were precompiled in native code before they were installed in the GAC. The advantage of using a native image is that even the first call of any method in an assembly will be as fast as its subsequent calls. You too can create a native image for your assembly by using the Native Image Generator tool (NGEN.EXE), which is installed as part of .NET Framework SDK.

Here are some fast facts about shared assemblies and the Global Assembly Cache:

- All assemblies that are installed in the GAC must have a strong name. A *strong name* consists of an assembly's name, a version number, a culture, a public key, and a digital signature. Having a strong name ensures an assembly's identity.
- The Common Language Runtime checks for the assembly's integrity before installing it in the GAC and ensures that an assembly has not been tampered with by checking the strong name of the assembly.
- The GAC is capable of maintaining multiple copies of an assembly with the same name but different versions.
- The runtime can determine what version of an assembly to load based on the information in an application's configuration file or the machine-wide configuration file (machine.config). You'll learn more about this in Chapter 15, "Configuring a Web Application."

To view the contents of the GAC, follow Step by Step 7.12.

STEP BY STEP

7.12 Viewing the Contents of Global Assembly Cache

1. Launch Windows Explorer and navigate to the system folder of your computer (such as `C:\Windows` or `C:\WINNT`). Open the subfolder named Assembly.
2. You are now seeing the contents of Global Assembly Cache, as shown in Figure 7.18. The .NET Framework installs a Windows shell extension called the Assembly Cache Viewer (Shfusion.dll) that allows you to easily view the contents of GAC. Select the System.Web assembly. Right-click it and select Properties from the Context menu to see information related to this assembly as shown in Figure 7.19.

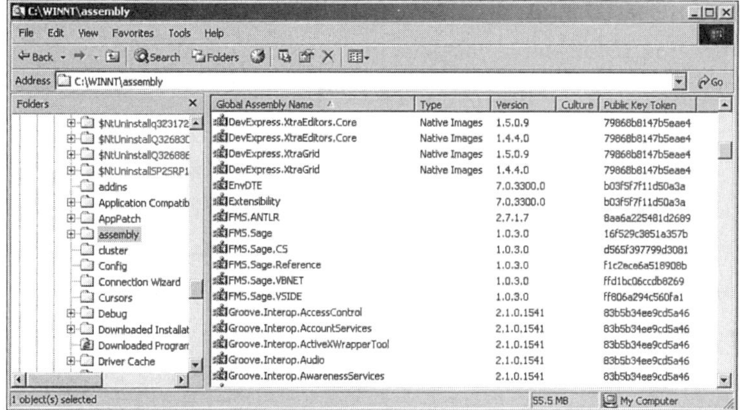

FIGURE 7.18
Viewing the Global Assembly Cache.

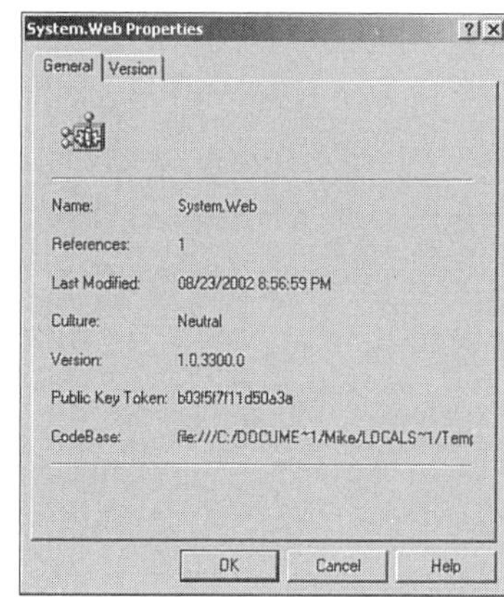

FIGURE 7.19
Properties for an assembly installed in Global Assembly Cache.

I'll talk more about the Global Assembly Cache in Chapter 13, in which you will learn how to deploy your own assemblies in the Global Assembly Cache. You'll also learn in Chapter 15, how to use configuration files to control which version of an assembly is loaded by your application.

Satellite and Resource-Only Assemblies

Create and modify a .NET assembly: Create and implement satellite assemblies.

Create and modify a .NET assembly: Create resource-only assemblies.

A Web application typically contains resources such as images and strings in addition to code. These resources can be translated into various cultures and languages. When you add these files to a Visual Studio .NET Project, their default Build type is Content. When you compile the project, the assemblies contain just code, metadata, and links to files that exist externally. This means that the resource files will be distributed with the application as separate files, and all these files must be available at runtime for your application to function correctly.

Another way to package the resource files with your application is to embed them into the assembly itself. To achieve this, when you add the resource files to your project, set their Build type to Embedded Resources instead of Content. You can do this through the Properties window by accessing the properties of these files.

When the Build type is set to Embedded Resources, the contents of the resource file will be included in the assembly itself at the compile-time. Visual Studio .NET does this in the following three steps:

1. It creates an XML resource file with an extension resx. This file stores the resources as key-value pairs—for example, the name of a resource file and its location.
2. At the time of compilation, all resources referenced by the resx file are embedded into a binary file with the extension resources.
3. The binary resource file is embedded into the code assembly.

Of course, all these steps can be done manually. The resx file is an XML file, so you can manually create it using any text editor. It can be compiled into a resources file using the Resource Generator tool (resgen.exe). A resources file can be embedded to an assembly using the VBC compiler's `/resource` option.

These steps create an assembly that contains both code and resources. Assemblies created in such a way are not dependent on external resource files but have all necessary information stuffed into themselves.

Another way to attach resources in an application is by creating resource-only assemblies. These assemblies just contain resources without any code.

With the exception of satellite assemblies, Visual Studio .NET does not allow you to create a resource-only assembly. However, you can use the command-line tools provided by the .NET Framework to create such assemblies.

The .NET Framework provides various classes in the System.Resources namespace that can be used to work with resource files. Some important classes of this namespace are listed in Table 7.1.

TABLE 7.1

SOME IMPORTANT CLASSES THAT DEAL WITH RESOURCES

Class	*Explanation*
`ResourceManager`	Provides access to resources at runtime. You can use this class to read information from resource-only assemblies.
`ResourceReader`	Enables you to read resources from a binary resource file.
`ResourceWriter`	Enables you to write resources to a binary resource file.
`ResXResourceReader`	Enables you to read resource information from an XML-based resx file.
`ResXResourceWriter`	Enables you to write resource information to an XML-based resx file.

Step by Step 7.13 will use some of these classes to write an application that will show how to programmatically generate resx and resource files from given resources. The objective is to create resource files for storing the flags of different countries. You can get these graphics from the common7\graphics\icons\flag folder from your Visual Studio .NET installation. For the purposes of this example, I renamed those files with their corresponding two letter ISO country codes.

STEP BY STEP

7.13 Creating Resource Files

1. Add a new Windows Application project to your solution and name it `StepByStep7-13`. I'm using a Windows application for this purpose because this is something you'd do once during development, not a process that you want Web site visitors to trigger.

2. In the Solution Explorer window, right-click `Form1.vb` and rename it `GenerateResourceFiles.vb`. Open the Properties window for this form and change its Name and Text properties to `GenerateResourceFiles`.

continues

continued

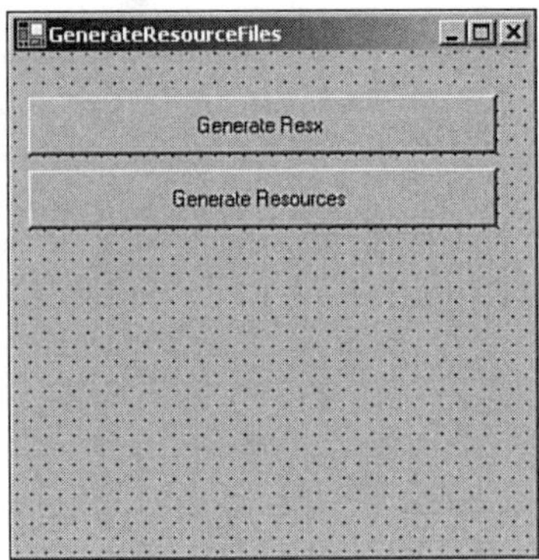

FIGURE 7.20
A form that generates Flags.resx and Flags.resources files.

3. In the Solution Explorer, right-click the project and select Add, New Folder. Name the folder `Flags`. Right-click the `Flags` folder and select Add, Add Existing Item and add all the icon files of the country flags to this folder.

4. Place two Button controls on the form as shown in Figure 7.20 and name them `btnGenerateResX` and `btnGenerateResources`.

5. Place the following directives at the top of the code:

```
Imports System.Resources
Imports System.IO
```

6. Add an event handler for the `Click` event of `btnGenerateResX` and add the following code to it:

```
Private Sub btnGenerateResx_Click( _
 ByVal sender As System.Object, _
 ByVal e As System.EventArgs) _
 Handles btnGenerateResx.Click
    ' Create a ResXResourceWriter object
    Dim rsxw As ResXResourceWriter = _
     New ResXResourceWriter("Flags.resx")
    ' the EXE will be placed in bin folder so refer to
    ' Flags folder from there
    Dim strFile As String
    Dim strCountryCode As String
    Dim img As Image
    For Each strFile In Directory.GetFiles( _
     "..\Flags", "*.ico")
        strCountryCode = _
         strFile.Substring(strFile.Length - 6, 2)
        img = Image.FromFile(strFile)
        ' Store the Key-Value pair.
        rsxw.AddResource(strCountryCode, img)
    Next
    rsxw.Close()
    MessageBox.Show("Flags.resx file generated")
End Sub
```

7. Add an event handler for the `Click` event of `btnGenerateResources` and add the following code to it:

```
Private Sub btnGenerateResources_Click( _
 ByVal sender As System.Object, _
 ByVal e As System.EventArgs) _
 Handles btnGenerateResources.Click
```

```
    ' Create a ResourceWriter object
    Dim rw As ResourceWriter = _
     New ResourceWriter("Flags.resources")
    ' The EXE will be placed in bin folder so refer to
    ' the Flags folder from there
    Dim strFile As String
    Dim strCountryCode As String
    Dim img As Image
    For Each strFile In Directory.GetFiles( _
     "..\Flags", "*.ico")
        strCountryCode = _
         strFile.Substring(strFile.Length - 6, 2)
        img = Image.FromFile(strFile)
        ' Store the Key-Value pair.
        rw.AddResource(strCountryCode, img)
    Next
    rw.Close()
    MessageBox.Show("Flags.resources file generated")
End Sub
```

8. Set the form as the startup object for the project and set the project as the startup project for the solution.

9. Run the Project. Click each of the buttons to create both a `Flags.resx` file and a `Flags.resources` file. The location of these files will be the same as the location of the project's EXE file. You can view the generated files in Solution Explorer by clicking the Show All Files toolbar button and browsing into the bin directory of the project.

This exercise creates both a RESX file and a resources file to demonstrate the capability of the ResXResourceWrite and ResourceWriter classes. Note that the Flags.resources file was not generated by compiling the Flags.resx file, but directly using the ResourceWriter class. You could also create a RESX file into a resources file from the command line by using the following command:

```
resgen Flags.resx
```

Although the Flags.resources file has resources embedded in binary format, it is not an assembly. To create an assembly from this file, you can use the Assembly Linker tool (al.exe) as shown in Step by Step 7.14.

STEP BY STEP

7.14 Creating a Resource-Only Assembly

1. Select Start, Programs, Microsoft Visual Studio .NET, Visual Studio .NET Tools, Visual Studio .NET Command Prompt to open a command window ready to execute .NET Framework command-line tools.
2. Change directory to where the Flags.resources file is stored. Give the following command to compile the Flags.resources file as a resource-only assembly.

```
al /embed:Flags.resources /out:Flags.Resources.dll
```

Now that you know how to create a resource-only assembly, let me show how to use it from a Web application. I'll demonstrate this in Step by Step 7.15. In this exercise you should especially focus on the use of the ResourceManager class to load the resources from resource-only assemblies.

STEP BY STEP

7.15 Using a Resource-Only Assembly

1. Crete a new Visual Basic ASP.NET project and name it `StepByStep4-18`.
2. Add a new Web Form to the project and name it `GetCountryFlag.aspx`. Delete the default `WebForm1.aspx` Web Form.
3. Add a `TextBox` control with the ID of `txtCountryCode`, an `Image` control with the ID of `imgFlag`, a `Button` control with the ID of `btnGetFlag`, and a `Label` control to the Web Form. Arrange the controls on form as shown in Figure 7.21. Set the `ImageUrl` property of `imgFlag` to `Image.aspx`.

4. Add the following code to the page's `Load` event handler:

```
Private Sub Page_Load(ByVal sender As System.Object, _
 ByVal e As System.EventArgs) Handles MyBase.Load
    If Not IsPostBack Then
        Session("Country") = "US"
    Else
        Session("Country") = _
         txtCountryCode.Text.ToUpper()
    End If
End Sub
```

5. Add another Web Form to the project. Name the new Web Form `Image.aspx`.

6. Switch to code view of `Image.aspx` and add the following code at the top of the module:

```
Imports System.Reflection
Imports System.Resources
```

7. Add an event handler for the `Load` event of the `Image.aspx` Web Form:

```
Private Sub Page_Load(ByVal sender As System.Object, _
 ByVal e As System.EventArgs) Handles MyBase.Load
    Dim bmp As Bitmap = New Bitmap(32, 32)
    ' Build a new resource manager on the
    ' resource-only assembly
    Dim rm As ResourceManager = _
        New ResourceManager("Flags", _
        System.Reflection.Assembly.LoadFrom( _
        Server.MapPath("Flags.resources.dll")))
    ' Use the session variable to retrieve the
    ' appropriate bitmap
    bmp = CType(rm.GetObject( _
        Session("Country")), Bitmap)
    ' And stream it back as the result of this page
    Response.ContentType = "image/Gif"
    bmp.Save(Response.OutputStream, _
        System.Drawing.Imaging.ImageFormat.Gif)
    ' Cleanup
    bmp.Dispose()
End Sub
```

8. Set the `GetCountryFlag.aspx` Web Form as the start page for the project and set the project as the startup project for the solution.

9. Copy the `Flags.resources.dll` file to the root folder for this project where the Image.aspx page is stored.

continues

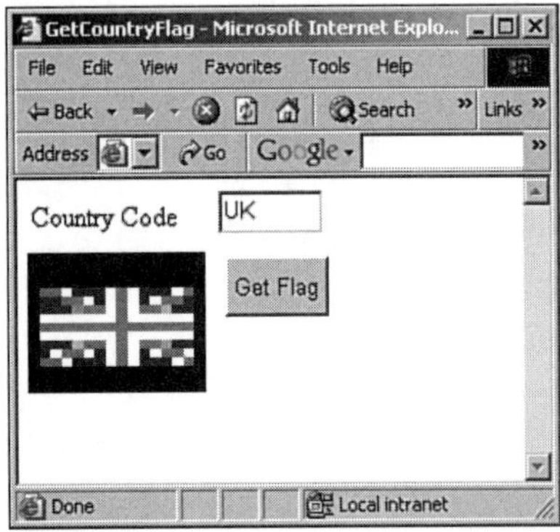

FIGURE 7.21
Reading resources from a resource-only assembly.

10. Run the project. It will default to displaying the U.S. flag. Enter another country code in the text box and click the Get Flag button. The appropriate flag will be loaded into the Image control from the resource assembly, as shown in Figure 7.21.

A common use of resource-only assemblies is to store language and culture-specific information. A Web application designed for international usage might package resource information for each locale in a separate assembly file. When a user downloads the application, she can ignore the assemblies for other cultures. Skipping the unnecessary files can significantly reduce the user's download time for the application.

Resource-only assemblies that store culture-specific information are also known as *satellite assemblies*. Visual Studio .NET offers user interface support for creating and using satellite assemblies for Windows forms, but not for Web Forms. To use a satellite assembly for a Web Form, you'll need to build your own resource-only assembly and use custom code to retrieve the resources as in the previous Step by Step. I'll cover the topic of satellite assemblies and globalization of applications in more detail in Chapter 9, "Globalization."

REVIEW BREAK

- Assemblies are the basic unit for reuse, versioning, security, and deployment of components created using the .NET Framework. Each assembly includes an assembly manifest to store the assembly's metadata.
- Depending on the number of files that make up an assembly, it is a single-file or a multifile assembly.
- A private assembly is an assembly available only to clients in the same directory structure as the assembly, while a shared assembly can be referenced by more than one application and is stored in the machine-wide Global Assembly Cache. A shared assembly must be assigned a cryptographically strong name.
- Resource-only assemblies are those assemblies that contain just resources and no code. Resource-only assemblies that store culture-specific information are known as satellite assemblies.

CHAPTER SUMMARY

Building an efficient Visual Basic .NET Web application requires you to create and manage .NET components and assemblies. As applications grow more complex, it's necessary to build them effectively by creating reusable components. The Microsoft .NET Framework allows programmers to create reusable components. You can create reusable Web components by building either Web custom controls or Web user controls, both of which are supported by Visual Studio .NET.

Assemblies are the basic unit for reuse, versioning, security, and deployment of components created using the .NET Framework. Assemblies are self-describing. They store their metadata within themselves in the assembly manifest.

Assemblies can be classified various ways: single-file and multifile assemblies, static and dynamic assemblies, private and shared assemblies, and satellite and resource-only assemblies.

Shared assemblies can be shared across applications and are stored in the machinewide Global Assembly Cache. Resource-only assemblies are those assemblies that contain just resources and no code. Resource-only assemblies that store culture-specific information are known as satellite assemblies.

KEY TERMS

- Component
- Web user control
- Web custom control
- Derived control
- Assembly
- Assembly manifest
- Assembly metadata
- Global Assembly Cache (GAC)
- Metadata
- Private assembly
- Resource-only assembly
- Satellite assembly
- Shared assembly
- Strong name

APPLY YOUR KNOWLEDGE

Exercises

7.1 Events from a Composite Control

In Step by Step 7.8, you saw how you could create a Web custom control as a composite control made up of individual server controls. In that Step by Step, you handled the button's Click event within the code of the Web custom control. But what if you want the Web custom control itself to expose an event to the containing page? This exercise shows how you can implement a custom event for a Web custom control.

Estimated Time: 25 minutes.

1. Launch a new instance of Visual Studio .NET.
2. Click the New Project button on the Start Page. Select the Visual Basic Projects project type and create a new Web Control Library project named WebCustomControls2.
3. Right-click the project in Solution Explorer and select Add, Add Class. Name the new class CompositeControlWithEvents.vb.
4. Delete the WebCustomControl1.vb class from the project.
5. Enter the following code for the CompositeControlWithEvents.vb class:

```
Imports System.Web.UI
Imports System.Web.UI.WebControls
Imports System.ComponentModel

Public Class CompositeControlWithEvents

    Inherits Control
    Implements INamingContainer

    Public Sub New()
        ' Set default values for
        ' persisted properties
        ViewState("MinValue") = 0
        ViewState("MaxValue") = 1000
    End Sub
```

```
Protected Overrides Sub _
 CreateChildControls()
    ' Create the constituent controls
    Dim lbl As System.Web.UI. _
     WebControls.Label = _
     New Label()
    Dim btn As System.Web.UI. _
     WebControls.Button = _
     New Button()
    ' Set initial properties
    With lbl
        .Height = Unit.Pixel(25)
        .Width = Unit.Pixel(75)
        .Text = "0"
    End With
    With btn
        .Height = Unit.Pixel(25)
        .Width = Unit.Pixel(75)
        .Text = "Go"
    End With
    ' Add them to the controls
    ' to be rendered
    Controls.Add(lbl)
    Controls.Add(btn)
    ' Hook up an event handler
    AddHandler btn.Click, _
     AddressOf btnClick
End Sub

' Public properties to display
' in the Properties Window
<Category("Behavior"), _
 Description("Minimum value")> _
Public Property MinValue() As Integer
    Get
        MinValue = CType(ViewState( _
         "MinValue"), Integer)
    End Get
    Set(ByVal Value As Integer)
        ViewState("MinValue") = Value
    End Set
End Property

<Category("Behavior"), _
Description("Maximum value")> _
Public Property MaxValue() As Integer
    Get
        MaxValue = CType(ViewState( _
         "MaxValue"), Integer)
    End Get
    Set(ByVal Value As Integer)
        ViewState("MaxValue") = Value
    End Set
End Property
```

APPLY YOUR KNOWLEDGE

```
        ' Handle the constituent control event
        Public Sub btnClick( _
         ByVal sender As Object, _
         ByVal e As EventArgs)
            Dim r As System.Random = _
             New System.Random()
            Dim Value As Integer
            ' Generate a new random value based
            ' on the minimum and maximum
            ' stored in the state
            Value = CType(r.Next( _
             CType(ViewState("MinValue"), _
             Integer), _
             CType(ViewState("MaxValue"), _
             Integer)), String)
            ' Find the constituent
            ' label control
            Dim lbl As Label = Controls(0)
            ' Make sure the controls
            ' really exist
            Me.EnsureChildControls()
            ' And set the text to display
            lbl.Text = Value.ToString
            ' Finally, bubble an event
            ' up to the page
            OnChange(EventArgs.Empty)
        End Sub

        ' Custom event for the control and
        ' method to raise it
        Public Event Change( _
         ByVal sender As Object, _
         ByVal e As EventArgs)
        Protected Sub OnChange( _
         ByVal e As EventArgs)
            RaiseEvent Change(Me, e)
        End Sub

    End Class
```

6. Save and build the WebCustomControls2 project.

7. Close the WebCustomControls solution. Create a new Visual Basic ASP.NET Web Application project named WebCustomControlEventTest.

8. Delete the default WebForm1.aspx Web Form from the new project.

9. Add a Web Form named Exercise7-1.aspx to the project.

10. Select the Components tab in the Visual Studio .NET Toolbox. Right-click the tab and select Customize Toolbox. Select the .NET Framework Components tab in the Customize Toolbox dialog box. Click the Browse button and browse to the WebCustomControls2.dll file in the bin directory under the WebCustomControls2 project. Click OK. This will add the CompositeControlWithEvents control to the Toolbox.

11. Drag the CompositeControl control from the Toolbox and drop it on the Web Form.

12. Set the MinValue property of the new control to 500 and the MaxValue property of the new control to 1500 by changing the values in the Properties Window.

13. Add a Label control with the ID of lblResults to the Web Form.

14. Add an event handler for the custom control's Change event:

```
Private Sub _
 CompositeControlWithEvents1_Change( _
 ByVal sender As Object, _
 ByVal e As System.EventArgs) _
 Handles CompositeControlWithEvents1.Change
    lblResults.Text = _
     "New random number generated at " & _
     DateTime.Now.ToShortTimeString
End Sub
```

15. Set the Web Form as the start page for the project.

16. Run the project. Click the button. A new random number will appear on the form, along with the informational message shown in Figure 7.22.

APPLY YOUR KNOWLEDGE

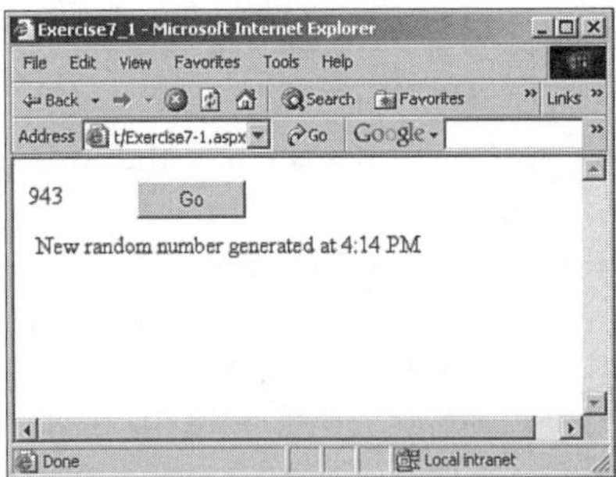

FIGURE 7.22
A composite control with events.

7.2 Getting Types in an Assembly

The classes in the System.Reflection namespace along with the System.Type class allow you to obtain information about loaded assemblies at runtime. This information includes the types defined within the assembly such as classes, interfaces, and value types. In this exercise you will use these classes to enumerate the types in an ASP.NET assembly

Estimated Time: 20 minutes.

1. Add a new Web Form named Exercise7-2.aspx to your project.
2. Place a ListBox control with the ID of lbTypes on the Web Form.
3. Switch to Code view and add the following line of code to the top of the Web Form's module:

```
Imports System.Reflection
```

4. Add code to handle the `Load` event of the Web Form:

```
Private Sub Page_Load( _
 ByVal sender As System.Object, _
 ByVal e As System.EventArgs) _
 Handles MyBase.Load
    ' Load the Assembly
    Dim assem As [Assembly] = _
    System.Reflection.Assembly. _
     GetExecutingAssembly()
    ' Get all the types in the assembly
    Dim types() As Type = assem.GetTypes()
    lbTypes.Items.Clear()
    Dim typ As Type
    For Each typ In types
        ' Dump the FullName of the
        ' Type to the ListBox
        lbTypes.Items.Add(typ.FullName)
    Next
End Sub
```

5. Set the Web Form as the start page for the project.
6. Run the project. All the types in the assembly with their full names will appear in the ListBox, as shown in Figure 7.23.

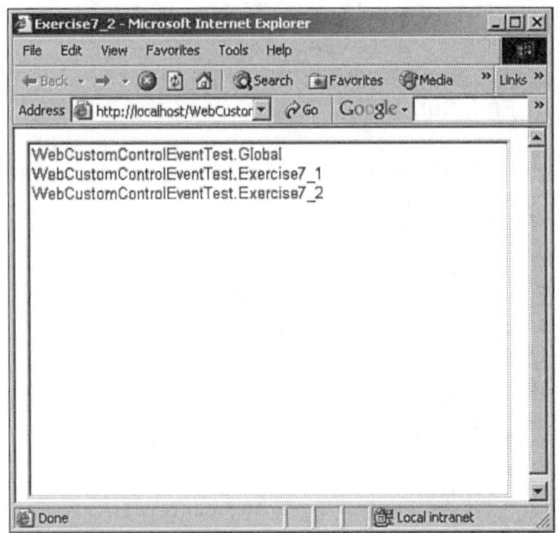

FIGURE 7.23
Getting the types from an assembly.

As you can see in Figure 7.23, ASP.NET compiles each Web Form into a separate class within the assembly. There's also one more class to hold global event handlers.

APPLY YOUR KNOWLEDGE

Review Questions

1. What are the benefits to using components in an application?
2. What is the difference between a Web user control and a Web custom control?
3. Name three types of Web custom controls.
4. What is the purpose of the EnsureChildControls method?
5. How can you provide design-time support for a composite control?
6. Where can you handle events from a Web custom control?
7. What is the purpose of the assembly manifest?
8. What type of assemblies should be stored in the Global Assembly Cache?
9. What are resource-only and satellite assemblies?

Exam Questions

1. You want to decrease the time it takes for a component to load for the first time. Which of the following tools can help you?

    A. gacutil.exe

    B. resgen.exe

    C. sn.exe

    D. ngen.exe

2. You have converted your application's assembly files to native images using the Native Image Generation tool (ngen.exe). Which of the following statements hold true for your assemblies? (Select two.)

    A. Applications that use a native assembly will run faster for the initial run.

    B. Applications using a native assembly will have consistently faster performance as compared to a JIT-compiled assembly.

    C. The native assemblies are portable. You should be able to use them on any machine that has the common language runtime installed on it.

    D. The native assemblies can be used in debugging scenarios.

3. You have developed a graphics application. Before you create a setup program you want to package some of the image files in a resource-only assembly. You have created an XML-based resource file for these files and named it App.resx. Which of the following steps would you take to convert this file into a resource-only assembly?

    A. Use the vbc.exe tool followed by the al.exe tool.

    B. Use the resgen.exe tool followed by the al.exe tool.

    C. Use the resgen.exe tool followed by the vbc.exe tool.

    D. Use the vbc.exe tool followed by the resgen.exe tool.

4. You have developed a utility network library that will be used by several applications in your company. How should you deploy this library?

    A. Sign the library using the Strong Name tool (sn.exe) and place it in Global Assembly Cache.

    B. Sign the library using the File Signing tool (signcode.exe) and place it in Global Assembly cache.

APPLY YOUR KNOWLEDGE

C. Sign the library using both the Strong Name tool and the File Signing tool and place it in the bin directory of each application using it.

D. Keep the library at a central place such as C:\CommonComponents and use each application's configuration files to point to it.

5. You have created a custom component that reads configuration information from a database. Because there may be many instances of this component in operation at any given time, you decide to implement a Dispose method in the component to close the database connection. How should you implement this method?

A.

```
Protected Overloads Overrides Sub Dispose( _
 ByVal disposing As Boolean)
    If Not disposing Then
        If Not (components Is Nothing) Then
            components.Dispose()
        End If
    End If
    mcnn.Close()
    mcnn = Nothing
    MyBase.Dispose(disposing)
End Sub
```

B.

```
Protected Overloads Overrides Sub Dispose( _
 ByVal disposing As Boolean)
    If disposing Then
        If Not (components Is Nothing) Then
            components.Dispose()
        End If
    End If
    mcnn.Close()
    mcnn = Nothing
    MyBase.Dispose(disposing)
End Sub
```

C.

```
Protected Overloads Overrides Sub Dispose( _
 ByVal disposing As Boolean)
    If Not disposing Then
        mcnn.Close()
        mcnn = Nothing
        MyBase.Dispose(disposing)
    End If
End Sub
```

D.

```
Protected Overloads Overrides Sub Dispose( _
 ByVal disposing As Boolean)
    If disposing Then
        components.Dispose()
    End If
    mcnn.Close()
    mcnn = Nothing
    MyBase.Dispose(disposing)
End Sub
```

6. You are developing a component that needs to expose a property named Count to its container. The Count property should be read-only. How should you implement this property?

A.

```
Public ReadOnly Property Count() As Integer
    Get
        Count = mCount
    End Get
End Property
```

B.

```
Public ReadOnly Count As Integer
```

C.

```
Public Property Count() As Integer
    Get
        Count = mCount
    End Get
End Property
```

D.

```
Public Readonly Property Count() As Integer
    Get
        Count = mCount
    End Get
    Set(ByVal Value As Integer)
    End Set
End Property
```

APPLY YOUR KNOWLEDGE

7. You have created a Web user control named menu.ascx that encapsulates the standard navigation menu to be used on your company's Web sites. You now want to use this control in Web applications other than the one where you built the control. What should you do?

   A. Install the control in the Global Assembly Cache (GAC).

   B. Include the control's project in the solution containing each application.

   C. Copy the control's files into each application.

   D. Compile the control and copy the compiled assembly into each application's bin folder.

8. You have created a Web custom control named menu.ascx that encapsulates the standard navigation menu to be used on your company's Web sites. You now want to use this control in Web applications other than the one where you built the control. What should you do?

   A. Install the control in the Global Assembly Cache (GAC).

   B. Include the control's project in the solution containing each application.

   C. Copy the control's files into each application.

   D. Compile the control and copy the compiled assembly into each application's bin folder.

9. The CreateChildControls method of your composite custom control uses this code to add four controls to its Controls collection:

```
Protected Overrides Sub _
 CreateChildControls()
    Dim lbl As System.Web.UI. _
     WebControls.Label = _
     New Label()
    Dim btn As System.Web.UI. _
     WebControls.Button = _
     New Button()
    Dim txt As System.Web.UI. _
     WebControls.TextBox = _
     New TextBox()
    Dim img As System.Web.UI. _
     WebControls.Image = _
     New Image()
    Controls.Add(lbl)
    Controls.Add(btn)
    Controls.Add(txt)
    Controls.Add(img)
End Sub
```

   In an event handler within the composite control class you need to refer to the TextBox control. How can you retrieve this control?

   A. Dim txt As TextBox = ViewState(txt)

   B. Dim txt As TextBox = New TextBox()

   C. Dim txt As TextBox = Controls(3)

   D. Dim txt As TextBox = Controls(2)

10. You are creating a Web custom control by inheriting directly from the System.Web.Ui.WebControls.WebControl class. What can you do to provide a design-time representation of your control? (Select two)

   A. Implement an Init method that returns HTML text.

   B. Implement a Render method that returns HTML text.

   C. Create a control designer class and specify it using attributes of the control class.

   D. Include a bitmap of the control in the assembly with the control's code.

APPLY YOUR KNOWLEDGE

11. You are creating an ASP.NET Web application to serve as the Web site for a small business client of yours. Each page in the site will have the same controls functioning as a menu. You won't need to reuse these controls for any other project. What sort of control should you create to represent the menu?

    A. Composite Web custom control

    B. Web custom control that inherits directly from Label

    C. Web custom control that inherits directly from WebControl

    D. Web user control

12. You are creating a specialized control that will manage image uploads for your company. This control must be installed into the Visual Studio toolbox so that it can be used in many projects. The control's user interface will be a single button that can be used to browse for a file. What sort of control should you create?

    A. Composite Web custom control

    B. Web custom control that inherits directly from Button

    C. Web custom control that inherits directly from WebControl

    D. Web user control

13. You are building a new control that will track Quality of Service (QoS) by issuing pings from the browser and uploading the results. The control will not have a run-time user interface. What sort of control should you create?

    A. Composite Web custom control

    B. Web custom control that inherits directly from Label

    C. Web custom control that inherits directly from WebControl

    D. Web user control

14. You have a standard set of controls that you use to implement menus in Web applications for a wide variety of customers. These controls include a series of LinkButtons, Images, and Labels. You've decided that you would like to encapsulate these controls for easy reuse. What sort of control should you create?

    A. Composite Web custom control

    B. Web custom control that inherits directly from Label

    C. Web custom control that inherits directly from WebControl

    D. Web user control

15. You have created a Web custom control that you will be using in numerous ASP.NET applications on multiple servers. You are considering installing the control in the Global Assembly Cache (GAC). What is a potential drawback of this action?

    A. Controls in the GAC cannot be used by ASP.NET applications.

    B. Controls in the GAC cannot be signed to ensure their security.

    C. You cannot deploy a control to the GAC via FTP or XCOPY.

    D. The GAC can only contain one version of any particular control.

APPLY YOUR KNOWLEDGE

Answers to Review Questions

1. Components have all the benefits of code reuse, including more rapid development and better testing. In addition, they support Visual Studio .NET features such as the Toolbox and the Properties window through the IComponent interface.

2. A Web user control is a piece of HTML code with associated VB .NET code, similar to a Web Form. A Web custom control is a compiled class that derives from the WebControl class.

3. Web custom controls can be composite controls composed of individual server controls, controls that derive directly from a specific control class such as the TextBox, or controls that derive directly from WebControl and implement all of their services from scratch.

4. The EnsureChildControls method prevents you from exceptions that would occur when trying to access child controls before they're created.

5. You can supply a custom designer class for any Web custom control, including a composite control.

6 You can handle events from a Web custom control directly in the control's own code, or you can bubble them up to the containing code, or both.

7. An assembly manifest stores the assembly's metadata. The metadata provides self-describing information like the name and version of the assembly, the files that are part of the assembly and their hash values, the files' dependencies on other assemblies, and so on. This subset of information in the manifest makes assemblies self-sufficient.

8. Shared assemblies (those used by more than one application) should be stored in the machinewide Global Assembly Cache. Shared assemblies are digitally signed and have a strong name.

9. Resource-only assemblies are those that contain just resources and no code. Resource-only assemblies that store culture-specific information are known as satellite assemblies.

Answers to Exam Questions

1. **D.** The Native Image Generator tool (ngen.exe) converts Microsoft intermediate language to processor-specific native code. These native assemblies will load faster the first time the code is called because the work the JIT compiler normally would do has been already done by the ngen tool. The other three choices are not relevant because gacutil.exe allows you to view and manipulate the contents of Global Assembly Cache. The resgen.exe is the Resource Generator tool that is used to compile XML-based resource files (resx files) into binary .resources files. The sn.exe is used to assign assemblies with a strong name so they can be placed in the Global Assembly Cache.

2. **A, D.** The native assemblies will load faster the first time because the work the JIT compiler normally would do has been already done by the ngen tool, but for subsequent usage the native assemblies would show the same performance as their JIT-compiled equivalents. The natively generated assemblies are processor-specific: They can't be ported across a different processor architecture. The ngen.exe tool provides a /debug switch to generate native assemblies for debugging scenarios.

APPLY YOUR KNOWLEDGE

3. **B.** To create a resource-only assembly, you first compile the XML-based resource file into a binary resource file using the Resource Generator tool (resgen.exe). Then you use the Assembly Generation tool (al.exe) to create a resource-only assembly.

4. **A.** If an assembly is used by several applications, it is a good idea to place the assembly in the Global Assembly Cache because GAC provides benefits, including versioning and security checks. To place an assembly in GAC you must assign a strong name to it. You can use the sn.exe tool to assign a strong name. The File Signing tool (signcode.exe) can digitally sign an assembly with a third-party software publisher's certification. It is not a requirement for an assembly to be placed in GAC.

5. **B**. The Dispose method should call Dispose on its own Components collection to make sure that any components in that collection are properly cleaned up. But you need to check two things before you launch this process. First, you should be sure that Dispose was called explicitly (rather than being called as part of the garbage collection process). Second, you need to make sure that the collection actually exists.

6. **A**. Read-only properties must be implemented using Property procedures rather than public variables. The procedure must be marked with the ReadOnly modifier and must contain only a Get procedure.

7. **C**. A Web user control can only be used by a project containing the control's files. You can compile the code-behind file, but the ascx file must still be copied to every application.

8. **A**. A Web custom control can be used by any application that can set a reference to the compiled version of the control. If you install a Web custom control in the Global Assembly Cache, it can be used by any application on the computer.

9. **D**. The constituent controls in a composite control are numbered in the order to which they were added to the Controls collection, starting at zero.

10. **B, C**. The design-time representation of a control is composed of HTML code representing the control. This HTML code can come from the control's Render method or from the GetDesignTimeHtml method of a control designer class.

11. **D**. For reuse in a single project, a Web user control is the quickest and easiest alternative.

12. **B.** For Toolbox support, you need to use a Web custom control. Because the user interface is similar to an existing control, you should derive your new control directly from that control.

13. **C**. This control doesn't require a user interface, so you can build it most simply by deriving it directly from the WebControl class.

14. **A.** You can encapsulate multiple controls in either a Web user control or a composite Web custom control. The composite control is a much better choice for use in multiple projects, because it can be added to the GAC and the Toolbox.

15. **C**. To deploy a control to the GAC, you must use a setup program, which can be a problem if you're managing multiple remote web servers. ASP.NET applications can use controls from the GAC without problems. Controls in the GAC must be signed. The GAC can host more than one version of the same control without conflicts.

APPLY YOUR KNOWLEDGE

Suggested Readings and Resources

1. Visual Studio .NET Combined Help Collection
   - ASP.NET Server Controls section
   - Developing ASP.NET Server Controls section
2. Jones, A. Russell, *Mastering ASP.NET with VB.NET.* Sybex, 2002.
3. Liberty, Jesse, and Hurwitz, Dan, *Programming ASP.NET,* O'Reilly, 2002.
4. Leinecker, Richard, *Special Edition Using ASP.NET*, Que Publishing, 2002.
5. Ahmed, Mesbah, et al, *ASP.NET Web Developer's Guide,* Syngress, 2002.

OBJECTIVES

This chapter covers the following Microsoft-specified objective for the Creating User Services section of the Visual Basic .NET Web Applications exam:

- **Instantiate and invoke a Web service.**

▶ Although the exam has only a single objective relating to Web services, this is a major area of .NET. With the release of .NET, it's become easier than ever to build, deploy, and use Web services (sometimes called *XML Web services* because they use XML to convey information). In this chapter you'll first learn what Web services are and how they fit into the overall .NET architecture. Then you'll see how to perform basic Web service tasks:

- Create a Web service.
- Discover a Web service.
- Instantiate and invoke a Web service.

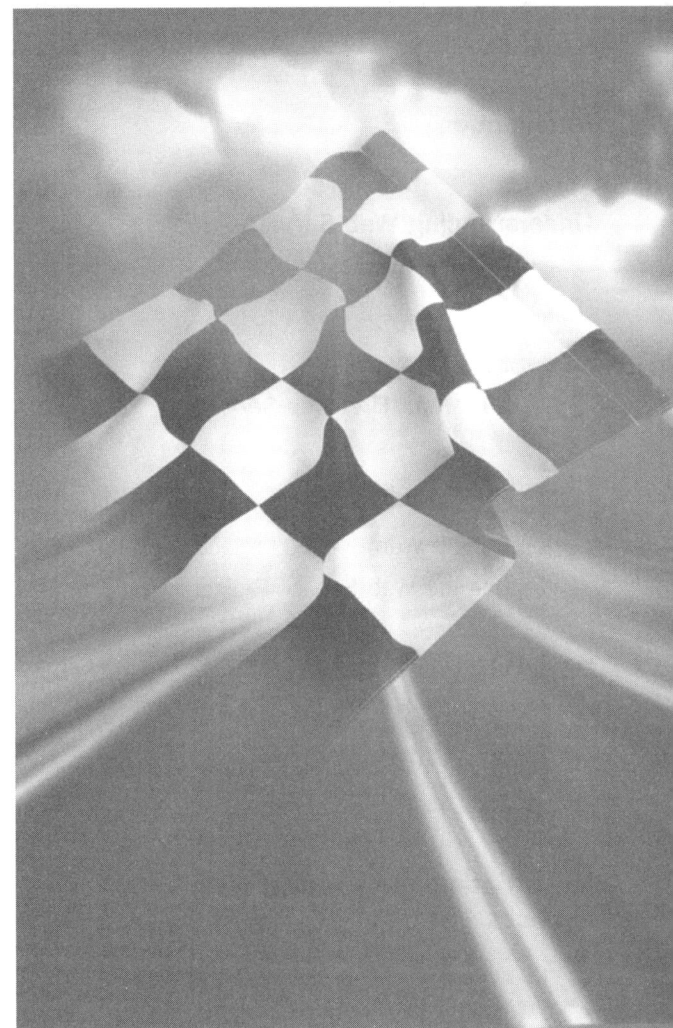

CHAPTER 8

Web Services

Outline

Study Strategies

- Use ASP.NET to create a simple Web service. Then use the wsdl.exe tool to create a proxy class for that Web service, and instantiate the Web service within another ASP.NET application. Make sure you understand how to make all of the pieces of the process work together.
- Use the registry at http://www.uddi.org/ to explore some available Web services.
- If you're reviewing references on Web services to study for the exam, make sure that they're specifically about Microsoft's approach to Web services. Although Web services are broadly interoperable between manufacturers, there are implementation differences.
- Use a tool such as the .NET WebService Studio to inspect SOAP message and WSDL files to see what's happening as you interact with a Web service.

NOTE

More Web Services As you progress toward the MCAD credential, you'll find that knowledge of Web services is essential. In particular, Web services are a major component of Exam 70-310, "Developing XML Web Services and Server Components with Microsoft Visual Basic .NET and the Microsoft .NET Framework."

INTRODUCTION

You've probably already heard quite a bit of hype about *Web services* in conjunction with .NET. In fact, Microsoft has gone so far as to sometimes describe the .NET Framework as "an XML Web services platform that will enable developers to create programs that transcend device boundaries and fully harness the connectivity of the Internet." You may also run across a lot of complex and confusing explanations of the architecture of these Web services. But at their most basic level, Web services are simple: They are a means for interacting with objects over the Internet.

Seen in that light, Web services are part of a natural progression:

1. Object-oriented languages such as C++ and C# let two objects within the same application interact.
2. Protocols such as COM let two objects on the same computer, but in different applications, interact.
3. Protocols such as DCOM let two objects on different computers, but the same local network, interact.
4. Web services let two objects on different computers, even if they're only connected by the Internet, interact.

In this chapter I'll introduce you to Web services as they exist in the .NET Framework. You'll see how to build and use Web services in your .NET applications, and you'll learn about the major protocols that are used when you communicate with a Web service.

UNDERSTANDING WEB SERVICES

Instantiate and invoke a Web service.

Before I get into the nuts and bolts of actually working with Web services, I'll give you an overview of the way they work. The key to understanding Web services is to know something about the protocols that make them possible:

- SOAP
- UDDI
- WSDL

One important thing to realize is that, by default, all communication between Web services servers and their clients is through XML messages transmitted over the HTTP protocol. This has two benefits. First, because Web services messages are formatted as XML, they're reasonably easy for human beings to read and understand. Second, because those messages are transmitted over the pervasive HTTP protocol, they can normally reach any machine on the Internet without worrying about firewalls.

SOAP

For Web services to manipulate objects through XML messages, there has to be a way to translate objects (as well as their methods and properties) into XML. This way is called SOAP, the Simple Object Access Protocol. SOAP is a way to encapsulate object calls as XML sent via HTTP.

> EXAM TIP
>
> **SOAP Over Other Protocols** You'll often read that SOAP messages travel over HTTP. While this is the default for SOAP as implemented by Visual Studio .NET, it's not a part of the SOAP specification. SOAP messages could be sent by email or FTP without losing their content. As a practical matter, SOAP today uses HTTP in almost all cases.

There are two major advantages to using SOAP to communicate with Web services. First, because HTTP is so pervasive, it can travel to any point on the Internet, regardless of intervening hardware or firewalls. Second, because SOAP is XML-based, it can be interpreted by a wide variety of software on many operating systems. Although you'll only work with the Microsoft implementation of Web services in this chapter, numerous Web services tools from other vendors can interoperate with Microsoft-based Web services.

Here's a typical SOAP message sent from a Web services client to a Web services server:

```
<?xml version="1.0" encoding="utf-8"?>
<soap:Envelope
  xmlns:soap="http://schemas.xmlsoap.org/soap/envelope/"
  xmlns:soapenc=
"http://schemas.xmlsoap.org/soap/encoding/"
  xmlns:tns=
"http://www.capeclear.com/AirportWeather.wsdl"
  xmlns:types="http://www.capeclear.com/
    AirportWeather.wsdl/encodedTypes"
  xmlns:xsi="http://www.w3.org/2001/XMLSchema-instance"
  xmlns:xsd="http://www.w3.org/2001/XMLSchema">
  <soap:Body soap:encodingStyle=
    "http://schemas.xmlsoap.org/soap/encoding/">
    <q1:getLocation
      xmlns:q1="capeconnect:AirportWeather:Station">
      <arg0 xsi:type="xsd:string">KSEA</arg0>
    </q1:getLocation>
  </soap:Body>
</soap:Envelope>
```

Even without digging into this file in detail, you can see some obvious points:

- The SOAP message consists of an envelope and a body.
- This particular message invokes a method named `getLocation` from a specified URL.
- The method takes a single parameter, `arg0`, which is transmitted as an XML element.

> **NOTE** **XML Files** If you need a refresher on the parts of an XML file, see Chapter 6, "Consuming and Manipulating Data."

Here's the SOAP message back from the server:

```
<?xml version="1.0" encoding="utf-8"?>
<SOAP-ENV:Envelope
  xmlns:SOAP-ENV=
"http://schemas.xmlsoap.org/soap/envelope/"
  xmlns:xsd="http://www.w3.org/2001/XMLSchema"
  xmlns:cc1=
"http://www.capeclear.com/AirportWeather.xsd"
  xmlns:xsi="http://www.w3.org/2001/XMLSchema-instance"
  xmlns:SOAP-ENC=
     "http://schemas.xmlsoap.org/soap/encoding/">
  <SOAP-ENV:Body SOAP-ENV:encodingStyle=
    "http://schemas.xmlsoap.org/soap/encoding/">
    <cc2:getLocationResponse
      xmlns:cc2="capeconnect:AirportWeather:Station"
      SOAP-ENC:root="1">
      <return xsi:type="xsd:string">
        Seattle, Seattle-Tacoma International Airport,
        WA, United States</return>
    </cc2:getLocationResponse>
  </SOAP-ENV:Body>
</SOAP-ENV:Envelope>
```

In the response message, the `getLocationResponse` element is the result of the call to the object on the server. It includes a string wrapped up as an XML element.

Disco and UDDI

Before you can use a Web service, you need to know where to find the service. Handling such requests is the job of several protocols, including Disco and UDDI. These protocols allow you to communicate with a Web server to discover the details of the Web services that are available at that server.

WSDL

The other prerequisite for using a Web service is knowledge of the SOAP messages that it can receive and send. You can obtain this knowledge by parsing WSDL files. WSDL stands for *Web Services Description Language*, a standard by which a Web service can tell clients what messages it accepts and which results it will return.

Here's a portion of a WSDL file:

```
<?xml version="1.0" encoding="utf-16"?>
<definitions
  xmlns:http="http://schemas.xmlsoap.org/wsdl/http/"
  xmlns:soap="http://schemas.xmlsoap.org/wsdl/soap/"
  xmlns:s="http://www.w3.org/2001/XMLSchema"
  xmlns:s0="http://www.capeclear.com/AirportWeather.xsd"
  xmlns:soapenc=
"http://schemas.xmlsoap.org/soap/encoding/"
  xmlns:tns=
"http://www.capeclear.com/AirportWeather.wsdl"
  xmlns:tm=
"http://microsoft.com/wsdl/mime/textMatching/"
  xmlns:mime="http://schemas.xmlsoap.org/wsdl/mime/"
  targetNamespace=
    "http://www.capeclear.com/AirportWeather.wsdl"
  name="AirportWeather"
  xmlns="http://schemas.xmlsoap.org/wsdl/">
  <types>
    <s:schema targetNamespace=
      "http://www.capeclear.com/AirportWeather.xsd">
      <s:complexType name="WeatherSummary">
        <s:sequence>
          <s:element minOccurs="1" maxOccurs="1"
            name="location" nillable="true"
            type="s:string" />
          <s:element minOccurs="1" maxOccurs="1"
            name="wind" nillable="true"
            type="s:string" />
          <s:element minOccurs="1" maxOccurs="1"
            name="sky" nillable="true" type="s:string" />
          <s:element minOccurs="1" maxOccurs="1"
            name="temp" nillable="true"
            type="s:string" />
          <s:element minOccurs="1" maxOccurs="1"
            name="humidity" nillable="true"
            type="s:string" />
          <s:element minOccurs="1" maxOccurs="1"
            name="pressure" nillable="true"
            type="s:string" />
          <s:element minOccurs="1" maxOccurs="1"
            name="visibility" nillable="true"
            type="s:string" />
        </s:sequence>
      </s:complexType>
    </s:schema>
  </types>
```

> **EXAM TIP**
>
> **Exposure Is Optional** Although UDDI and WSDL files make it possible to interact with Web services without any prior knowledge, these files are not required for a Web service to function. You can make a Web service available on the Internet without any UDDI or WSDL file. In that case, only clients who already know the expected message formats and location of the Web service will be able to use it.

```
<message name="getHumidity">
  <part name="arg0" type="s:string" />
</message>
<message name="getHumidityResponse">
  <part name="return" type="s:string" />
</message>
<message name="getLocation">
  <part name="arg0" type="s:string" />
</message>
<message name="getLocationResponse">
  <part name="return" type="s:string" />
</message>
<message name="getOb">
  <part name="arg0" type="s:string" />
</message>
...
```

WSDL files define everything about a Web service: the data types that it can process, the methods that it exposes, and the URLs through which those methods can be accessed.

> **WARNING**
>
> **Working with the Internet** Most of the examples in this chapter assume that you're working on a computer that is connected to the Internet. It's okay if there's a proxy server between you and the Internet, as long as you can connect to Web sites.

Invoking Your First Web Service

At this point, I'd like to show you a Web service in action. Step by Step 8.1 shows how you can use a Web service, in this case one supplied by Microsoft's TerraService geographical information server.

> **NOTE**
>
> **Airport Codes** You can find a list of four-letter ICAO airport codes to use with this Web service at `http://www.house747.freeserve.co.uk/aptcodes.htm`. Codes for airports in the United States all start with K; codes for Canadian airports all start with C.

STEP BY STEP

8.1 Invoking a Web Service

1. Open a Visual Basic .NET Web Application in the Visual Studio .NET IDE.
2. Right-click the References folder in Solution Explorer and select Add Web Reference. This opens the Add Web Reference dialog box.
3. Type `http://live.capescience.com/wsdl/AirportWeather.wsdl` into the Address bar of the Add Web Reference dialog box and press Enter. This connects to the Airport Weather Web service and downloads the information shown in Figure 8.1.

> **WARNING**
>
> **Web Service Stability** Web services come and go, and there's no guarantee that the one I'm using in this chapter will still be available when you go to test it. If the Airport Weather Web service doesn't seem to be available, one good way to find others is to use your favorite search engine to look for the term "Web service examples."

continues

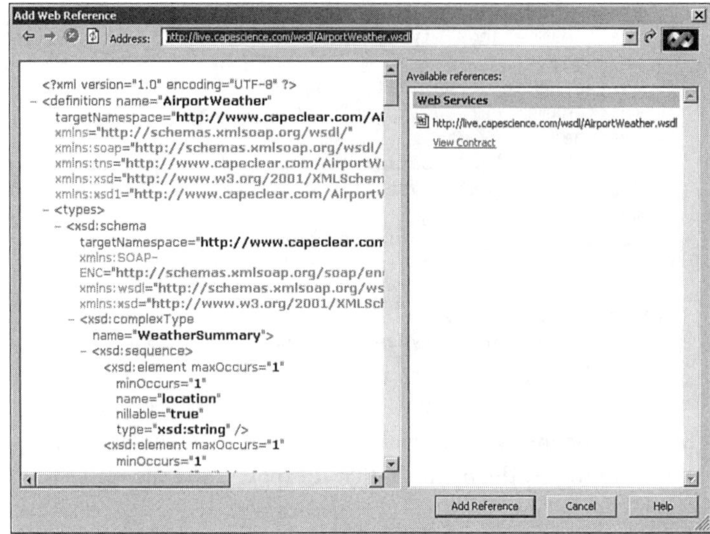

FIGURE 8.1
Connecting to a Web service over the Internet.

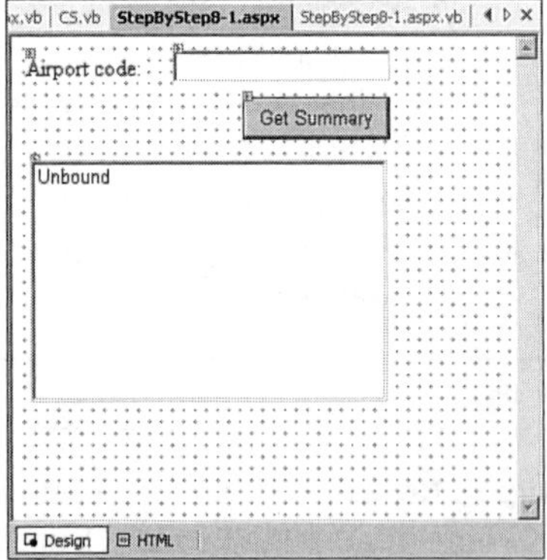

FIGURE 8.2
Creating a form to invoke a Web service.

4. Click the Add Reference button.

5. Add a new Web Form to your Visual Basic .NET project.

6. Place a Label control, a TextBox control with the ID of `txtCode`, a Button control with the ID of `btnGetSummary`, and a ListBox control with the ID of `lbResults` on the Web Form. Figure 8.2 shows this form in design view.

7. Double-click the Button control to open the form's module. Enter this code to invoke the Web service when the user clicks the button:

```
Private Sub btnGetSummary_Click( _
 ByVal sender As System.Object, _
 ByVal e As System.EventArgs) _
 Handles btnGetSummary.Click
    ' Connect to the Web service by declaring
    ' a variable of the appropriate type
    Dim aw As com.capescience.live.AirportWeather = _
     New com.capescience.live.AirportWeather()

    ' Call the Web service to get the summary
    ' for the entered airport
    Dim ws As com.capescience.live.WeatherSummary = _
     aw.getSummary(txtCode.Text)
```

NOTE

IntelliSense with Web Services
You'll see as you type this code that IntelliSense operates even though the objects you're working with are on the remote server.

```
    ' Display some of the properties
    ' filled in by the Web service
    With lbResults.Items
        .Clear()
        .Add(ws.location)
        .Add("Temperature: " & ws.temp)
        .Add("Visibility: " & ws.visibility)
        .Add("Wind: " & ws.wind)
    End With
End Sub
```

8. Set the Web Form as the start page for the project.

9. Run the project and fill in a value for the airport code. Click the button. After a brief pause while the Web service is invoked, you'll see some information in the `ListBox` control, as shown in Figure 8.3. This information is delivered from the server where the Web service resides, as properties of the `WeatherSummary` object.

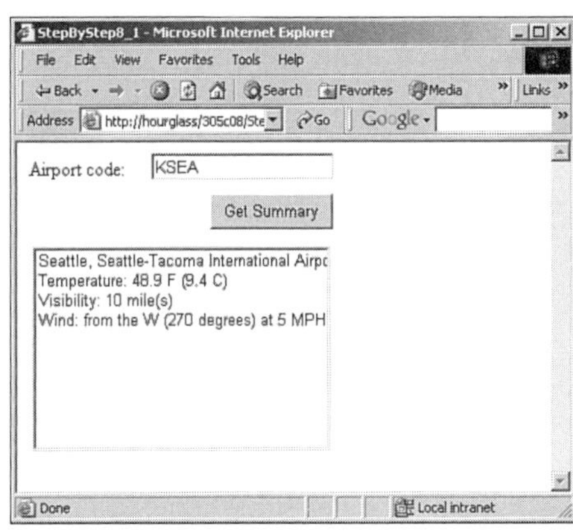

FIGURE 8.3
Invoking a Web service from a Web Form.

You'll learn more about the techniques in this Step by Step in the rest of the chapter, but you should be able to see the broad outlines of Web services already. In one sense, there's not much new here, compared to invoking any other object. After you've set a reference to the server, you can create objects from that server, invoke their methods, and examine the results. You could do the same with objects from a .NET library on your own computer.

But in another sense, there's a lot of revolutionary work going on here, even though you don't see most of it happening. When you create the Web reference, for example, Visual Studio .NET reads the appropriate WSDL file to determine which classes and methods are available from the remote server. When you call a method on an object from that server, the .NET infrastructure translates your call and the results into SOAP messages and transmits them without any intervention on your part.

REVIEW BREAK

- Web services provide you with the means to create objects and invoke their methods even though your only connection to the server is via the Internet.

continues

- Communication with Web services is via XML messages transported by the HTTP protocol.
- Because they communicate over HTTP, Web services are typically not blocked by firewalls.
- The Simple Object Access Protocol (SOAP) encapsulates object-oriented messages between Web service clients and servers.
- The Universal Description, Discovery, and Integration protocol (UDDI) allows you to find Web services by connecting to a directory.
- The Web Services Description Language (WSDL) lets you retrieve information on the classes and methods that are supported by a particular Web service.

CREATING WEB SERVICES

To better understand Web services, you should be familiar with both sides of the conversation. In this section, you'll learn how to create a Web service by using the tools built into ASP.NET. Although this material won't appear directly on the exam, it will help enhance your understanding of the skills that the exam does measure.

NOTE **Web Server Required** You'll need to have a Web server available to you to complete these exercises.

Creating a Web Service Project

To create a Web service, you can build an ASP.NET project in Visual Studio .NET.

STEP BY STEP

8.2 Creating a Web Service

1. Create a new project in Visual Studio .NET. Select the ASP.NET Web Service template and name the new project `StringProc`, as shown in Figure 8.4. You should replace HOURGLASS by the name of your own Web server.

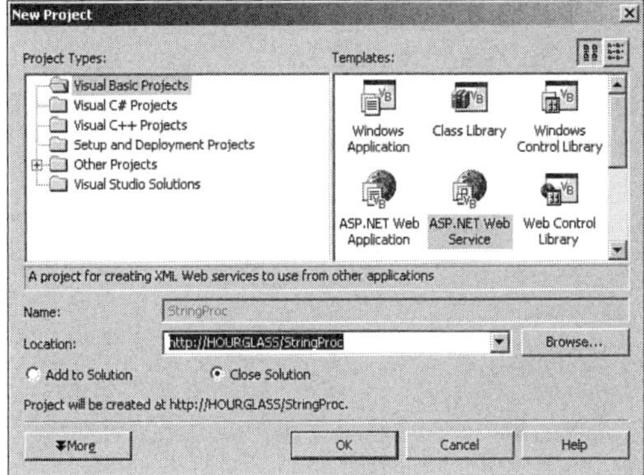

FIGURE 8.4
Creating a new Web service project.

2. Right-click the `Service1.asmx` file in Solution Explorer and rename it to `Strings.asmx`.

3. Click the hyperlink on the `Strings.asmx` design surface to switch to code view. Enter this code for the class (don't alter the Web Services designer generated code):

```
Imports System.Web.Services

<WebService(Namespace:= _
 "http://NetExam.org/StringProc")> _
Public Class Strings
    Inherits System.Web.Services.WebService

    <WebMethod()> Public Function ToUpper
➥(ByVal inputString As String) _
     As String
        ToUpper = inputString.ToUpper()
    End Function

    <WebMethod()> Public Function ToLower
➥(ByVal inputString As String) _
     As String
        ToLower = inputString.ToLower()
    End Function

End Class
```

4. Save the project.

5. Select Build, Build Solution to create the Web service on the server.

EXAM TIP

The Web Service Namespace The `WebService` attribute requires you to supply a value for the `Namespace` property. This value (`http://NetExam.org/StringProc` in this example) is purely arbitrary. It doesn't have to resolve to any actual Web site. This string is just a unique identifier for your Web service. If you leave the default value instead of changing it, you'll get a warning from Visual Studio .NET.

You now have a functioning Web service on your Web server. Congratulations! Although there is lots of plumbing involved in properly hooking up a Web service, Visual Studio .NET protects you from having to set up any of this plumbing. Instead, you only have to do three things:

1. Build your project from the ASP.NET Web Service template.
2. Mark the classes that should be available via the Web service with the `WebService` attribute.
3. Mark the methods that should be available via the Web service with the `WebMethod` attribute.

Testing the Web Service Project

Visual Studio .NET includes built-in tools, hosted on an HTML test page, for testing a Web service project without building any client applications for the Web service. Step by Step 8.3 shows you how to use these tools, which can save you time when you're debugging a Web service.

STEP BY STEP

8.3 Testing a Web Service

1. Start with the Web Service project from Step by Step 8.2. Run the project. This launches a browser and opens the test page shown in Figure 8.5.

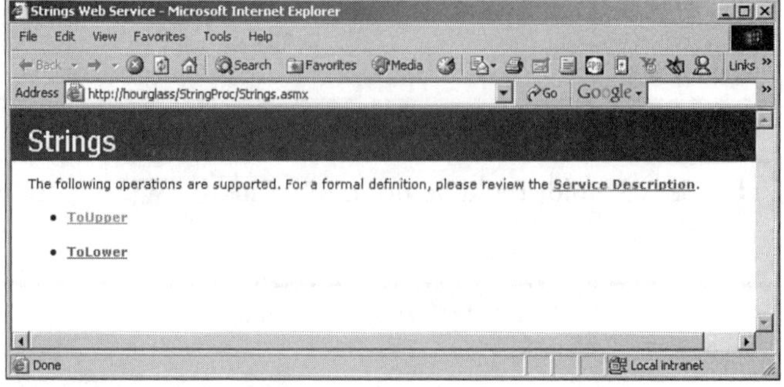

FIGURE 8.5
Web service test page.

2. Click the Service Description link on the test page. This lets you view the WSDL for this Web service. Click the Back button in the browser to return to the test page.

3. Click the ToUpper link on the test page. This opens a page for testing the `ToUpper` method, as shown in Figure 8.6.

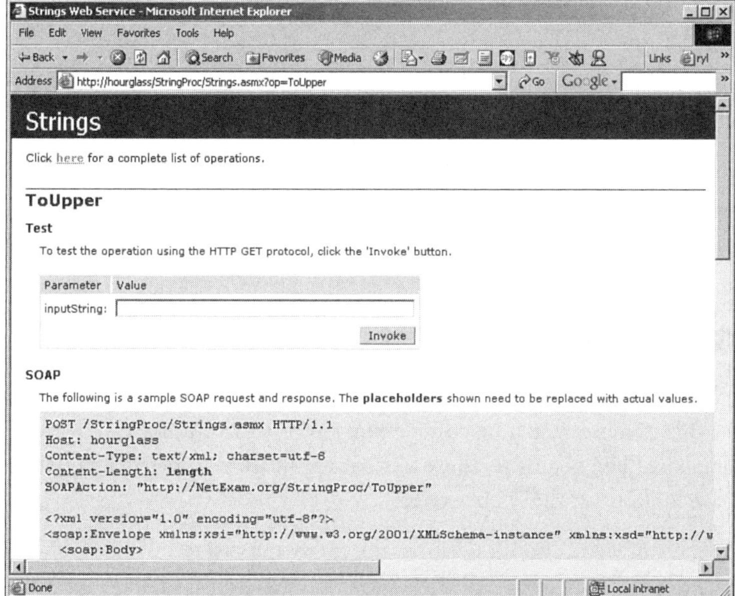

FIGURE 8.6
Test page for a Web method.

4. The Web method test page shows the SOAP and other messages that the Web service understands. It also contains a form to allow you to test the Web method.

5. Enter a string with mixed uppercase and lowercase characters in the `inputString` prompt.

6. Click the Invoke button. A second browser window opens, as shown in Figure 8.7, with the XML message that the Web service sends back when you call the `ToUpper` method on your test string.

continues

continued

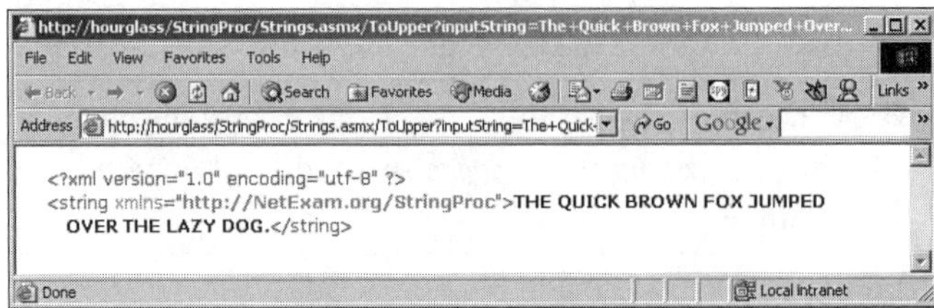

FIGURE 8.7
Testing a Web method.

7. You can also experiment with the `ToLower` method in the same way. When you click the Invoke button, the test page constructs the appropriate XML message and passes it to the Web service, which returns the results.

GUIDED PRACTICE EXERCISE 8.1

In this exercise, you'll be connecting a Web service to a SQL Server database. The goal is to allow a client application to perform a database lookup via the Web service.

Specifically, you should perform the following tasks:

1. Build a Web service that exposes a single class named `Customer`. The `Customer` class should expose a Web method named `GetCustomers`. The `GetCustomers` Web method should accept a country name and return a `Dataset` that contains all the customers from that country. Use the data from the Customers table of the Northwind sample database.
2. Build a client application that uses the Web service from step 1. The user should be able to enter a country name and see all the customers from that country.

You should try doing this on your own first. If you get stuck, or you'd like to see one possible solution, follow these steps:

1. Create a new project in Visual Studio .NET. Select the ASP.NET Web Service template and name the new project NorthwinD.

2. Right-click the `Service1.asmx` file in Solution Explorer and rename it to `Customer.asmx`.

3. Click the hyperlink on the `Strings.asmx` design surface to switch to code view. Change the name of the class to `Customer` and enter this code at the top of the file:

```
Imports System.Web.Services
Imports System.Data
Imports System.Data.SqlClient
```

4. Enter this code to create the `GetCustomers` Web method:

```
<WebMethod()> Public Function GetCustomers( _
 ByVal Country As String) As DataSet
    ' Create a SqlConnection
    Dim cnn As SqlConnection = _
     New SqlConnection("Data Source=(local);" & _
     "Initial Catalog=Northwind;" & _
     "Integrated Security=SSPI")
    ' Create a SqlCommand
    Dim cmd As SqlCommand = cnn.CreateCommand()
    cmd.CommandType = CommandType.Text
    cmd.CommandText = _
     "SELECT * FROM Customers WHERE Country = '" & _
     Country & "'"
    ' Set up the DataAdapter and fill the DataSet
    Dim da As SqlDataAdapter = New SqlDataAdapter()
    da.SelectCommand = cmd
    Dim ds As DataSet = New DataSet()
    da.Fill(ds, "Customers")
    ' And return it to the client
    GetCustomers = ds
End Function
```

5. Select Build, Build Solution to create the Web service on the server.

6. Now you can build the client application. Open your Web application for this chapter and add a new Web Form to the project.

7. Place a `Label` control, a `TextBox` control with the ID of `txtCountry`, a `Button` control with the ID of `btnGetCustomers`, and a `DataGrid` control with the ID of `dgCustomers` on the form. Figure 8.8 shows the design of this form.

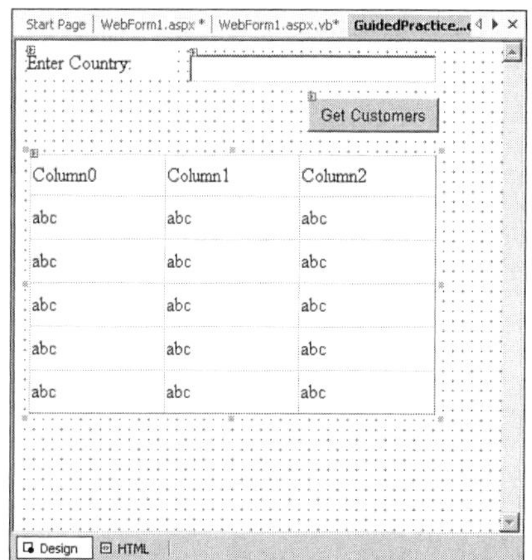

FIGURE 8.8
Designing a form to test the `GetCustomers` Web method.

continues

continued

8. Right-click the References folder in Solution Explorer and select Add Web Reference. This will open the Add Web Reference dialog box.

9. Type `http://YourServerName/Northwind/Customer.asmx` (substituting your own Web server name) into the Address bar of the Add Web Reference dialog box and press Enter. This connects to the server and downloads the information about the Northwind Web service.

10. Click the Add Reference button.

11. Double-click the `Button` control on the Web Form to open the Web Form's module. Enter this code at the top of the module:

```
Imports System.Data
Imports System.Data.SqlClient
```

12. Enter this code to handle the Button's `Click` event. You'll need to replace "hourglass" with the name of your own Web server:

```
Private Sub btnGetCustomers_Click( _
 ByVal sender As System.Object, _
 ByVal e As System.EventArgs) _
 Handles btnGetCustomers.Click
    ' Create a DataSet to hold
    ' the customers of interest
    Dim dsCustomers As DataSet
    ' Connect to the Web service
    ' and retrieve customers
    Dim cust As hourglass.Customer = _
     New hourglass.Customer()
    dsCustomers = cust.GetCustomers(txtCountry.Text)
    ' Bind the results to the user interface
    dgCustomers.DataSource = dsCustomers
    dgCustomers.DataMember = "Customers"
    dgCustomers.DataBind()
End Sub
```

13. Set the Web Form as the start page for the project.

14. Run the project and enter a country name (such as France). Click the button. After a brief delay while the project contacts the Web service, the `DataGrid` will fill with data as shown in Figure 8.9.

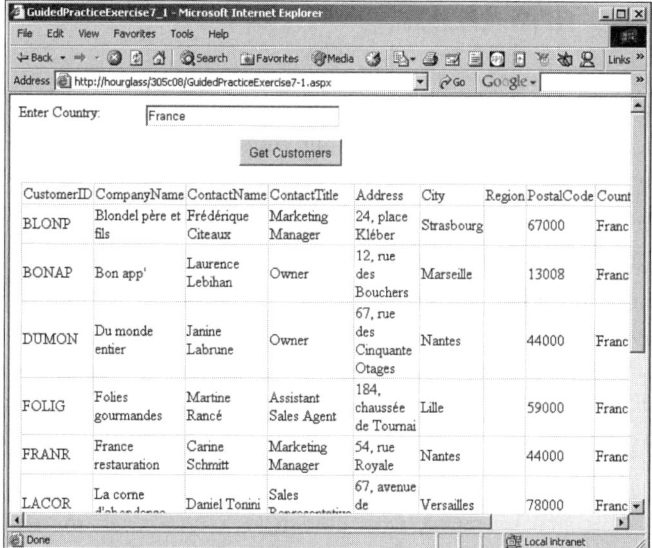

FIGURE 8.9
Data supplied by the `GetCustomers` Web method.

As this exercise shows, you can return complex objects from a Web service as easily as you can return simple types. The Web service takes care of all the details of converting the `DataSet` to an XML representation, wrapping it in a SOAP message, sending it to the client, and reconstituting the `DataSet` there.

Discovering Web Services

One of the problems with Web services is simply finding them. Because Web services aren't installed on your computer, you need some way to determine the messages that they accept and the services that they provide. The usual term for this process is *discovery*, which encompasses both finding Web services and determining their interfaces. You should know about three protocols in this area:

- Disco
- UDDI
- WSDL

Disco and UDDI

Disco is a Microsoft standard for the creation of discovery documents. A Disco document is kept at a standard location on a Web services server and contains paths and other information for retrieving other useful information, such as the WSDL file that describes a service.

UDDI (Universal Description, Discovery, and Integration) is a method for finding services by referring to a central directory. These can be Web services, URLs for information, or any other online resource. UDDI registries are sites that contain information available via UDDI; you can search such a registry to find information about Web services.

> NOTE
>
> **The UDDI Project** The UDDI specification is being developed jointly by several industry partners including Microsoft and IBM. For more information and a public directory, visit `http://www.uddi.org`.

UDDI registries come in two forms, *public* and *private*. A public UDDI registry is available to all comers via the Internet, and serves as a central repository of information about Web and other services for businesses. A private UDDI registry follows the same specifications as a public UDDI registry, but is located on an intranet for the use of workers at one particular enterprise.

Using the Web Services Discovery Tool (`disco.exe`)

When you set a Web reference inside of Visual Studio .NET, the software handles the details of discovery automatically for you. But you can also get into the details of the process yourself. One of the tools included in the .NET Framework SDK (and also in Visual Studio .NET) is the Web Services Discovery Tool, `disco.exe`. This is a command-line tool that will assist you in the discovery process, as seen in Step by Step 8.4.

STEP BY STEP

8.4 Using the Web Services Discovery Tool

1. Select Start, Programs, Microsoft Visual Studio .NET, Visual Studio .NET Tools, Visual Studio .NET Command Prompt. This opens a command prompt window and sets up the environment so that you can use any of the command-line tools from the .NET Framework SDK.

2. Enter the following command to discover the details of the Airport Weather Web service:

```
disco http://live.capescience.com/wsdl/
AirportWeather.wsdl
```

   As you can see, you need to know the base address of the Web service to use this tool.

3. The tool contacts the Web service and (in this case) creates two files of results: `CensusService.wsdl` and `results.discomap`.

4. Open the files in Visual Studio .NET to see the results of the discovery process.

5. The `results.discomap` file is an XML file that shows you the name of the other file and the URL from which its contents were retrieved.

6. The `AirportWeather.wsdl` file is an XML file that contains information on the interface of the Web service. This includes details of the messages, parameters, and objects with which you can interact. It's this file that gives Visual Studio .NET the details that it needs to let you use a Web service from your code.

REVIEW BREAK

- Disco is Microsoft's standard format for discovery documents, which contain information on Web services.
- UDDI, the Universal Description, Discovery, and Integration protocol, is a multi-vendor standard for discovering online resources, including Web services.
- The Web Services Discovery Tool, `disco.exe`, can retrieve discovery information from a server that exposes a Web service.

INSTANTIATING AND INVOKING WEB SERVICES

After you've discovered a Web service and retrieved information about its interface, you can instantiate an object representing that Web service and then invoke its methods. In this section you'll see two methods to integrate Web services into your applications, and you'll learn about testing a Web service as a consumer.

Creating Proxy Classes With the Web Services Description Language Tool (`wsdl.exe`)

The .NET Framework SDK includes the Web Services Description Language Tool, `wsdl.exe`. This tool can take a WSDL file and generate a corresponding proxy class that you can use to invoke the Web service, as seen in Step by Step 8.5.

STEP BY STEP

8.5 Using the Web Services Description Language Tool

1. Select Start, Programs, Microsoft Visual Studio .NET, Visual Studio .NET Tools, Visual Studio .NET Command Prompt. This opens a command prompt window and sets up the environment so that you can use any of the command-line tools from the .NET Framework SDK.
2. Navigate to the folder that contains the WSDL file that you created in Step By Step 8.4.
3. Enter the following command to create a proxy class to call the Airport Weather Web service:

```
wsdl /language:VB /out:aw.vb AirportWeather.wsdl
```

4. The tool reads the WSDL file and creates a new file named `aw.vb`.

5. Add the `aw.vb` file to your Visual Studio .NET Web application project by selecting File, Add Existing Item.

6. Add a new Web Form to your Visual Basic .NET Web project.

7. Place a Label control, a TextBox control with the ID of `txtCode`, a Button control with the ID of `btnGetSummary`, and a ListBox control with the ID of `lbResults` on the Web Form. Use the same form design that you saw in Figure 8.2.

8. Double-click the `Button` control to open the Web Form's module. Enter this code to invoke the Web service when the user clicks the button:

```
Private Sub btnGetSummary_Click( _
 ByVal sender As System.Object, _
 ByVal e As System.EventArgs) _
 Handles btnGetSummary.Click
    ' Connect to the Web service by declaring
    ' a variable of the appropriate type
    Dim aw As AirportWeather = _
     New AirportWeather()

    ' Call the Web service to get the summary
    ' for the entered airport
    Dim ws As WeatherSummary = _
     aw.getSummary(txtCode.Text)

    ' Display some of the properties
    ' filled in by the Web service
    With lbResults.Items
        .Clear()
        .Add(ws.location)
        .Add("Temperature: " & ws.temp)
        .Add("Visibility: " & ws.visibility)
        .Add("Wind: " & ws.wind)
    End With
End Sub
```

9. Set the Web Form as the start page for the project.

10. Run the project and fill in a value for the airport code. Click the button. After a brief pause while the Web service is invoked, you'll see some information in the `ListBox` control, as shown in Figure 8.3. This information is delivered from the server where the Web service resides, as properties of the `AirportWeather` object.

continues

continued

The difference between this and the version that you saw at the start of the chapter is that this code defines the objects that it uses explicitly rather than discovering them at runtime. The `AirportWeather` and `WeatherSummary` objects are proxy objects that pass calls through to the Web service and return results from the Web service.

Table 8.1 shows some of the command-line options that you can use with `wsdl.exe`. You don't need to memorize this material, but you should be familiar with the overall capabilities of the tool. You can use either the path to a local WSDL or Disco file or the URL of a remote WSDL or Disco file with this tool.

TABLE 8.1

COMMAND-LINE OPTIONS FOR WSDL.EXE

Option	*Meaning*
`/domain:`*`DomainName`*	Domain name to use when connecting to a server that requires authentication.
`/language:`*`LanguageCode`*	Specifies the language for the generated class. The `LanguageCode` parameter can be CS (for C#), VB (for VB .NET) or JS (for Jscript).
`/namespace:`*`Namespace`*	Specifies a namespace for the generated class.
`/out:`*`Filename`*	Filename for the generated output. If not specified, the filename will be derived from the Web service name.
`/password:`*`Password`*	Password to use when connecting to a server that requires authentication.
`/server`	Generates a class to create a server based on the input file. By default, the tool generates a client proxy object.
`/username:`*`Username`*	Username to use when connecting to a server that requires authentication.
`/?`	Displays full help on the tool.

Using Web References

As an alternative to using the Web Service Discovery Tool and the Web Service Description Language Tool to create explicit proxy classes, you can simply add a Web reference to your project to enable the project to use the Web service. You've seen Web references several times in this chapter, starting with Step By Step 8.1.

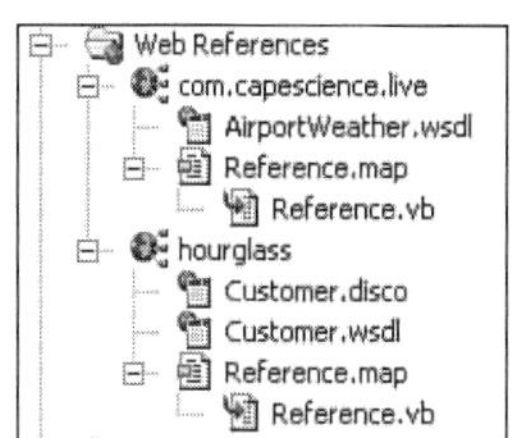

FIGURE 8.10
Files generated by adding a Web reference.

In fact, there's no difference in the end result between using the tools to create a proxy class and adding a Web reference. That's because, behind the scenes, the Web reference creates its own proxy class. To see this, click the Show All Files toolbar button within Solution Explorer, and then expand the Solution Explorer node for a Web reference. You'll see a set of files similar to that shown in Figure 8.10.

> **EXAM TIP**
>
> **Why Use a Web Reference?** The major benefit of using a Web reference (as compared to constructing proxy classes with the command-line tools) is that it's easier to update the proxy classes if the Web service changes. All that you need to do in that case is right-click the Web Reference node in Solution Explorer and select Update Web Reference.

The `.disco`, `.wsdl`, and `.map` files are the same files that would be generated by running the Web Service Discovery Tool on the URL of the Web reference. The `.vb` file defines the proxy objects to be used with the Web service represented by this Web reference, as you can see by opening this file. The major difference between this file and the proxy that you generated with the Web Services Description Language Tool is that the auto-generated file uses a namespace based on the name of the Web reference.

Testing a Web Service

If you'd like to test a Web service without building an entire client application, you can use a testing tool. Several such tools are easily available:

- NetTool is a free Web services proxy tool from CapeClear. You can get a copy from `http://capescience.capeclear.com/articles/using_nettool/`.
- The .NET WebService Studio tool comes from Microsoft. You can download a free copy from `http://www.gotdotnet.com/team/tools/web_svc/default.aspx`.

- XML Spy includes a SOAP debugger that can be used to test Web services. You can download a trial copy of this XML editor and toolkit from `http://www.xmlspy.com/default.asp`.

All three of these tools work in the same basic way: they intercept SOAP messages between Web services clients and servers so that you can inspect, and if you like, alter the results. In Step By Step 8.6 you'll use one of these tools to see a Web service in action.

STEP BY STEP

8.6 Testing a Web Service Without a Client Project

1. Download the .NET WebService Studio tool from `http://www.gotdotnet.com/team/tools/web_svc/default.aspx` and install it on your computer.
2. Launch the WebServiceStudio.exe application.
3. Enter `http://live.capescience.com/wsdl/AirportWeather.wsdl` as the WSDL endpoint and click the Get button.
4. The tool reads the WSDL file from the Web service and constructs the necessary proxy classes to invoke it. Click the GetSummary entry on the Invoke tab to use the GetSummary Web method.
5. In the Input section, select the arg0 item. You can now enter a value for this item in the Value section. Enter an airport code such as "KSEA" for the value.
6. Click the Invoke button. The tool sends a SOAP message to the Web service using your chosen parameters and then displays the results, as shown in Figure 8.11.

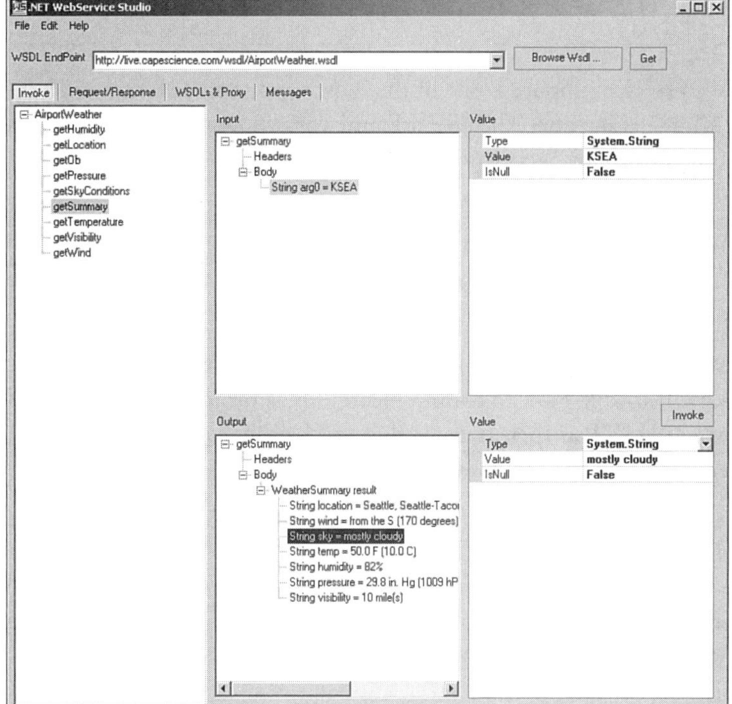

FIGURE 8.11
Invoking a Web service with the .NET WebService Studio Tool.

7. Click the Request/Response tab to view the outgoing and incoming SOAP messages.
8. Click the WSDLs & Proxy tab to see the WSDL file and the generated proxy class for this Web service.

REVIEW BREAK

- You can generate proxy classes for a Web service manually by using the Web Services Description Language tool.
- You can generate proxy classes for a Web service automatically by setting a Web reference to point to the Web service.
- You can test and debug a Web service without a client application by using one of several SOAP proxy tools.

CHAPTER SUMMARY

KEY TERMS

- Web service
- SOAP
- Disco
- UDDI
- WSDL
- Web method
- Web reference

Web service support is one of the most significant advances in the .NET architecture. The .NET Framework supports both creating and consuming Web services through command-line tools as well as the Visual Studio .NET IDE.

Web services provide you with a way to invoke objects over the Internet. A Web service can expose one or more Web methods, each of which can accept parameters and return objects.

Web services use protocols and standards including SOAP, Disco, UDDI, and WSDL to communicate. These protocols are designed to use HTTP as their transmission mechanism so that they are generally not blocked by firewalls.

The .NET Framework includes command-line tools to aid in the discovery and use of Web services. Visual Studio .NET wraps these tools in the simple act of setting a Web reference. Either method produces local proxy classes that you can use to send messages to a Web service and that will return the results from the Web service to the rest of your application.

APPLY YOUR KNOWLEDGE

Exercises

8.1 Calling a Web Service Asynchronously

Depending on the speed of your Internet connection, you may have noticed that the Web service client applications you constructed earlier in this chapter take a long time to reload when you invoke the Web service. That's because by default these applications use synchronous methods to communicate with the Web service, waiting for the SOAP response before allowing any other code to execute. But the proxy classes constructed by .NET include asynchronous methods as well. In this exercise, you'll learn how to call a Web service asynchronously.

Estimated Time: 30 minutes.

1. Open a Visual Basic .NET Web Application in the Visual Studio .NET IDE.

2. Right-click the References folder in Solution Explorer and select Add Web Reference. This opens the Add Web Reference dialog box.

3. Type `http://hourglass/StringProc/Strings.asmx?wsdl` into the Address bar of the Add Web Reference dialog box and press Enter. This connects to the StringProc Web service and creates the appropriate proxy classes, as you learned in this chapter. Of course, you should substitute the name of your own test server.

4. Click the Add Reference button.

5. Add a new Web Form to your Visual Basic .NET project.

6. Place a TextBox control with the ID of `txtInput`, a Button control with the ID of `btnUpperCase`, and a TextBox control with the ID of `txtOutput` on the Web Form.

7. Double-click the `Button` control to open the Web Form's module. Enter this code to invoke the Web service when the user clicks the button:

```
Private strUpperCase As String

Private Sub btnUpperCase_Click( _
 ByVal sender As System.Object, _
 ByVal e As System.EventArgs) _
 Handles btnUpperCase.Click
    ' Check for results from
    ' a previous call
    If Not Application("UpperCase") _
     Is Nothing Then
        txtOutput.Text = _
         Application("UpperCase")
    Else
        ' Connect to the Web service
        Dim objStrings As _
         hourglass.Strings = _
         New hourglass.Strings()

        ' Invoke the Web service.
        ' This may take some time
        ' so call it asynchronously.
        ' First, create a callback function
        Dim wcb As New AsyncCallback( _
         AddressOf WebServiceCallback)
        ' And then initiate the
        ' asynchronous call
        objStrings.BeginToUpper( _
         txtInput.Text, wcb, objStrings)
    End If
End Sub

Public Sub WebServiceCallback( _
 ByVal ar As IAsyncResult)
    ' This function will get
    ' called when the
    ' Web service call is done

    ' Retrieve the state of
    ' the proxy object
    Dim objStrings As hourglass.Strings = _
     ar.AsyncState
    ' Call the End method to
    ' finish processing
    Application("UpperCase") = _
     objStrings.EndToUpper(ar)

End Sub
```

APPLY YOUR KNOWLEDGE

8. Set the Web Form as the start page for the project.
9. Run the project and fill in a value for the input string. Click the button. The page should reload quickly, without waiting for the Web service to complete its work. Wait a few moments, and click the button again. This time the output box will show the uppercase version of the input string.

If you compare the code for this exercise with the code that you saw in Step By Step 8.1, you'll find some significant changes. In the .NET Framework, asynchronous Web service calls are managed by callback functions. When you add a Web reference, the proxy class includes `Begin` and `End` methods for each Web method. In this case, those are the `BeginToUpper` and `EndToUpper` methods.

The `Begin` method takes all the same parameters as the underlying Web method, plus two others. The first is the address of a callback function, and the second is an object whose properties should be available in the callback function. When you call the `Begin` method, the .NET Framework launches the call to the Web service in the background. When the Web method call completes, the `Callback` function will be invoked. The code in this exercise shows how you can then retrieve the original object and use its `End` method to finish the work of using the Web service.

> **WARNING**
>
> **Non-scaleable Technique** This exercise uses the Application object to store information until it's called for. There's only one Application object, shared by all users, so this isn't a good alternative for a real application. You'll learn about some other alternatives for storing state information in Chapter 15, "Configuring a Web Application."

Review Questions

1. What is the purpose of a Web service proxy class?
2. Describe the general purpose of SOAP.
3. Describe the general purpose of Disco and UDDI.
4. Describe the general purpose of WSDL.
5. Can a Web service exist without a WSDL file?
6. Explain two ways in which you can create proxy classes for a Web service.
7. List three steps involved in building a Web service using Visual Studio .NET.
8. What tools can you use to make local copies of the configuration files for a Web service?
9. How can you test a Web service without building a client application?
10. What is the advantage of sending SOAP messages over the HTTP protocol?

Exam Questions

1. You want to use a Web service that supplies inventory level information in your application. You know the URL of the .asmx file published by the Web service. What step should you take first?

   A. Open the .asmx file in a Web browser.

   B. Run the XML Schema Definition Tool.

   C. Run the Web Service Discovery Tool.

   D. Copy the .asmx file to your client project.

APPLY YOUR KNOWLEDGE

2. Your application includes a Web reference to a Web service that delivers customer information as an object with multiple properties. The developer of the Web service has added a new property named CreditRating to the object. What should you do to be able to use the CreditRating property in your code?

   A. Create an entirely new client application, and add a Web reference for the Web service to the new application.

   B. Delete and re-create the Web reference in the existing application.

   C. Update the Web reference in the existing application.

   D. Use a generic Object variable to hold customer information, so you can call any property you like.

3. You have created a Web service to return financial information using ASP.NET. One of the methods in your Web service is defined with this code:

```
Public Function Cash() As Double
    ' Calculations omitted
End Function
```

   Potential consumers of your Web service report that although they can set a reference to the Web service, the Cash method is not available. What could be the problem?

   A. The .asmx file for the Web service is not available on your Web server.

   B. The Web service class is not marked with the <WebService> attribute.

   C. The Cash method is not marked with the <WebMethod> attribute.

   D. Web services can only return string values.

4. You have created a new Web service to perform financial calculations. You're working in an ASP.NET project within the Visual Studio .NET environment. What's the easiest way to test your new Web service to make sure that it's returning the proper results?

   A. Cut and paste the code into a Windows application project, and test it in the new project.

   B. Run the Web service project and use the test page that it opens in the browser.

   C. Use a tool such as WebServicesStudio to send SOAP requests directly to the server.

   D. Have a large number of beta testers use the application, and monitor the server for odd behavior.

5. Your application uses a Web service named NorthwinD. The Northwind Web service includes a Web method named Suppliers that returns a DataSet containing all the company's suppliers. What data type should you use to declare an object to hold the result of the Suppliers method?

   A. Suppliers.DataSet

   B. DataSet

   C. NorthwinD.DataSet

   D. DataRow()

APPLY YOUR KNOWLEDGE

6. You're using the Web Services Discovery Tool to determine information about a Web service on a particular server. You receive the error message "The HTML document does not contain Web service discovery information." What could be the problem?

   A. The server address that you typed does not exist.

   B. The server requires authentication and you have entered improper credentials.

   C. The Web Services Discovery Tool works only on your local computer.

   D. There is no WSDL or Disco file available at the address that you typed.

7. You are using the Web Services Description Language Tool to create a proxy class for a Web service. The Web service exposes a class named Customer. You already have a Customer class in your application. What should you do to allow both classes to coexist in the same application?

   A. Use the /namespace option of the Web Services Description Language Tool to specify a unique namespace for the new class.

   B. Rename the existing class.

   C. Use the /out option of the Web Services Description Language Tool to specify a unique output file name for the new class.

   D. Manually edit the generated proxy class to change the class name that it contains.

8. You have used a UDDI registry to locate a Web service that might be able to supply information for your business. You want to test the interface of the Web service to make sure that it meets your requirements before you invest the effort to build a client application. How should you proceed?

   A. Use the Web Service Discovery Tool to download the WSDL file for the Web service and inspect it in an XML editor.

   B. Use the Web Service Description Language Tool to create a proxy class for the Web service and inspect the class using a text editor.

   C. Craft SOAP messages in an XML editor and use them to test the Web service.

   D. Use a tool such as the .NET WebService Studio to exercise the interface of the Web service.

9. Your application calls a Web service that performs complex, time-consuming calculations. Users complain that the user interface of the application freezes while it's recalculating. What can you do to fix this problem?

   A. Move the application to a faster computer.

   B. Install a faster link to the Internet.

   C. Install more memory in the computer.

   D. Use asynchronous calls to invoke the Web service.

10. One of your partner businesses has informed you that it is making its inventory information available via a Web service. You do not know the URL of the Web service. How can you discover the URL?

    A. Use the Web Service Discovery Tool to download the information.

    B. Use the Web Service Description Language Tool to create a proxy class.

    C. Use a UDDI Registry to locate the Web service.

    D. Use a search engine to explore your partner's Web site.

APPLY YOUR KNOWLEDGE

11. What must a developer do to make a Web service available asynchronously?

    A. Nothing. The client can always call a Web service asynchronously.

    B. Use a separate Thread object for each invocation of the Web service.

    C. Provide callback functions to invoke the Web service.

    D. Use only Sub procedures rather than Function procedures as Web methods.

12. You are invoking a Web service that returns a DataSet object. Your client application is written in Visual Basic .NET, while the Web service itself is written in C#. The Web service is outside of your corporate firewall. You receive an "object not found" error when you call the method that returns the DataSet. What could be the problem?

    A. The client project and the Web service project must use the same language.

    B. Objects supplied by a Web service cannot cross a firewall.

    C. The client project does not contain a reference to the System.Data namespace.

    D. Web services cannot properly serialize a complex object such as the DataSet object.

13. Your application invokes a Web service named Northwind that includes a Web method named GetOrders. GetOrders returns a DataSet containing order information. What must you do to use this DataSet in your client application?

    A. Create a new DataSet object and use the ReadXml method of the DataSet to initialize it from the returning SOAP message.

    B. Obtain an XSD file that specifies the schema of the DataSet. Use this XSD file to instantiate a DataSet from the returned data from the GetOrders methoD.

    C. Assign the return value from the GetOrders method to an array of DataRow variables. Loop through the array to build the DataSet.

    D. Assign the return value from the GetOrders method to a DataSet variable.

14. You have used the Web Services Discovery Tool to retrieve information about a Web service named ZipcodeService. Which file will contain the URL for any documentation of the ZipcodeService Web service?

    A. disco.exe

    B. results.discomap

    C. ZipcodeService.wsdl

    D. ZipcodeService.disco

15. You have used the Web Services Description Language Tool to create a proxy class for a Web service. When you add the proxy class to your project, you discover that it is coded in the C# language. What must you do to get the proxy class in VB .NET instead of C#?

    A. Manually convert the C# code to VB .NET code.

    B. Rerun the tool, specifying the /language:VB option.

    C. Rerun the tool, specifying the /namespace:VB option.

    D. Select File, Save As and save the file with the .vb extension.

APPLY YOUR KNOWLEDGE

Answers to Review Questions

1. A Web service proxy class is an object that you can create on the client to communicate with a Web service. The proxy accepts messages, forwards them to the Web service, and returns the results of those messages.
2. SOAP is designed to encapsulate objects as XML messages. These objects can then be sent via HTTP or other standard communications channels.
3. Disco and UDDI are designed to help you discover the interface details of a Web service.
4. WSDL exists to supply information on the interface of a Web service.
5. A Web service can exist without a WSDL file, but you must then know the exact incoming SOAP message that the Web service expects before you can use it.
6. You can create proxy classes for a Web service by using the disco.exe and wsdl.exe tools, or by creating a Web reference within Visual Studio .NET.
7. To build a Web service you must create a new Web service application, mark the classes to be exposed with the <WebService> attribute, and mark the methods to be exposed with the <WebMethod> attribute.
8. The disco.exe tool will make local copies of the configuration files for a Web service. Creating a new Web reference will also create these files.
9. You can use a tool such as .NET WebService Studio to test a Web service without building a client application.
10. Using HTTP as the transport protocol for SOAP messages means that these messages can take advantage of pervasive Internet connectivity to reach their destination.

Answers to Exam Questions

1. **C.** The Web Service Discovery Tool retrieves copies of the files that you need to proceed with this project.
2. **C.** The Update Web Reference menu item for a Web reference refreshes local configuration information from the server that hosts the Web service.
3. **C.** All exposed methods of a Web service must be marked with the <WebMethod> attribute.
4. **B.** When you're creating a Web service in ASP.NET, running the project will open a testing form in a browser window.
5. **B.** The client needs to declare the same data type that the server is returning, in this case the DataSet object.
6. **D.** The Web Services Discovery Tool requires the URL to a Disco or WSDL file to function.
7. **A.** Specifying a unique namespace for the new object removes the chance that it can clash with a pre-existing object name.
8. **D.** By using an automated tool you can avoid tedious and error-prone inspection of the XML files.
9. **D.** Speeding up the client computer will do nothing to speed up the Web service, which runs on the server computer.

APPLY YOUR KNOWLEDGE

10. **C**. UDDI Registries exist so that you can find business services by browsing or searching.

11. **A**. Building the proxy class, either with wsdl.exe or by setting a Web reference, automatically creates methods to invoke the Web service asynchronously.

12. **C**. Web services client and server applications must agree on the definition of the data to be exchangeD.

13. **D**. The only thing that you need to do to use a complex variable returned by the Web service is to declare an instance of the same data type in the client application.

14. **D**. The Disco file is the only one that contains pointers to non-XML resources.

15. **B**. The /language option controls the output language of the wsdl.exe tool.

Suggested Readings and Resources

1. Visual Studio .NET Combined Help Collection
2. .NET Framework SDK Documentation
   - XML Web Services Created Using ASP.NET and XML Web Service Clients
3. Scribner, Kenn and Stiver, Mark C. *Applied Soap: Implementing .NET XML Web Services.* Sams Publishing, 2001.
4. Cerami, Ethan. *Web Services Essentials.* O'Reilly, 2002.
5. Short, Scott. *Building XML Web Services for the Microsoft .NET Platform.* Microsoft Press, 2000.
6. Basiura, Russ, et al. *Professional ASP.NET Web Services.* Wrox, 2001.

OBJECTIVES

This chapter covers the following Microsoft-specified objectives for the Creating User Services section of the Visual Basic .NET Web-Based Applications exam:

Implement Globalization.

- **Implement localizability for the user interface**
- **Convert existing encodings**
- **Implement right-to-left and left-to-right mirroring**
- **Prepare culture-specific formatting**

Validate User Input

- **Validate non-Latin user input**

▸ The goal of this particular exam objective is to test your ability to produce what Microsoft calls "world-ready" applications. A world-ready application is one which can be translated for a new culture with a minimum of recoding (ideally, with no recoding at all). This means that you'll need some way to deal with issues such as these:

  - Different currency symbols for different countries
  - Changes of language on the user interface
  - Cultures that read right-to-left instead of left-to-right

▸ The .NET Framework offers good support for the process of producing world-ready applications.

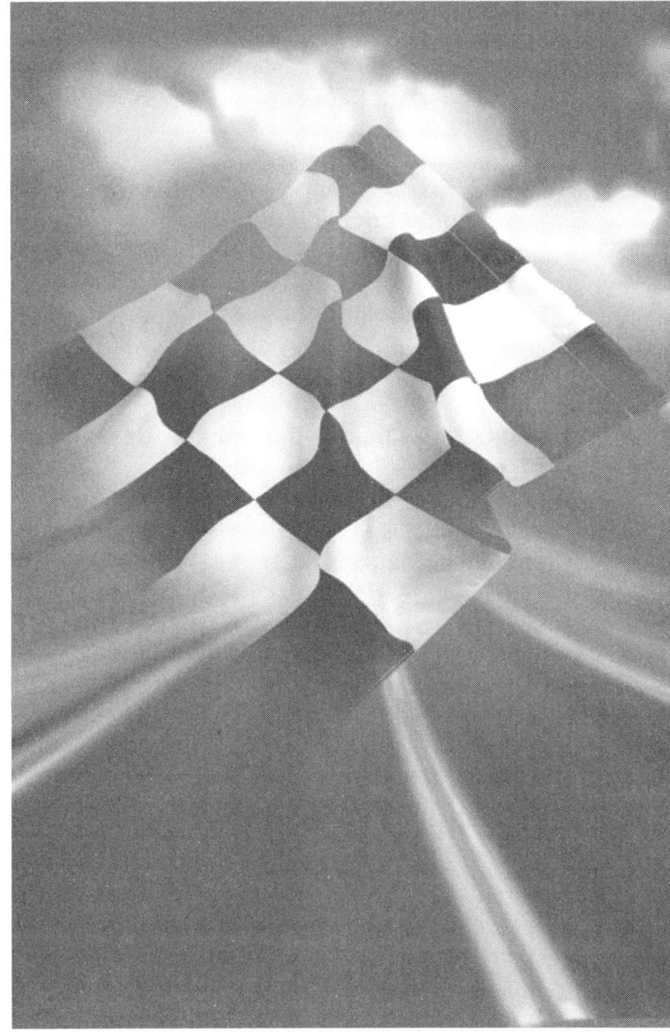

CHAPTER 9

Globalization

OUTLINE

STUDY STRATEGIES

- Review the "Globalization" section of the Common Tasks QuickStart tutorial. The QuickStart tutorials are installed as part of the .NET Framework installation.
- Experiment with code that uses the CurrentCulture and CurrentUICulture properties. Set these cultures to several different values and inspect the differences in your code's output.
- Change the mirroring of a complex form from one of your own applications and watch how its properties change at runtime.

INTRODUCTION

In the pre-Internet days, it wasn't unusual to design an application to be used in only a single country. Large companies such as Microsoft might produce Windows or Office in a dozen or more languages, but that was unusual. The majority of applications were written in a single human language, and all the users and developers spoke the same language.

These days, though, that approach can seriously limit the market for your software. Most developers need to think from the beginning of a project about translating a user interface into multiple languages a process known as *localization*. With the Internet as a marketing tool, there's no telling where your next customer will come from. If your application runs on the Internet (as many ASP.NET applications will), this is even more true.

In support of this new way of working, the .NET Framework provides excellent capabilities for localizing applications. Localization goes far beyond simply translating the text on a user interface. Some of the topics you need to consider include

- Translating user interface text, message boxes, and so on
- Using encodings to translate characters from one representation to another
- Using mirroring to change the direction of text in controls on the user interface
- Formatting things such as currency and dates that are presented in different ways in different locales
- Managing data sorts to take different alphabets into account

In this chapter, you'll learn about the concepts and techniques that the .NET Framework makes available for localization. You'll need a basic understanding of the entire process to pass the globalization section of the certification exam.

UNDERSTANDING LOCALIZATION AND GLOBALIZATION

If you consider the process of developing an application for multiple locations around the world (say, the United States, Singapore, and Peru), you can see two basic ways to undertake the job:

- Write three completely different sets of source code, one for each location where the application will be used.
- Write one set of source code, and build in the ability to customize the application for different locations.

The first of these alternatives is likely to be prohibitively expensive. Using three different sets of source code will require three times as many developers, testers, and managers as building a single version of the application. Perhaps worse, a bug that's found and fixed in one version might slip through the cracks and ship in another version. If you later needed to ship a version for a fourth location, you'd have to repeat the entire process again.

Not surprisingly, Visual Basic .NET encourages you to take the second approach. An application built from a single code base can be easily customized for multiple locations by using techniques such as locale-aware formatting functions and resource files. You don't have to worry about different versions getting "out of synch" (because they're all built from the same source code) and building a new version requires no work beyond translating strings into a new language.

> EXAM TIP
>
> **Where Are Your Users?** Another reason to use a single code base with translated resources for an Internet application is that it's very difficult to tell where a visitor to your Web site is located. This makes it extremely difficult to serve different versions of the code to different users.

The Localization Process

The technical term for the entire process of preparing an application for shipment in a new location-specific version is *localization.* Microsoft divides this process of preparing a "world-ready application" into three phases:

1. Globalization
2. Localizability
3. Localization

WARNING

Flexible Terms Although in theory the terms *globalization*, *localizability*, and *localization* are precise and distinct, in practice they tend to be used interchangeably. Indeed, even the objectives for the certification exam are not careful in the way that they use these terms.

Globalization is the first step in the process. In the globalization stage, you identify all the localizable resources in the application, and separate them from the executable code so that they can be modified easily. Ideally, you'll perform the globalization step during the design phase, so that the resources will always remain separate from the code.

Localizability is the second step in the process. In the localizability stage, you check to make sure that translating the application for a new location won't require design changes. If you've planned for localization from the beginning, localizability will typically be part of your quality assurance (QA) process.

Localization is the final step in the process. In the localization phase, you customize your application for new locales. This consists primarily of translating resources that you identified during the globalization phase.

What Should be Localized?

Obviously, you must modify text that shows on the user interface when you're localizing an application. This includes text on Web Forms, in error messages, and any other text that is show to the user. But there are many other things that you might need to localize in any given application. Here's a list of resources that are commonly localized, depending on the target locale:

- Menu item text.
- Form layouts. Text in German, for example, averages nearly twice as long as the same text in English. You may need to move and resize controls to accommodate this.
- The display format for dates and times.
- The display format for currency.
- The display format for numbers (for example, some countries use commas as the thousands separator in long numbers).
- Data input fields (what if you're asking for a Zip Code in a country other than the United States?).
- Maps, road signs, photos, or other graphics with local content.

- Shortcut keys. Not every character you know appears on every keyboard.
- Calendars. Countries such as Korea or Saudi Arabia use completely different calendars from each other.
- Alphabetical order.

You'll need to use some judgment in deciding which of these things really need to be localized in your application. You might decide, for example, that a set of general-purpose data entry fields can serve your needs for collecting addresses, rather than trying to research address formats worldwide.

IMPLEMENTING LOCALIZATION FOR THE USER INTERFACE

Implement localizability for the UI.

Prepare culture-specific formatting.

The System.Globalization namespace in the .NET Framework provides most of the support in .NET for localization in Visual Basic .NET applications. I'll start looking at localization code by exploring some of the concepts and classes that you'll need to understand to build your own world-ready applications.

The two key pieces to keep in mind are cultures and resource files. A *culture*, as you'll see, is an identifier for a particular locale. A *resource file* is a place where you can store some culture-dependent resources such as strings and bitmaps (.NET handles translating other resources, such as date formats, automatically).

Understanding Cultures

Before you can start localizing applications, you need to understand the concept of a *culture*. A culture, in .NET terms, is a more precise identifier than a location or a language. A culture identifies all the things that might need to be localized in an application, which requires you to know more than just the language.

For example, just knowing that an application uses English as its user interface language doesn't give you enough information to completely localize it: should you format dates and currency amounts in that application in a way appropriate to the United States, the United Kingdom, Canada, Australia, or New Zealand (among other possibilities)? Similarly, just knowing the location isn't enough: if an application will be used in Switzerland, there are four possibilities for the user interface language. Each combination of location and language identifies a culture.

About Culture Codes

Cultures are identified by abbreviations called *culture codes*. A full culture code consists of a neutral culture code (written in lowercase), followed by one or more subculture codes (written in mixed case or uppercase). Here are a few culture codes as samples:

- de identifies the German culture. This is a neutral culture—a culture that does not specify a subculture code. Neutral cultures generally do not provide sufficient information to localize an application.
- en-GB identifies the English (United Kingdom) culture. This is a specific culture—a culture that provides enough information to localize an application (in this case, for English speakers in Great Britain).
- az-AZ-Cyrl is an example of a specific culture with two subculture codes. This particular culture refers to the Azeri language in Azerbaijan, written with Cyrillic characters.

The `CultureInfo` Class

The .NET Framework represents cultures with the `System.Globalization.CultureInfo` class. This class lets you retrieve a wide variety of information about any particular culture.

STEP BY STEP

9.1 Retrieving Culture Information

1. Open a Visual Basic ASP.NET Web Application in the Visual Studio .NET IDE.

2. Add a new Web Form to your Visual Basic .NET project.

3. Place a `Button` control with the ID of `btnGetInfo`, a `TextBox` control with the ID of `txtCulture`, and a `ListBox` control with the ID of `lbInfo` on the form.

4. Double-click the `Button` control to open the form's module. Enter a reference to the `System.Globalization` namespace at the top of the code module:

```
Imports System.Globalization
```

5. Enter code to handle the button's `Click` event:

```
Private Sub btnGetInfo_Click( _
 ByVal sender As System.Object, _
 ByVal e As System.EventArgs) Handles btnGetInfo.Click
    ' Create a CultureInfo object
    ' for the specified culture
    Dim ci As CultureInfo = _
     New CultureInfo(txtCulture.Text)
    ' Dump information about the culture
    With lbInfo.Items
        .Clear()
        .Add("Display Name: " & ci.DisplayName)
        .Add("English Name: " & ci.EnglishName)
        .Add("Native Name: " & ci.NativeName)
        ' Get day names
        .Add("Day Names:")
        Dim strDayNames() As String = _
         ci.DateTimeFormat.DayNames
        Dim strDay As String
        For Each strDay In strDayNames
            .Add("  " & strDay)
        Next
        ' Get the current year
        .Add("Current year: " & ci.Calendar. _
         GetYear(DateTime.Today))
        ' And the currency symbol
        .Add("Currency symbol: " & _
         ci.NumberFormat.CurrencySymbol)
    End With
End Sub
```

6. Set the Web Form as the start page for the project.

7. Run the project and enter the name of a culture in the `TextBox`. Click the button. The form will retrieve and display some of the information that the `CultureInfo` object can return, as shown in Figure 9.1.

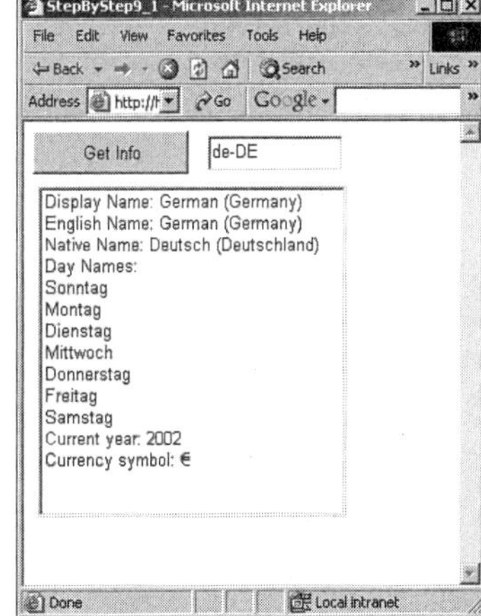

FIGURE 9.1
Retrieving information about a culture.

EXAM TIP

Enumerating Cultures You may have occasion to want a list of all supported cultures. The static CultureInfo.GetCultures method returns an array of CultureInfo objects that you can enumerate to get that list.

This example works by creating a `CultureInfo` object to represent the specified culture. It then uses properties of the `CultureInfo` object (and of the objects that it contains, such as the `DateTimeFormat`, `NumberFormat`, and `Calendar` objects) to retrieve information about that culture. This information is useful in localizing applications, and it's all built right into the .NET Framework.

The `CultureInfo` class is the key to localizing your applications. After you've retrieved the proper `CultureInfo` object, you can derive a wide variety of information from it.

The `CurrentCulture` and `CurrentUICulture` Properties

NOTE

The Thread Object The Thread object is a member of the System.Threading namespace, which allows you to write multithreaded applications. Multithreading is an advanced topic that I won't cover in this book. For a normal Windows application, there is a single thread of execution, represented by the Thread.CurrentThread object.

The .NET Framework handles localization on a thread-by-thread basis. Each thread has two properties that are used for determining the culture to use: `CurrentCulture` and `CurrentUICulture`. You can set or view these properties on the `Thread.CurrentThread` object.

The `CurrentUICulture` property tells the CLR which culture to use when choosing resources for the user interface. You'll see later on in this chapter how to provide multiple sets of resources for the CLR to use.

The `CurrentCulture` property is also used by the CLR to manage localization, but in a different way. The `CurrentCulture` property dictates the format for dates, times, currency, and numbers, as well as other culture-specific functionality, such as string comparison rules and casing rules.

The Invariant Culture

There's one more culture that you should know about: the invariant culture. This is a special culture that doesn't have an abbreviation. The invariant culture has two purposes:

- Interacting with other software, such as system services, where no user is directly involved.
- Storing data in a culture-independent format that won't be displayed directly to end users.

There are two ways to create a `CultureInfo` object that represents the invariant culture:

```
Dim ciInv As CultureInfo = New CultureInfo("")
Dim ciInv As CultureInfo = CultureInfo.InvariantCulture
```

REVIEW BREAK

- Localization is a three-step process that consists of globalization (identifying resources), localizability (verifying separation of resources from code), and localization (translating resources).
- Many resources may need to be localized, including user interface text, dates, times, currency amounts, and calendars.
- Cultures are identified by culture codes. Neutral culture codes specify only a location, and cannot be used for localization. Specific culture codes specify both a location and a language, and provide enough information for localization.
- The `CultureInfo` object represents a culture in the .NET Framework.

Displaying Localized Information

Now that you know how culture information is stored in the .NET Framework, you're ready to see its use in code.

STEP BY STEP

9.2 Displaying Localized Information

1. Add a new Web Form to your Visual Basic ASP.NET project.
2. Place a `Label` control, a `DropDownList` control (`ddlSelectCulture`), and four `TextBox` controls (`txtCulture`, `txtDate`, `txtCurrency`, and `txtNumber`) on the form. Set the `AutoPostBack` property of the `DropDownList` control to `True`.

continues

continued

3. Double-click the `DropDownList` control to open the form's module. Enter references at the top of the code module:

```
Imports System.Globalization
Imports System.Threading
```

4. Enter code to handle events in the form's module:

```
Private Sub Page_Load(ByVal sender As System.Object, _
 ByVal e As System.EventArgs) Handles MyBase.Load
    ' Stock the combo box
    If Not IsPostBack Then
        Dim ci As CultureInfo
        For Each ci In CultureInfo.GetCultures( _
         CultureTypes.SpecificCultures)
            ddlSelectCulture.Items.Add(ci.Name)
        Next
    End If
End Sub

Private Sub ddlSelectCulture_SelectedIndexChanged( _
 ByVal sender As System.Object, _
 ByVal e As System.EventArgs) _
 Handles ddlSelectCulture.SelectedIndexChanged
    ' Create an appropriate CultureInfo
    ' object for the thread
    Thread.CurrentThread.CurrentCulture = _
     New CultureInfo(ddlSelectCulture.SelectedItem.Text)
    ' Display the name of the culture
    txtCulture.Text = Thread.CurrentThread. _
     CurrentCulture.EnglishName
    ' Refresh the display of the data
    DisplayData()
End Sub

Private Sub DisplayData()
    Dim dtNow As Date = DateTime.Now
    Dim dblcurrency As Double = 13472.85
    Dim dblnumber As Double = 1409872.3502

    txtDate.Text = dtNow.ToLongDateString()
    txtCurrency.Text = dblcurrency.ToString("c")
    txtNumber.Text = dblnumber.ToString("n")
End Sub
```

5. Set the Web Form as the start page for the project.

6. Run the project. Select a culture from the combo box. The form refreshes to display localized information, as shown in Figure 9.2.

FIGURE 9.2
Displaying localized information.

When you select a culture from the `DropDownList`, the code uses that information to create a `CultureInfo` object assigned to the `CurrentCulture` property of the `CurrentThread`. It then calls a method to display some data on the form. Note that the display method simply uses the `ToLongDateString` and `ToString` methods to format the data that it displays. You don't have to do anything special to tell these methods which culture to use. They automatically use the culture specified by the `CurrentCulture` property.

> NOTE
> **No Localized Business Rules**
> Although this sample code changes the currency symbol when you select a new culture, it makes no attempt to convert the currency value into local units. The built-in localization support in the .NET Framework deals strictly with the user interface, not with business rules.

Setting Culture Properties

When you're setting the `CurrentCulture` and `CurrentUICulture` properties, you have two choices. You can set them based on information stored in the user's operating system, or you can provide a user interface to let the user choose a culture for formatting.

To use the culture of the operating system, you don't have to do anything. If the application is being executed on the Multiple User Interface (MUI) version of Windows 2000 or Windows XP, the .NET Framework automatically defaults to the culture that's currently selected. If the application is being executed on another version of Windows, the .NET Framework automatically defaults the culture to the language used by the operating system.

Although letting the .NET Framework choose the appropriate culture is the easy way to handle things, this strategy does not work well in ASP.NET applications. That's because the culture that the .NET Framework detects will be the culture on the Web server, not the culture on the user's computer! Remember, ASP.NET applications execute entirely on the server, and only the resulting HTML is sent to the client.

You can also code your ASP.NET application to sense the culture from the user's browser. To do this, you can retrieve the value of `Request.UserLanguages(0)` when you're processing a page. The ASP.NET Request object returns an array of strings specifying the language that the user's browser has set. The first member of this array will be the default language of the browser, in the standard culture code format. You can use this value to create an appropriate `CultureInfo` object for the current thread. For example:

```
Thread.CurrentThread.CurrentCulture = _
 New CultureInfo(Request.UserLanguages(0))
```

Attractive though this strategy sounds, there are several reasons why it doesn't work well in practice:

- Web browsers aren't required to specify a user language when sending an HTTP request for a Web page.
- Even if a Web browser specifies one or more acceptable languages, there's no guarantee that any of those languages will exactly match a culture that the .NET Framework makes available.
- The user may well be using a Web browser whose language doesn't match the user's own preferred language.

I think the best bet is generally to let the user choose the culture that the application should use. If you want to let the user choose the culture to use, you can follow a strategy similar to the one you just saw: Provide a control to select a culture, and update the `CurrentCulture` property when the user makes a selection from this control.

Working with Resource Files

So far you've seen how to use the `CurrentCulture` property to handle localized formatting of things such as currency, dates, and numbers. But localizing the text displayed on the user interface is perhaps even more important. The .NET Framework offers support for user interface localization through its ability to select a set of user interface resources at runtime.

The resources that you select at runtime will be contained in assembly resource files. Assembly resource files are specially formatted XML files that contain localized text. Visual Studio .NET allows you to work directly with assembly resource files.

In this section, I'll demonstrate how to use Visual Studio .NET to localize the user interface of a simple application.

STEP BY STEP

9.3 Localizing a Form with Resource Files

1. Add a new Web Form to your Visual Basic ASP.NET project.

2. Place a `Label` control with the ID of `lblFolder`, three `RadioButton` controls (`rbMyDocuments`, `rbDesktop`, and `rbNewFolder`), a `DropDownList` control with the ID of `ddlCulture`, and a `Button` control with the ID of `btnSave` on the form. Set the `AutoPostBack` property of the `DropDownList` control to True. Figure 9.3 shows this Web Form in design view.

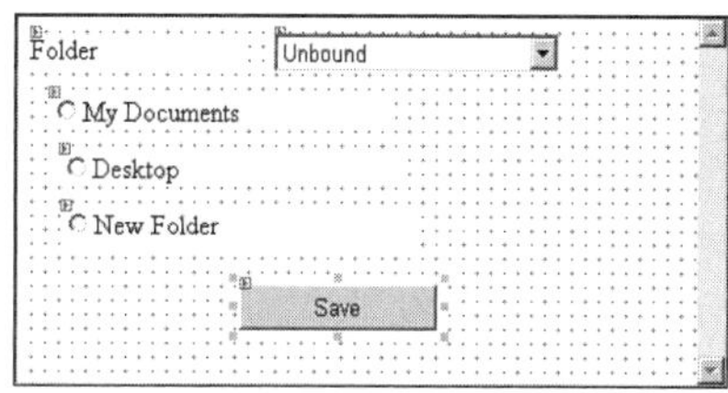

FIGURE 9.3
A Web Form to be localized at runtime.

3. Select Project, Add New Item. Select the Assembly resource file template. Name the new item `AppStrings.resx` and click Open to create the file.

4. The new file opens in the Visual Studio IDE with a grid-based editing interface. Enter names and values to identify all of the text strings on the user interface, as shown in Figure 9.4. You can optionally enter a comment for each string. The `Type` and `Mimetype` columns are not used for localizing strings.

Data for data

name	value	comment	type	mimetype
Folder	Folder	(null)	(null)	(null)
My_Documen	My Document	(null)	(null)	(null)
Desktop	Desktop	(null)	(null)	(null)
New_Folder	New Folder	(null)	(null)	(null)

FIGURE 9.4
Entering invariant resources.

5. Add two more Assembly resource files to your project. The first, named `AppStrings.en-US.resx`, should contain another copy of the strings in English. The second, named `AppStrings.fr-FR.resx`, should contain the strings in French, as shown in Figure 9.5. Note that the `Name` column is the same in the English and French version; only the value column changes.

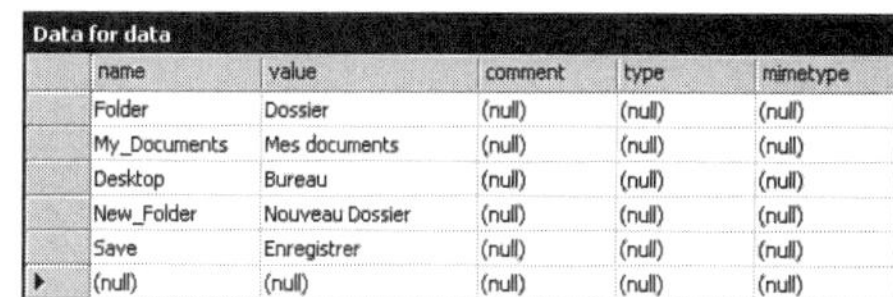

Data for data

name	value	comment	type	mimetype
Folder	Dossier	(null)	(null)	(null)
My_Documents	Mes documents	(null)	(null)	(null)
Desktop	Bureau	(null)	(null)	(null)
New_Folder	Nouveau Dossier	(null)	(null)	(null)
Save	Enregistrer	(null)	(null)	(null)
(null)	(null)	(null)	(null)	(null)

FIGURE 9.5
Entering French resources.

6. Double-click the `DropDownList` control to open the form's module. Enter references at the top of the code module:

```
Imports System.Globalization
Imports System.Resources
Imports System.Threading
```

7. Enter code to handle events in the form's module:

```
Private Sub Page_Load(ByVal sender As System.Object, _
 ByVal e As System.EventArgs) Handles MyBase.Load
    If Not IsPostBack Then
        ' Put language choices in the combo box
        ddlCulture.Items.Add("English")
        ddlCulture.Items.Add("French")
        ' Initialize the UI text
        SetUIText()
    End If
End Sub
```

continues

continued

```
Private Sub ddlCulture_SelectedIndexChanged( _
 ByVal sender As System.Object, _
 ByVal e As System.EventArgs) _
 Handles ddlCulture.SelectedIndexChanged
    ' When the user selects a language,
    ' change the UI culture
    Select Case ddlCulture.SelectedItem.Text
        Case "English"
            Thread.CurrentThread.CurrentUICulture = _
             New CultureInfo("en-US")
        Case "French"
            Thread.CurrentThread.CurrentUICulture = _
             New CultureInfo("fr-FR")
    End Select
    ' Initialize the UI text
    SetUIText()
End Sub

Private Sub SetUIText()
    Dim rm As ResourceManager = _
     New ResourceManager("_305Ch09.AppStrings", _
     GetType(StepByStep9_3).Assembly)
    lblFolder.Text = rm.GetString("Folder")
    rbMyDocuments.Text = rm.GetString("My_Documents")
    rbDesktop.Text = rm.GetString("Desktop")
    rbNewFolder.Text = rm.GetString("New_Folder")
    btnSave.Text = rm.GetString("Save")
End Sub
```

NOTE

Finding the Project Namespace

This code assumes that your VB .NET project is named 305Ch09. If it has some other name, you'll need to alter the first parameter to the constructor for the ResourceManager object. For this example, that parameter is set to _305Ch09.AppStrings (Visual Studio .NET adds an underscore to the name of the project in assigning a name to the namespace if the project name starts with a numeral). This parameter is the root namespace of your project. You can find the name of the root namespace by right-clicking the project node in Solution Explorer. Select Properties, and you'll find the root namespace in the General section. The second parameter to the ResourceManager constructor is the specific type of the executing code, as determined by the GetType method.

8. Set the Web Form as the start page for the project.

9. Run the project. As you select languages in the combo box, the user interface is refreshed with the appropriate resources.

The naming of the resource files in this example follows a required pattern. The .NET Framework looks for several specific files when it's loading resources, depending on the base name of the resources and the selected culture. The base name is the second part of the first parameter to the `ResourceManager` constructor, in this case `AppStrings`. When the `CurrentUICulture` is set to a `CultureInfo` object representing the `fr-FR` (French in France) culture, the .NET Framework checks for resources in three possible files, in this order:

1. A specific culture file, in this case `AppStrings.fr-FR.resx`.
2. A neutral culture file, in this case `AppStrings.fr.resx`.
3. An invariant culture file, in this case `AppStrings.resx`.

In other words, the .NET Framework falls back on increasingly more general resources in trying to load resources for a form.

Localizing Resources at Runtime

Runtime user interface resources are actually loaded by an instance of the `System.Resources.ResourceManager` class. After you've initialized a `ResourceManager` object by calling one of the class's constructors, there are two methods that you can use to retrieve localized resources:

- `GetObject` returns an object from the appropriate resource file.
- `GetString` returns a string from the appropriate resource file.

GUIDED PRACTICE EXERCISE 9.1

In this exercise, you'll combine the two types of localization that you've seen in this chapter, by using both the `CurrentCulture` and the `CurrentUICulture` properties in a single project.

The goal of this exercise is to build a form that displays the current date. The form should offer two choices:

1. A choice between two different cultures on the user interface.
2. A choice between long date and short date display formats.

You should try doing this on your own first. If you get stuck, or you'd like to see one possible solution, follow these steps:

1. Add a new Web Form to your Visual Basic ASP.NET Project. Name the form `GuidedPracticeExercise9-1.aspx`.
2. Place a `DropDownList` control with the ID of `ddlCulture`, two `RadioButton` controls with the IDs of `rbLongDate` and `rbShortDate`, and a `TextBox` control with the ID of `txtDate` on your Web Form. Set the `Checked` property of `rbLongDate` to `True`. Set the `GroupName` property of both `RadioButton` controls to `DateGroup`. Set the `AutoPostBack` properties of `ddlCulture` and of both `RadioButton` controls to True. Figure 9.6 shows a design for this form.

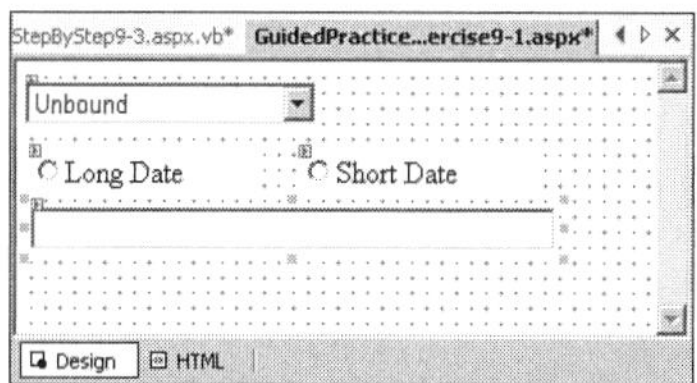

FIGURE 9.6
A Web Form to display localized dates.

continues

continued

3. Add a new Assembly resource file to your project. Name the file `GPE1.resx`. Enter two strings in the file. The first should be named `strLongDate` and have the value of `Long Date`. The second should be named `strShortDate` and have the value of `Short Date`.

4. Add a second Assembly resource file to your project. Name the file `GPE1.en-US.resx`. This file should have the same contents as the `GPE1.resx` file.

5. Add a third Assembly resource file to your project. Name the file `GPE1.de-DE.resx`. In this file, use the value `Langes Datum` for the `strLongDate` resource and the value `Kurzes Datum` for the `strShortDate` resource.

6. Double-click the `DropDownList` control to open the form's code module. Enter these references at the top of the file:

```
Imports System.Globalization
Imports System.Resources
Imports System.Threading
```

7. Enter this code to manage events on the form. Remember to modify the ResourceManager constructor if you've created your own project with a custom name:

```
Private Sub Page_Load(ByVal sender As System.Object, _
 ByVal e As System.EventArgs) Handles MyBase.Load
    If Not IsPostBack Then
        ' Put some choices in the combo box
        ddlCulture.Items.Add("en-US")
        ddlCulture.Items.Add("de-DE")
        ' Refresh the display
        DisplayData()
    End If
End Sub

Private Sub ddlCulture_SelectedIndexChanged( _
 ByVal sender As System.Object, _
 ByVal e As System.EventArgs) _
 Handles ddlCulture.SelectedIndexChanged
    ' Refresh the display
    DisplayData()
End Sub

Private Sub rbLongDate_CheckedChanged( _
 ByVal sender As System.Object, _
 ByVal e As System.EventArgs) _
 Handles rbLongDate.CheckedChanged
```

```
        ' Refresh the display
        DisplayData()
    End Sub

    Private Sub rbShortDate_CheckedChanged( _
     ByVal sender As System.Object, _
     ByVal e As System.EventArgs) _
     Handles rbShortDate.CheckedChanged
        ' Refresh the display
        DisplayData()
    End Sub

    Private Sub DisplayData()
        ' Set the current cultures to the selected culture
        Thread.CurrentThread.CurrentCulture = _
         New CultureInfo(ddlCulture.SelectedItem.Text)
        Thread.CurrentThread.CurrentUICulture = _
         New CultureInfo(ddlCulture.SelectedItem.Text)
        ' Reformat the date according to the user's choices
        If rbLongDate.Checked Then
            txtDate.Text = DateTime.Today.ToLongDateString()
        Else
            txtDate.Text =
     DateTime.Today.ToShortDateString()
        End If
        ' Update the user interface text
        Dim rm As ResourceManager = _
         New ResourceManager("_305Ch09.GPE1", _
         GetType(GuidedPracticeExercise9_1).Assembly)
        rbLongDate.Text = rm.GetString("strLongDate")
        rbShortDate.Text = rm.GetString("strShortDate")
    End Sub
```

8. Set the Web Form as the start page for the project.

9. Run the project and experiment with the user interface. You'll find that you can select either English or German, and that both the user interface text and the date formats change accordingly.

CONVERTING EXISTING ENCODINGS

Convert existing encodings.

Many different schemes have been developed for representing the characters in a language as numeric codes within a computer.

These schemes are referred to as encodings. For example, the venerable ASCII encoding represents common Latin characters as numeric codes ranging from 0 to 127. The .NET Framework provides support for encodings through the `System.Text.Encoding` class.

Understanding Unicode and Encodings

Internally, the .NET Framework's preferred encoding for characters is 16-bit Unicode, otherwise known as UTF-16. This encoding represents characters as 16-bit numbers, giving it the ability to represent approximately 65,000 distinct characters. That's enough to represent every character commonly in use. Additional features of the full Unicode specification allow for the representation of another million characters.

Over time, Windows has been moving toward Unicode as the basis for encoding characters, but that wasn't always the case. Earlier versions of Windows used code pages to represent character sets. A code page could hold 256 characters, and the system supplied different code pages for different character sets such as Greek characters or Latin characters.

Although Unicode is the native character encoding for .NET, the .NET Framework supports conversion to and from older encodings, such as ASCII or code pages, for compatibility with other applications. For example, Web services constructed with tools other than .NET may not be able to accept the full range of Unicode characters. In that case, you might want to use a more restrictive encoding, such as ASCII, for communication with the Web service, which retain the Unicode strings for internal processing in your own application.

> NOTE
> **Unicode Details** You can find everything that you'll ever need to know about Unicode at the Unicode home page, `http://www.unicode.org`.

Converting Encodings

The `System.Text` namespace contains classes that are designed to let you convert characters from the UTF-16 Unicode encoding to other encodings, and vice versa.

STEP BY STEP

9.4 Converting Character Encodings

1. Add a new Web Form to your Visual Basic ASP.NET project.

2. Place two `Label` controls, a `TextBox` control with the ID of `txtUnicode`, a `Button` control with the ID of `btnConvert`, and a `ListBox` control with the ID of `lbAscii` on the form.

3. Double-click the `Button` control to open the form's module. Enter a reference at the top of the code module:

```
Imports System.Text
```

4. Enter code to handle the `Button`'s click event:

```
Private Sub btnConvert_Click( _
 ByVal sender As System.Object, _
 ByVal e As System.EventArgs) Handles btnConvert.Click
    ' Get an encoding object for ascii
    Dim encASCII As ASCIIEncoding = _
     New ASCIIEncoding()
    ' Convert the string to an array of ASCII bytes
    Dim bytEncodedCharacters() As Byte
    bytEncodedCharacters = _
     encASCII.GetBytes(txtUnicode.Text)
    Dim i As Integer
    For i = 0 To bytEncodedCharacters.Length - 1
        lbASCII.Items.Add(bytEncodedCharacters(i))
    Next
End Sub
```

5. Set the Web Form as the start page for the project.

6. Run the project. Enter some text in the `TextBox` control and click the button. This converts the Unicode text from the `TextBox` into a series of ASCII byte codes and display those codes in the `ListBox`, as shown in Figure 9.7.

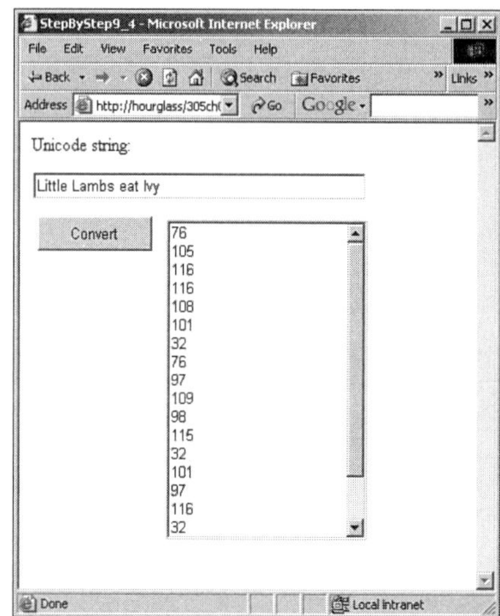

FIGURE 9.7
Converting Unicode characters to ASCII bytes.

This code sample uses the `GetBytes` method of the `ASCIIEncoding` object to convert a Unicode string into an array of ASCII bytes. Although I didn't use it in this example, there's a matching `GetChars` method that converts ASCII bytes into Unicode text.

The `ASCIIEncoding` class is a subclass of `System.Text.Encoding`. Table 9.1 lists the other available subclasses that help you convert to and from other encodings.

TABLE 9.1

ENCODING CLASSES IN THE `System.Text` NAMESPACE

Class	*Use*
`ASCIIEncoding`	Converts characters between Unicode and ASCII.
`Encoding`	General-purpose class. The `Encoding.GetEncoding` static method returns encodings that can be used for legacy code page compatibility.
`UnicodeEncoding`	Converts characters to and from Unicode encoded as consecutive bytes in either big-endian or little-endian order.
`UTF7Encoding`	Converts characters to and from 7-bit Unicode encoding.
`UTF8Encoding`	Converts characters to and from 8-bit Unicode encoding.

IMPLEMENTING MIRRORING

Implement right-to-left and left-to-right mirroring.

There are many differences between human languages. Of course different languages use different character sets, but there are differences beyond that. One of the most important differences is whether the language reads from left-to-right (like English) or from right-to-left (like Arabic). The .NET Framework supports both reading directions.

Understanding Mirroring

The process of switching a user interface between a left-to-right language such as German or English and a right-to-left language such as Hebrew or Arabic is called mirroring. Mirroring in the Windows environment involves changes beyond simply reversing the order of text strings. Figure 9.8, for example, shows part of the user interface from Arabic Windows.

As you can see, the entire format of the Windows user interface is reversed when you use mirroring. The close, minimize, and other buttons appear at the upper left of the window. Menus appear to the right of the menu bar. Combo box arrows are located to the left of the combo box, and checkbox text to the left of the textbox.

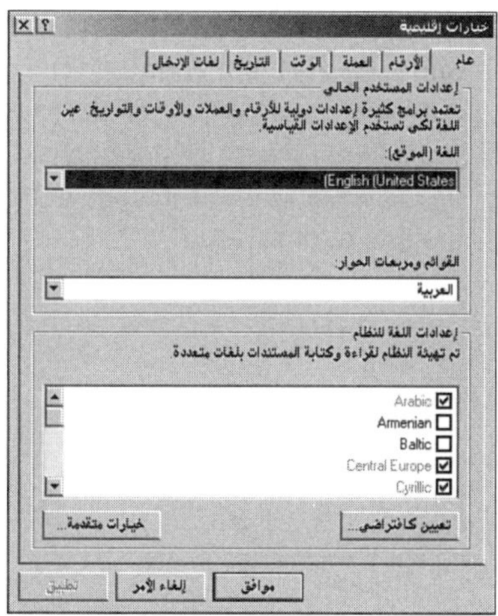

FIGURE 9.8
Mirroring in the Windows user interface.

Mirroring in .NET

The .NET Framework offers partial support for mirroring through the HTML `dir` attribute.

STEP BY STEP

9.5 Mirroring a Web Form

1. Add a new Web Form to your Visual Basic ASP.NET project.
2. Place a `TextBox` control, a `DropDownList` control, a `CheckBox` control, and a `RadioButton` control on the form. Figure 9.9 shows what the form might look like in design mode.
3. Switch to HTML view. Modify the HTML tag of the document as follows:

```
<HTML dir="rtl">
```

   Alternatively, you can select the `DOCUMENT` object in the Properties window and set the dir property of this object to `rtl`.
4. Set the Web Form as the start page for the project.
5. Run the project. You'll see that the form is partially mirrored, as shown in Figure 9.10. You may receive slightly different results if you're running on a version of Windows other than the U.S. English version.

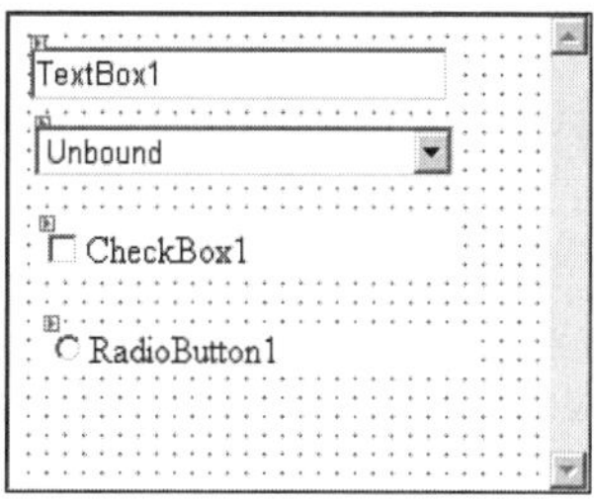

FIGURE 9.9
Preparing a Web Form to test mirroring.

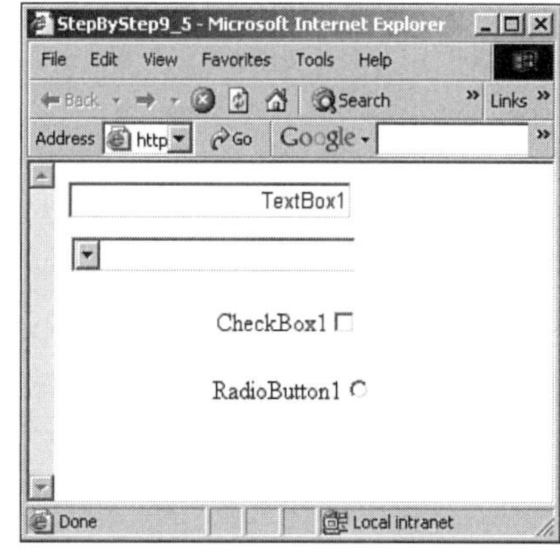

FIGURE 9.10
Right-to-left Web Form.

Setting the HTML `dir` attribute (which can also be set on individual controls) handles most of the facets of the mirroring process automatically. Controls fill from right-to-left as you enter text. `DropDownList`, `RadioButton`, and `CheckBox` controls reverse their appearance as well.

EXAM TIP

Mirroring Part of a Form If you only want to mirror part of a form, you can set the dir property to rtl on individual controls instead of on the entire form.

But the mirroring support is imperfect. The system menu and the other window buttons (such as the close and minimize buttons) don't switch positions. Controls are not mirrored to the opposite position on the form from their initial design (though, of course, you can manage that by manipulating the control panels at runtime from VB .NET code).

VALIDATING NON-LATIN USER INPUT

Validate non-Latin user input.

Another area where world-ready applications may require code changes is in handling character strings. I'll look at two areas where different alphabets may require you to implement code changes: string indexing and data sorting. These areas require the most coding attention for non-Latin characters (such as Arabic, Hebrew, or Cyrillic characters), but can be important when dealing with Latin characters as well.

String Indexing

String indexing refers to the process of extracting single characters from a text string. You might think that you could simply iterate through the data that makes up the string 16 bits at a time, treating each 16 bits as a separate character. But it turns out that things aren't that simple in the Unicode world.

Unicode supports surrogate pairs and combining character sequences. A surrogate pair is a set of two 16-bit codes that represent a single character from the extended 32-bit Unicode character space. A combining character sequence is a set of more than one 16-bit codes that represents a single character. Combining character sequences are often used to combine diacritical marks such as accents with base characters.

This presents a problem: If characters in a string aren't all the same length, how can you move smoothly from one to the next? The answer, of course, is to use a class from the .NET Framework that knows how to perform this task. The `System.Globalization.StringInfo` class is designed to be able to iterate through the elements in a string.

STEP BY STEP

9.6 Iterating with the `StringInfo` Class

1. Add a new Web Form to your Visual Basic ASP.NET project.

2. Place a `TextBox` control with the ID of `txtText`, a `Button` control with the ID of `btnIterate`, and a `ListBox` control with the ID of `lbIterate` on the form.

3. Double-click the button to open the form's module. Enter a reference at the top of the module:

```
Imports System.Globalization
```

4. Add code to handle the Click event of the button:

```
Private Sub btnIterate_Click( _
 ByVal sender As System.Object, _
 ByVal e As System.EventArgs) Handles btnIterate.Click
    lbIterate.Items.Clear()
    ' Get an iterator for the entered text
    Dim iter As TextElementEnumerator = _
     StringInfo.GetTextElementEnumerator(txtText.Text)
    ' The iterator starts before
    ' the string, have to move
    ' it forward once to reach the first element
    iter.MoveNext()
    Do
        lbIterate.Items.Add("Element " & _
         iter.ElementIndex & _
         ": " & iter.Current)
    Loop While (iter.MoveNext)
End Sub
```

5. Set the Web Form as the start page for the project.

6. Run the project. Paste or enter any text you like in the `TextBox` and then click the `Button` control. The code splits the string into its constituent characters, as shown in Figure 9.11.

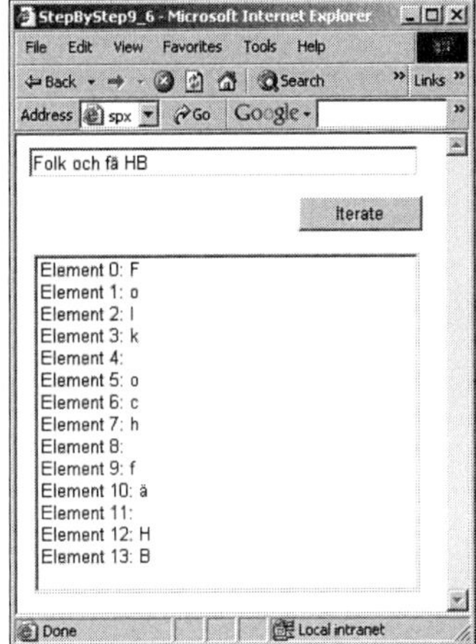

FIGURE 9.11
String decomposed by the `StringInfo` class.

This code uses the static `GetTextElementEnumerator` method of the `StringInfo` class. Given any Unicode string, this method returns an iterator that you can use to move through the string one character at a time, properly handling surrogate pairs and combining characters.

The iterator has a MoveNext method that returns True when there are more characters to be read, or False when it has exhausted the characters in the string. The Current property of the iterator returns a single character from the current position of the iterator.

Comparing and Sorting Data

Another area where you may need to alter code to produce a world-ready application is in working with strings. Different cultures use different alphabetical orders to sort strings, and different cultures compare strings differently. For example, the single-character ligature "AE" is considered to match the two characters "AE" in some cultures but not in others.

For the most part, you don't have to do any special programming to account for these factors in the .NET Framework. To make your application world-ready, you're more likely to need to remove old code—for example, code that assumes that characters are properly sorted if you sort their ASCII character numbers. Specifically, the .NET Framework provides these culture-aware features:

- The String.Compare method compares strings according to the rules of the CultureInfo referenced by the CurrentCulture property.
- The CultureInfo.CompareInfo object can search for substrings according to the comparison rules of the current culture.
- The Array.Sort method sorts the members of an array by the alphabetical order rules of the current culture.
- The SortKey.Compare method also compares strings according to the rules of the current culture.

REVIEW BREAK

- Internally, .NET applications use 16-bit Unicode (UTF-16) as their preferred character encoding.
- The System.Text.Encoding class and its subclasses allow you to convert text from one encoding to another.
- In some languages, the user interface is read from right to left instead of from left to right. Converting a form for one of these languages is referred to as mirroring.

- The .NET Framework provides partial support for mirroring through the `dir` attribute in HTML.
- To iterate through the elements of a string in a world-ready application, you should use the `GetTextElementEnumerator` method of the `StringInfo` class.
- Searching, sorting, and comparing strings in a world-ready application requires using standard objects and methods rather than clever programming tricks.

CHAPTER SUMMARY

The .NET Framework was designed to help you develop world-ready applications quickly and consistently. The localization process includes globalization (planning for localized versions), localizability (testing to make sure resources can be localized), and localization (actually translating the resources).

The .NET Framework contains a number of useful localization classes in the `System.Globalization` namespace. Key among these classes is the `CultureInfo` class, which provides the ability for .NET applications to properly display dates, times, currencies, and other culture-specific data properly.

Visual Studio .NET provides you with a straightforward way to localize the user interface of an application. These include satellite assemblies and assembly resource files. Assembly resource files, which contain localized resources, can be loaded at runtime.

Other important globalization topics include encoding (translating from one representation of text characters to another), mirroring (handling right-to-left language input and output), and working with character sorts, comparisons, and iteration.

KEY TERMS

- Globalization
- Localization
- Localizability
- Culture
- Resource file
- Culture code
- Unicode
- Encoding

APPLY YOUR KNOWLEDGE

Exercises

9.1 Using Localized Calendars

In addition to the features that you saw earlier in the chapter, the `CultureInfo` class can supply localized calendars for different cultures. In this exercise, you'll see how you can retrieve culture-specific calendar information.

Estimated Time: 20 minutes.

1. Open a Visual Basic .NET Web Application in the Visual Studio .NET IDE.

2. Add a new Web Form to the application.

3. Place a `Label` control, a `DropDownList` control with the ID of `ddlCultures`, and a `ListBox` control with the ID of `lbInfo` on the form. Set the `AutoPostBack` property of the `DropDownList` control to True.

4. Double-click the `DropDownList` control to open the form's module. Add a line of code to the top of the module:

```
Imports System.Globalization
```

5. Add code to handle the Load event of the Form and the `SelectedIndexChanged` event of the `DropDownList` control:

```
Private Sub Page_Load( _
 ByVal sender As System.Object, _
 ByVal e As System.EventArgs) _
 Handles MyBase.Load
    If Not IsPostBack Then
        ' Fill the combo box with cultures
        Dim ci As CultureInfo
        For Each ci In CultureInfo. _
         GetCultures( _
         CultureTypes.SpecificCultures)
            ddlCultures.Items.Add(ci.Name)
        Next
    End If
End Sub

Private Sub _
 ddlCultures_SelectedIndexChanged( _
 ByVal sender As System.Object, _
 ByVal e As System.EventArgs) _
 Handles ddlCultures.SelectedIndexChanged
    ' Get the selected CultureInfo
    ' and some other objects
    Dim ci As CultureInfo = _
     New CultureInfo(ddlCultures. _
     SelectedItem.Text)
    Dim cal As Calendar = ci.Calendar
    Dim dtfi As DateTimeFormatInfo = _
     ci.DateTimeFormat
    lbInfo.Items.Clear()
    Dim dt As DateTime = DateTime.Today
    ' List the culture and the calendar
    With lbInfo.Items
        .Add("The culture is " & _
         ci.EnglishName)
        .Add("The calendar is " & _
         cal.GetType.ToString)
        ' Get the current day,
        ' month, and year
        .Add("Today is day " & _
         cal.GetDayOfMonth(dt))
        .Add(" of month " & _
         cal.GetMonth(dt))
        .Add(" of year " & cal.GetYear(dt))
        .Add("This is day " & _
         cal.GetDayOfWeek(dt) & " _
         of the week")
        .Add("The day name is " & _
         dtfi.DayNames( _
         cal.GetDayOfWeek(dt)))
        .Add("The month name is " & _
         dtfi.MonthNames( _
         cal.GetMonth(dt) - 1))
        .Add("There are " & _
         cal.GetMonthsInYear( _
         cal.GetYear(dt)) & _
         " months in this year")
    End With
End Sub
```

6. Set the Web Form as the start page for the project.

7. Run the project. Select cultures from the combo box to see some of their calendar information in the `ListBox` control, as shown in Figure 9.12. You might try `ar-SA`, `he-IL`, and `th-TH` to get some sense of the calendars that the .NET Framework supports.

APPLY YOUR KNOWLEDGE

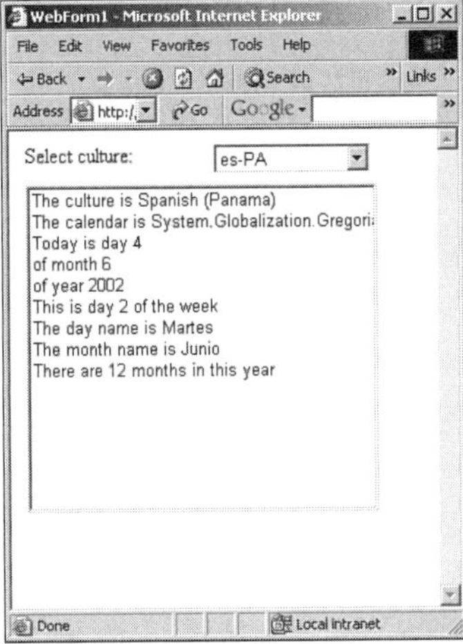

FIGURE 9.12
Calendar information from the `CultureInfo` class.

This exercise shows you some of the methods available from the `Calendar` class (and its subclasses such as `GregorianCalendar`. Here's a more extensive list of the available methods of the `Calendar` class. Their use should be self-evident from their names.

- `AddDays`
- `AddHours`
- `AddMilliseconds`
- `AddMinutes`
- `AddMonths`
- `AddSeconds`
- `AddWeeks`
- `AddYears`
- `GetDayOfMonth`
- `GetDayOfWeek`
- `GetDayOfYear`
- `GetDaysInMonth`
- `GetDaysInYear`
- `GetEra`
- `GetHour`
- `GetMilliseconds`
- `GetMinute`
- `GetMonth`
- `GetMonthsInYear`
- `GetSecond`
- `GetWeekOfYear`
- `GetYear`
- `IsLeapDay`
- `IsLeapMonth`
- `IsLeapYear`
- `ToDateTime`
- `ToFourDigitYear`

9.2 Retrieving Region Information

Another part of the `System.Globalization` namespace is the `RegionInfo` object. This object provides some additional information on a particular geographic region. In this exercise, you'll see how to retrieve the information that's available from the `RegionInfo` object.

Estimated Time: 15 minutes.

1. Open a Visual Basic .NET Web Application in the Visual Studio .NET IDE.
2. Add a new Web Form to the application.

APPLY YOUR KNOWLEDGE

3. Place a `Label` control, a `DropDownList` control with the ID of `ddlCultures`, and a `ListBox` control with the ID of `lbInfo` on the form. Set the `AutoPostBack` property of the `DropDownList` control to `True`.

4. Double-click the `DropDownList` control to open the form's module. Add a line of code to the top of the module:

```
Imports System.Globalization
```

5. Add code to handle the Load event of the Web Form and the `SelectedIndexChanged` event of the `DropDownList` control:

```
Private Sub Page_Load( _
 ByVal sender As System.Object, _
 ByVal e As System.EventArgs) _
 Handles MyBase.Load
    If Not IsPostBack Then
        ' Fill the combo box with cultures
        Dim ci As CultureInfo
        For Each ci In CultureInfo. _
         GetCultures( _
         CultureTypes.SpecificCultures)
            ddlCultures.Items.Add(ci.Name)
        Next
    End If
End Sub

Private Sub _
 ddlCultures_SelectedIndexChanged( _
 ByVal sender As System.Object, _
 ByVal e As System.EventArgs) _
 Handles ddlCultures.SelectedIndexChanged
    ' Attempt to get the correct RegionInfo
    Dim rgi As RegionInfo = _
     New RegionInfo( _
     ddlCultures.SelectedItem. _
     Text.Substring( _
     ddlCultures.SelectedItem. _
     Text.Length - 2))
    lbInfo.Items.Clear()
    ' List the regioninfo
    With lbInfo.Items
        .Add("The region is " & rgi.Name)
        .Add("Display Name: " & _
         rgi.DisplayName)
        .Add("English Name: " & _
         rgi.EnglishName)
        .Add("Currency symbol: " & _
         rgi.CurrencySymbol)
        If rgi.IsMetric Then
            .Add("Region uses metric " & _
             "measurements.")
        Else
            .Add("Region does not use " & _
             "metric measurements.")
        End If
        .Add("ISO Currency symbol: " & _
         rgi.ISOCurrencySymbol)
        .Add("ISO three-letter code: " & _
         rgi.ThreeLetterISORegionName)
    End With
End Sub
```

6. Set the Web Form as the start page for the project.

7. Run the project. Select cultures from the combo box to see some of their region information in the `ListBox` control, as shown in Figure 9.13.

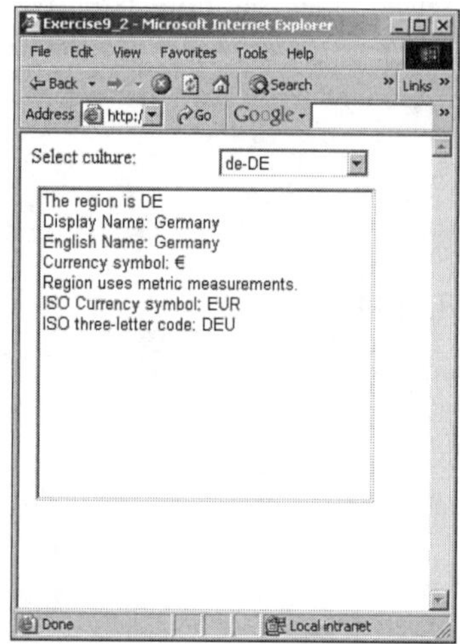

FIGURE 9.13
Region information from the `RegionInfo` class.

APPLY YOUR KNOWLEDGE

Regions are identified by two-letter codes assigned by the International Standards Organization, ISO. These codes usually match the subculture codes, so this example cheats and uses the rightmost two characters of culture codes to locate regions.

> EXAM TIP
>
> **CurrentRegion** To retrieve the region being used by the operating system, you can read the static Thread.CurrentThread.CurrentRegion property.

Review Questions

1. List some things that might need to be localized in a world-ready application.
2. Name and briefly describe the three steps of the localization process.
3. Describe the differences between neutral, specific, and invariant cultures.
4. What is the difference between the CurrentCulture property and the CurrentUICulture property of the currently executing thread?
5. Explain the naming standard for resx files.
6. What advantages do Assembly resource files have over satellite assemblies?
7. How many bits does a single UTF-16 character consist of?
8. Name some things that should change when a form is mirrored.
9. What class can you use to iterate through a string character-by-character in all cases?

Exam Questions

1. Your application displays order information including the total cost of each order. You are beginning to sell this application in multiple countries. How should you ensure that the correct currency symbol is used in all cases?

   A. Allow the user to select a culture from a list. Create a CultureInfo object based on the user's selection and assign it to the Thread.CurrentThread.CurrentCulture property. Use the ToString method to format currency amounts.

   B. Accept the Thread.CurrentThread.CurrentCulture property as it is set when you run your application. Use the ToString method to format currency amounts.

   C. Prompt the user for a currency symbol and store it in the registry.

   D. Allow the user to select a currency symbol from a list of supported symbols.

2. Your application allows users to select a culture such as English, French, or Spanish from an options dialog box. Users complain that some information is not displayed correctly, even after selecting the proper culture. What could be the problem?

   A. They are running your application on an English-only version of Windows.

   B. You're using a neutral CultureInfo to retrieve information instead of a specific CultureInfo.

   C. The users have not yet installed .NET Framework SP1.

   D. Your application is constructed as an executable file rather than a satellite library.

APPLY YOUR KNOWLEDGE

3. Users would like to include the day of the week when your application displays dates. They want this to be in the language of their Windows installation. What can you do to address this need? (Select two)

   A. Use the DateTime.ToLongDateString() method to format dates.

   B. Use the CultureInfo.DateTimeFormat property to retrieve the names of the weekdays, and select the proper name from that array.

   C. Force the user to enter the day of the week whenever they enter a date into the system.

   D. Use the RegionInfo object to retrieve the names of the weekdays, and select the proper name from that array.

4. Your user would like to see French dates and currencies displayed in an application, but wants the user interface to remain in English. How can you accomplish this?

   A. Set the CurrentCulture property to a CultureInfo representing the fr-FR culture and set the CurrentUICulture property to a CultureInfo representing the en-US culture.

   B. Set the CurrentCulture property to a CultureInfo representing the en-US culture, and set the CurrentUICulture property to a CultureInfo representing the fr-FR culture.

   C. Set the CurrentCulture property to a CultureInfo representing the fr-FR culture, and set the CurrentUICulture property to a CultureInfo representing the fr-FR culture.

   D. Set the CurrentCulture property to a CultureInfo representing the en-US culture, and set the CurrentUICulture property to a CultureInfo representing the en-US culture.

5. Your application is named 1st_Class_Tracer. You are using embedded Assembly resource files to localize the application. When you try to compile the localized application, you receive an error message. What could be the problem?

   A. This application must use satellite assemblies rather than Assembly resource files.

   B. You did not include resources for every possible culture in your application.

   C. You did not include a way for the user to switch cultures in your application.

   D. You used 1st_Class_Tracer rather than _1st_Class_Tracer as the namespace for your resources.

6. Your application's main form includes a group of radio buttons that lets users select English, French, Spanish, or German as the user interface language. When the user makes a selection, your code creates an appropriate CultureInfo object and assigns it to the Thread.CurrentThread.CurrentUICulture property.

   Users report that the user interface does not change languages when they make a selection from the radio buttons. What should you do to implement this functionality?

   A. Instruct the users to close and reopen the application after making a selection.

   B. Create Assembly resource files to hold the resources. Use a ResourceManager object to extract the resources whenever they're needed.

   C. Verify that your code contains the correct Namespace name for your application in the module that selects the resources to use.

   D. Spawn a second copy of the main form, this one with the correct user interface language.

APPLY YOUR KNOWLEDGE

7. Your application includes three Assembly resource files: Strings.resx contains the default (English) resources; Strings.en-US.resx contains the English resources; Strings.France.resx contains the French resources. Users report that they are getting the default English user interface when they've selected the option for a French user interface. What should you do?

   A. Instruct users to close and reopen the application after selecting a new user interface language.

   B. Add French resources to the Strings.resx file.

   C. Rename the French resource file to Strings.fr-FR.resx.

   D. Delete the Strings.en-US.resx file from the project.

8. Your application contains Unicode strings encoded in the UTF-16 format. You'd like to save a copy of those strings to disk in the UTF-8 format. What should you do?

   A. Use the Unicode.GetBytes method to perform the conversion.

   B. Use the Unicode.GetChars method to perform the conversion.

   C. Use the UTF8Encoding.GetBytes method to perform the conversion.

   D. Use the UTF8Encoding.GetChars method to perform the conversion.

9. You are localizing a Web Form for use in Saudi Arabia (the ar-SA culture). Which of these steps should you perform as part of the process? (Select two)

   A. Set the Tag property to ar-SA.

   B. Set the current thread's CurrentUICulture property to Arabic (Saudi Arabia).

   C. Set the Text property to ar-SA.

   D. Add the dir="rtl" attribute to the page's HTML tag.

10. A Label control in your application reports the number of characters in a particular data entry form. You're dividing the number of bits taken up by the data by 16 to arrive at this figure. Users of the localized version in Saudi Arabia complain that the number of characters is persistently overestimated, What should you do?

    A. Divide the number of bits by 32 to arrive at a more accurate figure.

    B. Use the String.Length method to retrieve the actual length of the string.

    C. Divide the number of bits by 8 to arrive at a more accurate figure.

    D. Use a GetTextElementEnumerator object to enumerate the characters.

11. Arabic-speaking users of your application would like to see dates displayed with the Arabic calendar. How can you accomplish this?

    A. Retrieve a Calendar object from Thread.CurrentThread.CurrentCulture, and use its methods to format the dates.

    B. Retrieve a Calendar object from Thread.CurrentThread.CurrentUICulture, and use its methods to format the dates.

    C. Retrieve a DateTime object from Thread.CurrentThread.CurrentCulture, and use its methods to format the dates.

    D. Retrieve a DateTime object from Thread.CurrentThread.CurrentCulture, and use its methods to format the dates.

APPLY YOUR KNOWLEDGE

12. You are shipping an application to France and Russia, and using Assembly resource files to hold localization resources. Now you need to start shipping to Spain. If the application is run on the Spanish version of Windows, you want to show the user interface in Spanish. What should you do? (Select two)

    A. Create an Assembly resource file to hold the user interface text translated into Spanish.

    B. Build a new project containing only the Spanish version of the form, and build this new project to sell in Spain.

    C. Use a ResourceManager object to assign resources from the new Assembly resource file at runtime.

    D. Create a new CultureInfo object for the Spanish (Spain) culture. Assign this object to the Thread.CurrentThread.CurrentUICulture property.

13. Your application contains an Options form that allows the user to select a culture for localizing dates, times, and currency. What should you do to make sure that all possible valid choices are available on this form?

    A. Retrieve the list of supported cultures by using the static CultureInfo.GetCultures method.

    B. Look up the list of available cultures in the .NET Framework help, and hard-code that list into your application.

    C. Retrieve the list of supported cultures from the Windows Registry.

    D. Allow users to enter cultures as they need them, and store a list of entered cultures for future use.

14. You are writing an application on a system that uses US English Windows (culture code en-US). The application will run on a system that uses Japanese Windows (culture code jp-JP). The application will send information to Windows services on the target computer. Which culture should you use to format your application's output?

    A. en-US

    B. jp-JP

    C. jp

    D. The invariant culture

15. Your application needs to search for substrings in longer strings. This searching should be culture-aware. What should you use to perform these searches?

    A. CultureInfo.CompareInfo

    B. Array.Sort

    C. InStr

    D. IndexOf

Answers to Review Questions

1. Items that may need to be localized include text on the user interface; form layouts; date, time, and currency formats; data input fields; graphics with local content shortcut keys; calendars; and alphabetical order.

2. The three steps are globalization (identification of resources to be localized), localizability (verification that localizable resources have been separated from code), and localization (translation of localized resources).

APPLY YOUR KNOWLEDGE

3. A neutral culture specifies a culture but not a subculture. A specific culture specifies a culture and one or more subcultures. The invariant culture does not specify either a culture or a subculture.
4. The CurrentCulture property is used by culture-aware functions such as ToString(). The CurrentUICulture is used to locate appropriate resources to display on the user interface.
5. A default resource file has a name such as MyResources.resx. A neutral resource file has a name such as MyResources.fr.resx. A specific resource file has a name such as MyResources.fr-FR.resx. When searching for resources to load, the .NET runtime will first try to find a specific resource file, then a neutral resource file, and then a default resource file.
6. You can extract resources from an Assembly resource file via a ResourceManager object at any time. Satellite assemblies are only used when a form is loaded.
7. Usually, a single UTF-16 character consists of 16 bits. However, surrogate characters and composed characters mean that a single UTF-16 character may consist of 32 bits or more.
8. When a form is mirrored, the location of controls should be flipped from one side of the form to the other, menus and the caption bar text should move to the right, and controls should fill with data starting at the right.
9. The StringInfo class supports iterating through any string, regardless of culture.

Answers to Exam Questions

1. **A.** Allowing the user to choose a culture is better than accepting the existing culture of the application, because the user might be running on a version of Windows that's not appropriate for his or her culture. There's no need to prompt or store a currency symbol when all necessary currency symbols are stored in the .NET Framework.
2. **B**. Neutral cultures do not contain enough information to properly localize an application. You should be using the appropriate specific culture instead.
3. **A, B**. The RegionInfo object does not expose weekday names, and there's no point in forcing the user to enter days when you've already got them available. Both the DateTime class and the CultureInfo class can supply the information that you need here.
4. **A**. The CurrentCulture property controls formatting, and the CurrentUICulture property controls user interface resource loading.
5. **D**. The namespace for resources must exactly match the namespace that .NET assigns to the project. In the case of a project whose name begins with a digit, .NET prepends an underscore to come up with the project name.
6. **B**. Satellite assemblies are only used when a form is first opened. For more responsive resource switching you should switch to using Assembly resource files.
7. **C**. Naming for Assembly resource files must follow the scheme that the .NET Framework is expecting. Otherwise, it won't be able to find the resource file.

APPLY YOUR KNOWLEDGE

8. **C**. The GetBytes method translates from Unicode characters to bytes that are appropriate for the Encoding object that's in use.
9. **B, D**. The Tag property has no effect on the localization process (or on anything else) and the Text property simply sets the caption for the form.
10. **D.** The problem is that the simple division by sixteen algorithm does not take into account composed characters.
11. **A**. The Calendar object contains localized date and time formatting resources. The CurrentCulture property, not the CurrentUICulture property, controls which CultureInfo object is used to supply formatting information.
12. **A, C**. To display a translated user interface on a form, you must supply a translated resource file and use code to move the resources to the form at runtime.
13. **A**. To get a list of cultures that .NET can work with, you should retrieve .NET's own list by iterating over the CultureInfo.GetCultures property.
14. **D**. You should always use the invariant culture for communication with Windows services, no matter what language-specific version of Windows is involved.
15. **A**. Array.Sort does not locate substrings. The Instr() method is obsolete and only works in VB6 or earlier versions. IndexOf can find substrings, but it is not culture-aware.

Suggested Readings and Resources

1. Visual Studio .NET Combined Help Collection
   - Developing World Ready Applications topic
2. Symmonds, Nick, *Internationalization and Localization Using Microsoft .NET*. Apress, 2001

OBJECTIVES

This chapter covers the following Microsoft-specified objectives for the Creating User Services section of the Visual Basic .NET Web-Based Applications exam:

Incorporate existing code into ASP.NET pages.

- **Instantiate and invoke an ActiveX control.**

Instantiate and invoke Web services or components.

- **Instantiate and invoke a COM or COM+ component.**
- **Call native functions by using platform invoke.**

▶ Although the .NET Framework can handle nearly all your application development needs, most organizations will already have accumulated a large amount of useful code. It doesn't make sense to simply throw away this legacy code and rewrite everything from scratch. Fortunately, if you've followed recommendations to encapsulate your code into components over the years, you don't need to abandon old code to start getting the benefits of .NET. Instead, you can make use of .NET's interoperability features to use several types of legacy code:

- ASP pages and ASP.NET pages can coexist.
- ActiveX controls can be placed on Web forms.
- COM and COM+ components can be instantiated and invoked by .NET code.
- The .NET platform invoke capability (usually referred to as PInvoke) can be used to call the Windows API.

▶ By using these interoperability features, you can ease your migration to .NET development. Using legacy components from .NET code means that you can migrate an application piecemeal rather than trying to do it all at once.

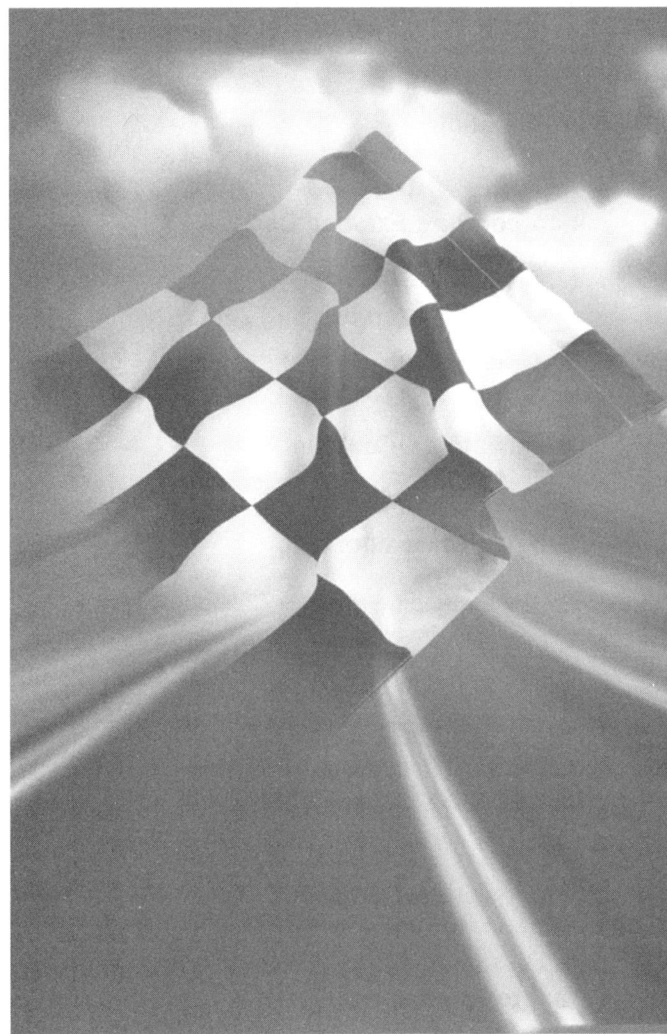

CHAPTER 10

Working with Legacy Code

OUTLINE

STUDY STRATEGIES

- If you have an existing ASP application, import the pages to an ASP.NET application and make the changes necessary to run them under ASP.NET.
- Convert several ActiveX controls for use in .NET. Try out the Visual Studio .NET tools for converting the ActiveX controls.
- If you have an existing COM or COM+ object to work with, create a runtime callable wrapper for the object to investigate the conversion process. If you don't have any existing objects, you can build one with older versions of Visual Basic.
- Experiment with PInvoke to invoke some common Windows API calls.

INTRODUCTION

Migrating to a new development platform can be a painful process. In extreme cases, you might have to throw away the results of years of work when you decide that it's time for a new set of tools. This can make switching to a new platform a very difficult decision.

Fortunately, Microsoft recognized the need to provide easy migration paths from previous versions of its tools to the .NET world. In particular, if you heeded the advice to use COM for intercomponent communications and to design your applications as a set of COM servers and clients, you'll find the upgrade path to .NET much smoother. That's because the .NET Framework includes good support for interoperating with existing COM-based code.

From .NET components, you can easily instantiate and call COM components such as ActiveX controls or COM libraries. (In fact, interoperability works in the other direction too, with COM components able to call .NET code, though I won't cover those techniques here.) Combine this with an existing modular architecture, and you get an easy migration path: Move one module at a time from COM to .NET, and use the .NET interoperability features so that the components can continue to talk to one another.

In this chapter, you'll learn about the facilities that the .NET Framework provides for using COM components and other legacy code. In particular, you'll learn about the tools and techniques that are necessary to call ActiveX controls, COM components, or Windows API code from the .NET Framework. You'll also see how you can move an existing ASP application to ASP.NET.

INCORPORATING EXISTING CODE

Incorporate existing code into ASP.NET pages.

Sometimes you have the luxury of starting a new project from scratch, and sometimes you don't. Many organizations will be implementing ASP.NET on the same servers that already host existing ASP applications. Fortunately, ASP and ASP.NET work fine together.

You can continue to run existing ASP pages on your ASP.NET servers, convert the pages to the new format, or move COM components from ASP pages to ASP.NET pages. In this section, you'll learn about this level of interoperability.

Running ASP and ASP.NET Together

ASP and ASP.NET run perfectly well together on the same server. That's a fundamental consequence of the architecture of the two systems. When you install Internet Information Services (IIS), it associates each file extension that the server understands with a particular application. ASP pages are handled by `c:\WINNT\System32\inetsrv\asp.dll`, whereas ASP.NET pages are handled by `C:\WINNT\Microsoft.NET\Framework\v1.0.3705\aspnet_isapi.dll`. Thus there's no confusion on the part of the server between the two file types, and no need to worry that old pages will be executed incorrectly after you install ASP.NET.

ASP pages and ASP.NET pages can even be incorporated into the same ASP.NET application, as you'll see in the following Step by Step.

STEP BY STEP

10.1 Running ASP and ASP.NET Pages Together

1. Open a Visual Basic ASP.NET Web Application in the Visual Studio .NET IDE.
2. Add a new Web Form to your Visual Basic .NET project. Name the new Web Form `StepByStep10-1.aspx`.
3. Add two `Label` controls and a `HyperLink` control to the Web Form. Set the ID properties of the `Label` controls to `lblDate` and `lblSession`. Set the Text property of the `HyperLink` control to "Go to Classic ASP page" and set its `NavigateUrl` property to `StepByStep10-1.asp`.
4. Add a new text file to your Visual Basic .NET project. Name the new text file `StepByStep10-1.asp`. This will make the file an ASP file.

5. Make sure that the ASP file is in HTML view in the designer and add this code to it:

```
<html>
<head>
<title>Classic ASP page</title>
<%@ Language=VBScript %>
</head>
<body>
<%
Dim vToday
Dim sSession

vToday = Date()
sSession = Session("RandomVar")
%>
<p>Today's date is: <%= vToday %></p>
<p>The random session variable is: <%= sSession %></p>
<p><a href="StepByStep10-1.aspx">
Return to ASP.NET page</a></p>
```

6. Double-click the ASP.NET Web Form to open its module. Enter code to handle the Page Load event:

```
Private Sub Page_Load(ByVal sender As System.Object, _
 ByVal e As System.EventArgs) Handles MyBase.Load
    lblDate.Text = "Today's date is: " & _
     DateTime.Today
    Dim r As Random = New Random()
    Session("RandomVar") = r.Next(1, 1000)
    lblSession.Text = "The random session
variable is: " & Session("RandomVar")
End Sub
```

7. Set the ASP.NET Web Form as the start page for the project.

8. Run the project to display the ASP.NET page. Click the hyperlink to go to the ASP page. You can click the hyperlink on that page to return to the original page.

EXAM TIP

No Shared State If you run this example, you'll discover one of the major problems in using ASP and ASP.NET pages together in the same application. Session and application state is not shared between the two types of pages. If you set a session or application variable in ASP.NET code, there's no way to retrieve it from ASP code, and vice versa.

Being able to run both types of pages on the same server is a useful technique, but in the long run you'll probably want to migrate all your ASP code to ASP.NET code. That will allow you to make use of the improved features of ASP.NET in your applications.

Converting ASP Pages to ASP.NET

One strategy for migrating an existing ASP application to ASP.NET is to rename the existing files so that they have the `aspx` extension instead of the `asp` extension. As soon as you do this, the pages will be delivered by ASP.NET instead of ASP.

The syntax of ASP.NET pages is very close to the syntax of ASP pages. But it's not identical. Here's a partial list of things you may need to change if you want to convert an existing ASP page to run as an ASP.NET page.

- In ASP, you could declare global variables and procedures in `<%...%>` blocks and they would be visible to all code on the page. In ASP.NET, such variables and procedures should be declared inside of a `<script runat=server>` block. ASP.NET will still execute code inside of `<%...%>` blocks, but such code is executed at render time, after all the code behind the page is already finished executing.
- In ASP, you could mix programming languages within a single page. ASP.NET requires each page to use a single programming language.
- ASP used scripting languages such as VBScript. ASP.NET uses the .NET languages such as Visual Basic .NET and C#. Although VBScript syntax is close to Visual Basic .NET syntax, it is not identical.
- ASP used the Variant data type for all variables. ASP.NET uses strong data types. You can use the `Object` data type when you do not know the exact type for a variable.
- ASP defaulted to passing parameters by reference. ASP.NET defaults to passing parameters by value.
- The `Set` keyword, the `Let` keyword, and default properties have been removed from ASP.NET.
- Arguments to methods in ASP.NET must be enclosed in parentheses, even if there is no return value.
- ASP would allow you to use nondeclared variables. ASP.NET requires you to declare all variables by default.

Using Late-Bound COM Components

The ASP.NET processor understands nearly all the syntax and all the objects that ASP itself supported. In particular, ASP.NET still supports the `Server.CreateObject` method for creating late-bound COM components. For example, you can create an ADO Connection object in either an ASP page or an ASP.NET page with this line of code:

```
cnn = Server.CreateObject("ADODB.Connection")
```

Not all COM components can be instantiated in ASP.NET this way. In particular, components that use the Single-Threaded Apartment (STA) threading model will not function properly in ASP.NET pages unless you add a compatibility directive to the page:

```
<%@Page aspcompat=true%>
```

STEP BY STEP

10.2 Converting an ASP Page to ASP.NET.

1. Add a new text file to your Visual Basic .NET project. Name the new text file `StepByStep10-2.asp`. This will make the file an ASP file.

2. Make sure that the ASP file is in HTML view in the designer and add this code to it:

```
<html>
<head>
<title>Customers</title>
<%@ Language=VBScript %>
</head>
<body>
<%
strConn = "Provider=SQLOLEDB;
Data Source=(local);
➥Database=Northwind;Integrated Security=SSPI"
Set cnn = Server.CreateObject("ADODB.Connection")
cnn.Open  strConn
strQuery = "SELECT CompanyName FROM Customers"
Set rstCust = cnn.Execute(strQuery)
%>
<table>
<tr>
   <td><b>Customers</b></td>
</tr>
```

continues

continued

```
<% Do While Not rstCust.EOF %>
<tr>
  <td> <%= rstCust("CompanyName") %> </td>
</tr>
<%
   rstCust.MoveNext
Loop
rstCust.Close
%>
</table>
<%
cnn.Close
Set rstCust = Nothing
Set cnn = Nothing
%>
</body>
</html>
```

3. Set this ASP page as the start page for the project.

4. Run the project. Your browser will open and display a list of customers from the Northwind database.

5. Stop the project.

6. Add a new ASP.NET Web Form to the project. Switch the form to HTML view in the designer.

7. Cut and paste the code from the ASP page to the ASP.NET page. Modify the code as follows (the boldfaced type indicates sections of the page that were changed):

```
<html>
<%@Page aspcompat=true%>
<head>
<title>Customers</title>
</head>
<body>
<%
Dim strConn As String
Dim cnn As Object
Dim strQuery As String
Dim rstCust as Object

strConn = "Provider=SQLOLEDB;Data Source=(local);
➥Database=Northwind;
➥Integrated Security=SSPI"
cnn = Server.CreateObject("ADODB.Connection")
cnn.Open(strConn)
strQuery = "SELECT CompanyName FROM Customers"
rstCust = cnn.Execute(strQuery)
%>
```

```
<table>
<tr>
   <td><b>Customers</b></td>
</tr>
<% Do While Not rstCust.EOF %>
<tr>
  <td> <%= rstCust("CompanyName").Value %> </td>
</tr>
<%
   rstCust.MoveNext
Loop
rstCust.Close
%>
</table>
<%
cnn.Close
rstCust = Nothing
cnn = Nothing
%>
</body>
</html>
```

8. Set the ASP.NET Web Form as the start page for the project.

9. Run the project to display the ASP.NET page, which will also show the customers from the Northwind sample database.

As you can see, it's pretty simple to convert an ASP page to an ASP.NET page. But you should still consider this only a temporary measure. Although the new page will be executed by the ASP.NET engine, it won't benefit from any of the new capabilities of the .NET Framework. In this particular case, for example, you could get better performance by switching to ADO.NET for data access. You could also make the page more maintainable by switching to a code-behind structure instead of intermingling code and HTML.

> **NOTE** **Early-bound COM Objects** COM objects that are initialized with `Server.CreateObject` are always late bound. You can also use COM objects as early-bound objects if you wrap them in .NET assemblies. You'll see this technique, which enhances performance, later in this chapter.

Using ActiveX Controls

Instantiate and invoke an ActiveX control.

With their roots in the Visual Basic custom control standard, ActiveX controls have become a major means of delivering encapsulated functionality to Windows and Web applications.

The key advance underlying ActiveX controls is that they have a standard set of interfaces through which they communicate with the hosting form. By supporting these interfaces, any application can make use of any ActiveX control, without any knowledge of the internal workings of that control.

This concept has turned out to be so popular that thousands of ActiveX controls are available commercially. You can find controls to display unusual graphs, controls that implement common Internet protocols, controls that emulate spreadsheets, and many more.

With the success of ActiveX controls in the Windows environment, it was only a matter of time before Microsoft found a way to bring them to the Web as well. It did this by making Internet Explorer an ActiveX container. A Web page can specify (by means of a GUID) an ActiveX control that should be instantiated and displayed in the browser.

But in the .NET world, an ActiveX control is useless. Web Forms can only contain instances of controls derived from the `System.Web.UI.Control` class. ActiveX controls, being built using previous technologies, do not derive from this class. So how can you possibly use an ActiveX control on a Web Form?

> **WARNING**
>
> **IE Only** Internet Explorer functions as an ActiveX host, but other browsers offer little or no support for ActiveX controls. You should only consider ActiveX controls a solution for situations where you control the choice of browser. Usually this means that ActiveX controls are only suitable for intranet applications.

The answer is that ActiveX controls are a client-side technology, not a server-side technology. Unlike a regular ASP.NET Server Control, which is compiled into HTML before the page is sent to the client, an ActiveX control is actually instantiated on the client. It doesn't matter whether the original page was HTML, ASP, or ASP.NET; in every case, it's up to the browser to handle the ActiveX control.

You can actually add ActiveX controls to the Web Forms toolbox in Visual Studio .NET. This makes it easy to add them to a Web Form, though the support the VS .NET supplies for actually using these controls is minimal.

STEP BY STEP

10.3 Using the Toolbox to Add an ActiveX Control

1. Create a new Web Form in your Visual Basic ASP.NET application.

2. Right-click the Toolbox and select Customize Toolbox.

3. Select the COM components tab in the Customize Toolbox dialog box.

4. Scroll down the list of components, which will include all the ActiveX controls that are registered on your computer, until you find the control you'd like to add to your project. Click the checkbox for the control. Figure 10.1 shows the process of adding the Microsoft Forms 2.0 `CommandButton` control.

EXAM TIP

Control Locations Remember, any ActiveX control that you use on a Web Form must be present on the client's computer to function. You can include a codebase tag that specifies a download location for the control if necessary.

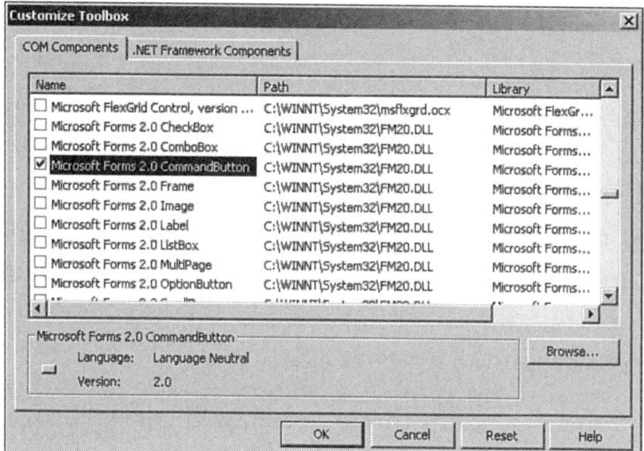

FIGURE 10.1◀
Adding an ActiveX control to the Visual Studio .NET Toolbox.

5. Click OK to add the control to the Toolbox.

6. The new control will show up at the bottom of the Toolbox, as shown in Figure 10.2. You can click and drag the control to a form just like any native .NET control. Place an instance of the `CommandButton` control on your form. Set the `id` property of the `CommandButton` control to `cmd1`.

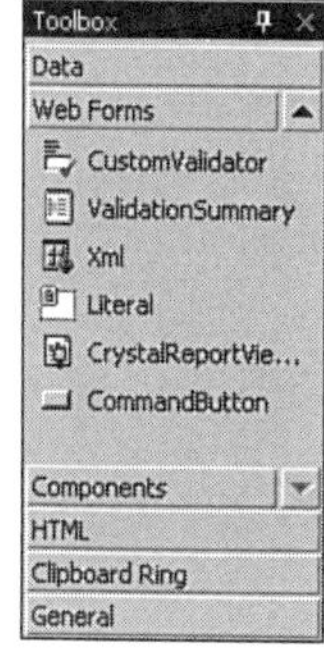

FIGURE 10.2▲
An ActiveX control in the Visual Studio .NET Toolbox.

7. Switch the form to HTML view in the designer. You'll find that the ActiveX control is represented as a collapsed region with an `OBJECT` tag. Expand the region. Modify the `PARAM` tag for the control's caption as follows:

```
<PARAM NAME="Caption" VALUE="Click Me">
```

continues

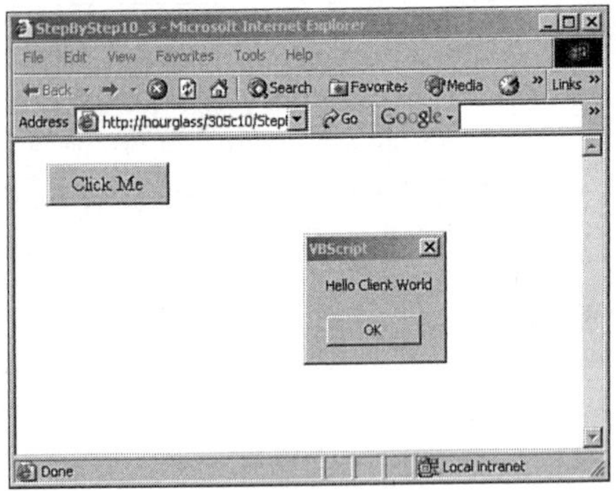

FIGURE 10.3
An ActiveX control in the browser.

continued

8. Add a script section to the HTML, just above the `</HEAD>` tag:

```
    <script language="vbscript">
Sub cmd1_Click()
    MsgBox "Hello Client World"
End Sub
    </script>
```

9. Run the project. Your browser will instantiate and display the ActiveX control. Click the button to display the message box, as shown in Figure 10.3.

When you run this sample, ASP.NET sends the `classid` value for the ActiveX control to the browser. It's up to the browser to check the registry on the computer where it is running, and to create the corresponding ActiveX control. The VBScript procedure that's tied to the control's click event is also sent to the browser. When the user clicks the control, the VBScript is executed on the client. This code doesn't interact with the server at all.

To sum up, there are a few things you should consider before you use ActiveX controls in your .NET applications.

Realize that ActiveX controls may impose a performance penalty on your ASP.NET applications. If the control isn't already present on the client, it will need to be downloaded when your page is sent to the client, potentially involving a long delay.

Because ActiveX controls are not managed code, they don't get any of the protection that the CLR brings to your .NET applications. An ActiveX control is free to access memory that doesn't belong to it or indulge in other buggy behavior that may crash your entire application.

Also remember that ActiveX controls will only function reliably in Internet Explorer. Other browsers support some ActiveX controls, but this support is imperfect.

Because of these drawbacks, you should use ActiveX controls sparingly (if at all). Before importing an ActiveX control into your project, you should consider whether a native .NET control can fill your requirements.

REVIEW BREAK

- You can import an ActiveX control to a Visual Studio .NET project by adding it to the Toolbox.
- After they're imported, ActiveX controls can be placed on a Web Form just like native .NET controls.
- ActiveX controls are instantiated on the client, not the server. Any event handlers for the control must be written in a scripting language and will also execute on the client.
- ActiveX controls impose a performance penalty and have other drawbacks.

USING COM COMPONENTS

Instantiate and invoke a COM or COM+ component.

Using ActiveX controls on a Web form is a special case of a more general problem: using legacy COM code from a .NET application. To see why you might want to do this, consider the task of migrating an entire application from ASP to ASP.NET. A full-fledged application will likely involve custom objects (perhaps a data access layer or a business rules layer) as well as ASP code. You're likely to spend a considerable amount of time cleaning up and fixing migrated code. For a large application, this can represent a formidable barrier to migration.

Fortunately, if you implemented your ASP project using a component architecture, you don't have to do a "big bang" migration all at once. .NET components can call COM components, and COM components can call .NET components. This means that you can migrate one component (a control, a class library, and so on) at a time, and still keep all of your code working together.

Why might you want to undertake such a gradual migration? There are four basic reasons for maintaining part of a system in COM components while moving other parts to .NET components:

- It takes time to learn enough about Visual Basic .NET, ASP.NET, and the .NET Framework to be productive.

While you're making your way up the learning curve, you may have to continue development of existing COM components.

- You may have components that can't be easily moved to .NET, because they use language features that are no longer supported or because of other implementation quirks.
- It takes time to move code from one system to the other. Unless you can afford extended downtime, a gradual move lets you write the converted code at a slower pace.
- Your application may depend on third-party controls or libraries for which you do not have the source code.

In this section of the chapter, you'll learn how you can encapsulate COM components for use from .NET applications. There are both command-line and GUI tools for working with COM components. Before seeing those tools, though, you should know a bit about wrapper classes.

Understanding Runtime Callable Wrappers

As you probably already know, Visual Basic .NET creates code that operates within the .NET Common Language Runtime (CLR). Code that operates within the CLR is called *managed code.* Managed code benefits from the services that the CLR offers, including garbage collection, memory management, and support for versioning and security.

Code that does not operate within the CLR is called *unmanaged code.* Code that was created by tools before .NET is by definition unmanaged code. COM components are unmanaged code, because COM was designed before the CLR existed, and COM components don't make use of any of the services of the CLR.

Managed code expects that all the code with which it interacts will use the CLR. This is an obvious problem for COM components. How can you take a component that was developed before the advent of .NET and make it look like a .NET component to other .NET components? The answer is to use a proxy. In general terms, a proxy accepts commands and messages from one component, modifies them, and passes them to another component.

The particular type of proxy that allows you to use COM components within a .NET application is called a runtime-callable wrapper. That is, it's a proxy that can be called by the CLR.

Figure 10.4 shows schematically how the pieces fit together.

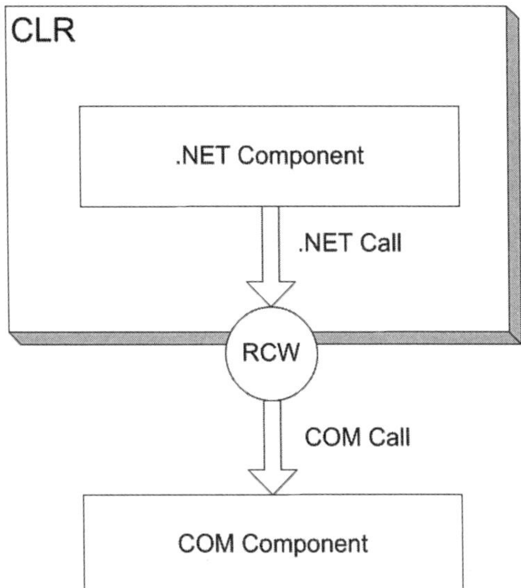

FIGURE 10.4
The architecture of a runtime-callable wrapper.

To see how COM interoperability works, you'll need a COM library. This Step by Step shows you how to build a simple one.

STEP BY STEP

10.4 Building a COM DLL

1. Launch Visual Basic 6.0. Create a new ActiveX DLL project.
2. Select the `Project1` node in the Project Explorer window and rename it `MyCustomer`.
3. Select the `Class1` node in the Project Explorer window and rename it `Balances`.

continues

continued

4. Add this code to the `Balances` class:

```
Option Explicit

Private mintCustomerCount As Integer
Private macurBalances(1 To 10) As Currency

' Create a read-only CustomerCount property
Public Property Get CustomerCount() As Integer
    CustomerCount = mintCustomerCount
End Property

' Create a GetBalance method
Public Function GetBalance(
CustomerNumber As Integer) As Currency
    GetBalance = macurBalances(CustomerNumber)
End Function

' Initialize the data
Private Sub Class_Initialize()
    Dim intI As Integer

    mintCustomerCount = 10

    For intI = 1 To 10
        macurBalances(intI) = Int(Rnd(1) _
         * 100000) / 100
    Next intI

End Sub
```

5. Save the Visual Basic project.
6. Select File, Build MyCustomer.dll to create the COM component.

> **NOTE**
> **If You Don't Have VB 6.0** You can still test COM interoperability by working with a COM library that's already installed on your computer. A variety of Microsoft components, including Office, SQL Server, and ADO, install COM libraries.

Using TLBIMP

The task of using COM components from .NET is made substantially easier by the fact that COM components, like .NET components, have metadata that describe their interfaces. For .NET components, this metadata is embedded in the assembly manifest. For COM components, the metadata is stored in a type library. A type library can be a separate file, or (as with Visual Basic 6 class libraries) it can be embedded within another file.

The .NET Framework includes a tool, the Type Library Importer, that can create an RCW from COM metadata contained in a type library.

STEP BY STEP

10.5 Using the Type Library Importer

1. Launch a .NET command prompt by selecting Start, Programs, Microsoft Visual Studio .NET, Visual Studio .NET Tools, Visual Studio .NET Command Prompt.

2. Inside the command prompt window, navigate to the folder that contains the MyCustomers.dll COM library.

3. Enter this command line to run the Type Library Importer:

```
tlbimp MyCustomer.dll /out:NETMyCustomer.dll
```

4. Add a new Web Form to your Visual Basic ASP.NET application.

5. Place three labels on the form: a `TextBox` control with the id of `txtCustomerCount`, a `TextBox` control with the id of `txtCustomerNumber`, a `Button` control with the id of `btnGetBalance`, and a `TextBox` control with the id of `txtBalance`. Figure 10.5 shows the design of this form.

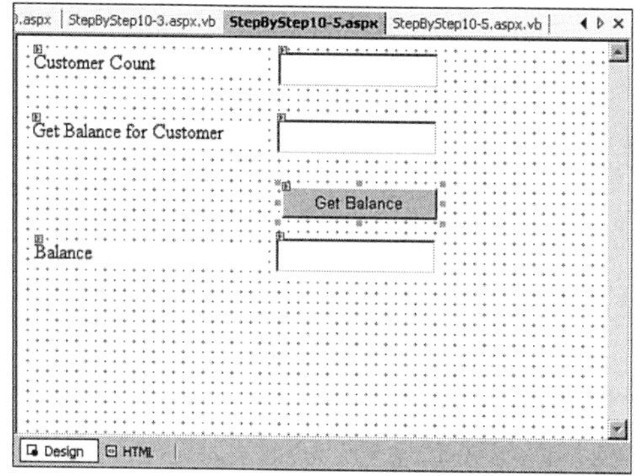

FIGURE 10.5
A form to test the use of a COM component.

6. Right-click the References node in Solution Explorer and select Add Reference.

7. Click the Browse button in the Add Reference dialog box. Browse to the NETMyCustomer.dll file that you created in step 3. Click OK to add the reference to the project.

8. Double-click the `Button` control to open the form's module. Enter this line of code at the top of the module:

```
Imports NETMyCustomer
```

9. Enter this code within the module:

```
Dim B As Balances

Private Sub Page_Load(ByVal sender As System.Object, _
 ByVal e As System.EventArgs) Handles MyBase.Load
    B = New Balances()
    txtCustomerCount.Text = B.CustomerCount
End Sub
```

continues

continued

```
Private Sub btnGetBalance_Click( _
 ByVal sender As System.Object, _
 ByVal e As System.EventArgs) _
 Handles btnGetBalance.Click
    txtBalance.Text = B.GetBalance( _
     txtCustomerNumber.Text)
End Sub
```

10. Set the Web Form as the start page for the project.

11. Run the project. The form will display the customer count in the first `TextBox` control. Enter a number between 1 and 10 in the customer number `TextBox` control and click the `Button` control to see that customer's balance.

In this Step by Step, you used the Type Library Importer to create a Runtime Callable Wrapper for the COM type library. This RCW is a library that you can add to your .NET project as a reference. After you've done that, the classes in the COM component can be used just like native .NET classes. When you use a class from the COM component, .NET makes the call to the RCW, which in turn forwards the call to the original COM component and returns the results to your .NET managed code.

The Type Library Importer supports a set of command-line options. Table 10.1 shows the available options.

TABLE 10.1

OPTIONS FOR THE TYPE LIBRARY IMPORTER

Option	*Meaning*
`/asmversion:`*`versioNumber`*	Specifies the version number for the created assembly.
`/delaysign`	Prepares the assembly for delay signing.
`/help`	Displays help on command-line options.
`/keycontainer:`*`containerName`*	Signs the assembly with the strong name from the specified key container.
`/keyfile:`*`filename`*	Signs the assembly with the strong name from the specified key file.

Option	*Meaning*
`/namespace:`*`namespace`*	Specifies the namespace for the created assembly.
`/out:`*`filename`*	Specifies the name of the created assembly.
`/primary`	Produces a primary interop assembly.
`/publickey:`*`filename`*	Specifies the file containing a public key used to sign the resulting file.
`/reference:`*`filename`*	Specifies a file to be used to resolve references from the file being imported.
`/silent`	Suppresses information that would otherwise be displayed on the command line during conversion.
`/strictref`	Refuses to create the assembly if one or more references cannot be resolved.
`/sysarray`	Imports COM `SafeArrays` as instances of the `System.Array.Class` type.
`/unsafe`	Creates interfaces without net security checks.
`/verbose`	Displays additional information on the command line during conversion.
`/?`	Displays help on command-line options.

EXAM TIP

Options overview You don't need to memorize all the options to the Type Library Importer. You should know that most of the options deal with the security of the resulting RCW and the code that it contains.

Using COM Components Directly

As with ActiveX controls, the Visual Studio .NET interface provides a streamlined way to use a COM component from your .NET code.

STEP BY STEP

10.6 Using Direct Reference with a COM Library

1. Add a new form to your Visual Basic .NET application.
2. Place three labels on the form: a `TextBox` control with the id of `txtCustomerCount`, a `TextBox` control with the id of `txtCustomerNumber`, a `Button` control with the id of `btnGetBalance`, and a `TextBox` control with the id of `txtBalance`. Refer back to Figure 10.5 for the design of this form.

continues

continued

3. Right-click the References node in Solution Explorer and select Add Reference.

4. Select the COM tab in the Add Reference dialog box. Scroll down the list of COM components until you come to the `MyCustomer` library. Select the `MyCustomer` library, click Select, and then click OK.

5. Double-click the `Button` control to open the form's module. Enter this line of code at the top of the module:

```
Imports MyCustomer
```

6. Enter this code within the module:

```
Dim B As MyCustomer.Balances

Private Sub Page_Load(ByVal sender As System.Object, _
 ByVal e As System.EventArgs) Handles MyBase.Load
    B = New MyCustomer.Balances()
    txtCustomerCount.Text = B.CustomerCount
End Sub

Private Sub btnGetBalance_Click( _
 ByVal sender As System.Object, _
 ByVal e As System.EventArgs) _
 Handles btnGetBalance.Click
    txtBalance.Text = _
     B.GetBalance(txtCustomerNumber.Text)
End Sub
```

7. Set the form as the startup object for the project.

8. Run the project. The form will display the customer count in the first `TextBox` control. Enter a number between 1 and 10 in the customer number `TextBox` control and click the `Button` control to see that customer's balance.

When you directly reference a COM library from the Visual Studio .NET IDE, the effect is almost the same as if you had used the Type Library Importer to import the same library. Visual Studio .NET creates a new namespace with the name of the original library and then exposes the classes from the library within that namespace.

Although you can use either of the two methods you've seen to call a COM component from a .NET component, there are reasons to prefer one method over the other:

- For a COM component that will only be used in a single Visual Basic .NET project, and which you wrote yourself, use the easiest method: direct reference from your .NET project. This method is only suitable for a truly private component that does not need to be shared.
- If a COM component is shared among multiple projects, use the Type Library Importer so that you can sign the resulting assembly and place it in the Global Assembly Cache. Shared code must be signed.
- If you need to control details of the created Assembly, such as its name, namespace, or version number, you must use the Type Library Importer. The direct reference method gives you no control over these details.

> **WARNING**
>
> **Only Import Your Own Code** You should not use either one of these methods on code written by another developer. That's because you are not allowed (according to Microsoft's recommendations on how to proceed) to sign code written by someone else. If you need to use a COM component from another developer, you should obtain a Primary Interop Assembly (PIA) from the original developer of the component. Microsoft supplies PIAs for all its common libraries.

USING COM+ COMPONENTS

COM+ is the Component Services layer of Windows 2000 and later operating systems. COM+ supplies a number of services to components running under Windows. These include

- Role-based security
- Object pooling and reusability
- Queued components for asynchronous calls
- Transactional processing
- A publish-and-subscribe events model

Despite the significant differences between COM+ and straight COM, you don't have to do anything different to use a COM+ component than to use a COM component. To the consumer, a COM+ component looks much like a COM component. The Type Library Importer and Visual Studio .NET can both create wrappers for COM+ components using the same procedures that they use for COM components.

GUIDED PRACTICE EXERCISE 10.1

EXAM TIP

Timing Code To tell how long a piece of code takes to run, you can use arithmetic with two instances of the `DateTime` class to produce a `TimeSpan` object.

In this exercise, you'll compare the performance of two implementations of the same code, using a COM library for one implementation and a native .NET class for the other implementation. You should pick some code that takes a reasonably long time to run, so that you can detect any differences between the two.

You should try doing this on your own first. If you get stuck, or you'd like to see one possible solution, follow these steps:

1. Launch Visual Basic 6.0. Create a new ActiveX DLL project.
2. Select the `Project1` node in the Project Explorer window and rename it `Numeric`.
3. Select the `Class1` node in the Project Explorer window and rename it to `Primes`.
4. Add this code to the `Primes` class:

```
Option Explicit

Public Function HighPrime(Max As Long) As Long
        Dim a() As Byte
        Dim lngI As Long
        Dim lngJ As Long

        ReDim a(Max)

        ' In the array, 1 indicates a prime,
        ' 0 indicates nonprime.
        ' Start by marking multiples
        ' of 2 as nonprime
        For lngI = 0 To Max
            If lngI Mod 2 = 0 And lngI <> 2 Then
                a(lngI) = 0
            Else
                a(lngI) = 1
            End If
        Next lngI
        ' Now execute the usual sieve of
        ' erasthones algorithm
        For lngI = 3 To Sqr(Max) Step 2
            If a(lngI) = 1 Then
                ' This is a prime, so eliminate
                '  its multiples
                For lngJ = lngI + lngI _
                 To Max Step lngI
                    a(lngJ) = 0
                Next lngJ
            End If
```

```
        Next lngI
        ' Find the largest prime by working backwards
        For lngI = Max To 1 Step -1
            If a(lngI) = 1 Then
                HighPrime = lngI
                Exit For
            End If
        Next lngI

End Function
```

5. Save the Visual Basic project.
6. Select File, Build Numeric.dll to create the COM component.
7. In your Visual Basic ASP .NET project, right-click the References node of Solution Explorer and select Add Reference.
8. Select the COM tab in the Add Reference dialog box. Scroll down the list of COM components until you come to the Numeric library. Select the Numeric library, click Select, and then click OK.
9. Add a new class to your Visual Basic ASP.NET project. Name the class `Primes.vb`.
10. Add this code to the `Primes.vb` class:

```
Public Class Primes
    Public Function HighPrime( _
     ByVal Max As Long) As Long
        Dim a() As Byte
        Dim intI As Integer
        Dim intJ As Integer

        ReDim a(Max)

        ' In the array, 1 indicates a prime,
        ' 0 indicates nonprime.
        ' Start by marking multiples
        ' of 2 as nonprime
        For intI = 0 To Max
            If intI Mod 2 = 0 And intI <> 2 Then
                a(intI) = 0
            Else
                a(intI) = 1
            End If
        Next intI
```

continues

continued

```
        ' Now execute the usual sieve of
        ' erasthones algorithm
        For intI = 3 To System.Math.Sqrt(Max) Step 2
            If a(intI) = 1 Then
                ' This is a prime, so eliminate
                ' its multiples
                For intJ = intI + intI  _
                 To Max Step intI
                    a(intJ) = 0
                Next intJ
            End If
        Next intI
        ' Find the largest prime by working backwards
        For intI = Max To 1 Step -1
            If a(intI) = 1 Then
                HighPrime = intI
                Exit For
            End If
        Next intI

    End Function

End Class
```

11. Add a new Web Form to your Visual Basic ASP.NET Project. Name the form `GuidedPracticeExercise10-1.aspx`.

12. Place five `Label` controls, a `Button` control, and a `TextBox` control on the form. Give the two blank `Label` controls the `id` properties of `lblCOMresults` and `lblNETresults`. Set the `id` of the `Button` control to `btnGo`, and set the `id` of the `TextBox` control to `txtMaximum`. Figure 10.6 shows a design for this form.

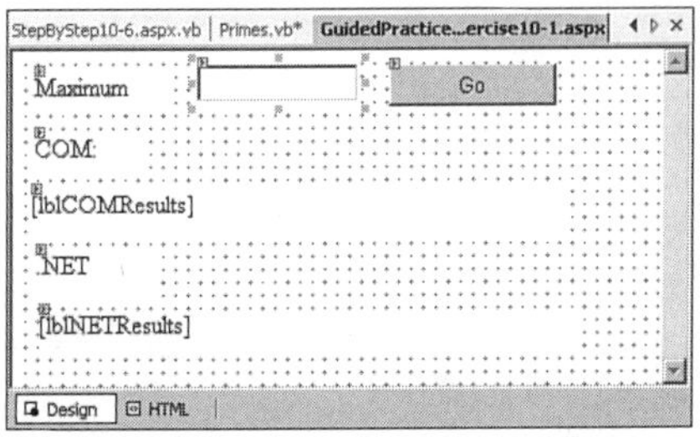

13. Double-click the `Button` control to open the form's module. Add this statement to the top of the module:

```
Imports Numeric
```

14. Add this code to run the code when the `Button` control is clicked:

```
Private Sub btnGo_Click( _
 ByVal sender As System.Object, _
 ByVal e As System.EventArgs) Handles btnGo.Click
    Dim lngHighPrime As Long

    Dim COM_Primes As Numeric.Primes = _
     New Numeric.Primes()
    Dim dt1 As DateTime = DateTime.Now
    lngHighPrime = COM_Primes.HighPrime( _
     txtMaximum.Text)
```

FIGURE 10.6
A form to compare execution speed

WARNING

The Pitfalls of Performance In this particular example, the .NET class was much faster than the COM class. But timing performance on Windows is notoriously difficult, for several reasons. First, although you can measure things down to the timer tick, the hardware does not provide precise-to-the-tick numbers. Second, because of caching and other programs being in memory, timings tend not to be repeatable. Finally, it's hard to write exactly equivalent COM and .NET code. Nevertheless, repeated runs of a program such as this example can give you general information on which of two alternatives is faster.

```
    Dim ts1 As TimeSpan = DateTime.Now.Subtract(dt1)
    lblCOMResults.Text = "High prime = " &
        ➥lngHighPrime.ToString() & _
     " took " & ts1.Ticks.ToString & " ticks"

    Dim NET_Primes As Primes = New Primes()
    Dim dt2 As DateTime = DateTime.Now
    lngHighPrime = _
     NET_Primes.HighPrime(txtMaximum.Text)
    Dim ts2 As TimeSpan = DateTime.Now.Subtract(dt2)
    lblNETResults.Text = "High prime = " &
        ➥lngHighPrime.ToString() & _
     " took " & ts2.Ticks.ToString & " ticks"
End Sub
```

15. Set the form as the start page for the project.
16. Run the project. Enter a fairly large number in the `TextBox` control and click the `button` control. The code will find the largest prime number that is smaller than the number you entered, first with the COM library and then with the native .NET class. It will display the relative execution times for the two versions, as shown in Figure 10.7.

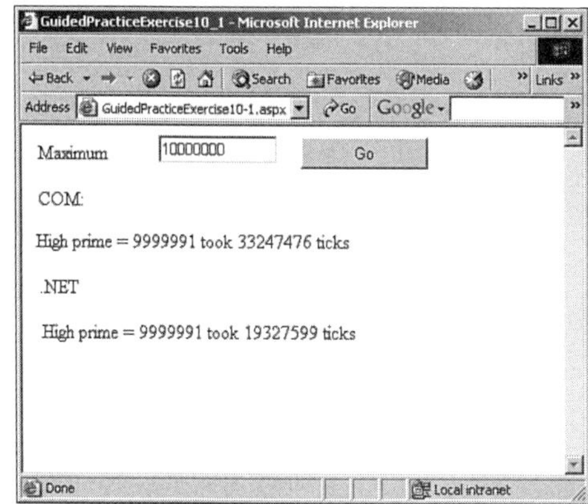

FIGURE 10.7
Comparing the execution speed of two classes.

Using Platform Invoke

Call native functions by using platform invoke.

So far, you've seen interoperability between managed code and unmanaged code by way of method calls to classes in COM libraries. There's a second way that .NET can interoperate with unmanaged code, though: through functional calls to unmanaged libraries. The *platform invoke* (often abbreviated as c) feature of .NET allows .NET code to call functions from unmanaged libraries such as the Windows API.

STEP BY STEP

10.7 Using Platform Invoke with the Windows API

1. Add a new module to your Visual Basic .NET application. Name the new module `API.vb`.

2. Add this code to the `API.vb` module:

```
Public Module API

    Declare Auto Function GetComputerName _
     Lib "kernel32" ( _
     ByVal lpBuffer As String, _
     ByRef nSize As Integer) As Integer

End Module
```

3. Add a new Web Form to your Visual Basic ASP.NET application.

4. Place a `Label` control named `lblComputerName` on the form.

5. Double-click the Form to open its module. Enter this line of code at the top of the module:

```
Imports System.Text
```

6. Enter this code within the module:

```
Private Sub Page_Load(ByVal sender As System.Object, _
 ByVal e As System.EventArgs) Handles MyBase.Load
    Dim buf As String = New String(CChar(" "), 128)
    Dim len As Integer = buf.Length
    Dim ret As Integer
    ret = GetComputerName(buf, len)
    lblComputerName.Text = _
     "This computer is named " & _
     buf.ToString.Substring(0, len)
End Sub
```

7. Set the Web Form as the start page for the project.

8. Run the project. The form will display the name of the computer where the code is run, as shown in Figure 10.8. Remember, if you're using a client on one computer and a server on another, the ASP.NET code executes on the server. So in that case the browser will display the name of the server, not the name of the client.

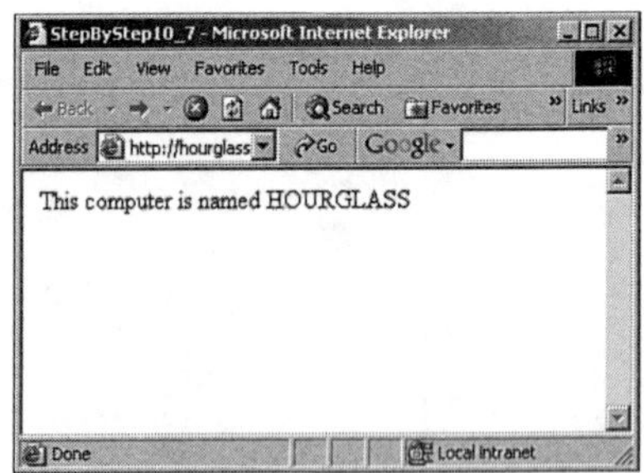

FIGURE 10.8
Calling the Windows API.

If you've used the Windows API from Visual Basic 6.0, PInvoke will look very familiar. The `Declare` statement (which must be contained in a module or a class module) tells the CLR where to find an API function by specifying the name of the library (in this case `kernel32.dll`) and the name of the function (in this case `GetComputerName`). Once the function is declared, you can use it within Visual Basic .NET just like any other function.

Note the use of the `Auto` modifier in the function declaration. You may know that many Windows API calls come in two versions, depending on the character set that you're using. For example, `GetComputerName` really exists as `GetComputerNameA` (for ANSI characters) and `GetComputerNameW` (for Unicode characters). The Auto modifier instructs the .NET Framework to use the appropriate version of the API call for the platform where the code is running.

PInvoke can also handle API calls that require structures as parameters. For example, many API calls require a `Rect` structure, which consists of four longs that are filled in with the co-ordinates of a rectangle. In Visual Basic .NET, you can declare a structure with explicit byte offsets for each member, which lets you define any structure that the Windows API requires:

```
<StructLayout(LayoutKind.Explicit)> _
Public Structure Rect
    <FieldOffset(0)> Public left As Integer
    <FieldOffset(4)> Public top As Integer
    <FieldOffset(8)> Public right As Integer
    <FieldOffset(12)> Public bottom As Integer
End Structure
```

The `StructLayout` attribute tells the VB .NET compiler that you'll explicitly specify the location of the individual fields within the structure. The `FieldOffset` attribute specifies the starting byte of each field within the structure. By using these attributes, you can ensure that .NET constructs the same structure that the API function is expecting to receive.

REVIEW BREAK

- Using COM or COM+ components from .NET managed code requires the creation of a runtime-callable wrapper (RCW).

continues

continued

- You can create an RCW for a COM component by using the Type Library Importer, or by directly referencing the COM component from your .NET code.
- To use COM components that you did not create, you should obtain a Primary Interop Assembly (PIA) from the creator of the component.
- RCWs impose a performance penalty on COM code.
- You can use the .NET Platform Invoke (PInvoke) facility to call functions from Windows libraries, including the Windows API.

CHAPTER SUMMARY

KEY TERMS

- Runtime Callable Wrapper (RCW)
- Managed Code
- Unmanaged Code
- Platform invoke

Although the .NET Framework is extensive, it is not all-encompassing. Many projects will need to use a mix of old (ASP, COM, or Windows) components and new (.NET) components. Even if all of the necessary facilities are available within the .NET Framework, it may not be feasible to migrate an entire existing application to .NET all at once.

The .NET Framework and Visual Studio .NET include a variety of features designed to make it easier to use legacy components. In this chapter, you saw four of those features:

- The ability to quickly convert ASP code to ASP.NET code.
- The ability to use ActiveX controls on a Web form.
- The ability to instantiate and invoke objects from a COM component.
- The ability to call functions from a Windows API or other DLL.

You can import an ActiveX control directly to the toolbox, and use it on a Web Form like any other control.

CHAPTER SUMMARY

COM components depend on wrappers, called Runtime-Callable Wrappers (RCW) to work with .NET. An RCW is a proxy that sends data back and forth between the COM component and .NET components. You can create RCWs with the Type Library Importer command-line tool, or by adding the COM component to the references collection of your .NET project.

You may also need to call functions from the Windows API or other DLLs. The .NET Platform Invoke functionality lets you do this. By using the `Declare` keyword, you can tell the .NET Framework where to find a function call and what parameters to send to the call.

APPLY YOUR KNOWLEDGE

Exercises

10.1 Finishing the Conversion

In Step by Step 10.2, you converted an ASP page to an ASP.NET page. The ASP.NET page, though, still depends on the COM components from the ADO library to do its work. In this exercise, you'll see the additional work necessary to finish the conversion, replacing the ADO components with ADO.NET components.

Estimated Time: 15 minutes.

1. Open a Visual Basic ASP.NET Web Application in the Visual Studio .NET IDE.
2. Add a new Web Form to the Visual Basic ASP.NET application.
3. Set the title property of the page to `Customers` to match the original page.
4. Double-click the page to open the form's module.
5. Add two lines of code to the top of the module to use the ADO.NET namespace:

```
Imports System.Data
Imports System.Data.SqlClient
```

6. Copy the code that opens the Recordset from Step by Step 10.2 and paste it in the form's Load event handler. Alter the code to use ADO.NET instead of ADO:

```
Private Sub Page_Load( _
 ByVal sender As System.Object, _
 ByVal e As System.EventArgs) _
 Handles MyBase.Load
    Dim cnn As SqlConnection = _
     New SqlConnection( _
     "Data Source=(local);
     ➥Database=Northwind;
     ➥Integrated Security=SSPI")
    Dim cmd As SqlCommand = _
     cnn.CreateCommand()
    cmd.CommandType = CommandType.Text
    cmd.CommandText = _
     "SELECT CompanyName FROM Customers"
    cnn.Open()
    Dim dr As SqlDataReader = _

     cmd.ExecuteReader
```

7. The original form used a loop to dump the contents of the Recordset to the Web page at render time. You can replace this with a bound `DataGrid` control to build the page at load time. Place a `DataGrid` control on the form and name it `dgCustomers`.
8. Finish the Load event handler by adding code to bind the data to the `DataGrid`:

```
Private Sub Page_Load( _
 ByVal sender As System.Object, _
 ByVal e As System.EventArgs) _
 Handles MyBase.Load
    Dim cnn As SqlConnection = _
     New SqlConnection( _
     "Data Source=(local); " & _
     "Database=Northwind; " & _
     "Integrated Security=SSPI")
    Dim cmd As SqlCommand = _
     cnn.CreateCommand()
    cmd.CommandType = CommandType.Text
    cmd.CommandText = _
     "SELECT CompanyName FROM Customers"
    cnn.Open()
    Dim dr As SqlDataReader =_
     cmd.ExecuteReader()

    dgCustomers.DataSource = dr
    dgCustomers.DataBind()
    cnn.Close()
End Sub
```

9. Set the form as the start page for the project.
10. Run the project. You'll see the customer list from the Northwind database, just as the original ASP page displayed. Figure 10.9 shows the finished page.

APPLY YOUR KNOWLEDGE

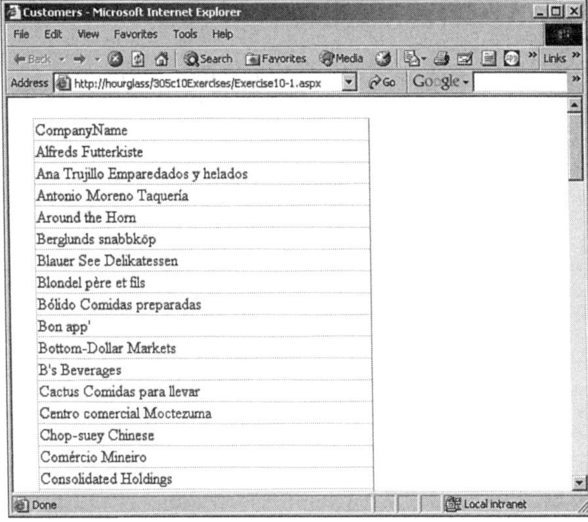

FIGURE 10.9
ASP page converted to ASP.NET.

10.2 Using StringBuilder with API Calls

You may already know that instances of the String class in .NET are immutable. The .NET Framework allows you to pass a string as a buffer to an API call, but for the return value to be properly displayed in the string, it has to destroy the variable and create a new one. In this exercise, you'll rewrite the code from Step by Step 10.7 to use a `StringBuilder` instead of a `String`. The advantage of the `StringBuilder` class is that it allows modifying an existing string.

Estimated Time: 15 minutes.

1. Add a new module to your Visual Basic ASP.NET application. Name the new module `API.vb`.

2. Add this code to the `API.vb` module:

```
Imports System.Text

Module API

    Declare Auto Function _
     GetComputerName Lib _
     "kernel32" ( _
     ByVal lpBuffer As StringBuilder, _
     ByRef nSize _
     As Integer) As Integer

End Module
```

3. Add a new form to your Visual Basic ASP.NET application.

4. Place a `Label` control named `lblComputerName` on the form.

5. Double-click the Form to open its module. Enter this line of code at the top of the module:

```
Imports System.Text
```

6. Enter this code within the module:

```
Private Sub Page_Load( _
 ByVal sender As System.Object, _
 ByVal e As System.EventArgs) _
 Handles MyBase.Load

    Dim buf As StringBuilder = _
     New StringBuilder(128)
    Dim len As Integer = buf.Capacity
    Dim ret As Integer

    ret = GetComputerName(buf, len)

    lblComputerName.Text = _
     "This computer is named " & _
     buf.ToString

End Sub
```

7. Set the form as the start page for the project.

8. Run the project. The form will display the name of the computer where the code is run.

Apply Your Knowledge

> **EXAM TIP**
>
> **`StringBuilder` Convenience**
> When you use a `StringBuilder` object as a buffer for a Windows API call, you don't have to worry about the length of the returned string. The .NET Framework automatically truncates the returned string at the first null character.

Review Questions

1. What do you need to do to use an ActiveX control on a Web Form in a Visual Basic ASP.NET application?
2. What are the advantages and disadvantages of using ActiveX controls on an ASP.NET Web Form?
3. Name some reasons to use COM components in a .NET project.
4. What is the purpose of a Runtime Callable Wrapper?
5. How can you create a Runtime Callable Wrapper?
6. What should you consider when choosing how to create a Runtime Callable Wrapper?
7. What extra steps do you need to take to use a COM+ component in a .NET application, as compared to using a COM component?
8. What's the difference between COM interoperability and `PInvoke`?
9. What is the purpose of the `Auto` modifier in a `Declare` statement?

Exam Questions

1. Your application uses an instance of the Microsoft Masked Edit ActiveX control to collect data from users. Some of the users report that the page containing this control won't load. You've checked, and those users do have the .NET Framework installed. What could be the problem?

   A. The Microsoft Masked Edit control is not installed on the problem computers, and you did not provide a codebase tag to indicate a download location.

   B. The RCW for the ActiveX control needs to be registered on the problem computers.

   C. The problem computers are not connected to the Internet.

   D. Service Pack 1 for the .NET Framework is not installed on the problem computers.

2. You're moving a legacy ASP application to ASP.NET. Some of the pages use ADO to load data. Other parts of the application work fine, but those pages will not load. What must you do to use the ADO objects in your ASP.NET application?

   A. Use a Page directive to set ASP compatibility mode.

   B. Build a Runtime Callable Wrapper for the ADO objects.

   C. Convert the ADO objects to ADO.NET.

   D. Use a Page directive to set the page language to VBScript.

APPLY YOUR KNOWLEDGE

3. You are responsible for migrating an existing ASP application to ASP.NET. The existing application consists of eight COM server components and a single client user interface component (written as a set of ASP pages) that instantiates and invokes objects from the server components. You'd like to give the user interface of the application an overhaul and migrate to ASP.NET with low risk and minimal downtime. How should you proceed?

   A. Use the Visual Basic Migration Wizard to bring all of the existing server components into Visual Basic .NET. Convert the user interface component from ASP to ASP.NET.

   B. Convert the user interface component from ASP to ASP.NET. Use COM interop to call the existing COM servers form the .NET user interface code. Migrate the servers one by one.

   C. Convert all the servers into Visual Basic .NET. Use COM interop to call the converted servers from the existing ASP pages.

   D. Use the Visual Basic Migration Wizard to bring all the ASP pages into ASP.NET. Use COM interop to call the existing COM servers from the .NET user interface code. Migrate the servers one by one.

4. Your company supplies a COM component to provide advanced data analysis for your clients. Some of your clients are moving to .NET, and require a Runtime Callable Wrapper for your component. How should you proceed?

   A. Use the Visual Basic Migration Wizard to bring the code into .NET, and recompile it.

   B. Use the Type Library Importer to create and sign a Primary Interop Assembly for your component.

   C. Set a reference to your component from any Visual Basic .NET project to create the Runtime Callable Wrapper for your component.

   D. Create a class that uses `PInvoke` to call functions from your component.

5. You wrote a COM component to supply random numbers in a specific distribution to a simple statistical client program. Now you're moving that client program to .NET. The COM component is used nowhere else, and you have not shipped copies to anyone else. You want to call the objects in the COM server from your new .NET client. How should you proceed?

   A. Set a direct reference from your .NET client to the COM server.

   B. Use the Type Library Importer to create an unsigned RCW for the COM component.

   C. Use the Type Library Importer to create a signed RCW for the COM component.

   D. Use `PInvoke` to instantiate classes from the COM component.

6. You have written several applications for your own use, all of which share classes from a COM component that you also wrote. You are moving the applications to .NET, but you intend to leave the COM component untouched. How should you proceed?

   A. Set a direct reference from each application to the existing COM component.

   B. Use the Type Library Importer to create an unsigned RCW for the COM component. Place a copy of this RCW in each application's directory.

APPLY YOUR KNOWLEDGE

C. Use PInvoke to call functions from the existing COM component in each application.

D. Use the Type Library Importer to create a signed RCW for the COM component. Place this RCW in the Global Assembly Cache.

7. Your application uses a communications library from a third-party developer. This library is implemented as a COM component. You are migrating your application to .NET. What should you do to continue to use the classes and methods within the communications library?

   A. Obtain a Primary Interop Assembly from the developer of the library. Install the PIA in the Global Assembly Cache.

   B. Use the Type Library Importer to create a signed Runtime Callable Wrapper for the library. Install the RCW in the Global Assembly Cache.

   C. Use the Type Library Importer to create an unsigned Runtime Callable Wrapper for the library. Install the RCW in the global assembly cache.

   D. Create wrapper code that uses `PInvoke` to call functions from the library. Import this wrapper code into your application.

8. Your Visual Basic ASP.NET application uses functions from a Visual Basic 6.0 COM library implemented as a DLL via a Runtime Callable Wrapper. You built the RCW by directly referencing the COM DLL. Users are complaining of poor performance. Which of these changes is most likely to improve the performance of your application?

   A. Recompile the Visual Basic 6.0 library as an EXE file.

   B. Switch your .NET application from Visual Basic .NET to C#.

   C. Use the Type Library Importer to create a new Runtime Callable Wrapper.

   D. Rewrite the Visual Basic 6.0 library as a native .NET library.

9. Your project contains the following API declaration:

```
Declare Auto Function _
 GetComputerName Lib "kernel32" ( _
 ByVal lpBuffer As String, _
 ByRef nSize As Integer) As Integer
```

   The project also contains code to use this API to display the computer name:

```
Private Sub ShowName()
    Dim buf As String = New String("")
    Dim len As Integer
    Dim ret As Integer
    ret = GetComputerName(buf, len)
    Label1.Text = buf.ToString
End Sub
```

   Users report that no computer name is displayed. What could be the problem?

   A. You used an immutable `String` rather than a `StringBuilder` to hold the computer name.

   B. The users' computers have no name set in their network properties.

   C. You neglected to initialize the `String` to hold any characters.

   D. You are not truncating the returned string at the returned length.

10. Your application uses the `GetComputerName` API function. This function exists in `kernel32.dll` in both ANSI and Unicode versions. Your declaration is as follows:

APPLY YOUR KNOWLEDGE

```
Declare Function GetComputerName _
 Lib "kernel32" ( _
 ByVal lpBuffer As String, _
 ByRef nSize As Integer) As Integer
```

Your code is failing with a `System.EntryPointNotFoundException` exception whenever you call this function. What should you do to fix this failure?

A. Supply the full path for kernel32.dll.

B. Add the `Auto` modifier to the declaration.

C. Declare the function as `GetComputerNameA` instead of `GetComputerName`.

D. Declare the function as `GetComputerNameW` instead of `GetComputerName`.

11. You want to use the `CommandButton` ActiveX control in your Visual Basic ASP.NET application. How can you make this control available for your Web forms? (Choose two)

A. Use the Type Library Importer.

B. Use HTML view to author the control's `classid` directly into your page's code.

C. Add the control directly to the Visual Basic .NET Toolbox.

D. Add a reference to the control's library.

12. You are using three classes from a COM component in your Visual Basic ASP.NET application. You'd like to give the Runtime Callable Wrapper for the COM component the same version number as the rest of your components when you ship your application. What should you do?

A. Use PInvoke to call functions from the COM component, thus eliminating the RCW.

B. Directly import the COM component into the References list. Right-click the reference and select Properties to set the version number.

C. Recompile the existing COM library with the desired version number before creating the RCW.

D. Use the Type Library Importer with the `/asmversion` option to explicitly set the version of the RCW.

13. You are planning to use two classes from a COM component in your ASP.NET application. You'd like to place these two classes into a namespace named `ComComponents`. What must you do?

A. Set a direct reference to the COM component. Create an empty class file in your .NET project. Specify the `ComComponents` namespace in that file and import the wrapper class.

B. Use the Type Library Importer with the `/namespace` option to set the namespace within the RCW.

C. Use the Type Library Importer with the `/out` option to create a file with the desired name.

D. Use PInvoke within a Namespace declaration to import the classes.

14. Your application will use functions from a COM+ component that uses COM+ for publish-and-subscribe events and object pooling. Which of these methods can you use to access the classes in the COM+ component ? (Select two)

A. Use `PInvoke` to declare the functions within the COM+ component.

B. Add the COM+ component directly to the Visual Basic .NET Toolbox.

APPLY YOUR KNOWLEDGE

C. Set a direct reference to the COM+ component.

D. Use the Type Library Importer to create a Runtime Callable Wrapper for the COM+ component.

15. You have an existing COM component that contains shared classes. These classes encapsulate functionality that you want to use in your ASP.NET application. How can you use these classes while maintaining the benefits of managed code such as type safety and automatic garbage collection?

    A. Use the Type Library Importer with the `/strictref` option to create a Runtime Callable Wrapper for the COM component.

    B. Call the methods from the COM component directly via Platform Invoke.

    C. Add a direct reference to the COM component.

    D. Rewrite the COM component as a .NET component.

Answers to Review Questions

1. Add the control directly to the Visual Studio .NET Toolbox. You can also simply use the OBJECT tag with the control's `classid` to create the control directly in the HTML code for a page.

2. The advantage of using an ActiveX control is that it may provide functionality that is not otherwise available to .NET applications. The disadvantages are that ActiveX controls impose a performance penalty, that they are unmanaged code, and that they make the distribution of your application more complex. They also tie you to Internet Explorer as a browser.

3. You might use COM components in a .NET project because you need to migrate an existing application in small pieces, or because the COM components contain unique functionality for which you do not have source code.

4. Runtime Callable Wrappers provide a proxy between .NET applications and COM components. The RCW translates .NET calls into COM calls, and returns the COM results as .NET results.

5. You can create a Runtime Callable Wrapper by using the Type Library Importer, or by adding a direct reference to the COM component.

6. When deciding how to create an RCW, you should consider whether you own the source code for the COM component, whether the RCW needs to go into the Global Assembly Cache, and how many .NET applications will make use of the COM component.

7. You don't need to take any extra steps. For purposes of calling from a .NET application COM components and COM+ components are identical.

8. COM interoperability allows you to instantiate COM classes within a .NET application and to invoke their members. `PInvoke` allows you to call functions from a DLL.

9. The Auto modifier tells the CLR to choose the correct version, ANSI or Unicode, of an API for the particular platform where you are running the code.

APPLY YOUR KNOWLEDGE

Answers to Exam Questions

1. **A.** ActiveX controls are a client-side technology, so they do not require an RCW. .NET does not require the Internet to run, nor does instantiating an ActiveX control depend on Service Pack 1. When you add an ActiveX control to your application, you must make sure that that ActiveX control is installed on the target computers. If it's not already there, you must provide a download location in a codebase tag.
2. **A**. The ADO library uses STA as its threading model. The .NET Framework only allows STA components on a page that's set to ASP compatibility mode.
3. **B**. Moving all the code will take longer than moving part of the code, and introduces additional risk. Because you'd like to rewrite the user interface you should move that component to .NET before the server components.
4. **B**. As the vendor of the component, it's your responsibility to supply the PIA.
5. **A**. For components that are used in a single project, and which you wrote, the simplest method of creating the RCW is best.
6. **D**. Shared libraries should be places in the Global Assembly Cache. Code must be signed before it can be placed in the GAC, and only the Type Library Importer can sign an RCW.
7. **A**. Because you did not write the code for the communications library, the proper way to proceed is to obtain a PIA from the original author.
8. **D**. Changing from a DLL to an EXE or from VB .NET to C# will have no significant effect on performance. RCWs are the same no matter how they're created. But rewriting the library into .NET will probably speed it up because it eliminates the extra calls in the proxy layer.
9. **C**. Although strings are generally immutable, the .NET Framework lets them change in `PInvoke` calls. All computers must have a name set. Not truncating the string might display bad data, but it would display some data. The code as it exists supplies a zero-character buffer to the API call.
10. **B**. The Auto modifier is necessary to tell the CLR to use the ANSI or Unicode versions of the function as appropriate to the operating system.
11. **B, C**. These are the two methods for using an ActiveX control within an ASP.NET project. The ToolBox is just a convenience; authoring the proper code directly has the same effect.
12. **D**. Only the Type Library Importer can explicitly set the version number for an RCW.
13. **B**. Only the Type Library Importer can set the namespace for an RCW.
14. **C, D**. You can use COM+ components through the same techniques that you use with COM components.
15. **D**. Only managed code benefits from the features of the CLR. The only way to turn the component into managed code is to rewrite it in .NET.

APPLY YOUR KNOWLEDGE

Suggested Readings and Resources

1. Visual Studio .NET Combined Help Collection
   - Interoperating with Unmanaged Code topic
   - Migrating ASP Pages to ASP.NET
2. Nathan, Adam, *.NET AND COM: The Complete Interoperability Guide.* Sams Publishing, 2002.
3. Jones, A. Russell, Mastering ASP.NET with Visual Basic. NET. Sybex, 2002.

OBJECTIVES

This chapter covers the following Microsoft-specified objectives for the Creating User Services section of the Visual Basic .NET Web-Based Applications exam:

Implement online user assistance.

Implement accessibility features.

- Perhaps at one time an application was finished when the code functioned properly, but that is certainly no longer the case. Users and managers alike expect more than properly functioning code in a useful and usable application. From the process of defining requirements right through the necessity to supply post-installation support, applications exist as part of a wide range of features and activities. In this chapter, I'll look at two necessary parts of shipping any complex application:
  - User assistance   The process of providing help within an application through a variety of means.
  - Accessibility   The coding that you must do to make your application usable by those with disabilities.

- Developers sometimes think of user assistance and accessibility features as being the "icing on the cake" that can be left out if they're in a hurry. That's a fundamental misunderstanding of the importance of these features. User assistance and accessibility should be designed into your applications right from the start and implemented as a matter of course with each new feature that you add.

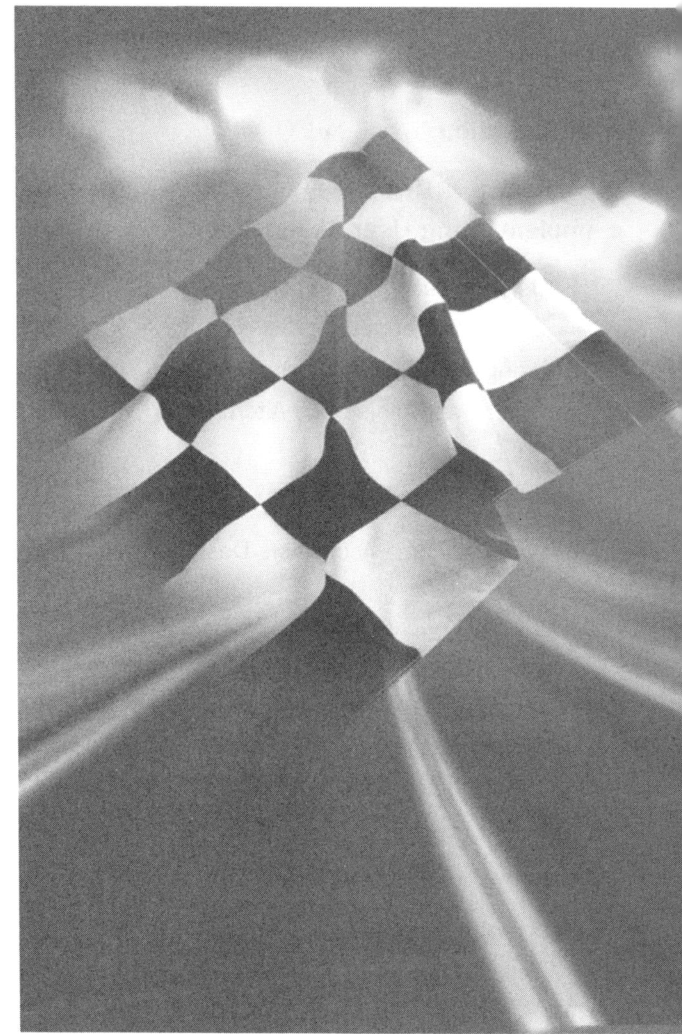

CHAPTER 11

User Assistance and Accessibility

OUTLINE

STUDY STRATEGIES

- Refer to the topic "Walkthrough: Creating an Accessible Web Application" in the Visual Studio .NET Combined Help Collection for another example of setting accessibility properties.
- Follow the accessibility guidelines in this chapter to make one of your own Web applications accessible.
- Use the testing strategies described in this chapter to evaluate some existing Web applications for accessibility.

INTRODUCTION

Building the best program in the world is useless if no one but the original developer can use it. As applications grow ever more complex, it's incumbent upon their developers to provide help for end users of the applications. Such help comes in two forms: user assistance and accessibility.

User assistance refers to the type of help that you get from the traditional help file: a set of short topics designed to teach you what you need to know to effectively use the capabilities of an application. Although there is no standard for user assistance with Web applications, you can make assistance available in a number of ways. For example, you can display help topics in a separate browser window or within a pane in the main browser window.

Accessibility refers to making sure that users with disabilities can work with your application. In the United States alone there are over thirty million people with some disability that can affect their ability to use software, according to government figures. Windows and the .NET Framework include a variety of tools and techniques to help you make your application accessible to these users.

In this chapter, you'll learn how to integrate help files with your Web applications. You'll also learn how to design an application for accessibility, as well as methods for implementing and testing accessibility.

IMPLEMENTING USER ASSISTANCE

"User assistance" refers to the techniques used to deliver helpful information to the users of an application. For Windows applications, there are well-defined standard ways to do this. For example, help files are written using HTML Help, a Microsoft standard for combining a set of HTML pages into a single file that can be browsed in a help viewer.

With Web applications, things are considerably less standardized. Even though HTML Help starts with HTML topics, it's not suitable for Web applications. The entire HTML Help file must be present on the client computer, which must also have a help viewer installed, for HTML Help to function properly. This poses a problem if you can't guarantee that all of your application's clients will be using the Windows platform, or if the entire help file is prohibitively large to download.

For Web applications, you'll need to get creative to deliver user assistance. In the first part of this chapter, I'll show you several alternatives for delivering user assistance with Web applications, including

- Help in a separate browser window
- Help in a browser pane
- Embedding Help

But before I can show you any user assistance techniques, I need to build an application that can be used to demonstrate these techniques. That's the purpose of Step By Step 11.1.

STEP BY STEP

11.1 Creating a Simple Web Application

1. Create a new Visual Basic .NET Web Application.
2. Rename the default form in the application to `StepByStep11-1.aspx`. Set the `pageLayout` property of the form to `FlowLayout`.
3. Arrange two `Label` controls (`lblHeadline` and `lblInstructions`), an `Image` control with the ID of `imgDecor`, a `TextBox` control with the ID of `txtRandomNumber`, a `Button` control with the ID of `btnGetRandom`, and a `Hyperlink` control with the ID of `hlOptions` on the Web Form. Figure 11.1 shows a design for this form.

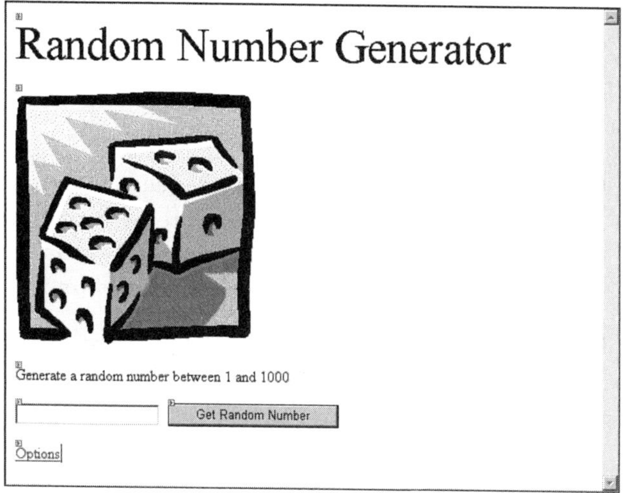

FIGURE 11.1
A sample Web application.

4. Set the `NavigateUrl` property of the `hlOptions` control to `Options.aspx`.

5. Double-click the form to open the form's module. Add this code to handle the form's `Load` event:

```
Private Sub Page_Load(ByVal sender As System.Object, _
 ByVal e As System.EventArgs) Handles MyBase.Load
    ' First time in, initialize the session variables
    If CStr(Session("Maximum")) = "" Then
        Session("Maximum") = 1000
    End If
    If CStr(Session("Minimum")) = "" Then
        Session("Minimum") = 1
    End If
    lblInstructions.Text = _
     "Generate a random number between " & _
     Session("Minimum") & " and " & Session("Maximum")
End Sub
```

6. Add code to handle the `Button` control's `Click` event:

```
Private Sub btnGetRandom_Click( _
 ByVal sender As System.Object, _
 ByVal e As System.EventArgs) _
 Handles btnGetRandom.Click
    Dim r As Random = New Random()
    txtRandomNumber.Text = r.Next( _
     Session("Minimum"), Session("Maximum"))
End Sub
```

continues

continued

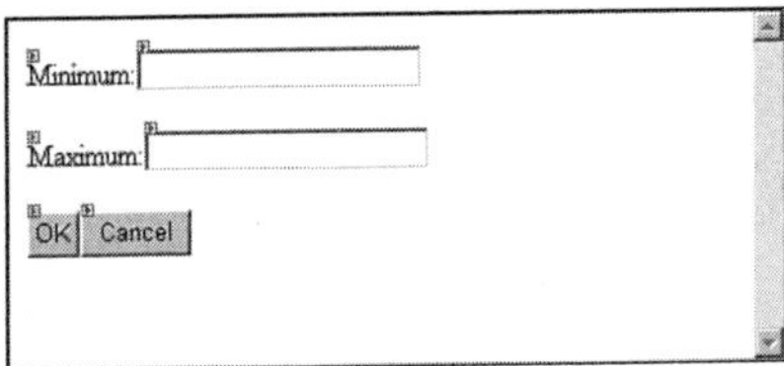

FIGURE 11.2
A design for the Options form.

7. Add a second Web Form to the application. Name the new form `Options.aspx`. Set the `pageLayout` property of the form to `FlowLayout`.

8. Place two Label controls (`lblMinimum` and `lblMaximum`), two `TextBox` controls (`txtMinimum` and `txtMaximum`), and two `Button` controls (`btnOK` and `btnCancel`) on the form. Figure 11.2 shows a design for the options form.

9. Double-click the form to open the form's module. Enter this code to handle events on this form:

```
Private Sub Page_Load(ByVal sender As System.Object, _
 ByVal e As System.EventArgs) Handles MyBase.Load
    ' Initialize the textboxes
    If Not IsPostBack Then
        txtMinimum.Text = Session("Minimum")
        txtMaximum.Text = Session("Maximum")
    End If
End Sub

Private Sub btnCancel_Click( _
 ByVal sender As System.Object, _
 ByVal e As System.EventArgs) Handles btnCancel.Click
    ' No changes, just redirect back to main page
    Response.Redirect("StepByStep11-1.aspx")
End Sub

Private Sub btnOK_Click( _
 ByVal sender As System.Object, _
 ByVal e As System.EventArgs) Handles btnOK.Click
    ' Save changes and redirect
    Session("Minimum") = txtMinimum.Text
    Session("Maximum") = txtMaximum.Text
    Response.Redirect("StepByStep11-1.aspx")
End Sub
```

10. Set the `StepByStep11-1.aspx` form as the start page for the project.

11. Run the project. Click the button to retrieve a random number. Click the hyperlink to go to the options form. Change the minimum and maximum, then verify that random numbers within the new range are being generated.

Using a Second Browser Window

Now that I've built a simple Web application, the next step is to deliver user assistance. The simplest way to do this is to just show the user instructions on Web pages. After all, if he's running a Web application, he certainly has a Web browser available.

STEP BY STEP

11.2 Using a Second Browser Window for User Assistance

1. Add a new Web Form to your application. Name it `MainHelp.aspx`.

2. Switch to HTML view and modify `MainHelp.aspx` as follows:

```
<%@ Page Language="vb" AutoEventWireup="false"
Codebehind="MainHelp.aspx.vb"
 Inherits="_305c11.MainHelp"%>
<!DOCTYPE HTML PUBLIC
"-//W3C//DTD HTML 4.0 Transitional//EN">
<HTML>
    <HEAD>
        <title>Main Help</title>
        <meta name="GENERATOR"
content="Microsoft Visual Studio.NET 7.0">
        <meta name="CODE_LANGUAGE"
content="Visual Basic 7.0">
        <meta name="vs_defaultClientScript"
content="JavaScript">
        <meta name="vs_targetSchema"
         content=
"http://schemas.microsoft.com/intellisense/ie5">
    </HEAD>
    <body>
    <h1>Welcome to the Random Server</h1>
    <p>The Random Server application
    is designed to serve all of
    your integer random number needs.
    Just run the program and click
    to get as many random numbers as
    you would like. The numbers can be
    in any range you like. Randomness
    guaranteed or your money back
    (this application is 100% free)!</p>
    <a href="OptionsHelp.aspx">Help on Options</a>
    </body>
</HTML>
```

continues

continued

3. Add another new Web Form to your application. Name it `OptionsHelp.aspx`.

4. Switch to HTML view and modify `OptionsHelp.aspx` as follows:

```
<%@ Page Language="vb" AutoEventWireup="false"
Codebehind="OptionsHelp.aspx.vb"
 Inherits="_305c11.OptionsHelp"%>
<!DOCTYPE HTML PUBLIC
"-//W3C//DTD HTML 4.0 Transitional//EN">
<html>
    <head>
        <title>Options Help</title>
        <meta name="GENERATOR"
content="Microsoft Visual Studio.NET 7.0">
        <meta name="CODE_LANGUAGE"
content="Visual Basic 7.0">
        <meta name="vs_defaultClientScript"
content="JavaScript">
        <meta name="vs_targetSchema"
         content=
"http://schemas.microsoft.com/intellisense/ie5">
    </head>
    <body>
    <p>This is the options form of the
    Random Number server. Enter the
    minimum and maximum values you
    would like to set for random numbers
    and click OK. You can also click
    Cancel to keep the settings
    unchanged.</p>
    </body>
</html>
```

5. Add a `HyperLink` control to the bottom of the `StepByStep11-1.aspx` page. Set the ID of this control to `hlHelp`, set its `Text` property to `Help`, set its `NavigateUrl` property to `MainHelp.aspx`, and set its `Target` property to `_blank`.

6. Add a `HyperLink` control to the bottom of the `Options.aspx` page. Set the ID of this control to `hlHelp`, set its `Text` property to `Help`, set its `NavigateUrl` property to `OptionsHelp.aspx`, and set its `Target` property to `_blank`.

7. Run the project. When you click the Help hyperlink on either form in the project, it will open the corresponding link in another browser window.

This method of displaying user assistance uses the `target="_blank"` attribute to open help pages in a second browser window. Although this method should work with nearly any browser, it has some problems. Users may become confused with multiple browser windows open, and it can be annoying to have the help window overlap the window where you are trying to do work.

Using the Search Pane

One way to address the problems of using a separate browser window for user assistance is to use the Internet Explorer search pane instead. Step By Step 11.3 shows you how to do this.

STEP BY STEP

11.3 Using the Search Pane for User Assistance

1. Open the `StepByStep11-1.aspx` Web Form in your application. Modify the `hlHelp` `HyperLink` control by changing its `Target` property to `_search`.
2. Open the `Options.aspx` Web Form in your application. Modify the `hlHelp` `HyperLink` control by changing its `Target` property to `_search`.
3. Run the project. When you click the Help hyperlink on either form in the project, it opens the corresponding link in the browser's search pane, as shown in Figure 11.3.

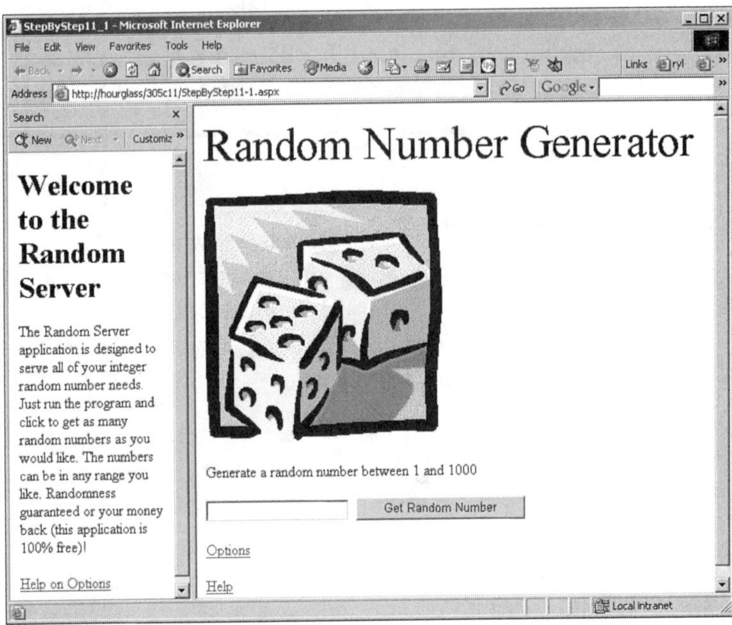

FIGURE 11.3
User assistance in the search pane.

Although using the search pane does address the problem of keeping the help with the application, it raises other issues. If your users are sophisticated enough to actually use the search pane (for search, history, or favorites, for example), they may not be pleased at having it hijacked by your application's help pages. Worse, though, is the fact that the `_search` target is specific to Internet Explorer. This technique won't work properly in other browsers such as Netscape, Mozilla, or Opera; instead, your help content will replace the page that the user was looking at. This makes using the Search pane a reasonable technique only if you have a captive audience that you know is using Internet Explorer for Web browsing.

Embedding Help

To avoid the problems with extra browser windows or with the search pane, you may choose to embed the user assistance directly in your Web pages. Step by Step 11.4 suggests a way to do this.

STEP BY STEP

11.4 Embedding User Assistance in an Application

1. In Solution Explorer, right-click `StepByStep11-1.aspx` and select Copy. Then right-click your project and select Paste. Rename the pasted Web Form to `StepByStep11-4.aspx`. Open the `aspx` and `vb` files for the new Web Form and change all references to `StepByStep11-1` to refer to `StepByStep11-4` instead. Change all references to StepByStep11_1 to StepByStep11_4 instead (Visual Studio .NET substitutes an underscore for the dash in the class name).

2. On the new Web Form, delete the `hlHelp Hyperlink` control. Replace it with a `LinkButton` control with the ID of `lbtnHelp`. Set the `Text` property of the `LinkButton` control to `Help`.

3. Add a `Label` control to the page after the `LinkButton` control. Set the `Label` control's ID property to `lblHelp` and set its `Visible` property to `False`. Set the `Text` property of the `Label` control to

```
Welcome to the Random Server. The Random Server
Application is designed to serve all of your
integer random number needs. Just run the program
and click to get as many random numbers as you
would like. The numbers can be in any range you
like. Randomness guaranteed or your money back
(this application is 100% free)!
```

4. Switch to the code view of the Web Form. Enter this code to handle the `Click` event of the `lbtnHelp` control:

```
Private Sub lbtnHelp_Click(ByVal sender As
System.Object, _
 ByVal e As System.EventArgs) Handles lbtnHelp.Click
    lblHelp.Visible = True
End Sub
```

5. Set `StepByStep11-4.aspx` as the start page for the project.

6. Run the project. When you click the `Help` hyperlink on the main page, it will display the help directly on the page, as shown in Figure 11.4.

FIGURE 11.4
Embedded user assistance.

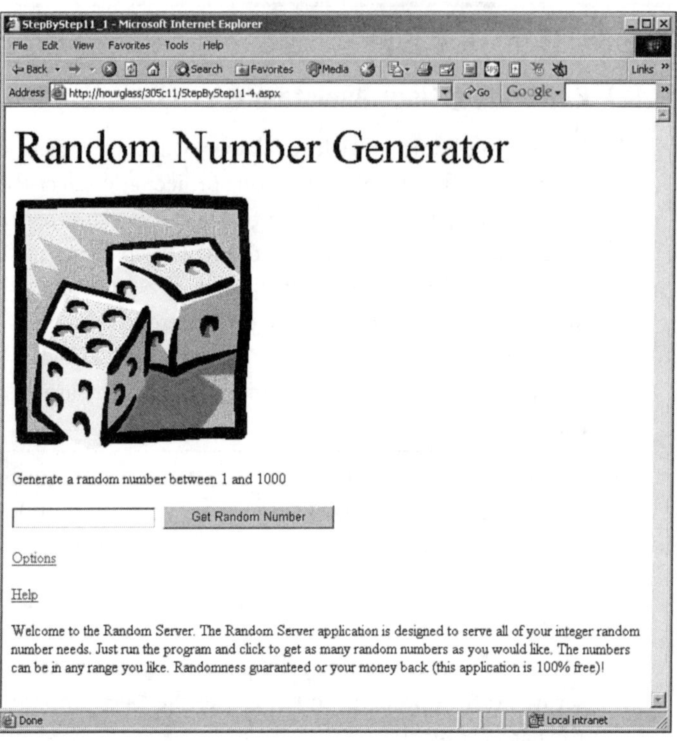

> **NOTE**
>
> **Embedded Help with DHTML** If you want, you can ship the user assistance embedded on the page and use DHTML behaviors to hide and show the information that's already in the user's browser. However this technique is not widely compatible with all browsers, and it increases the size of your Web pages by sending the help to the browser whether or not it's needed.

Embedding user assistance directly in the Web page is a good solution in many ways. It's compatible with all browsers (because the .NET Framework is delivering pure HTML when you show the `Label` control), and doesn't require opening a new browser window. Unfortunately, it does require a round-trip to the server to redraw the page when the user clicks the link.

Other User Assistance Alternatives

Although Microsoft does not offer a standard browser-based help solution, a number of companies have stepped into the gap. These companies can sell you software to create help files in pure HTML that still have nice features such as tables of contents and search panes. Choices in this area include

- eHelp's WebHelp (`http://www.ehelp.com/products/robohelp/formats.asp?WebHelp`)

- Deva Tools for DreamWeaver (`http://www.devahelp.com/devatools.htm`)
- WebWorks Help 3.0 (`http://www.webworks.com/products/wwp_pro/features4.asp`)

Although I'm focusing on the mechanics of providing user assistance in code, you should consider this just one facet of an overall user assistance strategy. Depending on your organization and the applications involved, user assistance may include any or all of the following:

- A Readme file or other introductory material for the user to refer to even before installing the application.
- Printed, online, or electronic documentation.
- Email, telephone, or on-site support from a product specialist.
- Wizards, builders, and other user interface components designed to guide the user through a process.

IMPLEMENTING ACCESSIBILITY FEATURES

Implement accessibility features.

According to Microsoft, there are over thirty million people in the United States alone with disabilities that can be affected by the design of computer hardware and software. Although software developers have long ignored this issue, modern software design takes accessibility strongly into account. From both ethical and economic standpoints, as well as to comply with the law, designing software for accessibility simply makes sense. In fact, Microsoft has made accessibility a key feature of the Windows logo certification program, which allows applications to display the "designed for Windows" logo.

There are five basic principles to accessible design:

- *Flexibility* The user interface should be flexible and customizable, so that users can adjust it to their own individual needs and preferences.

- *Choice of Input Methods* Different users have different abilities and preferences when it comes to choosing mouse or keyboard to perform tasks. All operations in your application should be accessible to the keyboard, and basic operations should be available via the mouse as well. In the future, voice and other types of input may also be considered here.
- *Choice of Output Methods* You should not depend on a single method of output (such as sound, color, or text) for important information.
- *Consistency* Your application should be consistent with the Windows operating system and other applications to minimize difficulties in learning and using new interfaces.
- *Compatibility with Accessibility Aids* Windows includes a number of accessibility aids such as the Magnifier (which can blow up text or graphics to a larger size) and the On-Screen Keyboard (which enables keyboard input via the mouse). Users may also be using specialized browsers that render pages as pure text, read the text aloud, or assist in other ways. Your application should not circumvent these accessibility aids.

As an example of implementing these principles, the Windows logo certification requirements includes these items:

- Support the standard system size, color, font, and input settings.
- Ensure compatibility with the High Contrast display setting. With this setting, the application can only use colors from the Control Panel or colors explicitly chosen by the user.
- Provide documented keyboard access to all features.
- It must always be obvious to both the user and programmatically where the keyboard focus is located. This is necessary for the Magnifier and Narrator accessibility aids to function properly.
- Do not convey information by sound alone.

In this section, you'll learn more about accessible design guidelines, and see how to implement those guidelines for a Visual Basic .NET Web application. I'll also look at some of the other accessibility standards that apply to Web applications, such as the W3C standards and the Section 508 standards.

EXAM TIP

Accessibility on the Web You can find much information on accessibility on the Microsoft Accessibility Web site. A good starting point for developers is `http://www.microsoft.com/enable/dev/`.

Understanding Accessible Design Guidelines

Table 11.1 lays out some of the important accessibility guidelines that you should consider for any application.

TABLE 11.1

ACCESSIBILITY GUIDELINES FOR WEB APPLICATION DESIGN

Area	*Guidelines*
ALT text	Every graphic should have ALT text. ALT text should convey the important information about an image. For large and complex images, you might want to include a link to a page that explains the image in text.
Imagemaps	Do not depend on imagemaps for navigation; also include a set of text links for those who cannot use the images.
Link Text	Link text should be useful in isolation, because some accessible browsers present a list of links with no context for fast navigation. If this isn't possible, use the TITLE attribute of the link to provide a more descriptive string.
Keyboard Navigation	The tab key will move between all links and imagemap areas in the order that they're defined in the HTML. Use the TABINDEX attribute where appropriate to override this.
Access Keys	All controls and links that act as controls should have an ACCESSKEY attribute. Underline the access key in the control's label.
Control Identification	Use the TITLE attribute or LABEL tags to associate a name with every control.
Frames and Tables	Provide alternative pages that do not use frames or tables.
Support Formatting Options	Do not assume that text will be in a specific font, color, or size. Do not assume that things will line up because the width may change. Use heading tags such as <TH> rather than specially formatted text.
Style Sheets	Make sure the page works even if the style sheet is turned off. Otherwise, offer an alternative page that is designed to work without a style sheet.
Audio and Video	Provide captions or transcripts for audio and video content.

The W3C Guidelines

The World Wide Web Consortium (better known as the W3C) is the body that governs standards for the Internet. The W3C has invested considerable effort in defining accessibility guidelines. You can find the home page of the W3C Web Accessibility Initiative at `http://www.w3.org/WAI/`. From that page, you can navigate through the W3C WAI's extensive list of resources, which should be required reading if you're concerned about Web site accessibility.

The W3C WAI has an extensive set of guidelines for accessibility available from its Web site. Here's a summary of their priority 1 guidelines, which they say that Web content developers *must* satisfy:

- Provide a text equivalent for every non-text element (for example, using `ALT`, `LONGDESC`, or in-element content). Non-text elements include images, graphical representations of text (including symbols), imagemap regions, animations (for example, animated GIFs), applets and programmatic objects, ASCII art, frames, scripts, images used as list bullets, spacers, graphical buttons, sounds (played with or without user interaction), stand-alone audio files, audio tracks of video, and video.
- Don't use color as the sole means to convey information. Always provide an alternative in content or markup.
- Clearly identify any changes in the document's natural language.
- Make sure documents are still readable in the absence of any style sheet.
- Ensure that equivalents for dynamic content are updated when the dynamic content changes.
- Avoid causing the screen to flicker.
- Use the clearest and simplest language appropriate to the site's content.
- Provide redundant text links for each active region of a server-side imagemap.
- Provide client-side imagemaps instead of server-side imagemaps except where the regions cannot be defined with an available geometric shape.

- Identify row and column headers in tables.
- Use markup to associate data cells and header cells.
- Use `TITLE` tags for all frames.
- Ensure that pages are usable when scripts, applets, or other programmatic objects are turned off or not supported. If this is not possible, provide equivalent information on an alternative accessible page.
- Provide an auditory description of any important video information.
- Synchronize captions with movies or animations.
- If, after best efforts, you cannot create an accessible page, provide a link to an alternative page that uses W3C technologies, is accessible, has equivalent information (or functionality), and is updated as often as the inaccessible (original) page.

The Section 508 Guidelines

Section 508 of the Rehabilitative Act sets standards for all U.S. agencies that maintain Web sites. This gives accessibility the force of law for federal Web sites (and serves to emphasize that it's a good idea for all Web sites).

There's an excellent discussion of the Section 508 standards at `http://www.access-board.gov/sec508/guide/1194.22.htm`. Here's a summary of the guidelines that Web sites must comply with. You'll see that there is considerable overlap with the Microsoft and W3C guidelines.

- A text equivalent for every non-text element shall be provided (for example, using `alt`, `longdesc`, or in-element content).
- Equivalent alternatives for any multimedia presentation shall be synchronized with the presentation.
- Web pages shall be designed so that all information conveyed with color is also available without color, for example from context or markup.
- Documents shall be organized so they are readable without requiring an associated style sheet.

- Redundant text links shall be provided for each active region of a server-side imagemap.
- Client-side imagemaps shall be provided instead of server-side imagemaps except where the regions cannot be defined with an available geometric shape.
- Row and column headers shall be identified for data tables.
- Markup shall be used to associate data cells and header cells for data tables that have two or more logical levels of row or column headers.
- Frames shall be titled with text that facilitates frame identification and navigation.
- Pages shall be designed to avoid causing the screen to flicker with a frequency greater than 2Hz and lower than 55Hz.
- A text-only page, with equivalent information or functionality, shall be provided to make a Web site comply with the provisions of these standards, when compliance cannot be accomplished in any other way. The content of the text-only page shall be updated whenever the primary page changes.
- When pages utilize scripting languages to display content, or to create interface elements, the information provided by the script shall be identified with functional text that can be read by assistive technology.
- When a Web page requires that an applet, plug-in, or other application be present on the client system to interpret page content, the page must provide a link to a plug-in or applet that complies with [the standards of the Act].
- When electronic forms are designed to be completed online, the form shall allow people using assistive technology to access the information, field elements, and functionality required for completion and submission of the form, including all directions and cues.
- A method shall be provided that permits users to skip repetitive navigation links.
- When a timed response is required, the user shall be alerted and given sufficient time to indicate more time is required.

EXAM TIP

Bobby Bobby is an automated tool that can check Web pages for compliance with the W3C WAI or the Section 508 guidelines. There's an online version that you can use to check a single page, and a downloadable version that will run in batch mode. The Bobby World Wide Web site is at `http://bobby.cast.org/html/en/index.jsp`.

Making a Web Application Accessible

If at all possible, you should plan to make your Web applications accessible right from the start. Sometimes, though, you won't have any choice except to add accessibility features after the fact. In this Step by Step, you'll modify the random number application for accessibility.

STEP BY STEP

11.5 Setting Control Properties for Accessibility

1. Open the `StepByStep11-1.aspx` Web Form in Visual Studio .NET.
2. Set the `TabIndex` property of `lblHeadline` to 0.
3. Set the `TabIndex` property of `imgDecor` to 1, and set its `AlternateText` property to `[Dice Image]`.
4. Set the `TabIndex` property of `lblInstructions` to 2.
5. Insert a Label control before the `txtRandomNumber TextBox` control. Set its `Text` property to `<u>R</u>andom Number` and set its `TabIndex` property to `3`.
6. Set the `TabIndex` property of `txtRandomNumber` to `4`, and set its `AccessKey` property to `R`.
7. Set the `TabIndex` property of `btnGetRandom` to `5`, and set its `AccessKey` property to `G`.
8. Set the `TabIndex` property of `hlOptions` to `6`, and set its `AccessKey` property to `O`.
9. Set the `TabIndex` property of `hlHelp` to `7`, and set its `AccessKey` property to H.
10. Set the Web Form as the start page for the project.
11. Run the project. Verify that the tab order and access keys work as designed.

> **NOTE**
>
> **AccessKey on a Button Control** In Windows applications, the access key for a control is normally indicated with an underlined character. The Button Web server control does not support underlined text. If you want to show underlined text on a button, you can use an HTML Button control, in which case you can use the `Accesskey` property to specify the character to be underlined. In that case, though, you'll need to move any processing from the button's click event to the `Postback` portion of the page's `Load` event.

Testing Application Accessibility

Before shipping an application, you should test the accessibility features. Here are some tests that you should perform:

- Navigate your user interface using only the keyboard. Make sure that all functionality is accessible by using the keyboard alone. Test all access keys. Press Enter to follow a selected link.
- View the page with graphics turned off to make sure the ALT tags are a good substitute. In Internet Explorer, you can turn off graphics from Tools, Internet Options, Advanced.
- Use the application with sound turned off to make sure that no important information is lost.
- Turn on the High Contrast option under Control Panel, Display and make sure the page is still readable.
- Alter the page's font size (you can do this with View, Text Size in Internet Explorer) and make sure the page is still readable.
- Resize the browser window and check for readability.

CHAPTER SUMMARY

KEY TERMS

- User assistance
- Accessibility

User assistance and accessibility are important parts of building an application. Just having code that performs properly isn't enough. You must also help the user understand how to use your application effectively and accommodate users who may have disabilities that affect their use of software and hardware.

Web applications offer you several ways to display user assistance text, though there is no universal standard for such text. You can choose to display user assistance in a second browser window, in the search pane within Internet Explorer, or dynamically on a Web page that also contains other controls.

Accessibility guidelines dictate the design of your application in certain areas. You must be prepared to handle either keyboard or mouse input, accessibility aids, different color schemes, and users who may not be able to process information provided in various ways. Visual Studio .NET offers excellent support for accessibility programming, and there are a number of excellent resources to help you design more accessible Web sites.

APPLY YOUR KNOWLEDGE

Exercises

11.1 Using ToolTips for User Assistance

ASP.NET offers a variety of properties for server controls. One of these, the ToolTip property, can be used to display brief help strings to the user when he hovers his mouse pointer over a control.

Estimated Time: 10 minutes.

1. Open a Visual Basic .NET Windows Application in the Visual Studio .NET IDE. Add a new form to the application.
2. Add a `TextBox` control, an `Image` control, and a `Button` control to the form. Arrange them however you like. Add text to the ToolTip property for each of these controls.
3. Set the Web Form as the start page for the project.
4. Run the project. Hover your mouse over one of the controls. After a few moments, the text from the ToolTip property for that control will appear in a small window, as shown in Figure 11.5.

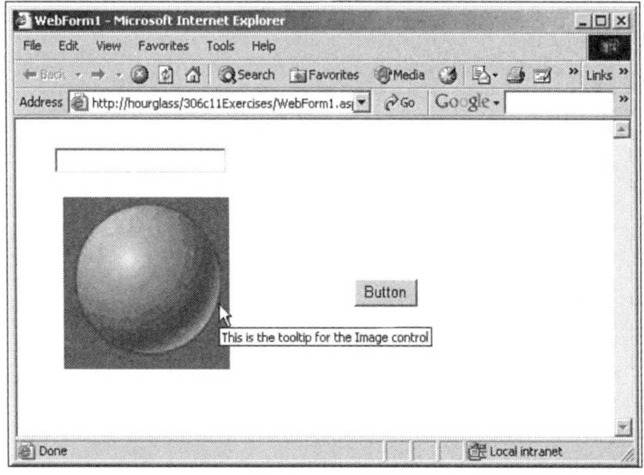

FIGURE 11.5
ToolTip on a Web Form.

ASP.NET renders ToolTips by using the `TITLE` attribute of HTML control tags. This solution is portable among all reasonably current browsers, although some older browsers (such as Netscape Communicator 4.79) will not display this information. In addition, some controls (notably the DropDownList control) do not support ToolTips.

11.2 Row and Column Headers for Tables

One of the accessibility guidelines states that you should supply row and column headers for data tables. This facilitates specialized browsers that are designed to help users understand the structure of tabular information. In this exercise, you'll learn how to properly format a data table for accessibility.

Estimated Time: 10 minutes.

1. Add a new Web Form to your Visual Basic ASP.NET application.
2. Set the form's `pageLayout` property to `FlowLayout`.
3. Select Table, Insert, Table. Select a table of three rows and three columns and click OK.
4. Fill in data as shown in Figure 11.6.

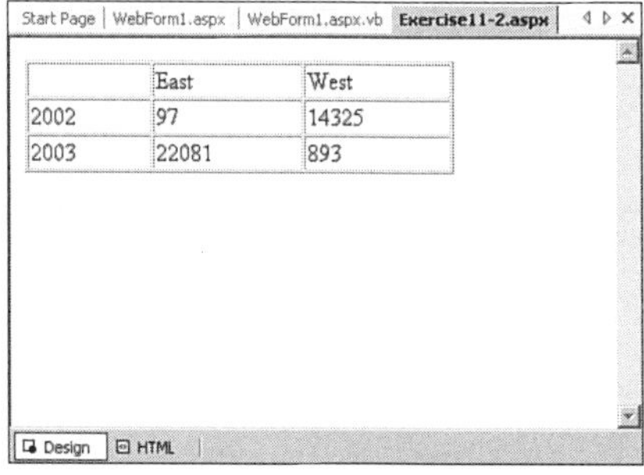

	East	West
2002	97	14325
2003	22081	893

FIGURE 11.6
A table on a Web Form.

APPLY YOUR KNOWLEDGE

5. Set the Web Form as the Start Page for the project. Run the project. Select View, Source in your Web browser. You'll find that the table portion of the page is formatted with this HTML markup:

```
<TABLE id="Table1" cellSpacing="1"
cellPadding="1" width="300" border="1">
    <TR>
        <TD></TD>
        <TD>East</TD>
        <TD>West</TD>
    </TR>
    <TR>
        <TD>2002</TD>
        <TD>97</TD>
        <TD>14325</TD>
    </TR>
    <TR>
        <TD>2003</TD>
        <TD>22081</TD>
        <TD>893</TD>
    </TR>
</TABLE>
```

6. Stop the project. Switch to HTML view of the Web Form and alter the HTML as follows:

```
<TABLE id="Table1" cellSpacing="1"
cellPadding="1" width="300" border="1">
    <TR>
        <TH></TH>
        <TH scope="col">East</TH>
        <TH scope="col">West</TH>
    </TR>
    <TR>
        <TD scope="row">2002</TD>
        <TD>97</TD>
        <TD>14325</TD>
    </TR>
    <TR>
        <TD scope="row">2003</TD>
        <TD>22081</TD>
        <TD>893</TD>
    </TR>
</TABLE>
```

7. Run the project again. You'll see that the information still appears on the Web page much as it did before.

The changes that you made to the Web page help to make the page more accessible. First, by using the `<TH>` rather than the `<TD>` tag for the header row of the table, you explicitly indicate to the browser that this is a header row; a user can use a local style sheet to format such rows prominently if they so desire. Second, by using the `scope` attribute you associate the row and column headers explicitly with the data in the rows and columns. This makes it much easier for screen reader software to tell a visually impaired user which row and column are associated with a particular data value.

Review Questions

1. What methods can you use to provide user assistance within a .NET Web application?
2. Name the five basic principles of accessible design.
3. Name some of the Windows Logo certification program accessibility requirements.
4. What are some of the major standards governing accessible Web page design?

Exam Questions

1. You are deploying a Web application on your company's intranet. Your company has selected Internet Explorer 5.5 as its standard Web browser. Users would like to have online help available for your application with minimal overhead and without needing to manage additional windows. How should you implement user assistance for this application?

   A. Display help in a second browser window.

   B. Display help by using control properties to hide and show Label controls.

APPLY YOUR KNOWLEDGE

C. Display help in the Internet Explorer search pane.

D. Display help using DHTML to hide and show controls.

2. Users with certain browsers report that they are having difficulty using your Web application because they are browsing without graphics. What should you do to make your application more accessible in this situation?

    A. Ensure that the graphics are saved in GIF format so that they will be quick to download.

    B. Add ALT text to all graphics to indicate their purpose.

    C. Use the AccessKey property to associate access keys with all graphics.

    D. Provide an alternative version of the page with no graphics.

3. Your Web application includes this table of information:

```
<TABLE id="Table1">
    <TR>
        <TD></TD>
        <TD>Oxygen</TD>
        <TD>Nitrogen</TD>
    </TR>
    <TR>
        <TD>Amount</TD>
        <TD>21</TD>
        <TD>79</TD>
    </TR>
</TABLE>
```

How should you alter the markup of this table to make it more accessible?

A.

```
<TABLE id="Table1">
    <TR>
        <TD></TD>
        <TD><B>Oxygen</B></TD>
        <TD><B>Nitrogen</B></TD>
    </TR>
    <TR>
        <TD>Amount</TD>
        <TD>21</TD>
        <TD>79</TD>
    </TR>
</TABLE>
```

B.

```
<TABLE id="Table1">
    <TR>
        <TD></TD>
        <TD scope="col">Oxygen</TD>
        <TD scope="col">Nitrogen</TD>
    </TR>
    <TR>
        <TD scope="row">Amount</TD>
        <TD>21</TD>
        <TD>79</TD>
    </TR>
</TABLE>
```

C.

```
<TABLE id="Table1">
    <TR>
        <TH></TH>
        <TH scope="col">Oxygen</TH>
        <TH scope="col">Nitrogen</TH>
    </TR>
    <TR>
        <TD scope="row">Amount</TD>
        <TD>21</TD>
        <TD>79</TD>
    </TR>
</TABLE>
```

D.

```
<TABLE id="Table1" ALT="Table of Elements">
    <TR>
        <TD></TD>
        <TD">Oxygen</TD>
        <TD>Nitrogen</TD>
    </TR>
    <TR>
        <TD>Amount</TD>
        <TD>21</TD>
        <TD>79</TD>
    </TR>
</TABLE>
```

APPLY YOUR KNOWLEDGE

4. Which of these Web pages violate common accessibility guidelines? (Choose two)

   A. A page that supplies a link to a transcript in addition to an audio file.

   B. A page that beeps and waits for a correction when the user enters an invalid date on a form.

   C. A page that uses the <H1> and <H2> tags for two levels of outlining.

   D. A page that shows a red bullet for bad values and a green bullet for good values in a complex table.

5. You are designing a Web application that will be used by your company's business partners worldwide. The users will be using a variety of browsers on a variety of operating systems. Some will be connected to your server with very slow links. How should you provide user assistance for this application?

   A. HTML Help

   B. In the search pane

   C. In a separate browser window

   D. Using dynamic controls

6. Your Web application contains a Button server control that has its Text property set to Submit. You'd like to show the S underlined as an accelerator key. What should you do?

   A. Replace the Button server control with a Button HTML control.

   B. Set the control's AccessKey property to S.

   C. Set the control's Text property to &Submit.

   D. Set the control's Text property to <U>S</U>ubmit.

7. Your Web application allows data entry through a form. The form uses the browser's default colors and fonts throughout. When the user makes a data entry mistake, the computer beeps and the cursor remains in place. When the user saves a record, the entry colors are cleared and the cursor is returned to the first control on the form.

   What should you do to make this form more accessible?

   A. Prompt the user before clearing the form.

   B. Set the form's bgColor to white instead of depending on the system properties.

   C. Provide audio notification of saves.

   D. Provide an additional, non-audio, means of notification for data entry errors.

8. Your application will be used by people who depend on accessibility aids such as screen readers. Which properties should you explicitly set for controls in this application? (Choose two)

   A. bgColor property of the Document object

   B. ALT text for Image controls

   C. Scope property for table header cells

   D. AccessKey properties for label controls

9. Your group is designing a new Web application to be deployed on your company's Internet site. The project lead proposes to use Microsoft's new HTML Help 2.0 for user assistance in this application. Should you endorse this proposal?

   A. Yes, because HTML Help is the standard help for Visual Studio .NET applications.

   B. Yes, because HTML Help can be viewed in any Web browser.

APPLY YOUR KNOWLEDGE

C. No, because HTML Help cannot use the full range of standard HTML 4.01 tags.

D. No, because HTML Help is only available on the Microsoft Windows operating system.

10. Your Web application includes a Label control with the ID of lblCaption and a TextBox control with the ID of txtData. The Text property of the Label control is set to Enter Data. Which two properties of the TextBox control should you set to ensure that it can be accessed by the expected keyboard actions?

    A. TabIndex

    B. AccessKey

    C. CssClass

    D. TextMode

11. You are developing an online checkbook application. Currently, the application plays a music file when the checkbook is in balance. Which of these modifications would make the application more accessible? (Select two)

    A. Add a message box that is also displayed when the checkbook is in balance.

    B. Allow the user to select a custom music file to play when the checkbook is in balance.

    C. Allow the user to set the volume of the music played when the checkbook is in balance.

    D. Display a checkmark graphic when the checkbook is in balance.

12. You have designed a complex Web application that spreads across many pages. Which of these elements should always be accompanied by an alternative text link?

    A. Graphic

    B. Imagemap

    C. Table

    D. Frame

13. You'd like to highlight some information on a Web page. Which of these tags is suitable for highlighting from an accessibility point of view? (Select two)

    A. <B>

    B. <U>

    C. <BLINK>

    D. <MARQUEE>

14. Your Web application uses a frame set to organize information. What must you do to comply with Section 508 accessibility guidelines?

    A. Provide Title text for each frame.

    B. Provide a link to an alternative, non-framed page.

    C. Replace the frame set with a table.

    D. Add an ALT text tag to the FRAMESET tag.

15. Your Web site includes a text-only version of its main page to comply with accessibility guidelines. How often must you update the text-only version of the page?

    A. Every time that the normal main page is updated.

    B. Every time that the normal main page is completely redesigned.

    C. Within two weeks of every change to the normal main page.

    D. Every six months.

APPLY YOUR KNOWLEDGE

Answers to Review Questions

1. You can use HTML pages to provide user assistance to a Web application. These pages can be displayed in their own browser window, in a pane within an existing browser window, or merged with the pages that make up a Web application.
2. The basic principles of accessible design are flexibility, choice of input methods, choice of output methods, consistency, and compatibility with accessibility aids.
3. The Windows Logo certification program accessibility requirements include support for system size, color, font, and input settings, compatibility with the High Contrast display setting, keyboard access to all features, obvious keyboard focus, and alternatives to sound for conveying information.
4. Section 508 of the Rehabilitation Act specifies accessibility guidelines for Web sites run by agencies of the Federal government. The Web Accessibility Initiative of the World Wide Web Consortium has produced an extensive set of recommendations for accessible design.

Answers to Exam Questions

1. **C.** With Internet Explorer as a standard browser, you can use the IE search pane to display help. This avoids the overhead of solutions that require a round trip to the server to download the help.
2. **B.** All graphics should have an ALT tag that conveys the important information about the image. Providing an entirely separate page should be viewed as a last resort, because it can be difficult to keep the regular and alternate pages synchronized.
3. **C.** The <TH> and Scope elements provide important context information for users who access your Web page with screen readers.
4. **B, D.** Accessibility guidelines specify that you should not use only sound or only color to convey information.
5. **C.** HTML Help requires the Windows operating system, and search pane help requires Internet Explorer. Dynamic help tends to increase page sizes and download times, which can be a problem over slow links.
6. **A.** The Button server control does not support displaying underlined text. If you require underlined text, you'll need to use a Button HTML control with its accesskey property set to the character to be underlined.
7. **D.** Accessible applications should not depend on sound as the sole means of feedback.
8. **B, C.** All graphics require an ALT text to be accessible to those who are browsing with graphics turned off. Table header cells should have a Scope attribute to indicate that their contents apply to the entire column in the table.
9. **D.** Although the topics in an HTML Help file can use any valid HTML markup, the HTML Help viewer is a Windows-only technology.
10. **A, B.** The TabIndex property is important to make sure that the control can be accessed by the tab key, and the AccessKey property is important to make sure that the control can be accessed by an accelerator key.
11. **A, D.** To make an application that depends on sounds for notification more accessible, you must add a non-audio means of notification.

APPLY YOUR KNOWLEDGE

12. **B**. Imagemaps must always be accompanied by alternative text navigation links, because screen readers may not be able to represent graphics to a visually impaired user. Navigation that depends on images is unusable in this situation.

13. **A, B**. Blinking or moving text can pose problems for many users and accessibility aids.

14. **A**. Frames can be used in accessible sites so long as frames are titled with text that makes it easy to identify and navigate between frames.

15. **A**. Accessible portions of a Web site should be kept up-to-date with the rest of the Web site.

Suggested Readings and Resources

1. Visual Studio .NET Combined Help Collection
   - Designing Accessible Applications topic
2. W3C WAI Web site, `http://www.w3.org/WAI/`.
3. Section 508 Web site, `http://www.section508.gov/`.

PART II

Testing, Debugging, and Deploying a Web Application

OBJECTIVES

This chapter covers the following Microsoft-specified objective for the Testing and Debugging section of the Visual Basic .NET Web-Based Applications exam:

Create a unit test plan.

- Before releasing an application, it needs to pass through different types of tests. This objective requires you to know the different types of testing that a product should undertake to verify its robustness, reliability, and correctness. These tests should be executed with a designed test plan that ensures that the product thoroughly meets its goals and requirements.

Implement tracing.

- **Add trace listeners and trace switches to an application.**
- **Display trace output.**

- Tracing helps in displaying informative messages during the application's runtime to get a fair idea of how the application is progressing. This objective requires you to know how to use various classes available for tracing an application, attach trace listeners, and apply trace-switches.

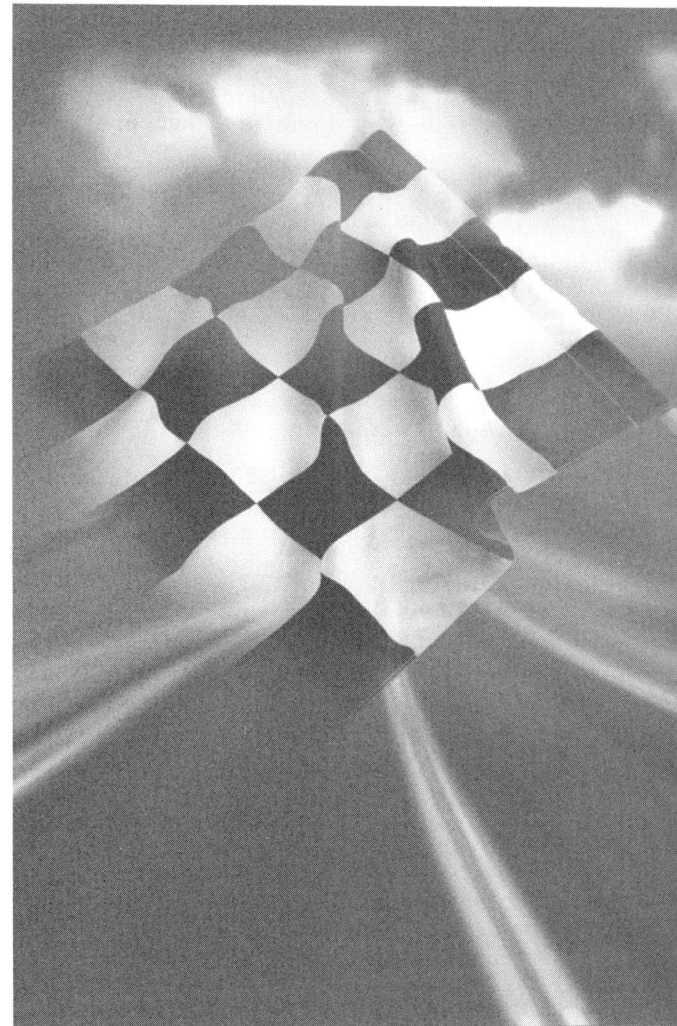

CHAPTER 12

Testing and Debugging a Web Application

OBJECTIVES

Debug, rework, and resolve defects in code.

- **Configure the debugging environment.**
- **Create and apply debugging code to components, pages, and applications.**
- **Provide multicultural test data to components, pages, and applications.**
- **Execute tests.**
- **Resolve errors and rework code.**

▶ Debugging is the process that helps you to locate logical or runtime errors in an application. This objective requires you to know the various tools and windows available in Visual Basic .NET to enable easy and effective debugging. These debugging tools and windows help a great deal in determining errors, executing test code, and resolving the errors.

OUTLINE

STUDY STRATEGIES

- Review the "ASP.NET Trace," "Introduction to Instrumentation and Tracing," and the "Using the Debugger" sections of the Visual Studio .NET Combined Help Collection.
- Experiment with the web.config file to enable tracing for an application. Also, work with setting tracing at the page-level.
- Try calling different methods of the Trace and Debug classes. Note the difference in output when you run a program using the Debug and Release configurations.
- Experiment with attaching predefined and custom-made listeners to the Trace object. Refer to Step by Step 12.4 and Guided Practice Exercise 12.1 for examples.
- Know how to implement trace switches and conditional compilation in a Web application. Refer to Step by Step 12.5 and 12.6 for examples.
- Experiment with the different types of debugging windows available in Visual Basic .NET. Understand their advantages and learn to use them effectively. They can be a great help in resolving errors.
- Experiment with various techniques of debugging—such as local and remote debugging, debugging client side scripting, and debugging SQL Server stored procedures.

INTRODUCTION

Building a quality Web application requires thorough testing to ensure that the application has a minimum of possible defects. To ensure this, you need to chart an effective test plan. Complex applications require multiple levels of testing—unit testing, integration testing, and regression testing.

Tracing is the process of monitoring an executing program. Tracing in ASP.NET can be done using two different and complementary approaches. The first approach is to use the TraceContext class available in the System.Web namespace. The other approach is to use the Trace and Debug classes of System.Diagnostics namespace. The former approach allows you to view diagnostics information and trace messages along with the page output or through a separate trace viewer utility (trace.axd). The latter approach allows you to send the tracing messages to a variety of destinations such as the Output window, a text file, an event log, or any other custom-defined trace listener. These messages can be recorded to analyze the behavior of the program. Trace switches can be used to change the types of messages being generated without recompiling the application.

The process of testing may reveal various logical errors or bugs in a program. The process of finding the exact location of these errors may be time-consuming. Visual Basic .NET provides a rich set of debugging tools that makes this process very convenient.

In this chapter I'll first discuss test plans and various common testing techniques. I'll then show you how to put tracing code in a program to monitor its execution. Finally I'll talk about the debugging capabilities of Visual Studio .NET.

> NOTE
>
> **Correctness, Robustness, and Reliability** *Correctness* refers to the ability of a program to produce expected results when program is given a set of valid input data. *Robustness* is the ability of a program to cope up with invalid data or operation. Reliability is the ability of a program to produce consistent results on every use.

TESTING

Testing is the process of executing a program with the intention of finding errors (bugs). By "error," I mean any case where the program's actual results failed to match the expected results. Expected results may include not just the correctness of the program but may also include other attributes such as usability, reliability, and robustness. The process of testing may be manual, automated, or a mix of both techniques.

In the world of increasing competition, testing is more important than ever. A software company cannot afford to ignore the importance of testing. If a company releases buggy code not only will it end up spending more time and money in fixing and redistributing the corrected code, it will also lose the goodwill and business of potential customers. In the Internet world, the competition is not even next-door but is just a click away!

Creating a Test Plan

Create a unit test plan.

A test plan is a document that guides the whole process of testing. A good test plan will typically include the following information:

- Which software component needs to be tested?
- What parts of a component's specification are to be tested?
- What parts of a component's specification are not to be tested?
- What approach needs to be followed for testing?
- Who will be responsible for each task in the testing process?
- What is the schedule for testing?
- What are the criteria for a test to fail or pass?
- How will the test results be documented and disseminated?

Executing Tests

Debug, rework, and resolve defects in code

- **Execute tests.**

Incremental testing (sometime also called evolutionary testing) is a modern approach to testing that has proven very useful for Rapid Application Development (RAD). The idea here is to test the system as you build it. There are three levels of testing involved:

- **Unit Testing**: Involves testing elementary unit of the application (usually a class).
- **Integration Testing**: Tests the integration of two or more units or integration between subsystems of those units.

- **Regression Testing**: Usually involves the process of repeating the unit and integration tests whenever a bug is fixed to ensure that no old bugs have recurred and that no new bugs have been introduced. You should also run your regression tests when you have modified or added code, to make sure that the new code does not have unintended consequences.

Unit Testing

Units are the smallest building blocks of an application. In Visual Basic .NET these building blocks are often a component or a class definition. Unit tests involve performing basic tests at the component level to ensure that each unique execution path in the component behaves exactly as documented in its specifications.

> NOTE
>
> **NUnit** NUnit is a simple framework that enables you to write repeatable tests in any .NET language. For more information visit http://www.nunit.org/.

Often the same person who writes the component also does unit testing for it. Unit testing typically require writing special programs that uses the component or class under test. These programs are called test drivers and they are used throughout the testing process but are not part of the final product.

Some of the major benefits of unit testing are as follows:

- It allows you to test parts of an application without waiting for the other parts to be available.
- It allows you to test those exceptional conditions that are not easily reached by external inputs in a large integrated system.
- It simplifies the debugging process by limiting the search for bugs to a small unit when compared to the complete application.
- It avoids lengthy compile-build-debug cycles when debugging difficult problems.
- It enables you to detect and remove defects at a much lower cost compared to other, later stages of testing.

Integration Testing

Integration testing verifies that the major subsystems of an application work well with each other. The objective of integration testing is to uncover the errors that might result because of the way units integrate or interface with each other.

If you visualize the whole application as a hierarchy of components, integration testing can be performed in any of the following ways:

- **Bottom-Up Approach:** In this approach, testing progresses from the smallest subsystem and then gradually progresses up in the hierarchy to cover the whole system. This approach may require you to write a number of "test-driver" programs that test the integration between subsystems.
- **Top-Down Approach**: This approach starts with the top-level system to test the top-level interfaces and gradually comes down and tests smaller subsystems. You might be required to write stubs (dummy modules that just mimic the interface of a module but that have no functionality) for the modules that are not yet ready for testing.
- **Umbrella Approach**: This approach focuses more on testing those modules that have a high degree of user interaction. Normally stubs are used in place of process-intensive modules. This approach enables you to release GUI-based applications early allowing you to gradually increase functionality. The reason it is called "umbrella" is that when you look at the application hierarchy (as shown in Figure 12.1), the input/output modules are generally present on the edges forming an umbrella shape.

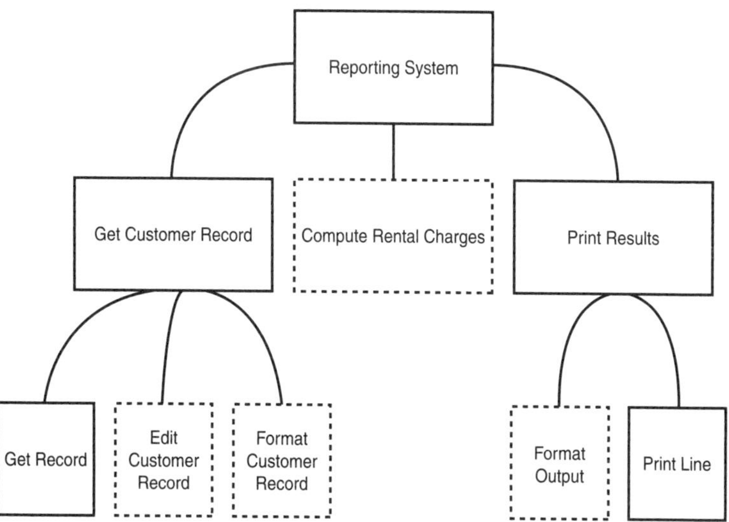

FIGURE 12.1
Hierarchy of subsystems to be tested.

NOTE

Limitations of Testing Testing can only show the presence of errors but can never confirm their absence. Various factors such as the complexity of the software, requirements like interoperability with various software and hardware, and globalization issues like support for various languages and culture, can create excessive input data and too many execution paths to be tested. Many companies do their best to capture most of the test cases by using automation (using computer programs to find errors) and beta-testing (involving product enthusiasts to find errors). Despite the effort invested errors still exist in shipping products, as any user of software well knows.

Regression Testing

Regression testing should be performed any time a program is modified, either to fix a bug or to add a feature. The process of regression testing involves running all the previous tests plus any newly added test cases to test the added functionality. Regression testing has two main goals:

- Verify that all known bugs are corrected.
- Verify that the program has no new bugs.

Testing International Applications

Debug, rework, and resolve defects in code

- **Provide multicultural test data to components, pages, and applications.**

Testing an application designed for international usage involves checking the country and language dependencies of each locale for which the application has been designed. While testing international applications you need to consider the following guidelines:

- Test the application's data and user interface to make sure that they conform to the locale's standards for date and time, numeric values, currency, list separators, and measurements.
- If you are developing for Windows 2000 or Windows XP, test your application on as many language and culture variants as necessary to cover your entire market for the application. These operating systems support the languages used in more than 120 cultures/locales.
- Prefer using Unicode for your application. Applications using Unicode will run fine without making any changes on Windows 2000 and XP. If instead your application uses Windows code pages, you will need to set the culture/locale of operating system according to the localized version of application that you are testing, and reboot after each change.
- Carefully test your application's logic for setting an appropriate language. It may be difficult to determine the user's preferred language from their Web browser settings. You may wish to allow the user to select a language instead.

- While testing a localized version of an application make sure that you use input data in the language supported by the localized version. This will make testing scenario close to the scenario in which application will be actually used.

For more discussion on support for Globalization in a Window application, refer to Chapter 9, "Globalization."

REVIEW BREAK

- Testing is the process of executing a program with the intention of finding errors. You should design an effective test plan to ensure that your application is free from all detectable defects and errors.
- Unit testing ensures each unit of an application function perfectly as desired. It is the lowest level of testing.
- Integration testing ensures that different units of an application function as expected by the test plan after being integrated.
- Whenever the code is modified or a new feature is added in an application, you should run all the existing test cases along with a new set of test cases to check the new feature. This regression testing helps in developing robust applications.

TRACING

The process of testing can reveal presence of errors in the program, but for finding the actual cause of problem, you may need the program to generate information about its own execution. Analysis of this information may help you to understand why the program is behaving in a particular way and may lead to possible resolution of the error.

This process of collecting information about a program's execution is called tracing. In this section I'll tell you about two different ways for tracing:

- **Using the System.Web.TraceContext class**: This class allows you to view diagnostic information and trace messages along with the page output or through a separate trace viewer utility (trace.axd).

NOTE

Tracing Helps in Resolving "Hard to Reproduce" Errors When programs run in the production environment they may sometime report errors (mostly related to performance or threading problems) that are difficult to reproduce in a simulated testing environment. Tracing the production application can help you to get runtime information that may help you in trapping these hard to reproduce errors.

- **Using the System.Diagnostics.Trace and System.Diagnostics.Debug classes**: By default these classes display trace messages in the Output window, but you can use the TraceListener class to send output to additional destinations like text files, event logs, or other custom-defined trace listeners.

Using the TraceContext Class

Implement tracing: Display trace output.

The TraceContext class is responsible for gathering the execution details of a Web request. You can access the TraceContext object for the current request through the Trace property of the Page class. Once you have the TraceContext object, you can invoke its member methods to write trace messages to the trace log. Table 12.1 lists some of the important members of the TraceContext class that you should be familiar with.

NOTE

Tracing Beyond a Page The Page class exposes a Trace property that gives you access to the TraceContext object. If you want to write messages from outside the page (for example, from the global.asax file or from custom server controls) you can access the Trace property of the HttpContext object via Control.Context or HttpContext.Current property.

TABLE 12.1

IMPORTANT MEMBERS OF TRACECONTEXT CLASSES

Member	*Type*	*Description*
`IsEnabled`	Property	Specifies whether tracing is enabled for a request.
`TraceMode`	Property	Indicates the sort order in which the messages should be displayed. It can have one of three values—Default, `SortByCategory` and `SortByTime`.
`Warn`	Method	Writes messages to the trace log in red, to indicate them as warnings. It has three overloads—one with message, one with category and message, and the last one with category, message, and exception object.
`Write`	Method	Writes the messages to the trace log. It has the same three overloads as the `Warn` method.

EXAM TIP

IsEnabled Property The IsEnabled property can be dynamically assigned to turn on or off tracing for a page. It can also be used include or exclude code based on the Trace setting for a page.

By default, tracing is not enabled. Thus trace messages are not displayed. You can enable tracing for a Page by using the Trace attribute of the Page directive. When the Trace attribute is set to True, the page appends the tracing information of the current Web request to its output.

You can also enable tracing by setting the DOCUMENT object's Trace property to True. Step by Step 12.1 demonstrates how to enable tracing in a page and how to write trace messages in to the trace log.

STEP BY STEP

12.1 Using the TraceContext Class to Display Debugging Information

1. Launch a new Visual Basic ASP.NET Web Application project. Name it `305C12`.

2. Add a new Web Form to the project. Name the Web Form `StepByStep12-1.aspx`. Set the page to `FlowLayout` mode.

3. Place two `TextBox` controls (`txtNumber` and `txtFactorial`), three `Label` controls, and a `Button` control (`btnCalculate`) on the Web Form and arrange the controls as shown in Figure 12.2.

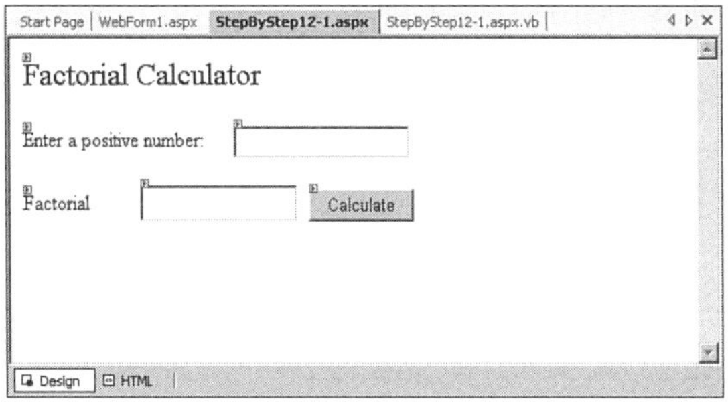

FIGURE 12.2
Factorial calculator.

4. Switch to HTML view of the form in the designer. Add the `Trace="True"` attribute to the `Page` directive:

```
<%@ Page Language="vb" AutoEventWireup="false"
 Codebehind="StepByStep12-1.aspx.vb"
 Inherits="_305C12.StepByStep12_1" Trace="True"%>
```

5. Switch back to design view of the form. Double-click the button control and add the following code to the event handler to handle the `Click` event:

continues

continued

```
Private Sub btnCalculate_Click( _
 ByVal sender As System.Object, _
 ByVal e As System.EventArgs) _
 Handles btnCalculate.Click
    ' Write a trace message
    Trace.Write("Factorial", _
     "Inside Button Click event handler")
    Dim intNumber As Integer
    Try
        intNumber = Convert.ToInt32(txtNumber.Text)
    Catch ex As Exception
        Trace.Warn("Factorial", "Invalid value", ex)
        Exit Sub
    End Try
    If intNumber < 0 Then
        Trace.Warn("Factorial", _
         "Invalid negative value")
    End If
    Dim intFac As Integer = 1
    Dim i As Integer
    Try
        For i = 2 To intNumber
            intFac = intFac * i
            Trace.Write("Factorial", _
             "Value of i: " & i)
        Next
    Catch ex As Exception
        Trace.Warn("Factorial", _
         "There was an overflow")
    End Try

    txtFactorial.Text = intFac.ToString()
    Trace.Write("Factorial", _
     "Done with computations, returning...")
End Sub
```

6. Set the Web Form as the start page for the project.

7. Run the project. You will notice that the page displays a wide range of information after its general output. Enter a value into the number textbox and click Calculate button. You will see the factorial value displayed in the factorial textbox along with some trace messages in the Trace Information section as shown in Figure 12.3.

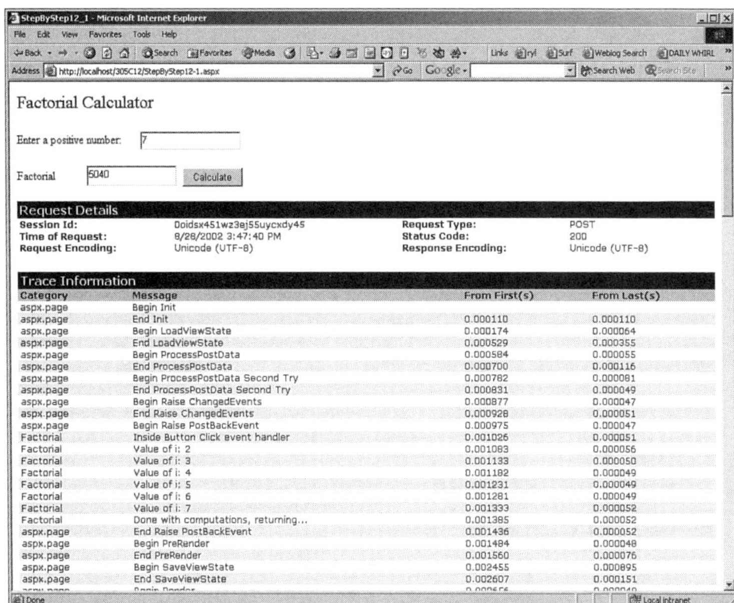

FIGURE 12.3
Tracing information.

8. Try entering a negative value or a large value (say, 100). You'll see the trace messages displayed in the trace log. You will see that warning messages are displayed in red.

As you can see, when tracing is enabled, ASP.NET displays a great deal of information related to the request in addition to messages written by you. The information is displayed by grouping it in different tables:

- **Request Details**: Includes the session identifier, the time the request was made, the request character encoding, the type of HTTP request (GET or POST), the HTTP response status code, and the response character encoding.
- **Trace Information**: Includes the messages and warnings generated by the ASP.NET engine or by you by making calls to the Write or Warn methods of the TraceContext class. It displays the information in four columns—the category of the message, the trace message, the number of seconds since the first trace message was displayed, and the number of seconds since the most recent trace message was displayed.

- **Control Tree**: Includes the entire collection of controls in the ASP.NET page hierarchically. The information is displayed in four columns—the control identifier, the fully qualified type of the control, the size (in bytes) of the rendered control, including its child controls, and the size (in bytes) of the view state of the control, excluding its child controls.
- **Session State**: Includes the session state only if any data is stored in the session. The Session State table displays the session key, the fully qualified type of the session data stored, and the value of the session data.
- **Cookies Collection**: Includes the cookies associated with the application. The information displayed is the name of the cookie, the value of the cookie, and its size.
- **Headers Collection**: Includes the HTTP headers passed to the Web page. It displays the name of the header and its value.
- **Form Collection**: Includes the form collection. It is displayed only if there is a Web Form defined in the page and the form is posting back from the server. It displays the name of the control in the form and its value.
- **Querystring Collection**: Includes the querystring collection only if any querystring parameters are passed while requesting the page. It displays the name of the querystring parameter and its value.
- **Server Variables**: Includes all the server variables associated with the page. It displays the name of the server variable and its value.

As apparent from the preceding list, the trace log definitely helps a great deal to understand the program's execution path. It provides various state information, page control's structure information, and performance information. This information can be of great help in debugging and improving the quality of the program.

You can enable tracing for an entire Web application using the application configuration (web.config) file in the application's root directory. Enabling tracing through web.config file allows you to view the trace information using trace viewer in a separate page instead of displaying it with the page output.

The <trace> element is used to configure tracing for an application. The attributes of the <trace> element are

- **enabled**: Indicates whether tracing is enabled for an application. If enabled, trace information can be viewed using trace viewer.
- **localOnly**: Indicates whether trace viewer can be viewed by only the local client (running on the Web server itself) or by any client.
- **pageOutput**: Indicates whether the trace information should be displayed along with the page output.
- **requestLimit**: Indicates the number of requests whose trace information should be stored on the server. Tracing gets disabled when the request limit is reached.
- **traceMode**: Indicates the order in which the trace messages should be displayed in the Trace Information section. It can be either SortByCategory (sorted by the Category column) or SortByTime (sorted by the First(s) column).

EXAM TIP

Page-Level Tracing Overrides The page-level trace setting overrides the trace setting for the application. For example, if the pageOutput is set to False in the web.config file and if the trace attribute is enabled at page level, the trace information is still displayed along with the page output.

Thus when the tracing is enabled for an application, request for each of its pages can be viewed using Trace Viewer (unless the Page directive's trace attribute is set to false). Trace Viewer can be viewed by navigating to trace.axd from any directory in an application. You will notice there is no trace.axd file in the application directory structure. This request is rather handled by TraceHandler defined in the machine.config file's <httpHandlers> element. Trace Viewer lists all the page requests in an application along with the time of request, the filename, an HTTP status code, the type of request, and a link to view the trace log of the request. It also contains a link to clear the current trace information of all page requests.

STEP BY STEP

12.2 Setting Application-Level Tracing

1. Open the `web.config` file from the Solution Explorer. Modify the `<trace>` element defined in the `<system.web>` element as follows:

continues

continued

```
<trace
    enabled="true"
    requestLimit="10"
    pageOutput="false"
    traceMode="SortByTime"
    localOnly="true"
      />
```

2. Remove the `Trace="True"` attribute from the Page directive of the form `StepByStep12_1`.

3. Run the project. You will notice that there is no trace information along with the page display. Enter a value into the number textbox and click the Calculate button. You will see the factorial value displayed in the factorial textbox.

4. Now navigate to `trace.axd` under your application directory by typing `http://localhost/305C12/Trace.axd` (assuming the Web server and the development machine are the same box). This will load the Application Trace page as shown in Figure 12.4.

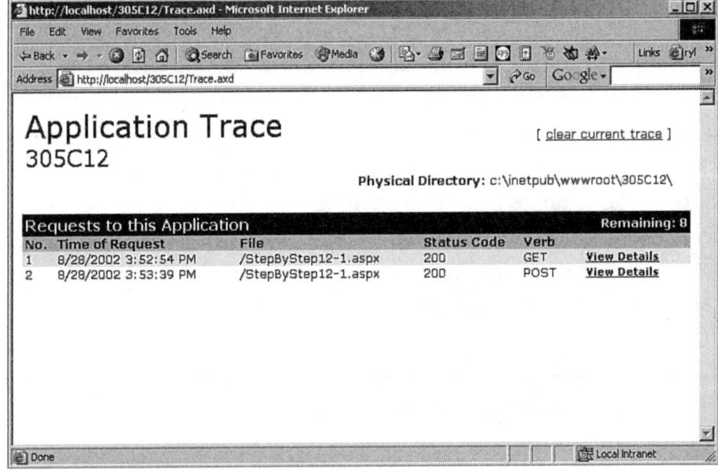

FIGURE 12.4
Application Trace page viewed using trace viewer.

5. Click the View Details link in the second row (the one with the POST request). You will notice that the entire trace log for that page request is displayed as shown in Figure 12.5.

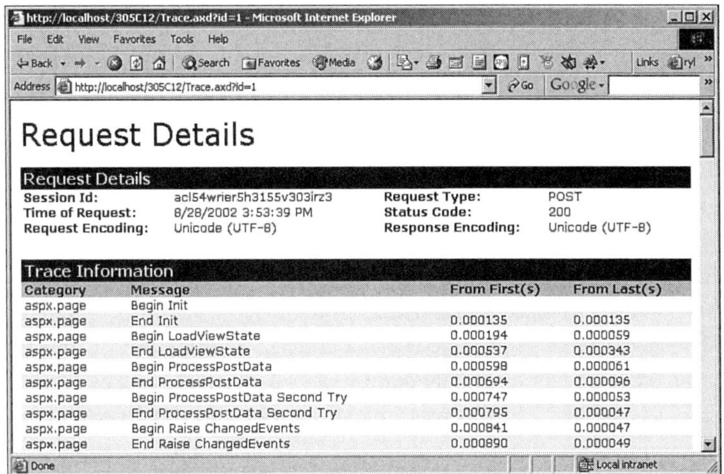

FIGURE 12.5

Viewing trace log with the help of trace Viewer.

6. Now open the `web.config` file and change the `pageOutput` attribute to `true`. Run the project. Enter a value into the number textbox and click the Calculate button. You will see the factorial value being displayed in the factorial textbox along with the entire trace log being appended to the trace output. You can also view the trace log with the help of trace viewer as shown in Step 4 and 5.

7. Now open the form in HTML view in the designer. Add `trace="false"` attribute in the Page directive. Run the project. Enter a value into the number textbox and click the Calculate button. You will see the factorial value displayed in the factorial textbox. You will notice that neither the page output nor the trace viewer displays the trace information. This is because the page-level directive overrides the settings in the `web.config` file.

8. Set the enabled attribute to false in the `web.config` file.

Using the Trace and Debug Classes

Debug, rework, and resolve defects in code

- **Create and apply debugging code to components, pages, and applications.**

Implement tracing: Display trace output.

Tracing in Visual Basic .NET can also be done by generating messages about the program's execution with the use of Debug and Trace classes. The messages generated by these classes by default can be viewed in the Output Window.

The Trace and Debug classes have several things in common—both belong to the System.Diagnostics namespace, they have members with the same names, all their members are static, and they are conditionally compiled (that is, their statements will be included in the object code only if a certain symbol is defined). The only difference between the Debug and Trace classes is that, the members of the Debug class are conditionally compiled only when the DEBUG symbol is defined. On the other hand, members in the Trace class are conditionally compiled only if the TRACE symbol is defined.

Visual Basic .NET provides two basic configurations for a project, Debug and Release. Debug is the default configuration, as shown in Figure 12.6. When you compile a program using the Debug configuration, both the TRACE and DEBUG conditional compilation symbols are defined. You'll learn how to specify other conditional compilation symbols later in the chapter. When you compile a program in the Release configuration, only the TRACE symbol is defined. You can switch between Debug and Release configurations using the Solution Configurations combo box on the standard toolbar (as shown in Figure 12.7) or using the Configuration Manager (as shown in Figure 12.8) from the project's property pages.

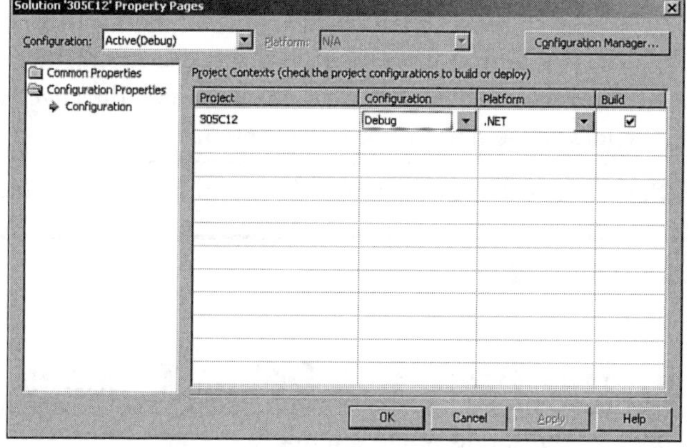

FIGURE 12.6
Project Property Pages.

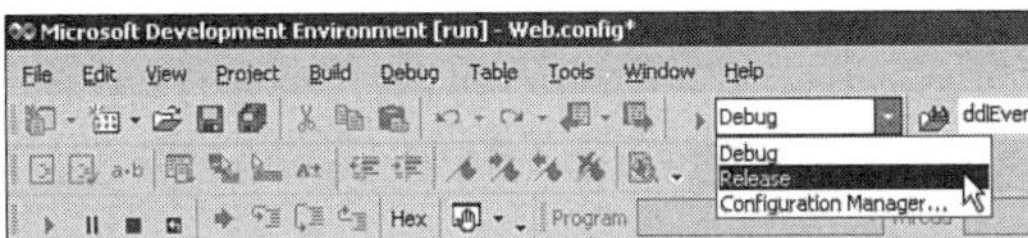

FIGURE 12.7
Solutions Configuration combo box on the standard toolbar.

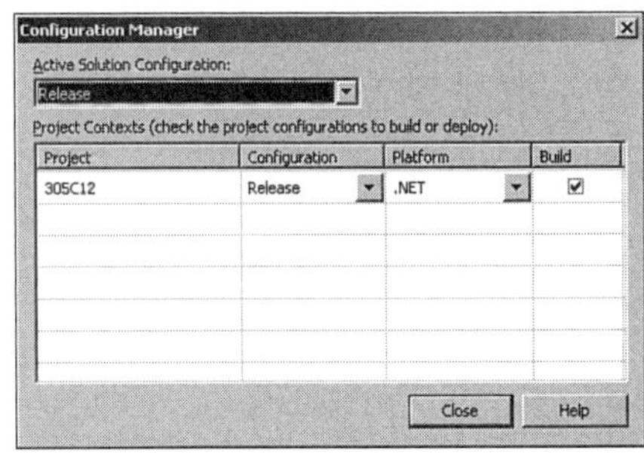

FIGURE 12.8
Configuration Manager.

You can of course change the symbols that are available for a configuration by making changes to the project's configuration. Later in this section, I will show you how to make those changes from within the program and through the command line compilation options.

You should note here that when you compile a program using the Debug configuration, code using Debug as well as Trace is included in the compiled code. When you run such a program, you will get messages generated using both Debug and Trace classes. As opposed to this, when a program is compiled using the Trace configuration, it will not include any calls to Debug class. Thus when such a program is executed, you only get the messages generated using the Trace class. Table 12.2 summarizes the members of both Trace and Debug classes.

TABLE 12.2

MEMBERS OF DEBUG AND TRACE CLASSES

Member	*Type*	*Description*
`Assert`	Method	Checks for a condition, and displays a message if the condition is false.
`AutoFlush`	Property	Specifies whether `Flush` should be called on the Listeners after every write.
`Close`	Method	Flushes the output buffer and then closes the `Listeners`.
`Fail`	Method	Displays an error message.
`Flush`	Method	Flushes the output buffer and causes buffered data to be written to the `Listeners`.
`Indent`	Method	Increases the current `IndentLevel` by one.
`IndentLevel`	Property	Specifies the indent level.
`IndentSize`	Property	Specifies the number of spaces in an indent.
`Listeners`	Property	\Collection of listeners that is monitoring the trace output.
`Unindent`	Method	Decreases the current `IndentLevel` by one.

continues

TABLE 12.2 *continued*

MEMBERS OF DEBUG AND TRACE CLASSES

Member	*Type*	*Description*
`Write`	Method	Writes the given information to the trace listeners in the `Listeners` collection.
`WriteIf`	Method	Writes the given information to the trace listeners in the `Listeners` collection only if a condition is true.
`WriteLine`	Method	Same as `Write` but appends the information with a newline character.
`WriteLineIf`	Method	Same as `WriteIf` but appends the information with a newline character.

Step by Step 12.3 demonstrates how to use some of the methods of the Trace and Debug classes.

STEP BY STEP

12.3 Using the Trace and Debug Classes to Display Debugging Information

1. Add a new Web Form to the Visual Basic ASP.NET project. Name it `StepByStep12-3.aspx`.

2. Place two `TextBox` controls (`txtNumber` and `txtFactorial`), three `Label` controls, and a `Button` control (`btnCalculate`) on the Web Form and arrange the controls as shown in Figure 12.2.

3. Add the following code to the top of the Web Form's module:

```
Imports System.Diagnostics
Imports System.Diagnostics.Trace = _

 System.Diagnostics.Trace
```

4. Add the following code to the `Click` event handler of `btnCalculate`:

```
Private Sub btnCalculate_Click( _
 ByVal sender As System.Object, _
 ByVal e As System.EventArgs) _
 Handles btnCalculate.Click
```

```
    ' Write a debug message
    Debug.WriteLine( _
     "Inside Button Click event handler")
    ' Start indenting messages now
    Debug.Indent()
    Dim intNumber As Integer = _
     Convert.ToInt32(txtNumber.Text)
    ' Make a debug assertion
    Debug.Assert(intNumber >= 0, "Invalid value", _
     "negative value in debug mode")
    ' Write a trace assertion
    DiagnosticTrace.Assert(intNumber >= 0, _
     "Invalid value", _
    "negative value in trace mode")

    Dim intFac As Integer = 1
    Dim intI As Integer
    Try
        For intI = 2 To intNumber
            intFac = intFac * intI
            ' Write a debug message
            Debug.WriteLine(intI, _
             "Factorial Program Debug, Value of intI")
        Next
    Catch ex As Exception
        ' Write a trace message
        ' if the condition is true
        DiagnosticTrace.WriteLineIf( _
         TypeOf ex Is System.OverflowException, _
         "There was an overflow", _
         "Factorial Program Trace")
        ' Write a debug message
        ' if the condition is true
        Debug.WriteLineIf( _
         TypeOf ex Is System.OverflowException, _
         "There was an overflow", _
         "Factorial Program Debug")
    End Try

    txtFactorial.Text = intFac.ToString()
    ' Decrease the indent level
    Debug.Unindent()

    ' Write a debug message
        Debug.WriteLine( _
     "Done with computations, returning...")

End Sub
```

5. Set the Web Form as the start page for the project.

6. Run the Project in Debug mode. Keep the program running and switch to the Visual Studio .NET IDE. Select View, Other Windows, Output. Push the pin on the output window so that it does not auto-hide.

continues

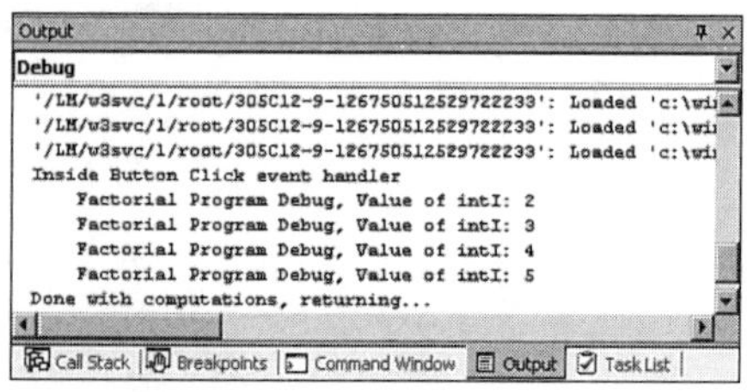

FIGURE 12.9
The Output window.

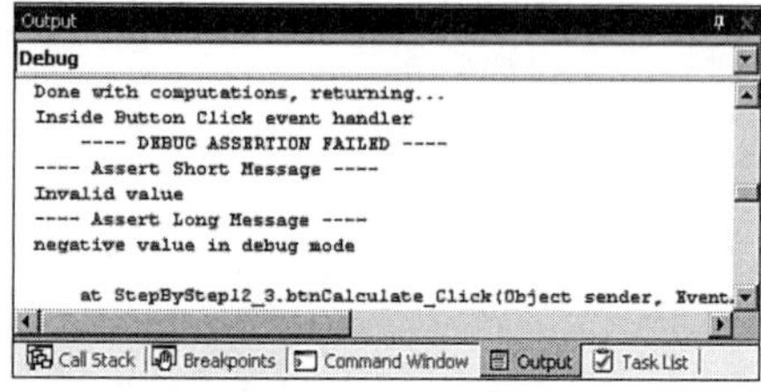

FIGURE 12.10
Assertion Failed messages in the Output window.

continued

Now switch to the running program, enter 5 in the textbox, and click the Calculate button. You will see the debug messages generated by the program as shown in Figure 12.9.

7. Enter a value of 100 and click the Calculate button; you will now see that messages displayed by both `Debug` class as well as `Trace` class are displayed in the Output window. Note that the default configuration is the Debug configuration where both `TRACE` and `DEBUG` symbols are defined.

8. Enter a negative value—say, –1—and click the Calculate button. This will cause the assertion to fail and you will see assertion-failed debug and trace messages in the output window as shown in Figure 12.10.

9. Stop the project. From the Solution Configurations combo-box, select the Release configuration so that only the TRACE symbol is defined. Run the project. Enter value 5 and click the Calculate button. The factorial will be calculated but there are no trace messages in the output window. Enter the value 100 and click the Calculate button. You will now see the trace message about overflow in the Output window. Finally try calculating the factorial of –1; you will see just one trace assertion-failed message.

As I demonstrated in this exercise, you can also use Debug and Trace methods to display messages based on a condition (using their WriteIf and WriteLineIf methods). This can be a very useful technique if you are trying to understand the flow of logic of a program. Also note the use of DiagnosticsTrace in the Imports directive as an alias for System.Diagnostics.Trace class. I have used it to remove the naming conflict between the Trace class and the Trace property of the Page class. Alternatively, you could use the fully qualified name for the System.Diagnostics.Trace class.

Trace Listeners

Implement tracing

- **Add trace listeners to an application.**

Listeners are the classes responsible for forwarding, recording, or displaying the messages generated by the Trace and Debug classes. You can have multiple listeners associated with the Trace and Debug classes by adding multiple Listener objects to their Listeners property. The Listeners property is a collection capable of holding objects of any type derived from the TraceListener class. The TraceListener class is an abstract class that belongs to the System.Diagnostics namespace, which has three implementations in the FCL:

- **DefaultTraceListener**: An object of this class is automatically added to the Listeners collection of Trace and Debug classes. Its behavior is to write messages on the Output window.
- **TextWriterTraceListener**: Writes the messages to any class that derives from Stream class. This includes the console or a file.
- **EventLogTraceListener**: Writes the messages to the Windows Event Log.

> EXAM TIP
>
> **Same Listeners for Debug and Trace** Messages sent through the Debug and Trace objects are directed through each Listener in the Listeners collection. Debug and Trace share the same Listeners collection, so any Listener defined in the Trace.Listeners collection will also be defined in the Debug.Listeners collection.

If you want a listener object to perform differently than the previously mentioned listener classes, you can create your own class that inherits from the TraceListener class. When doing so you must at least implement the Write and WriteLine methods.

Step by Step 12.4 creates a custom listener class that implements the TraceListener class to send debug and trace messages through email.

STEP BY STEP

12.4 Creating a Custom TraceListener

1. Add a new class to your ASP.NET project. Name the class `EmailTraceListener.vb` and add the following code to it:

```
Imports System
Imports System.Diagnostics
Imports System.Text
Imports System.Web.Mail

Public Class EmailTraceListener
    Inherits TraceListener

    ' Mmessage log will be sent to this address
    Private mstrMailTo As String
```

continues

continued

```
    ' Storage for the message log
    Private mmessage As StringBuilder

    Public Sub New(ByVal MailTo As String)
        mstrMailTo = MailTo
    End Sub

    ' A custom listener must override Write method
    Public Overloads Overrides Sub Write( _
     ByVal message As String)
        If mmessage Is Nothing Then
            mmessage = New StringBuilder()
        End If
        mmessage.Append(message)
    End Sub

    ' A custom listener must override WriteLine method
    Public Overloads Overrides Sub WriteLine( _
     ByVal message As String)
        If mmessage Is Nothing Then
            mmessage = New StringBuilder()
        End If
        mmessage.Append(message)
        mmessage.Append(vbCrLf)
    End Sub

    ' Use the close method to send the mail.
    Public Overrides Sub Close()
        Flush()
        Dim msg As MailMessage = New MailMessage()
        msg.To = mstrMailTo
        msg.Subject = _
         "Factorial Program Debug/Trace output"
        If Not mmessage Is Nothing Then
            msg.Body = mmessage.ToString()
        Else
            msg.Body = ""
        End If
        ' Send the mail
        SmtpMail.Send(msg)
    End Sub

    Public Overrides Sub Flush()
        ' Nothing much to do here
        ' Just call the base class's implementation
        MyBase.Flush()
    End Sub

End Class
```

2. In Solution Explorer, right-click StepByStep12-3.aspx and select Copy. Right-click your project and select Paste.

Rename the pasted Web Form to StepByStep12-4.aspx. Open the aspx (HTML view) and vb files of the new Web Form and change all references referring to StepByStep12_3 to StepByStep12_4 instead.

3. Add the following code to the Page_Load event. Change the email address to a real address where you can receive email:

```
Private Sub Page_Load( _
 ByVal sender As System.Object, _
 ByVal e As System.EventArgs) Handles MyBase.Load
    If Not IsPostBack Then
        ' Add a custom listener to
        ' the Listeners collection
        DiagnosticTrace.Listeners.Add( _
         New EmailTraceListener( _
         "Insert@youraddress.here"))
    End If
End Sub
```

4. Add the following code at the end of the Click event handler of the btnCalculate control:

```
' Call the close methods for all listeners
DiagnosticTrace.Close()
```

5. Set the Web Form as the start page for the project.

6. Run the project using the default Debug configuration. Enter a value and click the Calculate button. You will note that both Debug and Trace messages appear on the Output window. The messages will also be emailed to the specified address using the local SMTP server. Run the project again in the Release mode. Enter a large value, say 100, and click the Calculate button. You will see the overflow message in the Output window and also an email will be sent to the specified email address containing the trace overflow message.

Trace Switches

Implement tracing

- **Add trace switches to an application.**

So far, you have learned that the Trace and Debug classes can be used to display valuable information related to program execution. You also learned that it is possible to capture the messages in a variety of formats by using TraceListener objects. In this section, you'll learn how to control the nature of messages that you get from a program.

Trace switches allow you to set the parameters that can control the level of tracing that needs to be done on a program. These switches are set in an XML-based external configuration file. This is especially useful when the application is in production mode. You may not normally want your application to generate any trace messages. However, if the application has problems, or you just want to check on the health of the application you may instruct the application to write a particular type of trace information by just changing the configuration file. There's no need to recompile the application. The application will automatically pick up the changes from the configuration file the next time you run the application.

There are two predefined classes for creating trace switches: the BooleanSwitch class, and the TraceSwitch class. Both classes derive from the abstract Switch class. You can also define your own trace switch class by deriving a class from the Switch class.

The BooleanSwitch class differentiates between two modes of tracing: trace-on or trace-off. Its default value is zero. This corresponds to the trace-off state. If the value of the class is set to any non-zero value, this corresponds to a trace-on state.

Unlike the BooleanSwitch class, the TraceSwitch class provides you with five different levels of tracing switches. These levels are defined by the TraceLevel enumeration, listed in Table 12.3. The default value of TraceLevel for a TraceSwitch is 0 (Off).

TABLE 12.3

THE TRACELEVEL ENUMERATION

Enumerated Value	*Integer Value*	*Type of tracing*
`Off`	0	None
`Error`	1	Only error messages
`Warning`	2	Warning messages and error messages

Enumerated Value	*Integer Value*	*Type of tracing*
`Info`	3	Informational messages, warning messages, and error messages
`Verbose`	4	Verbose messages, informational messages, warning messages, and error messages

Table 12.4 displays the important properties of the TraceSwitch class.

TABLE 12.4

IMPORTANT PROPERTIES OF THE TRACESWITCH CLASS

Property	*Description*
`Description`	Description of the switch (inherited from Switch).
`DisplayName`	A name used to identify the switch (inherited from Switch).
`Level`	Specifies the trace level that helps in selecting which trace and debug messages will be processed. Its value is one of the `TraceLevel` enumeration values (refer Table 12.2).
`TraceError`	Returns true if the `Level` is set to Error, Warning, Info, or Verbose, otherwise a false value.
`TraceInfo`	Returns true if the `Level` is set to Info or Verbose, otherwise a false value.
`TraceVerbose`	Returns true if the `Level` is set to Verbose, otherwise a false value.
`TraceWarning`	Returns true if the `Level` is set to Warning, Info, or Verbose, otherwise a false value.

EXAM TIP

Out-of-range Values for BooleanSwitch and TraceSwitch
For a BooleanSwitch object, if any non-zero (negative or positive) value is specified in the configuration file, the Enabled property of the object is set to True. For a TraceSwitch object, if a value greater than 4 is specified, the Level property of the object is set to TraceLevel.Verbose (4). But if a negative value is specified for a TraceSwitch, a StackOverflow exception will occur at runtime.

Step by Step 12.5 demonstrates how to use trace switches in a Web application.

STEP BY STEP

12.5 Using the TraceSwitch Class

1. In Solution Explorer, right-click StepByStep12-3.aspx and select Copy. Right-click your project and select Paste. Rename the pasted Web Form to StepByStep12-5.aspx.

continues

continued

Open the aspx (HTML view) and vb files of the new Web Form and change all references to StepByStep12_3 to refer to StepByStep12_5 instead.

2. Change the `Click` event handler of the Calculate button as follows:

```
Private Sub btnCalculate_Click( _
 ByVal sender As System.Object, _
 ByVal e As System.EventArgs) _
 Handles btnCalculate.Click
    Dim ts As TraceSwitch = _
       New TraceSwitch("FactorialTrace", _
        "Trace the factorial application")
    If ts.TraceVerbose Then
        ' Write a debug message
        Debug.WriteLine( _
         "Inside Button Click event handler")
    End If

    ' Start indenting messages now
    Debug.Indent()
    Dim intNumber As Integer = _
     Convert.ToInt32(txtNumber.Text)

    If ts.TraceError Then
        ' Make a debug assertion
                Debug.Assert(intNumber >= 0, _
         "Invalid value", _
         "negative value in debug mode")
    End If

    Dim intFac As Integer = 1
    Dim i As Integer
    Try
        For i = 2 To intNumber
            intFac = intFac * i
            ' Write a debug message
            If ts.TraceInfo Then
                Debug.WriteLine(i, _
                 "Factorial Program Debug, " & _
                 " Value of i")
            End If
        Next
    Catch ex As Exception
        If ts.TraceWarning Then
            ' Write a debug message
            ' if condition is true
            Debug.WriteLineIf( _
             TypeOf ex Is System.OverflowException, _
             "There was an overflow", _
             "Factorial Program Debug")
        End If
    End Try
```

```
        txtFactorial.Text = intFac.ToString()
        ' Decrease the indent level
        Debug.Unindent()

        If ts.TraceVerbose Then
            ' Write a debug message
            Debug.WriteLine( _
             "Done with computations, returning...")
        End If
    End Sub
```

3. Open the `web.config` file from the Solution Explorer. Insert the `<system.diagnostics>` element after the `<system.web>` element definition in the `<configuration>` element (that is in between the `</system.web>` and `</configuration>` element) as shown here:

```
<configuration>
   <system.web>
   ...
         </system.web>
    <system.diagnostics>
        <switches>
            <add name="FactorialTrace" value="4" />
        </switches>
    </system.diagnostics>
</configuration>
```

4. Set the Web Form as the start page for the project.

5. Run the project using the default Debug configuration. Enter a value of 5; you will note that all messages appear on the Output Window. Try again with a negative value and a large value, you will see all errors as well as warning messages. Close the form. Modify the XML file to change the value of `FactorialTrace` to 3. You will now see all messages except the one set with `TraceLevel` as `Verbose`. Repeat the process with values of `FactorialTrace` in the configuration file changed to 2, 1, and 0.

6. Modify the program to change all Debug statements to the `DiagnosticsTrace` (`System.Diagnostics.Trace`) statements. Run the project using the Release configuration. Change the trace attribute's value to 4 and then repeat the whole process discussed in step 6.

NOTE

The VB Preprocessor There is no separate preprocessor in the Visual Basic .NET compiler. The lexical analysis phase of compiler processes all the preprocessing directives. This contrasts with languages like C and C++ that use a separate preprocessor to take care of conditional compilation.

Conditional Compilation

The Visual Basic .NET programming language provides a set of preprocessing directives. You can use these directives to skip sections of source files for compilation (for example, you may not want to include testing code in the released version of your software), to report errors and warnings, or to mark distinct regions of the source code.

Table 12.5 summarizes the preprocessing directives available in Visual Basic .NET.

TABLE 12.5

VISUAL BASIC .NET PREPROCESSING DIRECTIVES

Directives	*Description*
`#If`, `#Else`, `#ElseIf`, and `#End If`	These directives conditionally skip sections of code. The skipped sections are not the part of compiled code.
`#Const`	This directive defines a preprocessor constant. This constant can only be used within a conditional compilation directive, not in regular code.
`#ExternalSource` and `#End ExternalSource`	These directives are used by the compiler to track line numbers for compiler error messages. You won't use them in your own code.
`#Region` and `#End Region`	These directives mark sections of code. A common example of these directives is the code generated by Windows Forms Designer. This marking can be used by visual designers such as Visual Studio .NET to show, hide, and format code.

In addition to the preprocessing directives, Visual Basic .NET also provides you with a ConditionalAttribute class.

A method can be marked as conditional by applying the Conditional attribute to it. The Conditional attribute takes one argument that specifies a symbol. A symbol is just an arbitrary name that the conditional compilation can use to make decisions. The conditional method is either included or omitted from the compiled code depending on the definition of the specified symbol at that point. If the symbol definition is available, then the call to that method is included; otherwise, the method call is excluded from the compiled code.

Careful use of conditional compilation directives as well as methods with Conditional attribute allows you to keep debugging related code in the source code while you're developing an application, but exclude it from the compiled version. That way, no extraneous messages are generated in shipping code, and production programs do not encounter a performance hit due to processing of additional code. If you want to resolve some errors, then the debugging code can be easily activated by defining a symbol and recompiling the program.

Step by Step 12.6 demonstrates the use of ConditionalAttribute with the usage of conditional compilation directives.

> **EXAM TIP**
>
> **Conditional Method** A method must be a Sub rather than a Function to have the Conditional attribute applied to it.

STEP BY STEP

12.6 Using Conditional Compilation

1. In Solution Explorer, right-click `StepByStep12-3.aspx` and select Copy. Right-click your project and select Paste. Rename the pasted Web Form to `StepByStep12-6.aspx`. Open the `aspx` (HTML view) and `vb` files of the new Web Form and change all references to `StepByStep12_3` to refer to `StepByStep12_6` instead. Name the Label control at the top of the Web Form `lblHeading`.

2. Switch to code view. Add the following two conditional methods to the class definition:

```
<Conditional("DEBUG")> _
Public Sub InitializeDebugMode()
    lblHeading.Text =_
    "Factorial Calculator: Debug Mode"
End Sub

<Conditional("TRACE")> _
Public Sub InitializeReleaseMode()
    lblHeading.Text = _
     "Factorial Calculator Version 1.0"
End Sub
```

3. Add the following code in the `Page_Load` event of the form:

```
Private Sub Page_Load( _
 ByVal sender As System.Object, _
 ByVal e As System.EventArgs) _
 Handles MyBase.Load
```

continues

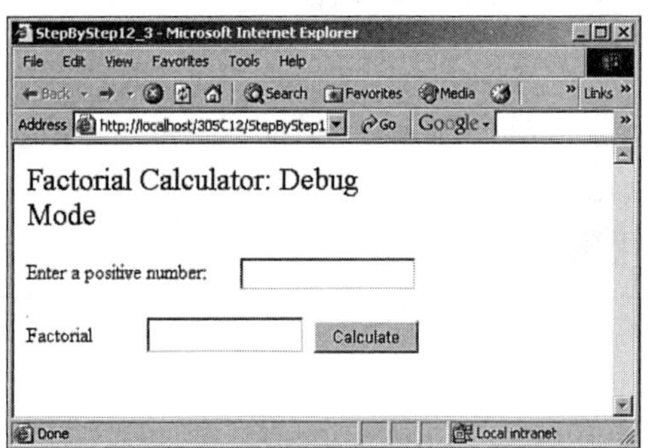

FIGURE 12.11
A program conditionally compiled for Debug configuration.

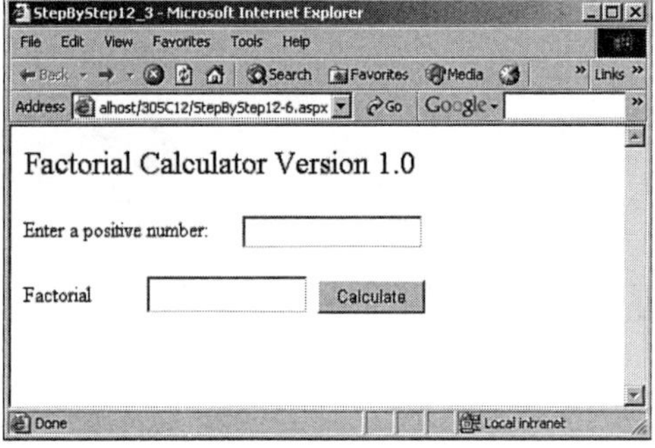

FIGURE 12.12
A program conditionally compiled for Release configuration.

continued

```
#If Debug Then
                Debug.WriteLine( _
          "Program started in debug mode")

        InitializeDebugMode()
#Else
        DiagnosticTrace.WriteLine _
         ("Program started in release mode")
        InitializeReleaseMode()
#End If
    End Sub
```

4. Set the Web Form as the start page for the project.

5. Run the project using the default Debug configuration. You will see that the heading of the form displays "Factorial Program: Debug Mode" as shown in Figure 12.11. The Output window also displays a string, "Program started in debug mode." Stop the project, and start it again in the Release mode. You will see a different heading for the form as shown in Figure 12.12 and a different message in the Output window.

The DEBUG and TRACE symbols can be defined for the compiler in the following ways:

- Modifying the project's property pages.
- Using the #Const directive in the beginning of the code file.
- Using the /define (/d for short) option with the command-line Visual Basic .NET compiler, vbc.exe.

Step by Step 12.6 demonstrated conditional compilation with DEBUG and TRACE symbols. You can also use conditional compilation with any other custom defined symbols to perform conditional compilation, as you want.

GUIDED PRACTICE EXERCISE 12.1

In this exercise, you will add an EventLogTraceListener to the Factorial Calculator program so that it writes all Trace and Debug messages to the System event log.

This exercise will give you a good practice on using trace listeners. I would recommend that you should first attempt doing this exercise on your own, if you would later like to see one of the possible solutions, follow these steps.

1. In Solution Explorer, right-click StepByStep12-3.aspx and select Copy. Right-click your project and select Paste. Rename the pasted Web Form to GuidedPracticeExercise12-1.aspx. Open the aspx (HTML view) and vb files of the new Web Form and change all references to StepByStep12_3 to refer to GuidedPracticeExercise12_1 instead.

2. Add the following code to the Page_Load event handler:

```
Private Sub Page_Load( _
 ByVal sender As System.Object, _
 ByVal e As System.EventArgs) Handles MyBase.Load
    If Not IsPostBack Then
        ' Add an event log listener tion
        DiagnosticTrace.Listeners.Add( _
                  New EventLogTraceListener( _
         "FactorialCalculator"))
    End If
End Sub
```

3. Set the Web Form as the start page for the project.

4. Run the project. Enter a value for finding factorial. Click the Calculate button. Close the program. Select View, Server Explorer in Visual Basic .NET. Navigate to your computer, and expand the Event Logs, Application, FactorialCalculator node. You will see that the messages generated by Trace and Debug classes have been added to the Application event log as shown in Figure 12.13.

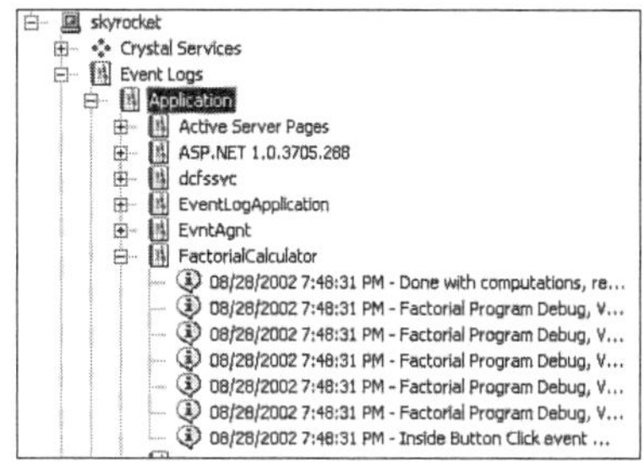

FIGURE 12.13
Viewing the System Event Log from Server Explorer.

REVIEW BREAK

- The System.Web.TraceContext class can be used to display trace messages in an application. These messages can be easily viewed by using the trace viewer or at the end of the page output. ASP.NET displays various page request details along with custom trace messages displayed by you.

continues

continued

- Tracing can be enabled at the application-level by setting the trace element enabled attribute to true in the application-wide web.config file. To enable tracing for an individual page, set the trace attribute to true in the Page directive.
- The Trace and Debug classes from System.Diagnostics can be used to display informative messages in an application when the DEBUG and TRACE symbols are defined respectively at the time of compilation.
- By default, both TRACE and DEBUG symbols are defined in the Debug Configuration for compilation and only the TRACE symbol is defined for the Release configuration of compilation.
- Listeners are objects that receive trace and debug output. By default, there is one listener attached to the Trace and Debug classes, DefaultTraceListener, that displays the messages in the Output window.
- Debug and Trace objects share the same Listeners collection. Therefore any Listener added to the Trace.Listeners collection will also be added to the Debug.Listeners collection.
- Trace switches provide a mechanism that allows you to change the type of messages traced by a program depending upon the value stored in XML configuration file. You need not recompile the application for this change to take effect, just restart it. You need to implement code to display the messages depending up on the value of the switch.
- Visual Basic .NET preprocessor directives allow you to define and undefine symbols in an application, report errors or warnings, mark regions of code, and allow you to conditionally skip code for compilation.
- Conditional attribute allows you to conditionally add or skip a method for compilation depending on the value of the symbol passed as a parameter to the attribute.

DEBUGGING

Debug, rework, and resolve defects in code

- **Configure the debugging environment.**

Debugging is the process of finding the cause of errors in a program, locating the lines of code causing the error, and then fixing those errors.

Without good tools, the process of debugging can be very time-consuming and tedious. Thankfully, Visual Studio .NET comes loaded with a large set of tools to help you with various debugging tasks.

Due to the compiled nature of ASP.NET applications, the process of debugging Web applications is almost the same as the process of debugging any other managed application. To enable debugging in an ASP.NET application be sure that the debug attribute of the <compilation> element in the web.config file is set to true.

```
<compilation>
     debug="true"
</compilation>
```

NOTE

Runtime Errors and Compile-time Errors Compile-time errors are produced when a program does not comply with the syntax of the programming language. These errors are trivial to find and are generally pointed out by compilers themselves. Runtime errors occur in those programs that are compiled successfully but do not behave as expected. The process of testing and debugging applies to runtime errors only. Testing reveals these errors and debugging repairs them.

WARNING

Applications Will Run Significantly Slower in Debug Mode When debugging is enabled for an application, the compiler will include extra debugging information in the page, creating a large executable file that executes slowly. When you deploy your application make sure you set the debug attribute in the <compilation> element in the web.config file to false.

Setting Breakpoints and Stepping Through Program Execution

A common technique for debugging is the step-by-step execution of a program, sometimes called *stepping*. This systematic execution allows you to track the flow of logic to ensure that the program is following the path of execution that you expect it to follow. If there is a difference, you can immediately identify the location of problem.

Stepping also gives you an opportunity to monitor its state before and after a statement is executed. This includes checking the values in variables, the records in a database, and other changes in environment. Visual Studio .NET provides you tools to make these tasks convenient.

The Debug menu provides three options for step execution of a program, as listed in Table 12.6. The Keyboard shortcuts listed in the table correspond to the Visual Basic settings of the Visual Studio IDE.

If you have personalized the keyboard scheme either through the Tools, Options, Environment, Keyboard menu or through the VS.NET Start Page, you might have a different keyboard mapping. You can check out the keyboard mappings available for your customization through VS.NET's context sensitive help.

TABLE 12.6

DEBUG OPTIONS FOR STEP EXECUTION

Debug Menu Item	*Keyboard Shortcut*	*Purpose*
Step Into	F8	Executes the code in step mode. If a method call is encountered, the program execution steps into the code of the function and executes the method in step mode.
Step Over	Shift+F8	Use this key when a method call is encountered and you do not want to step into the method code. When this key is pressed the debugger will execute an entire method without any step-by-step execution (interruption) and then step to the next statement after the method call.
Step Out	Ctrl+Shift+F8	Use this key inside a method call to execute the rest of the method without stepping and resume step execution mode when the control reaches back to the calling method.

Breakpoints are markers in the code that signal the debugger to pause execution as soon as it encounters one. Once the debugger pauses at a breakpoint, you can take your time to analyze variables, data records, and other settings in environment to determine the state of the program. You can choose to execute the program in step mode from this point onward.

If you have placed a breakpoint in the Click event handler of a button, the program will be paused when you click the button and the execution reaches the point where you have marked the breakpoint. You can now step through the execution for rest of the event handler. Once the handler code is over, control will be transferred back to the form under execution. This time if the user clicks another button and if you don't have a breakpoint set in its event handler, then the program is no longer under step execution. Be sure to insert breakpoints wherever you want execution to pause for debugging.

STEP BY STEP

12.7 Setting Breakpoints and Performing Step-by-Step Execution

1. In Solution Explorer, right-click `StepByStep12-3.aspx` and select Copy. Right-click your project and select Paste. Rename the pasted Web Form to `StepByStep12-7.aspx`. Open the `aspx` (HTML view) and `vb` files of the new Web Form and change all references to `StepByStep12_3` to refer to `StepByStep12_7` instead.

2. Add the following method to the class:

```
Private Function Factorial( _
 ByVal intNumber As Integer) As Integer
    Dim intFac As Integer = 1
    Dim i As Integer
    For i = 2 To intNumber
        intFac = intFac * i
    Next
    Factorial = intFac
End Function
```

3. Modify the `Click` event handler of `btnCalculate` to the following:

```
Private Sub btnCalculate_Click( _
 ByVal sender As System.Object, _
 ByVal e As System.EventArgs) _
 Handles btnCalculate.Click
    Dim intNumber, intFactorial As Integer
    Try
        intNumber = Convert.ToInt32(txtNumber.Text)
        intFactorial = Factorial(intNumber)
        txtFactorial.Text = intFactorial.ToString()
    Catch ex As Exception
        Debug.WriteLine(ex.Message)
    End Try
End Sub
```

4. In the preceding event handler, right-click the beginning of the line that makes a call to the Factorial method and select Insert Breakpoint from the context menu. You will note that the line of code is highlighted with red and also a red dot appears on the left margin as in Figure 12.14. You can alternatively create a breakpoint by clicking the left margin next to a line of code.

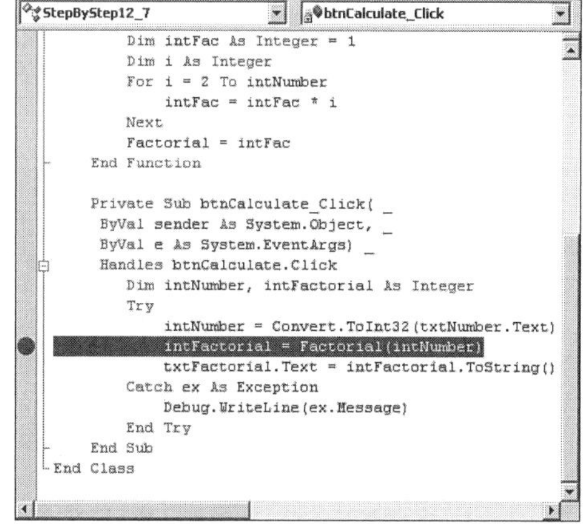

FIGURE 12.14
Setting a breakpoint.

continues

5. Set the Web Form as the start page for the Project.

6. Run the project. Enter a value and click the Calculate button. You will note that the execution pauses at the location where you have marked the breakpoint. You will also see an arrow on the left margin of the code as shown in Figure 12.15. This arrow points to the next statement to be executed.

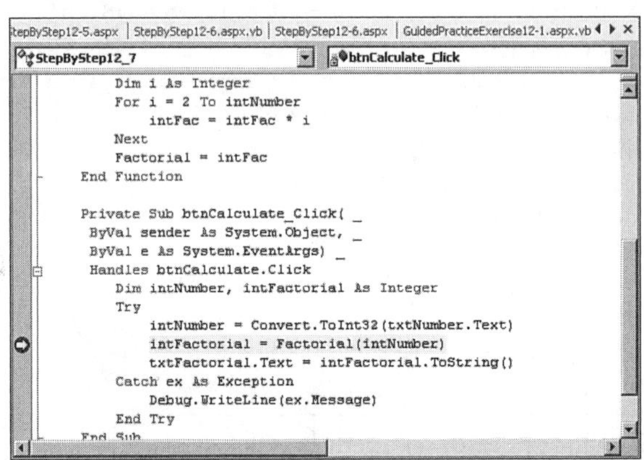

FIGURE 12.15
Stepping through a program's execution.

> **NOTE**
>
> **Disassembly Window Shows Assembly Code Instead of MSIL**
> Although Visual Basic .NET programs are compiled to the MSIL, they are Just-in-Time compiled to native assembly code only at the time of their first execution. This means the executing code is never in IL, it is always in native code. Thus you will always see native code instead of IL in the Disassembly window.

7. Press the F8 key to step into the code of Factorial function. Hover the mouse-pointer over various variables in the Factorial function. You will see the current values of the variables.

8. Select Debug, Windows, Breakpoints. This will open up the Breakpoints window as shown in Figure 12.16. Right-click the breakpoint listed in the window and select, Goto Disassembly. This will open up the diassembler, showing you the object code of the program along with the disassembled source code.

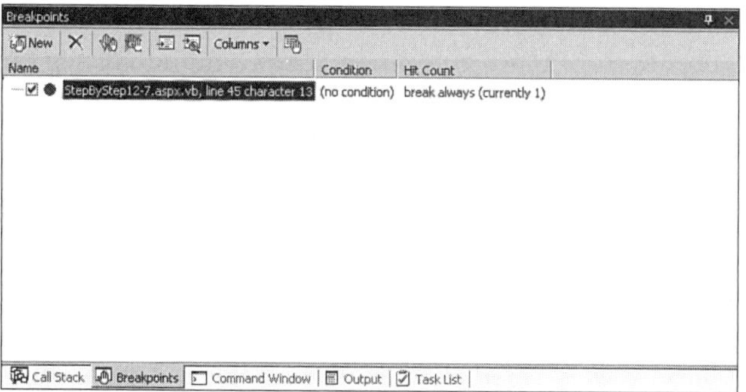

FIGURE 12.16
The Breakpoints window gives you convenient access to all breakpoint-related tasks at one place.

> NOTE
> **Debug Configuration** Breakpoints and other debugging features are only available when you run your project using the Debug configuration.

9. Close the Disassembly window. From the Debug menu, select Step Out to automatically execute the rest of the factorial function and start the step mode again in the event handler at the next statement. Step through the execution until you see the form again.
10. Select Stop Debugging from the Debug menu. This will end the debugging session and close the Web page.
11. In the code view, right-click the statement where you have set the breakpoint and select Disable Breakpoint from the context menu.

> NOTE
> **Disabling Versus Removing a Breakpoint** When you remove a breakpoint, you lose all information related to it. Alternatively, you can choose to disable the breakpoint. Disabling a breakpoint will not pause the program at that point but still, Visual Basic .NET will remember the breakpoint settings. At any time you can select Enable Breakpoint to reactivate the breakpoint.

For setting advanced options in a breakpoint, you can choose to create a new breakpoint by selecting this option from the context menu of the code or from the toolbar in the Breakpoints window. The New Breakpoint dialog box as shown in Figure 12.17 has four different tabs that allow you to set a breakpoint in a function, in a file, at an address in the object code and when the data value (value of a variable) changes.

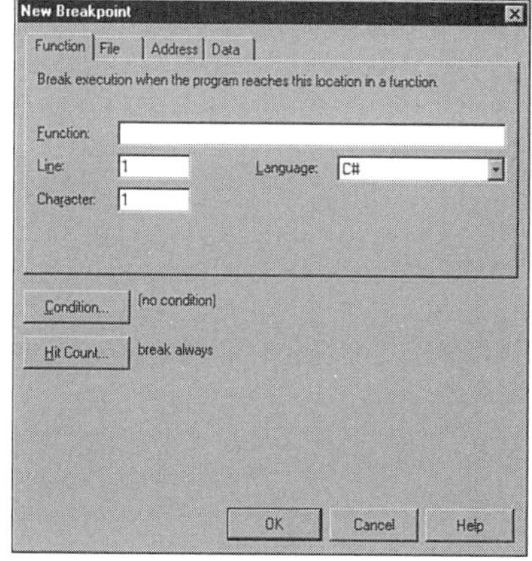

FIGURE 12.17
New Breakpoint dialog box.

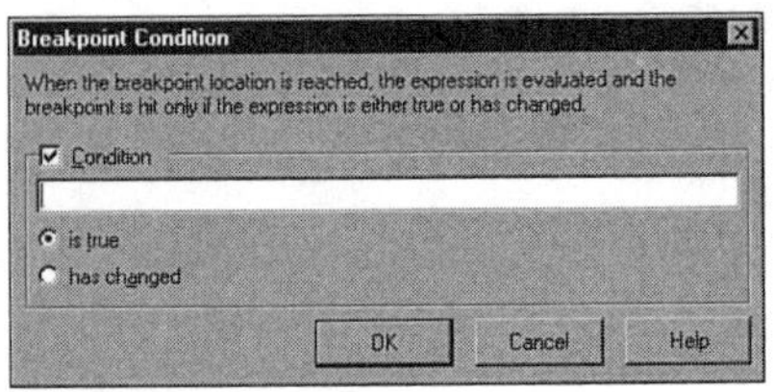

FIGURE 12.18
Breakpoint Condition.

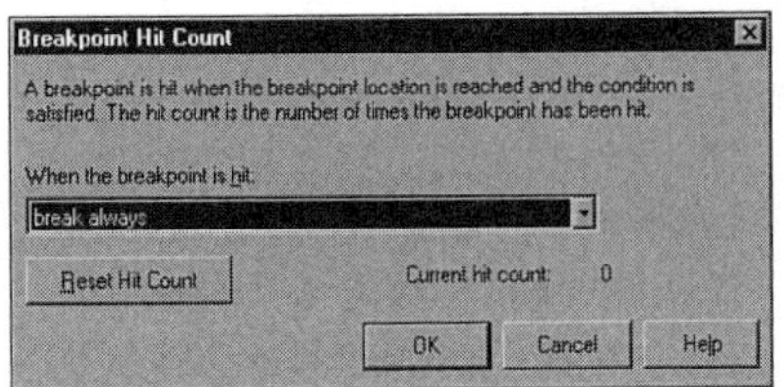

FIGURE 12.19
Breakpoint Hit Count.

Clicking the Condition button will open a Breakpoint Condition dialog box, as shown in Figure 12.18. The Condition dialog box allows you to set a breakpoint that is based on a value of an expression at runtime.

Clicking the Hit Count button will open a Hit Count dialog box, as shown in Figure 12.19. This dialog box gives you a facility to break the program execution only if the specified breakpoint has been hit a given number of times. This can be especially helpful if you have a breakpoint inside a lengthy loop and you want to step-execute the program only toward the end of the loop.

Analyzing Program State to Resolve Errors

Debug, rework, and resolve defects in code: Resolve errors and rework code.

When you break the execution of a program, you have a program at a particular state in its execution cycle. You can use various debugger tools to analyze the values of variables, result of expressions, path of execution, and so on, to help you identify the cause of error that you are debugging.

Step by Step 12.8 demonstrates the usage of various Visual Basic .NET debugging tools such as the Watch, Autos, Locals, Me, Immediate, and the Call Stack windows.

STEP BY STEP

12.8 Analyzing Program State to Resolve Errors

1. In Solution Explorer, right-click `StepByStep12-7.aspx` and select Copy. Right-click your project and select Paste. Rename the pasted Web Form to `StepByStep12-8.aspx`. Open the `aspx` (HTML view) and `vb` files of the new Web Form and change all references to `StepByStep12_7` to refer to `StepByStep12_8` instead.

2. Change the code in the Factorial method to the following (note that I have introduced a logical error that I will later "discover" through debugging):

```
Private Function Factorial( _
 ByVal intNumber As Integer) As Integer
    Dim intFac As Integer = 1
    Dim i As Integer

    For i = 2 To intNumber + 1
        intFac = intFac * i
    Next
    Factorial = intFac
End Function
```

3. Set the Web Form `StepByStep12_8` as the start page for the project.

4. Run the project. Enter a value `5` in the text box and click the calculate button. Hmmm…the result is not correct; this program needs to be debugged.

5. Set a breakpoint in the `Click` event handler of `btnCalculate` at the line where a call to Factorial function is being made. Execute the program, enter the value `5` again, and click the Calculate button.

6. Press the F8 key to step into the Factorial function. Select Debug, Windows, Watch, Watch1 to add a watch window. Similarly, select the Debug, Windows menu and add the Locals, Autos, Me, Immediate and Call Stack Windows. Pin down the windows so that they always remain in view and are easy to watch as you step through the program.

7. Look at the Call Stack window shown in Figure 12.20. It shows you the method call stack, giving you information about the path taken by the code to reach at its current point of execution. The currently executing method is at the top of the stack pointed by a yellow arrow. When this method quits, the next entry in the stack will be the method receiving the control of execution.

continues

continued

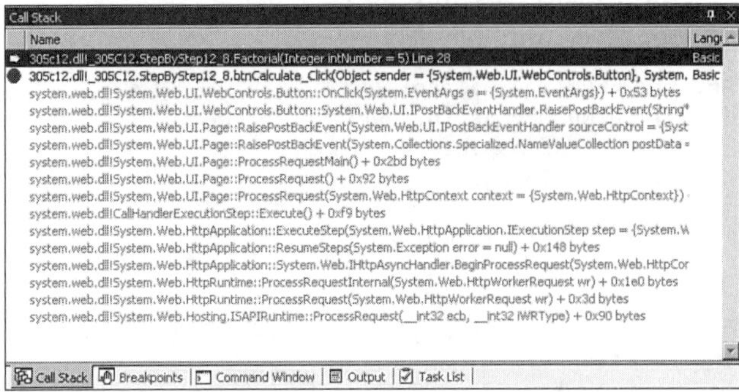

FIGURE 12.20
Call Stack window.

8. Next, look at the Me window shown in Figure 12.21. This will allow you to examine the members associated with the current object (the Web Form). You can scroll down to find txtNumber object. If you need you can change the values of these objects here. Though you don't need to change values at this point.

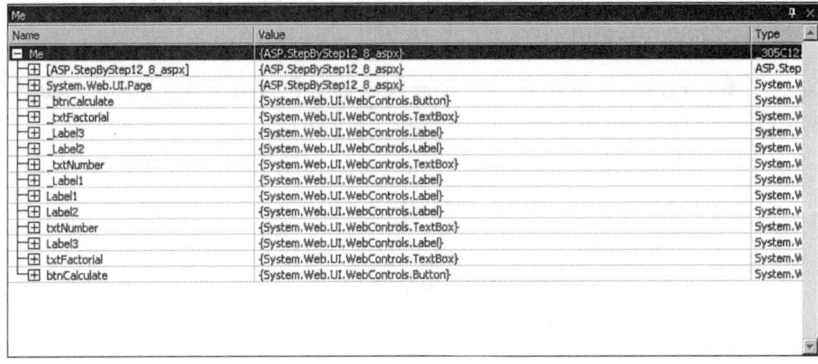

FIGURE 12.21
This window.

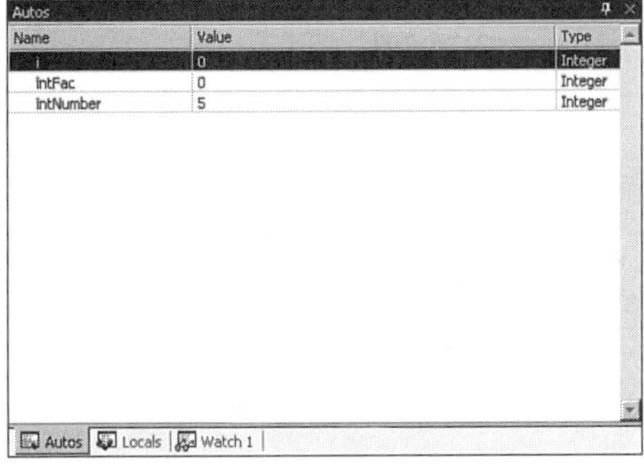

FIGURE 12.22
Autos window.

9. Activate the Autos window shown in Figure 12.22. It displays the variables in the current statement and in the previous statement. Debugger determines this for you automatically, therefore the name of this window is Autos.

10. Next, invoke the Locals window shown in Figure 12.23. It displays the variables local to the current context (the current method under execution) with their current values. The figure shows the local variables in the Factorial method.

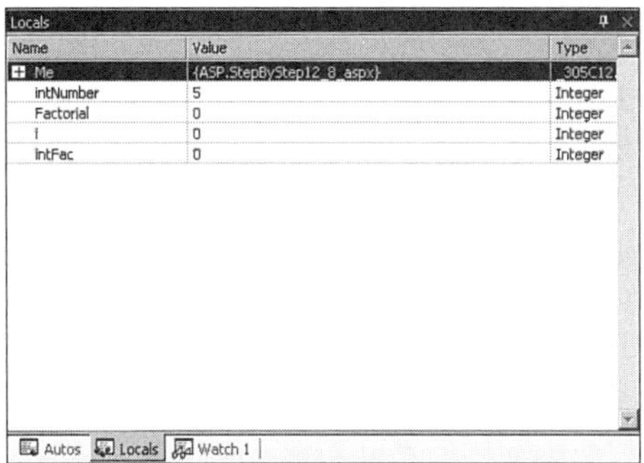

FIGURE 12.23
Locals window.

> **NOTE**
>
> **Two Modes of Command Window**
> The Command window has two modes, the command mode and the immediate mode. When you invoke the command window from View, Other Windows, Command Window, it is invoked in command mode. In command mode, the window can be used to issue commands such as Edit to edit text in file. You can use regular expressions with Edit command to make editing operations extremely quick and effective. The command window shows you a > prompt (see Figure 12.24).
>
> On the other hand when you invoke the Command window from Debug, Window, Immediate menu option, you can use it to evaluate expressions in the currently debugged program. The immediate mode does not show any prompt. You can switch from the immediate mode to command mode by typing >cmd and can switch from command mode to immediate mode by typing `immed` command (see Figure 12.24).

11. Now, activate the Immediate window. Type `?intNumber` and press Enter. The current value of this variable will immediately be evaluated and displayed in the next line. Now type the expression `Factorial(intNumber)`. The immediate window will call the Factorial function for given value and print the result. So this Immediate window can be used to print values of variables and expressions while you are debugging the program.

12. Finally, invoke the Watch1 window. Select the variable `intFac` in the code and drag and drop in the Watch1 window. You can also double-click the next available row and add a variable to it. Add the variables `i` and `intNumber` to the Watch1 window shown in Figure 12.25.

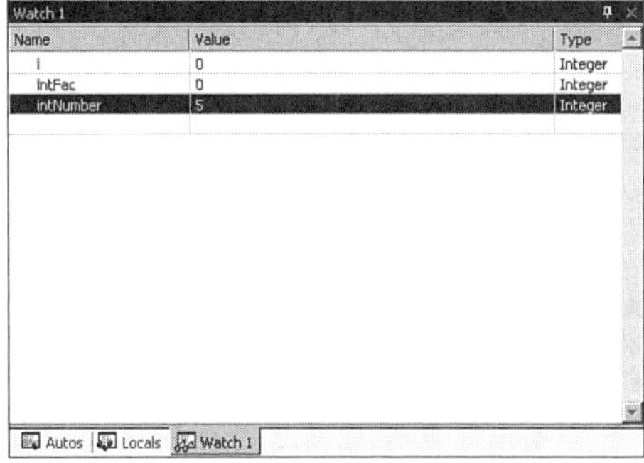

FIGURE 12.25
Watch window.

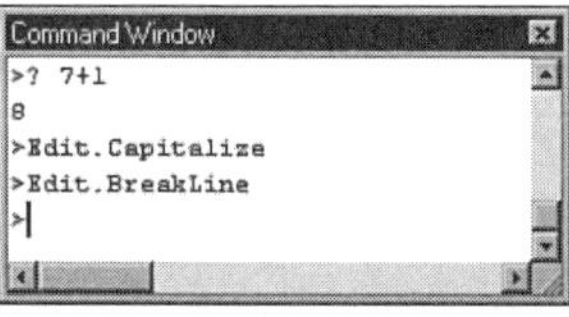

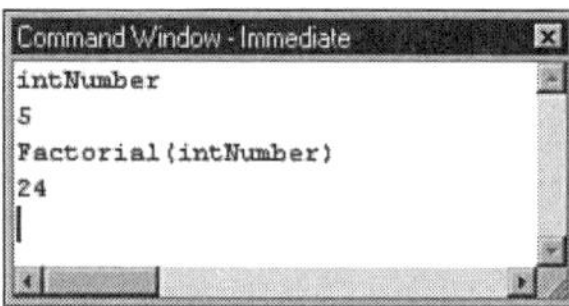

FIGURE 12.24
Two modes of the Command window.

continues

continued

13. Step through the execution of the program by pressing the F8 key, and keep on observing the way value changes in the Watch1 (or Autos or Locals Window). After a few steps the method will terminate but you will note that it only executes until the value of `i` is 4; the loop is not iterated back when the value of i is 5. And that's the cause of the wrong output in your program.

14. Change the condition in the For loop to use `intNumber` rather than `intNumber + 1` as the ending condition and press F8 to step through. You will see the Unable to Apply Code Changes dialog box as shown in Figure 12.26. The dialog box appears because after you have identified the problem and corrected the code, the source code is different from the compiled version of the program. If you choose to continue at this stage, your source code and program in execution are different and this may mislead you. I would recommend to always restart the execution in this case. Click the Restart button. The code will be recompiled and the program will be started again.

15. Enter the value `5` and click the Continue button. The program will break into debugger again because the breakpoint is still active. Step through the program and watch the value of variables. The loop will be executed for the correct number of times and you will get the correct factorial value.

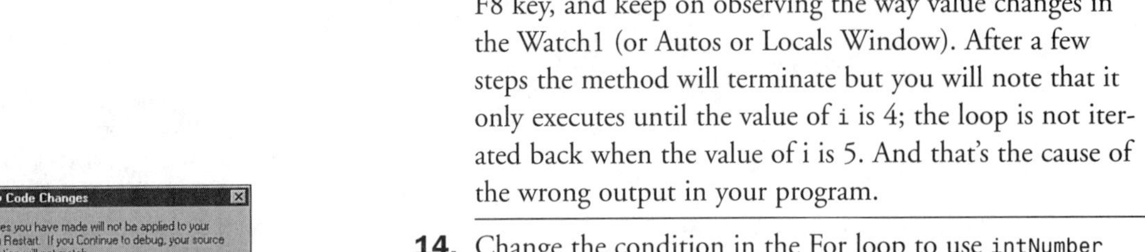

FIGURE 12.26
Unable to Apply Code Changes dialog box.

> NOTE
>
> **Support for Cross-Language Debugging** Visual Studio .NET supports debugging the projects that contain code written in several managed languages. The debugger can transparently step in and step out from one language to another making the debugging process smooth for you as a developer. Visual Studio .NET also extends this support to nonmanaged languages too but with minor limitations.

Debugging on Exceptions

You can control the way the debugger behaves when it encounters a line of code that throws an exception. You can control this behavior through the Exceptions dialog box shown in Figure 12.27, which is invoked from the Debug, Exceptions menu option. The Exception dialog box allows you to control the debugger's behavior for each different type of exception defined in the system. In fact, if you have defined your own exceptions, you can also add them to this dialog box.

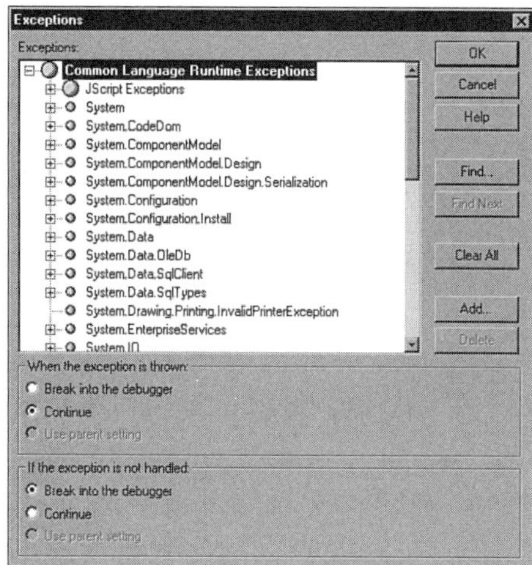

FIGURE 12.27
The Exceptions dialog box.

There are two levels at which you can control behavior of the debugger for exceptional code:

- **When the exception is thrown** You can instruct the debugger to either continue or break the execution of program when an exception is thrown. The default setting for CLR exceptions is to continue the execution possibly in the anticipation that there will be an exception handler.
- **If the exception is not handled** If the program that you are debugging fails to handle an exception, you can instruct the debugger to either ignore it and continue or break the execution of program. The default setting for CLR exceptions is to break the execution alarming the programmer for a possible problematic situation.

GUIDED PRACTICE EXERCISE 12.2

The Factorial Calculator created in Step by Step 12.6 throws exceptions of type System.FormatException and System.OverflowException when users are not careful about the data that they enter.

continues

continued

The later versions of this program (Step by Steps 12.7 and 12.8) catch the exception so that the users don't complain about the annoying exception messages. In this exercise you will configure the debugger in Step by Step 12.8 so that when the reported exception occurs you get an opportunity to analyze the program.

This exercise will give you a good practice on configuring the exception handling for the VS.NET debugger environment. I would recommend that you should first attempt doing this exercise on your own, if you would later like to see one of the possible solutions, follow these steps:

1. Set the Web Form StepByStep12-8 as the start up page for the project.
2. Activate the Exceptions dialog box by selecting Debug, Exceptions.
3. On the Exceptions dialog box, click the Find button. Enter System.FormatException and click OK. This will quickly take you to the desired exception in the exception tree view.
4. In the When the Exception is Thrown group box, select Break into the Debugger.
5. Repeat the preceding two steps for System.OverFlowException.
6. Run the project, enter a non-numeric value for finding factorial. This will cause a System.FormatException and debugger will prompt you to either break or continue the execution. Select Break. You can now note the values of various variables at this stage either by taking the mouse pointer over them or by adding the variables to the watch window. On the next run of the program, enter a very large value. This will cause System.OverFlowException; select Break when prompted by the debugger and analyze the value of various variables.

Debugging a Running Process

Until this point, you have only seen debugging programs by starting them from the VS.NET environment. The Visual Studio .NET debugging environment also allows you to debug the processes that are running outside the debugging environment. This feature can be quite helpful for debugging already deployed applications.

When a Web page is requested from the Web server, the ASP.NET worker process (aspnet_wp.exe) serves the request. To debug a running page you need to attach the VS .NET debugger to the aspnet_wp.exe process running on the Web server. In addition to this you also need to open the source files for the Web page in VS .NET and set a breakpoint in it at the desired location. Once this debugging setup is done, when you interact with the already running Web page, it will break into the debugger whenever the breakpoint is hit. Step by Step 12.9 demonstrates how to attach a debugger to a process under execution.

STEP BY STEP

12.9 Attaching a Debugger to a Process in Execution

1. Launch Internet Explorer. Navigate to `http://localhost/305C12/StepByStep12-8.aspx` (you can change `localhost` to the name of your Web server).

2. Start a new instance of Visual Studio .NET. Select Tools, Debug Processes. You will now see the Processes dialog box as shown in Figure 12.28. Change the Name field to point to the Web server used in Step 1. Make sure you check the Show system processes option. In the Available Processes list, you may have different processes from what is shown in the figure, but in particular you want to look for a process named aspnet_wp.exe.

continues

continued

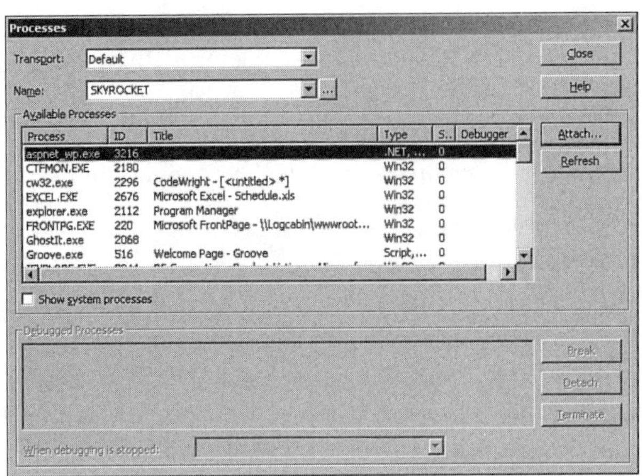

FIGURE 12.28
The Processes dialog box.

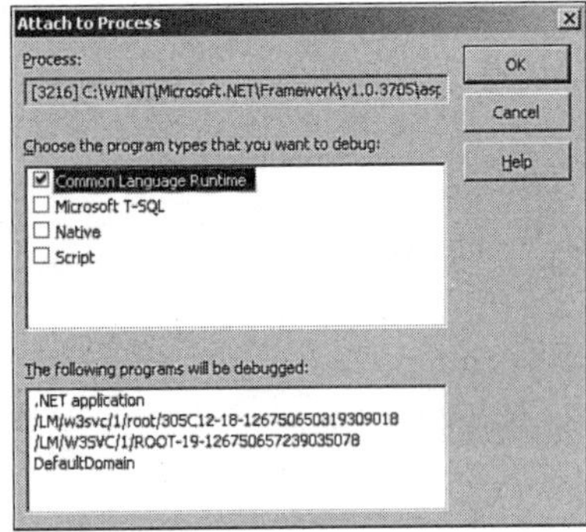

FIGURE 12.29
Attach to Process dialog box.

3. Select the process named `aspnet_wp.exe` and click the Attach button. This will invoke an Attach to Process dialog box as shown in Figure 12.29. Select the Common Language Runtime as your program type. Click the OK button. You will now see the selected process in the Debugged Processes section of the Processes dialog box. Click the Close button to close the Processes dialog box for now.
4. Now open `StepByStep12_8.aspx.vb` file in the new instance of VS.NET. Set a breakpoint on the line of code making a call to the Factorial method.
5. Enter a value 5, in the running Web Form and click the Calculate button. You will see that debugger will break the execution when the breakpoint is reached.
6. Use Watch, Locals, Autos windows to analyze variables and step through the program execution.
7. When the factorial result is displayed. Invoke Processes window again by select Debug, Processes. From the List of Debugged Processes, select `aspnet_wp.exe` and click the Detach button.

WARNING

Terminating aspnet_wp.exe The ASP.NET worker process (aspnet_wp.exe) processes requests from all ASP.NET applications. If after debugging you choose to terminate the aspnet_wp.exe process, it will affect all Web applications running on the server. You need to be especially careful when selecting this option on a production/shared server.

EXAM TIP

Don't Debug on a Production Server When you attach a debugger to the Aspnet_wp.exe process, it will freeze the execution of all other applications on that server. This may cause undesirable effects on a production server.

8. Click the Close button to dismiss the Processes dialog box. You will note that the Web Form StepByStep12_8.aspx is still executing as it was when you initiated the debugging process.

NOTE

Microsoft CLR Debugger(DbgClr.exe) The .NET Framework provides a tool called the Microsoft CLR Debugger (DbgClr.exe). This tool is based on Visual Studio .NET debugger and has almost the same features. This tool is especially useful if you are not using Visual Studio .NET for developing your applications and still want all the powerful GUI-based debugging capabilities.

Debugging a Remote Process

The process of debugging a Remote process is almost same as debugging an already running process. The only difference is that, prior to selecting a running process from the Processes dialog box, you must select the remote machine name from the Name list in the Processes dialog box.

Before you can debug a process remotely, you need to perform a one-time configuration on the remote machine (where the processes are running). You can do this in either of two ways:

- Install Visual Studio .NET on the remote machine.
- Install the Remote Components Setup on the remote machine (you can start this from the Visual Studio .NET Setup Disc 1).

The preceding steps will set up Machine Debug Manager (mdm.exe) on the remote computer. Mdm.exe will run as a background service on the computer and will provide remote debugging support. In addition to this, the above steps will also add the logged-on user to the Debugger Users group. You need to be a member of this group if you want to remotely access this computer. If the name is not added directly you can always add a username to this group by using the Computer Management MMC Snap-in. By default, the aspnet_wp.exe runs as a MACHINE process so you must also have Administrator privileges on the remote machine to debug it.

EXAM TIP

DCOM Error While Debugging If you get a DCOM configuration error while debugging, possibly you are not a member of the Debugger Users group on the remote machine.

If SQL Server is installed on the remote machine, the preceding setup process will also configure the machine for SQL Server Stored Procedures debugging. I'll demonstrate SQL Server Stored Procedure debugging in Exercise 12.2.

For a different configuration or requirement, you may like to refer to the "Setting up Remote Debugging" topic in the VS .NET combined help collection.

Debugging Code in DLL Files

The process of debugging a DLL file for which you have the source code is similar to debugging a Web Form. There is one difference though; the code in a DLL file cannot be directly invoked, so you need to have a Web Form that calls various methods from the DLL files.

You typically need to take the following steps for debugging code in a DLL file:

- Launch the Web Form that uses the methods in the DLL file.
- Launch Visual Studio .NET and attach the debugger on the Web Form. Set a breakpoint where the method in DLL file is called. Continue with the execution.
- The execution will break when the breakpoint is reached. At this point, select Step Into from the Debug menu to step into the source code of DLL file. Execute the code in the DLL file in step mode while you watch the value of its variables.

In addition to this, if the code files are executing on a remote machine, make sure that the remote machine is setup with Remote Debugging support as explained in the previous section.

Debugging Client-side scripts

Visual Studio .NET also allows you to debug client-side scripts. The process still is similar to the process that I discussed earlier for ASP.NET Web forms. However, you must note the following points for client-side scripting:

- Client-side debugging only works with Microsoft Internet Explorer.
- You have to enable script debugging in Internet Explorer. To do this, select Tools, Internet Options. Select the Advanced tab and uncheck the Disable script debugging option in the Browsing section.

- Attach the debugger to the iexplore.exe process displaying the Web Form. This is only required if you are debugging an already running process. While attaching the process, in the Attach to Process dialog box make sure you also select the Script option.

REVIEW BREAK

- Debugging is the process of finding the cause of errors in a program, locating the lines of code causing the error, and then fixing those errors.
- The three options available while performing step-by-step execution are Step Into, Step Over, and Step Out.
- Breakpoints allow you to mark code that signals the debugger to pause execution when it encounters them. When code is paused, you can choose to continue step-by-step execution with Step Into, Step Over, or Step Out. You can also resume normal execution by pressing F5 or clicking the Continue button.
- The various tool windows like This, Locals, Autos, Watch, Call Stack can be of great help in tracking the execution path and the status of variables in the process of debugging an application in Visual Studio .NET.
- When an exception is thrown by an application, you can choose to either continue execution or break into debugger (start debugging operations like step-by-step execution). You can customize this behavior for each exception object using the Exceptions dialog box.
- You can attach a debugger to a running process (local or remote) with the help of Processes dialog box.

CHAPTER SUMMARY

KEY TERMS

- Debugging
- Testing
- Tracing

The chapter started by discussing the various types of tests and how important testing is for an application. You learned that designing and executing a comprehensive test plan is desirable to ensures that application is robust, correct, and reliable.

The .NET Framework provides various classes and techniques to instrument tracing in Web applications. Tracing helps in displaying informative messages during execution of the program.

The System.Web.TraceContext class can be used to display trace messages in an application. These messages can be easily viewed by using trace viewer or at the end of the page output. ASP.NET displays various Web page request details along with custom trace messages displayed by you.

The Trace and Debug classes of System.Diagnostics namespace provide different methods to generate messages at specific location in the code. Classes derived from the TraceListener class process these messages, by default these messages are displayed in the Output window. You also saw how Trace switches could be applied to an application to give you a control over the type of tracing information generated by an application without even recompiling the application. Later in the chapter, I discussed various preprocessor directives available in Visual Basic .NET. You also saw how methods could be conditionally compiled using Conditional attribute.

The compiler helps in removing the syntactical errors at compile-time itself. The tough job is to find logical and runtime errors in the application. Visual Basic .NET offers some powerful tools for debugging. In this chapter, you've seen a broad survey of various tools available for debugging. You also saw how to debug an already running process, debug from a remote machine, debug DLL files, debug client-side scripts, and debug SQL Server stored procedures. As you continue to work with Visual Basic .NET, you'll discover more benefits from debugging in all of these areas.

APPLY YOUR KNOWLEDGE

Exercises

12.1 Creating a Custom Trace Switch

The TraceSwitch and BooleanSwitch classes are two built-in classes that provide trace switch functionality. If you need different trace levels or different implementation of Switch class you can inherit from Switch class and implement your own custom trace switch.

In this exercise I show you how to create custom switch. I will create a FactorialSwitch class that can be set with four values—Negative (-1), Off (0), Overflow (1), and Both (2)—for the Factorial Calculator form. The class has will have two properties, Negative and Overflow.

Estimated Time: 25 minutes.

1. Create a Visual Basic ASP.NET Web application and name it 305C12Exercises.

2. Add a new class to the project. Name the class FactorialSwitch and modify the class definition with the following code:

```
Imports System
Imports System.Diagnostics

Public Enum FactorialSwitchLevel
    Negative = -1
    Off = 0
    Overflow = 1
    Both = 2
End Enum

Public Class FactorialSwitch
    Inherits Switch

    Public Sub New( _
     ByVal DisplayName As String, _
     ByVal Description As String)
        MyBase.New(DisplayName, _
         Description)
    End Sub

    Public Property Negative() As Boolean
        Get
                            ' Return true if
            ' the SwitchSetting
            ' is Negative or Both
            If ((SwitchSetting = -1) Or _
             (SwitchSetting = 2)) Then
                Return True
            Else
                Negative = False
            End If
        End Get
        Set(ByVal Value As Boolean)

        End Set
    End Property

    Public Property Overflow() As Boolean
        Get
            ' Return true if
            ' the SwitchSetting
            ' is Overflow or Both
            If ((SwitchSetting = 1) Or _
             (SwitchSetting = 2)) Then
                Return True
            Else
                Negative = False
            End If
        End Get
        Set(ByVal Value As Boolean)

        End Set
    End Property
End Class
```

3. Add a new Web Form to the project. Name it Exercise12-1.

4. Place two TextBox controls (txtNumber and txtFactorial), three Label controls, and a Button control (btnCalculate) to the Form and arrange the controls as shown in Figure 12.2.

5. Switch to code view. Add the following line of code at the top of the module:

```
Imports System.Diagnostics
```

APPLY YOUR KNOWLEDGE

6. Add the following code to the Click event handler of the btnCalculate control:

```
Private Sub btnCalculate_Click( _
 ByVal sender As System.Object, _
ByVal e As System.EventArgs) _
 Handles btnCalculate.Click
    Dim facSwitch As FactorialSwitch = _
     New FactorialSwitch( _
     "FactorialTrace", _
    "Trace using Factorial Switch")
    Dim intNumber As Integer = _
     Convert.ToInt32(txtNumber.Text)

    If facSwitch.Negative Then
        ' Make a debug assertion
        Debug.Assert(intNumber >= 0, _
         "Invalid value", _
         "negative value in debug mode")
    End If

    Dim intFac As Integer = 1
    Dim i As Integer
    Try
        For i = 2 To intNumber
            intFac = intFac * i
        Next
    Catch ex As Exception
        If (facSwitch.Overflow) Then
            ' Write a debug message
                      Debug.WriteLine( _
             "There was an overflow", _
             "Factorial Program Debug")
        End If
    End Try
    txtFactorial.Text = intFac.ToString()

End Sub
```

7. Open the web.config file from the solution explorer. Insert the <system.diagnostics> element after the <system.web> element definition in the <configuration> element (that is in between the </system.web> and </configuration> element) as shown here:

```
<configuration>
   <system.web>
   ...
       </system.web>
    <system.diagnostics>
        <switches>
                                <add name="Factorial-
Trace"
                    value="2" />
        </switches>
    </system.diagnostics>
</configuration>
```

8. Set the Web Form as the start page for the project.

9. Run the project using the default Debug configuration. You will notice that Negative assertion dialog box is displayed only if the switch is set with the value –1 or 2. Similarly, the Overflow message is displayed in the Output window only if the switch value is set to 1 or 2.

10. Modify the program to change all Debug statements to the System.Diagnostics.Trace statements. Run the project using Release configuration. Experiment modifying the FactorialTrace switch value with different possible values.

The value set in the configuration file can be accessed through the SwitchSetting property of the Switch class. The property's Negative and Overflow properties return True or False depending upon the value of the SwitchSetting property.

12.2 Debugging SQL Server Stored Procedures Using Visual Basic .NET

Yes, you can even perform step-by-step execution of SQL Server Stored Procedures in Visual Basic .NET. This exercise shows you how to perform debugging with stored procedures.

Estimated Time: 30 minutes.

1. Add a new Web Form Exercise12-2.aspx to the project.

APPLY YOUR KNOWLEDGE

2. Right-click the project in the Solution Explorer and select Properties from the context menu. Select Debugging under the Configuration Properties node in the left pane of the Property Pages window. In the right pane, in the Debuggers section, check the box to enable SQL Server Debugging as shown in Figure 12.30.

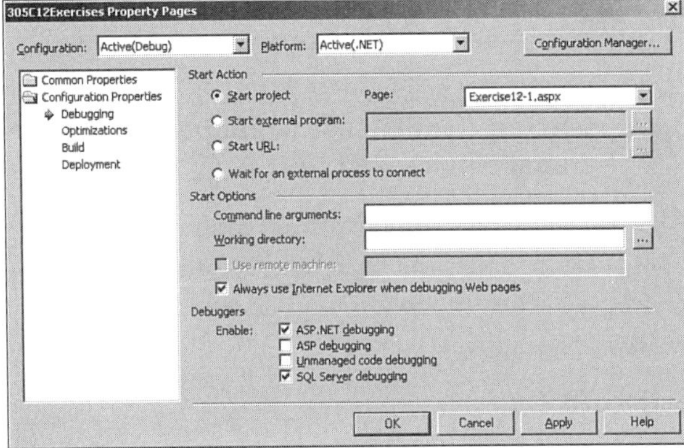

FIGURE 12.30
Property pages showing Debugging properties.

3. Drag a SqlDataAdapter component from the Data tab of the Toolbox to the form. This will activate the Data Adapter Configuration Wizard. Click Next. Select the Northwind database connection already created in the earlier chapters (Chapters 5 and 6) or click the New Connection button to create a Northwind database connection. Click Next.

4. Choose "Use existing stored procedures" option in the Choose a Query type page. Click Next. Select "Ten Most Expensive Products" from the select combo box as shown in Figure 12.31. Click Next and then Finish. This will create SqlConnection and SqlDataAdapter components in the component tray.

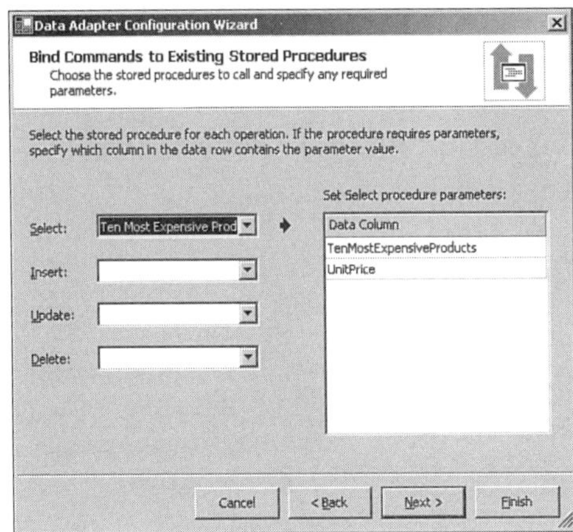

FIGURE 12.31
Bind commands to Existing Stored Procedures.

5. Select the SqlDataAdapter1 component, right-click and select Generate DataSet from the context menu. Create a new DataSet1 and choose the Ten Most Expensive Products from the checked listbox. Click OK and this will create a DataSet11 component in the component tray.

6. Place a Button control(btnGetProducts) and a DataGrid control(DataGrid1) on the form. Change the DataSource property of the DataGrid control to DataSet1 and the DataMember property to Ten Most Expensive Products.

7. Add the following code to the Click event of the Button control:

```
Private Sub btnGetProducts_Click( _
 ByVal sender As System.Object, _
 ByVal e As System.EventArgs) _
 Handles btnGetProducts.Click
    SqlDataAdapter1.Fill(Me.DataSet11)
End Sub
```

8. Insert a Breakpoint in the Click event handler, at the place of the call to the Fill method of the SqlDataAdapter1 object.

APPLY YOUR KNOWLEDGE

9. Open the Server Explorer, open the Data Connections node, select the Stored Procedure Ten Most Expensive Products. Right-click the Stored Procedure and select Edit Stored Procedure. Insert a Breakpoint in the starting code line of the Stored Procedure as shown in Figure 12.32.

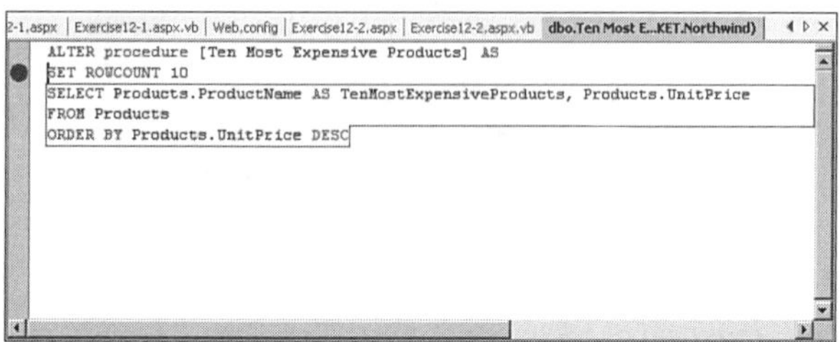

FIGURE 12.32
Property pages showing Debugging properties.

10. Set the Web Form as the start page for the project.

11. Run the project. Click the button. You will notice that the program starts step-by-step execution as soon as it encounters a breakpoint in the Fill method call line. Press F8. You will be taken to the stored procedure code where you can perform step-by-step execution.

This exercise teaches you how to debug SQL Server Stored Procedures using step-by-step execution. In Figure 12.32, you will notice Select statement enclosed in blue outline, this represents each step in the stored procedure (if the step occupies more than a line) that you can execute in step mode.

> **EXAM TIP**
>
> **Watching SQL Server Variables**
> You can use various tools like Watch and Locals windows to keep track of the values of the variables defined in the Stored Procedures during its step-by-step execution. These tools will prove to be of great help while debugging complex stored procedures.

12.3 Setting Conditional Breakpoints Using Visual Basic .NET

This exercise shows you how to set conditional breakpoints. I'll set a breakpoint in the Factorial calculation that breaks when the Factorial value overflows (that is, it becomes negative).

Estimated Time: 30 minutes.

1. Add a new Web Form Exercise12-3 to the project.

2. Place two TextBox controls (txtNumber and txtFactorial), three Label controls, and a Button control (btnCalculate) to the Form and arrange the controls as shown in Figure 12.2.

3. Add the following code to the Click event handler of the btnCalculate control:

```
Private Sub btnCalculate_Click( _
 ByVal sender As System.Object, _
 ByVal e As System.EventArgs) _
 Handles btnCalculate.Click
    Dim intNumber As Integer = _
     Convert.ToInt32(txtNumber.Text)

    Dim intFac As Integer = 1
    Dim i As Integer
    For i = 2 To intNumber
        intFac = intFac * i
    Next
    txtFactorial.Text = intFac.ToString()
End Sub
```

APPLY YOUR KNOWLEDGE

4. Set a breakpoint on the line shown below in the button click event handler. Then right-click on the line and select Breakpoint Properties from the context menu.

```
intFac=intFac*i
```

This will open the Breakpoint Properties dialog box. Select the File tab. You will note that File, Line, and Character position are already marked correctly. Click the Condition button. This will open the Breakpoint Condition dialog box. Set the values in the dialog box as shown in Figure 12.33. Select the Condition checkbox. Enter "intFac < 1" in the Condition text box and select "is true" option. Click OK twice to dismiss the New Breakpoint dialog box.

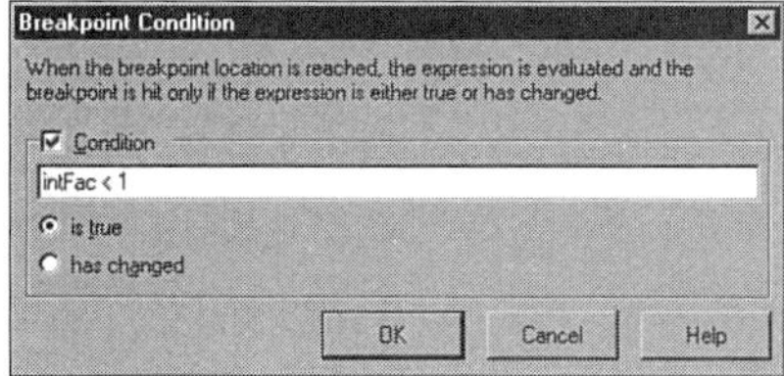

FIGURE 12.33
Setting Conditional Breakpoints with Breakpoint Condition dialog box.

5. Set the Web Form as the start page for the project.
6. Run the project using the default Debug configuration. Enter a bigger number, say 50, and click the Calculate button. You will notice that the running page will break into debugger when intFac has a negative value when the breakpoint is reached.

Review Questions

1. What is the use of a test plan?
2. What types of tracing can be implemented in ASP.NET?
3. What is the main purpose of the TraceListener class? What are the classes that implement TraceListener in the Framework Class Library?
4. What are the two built-in trace switches in the .NET Framework class library?
5. What is the main advantage of trace switches?
6. What types of methods can be marked with the Conditional attribute?
7. What is the purpose of the #const preprocessor directive?
8. What are the three commands for stepping through code while debugging?
9. What happens when you put a breakpoint in your code?
10. Name some of the different tool windows available for debugging.
11. How can you attach the debugger to a running process in Visual Basic .NET?
12. In order to verify that remote debugging is enabled on a system, what should you check?

APPLY YOUR KNOWLEDGE

Exam Questions

1. Which of the following correctly defines a typical unit test?

   A. Locate and fix errors.

   B. Run the application with carefully planned test data and check if it works according to its specification.

   C. Run a module with carefully planned test data and check if it works according to its specification.

   D. Verify that a program module integrates well with other modules in an application.

2. You want to view the trace output for your Web application. The Web application root directory is at http://localhost/myapplication. Which of the following URL would you type in the Internet Explorer to view the trace result for this application?

   A. http://localhost/myapplication?trace=true

   B. http://localhost/myapplication/trace

   C. http://localhost/myapplication?trace=ON

   D. http://localhost/myapplication/trace.axd

3. While debugging your ASP.NET Web Form you want to display the trace messages as part of the Page execution details. Which of the following commands should you use? (Select two.)

   A. TraceContext.Write

   B. TraceContext.Warn

   C. System.Diagnostics.Trace.Write

   D. System.Diagnostics.Debug.Write

4. You are developing a Web application using Microsoft Visual Studio .NET. You have included the following line at the top of the source code.

   ```
   #const TRACE
   ```

   Which of the following statements are true with respect to program execution? (Select all that apply.)

   A. You will see the trace messages while running the program in the Debug configuration.

   B. You will see the trace messages while running the program in the Release configuration.

   C. You will only see the trace messages generated by the methods of Debug class.

   D. You will not see any trace messages.

5. You have added the following statement to the Load event handler of a single-page Web application.

   ```
   Trace.Listeners.Add( _
    New TextWriterTraceListener( _
    "TraceLog.txt"))
   ```

   Which of the following statements are true with respect to program execution? (Select all that apply.)

   A. TextWriterTraceListener will listen to all messages generated by the methods of Debug and Trace classes.

   B. TextWriterTraceListener will listen only to the messages generated by the methods of Trace classes.

   C. All the trace messages will get stored in a file named “TraceLog.txt”.

   D. The trace messages are displayed in the Output window while running the program in either Debug or Release configurations.

APPLY YOUR KNOWLEDGE

6. In your Visual Basic .NET program you have the following lines of code

```
Dim myTraceSwitch As TraceSwitch = _
New TraceSwitch("SwitchOne", _
 "The first switch")
myTraceSwitch.Level = TraceLevel.Info
```

Which of the following expressions in your program will evaluate to false?

A. myTraceSwitch.TraceInfo

B. myTraceSwitch.TraceWarning

C. myTraceSwitch.TraceError

D. myTraceSwitch.TraceVerbose

7. You want to control the tracing and debug output of a Web application without recompiling your code. Which of the following classes will enable you to do this?

A. TraceListener

B. TraceSwitch

C. Trace

D. Debug

8. You are given a task to implement tracing in a Web application such that the application displays both warning and error messages when the application is run using the Debug configuration and should only display error message when run using the Release configuration of Visual Basic .NET. Which of the following code segment best solves this requirement?

A.

```
Dim ts As TraceSwitch = Nnew TraceSwitch( _
 "MySwitch", "Error and Warning Switch")

#If DEBUG
   ts.Level = TraceLevel.Warning
#Else
   ts.Level = TraceLevel.Error
#End If

Trace.WriteLineIf( _
 ts.TraceWarning, "Warning Message")
Trace.WriteLineIf( _
 ts.TraceError, "Error Message")
```

B.

```
Dim ts As TraceSwitch = Nnew TraceSwitch( _
 "MySwitch", "Error and Warning Switch")
#If DEBUG
   ts.Level = TraceLevel.Warning
#else
   ts.Level = TraceLevel.Error
#End If

Debug.WriteLineIf( _
 ts.TraceWarning, "Warning Message")
Debug.WriteLineIf( _
 ts.TraceError, "Error Message")
```

C.

```
Dim ts As TraceSwitch = Nnew TraceSwitch( _
 "MySwitch", "Error and Warning Switch")

#If TRACE
   ts.Level = TraceLevel.Warning
#else
   ts.Level = TraceLevel.Error
#End If

Trace.WriteLineIf( _
 ts.TraceWarning, "Warning Message")
Trace.WriteLineIf( _
 ts.TraceError, "Error Message")
```

D.

```
Dim ts As TraceSwitch = Nnew TraceSwitch( _
 "MySwitch", "Error and Warning Switch")

#If TRACE
   ts.Level = TraceLevel.Error
#Else
    ts.Level = TraceLevel.Warning
#End If

Trace.WriteLineIf( _
 ts.TraceWarning, "Warning Message")
Trace.WriteLineIf( _
 ts.TraceError, "Error Message")
```

APPLY YOUR KNOWLEDGE

9. The configuration file of a Web application has the following contents:

```
<system.diagnostics>
   <switches>
      <add name="BooleanSwitch"
           value="-1" />
      <add name="TraceLevelSwitch"
           value="33" />
   </switches>
</system.diagnostics>
```

You are using the following statements to create switch objects in your code:

```
Dim bSwitch As BooleanSwitch = _
New BooleanSwitch( _
"BooleanSwitch", "Boolean Switch")
Dim tSwitch As TraceSwitch = _
 New TraceSwitch("TraceLevelSwitch", _
 "Trace Switch")
```

Which of the following options is correct regarding the values of these switch objects?

A. bSwitch.Enabled property is set to false and tSwitch.Level is set to TraceLevel.Verbose.

B. bSwitch.Enabled property is set to true and tSwitch.Level is set to TraceLevel.Verbose.

C. bSwitch.Enabled property is set to false and tSwitch.Level is set to TraceLevel.Error.

D. bSwitch.Enabled property is set to false and tSwitch.Level is set to TraceLevel.Info.

10. You are developing a Web application. Your application's configuration files have the following code:

```
<system.diagnostics>
    <switches>
            <add name="TraceLevelSwitch"
         value="3" />
    </switches>
</system.diagnostics>
```

You have written the following tracing code in your program:

```
<Conditional("DEBUG")> _
Private Sub Method1()
    Trace.WriteLineIf(ts.TraceError, _
     "Message 1", "Message 2")
End Sub

<Conditional("TRACE")> _
Private Sub Method2()
    Trace.WriteLine("Message 3")
End Sub

Private Sub btnCalculate_Click( _
 ByVal sender As Object, _
 ByVal e As, System.EventArgs)
Dim ts As TraceSwitch = New TraceSwitch( _
 "TraceLevelSwitch", _
 "Trace the application")
    If ts.TraceWarning Then
        Trace.WriteLine("Message 10")
        Method1()
    Else
        Trace.WriteLineIf( _
         ts.TraceInfo, "Message 20")
        Method2();
    End If

    If (ts.TraceError)
        Trace.WriteLineIf( _
         ts.TraceInfo, "Message 30")
    End If
        Trace.WriteLineIf( _
     ts.TraceVerbose, "Message 40")
End Sub
```

What tracing output will be generated when you run your program in debug mode and click the btnCalculate button?

A.

```
Message 10
Message 1
Message 2
Message 30
```

B.

```
Message 10
Message 2: Message 1
Message 30
```

APPLY YOUR KNOWLEDGE

C.

```
Message 10
Message 2
Message 30
Message 40
```

D.

```
Message 20
Message 3
Message 30
Message 40
```

11. You have following segment of code in your program:

```
Dim tl As EventLogTraceListener = _
 new EventLogTraceListener("TraceLog")

Trace.Listeners.Add(tl)
Debug.Listeners.Add(tl)

Trace.WriteLine("Sample Message")
Debug.WriteLine("Sample Message")
```

When you debug the program through Visual Studio .NET, how many times will the message "Sample Message" be written to the TraceLog?

A. 1

B. 2

C. 3

D. 4

12. You are debugging a Web Form. The form involves long calculation and iterations. You want to break into the code to watch the value of variables whenever the value of intValue changes in the following statement:

```
intValue = ProcessValue(intValue)
```

Which of the following option will quickly allow you do achieve this?

A. Run the application using step execution mode. Use Step Out key to step out of execution from the ProcessValue function. Use the Immediate window to display the value of intValue before and after this line of code executes.

B. Set a Breakpoint at the given statement. Set the Hit Count option "break when hitcount is equal to" to 1.

C. Set the Breakpoint at the given statement. In the Breakpoint condition dialog enter intValue () intValue and check the "is true" option.

D. Set the Breakpoint at the given statement. In the Breakpoint condition dialog enter intValue and check the "has changed" option.

13. Which of the following statements are true for remote debugging of processes?

A. Both local as well as remote machine should have Visual Studio.NET installed.

B. Only the local machine needs Visual Studio.NET.

C. Remote Components setup is required on local machine.

D. Remote Components setup is required on the remote machine.

14. You are trying to debug a Web application using Visual Studio .NET installed on your local machine. The Web application is deployed on a remote server. When you attempt to debug the application, you get DCOM configuration error. Which step should you take to resolve this problem?

A. Add your account to the Power Users group on the local computer.

B. Add your account to the Power Users group on the remote computer.

APPLY YOUR KNOWLEDGE

C. Add your account to the Debugger Users group on the local computer.

D. Add your account to the Debugger Users group on the remote computer.

15. While you are debugging in Visual Studio .NET, you only want to watch the value of those variables that you are using in the current statement and its previous statement. Which of the following debugger window is the easiest way to watch these variables?

A. Autos

B. Locals

C. Me

D. Watch

16. You have developing a Web application for an airline's ticketing system. The Web Form in the Web application also has some client side scripting code written in JavaScript. You want to step through this code to understand its execution. Which of the following steps would you take? (Select three.)

A. Set breakpoint in the client side scripting code where you want the application to pause execution.

B. Attach the debugger to the aspnet_wp.exe process executing the Web Form.

C. Attach the debugger to the iexplore.exe process displaying the Web Form.

D. Enable script debugging in the Internet Explorer.

17. You are developing a Web application that heavily uses SQL Server stored procedures. You are debugging a Web Form that calls the YTDSales stored procedure. The stored procedure uses a variable named @Sales. You want to see how the value of this variable changes as the code in the stored procedure executes. Which of the following option will allow you to do this?

A. Use SQL Server PRINT command to display the value of @Sales variable at different places.

B. Use Debug.Write statement to print the value of @Sales variable.

C. Use Trace.Write statement to print the value of @Sales variable.

D. Use the Locals window to monitor the value of @Sales as you step through the stored procedure.

Answers to Review Questions

1. Test plan is a document that guides in the process of testing. The document clearly specifies the different approaches of testing, the test–cases, the validation criteria of the tests, and so on.

2. System.Web.Trace class and Trace and Debug classes of System.Diagnostics can be used to implement tracing in ASP.NET. Both the namespaces implement different types of tracing.

3. TraceListener is an abstract class that provides the functionality to receive trace and debug messages. DefaultTraceListener, TextWriterTraceListener and EventLogTraceListener are the three built-in classes that implement TraceListener.

APPLY YOUR KNOWLEDGE

4. BooleanSwitch and TraceSwitch.
5. You can easily change the value of trace switches by editing the application configuration (XML) file using any text editor. To bring these changes in effect, you need not recompile the application.
6. To apply Conditional attribute to a method, the method should be a Sub rather than a Function.
7. The #Const preprocessing directive lets you define a constant in code. This constant can only be used by other preprocessor directives, not by regular Boolean statements.
8. The three commands that allow you to step through code are Step Into (steps into each statement of the method called), Step Over (performs the entire method call in one step), and Step Out (step out of the method call).
9. When the debugger encounters a breakpoint in the code, it pause the execution of the application. The execution then can be resumed using through stepping commands.
10. Visual Studio .NET provides a variety of tools to ease debugging process like This, Locals, Autos, Watch, Immediate, Call Stack, and Breakpoints, and so on.
11. To attach the debugger to a running process open Visual Basic .NET, invoke the processes dialog, select the process from the list of processes, and click the Attach button. You also need to open the source file in Visual Studio .NET and set a break point in it.
12. You should verify that remote machine has Machine Debug Manager (mdm.exe) running as a background process to enable debugging support. You should verify that you are a member of "Debugger Users" group in order to remotely access the machine for debugging. You should also have Administrator privileges on the remote machine to perform remote debugging.

Answers to Exam Questions

1. **C.** A unit test involves running a module against carefully planned test data and check if it works according to its specification. The process of locating and fixing errors defines the process of debugging. When you run complete application against test data, you are performing system testing. Checking if the modules integrate well is a task that belongs to integration testing.
2. **D.** Once you have enabled tracing for a Web application, when each page in the application is requested, the trace statements in the Web page will be executed. You can view trace information in the trace viewer. You can view the trace viewer by requesting trace.axd from the application directory.
3. **A** and **B**. The trace messages written using TraceContext.Write and TraceContext.Warn can append your trace messages along with other tracing information of the current Web request to the page output. However, the trace messages written using Trace and Debug classes of System.Diagnostics namespace are written by default to the Output window.
4. **A** and **B**. When you define the TRACE symbol, you'll always see tracing messages, regardless of the configuration you use to run the program.

APPLY YOUR KNOWLEDGE

5. **A**, **C**, and **D**. When you add a listener to Trace.Listeners collection, it listens to the messages generated by both Trace and Debug classes. When the new listener is added it will get added to the Listeners collection, it already has a DefaultTraceListener that sends messages to the Output window, and it will be still active and listening to the Trace messages. Therefore, you will have messages in TraceLog.txt as well as on the Output window.

6. **D**. Setting the Level property of a TraceSwitch to TraceLevel.Info will allow it to capture all informational, warning, and error messages, but not the verbose messages. Thus the TraceInfo, TraceWarning, and TraceError properties of the switch will result to true but the TraceVerbose property will result to false.

7. **B**. The TraceSwitch class provides a multilevel switch that allows you to control tracing and debug output of a Web application without recompiling the code. The changes in behavior can be instrumented, by just changing the application's configuration file.

8. **A**. In this option, for the Debug configuration where DEBUG symbol is defined, the Level property of traceSwitch is set to TraceLevel.Warning. This will cause both TraceWarning and TraceError properties of this object to be true using the Debug configuration causing both the messages to be displayed. In the Release configuration where only TRACE symbol is defined, the Level property of traceSwitch is set to TraceLevel.Error. This will cause TraceWarning property to result a false value and TraceError property to return a true value causing only the error messages to be displayed.

9. **B**. For BooleanSwitch, a value of 0 corresponds to Off, and any nonzero value corresponds to On. For TraceSwitch any number greater than 4 is treated as Verbose. From the given values in the configuration file, the booleanSwitch object will have its Enabled property set as true and the traceSwitch object will have its Level property set to TraceLevel.Verbose.

10. **B**. The XML file has the value for the TraceLevelSwitch as 3, this will set the Level property as TraceLevel.Info. This will cause TraceError, TraceWarning, and TraceInfo properties of the traceSwitch to be true, only the TraceVerbose property will evaluate to false. Also, the third parameter to the WriteLineIf method is used to categorize the output by placing its value followed by a colon (:) and then the trace message.

11. **D**. The message SampleMessage will be written four times. This is because two instances of EventLogTraceListeners are added to the Listeners collection. So any message generated by Trace and Debug classes will be listened twice. Now the program is running in Debug mode so both Trace and Debug statements will get executed. The net effect is that Trace.WriteLine and Debug.WriteLine messages will be both written twice making it four entries in TraceLog.

12. **D**. When you want to break into the code when the value of a variable changes, the quickest approach is to set a conditional breakpoint where you specify the variable name and check the "has changed" option.

APPLY YOUR KNOWLEDGE

13. **B** and **D**. For remote debugging Visual Studio .NET is not required on the remote machine but in that case you need to run Remote Components setup on the remote machine. For local machine you need to have Visual Studio .NET to be able to debug the remote processes.
14. **D**. If you get a DCOM configuration error while debugging, possibly you are not the member of the Debugger Users group on the remote machine. To resolve this, add your account on the remote machine to the Debugger Users group.
15. **A**. The Autos windows gives you the most convenient access as it at every step displays name and values of all variables in the current statement and the previous statement.
16. **A**, **C** and **D**. To enable client-side script debugging, you need to set a breakpoint in the client-side script. In addition to this you will attach the debugger to the Iexplore.exe process running the Web Form. Also make sure to enable script debugging in Internet Explorer.
17. **D**. You can use the Locals window to keep track of the values of the variables defined in the Stored Procedures during its step-by-step execution.

Suggested Readings and Resources

1. ASP.NET QuickStart Tutorial
   - The Microsoft .NET Framework SDK Debugger
2. Visual Studio .NET Combined Help Collection
   - ASP.NET Trace.
   - Introduction to Instrumentation and Tracing.
   - Using the Debugger.
   - Debugging ASP.NET Applications.
3. Burton, Kevin. *.NET Common Language Runtime Unleashed*, Sams Publishing, 2002.

OBJECTIVES

This chapter covers the following Microsoft-specified objectives for the "Deploying a Web Application" section of the Visual Basic .NET Web Applications exam:

Deploy a Web application.

- Microsoft Visual Basic .NET ships with a new project category, Setup and Deployment projects. These projects contain templates that help in building user-friendly installation packages for different types of applications. This objective requires you to know how to create various Setup projects that help in deploying Web applications.

Create a Setup program that installs a Web application and allows for the application to be uninstalled.

- Visual Studio .NET creates installation packages based on the Microsoft Windows Installer technology. The Microsoft Windows Installer 2.0 takes care of handling the execution of tasks involved in installing, uninstalling, and repairing Windows applications. You have to just focus on what files need to be installed, where they should be located, what registry entries need to be made, what type of user interface should be displayed to the end user during the installation, and whether any custom code should be executed during the installation.

Add assemblies to the Global Assembly Cache.

- The .NET Framework allows you to place shared assemblies (assemblies intended to be used by more than one application) in a central location called the Global Assembly Cache (GAC). Assemblies that are placed in GAC must have a strong name. This objective requires you to know how to assign a strong name to an assembly and how to install files in the GAC on the target machine during deployment.

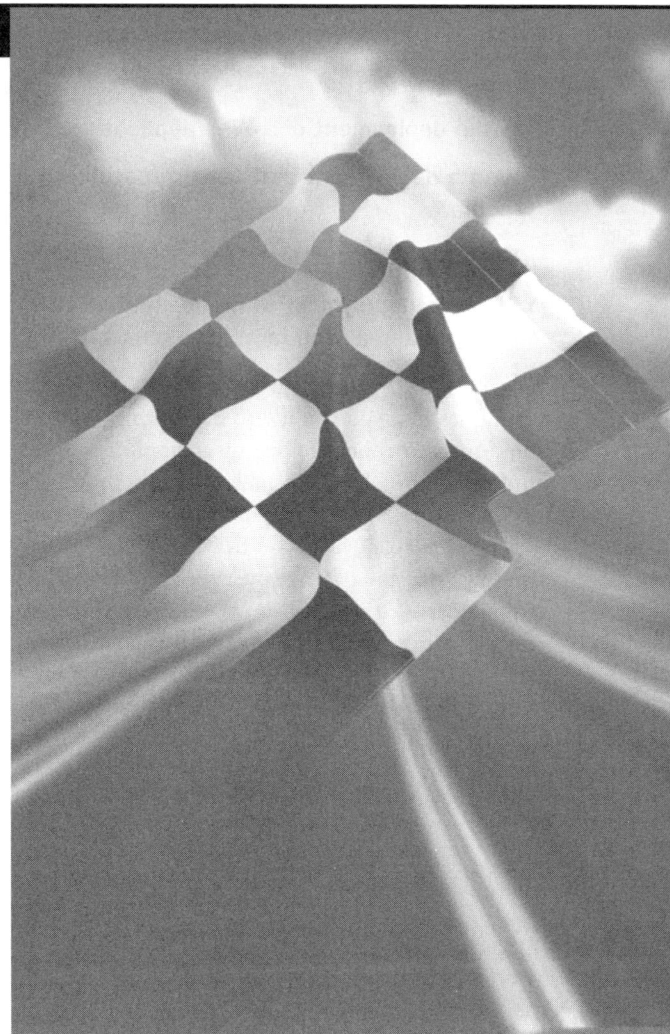

CHAPTER 13

Deploying a Web Application

Objectives

Plan the deployment of a Web application.

- **Plan a deployment that uses removable media.**
- **Plan a Web-based deployment.**
- **Plan the deployment of an application to a Web garden, a Web farm, or a cluster.**

▶ This objective requires you to know the various techniques that you can use to deploy your applications. You can choose to deploy an application through removable media such as floppy disks, CDs, or DVDs, or you can have your installation package available over the Web where the end user can download the package over the Internet. When deploying a Web application, you also need to consider scalability and reliability requirements. This may require deploying your application to a Web garden (multi-processor server), Web farm (multiple servers), or a cluster of Web servers.

Outline

Outline

Study Strategies

- Review the "Deployment Concepts" and the "Deploying Applications" section of the Visual Studio .NET Combined Help Collection.
- Experiment with using Setup projects and Merge Module projects to deploy Web applications. Understand when you should choose to create a Setup project rather than a Merge Module project.
- Work with the different editors available in the Setup and Merge Module projects and thoroughly understand the purpose of each of these editors.
- Experiment with the Strong Name Tool (sn.exe) to create a public/private key pair and then use the key pair to assign a strong name to an assembly. Work with the delay-signing feature and understand the scenarios in which it can be helpful.
- Experiment with placing assemblies in the Global Assembly Cache (GAC). Understand the steps performed by the runtime to locate assemblies.
- Experiment with the creation of a custom action to compile assemblies into machine specific code at install time.
- Understand the various ways to deploy a Web application, their benefits and shortcomings. Understand when you would use XCOPY or FTP deployment or a Windows Installer-based installation package.
- Understand the requirements of Windows Logo Program.

INTRODUCTION

Once you have developed and tested a Web application the next step is to deploy the application so that the end user can run it. The complexity and requirements of the application should be kept in mind in order to choose the right deployment tool. The .NET Framework simplifies the deployment model by making it possible to deploy simple applications by using nothing more than an XCOPY or FTP command. However, for applications that are packaged and shipped to the user, Microsoft recommends the use of Microsoft Windows Installer technology. With Web applications, of course, most users are simply downloading HTML from a Web server. Those are not the users that this chapter is concerned with. Rather, I'll be considering the situation where you're deploying a Web application to a new Web server. This might be the case, for example, when you're moving from a test server to a deployment server. It can also happen if you're selling a turnkey Web application (such as an e-commerce store or a discussion board) to external customers.

This chapter discusses how to use Visual Studio .Net to create Windows Installer-based Setup and Deployment projects. You'll learn about both Setup projects (used to package applications) and Merge Module projects (used to package shared components).

Chapter 7, "Creating and Managing .NET Components and Assemblies," introduced you to the concept of shared assemblies. Shared assemblies are components that are shared between several applications. In this chapter I'll delve into the details of creating and installing shared assemblies.

I'll also talk about various ways in which an application can be deployed. Web applications can have unusual deployment requirements to achieve reliability and scalability. I'll end the chapter with a look at the use of Web gardens, Web farms, and clustering to address these requirements.

Deployment Tools

A deployment tool helps you to set up an application on the user's computer. Choosing the right deployment tool is important because the correct tool will not only make the process of deployment simpler but will also minimize the total cost of ownership for the application's users. The choice of tool will also depend on the nature of your application. For installing simple applications, a tool as simple as the XCOPY or FTP command can be used. For sophisticated requirements, you may want to use a tool that creates a Windows Installer–based setup package for your application.

XCOPY Deployment

The .NET Framework simplifies deployment by making zero-impact install and XCOPY deployment feasible. For a .NET application that only uses managed code and private assemblies, the application can be installed by just copying all files to the desired destination. You do not need to create registry entries or copy files to the Windows system directory (thereby causing zero-impact on the configuration of user's computer).

However, there are scenarios where XCOPY is not sufficient as a deployment tool. Here is a list of some common installation tasks that are difficult or impossible to perform through an XCOPY command:

- Creating IIS sites or virtual directories
- Creating shortcuts
- Allowing users to select features during installation
- Copying files to relative paths on the target machine that differ from the paths on the source machine
- Adding assemblies to the Global Assembly Cache (GAC)
- Creating or configuring databases during the installation
- Adding custom event logs or performance counters to the target machine

- Checking whether the .NET Framework redistributable is installed on the target machine
- Presenting a user-friendly and branded user interface
- Allowing license key management and user registration

For the scenarios listed previously, the preferred alternative is to use Microsoft Windows Installer–based installation program instead of using XCOPY for deploying an application.

FTP Deployment

When you're deploying a Web application to a Web server to which you don't have a direct network connection, you can still achieve a simple file copy deployment by using FTP. If you have remote access via FTP to the directory on your Web server where an ASP.NET application is located, you can upgrade that application just by using FTP to copy the new version of the application over the old version.

ASP.NET is designed to allow this sort of passive upgrade without restarting an application. This is a consequence of the lifecycle of an ASP.NET page:

1. The page is initially deployed as MSIL code on the Web server.
2. The first time a user requests the page in her browser, the MSIL version is Just-in-Time compiled to native code. This JIT-compiled version generates the HTML that is delivered to the end user.
3. The JIT-compiled version is cached in memory by ASP.NET. Future requests for the page are satisfied by the cached version.
4. ASP.NET monitors the original source code and its dependencies. If any of these files change, the cached copy is invalidated. The next end-user request causes the page to be recompiled from the new sources.

FTP deployment is logically the same as XCOPY deployment; both are merely ways to move a file or set of files to a deployment location. FTP deployment suffers from the same lack of advanced features as XCOPY deployment. To satisfy advanced requirements, you'll still need to use the Windows Installer.

Microsoft Windows Installer

The Microsoft Windows Installer is an installation and configuration service built in to the Windows operating system. It gives you complete control over installation of an application, a component, or an update.

The Windows Installer includes many built-in actions for performing the installation process. In addition to the standard actions such as installing files, creating shortcuts to files, making Start menu entries, and writing registry entries, it also offers several advanced features, some of which are listed as here:

- Provides the ability to take custom actions while installing the application. For example, you might want to run a SQL script to install a database during the application installation.
- Provides "on-demand" installation of features. This capability allows the user to install a feature at a later stage that was not installed during the application's original installation. On-demand installation does not force the user to run the entire installation package just to add a single feature.
- Provides the ability to roll back an installation. The Windows Installer maintains an "undo operation" for every operation that was performed during an application installation. If it encounters any error while installing the application, it can uninstall everything that was installed during the installation.
- Allows uninstalling an application without breaking any other application which depends on it.
- Allows fixing an application or one of its components if they become corrupted. This way, users spend less time uninstalling and reinstalling an application.

The Windows Installer Service manages all installed components on a system by keeping a database of information about every application that it installs, including files, registry keys, and components.

When you create an installation program for the Windows Installer service, you will create a Windows Installer (.msi) package. This package includes a number of database tables that describes the application to the Windows Installer service. When this package is executed on the target machine, the Windows Installation service will install the program by reading the installation information stored in the Windows Installer package.

> NOTE
>
> **Microsoft Windows Installer**
> Although the Windows Installer Service is included in all current versions of Windows, you may need to install a redistributable to have its latest version. Later in this chapter you will see how to create a Windows Installer bootstrapper to ensure that the Windows Installer Service is updated (if necessary) on target machines.

> NOTE
>
> **Windows Installer Requirements**
> Windows Installer version 2.0 (the version used to install .NET applications) requires Windows NT 4.0 with Service Pack 6 or later, Windows XP, Windows .NET Server, Windows 2000, or Windows Me. Earlier Windows Installer versions require Windows NT 4.0 with Service Pack 3 or later, Windows XP, Windows 2000, or Windows Me. Windows Installer is also available as a redistributable for Windows NT 4.0, Windows 95, and Windows 98. It can be downloaded from `http://www.microsoft.com/msdownload/platformsdk/sdkupdate/psdkredist.htm`.

> NOTE
>
> **Using Windows Installer** Microsoft recommends the use of Windows Installer Service to install and configure .NET applications on an end user's system.

There are several ways to create a Windows Installer package. The most basic option is to manually create it using the Windows Installer SDK but for most practical requirements you should instead use a visual tool that can help you with the process. In this chapter, I will use Setup and Deployment Visual Studio .NET projects to create setup packages using the Windows Installer technology. A lot of people also use installation tools from independent vendors such as InstallShield or Wise Solutions. Specialized tools from these vendors provide you with a much higher level of customization and ease for creating Windows Installer–based setup programs.

CAB Files

When you create a setup project in Visual Studio .NET, you'll notice an option to create a CAB project. A CAB project is used to package a control in a cabinet file. Cabinet files are an older standard for delivering code over the Internet, designed to deploy ActiveX controls into a Web browser such as Internet Explorer.

In Visual Studio .NET, CAB files have been largely superseded by Windows Installer packages. CAB files are still used when delivering controls written using unmanaged C++ and technologies such as MFC or ATL. But you won't need to know the details of this method of deployment if you're using Visual Basic .NET.

DEPLOYING A WEB APPLICATION

Deploy a Web application.

Microsoft Visual Studio .NET allows you to create Windows Installer–based installation packages. It offers four types of deployment project templates:

- **Setup Project**: Used to create installation packages for deploying Windows-based applications.
- **Web Setup Project**: Used to create installation packages for deploying Web-based applications.
- **Merge Module Project**: Used to create installation packages for components that may be shared by multiple applications.

- **Cab Project**: Used to package ActiveX components so that they can be downloaded over the Internet.

Before you delve into the details of creating deployment projects with the help of Visual Studio .NET, you will sure need to create an application that can be deployed. In Step by Step 13.1, you will create a simple Windows application named WebSql that returns the result of any SELECT query from the SQL Server Northwind database. This application will then serve as a testbed for exploring various deployment features over the course of this chapter.

STEP BY STEP

13.1 Building an Application That Requires Deployment

1. Launch Visual Studio .NET. From the menu, select File, New, Blank Solution and name it `305C13`.

2. In the Solution Explorer window. Add a Visual Basic ASP.NET Web application project to the solution. Name the project `WebSql`.

3. Delete the default `WebForm1.aspx`. Add a new Web form named `WebSql.aspx`.

4. Open Server Explorer. Expand the tree under Data Connections to show a SQL Server data connection that points to the `Northwind` sample database. Drag and drop the data connection to the form. This will create a `SqlConnection1` object on the form. This object represents a connection to SQL Server. The `SqlConnection` object will use the name of the actual server that you chose in Server Explorer. If you'd like the deployed application to always look on the Web server's computer for an instance of SQL Server, use the Properties window to change the Data Source portion of the `ConnectionString` property to this string:

```
Data Source=(local)
```

continues

continued

5. Place a `TextBox` control with the `id` of `txtQuery`, a `TextBox` control with the `id` of `txtFile`, a `Button` control with the `id` of `btnLoad`, a `Button` control with the `id` of `btnExecute`, a `Label` control with the `id` of `lblError`, and a `DataGrid` control with the `id` of `dgResults` on the form. Set the `TextMode` property of `txtQuery` to `MultiLine`. Set the Visible property `lblError` to False.

6. Switch to code view. Add these statements at the top of the form's module:

```
Imports System.Data.SqlClient
Imports System.IO
```

7. Add the following code to the `Click` event handler of the `btnLoad` control:

```
Private Sub btnLoad_Click( _
 ByVal sender As System.Object, _
 ByVal e As System.EventArgs) Handles btnLoad.Click
    ' Load the specified file from the same folder
    ' where this page is located on the server
    Try
        Dim sr As StreamReader = _
         New StreamReader( _
          Server.MapPath(txtFile.Text))
        txtQuery.Text = sr.ReadToEnd()
        sr.Close()
    Catch ex As Exception
        lblError.Text = "Error loading query: " & _
         ex.Message
        lblError.Visible = True
    End Try
End Sub
```

8. Enter this code to execute the query when you click the `btnExecute` control:

```
Private Sub btnExecute_Click( _
 ByVal sender As System.Object, _
 ByVal e As System.EventArgs) Handles btnExecute.Click
    ' Create a SqlCommand to represent the query
    Dim cmd As SqlCommand = _
     SqlConnection1.CreateCommand()
    cmd.CommandType = CommandType.Text
    cmd.CommandText = txtQuery.Text
    ' Create a SqlDataAdapter to talk to the database
    Dim da As SqlDataAdapter = New SqlDataAdapter()
    da.SelectCommand = cmd
```

```
    ' Create a DataSet to hold the results
    Dim ds As DataSet = New DataSet()
    Try
        ' Fill the DataSet
        da.Fill(ds, "Results")
        ' And bind it to the DataGrid
        dgResults.DataSource = ds
        dgResults.DataMember = "Results"
        dgResults.DataBind()
    Catch ex As Exception
        lblError.Text = "Error executing query: " & _
         ex.Message
        lblError.Visible = True
    End Try
End Sub
```

9. Change the solution configuration to `Release` mode. Run the application. Enter a select query for the `Northwind` database in the textbox.

10. Click the Execute button. This will run the code, retrieving the results to the data grid, as shown in Figure 13.1.

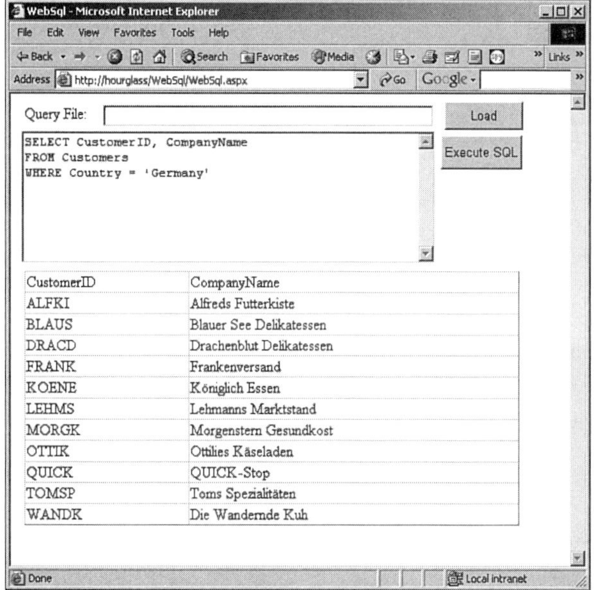

FIGURE 13.1
WebSql application returning SELECT query results from Northwind database.

continues

continued

11. Now you'll add few files that will be required when you deploy this application. Launch WordPad. Create a `ReadMe.rtf` file with the following text:

```
WebSql Version 1.0
This application allows you to SELECT data from the
Northwind database. Just type any valid SELECT
statement and you will see the results of the
query instantly!
```

12. Create another file with the name, `License.rtf` having the following text:

```
WebSql End User License Agreement
You should carefully read the following terms
and conditions before using this software.
If you do not agree to any of the terms of
this License, then do not install, distribute
or use this copy of WebSql.
This software, and all accompanying files,
data and materials, are distributed "AS IS"
and with no warranties of any kind, whether
express or implied. Good data processing
procedure dictates that any program be
thoroughly tested with non-critical data
before relying on it.  The user must assume
the entire risk of using the program.
© All rights reserved.
```

13. Add the two rtf files to your project by selecting Add, Existing Item in Solution Explorer. Browse to the files and then click OK.

Now that you have created an application, in the following section I will demonstrate how to create a setup project for installing this application.

Creating a Setup Project

Visual Studio .NET provides the Setup project template to create an installer for a Web application. It also provides a Setup Wizard that helps you in creating different types of setup and deployment projects using an interactive interface. Step by Step 13.2 guides through the process of creating a simple installer using the Setup Wizard for the WebSql application that you created in the previous exercise.

STEP BY STEP

13.2 Creating a Setup Project for the `WebSql` Project Using the Setup Wizard

1. In the Solution Explorer window, right-click Solution and select Add, New Project. Select Setup and Deployment projects from the Project Types tree and then select Setup Wizard from the list of templates on the right, as shown in Figure 13.2.

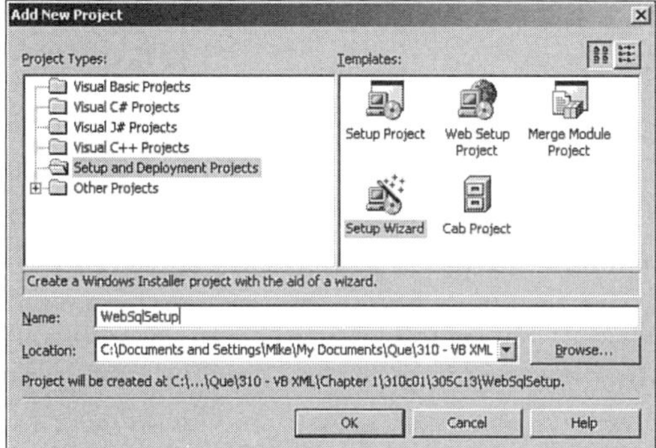

FIGURE 13.2
Adding new Setup Project via a Setup Wizard.

2. Name the project `WebSqlSetup`. Click OK. This will launch the Setup Wizard. The first screen that will appear is the Welcome screen. Click Next.

3. The second page will show the Choose a project type screen. Choose Create a Setup for a Web application in the first group of options as shown in Figure 13.3. Click Next.

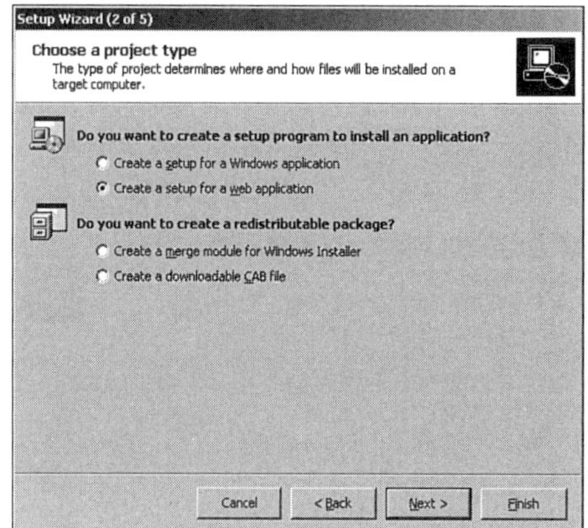

FIGURE 13.3
Choose a project type Setup Wizard screen.

4. The third page will show the Choose project outputs to include screen. Select Primary output from `WebSql` and Content Files from `WebSql` as shown in Figure 13.4. Click Next.

continues

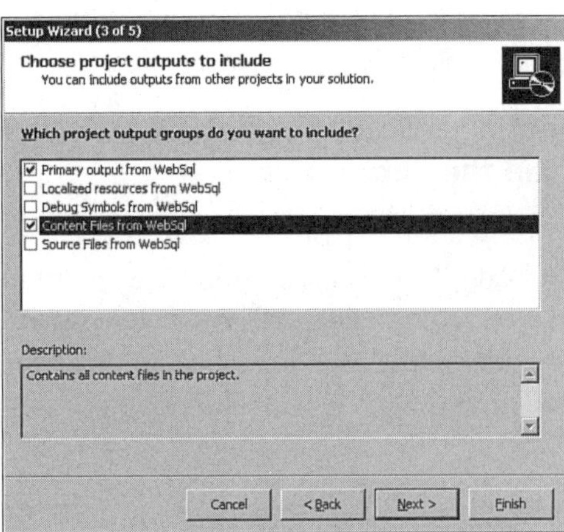

FIGURE 13.4▶
Choose project outputs to include Setup Wizard screen.

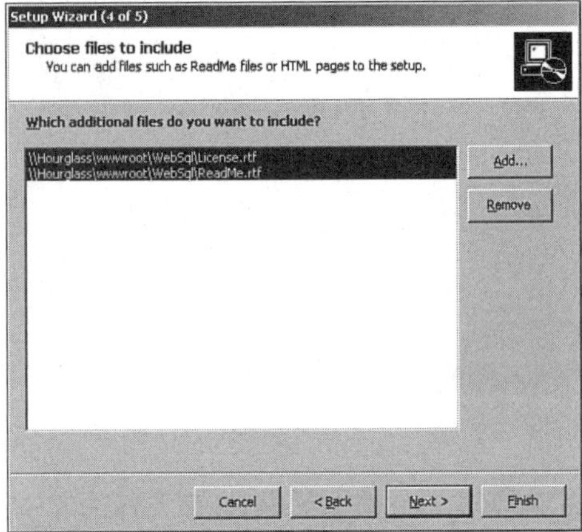

FIGURE 13.5▲
Choose files to include Setup Wizard screen.

5. The fourth page will show the Choose files to include screen. Click the Add button and include the `Readme.rtf` and `License.rtf` files from the `WebSql` project folder. After including the files the screen will appear as shown in Figure 13.5. Click Next.

6. The fifth and last page will show the Project Summary screen as shown in Figure 13.6. Click Finish to create the project.

7. Select the new project `WebSqlSetup` in Solution Explorer. Activate the Properties window. Set the `Manufacturer` to `WebSql Software`, `ProductName` to `WebSql`, and `Title` to `WebSql Installer`, as shown in the Figure 13.7.

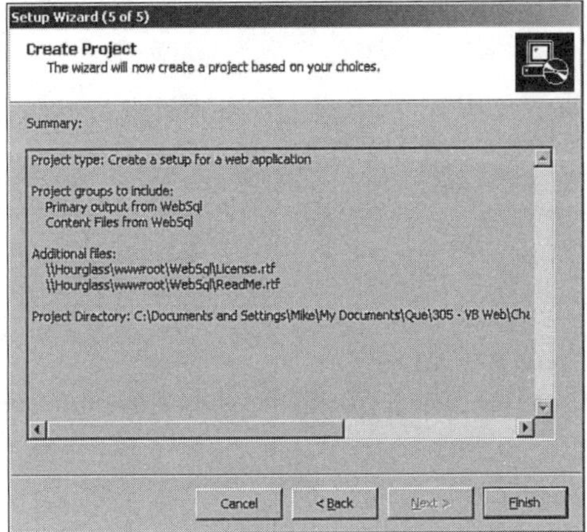

FIGURE 13.6▲
Project Summary Setup Wizard screen.

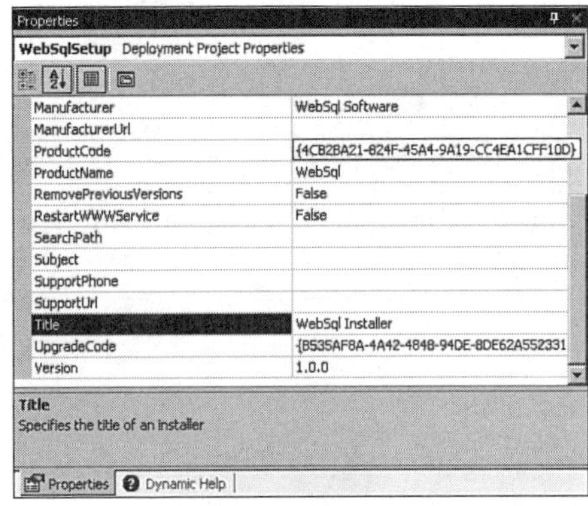

FIGURE 13.7▶
Project properties of the WebSqlSetup Deployment project.

8. Select the Web Application Folder node in the File System Editor. Change its `VirtualDirectory` property to `WebSql`.

9. Set the solution configuration to Release. Build the `WebSqlSetup` project. Open Windows Explorer and navigate to the `Release` folder inside the project folder. Run the `Setup.exe`. Alternatively, on the development machine, you can also install by right-clicking the project in the Solution Explorer and choosing the `Install` option from its context menu. This will open the `WebSql` Setup wizard with a Welcome screen. Click Next. The Select Installation Address screen will appear as shown in Figure 13.8. Select the default settings and click Next. Click Next again to start the installation. Click Close.

10. Open Internet Explorer and navigate to `http://localhost/WebSql/WebSql.aspx` (if you installed on a server other than the one where you're developing code, substitute the server name for `localhost`). Enter a query and click the button to get the results of the query.

11. Select Settings, Control Panel, Add/Remove Programs from the Windows Start menu to open the Add/Remove Programs dialog box. Select the Change or Remove Programs icon from the left pane and select `WebSql` application from the right pane. Click the Remove button to uninstall the WebSql application and click Yes. The `WebSql` application will be uninstalled from your application. Alternatively, on the development machine, you can also uninstall by right-clicking the setup project in the Solution Explorer and choosing the Uninstall option from its context menu.

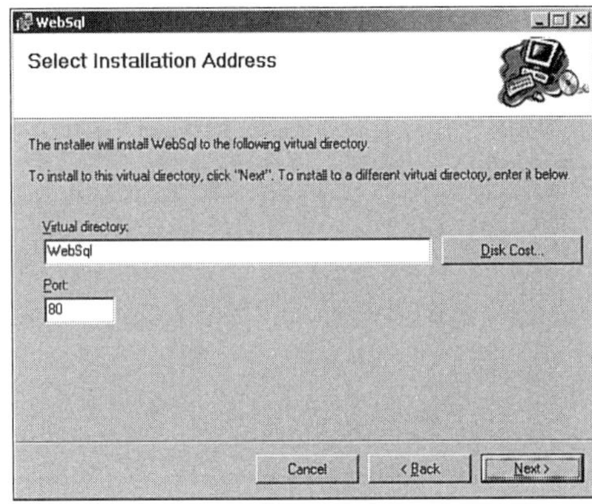

FIGURE 13.8
Select Installation Folder screen during installation process.

The previous exercise illustrated the process of creating a Setup project. When the project is compiled, the output files are placed in the Release or Debug folder, depending on the active configuration. The contents of the folder are an installer package (.msi), executables (.exe) and initialization (.ini) files. The .msi file is the installation package in the Microsoft Windows Installer format.

If the Windows Installer Service is installed on your computer, you can directly start the installation by double-clicking this file. The executable files consist of Setup.exe, InstMsiA.exe, and InstMsiW.exe. Setup.exe (also called the Windows Installer Bootstrapper) bootstraps the installation process by first testing for the presence of Windows Installer service on the target machine. If the Windows Installer service is not installed, the bootstrapper will first install it using either InstMsiA.exe (for Windows 9x and Me) or InstMsiW.exe (for Windows NT/2000/XP/.NET) and then will instruct the Windows Installer service to execute the installation based on the information stored in the installation package (.msi file). The setup.ini file stores the initialization settings such as name of the installation database, for the bootstrap file setup.exe.

But there is one catch here. This setup project will only work on the computers where the .NET Framework runtime has been already installed. In fact, when you build the setup project, you will see the following message in the Output window of Visual Studio .NET:

"WARNING: This setup does not contain the .NET Framework which must be installed on the target machine by running dotnetfx.exe before this setup will install. You can find dotnetfx.exe on the Visual Studio .NET 'Windows Components Update' media. Dotnetfx.exe can be redistributed with your setup."

On the other hand when you look at the Setup project folder in the Solution Explorer window, you will see that it had created a Detected Dependencies folder and included a file named "dotnetfxredist_x86_enu.msm" in it. But the Exclude property of this file is set to True. This is basically just a placeholder module that stops Visual Studio .NET from automatically including the .NET Framework files from your installation of the .NET Framework into the project. If you try changing the Exclude property of dotnetfxredist_x86_enu.msm file to False, Visual Studio .NET won't allow you and you will get an error at the time of building the project. The Error message would say "ERROR: dotNETFXRedist_x86_enu.msm must not be used to redistribute the .NET Framework. Please exclude this merge module." Ideally, you should leave the Exclude property at its default value of True for the dotNETFXRedist_x86_enu.msm dependency.

The .NET Framework cannot be included in a Windows Installer setup package created using the Visual Studio .NET deployment tools. It must be installed separately. There are several ways you can do this:

- Ask the user to run setup for .NET Framework from the Windows Component Upgrade CD that comes with Visual Studio .NET.
- Ask the user to download the .NET Framework from the Microsoft MSDN Download Center or from the Microsoft Windows Update Website, http://windowsupdate.microsoft.com.
- Use the .NET Framework bootstrapper (Setup.exe), that checks for the availability of the .NET Framework and installs it if it is not already installed.

Of course, for a professional installation you would not like to leave it to the users to perform a manual installation of the .NET Framework, so the last method is the most attractive. Using a bootstrapper Setup.exe is a good idea. Microsoft provides a sample bootstrapper Setup.exe that you can readily use in your projects. I will tell you where to get and how to use this bootstrapper Setup.exe later in this chapter in Exercise 1. For now I will assume that the .NET Framework is available on the machine where you will deploy your applications.

You can modify the configuration settings for a setup project by selecting the project in Solution Explorer and choosing Project, Properties from the main menu. This opens up the Project Property Pages dialog box as shown in Figure 13.9.

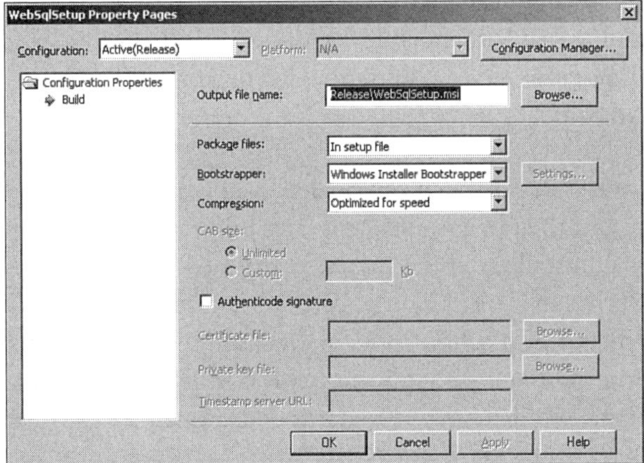

FIGURE 13.9

Property pages showing configuration properties of the WebSqlSetup project.

There are five main configuration properties:

- **Output file name**—Specifies the output filename of the installation package (.msi file).
- **Package files**—Specifies how to package the files. The options are "As loose uncompressed files," "In setup file," and, "In cabinet file(s)." If the "In cabinet file(s)" option is selected, you can also specify the maximum size of the cab files.
- **Bootstrapper**—Specifies whether any bootstrap file needs to be created for launching the installation program. A bootstrap is required when the target machine does not have Windows Installer service already installed. The None option generates only the installation package (.msi file). The Windows Installer Bootstrapper option creates a Setup.exe file capable of installing the Windows Installer service if that is not already installed.
- **Compression**—Specifies whether to optimize the installation files for size or speed or if no optimization is required. The value "Optimized for speed" will use a faster compression algorithm that will unpack the files quickly at install time. A faster compression algorithm will usually result in a larger installation file. The value "Optimized for size" will use a compression algorithm that will run slowly but tightly pack the files. If the value "None" is selected, no optimization is performed.
- **Authenticode signature**—Allows you to specify the file containing the Authenticode certificate, Private key file, and the Timestamp server URL (provided by the certification authority).

The output files generated can be deployed (copied) to any target machine and then be installed and later uninstalled. When an application is uninstalled, all the actions performed by the installer application during the installation on the target machine are undone, leaving the target machine to its original state. You can also choose to repair or reinstall the application installed by clicking the Change button in the Add/Remove Programs dialog box.

REVIEW BREAK

- Although .NET supports XCOPY and FTP deployment, this is not sufficient for advanced deployment requirements. For advanced requirement, you should instead choose a Microsoft Windows Installer–based installation package to deploy your applications.
- Microsoft Windows Installer 2.0 is the built-in installation and configuration service of the Windows operating system. It addition to several advanced installation features it also provides features such as the ability to rollback the installation process, uninstalling an application, and repairing a component or an application.
- Visual Studio .NET provides four types of deployment templates: Setup Project (for Windows-based applications), Web Setup Project (for Web-based applications), Merge Module Project (for shared components and assemblies), and CAB project (ActiveX components to be downloaded over the Internet). It also provides a Setup Wizard that helps in creating installation package for any of these deployment projects.

Customizing Setup Projects

When you are creating a professional application you don't want the user to have to navigate to the installation folder to run the application. You would instead like to create menu options and shortcuts in the target machine so that the end user can easily run the application. You may also like the installation program to provide different custom features and actions while performing installation.

Visual Studio .NET provides several different editors to customize various aspects of the installation process:

- File System Editor
- Registry Editor
- File Types Editor
- User Interface Editor

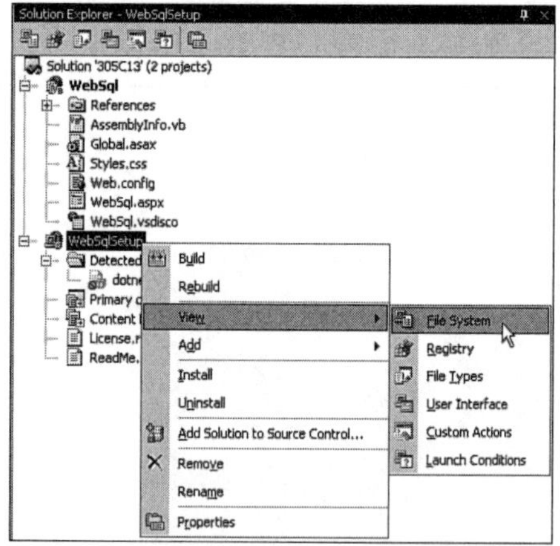

FIGURE 13.10
You can launch various editors for a Setup project via the Solution Explorer.

- Custom Actions Editor
- Launch Conditions Editor

You can view an editor by either choosing its icon from the Solution Explorer or selecting the Project in Solution Explorer and choosing View and the respective editor option from its shortcut menu as shown in Figure 13.10.

Using the File System Editor

The File System Editor provides a mapping of the file system on the target machine. The folders are referred to by special names that are converted to represent the folder on the target machine during the installation process. For example, the special folder User's Desktop will be converted to the actual desktop path on the target machine at the time of installation.

You can add special folders by selecting the File System on Target Machine node in the left pane and choosing Add Special Folder option from its context menu. There are many types of special folders such as Application Folder, Common Files Folder, Program Files Folder, User's Desktop, System Folder, User's Startup Folder, and many others, each of which represents a particular folder on the target machine.

In Step by Step 13.3, you will add a menu option to the Windows program menu to display the contents of the ReadMe.rtf file.

STEP BY STEP

13.3 Using the File System Editor

1. Right-click the `WebSqlSetup` project in the Solution Explorer and select View, File System. In the editor, select the Application Folder under the File System on Target Machine node in the left pane of the editor.
2. Right-click the File System on Target Machine node and select Add Special Folder, User's Programs Menu.

3. Right-click the User's Programs Menu folder in the left pane of the editor and select Add, Folder. Rename the new folder to `WebSql`. Figure 13.11 shows the folder structure in the File System Editor.

4. Select the Web Application Folder in the tree view. Right-click the `ReadMe.rtf` and select Create Shortcut to `ReadMe.rtf`, as shown in Figure 13.12.

5. Move the shortcut created to the WebSql folder either by dragging and dropping it or by choosing Cut and Paste from the context menu.

6. Build the `WebSqlSetup` project. Right-click the project in Solution Explorer and select the Install option. Install the project.

7. Select Start, Programs, WebSql and you'll find a shortcut to the readme file. Click it to verify that it works as desired.

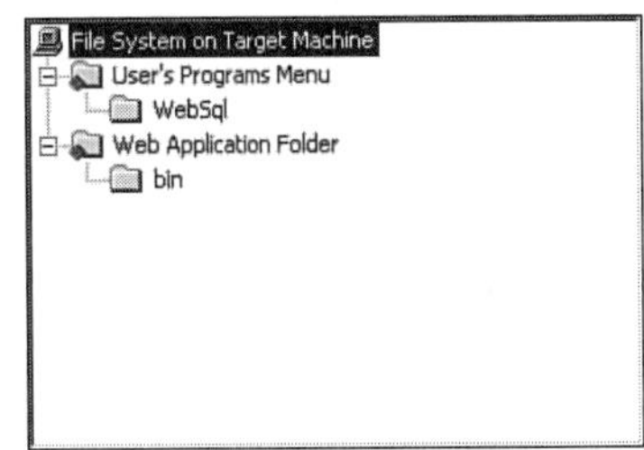

FIGURE 13.11
Folder in the File System Editor.

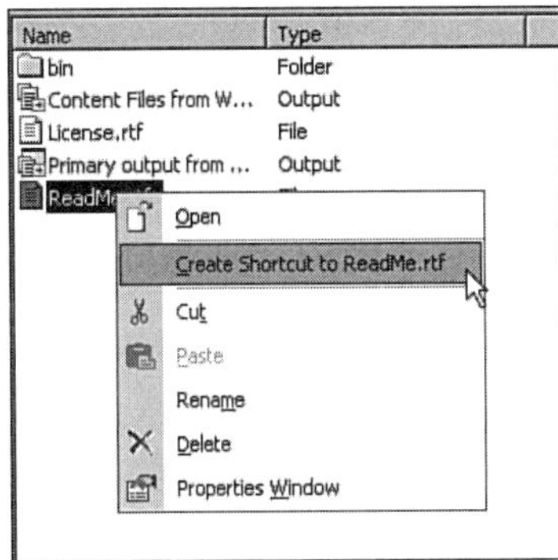

FIGURE 13.12
Creating shortcuts via the File System Editor.

GUIDED PRACTICE EXERCISE 13.1

In this exercise, you will create a Setup Project using the Setup Project template rather than the Setup Wizard. The project will install the WebSql application and create a shortcut for the ReadMe.rtf file on the user's desktop.

This exercise will give you practice on creating Setup projects using the Setup project template. I would recommend that you should first attempt doing this exercise on your own; if you would later like to see one of the possible solutions, follow these steps:

1. In the Solution Explorer window, right-click the Solution and select Add, New Project. Select Setup and Deployment projects from the Project Types tree and then select Setup Project from the list of templates on the right. Name the project GuidedPracticeExercise13-1.

continues

continued

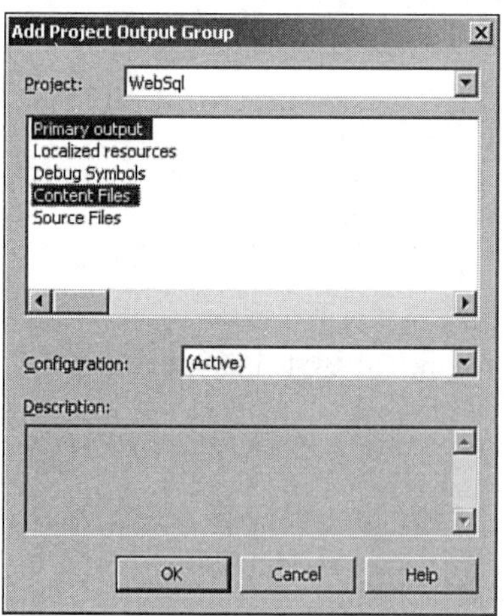

FIGURE 13.13
Add Project Output Group dialog box.

2. In the Solution Explorer window, right-click the project and select Add, Project Output from the context menu. This will open Add Project Output Group dialog box as shown in Figure 13.13. Select WebSql as Project and select Primary Output and Content Files from the list box. Click OK.
3. Now select Add, File from the context menu. This will open Add Files dialog box. Navigate to the WebSql project folder and add the ReadMe.rtf file.
4. Open the File System Editor by clicking the File System Editor icon in the Solution Explorer. Select the Application Folder under the File System on Target Machine node in the left pane of the editor.
5. Right-click the ReadMe.rtf and select Create Shortcut to ReadMe.rtf. Rename the Shortcut to Read Me. Move the Shortcut created to the User's Desktop folder.
6. Select the new project in the Solution Explorer. Activate Properties Window. Set the Manufacturer to "WebSql SoftwareGPE," and the ProductName to "WebSqlGPE."
7. Build the GuidedPracticeExercise13_1 project. Right-click the project in Solution Explorer and select the Install option. Install the project.
8. The desktop will now contain a shortcut to the readme file. Double-click the shortcut to verify that it performs as expected.

Using the Registry Editor

The Registry Editor allows you to specify registry keys, subkeys, and values that are added to the registry in the target machine during installation. You can also import registry files to the Registry editor.

STEP BY STEP

13.4 Using the Registry Editor

1. Select the `WebSqlSetup` project in the Solution Explorer. Open the Registry Editor by clicking the Registry Editor icon in the Solution Explorer.

2. In the left pane, right-click the `HKEY_LOCAL_MACHINE` node and select New Key. Name the new key Software. Add a second new key as a child of the Software key and name it WebSql Software. Right-click this key and select New, DWORD Value as shown in Figure 13.14. Name the key value `FreeWare`. Change the `Value` property of the `FreeWare` key to 1 in the Properties Window.

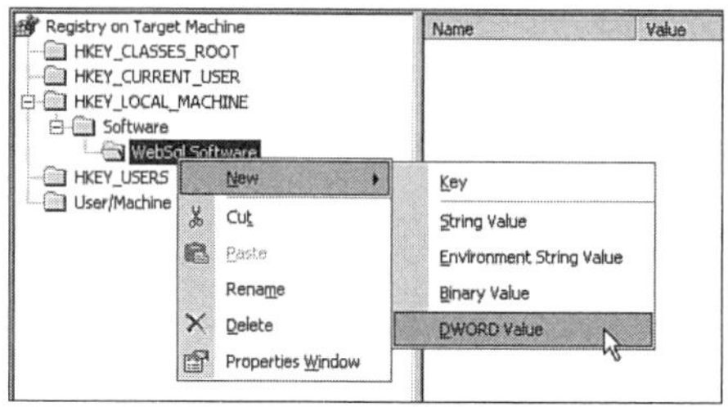

FIGURE 13.14
Adding Registry Keys via Registry Editor.

3. Build the `WebSqlSetup` project. Right-click the project in Solution Explorer and select the Install option. Install the project.

4. Select Run from the Windows Start menu and type `regedit` in the Open textbox. Click OK. This will launch the Windows Registry Editor. In the left pane, select My Computer, HKEY_LOCAL_MACHINE, Software, WebSql Software to view the `FreeWare` value added as shown in Figure 13.15.

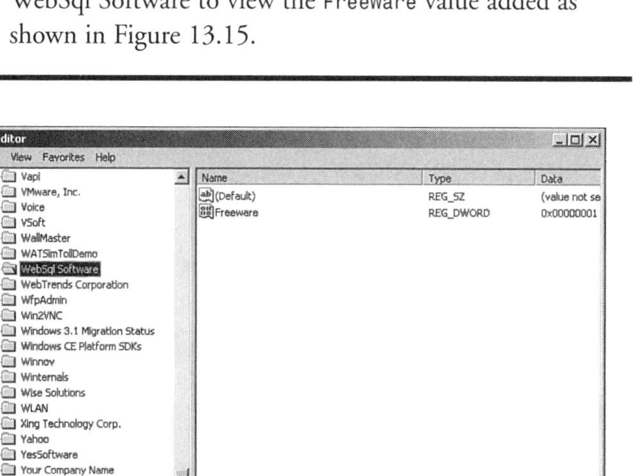

FIGURE 13.15
Viewing the registry key value added in the Registry Editor.

WARNING

Working With the Registry Be careful when working with Windows Registry. Take special care with the DeleteAtUninstall property of Registry Settings Properties. If you end up setting DeleteAtUninstall to True for a wrong key (such as HKEY_LOCAL_MACHINE\SOFTWARE), it might have very bad consequences for your computer.

Using the File Types Editor

The File Types Editor provides the facility to associate file extensions and actions with an application. For example, files with the extension doc are normally associated with Microsoft Word or WordPad. I'm mentioning this editor only for the sake of completeness. You're unlikely to need the File Types Editor for an ASP.NET application because all the file types that your application uses will be processed by ASP.NET.

Using the User Interface Editor

The User Interface Editor allows you to customize the user interface that is provided to the user during the installation process. The user interface is nothing but the various dialog boxes that appear during the installation process. The user interface provided to the user is divided into three stages—Start, Progress, and End. You can add different types of dialog boxes at each stage. Each stage allows only certain types of dialog boxes to be added.

The User Interface editor displays the user interface applicable to both end-user installation and administrative. You can customize the user interface for both types of installations. The administrative installation occurs when you run the msiexec command line tool with /a option. This is the type of installation you can use to make an application available for installation over a network.

STEP BY STEP

13.5 Using User Interface Editor.

1. Select the `WebSqlSetup` project in the Solution Explorer. Open the User Interface Editor by clicking the User Interface Editor icon in the Solution Explorer.
2. Right-click the `Start` node under the `Install` tree and select Add Dialog from the context menu. This will open the Add Dialog box. Select License Agreement as shown in Figure 13.16. Click OK. Right-click the License Agreement and choose Move Up twice to move the License Agreement dialog box to appear directly after the Welcome dialog box.

NOTE

LicenseFile and ReadmeFile Property The LicenseFile and ReadmeFile properties of the User Interface Dialog only work with the Rich Text Format (RTF) files. If you specify a file of any other format, you won't get any error but the contents of the file will not be displayed.

Select the LicenseFile property in the Properties Window, Select (Browse...) from the drop-down list. This will open the Select Item in Project dialog box. Navigate to the Web application folder and select `License.rtf`.

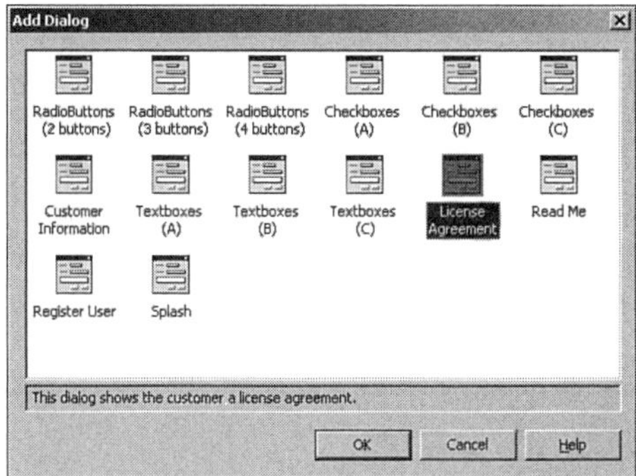

FIGURE 13.16
The Add Dialog box adds dialog boxes in the User Interface Editor.

3. Similarly, add a Read Me dialog box to the End node under the Install Tree. Move the Read Me dialog box before the Finished dialog box. The dialog boxes should appear in the User Interface Editor as shown in Figure 13.17. Set the `ReadmeFile` property to the `ReadMe.rtf` file.

4. Build the `WebSqlSetup` project. Right-click the project in Solution Explorer and select the Install option. Install the project. You will notice a License Agreement screen; only when you select the "I Agree" option is the Next button enabled, as shown in Figure 13.18. You will also notice the Read Me screen before the Close screen being shown.

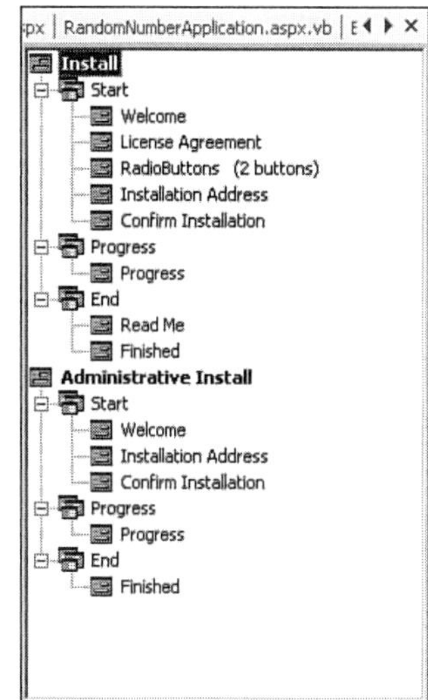

FIGURE 13.17
Customizing the user interface of the installation program via User Interface Editor.

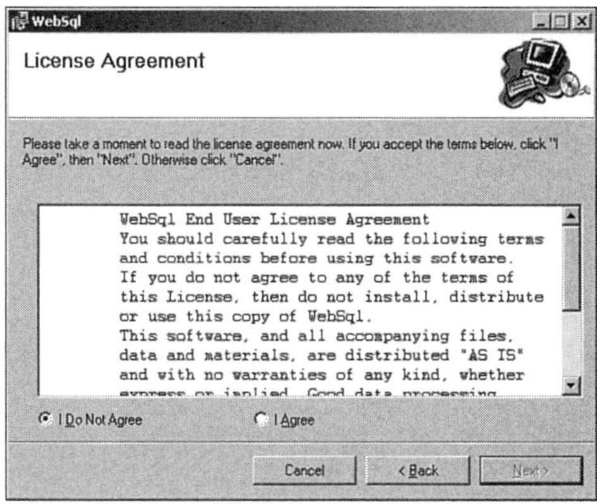

FIGURE 13.18
License Agreement screen appearing during Installation process.

Using the Custom Actions Editor

The Custom Actions Editor allows you to run compiled dll or exe files, or assemblies at the end of the installation. These files can be used to perform custom actions that are vital but were not carried out during the installation. If the custom action fails, then the entire installation process is rolled back. For example, you may have to install the database required by your application during the installation process.

There are four phases in which custom action can be performed—Install, Commit, Rollback, and Uninstall. In Step by Step 13.6 you will create a simple custom action to launch the WebSql application when the installation ends.

NOTE

The Process and ProcessInfo Classes I'll discuss the Process and ProcessInfo classes in detail in Chapter 14, "Maintaining and Supporting a Web Application."

STEP BY STEP

13.6 Using the Custom Action Editor.

1. In the Solution Explorer window, right-click Solution and select Add, New Project. Select Visual Basic Projects from the Project Types tree and then select Empty Project from the list of templates on the right. Name the project `LaunchWebSql`.
2. Right-click the new project in the Solution Explorer and select Add, Add Module from the context menu. Name the module `LaunchWebSql.vb`.
3. Right-click the References node in Solution Explorer and select Add Reference. Add a reference to System.dll.
4. Modify the module as follows:

```
Imports System
Imports System.Diagnostics

Module LaunchWebSql
    Public Sub Main()
        ' Create a ProcessStartInfo object
        Dim psi As _
          System.Diagnostics.ProcessStartInfo = _
         New ProcessStartInfo()
        psi.FileName = "iexplore"
        psi.Arguments = _
         "http://localhost/websql/websql.aspx"
        Process.Start(psi)
    End Sub
End Module
```

5. Right-click the `LaunchWebSql` project in the Solution Explorer and select Properties. This will open the Project Property Pages dialog box. In the left pane select the `General` node under the `Common Properties` tree. Set the Output Type property to `Windows Application`. Also set the startup object of the project to `LaunchWebSql`. Click OK. Build the LaunchWebSql project.

6. In the Solution Explorer window, right-click the `WebSqlSetup` project and select Add, Project Output from the context menu. This will open Add Project Output Group dialog box. Select the `LaunchWebSql` as Project and select `Primary Output` from the list box. Click OK.

7. Select the `WebSqlSetup` project in the Solution Explorer. Open the Custom Actions Editor by clicking the Custom Actions Editor icon in the Solution Explorer.

8. Select the `Install` node under the Custom Actions tree. Select Add Custom Action from the Action menu. This opens the Select Item in Project dialog box. Navigate to the Web Application folder and select `Primary Output from LaunchWebSql (Active)`. Rename the action to `LaunchWebSql`.

9. Select the custom action `LaunchWebSql` and open the Properties Window. Set the `InstallerClass` property to `False` as shown in Figure 13.19.

10. Build the `WebSqlSetup` project. Right-click the project in Solution Explorer and select the `Install` option. Install the project. The WebSql application will be launched after the installation process is completed.

FIGURE 13.19
Adding the Custom Actions via Custom Actions Editor.

The `Arguments` property is used to pass any command-line arguments to the custom action launched. In this particular case, we didn't pass any arguments. You will also note that the `InstallerClass` property is set to False. This is because the `LaunchWebSql` class did not inherit from the `Installer` class. The .NET Framework provides the Installer class to provide a base for custom installations. I'll talk more about the `Installer` class later in the chapter.

Using the Launch Conditions Editor

The Launch Conditions editor allows you to set conditions to be evaluated when the installation begins on the target machine. If the conditions are not met, the installation stops. For example, you would like to install your Visual Basic .NET application only if the .NET Framework runtime exists on the target machine. This condition is by default added by Visual Studio .NET. You may also need to perform other checks such as whether a particular file exists on the target machine or verify a particular registry key value on the target machine.

The Launch Conditions Editor allows you to perform searches on the target machine for a file, or registry key or Windows Installer components. For example, you can determine whether MDAC is installed on the target machine by making a search in the registry for the particular registry key value shown in Figure 13.20.

You can add conditions to be evaluated for the search performed on the target machine. If the conditions fail, the installation ends. For example, you can add a condition that MDAC installed should be 2.7 or higher to continue with the installation, by checking against the registry key value retrieved by the registry search as shown in Figure 13.21. Step by Step 13.7 demonstrates the use of the Launch Conditions Editor.

STEP BY STEP

13.7 Using the Launch Conditions Editor

1. Select the `WebSqlSetup` project in the Solution Explorer. Open the Launch Conditions Editor by clicking the Launch Conditions Editor icon in the Solution Explorer.

2. Select the `Requirements on Target Machine` node and select `Add Registry Launch Condition` from the `Action` menu. This adds two nodes, one under the `Search Target Machine` node and another under the `Launch Conditions` node.

3. Select the newly created node under the Search Target Machine Node and open the Properties window. Set the `Name` property to `Search for MDAC Support`, the `Property` property to `MDACSUPPORT`, the `Root` property to `vsdrrHKLM`, the `RegKey` property to `Software\Microsoft\DataAccess`, and the `Value property` to `FullInstallVer` as shown in Figure 13.20.

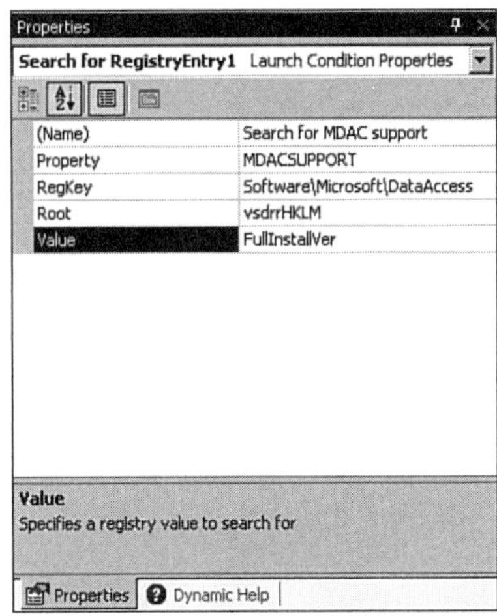

FIGURE 13.20
Adding a Registry Search via Launch Conditions Editor.

4. Select the newly created node under the Launch Conditions Node and open the Properties window. Set the `Name` property to `MDACSupport`, the `Condition` property to `MDACSUPPORT >= "2.7"` and the `Message` property to "You must have MDAC version 2.7 or higher installed on this computer. Please contact the administrator for installation information." as shown in Figure 13.21.

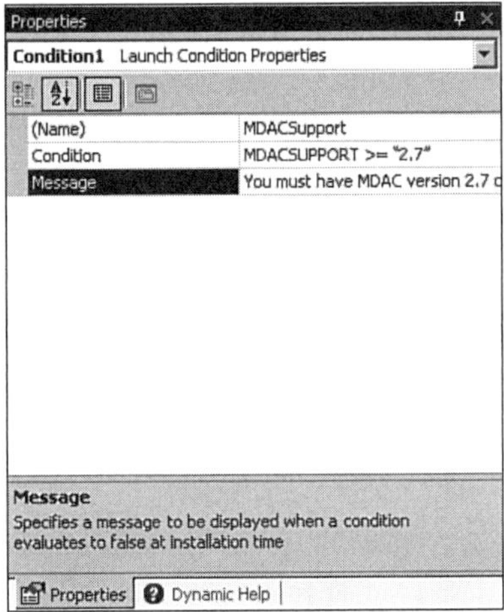

FIGURE 13.21
Adding a Launch Condition via Launch Conditions Editor.

5. Build the `WebSqlSetup` project. Right-click the project in Solution Explorer and select the `Install` option. Install the project. If the target computer does not have MDAC 2.7 or higher installed, the installation process of the `WebSql` project fails. Instead you'll get the error message set in the `Message` property of the Launch condition.

NOTE

Condition Property Setup and Deployment Project Editor elements such as folders, files, registry keys, custom actions, launch conditions, and so on have this property. The Condition property consists of a valid conditional statement in form of a string that evaluates to either true or false.

The conditional statement is executed during installation and if it returns True then the action associated with that particular element is performed on the target machine. For example, a condition is applied to registry key value and if it evaluates to False during installation, the particular key value will not be entered in the registry on the target machine.

GUIDED PRACTICE EXERCISE 13.2

In this exercise, you will add a few sample files to the `WebSqlSetup` project and then provide an option to include or omit installation of sample files on the target machine. You will use the User Interface Editor to provide the user interface to select or deselect this option. You will use the `Condition` property of the files to check whether the samples option is selected by the end user.

This exercise will give you good practice on how to perform conditional deployment. I would recommend that you should first attempt doing this exercise on your own; if you would later like to see one of the possible solutions, follow these steps:

1. Open the `WebSql` project in the Solution Explorer.
2. Add a sample query file `CustomersFromBrazil.qry` with the following text to the `WebSql` project:

   ```
   SELECT *
   FROM Customers
   WHERE Country = 'Brazil'
   ORDER BY CompanyName
   ```

3. Add another sample query file `TenMostExpensiveProducts.qry` with the following text to the `WebSql` project:

   ```
   SELECT TOP 10
   Products.ProductName AS TenMostExpensiveProducts, Prod-
   ucts.UnitPrice
   FROM Products
   ORDER BY Products.UnitPrice DESC
   ```

4. Open the File System Editor of the `WebSqlSetup` project. Select the `Web Application Folder`.
5. Select Add, File from the context menu. This will open the Add Files dialog box. Navigate to the sample query files created in the previous steps and add them to the folder.
6. Open the User Interface Editor of the `WebSqlSetup` project. Right-click the `Start` node under the `Install` tree and select Add Dialog from the context menu. This will open Add Dialog box. Select Radio Buttons (2 Buttons) dialog. Click OK. Place the newly added dialog in between the License Agreement and Installation Folder dialog.

7. Set the properties `BannerText` to `WebSql Samples`, `BodyText` to `Do you want to install Samples?`, `Button1Label` to `Yes`, `Button1Value` to `1`, `Button2Label` to `No`, `Button2Value` to `2`, `ButtonProperty` to `WEBSQLSAMPLES`, and `DefaultValue` to 1 as shown in Figure 13.22.

8. Open the File System Editor. Change the `Condition` property of each of the sample files to `WEBSQLSAMPLES=1`.

9. Build the `WebSqlSetup` project. Right-click the project in Solution Explorer and select the `Install` option. Install the project. You'll see the Samples dialog box being displayed with `Yes` option selected as shown in Figure 13.23 during the installation process.

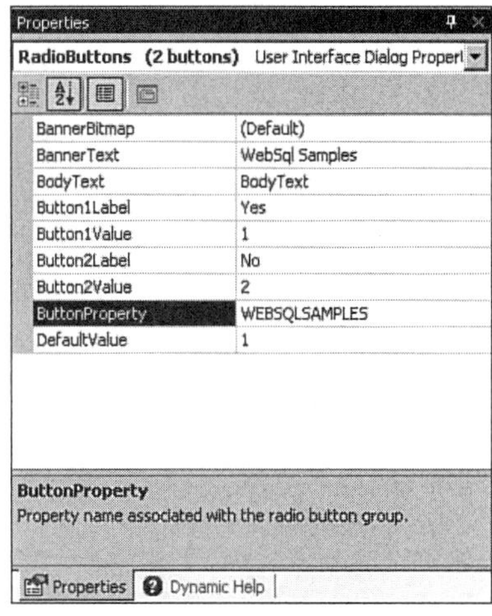

FIGURE 13.22▲
Properties of the Radio Buttons dialog box.

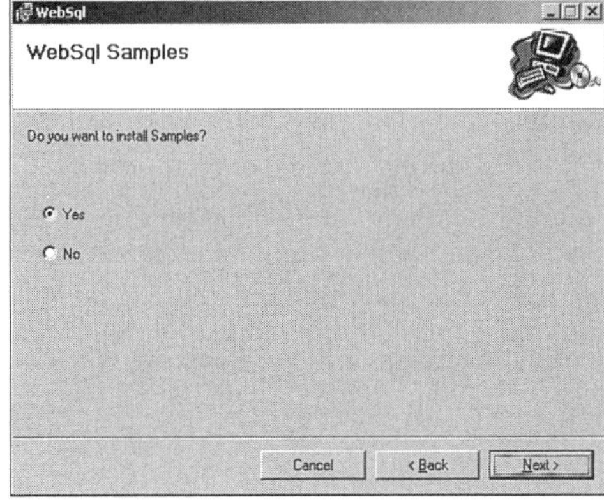

FIGURE 13.23◀
Customized Samples dialog box appears during the installation process.

10. If you choose the option `Yes`, the samples will be installed.

REVIEW BREAK

- The File System Editor provides a mapping of the file system on the target machine. The folders are referred to by special names that during the installation process are converted to represent the folder as per the file system on the target machine.

continues

continued

- The Registry Editor allows you to specify registry keys, sub keys, and values that are added to the registry on the target machine during installation.
- The File Types Editor allows you to register one or more file extensions with your Windows application.
- The User Interface Editor allows you to customize the user interface that is provided to the user during the installation process. There are different types of user interfaces available for end user installation and administrative installation.
- The User Interface Editor and Launch Conditions Editor provide special properties (like Property, ButtonProperty) whose value can be evaluated to perform the installation as per the end-user's choice.
- The Custom Actions Editor allows you to add custom actions to be performed during the installation process. It allows you to run .dll, .exe, assembly, and scripts files. There are four phase when custom action can be performed—Install, Commit, Rollback, and Uninstall.
- The Launch Conditions editor allows you to set conditions to be evaluated when the installation begins on the target machine. If the conditions are not met, then the installation stops.

SHARED ASSEMBLIES

Add assemblies to the Global Assembly Cache.

In Chapter 7, "Creating and Managing Components and .NET Assemblies," I briefly discussed shared assemblies. In this section I will explore more about shared assemblies and how to deploy them.

A shared assembly is shared among multiple applications on a machine. It is therefore stored at a central location called the Global Assembly Cache (GAC) and enjoys special services such as file security, shared location, and side-by-side versioning.

Since shared assemblies are all installed at a central location, distinguishing them with just a filename is not enough. You would not like your application to break when some other vendor installs an assembly with the same name in the GAC. To avoid this possibility, Microsoft requires you to assign a strong name to each assembly before placing it in the GAC.

Assigning a Strong Name to an Assembly

An assembly is identified by its text name (usually the name of the file without the file extension), version number, and culture information. However, these pieces of information do not guarantee that an assembly will be unique. There might be a case where two software publishers end up using the same identity for an assembly thereby causing applications using those assemblies to behave abnormally. This problem can be greatly reduced by assigning a strong name to an assembly. A strong name strengthens an assembly's identity by qualifying it by the software publisher's identity. The .NET Framework uses a standard cryptography technique known as digital signing to ensure uniqueness of an assembly.

The process of digital signing involves two related pieces of binary data known as the public key and private key. The public key represents the software publisher's identity and is freely distributed. While creating a strong named assembly, the public key is stored in the assembly manifest along with other identification information such as the name, version number, and culture of the assembly. This scheme does not look foolproof because after all the public key is available freely and nobody can stop a software publisher from using some other company's public key. To verify that only the legitimate owner of the public key has created the assembly, an assembly is signed using the publisher's private key. The private key is assumed to be only known to the publisher of the assembly. The process of signing an assembly and verifying its signature works like this:

- **Signing an Assembly**: A signature is created by computing a crptographic hash from the contents of the assembly. The hash is encoded with the private key. This signature is then stored within the assembly.

NOTE

Signing a Multi-File Assembly If your assembly consists of multiple files, just the file containing the assembly manifest needs to be signed. This is because the assembly manifest already contains file hashes for all the files that constitute the assembly implementation. You can easily determine whether a file has been tampered with by matching its actual hash with what is stored in the assembly manifest.

- **Verifying the Signature**: Later when the CLR verifies an assembly's identity, it will read its public key from the assembly manifest and use it to decrypt the cryptographic hash stored in the assembly. It will then recalculate the hash for the current contents of the assembly. If the two hashes match, it ensures two things: first, the contents of the assembly were not tampered with after it was signed and, second, only the person having a private key associated with the public key stored in the assembly has signed the assembly.

Public/private key pairs can be easily generated using the Strong Name tool (`sn.exe`) available in the .NET Framework SDK.

STEP BY STEP

13.8 Creating a Public/Private Key Pair Using the Strong Name Tool (sn.exe)

1. From the Visual Studio .NET program group in the Windows Start menu, launch the Visual Studio .NET command prompt.

2. Issue the following command to create a pair of public/private keys.

```
sn -k RandNumCorpKeys.snk
```

3. Both the public as well as private keys will be created and stored in a file named `RandNumCorpKeys.snk` as shown in Figure 13.24. Note the directory where this file is created, because you will be using it in Step by Step 13.9.

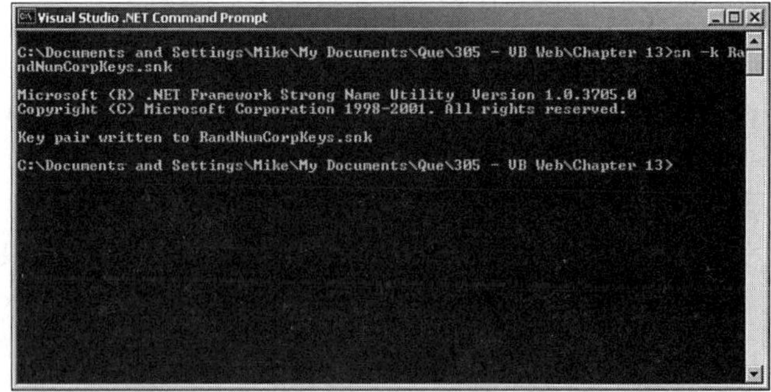

FIGURE 13.24
Creating public/private key pair using Strong Name tool.

I will now create a strong named assembly where I will use the key file generated previously to digitally sign it.

STEP BY STEP

13.9 Creating a Component with Strong Name

1. Create a new Visual Basic .NET Class Library project in the solution `305C13`. Name the project `RandomNumberGenerator`.

2. Add a Class to the project and name it `RandomNumberGenerator.vb`. Delete `Class1.vb`.

3. Modify the code for the class as follows:

```
Public Class RandomNumberGenerator

    Private mminValue As Integer = 1
    Private mmaxValue As Integer = 100

    Public Property MinValue() As Integer
        Get
            MinValue = mminValue
        End Get
        Set(ByVal Value As Integer)
            mminValue = Value
        End Set
    End Property

    Public Property MaxValue() As Integer
        Get
            MaxValue = mmaxValue
        End Get
        Set(ByVal Value As Integer)
            mmaxValue = Value
        End Set
    End Property

    Public Function GetRandomNumber() As Integer
        Dim r As Random = New Random()
        GetRandomNumber = r.Next(MinValue, MaxValue)
    End Function

End Class
```

4. Add the existing `RandNumCorpKeys.snk` file that was generated in Step by Step 13.8 to this project.

continues

continued

5. Open the `AssemblyInfo.vb` file. Scroll down the file and change the `AssemblyVersion` and `AssemblyKeyFile` attributes as shown here:

```
<Assembly: AssemblyVersion("1.0")>
<Assembly: AssemblyKeyFile( _
 "..\..\RandNumCorpKeys.snk")>
```

6. Build the project. This will generate a RandomNumberGenerator.dll and assign a strong name to it based on the specified key file.

Note that I have changed the `AssemblyVersion` attribute of the assembly from "1.0.*" to "1.0". The assembly's version consists of up to four parts:

```
<major>.<minor>.<build>.<revision>
```

If you want to use a fixed value, you can hard-code it. The default value of this version uses an asterisk in place of build and revision number. This changes the build and revision each time you compile the project. The build will be calculated as the number of days since January 1 2000, and the revision will be calculated as the number of seconds since midnight modulo 2.

At runtime the CLR will use this information to load this assembly. In next few examples, you will frequently compile the projects thereby changing the version of the assembly if you use the default version property. The Global Assembly Cache allows you to install multiple versions of the same assembly. For this chapter, I'll hard-code the version of the application's assembly to keep matters simple.

I have used Visual Studio .NET to attach a strong name with an assembly. If you want to do this manually you can use the Assembly Linker tool (al.exe) with its –keyfile option.

Adding an Assembly to the Global Assembly Cache

Once you have associated a strong name with an assembly, you can place it in the GAC. There are several ways in which you can add an assembly to the global assembly cache. Using the Windows Installer is the recommended approach but there are some quick alternatives too. However, these quick approaches should only be used for development purpose and are not recommended for installing assemblies on the end-user's computer.

> NOTE
>
> **Working with the GAC** You need to have administrative privileges on a computer to manage its Global Assembly Cache.

Using Windows Installer

Using Microsoft Windows Installer is the preferred way of adding assemblies to the global assembly cache. It maintains a reference counting for assemblies in the GAC and provides uninstallation support. I will tell you how to add assemblies using Windows Installer technology through the Setup and Deployment projects of Visual Stuido .NET a little later in this chapter.

Using Windows Explorer

When the .NET Framework is installed, it also installs the Assembly Cache Viewer Shell Extension (shfusion.dll). This extension allows you to view the complex structure of the GAC folder in a much more navigable and understandable manner. Since it is integrated with Windows Shell, you can view and manage GAC contents with the help of Windows Explorer.

STEP BY STEP

13.10 Adding an Assembly to GAC Using Windows Explorer

1. Open Windows Explorer. Navigate to the assembly cache folder. It is usually `c:\WINNT\assembly` or `C:\Windows\assembly` (as shown in Figure 13.25).

continues

continued

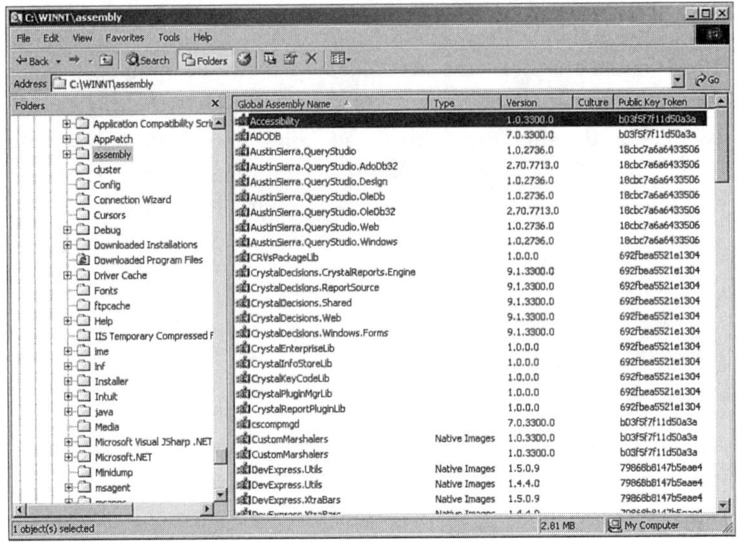

FIGURE 13.25
The Assembly Cache Viewer Shell Extension enables you to view and manage the contents of Assembly Cache using Windows Explorer.

NOTE

Assembly Cache Folder The Assembly Cache Folder actually contains two caches, the Global Assembly Cache and the Native Image Cache. When you view the Assembly Cache Folder using the Windows Explorer, the Assembly Cache Viewer Shell Extension will show you a combined list of both caches. You can identify whether the assembly is from the GAC or from the Native Image Cache from the Type field in the list. When you add an assembly to this folder using Windows Explorer, it will be added to the GAC. You will learn about the Native Image Cache and how to add assemblies to it, later in this chapter.

2. Using Windows Explorer, drag the `RandomNumberGenerator.dll` created in the previous Step by Step and drop it in the Assembly Cache folder.

3. In the Assembly Cache folder, select Properties from the shortcut menu of `RandomNumberGenerator.dll`, you will see the Properties dialog box as shown in Figure 13.26.

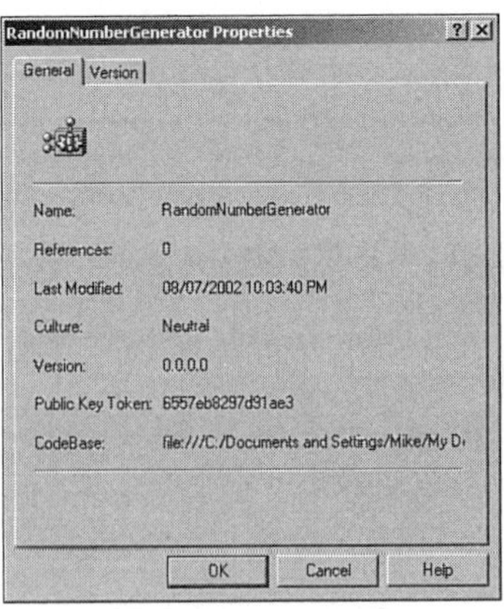

FIGURE 13.26
Viewing properties of RandomNumberGenerator assembly installed in the Global Assembly Cache.

If you want to remove a file from the GAC, just delete it from the Windows Explorer by selecting the delete option from the File menu or the shortcut menu.

Using .NET Framework Configuration Tool

You can also use the .NET Framework Configuration Tool (mscorcfg.msc) to manage an assembly in the GAC. Step by Step 13.11 guides you through the process of adding an assembly using .NET Framework Configuration Tool.

STEP BY STEP

13.11 Adding an Assembly to the GAC Using the .NET Framework Configuration Tool

1. Open the Administrative Tools section of the Windows Control Panel. Open the tool named Microsoft .NET Framework Configuration. Select the Assembly Cache folder on the left pane under the `My Computer` node. See Figure 13.27.

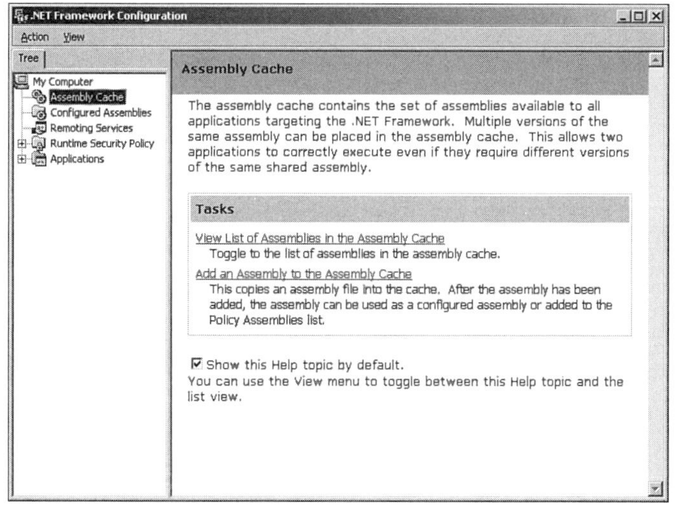

FIGURE 13.27
The .NET Framework Configuration Tool allows you to manage Assembly Cache.

continues

continued

2. On the right pane, click the hyperlink titled Add an Assembly to the Assembly Cache. This will open up a Add an Assembly dialog box. Navigate to the `RandomNumberGenerator.dll` in the `RandomNumberGenerator` project and click the OK button.
3. Click the other hyperlink titled View List of Assemblies in the Assembly Cache. You will see list of installed assemblies. Ensure that `RandonNumberGenerator` is in this list as shown in Figure 13.28.

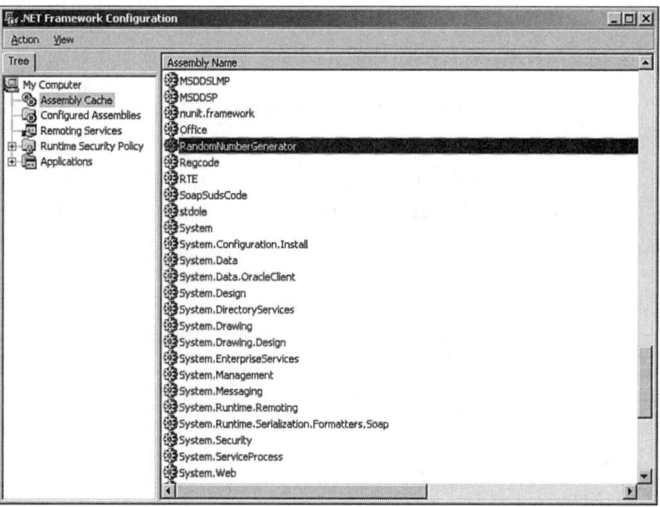

FIGURE 13.28
The .NET Framework Configuration Tool showing the list of assemblies in the Assembly Cache.

To uninstall an assembly using this tool, just select delete from the Action menu or from the assembly's shortcut menu.

In addition to adding or removing assemblies, this tool also helps you to configure an assembly and manage its runtime security policy.

Using Global Assembly Cache Tool (GacUtil.exe)

GacUtil.exe is a command line tool that is especially useful to add or remove assemblies from the GAC from a program script or a batch file.

STEP BY STEP

13.12 Adding an Assembly to GAC using the Global Assembly Cache Tool

1. From the Visual Studio .NET program group in the Windows Start menu, launch the Visual Studio .NET command prompt.
2. Change the directory to the folder where the `RandomNumberGenerator.dll` resides in the `RandomNumberGenerator` project, in this case, project's `bin` directory.
3. Issue the following command to install the assembly to the GAC as shown in Figure 13.29.

```
gacutil /i RandomNumberGenerator.dll
```

```
Visual Studio .NET Command Prompt
C:\Documents and Settings\Mike\My Documents\Que\305 - VB Web\Chapter 13\305C13\R
andomNumberGenerator>cd bin

C:\Documents and Settings\Mike\My Documents\Que\305 - VB Web\Chapter 13\305C13\R
andomNumberGenerator\bin>gacutil /i RandomNumberGenerator.dll

Microsoft (R) .NET Global Assembly Cache Utility.  Version 1.0.3705.0
Copyright (C) Microsoft Corporation 1998-2001. All rights reserved.

Assembly successfully added to the cache

C:\Documents and Settings\Mike\My Documents\Que\305 - VB Web\Chapter 13\305C13\R
andomNumberGenerator\bin>_
```

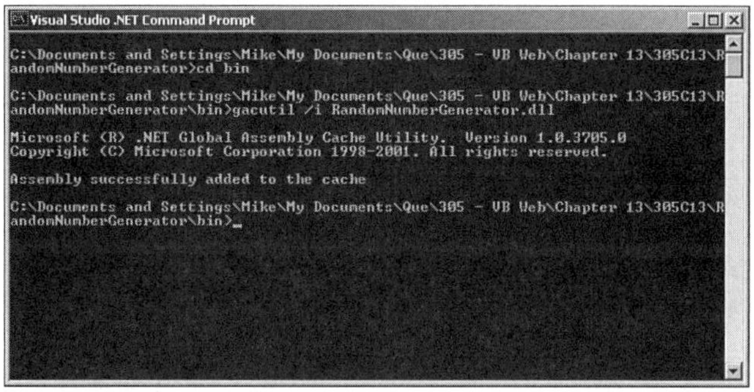

FIGURE 13.29
Adding an assembly to the GAC using Global Assembly Cache tool.

You can list all the assemblies in the GAC using the gacutil.exe tool with the /l option. You can use the /u option with the name of the assembly (without file extension) to uninstall the assembly from the GAC.

```
gacutil /u RandomNumberGenerator
```

You can also choose to uninstall an assembly of a specific version and specific culture from the GAC by specifying its version, culture, and public key along with the name of the assembly.

```
gacutil /u RandomNumberGenerator,Version=1.0.0.0,
➥Culture=neutral,PublicKeyToken=f26af4dbb33881b1
```

Referencing an Assembly from the GAC

Normally when you refer an assembly in a Windows application project, you can invoke the Add Reference dialog box and browse to the desired assembly. But once you have added an assembly to the GAC, this approach won't work. This is because the GAC has a complex structure that cannot be directly enumerated by the Add Reference dialog box.

When you view the GAC using tools mentioned in the previous section you see an abstraction of its structure. If you instead switch to the command prompt and change the directory to the GAC folder, you will see that GAC is actually made up of various subdirectories—one for each assembly. Each of these directories further has subdirectories whose name depends on assembly's version and public key. Finally, each subdirectory will store the actual assembly file with some additional assembly information. Figure 13.30 shows how the GAC entry is made for the RandomNumberGenerator component on my computer.

```
Visual Studio .NET Command Prompt
C:\WINNT\assembly\GAC\RandomNumberGenerator>dir
 Volume in drive C has no label.
 Volume Serial Number is 44A8-6214

 Directory of C:\WINNT\assembly\GAC\RandomNumberGenerator

08/07/2002  10:11p      <DIR>          .
08/07/2002  10:11p      <DIR>          ..
08/07/2002  10:11p      <DIR>          0.0.0.0__6557eb8297d91ae3
               0 File(s)              0 bytes
               3 Dir(s)   4,308,631,552 bytes free

C:\WINNT\assembly\GAC\RandomNumberGenerator>cd 0.0.0.0__6557eb8297d91ae3

C:\WINNT\assembly\GAC\RandomNumberGenerator\0.0.0.0__6557eb8297d91ae3>dir
 Volume in drive C has no label.
 Volume Serial Number is 44A8-6214

 Directory of C:\WINNT\assembly\GAC\RandomNumberGenerator\0.0.0.0__6557eb8297d91
ae3

08/07/2002  10:11p      <DIR>          .
08/07/2002  10:11p      <DIR>          ..
08/07/2002  10:11p               7,168 RandomNumberGenerator.dll
08/07/2002  10:11p                 305 __AssemblyInfo__.ini
               2 File(s)          7,473 bytes
               2 Dir(s)   4,309,045,248 bytes free
```

FIGURE 13.30
Exploring the Global Assembly Cache using the Command window.

A better practice is to keep a copy of the assemblies installed in GAC, somewhere outside it where it is easily accessible by a path name. These assemblies can then easily be referenced through the Add Reference dialog box by browsing to that path. In fact the .NET Framework uses the same techniques for all its assemblies stored in the GAC, It also stores a copy of those files in the folder where the .NET Framework is installed. By installing the assemblies both inside and outside the GAC, you share the running code while making it easier to reference the code from within a project.

You don't need to worry about the versions getting out of synch because Visual Studio .NET will only use the GAC version if it's the same as the other version.

The following exercise shows you how to instruct Visual Studio .NET to add assemblies stored in a custom folder to its Add Reference dialog box:

STEP BY STEP

13.13 Displaying an Assembly in the Add Reference Dialog

1. Open Registry Editor by launching `Regedit.exe` from Windows Start, Run dialog box.
2. In the Registry Editor, browse to the key named `HKEY_LOCAL_MACHINE\SOFTWARE\Microsoft\.NETFramework\AssemblyFolders`.
3. At this level create a new key, and name it `MyAssemblies`.
4. Double-click the `Default` value in this key and change its value data to the location of `RandomNumberGenerator.dll` in the `bin\Release` folder of `RandomNumberGenerator` project as shown in Figure 13.31.

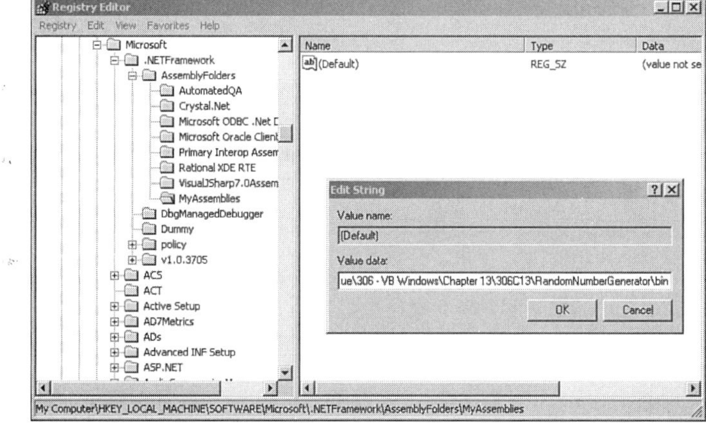

FIGURE 13.31
Setting the Default value via Edit String dialog box.

5. Close Registry Editor. Close all instances of Visual Studio .NET.

I'll now create a small Web application that when executed will load the component installed in the global assembly cache. Before starting with these steps, make sure that you have already installed the RandomNumberGenerator.dll in the GAC.

STEP BY STEP

13.14 Creating a Web Application that Uses the `RandomNumberGenerator` Component

1. Add a new Visual Basic ASP.NET Web application project to the solution 305C13 and name it `RandomNumberApplication`.

2. In the Solution Explorer window, add a new Web form named `RandomNumberApplication.aspx`. Delete the default `WebForm1.aspx`.

3. Using the Add Reference dialog box window, add a reference to `RandomNumberGenerator.dll`. Set the `Copy Local` property of the `RandomNumberGenerator.dll` to `False`.

4. Add a `Label` (`lblResults`) and a `Button` (`btnGenerate`) to the Web Form. Set the label's text property to empty and button's `Text` property to `Generate a Random Number!`. Double-click the button control to add an event handler for its `Click` event. Add the following code to the event handler:

```
Private Sub btnGenerate_Click( _
 ByVal sender As System.Object, _
 ByVal e As System.EventArgs) _
 Handles btnGenerate.Click
    Dim r As New RandomNumberGenerator. _
     RandomNumberGenerator()
    r.MinValue = 500
    r.MaxValue = 1000
    lblResults.Text = String.Format( _
     "The next random number is: {0}", _
     r.GetRandomNumber())
End Sub
```

5. Set the project `RandomNumberApplication` as the Startup Project and set the Web form as the start page for the project.

6. Run the Solution. Click the button, and you will get a random number in range of `500` and `1000` every time you press the button, as shown in Figure 13.32.

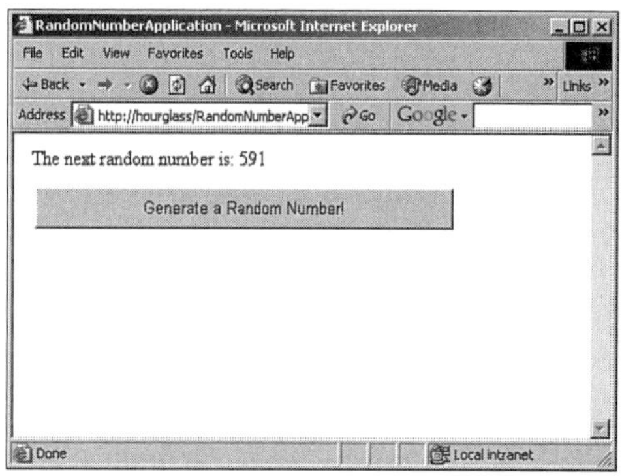

FIGURE 13.32
A form generating random numbers using the RandomNumberGenerator component installed in the GAC.

No matter which copy of the assembly you use to add the reference, the application will load the assembly from the global assembly cache instead of the copy in the application folder. To understand what I mean, you need to understand how the runtime locates assemblies.

How the Runtime Locates Assemblies

The CLR uses the following steps to locate an assembly:

- Try to determine the version of assembly to be located. (This information may be available in the application's configuration files.)
- Check to see if the assembly is already loaded. If the requested assembly has been loaded in one of the previous calls, then use the already loaded assembly.
- Check the Global Assembly Cache. If the assembly is in the GAC, load it from there.
- If there is a <codebase> element specified in the application's configuration file, locate the assembly using the path specified by the <codebase>.
- If there is no <codebase> element specified in the configuration files and if there is no culture information available for the assembly, check the following locations (in the given order) for the assembly:

```
[ApplicationBase]\[AssemblyName].dll
[ApplicationBase]\[AssemblyName]\[AssemblyName].dll
[ApplicationBase]\[PrivatePath1]\[AssemblyName].dll
[ApplicationBase]\[PrivatePath1]\[AssemblyName]\
➥[AssemblyName].dll
```

```
[ApplicationBase]\[PrivatePath2]\[AssemblyName].dll
[ApplicationBase]\[PrivatePath2]\[AssemblyName]\
➥[AssemblyName].dll
.
.
.
```

Here ApplicationBase is the root directory where the application is installed. AssemblyName is the text name of the assembly. PrivatePath1, PrivatePath2, and so on are the user-defined list of subdirectories specified either in the application's configuration file using the <probing> element or via the AppendPrivatePath property for an application domain.

- If there is no <codebase> element specified in the configuration files and if the culture information is available, then check the following locations (in the given order) for the assembly:

```
[ApplicationBase]\[culture]\[AssemblyName].dll
[ApplicationBase]\[culture]\[AssemblyName]\
➥ [AssemblyName].dll
[ApplicationBase]\[culture]\[PrivatePath1]\
➥ [AssemblyName].dll
[ApplicationBase]\[culture]\[PrivatePath1]\
➥ [AssemblyName]\[AssemblyName].dll
[ApplicationBase]\[culture]\[PrivatePath2]\
➥ [AssemblyName].dll
[ApplicationBase]\[culture]\[PrivatePath2]\
➥ [AssemblyName]\[AssemblyName].dll
.
.
.
```

Here ApplicationBase is the root directory where the application is installed. AssemblyName is the text name of the assembly. PrivatePath1, PrivatePath2, etc. are the user-defined list of subdirectories specified either in the application's configuration file using the <probing> element or via the AppendPrivatePath property for an application domain.

In the case of an assembly that is stored in the GAC, these rules ensure that the GAC copy is always the one used. Installing an assembly in the GAC overrides all other rules. Thus you can be sure that assemblies you place in the GAC are the copies that applications are actually using.

Delay Signing an Assembly

In Step by Step 13.9, when you signed an assembly you used a key file that contained both the public key and the private key for a company. But the private key ensures that the assembly is signed only by its advertised publisher. Thus in most companies the private key is stored securely and only a few people have access to it.

If the keys are highly protected, it might be difficult to frequently access the private key when multiple developers of a company are building assemblies several times a day. To solve this problem, .NET Framework uses a technique of delay signing an assembly.

Using delay signing you will only use the public key to build an assembly. Associating public keys with an assembly will allow you to place the assembly in the GAC and complete most of the development and testing tasks with the assembly. Later, when you are ready to package the assembly, someone who is authorized will sign the assembly with the private key. Signing with the private key will ensure that CLR will provide tamper protection for your assembly. The following list summarizes the various steps involved with delay signing:

- **Extracting a public key from the public/private key pair**: To extract the public key from a file storing the public/private key pair, you can use the strong name tool:

  ```
  sn.exe -p RandNumCorpKeys.snk RandNumCorpPublicKey.snk
  ```

  At this stage, the RandNumCorpPublicKey.snk file can be freely distributed to the development team while the RandNumCorpKeys.snk file that contains both private and public keys can be stored securely (possibly on a hardware device such as smart card).

- **Delay Signing an assembly using Visual Studio .NET**: To use delay signing in a Visual Studio .Net project modify the following two attributes of the project's Assemblyinfo.cs file and build the assembly:

  ```
  [<Assembly: AssemblyDelaySign(True)>
  <Assembly: AssemblyKeyFile( _
   "RandNumCorpPublicKey.snk")>
  ```

- **Turning off verification for an assembly in the GAC**: The default nature of GAC is to verify each assembly for its strong name. If the assembly is not signed using the private key, this verification will fail. So for development and testing purpose you can relax this verification for an assembly by issuing the following command:

  ```
  sn.exe -Vr RandomNumberGenerator.dll
  ```

  When you execute this command, GAC will always skip the verification for this assembly in future.

- **Signing a delay signed assembly with the private key**: When you are ready with the deployment of a delay signed assembly, you need to sign it with the company's private key.

  ```
  sn.exe -R RandomNumberGenerator.dll
  ➥RandNumCorpKeys.snk
  ```

- **Turning-on verification for an assembly in the GAC**: Finally you can instruct the GAC to turn-on verification for an assembly by the following command:

  ```
  sn.exe -Vu RandomNumberGenerator.dll
  ```

Delay Signing Using Assembly Linker Tool

The Assembly Linker Tool (al.exe) generates an assembly with an assembly manifest from the given modules or resource files. You will recall that a module is a MSIL file without an assembly manifest.

While generating an assembly, you can also instruct the Assembly Linker Tool to sign or delay sign an assembly with the given public/private key file. When using al.exe for delay signing, you will use the arguments listed in Table 13.1 with the command.

TABLE 13.1

ARGUMENTS PASSED TO AL.EXE FOR DELAY SIGNING

Arguments	*Description*
`<sourcefiles>`	In place of `<sourcefiles>` specify one or more complied modules that will be the parts of the resulting assembly.

Arguments	*Description*
`/delay[sign][+|-]`	You can use either the `delay` argument or the `delaysign` argument for delay signing. The option + is used to delay sign the assembly by storing just the public key manifest in the assembly manifest. The - option is used to fully sign an assembly using both public and private keys. Thus, `delaysign-` is the same as not specifying delay signing at all. If you do not use either + or -, the default value of - will be assumed.
`/keyf[ile]:<filename>`	You can use either `keyf` or `keyfile` to specify the keyfile. Replace `<filename>` with the name of the file storing the key(s).
`/out:<filename>`	Replace `<filename>` with the desired name of the output assembly file.

EXAM TIP

Strong Name and Authenticode Signature Assemblies signed with a strong name do not automatically assert a company's identity such as its name. For that purpose you can use an Authenticode signature where the company's identity is asserted by a third-party certification authority (like Verisign or Thawte). You can use the File signing tool (signcode.exe) to attach an authenticode signature with your assembly.

An important thing to know is the order of commands when signing an assembly using both sn.exe and signcode.exe. In this case, you must sign your assembly using Strong Name Tool (sn.exe) before signing it using the File Signing Tool (signcode.exe).

Assuming that you want to create an assembly by linking two modules, Sample1.netmodule and Sample2.netmodule. The public key file is SamplePublicKey.snk and the name of the desired output assembly is SignedSample.exe. You will use the al.exe command in the following form:

```
al.exe Sample1.netmodule,Sample2.netmodule /delaysign+
➥/keyfile:SamplePublicKey.snk
➥/out:SignedSample.exe
```

Creating a Setup Project for Distributing Components

You will now see how to create a setup project for distributing a component such as the RandomNumberGenerator component. The process of packaging a component is different from the process of packaging Windows applications. When you have a component that will be shared among multiple applications, you should package it as a merge module (.msm file). A merge module will include the actual component such as a .dll along with any related setup logic like adding resources, registry entries, custom actions, and launch conditions.

When you modify a component to release new versions, you will create a new merge module for each of its new versions. A new merge module should be created for each successive version of a component in order to avoid version conflicts.

Merge modules cannot be directly installed. They need to be merged with installers of applications that use the component packed into a merge module.

STEP BY STEP

13.15 Creating a Merge Module Project Using Setup Wizard to Package a Shared Component for Deployment

1. In the Solution Explorer window, right-click Solution and select Add, New Project. Select Setup and Deployment projects from the Project Types tree and then select Setup Wizard from the list of templates on the right. Name the project `RandomNumberMergeModule`.

2. The first screen that will appear is the Welcome screen. Click Next. The second page will show the Choose a project type screen. Choose Create a merge module for Windows Installer option in the second group (Do you want to create a redistributable package?). Click Next.

3. The third page will show the Choose project outputs to include screen. Select Primary output from `RandomNumberGenerator`. Click Next. Click Next on the fourth page and then click Finish.

4. Open the File System Editor for the merge module project. Add a new folder `RandNumCorp` to the `Common Files Folder`. Move the `Primary Output from RandomNumberGenerator (Active)` file in the `Common Files Folder` to the `RandNumCorp` folder.

5. Select the `File System on Target Machine` node and choose Add Special Folder – Global Assembly Cache Folder from the context menu. Select the `Global Assembly Cache` Folder and select Add – Project Output from the context menu.

6. This will open the Add Project Output Group dialog box. Select `RandomNumberGenerator` project and `Primary Output` from the list of items to be added and click OK.

7. Open the Registry Editor. Select `HKEY_LOCAL_MACHINE` node and add new keys hierarchically to the node in the order `HKEY_LOCAL_MACHINE - Software - Microsoft - .NETFramework - AssemblyFolders - RandNumCorp` as shown in Figure 13.33.

8. Add a new `String Value` to the newly added `RandNumCorp` key. Select the value and invoke the Properties window. Empty out the `Name` property. You will notice that when you empty out the `Name` property the [Default] name of the value is set as shown in Figure 13.33. Set the Value property to `[CommonFilesFolder]RandNumCorp\` where the assembly file copy is stored.

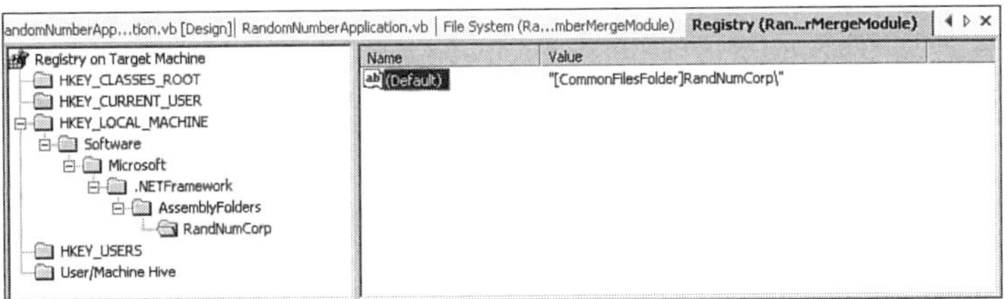

FIGURE 13.33
Setting the keys and value in the Registry Editor to add the assembly into Add Reference dialog box.

9. Build the `RandomNumberMergeModule` project. Open Windows Explorer and navigate to the `Release` folder inside the project folder. You will notice that the merge module `RandomNumberMergeModule.msm` is created.

If you want to distribute this component later with a Windows application, you can just add the merge module to your application's setup project. Guided Practice Exercise 13.3 shows how you can do this.

GUIDED PRACTICE EXERCISE 13.3

In this exercise, you will create a Setup Project that will install the Web application RandomNumberApplication and include the merge module RandomNumberMergeModule to install the component RandomNumberGenerator.dll.

continues

continued

This exercise will give you a good practice on how to create installers for applications that have components that are packaged as merge modules. I would recommend that you should first attempt doing this exercise on your own; if you would later like to see one of the possible solutions, follow these steps:

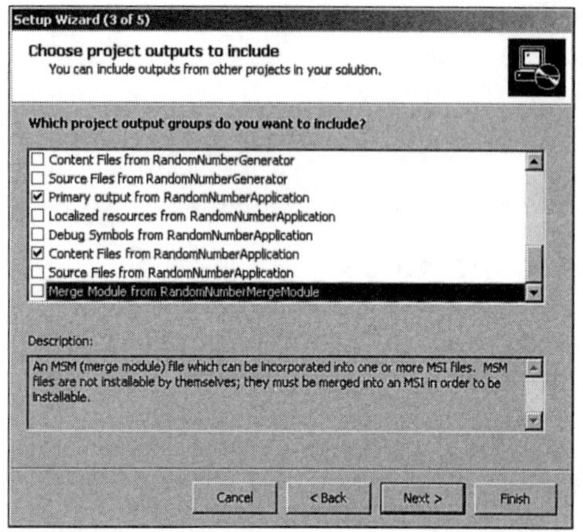

FIGURE 13.34
Choose project outputs to include Setup Wizard screen.

1. In the Solution Explorer window, right-click Solution and select Add, New Project. Select Setup and Deployment projects from the Project Types tree and then select Setup Wizard from the list of templates on the right. Name the project as RandomNumberAppSetup. Click OK. This will launch the Setup Wizard. The first screen that will appear is the Welcome screen. Click Next.
2. The second page will show the Choose a project type screen. Choose Create a Setup for a Web application in the first group of options. Click Next.
3. The third page will show the Choose project outputs to include screen. Select Primary output from RandomNumberApplication, Content Files from RandomNumberApplication, and Merge Module from RandomNumberMergeModule as shown in Figure 13.34. Click Next, Next, and then Finish to create the project.
4. You'll see that Application Folder in the File System Editor has two files: the Primary Output from RandomNumberApplication (Active) and Content Files From RandomNumberApplication (Active). The bin folder beneath this includes a copy of RandomNumberGenerator.dll. The RandomNumberGenerator.dll is included because by default the dependencies of the RandomNumberApplication project are included as well. Set the Exclude property of the RandomNumberGenerator.dll to True as the RandomNumberMergeModule already places the assembly copy into GAC.
5. Select the setup project RandomNumberAppSetup in the Solution Explorer. In the Properties Window, set the Manufacturer to "Random Number Corporation," ProductName to "Random Number Application" and Title to "Random Number Application."

6. Build the RandomNumberAppSetup project. Open Windows Explorer and navigate to the Release folder inside the project folder. Run the Setup.exe to install the project.
7. Open Windows Explorer and navigate to Assembly Cache folder path (typically it is C:\Winnt\assembly or C:\Windows\assembly). Scroll down the assemblies and you will notice that RandomNumberGenerator assembly is added into the GAC. Now navigate to C:\Program Files\Common Files\RandNumCorp ([CommonFilesFolder]RandNumCorp), where you will find a copy of the RandomNumberGenerator.dll in this folder.
8. Open Registry Editor by launching Regedit.exe from Windows Start, Run dialog box. In the registry editor, browse to the key named: HKEY_LOCAL_MACHINE\SOFTWARE\Microsoft\.NETFramework\AssemblyFolders. You will notice that a key with RandNumCorp is created with default value being C:\Program Files\Common Files\RandNumCorp path ([CommonFilesFolder]RandNumCorp). This all happens due to the actions performed in the Step by Step 13.15.
9. Now close all instances of Visual Studio .NET (if any were opened). Launch Visual Studio .NET. Open the Add Reference dialog box by loading any Windows application. Select the .NET tab, and browse through to find. You will notice that a reference to the C:\Program Files\Common Files\RandNumCorp\RandomNumberGenerator.dll is added as shown in Figure 13.35.

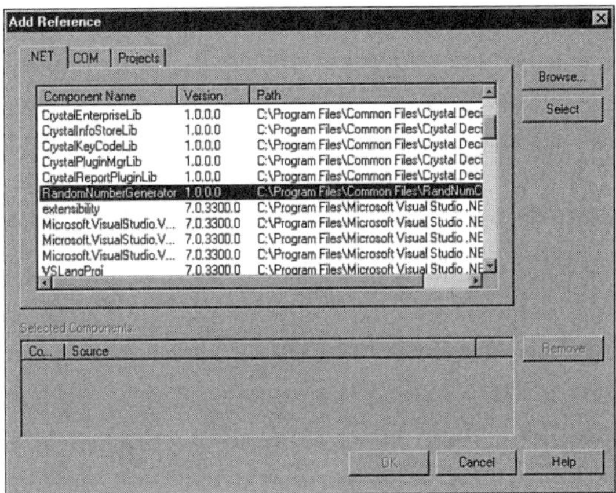

FIGURE 13.35
Add Reference dialog box showing reference to RandomNumberGenerator component.

REVIEW BREAK

- Shared assemblies are used by multiple applications on a machine. They are placed in the GAC and enjoy special priviliges such as file security (as they are placed in the System folder), shared locations and side-by-side versioning.
- Public/private key pairs are generated using the Strong Name tool (sn.exe). These pairs then can be used to digitally sign an assembly.
- A shared assembly can be added to GAC by using Windows Explorer, .NET Framework Configuration tool, Global Assembly Cache Tool (gacutil.exe), or the Installer tool.
- The best way to add an assembly during deployment is using Microsoft Windows Installer as it provides an assembly reference-counting feature and manages removal of the assembly at the time of uninstallation, when the reference-counting is just referring to the application being uninstalled.
- The Assembly Cache folder in the System folder when viewed in Windows Explorer displays assemblies from Global Assembly Cache and Native Image Cache.
- The CLR first searches the GAC to locate assemblies before looking into the files and folders where the assembly is installed. Thus shared assemblies placed in GAC are more efficient because the CLR does not engage itself in looking into <codebase> and <probing> elements of the applicable configuration files.
- Delay signing allows a shared assembly to be placed in the GAC by just signing the assembly with the public key. This allows the assembly to be signed with private key at a later stage when the development process is complete and the component or assembly is ready to be deployed. This process allows developers to work with shared assemblies as if they are strongly named and yet also secure the private-key of the signature from being accessed at different stages of development.
- Merge Module allows you to create reusable components that helps in deploying shared components. The Merge Modules cannot be directly installed. They need to be merged with installer programs of applications that use the component packed into a merge module.

CREATING INSTALLATION COMPONENTS

Create a Setup program that installs a Web application and allows for the application to be uninstalled.

When you develop an application using Visual Studio .NET, you may use several resources at the time of development, such as databases, event logs, performance counters, message queues, and so on. However, when you install the program on a user's machine, these resources might not be present there. A good installation program ensures that all necessary resources that are required by an application exist on the target machine.

The .NET Framework provides you with an Installer class that is defined in the System.Configuration.Install namespace. This class is specifically designed to help you perform customized installation actions like those mentioned previously. In this section I will explore various ways in which you can use the Installer class to create powerful installation programs.

I will show you how to use the predefined installation classes that are available with several components of Visual Studio .NET. I will also show you how to create your own classes that extend the Install class to perform specialized tasks at the time of installation.

Understanding the Installer Class

The System.Configuration.Install.Installer class works as a base class for all the custom installers in the .NET Framework. Some of the important members of Installer class that I will discuss in this chapter are listed in Table 13.2.

TABLE 13.2

IMPORTANT MEMBERS OF THE INSTALLER CLASS

Member Name	*Type*	*Description*
`Commit`	Method	The code in the `Commit()` method is executed if the `Install()` method executes successfully.
`Install`	Method	Performs the specified actions during an application's installation.

continues

TABLE 13.2 *continued*

IMPORTANT MEMBERS OF THE INSTALLER CLASS

Member Name	*Type*	*Description*
`Installers`	Property	Collection of `Installer` objects that are needed for this `Installer` instance to successfully install a component.
`Rollback`	Method	If the `Install()` method fails for some reason, the code in `Rollback()` method is called to undo any custom actions performed during the Install method.
`Uninstall`	Method	Perform the specified actions when a previously installed application is uninstalled.

You can derive a class from the Installer class and override the methods given in Table 13.2 to perform any custom actions.

If you want the derived Installer class to execute when an assembly is installed using a Setup project or by using the Installer Tool (InstallUtil.exe), you need to decorate the class with RunInstallerAttribute set to true:

```
<RunInstaller(true)>
```

The Installer classes provide the infrastructure for making installation a trasactional process. If an error is encountered during the Install( ) method, the Rollback( ) method will track back all the changes and undo them to leave the machine in the clean state as it was before the process of installation started. The Rollback( ) method must know the order in which the installation steps were performed and exactly what changes were made so that it can undo those changes in right order.

Similarly when an application is uninstalled, the Uninstall( ) method of the Installer class is called. The responsibility of the Uninstall method is again to undo the changes done by the installation process so that machine is left clean as if the program were never installed on it.

A question that arises is how does the Install( ) method communicate its installation information with the Rollback( ) and Uninstall method( )? This question becomes even more interesting when you see that the Install( ) and Uninstall( ) methods are not called in the same process. Install( ) is called when the application is installed, whereas Uninstall( ) is called when the application is uninstalled.

These two events might occur between several days and computer restarts.

The Install( ) method communicates the installation state by persisting it in a file with extension .InstallState. This file is placed in the installation directory of the application. The Installer class makes this file available to each of the Install( ), Commit( ), Rollback( ), and Uninstall( ) methods by passing an IDictionary object to the contents of this file. Content in the .InstallState file is used by the Rollback( ) and Uninstall( ) methods to perform the required cleanup operation.

Working with Predefined Installation Components

Most of the components available through the Server Explorer have a predefined installation component associated with them. For example, creating an instance of the EventLog component in your project allows you to add an installer corresponding to it with your project. When you set the properties of an EventLog object in your program, those properties will be remembered by the Installer component and will be reproduced on the target machine when the application is deployed.

In Step by Step 13.16, I'll show you how to create the required event log resources on the target machine at the times of installation with the help of predefined installation components.

STEP BY STEP

13.16 Using Predefined Components to Install an Event Source on a Target Computer

1. Add a new Visual Basic ASP.NET Web application project to the solution `305C13`. Name the project `EventLogApplication`.

2. Rename `WebForm1.aspx` to `EventLogApplication.aspx` in the project. Switch to the code view of the form and modify all references to WebForm1 to refer to `EventLogApplication` instead.

continues

continued

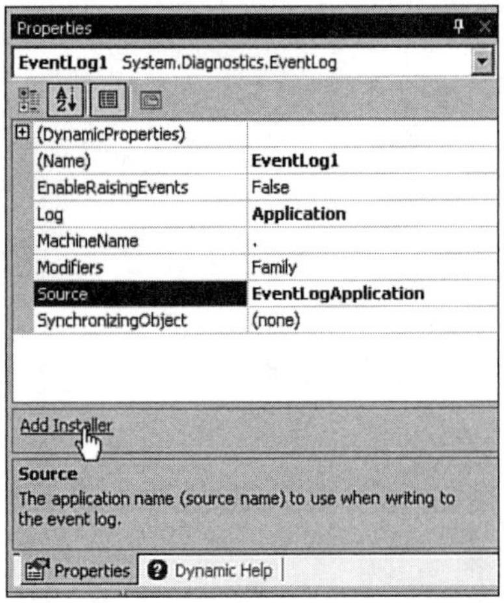

FIGURE 13.36
You can add an Installer class for EventLog component through the Add Installer hyperlink in the Properties Window.

> **WARNING**
>
> **Event Log Security** Allowing event log access to ASP.NET forms can be a security risk. If you're running ASP.NET as the untrusted machine account, this code won't run. You'll need to configure ASP.NET to use the trusted System account to complete this example. See Chapter 15, "Configuring a Web Application," for more details.

3. Open Server Explorer. Expand the tree under Event Logs. Drag and drop the Application event log to the Web form. This will create an `EventLog1` object that you will see in the component tray.

4. Access the properties of the `EventLog1` object and change its `Source` property to `EventLogApplication`. Change the `MachineName` property to `.` (a single dot), so that it will refer to the local computer no matter what computer the application is installed on. Click the Add Installer link just above the description area in the Properties window as shown in Figure 13.36. This will add a new class named `ProjectInstaller.vb` to the project. You will see that in design mode, `ProjectInstaller.vb` contains an object named `EventLogInstaller1`. This is the installation component for the event log created in the `EventLogApplication.cs` form.

5. Switch to the code view of `ProjectInstaller.vb`. You will note the use of the following attribute with the `ProjectInstaller` class.

```
<RunInstaller(true)>
```

   This attribute specifies whether this should be invoked during the execution of an assembly. View the component designer–generated code for this class. You will find all the necessary coding for installing an event log or event source on the target machine.

6. Switch to the design view of `EventLogApplication.aspx`, and add a `TextBox` (`txtMessage`) and a `Button` (`btnWrite`) control to the Form. Double-click the button control to attach an event handler to its `Click` event. Add the following code to the event handler:

```
Private Sub btnWrite_Click( _
 ByVal sender As System.Object, _
 ByVal e As System.EventArgs) Handles btnWrite.Click
    EventLog1.WriteEntry(txtMessage.Text)
End Sub
```

7. Build your project using the `Debug` mode. Run the project. Enter a value in the textbox and click the button. Open Server Explorer. Expand the Event Logs and the Application node. You will see a new source added to the Application event log on the Web server with a message that you give when you run the program.

8. Build your project using the `Release` mode. This project is now ready for deployment.

As you have observed in this Step by Step, when you click the Add Installer link for an `EventLog` component, a `ProjectInstaller` class is created in your project and the installation component for the `EventLog` component is added to this class. If you add additional installation components (for example, a `PerformanceCounter` installation component) to this project, they will be all added to this `ProjectInstaller` class. These are actually added to the `Installers` collection of this class. When you compile the project to build an `EXE` or a `DLL` file, the ProjectInstaller class is now part of the output assembly.

Deploying an Assembly Containing the Installation Components

There are two ways in which an assembly containing installation components can be deployed:

- Using a setup and deployment project
- Using the installer tool (InstallUtil.exe)

I will show you how to deploy an application containing installation components using both the techniques in the following sections.

Deploying an Installation Component Using the Setup Project

To deploy an application that consists of installation components, you will create a setup project as you would do normally.

But this time, you will use the Custom Actions Editor to deploy the additional resources needed for the application. At the time of deployment, the deployment project will execute the `ProjectInstaller` class as a part of its custom installation action to create component resources. Step by Step 13.17 shows you how.

STEP BY STEP

13.17 Using a Setup Project to Install Component Resources

1. Add a New Web Setup project to the solution. Name the project `EventLogApplicationSetup`.
2. Right-click the `EventLogApplicationSetup` project in the Solution Explorer. Select Add, Project Output from its shortcut menu. In the Add Project Output Group dialog Box, select `Primary Output` and `Content Files` of the `EventLogApplication` project.
3. Open the Custom Actions Editor for the `EventLogApplicationSetup` project. Select the Custom Actions node, and select Add Custom Action from its shortcut menu. This will open Select Item in Project dialog box. Look in the Web Application Folder and select `Primary Output from EventLogApplication(Active)`. Click OK. The primary output will be added to all the four nodes under Custom actions `Install`, `Commit`, `Rollback`, and `Uninstall`.
4. Select the new project in the Solution Explorer. Activate the Properties Window. Set the `Manufacturer` to `EventLog Application`, and the `ProductName` to `EventLogApplication`.
5. Build the `EventLogApplicationSetup` project. Take the project's output to a computer that does not already have an event source for the `EventLogApplication`. Alternatively, clear out the event log to wipe out previous traces of the program. Run the installation. You will note that setup program will install the `EventLogApplication` along with required event source.

6. Run the application's executable from the installation folder. Enter some text and click the button. Launch the Event Viewer from the Administrative Tools section of the Windows Control Panel. Select the Application log under Event Viewer node. You will notice your event log entries in the right pane of the event viewer.

Deploying an Installation Component Using the Installer Tool (InstallUtil.exe)

You can also use the command line Installer Tool (installutil.exe) to install the assemblies that contain additional component resources.

To install the resources contained in an assembly named Assembly1.dll, you can use the following form of InstallUtil.exe command:

```
InstallUtil.exe Assembly1.dll
```

You can also install resources contained in multiple assemblies together:

```
InstallUtil.exe Assembly1.dll Assembly2.dll Assembly3.dll
```

If you instead want to launch the uninstaller for installation classes stored in an assembly, you will use the /u or /uninstall option with the command:

```
InstallUtil.exe /u Assembly1.dll
```

EXAM TIP

InstallUtil.exe Performs Installation in a Transactional Manner If you are installing components from multiple assemblies using the InstallUtil.exe command, and any of the assemblies fails to install, InstallUtil.exe will roll back the installations of all the assemblies.

Working With Installer Classes

You can add your own Installer classes to a project to perform custom actions during installation, such as compiling the code to native image or creating a database on a target computer. These compiled installer classes from your project are then added to the deployment project as custom actions that are run at the end of the installation. The following are typical actions you would perform while creating a Custom Installer class:

- Inherit a class from the Installer class.
- Make sure that the RunInstallerAttribute is set to true in the derived class.

- Override the Install(), Commit(), Rollback(), and Uninstall() methods to perform any custom actions.
- In a Setup project, use the custom action editor to invoke this derived class to do the required processing.
- If needed, pass arguments from the Custom Actions Editors to the custom Installer class using the CustomActionData property.

In the following section, I'll show you how to use the preceding steps to create a custom installation program that translate the MSIL assemblies to native images using the ngen.exe tool.

Performing Install-time Compilation

Create a setup program that installs an application and allows for the application to be uninstalled: Perform an install-time compilation of a Windows-based application.

When assemblies are loaded at runtime, the CLR compiles the requested MSIL code into native code using a technique known as Just-In-Time (JIT) compilation. The advantage is that the next time a piece of code is called, it need not be converted again to the native code and will in turn execute faster.

Because of JIT compilation, an application that executes a lot of startup code will be slower when it starts. This problem can be solved by precompiling the MSIL code to the native code. The best place to do this conversion is at installation time because at that time the compilation can be done according to the exact architecture of the machine that will execute the code.

The compilation from MSIL to native code can be done using the Native code generation tool (ngen.exe) installed on the target machine. If you are using this at the install time, you will have to typically take the following steps:

- Find the location where the .NET Framework Runtime is installed on the target computer. This is the path where ngen.exe is located.

- Execute ngen.exe for each assembly that you wish to compile into native code. Your assemblies may be present either in a common location such as the Common Files folder or in a location specified by the user at the time of compilation. You need to find out this path so that you can create the correct command line for calling ngen.exe.

Step by Step 13.18 shows you how to create a custom installer class that will run ngen.exe and how to call the class from a setup project.

STEP BY STEP

13.18 Adding Custom Action to Perform Install-time Compilation

1. In the Solution Explorer window, add a Visual Basic Class Library project to the solution. Name the project `GenerateNativeImage`.

2. Right-click the project `GenerateNativeImage` and choose Add, Add New Item from the context menu. This will open Add New Item dialog box. Select `Installer` Class from the right pane as shown in Figure 13.37. Name it `GenerateNativeImage.vb`.

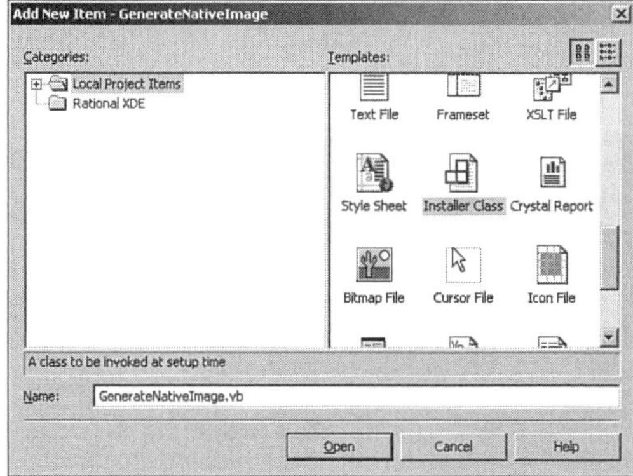

FIGURE 13.37
Adding Installer Class via Add New Item dialog box.

continues

continued

3. Open `GenerateNativeImage.vb` in code view. Add the following code at the top of the file:

```
Imports System.Diagnostics
Imports System.Text
Imports System.Runtime.InteropServices
```

4. Add the following code after the Component Designer generated code in the class definition:

```
' Gets the install directory for the version of the
' runtime that is loaded in the current process
Private Declare Function GetCORSystemDirectory Lib _
 "mscoree.dll" (<MarshalAs(UnmanagedType.LPWStr)> _
 ByVal Buffer As System.Text.StringBuilder, _
 ByVal BufferLength As Integer, _
 ByRef Length As Integer) As Integer

Public Overrides Sub Install( _
 ByVal savedState As System.Collections.IDictionary)
    ' Call the Install method of the base class
    MyBase.Install(savedState)
    ' Get the arguments to pass to the class
    Dim strArgs As String = _
     Me.Context.Parameters.Item("Args")
    If strArgs = "" Then
        Throw New InstallException( _
         "No arguments specified")
    End If

    ' Declare a StringBuilder to hold the path
    'of the ngen.exe on the target machine
    Dim strPath As StringBuilder = _
     New StringBuilder(1024)
    Dim intSize As Integer

    ' Call the mscoree.dll's _
    ' GetCORSystemDirectory method
    GetCORSystemDirectory(strPath, _
     strPath.Capacity, intSize)

    ' Run the ngen process with the
    ' arguments passed to the class
    Dim si As ProcessStartInfo = _
     New ProcessStartInfo(strPath.ToString() & _
        "ngen.exe ", "\"" & strArgs & " \ "")
    si.WindowStyle = ProcessWindowStyle.Hidden
    Try
        Dim p As Process = Process.Start(si)
        p.WaitForExit()
    Catch ex As Exception
        Throw New InstallException(ex.Message)
    End Try
End Sub
```

```
Public Overrides Sub Commit( _
 ByVal savedState As System.Collections.IDictionary)
    ' Call the Commit method of the base class
    MyBase.Commit(savedState)
End Sub

Public Overrides Sub Rollback( _
 ByVal savedState As System.Collections.IDictionary)
    ' Call the Rollback method of the base class
    MyBase.Rollback(savedState)
End Sub

Public Overrides Sub Uninstall( _
 ByVal savedState As System.Collections.IDictionary)
    ' Call the Uninstall method of the base class
    MyBase.Uninstall(savedState)
End Sub
```

5. Build the `GenerateNativeImage` project.

6. Select the `RandomNumberMergeModule` project in the Solution Explorer. Open the File System Editor for the merge module project. Move to the `RandNumCorp` folder in the `Common Files Folder` node. Add the `Primary Output from GenerateNativeImage (Active)` to the folder by selecting Add, Project Output from the Action menu.

7. Open the Custom Actions Editor for the merge module project. Select the Custom Actions node and select Add Custom Action from the context menu. This will open the Select Item in Project dialog box. Select `Primary Output from GenerateNativeImage (Active)` by navigating to the Common Files Folder – RandNumCorp folder. Click OK. This will add `Primary Output from GenerateNativeImage (Active)` to all the four nodes under Custom Actions.

8. Select the newly added custom action under the Install node. Open the Properties Window and set the `CustomActionData` property to `/Args="[CommonFilesFolder]RandNumCorp\RandomNumberGenerator.dll"`.

9. Build the `RandomNumberAppSetup` project. Install the project.

10. You will notice that a precompiled Native Image of `RandomNumberGenerator` assembly is added to the Native Image Cache as shown in Figure 13.38.

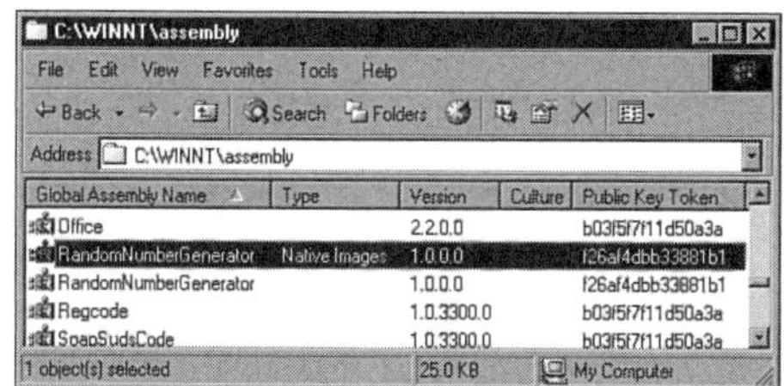

FIGURE 13.38
The Native Image Cache is centrally stored in the Assembly Cache along with the Global Assembly Cache.

In the preceding program note the use of CustomActionData property of the Custom Actions Editor. This property is used to pass installation data from a setup program to the custom installer class.

Another important thing to note from the preceding exercise is the use of the term Native Image Cache. The runtime stores all natively compiled assemblies in a central area called as Native Image Cache. The Native Image Cache is stored in a separate folder inside the Assembly Cache folder (usually c:\WINNT\assembly or c:\Windows\assembly) along with the Global Assembly Cache as shown in Figure 13.38. You can identify whether the assembly is from the GAC or from the Native Image Cache from the Type field in the list. You can also list the contents of Native Image Cache using the /show option with ngen.exe as shown in Figure 13.39.

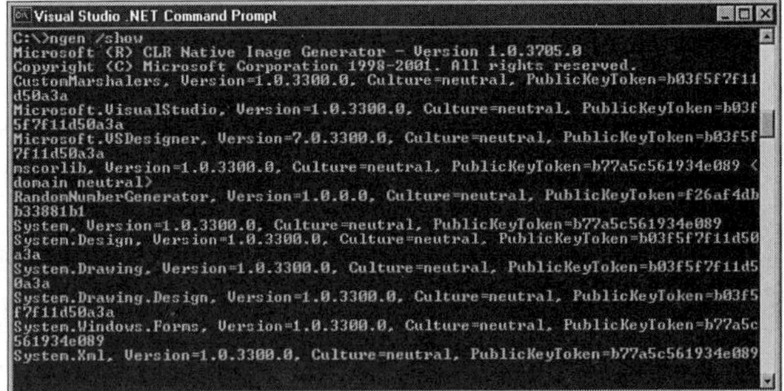

FIGURE 13.39
You can also use ngen.exe to view the contents of Native Image Cache.

REVIEW BREAK

- The System.Configuration.Install.Installer class works as a base class for all the custom installers in the .NET Framework.
- The Installer class method Install( ) is called when the application is installed, while Uninstall( ) is called when the application is uninstalled. The Commit( ) method is executed if the Install( ) method executes successfully and the Rollback( ) method is executed if the Install( ) method is not executed successfully.
- If you add predefined installation components (for example, a PerformanceCounter installation component) to the Setup project, they will be all added to the ProjectInstaller class. These are actually added to the Installers collection of this class.

- You can add your own custom Installer classes to a project to perform custom actions through the Custom Actions Editor during installation such as compiling the code to native image or creating a database on a target computer.
- The compilation from MSIL to the native code can be done using the Native Image Generator tool (ngen.exe). The assemblies that are compiled into machine-specific native code are placed in the Native Image Cache.

SCALABLE AND RELIABLE DEPLOYMENT

Plan the deployment of a Web Application: Plan the deployment of an application to a Web garden, a Web farm, or a cluster.

Web applications can be subject to considerable traffic. A popular Web site might have to support hundreds or thousands of simultaneous users. To handle this load reliably, designers have developed several server architectures. You should be aware of the differences between these architectures and their uses:

- Web garden
- Web farm
- Cluster

> **WARNING**
>
> **Beware of Tradeoffs** Although Web gardens and Web farms offer increased scalability for your application, they can involve other tradeoffs. In particular, if your application is distributed across multiple processors or multiple computers, you can't use simple session state to store user-related information; you'll need to move to using the State Service or a SQL Server database to store session state. See Chapter 15, "Configuring a Web Application," for more details on session state.

Web Gardens

A *Web garden* is a Web application that is distributed across more than one processor on a multiprocessor computer. Web gardening is the default behavior for ASP.NET. For example, suppose you install an ASP.NET application on a computer with eight CPUs. In this case, ASP.NET will automatically launch eight worker processes to handle incoming Web requests, and assign one of these processes to each CPU (a procedure known as setting the affinity of the process).

Web gardens offer the benefit of faster response times on a multiple CPU computer. In particular, if one worker process hangs or slows down due to programming errors or unexpected input, the Web garden can continue serving requests from the other worker processes.

Because ASP.NET enables this behavior automatically, you don't have to do anything to gain the benefit of a Web garden. However, you may want to configure your Web server to not use every processor for Web gardening. To do this, you can set the value of two attributes within the processModel element of the web.config file:

- webGarden. When set to True, this attribute directs Windows to schedule processes to CPUs (thus enabling the default behavior of Web gardening). When set to False, this attribute uses the cpuMask attribute to determine which processors should participate in a Web garden.
- cpuMask. This attribute is a bitmask indicating which processors should participate in a Web garden. For example, setting cpuMask to 7 would indicate that processors 0, 1, and 2 (and no others) should participate in a Web garden.

> NOTE **Configuration Files** See Chapter 15 for more details on using configuration files with ASP.NET.

Changes to the processModel element only take effect when IIS is restarted, and are only effective in the top-level web.config file. For these reasons, Web gardening is best customized by the system administrator rather than as part of a setup package.

Web Farms

A *Web farm* takes the concept of a Web garden and extends it to multiple computers. In a Web farm, your application runs on multiple Web servers at the same time. Some mechanism outside of the Web servers is used to distribute requests to the individual servers.

Web farms offer the benefits of both scalability and reliability. Your application is more scalable because you can increase its capacity by adding more computers to the Web farm. Your application is more reliable because a failure of any one server does not affect the other servers. Although requests that were in process at the failing server may not receive responses, the other computers in the Web farm can continue running despite the failure.

Web farms are typically enabled by a technique known as Network Load Balancing (NLB). NLB can be implemented in either hardware or software. Hardware devices, such as Cisco LocalDirector or F5 Networks' BIG-IP, distribute incoming HTTP requests among a pool of Web servers. Software NLB is built into the Windows 2000 Advanced Server operating system and is available for the Windows 2000 Server operating system as part of Microsoft Application Server. Software NLB, although not supporting quite as many computers as hardware NLB, is less expensive to implement.

Provided that you've chosen an appropriate option for storing session state, you do not need to change your application at all for deployment on a Web farm. Your system administrator can simply run the setup program for your application on each server in the Web farm, and then configure the Web farm using the tools built into Windows 2000 or Application Center.

Clusters

Clustering provides a second method of combining multiple computers for a single purpose. The goal of clustering is not to provide additional scalability, but to provide additional reliability. In a cluster, multiple computers are configured using the same software, but only one of these computers is active at any given time. The active server handles all requests unless it experiences a hardware or software failure. At that point, the clustering software automatically directs requests to the standby server, which becomes the new active server.

Clustering solutions are typically implemented with hardware that includes shared storage. You might, for example, have two computers sharing the same external array of hard drives to store information. If the active server fails, the standby server can pick up where the active server left off, using the same disks for storing application data.

Clustering is a built-in feature of the Windows server operating systems. You can also use products such as Microsoft Application Center to make it easier to manage software on a cluster. But like Web farms, clusters have no impact on the coding of your Visual Basic .NET applications.

Methods of Deployment

After you have created a setup package, you can deploy your application from any location that's accessible to all its potential users. The Web-based applications exam requires you to know about two types of deployment:

- Deployment via removable media
- Web-based deployment

The following sections discuss each of these deployment options.

Deployment via Removable Media

Plan the deployment of a Web application: Plan a deployment that uses removable media.

The most common examples of removable media are floppy disks, CD-ROMs, and DVDs. Deployment via removable media is suitable under the following conditions:

- Users are in many locations without any common central connection.
- Not all the users have access to the Internet.
- Application size is huge and not all users have access to a high-speed Internet connection.

Deployment via removable media is becoming more outdated with every new day. It involves costs for media, replication, and distribution that can be easily eliminated by other deployment options. But deployment via removable media is still the "lowest common denominator" solution and will cover the maximum number of users.

Deployment projects in Visual Studio .NET can be used to create packages divided across multiple files each with small size as specified by the developer. These small-sized files then can be copied to floppy disks or CD-ROM and distributed to the users.

To create a setup project for removable media, create a setup project as you would normally do. Right-click the project in the Solution Explorer window and select Properties from its shortcut menu.

In the Properties page, change Package files to "In cabinet file(s)". This will enable the CAB size option. Set the CAB size to custom and set the size depending on your media size as shown in Figure 13.40.

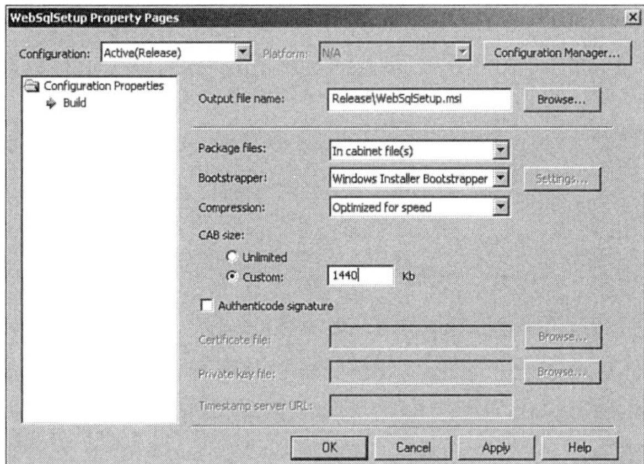

FIGURE 13.40
Setting the Setup project configuration properties to create an installation package in cabinet files of size 1440KB.

Now build the setup project. It will create a Windows Installer package (MSI file) and one or more CAB files depending on the size of the application. If the Bootstrapper option was set to Windows Installer Bootstrapper, it will also create a Setup.exe file. When you copy all these files to the removable media, copy Setup.exe and the MSI file to the first disk and then copy each CAB file to a separate disk.

Web-based Deployment

Plan the deployment of a Web application: Plan a Web-based deployment.

Web-based deployment is the most popular form of deployment especially for small-sized applications. With the growth of high-speed Internet connections, you will see this form of deployment in higher demand as compared to removable media. It offers several advantages over other forms of application deployment:

- It reduces the cost of media, replication, and distribution.
- Management of software updates is simple. You can program an application so that it can check for updates automatically on the Web or you can instruct users to download the setup from a Web page.

Creating a setup package for Web-based deployment is the same as creating a setup package for direct deployment, just as you did for most of the applications in this chapter. Once the setup files are created, rather than copying them to a network share or directly to the target computer, you will copy them to a virtual directory on a Web server. You may also want to password protect the deployment Web site so that only authorized users are able to download your application. You can then install the application by navigating to the virtual directory and executing the setup.exe program that you find there.

REVIEW BREAK

- You should select a deployment method that is convenient and accessible to all the product's users.
- You can create installation packages in multiple cabinet files by choosing the "In cabinet file(s)" option in the Project Property pages.
- Web-based deployment reduces the cost of media, replication, and distribution. It also makes the management of software updates simple.

CHAPTER SUMMARY

The chapter focused on how to deploy Web-based applications. Some simple applications will be as easy to deploy as just copying the files from one location to another, whereas some applications may be complex and may require reliance on Microsoft Windows Installer Service. I discussed how to create Setup projects to deploy Web-based applications. I also discussed how to use various types of editors provided in the Setup and Deployment projects to perform specific types of tasks. Through these editors you can perform various tasks on the target machine such as placing files in multiple folders including the GAC, creating registry keys and values in the registry editor, associating file types with the application, checking on dependencies, performing custom actions at different phases like during Install, Commit, Rollback and Uninstall, customizing the user-interface of the installation process, and many more.

Later in the chapter, I discussed shared assemblies. You saw how to use the Strong Name tool (sn.exe) to digitally sign an assembly. Strong Name tools can be also used to perform delayed signing for an assembly. I also discussed how you can add assemblies to the GAC through Windows Explorer, Microsoft .NET Framework Configuration Tool, Global Assembly Cache tool, (gacutil.exe) and through Microsoft Windows Installer by using the Setup and Deployment projects.

I also discussed how to precompile a Windows application during installation by creating an Installer class and adding the class to the custom actions. Finally, I discussed alternative architectures for more reliable and scalable Web applications, and summarized the different ways in which Web applications can be deployed.

KEY TERMS

- Delayed signing
- Deployment
- Merge module
- Native compilation
- Native Image Cache

APPLY YOUR KNOWLEDGE

Exercises

13.1 Using Microsoft's Sample .NET Framework Bootstrapper

The setup projects created in the chapter assume that the .NET Framework is already installed on the target machine. You cannot use Visual Studio .NET Setup and Deployment projects to package the required .NET Framework along with a setup package. The .NET Framework has to be installed on target machine using a .NET Framework redistributable file (dotnetfx.exe) that is available through

- The Windows Component Upgrade CD that comes with Visual Studio .NET
- The Microsoft MSDN Download Center (http://msdn.microsoft.com/downloads/sample.asp?url=/MSDN-FILES/027/001/829/msdncompositedoc.xml) or from the Microsoft Windows Update Website (http://windowsupdate.microsoft.com)

Ideally you would like a Web application's installation program to perform a test for availability of the .NET Framework on the target machine. If the .NET Framework is not already installed, install it using the .NET Framework redistributable file (dotnetfx.exe).

In this exercise I will show you how to use the Microsoft's sample .NET Framework bootstrapper Setup.exe file along with a setup package generated through Visual Studio .NET to check for the availability of the .NET Framework on a user's machine and install it using the .NET Framework redistributable, if it is not already installed.

Estimated Time: 20 minutes.

1. Open the solution 305C13. In the Solution Explorer, select the WebSqlSetup Project.
2. Right-click the project and select Properties from the shortcut menu. In the WebSqlSetup Project Property Pages, change the Bootstrapper option to None. Click OK and build the project.
3. You will notice that only WebSqlSetup.msi file has been created in the bin\Release folder of the WebSqlSetup project.
4. Download the Setup.exe Bootstrapper sample from http://msdn.microsoft.com/downloads/sample.asp?url=/msdn-files/027/001/830/msdncompositedoc.xml.
5. Install the downloaded sample. It will install two files on your computer, Setup.exe and settings.ini. Copy both the files to the bin\Release folder of the WebSqlSetup project.
6. Open the settings.ini file in any text editor. Change its contents with the text as follows:

   ```
   [Bootstrap]
   Msi=WebSqlSetup.msi
   'LanguageDirectory=jpn
   'ProductName=testproductname
   'DialogText=
   'CaptionText=
   'ErrorCaptionText=
   FxInstallerPath=d:\dotNetFramework
   ```

   The value of FxInstallerPath is the path where you have stored the .NET Framework re-distributable file dotnetfx.exe. You can change the value to the actual path that you're using.
7. Open the setup.exe file. The installation is now bootstrapped by the sample setup.exe file. It will first test for the availability of the .NET Framework; if not, it will use the path specified in the FxInstallerPath to install the .NET Framework. Here you would note that there are no bootstrap files for installing Microsoft Windows Installer. This is because that check is a part of the .NET Framework installation and will be automatically performed by dotnetfx.exe.

APPLY YOUR KNOWLEDGE

13.2 Creating Database Scripts During Installation

You have already seen that the Custom Actions Editor allows you to perform custom actions during the installation process. In this exercise, you will create a custom action to run the Northwind database installation script during installation of WebSql project. You will use osql, a command-line utility to run the sql script. This exercise assumes that you have Microsoft SQL Server installed on your machine.

Estimated Time: 20 minutes.

1. Open the solution 305C13. Add a Visual Basic .NET Class Library project to the solution. Name the project InstallNorthwind.

2. Add the Northwind database installation script "instnwnd.sql" (usually available in the Microsoft SQL Server installation directory) file to the project.

3. Right-click the project InstallNorthwind and choose Add, Add New Item from the context menu. This will open the Add New Item dialog box. Add an installer class named InstallNorthwind.vb to the project.

4. Open `InstallNorthwind.vb` file in the code view. Add the following directive:

   ```
   Imports System.Diagnostics
   ```

5. Add the following code after the Component Designer generated code in the class definition:

   ```
   Public Overrides Sub Install( _
    ByVal savedState As _
    System.Collections.IDictionary)
       ' call the Install method
       ' of the base class
       MyBase.Install(savedState)
       Dim strSqlFilePath As String = _
        Me.Context.Parameters.Item("Args")
       ' Run the osql process to run
       ' the database script
       Dim psi As ProcessStartInfo = _
        New ProcessStartInfo("osql.exe ", _
        "-E -i " & "\"" & _
        strSqlFilePath & " \ "")
       psi.WindowStyle = _
        ProcessWindowStyle.Hidden
       Try
           Dim p As Process = _
            Process.Start(psi)
           p.WaitForExit()
       Catch e As Exception
           ' throw InstallException with
           ' the original exception message
           Throw New InstallException( _
            e.Message + strSqlFilePath)
       End Try
   End Sub

   Public Overrides Sub Commit( _
    ByVal savedState As _
    System.Collections.IDictionary)
       ' Call the Commit method
       ' of the base class
       MyBase.Commit(savedState)
   End Sub

   Public Overrides Sub Rollback( _
    ByVal savedState As _
    System.Collections.IDictionary)
       ' Call the Rollback method
       ' of the base class
       MyBase.Rollback(savedState)
   End Sub

   Public Overrides Sub Uninstall( _
    ByVal savedState As _
    System.Collections.IDictionary)
       ' Call the Uninstall method
       ' of the base class
       MyBase.Uninstall(savedState)
   End Sub
   ```

6. Build the InstallNorthwind project.

7. Select the WebSqlSetup project in the Solution Explorer. Open the File System Editor for the project. Select the Application Folder node and add the Primary Output from InstallNorthwind (Active) to the folder by selecting Add, Project Output from the Action menu.

APPLY YOUR KNOWLEDGE

8. Open the Custom Actions Editor for the WebSqlSetup project. Select Custom Actions node and select Add Custom Action from the context menu. This will open the Select Item in Project dialog box. Select Primary Output from InstallNorthwind (Active) by navigating to Application Folder. Click OK. This will add Primary Output from InstallNorthwind (Active) to all the four nodes under Custom Actions.
9. Select the newly added custom action under the Install node. Move it before the Launch WebSql custom action. Open Properties Window and set the CustomActionData property to /Args="[TARGETDIR]instnwnd.sql".
10. Build the WebSqlSetup project. Install the project.
11. You will notice that this time during installation the Northwind database installation script is also executed.

Review Questions

1. What are the advantages and disadvantages of XCOPY and FTP deployment?
2. What are the different parts of an assembly version?
3. What is the purpose of the File System Editor?
4. How can you customize the user interface of an installation process?
5. When can you call the custom actions to be performed?
6. What are shared assemblies?
7. Where is the GAC located on a machine? How can you add items to the GAC?
8. What is the use of delay signing?
9. When should you use a Merge Module project?
10. How can you convert code into native code? Where are the precompiled assemblies placed?
11. What is the purpose of the CustomActionData property in the Custom Actions Editor?

Exam Questions

1. You have created a database-driven Windows application. Using Microsoft SQL Server, you have also generated an installation script for your database. This script is stored in a file named InstData.sql. You want to deploy this application on a Web server. When the application is deployed, the database should also be created on the same server. You are creating a Setup project using Visual Studio .NET. Which of the following actions should you take to create the database while deploying your application on the Web server?

   A. Create a component that derives from the Installer class. Override its Install method to create the database. Add the component to the Install node of the Custom Actions editor in the Setup project.

   B. Create a component that derives from the Installer class. Override its Install method to create the database. Add the component to the Commit node of the Custom Actions editor in the Setup project.

APPLY YOUR KNOWLEDGE

C. Copy the InstData.sql file to the Application Folder on the File System on Target Machine using the File System Editor. Add InstData.sql to the Install node of the Custom Actions editor in the Setup project.

D. Create a component that derives from the Installer class. Override its Install method to create the database. Add the component to the Launch Conditions editor in the Setup project.

2. You are creating a Setup project for a Web application. In the Property Pages for the Setup project you have set the compression property to "Optimized for speed." Which of the following options will be true as a result of this configuration option? (Choose two.)

   A. All assemblies in the application will be precompiled to native code so that they run faster.

   B. Resulting assemblies will be of larger size.

   C. The setup package will be larger.

   D. The setup project will run faster.

3. You have developed a database-intensive Web application. When the application is installed on the user's computer, it must also install the required database. The execution of the program cannot continue without the database. Therefore, if the setup of database fails, you would like to rollback the installation process. Which of the following editor would you use in the Setup project to ensure that database is properly installed on the target machine?

   A. File System Editor.

   B. Custom Actions Editor.

   C. Launch Conditions Editor.

   D. Registry Editor.

4. You have created a Web application that uses some components that are not shared by other applications. Each component creates its own assemblies and all these assemblies have a strong name associated with them. The application that uses these components is not required to load a specific version of these components. You do not want to store the assembly directly under the application's installation folder. Which of the following options is the best approach to store the assembly files for the application's components?

   A. Store the components in Global Assembly Cache.

   B. Store the components anywhere you like and specify the path to them using the <codebase> element in the application's configuration file.

   C. Store the assemblies in one of the subdirectories under the application's installation directory and specify this subdirectory as part of the <probing> element in the application's configuration file.

   D. Store the components in the Windows System directory.

5. When you install a Web application on a target machine, you want to store the Readme.txt file in the directory selected by the user to install the application. You also want to create a shortcut for the Readme.txt file on the desktop of the target machine. While creating a Setup project, which of the following actions will you take in the File System Editor to achieve this? (Select all that apply.)

APPLY YOUR KNOWLEDGE

A. Move the shortcut to Readme.txt file from the application folder to the user's desktop in the file system on the target machine.

B. Add the Readme.txt file to the Application Folder node of the file system on the target machine.

C. Create a shortcut to Readme.txt file available in the Application Folder node of the file system on the target machine.

D. Add the Readme.txt file to the user's desktop in the file system on the target machine.

E. Move the shortcut to Readme.txt file from the user's desktop to the application folder in the file system on the target machine.

6. You have written a component that will be shared among multiple applications. You want to install the component to the Global Assembly Cache. Which of the following tools will you use to achieve this? (Choose two.)

   A. sn.exe

   B. gacutil.exe

   C. ngen.exe

   D. installUtil.exe

7. You are a developer in a large manufacturing company. You are developing a complex inventory control application with a team of 15 other developers. You have written two program modules, inv1234.vb and inv5678.vb, that are generic and will be used from several other applications within the company. You compiled both the program modules using the Visual Basic .NET compiler, producing inv1234.netmodule and inv5678.netmodule files. You now want to link both the compiled modules into an assembly that you would install in the Global Assembly Cache to test some Windows forms that depend on this assembly.

   You have decided to keep the name of the assembly as InvLib.dll. You do not have access to the private key of the company, although you have access to company's public key. The public key is stored in a file named BigCoPublic.snk. When the testing is completed, your project manager will use the private key (stored in BigCoPrivate.snk file) to fully sign all the assemblies in the accounting software application. Which of the following commands will you choose to successfully sign your assembly?

   A.

   ```
   al.exe inv1234.netmodule,inv5678.netmodule
   ➥ /delaysign /keyfile:
   ➥BigCoPublic.snk /out:InvLib.dll
   ```

   B.

   ```
   al.exe inv1234.netmodule,inv5678.netmodule
   ➥ /delaysign+ /keyfile:
   ➥BigCoPublic.snk /out:InvLib.dll
   ```

   C.

   ```
   al.exe inv1234.netmodule,inv5678.netmodule
   ➥ /delaysign- /keyfile:
   ➥BigCoPublic.snk /out:InvLib.dll
   ```

   D.

   ```
   csc.exe inv1234.cs,inv5678.cs /delaysign
   ➥ /keyfile:BigCoPublic.snk
   ➥ /out:InvLib.dll
   ```

8. You are using the Installer Tool (installutil.exe) to install server resources by executing the installer components in three assemblies. You issued the following command:

   ```
   installutil Assembly1.exe Assembly2.exe
   ➥ Assembly3.exe
   ```

   While executing this command, the installation of Assembly3 failed. Which of the following will happen?

   A. Only Assembly1.exe will be installed.

   B. Only Assembly2.exe will be installed.

APPLY YOUR KNOWLEDGE

C. Both Assembly1.exe and Assembly2.exe will be installed.

D. None of the assemblies will be installed.

9. You have developed a Web control that will be used to provide consistent navigation links across all your company's Web applications. These applications will be developed by many different developers and deployed across multiple servers. The Web control should be installed in the GAC. Which method should you use for deploying this control?

   A. Merge module

   B. FTP deployment

   C. Windows setup project

   D. Web setup project

10. You are deploying a mission-critical Web application for your company. Which of these configurations will enable your application to continue functioning even if a critical hardware component such as a power supply fails? (Select two.)

    A. Single-server deployment

    B. Web farm deployment

    C. Web garden deployment

    D. Cluster deployment

11. You want to create a customized setup program for a Web application. One of the screens shown during installation should be available only from the administrative installation of the Microsoft Windows Installer package. Other setup options are available for both regular as well as administrative installations. Which of the following editors will allow you to create such an installation program?

    A. File System Editor

    B. User Interface Editor

    C. Custom Actions Editor

    D. Launch Conditions Editor

12. You have used a native compilation option for several assemblies in your Web application. During the testing of the application it was reported that one of the several parameters on the Order Entry Forms are displayed incorrectly. You determine that the classes involved in the problem are part of the Native Image Cache. You want to analyze the contents of the Native Image cache on the Web server to see if the correct versions of the assemblies are installed there. Which of the following methods can you use to view the contents of the Native Image Cache? (Select all that apply.)

    A. Use Assembly Cache Viewer (shfusion.dll) shell extension.

    B. Use Global Assembly Cache Tool (GacUtil.exe).

    C. Use Native Image Generator Tool (ngen.exe).

    D. Use Assembly Binding Log Viewer (fuslogvw.exe).

13. You work as a software developer for a big pharmacy. You are writing some components that will be shared across several applications throughout the company. You want to place an assembly named CommonComponents.dll in the global assembly cache for testing purpose. You do not have access to the company's private key but you have stored the company's public key in the assembly manifest of CommonComponents.dll.

APPLY YOUR KNOWLEDGE

Which of the following commands you are required to run to place your assembly in the GAC. (Select all that apply.)

A. sn.exe –Vr CommonComponents.dll

B. sn.exe –Vu CommonComponents.dll

C. gacutil.exe /i CommonComponents.dll

D. gacutil.exe /u CommonComponents.dll

14. Your Web application is already deployed to your company's production Web server when you discover a logic error in the Visual Basic .NET code behind one of the application's Web Forms. You have corrected the error and rebuilt the application on the test server. What is the easiest way to transfer the changes to the production server?

A. Use FTP to move the changed files to the production server. Restart the WWW service on the production server.

B. Build a Windows Installer project to install the entire application. Run the Installer project on the production server. Restart the WWW service on the production server.

C. Use FTP to move the changed files to the production server. Do not restart the WWW service on the production server.

D. Build a Windows Installer project to install the entire application. Run the Installer project on the production server. Do not restart the WWW service on the production server.

15. You are designing a Web application that will be deployed to multiple Web servers owned by independent software vendors (ISVs). The application uses several components that need to be installed on the Global Assembly Cache on the Web server. You want to sign your components with a cryptographic digital signature as well with an Authenticode signature where the Identity of your company is certified through an independent certifying authority. Which of the option will you use for signing the components before they are packaged for deployment.

A. Use sn.exe to sign the assemblies.

B. Use signcode.exe to sign the assemblies.

C. Use sn.exe followed by signcode.exe to sign your assemblies.

D. Use signcode.exe followed by sn.exe to sign your assemblies.

Answers to Review Questions

1. XCOPY deployment is suitable for deploying small and simple applications that contain private assemblies. XCOPY deployment makes zero impact on the configuration of the target machine. However, it lacks most of the amenities provided by the Microsoft Windows Installer, such as copying files and shortcuts on different places in the target machine, associating file types with the extensions, allowing custom actions to be performed during installation process, providing ability to rollback the installation process, uninstalling an application, repairing a component or an application, checking for dependencies and rollback the installation process when the dependencies do not exists, providing a user-interface and many more. Further, XCOPY deployment is also not suitable when you want to place components or assemblies of an application in the GAC. FTP deployment has the same advantages and drawbacks as XCOPY deployment, with the benefit that you can use FTP deployment over the Internet.

APPLY YOUR KNOWLEDGE

2. The different parts of an assembly version are: <major>.<minor>.<build>.<revision>
3. The File System Editor provides a mapping of the file system on the target machine. The folders are referred to by special names that during the installation process are converted to represent the folder as per the file system on the target machine.
4. The User Interface Editor allows you to create your own user-interface for the installation process. There are three stages of installation: Start, Progress, and End. The editor allows you to add different varieties of dialog boxes to each of the different stages. It provides special properties whose values can be evaluated to perform the installation as per the end user's choice.
5. Custom actions can be performed in four phases—Install, Commit, Rollback, and Uninstall.
6. Shared assemblies are shared by multiple applications on a machine and are placed in GAC. A shared assembly should have a strong name consisting of its text name (usually the name of the file without the file extension), version number, culture information, and the public key token. The public key token is retrieved by digitally signing an assembly.
7. The GAC is located in the assembly folder under the system folder (/WINNT or /WINDOWS) on a machine. Shared assemblies in the GAC can be viewed by navigating to the assembly folder in the Windows Explorer. You can add shared assemblies to the GAC through Windows Explorer, or the .NET Framework Configuration tool (mscorcfg.msc), or the Global Assembly Cache command-line tool (gacutil.exe) or through the Windows Installer technology.
8. Delay signing is a process that allows a shared assembly to be placed in the GAC by just signing the assembly with the public key. This allows the assembly to be signed with private key at a later stage when the development process is complete and the component or assembly is ready to be deployed.
9. Merge Modules should be used to package components with their related resources, registry entries, custom actions and launch conditions. Merge modules cannot be installed directly but rather are merged with into an installer project.
10. Compilation from MSIL to the native code can be done using the Native Image Generator tool (ngen.exe). The assemblies that are compiled into machine-specific native code are placed in the Native Image Cache.
11. The CustomActionData property is used to pass custom data from a setup program to the custom installer class.

Answers to Exam Questions

1. **A.** You can use the Custom Actions editor to take custom actions like database installation during the application setup. If you have an Installer class or program that creates database that must be added to the Install node of the Custom Actions editor.
2. **C** and **D**. When you modify a setup project's property it will not affect the size or the speed of the installed assemblies. Instead, the setup program will compress the assemblies using a compression algorithm optimize for speed. As a result, you will have a lower compression ratio resulting in large size setup package but that will execute faster.

APPLY YOUR KNOWLEDGE

3. **B**. The Custom Actions editor allows you to execute custom actions like database installations while running the setup program. It also has provisions for performing an installation rollback if the installation operation fails.

4. **C**. If the components are not shared between applications then it is not a good idea to store it in the Global Assembly Cache. You could have used the <codebase> element in the application's configuration file but in that case you must specify a version of assembly. The applications in question are not specific about versions so a good place to store the assemblies is a folder inside the application's installation folder and specify its location via the <probing> element in the application's configuration file.

5. **A, B,** and **C**. To copy the Readme.txt file to the installation directory selected by user at install time, you would add it to the application folder in the file system on the target machine. To create a shortcut, you will first create a shortcut to the Readme.txt file stored in the application folder in the file system on the target machine. Then, you will move this shortcut from the application folder to the user's desktop in the file system on the target machine.

6. **A** and **B**. When you want to install a component to the GAC, you will first assign it with a strong name. This is done using the Strong Name tool (sn.exe). A strong named assembly can be placed in the GAC using the Global Assembly Cache Tool (gacutil.exe).

7. **B**. The al.exe command can be used to link already compiled modules into an assembly. The process of including a public key in the assembly and signing it with a private key at a later stage is called delay signing. The delay signing can be perform with al.exe on an assembly by using /delay+ switch.

8. **D**. InstallUtil.exe performs installation in a transactional manner. If one of the assemblies fails to install, it rolls back the installations of all other assemblies. So if Installation of Assembly3.exe fails, none of the assemblies will be installed.

9. **A**.The merge module can be incorporated into many different application setup projects, and can perform advanced operations, such as inserting assemblies in the GAC. XCOPY deployment cannot register the control in the GAC. A Windows or Web setup project cannot be merged with other setup projects.

10. **B** and **D**. Single-server and Web garden installations place the application on a single physical server, where a failure of a critical hardware component can bring down the whole application. Web farm and cluster deployments use multiple servers to provide redundancy and hardware fault tolerance to an application.

11. **B**. You can customize the user-interface of an installation program by using the User Interface editor for both the regular installation and administrative installation.

12. **A, B,** and **C**. The Native Image Cache can be viewed with all of the above tools except for the Assembly Binding Log Viewer (fuslogvw.exe) that is used to display failed assembly binds.

13. **A** and **C**. You will have to first turn off the verification for partially signed assemblies. This can be done by using the sn.exe tool with the –Vr switch.

APPLY YOUR KNOWLEDGE

Next the assembly can be installed to the GAC using /i switch with the gacutil.exe command.

14. **C.** If a Web application is already installed on IIS, you can simply replace any updated files. ASP.NET will detect the changed files and automatically recompile the pages as they are requested by clients.

15. **C.** sn.exe is used to sign assemblies with a cryptographic digital certificate where signcode.exe is used to sign assemblies with an Authenticode signature. When both are used together to sign an assembly, you should always use sn.exe before using signcode.exe.

Suggested Readings and Resources

1. The Visual Studio .NET Combined Help Collection, including the following:
   - Deploying Applications and Components
   - Deployment Walkthroughs
   - Creating Installation Components
2. Jeffery Ritcher. *Applied Microsoft .NET Framework Programming.* Microsoft Press, 2002
3. `http://msdn.microsoft.com/library/en-us/dnnetsec/html/v1securitychanges.asp`
4. `http://msdn.microsoft.com/certification`
5. `http://www.microsoft.com/winlogo`
6. `http://www.microsoft.com/net/logo`

PART 

Maintaining and Configuring a Web Application

Objectives

This chapter covers the following Microsoft-specified objectives for the Maintaining and Supporting a Web Application section of the Visual Basic .NET Web-Based Applications exam:

Optimize the performance of a Web application.

- This exam objective requires you to know about the techniques of optimizing a Web application for performance.

Diagnose and resolve errors and issues.

- Once an application has been deployed, you would ideally expect it to run smoothly. However, experience shows that even a well-tested application may misbehave due to various reasons. It's helpful to be able to log the behavior of your application. You might also like to design applications that can fine-tune themselves according to their environment. For example, an application might start or stop itself in response to performance measurements. The .NET Framework provides you with a variety of components and tools to publish, record, and analyze an application's performance. This exam objective requires you to know about the classes in the System.Diagnostics namespace that help you design an application that is easy to manage and maintain.

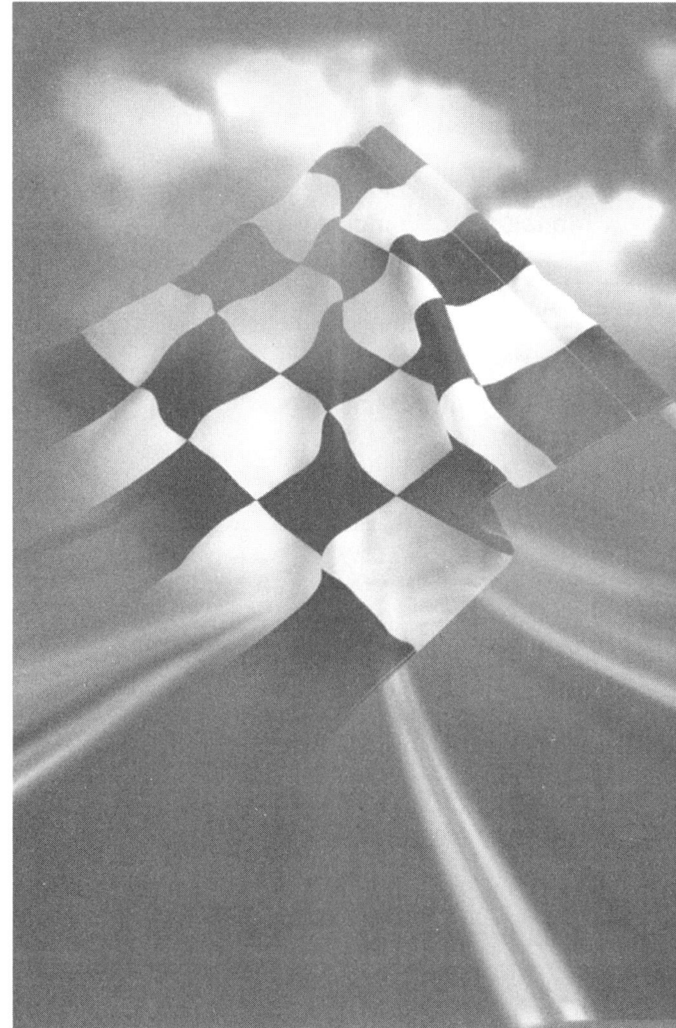

CHAPTER 14

Maintaining and Supporting a Web Application

OUTLINE

STUDY STRATEGIES

- Review the "Performance Tips and Tricks in .NET Applications" White paper from the Visual Studio .NET Combined Help Collection. This paper is also available online at `http://msdn.microsoft.com/library/en-us/dndotnet/html/dotnetperftips.asp`.
- Try out the walkthrough exercises related to the Process, EventLog, and PerformanceCounter classes from the "Visual Basic and Visual C# Walkthroughs" section of the Visual Studio .NET Combined Help Collection.
- Review the Design Goals - Performance section of the Designing Distributed Applications topic from the Visual Studio .NET Combined Help Collection.

INTRODUCTION

The System.Diagnostics namespace provides various classes that help in managing and monitoring a Web application. In this chapter, I'll focus on three of these classes:

- **Process** The Process class provides information about the processes running on a computer. You can also access process information for computers across the network. This class also facilitates starting and stopping a process on a local computer.
- **EventLog** The EventLog class allows you to read from and write to a Windows Event log. Your applications can monitor an event log to take action when an entry is written to the log. An application may also publish its own events that may be of interest to other applications or to the system administrator.
- **PerformanceCounter** The PerformanceCounter class can be used to get performance data for running processes. You can also use this class to publish performance data over a network.

In addition to these classes, I'll use a whole bunch of supporting classes to monitor and manage processes, event logs and performance counters. The System.Diagnostics namespace also provides other classes such as Trace and Debug that helps you to test and debug an application. For more information on the Trace and Debug classes see Chapter 12, "Testing and Debugging a Web Application."

In the latter part of this chapter, I'll also discuss various techniques that may help you in improving the performance of your applications.

> NOTE
>
> **Security Issues** Many of the techniques in this chapter require the ASP.NET process to have access to system resources that are ordinarily secured. The easiest way to ensure this in testing is to configure ASP.NET to use the system account rather than the machine account. Alternatively, you can use .NET's security facilities to grant permissions on an assembly-by-assembly basis. For more details on these topics, see Chapter 15, "Configuring a Web Application."

MANAGING A WINDOWS PROCESS

Diagnosing and resolving errors and issues.

A process is an application under execution. Each running process is uniquely identified on a computer with a Process Identifier (PID). When a process executes, it consumes resources such as processor time and memory. Managing a Windows process involves getting execution information about the running processes. You may also want to programmatically start or stop processes.

The System.Diagnostics namespace provides several classes that help you with process management. The key to working with processes is the Process class. This class represents an instance of a process. You can create instances of the Process class programmatically, or you can use the Process component from the Windows Forms Designer's Toolbox. Programmatic access is especially useful for dynamically representing multiple running processes.

Starting and Stopping Processes

To start a process you can call the Start method of the Process class. This method is available in both static and non-static versions. To use the non-static version of the Start method, you must first create an instance of the Process class, set its StartInfo property to specify the necessary startup information (such as the executable filename, arguments, environment variables, working directory, and so on), and finally call the Start method of this instance. The static version of the Start method returns an instance of a created process. You pass the static version a ProcessStartupInfo object or other arguments such as the application's filename and environment.

NOTE

Starting and Stopping a Process The Process class only allows you to start and stop processes on the local machine where the code is running. For ASP.NET applications, this will be the Web server. Although you can access process information for remote machines, you cannot start or stop processes on a remote machine using this class.

WARNING

Be Careful with Kill The Kill method is the equivalent of using Task Manager to kill a process that is hung. If you use this method to kill a process, it won't have a chance to save data or clean up resources that it's using.

There are two methods that can stop a process: CloseMainWindow and Kill. The CloseMainWindow method requests a normal shutdown of the program. This is equivalent to closing an application by clicking on the close icon in its main window. CloseMainWindow can only stop processes that participate in the Windows message loop and that have a user interface. On the other hand, the Kill method causes an abnormal program termination by forcedly killing an application. Kill is the way to stop processes that do not have a user interface, or those which do not participate in the Windows message loop (such as MS-DOS based programs).

Table 14.1 lists the members of the Process class that are useful for starting or stopping processes.

TABLE 14.1

Members of the Process Class That Are Useful for Starting or Stopping Processes

Member	*Type*	*Description*
`CloseMainWindow`	Method	Closes a process that has a user interface by sending a close message to its main window
`EnableRaisingEvents`	Property	Specifies whether the Exited event should be raised when the process terminates
`ExitCode`	Property	Value specified by a process when it exits
`Exited`	Event	Occurs when a process exits
`ExitTime`	Property	Time at which the process exited
`GetProcessById`	Method	Returns a Process object that represents an already running process with the given Process Identifier (PID)
`GetProcesses`	Method	Returns an array of Process objects where each element represents an already existing process
`GetProcessesByName`	Method	Returns an array of Process objects where each element represents an already running process with the specified process name
`HasExited`	Property	Indicates whether the process has been terminated
`Id`	Property	The unique identifier of the process
`Kill`	Method	Immediately stops the process
`Start`	Method	Start a new process
`StartInfo`	Property	Specifies the properties to pass to the Start method of the Process
`WaitForExit`	Method	Sets the period to wait for the process to exit and blocks the current thread of execution until the time has elapsed or the process has exited
`WaitForInputIdle`	Method	Causes a Process object to wait for the process to enter an idle state

NOTE

Processes in ASP.NET Applications You're unlikely to need to manipulate processes in ASP.NET applications. That's because the only process on the server that the client communicates with is the ASP.NET process. I'm including the bare details of working with processes here, so that you can understand them when you run across them. You should not expect much of this content to appear on the exam.

Getting Process Information

You can create an instance of the Process class for any of the processes running on the local or a remote machine. This object can then be used to get details about the running process. Some examples of execution details include the current processor usage, memory usage, and whether the process is responding.

In your application, access to this information may help you decide whether you need to increase or decrease processing in your application based on the current system load. This information may also help you terminate or restart misbehaving processes. Table 14.2 lists some important properties of the Process class for getting process information.

TABLE 14.2

IMPORTANT PROPERTIES OF THE Process CLASS FOR GETTING INFORMATION ABOUT PROCESSES

Property	*Description*
`MachineName`	Name of the computer on which the process is running
`MainModule`	Main module of the process
`MainWindowTitle`	Caption of the main window of the process
`Modules`	Modules that have been loaded by the associated process
`PriorityClass`	Priority class for the process
`ProcessName`	Name of the process
`ProcessorAffinity`	Specifies the processors on which the threads in this process can be scheduled to run
`Responding`	Indicates whether the user interface of the process is responding
`StandardError`	Provides access to a `StreamReader` object through which you can read error output from the process
`StandardInput`	Provides access to a `StreamWriter` object through which you can write input to the process
`StandardOutput`	Provides access to a `StreamReader` object through which you can read output from the process
`StartTime`	Time at which the process was started

Property	*Description*
`Threads`	Gets the threads that are running in the associated process
`TotalProcessorTime`	Total processor time spent on this process
`UserProcessorTime`	Total user processor time spent on this process
`VirtualMemorySize`	Size of the process's virtual memory
`WorkingSet`	Process's physical memory usage

NOTE

Processes on a Remote Computer You must have administrative privileges on the remote computer to get process information for that computer.

Working with Event Logs

Event logging is the standard way in Windows for applications to leave a record of their activities. A system administrator can easily monitor the behavior of an application by analyzing its messages in the event log with the Event Viewer utility. You can also view events from within the Visual Studio .NET environment. You can access event logs through Server Explorer.

The Framework Class Library provides you with a set of classes designed to work with event logs. With the help of these classes, you can programmatically read from or write to the event logs. Programmatic access may even allow you to automate some of the administrative tasks associated with the application.

By default three event logs are available: Application, Security, and System. Other applications (including .NET applications) or operating system components such as Active Directory may add other event logs. Table 14.3 lists the important members of the EventLog class.

TABLE 14.3

Important Members of the EventLog Class

Member	*Type*	*Description*
`CreateEventSource`	Method	Open an event source for an application to write event information
`Delete`	Method	Removes a log resource

continues

TABLE 14.3 *continued*

IMPORTANT MEMBERS OF THE EventLog CLASS

Member	*Type*	*Description*
DeleteEventSource	Method	Removes an application's event source from the event log
EnableRaisingEvents	Property	Specifies whether the EventLog object receives notifications for the EntryWritten event
Entries	Property	Gets the contents of the event log
EntryWritten	Event	Occurs when an entry is written to an event log on the local computer
Exists	Method	Determines whether the specified log exists
GetEventLogs	Method	Creates an array of the event logs
Log	Property	Specifies the name of the log to read from or write to
LogDisplayName	Property	An event log's friendly name
LogNameFromSourceName	Method	Gets the name of the log to which the specified source is registered
MachineName	Property	Name of the computer on which to read or write events
Source	Property	Specifies the source to register and use when writing to the event log
SourceExists	Method	Finds whether a given event source exists
WriteEntry	Method	Writes an entry in the event log

Each application that is interested in interacting with an event log must register an event source with it. Once an event source is registered, its information is stored in the system registry and is available across application restarts.

The CreateEventSource method allows you to register the application with an event log, If the event log does not already exist, the CreateEventSource method will create it for you.

Writing to Event Logs

The WriteEntry method of the EventLog object allows you to write messages to the event log specified by the event source. If you haven't called CreateEventSource, WriteEntry will create the event source for you.

You can write different types of messages (information, error, and so on) to an event log. These types are specified by the values in EventLogEntryType enumeration.

The sample application in Step by Step 14.1 demonstrates creating an event log, registering an application with the event log, un-registering an application with an event log, writing to an event log, and deleting an event log.

STEP BY STEP

14.1 Creating and Writing to an Event Log

1. Create a new blank solution in Visual Studio .NET. Add a Visual Basic ASP.NET Web Application project to the solution. Name the project `StepByStep14-1`.

2. Rename `WebForm1.aspx` to `StepByStep14-1.aspx` in the project. Switch to the code view of the form and modify all references to `WebForm1` to refer to `StepByStep14_1` instead.

3. Place five `Label` controls, two `TextBox` control (`txtMessage`, with its `TextMode` property set to `MultiLine`, and `txtLogName`), four `Button` controls (`btnCreate`, `btnRemoveSource`, `btnRemoveLog`, and `btnWrite`), one `DropDownList` control (`ddlEventLogs`) and five `RadioButton` controls (`rbError`, `rbInformation`, `rbFailureAudit`, `rbSuccessAudit`, and `rbWarning`) on the form. Set the `GroupName` property for each of the `RadioButton` controls to `EventType`. Arrange the controls as shown in Figure 14.1.

continues

continued

FIGURE 14.1
Form to create and write to Event Log.

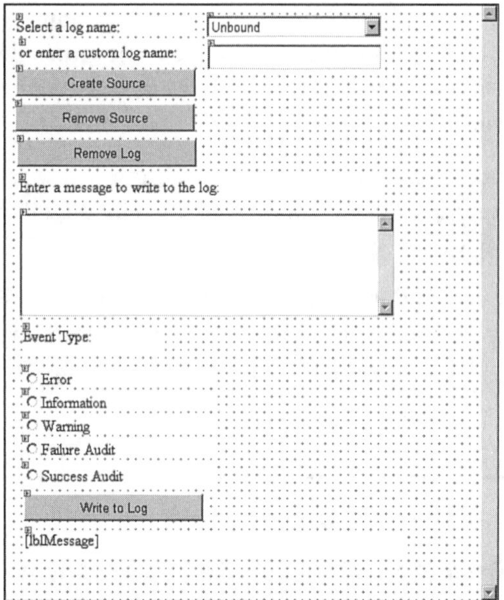

4. Switch to code view. Add this code to the top of the form's module:

```
Imports System.Diagnostics
```

5. Add a new methods named `PopulateLogNames` and `GetLogName` and an event handler for the page's `Load` event:

```
Private Sub PopulateLogNames()
    cbEventLogs.Items.Clear()
    ' Add eventlogs in to the combo box.
    Dim el As EventLog
    For Each el In EventLog.GetEventLogs()
        ddlEventLogs.Items.Add(el.Log)
    Next
End Sub

Private Function GetLogName() As String
    ' Use a custom log name if entered, otherwise
    ' use the selected log name in the DropDownLost
    If txtLogName.Text <> "" Then
        GetLogName = txtLogName.Text
    Else
        GetLogName = ddlEventLogs.SelectedItem.Text
    End If
End Function
```

```
Private Sub Page_Load( _
 ByVal sender As System.Object, _
 ByVal e As System.EventArgs) _
 Handles MyBase.Load
    PopulateLogNames()
End Sub
```

6. Add handlers for the `Click` events of the button controls:

```
Private Sub btnCreate_Click( _
 ByVal sender As System.Object, _
 ByVal e As System.EventArgs) _
 Handles btnCreate.Click
    If ddlEventLogs.SelectedItem.Text <> "" Then
        Dim strSourceName As String = _
         "StepByStep14-1_" & GetLogName()
        ' Check whether the Source already exists
        If Not EventLog.SourceExists( _
         strSourceName) Then
            Try
                ' Create event source
                ' and the event log
                EventLog.CreateEventSource( _
                 strSourceName, _
                 GetLogName())
                PopulateLogNames()
                lblMessage.Text = _
                 "Created EventSource for " & _
                 "Selected EventLog"
            Catch ex As Exception
                lblMessage.Text = ex.Message
            End Try
        Else
            lblMessage.Text = _
             "EventSource already attached"
        End If
    End If
End Sub

Private Sub btnRemoveSource_Click( _
 ByVal sender As System.Object, _
 ByVal e As System.EventArgs) _
 Handles btnRemoveSource.Click
    If GetLogName() <> "" Then
        Dim strSourceName As String = _
         "StepByStep14-1_" & GetLogName()
        If EventLog.SourceExists(strSourceName) Then
            ' Delete the Event Source
            EventLog.DeleteEventSource(strSourceName)
            lblMessage.Text = _
             "Deleted the EventSource"
        Else
            lblMessage.Text = _
             "No EventSource for the EventLog"
        End If
    End If
End Sub
```

continues

continued

```
Private Sub btnRemoveLog_Click( _
 ByVal sender As System.Object, _
 ByVal e As System.EventArgs) _
 Handles btnRemoveLog.Click
    Dim strLogName As String = _
     GetLogName().ToUpper()
    ' Do not delete system created logs
    If strLogName = "APPLICATION" Or _
     strLogName = "SECURITY" Or _
      strLogName = "SYSTEM" Then
        lblMessage.Text = _
         "You cannot delete system" & _
         "created event logs"
        Exit Sub
    End If
    ' If the log exists
    If EventLog.Exists(GetLogName()) Then
        Try
            ' Delete the Event Log
            EventLog.Delete(GetLogName())
            PopulateLogNames()
        Catch ex As Exception
            lblMessage.Text = _
             "Error Deleting EventLog"
        End Try
    Else
        lblMessage.Text = _
         "Cannot Delete EventLog"
    End If
End Sub

Private Sub btnWrite_Click( _
 ByVal sender As System.Object, _
 ByVal e As System.EventArgs) _
 Handles btnWrite.Click
    Dim eletEntryType As EventLogEntryType

    eletEntryType = EventLogEntryType.Error

    If rbInformation.Checked Then
        eletEntryType = EventLogEntryType.Information
    End If
    If rbError.Checked Then
        eletEntryType = EventLogEntryType.Error
    End If
    If rbWarning.Checked Then
        eletEntryType = EventLogEntryType.Warning
    End If
    If rbFailureAudit.Checked Then
        eletEntryType = EventLogEntryType.FailureAudit
    End If
```

```
    If rbSuccessAudit.Checked Then
        eletEntryType = EventLogEntryType.SuccessAudit
    End If

    If GetLogName() <> "" Then
        Dim strSourceName As String = _
         "StepByStep14-1_" & _
         GetLogName()
        ' If Source exists
        If EventLog.SourceExists(strSourceName) Then
            Try
                ' Write an entry into event log
                EventLog.WriteEntry(strSourceName, _
                 txtMessage.Text, _
                 eletEntryType)
                lblMessage.Text = _
                 "Entry Written Successfully"
            Catch ex As Exception
                lblMessage.Text = _
                 "Cannot Write to selected EventLog"
            End Try
        Else
            lblMessage.Text = "No such event source"
        End If
    Else
        lblMessage.Text = _
         "Please Select a log to write to."
    End If
End Sub
```

7. Set the project `StepByStep14_1` as the start up project.

8. Run the project. Enter a name such as "MyLogEntry" in the `DropDownList` control to create a source and connect to the event log. Select the log from the combo box that you want to write to, enter a message in the message textbox and select the type of the message from the radio button options. Click the Write button to write to the event log.

9. To view the logged messages, navigate to Server Explorer, expand the Servers node, select the node corresponding to your computer and expand it. Right-click on the Events node and select Launch Event Viewer from its shortcut menu. Figure 14.2 shows a custom event log created with this application.

WARNING

Deleting an Event Log You should use the Delete method to delete an EventLog cautiously. When an event log is deleted it deletes all event sources registered with it, so no application can continue writing to this log. Do not attempt to delete an event log created by Windows or any other important application; this may cause those applications to crash or behave in unexpected ways.

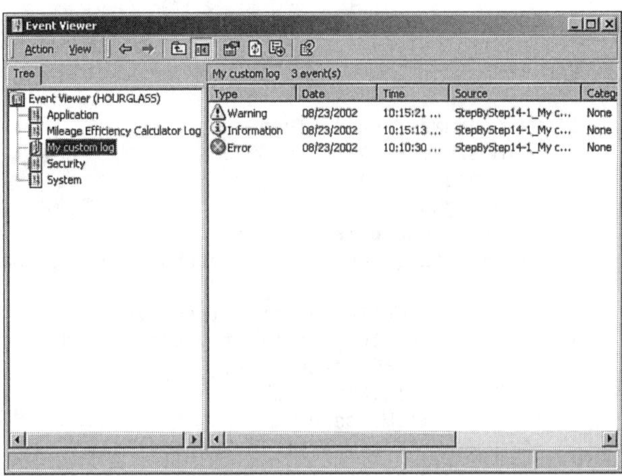

FIGURE 14.2
Event Viewer showing the Event Logs.

> NOTE
> **Security Log** The Security log is read-only.

Reading and Monitoring Event Logs

To read the contents of an event log, you can access the Entries property of the EventLog object. The Entries property returns an EventLogEntryCollection object, each of whose elements gives you access to an individual event log entry. Guided Practice Exercise 14.1 will help you experiment with this process.

> NOTE
> **Reading Entries from Remote Machines** Although the EventLog class allows you to access event log entries for the remote machines, it does not allow you to dynamically get notification for entries written to event logs on remote machines. You can only attach an event handler to the EntryWritten event for the event logs on the local computer.

You can also monitor an event log by registering an event handler for its EntryWritten event. But before that you will have to set the EnableRaisingEvents property of the Event Log object to true. If you do this, your event handler will be called each time a new entry is written to the specified event log.

GUIDED PRACTICE EXERCISE 14.1

In this exercise, you will create a Web form as shown in Figure 14.3. Your objective is to select an event log and get its content.

You should try doing this on your own first. If you get stuck, or you'd like to see one possible solution, follow these steps:

1. Add a Visual Basic ASP.NET Web Application project to the solution. Name the project GuidedPracticeExercise14-1.

2. Rename WebForm1.aspx to GuidedPracticeExercise14-1.aspx in the project. Switch to the code view of the form and modify all references to Form1 to refer to GuidedPracticeExercise14_1 instead.

3. Place four Label controls, one TextBox control (txtMachineName), one Button control (btnGetEvents), one DropDownList control (ddlEventLogs) and one ListBox control (lbEvents) on the form. Set the AutoPostBack property of txtMachineName to True. Set the Text property of txtMachineName to a single dot (.). Arrange the controls as shown in Figure 14.3.

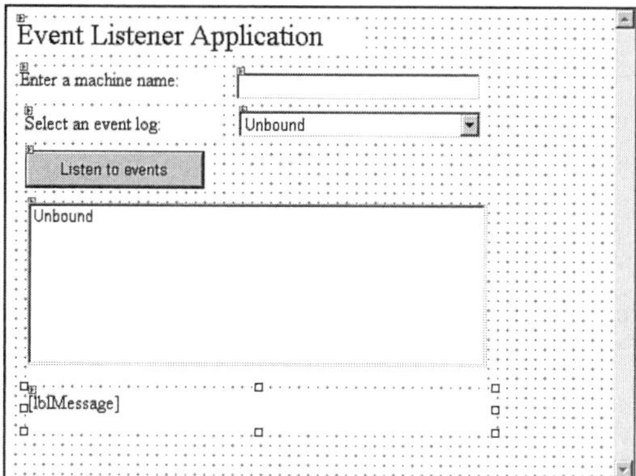

FIGURE 14.3
Form to listen to events from an Event Log.

4. Add this line of code to the top of the form's module:

```
Imports System.Diagnostics
```

5. Add a 7new method named PopulateLogNames and a handler for the form's Load event:

```
Private Sub PopulateLogNames()
    ddlEventLogs.Items.Clear()
    Dim el As EventLog
    For Each el In EventLog.GetEventLogs( _
     txtMachineName.Text)
        ddlEventLogs.Items.Add(el.Log)
    Next
End Sub

Private Sub GuidedPracticeExercise14_2_Load( _
 ByVal sender As System.Object, _
 ByVal e As System.EventArgs) Handles MyBase.Load
    If Not IsPostBack Then
        ' Add eventlogs in to the combo box.
        PopulateLogNames()
    End If
End Sub
```

NOTE

Referring to the Local Machine You can easily refer to the local machine in all Event Log related classes by using a single dot "." as the name.

continues

continued

6. Attach an event handler to the TextChanged event of the txtMachineName control:

```
Private Sub txtMachineName_TextChanged( _
 ByVal sender As System.Object, _
 ByVal e As System.EventArgs) _
 Handles txtMachineName.TextChanged
    Try
        ' Add event logs in to the combo box.
        PopulateLogNames()
    Catch ex As Exception
        lblMessage.Text = _
         "Please try a different machine"
    End Try
End Sub
```

7. Add an event handler for the Button control:

```
Public Sub AddEntryToList(ByVal ele As EventLogEntry)
    Try
        Dim strEntry As String = _
         ele.EntryType.ToString() & ": " & _
         ele.Message.Trim() & " from " & _
         ele.Source & " at " & _
        ele.TimeGenerated.ToString()
        lbEvents.Items.Add(strEntry)
    Catch ex As Exception
        lblMessage.Text = ex.Message
    End Try
End Sub

Private Sub btnGetEvents_Click( _
 ByVal sender As System.Object, _
 ByVal e As System.EventArgs) _
 Handles btnGetEvents.Click
    Dim el As EventLog = New EventLog( _
     ddlEventLogs.SelectedItem.Text, _
     txtMachineName.Text)
    lbEvents.Items.Clear()

    Dim ele As EventLogEntry
    For Each ele In el.Entries
        ' Add the entry in to the list view
        AddEntryToList(ele)
    Next
End Sub
```

8. Set the form as the startup object for the project, and set the project as the startup project for the solution.

9. Run the application. Enter a machine name and select a log name. You will see a list of events that are already in the log, as shown in Figure 14.4.

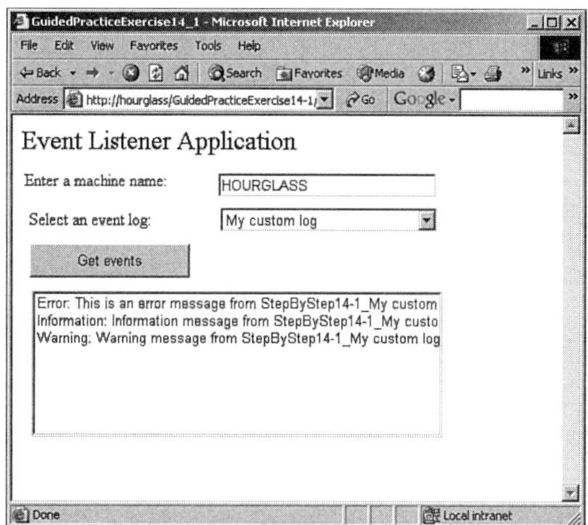

FIGURE 14.4
Retrieving events from an event log.

WORKING WITH PERFORMANCE COUNTERS

Performance counters are the Windows way of collecting performance data from running processes. Microsoft Windows itself provides several hundred performance counters, each monitoring a particular system parameter. In addition to this, the various .NET server products such as SQL Server and Exchange Server, and applications such as the .NET Framework, also publish their own custom performance counters.

Windows organizes performance counters in categories. Each category defines a specific set of performance counters. For example, there are categories like Memory, Process, Processor, and PhysicalDisk. The Memory category has various counters such as Available Bytes, Cache Bytes, Committed Bytes, and so on.

Some categories are further divided into instances. For example, the Process category is divided into several instances each representing a running process on the computer. A new instance is added to the category whenever a new process is started and removed when a process is killed. Each instance can have performance counters such as I/O Read Bytes/sec that specify the activity of that particular process. Usually all instances in a category will have the same list of performance counters. Of course, each of the performance counters will have separate performance data associated with it.

The PerformanceCounter class allows you to read performance samples for processes running on the local computer or remote machines. By using this class an application can even publish its own performance counters, informing the world about its performance level.

Table 14.4 lists the important members of the PerformanceCounter class.

TABLE 14.4

IMPORTANT MEMBERS OF THE PerformanceCounter CLASS

Member	*Type*	*Description*
`CategoryName`	Property	Performance Counter category name
`Close`	Method	Closes the performance counter and frees all the resources
`CounterHelp`	Property	Performance counter description
`CounterName`	Property	Performance counter name
`CounterType`	Property	Performance counter type
`Decrement`	Method	Decrements the performance counter value by one
`Increment`	Method	Increments the performance counter value by one
`IncrementBy`	Method	Increments or decrements the value of the performance counter by a specified amount
`InstanceName`	Property	Instance name
`MachineName`	Property	Computer name
`NextSample`	Method	Gets a sample for the performance counter and returns the raw, or uncalculated, value for it
`NextValue`	Method	Gets a sample for the performance counter and returns the calculated value for it
`RawValue`	Property	Gets a sample for the performance counter and returns its raw or uncalculated value
`ReadOnly`	Property	Indicates whether the `PerformanceCounter` is in read-only mode
`RemoveInstance`	Method	Deletes an instance from the `PerformanceCounter` object

NOTE

Performance Counters on Remote Machines You can read existing performance counters on remote computers, but you can only create custom performance counters on the local machine.

Reading Performance Data of Running Processes

The process of reading a performance counter value is also referred to as *sampling* the performance counter. When you sample a performance counter, it gives you a value specifying its performance level at that particular instant. The value of a performance counter may vary rapidly. A good way to analyze a performance counter is to graph the sample values over a period. Windows provides you a Performance monitoring tool (perfmon.exe) exactly for this purpose. This tool can be quickly launched by executing perfmon.exe from the Windows Start, Run dialog box. You can also access it through the Performance option in the Administrative Tools section of the Windows Control Panel.

Although tools like perfmon.exe make it simple for administrators to monitor the performance of an application, it is sometimes also useful to read the values programmatically. This can be useful when a program wants to monitor the performance of another program and take actions depending on the performance data from that program. For example, you may want to run a processor-intensive SalesAnalysis application at a time when the critical DownloadWebOrders process is idle.

The performance monitors installed on a computer can be easily accessed through Server Explorer in Visual Studio. NET. You can drag and drop the performance counter of your choice to create an instance of the PerformanceCounter component. Step by Step 14.2 demonstrates how to use an instance of PerformanceCounter component to monitor the currently available memory on the Web server computer.

STEP BY STEP

14.2 Reading Performance Data

1. Add a Visual Basic ASP.NET Web Application project to the solution. Name the project `StepByStep14-2`.

continues

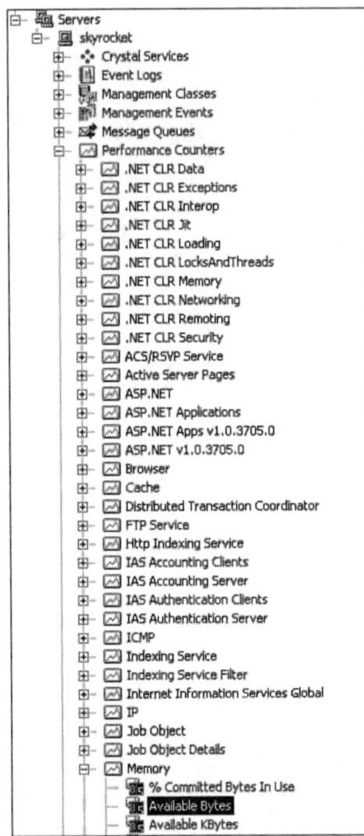

FIGURE 14.5
Available Bytes performance counter in Server Explorer.

continued

2. Rename `WebForm1.aspx` to `StepByStep14-2.aspx` in the project. Switch to the code view of the form and modify all references to `WebForm1` to refer to `StepByStep14_2` instead.

3. Place a Label control, a `Button` control (`btnSample`) and a `ListBox` control (`lbPerformance`) on the form.

4. Open Server Explorer and select the server from the Servers node. Select Available Bytes performance counter by navigating to Performance Counters, Memory, Available Bytes from the server node (see Figure 14.5). Drag the Available Bytes counter to the form. Name the counter `pcMemory`. Change the `MachineName` property of the counter to a single dot (.) to refer to the Web server where the code is running.

5. Switch to code view. Add the following code to the top of the form's module:

```
Imports System.Diagnostics
```

6. Attach an event handler to the `Click` event of the `Button` control and add the following code in the event handler:

```
Private Sub btnSample_Click( _
 ByVal sender As System.Object, _
 ByVal e As System.EventArgs) Handles btnSample.Click
    ' Get the next performance data
    ' Add the data to the listview
    Dim csSample As CounterSample = _
     pcMemory.NextSample()
    lbPerformance.Items.Add( _
     pcMemory.CounterName & ": " & _
     csSample.RawValue.ToString() & " at " & _
     csSample.TimeStamp.ToString())
End Sub
```

7. Set the form as the start object for the project and set the project as the start project for the solution.

8. Run the Project. Each time you click the button, a new performance value will be added as a new row to the `ListBox` control, as shown in Figure 14.6.

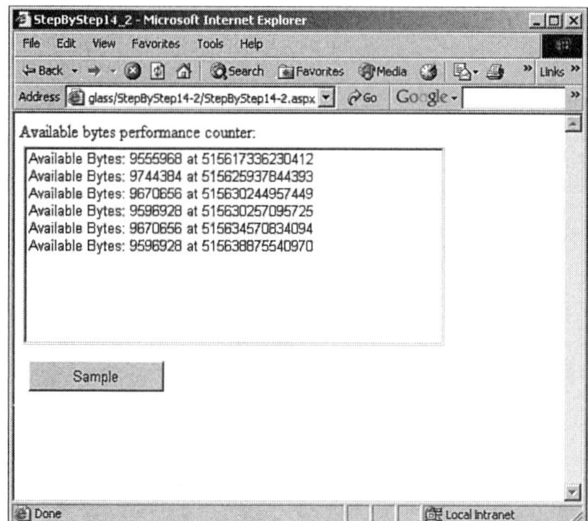

FIGURE 14.6
Monitoring the Available Bytes Performance Counter.

Publishing Performance Data

The .NET Framework also allows applications to create their own custom performance counter and publish their performance data. This performance data can be then monitored from the Performance Monitoring tool (perfmon.exe) or can be monitored through any other application like the one you will create later in Exercise 14.2.

Step by Step 14.3 demonstrates programmatic creation of a performance counter, and then demonstrates setting the value of the resulting counter.

NOTE

Performance Counter Builder Wizard Visual Studio .NET makes it easy for you to create new local performance categories and counters through the Performance Counter Builder Wizard available via Server Explorer. To launch the wizard, right-click on the Performance Counters node and select New Category. But this wizard isn't available if you're dealing with a remote server such as a Web server.

STEP BY STEP

14.3 Publishing Performance Data

1. Add a Visual Basic ASP.NET Web Application project to the solution. Name the project `StepByStep14-3`.

2. Rename `WebForm1.aspx` to `StepByStep14-3.aspx` in the project. Switch to the code view of the form and modify all references to `WebForm1` to refer to `StepByStep14_3` instead.

3. Place three `Label` controls (one named `lblCurrentLevel`), one `TextBox` control (`txtLevel`) and three `Button` controls (`btnInc`, `btnDec`, and `btnSet`) on the form. Arrange the controls as shown in Figure 14.7.

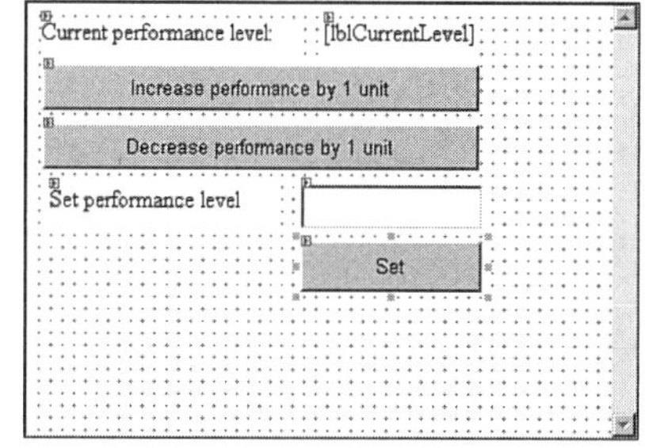

FIGURE 14.7
A form to manipulate a performance counter.

continues

continued

4. Switch to code view. Add a line of code to the top of the form's module:

```
Imports System.Diagnostics
```

5. Add code to create the performance counter if necessary:

```
Private Sub Page_Load(ByVal sender As System.Object, _
 ByVal e As System.EventArgs) Handles MyBase.Load
    ' Make sure custom category & counter exist
    If Not IsPostBack Then
        If Not PerformanceCounterCategory. _
         Exists("StepByStep14-3") Then
            Dim ccd(0) As CounterCreationData
            ccd(0) = New CounterCreationData()
            ccd(0).CounterName = "Performance"
            Dim ccdcoll As New _
             CounterCreationDataCollection(ccd)
            PerformanceCounterCategory.Create( _
             "StepByStep14-3", _
             "Counters for StepByStep14-3", ccdcoll)
            Dim pc As PerformanceCounter = _
             New PerformanceCounter( _
             "StepByStep14-3", _
             "Performance", "", False)
        End If
    End If
End Sub
```

6. Add code to handle the `Button` events:

```
Private Sub btnInc_Click( _
 ByVal sender As System.Object, _
 ByVal e As System.EventArgs) Handles btnInc.Click
    Dim pc As PerformanceCounter = _
     New PerformanceCounter()
    pc.CategoryName = "StepByStep14-3"
    pc.CounterName = "Performance"
    pc.ReadOnly = False
    pc.Increment()
    lblCurrentLevel.Text = pc.NextValue().ToString()
End Sub

Private Sub btnDec_Click( _
 ByVal sender As System.Object, _
 ByVal e As System.EventArgs) Handles btnDec.Click
    Dim pc As PerformanceCounter = _
     New PerformanceCounter()
    pc.CategoryName = "StepByStep14-3"
    pc.CounterName = "Performance"
    pc.ReadOnly = False
    pc.Decrement()
    lblCurrentLevel.Text = pc.NextValue().ToString()
End Sub
```

```
Private Sub btnSet_Click( _
 ByVal sender As System.Object, _
 ByVal e As System.EventArgs) Handles btnSet.Click
    Dim pc As PerformanceCounter = _
     New PerformanceCounter()
    pc.CategoryName = "StepByStep14-3"
    pc.CounterName = "Performance"
    pc.ReadOnly = False
    pc.RawValue = Int32.Parse(txtLevel.Text)
    lblCurrentLevel.Text = pc.NextValue().ToString()
End Sub
```

7. Set the form as the startup object for the project and set the project as the startup project for the solution.

8. Run the project. Enter a number in the textbox and click on the set button. The label will immediately reflect this as the current value of the performance counter. Click on the increment and decrement buttons and notice the value changing in the label.

   To create the performance counter, this code first builds an array of CounterCreationData objects. In this particular case, the array has a single member, but you can use a larger array to create more than one counter at the same time. This array is used as input to the constructor for a CounterCreationDataCollection object. This object in turn goes to the constructor for a PerformanceCounterCategory object, which also takes as parameters the name of the new category and a description of the category that other tools can use.

REVIEW BREAK

- A process is an application under execution. Each running process is uniquely identified on a computer with a Process Identifier (PID).
- The Process class provides a large set of properties to get information about running processes on a local or remote machine.
- The Event Log provides a central repository for various issues that an application may encounter while they are executing.

continues

continued

Using an event log to record such messages not only makes the job of system administrator easier, but also allows other applications to take appropriate action when an entry is written to a log.

- Multiple event sources can write into an event log. However, an event source can only be used to write into one event log.
- By default, events of the Process and EventLog class are not enabled. You can set the EnableRaisingEvents property to True in order to instruct them to raise events.
- Performance counters are organized in categories. Each category defines a specific set of performance counters.
- The process of reading a performance counter value is called sampling the performance counter. The process of updating a performance counter value is called publishing a performance counter.

DESIGNING A WEB APPLICATION FOR PERFORMANCE

Optimizing the performance of a Web-based application.

You should design and develop an application for performance early in its development cycle. Removing any performance glitches early in the development cycle is the cheapest solution. The cost of rewriting modules, modifying code, or redistributing applications goes up as the application moves beyond design and into implementation.

A common practice for ensuring the quality of code is to do frequent code reviews. You can should also plan to test alternative ways of implementing your code to determine the performance impact of your choices.

I have listed some of the commonly acknowledged best practices for writing high performing applications using the .NET Framework here.

- **Use Caching to Store Content** ASP.NET allows you to cache entire pages, fragments of pages, or controls. You can also cache variable data by specifying the parameters that the data depends on. Using caching makes it quicker for the ASP.NET engine to return data in response to repeated requests for the same page.
- **Avoid Session State** Whether you store it in-process, in State Server, or in a SQL Server database, session state takes memory and requires processing time to store and receive. If your application doesn't depend on session state, disable it with the <@% EnableSessionState=False %> directive.
- **Avoid ViewState** ViewState lets you persist the contents of a control across trips to a server. This comes at the cost of additional bytes traveling in each direction, and hence imposes a speed hit. You can avoid this penalty by setting the EnableViewState property of controls to False when you don't need their contents to persist.
- **Use Low Cost Authentication** Passport authentication is slower than forms-based authentication, which is slower than Windows authentication. Not authenticating users at all is the fastest choice.
- **Boxing and Unboxing** When a value type (such as a Structure) is copied to a reference type (such as a class), the compiler needs to create an object on the heap and copy the value of the value type from the stack to this newly created object on the heap. This process is called boxing and requires more overhead than a simple copy from value type to value type. On the other hand, when you copy a reference type to a value type, the value of object from the heap is copied to the value type in stack. This process is called unboxing. You should be aware of this overhead involved in boxing and unboxing, and while designing the application, choose data types to minimize this overhead.
- **Using StringBuilder** The String type is immutable. That means that once a string is created it can't be modified. When you modify a string, the runtime will in fact create a new string based on your modifications and return it. The original string still hangs around in memory waiting to be garbage-collected.

If your application is extensively modifying strings, you should consider using the System.Text.StringBuilder class. The StringBuilder class stores the string as an array of characters. The StringBuilder object is mutable and does in-place modification of strings. Using StringBuilder may help you achieve noticeable performance gains in an application using extensive string manipulations.

- **Use AddRange with collections** A large number of collection classes provide an AddRange method to add an array of items to the collection. Using AddRange is much faster than adding elements by repeatedly calling the Add method inside a loop.
- **Native compilation reduces startup time** When you compile a program using the VB .NET compiler, it generates the MSIL (Microsoft Intermediate Language) code. When the program is loaded, this MSIL code is compiled into the native code by the Just-in-time (JIT) compiler as it executes. When a method is called for the first time, it will be slower because of the additional step of compilation. Successive calls to the method will be faster because the code is already converted to the native code. Although this behavior will meet your requirements most of the time, you might want to optimize your application's performance even when the functions are loaded for the first time. In these cases, you should consider using the native code compilation tool (ngen.exe) to convert an application to native code before deploying it on the target machine. This way you will get maximum performance at all the times. As an example, Microsoft precompiles several libraries of the .NET Framework, including mscorlib.dll, System.Drawing.dll, System.Windows.Forms.dll, and others before deploying them on your machine because these classes are used by most applications.
- **Throwing exceptions** Throwing exceptions is a costly operation. You should be very careful when you throw exceptions from programs; use them only to signify exceptional error cases. Don't use exceptions just to manage normal program flow.

- **Unmanaged code** Calls to unmanaged components involves costly marshaling operations and therefore these programs may see deteriorated performance. For maximum performance, rewrite the unmanaged components using one of the languages supported by the CLR. If a rewrite is not possible, monitor the use of unmanaged components and see if you can reduce the number of calls between the managed and unmanaged code, possibly by doing more work in each call rather than making frequent calls for doing small tasks.
- **Make fewer calls across processes** Working with distributed applications involves the additional overhead of negotiating network and application level protocols. Network speed may also be a bottleneck. The best approach is to get more done with fewer calls across the network. Reducing the number of calls is critical in the creation of high-performance distributed applications.
- **Compile the application using the Release Configuration** When you are ready to deploy your application, compile it in release mode rather than the default Debug mode. Deploying an application compiled using Debug mode may cause it to run slowly because of the presence of extra debugging code.
- **Use the optimized managed providers** System.Data.OleDb is a generic provider that can access data exposed by any OleDb provider. For some database you have managed providers specifically optimized for them. For example when you use System.Data.OleDb to connect to SQL Server database, it first passes your request to the OLE DB COM components that in turn translate the requests to SQL Server's native Tabular Data Stream (TDS) format. When you use System.Data.SqlClient, it directly constructs the TDS packets and communicates with SQL Server. The removal of the extra translation step increases data access performance significantly. So if you are connecting to a SQL Server database prefer System.Data.SqlClient to the generic System.Data.OleDb. Similarly use System.Data.OracleClient for connecting to Oracle database.

> NOTE
>
> **Managed Provider for Oracle** The Oracle-managed provider is an add-on to the .NET Framework. You can download it from `http://www.microsoft.com/downloads/release.asp?releaseid=40032`.

- **Prefer stored procedures over SQL Statements** When working with SQL Server, I prefer using stored procedures over a set of SQL statements given as a text command. This is because stored procedures are highly optimized for server-side data access and their use will usually improve the data access performance significantly.

- **Tune the database** Keeping up-to-date indexes also greatly helps in improving performance for a database-intensive Web application. You can run SQL Server's Profiler and Index Tuning Wizard to avoid any bottlenecks because of indexing. Also, use SQL Server Query Analyzer to optimize a query's performance.

- **DataReader versus DataSet** If you are reading a table sequentially, I prefer using DataReader over DataSet. DataReader is a read-only, forward-only stream of data. This increases application performance and reduces system overhead because only one row is in memory at a time.

- **Connection pooling for SQL Server .NET Data provider** The slowest database operation is establishing a connection with the database. The SQL Server .NET Data provider provides connection pooling to improve performance when connecting to a database. This stores old connection information in a connection pool and reuses this information when connecting the next time, thereby allowing significant performance gains. A connection pool is created based on the connection string in the connection. Each connection pool is associated with a distinct connection string. When a new connection is opened, if the connection string is not an exact match to an existing pool, a new pool is created.

- **Auto-fenerated commands** The SqlCommandBuilder and OleDbCommandBuilder classes provide a means of automatically generating commands used to reconcile changes made to a DataSet. Although automatic generation of INSERT, UPDATE, and DELETE statements for changes to the DataSet makes database updates very convenient, it makes extra trips to the server to get the schema information.

> **EXAM TIP**
>
> **User Identity and Connection Pooling** For Connection pooling to work, multiple connections to a database must use the same connection strings. If you are including user identity and password information in the connection string, the connection string for user Mahesh will not match with user Mary. This will instead form two separate connection pools. To gain maximum performance gains, you must use a single identity and password in the connection string to a database.

- **Using transactions** Distributed transactions may have significant performance overhead. As a rule of thumb, use transactions only when required and keep transactions as short-lived as possible.
- **Improving perceived performance** This last technique has more to do with human behavior than actual performance of the application. Studies have shown that showing an active splash screen at the application startup may make your application appear as if it is loading faster. Similarly showing a progress bar for a long operation keeps users informed and in communication with the application. Use these techniques to improve the perceived performance of your application.

Chapter Summary

This chapter discussed the use of the Process, EventLog, PerformanceCounter, and related classes that helps in managing and monitoring a Windows application.

This chapter also discussed some of the well-known techniques to optimize the performance of a Web application. If you judiciously use these techniques while designing and developing your application, you may see a significant performance gain in your application.

KEY TERMS

- Boxing
- Performance Counter
- Process
- Unboxing

APPLY YOUR KNOWLEDGE

Exercises

14.1 Getting Module Information for a Process

When a process executes, it will usually load several other modules (generally dll files) to help it perform its functions. Using the Process class, you can also determine the modules loaded by an application. For each module, you can also determine various details such as version number, entry point address, and memory size.

In this exercise, I will show you how to work with the ProcessModule class and the ProcessModuleCollection class to get information about the modules loaded by a process in execution.

Estimated Time: 25 minutes.

1. Launch Visual Studio .NET. Select File, New, Blank Solution and name the new solution 305C14Exercises.

2. Add a new Visual Basic ASP.NET Web application project to the solution. Name the project Exercise14-1.

3. Rename WebForm1.aspx to Exercise14-1.aspx in the project. Switch to the code view of the form and modify all references to WebForm1 to refer to Exercise14_1 instead.

4. Place four Label controls, two TextBox controls (txtMachine and txtModuleInfo), one Button control (btnLoad), and two ListBox controls (lbModules and lbProcesses) on the form. Set the TextMode property of txtModuleInfo to MultiLine. Set the AutoPostBack property of both ListBox controls to True. Arrange the controls as shown in Figure 14.8.

5. Switch to code view. Add the following code at the top of the form's module:

```
Imports System.Diagnostics
Imports System.Text
```

6. Add code to handle events on the form:

```
Private Sub Page_Load( _
 ByVal sender As System.Object, _
 ByVal e As System.EventArgs) _
 Handles MyBase.Load
    If Not IsPostBack Then
        ' Set the textbox with
        ' the System ComputerName
        txtMachine.Text = _
         Server.MachineName
    End If
End Sub

Private Sub btnLoad_Click( _
 ByVal sender As System.Object, _
 ByVal e As System.EventArgs) _
 Handles btnLoad.Click
    ' Clear the listbox
    ' and textbox controls
    lbProcesses.Items.Clear()
    lbModules.Items.Clear()
    txtModuleInfo.Text = ""
    ' Get all the processes
    Dim arrProcesses() As Process = _
     Process.GetProcesses(txtMachine.Text)
    Dim p As Process
    For Each p In arrProcesses
        ' Add each process to the list
        lbProcesses.Items.Add( _
         p.Id.ToString & _
         " " & p.ProcessName)
    Next
End Sub

Private Sub _
 lbProcesses_SelectedIndexChanged( _
 ByVal sender As System.Object, _
 ByVal e As System.EventArgs) _
 Handles lbProcesses.SelectedIndexChanged
    lbModules.Items.Clear()
    txtModuleInfo.Text = ""
    Dim intSpace As Integer = _
     lbProcesses.SelectedItem. _
      Text.IndexOf(" ")
```

APPLY YOUR KNOWLEDGE

```
        Dim intProcessId As Integer = _
         Convert.ToInt32( _
          lbProcesses.SelectedItem. _
         Text.Substring(0, intSpace))
        Try
            Dim p As Process = _
             Process.GetProcessById( _
             intProcessId, txtMachine.Text)
            Dim pm As ProcessModule
            For Each pm In p.Modules
                lbModules.Items.Add( _
                 pm.ModuleName)
            Next
        Catch ex As Exception
            Debug.WriteLine(ex.Message)
        End Try
    End Sub

    Private Sub _
     lbModules_SelectedIndexChanged( _
     ByVal sender As System.Object, _
     ByVal e As System.EventArgs) _
     Handles lbModules.SelectedIndexChanged

        txtModuleInfo.Text = ""
        Dim intSpace As Integer = _
         lbProcesses.SelectedItem. _
          Text.IndexOf(" ")
        Dim intProcessId As Integer = _
         Convert.ToInt32(lbProcesses. _
         SelectedItem. _
         Text.Substring(0, intSpace))
        Try
            ' Get the selected process
            Dim p As Process = _
             Process.GetProcessById( _
             intProcessId, txtMachine.Text)
            ' Get the Modules of
            ' the selected process
            ' Display module information
            Dim pm As ProcessModule
            For Each pm In p.Modules
                If pm.ModuleName = _
                 lbModules.SelectedItem. _
                 ToString() Then
                    Dim sb As StringBuilder = _
                     New StringBuilder()
                    sb.Append(String.Format( _
                     "Base Address : {0}" & _
                      vbCrLf, _
                      pm.BaseAddress. _
                      ToString()))
                    sb.Append(String.Format( _
                     "EntryPointAddress: {0}" _
                     & vbCrLf, _
                      pm.EntryPointAddress))
                    sb.Append(String.Format( _
                    "FileVersionInfo  : {0}" _
                     & vbCrLf, _
                      pm.FileVersionInfo._
                      ToString()))
                    sb.Append(String.Format( _
                     "ModuleMemorySize : {0}", _
                      pm.ModuleMemorySize. _
                      ToString()))
                    txtModuleInfo.Text = _
                     sb.ToString()
                    Exit For
                End If
            Next
        Catch ex As Exception
            Debug.WriteLine(ex.Message)
        End Try
    End Sub
```

7. Set the form as the start page for the project, and set the project as the startup project for the solution.

8. Run the project. You'll see your Web server's name in the machine name textbox. Change the value if you want and then click the load button. You will see a list of all the running processes in the process list. Select a process in the list; you will see that its modules are listed in the list box. Select a module in the list box to obtain its information as shown in Figure 14.8.

APPLY YOUR KNOWLEDGE

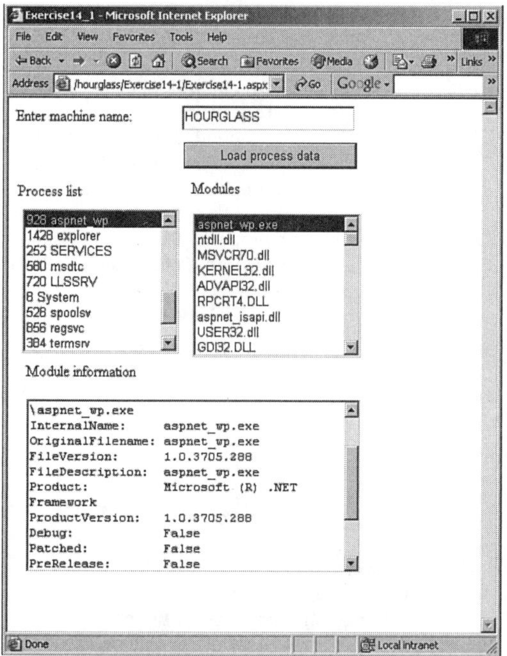

FIGURE 14.8
Process modules information.

14.2 Getting Performance Information

Performance counters are categorized either by the operating system or by the application that created them. Each performance counter category may also have zero or more instances. When a category has instances you must specify the instance name along with the category when you want to read the value of a performance counter.

In this exercise, I'll create a performance counter explorer that is similar to perfmon.exe. Rather than display graphs, though, it will just list the raw value of the performance counter when you ask for a sample.

Estimated Time: 35 minutes.

1. Add a new Visual Basic ASP.NET Web application project to the solution. Name the project Exercise14-2.

2. Rename WebForm1.aspx to Exercise14-2.aspx in the project. Switch to the code view of the form and modify all references to WebForm1 to refer to Exercise14_2 instead.

3. Place eight Label controls (including lblMessage), two TextBox controls (txtMachineName and txtDescription), one DropDownList control (ddlCategories), three ListBox controls (lbCounters, lbInstances, and lbPerformance) and a Button control (btnGetSample) on the Form. Set the TextMode property of txtDescription to MultiLine. Set the AutoPostBack property of txtMachineName, ddlCategories, lbCounters, and lbInstances to True. Arrange the controls as shown in Figure 14.9.

4. Switch to code view. Add this code at the top of the form's module:

```
Imports System.Diagnostics
```

5. Add the following code directly after the Web Form Designer–generated code:

```
Private Sub PopulateCategoryList()
    ddlCategories.Items.Clear()
    lbPerformance.Items.Clear()
    lbCounters.Items.Clear()
    lbInstances.Items.Clear()

    ' Get all the Performance
    ' Counter category
    ' objects for the given machine
    Dim pcc() As _
     PerformanceCounterCategory = _
     PerformanceCounterCategory. _
     GetCategories( _
     txtMachineName.Text)
    ' Populate the category list
    ' with category names
```

APPLY YOUR KNOWLEDGE

```
        Dim p As PerformanceCounterCategory
        For Each p In pcc
            ddlCategories.Items. _
             Add(p.CategoryName)
        Next
    End Sub
```

6. Add event-handling code to the form:

```
Private Sub Page_Load( _
 ByVal sender As System.Object, _
 ByVal e As System.EventArgs) _
 Handles MyBase.Load
    If Not IsPostBack Then
        ' Get the name of the
        ' Web server computer
        txtMachineName.Text = _
         Server.MachineName
        ' Populate performance
        ' category list
        PopulateCategoryList()
    End If
End Sub

Private Sub txtMachineName_TextChanged( _
 ByVal sender As System.Object, _
 ByVal e As System.EventArgs) _
 Handles txtMachineName.TextChanged
    Try
        ' Re-populate the category
        ' list if a machine name
        ' is changed
        PopulateCategoryList()
    Catch ex As Exception
        ' Alert user about
        ' incorrect machine name
        lblMessage.Text = _
         "Please try a different name"
    End Try
End Sub

Private Sub _
 ddlCategories_SelectedIndexChanged( _
 ByVal sender As System.Object, _
 ByVal e As System.EventArgs) _
 Handles ddlCategories.SelectedIndexChanged
    lbCounters.Items.Clear()
    lbInstances.Items.Clear()
    lbPerformance.Items.Clear()
    Dim pcc As _
     PerformanceCounterCategory = _
     New PerformanceCounterCategory( _
     ddlCategories.SelectedItem.Text, _
     txtMachineName.Text)

    Dim arrInstanceNames() As String = _
     pcc.GetInstanceNames()
    Dim strInstanceName As String
    For Each strInstanceName _
     In arrInstanceNames
        lbInstances.Items.Add( _
         strInstanceName)
    Next

    Dim pc As PerformanceCounter
    If arrInstanceNames.Length = 0 Then
        For Each pc In pcc.GetCounters()
            lbCounters.Items.Add( _
             pc.CounterName)
        Next
    Else
        For Each pc In _
         pcc.GetCounters( _
         arrInstanceNames(0))
            lbCounters.Items.Add( _
             pc.CounterName)
        Next
    End If
End Sub

Private Sub btnGetSample_Click( _
 ByVal sender As System.Object, _
 ByVal e As System.EventArgs) _
 Handles btnGetSample.Click
    ' Get the current performance data
    ' for the selected counter
    Dim pcc As _
     PerformanceCounterCategory = _
     New PerformanceCounterCategory( _
     ddlCategories.SelectedItem. _
     ToString(), _
     txtMachineName.Text)
    Dim pcCurrent As PerformanceCounter
    If lbInstances.Items.Count > 0 Then
        pcCurrent = _
         New PerformanceCounter( _
         pcc.CategoryName, _
         lbCounters.SelectedItem.Text, _
         lbInstances.SelectedItem.Text, _
         txtMachineName.Text)
```

Apply Your Knowledge

```
        Else
            pccurrent = _
             New PerformanceCounter( _
             pcc.CategoryName, _
             lbCounters.SelectedItem.Text, _
             "", txtMachineName.Text)
        End If

        Dim csSample As CounterSample = _
         pcCurrent.NextSample()
        ' Display details
        lbPerformance.Items.Add( _
         pcCurrent.CounterName & ": " & _
         csSample.RawValue.ToString() & _
         " at " & _
         csSample.TimeStamp.ToString())

    End Sub

    Private Sub _
     lbCounters_SelectedIndexChanged( _
     ByVal sender As System.Object, _
     ByVal e As System.EventArgs) _
     Handles lbCounters.SelectedIndexChanged
        If lbInstances.Items.Count > 0 And _
         lbInstances.SelectedIndex = -1 Then
            lbInstances.SelectedIndex = 0
        End If
        lbPerformance.Items.Clear()
        Dim pcc As _
         PerformanceCounterCategory = _
         New PerformanceCounterCategory( _
         ddlCategories.SelectedItem.Text)
        Dim pc As PerformanceCounter
        ' get the PerformanceCounter object
        ' based on current selections
        If lbInstances.Items.Count > 0 Then
            pc = New PerformanceCounter( _
             pcc.CategoryName, _
             lbCounters.SelectedItem.Text, _
             lbInstances.SelectedItem.Text, _
             txtMachineName.Text)
        Else
            pc = New PerformanceCounter( _
             pcc.CategoryName, _
             lbCounters.SelectedItem.Text, _
             "", txtMachineName.Text)
        End If
        ' Display Description of
        ' selected counter
        txtDescription.Text = pc.CounterHelp
    End Sub

    Private Sub _
     lbInstances_SelectedIndexChanged( _
     ByVal sender As System.Object, _
     ByVal e As System.EventArgs) _
     Handles lbInstances.SelectedIndexChanged
        If lbCounters.Items.Count > 0 And _
         lbCounters.SelectedIndex = -1 Then
            lbCounters.SelectedIndex = 0
        End If
        lbPerformance.Items.Clear()
        Dim pcc As _
         PerformanceCounterCategory = _
         New PerformanceCounterCategory( _
         ddlCategories.SelectedItem.Text)
        Dim pc As PerformanceCounter
        ' get the PerformanceCounter object
        ' based on current selections
        If lbInstances.Items.Count > 0 Then
            pc = New PerformanceCounter( _
             pcc.CategoryName, _
             lbCounters.SelectedItem.Text, _
             lbInstances.SelectedItem.Text, _
             txtMachineName.Text)
        Else
            pc = New PerformanceCounter( _
             pcc.CategoryName, _
             lbCounters.SelectedItem.Text, _
             "", txtMachineName.Text)
        End If
        ' Display Description
        ' of selected counter
        txtDescription.Text = pc.CounterHelp
    End Sub
```

7. Set the form as the startup object for the project and set the project as the startup project for the solution.

8. Run the project. You'll see your Web server's computer name in the computer name textbox. Change the value if you want and then select a performance category from the combo box. You will see a list of all the performance counters of the performance category selected in the Performance Counters list box, and Instances listed in the Instances List. Select the desired performance counter and instance. Click the button to add a performance sample to the ListBox control, as shown in Figure 14.9.

APPLY YOUR KNOWLEDGE

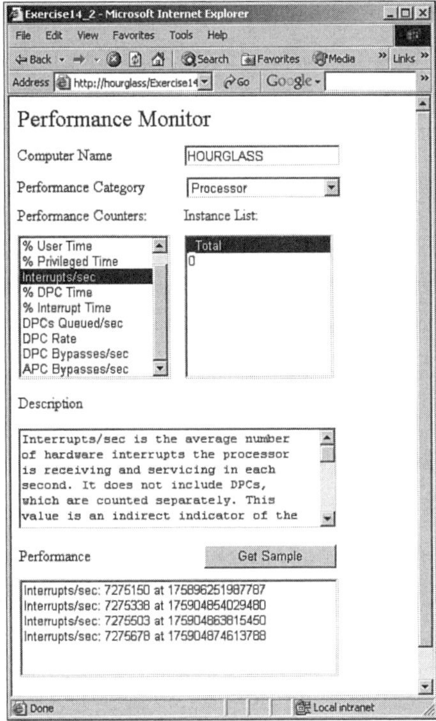

FIGURE 14.9
Performance Monitor.

Review Questions

1. How do you stop a process that has a user interface and how do you stop a process that does not have a user interface?

2. What types of messages can you write into an event log?

3. Explain the terms sampling a performance counter and publishing a performance counter.

4. What is the purpose of the Native Code Generation Tool (ngen.exe)?

5. When should you prefer using a SqlDataReader to a DataSet for reading data?

Exam Questions

1. You have developed a database-intensive ASP.NET application for a large pharmaceutical company. The database for the application uses SQL Server 2000. Users of your application are complaining about the consistently slow nature of some reports. Which of the following actions would you take to increase the performance of this application? (Select two.)

   A. Compile the application to native code using ngen.exe.

   B. Run the SQL Server Index Tuning Wizard.

   C. Convert all ad-hoc SQL statements to SQL Server stored procedures.

   D. Add a PerformanceMonitor component to the code.

2. You have recently deployed an expense-reporting system in your company. The application relies heavily on its SQL Server database. All employees in the company have similar access permissions to the database. You have created the application in such a way that it uses the employee's logon name and password in the connection string to connect to SQL Server. Users of the application have reported significantly slow performance. Your task is to optimize the performance of this application. Which of the following steps should you take?

   A. Compile the application to native code using ngen.exe.

   B. Run the SQL Server Index Tuning Wizard.

APPLY YOUR KNOWLEDGE

C. Increase the maximum size of the connection pool.

D. Use the same connection string for all users.

3. You are designing a database-intensive Web application for a large publishing house. You want to get maximum performance from the SQL queries that run to populate a combo box from a SQL Server database. Which of the following code segment will give you the fastest performance?

A.

```
Dim conn As SqlConnection = _
 New SqlConnection(connStr)
conn.Open()
Dim ds As DataSet = New DataSet()
Dim ad As SqlDataAdapter = _
 New SqlDataAdapter( _
 "SELECT * FROM authors", conn)
ad.Fill(ds)
End Sub
```

B.

```
Dim conn As OleDbConnection = _
 New OleDbConnection(connStr)
conn.Open()
Dim ds As DataSet = New DataSet()
Dim ad As OleDbDataAdapter = _
 New OleDbDataAdapter( _
 "SELECT * FROM authors", conn)
ad.Fill(ds)
```

C.

```
Dim conn As SqlConnection = _
 New SqlConnection(connStr)
Dim cmd As SqlCommand = _
 New SqlCommand("SELECT * FROM authors", _
 connStr)
conn.Open()
Dim rdr As SqlDataReader
rdr = cmd.ExecuteReader()
```

D.

```
Dim conn As OleDbConnection = _
 New OleDbConnection(connStr)
Dim cmd As OleDbCommand = _
 New OleDbCommand( _
 "SELECT * FROM authors", connStr)
conn.Open()
Dim rdr As OleDbDataReader
rdr = cmd.ExecuteReader()
```

4. Your Web application provides information on your company's office locations. Users can select a state from a DropDownList control, and are then shown a list of all the offices in that state. The list is stored in a database, and changes very infrequently. You are concerned about the performance of the application when the Web server is under very heavy load. Which of these actions should you take to improve application performance?

A. Use State Server to store the information for each user between requests.

B. Use caching with the VaryByParam attribute to hold the delivered page in memory between requests.

C. Use thread pooling to ensure that the application will always have available threads.

D. Migrate the results page from ASP.NET to ASP.

5. Your Web application displays routing and timing information related to your company's Internet connections. Each time a new page is loaded, it makes entirely new calculations to determine which information to display. No page in the application passes any information to another page in the application. Which alternative should you use for session state in this application to maximize performance?

A. Disable session state.

B. In-process session state

APPLY YOUR KNOWLEDGE

C. State Server session state

D. SQL Server session state

6. Your application includes a complex Web page with approximately fifty TextBox controls. The data in three of these controls is important in determining the proper navigation path when the page is posted back to the server; the others are only used by client-side JavaScript code. What should you do to improve performance on this page?

   A. Set the Enabled property of the TextBox controls that are not used by server-side code to False.

   B. Set the ViewState property of the TextBox controls that are not used by server-side code to False.

   C. Set the ViewState property of the TextBox controls that are used by server-side code to False.

   D. Set the Enabled property of the TextBox controls that are used by server-side code to False

7. Which of the following statements are true with respect to Windows Performance counters? (Select two.)

   A. Performance counters are categorized into performance counter categories.

   B. Each performance counter category has zero or more Instances associated with it.

   C. Each performance counter category has one or more Instances associated with it.

   D. Each performance counter must have an instance associated with it.

8. Which of the following statements is false with respect to the EventLog class?

   A. You cannot write to any event log on the remote machine.

   B. You can write to all event logs on a local machine.

   C. You cannot get event-driven notifications when an entry is written to an event log on remote machine.

   D. You can get event-driven notifications when an entry is written to an event log on local machine.

9. Your Web application requires users to be authenticated before they can view information. Each user has an account on your Windows servers. Which form of authentication should you use for best performance?

   A. Default authentication

   B. Windows authentication

   C. Forms-based authentication

   D. Passport authentication

10. Your e-commerce store is about to launch, and you want to be able to quickly increase the processing power available if the number of users is larger than planned. Which server configuration offers you the most flexibility for adding additional power?

   A. Single server

   B. Web garden

   C. Web farm

   D. Cluster

APPLY YOUR KNOWLEDGE

11. You recently developed an Expense Reporting System. When you deployed the application, you found that some of the features of the application are not working as expected. You suspect that the application is using old version for some of its components. You then created a small test application to get all the modules loaded by the application; your program contains the following segment of code (line numbers are for reference only):

```
1  Dim p As Process = Process.Start(new _
2   ProcessStartInfo("ExpenseReport.exe "))
3
4  Dim pmc As ProcessModuleCollection = _
5      Process.GetProcessById(p.Id).Modules
```

    However when you analyze the resulting collection of modules, you noted that not all the modules actually being used by the application are added to the ProcessModuleCollection object. Which of the following statements should you add as line 3?

    A. p.Refresh()

    B. p.WaitForInputIdle()

    C. p.WaitForExit()

    D. p.CreateObjRef()

12. You have written an application that publishes its own custom performance counter. You want to decrease the value of a performance counter by 5, which of the following methods will allow you to do this with the least code?

    A. Decrement

    B. Increment

    C. IncrementBy

    D. NextValue

13. You want to determine if a given event log exists on a remote machine. Which of the following methods is the most efficient way of determining this?

    A. Exists

    B. SourceExists

    C. GetEventLogs

    D. LogNameFromSourceName

14. Your Web application uses a legacy COM component to perform calculations. Ten different values need to be passed to the COM component. You have the choice of several methods to communicate with the COM component. Which method should you select for best performance?

    A. Call individual Property Set procedures to pass the ten values. Then call a single method with no parameters that returns the answer.

    B. Call ten individual methods, each of which takes a single value as a parameter and each of which returns part of the required information.

    C. Call a single method that takes all ten values as parameters and then returns the required information.

    D. Call one method that takes an array of all ten values as a parameter, and then call a second method that returns the required information.

15. Which of the following coding constructs will have a major impact on an application's performance and should therefore be used cautiously?

    A. `Try`

    B. `Catch`

APPLY YOUR KNOWLEDGE

C. `Finally`

D. `Throw`

Answers to Review Questions

1. The CloseMainWindow method of the Process class stops the processes that participate in the Windows message loop and have a user interface, and the Kill method of the Process class stops processes that do not have a user interface or those which do not participate in Windows message loop. You can also use the Kill method to kill applications with an interface.

2. The different types of messages that can be written into an event log are specified by the EventLogEntryType enumeration. The possible types are Error, FailureAudit, Information, SuccessAudit, and Warning.

3. The process of reading a performance counter value is called sampling the performance counter. The process of updating a performance counter value is called publishing a performance counter.

4. The Native Code Generation Tool (ngen.exe) is used to convert an application to native code before deploying it on the target machine.

5. The SqlDataReader provides high performance data access for reading forward only, read-only data. So you will use SqlDataReader instead of a DataSet when you are reading data sequentially and updates are not required.

Answers to Exam Questions

1. **B** and **C.** SQL Server's Index Tuning Wizard will identify any bottlenecks because of indexing. Using SQL Server stored procedure improves data access performance significantly.

2. **D.** Using different user names and passwords when connecting to SQL Server creates a unique connection string at each database connection. This eliminates any gain that you may have because of connection pooling. To get the maximum benefit from connection pooling you must use the same connection string every time you connect to the database.

3. **C.** When working with a SQL Server database, using the SQL Server managed provider will give better performance than its OleDb counterpart. Also when doing sequential read-only operations like populating a ComboBox, the SqlDataReader gives better performance than the SqlDataAdapter.

4. **B.** By using the VaryByParam attribute with page-level caching, you can cache a separate copy of the results page for each input state. These copies can be delivered by the server quickly because no database access or other processing is involved in satisfying subsequent requests.

5. **A.** Nothing in this application requires knowledge of session state. To maximize performance, you should disable session state tracking.

6. **B.** When you set the ViewState property for a TextBox control to True, the contents of the textbox are passed between client and server in a hidden form field. Setting ViewState to False removes this information, and hence cuts down on download times.

APPLY YOUR KNOWLEDGE

7. **A** and **B.** The Performance counters are categorized into various performance counter categories. Each performance counter category has zero or more Instances associated with it.

8. **B.** Although it is possible to write to the event logs on the local machine, it's not possible to write to all of them. The Security log created by the operating system itself, and is read-only. You cannot write to it even on a local machine.

9. **B.** The default for Web applications is no authentication at all, which does not fulfill the requirements. Passport authentication is slower than forms-based authentication, which is slower than Windows authentication.

10. **C.** A Web farm lets you quickly add more processing power by installing additional computers. Web gardens are limited in their scalability by the number of CPUs available in a single computer. Clusters add reliability, but do not add scalability.

11. **B.** You should always retrieve the modules used by an application when it is completely loaded. You can ensure that an application is loaded and is ready to start by calling the WaitForInputIdle method on its Process object.

12. **C.**The IncrementBy method is the most efficient method to increase or decrease the value of a counter by the specified unit.

13. **A.** The easiest and the most efficient way to find out whether a log exists on a local or a remote machine is to use the static Exists method of the EventLog class.

14. **C.** Communication with legacy COM components must cross process boundaries. To speed up this communication, you need to minimize the number of calls between your application and the COM component.

15. **D.** The Throw statement has the maximum performance penalty and should be used cautiously.

Suggested Readings and Resources

1. Visual Studio .NET Combined Help Collection
   - Managing Processes
   - Logging Application, Server, and Security events.
   - Monitoring Performance Thresholds.
   - Performance Tips and Tricks in .NET Applications.
   - Performance Considerations for Run-Time Technologies in the .NET Framework.
2. Burton, Kevin. *.NET Common Language Runtime Unleashed*, Sams Publishing, 2002.

OBJECTIVES

This chapter covers the following Microsoft-specified objective for the Configuring and Securing a Web Application section of the Visual Basic .NET Web-Based Applications exam:

Configure a Web application.

- **Modify the `web.config` file.**
- **Modify the `machine.config` file.**
- **Add and modify application settings.**

Configure security for a Web application.

- **Select and configure authentication types. Authentication types include Windows authentication, none, forms-based, Microsoft Passport, Internet Information Services (IIS) authentication, and custom authentication.**

Configure authorization. Authorization methods include file-based methods and URL-based methods.

- **Configure role-based authorization.**
- **Implement impersonation.**

Configure and implement caching. Caching types include output, fragment, and data.

- **Use a cache object.**
- **Use cache directives.**

Configure and implement session states in various topologies such as a Web garden and a Web farm.

- **Use session state within a process.**
- **Use session state with session state service.**
- **Use session state with Microsoft SQL Server.**

CHAPTER 15

Configuring a Web Application

OBJECTIVES

Install and configure server services.

- **Install and configure a Web server.**
- **Install and configure Microsoft FrontPage Server Extensions.**

- Web servers are complex pieces of software, and ASP.NET adds an additional layer of complexity to Microsoft Internet Information Services, the Web server that ASP.NET uses. With this complexity, it's not surprising that there are many configuration options for ASP.NET. In a large organization, configuration may be the job of a dedicated systems administrator, but in a small organization you may be responsible for configuring your own servers. In any case, you should understand the options that can be used to change the behavior of ASP.NET and your applications.

- The first objective covers configuration options for ASP.NET itself and for ASP.NET applications. You'll see that these options are stored in a complex series of nested XML configuration files. Configuration files are hierarchical so you can configure an application or even part of an application without affecting other software running on the same server.

- Security is another area where configuration is necessary. Configuration tasks in this area center around authentication (verifying a user's identity) and authorization (determining what an authenticated user is allowed to do).

- Caching and session state are two other important areas of configuration. Caching options let you control when content is stored for future delivery instead of being generated every time the page is requested. Session state lets you store user-related information as the user navigates between pages in your application. ASP.NET offers several options for both caching and session state.

- Finally, you should understand how to set up a new server and how to install the essential software on which ASP.NET relies to do its job.

OUTLINE

Study Strategies

- Inspect the `web.config` and `machine.config` files on your Web server to understand their default contents. Read the comments in the files to see what you can change.
- Build static and dynamic pages and change the caching options to see their effect.
- Use Session variables to store information in an application. Experiment with the various choices for storing session state.
- Configure a new Web on an IIS server, and install and configure the FrontPage Server Extensions on that Web.

INTRODUCTION

Developing ASP.NET applications offers challenges that are not present when working on simple Windows applications. When you need to develop applications on a Web server, you need to worry about configuring that server. In addition to configuring Microsoft Internet Information Services (IIS), there are also numerous settings you can make to configure ASP.NET.

Administrators, too, will want to configure applications. Administrative configuration often takes the form of setting up security. In some cases, this will be computer security, designed to keep untrusted applications from harming the operating system or the user's critical data files. In others, this will be user security, designed to control who can use a particular application.

You'll also need to worry about configuring caching and session state. With caching, you can control whether pages are constructed every time they're requested by a user, or whether they should be delivered from saved copies instead. Session state allows you to save user information as the user navigates between the pages in your application.

The .NET Framework offers you substantial control of these (and other) types of configuration. Configuration files make most runtime configuration tasks a simple matter of editing XML files. The .NET Framework also includes a complete security system with flexible authentication and authorization options.

In this chapter, you'll learn how you can configure your ASP.NET environment for our own needs, both as a developer and as an administrator.

CONFIGURING A WEB APPLICATION

Configure a Web application

- **Modify the `web.config` file.**
- **Modify the `machine.config` file.**
- **Add and modify application settings.**

ASP.NET offers a number of ways for the administrator to configure its workings. You can specify such things as custom error pages, authentication methods, browser detection methods, or the timeout period for HTTP requests on a server-by-server, an application-by-application, or even a folder-by-folder basis.

All these settings are stored in a set of external configuration files. These files are plain-text XML files. Using external XML files for configuration settings offers several advantages for server administration:

- Because they're XML files, they can be modified by any editor that understands the XML file format.
- Because XML files are also plain-text files, configuration files can even be modified with a text editor such as Notepad (as long as you know what you're doing).
- There's no need for direct access to the server to change configuration; you can just apply a new configuration file via FTP or any other means that you have for transferring files to the server.

> NOTE
>
> **One Reboot Necessary** If you change the `processModel` element in the `machine.config` file, you must restart IIS to have the changes take effect. This element controls internal IIS settings such as which processors to use on a multiprocessor computer and the number of threads to allocate to ASP.NET.

> EXAM TIP
>
> **Loss of State** Although changes to configuration files are picked up automatically by ASP.NET, that doesn't mean you can change things without consequences. When you change a configuration file, ASP.NET clears all the application state and session state variables for the affected site. If you change the `machine.config` file, you'll lose all the state settings for every site on the Web server.

Configuration files are treated as a hierarchy by ASP.NET. One configuration file controls settings for the entire computer. Any of these settings can be overridden for a particular Web site hosted on the computer by a configuration file located in the root folder of that Web site. Those settings themselves can be overridden for a particular Web application (virtual directory) by an application-specific configuration file. These settings in turn can be overridden by other configuration files that apply to only part of an application. I'll discuss this hierarchy in more detail a bit later in this chapter.

ASP.NET automatically monitors configuration files for changes. If you change a configuration file, the new settings automatically take effect. There's no need to stop and restart the ASP.NET process or to reboot the computer.

Anatomy of a Configuration File

The easiest way to learn about the structure of configuration files is to look inside of one. I'll start with the master configuration file that controls ASP.NET's operations on the computer.

This file is named `machine.config`, and you'll find it in a directory underneath your Windows installation directory, whose name is based on the version of the .NET Framework installed. For example, on a Windows 2000 computer with the initial release of the .NET Framework installed, this file is at

```
C:\WINNT\Microsoft.NET\Framework\
[ic:lcc]v1.0.3705\CONFIG\machine.config
```

> **WARNING**
>
> **Work From a Backup** Because the `machine.config` file is critical to the workings of ASP.NET, I recommend that you explore a copy of this file rather than the actual file. Any changes to `machine.config` should be made very cautiously, and you should always keep a copy of the unchanged file in case you need to reverse the changes.

Like any other XML file, the `machine.config` file starts with an XML declaration. Then comes a root element named `<configuration>` that brackets the entire contents of the XML file. Then comes a single `<configSections>` element. This element contains entries that identify all the types of configuration settings that the file can manage. Here's a portion of the `<configSections>` element (I've reformatted a bit to fit on the page; ellipses indicate where I've omitted sections of the file):

```
<configSections>
    <!-- tell .NET Framework to ignore CLR sections -->
    <section name="runtime"
     type="System.Configuration.IgnoreSectionHandler,
     System, Version=1.0.3300.0,
     Culture=neutral,
     PublicKeyToken=b77a5c561934e089"
     allowLocation="false"/>
...
    <section name="appSettings"
     type="System.Configuration.
     NameValueFileSectionHandler,
     System, Version=1.0.3300.0,
     Culture=neutral,
     PublicKeyToken=b77a5c561934e089"/>
    <sectionGroup name="system.net">
        <section name="authenticationModules"
         type="System.Net.Configuration.
         NetAuthenticationModuleHandler,
         System, Version=1.0.3300.0,
         Culture=neutral,
         PublicKeyToken=b77a5c561934e089"/>
...
    </sectionGroup>
...
</configSections>
```

The purpose of the `<configSections>` element is to tell the .NET Framework what sorts of settings are contained within the rest of the file. As you can see, there are both `<sectionGroup>` and `<section>` elements within this section of the file.

The `<sectionGroup>` element defines a namespace within the configuration file. This allows you to keep section names from conflicting with one another. For example, in the part of the file shown here, the `system.net` section group contains an `authenticationModules` section. You could also have an `authenticationModules` section in another section element group.

The `<section>` element defines a section of the configuration file. Each section has an arbitrary name and a type. The type of a section defines a class within the .NET Framework that will be used to read settings from the specified section. As you can see, types are specified with complete information, including a public key token to ensure their identity.

There are also two optional attributes that you can add to the section tag. The `allowDefinition` attribute specifies which configuration files can contain a particular section. The values for this attribute are `Everywhere` (the default), `MachineOnly` (which allows defining the section in the `machine.config` file only), or `MachineToApplication` (which allows defining the section in the `machine.config` file or application configuration files). The other optional attribute is `allowLocation`, which can be set to true or false. If you set `allowLocation` to false, it prevents this section from appearing further down in the configuration file hierarchy. In the section of the file above, this setting is used to prevent other files from defining a section that might substitute a malicious .NET runtime file.

After element (machine.config)>the `<configSections>` element, you'll find the actual sections themselves. For example, this `<configSections>` defines a section named `appSettings`, and farther down in the file you'll find the corresponding `<appSettings>` element. Within that element you would place any configuration settings defined for applications.

If you browse through the `machine.config` file on your computer, you'll get a sense of what you can configure in this fashion. The file includes some comments to show you the allowable options for settings. Table 15.1 lists the various sections that you can specify in this and other configuration files.

TABLE 15.1

CONFIGURATION FILE SECTIONS

Section	*Used for*
`<allow>`	Allows access to a resource.
`<assemblies>`	Assemblies to use for dynamic compilation.
`<authentication>`	Configures authentication.
`<authorization>`	Configures authorization.
`<browserCaps>`	Detecting the user's browser type.
`<clientTarget>`	Specifies user agent aliases.
`<compilation>`	Compiler settings.
`<compilers>`	Supported compilers.
`<credentials>`	Name and password credentials for authenticating users.
`<customErrors>`	Custom error messages.
`<deny>`	Denies access to a resource.
`<forms>`	Configures forms-based authentication.
`<globalization>`	Configures globalization settings.
`<httpHandlers>`	Maps incoming requests to HTTP handlers.
`<httpModules>`	Manages HTTP modules within an application.
`<httpRuntime>`	Configures the HTTP runtime.
`<identity>`	Configures application identity.
`<pages>`	Page-specific configuration information.
`<processModel>`	Controls the ASP.NET process model.
`<protocols>`	Protocols used to decrypt client data.
`<securityPolicy>`	Maps security levels to policy files.
`<serviceDescription FormatExtensionTypes>`	Specifies service description format extensions.
`<sessionState>`	Configures session state options.
`<soapExtensionTypes>`	Specifies SOAP extensions.
`<trace>`	Configures application tracing.
`<trust>`	Configures code access security.
`<user>`	Defines users.
`<webServices>`	Settings for Web services.

NOTE

Other Settings Some of these sections can include other tags for more detail. For a complete list of what may appear in each element within a config file, see the Configuration File Schema setting of the Reference information in the .NET Framework SDK documentation.

The Configuration File Hierarchy

As I mentioned previously, configuration files are arranged in a hierarchy. This means that individual applications can supplement or even override the configuration defined in the `machine.config` file. Step by Step 15.1 shows you how this works.

STEP BY STEP

15.1 Configuring an Individual Application

1. Create a new Visual Basic ASP.NET application. Add a new Web Form to the application.
2. Add a `HyperLink` control to the Web Form and set its `NavigateUrl` property to `NonexistentPage.aspx`. Set this form as the start page for the application.
3. Open the `machine.config` file on your Web server and scroll down until you find the `<customErrors>` section. If you have not edited this section since the file was installed, it will contain this setting:

```
<customErrors mode="RemoteOnly"/>
```

   This setting tells ASP.NET to display any custom errors to remote clients and to use ASP.NET native errors if the application is running on the local host. See Chapter 4 "Error Handling for the User Interface" for more information on custom and native errors.

4. Double-click the `web.config` file in Solution Explorer. This is the configuration file that contains settings for the local application. By default, it has the same custom error setting that the `machine.config` file contains. Change the setting in the `web.config` file so that it reads

```
<customErrors mode="On">
    <error statusCode="404" redirect="404.aspx" />
</customErrors>
```

   This tells ASP.NET to display custom errors regardless of whether you're executing the application from a remote client or a local client, and to display a page named `404.aspx` in response to 404 (page not found) errors.

5. Add a new Web Form to the application. Name the new form `404.aspx`. Change the `pageLayout` property of the page to `FlowLayout`. Type this text directly on the page:

```
The page you were trying to open was not found.
```

6. Run the project. Click the `HyperLink` control. Your custom error page will appear in the browser window.

7. Stop the project. Right-click the project in Solution Explorer and select Add, New Folder. Name the new folder `SubDir`.

8. Right-click the `SubDir` folder and select Add, Add New Item. Add a new Web Form to this folder.

9. Add a `HyperLink` control to the Web Form and set its `NavigateUrl` property to `NonexistentPage.aspx`. Set this form as the start page for the application.

10. Run the project. Click the `HyperLink` control. Your custom error page will once again appear in the browser window.

11. Stop the project. Right-click the `SubDir` folder and select Add, Add New Item. Add a Web configuration file with the default name of `web.config` to the folder. The new file will be created with the default `customErrors` setting. Open the new `web.config` file and edit it so that it contains only the `customErrors` setting:

```
<?xml version="1.0" encoding="utf-8" ?>
<configuration>
  <system.web>
    <customErrors mode="Off" />
  </system.web>
</configuration>
```

12. Run the project again. Click the `HyperLink` control. Instead of your custom error page, you'll see the default error message shown in Figure 15.1.

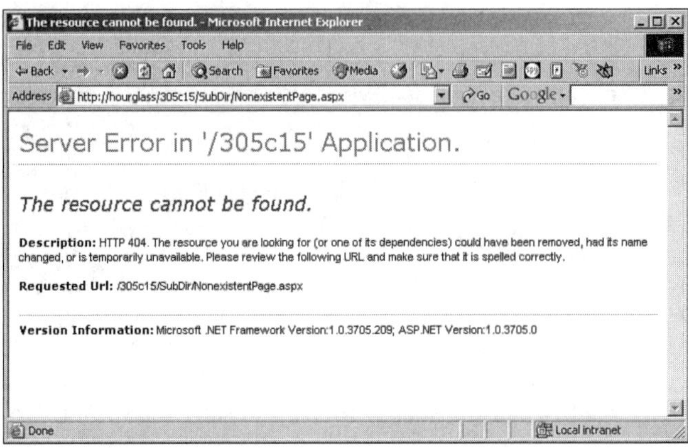

FIGURE 15.1
Default error for a nonexistent ASPX file.

This example demonstrates the essentials of hierarchical configuration files. When you ran the project in Step 6, ASP.NET found the default `machine.config` file, but it also found the `web.config` file in the same folder as the Web page that you were displaying. The more specific custom error setting in the `web.config` file overrides the setting in the general `machine.config` file, and so the custom 404 page was displayed.

When you ran the project the second time, in step 10, ASP.NET did not find a `web.config` file in the same folder as the Web page that you were working with. Therefore, the page inherited the settings from the `web.config` file in the parent folder, and the custom error page was displayed again.

The third time, the `web.config` file in the `SubDir` folder overrode the `machine.config` file and the `web.config` file in the parent folder, and so the default error message came up in the browser instead.

At any time, the `web.config` file closest in the folder chain to the page being displayed controls the settings used by ASP.NET. Note that not every setting comes from the same file. For example, in the final part of Step by Step 15.1 only the custom error setting comes from the most specific `web.config` file. Other settings, such as the tracing and session state settings, come from the parent `web.config` file or even from the `machine.config` file.

Several other factors complicate this simple picture of how things work:

- The parent folder that matters is not the physical folder on the hard drive, but the virtual folder in IIS. In the final example shown previously, if the page were displayed from a virtual root that was pointed directly at the `SubDir` folder, none of the settings in the parent `web.config` file would apply.
- A setting in a configuration file can be marked with a location element. For example, you might tag a particular section with the element `<location path="Subdir1">`. Settings contained within this element will apply only to pages stored within the `Subdir1` subdirectory of the application.
- ASP.NET configuration files only apply to ASP.NET resources. So, for example, if the bad link had pointed to `NonexistentPage.htm`, the custom error setting would never be invoked (because ASP.NET does not manage HTML files).
- Any configuration file can mark a section with the `allowOverride="false"` attribute. In this case, more specific configuration files cannot override this setting.

EXAM TIP

Dedicated Editor It can be difficult to determine which settings actually apply to a particular resource. If you plan to work extensively with ASP.NET configuration files, you might check out the Web Config Editor from Hunter Stone, `http://hunterstone.com/default.htm`.

Reading Configuration Settings from Code

All the settings that you've seen in the ASP.NET configuration files so far are used by ASP.NET itself. Your code can also use the configuration files to store information. The .NET Framework provides you with programmatic access to both the existing information and your own custom information in these files.

STEP BY STEP

15.2 Reading from Configuration Files

1. Add a new Web form to your Visual Basic ASP.NET application.

continues

2. Arrange two `Label` controls and two `TextBox` controls on the Web Form as shown in Figure 15.2. Set the ID properties of the `TextBox` controls to `txtBuiltin` and `txtCustom`.

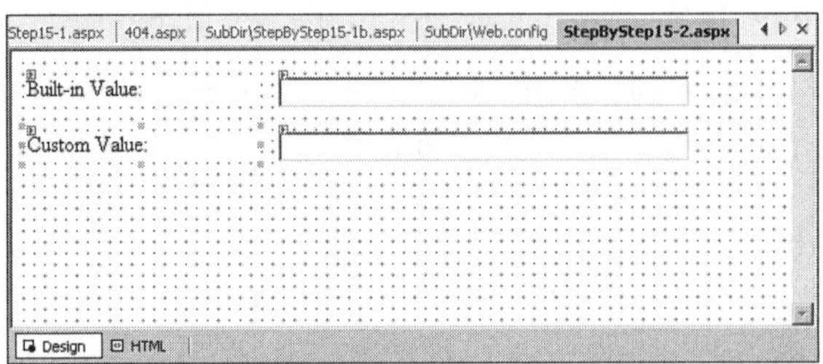

FIGURE 15.2
Web Form for testing configuration values.

3. Add a section to the `web.config` file, directly after the `<configuration>` element:

```
<appSettings>
  <add key="Custom"
   value="Custom configuration value" />
</appSettings>
```

4. Double-click the Web Form to open the form's module. Add code to read settings when the form is loaded:

```
Private Sub Page_Load(ByVal sender As System.Object, _
 ByVal e As System.EventArgs) Handles MyBase.Load
    txtCustom.Text =
    ConfigurationSettings.AppSettings("Custom")
    txtBuiltIn.Text = Session.Mode.ToString()
End Sub
```

5. Set the form as the start page for the project.

6. Run the project. The page will display settings from the configuration file as shown in Figure 15.3.

EXAM TIP

Flexible Settings Although the `appSettings` section is defined for you, and the `ConfigurationSettings.AppSettings` property provides convenient access to this portion of the configuration file, you're not limited to storing settings in this one specific place. If you prefer, you can define a custom configuration handler and store settings in your own custom section. See the .NET Framework SDK Help topic "Creating New Configuration Sections" for details on this technique.

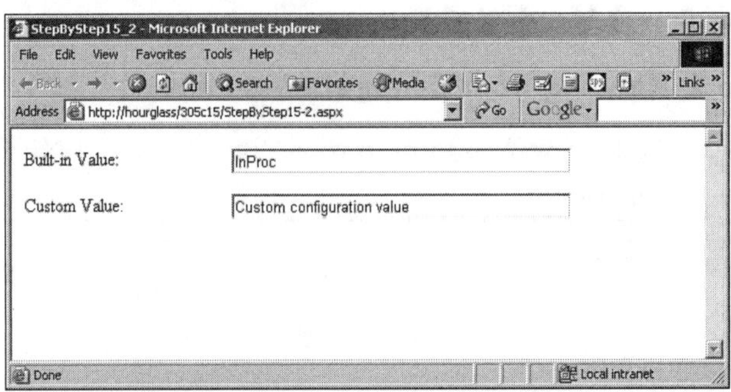

FIGURE 15.3
Configuration values retrieved at runtime.

To read a value from the `appSettings` section of a config file, you can use the static `AppSettings` property of the `ConfigurationSettings` object. To read one of the built-in values, you need to know which object within the ASP.NET object model consumes that setting. In this case, the `Mode` property of the `Session` object exposes the value of the `Mode` tag in the `sessionState` section of the configuration file.

REVIEW BREAK

- ASP.NET stores configuration information in XML files.
- Configuration files form a hierarchy. Settings are generally retrieved from the configuration file most local to the current page.
- You can use the `ConfigurationSettings` object to retrieve custom information from a configuration file.
- Configuration files are automatically reread by ASP.NET when they are changed, without a restart or a reboot.

Configuring Security

When you're developing ASP.NET applications, you need to configure two aspects of security: *authentication* and *authorization*. Authentication refers to the process of obtaining credentials from a user and verifying their identity. After an identity has been authenticated, it can be authorized to use various resources.

ASP.NET supports a number of methods of authentication. These methods of authentication include

- None In many cases, there's no need for users of an ASP.NET application to be authenticated at all. Pages can simply be delivered to all comers.
- Windows ASP.NET applications can use the Windows authentication methods built into IIS to authenticate users in a Windows domain.

- Forms-based This form of authentication uses an HTML form to request credentials from the user. If the credentials are acceptable, the application sends back an identity key.
- Passport Microsoft Passport provides a centralized authentication and profile service for member sites.
- IIS Authentication IIS supports several alternative methods for authentication. These methods interact with the authentication choices within ASP.NET. IIS authentication can also protect resources that are not controlled by ASP.NET.
- Custom You can develop your own custom authentication scheme if you like. You should be aware, though, that it is very difficult to design a secure authentication scheme.

After you've authenticated a user, you can use his or her identity to authorize access to resources. One way to do this is by using .NET's own role-based security, which allows you to dictate in code which users should have access to which resources. As an alternative, you can allow the ASP.NET process to impersonate the authenticated user, and rely on the security mechanisms in Windows to determine access to resources.

Configuring Authentication

Configure security for a Web application:

Select and configure authentication type. Authentication types include Windows authentication, none, forms-based, Microsoft Passport, Internet Information Services (IIS) authentication, and custom authentication.

Authentication is the process of obtaining credentials from a user and validating those credentials against some authority. If the validation succeeds, the user's identity is considered authenticated, and you can proceed to use that identity to authorize access to resources.

ASP.NET provides you with flexible alternatives for authentication. You can perform authentication yourself in code, or delegate authentication to other authorities. Settings in the `web.config` file control the method of authentication that will be used for any given request.

No Authentication

The simplest form of authentication is no authentication at all. To enable an application to execute without authentication, you add this section to its configuration file:

```
<authentication mode="None" />
```

Setting the mode to `None` tells ASP.NET that you don't care about user authentication. The natural consequence of this, of course, is that you can't base authorization on user identities, because users are never authenticated.

IIS and ASP.NET Authentication

One thing that trips up some developers is that there are actually two separate authentication layers in an ASP.NET application. That's because all requests flow through IIS before they're handed to ASP.NET, and IIS can decide to deny access before the ASP.NET process even knows about the request. Here's a rundown on how the process works:

1. IIS first checks to make sure that the incoming request comes from an IP address that is allowed access to the domain. If not, the request is denied.
2. Next, IIS performs its own user authentication, if it's configured to do so. I'll talk more about IIS authentication later in the chapter. By default, IIS allows anonymous access, so requests are automatically authenticated.
3. If the request is passed to ASP.NET with an authenticated user, ASP.NET checks to see whether impersonation is enabled. If impersonation is enabled, ASP.NET acts as though it were the authenticated user. If not, ASP.NET acts with its own configured account.
4. Finally, the identity from step 3 is used to request resources from the operating system. If all the necessary resources can be obtained, the user's request is granted; otherwise, it is denied.

As you can see, several security authorities interact when the user requests a resource or a Web page. If things aren't behaving the way that you think they should, it can be helpful to review this list and make sure you've considered all the factors involved.

Authentication Providers

So what happens when a request gets to ASP.NET? The answer depends on the site's configuration. The ASP.NET architecture delegates authentication to an authentication provider—a module whose job it is to verify credentials and provide authentication. ASP.NET ships with three authentication providers:

- The Windows authentication provider allows you to authenticate users based on their Windows accounts. This provider uses IIS to perform the actual authentication and then passes the authenticated identity to your code.
- The Passport authentication provider uses Microsoft's Passport service to authenticate users.
- The Forms authentication provider uses custom HTML forms to collect authentication information and allows you to use your own logic to authenticate users. Credentials are then stored in a cookie.

To select an authentication provider, you make an entry in the `web.config` file for the application. You can use any of these entries to select one of the built-in authentication providers:

```
<authentication mode="Windows" />

<authentication mode="Passport" />

<authentication mode="Forms" />
```

You can also create your own custom authentication provider. This doesn't mean that you plug a new module in place of the supplied provider; it means that you write custom code to perform authentication,] and set the authentication mode for the application to `None`. For example, you might depend on an ISAPI filter to authenticate users at the level of incoming requests. In that case, you wouldn't want to use any of the .NET authentication providers.

Configuring IIS Authentication

If you decide to use Windows authentication within your applications, you'll need to consider how to configure IIS authentication. That's because the Windows identities are actually provided by IIS. IIS offers four different authentication methods:

- If you select anonymous authentication, IIS does not perform any authentication. Anyone is allowed access to the ASP.NET application.
- If you select basic authentication, users must provide a Windows username and password to connect. However, this information is sent across the network in clear text, making basic authentication dangerously insecure on the Internet.
- If you select digest authentication, users must still provide a Windows username and password to connect. However, the password is hashed (scrambled) before being sent across the network. Digest authentication requires that all users be running Internet Explorer 5 or later, and that Windows accounts are stored in Active Directory.
- If you select Windows integrated authentication, passwords never cross the network. Users must still have a Windows username and password, but either the Kerberos or challenge/response protocols are used to authenticate the user. Windows-integrated authentication requires that all users be running Internet Explorer 3.01 or later.

STEP BY STEP

15.3 Configuring IIS Authentication

1. Open the `web.config` file for your Visual Basic ASP.NET application and verify that the authentication mode is set to Windows.
2. In Windows, select Start, Programs, Administrative Tools, Internet Services Manager.
3. In Internet Services Manager, drill-down into the tree view until you find the node that corresponds to your Visual Basic ASP.NET application. This node will have the same name as the application and will be located beneath the Default Web Site node. Right-click the application node and select Properties.

continues

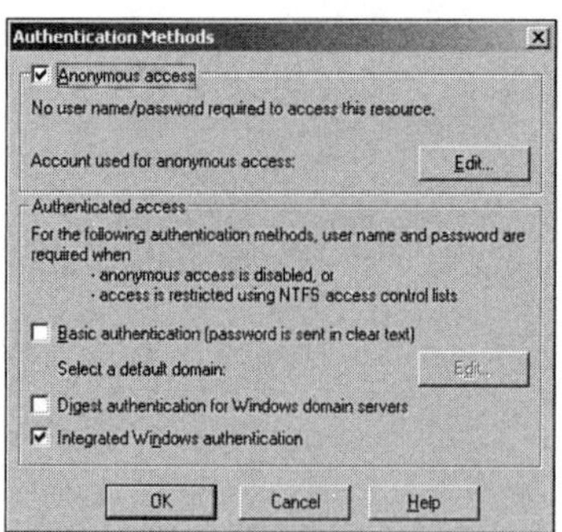

FIGURE 15.4
Editing IIS authentication methods.

FIGURE 15.5
Logging on with basic authentication.

continued

4. In the Properties dialog box, click the Directory Security tab. Click the Edit button in the anonymous access and authentication methods section to open the Authentication Methods dialog box, shown in Figure 15.4.
5. Uncheck the Anonymous Access checkbox and the Integrated Windows Authentication checkbox.
6. Check the Basic Authentication checkbox. Click Yes and then click OK twice to save your changes.
7. In Visual Studio .NET, select Debug, Run Without Debugging to run the project. You'll see the Enter Network Password dialog box shown in Figure 15.5. Enter your username and password to see the start page for the application. To log on to a domain account, enter the username as `DOMAIN\User`.

Passport Authentication

ASP.NET has built-in connections to Microsoft's Passport authentication service. If your users have signed up with Passport, and you configure the authentication mode of the application to be Passport authentication, then all authentication duties are offloaded to the Passport servers.

Passport uses an encrypted cookie mechanism to indicate authenticated users. If users have already signed in to Passport when they visit your site, they'll be considered authenticated by ASP.NET. Otherwise, they'll be redirected to the Passport servers to log in.

To use Passport authentication, you'll need to download the Passport Software Development Kit (SDK) and install it on your server. The SDK can be found at `http://msdn.microsoft.com/downloads/default.asp?URL=/downloads/sample.asp?url=/msdn-files/027/001/885/msdncompositedoc.xml`.

You'll also need to license Passport authentication. Currently the license fees are $10,000 per year plus a periodic $1,500 testing fee. You can get details on licensing Passport at `http://www.microsoft.com/netservices/passport/`.

Forms Authentication

Forms authentication provides you with a way to handle authentication using your own custom logic within an ASP.NET application (note that this is different from custom authentication using an ISAPI filter, which takes place before the request ever gets to ASP.NET). With forms authentication, the logic of the application goes like this:

1. When a user requests a page from the application, ASP.NET checks for the presence of a special cookie. If the cookie is present, the request is processed.
2. If the cookie is not present, ASP.NET redirects the user to a Web Form that you provide.
3. You can carry out whatever authentication checks you like in your form. When the user is authenticated, you indicate this to ASP.NET, which creates the special cookie to handle subsequent requests.

STEP BY STEP

15.4 Implementing Forms Authentication

1. In Windows, select Start, Programs, Administrative Tools, Internet Services Manager.
2. In Internet Services Manager, drill-down into the tree view until you find the node that corresponds to your Visual Basic ASP.NET application. This node will have the same name as the application and will be located beneath the Default Web Site node. Right-click the application node and select Properties.
3. In the Properties dialog box, click the Directory Security tab. Click the Edit button in the Anonymous Access and Authentication Methods section to open the Authentication Methods dialog box.
4. Check the Anonymous Access checkbox. This will cause IIS to pass all requests directly to ASP.NET for processing.

continues

continued

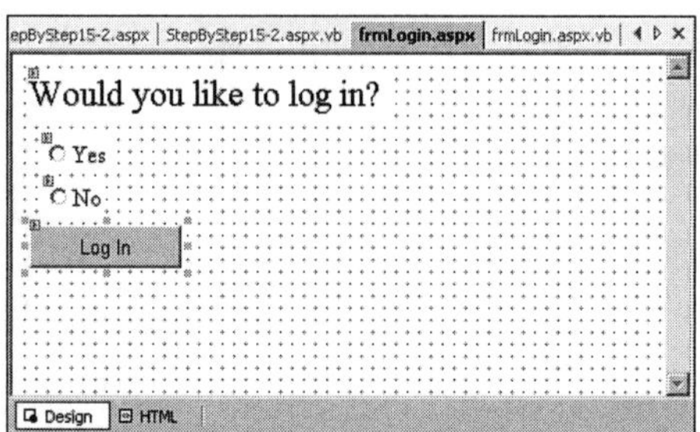

FIGURE 15.6
Testing forms authentication.

5. If you receive a security warning, Click Yes and then click OK twice to save your changes.

6. Add a new Web Form to your Visual Basic ASP.NET application. Name the new form `frmLogin.aspx`.

7. Place a `Label` control, two `RadioButton` controls (`rbYes` and `rbNo`), and a `Button` control with the ID of `btnLogin` on the form. Figure 15.6 shows a design for this form.

8. Double-click the `Button` control to open the form's module. Add a reference at the top of the module:

```
Imports System.Web.Security
```

9. Add this code to handle the `Button` control's `Click` event:

```
Private Sub btnLogin_Click( _
 ByVal sender As System.Object, _
 ByVal e As System.EventArgs) Handles btnLogin.Click
    If rbYes.Checked Then
        FormsAuthentication. _
         RedirectFromLoginPage("Admin", False)
    End If
End Sub
```

10. Edit the `web.config` file to replace both the authentication and authorization sections as follows:

```
<authentication mode="Forms">
<forms loginUrl="frmLogin.aspx"
 name="305c15"
 timeout="1" />
</authentication>

<authorization>
   <deny users="?" />
</authorization>
```

11. Run the project. Instead of the start page of the application, your browser will display the custom login form. To proceed further, you'll need to select the Yes radio button and click the Login button.

Of course, in a real application you'd likely implement a more sophisticated authentication scheme than just making users select a radio button! But in forms-based authentication, you can use any login scheme you can code. You might, for example, store usernames and IP addresses in a database, and only allow users who connect from their registered IP address. Or you might develop a Web service that allows authenticating users over the Internet.

Note the change to the authorization section of the configuration file in this example. By default, the authorization section contains an `allow` element:

```
<allow users="*" />
```

With that authorization setting, ASP.NET allows all users—even unauthenticated users—access to application resources. The `*` wildcard matches any user. For this example, I changed this to a deny element:

```
<deny users="?" />
```

The `?` wildcard matches only unauthenticated users. The net effect is to allow authenticated users access to all resources, while denying unauthenticated users access to any resources.

The `<forms>` element contains the name of the URL of the form to use for login authentication, the name of the cookie to use, and a timeout that controls how long a user can work with the application before being directed back to the login page (here set to the very low value of one minute for testing).

When the user is authenticated, the form calls the `RedirectFromLoginPage` method of the `FormsAuthentication` object. The two parameters to this method are the name of the authenticated user and a Boolean value that controls whether to save a permanent (cross-session) cookie. In this case the second parameter is `False`, so the cookie is stored in memory, and only for the length of the browser session.

Note that the login form doesn't contain any reference to the page where the user will go after authenticating. The forms authentication provider automatically keeps track of the name of the page that the user was trying to access and sends her there when you call the `RedirectFromLoginPage` method.

Configuring Authorization

After your application has authenticated users, you can proceed to authorize their access to resources. But there's a question to answer first: Just who is the user who you are granting access to? It turns out that there are different answers to that question, depending on whether you implement impersonation. With impersonation, the ASP.NET process can actually take on the identity of the authenticated user.

Once a user has been authenticated and you've decided whether to use impersonation, you can proceed to grant access to resources. ASP.NET uses the role-based authorization features of the .NET Framework for this purpose.

In this section I'll discuss both impersonation and role-based authorization.

Implementing Impersonation

Configure authorization: Implement impersonation.

ASP.NET impersonation is controlled by entries in the applicable `web.config` file. The default setting is no impersonation. You can also explicitly specify this setting by including this element in the file:

```
<identity impersonate="false"/>
```

With this setting, ASP.NET does not perform user impersonation. What does that mean? It means that ASP.NET will always run with its own privileges. By default, ASP.NET runs as an unprivileged account named `ASPNET`. You can change this by making a setting in the `processModel` section of the `machine.config`. This setting can only be changed in `machine.config`, so any change automatically applies to every site on the server. To use a high-privilege system account instead of a low-privilege account, set the `userName` attribute of the `processModel` element to `SYSTEM`.

So when impersonation is disabled, all requests will run in the context of the account running ASP.NET, either the `ASPNET` account or the system account. This is true whether you're using anonymous access or authenticating users in some fashion.

The second possible setting is to turn on impersonation:

```
<identity impersonate="true"/>
```

In this case, ASP.NET takes on the identity passed to it by IIS. If you're allowing anonymous access in IIS, that means that ASP.NET will impersonate the `IUSR_ComputerName` account that IIS itself uses. If you're not allowing anonymous access, ASP.NET will take on the credentials of the authenticated user and make requests for resources as if it were that user.

Finally, you can specify a particular identity to use for all authenticated requests:

```
<identity impersonate="true"
 name="DOMAIN\username" password="password"/>
```

With this setting, all requests are made as the specified user (assuming that the password is correct in the configuration file).

STEP BY STEP

15.5 Using Impersonation

1. In Windows, select Start, Programs, Administrative Tools, Internet Services Manager.
2. In Internet Services Manager, drill-down into the tree view until you find the node that corresponds to your Visual Basic ASP.NET application. This node will have the same name as the application and will be located beneath the Default Web Site node. Right-click the application node and select Properties.
3. In the Properties dialog box, click the Directory Security tab. Click the Edit button in the anonymous access and authentication methods section to open the Authentication Methods dialog box.
4. Uncheck the Anonymous Access checkbox. Check the Basic authentication checkbox.
5. Click Yes and then click OK twice to save your changes.
6. Add a new Web Form to your Visual Basic ASP.NET application. Name the new form `StepByStep15-5.aspx`.

continues

continued

7. Place a TextBox control with the ID of txtAuthenticatedUser on the form.

8. Double-click the form to open its module. Add a reference at the top of the module:

```
Imports System.Security.Principal
```

9. Add this code to run when the page is loaded:

```
Private Sub Page_Load(ByVal sender As System.Object, _
 ByVal e As System.EventArgs) Handles MyBase.Load
    Dim wi As WindowsIdentity = _
     WindowsIdentity.GetCurrent()
    txtAuthenticatedUser.Text = wi.Name
End Sub
```

10. Edit the web.config file to replace both the authentication and authorization sections as follows:

```
<authentication mode="Windows">
</authentication>

<authorization>
   <allow users="*" />
</authorization>
```

11. Run the project. Log in using a Windows username and password (depending on your network configuration, you may not receive a login prompt at this point). The form will display the name of the ASP.NET user (which will be something like DOMAIN\ASPNET). That's because you don't have impersonation turned on at this point.

12. Stop the project. Edit the web.config file to include impersonation:

```
<authentication mode="Windows">
</authentication>
<identity impersonate="true" />

<authorization>
   <allow users="*" />
</authorization>
```

13. Run the project again. Log in using a Windows username and password. The form will display the username and domain that you supplied to authenticate, indicating that the ASP.NET process has taken on the identity of the authenticated user.

Using Role-based Authorization

Configure authorization: Configure role-based authorization.

If you like, you can use the security mechanisms in Windows to authorize access to resources once you've authenticated a user. For example, you can give a Windows account permissions to log on to a SQL Server or to open a particular file. These permissions can be granted to the `ASPNET` user (if you're not using impersonation) or to individual domain users or groups (if you are using impersonation).

But you can also control access to resources directly in your .NET code. Within a Visual Basic .NET Windows application, authorization is handled by the role-based security system. Role-based security revolves around two interfaces: `IIdentity` and `IPrincipal`. For applications that use Windows accounts in role-based security, these interfaces are implemented by the `WindowsIdentity` and `WindowsPrincipal` objects, respectively.

> NOTE
> **Custom Authorization** If for some reason you want to develop a custom authorization scheme, you can implement `IIdentity` and `IPrincipal` in your own classes. In use, these classes will function very much like the Windows-based classes.

The `WindowsIdentity` object represents the Windows user who is running the current code. The properties of this object allow you to retrieve such information as the username and his or her authentication method.

The `WindowsPrincipal` object adds functionality to the `WindowsIdentity` object. The `WindowsPrincipal` object represents the entire security context of the user who is running the current code, including any roles to which he belongs. When the CLR decides which role-based permissions to assign to your code, it inspects the `WindowsPrincipal` object.

STEP BY STEP

15.6 WindowsIdentity and WindowsPrincipal

1. Add a new form to your Visual Basic ASP.NET application. You should leave the application set to perform Windows authentication with impersonation, as it is at the end of Step by Step 15.5.
2. Place a `ListBox` control with the ID of `lbProperties` on the form.

continues

continued

WARNING

Modify the Domain Name This code contains a reference to a specific domain named `LARKGROUP` in its call to the `IsInRole` method. You should change that to the name of your own domain to test this code.

3. Double-click the form to open its module. Add this statement to the top of the module:

```
Imports System.Security.Principal
```

4. Add this code to retrieve properties when you load the form:

```
Private Sub Page_Load(ByVal sender As System.Object, _
 ByVal e As System.EventArgs) Handles MyBase.Load
    ' Tell the CLR which principal policy is in use
    AppDomain.CurrentDomain.SetPrincipalPolicy( _
     PrincipalPolicy.WindowsPrincipal)
    lbProperties.Items.Clear()

    ' Get the current identity
    Dim wi As WindowsIdentity = _
     WindowsIdentity.GetCurrent()
    ' Dump its properties to the listbox
    With lbProperties.Items
        .Add("WindowsIdentity:")
        .Add("  Authentication type: " & _
         wi.AuthenticationType)
        .Add("  Is Anonymous: " & wi.IsAnonymous)
        .Add("  Is Authenticated: " & _
         wi.IsAuthenticated)
        .Add("  Is Guest: " & wi.IsGuest)
        .Add("  Is System: " & wi.IsSystem)
        .Add("  Name: " & wi.Name)
        .Add("  Token: " & wi.Token.ToString)
    End With

    ' Get the current principal
    Dim prin As WindowsPrincipal = _
     New WindowsPrincipal(wi)
    ' Dump its properties to the listbox
    With lbProperties.Items
        .Add("  Authentication Type: " & _
         prin.Identity.AuthenticationType)
        .Add("  Is Authenticated: " & _
         prin.Identity.IsAuthenticated)
        .Add("  Name: " & prin.Identity.Name)
        .Add("  Member of Domain Users: " & _
         prin.IsInRole("LARKGROUP\Domain Users"))
    End With
End Sub
```

5. Set the Web Form as the start page for the project.

6. Run the project and log in to the application. You'll see output similar to that in Figure 15.7. Your output may differ depending on the way that users and groups are set up on your network.

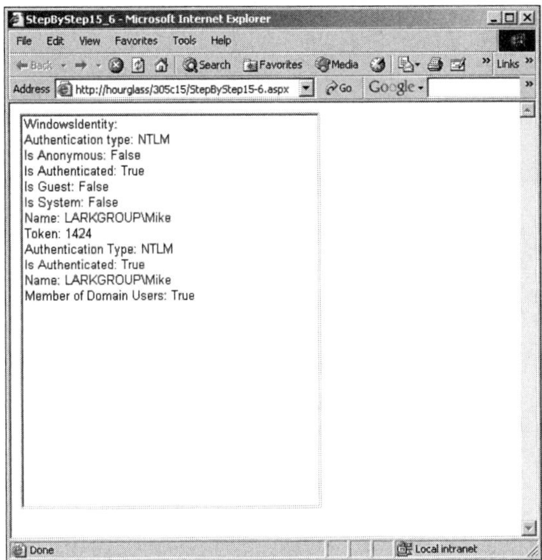

FIGURE 15.7
`WindowsIdentity` and `WindowsPrincipal` properties.

This code first tells the CLR that you're using the standard Windows authentication method by calling the `SetPrincipalPolicy` method of the current `AppDomain`. It then retrieves the `WindowsIdentity` of the current user through the static `GetCurrent` method of the `WindowsIdentity` object. After displaying some of the properties of the `WindowsIdentity` object, it gets the corresponding `WindowsPrincipal` object by passing the `WindowsIdentity` object to the constructor of the `WindowsPrincipal` class.

Note that the properties of the `WindowsIdentity` are somewhat richer than those of the `WindowsPrincipal` object, but that the `WindowsPrincipal` object lets you evaluate role membership for the current user. If you only want to work with the `WindowsPrincipal` object, you can also retrieve it from the `Thread.CurrentPrincipal` static method.

One way to manage role-based security is to use the `IsInRole` method of the `WindowsPrincipal` object to determine whether the current user is in a specific Windows group. The results of this method call can be used to modify your application's user interface or to perform other tasks.

STEP BY STEP

15.7 Verifying Role Membership

1. Add a new Web Form to your Visual Basic ASP.NET application.
2. Place a `Label` control with the ID of `lblMembership` on the form.
3. Double-click the form to open its module. Add these statements to the top of the module:

```
Imports System.Security.Principal
Imports System.Threading
```

4. Add this code to run when you load the form:

```
Private Sub Page_Load(ByVal sender As System.Object, _
 ByVal e As System.EventArgs) Handles MyBase.Load
    ' Tell the CLR to use Windows security
    AppDomain.CurrentDomain.SetPrincipalPolicy( _
     PrincipalPolicy.WindowsPrincipal)
    ' Get the current principal object
    Dim prin As WindowsPrincipal = _
     Thread.CurrentPrincipal
    ' Determine whether the user is an admin
    Dim fAdmin As Boolean = _
     prin.IsInRole(WindowsBuiltInRole.Administrator)
    ' Display the results on the UI
    If fAdmin Then
        lblMembership.Text = _
         "You are in the Administrators group"
    Else
        lblMembership.Text = _
         "You are not in the Administrators group"
    End If
End Sub
```

5. Set the Web Form as the start page for the project.
6. Run the project. The form will tell you whether you're in the Administrators group.

There are three available overloaded forms of the `IsInRole` method:

- `IsInRole(WindowsBuiltInRole)` uses one of the `WindowsBuiltInRole` constants to check for membership in the standard Windows groups.

- `IsInRole(String)` checks for membership in a group with the specified name.
- `IsInRole(Integer)` checks for membership in a group with the specified Role Identifier (RID). RIDs are assigned by the operating system and provide a language-independent way to identify groups.

REVIEW BREAK

- ASP.NET security is divided into authentication (verifying a user's identity) and authorization (allowing an authenticated user to access resources).
- Users must satisfy any IIS authentication requirements before ASP.NET authentication takes over.
- ASP.NET authentication uses interchangeable authentication providers. You can choose Windows authentication, Passport authentication, or forms-based authentication.
- Identity impersonation lets the ASP.NET process act as the authenticated user.
- Role-based security allows you to authorize access to resources based on user identity or group membership.

USING CACHING

Caching refers to storing information for later retrieval, rather than generating it anew every time it's requested. For instance, a Web page can be cached so that it's quicker to deliver when requested a second time. ASP.NET supplies detailed control over caching in Web applications. You can control what should be cached, how long it should be cached, and whether the cached item depends on particular data. In this section I'll discuss the options that ASP.NET offers for caching in your code.

> **EXAM TIP**
>
> **Caching Tradeoffs** Caching represents a tradeoff in any dynamic application. By caching output, you can ease the load on the server, because it does not have to regenerate the output for every page request. But this means that the output sent to a client might not be identical to what the client would have received if there were no caching in place. You need to balance your needs for current data against server load by specifying an appropriate expiration time for any cached content.

Types of Caching

Configure and implement caching. Caching types include output, fragment, and data.

ASP.NET implements three types of caching: *output*, *fragment*, and *application data.*

Output caching refers to caching the entire output of a page request. When you cache a page's output, there are two things that you need to specify. The first is an expiration policy for the cache; you can choose how long a cached page is considered valid before ASP.NET will generate a new version of the page instead of returning the cached page. The second thing to specify is any parameter dependence of the page. For example, suppose your application includes a Web page that generates statistics for voter registrations by state. You could specify that the output varies by state, so that pages for California and Connecticut (and any other states) will be cached separately.

> NOTE
> **User Controls** For more information on user controls, refer to Chapter 2, "Controls."

Fragment caching refers to caching part of a page. ASP.NET enables fragment caching by allowing you to specify cache rules for Web Forms user controls. You can encapsulate a portion of a page into a user control and cache that portion of the page, while still making the rest of the page be dynamically generated for each request. The `@OutputCache` directive will also cache user controls.

Application data caching refers to caching arbitrary data. You can cache any object you like in ASP.NET by calling the `Add` or `Insert` methods of the `Cache` object. Later, you can retrieve the object programmatically by supplying its key. Cached data can be set to expire in a fixed amount of time, but it can also be made dependent on an external resource. For example, you could cache a connection string with instructions to invalidate the cache if a particular XML file were ever changed.

Using the `Cache` Object

Configure and implement caching: Use a cache object.

One way to manage caching is to use the `Cache` object. The `Cache` object is a static class that's always available to your code.

STEP BY STEP

15.8 Using the Cache Object

1. Add a new Web Form to your Visual Basic ASP.NET application.

2. Place a `Label` control with the ID of `lblGenerateTime` on the form.

3. Double-click the form to open its module. Add this code to run when you load the form:

```
Private Sub Page_Load(ByVal sender As System.Object, _
 ByVal e As System.EventArgs) Handles MyBase.Load
    lblGenerateTime.Text = _
     DateTime.Now.ToLongTimeString()
End Sub
```

4. Set the Web Form as the start page for the project.

5. Run the project. The form will be displayed with the current time. Refresh the page several times and note that the displayed time changes every time that you refresh the page.

6. Stop the project. Modify the `Page_Load` code as follows:

```
Private Sub Page_Load(ByVal sender As System.Object, _
 ByVal e As System.EventArgs) Handles MyBase.Load
    lblGenerateTime.Text = _
     DateTime.Now.ToLongTimeString()
    Response.Cache.SetExpires( _
     DateTime.Now.AddSeconds(15))
    Response.Cache.SetCacheability( _
     HttpCacheability.Public)
    Response.Cache.SetValidUntilExpires(True)
End Sub
```

7. Run the project. The form will be displayed with the current time. Refresh the page several times and note that the displayed time does not change until you refresh the page more than 15 seconds after the original request.

This example uses three properties of the `Cache` object. The `SetExpires` method specifies an expiration time for the cached version of the page; in this case, 15 seconds from the time that the page is generated.

The SetCacheability method specifies where output can be cached: NoCache for no caching at all, Private to allow caching only on the client (the default value), Public to allow caching on any proxy server as well as on the client, and Server to cache the document on the server only. Finally, the SetValidUntilExpires(true) method tells the server to ignore client-side attempts to refresh the cached content until it expires.

Using a Cache Directive

Configure and implement caching: use a cache directive.

Alternatively, you can specify the cacheability of a page by using the @OutputCache directive.

STEP BY STEP

15.9 Using a Cache Directive

1. Add a new Web Form to your Visual Basic ASP.NET application.
2. Place a Label control with the ID of lblGenerateTime on the form.
3. Switch the form to HTML view in the designer. Add this directive directly after the @Page directive at the top of the file:

```
<%@ OutputCache Duration="15" VaryByParam="None" %>
```

4. Double-click the form to open its module. Add this code to run when you load the form:

```
Private Sub Page_Load(ByVal sender As System.Object, _
 ByVal e As System.EventArgs) Handles MyBase.Load
    lblGenerateTime.Text = _
     DateTime.Now.ToLongTimeString()
End Sub
```

5. Set the Web Form as the start page for the project.
6. Run the project. The form will be displayed with the current time. Refresh the page several times and note that the displayed time does not change until you refresh the page more than 15 seconds after the original request.

In this case, the `@OutputCache` directive has exactly the same effect as manipulating the cache object did in the previous example. Note that the `@OutputCache` directive requires the `VaryByParam` attribute. If the page output doesn't depend on any input parameters, you can use `None` as the value of this attribute; otherwise, use the name of the parameter to cause caching to be done on a per-parameter-value basis. You can get the same effect programmatically with the cache object by using the `Cache.VaryByParams` property.

GUIDED PRACTICE EXERCISE 15.1

Caching multiple versions of a page is useful any time that you have a page whose output depends on an input parameter. You can base such multiple-version caching on any HTTP header or browser attribute, but most commonly you'll use the `VaryByParams` attribute to cache multiple values depending on a query string or form POST parameter. In this exercise, you'll build a page that caches multiple versions depending on an input parameter.

You should try doing this on your own first. If you get stuck, or you'd like to see one possible solution, follow these steps:

1. Add a new form to your Visual Basic ASP.NET application. Name the form `GuidedPracticeExercise15-1.aspx`.

2. Place a `Label` control with the ID of `lblGenerateTime` and two `HyperLink` controls (`hlCache1` and `hlCache2`) on the form. Set the `NavigateUrl` property of the `hlCache1` control to `GuidedPracticeExercise15-1.aspx?Cache=1` . Set the `NavigateUrl` property of the `hlCache2` control to `GuidedPracticeExercise15-1.aspx?Cache=2`.

3. Switch the form to HTML view in the designer. Add this directive directly after the `@Page` directive at the top of the file:

```
<%@ OutputCache Duration="15" VaryByParam="Cache" %>
```

4. Add code to handle the page's `Load` event:

```
Private Sub Page_Load(ByVal sender As System.Object, _
 ByVal e As System.EventArgs) Handles MyBase.Load
    lblGenerateTime.Text = _
     DateTime.Now.ToLongTimeString()
End Sub
```

continues

continued

5. Set the Web Form as the start page for the project.
6. Run the project. Click the first `HyperLink` control and note the displayed time. Now click the second `HyperLink` control. Note that the displayed time is updated. Click the first `HyperLink` control again and the original displayed time will be returned from the cache. You'll find that both versions of the page are cached for 15 seconds each.

In this exercise, the `VaryByParam` attribute of the `@OutputCache` directive specifies the name of a query string parameter on which the results of the page depend. Each time a new value of that query parameter is sent, a new output page is created and cached. The various cached pages all expire independently in the specified length of time.

HANDLING SESSION STATE

You probably already know about the use of Session variables to store information in an ASP.NET application. HTTP is, of course, a stateless protocol—meaning that the browser has no way of associating information from one page to another of an ASP.NET application. With Session variables, you store this information on the server. The server sends a cookie or a specially munged URL to the browser with each request, and then uses this value to retrieve session state information when the browser returns a new request.

But have you ever thought about just where the server stores this information? In this, as in many other ways, ASP.NET offers several configuration options. In this section, I'll show you three different ways to store session information, and discuss the tradeoffs among them:

- In-process storage
- Session state service
- SQL Server

Using Session State Within a Process

Configure and implement session state: Use session state within a process.

The default location for session state storage is in the ASP.NET process itself. This Step by Step shows you the consequences of this choice.

NOTE

Cookies Required You'll need to accept cookies from your Web server to try any of the session state examples.

STEP BY STEP

15.10 Storing Session State In-Process

1. Add a new Web Form to your Visual Basic ASP.NET application. Name the new form `State1.aspx`.
2. Place a `TextBox` control with the ID of `txtName`, a `Button` control with the ID of `btnSubmit`, and a `HyperLink` control on the form. Set the `NavigateUrl` property of the `HyperLink` control to `State2.aspx`.
3. Switch the form to HTML view in the designer. Add this code to run when you click the button:

```
Private Sub btnSubmit_Click( _
 ByVal sender As System.Object, _
 ByVal e As System.EventArgs) Handles btnSubmit.Click
    Session("Name") = txtName.Text
End Sub
```

4. Set the Web Form as the start page for the project.
5. Add a second new Web Form to the project. Name this form `State2.aspx`.
6. Place a `Label` control named `lblName` on the `State2.aspx` Web Form.
7. Switch the form to HTML view in the designer. Add this code to run when you load the form:

```
Private Sub Page_Load(ByVal sender As System.Object, _
 ByVal e As System.EventArgs) Handles MyBase.Load
    lblName.Text = Session("Name")
End Sub
```

continues

continued

8. Run the project. Enter a name in the `TextBox` control and click the button. Then click the `HyperLink` control to proceed to the second page. The label shows the name that you entered.
9. Close the browser session. Run the project again to load the page into a fresh session. Enter a name and click the button, but do not click the hyperlink.
10. Select Start, Programs, Administrative Tools, Services on the computer where the Web server for the project is located. Stop and restart the World Wide Web Publishing Service.
11. Click the `HyperLink` control. The second page will show, but the name that you entered will not be in the label.

By default, session state information is stored in memory as part of the ASP.NET process itself. If you stop the WWW server (or if it crashes for some reason), all this information is lost.

Using Session State Service

Configure and implement session state: Use session state with session state service.

As an alternative to using in-process storage for session state, ASP.NET provides the ASP.NET State Service.

STEP BY STEP

15.11 Storing Session State in State Service

1. Select Start, Programs, Administrative Tools, Services on the computer where the Web server for the project is located. Make sure that ASP.NET State Service is started.
2. Open your ASP.NET application's `web.config` file. Edit the `sessionState` element as follows:

```
<sessionState
        mode="StateServer"
        stateConnectionString="tcpip=127.0.0.1:42424"
        sqlConnectionString=
         "data source=127.0.0.1;user id=sa;password="
        cookieless="false"
        timeout="20"
/>
```

3. Run the project. Enter a name in the `TextBox` control and click the button. Then click the `HyperLink` control to proceed to the second page. The label will show the name that you entered.

4. Close the browser session. Run the project again to load the page into a fresh session. Enter a name and click the button, but do not click the hyperlink.

5. Select Start, Programs, Administrative Tools, Services on the computer where the Web server for the project is located. Stop and restart the World Wide Web Publishing Service.

6. Click the `HyperLink` control. The second page will show, and the name that you entered will be in the label.

7. Repeat the experiment, but this time stop and restart the ASP.NET State Service. The label will not show the name.

There are two main advantages to using the State Service. First, it is not running in the same process as ASP.NET, so a crash of ASP.NET will not destroy session information. Second, the `stateConnectionString` that's used to locate the State Service includes the TCP/IP address of the service, which need not be running on the same computer as ASP.NET. This allows you to share state information across a Web garden (multiple processors on the same computer) or even across a Web farm (multiple servers running the application). With the default in-process storage, you can't share state information between multiple instances of your application.

The major disadvantage of using the State Service is that it's an external process, rather than part of ASP.NET. That means that reading and writing session state is slower than it would be if you kept the state in-process.

> **WARNING**
>
> **Session State Patch** There is a bug in the initial release of the State service that allows a determined attacker to crash the ASP.NET process remotely. If you're using the State service to store session state, you should install the patch available from `http://www.microsoft.com/technet/treeview/default.asp?url=/technet/security/bulletin/MS02-026.asp`.

Using Microsoft SQL Server to Store Session State

Configure and implement session state: Use session state with Microsoft SQL Server.

The final choice for storing state information is to save it in a Microsoft SQL Server database. To use SQL Server for storing session state, follow these steps:

1. Run the `InstallSqlState.sql` script on the Microsoft SQL Server where you intend to store session state. This script will create the necessary database and database objects.
2. Edit the `sessionState` element in the `web.config` file for your application as follows:

```
<sessionState
        mode="SQLServer"
        stateConnectionString="tcpip=127.0.0.1:42424"
        sqlConnectionString=
        "data source=SERVERHAME;user id=sa;password="
        cookieless="false"
        timeout="20"
/>
```

   You'll need to supply the server name, username, and password for a SQL Server account in the `sqlConnectionString` attribute.

Like the State Service, SQL Server lets you share session state among the processors in a Web garden or the servers in a Web farm. But you also get the additional benefit of persistent storage. Even if the computer hosting SQL Server crashes and is restarted, the session state information will still be present in the database and will be available as soon as the database is running again.

Like the State Service, SQL Server is slower than keeping session state in process. You also need to pay additional licensing fees to use SQL Server for session state in a production application.

REVIEW BREAK

- Session variables let you store information across multiple browser requests.
- The default storage location for session state is in-process memory in the ASP.NET process itself.

- A second choice for storing session state is the ASP.NET Session Service, which provides an out-of-process location to store the information.
- A third choice for storing session state is a Microsoft SQL Server database.

INSTALLING AND CONFIGURING SERVER SERVICES

Finally, if you're responsible for ASP.NET applications you should understand the basic installation of the server software that ASP.NET depends on. This includes Internet Information Services (IIS) and the Microsoft FrontPage Server Extensions.

Installing and Configuring IIS

Install and configure server services: Install and configure a Web server.

Ordinarily installing IIS is simple: It's installed as part of the operating system. Although you can run some .NET code on IIS 4.0 on Windows NT 4.0, you'll lose substantial functionality that way; in particular, ASP.NET applications or Web Services won't run on that platform. The recommended platform is IIS 5.0 on Windows 2000 or Windows XP.

To check the status of an IIS installation on Windows 2000 (Windows XP is similar) follow these steps:

1. Select Start, Settings, Control Panel, Add/Remove Programs.
2. Click the Add/Remove Windows Components button on the left side bar of the dialog box.
3. In the Windows Component Wizard, check the checkbox for Internet Information Services (IIS). You can also click the Details button and select individual components. Make sure you install at least the common files, FrontPage 2000 Server Extensions, Internet Information Services Snap-In, and World Wide Web Server component.

NOTE

IIS 6.0 As of this writing, IIS 6.0 is in beta and is expected to ship as part of Windows .NET Server in 2003. IIS 6.0 should support ASP.NET excellently out of the box.

NOTE

ASP.NET Security By default, ASP.NET is installed using a low-security account. You'll usually need to configure ASP.NET before it will start delivering pages.

EXAM TIP

Install IIS First For proper functionality, you should install IIS before you install Visual Studio .NET. If you install IIS after Visual Studio .NET, you should reinstall Visual Studio .NET after the IIS installation.

4. Click Next to install the selected components.
5. Click Finish.

Installing and Configuring FrontPage Server Extensions

Install and configure server services: Install and configure Microsoft FrontPage Server Extensions.

Visual Studio .NET also depends on the FrontPage Server Extensions for access to ASP.NET projects on remote servers. If you're working with a server across the Internet, you need to be sure that FrontPage Server Extensions are installed and configured on that server. Even if the server is on the local intranet you can still use this method of access.

If you install IIS on a hard drive formatted with the NTFS file system, the FrontPage Server Extensions will automatically be installed and configured for you. If you install IIS on a hard drive formatted with the FAT16 or FAT32 file system, you need to follow these steps to configure the FrontPage Server Extensions:

1. Select Start, Settings, Control Panel, Administrative Tools, Computer Management.
2. Drill down into the tree via the Services and Applications node, and expand the Internet Information Services node.
3. Right-click the Default Web Server Site node and select All Tasks, Configure Server Extensions.
4. Complete the Server Extensions Wizard by clicking Next, then Yes, then Next, and then Finish.

REVIEW BREAK

- IIS is installed as part of the Windows operating system. For full ASP.NET functionality, you should install IIS 5.0 on Windows 2000 or a later version.
- Visual Studio .NET uses the FrontPage Server Extensions to access files on remote Web servers via HTTP.

- If your server's hard drive is NTFS-formatted, the FrontPage Server Extensions will be set up automatically when you install IIS. Otherwise, you can configure the FrontPage Server Extensions via the Computer Management control panel applet.

CHAPTER SUMMARY

After you've finished writing an application, you may still need to configure it. In this chapter, you learned about several broad areas of configurability that are supported by the .NET Framework for ASP.NET applications.

Configuration files let you control the parameters of ASP.NET applications even while those applications are running. You can edit configuration files with any text editor, and read them from code. Configuration files form a hierarchy where any setting can be made on a variety of levels.

Security in ASP.NET revolves around authentication and authorization. You can choose from several authentication providers, including Windows, forms, and Passport authentication. After you've authenticated a user, you can authorize his access to resources.

Role-based security allows you to make decisions in your code based on the user who is currently logged on. You can check for a particular username or for membership in a built-in or custom Windows group, and make decisions accordingly.

Two other areas you may need to configure are caching and session state. ASP.NET lets you decide which pages or fragments of pages to cache, and how long to cache them. You can store session state in-process, in a separate state server, or in a SQL Server database.

Finally, you may need to install and configure the software on which ASP.NET depends. This includes the IIS Web server and the FrontPage Server Extensions.

KEY TERMS

- Configuration file
- Authentication
- Authorization
- Role-based security
- Impersonation
- Caching
- Session state

APPLY YOUR KNOWLEDGE

Exercises

15.1 Variable Caching with the Cache Object

You've already seen that you can use an @OutputCache directive to dictate caching that varies by input parameter. In this exercise, you'll learn how to implement the same feature by using the Cache object.

Estimated Time: 15 minutes.

1. Open a Visual Basic ASP.NET Web Application in the Visual Studio .NET IDE. Add a new Web Form to the application. Name the new Web Form Exercise15-1.aspx.

2. Place a Label control with the ID of lblGenerateTime and two HyperLink controls (hlCache1 and hlCache2) on the form. Set the NavigateUrl property of the hlCache1 control to Exercise15-1.aspx?Cache=1 . Set the NavigateUrl property of the hlCache2 control to Exercise15-1.aspx?Cache=2.

3. Double-click the form to open its module. Add this code to run when you load the form:

```
Private Sub Page_Load( _
 ByVal sender As System.Object, _
 ByVal e As System.EventArgs) _
 Handles MyBase.Load
    lblGenerateTime.Text = _
     DateTime.Now.ToLongTimeString()
    Response.Cache.SetExpires( _
     DateTime.Now.AddSeconds(15))
    Response.Cache.SetCacheability( _
     HttpCacheability.Public)
    Response.Cache.VaryByParams( _
     "Cache") = True
    Response.Cache. _
     SetValidUntilExpires(True)
End Sub
```

4. Set the Web Form as the start page for the project.

5. Run the project. Click the first HyperLink control and note the displayed time. Now click the second HyperLink control. Note that the displayed time is updated. Click the first HyperLink control again and the original displayed time will be returned from the cache. You'll find that both versions of the page are cached for 15 seconds each.

The Cache.VaryByParams property specifies the parameters that this page's caching depends on. By setting this to the "Cache" query parameter, you've caused ASP.NET to cache two separate versions of the page. You can also vary by multiple parameters by separating names with a semicolon:

```
Response.Cache.VaryByParams("City;State") =
True
```

Or you can tell ASP.NET to vary with every parameter it receives by specifying an asterisk:

```
Response.Cache.VaryByParams("*") = True
```

15.2 Application Data Caching

Caching is not limited to the output of ASP.NET pages. Because you have programmatic access to the Cache object, you can place anything you like in the cache. You can set time-based expiration policies, or (as in the following exercise) you can tie the expiration of a cached item to an external resource such as a file

Estimated Time: 20 minutes.

1. Add a new Web Form to your Visual Basic ASP.NET application.

2. Add a Label control with the id of lblConfig to the form.

3. Double-click the form to open the form's module. Add this code to the top of the module:

```
Imports System.Web.Caching
```

APPLY YOUR KNOWLEDGE

4. Add this code to handle the `Load` event of the page:

```
Private Sub Page_Load( _
 ByVal sender As System.Object, _
 ByVal e As System.EventArgs) _
 Handles MyBase.Load
    lblConfig.Text = _
     CType(Cache("CacheValue"), String)
    If lblConfig.Text = "" Then
        lblConfig.Text = _
        ConfigurationSettings. _
        AppSettings("CacheValue")
        Cache.Insert("CacheValue", _
         lblConfig.Text, _
         New CacheDependency( _
          Server.MapPath("web.config")))
    End If
End Sub
```

5. Open the application's `web.config` file. Add an `appSettings` element between the configuration element and the `system.web` element:

```
<appSettings>
  <add key="CacheValue"
       value="Cache this value" />
</appSettings>
```

6. Set the Web Form as the start page for the project.

7. Run the project. The text from the `appSettings` element will be displayed on the page. Refresh the page several times and note that the data is delivered quickly (because it is in the cache). Now, without stopping the application, edit the value in the `web.config` file. Refresh the page and you'll see that the new value shows up, because saving the dependent file invalidated the cached value.

This example shows how you can cache arbitrary data, and how that data can be made to depend on a file.

The `Cache` object maintains an indexed collection of key-value pairs. If you supply the key, you'll get back the value (which can be any type of object), or Nothing if the key does not correspond to a value. This example retrieves a value, and if the value doesn't exist, it gets the value from the `ConfigurationSettings.AppSettings` method and stores it in the cache.

The `CacheDependency` object specifies that (in this case) the cache should be invalidated when a particular file changes. This object has a variety of constructors. You can specify a cache dependency on any of the following items:

- Changes to a file or directory.
- Changes to any of a number of files or directories specified in an array.
- Changes to a file or directory after a specified time.
- Changes to any of an array of files or directories after a specified time.
- Changes to an array of cache keys (so that one cache value can depend on another).

Review Questions

1. How many configuration files can apply to a single ASP.NET page?
2. Explain the use of the `allowDefinition` and `allowLocation` attributes in configuration file section tags.
3. What is the purpose of `allowOverride="False"` in a configuration file?
4. What are authentication and authorization?

APPLY YOUR KNOWLEDGE

5. What are the default accounts for the ASP.NET process?
6. Name four types of authentication that you can specify in an ASP.NET configuration file.
7. What is meant by impersonation in ASP.NET?
8. Name three types of caching.
9. Name three places that you can store session state information in ASP.NET.
10. What do the `WindowsIdentity` and `WindowsPrincipal` objects represent?

Exam Questions

1. You are adding a section to the `machine.config` file on your ASP.NET Web server. You want to ensure that this section cannot be defined in any other configuration file. Which declaration should you use?

   A.

```
<section name="customSection"
     type="CustomConfiguration Handler"
     allowDefinition=
     "MachineToApplication"/>
```

   B.

```
<section name="customSection"
     type="CustomConfiguration Handler"
     allowLocation="false"/>
```

   C.

```
<section name="customSection"
     type="CustomConfiguration Handler" />
```

   D.

```
<section name="customSection"
     type="CustomConfiguration Handler"
     allowOverride="false"/>
```

2. You have adjusted a setting in one of your ASP.NET application's configuration files by editing the file with Notepad. What must you do to have the new setting take effect?

   A. Restart the Web server.

   B. Reboot the computer that hosts the Web server.

   C. Open the file in Visual Studio .NET.

   D. Save the file.

3. Your ASP.NET application requires users to be authenticated with a strong identity. You must allow users with any version 4.x or better browser, and you want passwords to cross the network only with secure encryption. Which authentication should you use?

   A. Windows authentication with Basic IIS authentication.

   B. Windows authentication with digest IIS authentication.

   C. Windows authentication with integrated IIS authentication.

   D. Passport authentication with anonymous IIS authentication.

4. You have implemented forms-based authentication for your ASP.NET application. Some users report that they cannot access any resources on the site, even though you have verified that these users are entering correct authentication information. What could be the problem?

   A. These users are using a browser other than Internet Explorer.

   B. These users have disabled cookies for your Web site.

APPLY YOUR KNOWLEDGE

C. These users do not have a Microsoft Passport.

D. These users are connecting from the Internet rather than a local intranet.

5. Your application requires the user to be in the Domain Admins group to activate certain functions. Which ASP.NET security feature should you use to ensure that the user is in this group?

A. Passport authentication

B. Role-based security

C. Encryption

D. Type safety

6. You want to allow any authenticated user access to your ASP.NET application, but refuse access to all unauthenticated users. Which setting should you place in the application's `web.config` file?

A.

```
<deny users="?" />
```

B.

```
<deny users="*" />
```

C

```
<allow users="?" />
```

D.

```
<allow users="*" />
```

7. You are allowing anonymous or Windows-integrated authentication on your IIS server. Your ASP.NET application uses Windows authentication with impersonation enabled. What account will ASP.NET use when a user attempts to retrieve a page from the application?

A. The user's own Windows account

B. The `ASPNET` account

C. The `IUSR_ComputerName` account

D. An account in the local Administrators group

8. Your ASP.NET application contains this setting in the `web.config` file:

```
<identity impersonate="true"
name="MAIN\Charles"
password="CharlesPassword"/>
```

You are allowing only digest or Windows integrated authentication in IIS. What identity will ASP.NET use to authorize resources if a user with the Windows account Fred in the `MAIN` domain logs in?

A. `MAIN/Fred`

B. `ASPNET`

C. `MAIN/Charles`

D. `IUSR_ComputerName`

9. Your ASP.NET Web form includes a custom user control that displays company information. The rest of the page displays highly volatile stock ticker information. Which type of caching should you use to speed up this page?

A. Output

B. Varying

C. Application data

D. Fragment

10. Your application retrieves a connection string from a text file. Administrators can change the text file to add additional servers to the application. Which form of caching should you use to keep a copy of the most current connection string available?

A. Output

B. Application data

APPLY YOUR KNOWLEDGE

C. Fragment

D. Varying

11. Your server is experiencing performance problems due to excessive load. You trace the problem to users overriding the application's caching policy by sending `nocache` headers in their HTTP requests. What should you do?

    A. Use the `@OutputCache` directive to configure caching.

    B. Use the `Cache.SetExpires` method to set an extended cache period.

    C. Set the `Cache.SetCachability` property to `Private`.

    D. Set the `Cache.SetValidUntilExpires` property to `True`.

12. Your ASP.NET application runs in a four-processor Web garden. Requests are randomly balanced among the four processors. If the computer crashes, it's acceptable to lose state information. However, the state information must be available no matter which processor handles the next request. Which alternative should you use for storing state information?

    A. Session State service

    B. In-process storage

    C. Configuration files

    D. SQL Server storage

13. Your ASP.NET application uses a Web farm to maintain confidential financial information. It's critical that session state be maintained even in case of a server crash. Which alternative should you use for storing state information?

    A. Session State service

    B. In-process storage

    C. SQL Server storage

    D. Configuration files

14. You are preparing to set up a test bed to practice ASP.NET programming. Which of these server configurations can you use? (Select two)

    A. IIS 5.0 on Windows 2000

    B. Personal Web Services on Windows 98

    C. IIS 5.0 on Windows XP

    D. IIS 4.0 on Windows NT 4.0.

15. Your ASP.NET application will run on your company's intranet. The company has standardized on Internet Explorer 5.5 as a browser. All users of the application have Windows domain accounts. You need to track which user accesses certain critical resources. Which form of authentication should you use?

    A. None

    B. Forms

    C. Windows

    D. Passport

Answers to Review Questions

1. There can be a single `machine.config` file, an application-level `web.config` file, and one `web.config` file for every subdirectory in the path to the page.

APPLY YOUR KNOWLEDGE

2. The `allowDefinition` attribute specifies which configuration files can contain a particular section. The values for this attribute are `Everywhere` (the default), `MachineOnly` (which allows defining the section in the `machine.config` file only), or `MachineToApplication` (which allows defining the section in the `machine.config` file or application configuration files). The other optional attribute is `allowLocation`, which can be set to true or false. If you set `allowLocation` to false, it prevents this section from appearing further down in the configuration file hierarchy.

3. In this case, more specific configuration files cannot override this setting.

4. Authentication refers to verifying credentials to determine the identity of a user. Authorization refers to granting access to resources to an authenticated user.

5. By default ASP.NET runs as a low-privilege user named ASPNET. You can also configure ASP.NET to run as a high-privilege system account.

6. You can specify None, Windows, Passport, or Forms authentication in an ASP.NET configuration file.

7. If you enable ASP.NET impersonation, the ASP.NET user acts as the authenticated user when requesting access to resources.

8. The three types of caching are output, fragment, and application data caching.

9. You can store session state data in-process to the ASP.NET process, in the ASP.NET State Server service, or in a Microsoft SQL Server database.

10. The `WindowsIdentity` object represents a logged-on user; the `WindowsPrincipal` object represents the entire security context of the logged-on user.

Answers to Exam Questions

1. **B.** The `allowLocation` attribute lets you specify that this section should not appear beneath the file where it is defined. The `allowOverride` attribute applies to actual configuration data, not to section declarations. The `allowDefinition` attribute set to `MachineToApplication` allows defining this section on the application level; omitting all attributes allows it to be defined everywhere.

2. **D.** Changes to ASP.NET configuration files are automatically picked up by ASP.NET as soon as the files are saved.

3. **D.** Basic IIS authentication does not securely encrypt passwords. Digest and Windows integrated authentication require Internet Explorer as the browser. Only Passport authentication fulfills these requirements.

4. **B.** Forms authentication depends on cookies to indicate that a browser session has been authenticated.

5. **B.** Role-based security allows you to check whether a user is in a particular group.

6. **A.** The question mark wildcard matches unauthenticated users, whereas the asterisk wildcard matches all users (authorized or not). If you deny access to all unauthenticated users, only authenticated users will be able to use the application.

APPLY YOUR KNOWLEDGE

7. **C.** If you allow anonymous authentication in IIS, users will never be prompted for their Windows credentials. ASP.NET will impersonate the identity of IIS itself, the `IUSR_ComputerName` account.

8. **C.** If you specify an account name in the identity element, that account is used to impersonate all authenticated users.

9. **D.** In this case the user control is a good candidate for caching, but the rest of the page should not be cached. Fragment caching allows you to cache a single user control.

10. **B.** By using application data caching, you can cause ASP.NET to automatically invalidate the cache if the contents of a particular file change.

11. **D.** The `Cache.SetValidUntilExpires` property tells the server to ignore client-side refreshes as long as the cache is valid.

12. **A.** Either the Session State service or SQL Server is compatible with sharing state between processors in a Web garden. There's no need to use SQL Server to store session state unless you need to persist the information between logins.

13. **C.** By placing session state information in a SQL Server database, you get the benefit of SQL Server's transactional, logged storage which is guaranteed to keep the data in a consistent state even if the server crashes.

14. **A, C.** ASP.NET is not supported on Windows 9x servers or on Windows NT 4.0.

15. **C.** Because the browser is standardized and all users have Windows domain accounts, you can use Windows authentication (with IIS integrated or digest authentication) to track which users are accessing your data.

Suggested Readings and Resources

1. Visual Studio .NET Combined Help Collection
   - ASP.NET State Management section
   - ASP.NET Caching Features section
2. Jones, A. Russell, *Mastering ASP.NET with VB.NET,* Sybex, 2002.
3. Liberty, Jesse and Hurwitz, Dan, *Programming ASP.NET,* O'Reilly, 2002.
4. Goodyear, Jonathan, et al, *Debugging ASP.NET,* New Riders, 2002.
5. Leinecker, Richard, *Special Edition Using ASP.NET,* Que, 2002.
6. Ahmed, Mesbah et al, *ASP.NET Web Developer's Guide,* Syngress, 2002.

PART IV

Final Review

Fast Facts

Practice Exam

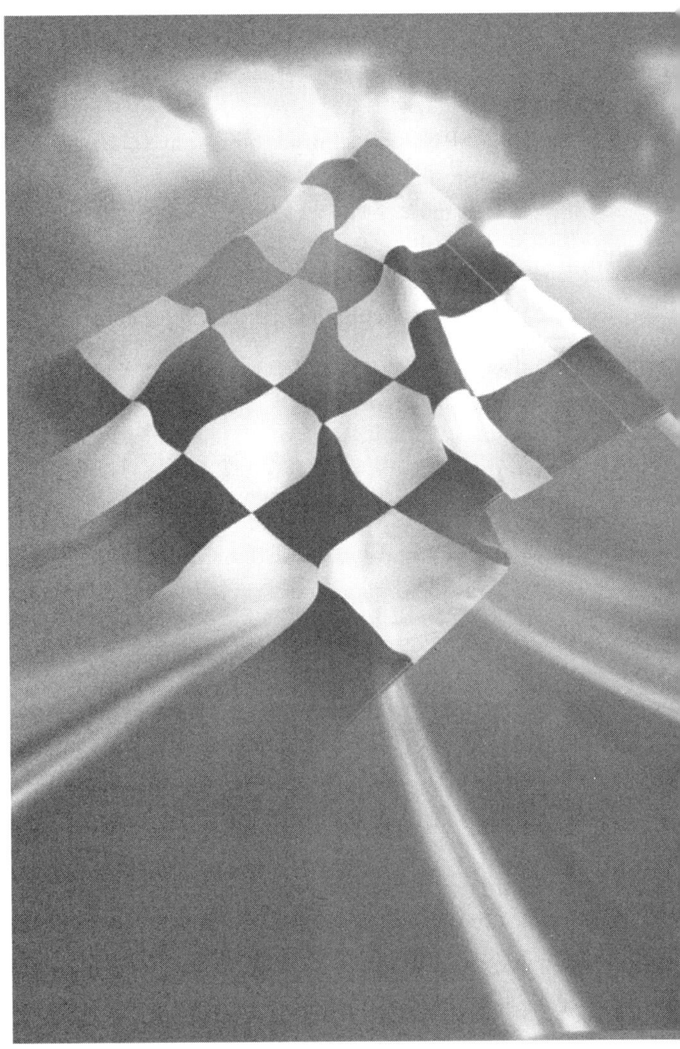

Fast Facts

70-305

Now that you've read this book, worked through the exercises and Step by Steps, and acquired as much hands-on experience using VB .NET with ASP.NET as you could, you are ready for the exam. This final review section is designed as a "final cram in the parking lot" before you walk in to the testing center. You can't reread the whole book in an hour, but you will be able to read this section in that time.

This chapter is organized by objective category, giving you not just a summary, but a review of the most important points from the book. Remember, this is just a review, not a replacement for the actual study material! It's meant to be a review of concepts and a trigger for you to remember useful bits of information you will need when taking the exam. If you know what is in here and the concepts that stand behind it, chances are that the exam will be a snap.

Creating User Services

Create ASP.NET pages.

- Active Server Pages .NET (ASP.NET) is the infrastructure built inside the .NET Framework for running Web applications.
- An ASP.NET Web application is executed through a series of HTTP request and response messages between the client browser and the Web server.
- Some of the advantages of ASP.NET are an enhanced application development model, rich class library support, performance, scalability, security, manageability, and extensibility.

- An ASP.NET Web page should have an .aspx extension. Typically, you will place the Web page in a virtual directory of a Web server. The name of the Web server and the path of virtual directory makes up the URL that users will use to request the Web page from the Web server.
- Each ASPX file is dynamically converted to a class that derives its basic functionality from the System.Web.UI.Page class. This class is compiled into a DLL file when the ASPX page is opened in the browser for the first time.
- You should take care not to define class level code such as the declaration of variables, methods, and so on between the <%…%> render blocks in an ASPX page.

Add and set directives on ASP.NET pages.

- ASP.NET directives allow you to specify various compiler options. Directives can modify caching options, set references, import namespaces, or register controls.
- The Page directive is used to specify page-related attributes that helps compilers know how an ASP.NET page is to be compiled and executed.

Separate user interface resources from business logic.

- ASP.NET provides a technique called code-behind to separate the user interface portion of a Web page from the business logic. The user interface is written in an aspx page (.aspx) and the business logic code is written in a Visual Basic .NET code file (.vb).
- The Src attribute of the Page directive specifies the name of the code-behind file. The Inherits attribute allows you to specify the name of the class that contains the code for the aspx page so that it can be compiled when the page is requested. If you are precompiling the code-behind file, you need not specify the Src attribute.
- Visual Studio .NET uses the code-behind with precompilation as the preferred way of creating Web forms.

Add Web server controls, HTML server controls, user controls, and HTML code to ASP.NET pages.

- HTML controls represent common HTML elements. You can access all the commonly used HTML controls through the HTML tab of the Visual Studio .NET Toolbox. The IDE allows you to visually work with HTML controls. However, HTML controls are not programmatically accessible on the Web server.
- ASP.NET provides server controls that are directly accessible on the Web server. There are two main categories of server controls—HTML server controls and Web server controls.
- The HTML server controls mainly exist to provide an easy migration path for existing Web forms. It is very easy to change an HTML control to run as a server control because all you need to do is to apply runat="server" attribute to every HTML control.

- For HTML server controls, ASP.NET analyzes the HTTP post to find if any events need to be raised at server side and raises all such events. Only some of the HTML server controls raise events on the server side and an HTML control can raise either a ServerClick event or a ServerChange event.
- Client-side event handling still proves helpful for handling frequently occurring events such as MouseMove or KeyPress. The traditional JavaScript-based event handling techniques still apply for handling client side events for HTML server controls.
- Web server controls provide a rich and consistent programming model of programming that integrates well with the rest of .NET Framework.
- Some Web server controls such as the DropDownList, RadioButton, and CheckBox have a property named AutoPostBack. When this property is set to True, it causes an immediate postback of the page when the value of control is changed. This allows the Web server to immediately respond to change events without waiting for a click event to cause a page postback.
- The preferred way to add client-side event handling code for Web server controls is via the use of the Attribute property of the Web server controls.
- A button is used to initiate a specific action when clicked by the user. There are three types of buttons—Button, LinkButton, and ImageButton. Each button has similar functionality but is different in its appearance and is rendered differently on the Web page.
- There are four list Web server controls—ListBox, DropDownList, CheckBoxList, and RadioButtonList. These controls are used to present a list of items of the user.
- Use the Placeholder and Panel controls as container controls. These controls can be used to organize other controls either at design time or dynamically through a program.
- Use the AdRotator control to display a randomly selected advertisement banner on the Web page. The advertisement is selected based on the settings stored in an XML advertisement file.
- Use the Calendar control to display a single month of a calendar on a Web page. The control allows you to select dates and move to the next or previous month.

Set properties on controls.

- You can set properties on controls either at design time or at runtime.
- To set properties on a control at design time, you specify the desired property value in the control's Properties window.
- To set properties on a control at runtime, you execute code that assigns a value to the property using the control.property = value syntax.

Load controls dynamically.

- To load controls dynamically on a Web Form, reserve space for the controls with a Placeholder or a Panel control. Then create the controls in code by declaring and instantiating variables of the proper class. Add the new controls to the Controls collection of the Panel or Placeholder control to display them on the Web Form.

Apply templates.

- The Repeater control uses templates to allow you to precisely format data from a collection.

- The DataBinder.Eval method is used to handle casts and formatting for data in a templated control.
- The DataList also uses templates, and supports formatting directly in the Visual Studio IDE.
- You can set the EditItemIndex property of a DataList control to show a particular row with edit controls.
- The EditCommand, UpdateCommand, and CancelCommand events of the DataList are used to control the editing process.

Set styles on ASP.NET pages by using cascading style sheets.

- The Style Builder dialog box provides a visual interface in Visual Studio .NET to build CSS styles.
- A custom style class is applied to the Web server control using the CssClass property and to the HTML server control using the Class property.

Instantiate and invoke an ActiveX control.

- You can import an ActiveX control to a Visual Studio .NET project by adding it to the Toolbox.
- After they're imported, ActiveX controls can be placed on a Web Form just like native .NET controls.
- ActiveX controls are instantiated on the client, not the server. Any event handlers for the control must be written in a scripting language and will also execute on the client.
- ActiveX controls impose a performance penalty and have other drawbacks.

Implement navigation for the user interface (UI).

- Web applications are disconnected in nature. That is, the values of a page's variables and controls are not preserved across the page requests.
- You can use the Page.IsPostBack property to determine whether a page is being loaded for the first time or in response to a postback operation.
- ASP.NET has a feature called smart navigation that can greatly enhance the user experience of a Web page for users of Internet Explorer 5.0 or higher browsers.
- The Response.Redirect() method can be used to connect to any specified URL. The specified URL can point to any resource and may also contain query strings. The use of Response.Redirect causes an additional roundtrip to the server.
- The Server.Transfer() method performs a server-side redirection of a page. The use of Server.Transfer() avoids an extra roundtrip but only works with an ASPX file residing on the same Web server. Also, you cannot pass a URL containing query string data as an argument to the Server.Transfer() method.
- The Server.Execute method is like a function call to an ASPX file. This method executes the specified ASPX file and then returns execution to the calling ASPX page. The file specified as an argument to the Server.Execute() must be an ASPX file residing on the same Web server and the argument should not contain query string data.

Manage the view state.

- ASP.NET uses a hidden input control named __VIEWSTATE to maintain state for all controls that are modified in the code, except for those that are normally sent as part of a postback operation. When ASP.NET executes a page, it collects values for all these controls and formats them into a single base64-encoded string. This string is then stored in the __VIEWSTATE control.
- You can use the ViewState property of the Page class to store page level values. ViewState property allows you to store structured data as long as the data is serializable.
- View state is easily configurable. ASP.NET provides configuration schemes for disabling, tamper-proofing, or protecting the contents of the view state.

Manage data during postback events.

Use session state to manage data across pages.

- ASP.NET provides session state to store session specific data for each user. The session state can be scaled to support multiple Web servers in a Web farm with just minor configuration changes.
- ASP.NET provides two ways to store data that is globally used throughout the application. One is Application state and the other is Application data cache. The application data cache provides all that the application state offers and also provides several other advanced features such as a cache expiration policy.

Validate user input.

- ASP.NET provides a set of Web server controls called validation controls that provide sophisticated validation on both the client side and the server side depending upon the validation settings and the browser's capabilities.
- The BaseValidator class serves as the base class for all the validation controls. This class provides the basic implementation of the validation controls.
- You can associate any number of validation controls to an input server control.
- The RequiredFieldValidator control can be used to check whether the input control contains an entry.
- The RegularExpressionValidator control ensures that the associated input control's value matches a specified regular expression.
- The RangeValidator control is used to check whether the input control contains value in the specified range.
- The CompareValidator control is used to compare the input server controls value against a data type, a fixed value, or another input control.
- The CustomValidator control allows you to specify custom validation code to be executed during validation.
- The ValidationSummary control is used to display summary of all the validation errors of a Web page.

Validate non-Latin user input.

- To iterate through the elements of a string in a world-ready application, you should use the GetTextElementEnumerator method of the StringInfo class.

Implement error handling in the user interface.

- An exception occurs when a program encounters any problem during normal execution.
- The Framework Class Library (FCL) provides two main types of exceptions, namely SystemException and ApplicationException. SystemException represents the exceptions thrown by the CLR where as ApplicationException represents the exceptions thrown by the user programs.
- The System.Exception class represents the base class for all CLS-compliant exceptions and provides the common functionality for exception handling.
- The try block consists of code that may raise an exception. A try block cannot exist on its own. It should be immediately followed by one or more catch blocks or a finally block.
- The catch block handles any exception raised by the code in the try block. The runtime looks for a matching catch block to handle the exception, which is the first catch block with either an exact same exception or any of the exception's base classes.
- If there are multiple catch blocks associated with a try block, then the catch blocks should be arranged in top-bottom order of specific to general exception types.
- The throw statement is used to raise an exception.
- The finally block is used to enclose the code that needs to be run irrespective of whether or not the exception is raised.

Configure custom error pages.

- If the existing exception classes do not meet your exception handling requirements, you can create new exception classes that are specific to your application by deriving from the ApplicationException class.
- Custom error pages can be used to display user-friendly messages rather than the default error page shown by ASP.NET. They can be set by configuring the customErrors element in the web.config file for all the Web pages in an application.

Implement Global.asax, application, page-level, and page event error handling.

- You can set a custom error Web page for individual pages in your application by using the ErrorPage attribute of the Page directive or the ErrorPage property of the Page class.
- You can handle any unhandled error that occurs in a page in its Error event handler.
- Unhandled exceptions for an entire application can be trapped in the Application_Error event handler in the global.asax file.

Implement online user assistance.

- User assistance refers to the process of providing help within an application through a variety of means.
- User assistance for a Web application can be delivered in a separate browser window, in a browser pane, or as embedded help that is dynamically displayed.

Incorporate existing code into ASP.NET pages.

- ASP and ASP.NET run perfectly well together on the same server. That's a fundamental consequence of the architecture of the two systems. When you install applications to Internet Information Services (such as ASP or ASP.NET), each such application is associated with a particular set of page extensions. ASP pages are handled by c:\WINNT\System32\inetsrv\asp.dll, while ASP.NET pages are handled by C:\WINNT\Microsoft.NET\Framework\v1.0.3705\aspnet_isapi.dll.
- The ASP.NET processor understands nearly all the syntax and all the objects that ASP itself supported. In particular, ASP.NET still supports the Server.CreateObject method for creating late-bound COM components.
- Not all COM components can be instantiated in ASP.NET with Server.CreateObject. In particular, components that use the Single-Threaded Apartment (STA) threading model will not function properly in ASP.NET pages unless you add a compatibility directive to the page: `%@Page aspcompat=true%`.

Display and update data.

Transform and filter data.

- The Server Explorer provides a powerful tool for working with SQL Server data.
- You can edit and design SQL Server objects directly within Visual Studio .NET.
- The DataView object offers sorting and filtering capabilities at the Web server (instead of on the database server) for data bound objects.
- Views on the server can be an efficient way to filter or transform data.

Bind data to the user interface.

- Simple data binding refers to connecting a single entity in the data model to a single property of a control on the user interface.
- Anything that will deliver data can be bound. This includes public Page properties, methods, public variables, and properties of other controls.
- You can bind to almost any property of any control.
- The DataBind method is used to bind data to an entire page or to any of the controls on the page. This method triggers a DataBinding event for the affected controls.
- The Data Form Wizard will help you create data-bound forms, both simple and complex, quickly. These forms will draw their data from a relational database such as SQL Server.
- Complex data binding binds a user interface control to an entire collection of data.

Use controls to display data.

- To use complex data binding with a list control (such as a ListBox, DropDownList, RadioButtonList, or CheckBoxList control), you set the control's DataSource and DataTextField properties.

- A list control can act to pull values from one data source and place them in another.
- You can cause a list control to display one value while binding another by using the DataTextField and DataValueField properties of the control.
- The DataGrid control displays an entire array of data in rows and columns. You specify the data to display by setting the DataSource property of the DataGrid control.
- The properties of the DataGrid control include many flexible formatting options.

Instantiate and invoke Web Service or components.

Instantiate and invoke a Web Service.

- Web Services provide you with the means to create objects and invoke their methods even though your only connection to the server is via the Internet.
- Communication with Web Services is via XML messages transported by the HTTP protocol.
- Because they communicate over HTTP, Web Services are typically not blocked by firewalls.
- The Simple Object Access Protocol (SOAP) encapsulates object-oriented messages between Web Service clients and servers.
- The Universal Description, Discovery, and Integration protocol (UDDI) allows you to find Web Services by connecting to a directory.
- The Web Services Description Language (WSDL) lets you retrieve information on the classes and methods that are supported by a particular Web Service.
- Disco is Microsoft's standard format for discovery documents, which contain information on Web Services.
- UDDI, the Universal Description, Discovery, and Integration protocol, is a multi-vendor standard for discovering online resources, including Web Services.
- The Web Services Discovery Tool, disco.exe, can retrieve discovery information from a server that exposes a Web Service.
- You can generate proxy classes for a Web Service manually by using the Web Services Description Language tool.
- You can generate proxy classes for a Web Service automatically by setting a Web Reference to point to the Web Service.
- You can test and debug a Web Service without a client application by using one of several SOAP proxy tools.

Instantiate and invoke a COM or COM+ component.

- Using COM or COM+ components from .NET managed code requires the creation of a runtime-callable wrapper (RCW).
- You can create an RCW for a COM component by using the Type Library Importer, or by directly referencing the COM component from your .NET code.
- To use COM components that you did not create, you should obtain a Primary Interop Assembly (PIA) from the creator of the component.
- RCWs impose a performance penalty on COM code.

Instantiate and invoke a .NET component.

- Components provide a way to encapsulate reusable code for use in multiple projects.
- In the .NET Framework, components are classes that derive from System.Component.
- Component classes enjoy features such as container support and resource management because they derive from System.Component.
- You can add methods and properties to a component class just as you can add them to any other class.

Call native functions by using platform invoke.

- You can use the .NET Platform Invoke (PInvoke) facility to call functions from Windows libraries including the Windows API.

Implement globalization.

- Localization is a three-step process that consists of globalization (identifying resources), localizability (verifying separation of resources from code), and localization (translating resources).
- Many resources may need to be localized, including user interface text, dates, times, currency amounts, and calendars.
- Cultures are identified by culture codes. Neutral culture codes specify only a location, and cannot be used for localization. Specific culture codes specify both a location and a language, and provide enough information for localization.
- The CultureInfo object represents a culture in the .NET Framework.

Convert existing encodings.

- Internally, .NET applications use 16-bit Unicode (UTF-16) as their preferred character encoding.
- The System.Text.Encoding class and its subclasses allow you to convert text from one encoding to another.

Implement right-to-left and left-to-right mirroring.

- In some languages, the user interface is read from right to left instead of from left to right. Converting a form for one of these languages is referred to as mirroring.
- The .NET Framework provides partial support for mirroring through the RightToLeft property on forms and controls.

Prepare culture-specific formatting.

- To iterate through the elements of a string in a world-ready application, you should use the GetTextElementEnumerator method of the StringInfo class.
- Searching, sorting, and comparing strings in a world-ready application requires using standard objects and methods rather than clever programming tricks.

Handle events.

Create event handlers.

- Event handling allows a program to respond to changes in the environment. Events in Visual Basic .NET are based on a publisher-subscriber model. The class that creates and implements an event is called the publisher of the event. A class that subscribes a published event by registering an appropriate event handler with the published event is called a subscriber of the event.
- You can respond to an event by overriding the On method corresponding to an event. When you use this method, you should be sure to call the corresponding On method for the base class so that you don't miss any of the functionality of the base class when the event is raised.
- Custom code can be executed when an event occurs if the code is registered with the event. The pieces of code that respond to an event are called event handlers. An event handler must have a prototype compatible with the event that it is handling.
- Event handlers can be registered with events through delegate objects. Delegates are special objects that are capable of storing references to methods with a particular prototype.
- You can also register events of Page class by defining event handlers with specific names such as Page_Init(), Page_Load(), and so on. and setting the AutoEventWireup attribute to true in the Page directive.
- The global.asax file is the appropriate place to handle global events that are not specific to a Web form but rather apply to an application as a whole.

Raise events.

- To raise an event, use the RaiseEvent statement with the name of the event, followed by any required event arguments in parentheses.

Implement accessibility features.

- Accessibility refers to the coding that you must do to make your application usable by those with disabilities.
- The basic principles of accessible design are flexibility, choice of input methods, choice of output methods, consistency, and compatibility with accessibility aids.
- The W3C Web Accessibility Initiative and the U.S. government have issued formal guidelines for accessible Web applications.

Use and edit intrinsic objects. Intrinsic objects include response, request, session, server, and application.

- ASP.NET provides intrinsic objects to enable low-level access to the Web application framework. With the help of these intrinsic objects you can work directly with the underlying HTTP request, HTTP response, server, session, and application objects.

Retrieve values from the properties of intrinsic objects.

- You can treat intrinsic objects like any other objects in code. The intrinsic objects are exposed through properties of the Page object. To retrieve values from an intrinsic object, use the value = object.property syntax.

Set values on the properties of intrinsic objects.

- You can treat intrinsic objects like any other objects in code. The intrinsic objects are exposed through properties of the Page object. To set values on an intrinsic object, use the object.property = value syntax.

Use intrinsic objects to perform operations.

- ASP.NET maintains a pool of HttpApplication objects. When a new HTTP request arrives, ASP.NET uses one of the objects from this pool rather than creating an HttpApplication object from the scratch.
- The Global.asax file can be used to define a customized HttpApplication class. When a global.asax file exists in the Web applications root directory, ASP.NET uses the HttpApplication-derived class defined in the global.asax file to serve the Web application.

Creating and Managing Components and .NET Assemblies

Create and modify a .NET assembly.

- Assemblies are the basic unit for reuse, versioning, security, and deployment of components created using the .NET Framework. Each assembly includes an assembly manifest to store the assembly's metadata.
- Depending on the number of files that make up an assembly, it is a single-file or a multifile assembly.
- A private assembly is an assembly available only to clients in the same directory structure as the assembly, while a shared assembly can be referenced by more than one application and is stored in the machinewide Global Assembly Cache. A shared assembly must be assigned a cryptographically strong name.

Create and implement satellite assemblies.

- Resource-only assemblies are those assemblies that contain just resources and no code.

Create resource-only assemblies.

- Resource-only assemblies that store culture-specific information are known as satellite assemblies.

Create Web custom controls and Web user controls.

- Web User Controls let you encapsulate common blocks of user interface functionality for reuse.
- You can create properties for a Web user control by creating public members for the control.
- Web user controls can handle the events of their own constituent controls in their own code-behind files.
- Web user controls must be contained within the project in which they are used.
- Web custom controls are compiled components that offer support for almost all the features of the server controls that ship with Visual Studio .NET.
- You can create a Web custom control by combining existing controls, by deriving from an existing control, or by inheriting directly from the WebControl class.
- Web custom controls offer full support for the Visual Studio .NET interface, including the Toolbox and the Properties window.
- You can create a designer class that handles the display of a Web custom control at design time.

CONSUMING AND MANIPULATING DATA

Access and manipulate data from a Microsoft SQL Server™ database by creating and using ad hoc queries and stored procedures.

- Transact-SQL is the Microsoft SQL Server dialect of the ANSI SQL-92 standard query language.
- You can execute T-SQL statements from a variety of interfaces, including the Visual Studio .NET IDE, osql, SQL Query Analyzer, or custom applications.
- SELECT statements retrieve data from tables in a database.
- INSERT statements add new data to tables in a database.
- UPDATE statements modify existing data in tables in a database.
- DELETE statements remove data from tables in a database.

Access and manipulate data from a data store. Data stores include relational databases, XML documents, and flat files. Methods include XML techniques and ADO .NET.

- The ADO.NET object model includes both database-specific data provider classes and database-independent DataSet classes.
- Data providers contain implementations of the Connection, Command, Parameter, DataReader, and DataAdapter objects optimized for a particular database product.
- The SqlConnection object represents a connection to a database.
- The SqlCommand object represents a command that can be executed.
- The SqlParameter object represents a parameter of a stored procedure.
- The SqlDataReader object provides a fast way to retrieve a result set from a command.
- The SqlDataAdapter object implements a two-way pipeline between the database and the data model.
- The DataSet represents an entire relational database in memory. It's composed of DataTable, DataRelation, DataRow, and DataColumn objects.
- The DataView object provides a filtered row of the data from a DataTable.
- Changing data in a DataSet can be done just by treating the items in the DataSet like any other variable.
- To persist changes from the data model to the underlying database you must call the Update method of the SqlDataAdapter object.
- The UpdateCommand property of the SqlDataAdapter object specifies a SqlCommand object to be executed for all changed rows.
- The InsertCommand property of the SqlDataAdapter object specifies a SqlCommand object to be executed for all new rows.
- The DeleteCommand property of the SqlDataAdapter object specifies a SqlCommand object to be executed for all deleted rows.
- The DataGrid control can provide a convenient way to handle data changes on the user interface.
- File-based input and output in the .NET Framework revolves around the twin concepts of *streams* and *backing stores*. A stream represents a flow of raw data. A backing store represents some place you can put data.
- The FileStream class gives you a stream-oriented view of a disk file. The FileStream class treats files as a raw, typeless stream of bytes.
- For cases where you know more about the structure of the file, you may find the BinaryReader and BinaryWriter, or StreamReader and StreamWriter classes to be more convenient to use. The StreamReader and StreamWriter classes are optimized for textual data, while the BinaryReader and BinaryWriter classes are optimized for structured binary data.
- Elements of an XML document can be represented by XmlNode objects. XmlNode objects are collected into an XmlDocument object. XmlDocument is the object in the System.Xml namespace that represents an entire XML document.

- You can also treat an XML document as relational data. To do this, you can use an XmlDataDocument class, which inherits from XmlDocument. The key feature of the XmlDataDocument class is that it can be synchronized with a DataSet.

Handle data errors.

- Every real-world application should include error trapping. Data manipulation adds some special requirements to error trapping code.
- The SqlException and SqlError objects provide you with the means to retrieve SQL Server specific error information.
- You can choose when you're designing update commands between optimistic concurrency and "last one wins" concurrency.

TESTING AND DEBUGGING

Create a unit test plan.

- Testing is the process of executing a program with the intention of finding errors. You should design an effective test plan to ensure that your application is free from all detectable defects and errors.
- Unit Testing ensures each unit of an application function perfectly as desired. It is the lowest level of testing.
- Integration Testing ensures that different units of an application function as expected by the test plan after being integrated.
- Whenever the code is modified or a new feature is added in an application, you should run all the existing test cases along with a new set of test cases to check the new feature. This regression testing helps in developing robust applications.

Implement tracing.

Add trace listeners and trace switches to an application.

- The System.Web.TraceContext class can be used to display trace messages in an application. These messages can be easily viewed by using the trace viewer or at the end of the page output. ASP.NET displays various page request details along with custom trace messages displayed by you.
- Tracing can be enabled at the application-level by setting the trace element enabled attribute to true in the applicationwide web.config file. To enable tracing for an individual page, set the trace attribute to true in the Page directive.
- Listeners are objects that receive trace and debug output. By default, there is one listener attached to the Trace and Debug classes, DefaultTraceListener, that displays the messages in the Output window.
- Debug and Trace objects share the same Listeners collection. Therefore any Listener added to the Trace.Listeners collection will also be added to the Debug.Listeners collection.
- Trace Switches provides a mechanism that allows you to change the type of messages traced by a program depending upon the value stored in XML configuration file. You need not recompile the application for this change to take effect, just restart it. You need to implement code to display the messages depending on the value of the switch.

Display trace output.

- The Trace and Debug classes from System.Diagnostics can be used to display informative messages in an application when the DEBUG and TRACE symbols are defined respectively at the time of compilation.
- By default, both TRACE and DEBUG symbols are defined in the Debug Configuration for compilation and only the TRACE symbol is defined for the Release configuration of compilation.

Debug, rework, and resolve defects in code.

Configure the debugging environment.

- VB .NET preprocessor directives allow you to define and undefine symbols in an application, report errors or warnings, mark regions of code, and allow you to conditionally skip code for compilation.
- Conditional attribute allows you to conditionally add or skip a method for compilation depending on the value of the symbol passed as a parameter to the attribute.

Create and apply debugging code to components, pages, and applications.

- Components and pages can make use of the full range of ASP.NET debugging objects. These include the Trace and Debug objects, as well as the TraceContext class.
- The global event handlers in the global.asax file provide a convenient place for application-level debugging code.

Provide multicultural test data to components, pages, and applications.

- Test the application's data and user interface to make sure that they conform to the locale's standards for date and time, numeric values, currency, list separators, and measurements.
- If you are developing for Windows 2000 or Windows XP, test your application on as many language and culture variants as necessary to cover your entire market for the application. These operating systems support the languages used in more than 120 cultures/locales.
- Use Unicode for your application. Applications using Unicode will run fine without making any changes on Windows 2000 and XP. If instead your application uses Windows code pages, you will need to set the culture/locale of operating system according to the localized version of application that you are testing, and reboot after each change.
- While testing a localized version of an application make sure that you use input data in the language supported by the localized version. This will make the testing scenario close to the scenario in which application will be actually used.

Execute tests.

- Debugging is the process of finding the cause of errors in a program, locating the lines of code causing the error, and then fixing those errors.

- The three options available while performing step-by-step execution are Step Into, Step Over, and Step Out.
- Breakpoints allow you to mark code that signals debugger to pause execution when it encounters them. You can choose to continue step-by-step execution or resume the normal execution by clicking F5 or the resume button by pressing the Continue button (alternatively, F5).
- The various tool windows like Me, Locals, Autos, Watch, Call Stack can be of great help in tracking the execution path and the status of variables in the process of debugging an application in Visual Studio .NET.
- When an exception is thrown by an application, you can either choose to continue execution or break into debugger (start debugging operations like step-by-step execution). You can customize this behavior for each exception object using the Exceptions dialog box.
- You can attach a debugger to a running process (local or remote) with the help of Processes dialog box.

Resolve errors and rework code.

- The most important thing about resolving errors is to be systematic. Use the ASP.NET debugging tools to verify the location of the error in your code. Then correct the code to remove the error.
- After reworking the code, it is crucial to run the same test that identified the error in the first place. The reworked code should pass the test without error.

Deploying a Web Application

Plan the deployment of a Web application.

- You should select a deployment method that is convenient and accessible to all the product's users.
- You can create installation packages in multiple cabinet files by choosing the "In cabinet file(s)" option in the Project Property pages.
- Web-based deployment reduces the cost of media, replication, and distribution. It also makes the management of software updates simple.

Plan a deployment that uses removable media.

- Deployment via removable media is suitable when users are in many locations without any common central connection, not all the users have access to the Internet, or the application is very large and not all users have access to a high-speed Internet connection.
- To create a setup for removable media, set the CAB size option of your setup project.

Plan a Web-based deployment.

- Web-based deployment is the most popular form of deployment, especially for small-sized applications.

- Once the setup files are created, rather than copying them to a network share or directly to the target computer, you will copy them to a virtual directory on a Web server. You may also want to password protect the deployment Web site so that only authorized users can download your application. You can then install the application by navigating to the virtual directory and executing the setup.exe program that you find there.

Plan the deployment of an application to a Web garden, a Web farm, or a cluster.

- A Web garden is a Web application that is distributed across more than one processor on a multiprocessor computer. Web gardening is the default behavior for ASP.NET. For example, suppose you install an ASP.NET application on a computer with eight CPUs. In this case, ASP.NET will automatically launch eight worker processes to handle incoming Web requests, and assign one of these processes to each CPU (a procedure known as setting the affinity of the process).
- You can set attributes in the web.config file to limit a Web garden to using only specific CPUs.
- In a Web farm, your application runs on multiple Web servers at the same time. Some mechanism outside of the Web servers is used to distribute requests to the individual servers.
- Provided that you've chosen an appropriate option for storing session state, you do not need to change your application at all for deployment on a Web farm. Your system administrator can simply run the setup program for your application on each server in the Web farm, and then configure the Web farm using the tools built into Windows 2000 or Application Center.
- In a cluster, multiple computers are configured using the same software, but only one of these computers is active at any given time. The active server handles all requests unless it experiences a hardware or software failure. At that point, the clustering software automatically directs requests to the standby server, which becomes the new active server.

Create a setup program that installs a Web application and allows for the application to be uninstalled.

- The File System Editor provides a mapping of the file system on the target machine. The folders are referred to by special names that during the installation process are converted to represent the folder as per the file system on the target machine.
- The Registry Editor allows you to specify registry keys, sub keys, and values that are added to the registry on the target machine during installation.
- The File Types Editor allows you to register one or more file extensions with your Windows application.
- The User Interface Editor allows you to customize the user interface that is provided to the user during the installation process. There are different types of user interfaces available for end user installation and administrative installation.
- The User Interface Editor and Launch Conditions Editor for Search elements provide special properties (like Property, ButtonProperty) whose value can be evaluated to perform the installation as per the end user's choice.

- The Custom Actions Editor allows you to add custom actions to be performed during the installation process. It allows you to run .dll, .exe, assembly, and scripts files. There are four phases when custom action can be performed—Install, Commit, Rollback, and Uninstall.
- The Launch Conditions editor allows you to set conditions to be evaluated when the installation begins on the target machine. If the conditions are not met, the installation stops.
- The System.Configuration.Install.Installer class works as a base class for all the custom installers in the .NET Framework.
- The Installer class method Install() is called when the application is installed, while Uninstall() is called when the application is uninstalled. The Commit() method is executed if the Install() method executes successfully and the Rollback() method is executed if the Install() method is not executed successfully.
- If you add predefined installation components (for example, a PerformanceCounter installation component) to the Setup project, they will be all added to the ProjectInstaller class. These are actually added to the Installers collection of this class.
- You can add your own custom Installer classes to a project to perform custom actions through the Custom Actions Editor during installation such as compiling the code to native image or creating a database on a target computer.

Deploy a Web application.

- Although .NET supports XCOPY and FTP deployment, this is not sufficient for advanced deployment requirements. For advanced requirement, you should instead choose a Microsoft Windows Installer–based installation package to deploy your applications.
- Microsoft Windows Installer 2.0 is the built-in installation and configuration service of the Windows operating system. It addition to several advanced installation features it also provide features such as the ability to rollback installation process, uninstalling an application, and repairing a component or an application.
- Visual Studio .NET provides four types of deployment templates:Setup Project (for Windows-based applications), Web Setup Project (for Web-based applications), Merge Module Project (for shared components and assemblies), and CAB project (ActiveX components to be downloaded over the Internet). It also provides a Setup Wizard that helps in creating installation package for any of these deployment projects.

Add assemblies to the Global Assembly Cache.

- Shared assemblies are used by multiple applications on a machine. They are placed in the GAC and enjoy special privileges such as file security (as they are placed in the System folder), shared location, and side-by-side versioning.
- Public/private key pairs are generated using the Strong Name tool (sn.exe). These pairs then can be used to digitally sign an assembly.

- A shared assembly can be added to GAC by using Windows Explorer, .NET Framework Configuration tool, Global Assembly Cache Tool (gacutil.exe), or the Installer tool.
- The best way to add an assembly during deployment is using Microsoft Windows Installer as it provides assembly reference-counting features. These features allow the Installer to uninstall an assembly when no further applications are using it.
- The Assembly Cache folder in the System folder when viewed in Windows Explorer displays assemblies from Global Assembly Cache and Native Image Cache.
- The CLR first searches the GAC to locate assemblies before looking into the files and folders where the assembly is installed. Thus shared assemblies placed in GAC are more efficient because the CLR does not engage itself in looking into <codebase> and <probing> elements of the applicable configuration files.
- Delay signing allows a shared assembly to be placed in the GAC by just signing the assembly with the public key. This allows the assembly to be signed with private key at a later stage when the development process is complete and the component or assembly is ready to be deployed. This process allows developers to work with shared assemblies as if they were strongly named and yet also secure the private key of the signature from being accessed at different stages of development.
- Merge Module allows you to create reusable components that help in deploying shared components. The Merge Modules cannot be directly installed. They need to be merged with installer programs of applications that use the component packed into a merge module.

MAINTAINING AND SUPPORTING A WEB APPLICATION

Optimize the performance of a Web application.

- ASP.NET allows you to cache entire pages, fragments of pages, or controls. You can also cache variable data by specifying the parameters that the data depends on. Using caching makes it quicker for the ASP.NET engine to return data in response to repeated requests for the same page.
- Whether you store it in-process, in State Server, or in a SQL Server database, session state takes memory and requires processing time to store and receive. If your application doesn't depend on session state, disable it with the <@% EnableSessionState=False %> directive.
- ViewState lets you persist the contents of a control across trips to a server. This comes at the cost of additional bytes traveling in each direction, and hence imposes a speed hit. You can avoid this penalty by setting the EnableViewState property of controls to False when you don't need their contents to persist.
- Passport authentication is slower than forms-based authentication, which is slower than Windows authentication. Not authenticating users at all is the fastest choice.
- Choose data types to minimize boxing and unboxing operations (copying data from reference types to value types and vice versa).

- Using StringBuilder may help you achieve noticeable performance gains in an application using extensive string manipulations.
- Using AddRange to add elements to collections is much faster than adding elements by repeatedly calling the Add method inside a loop.
- Throwing exceptions is a costly operation. Don't use exceptions just to manage normal program flow.
- Reduce the number of calls between the managed and unmanaged code, possibly by doing more work in each call rather than making frequent calls for doing small tasks.
- When you are ready to deploy your application, compile it in release mode rather than the default Debug mode. Deploying an application compiled using Debug mode may cause it to run slowly because of the presence of extra debugging code.
- Use the SqlClient and Oracle-managed providers rather than the generic OleDb managed provider to retrieve data from SQL Server and Oracle data sources. The specific drivers are optimized for communication with their particular databases.
- Use stored procedures over a set of SQL statements given as a text command. This is because stored procedures are highly optimized for server-side data access and their use will usually improve the data access performance significantly.
- Run SQL Server's Profiler and Index Tuning Wizard to avoid any bottlenecks because of indexing. Also, use SQL Server Query Analyzer to optimize a query's performance.
- If you are reading a table sequentially, use DataReader over DataSet. DataReader is a read-only, forward-only stream of data. This increases application performance and reduces system overhead because only one row is in memory at a time.
- The slowest database operation is establishing a connection with the database. The SQL Server .NET Data provider provides connection pooling to improve performance when connecting to database. This stores old connection information in a connection pool and reuses this information when connecting the next time, thereby allowing significant performance gains.
- The SqlCommandBuilder and OleDbCommandBuilder classes provide a means of automatically generating commands used to reconcile changes made to a DataSet. Although automatic generation of INSERT, UPDATE, and DELETE statements for changes to the DataSet makes database updates very convenient, it makes extra trips to server to get the schema information.
- Distributed transactions may have significant performance overhead. As a rule of thumb, use transactions only when required and keep transactions as short-lived as possible.

Diagnose and resolve errors and issues.

- A Process is an application under execution. Each running process is uniquely identified on a computer with a Process Identifier (PID).
- The Process class provides a large set of properties to get information about running processes on a local or remote machine.
- The Event Log provides a central repository for various issues that an application may encounter while it is executing. Use of an event log to record such messages not only makes the job of system administrator easier, but also allows other applications to take appropriate action when an entry is written to a log.

- Multiple event sources can write into an event log. However, an event source can only be used to write into one event log.
- By default, events of the Process and EventLog class are not enabled. You can set the EnableRaisingEvents property to True in order to instruct them to raise events.
- Performance counters are organized in categories. Each category defines a specific set of performance counters.
- The process of reading a performance counter value is called sampling the performance counter. The process of updating a performance counter value is called publishing a performance counter.

Configuring and Securing a Web Application

Configure a Web application.

Modify the web.config file.

- ASP.NET stores configuration information in XML files.
- Configuration files form a hierarchy. Settings are generally retrieved from the configuration file most local to the current page.
- You can use the ConfigurationSettings object to retrieve custom information from a configuration file.
- The web.config file contains settings that apply to all ASP.NET applications, such as the account under which the ASP.NET process executes.
- Configuration files are automatically reread by ASP.NET when they are changed, without a restart or a reboot.

Modify the Machine.config file.

- The machine.config file contains settings that control the operation of .NET on the entire computer. For example, compiler settings for the .NET Framework are stored in this file.

Add and modify application settings.

- Any Web application can have its own settings that override the global web.config file. These settings are stored in a web.config file specific to the application.

Configure security for a Web application.

Select and configure authentication type. Authentication types include Windows Authentication, None, forms-based, Microsoft Passport, and custom authentication.

- ASP.NET security is divided into authentication (verifying a user's identity) and authorization (allowing an authenticated user to access resources).
- Users must satisfy any IIS authentication requirements before ASP.NET authentication takes over.

- ASP.NET authentication uses interchangeable authentication providers. You can choose Windows authentication, Passport authentication, or forms-based authentication.

Configure authorization.

Configure role-based authorization.

- Role-based security allows you to authorize access to resources based on user identity or group membership.

Implement impersonation.

- Identity impersonation lets the ASP.NET process act as the authenticated user.

Configure and implement caching. Caching types include output, fragment, and data.

- Output caching refers to caching the entire output of a page request.
- Fragment caching refers to caching part of a page. ASP.NET enables fragment caching by allowing you to specify cache rules for Web forms user controls.
- Application data caching refers to caching arbitrary data. You can cache any object you like in ASP.NET by calling the Add or Insert methods of the Cache object.

Use a cache object.

- One way to manage caching is to use the Cache object. The Cache object is a static class that's always available to your code.
- The Cache.SetExpires method specifies an expiration time for the cached version of the page. The Cache.SetCacheability method specifies where output can be cached: NoCache for no caching at all, Private to allow caching only on the client (the default value), Public to allow caching on any proxy server as well as on the client, and Server to cache the document on the server only. The Cache.SetValidUntilExpires(true) method tells the server to ignore client-side attempts to refresh the cached content until it expires.

Use cache directives.

- You can specify the cacheability of a page by using the @OutputCache directive.
- The @OutputCache directive requires the VaryByParam attribute. If the page output doesn't depend on any input parameters, you can use None as the value of this attribute; otherwise, use the name of the parameter to cause caching to be done on a per-parameter-value basis.

Configure and implement session state in various topologies such as a Web garden and a Web farm.

Use session state within a process.

- Session variables let you store information across multiple browser requests.

- The default storage location for session state is in-process memory in the ASP.NET process itself.

Use session state with session state service.

- A second choice for storing session state is the ASP.NET Session Service, which provides an out-of-process location to store the information.

Use session state with Microsoft SQL Server.

- A third choice for storing session state is a Microsoft SQL Server database.

Install and configure server services.

Install and configure a Web server.

- IIS is installed as part of the Windows operating system. For full ASP.NET functionality, you should install IIS 5.0 on Windows 2000 or a later version.

Install and configure Microsoft FrontPage Server Extensions.

- Visual Studio .NET uses the FrontPage Server Extensions to access files on remote Web servers via HTTP.

- If your server's hard drive is NTFS-formatted, the FrontPage Server Extensions will be set up automatically when you install IIS. Otherwise, you can configure the FrontPage Server Extensions via the Computer Management control panel applet.

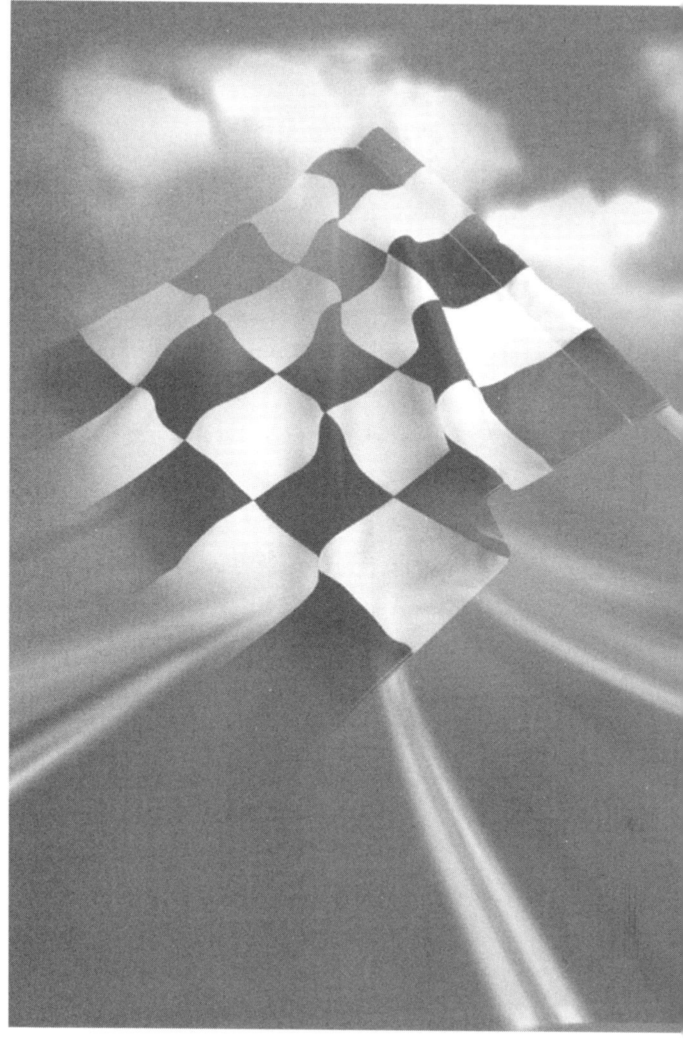

Practice Exam

This portion of the Final Review section consists of a practice exam containing 75 questions. These practice questions are representative of what you should expect on the actual exam. The answers are at the end of the exam. I strongly suggest that when you take this exam, you treat it just as you would the actual exam at the test center. Time yourself, read carefully, don't use any reference materials, and answer all the questions as best you can.

Some of the questions may be vague and require you to make deductions to come up with the best possible answer from the possibilities given. Others may be verbose, requiring you to read and process a lot of information before you come to the actual question. These are skills that you should acquire before attempting the actual exam. Run though the test, and if you miss more than 18 questions, try rereading the chapters containing information where you were weak. You can use the index to find keywords to point you to the appropriate locations.

EXAM QUESTIONS

1. You have inherited a large ASP.NET application because the original developer has left the company. You are concerned because there does not seem to be sufficient error trapping in the code-behind files to catch all likely errors. What is the easiest way for you to begin tracking all unhandled errors?

   A. Add error trapping to every procedure behind every page.

   B. Add a Page_Error event handler to each page's code-behind file.

   C. Add an Application_Error event handler to each page's code-behind file.

   D. Add an Application_Error event handler to the Global.asax file.

2. Which of the following ASP.NET applications requires you to use the Windows Installer rather than FTP to deploy to a Web server?

   A. An application that includes a Web user control that is not shared with other applications.

   B. An application that includes a composite Web custom control that is not shared with other applications.

   C. An application that upgrades an existing ASP.NET application.

   D. An application that includes a Web custom control that should be deployed to the GAC.

3. Your Web application is used to display product information from your company's database. The application consists of a set of pages, each of which uses ADO.NET objects to display data from a SQL Server database. No page in the application passes any information to another page in the application. Which alternative should you use for session state in this application to maximize performance?

   A. In-process session state

   B. State Server session state

   C. SQL Server session state

   D. <@% EnableSessionState=False %>

4. Your application requires the user to be in the Power Users group to activate certain functions. Which ASP.NET security feature should you use to ensure that the user is in this group?

   A. Code-access security

   B. Role-based security

   C. Encryption

   D. Passport authentication

5. You have created a SqlConnection object named SqlConnection1 and a SqlDataAdapter object named SqlDataAdapter1 by dragging the Orders table from your database in Server Explorer and dropping it on a Web Form. You have added a DataGrid control named dgOrders to the Web Form. You have selected the SqlDataAdapter1 object and created a DataSet object named DsOrders1 by using the Generate DataSet dialog box. The Page_Load procedure for your Web Form contains the following code:

```
Private Sub Page_Load(ByVal sender As
System.Object, _
 ByVal e As System.EventArgs) Handles
MyBase.Load
    ' Move the data from the database to
the DataGrid
    dgOrders.DataBind()
End Sub
```

   The Web Form loads without error, but the DataGrid does not display any data. What is the problem?

   A. You neglected to call the Fill method of the SqlDataAdapter object.

   B. You called the DataBind() method of the DataGrid control rather than the DataBind() method of the page.

C. You should have based your DataSet object on a view rather than basing it on a table.

D. You should have used a Repeater control rather than a DataGrid control.

6. Your application contains the following code:

```
Dim dr As SqlDataReader =
cmd.ExecuteReader()
Dim s As String
While dr.Read()
    s = s & dr.GetString(0)
End While
```

What can you do to optimize this portion of the application?

A. Replace the SqlDataReader object with a DataSet object.

B. Replace the SqlDataReader object with an OleDbDataReader object.

C. Replace the String object with a StringBuilder object.

D. Replace the While loop with a For Each loop.

7. You are using the command-line Installer tool to install three assemblies, with this command line:

```
InstallUtil.exe Assembly1.dll Assembly2.dll
Assembly3.dll
```

A problem occurs with the installation of Assembly2.dll, and that assembly cannot be installed. Which assembly or assemblies will be installed on the target machine?

A. Only Assembly1.dll will be installed.

B. Only Assembly3.dll will be installed.

C. No assemblies will be installed.

D. Assembly1.dll and Assembly3.dll will be installed.

8. You are designing the user assistance for an ASP.NET application that will be available over the Internet. You have no control over the browsers that users will use to view your application. Which form of user assistance can you use with this application?

A. HTML Help 1.3

B. HTML Help 2.0

C. User assistance displayed as separate Web pages

D. User assistance displayed in the Search pane

9. You are converting an existing HTML and Jscript-based application to use ASP.NET Web Forms instead. Which of these activities is not a good candidate for code in a code-behind file?

A. Tracking mouse movement over an image and displaying updated text in the browser status bar depending on the mouse location.

B. Retrieving a list of states or provinces when the user selects a country in a DropDownList control.

C. Storing information entered by the user in a database on the Web server.

D. Setting up the initial list of items in a data-drive ListBox control.

10. You are building a custom control for your company's ASP.NET Web applications. The control will contain the company's privacy policy and copyright notices in a standard set of labels. This control should be shared by multiple applications. Which type of control should you create?

A. Web user control

B. Composite Web custom control

C. Web custom control that inherits from Label

D. Web custom control that inherits from WebControl

11. The Orders table of your corporate database contains approximately 650,000 orders. The average customer has placed between 5 and 10 orders. You are designing a Web Form that will allow users to enter a customer ID. The form will then retrieve and display only the orders placed by that customer. What strategy should you use for retrieving the correct orders?

A. Retrieve the orders into a DataTable, and then use a DataView to filter the retrieved orders.

B. Retrieve the orders into a DataTable, and then use a For Each loop to move through all of the DataRows in the DataTable, selecting the proper rows.

C. Create a view on the server that will return only the desired orders.

D. Create a stored procedure on the server that will return only the desired orders.

12. You are designing a Web Form that will use a Repeater control to display information from several columns of the Employees table in your database. You want to display the column names at the top of the control. Which template should include Label controls with the column names?

A. ItemTemplate

B. AlternatingItemTemplate

C. HeaderTemplate

D. SeparatorTemplate

13. You are converting an existing ASP application to an ASP.NET application. The ASP application uses ADO extensively for data access. You do not yet want to convert the ADO code to ADO.NET code. What should you do to ensure that the ADO objects continue to function properly on the ASP.NET pages?

A. Build a Runtime Callable Wrapper for each ADO object that you use.

B. Use a Page directive to set the ASP.NET page language to VBScript.

C. Use the Type Library Importer to create a Primary Interop Assembly for the ADO objects.

D. Use a Page directive to set ASP compatibility mode on the ASP.NET pages.

14. You have deployed an ASP.NET application on your company's intranet. Your company has standardized on Internet Explorer 6.0 as the corporate browser. Users complain that when they use the Submit button to send their expense reports in via the application, the focus moves to the first control on the reporting form. This makes it difficult for users to edit their expense reports.

What is the easiest way to maintain focus across postback operations in this application?

A. Store the name of the current control in session state when the page is posted back, and use this name to set the focus when the page is re-created.

B. Store the name of the current control in application state when the page is posted back, and use this name to set the focus when the page is re-created.

C. Write client-side Jscript code that stores the focus control in a temporary cookie and retrieves this information when the page is re-created.

D. Set the SmartNavigation property of the Page class to True.

15. You have created a Web service named MedicalPolicies. Within the Web service class, you have a method named Reimbursables that returns a DataSet object. What must you do to make the information contained in this DataSet object available to clients of the Web service?

A. Mark the Reimbursables method with the <WebMethod> attribute.

B. Mark the Reimbursables method with the <WebService> attribute.

C. Call the WriteXml method of the DataSet object to serialize the object to the data stream.

D. Write a Function procedure that returns an individual DataRow from the DataSet. Call this function multiple times to transfer the DataSet.

16. Your ASP.NET page displays the orders for a particular customer in a DataGrid control. The orders are retrieved by constructing an ad-hoc SQL statement with a WHERE clause that specifies the customer. The application uses a SqlConnection object to connect to the database. The SQL statement is used to fill a DataSet, which is bound to the DataGrid control. What can you do to optimize this portion of your application? (Select two.)

A. Replace the ad-hoc SQL statement with a stored procedure.

B. Replace the DataGrid control with a DataList control.

C. Replace the DataSet object with a SqlDataReader object.

D. Replace the SqlConnection object with an OleDbConnection object.

17. Your ASP.NET application contains this setting in the web.config file:

```
<identity impersonate="true"
name="CORP\Auditing"
 password="Auditing"/>
```

You are allowing only digest or Windows integrated authentication in IIS. ASP.NET is running under the machine account. What identity will ASP.NET use to authorize resources if a user with the Windows account Shirley in the CORP domain logs in via digest authentication?

A. CORP\Shirley

B. ASPNET

C. IUSR_ComputerName

D. CORP\Auditing

18. Your Web application provides information on your company's shipping policies. Users can select a region of the country from a ListBox control, and are then shown a list of all the shipping choices for that region. The list is stored in a database, and changes very infrequently. You are concerned about the performance of the application when the Web server is under very heavy load. Which of these actions should you take to improve application performance?

A. Use the State Service to store the information for each user between requests.

B. Use SQL Server to store the information for each user between requests.

C. Use fragment caching to cache the ListBox control between requests.

D. Use caching with the VaryByParam attribute to hold the delivered page in memory between requests.

19. Your ASP.NET application is running on your company's production Web server. To fix a bug, you've modified one of the ASPX pages that is a part of this application. What must you do to ensure that the production Web server uses the modified page?

    A. Copy the modified ASPX page to the Web server in place of the original page. Restart IIS on the Web server.

    B. Copy the modified ASPX page to the Web server in place of the original page. IIS will automatically use the modified page.

    C. Copy the modified ASPX page to the Web server in a new directory. Use Internet Services Manager to change the IIS application to use the new directory.

    D. Copy the modified ASPX page to the Web server in place of the original page. Reboot the Web server.

20. You have designed a Web Form that includes a DropDownList control with the id of ddlSize. The Items property of the ddlSize control contains the following items:

```
-
9
10
11
12
```

    The Web Form also contains a RequiredFieldValidator control named rfvSize. You have set the ControlToValidate property of rfvSize to ddlSize. Your goal is to make sure that a non-default value is chosen from ddlSize before the Web Form is posted back to the server. What other property setting must you make on the rfvSize control?

    A. InitialValue = "-"

    B. Display = Dynamic

    C. Visible = True

    D. EnableClientScript = False

21. You have created a Web user control named signup.ascx that encapsulates the controls used within your enterprise for newsletter signup forms. Now you want to use this control in other Web applications. What must you do?

    A. Install the control in the Global Assembly Cache (GAC).

    B. Copy the control's files into each application.

    C. Include the control's project in the solution containing each application.

    D. Compile the control and copy the compiled assembly into each application's bin folder.

22. Your application connects to a database and adds employee names to a ListBox control in the Page.Load event. Supervisors can edit employee information on this page and submit the edits with a button on the page.

    Supervisors report that after they edit an employee's information, each employee name appears twice in the ListBox control. What should you do to fix this problem?

    A. Set the page's EnableViewState property to false.

    B. Check the IsPostBack property in the Page.Load event and only add names if IsPostBack is false.

    C. Add code to clear the Items collection of the ListBox control in the Page.Init event.

    D. Load a separate form after any editing operation with a hyperlink that goes back to the original page.

23. Your ASP.NET Web Form displays ordering information for 62 products in a DataGrid control. Your company is as yet unable to accept Web orders, so there are no controls on the page to post the data back to the server. What can you do to optimize the delivery of this page?

    A. Disable ViewState for the DataGrid control.

    B. Use GridLayout rather than FlowLayout for the page.

    C. Store state information in-process.

    D. Set the page to ASP compatibility mode.

24. Your ASP.NET application tracks donor contributions for non-profit organizations. Because of the nature of this data, you need to maintain session state even if the Web server crashes and needs to be restarted. Which alternative should you use to store session state for this application?

    A. Configuration files

    B. In-process storage

    C. Session Service

    D. SQL Server

25. Your application needs to search for substrings in longer strings. This searching should be culture-aware. What should you use to perform these searches?

    A. Array.Sort

    B. CultureInfo.CompareInfo

    C. InStr

    D. IndexOf

26. You are implementing server-to-server FTP functionality for use in your ASP.NET applications. You've decided to implement this functionality as a .NET component that inherits directly from the base Component class. How can you create a Transfer method in your component's code?

    A. Implement a Public field named Transfer.

    B. Implement a Public property named Transfer.

    C. Implement a Public Event named Transfer.

    D. Implement a Public Sub or Public Function named Transfer.

27. Your ASP.NET application allows the user to display all the orders that were placed by a particular customer. Your database contains 100 orders and 10 customers. Users of the application might want to see orders from several different customers during the course of a single session. Which ADO.NET object should you use to hold the orders?

    A. SqlDataAdapter

    B. SqlDataReader

    C. DataColumn

    D. DataView

28. You have created a Web custom control that handles file uploading with custom authentication. This control will be used in several of your company's ASP.NET Web applications. Which method should you use for deploying this control?

    A. XCOPY deployment

    B. FTP deployment

    C. Merge module

    D. Web setup project

29. Your application uses the GetSystemDirectory API function. This function exists in kernel32.dll in both ANSI and Unicode versions. Your declaration is as follows:

```
Declare Function GetSystemDirectory Lib
"kernel32" ( _
 ByVal lpBuffer As String, _
 ByRef nSize As Integer) As Integer
```

Your code is failing with a System.EntryPointNotFoundException exception whenever you call this function. What should you do to fix this failure?

A. Add the Auto modifier to the declaration.

B. Declare the lpBuffer parameter as a StringBuilder rather than as a String.

C. the function as GetSystemDirectoryA.

D. Declare the function as GetSystemDirectoryW.

30. You are developing an application to take orders over the Internet. When the user posts back the order form, you first check to see whether they are a registered customer of your company. If not, you must transfer control to the Register.html page. Which method should you use to effect this transfer?

A. Response.Redirect

B. Server.Transfer

C. Server.Execute

D. Page.ProcessRequest

31. Your application contains a DataSet consisting of patient and physician records. You wish to write this DataSet out to a disk file as an XML document. How should you proceed?

A. Synchronize the DataSet object with an XmlDataDocument object, and call the WriteXml method of the XmlDataDocument object.

B. Call the WriteXml method of the DataSet object.

C. Synchronize the DataSet object with an XmlDataDocument object, and then use an XmlTextWriter object to write the XML to disk.

D. Use a For Each loop to walk through the DataSet, and write the data to disk with a FileStream object.

32. You have created a new Web service to deliver stock recommendations to your customers. You're working in an ASP.NET project within the Visual Studio .NET environment. What's the easiest way to test your new Web service to make sure that it's returning the proper results?

A. Run the Web service project and use the test page that it opens in the browser.

B. Cut and paste the code into a Windows application project, and test it in the new project.

C. Cut and paste the code into an ASP.NET Web application project, and test it in the new project.

D. Use a tool such as WebServicesStudio to send SOAP requests directly to the server.

33. You are developing a Web Form that will be used as part of an online banking application. You have placed a set of RadioButton controls on the form to represent account types. Only one account type should be selected at a time. When you test the Web Form, you discover that you can select multiple account types at the same time, and you cannot deselect an account type after selecting it. How can you fix this problem? (Select two.)

A. Replace the RadioButton controls with CheckBox controls.

B. Assign an identical GroupName property value to each of the RadioButton controls.

C. Place the RadioButton controls on a Panel control.

D. Replace the RadioButton controls with a RadioButtonList control.

34. You have added an EventLogTraceListener object to the Debug.TraceListeners collection so that debug messages are written to the Application event log. You are finished debugging and set your application to the Release configuration. The application contains calls to the Trace object to write tracing messages. In this configuration, where will the trace messages appear?

    A. Only in the Output window.

    B. Only in the Application event log.

    C. In both the Output window and in email messages.

    D. In both the Output window and in the Application event log.

35. You have created and tested an ASP.NET application on your local development server. The application makes heavy use of Web server controls, along with static HTML text. Now you have deployed the application to your company's production server via FTP. The production server has IIS 5.0 installed. The pages in the application are displaying in a jumbled fashion, with text present but none of the Web server controls. What could be the problem?

    A. Applications containing Web server controls cannot be deployed via FTP.

    B. The ASP.NET worker process is not properly installed on the production server.

    C. Web server controls will not function properly on a page that also contains static HTML text.

    D. ASP.NET requires IIS 6.0 to function properly.

36. You are debugging your ASP.NET Web application and are concerned about the amount of time that it's taking to render a particular page. Which class can you use to obtain detailed timing information for the events on the page as it is rendered by the ASP.NET engine?

    A. System.Diagnostics.Trace

    B. System.Diagnostics.Debug

    C. System.Web.TraceContext

    D. System.Web.Ui.Page

37. You are deploying your ASP.NET application to a single Web server. However, you're preparing to move to a Web farm should traffic justify the additional hardware investment. What should you do to make sure your application is ready to move to a Web farm if need be?

    A. Use either the State Service or SQL Server to store session state.

    B. Use only static HTML pages in your application.

    C. Compile the application in release configuration.

    D. Remove all references to the Request and Response objects from your code.

38. Your application includes 4,500 double-precision floating point numbers that you want to write out to a disk file. You'd like to minimize the size of the disk file. Which object should you use to write the file?

    A. FileStream

    B. StreamWriter

    C. BinaryWriter

    D. XmlTextWriter

39. You are developing an ASP.NET application that can display its user interface in English, French, German, or Japanese. What strategy should you use to select the language to display?

 A. Retrieve the value of Request.UserLanguages(0) when you're processing the page and set the corresponding language.

 B. Allow the user to select a language by choosing a hyperlink or a selection in a DropDownList.

 C. Use the language returned by the CurrentThread.CurrentCulture property.

 D. Use the language returned by the CurrentThread.CurrentUiCulture property.

40. You have created an ASP.NET Web Form that displays parts stock information to your customers in a series of DropDownList and ListBox controls. This page is never posted back to your Web server. Which page directive can you use to optimize this page so that it does not download unnecessary data?

 A. WarningLevel = "0"

 B. Explicit = "True"

 C. AutoEventWireup = "False"

 D. EnableViewState = "False"

41. You are working with an ASP.NET custom validation control which is required to emit client-side script as part of page processing. Which is the last Page event that you can use to create this script?

 A. Init

 B. Load

 C. Prerender

 D. Render

42. You are developing a version of your ASP.NET application that will be shipped to a locale that uses right-to-left text ordering. What property should you set for controls on your Web Forms to ensure that they fill in the proper direction?

 A. Set the rtl attribute to "True" in the individual control tags.

 B. Set the dir attribute to "rtl" in the individual control tags.

 C. Set the rtl attribute to "True" in the HTML tag.

 D. Set the dir attribute to "rtl" in the HTML tag.

43. Your ASP.NET application allows the user to input the URL of a Web page, and then applies an XSLT file to show how that Web page looks on a mobile device. What sort of control should you use to validate the TextBox control where the user inputs the URL?

 A. RequiredFieldValidator

 B. RangeValidator

 C. RegularExpressionValidator

 D. CompareValidator

44. You have implemented a Web service that calculates shipping for your company's products and exposed this Web service to the Internet. However, you have removed the UDDI and WSDL files for the Web service. What is the consequence of this action?

 A. The Web service can only be used by applications that have knowledge of its interface.

 B. The Web service cannot be used by any application.

C. The Web service can only be used by applications on your intranet.

D. The Web service can be used by any application.

45. The login page for your Web application uses many PNG graphics to indicate what the user should do. Some users report difficulty with this page because they are browsing with graphics disabled. What should you do to make this page more accessible?

A. Use JPG graphics instead of PNG graphics for maximum browser compatibility.

B. Set the TabIndex property for all text controls on the page so that the page is more usable without instructions.

C. Use the AccessKey property for all graphical controls to make them more accessible.

D. Add ALT text to all graphics to indicate their purpose.

46. Your application uses a library of advanced mathematical functions from a third-party developer. This library is implemented as a COM component. You are migrating your application to .NET. What should you do to continue to use the classes and methods within the library?

A. Use the Type Library Importer to create a signed Runtime Callable Wrapper for the library. Install the RCW in the Global Assembly Cache.

B. Use the Type Library Importer to create an unsigned Runtime Callable Wrapper for the library. Install the RCW in the global assembly cache.

C. Obtain a Primary Interop Assembly from the developer of the library. Install the PIA in the Global Assembly Cache.

D. Use the Type Library Importer to create an unsigned Runtime Callable Wrapper for the library. Install the RCW in each application's directory.

47. One of your trading partners has sent you the URL to an ASMX file that specifies a Web service for you to use in communicating with his servers. Which tool can you use to construct a proxy class for calling this Web service?

A. Web Services Discovery Tool

B. Web Services Description Language Tool

C. Soapsuds Tool

D. XML Schema Definition Tool

48. You are deploying an ASP.NET application to multiple customer sites. You are not positive that all the bugs have been found in the application, and want to be able to retrieve debugging information from the deployed applications if necessary. You don't want the debugging information to impose any overhead when it's not needed. What should you do?

A. Compile the application in debug mode. When you need to debug the application, use remote debugging to connect to the server.

B. Supply debugging objects in a separate DLL. When you need to debug the application, use reflection to obtain debugging objects from the DLL.

C. Include calls to the Trace object in the application. Use a TraceSwitch object to control the output of the Trace object. When you need to debug the application, edit the config file to activate the TraceSwitch object.

D. Compile the application in both debug mode and release mode. When you need to debug the application, have the customer replace the release mode files with the debug mode files.

49. You have developed an ASP.NET Web Form that displays product information from your company's database. The database contains approximately 200 products. Each time the page is displayed, it retrieves information on one product specified by the user.

    What type of caching can you use to speed up the delivery of this page?

    A. Output

    B. Varying

    C. Application

    D. Fragment

50. Your application uses a SqlDataReader object to retrieve monthly shipping data from a SQL Server database. When you find a month with above-average sales, you invoke the ExecuteNonQuery method of a SqlCommand object to insert a row in another table using an INSERT INTO stored procedure.

    Calling the ExecuteNonQuery method is causing an error. What is the most likely reason for this error?

    A. You should use the ExecuteScalar method of the SqlCommand object, rather than the ExecuteNonQuery method, to execute the INSERT INTO stored procedure.

    B. You should use a DataAdapter object to insert the rows in the database, rather than a SqlCommand object.

    C. The database requires you to use an ad-hoc SQL statement instead of a stored procedure to insert rows.

    D. You are using the same SqlConnection object for both the SqlDataReader object and the SqlCommand object, and the SqlDataReader is still open when you try to execute the SqlCommand.

51. You have written a Visual Basic .NET procedure that opens a database connection using a SqlConnection object, retrieves some information from the database and then closes the connection. The information is retrieved using a stored procedure that may not always be available due to backup schedules. You have wrapped the code to call the stored procedure in a Try/Catch/Finally block. Where should you place the code to close the SqlConnection object?

    A. Inside the Try block, before the first Catch block.

    B. Inside the Catch block that will catch exceptions thrown by the SqlCommand object.

    C. Inside the Finally block.

    D. Outside of the Try/Catch/Finally block.

52. When a page cannot be found in your ASP.NET application (that is, when a 404 error occurs), you want to display a page named NotFound.aspx to the user. For all other errors, you want to display a page named GeneralError.aspx. Which settings should you make in the web.config file to ensure this?

    A.

```
<customErrors mode="Off"
 defaultRedirect="GeneralError.aspx">
    <error statusCode="404"
redirect="NotFound.aspx" />
</customErrors>
```

    B.

```
<customErrors mode="On"
 defaultRedirect="GeneralError.aspx">
    <error statusCode="404"
redirect="NotFound.aspx" />
</customErrors>
```

    C.

```
<customErrors mode="Off">
    <error statusCode="404"
redirect="NotFound.aspx" />
    <error statusCode="all"
redirect="GeneralError.aspx" />
</customErrors>
```

D.

```
<customErrors mode="On">
    <error statusCode="404"
redirect="NotFound.aspx" />
    <error statusCode="all"
redirect="GeneralError.aspx" />
</customErrors>
```

53. You are in the process of upgrading an existing ASP application to ASP.NET by converting pages one by one to the new architecture. The application currently uses an ASP.NET page to request the user's first name, which is stored in a session variable with this line of code:

```
Session("FirstName") = txtFirstName.Text
```

You run the application and enter a first name on the ASP.NET page. When you browse to an existing ASP page that uses the FirstName session variable, the first name is blank. What could be the problem?

A. You must explicitly use the Page.Session property to store shared session state.

B. The ASP page needs to explicitly retrieve the Value property of the Session item.

C. The ASP and ASP.NET engines do not share session state or application state.

D. You do not have cookies enabled on your computer.

54. Your ASP.NET Web Form includes a DataGrid control that contains data the user may wish to edit. You need to maintain the information in this control across page postbacks to the server. The information is not needed by any other page in the application. Which state management technique should you use for this control?

A. Query strings

B. Cookies

C. Session

D. ViewState

55. The machine.config file on your computer contains this setting:

```
<customErrors mode="RemoteOnly"/>
```

Your application's root directory contains a web.config file with this setting:

```
<customErrors mode="On">
    <error statusCode="404"
redirect="404.aspx" />
</customErrors>
```

Your application's /custom directory contains a web.config file with this setting:

```
<customErrors mode="Off" />
```

Your application's /custom/local directory contains a web.config file with this setting:

```
<customErrors mode="On">
    <error statusCode="404"
redirect="404.htm" />
</customErrors>
```

A user at a remote computer requests the file /custom/remote/bad_doc.aspx, which does not exist. What is the result?

A. The 404.aspx file is displayed.

B. The default ASP.NET error page is displayed.

C. The 404.htm file is displayed.

D. The stack trace information for the error is displayed.

56. Your ASP.NET application contains a Web Form named login.aspx. When this page is posted back to the server, you check the entered username and password against your corporate database. If the username and password match, you wish to display the accountdetails.aspx Web Form as the result in the user's browser. Execution of the application will proceed from that page. How should you transfer control in this case?

A. HyperLink control

B. Response.Redirect() method

C. Server.Transfer() method

D. Server.Execute() method

57. You have used the Setup Wizard to create a setup for your ASP.NET Web application and chosen to install a Bootstrapper in the setup. Which of these actions will the Bootstrapper *not* perform?

A. Install IIS.

B. Install the Windows Installer.

C. Install the .NET Framework.

D. Launch your application's setup.

58. You are developing an ASP.NET application that will display the strings on its user interface in any of five different languages, depending on the setting of the CurrentThread.CurrentUiCulture property. Where should you store the localized strings so that they can most easily be displayed?

A. In Assembly resource files

B. In XML Schema design files

C. In .resources files

D. In code-behind files

59. You have designed an ASP.NET Web form where you need to highlight important information within a table so that it stands out to the user. Which method of highlighting is most accessible?

A. <BGCOLOR>

B. <BLINK>

C. <B>

D. <MARQUEE>

60. You are creating a specialized control that will display text that rotates at an angle specified at design time. This control must be installed into the Visual Studio toolbox so that it can be used in many projects. The control's user interface will resemble that of a Label control, with one additional property named RotationAngle.

What sort of control should you create?

A. Web user control.

B. Composite Web custom control.

C. Web custom control that inherits from WebControl.

D. Web custom control that inherits from Label.

61. You have developed a Web Form that will display account information to sales representatives. You want your code to respond to the Page's Load event by running a procedure named LoadAccounts, which is defined as follows:

```
Private Sub LoadAccounts(ByVal sender As
System.Object, _
 ByVal e As System.EventArgs)
```

What statement should you use to attach this procedure to the Load event?

A.

```
Me.Load = EventHandler(LoadAccounts)
```

B.

```
Me.Load = New EventHandler(LoadAccounts)
```

C.

```
Me.Load = AddressOf LoadAccounts
```

D.

```
AddHandler Me.Load, AddressOf LoadAccounts
```

62. Your user would like to see German dates and currencies displayed in an application but wants the user interface to remain in English. How can you accomplish this?

A. Set the CurrentCulture property to a CultureInfo representing the en-US culture, and set the CurrentUICulture property to a CultureInfo representing the de-DE culture.

B. Set the CurrentCulture property to a CultureInfo representing the de-DE culture, and set the CurrentUICulture property to a CultureInfo representing the en-US culture.

C. Set the CurrentCulture property to a CultureInfo representing the de-DE culture, and set the CurrentUICulture property to a CultureInfo representing the de-DE culture.

D. Set the CurrentCulture property to a CultureInfo representing the en-US culture, and set the CurrentUICulture property to a CultureInfo representing the en-US culture.

63. Your ASP.NET application includes a Web page named AllErrors.htm that is displayed in response to any error. This page is configured using this code in the web.config file:

```
<customErrors mode="On"
 defaultRedirect="AllError.htm">
</customErrors>
```

The application includes a login page named Login.aspx. When an error occurs on the login page, you wish to display the page LoginInstructions.htm instead of AllErrors.htm. What should you do?

A. Add an <error> element as a child of the <customErrors> element in web.config. Specify the page name Login.aspx and the redirect page LoginInstructions.htm in the new element.

B. Add an ErrorPage attribute to the Page directive for Login.aspx. Set the value of this attribute to LoginInstructions.htm.

C. Create a new ASP.NET application. Place the Login.aspx and LoginInstructions.htm page in this application. Specify LoginInstructions.htm as the default error page for the new application.

D. Set a Session variable when the Login.aspx page is loaded. Check for the presence of this Session variable in AllErrors.htm and redirect to LoginInstructions.htm if the variable is set.

64. You allow users to edit Customer information on a DataGrid bound to a DataSet. When the user clicks the Update button on the form, you call the SqlDataAdapter.Update method to persist the changes from the DataSet to the underlying database.

Users report that updated records are saved properly, and deleted records are removed, but that new records are missing the next time they run the application. What could be the problem?

A. The users do not have permission to update the underlying table.

B. The Update method does not add rows.

C. The InsertCommand property of the SqlDataAdapter points to a SqlCommand object that does not properly add rows.

D. Someone is restoring an old version of the database between the two executions of the program.

65. Your company supplies a COM component to provide network connectivity services and peer-to-peer file sharing. Some of your clients are moving to .NET, and require a Runtime Callable Wrapper for your component. How should you proceed?

A. Use the Type Library Importer to create and sign a Primary Interop Assembly for your component.

B. Set a reference directly from the new ASP.NET applications to automatically create a Runtime Callable Wrapper.

C. Create a class that uses PInvoke to call functions from the existing component.

D. Supply your component's source code to your clients.

66. Your Web application uses a frame set to organize information. What must you do to comply with Section 508 accessibility guidelines?

   A. Add an Alt tag to each Frame element.

   B. Replace the frame set with a table.

   C. Provide a link to an alternative, non-framed version of the site.

   D. Provide Title text for each frame.

67. You are creating an ASP.NET Web application that displays a table representing your company's financial performance over the past eight quarters. The information is grouped into columns and subcolumns. Which attribute can you use in the <th> tags for the table to make it clear to screen readers which data cells the headers are associated with?

   A. colspan

   B. nowrap

   C. scope

   D. abbr

68. Your application uses a custom database to hold information on inventory levels. When an exception occurs during database processing, you want to make current database status information available to the Catch block. What should you do?

   A. Keep the status information in global variables that are available to the Catch block.

   B. Derive a custom exception class from the Exception class. Pass the information as properties of the custom exception class.

   C. Derive a custom exception class from the ApplicationException class. Pass the information as properties of the custom exception class.

   D. Keep the database connection in a global variable that is available to the Catch block.

69. You have designed a Web Form that uses a DropDownList control to allow the user to select a state containing their shipping address. In the code-behind file for the Web Form, you've implemented an event handler for the SelectedIndexChanged event to update the sales tax amount displayed on the Web Form when a new state is changed.

   Users report that the sales tax amount is not updated no matter which state they choose in the DropDownList. What must you do to fix this problem?

   A. Move the code to the PreRender event of the DropDownList control.

   B. Set the AutoPostBack property of the DropDownList control to True.

   C. Replace the DropDownList control with a ListBox control.

   D. Set the EnableViewState property of the DropDownList control to True.

70. You are designing a new control for use in ASP.NET applications. The new control will be used to load an image from a disk file to an Image control at runtime. The control will not need a runtime user interface, but it must allow you to select a filename in the Properties window at design time. Which type of control should you create?

   A. Web custom control that inherits directly from WebControl

   B. Web custom control that inherits directly from Label

   C. Composite Web custom control

   D. Web user control

71. Your application includes a ListBox control named lbCustomers that displays a list of customers. The DataTextField property of the ListBox is bound to the CompanyName column of the Customers database table. The DataValueField property of the ListBox is bound to the CustomerID column of the Customers database table.

    Your form also contains a TextBox control named txtCustomerID. This control uses simple data binding to the ListBox to display the SelectedItem.Value from the ListBox control.

    When the user selects a new company name in the ListBox, you wish to display the corresponding CustomerID value in the txtCustomerID control. What should you do?

    A. Call the DataBind method of the ListBox control in the SelectedIndexChanged event of the ListBox.

    B. Create a public property named CustomerID and return the SelectedItem.Value property of the ListBox as the value of the public property.

    C. Use simple data binding to bind the SelectedValue property of the ListBox to the CustomerID column of the Customers table.

    D. Call the DataBind method of the TextBox control in the SelectedIndexChanged event of the ListBox.

72. You have defined a function named DataLoad that makes a list of customers available by returning an ICollection interface. You have an ASP.NET Web Form with a ListBox control named lbCustomers. The Page_Load event handler for the Web Form contains this code:

```
    Private Sub Page_Load(ByVal sender As
System.Object, _
     ByVal e As System.EventArgs) Handles
MyBase.Load
        lbCustomers.DataSource = DataLoad()
        lbCustomers.DataTextField =
"CustomerName"
    End Sub
```

    The Web Form opens without error, but no customer names are displayed. What is the problem?

    A. You have neglected to call the DataBind() method of the page.

    B. A ListBox control cannot be bound to an ICollection interface.

    C. There is an untrapped error in the database code within the DataLoad() function.

    D. The data-binding code must be contained in a Try-Catch block.

73. You are invoking a Web service that returns a StringBuilder object. Which project requires a reference to the System.Text namespace?

    A. The client project.

    B. The Web service project

    C. Both the client project and the Web service project.

    D. The project that contains the WSDL file.

74. You are attempting to debug an ASP.NET application located on your company's production server. The server has the remote debugging components installed, and your local workstation has a full install of Visual Studio .NET. When you attempt to connect to the server process, you receive a DCOM error. What could be the problem?

    A. You are not a member of the Administrators group on the server.

    B. You are not a member of the Debugger Users group on the server.

C. You are not a member of the Debugger Users group on your workstation.

D. You do not have a NetBIOS connection to the server.

75. You are debugging an ASP.NET application. You want to write the value of a particular variable to a disk file whenever a page is loaded. You only want to record this information during debugging, not after the application has been released. Which object should you use?

  A. System.Web.TraceContext

  B. System.Diagnostics.Trace

  C. System.Diagnostics.Debug

  D. System.Io.FileStream

Answers to Exam Questions

1. **D.** An Application_Error event handler in the Global.asax file is automatically invoked for any error that is not caught in other error handlers.
2. **D.** You cannot use FTP to deploy components to the GAC.
3. **D.** The application as described does not use session state for any purpose, so the best-performing alternative is to disable session state entirely.
4. **B.** By using role-based security, you can base decisions about which code to run on the user's authenticated Windows identity. This includes both username and group membership.
5. **A.** Dragging and dropping a table from Server Explorer to a Web Form and using it as the basis for a DataSet sets up all the code necessary to retrieve the data, but it does not actually retrieve any data. The Fill method of the SqlDataAdapter object is used to move data from the database to the DataSet.
6. **C.** The String object must be destroyed and re-created whenever you concatenate new characters to the string. The StringBuilder object is designed to be modified in place.
7. **C.** InstallUtil.exe performs its work in a transactional fashion. If any part of a command-line operation cannot be completed than the entire operation is rolled back.
8. **C.** For widest availability, user assistance should be delivered as Web pages. HTML Help and the Search pane are Internet Explorer technologies that may not be available in other browsers.
9. **A.** Executing server-side code in a code-behind file requires a round trip from the browser to the server. Tracking mouse movements is not a good candidate for this architecture because mouse events occur too frequently and performance will suffer.
10. **B.** The composite control can encapsulate multiple Label controls into a single control easily. Because it's a custom control, it can be installed into the GAC and shared by multiple applications.
11. **D.** There are so many orders in the database that you need to do the filtering with a server-side object rather than with a client-side object. For such operations, a stored procedure will be moderately faster than a view because the code for a stored procedure can be precompiled.
12. **C.** The controls in the HeaderTemplate template are rendered once at the start of the Repeater control when it is converted to HTML.
13. **D.** The ADO library uses STA as its threading model. The .NET Framework only allows STA components on a page that's set to ASP compatibility mode.

14. **D.** SmartNavigation offers several benefits to users running Internet Explorer 5.0 or higher, including focus persistence, minimized screen flashing, persistent scroll positioning, and better history management.

15. **A.** You can return complex objects from a Web service as easily as you can return simple types. All you need to do is mark the procedure with the <WebMethod> attribute to indicate that its return value should be remotely available. The Web service takes care of all the details of converting the DataSet to an XML representation, wrapping it in a SOAP message, sending it to the client, and reconstituting the DataSet there.

16. **A, C.** Stored procedures have a performance advantage over ad-hoc SQL statements because they can be precompiled on the database server. The SqlDataReader object is the fastest way to retrieve SQL Server data that you don't need to edit.

17. **D.** When you enable impersonation, any authenticated user takes on the credentials of the specified account for purposes of authorizing resources.

18. **D.** By using the VaryByParam attribute, you can cache each regional version of the page, so that it can be delivered quickly from the cache if it's requested more than once.

19. **B.** ASP.NET monitors ASPX pages for changes. If a page is modified, ASP.NET automatically compiles the modified version and uses it to satisfy subsequent requests for the page.

20. **A.** The RequiredFieldValidator control checks to see whether the value in a control is different than the original value in the control. You must supply this original value as the InitialValue property of the RequiredFieldValidator control.

21. **B.** Web user controls can only be shared by copying their files into each application where you wish to use the control.

22. **B.** The IsPostBack property is set to False when a page is first loaded and to True if the page is loading because it was posted back from the client. This is useful for checking whether one-time initializations should be performed in your code.

23. **A.** By default, ASP.NET will save a copy of all the DataGrid information in the hidden ViewState control. Because the page will not be posted back, you don't need this information. Disabling ViewState will make the page smaller so that it will be delivered more quickly.

24. **D.** When you store session state data in SQL Server, you can take advantage of the robustness and data protection qualities of SQL Server. This includes the ability to preserve data even across server crashes.

25. **B.** The CultureInfo.CompareInfo method takes into account the lexical and character-matching rules of different cultures, as well as the differences in number of bytes needed to store a character.

26. **D.** The public Function and Sub procedures of a component class are the methods of the component.

27. **D.** By retrieving all the orders into a DataView object, you can quickly filter out the desired orders without requiring further interaction with the database server.

28. **C.** By packaging the control as a Merge module, you can perform advanced tasks (such as installing the control into the GAC) and be sure that all your applications install the control consistently.

29. **A.** Because GetSystemDirectory has both ANSI and Unicode versions, there isn't any entry point named just "GetSystemDirectory." Using the Auto modifier tells .NET to use the appropriate entry point, GetSystemDirectoryA or GetSystemDirectoryW, depending on the operating system.

30. **A.** To transfer execution to a page that is not processed by the ASP.NET process, you must use the Response.Redirect method.

31. **B.** You can use the WriteXml method of the DataSet object to persist a DataSet directly as XML.

32. **A.** When you're creating a Web service in ASP.NET, running the project will open a testing form in a browser window.

33. **B, D.** Although by convention radio buttons are mutually exclusive, this is not enforced for radio buttons on a Web Form by default. You can force a group of radio buttons to act as mutually exclusive choices by making them all part of the same group with the GroupName property, or by using a RadioButtonList control to group them.

34. **D.** The Debug and Trace classes share a single Listeners collection, so that adding a listener to the Debug.Listeners collection also adds it to the Trace.Listeners collection. In this case, messages will go to the default listener, which displays them in the Output window, and to the EventLogTraceListener.

35. **B.** You must install the ASP.NET software on the Web server before it will properly display ASP.NET Web server controls. If ASP.NET is not installed, the pages will be rendered by IIS as HTML pages, and the Web server controls will not be displayed.

36. **C.** The TraceContext class is responsible for providing detailed timing and other information in the browser window when you activate ASP.NET tracing.

37. **A.** Because multiple page requests during a session might be served by different computers within a Web farm, you must store any state information in a shared repository outside of ASP.NET itself.

38. **C.** The BinaryWriter class uses an efficient binary format to save data to disk. This format is not human-readable, but it does minimize storage requirements.

39. **B.** The CurrentThread culture properties in an ASP.NET application return culture information from the Web server, not from the browser. The value of the UserLanguages string is not a reliable indicator of the end user's preferred language because Web browsers are not required to set this property. The best solution is to let the user explicitly choose the language to use.

40. **D.** Web server controls use Viewstate to store information so that it will be available if the page is posted back to the server. This information can add many bytes to the page as it is sent to be browser. If a page will never be posted back, you can disable Viewstate for the page to avoid sending this unnecessary information.

41. **C.** The Prerender event occurs just before the page is completed to be sent to the browser. This is the final event in which you can modify the page.

42. **D.** Setting the dir attribute of the HTML tag to "rtl" causes all controls on the page to render right-to-left.

43. **C.** The RegularExpressionValidator control lets you check that the URL is in the proper format on the client side, before the page has been posted back to the server.

44. **A.** By removing the WSDL and UDDI files, you remove the ability for the Web service and its interface to be discovered. The Web service can still be used from any application that hard-codes knowledge of its interface.

45. **D.** In an accessible Web application, all graphics should have informative ALT text, to cater to those who cannot or will not view the graphics.

46. **C.** Because the component comes from another company, you should contact that company to obtain a Primary Interop Assembly. You should not create RCWs for another company's components.

47. **B.** The Web Services Description Language Tool can retrieve a WSDL file from an ASMX URL and use the information in the WSDL file to build a proxy class that invokes the Web service.

48. **C.** By using a TraceSwitch object to control debugging output, you can turn output on and off by simply editing a config file.

49. **B.** By using Varying caching you can place one copy of the page in RAM for each product in the database. These copies will quickly deliver information on the individual products without requiring a round trip to the database for each request.

50. **D.** The SqlDataReader object requires exclusive use of a SqlConnection object. If you need to perform other operations in the same database while the SqlDataReader object is open, you should open a second SqlConnection object to the same database.

51. **C.** The database connection should be closed whether or not the information can be retrieved. Code in the Finally block will be executed regardless of whether an exception is thrown by the rest of the code.

52. **B.** To display custom error pages, the mode attribute of the customErrors element must be set to "On" or "RemoteOnly." The defaultRedirect attribute of the customErrors element specifies the page to be displayed for any errors not listed. Error attributes specify an error status code and the resulting page to display.

53. **C.** This is one of the major problems in using ASP and ASP.NET pages together in the same application. Session and application state is not shared between the two types of pages. If you set a session or application variable in ASP.NET code, there's no way to retrieve it from ASP code, and vice versa.

54. **D.** ViewState provides automatic, compressed data management for information contained in Web Form controls. For data that does not need to be shared with other pages, it is the simplest state management technique.

55. **B.** The configuration settings most local to the requested page control the response of ASP.NET. In this case, that's the configuration file in the /custom directory, which specifies that no custom error page be shown.

56. **C.** The Server.Transfer() method provides a quick way to switch pages within the context of a single ASP.NET application.

57. **A.** The Bootstrapper will verify the Windows Installer version and upgrade it if necessary, install the .NET Framework redistributable package if necessary, and then launch the setup for your own application.

58. **A.** If you store user interface strings in properly named Assembly resource files, the CLR will automatically choose the proper set of strings to use at runtime based on the value of the CurrentThread.CurrentUiCulture property.

59. **C.** For compatibility with the largest number of accessibility aids, you should use bold or underlining to highlight information. It's okay to use color as well, but don't depend on only color to convey information in an accessible application.

60. **D.** Because this control is an extension of the Label control, it's easiest to create it by subclassing the existing Label control.

61. **D.** You can use the AddHandler statement to add an event handler to an event in Visual Basic .NET.

62. **B.** The CurrentCulture property controls formatting for items such as dates and currency, while the CurrentUiCulture property controls the choice of user interface languages.

63. **B.** The ErrorPage attribute in the Page directive overrides any default error page set for the application in the web.config file.

64. **C.** The Update method of the SqlDataAdapter calls the SqlCommand objects specified by its UpdateCommand, InsertCommand, and DeleteCommand methods. If one of these SqlCommand objects is improperly configured, the corresponding database operation will not be performed.

65. **A.** Because your company created the component, the right course of action is to create a Primary Interop Assembly. This will allow any .NET client application to use the component.

66. **D.** Accessible Web pages should use the Title tag and similar tags to make sure that there is a textual equivalent for every element on the Web page.

67. **C.** The scope attribute of the <th> tag associates a header with a column or a set of columns. This helps screen readers provide sensible context information when reporting the value of a cell in the table.

68. **C.** When you create a custom exception class, you can specify any properties you like for the class. Custom exceptions should be derived from the ApplicationException class rather than directly from the Exception class.

69. **B.** By default, the SelectedIndexChanged event of the DropDownList control is only fired when the page is posted back to the server. By setting the AutoPostBack property of the control to True, you cause the page to post back as soon as a selection is made in the list.

70. **A.** In this situation, you should create a Web custom control, so that you get the required Properties window support. Because the control does not need a runtime user interface, you can inherit it directly from the WebControl class.

71. **D.** As described, the controls already contain all the necessary property settings to transfer the data from the ListBox to the TextBox. But you must still call the DataBind method to actually perform the transfer.

72. **A.** Unlike Windows forms, Web Forms do not automatically bind data to controls. You must explicitly call the DataBind method of the Page or of the particular control to bind the data.

73. **C.** Both the client and server project must have access to the namespaces that declare any shared objects.

74. **B.** ASP.NET checks for membership in the Debugger Users group on the server to determine whether you are authorized to debug processes on that server.

75. **C.** Either the Trace or the Debug class can write values to a disk file by using a TextWriterTraceListener object. The Debug class will only write information when the application is in the Debug configuration.

PART V

APPENDIXES

APPENDIX A

Glossary

A

accessibility The process of making an application more readily available to users who may have disabilities that interfere with their use of computer hardware or software.

ad-hoc query A set of SQL statements that are executed immediately.

ASP.NET ASP.NET is a set of the .NET Framework that enables you to develop Web applications. Being a part of the .NET Framework, it enjoys all the advantages offered by the .NET Framework.

ASP.NET application An ASP.NET application is made up of the Web forms, assemblies, and other files stored within a virtual Web directory marked as an IIS application.

assembly A logical unit of functionality that can contain one or more files. Every type loaded in the Common Language Runtime belongs to precisely one assembly.

assembly manifest The assembly manifest stores the assembly's metadata. This subset of information in the manifest makes assemblies self-sufficient.

assembly metadata Assembly metadata provides the assembly's self-describing information such as the name and version of the assembly, the files that are part of the assembly and their hash values, the files' dependencies on other assemblies, and so on.

attribute A property of an XML object.

authentication Determining the identity of a user from his or her credentials.

authorization Allowing a user to use specific resources based on his or her authenticated identity.

B

backing store A place where you can store a file.

boxing A process of conversion of value type to a reference type where the value in the stack is copied into heap by creating a new instance of object to hold its data.

C

caching Caching refers to storing information for later retrieval, rather than generating it anew every time it's requested.

CDATA section Raw data within an XML file.

class A reference type that encapsulates its data (constants and fields) and behavior (methods, properties, indexers, events, operators, instance constructors, static constructors, and destructors).

CLR (Common Language Runtime) A program that executes all managed code and provides code with various services at runtime, such as automatic memory management, cross-language integration, code access security, and debugging and profiling support.

column All the values for one particular property in a table.

complex data binding Complex data binding means connecting a user interface control to an entire collection of data, rather than to a single data item.

component A package of reusable code that implements the IComponent interface.

configuration file ASP.NET configuration files are XML files that ASP.NET reads at runtime to determine configuration options.

CSS (Cascading Style Sheets) A cascading style sheet defines the style that are applied to elements in an HTML document. The CSS styles define how the HTML elements are displayed and where they are rendered in the Web browser.

culture A combination of language and location that is sufficient to dictate the formatting of resources.

culture code An abbreviation that identifies a particular culture.

D

data binding Data binding refers to the process of making a link between controls on the user interface and data stored in the data model.

data provider The server-specific ADO.NET classes that supply data.

DataSet The DataSet is a server-independent store that can hold multiple tables and their relations.

debugging A process of locating logical or runtime errors in an application. It involves finding the cause of the errors and fixing them.

delay signing A technique that allows a shared assembly to be placed in the GAC by just signing the assembly with the public key. This allows the assembly to be signed with private key at a later stage when the development process is complete and the component or assembly is ready to be deployed. This process allows developers to work with shared assemblies as if they are strongly named and yet also secure the private-key of the signature from being accessed at different stages of development.

delegate A reference type that stores references to a method with a specific signature. A delegate object can be used to dynamically invoke a method at runtime.

deployment A process by which a Windows application or component is distributed in the form of installation package files to be installed on the other computers.

derived control A control that inherits directly from a specific server control such as the TextBox or Label control.

Disco A Microsoft standard for Web service discovery.

E

element An XML tag together with its contents.

encoding An encoding is a scheme for representing textual characters as numeric codes.

event A message that is sent by an object to signal an action. The action can be a result of user interaction, such as a mouse click, or it can be triggered by any other program.

event handling The act of responding to an event. Event handling can be accomplished by writing methods called event handlers that are invoked in response to events.

exception An exception indicates a problem that occurred during normal execution of the program.

exception handling The process of handling exceptions that are raised when the program executes is called exception handling. You can choose to ignore an exception or respond to it by running your own code.

F

FCL (Framework Class Library) A library of classes, interfaces, and value types that are included in the Microsoft .NET Framework. This library provides access to the system functionality and is the foundation on which the .NET Framework applications, components, and controls are built.

field A variable that is associated with an object or a class.

foreign key The foreign key in a database table stores values from the primary key in another table. These values indicate which row in the primary table each row in the other table is related to.

G

GAC (Global Assembly Cache) The Global Assembly Cache is a cache of assemblies that can be shared by many applications on the computer.

globalization The process of identifying the resources to be localized in a particular application.

H

HTML controls HTML controls are the HTML elements. These controls are only used for client side rendering and are not directly accessible in the ASP.NET programs.

HTML server controls The HTML controls marked with runat="server" attributes are known as HTML server controls. These controls can be directly used in ASP.NET programs.

I

identity An identity column is one with a value that is automatically assigned by the server when a new row is entered.

IL (intermediate language) The language into which compilers that support the .NET Framework compile a program. IL has been ratified as an ECMA standard that calls IL common intermediate language (CIL). The Microsoft implementation of CIL is called Microsoft IL (MSIL).

impersonation ASP.NET uses impersonation to make requests for resources as if those requests were made by the authenticated user.

inheritance A process through which you create a new type based on an existing type. In an inheritance relationship, the existing type is called the base type and the new type is called the derived type. When you use inheritance, the derived type automatically gets all the functionality of the base type—without any extra coding.

input validation A process by which an application examines user input to determine whether it is acceptable for the application.

J-K

JIT (just-in-time) compilation The process of converting IL code into machine code at runtime, just when it is required.

L

"Last one wins" concurrency control With "last one wins" concurrency control, an update to a row always succeeds, whether or not another user has edited the row (as long as the row still exists).

localizability The process of verifying that all localizable resources have been separated from code.

localization The process of translating resources for another culture.

M

managed code The code that runs under the services provided by the CLR. Managed code must expose necessary metadata information to the CLR in order to enjoy these services. *See* CLR.

merge module Allows you to create reusable components that helps in deploying shared components. The merge modules cannot be directly installed. They need to be merged with installers of applications that use the component packed into a merge module.

metadata Information about elements such as assembly, type, method, and so on that helps the common language runtime manage garbage collection, object lifetime management, code access security, debugging, and other services.

N

namespace A naming scheme that provides a way to logically group related types. Namespaces have two benefits: They are used to avoid naming conflicts and they make it easier to browse and locate classes.

native compilation The process of precompiling assemblies in the processor specific machine code. This can be done with the help of Native Image Generator Tool (ngen.exe).

Native Image Cache A cache that contains precompiled assemblies.

.NET Framework A platform for building, deploying, and running XML Web services and applications. The .NET Framework consists of three main parts: the CLR, the FCL, and a set of language compilers.

O

one-way data binding In one-way data binding, the bound property of the control reflects changes to the data model, but changes to the control are not written back to the data model.

optimistic concurrency control With optimistic concurrency control, an update to a row will succeed only if no one else has changed that row after it was loaded into the DataSet.

OSQL A SQL Server command-line tool for executing queries.

P

parameter A piece of information that is passed to a stored procedure at runtime.

Performance Counter The method used by Windows to publish performance-related data for applications and its own components.

platform invoke The feature of the .NET Framework that allows you to call Windows API and other DLL procedures from managed code.

postback A postback occurs when the user submits a Web form to the server.

primary key The unique identifier for a row in a database table.

private assembly An assembly available only to clients in the same directory structure as the assembly.

process An application under execution.

property A class member that is like a public field but that can also encapsulate additional logic within its get and set accessor methods.

Q-R

relation A connection between two tables in a database.

relational database A relational database stores multiple tables and the relations between them.

resource file A file containing string, bitmap, or other resources that can differ between cultures.

resource-only assembly Assemblies that only contain resources and no executable code are called resource-only assemblies.

result set A result set is a collection of data arranged in rows and columns.

role-based security With role-based security, you authorize access to resources depending on the authenticated identity of the user running the code.

roundtrip A roundtrip is the combination of a Web page request and a postback operation.

row All the values in a table that describe one instance of an entity.

Runtime Callable Wrapper (RCW) A proxy that allows .NET code to make use of COM classes and members.

S

satellite assembly A resource-only assembly that contains culture-specific information.

schema The structure of a database or XML file.

session A session is a sequence of interaction between a client browser and a Web server. Each session is uniquely identified using a SessionID.

session state Session state information is persisted between individual stateless HTTP requests.

shared assembly A shared assembly can be referenced by more than one application. An assembly must be explicitly built to be shared by giving it a cryptographically strong name. Shared assemblies are stored in the machine-wide Global Assembly Cache.

simple data binding Simple data binding means connecting a single value from the data model to a single property of a control.

SOAP (Simple Object Access Protocol) A standard for transmitting objects as XML over HTTP.

SQL Query Analyzer A SQL Server graphical tool for executing queries.

SQL-92 An official ANSI specification for Structured Query Language.

stored procedure A set of SQL statements that are stored on the server for later execution.

stream A file viewed as a stream of bytes.

strong name A name that identifies an assembly globally. It consists of a simple text name, a version number, and culture information (if provided) that is signed by a digital signature and contains a public key of the assembly. If the assembly contains more than one file, it is sufficient to generate a digital signature just for the file that contains the assembly manifest.

structure A user-defined value type. Like a class, a structure has constructors, fields, methods, properties, and so on. However, structures do not support inheritance.

T

table A collection of data about instances of a single entity.

templated control A templated control is one whose display is entirely dictated by templates.

testing The process of executing programs and determining whether they worked as expected. It is the process of revealing errors by executing programs with various test cases and test-data.

tracing The process of displaying informative messages in an application at the time of execution. These messages can be helpful in checking the health of the program or finding out errors even though the program is in the production environment as well.

Transact-SQL Transact-SQL, also called T-SQL, is the SQL-92 dialect used in Microsoft SQL Server.

two-way data binding In two-way data binding, changes to the control are written back to the data model.

U-V

UDDI Universal Description, Discovery, and Integration, a standard for discovering details of Web services and other business services available via the Internet.

unboxing A process of conversion of a reference type to a value type where the value from the heap is copied back into stack.

unhandled exceptions When exceptions in a program are not handled within a Try...Catch block of the program, they are called unhandled exceptions.

Unicode A universal character set that can represent over a million characters. Unicode is the default internal language of .NET.

unmanaged code Code written in a non .NET environment that does not benefit from the services of the CLR.

user assistance Any means of providing information about your application to the user.

W

Web custom control A control that inherits from the WebControl class. Web custom controls can be compiled and support advanced features in Visual Studio .NET.

Web method A method of a Web service that can be invoked by client applications.

Web reference Information in a Visual Studio .NET project that allows you to use objects supplied by a Web service.

Web server controls The Web server controls, also known as the ASP.NET server controls, provides a large set of controls, provide richer functionality and consistent programming models.

Web service A Web service allows you to instantiate and invoke objects over the Internet.

Web user control A composite control implemented as an ascx file with an associated vb file.

WSDL (Web Services Description Language) Web Services Description Language, an XML language that describes the interface of a Web service.

X-Y-Z

XML (Extensible Markup Language) A standard for representing information as tagged elements that may contain untagged attributes.

XML declaration The line in an XML file that identifies the file as XML.

XML namespace A set of XML tags that is private to an application.

APPENDIX **B**

Overview of the Certification Process

You must pass rigorous certification exams to become a Microsoft Certified Professional. These closed-book exams provide a valid and reliable measure of your technical proficiency and expertise. Developed in consultation with computer industry professionals who have experience with Microsoft products in the workplace, the exams are conducted by two independent organizations. Prometric offers the exams at more than 3,500 Authorized Prometric Testing Centers around the world. Virtual University Enterprises (VUE) testing centers offer exams at over 3,000 locations.

To schedule an exam, call Prometric Testing Centers at 800-755-EXAM (3926) or VUE at 800-TEST-REG (837-8734) (or register online with Prometric at `http://www.2test.com/index.jsp` or with VUE at `http://www.vue.com/ms/`). Currently Microsoft offers seven types of certification, based on specific areas of expertise.

Types of Certification

- Microsoft Certified Professional (MCP). Qualified to provide installation, configuration, and support for users of at least one Microsoft product or technology. Candidates can take elective exams to develop areas of specialization. MCP is the base level of expertise.
- Microsoft Certified Systems Administrator (MCSA). Qualified to implement, manage, and troubleshoot existing network and system environments based on the Microsoft Windows 2000 and Windows .NET Server platforms.
- Microsoft Certified Systems Engineer (MCSE). Qualified to analyze business requirements and design and implement the infrastructure for business solutions based on the Microsoft Windows 2000 platform and Microsoft server software. The MCSE credential is the next step up from the MCSA.
- Microsoft Certified Application Developer (MCAD). Qualified to use Microsoft technologies to develop and maintain department level applications, components, Web or desktop clients, or back-end data services. This is the entry-level developer certification.
- Microsoft Certified Solution Developer (MCSD). Qualified to design and develop leading-edge business solutions by using Microsoft development tools, technologies, and platforms, including Microsoft Office and Microsoft BackOffice. MCSD is the highest level of expertise with a focus on software development.
- Microsoft Certified Database Administrator (MCDBA). Qualified to implement and administer Microsoft SQL Server databases.

- Microsoft Certified Trainer (MCT). Instructionally and technically qualified by Microsoft to deliver Microsoft Education Courses at Microsoft-authorized sites. An MCT must be employed by a Microsoft Solution Provider Authorized Technical Education Center or a Microsoft Authorized Academic Training site.

> **NOTE** Microsoft's certifications and the exams that lead to them are under constant revision. For up-to-date information about each type of certification, visit the Microsoft Training and Certification World Wide Web site at `http://www.microsoft.com/traincert/`. You must have an Internet account and a WWW browser to access this information. You also can contact the following sources:
>
> Microsoft Regional Education Service Center for North America: 800-635-7544.
>
> MCPHelp@Microsoft.com

Certification Requirements

An asterisk following an exam in any of the lists that follow means that it is slated for retirement.

How to Become a Microsoft Certified Professional

Passing any Microsoft exam (with the exception of exam 70-058, Networking Essentials) is all you need to do to become certified as a MCP.

How to Become a Microsoft Certified Systems Administrator

You must pass three core exams and one elective exam to become an MCSA. The following lists show both the core requirements and the electives you can take to earn this certification.

Core Exams

You must pass three core exams from the following list:

- Installing, Configuring, and Administering Microsoft Windows 2000 Professional, #70-210

  or Installing, Configuring, and Administering Microsoft Windows XP Professional, #70-270

- Installing, Configuring, and Administering Microsoft Windows 2000 Server, #70-215

  or Installing, Configuring, and Administering Microsoft Windows .NET Server, #70-275

- Managing a Microsoft Windows 2000 Network Environment, #70-218

  or Managing a Microsoft Windows 2000 Network Environment, #70-218

Elective Exams

You must pass any one of the exams from the following list:

- Administering Microsoft SQL Server 7.0, #70-028
- Implementing and Supporting Microsoft Exchange Server 5.5, #70-081*
- Implementing and Supporting Microsoft Systems Management Server 2.0, #70-086

- Implementing and Supporting Microsoft Proxy Server 2.0, #70-088*
- Implementing and Administering Security in a Microsoft Windows 2000 Network, #70-214
- Implementing and Administering a Microsoft Windows 2000 Network Infrastructure, #70-216
- Installing, Configuring, and Administering Microsoft Exchange 2000 Server, #70-224
- Installing, Configuring, and Administering Microsoft Internet Security and Acceleration (ISA) Server 2000, Enterprise Edition, #70-227.
- Installing, Configuring, and Administering Microsoft SQL Server 2000 Enterprise Edition, #70-228
- Supporting and Maintaining a Microsoft Windows NT Server 4.0 Network, #70-244
- A+ and Network+, CompTIA exams
- A+ and Server+, CompTIA exams

The MCSA is the first Microsoft certification to recognize some third-party certification exams as electives. Two particular combinations of exams from CompTIA qualify as MCSA objectives.

How to Become a Microsoft Certified Systems Engineer

You must pass five core exams (four operating system exams and one design exam) and two elective exams to become a MCSE.

The following lists show the core requirements and the electives that you can take to earn the MCSE certification.

Operating System Exams

The four core requirements for MCSE certification are as follows:

- Installing, Configuring, and Administering Microsoft Windows 2000 Professional, #70-210

  or Installing, Configuring, and Administering Microsoft Windows XP Professional, #70-270
- Installing, Configuring, and Administering Microsoft Windows 2000 Server, #70-215

  or Installing, Configuring, and Administering Microsoft Windows .NET Server, #70-275
- Implementing and Administering a Microsoft Windows 2000 Network Infrastructure, #70-216

  or Implementing and Administering a Microsoft Windows .NET Server Network Infrastructure, #70-276
- Implementing and Administering a Microsoft Windows 2000 Directory Services Infrastructure, #70-217

  or Implementing and Administering a Microsoft Windows .NET Server Directory Services Infrastructure, #70-277

Design Exam

You must pass one of the design electives on this list:

- Designing a Microsoft Windows 2000 Directory Services Infrastructure, #70-219

  or Designing Security for a Microsoft Windows 2000 Network, #70-220

  or Designing a Microsoft Windows 2000 Network Infrastructure, #70-221

  or Designing Highly Available Web Solutions With Microsoft Windows 2000 Server Technologies, #70-226

Elective Exams

You must pass two of the following elective exams for MCSE certification:

- Designing and Implementing Data Warehouses with Microsoft SQL Server 7.0, #70-019
- Administering Microsoft SQL Server 7.0, #70-028
- Designing and Implementing Databases with Microsoft SQL Server 7.0, #70-029
- Implementing and Supporting Web Sites Using Microsoft Site Server 3.0, #70-056*
- Implementing and Supporting Microsoft Internet Explorer 5.0 by Using the Microsoft Internet Explorer Administration Kit, #70-080*
- Implementing and Supporting Microsoft Exchange Server 5.5, #70-081*
- Implementing and Supporting Microsoft SNA Server 4.0, #70-085*
- Implementing and Supporting Microsoft Systems Management Server 2.0, #70-086
- Implementing and Supporting Microsoft Proxy Server 2.0, #70-088*
- Implementing and Administering Security in a Microsoft Windows 2000 Network, #70-214
- Managing a Microsoft Windows 2000 Network Environment, #70-218
- Designing a Microsoft Windows 2000 Directory Services Infrastructure, #70-219
- Designing Security for a Microsoft Windows 2000 Network, #70-220
- Designing a Microsoft Windows 2000 Network Infrastructure, #70-221
- Migrating from Microsoft Windows NT 4.0 to Microsoft Windows 2000, #70-222
- Installing, Configuring, and Administering Microsoft Clustering Services by Using Microsoft Windows 2000 Advanced Server, #70-223
- Installing, Configuring, and Administering Microsoft Exchange 2000 Server, #70-224
- Designing and Deploying a Messaging Infrastructure with Microsoft Exchange 2000 Server, #70-225
- Designing Highly Available Web Solutions With Microsoft Windows 2000 Server Technologies, #70-226
- Installing, Configuring, and Administering Microsoft Internet Security and Acceleration (ISA) Server 2000 Enterprise Edition, #70-227
- Installing, Configuring, and Administering Microsoft SQL Server 2000 Enterprise Edition, #70-228
- Designing and Implementing Databases with Microsoft SQL Server 2000 Enterprise Edition, #70-229
- Designing and Implementing Solutions With Microsoft BizTalk Server 2000 Enterprise Edition, #70-230
- Implementing and Maintaining Highly Available Web Solutions with Microsoft Windows 2000 Server Technologies and Microsoft Application Center 2000, #70-232
- Designing and Implementing Solutions with Microsoft Commerce Server 2000, #70-234
- Supporting and Maintaining a Microsoft Windows NT Server 4.0 Network, #70-244

You cannot count the same exam as both a core exam and an elective exam for the MCSE.

How to Become a Microsoft Certified Application Developer

You must pass two core exams and one elective exam to earn the MCAD certification.

The following lists show the core requirements and the electives that you can take to earn the MCAD certification.

Core Exams

The two core requirements for MCAD certification are as follows:

- Developing and Implementing Web Applications with Microsoft Visual Basic .NET and Microsoft Visual Studio .NET, #70-305

  or Developing and Implementing Windows-based Applications with Microsoft Visual Basic .NET and Microsoft Visual Studio .NET, #70-306

  or Developing and Implementing Web Applications with Microsoft Visual C# .NET and Microsoft Visual Studio .NET, #70-315

  or Developing and Implementing Windows-based Applications with Microsoft Visual Basic .NET and Microsoft Visual C# .NET, #70-316

- Designing XML Web Services and Server Components with Microsoft Visual Basic .NET and the Microsoft .NET Framework, #70-310

  or Designing XML Web Services and Server Components with Microsoft Visual C# .NET and the Microsoft .NET Framework, #70-320

Elective Exams

You must pass one of the following elective exams for MCAD certification:

- Designing and Implementing Databases with Microsoft SQL Server 2000 Enterprise Edition, #70-229
- Designing and Implementing Solutions With Microsoft BizTalk Server 2000 Enterprise Edition, #70-230
- Designing and Implementing Solutions with Microsoft Commerce Server 2000, #70-234

You may also count as elective one of the four core exams 70-305, 70-306, 70-315, and 70-316. The one you can count as an elective is the exam from the opposite technology and language as the exam that you counted for core. For example, if you take the VB Windows-based Applications exam (70-306) as a core exam, you can take the C# Web Applications exam (70-315) as an elective.

How to Become a Microsoft Certified Solution Developer

There are two different tracks for the MCSD certification. The new track is for the MCSD for Microsoft .NET certification, while the old track covers the previous round of Microsoft technologies. The requirements for both tracks are listed here.

New Track

For the new track, you must pass four core exams and one elective exam. Both the core and elective exams are listed here.

Core Exams

- Developing and Implementing Web Applications with Microsoft Visual Basic .NET and Microsoft Visual Studio .NET, #70-305

  or Developing and Implementing Web Applications with Microsoft Visual C# .NET and Microsoft Visual Studio .NET, #70-315

- Developing and Implementing Windows-based Applications with Microsoft Visual Basic .NET and Microsoft Visual Studio .NET, #70-306

  or Developing and Implementing Windows-based Applications with Microsoft Visual Basic .NET and Microsoft Visual C# .NET, #70-316

- Designing XML Web Services and Server Components with Microsoft Visual Basic .NET and the Microsoft .NET Framework, #70-310

  or Designing XML Web Services and Server Components with Microsoft Visual C# .NET and the Microsoft .NET Framework, #70-320

- Analyzing Requirements and Defining .NET Solution Architectures, #70-300

Elective Exams

You must pass one of the following elective exams:

- Designing and Implementing Databases with Microsoft SQL Server 2000 Enterprise Edition, #70-229
- Designing and Implementing Solutions With Microsoft BizTalk Server 2000 Enterprise Edition, #70-230
- Designing and Implementing Solutions with Microsoft Commerce Server 2000, #70-234

Old Track

For the old track, you must pass three core exams and one elective exam. Both the core and elective exams are listed here.

Core Exams

- Designing and Implementing Desktop Applications with Microsoft Visual C++ 6.0, #70-016

  or Designing and Implementing Desktop Applications with Microsoft Visual FoxPro 6.0, #70-156

  or Designing and Implementing Desktop Applications with Microsoft Visual Basic 6.0, #70-176

- Designing and Implementing Distributed Applications with Microsoft Visual C++ 6.0, #70-015

  or Designing and Implementing Distribute Applications with Microsoft Visual FoxPro 6.0, #70-155

  or Designing and Implementing Distributed Applications with Microsoft Visual Basic 6.0, #70-175

- Analyzing Requirements and Defining Solution Architectures, #70-100

Elective Exams

You must pass one of the following elective exams:

- Designing and Implementing Distributed Applications with Microsoft Visual C++ 6.0, #70-015
- Designing and Implementing Desktop Applications with Microsoft Visual C++ 6.0, #70-016

- Designing and Implementing Data Warehouses with Microsoft SQL Server 7.0, #70-019
- Implementing a Database Design on Microsoft SQL Server 7.0, #70-029
- Designing and Implementing Commerce Solutions with Microsoft Site Server 3.0, Commerce Edition, #70-057*
- Designing and Implementing Solutions with Microsoft Office 2000 and Microsoft Visual Basic for Applications, #70-091*
- Designing and Implementing Collaborative Solutions with Microsoft Outlook 2000 and Microsoft Exchange Server 5.5, #70-105
- Designing and Implementing Web Solutions with Microsoft Visual InterDev 6.0, #70-152
- Designing and Implementing Distribute Applications with Microsoft Visual FoxPro 6.0, #70-155
- Designing and Implementing Desktop Applications with Microsoft Visual FoxPro 6.0, #70-156
- Designing and Implementing Distributed Applications with Microsoft Visual Basic 6.0, #70-175
- Designing and Implementing Desktop Applications with Microsoft Visual Basic 6.0, #70-176
- Designing and Implementing Databases with Microsoft SQL Server 2000 Enterprise Edition, #70-229
- Designing and Implementing Solutions With Microsoft BizTalk Server 2000 Enterprise Edition, #70-230
- Designing and Implementing Solutions with Microsoft Commerce Server 2000, #70-234

You cannot count the same exam as both a core exam and an elective exam.

How to Become a Microsoft Certified Database Administrator

You must pass three core exams and one elective exam to earn the MCDBA certification.

The following lists show the core requirements and the electives that you can take to earn the MCAD certification.

Core Exams

The three core requirements for MCAD certification are as follows:

- Administering SQL Server 7.0, #70-028

  or Installing, Configuring, and Administering Microsoft SQL Server 2000 Enterprise Edition, #70-228
- Designing and Implementing Databases with Microsoft SQL Server 7.0, #70-029

  or Designing and Implementing Databases with Microsoft SQL Server 2000 Enterprise Edition, #70-229
- Installing, Configuring, and Administering Microsoft Windows 2000 Server, #70-215

  or Installing, Configuring, and Administering Microsoft Windows .NET Enterprise Server, #70-2715

Elective Exams

You must pass one of these elective exams:

- Designing and Implementing Distributed Applications with Microsoft Visual C++ 6.0, #70-015
- Designing and Implementing Data Warehouses with Microsoft SQL Server 7.0, #70-019
- Designing and Implementing Distribute Applications with Microsoft Visual FoxPro 6.0, #70-155
- Designing and Implementing Distributed Applications with Microsoft Visual Basic 6.0, #70-175
- Implementing and Administering a Microsoft Windows 2000 Network Infrastructure, #70-216
- Implementing and Administering a Microsoft .NET Server Network Infrastructure, #70-276

How to Become a Microsoft Certified Trainer

To understand the requirements and process for becoming a MCT, you need to obtain the Microsoft Certified Trainer Program Guide document from the following WWW site:

```
http://www.microsoft.com/traincert/mcp/mct/guid
es.asp
```

The MCT Program Guide explains the four-step process of becoming a MCT. The general steps for the MCT certification are as follows:

1. Obtain one of the Microsoft premier certifications: MCSE, MCSD, or MCDBA.
2. Attend a classroom presentation of a Microsoft course taught by a Microsoft Certified Trainer at a Microsoft Certified Technical Education Center (CTEC).
3. Demonstrate instructional presentation skills by attending a Train-the-Trainer course or providing proof of experience in technical training.
4. Complete the MCT application, which you can fill out on the MCT Web Site.

WARNING

Things Change Please consider this appendix to be a general overview of the Microsoft certification process. You'll find much more detailed information, as well as the latest program changes, on the Microsoft Training & Certification Web Site mentioned earlier in the appendix.

APPENDIX C

What's on the CD-ROM

This appendix is a brief rundown of what you'll find on the CD-ROM that comes with this book. For a more detailed description of the *PrepLogic Practice Tests, Preview Edition* exam simulation software, see Appendix D, "Using the *PrepLogic Practice Tests, Preview Edition* Software." In addition to the *PrepLogic Practice Tests, Preview Edition*, the CD-ROM includes the electronic version of the book in Portable Document Format (PDF), several utility and application programs, and a complete listing of test objectives and where they are covered in the book.

PrepLogic Practice Tests, Preview Edition

PrepLogic is a leading provider of certification training tools. Trusted by certification students worldwide, PrepLogic is, we believe, the best practice exam software available. In addition to providing a means of evaluating your knowledge of the Training Guide material, *PrepLogic Practice Tests, Preview Edition* features several innovations that help you to improve your mastery of the subject matter.

For example, the practice tests allow you to check your score by exam area or domain to determine which topics you need to study more. Another feature allows you to obtain immediate feedback on your responses in the form of explanations for the correct and incorrect answers.

PrepLogic Practice Tests, Preview Edition exhibits most of the full functionality of the *Premium Edition* but offers only a fraction of the total questions. To get the complete set of practice questions and exam functionality, visit PrepLogic.com and order the Premium Edition for this and other challenging exam titles.

Again for a more detailed description of the *PrepLogic Practice Tests, Preview Edition* features, see Appendix D.

APPENDIX D

Using *PrepLogic Practice Tests, Preview Edition* Software

This Training Guide includes a special version of *PrepLogic Practice Tests*—a revolutionary test engine designed to give you the best in certification exam preparation. PrepLogic offers sample and practice exams for many of today's most in-demand and challenging technical certifications. This special Preview Edition is included with this book as a tool to use in assessing your knowledge of the Training Guide material while also providing you with the experience of taking an electronic exam.

This appendix describes in detail what *PrepLogic Practice Tests, Preview Edition* is, how it works, and what it can do to help you prepare for the exam. Note that although the Preview Edition includes all the test simulation functions of the complete, retail version, it contains only a single practice test. The Premium Edition, available at PrepLogic.com, contains the complete set of challenging practice exams designed to optimize your learning experience.

Exam Simulation

One of the main functions of *PrepLogic Practice Tests, Preview Edition* is exam simulation. To prepare you to take the actual vendor certification exam, PrepLogic is designed to offer the most effective exam simulation available.

Question Quality

The questions provided in the *PrepLogic Practice Tests, Preview Edition* are written to highest standards of technical accuracy. The questions tap the content of the Training Guide chapters and help you review and assess your knowledge before you take the actual exam.

Interface Design

The *PrepLogic Practice Tests, Preview Edition* exam simulation interface provides you with the experience of taking an electronic exam. This enables you to effectively prepare for taking the actual exam by making the test experience a familiar one. Using this test simulation can help eliminate the sense of surprise or anxiety you might experience in the testing center because you will already be acquainted with computerized testing.

Effective Learning Environment

The *PrepLogic Practice Tests, Preview Edition* interface provides a learning environment that not only tests you through the computer, but also teaches the material you need to know to pass the certification exam.

Each question comes with a detailed explanation of the correct answer and often provides reasons the other options are incorrect. This information helps to reinforce the knowledge you already have and also provides practical information you can us on the job.

SOFTWARE REQUIREMENTS

PrepLogic Practice Tests requires a computer with the following:

- Microsoft Windows 98, Windows Me, Windows NT 4.0, Windows 2000, or Windows XP
- A 166MHz or faster processor is recommended
- A minimum of 32MB of RAM
- As with any Windows application, the more memory, the better your performance.
- 10MB of hard drive space

INSTALLING *PREPLOGIC PRACTICE TESTS, PREVIEW EDITION*

Install *PrepLogic Practice Tests, Preview Edition* by running the setup program on the *PrepLogic Practice Tests, Preview Edition* CD. Follow these instructions to install the software on your computer.

1. Insert the CD into your CD-ROM drive. The Autorun feature of Windows should launch the software. If you have Autorun disabled, click Start and select Run. Go to the root directory of the CD and select setup.exe. Click Open, and then click OK.
2. The Installation Wizard copies the *PrepLogic Practice Tests, Preview Edition* files to your hard drive; adds *PrepLogic Practice Tests, Preview Edition* to your Desktop and Program menu; and installs test engine components to the appropriate system folders.

Removing *PrepLogic Practice Tests, Preview Edition* from Your Computer

If you elect to remove the *PrepLogic Practice Tests, Preview Edition* product from your computer, an uninstall process has been included to ensure that it is removed from your system safely and completely. Follow these instructions to remove *PrepLogic Practice Tests, Preview Edition* from your computer:

1. Select Start, Settings, Control Panel.
2. Double-click the Add/Remove Programs icon.
3. You are presented with a list of software installed on your computer. Select the appropriate *PrepLogic Practice Tests, Preview Edition* title you want to remove. Click the Add/Remove button. The software is then removed from your computer.

USING *PREPLOGIC PRACTICE TESTS, PREVIEW EDITION*

PrepLogic is designed to be user friendly and intuitive. Because the software has a smooth learning curve, your time is maximized because you start practicing almost immediately. *PrepLogic Practice Tests, Preview Edition* has two major modes of study: Practice Test and Flash Review.

Using Practice Test mode, you can develop your test-taking abilities as well as your knowledge through the use of the Show Answer option. While you are taking the test, you can expose the answers along with a detailed explanation of why the given answers are right or wrong. This gives you the ability to better understand the material presented.

Flash Review is designed to reinforce exam topics rather than quiz you. In this mode, you will be shown a series of questions but no answer choices. Instead, you will be given a button that reveals the correct answer to the question and a full explanation for that answer.

Starting a Practice Test Mode Session

Practice Test mode enables you to control the exam experience in ways that actual certification exams do not allow:

- **Enable Show Answer Button**—Activates the Show Answer button allowing you to view the correct answer(s) and full explanation(s) for each question during the exam. When not enabled, you must wait until after your exam has been graded to view the correct answer(s) and explanation.
- **Enable Item Review Button**—Activates the Item Review button, allowing you to view your answer choices, marked questions, and to facilitate navigation between questions.
- **Randomize Choices**—Randomize answer choices from one exam session to the next. Makes memorizing question choices more difficult therefore keeping questions fresh and challenging longer.

To begin studying in Practice Test mode, click the Practice Test radio button from the main exam customization screen. This enables the options detailed in the preceding list.

To your left, you are presented with the option of selecting the preconfigured Practice Test or creating your own Custom Test. The preconfigured test has a fixed time limit and number of questions. Custom Tests allow you to configure the time limit and the number of questions in your exam.

The Preview Edition included with this book includes a single preconfigured Practice Test. Get the compete set of challenging PrepLogic Practice Tests at PrepLogic.com and make certain you're ready for the big exam.

Click the Begin Exam button to begin your exam.

Starting a Flash Review Mode Session

Flash Review mode provides you with an easy way to reinforce topics covered in the practice questions. To begin studying in Flash Review mode, click the Flash Review radio button from the main exam customization screen. Select either the preconfigured Practice Test or create your own Custom Test.

Click the Best Exam button to begin your Flash Review of the exam questions.

Standard *PrepLogic Practice Tests, Preview Edition* Options

The following list describes the function of each of the buttons you see. Depending on the options, some of the buttons will be grayed out and inaccessible or missing completely. Buttons that are appropriate are active. The buttons are as follows:

- **Exhibit**—This button is visible if an exhibit is provided to support the question. An exhibit is an image that provides supplemental information necessary to answer the question.

- **Item Review**—This button leaves the question window and opens the Item Review screen. From this screen you will see all questions, your answers, and your marked items. You will also see correct answers listed here when appropriate.
- **Show Answer**—This option displays the correct answer with an explanation of why it is correct. If you select this option, the current question is not scored.
- **Mark Item**—Check this box to tag a question you need to review further. You can view and navigate your Marked Items by clicking the Item Review button (if enabled). When grading your exam, you will be notified if you have marked items remaining.
- **Previous Item**—View the previous question.
- **Next Item**—View the next question.
- **Grade Exam**—When you have completed your exam, click to end your exam and view your detailed score report. If you have unanswered or marked items remaining you will be asked if you would like to continue taking your exam or view your exam report.

Time Remaining

If the test is timed, the time remaining is displayed on the upper-right corner of the application screen. It counts down minutes and seconds remaining to complete the test. If you run out of time, you will be asked if you want to continue taking the test or if you want to end your exam.

Your Examination Score Report

The Examination Score Report screen appears when the Practice Test mode ends—as the result of time expiration, completion of all questions, or your decision to terminate early.

This screen provides you with a graphical display of your test score with a breakdown of scores by topic domain. The graphical display at the top of the screen compares your overall score with the PrepLogic Exam Competency Score.

The PrepLogic Exam Competency Score reflects the level of subject competency required to pass this vendor's exam. Although this score does not directly translate to a passing score, consistently matching or exceeding this score does suggest you possess the knowledge to pass the actual vendor exam.

Review Your Exam

From Your Score Report screen, you can review the exam that you just completed by clicking on the View Items button. Navigate through the items, viewing the questions, your answers, the correct answers, and the explanations for those questions. You can return to your score report by clicking the View Items button.

Get More Exams

Each *PrepLogic Practice Tests, Preview Edition* that accompanies your training guide contains a single PrepLogic Practice Test. Certification students worldwide trust PrepLogic Practice Tests to help them pass their IT certification exams the first time. Purchase the Premium Edition of *PrepLogic Practice Tests* and get the entire set of all new challenging Practice Tests for this exam. PrepLogic Practice Tests—Because You Want to Pass the First Time.

Contacting PrepLogic

If you would like to contact PrepLogic for any reason including information about our extensive line of certification practice tests, we invite you to do so. Please contact us online at `www.preplogic.com`.

CUSTOMER SERVICE

If you have a damaged product and need a replacement or refund, please call the following phone number:

800-858-7674

Product Suggestions and Comments

We value your input! Please email your suggestions and comments to the following address:

`feedback@preplogic.com`

License Agreement

YOU MUST AGREE TO THE TERMS AND CONDITIONS OUTLINED IN THE END USER LICENSE AGREEMENT ("EULA") PRESENTED TO YOU DURING THE INSTALLATION PROCESS. IF YOU DO NOT AGREE TO THESE TERMS, DO NOT INSTALL THE SOFTWARE.

APPENDIX **E**

Suggested Reading and Resources

.NET User Assistance

Your first source for help with any aspect of Visual Basic .NET should be the user assistance resources that Microsoft ships with their .NET products:

- .NET Framework Documentation. All the classes, methods, properties, and other members of the .NET Framework Base Class Library are documented in this help file. This file is installed by the .NET Software Development Kit (SDK), and is also integrated into the Visual Studio .NET help file.
- Visual Studio .NET help file. This file includes help on all aspects of the Visual Studio interface, as well as a series of walkthroughs and samples that you can refer to for examples of using particular pieces of code.
- Samples and QuickStart Tutorials. These are installed by the .NET Framework SDK and are available through Start, Programs, Microsoft .NET Framework SDK, Samples and QuickStart Tutorials. This set of HTML pages shows examples of many aspects of the .NET Framework in both Visual Basic .NET and C#, and includes links to both working copies and source code for each example.

Books

Ahmed, Mesbah, *ASP.NET Web Developer's Guide.* Wrox, 2002.

Barwell, Fred, et al. *Professional VB.NET 2nd Edition.* Wrox, 2002.

Basiura, Russ, et al. *Professional ASP.NET Web Services.* Wrox, 2001.

Box, Don. *Essential .NET Vol.1: The Common Language Runtime.* Addison Wesley, 2002.

Burton, Kevin. *.NET Common Language Runtime Unleashed.* Sams Publishing, 2002.

Cerami, Ethan. *Web Services Essentials.* O'Reilly, 2002.

Chappell, David. *Understanding .NET.* Addison Wesley, 2001.

Cisco, Steve. *Migrating to Visual Basic .NET.* M&T Books, 2002.

Cornell, Gary, and Morrison, Jonathan. *Programming VB.NET: A Guide for Experienced Programmers.* Apress, 2002.

Delaney, Kalen. *Inside SQL Server 2000.* Microsoft Press, 2000.

Goodyear, Jonathan, et al. *Debugging ASP.NET.* New Riders, 2002.

Grimes, Richard. *Developing Applications with Visual Studio .NET.* Addison Wesley, 2002.

Grundgeiger, Dave. *Programming Visual Basic .NET.* O'Reilly, 2002.

Gunderloy, Mike. *ADO and ADO.NET Programming.* Sybex, 2002.

Jennings, Roger. *Visual Basic .NET XML Web Services Developer's Guide.* Osborne, 2002.

Jones, A. Russell. *Mastering ASP.NET with VB.NET.* Sybex, 2002.

LaMacchia, Brian A., et al. *.NET Framework Security.* Addison Wesley, 2002.

Leinecker, Richard. *Special Edition Using ASP.NET.* Que, 2002.

Liberty, Jesse, and Hurwitz, Dan. *Programming ASP.NET.* O'Reilly, 2002.

Nathan, Adam. *.NET and COM: The Complete Interoperability Guide.* Sams Publishing, 2002.

Richter, Jeffery. *Applied Microsoft .NET Framework Programming.* Microsoft Press, 2001.

Scribner, Kenn, and Stiver, Mark C. *Applied SOAP: Implementing .NET XML Web Services.* Sams Publishing, 2001.

Short, Scott. *Building XML Web Services for the Microsoft .NET Platform.* Microsoft Press, 2000.

Siler, Brian, and Spotts, Jeff. *Special Edition Using Microsoft Visual Basic .NET.* Que, 2002.

Symmonds, Nick. *Internationalization and Localization Using Microsoft .NET.* Apress, 2001.

Troelsen, Andrew. *Visual Basic .NET and the .NET Platform.* Apress, 2001.

Vaughn, Bill. *ADO.NET and ADO Examples and Best Practices for VB Programmers.* Apress, 2002.

WEB SITES

`http://msdn.microsoft.com/library/default.asp?url=/nhp/Default.asp?contentid=28000519`. The MSDN Web site contains extensive technical documentation on all aspects of .NET development.

`http://www.gotdotnet.com/`. The GotDotNet site is a Microsoft-sponsored community Web site that includes downloads and tools, samples, and user-contributed code.

`http://msdn.microsoft.com/vstudio/default.asp`. The Visual Studio home page will keep you up to date on new versions and fixes for all of the Visual Studio .NET applications.

`http://msdn.microsoft.com/architecture/`. The .NET Architecture Center contains a wealth of information on best practices for designing distributed .NET applications.

Index

SYMBOLS

A

B

C

D

E

J-K

L

M

N

O

P

Q

R

S

T

U

V

X-Z